Volume II

International Conference on Computers in Education

ICCE 2002

The Rigours of On-Line Student Assessment – Lessons from E-Commerce

George R S Weir
Department of Computer and Information Sciences
University of Strathclyde
Glasgow G1 1XH
UK
Email:gw@cis.strath.ac.uk

Abstract

Moving to Web-based student assessment is a natural progression from current deployment of Web-based delivery of teaching materials. This paper notes similarities in requirements between network-based student assessment and network-based e-commerce. The parallels are instructive since they indicate the stringent technical demands that must be met by both contexts if confidence is to be assured. Furthermore, we argue that the student assessment context faces more severe constraints than the e-commerce scenario. The paper concludes with proposed techniques that move toward the required levels of assurance, and indicates that adequate on-line student assessment is a loftier goal than secure e-commerce. Keywords: On-line assessment, e-commerce, security, student integrity.

1. Introduction

As pressures increase on academic institutions to provide quality education to growing numbers of students, often without corresponding increases in resources, there is a natural move toward technological means of achieving this goal. Available, low-cost solutions are always initially the most appealing and are pursued early with greatest vigour. The apparently wholesale adoption of the World Wide Web as an information delivery mechanism is testament to the seductive power of effective, accessible and inexpensive technologies.

Web-based delivery of coursework or other computer-based training is seen by many as a helpful strategy for enhancing efficiency and reducing perceived institutional load, whilst simultaneously enriching the overall learning experience for the target students. This approach is evident in trends toward so-called 'virtual universities' and the growing emphasis upon 'asynchronous learning networks' [1], [2].

2. On-line assessment

This paper is not concerned with the merits of computer-assisted teaching. Rather it seeks clarification of the rigorous requirements of on-line assessment. There are many ways in which networked computers may contribute to student assessment. The concern here is with a 'traditional' assessment context in which students must exhibit their knowledge or ability by individually engaging with a computer-based test. Frequently, the computer context for such assessments is a networked laboratory of multiple machines. In turn, this raises issues common to examination environments. Perhaps the technical context of computer assessment affords means to achieve safe and reliable assessment. In clarification of this question, we offer a contrast between the needs of on-line assessment and those of electronic commerce.

3. E-commerce

There is presently enormous growth in the area of e-commerce. This entails the use of distributed networks as a basis for the purchase and sale of goods and services. Underlying this development are mechanisms that enable secure exchange of information (secure electronic transactions). Security is a prevalent concern, since some of the exchanged information contains financial data that facilitates payments. Such information is protected from unauthorised view by means of encryption and authenticated through certification. Of special significance are the transactional constraints and technical means employed in the e-commerce setting in order to attain security, confidence and trust. These accomplishments shed light on the comparable demands of on-line student assessment and enable us to adjudge the technical viability of the latter prospect.

What are the requirements for secure on-line commercial transactions? Clearly, transactional integrity plays a role in this context, as it must for on-line assessment. A network user wishing to make an electronic purchase requires some assurance of the vendor's status. In addition, making a payment on-line is made secure by encrypting the details of the purchaser's credit card. These features are ensured through use of a 'public key infrastructure' (PKI). (This is usually implemented via the Secure Sockets Layer (SSL) protocol [3] and [4] or the emerging TLS standard [5].)

For secure Web transactions, the public key certification and encryption facilities are integrated within the Web server and Web client software. Thereby, the transition from an insecure to a secure Web page invokes the transfer of a digital certificate from the secure server to the Web client. This certificate is usually endorsed by a third-party (the so-called 'trusted third party') and serves to vouch for the vendor as genuine. Upon receipt of this certificate, an exchange of public keys takes place. This facilitates each side in creating a single shared key that can be used securely for data encryption and decryption (often using the Diffie-Hellman key management technique (cf. [6]). Thereupon, all data communicated between the Web browser and the Web server is encrypted and exchanged with confidence. Thus, the PKI environment provides surety for each party to the transaction.

3.1. Trust relationships

The mechanics of PKI support both buyer and seller. Each takes assurance from the technical context that the transaction can be completed securely. Elucidation of the locus of security is instructive here. In the e-commerce setting, the purchaser needs assurance that the seller is trustworthy. Additionally, the buyer needs assurance that their financial details will remain private. From the merchant's perspective, the privacy of exchanged financial data is important, if only for the sake of protecting the customer and maintenance of buyer confidence. Of primary concern to the seller is the validity of the customer's credit, i.e., that the credit card details afford the intended purchase.

A significant asymmetry is evident in this transactional setting. Generally, the buyer's identity need not be assured. (Only the buyer's *credit* must be substantiated. This is accomplished outwith the PKI context.) In contrast, the seller's identity (understood as a gauge of their trustworthiness) must be assured to the buyer. Notably, this context presumes the integrity of the 'user'. There is normally no question of the buyer proving either identity or good will (i.e., serious intent to engage in a purchase); rather, these features are assumed. (In a business-to-business (b2b) transaction, both parties would require proof of identity through digital certificates, e.g., over an extranet or virtual private network.) In this context, the locus of security lies in seller's identity, seller's integrity (trustworthiness) and data privacy. PKI is the technical means of meeting each of these requirements.

4. Requirements for secure on-line assessment

Parallels between e-commerce and on-line assessment may already be apparent. Specifically, identity, data security and participant integrity are vital for adequate on-line assessment, as they are for secure e-commerce. Yet the parallel is not precise and the differences are important.

In order for on-line interaction to provide a credible basis for student assessment, we require proof of student identity. In addition, we require warranty that, for the duration of the assessment, the student has no recourse to external sources of information. Thirdly, we need assurance that they cannot otherwise impair the integrity of the assessment. We suggest that most, but not all, of these requirements can be met through adoption of PKI in the assessment context. The fact that some requirements for on-line assessment cannot be satisfied by means of PKI indicates that adequate on-line assessment is more complex and technically more demanding than e-commerce.

Proof of student identity may be achieved through use of digital certificates. More plausibly, digital signatures, derived from public key encryption - for instance, by means of the RSA public key algorithm [7] - could authenticate each student. Although seldom used, SSL also supports client authentication via digital certificates [8, p.444ff.]. Secure distribution and collection of data is available through PKI-based encryption. This affords confidence in data privacy. Still, there is one vital factor that must be secured for on-line assessment, that is, *student integrity*. This discrepancy between the requirements for secure assessment and the requirements for e-commerce is highlighted in Figure 1, below. Here, the key elements for each scenario are noted against the technical means for their achievement.

We would expect the technical requirements for on-line assessment to be demanding. Where better to look for a technically demanding data exchange context than e-commerce? Yet, the undeniably stringent conditions for e-commerce prove less than adequate for on-line assessment. An asymmetry is apparent between the two scenarios. While the PKI basis for e-commerce goes a long way toward satisfying the needs of on-line assessment, it cannot guarantee student integrity.

	E-commerce	On-line assessment
Identity	PKI	PKI
Privacy	PKI	PKI
Integrity	PKI	?

Figure 1: Requirements for e-commerce versus on-line assessment

4.1 Student integrity

The on-line assessment setting demands that students cannot affect the clinical nature of the 'examination'. In any assessment context, the participant may be motivated to beat the system – aiming to achieve a better than accurate portrayal of ability. Ideally, the constraints of the assessment context will severely limit, if not remove, such a possibility. From our discussion thus far, it is clear that any technical solution to this student integrity problem lies beyond the scope of 'standard' transactional security. How then can we secure the required student integrity?

Some measure of protection will be gained by the use of data encryption derived from PKI. This precludes any threat from subjects snooping on network traffic [9] and gaining insight into other participant activities. The remaining concern relates to the accessibility of third-party information.

Any prospect that subjects may communicate with third parties, either in two-way dialogue or by accessing external sources of information, must be eliminated in our technical configuration for on-line assessment. Standard exam conditions may assist here but technical measures are a desirable precaution. Only through removal of this risk can we assure participant integrity.

Two strategies are available as technical constraints on student activity. The first measure is to restrict access solely to essential applications. Web browser access may be all that is required for on-line assessment. In which case, we aim to remove user access to other communication facilities, such as email, telnet, and FTP. Likewise, use of software that allows users to record their interaction, either dynamically or through text input, may be eliminated. Finally, steps must be taken to avoid users from installing any additional software. Precautions against such activities go a long way to securing proper student behaviour. Facilities for locking down the computer desktop are available for MS-Windows. (Restrictions can be applied to individual machines via the Windows registry.) Similar steps can be taken with open environments, such as Linux, in which the kernel may be customised to restrict functionality.

In principle, these steps go a long way toward imposing the necessary restrictions and assuring student integrity. Inevitably, the use of a Web browser as the primary vehicle for assessment delivery adds further to our integrity problem. The concern here is that students may simply address external web pages and gain access to third-party information sources, thereby contaminating the assessment. Likewise, savvy students may work directly from the operating system and gain network access to remote information resources or transmit sensitive information to subsequent examinees. For instance, many operating systems have native FTP or telnet client capability. Assuming that users are familiar with the requisite protocol, this may allow direct access to FTP, SMTP, or other information services. Similarly, restrictions may be required to prevent concurrent examinees from sharing access to each other's files, including Web cached information.

Some dangers can be removed by disconnecting the local network of computers from access to the external world. Physically unplugging the local area network from a network switch would secure this feature and seal the location against external communication.

4.2 Refining the assessment environment

Our comments above indicate that the inherent problem of student integrity is surmountable, but the cost and inconvenience may be unpalatable. In particular, network clusters intended for temporary use in assessment may not be alterable in the required manner without removing them from normal operation, both during and after reconfiguration. An alternative approach recommends itself by its limited disruptive impact. Traffic limitation can be imposed simply and quickly by means of a network firewall. This facilitates control of outgoing and incoming network traffic - usually, by means of packet filtering, or application proxying (cf. [10], [11]). Filtering may also be applied within specific application protocols. For example, Web access may be disallowed to all destinations save the assessment server. By this mechanism we may conveniently restrict student activity within the examination context.

With this conclusion we complete a circle. Our goal was to specify a setting in which on-line assessment may take place reliably and securely. Many of our requirements are satisfied through adoption of security facilities from e-commerce. In particular, a Public Key Infrastructure allows us to address the central issues of identity and data privacy. The final constraint on our assessment environment, the need for assurance of student integrity, is best accomplished through recourse to a further network security component, the firewall. Figure 2, portrays our technical solutions to the desired assessment scenario.

5. Conclusions

Establishing a context for localised on-line student assessment is far from simple. The situation is complicated by the core requirements of authentication (student identity), data privacy and student integrity. Exploring the parallels between these requirements and the stringent constraints of e-commerce indicates that on-line assessment is the more demanding context.

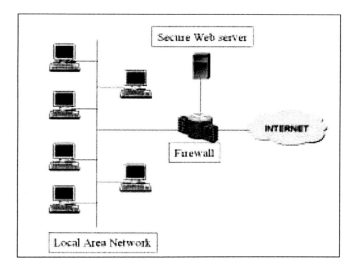

Figure 2: Architecture for secure on-line assessment

Ultimately, our requirements may be met through a combination of network security measures. A secure Web service with PKI, as found in e-commerce, in tandem with a traffic filtering firewall, will provide the necessary *environment* for secure on-line student assessment. Note, however, that our solution still presumes clinical exam conditions. We have yet to identify adequate technical means to guarantee full student integrity. Difficulties remain wherever collusion is an undesirable prospect.

References

[1] Thompson, M. M. & McGrath, J. W., Using ALNs to support a complete educational experience, *Journal of Asynchronous Learning Networks*, Vol.3 (2) November, 54-63, 1999.

[2] Turoff, M., 'Costs for the development of a virtual university', Journal of Asynchronous Learning Networks, Vol.1 (1) March, 23-28, 1997.

[3] Netscape Communications, *The SSL Protocol, Version 3*, November 1996.

[4] Netscape Communications, 'How SSL works', 1999, http://developer.netscape.com/tech/security/ssl/howitworks.html

[5] Dierks, T. & C. Allen, The TLS Protocol Version 1.0, RFC 2246, November 1998.

[6] Rescorla, E., *Diffie-Hellman Key Agreement Method*, RFC2631, 1999.

[7] Rivest R., Shamir A., & Adleman L. M., A Method for Obtaining Digital Signatures and Public-Key Cryptosystems, *Communications of the ACM*, Vol. 21 (2) February, 120-126, 1978.

[8] Stallings, W, *Cryptography and Network Security*, Prentice-Hall, New Jersey, 1998.

[9] Yu, J. H. & Le, T. K., ' Internet and Network Security', Journal of Industrial Technology, Vol.17 (1), 2001.

[10] Goncalves, M., *Check Point Firewalls An Administration Guide*, McGraw, 1999.

[11] Sonnenreich, W, *Building Linux and OpenBSD Firewalls*, Wiley, 2000.

Using the Inter- and Intranet in a University Introductory Psychology Course to Promote Active Learning

Dr. Sonya Symons & Dr. Doug Symons
Acadia University, Wolfville NS Canada B0P 1X0

Abstract

This paper reports on how a university Introductory Psychology course was restructured after a campus-wide information technology program was introduced at a small Canadian university. Our use of the campus Intranet and the Internet resulted in a technology-enhanced lecture environment, greater student exchange of ideas, greater and more efficient communication between the instructor and students, and more writing assignments than are typical of first year psychology courses. Evidence of success came from increased grades on examinations, positive course evaluations, and an increase in the numbers of students declaring psychology as their major. Technology was helpful in implementing aspects of undergraduate education that promote active learning.

Introduction

The purpose of this article is to report on the use of the Internet and Intranet in an the teaching of introductory psychology at Acadia University, a small liberal arts university in Eastern Canada. In 1996, the university implemented the "Acadia Advantage" program in which all students and faculty were provided with an IBM notebook computer and Internet access, classrooms were wired for high speed Internet access and data projection, and technical support services were increased. There are, for example, over 6000 ports around campus for the approximately 3700 students, including work stations in studio-style classrooms and all residence rooms. In part due to the Acadia Advantage, Acadia University is regularly rated in a national news magazine as being the most innovative university in Canada. (For details, see http://www.acadiau.ca/advantage/).

Our approach to incorporating computer technology into our teaching was to ask ourselves if the change would increase students' active engagement in the learning process. If the answer was "yes" then we were willing to make the investment to adapt our teaching methods. The goal was to encourage active and collaborative learning by creating a networked learning environment [1], given that technological upgrades provide an opportunity to revise course delivery and enhance instruction [2]. Introductory psychology is one of the highest enrolment courses at many universities and methods of course delivery including large lectures and multiple-choice examinations can encourage a very passive approach to learning. We aimed to encourage greater engagement in the learning process by using the Intranet and Internet to get students doing more learning activities, and to communicate with each other and their instructor.

Prior to 1996, the course was taught in 6 sections, with approximately 75 students receiving 3 lectures per week being evaluated with multiple-choice and sometimes brief written exams. Written work played a minimal role, which was problematic given that written assignments can enhance some aspects of student learning in introductory psychology [3,4]. With the advent of the Acadia Advantage program, we realized we had an opportunity to change our approach to teaching introductory psychology. We started by listing the kinds of learning experiences that we wanted to incorporate: Interactive learning to demonstrate concepts, discussion of ideas, expressing ideas in writing, and evaluation of learning using both multiple choice and written formats. We felt that student access to notebook computers and to the Internet and Intranet could facilitate some of these pedagogical goals.

Our revised course took the following form. The three hours of instruction per week were reorganized into two one-hour lectures and a one-hour discussion group. Students attended lecture classes of approximately 200-250. This size still permitted some questions and discussion, in addition to traditional lecturing, and there is little documentation relating instructional quality to class size [5,6]. Lecture outlines were posted on an Intranet-based course web page that students printed before attending class, permitting students who were new to university and to note-taking to elaborate on these outlines. The classroom was equipped with a state-of the-art teaching podium with notebook computer docking station and high-resolution data projection of computer and video images. The screen in the lecture hall was 30 feet tall and the audio system had excellent sound quality. Lecture preparation and planning had to be increased so "down time" was minimized: 200 students idle for 5 to 10 minutes can have disastrous consequences [6].

In the weekly discussion group, 20 – 30 students met with a graduate student teaching assistant to discuss the week's material. In addition, we implemented web-based assignments and activities using existing Internet resources to encourage interactive learning. Some of these came from commercial web sites such as "PSYCPLACE", but we created others ourselves. Each activity was followed by a specific explanation and discussion of what students were to take away from the activity. There were three written assignments required from students during the term that were based on discussion group activities. Finally, an online discussion group was created to help students with their assignments. They could post ideas, approaches to the assignment, or questions on the message board, and other students could provide feedback on the messages. Not only were students exchanging ideas in class, but they were also able to do so on-line, and in written form whenever it was convenient to them. Finally, we changed the structure of midterm examinations for the course. In addition to multiple-choice questions tapping content, we devoted about ¼ of the midterm to short answer questions based on the active learning experiences done in discussion groups.

In our first year of implementing discussion groups, the on-line discussion forum was rarely used and discussion group attendance was poor. Unfortunately student motivation is sometimes extrinsically related to "having to know things for tests" rather than inherent love of learning [4]. In response, in subsequent years we have devoted 10% of the final grade to discussion group participation. By participation, we included attending discussion groups, speaking up in the group, and participating in on-line discussion. There was a nice trade-off for shy students new to university in that if they were not yet comfortable speaking up in class, they could be involved in on-line activities

Why do we think our use of technology in Introductory Psychology has been effective in promoting learning? In the first year of implementation, we had the opportunity to conduct a quasi-experiment comparing students who were in the Acadia Advantage program to those who were not because students had the option of choosing the program. Those students who chose to enter the Acadia Advantage program did not have higher grades in high school courses. Yet, they had higher grades on their Introductory mid-term and final exams than did students who opted to not enroll in the Acadia Advantage program (mean difference 4%). In fact, only 27% of the Advantage students received a grade lower than C- (60%) compared to 43% of the students who were not enrolled in the Acadia Advantage program. Teaching evaluations indicate that students consistently rate introductory psychology as a very good course, (e.g., a mean over 4.0 on a five-point scale with 1 = very

poor, 3 = average, and 5 = very good). Only a very small percentage of students rate the course as below average. Anecdotally, many students have told us that introductory psychology was their favorite university course and that it had the best integration of material with new learning technologies. Third, grades on written work and participation in discussion groups are positively correlated with final exam grades the course ($r = .50$), reinforcing the importance of these components.

The university's investment in the Acadia Advantage program facilitated these changes to Introductory Psychology. But the improvements in student learning experience were possibly based on changes to course structure and activities. Some of these were facilitated by the use of technology. But others, such as having students do more written work, exchange ideas, and see concepts demonstrated, are tried and true methods of effective instruction. Technology helped us incorporate these valuable aspects of education in more ways than are usually possible in large classes. From a methodological viewpoint it is difficult to attribute changes in student achievement and course evaluations to technology because we implemented many changes to the course at the same time that we adopted computer technology. The first-year evidence is moderately convincing, however, since the comparison involved two groups of students who differed only in terms of whether they were given their own computer and in the type of discussion group that they participated in (traditional or computer-enhanced). Perhaps the most important impact of the decision to adopt computer technology is the opportunity it afforded to consider our pedagogy and its impact on student learning.

Reference
1. Harasim, L.M. (1996). *Computer networking for education.* In E. DeCorte & F.E. Weinert (Eds.), International encyclopedia of developmental and instructional psychology. Oxford, U.K.: Pergamon.
2. Brothen, T. (1991). Implementing a computer-assisted cooperative learning model for Introductory Psychology. *Teaching of Psychology, 18,* 183-185.
3. Boyes, M.P., Killian, P.W., & Rileigh, K.K. (1994). Learning by writing in Introductory Psychology. *Psychological Reports, 75,* 563-568.
4. Hinkle, S., & Hinkle, A. (1990). An experimental comparison of the effects of focused freewriting and other study strategies on lecture comprehension. *Teaching of Psychology, 17,* 31-35.
5. Glass, G.V., & Smith, M.L. (1979). Meta-analysis of research on class size and achievement. *Educational Evaluation and Policy Análisis, 1,* 2-16.
6. Jenkins, J.J. (1991). Teaching psychology in large classes: Research and personal experience. *Teaching of Psychology, 18,* 74-80.

Multimedia Enhanced Student Portfolios:
Providing Evidence of Competency in a Teacher Education Program

Jackie Stokes, The RITE Group, QUT

Abstract:

Changing life and work environments have led to a decline in permanency of employment within industrialised societies. The new millennium calls for portfolio workers with transportable skills. Skills and work practices heavily bound to one context are no longer considered as currency; employers are calling for generic attributes to be identified.

This paper discusses the second stage of a learning and development project at Queensland University of Technology (QUT), Brisbane, Australia. One of the projects the Faculty of Education's Flexible Pedagogies research team are investigating is the use of digital images to aid reflection. The paper will focus on how the taking of still and video images whilst on practicum placement aided reflection with two cohorts of pre-service teachers.

1. Defining teacher practitioner attributes

Changing life and work environments have led to a decline in permanency of employment within industrialised societies. The new millennium calls for portfolio workers with transportable skills. Skills and work practices heavily bound to one context are no longer considered as currency; employers are calling for generic attributes to be identified.

This paper discusses the second stage of a learning and development project at Queensland University of Technology (QUT), Brisbane, Australia. The Faculty of Education's Flexible Pedagogy research team is investigating how digital images taken on practicum placement can aid reflection. It relies on the Faculty of Education allowing pre-service teachers to store files on a student server accessed through its intranet, and to allow the pre-service teacher web folders to be accessed through the Internet.

2. Background information

The first stage of the project was to establish what 'generic attributes' were to be targeted. QUT (2000) had identified a set of generic attributes for all of its graduates, regardless of discipline [1]. These 21 attributes were listed under three headings: Knowledge/problem-solving (9), Ethical/attitudinal (6) and Social/relational (6). The Faculty of Education, QUT (2000a) had identified an additional set of 20 attributes under the same headings [2]. The largest employer of Queensland teachers, Education Queensland (1999), had a draft set of twelve professional standards for its teachers [3]. On a national level, the Federal Government (National Project on the Quality of Teaching and Learning, 1996) had issued a set of generic capabilities for beginning teachers [4].

After cross matching these 'attributes', 'capabilities' and 'standards' (Greishaber, Healy, Hoepper, Irving, Stokes & Hobart, 2000) the decision was made that the number of attributes nominated in any of these lists was too large to be effectively tracked [5]. Six major attributes were isolated as being important for developing in the education course - Discipline knowledge, Ethics and responsibility, Communication, Designing and problem-solving, Literacies, and Interpersonal skills.

The project's debates were informed by a key research document, *Generic capabilities of Australian Technology Network university graduates* (Bowden, Hart, Kelly, Trigwell, & Watts, 1999), QUT being one of the five universities involved in the research [6]. In the report Teaching and Learning Committee of the Australian Technology Network identified three reasons for the inclusion of generic attributes into higher education courses:

1. The historic role of universities to produce leaders of society who have a greater role in their community than mere discipline expertise;
2. The production of life-long learners with capabilities to face an unknown future; and
3. Employer expectations of a larger set of capabilities than discipline knowledge.

The report noted that an essential part of this was the need for tertiary students to be metacognitive in their approach to learning, aware of their strengths and areas that needed developing, and in determining how each aspect of course delivery contributed to their skill-set.

Within the research recorded in this paper the use of electronic portfolios provided pre-service teachers with an ongoing reflective device that allowed them to monitor their development of latest version of the Teacher Practitioner Attributes over the course of their study [7]. In terms of Barrett's stages of electronic portfolio development (2001) pre-service teachers are given the portfolio template and told of the *goal and context* [8]. The use of the TPAs as the framework enables the pre-service teachers whilst *working* on the portfolio to gain an understanding of how attainment of the indicator is embedded in the activities and assessment items of their course. Their selection of evidence is ongoing. This selection allows the pre-service teacher to be *reflective*, not only with regards to their attainment of attributes, but also with what the artefact tells about their ability to "understand and act appropriately in a variety of contexts", the relating stage of Bowden et al's, (1999) scale of attainment [6]. The advantage of a *connected portfolio* is that pre-service teachers can invite administration teams in schools and employing bodies to view their evidence, thus serving as a *presentation portfolio* in the interview situation.

1.1   Using the TPAs as a reflective device

In 2001 the TPAs were used as the basis of digital portfolio for the first year Bachelor of Education (Primary) students (n=300). At the end of semester one they were advised to place in an evidence folder any tasks undertaken during the semester that demonstrated their current attainment of that attribute. For example, Figures 1 and 2 show the homepage and Individual TPAs of a student who has linked two items of evidence to the page (pages used with permission).

**Figure 1. Student homepage
(used with permission)**

**Figure 2. Individual TPAs with evidence linked
(used with permission)**

The portfolio is not assessed. One of its aims is to allow students to be metacognitive about their learning, and reference to the TPAs on the portfolio pages encouraged the students to become familiar with the range of teacher practitioner attributes the Faculty of Education had deemed important.

2.0   Multimedia-enhanced student portfolios

In semester 2 2001 the project was further enhanced by the use of video segments and images. Two tutorial groups were chosen to trial the project. One tutorial group was clustered for practicum placement in a geographic region where the liaison academic had established rapport with the administration teams in five schools. These schools were approached and an acceptable user policy was devised. It was a stipulation of the project that:

- No image/movie can be published that has not been viewed and passed by the authorised person in the Cluster School.
- No image/movie can be published in which any student can be identified.
- All images where students can be identified MUST be destroyed before you leave your prac school.
  http://education.qut.edu.au/stokes/mesp/web [9]

2.1   Logistics

Seven digital cameras were purchased for the project. The Sony Mavica MVC-FD92 camera was chosen because of the ability to capture 60 seconds of video and record onto a 3.5 cm disk. The Sony CD Mavica, that saves digital media to mini CDs, was trialed but proved more cumbersome to use. The mini CDs had to be formatted in the camera prior to images being taken and a caddy was needed to hold the mini CDs before the images could be down-loaded onto the computer. Mini tripods that stood on desk-tops were also bought.

In recognition of the cooperation of the cluster school, equipment left at the school (camera, charger and tripod) could be used on days that the pre-service teachers were not attending practicum placement, on the proviso that the cameras would be ready for pre-service teacher use when needed.

3.0   Feedback

Feedback from pre-service teachers, supervising teachers and school administration teams was positive. Supervising teachers indicated that the process did not interfere with either student learning or pre-service teacher concentration on their teaching task. Whilst it was proposed that pre-service teachers cooperatively take the images of each other teaching often the supervising teacher was so enthralled by the project that they captured the images.

Administration teams indicated that they thought that the project was worthwhile, some lamenting the fact that their teachers were not as proficient as the pre-service teachers when it came to ICT use in constructing webpages.

Below are comments from pre-service teachers who responded to a survey sent at the end of their practice teaching placement:

- *I plan to add to it (my webpage) in the future;*
- *Good to reflect on my teaching strategies;*
- *This process provides a snapshot of the teacher's presence in the classroom and could prove beneficial to a prospective employer.*

4.0   Current state of project

In 2002 the project is being trialed again with a Master of Teaching cohort (n=41). These pre-service teachers are at a different stage of their teacher education from the previous cohort. The assessment for one of the units undertaken in their third semester is to prepare a portfolio that becomes the basis of their teaching portfolio for their employment interview with Education Queensland. Eleven of the cohort have elected to trial capturing multimedia elements whilst on practicum placement and to construct an electronic portfolio. The pre-service teachers have elected to use EQ's selection criteria as the basis of their portfolios (http://education.qld.gov.au/corporate/hr/pdfs/teach.pdf) [10].

In 2002 the project team will distribute the cameras and tripods to pre-service teachers on practicum placement during their third semester practicum but access to the equipment in semester four will be pre-service teacher initiated. Surveys will capture pre-service teacher use of equipment, reflections on the project and the use of the portfolio in the interview situation. This data will be ready for dissemination at the time of the conference.

5.0   References

[1] QUT. (2000). Manual of Policies and Procedures Chapter C - Teaching and learning 1.3 Generic attributes of QUT graduates, http://www.publications.qut.edu.au/ltd/qut/pubs/mopp/C/C_01_03.html (19/6/00).

[2] Faculty of Education, QUT. (2000a). Faculty of Education Generic Attributes http://www.fed.qut.edu.au/TPAproject/EDgenatt2000.html (2/2/01).

[3] Education Queensland. (1999). The professional standards for teachers. http://education.qld.gov.au/learning_ent/ldf/standards/teachers.html (9/8/02).

[4] National Project on the Quality of Teaching and Learning (1996). National competency framework for beginning teaching. AGPS: Canberra.

[5] Greishaber, S., Healy, A., Hoepper,B., Irving, K., Stokes, J., & Hobart, L. (2000). Bachelor of Education Review – October 2000.

[6] Bowden, J., Hart, G., Kelly, B., Trigwell, K., & Watts, O. (1999). Generic capabilities of ATN university graduates. Teaching and Learning Committee, Australian Technology Network. http://www.clt.uts.edu.au/ATN.grad.cap.project.index.html (24/4/02).

[7] Faculty of Education, QUT. (2000b). Teacher Practitioner Attributes. http://www.fed.qut.edu.au/tpaproject/index.html (2/2/01).

[8] Barrett, H. (2001). Electronic portfolios, In Educational Technology, ASBC-CLIO.

[9] Stokes, J. (2001). Multimedia enhanced student portfolios project. http://education.qut.edu.au/stokes/mesp/web.htm (24/4/02).

[10] Education Queensland. (2002). Employing for teacher employment booklet: March 2002. Avaliable from http://education.qld.gov.au/corporate/hr/pdfs/teach.pdf (24/4/02).

A "Low-Tech" Design Experiment Improving Student Work

Dr. David Walker, Executive Director LTRC, McMaster University, Hamilton, Canada

ABSTRACT

Following Collins' work [1,2], a design experiment had graduate music students create an on-line journal of peer-reviewed articles to introduce them to the professional process. The students reported learning a great deal and the professor found that most produced work that greatly exceeded his expectations. Positive results were independent of previous computing or subject matter experience, and improvement was noted in all but the lowest performing student.

1: Design experiment

Collins [1] suggests that we "begin to develop a science of education" on an experimental, rather than ad hoc basis. This science is to be a "design science" rather than an analytic one, and to achieve it we must "determine how different designs of learning environments contribute to learning, cooperation, motivation, etc." (p. 15). We can accomplish this through the careful planning and execution of design experiments, wherein the researchers solicit the active involvement of teachers who provide the courses. To this Brown [3] adds a holistic view of learning recognizing the many interwoven aspects in any learning situation that lead to "highly interdependent outcomes of a complex social and cognitive intervention" (pp. 166-7). This complexity strongly suggests that we are unlikely to hit upon a definitive experimental intervention on our first attempt, and that success will come with a series of refined experimental prototypes. This methodology is especially well adapted to the use of technology.

2: The Case Study

Many students find the transition from school to the working world difficult. I proposed a design experiment to a colleague to help bridge this gap, using a framework of Legitimate Peripheral Participation [4], in which the learner works as a novice professional (or apprentice) at the periphery of practice in their chosen field. Such a situated approach to learning builds on constructivism [5] and cognitive apprenticeship [6] but stresses the socially constructed nature of knowledge as situated in communities of individuals working at similar practices. Rather than "learning facts" the learner addresses the practices and skills of the community. This works

particularly well in graduate school, where an on-line community of scholars is possible. Here we gave them a common goal: create an on-line journal of peer-reviewed papers by the end of term (rather than doing term papers for the teacher's eyes only).

Qualitative methods of research have been shown effective in studying educational cases [7] and design experiments [2], and case study is particularly useful for exploratory studies [8,9]. Given the dearth of data from the student's point of view [10], ethnographically-informed approaches [11] using participant-observation, field notes, and grounded theory [12] are useful. Gardner [13] has shown that students attend to and want to learn different things, and they often are not aware of their own learning strategies and goals. Observation and careful interviewing can help uncover them. Belmont [14] points out that Vygotsky's Zone of Proximal Development is negotiated between learner and teacher, and may be most apparent to an observer.

Both classes studied met once per week for a three-hour seminar. Computer conferencing kept students in touch with the professor and each other between classes. My colleague taught the course, and I was free to study the class as a participant-observer, taking field notes during class sessions and on-line discussions; giving the students bi-weekly open-ended surveys; and triangulating this data with a 90-minute exit interview.

The first full experiment was conducted from September to December 1999 with a class of eight masters' students in a class of music analysis. The course was very popular with the students, and the professor considered it a success as 7 of 8 students produced work that significantly exceeded his expectations for them. He attributed this to the greater number of drafts written in response to peer review. The students were satisfied that they had learned computing skills that they wanted; that they learned analysis as a skill for their careers; and that they had a publication, albeit one in a journal of dubious importance in their own eyes.

The second experiment was conducted from September to December 2001, again with a class of eight masters' students in music analysis. This time the professor found that all students exceeded his expectations, although by a narrower margin. These students had better computing skills, but were still happy to have improved them; to have learned analysis as a career skill; to have a paper published; and to have improved the look of the journal.

Students formed communities in different ways. The first class split into two groups, but were more cohesive on-line, whereas the second class was more homogenous both in class and on-line. Both classes left the brunt of the technical work to one student: the first class to a former computer science student, the second to an interested computing novice. There were common factors in student success in both classes: the number of drafts, visibility of work on the web, peer pressure, personal interest, and publication.

A single study can only suggest the efficacy of a given intervention. The excellent results from the first study encouraged us to repeat it with minor modifications. The second study suggested that the efficacy of the student journal was independent of the individuals in the class. Personalities did enter into the efficiency with which the journal was run: the first class had two highly motivated and organized editors that kept the work on schedule, while the second class had less organized individuals.

3: What did we learn?

Strictly speaking we found that these two classes did well producing a student journal, and may have produced better work than in doing a normal term paper. Acknowledging that qualitative data is suggestive rather than definitive, the data from these studies suggests that students value their learning and produce very good work with a peer-reviewed web journal. This finding holds across different levels of previous computer experience, differing levels of analysis study, interest, and career goal. The only student in either class who did not flourish had extreme difficulty in passing the course, and the professor felt that no intervention would have helped this situation.

All students in both classes reported that a very important aid to their learning was the perspectives that other students had on the subject matter and their methodologies in doing their coursework. Even when the same advice was given by the professor, students gave it more credibility, and acted on it more often when it came from other students. This applied to subject matter learning as well as ad hoc computer tips and other operational concerns. Another vital factor was the students' own interest in developing a web journal. Over half of the students put in extraordinary amounts of time working on the journal, and their reported levels of absorption and feelings of empowerment are strongly reminiscent of Csikszentmihalyi's [15] concept of "flow."

I find the success of a relatively "low-tech" intervention gratifying; keeping the students central and using technology as a tool seems to have produced better results than we had dared hope for. This design experiment does need further refinement and extension into areas other than music analysis, and indeed outside of the humanities. Our data suggests that students considered this journal a stepping stone into the "real world" of work after university, and while such a project is not authentic to every discipline it surely must apply to many more than music.

REFERENCES

[1] Collins, A. (1992). "Toward a Design Science of Education." in New Directions in Educational Technology. E. Scanlon & T. O'Shea (Eds.) Berlin: Springer-Verlag.
[2] Collins, A. (1996). Design Issues for Learning Environments. In S. Vosniadou, E. DeCorte, R. Glaser, and H. Mandl (Eds.), International perspectives on the design of technology-supported learning environments. pp. 149-163. Mahwah, NJ: Lawrence Erlbaum Associates.
[3] Brown, A. (1992). Design experiments: Theoretical and methodological challenges in creating complex interventions in classroom settings. The Journal of the Learning Sciences, 2(2), pp. 141-178.
[4] Lave, J. & Wenger, E. (1991). Situated Learning: Legitimate Peripheral Participation. Cambridge: Cambridge University Press.
[5] Honebein, P. C., Duffy, T. M., and Fishman, B. J. (1993). Constructivism and the Design of Learning Environments: Context and Authentic Activities for Learning. In Designing Environments for Constructive Learning. (Duffy, T. M., Lowyck, J., and Jonassen, D. Eds.) Heidelberg: Springer Verlag.
[6] Collins, A., Brown, J. S., and Newman, S. E. (1989). Cognitive Apprenticeship: Teaching the Crafts of Reading, Writing, and Mathematics. In L. B. Resnick (Ed.) Knowing, Learning, and Instruction: Essays in Honor of Robert Glaser. Hillsdale, NJ: Lawrence Erlbaum Associates.
[7] Merriam, S. B. (1998). Qualitative Research and Case Study Applications in Education. San Francisco: Jossey-Bass.
[8] Stake, R. (1994) "Case Studies." in Handbook of Qualitative Research. N. Denzin & Y. Lincoln (Eds.) Thousand Oaks, CA: Sage Publications.
[9] Yin, R. (1994) Case Study Research: Design and Methods. Second Edition. Thousand Oaks, CA: Sage Publications.
[10] Lincoln, Y.S. (1995). In search of students' voices. Theory into Practice. 34, 2, Spring 1995.
[11] Spradley, J. P. (1980). Participant Observation. Toronto: Holt, Rinehart and Winston.
[12] Glaser, B.G., & Strauss, A. L. (1967). The discovery of grounded theory: Strategies for qualitative research. Chicago: Aldine.
[13] Gardner, H. (1983). Frames of mind: the theory of multiple intelligences. New York : Basic Books.
[14] Belmont, J. A. (1989). Cognitive Strategies and Strategic Learning: The Socio-Instructional Approach. American Psychologist, 44, 142-148.
[15] Csikszentmihalyi, M. (1990). Flow: The psychology of optimal experience. New York: Harper and Row.

Small-size Web-based Instructional System in Campus Network

Ruhui Ni , Fei Li

Abstract

In an analysis of the advantages and disadvantages of the large-scale platforms for teaching assistance, this paper intends to explore a small-size web-based instructional system in order to adapt the current situation of double-approach teaching model in university: at the same time, classroom teaching and web assistance.

Introduction

With the rapid development of campus network and popularity of Internet, the utilization of network including both of them is more and more prevalent in the campus. As a result of the peculiarity of network which is one of the communication media, the manners of application of which are consequentially numerous. As far as the assistance to teaching, after a long period of experimentation, both the requirement of different kinds of customers and the various models began to emerge definitely.

A lot of companies and national organizations developed a great deal number of large-scale platforms for distance learning and teaching assistance. These platforms sometimes were designed for whole university, or one province and even for country. Generally, the large-scale platforms of teaching assistance were provided with better universal functions, such as Bulletin, the delivery and checking of homework, discussion after class and so on. But, the virtues of large-scale platform may not be really beneficial to teachers who are teaching different course in school or university and hold maybe totally different applications concerning to their courses.

First of all, the large-scale platform provide so universal functions that it is difficult to satisfy the depth and individuation of demand. For example, when involved in the process of the delivery of instructional materials on network, large-scale platform always could not provide a real flexible instrument called authoring tool for web-based courseware but replaced by space on server for teachers to upload the courseware which is packed offline. Teachers could not hold enough capacity to dominate and rework the instructional materials which is delivered through this method. Most teachers require to utilize the trait of network to optimize their instructional materials from classroom. Secondly, considering the mechanism and management of large-scale platform, teachers sometimes would not feel convenience to control and use it, particularly, when teachers feel obliged to sacrifice some applications by reason of versatility of platform. If this sacrifice or concession exceeds the advantage of making use of the platform, teachers may have to abandon it.

In a word, what the teachers need is a very flexible and comparatively small method to use the network to assistant their classroom teaching. The depth of assistance is due to the situation of classroom teaching and the characteristics of course. We figure out that this method should be a small-size web-based instructional system based on campus network. Compared with the large-scale platform, the small-size system may not be in possession of all-purpose functions, but the flexibility and practicablity is its virtue and it gives more attention to the function of delivery instructional materials to net, so the small-size system could transfer and reflect more valuable peculiarity of classroom teaching. Specially, after the development of the small-size system, there is possibility that the teacher whose self could become the administrator of server and control every step of using this system, even during the process of delivery instructional materials. The feasibility lies on the customization and flexibility of system. It will take a great deal advantage for teachers who adopt the double-approach teaching model: at the same time, classroom teaching and web assistance.

Such consideration was taken as guide for the development of a relatively small web-based instructional system initiated in March 2001.

1. The campus Network Environment

An infrastructure for digital campus has been built at Tsinghua University. All students have received necessary training on computer skills and have guaranteed online time. In this case, it is technologically viable to adopt the web-based instructional system on campus.

2. Course Information & Assignment of Web-based Instructional system

Engineering Mechanics, a required course for majors such as Mechanical Engineering and Precision Instrument, is chosen for our project. The course is designed to equipped students with true mechanics quality through the large number of engineering cases as well as computer analysis introduced. The integration of theoretical and practical issues is intended to lay a good foundation for students' future engineering practice. Each semester there are usually 360 students registered for the course.

The teacher leads his class activity in an interactive fashion, in which students response is well encouraged and creativity appreciated. Questions are raised and analyzed in class to foster the capability of problem solving, meanwhile enough space is left after class for student to think, discuss, and reach conclusion by themselves.

The teacher has composed wonderful PowerPoint file, in which rich quantities of images, graphics and formula evolution are presented with mastery. The strong power of electronic presentation, combined with the vivid language of the teacher, has made abstract concept visible and accessible, thus creating good effect in classroom.

However several problems exist. First, not all students could understand the large volume of course content completely at first time in class. Second, only a small portion of students could actually take part in the classroom interaction with teacher, leaving the rest as static audience. At the same time, discussion and exchange of ideas are in fact indispensable to the inspiring teaching. Therefore, a network platform is in need for students to review and discuss what they've learnt in class, and the delivery of instructional materials on network and the management of that platform should be control by the responsible teacher or teaching assistants. To meet such needs, we have developed specifically for the course Engineering Mechanics a web-based instructional system based on the Tsinghua campus network.

The principal task of this system is to support the review of classroom instructional materials for students and maintain an environment under the control of teacher to supply the discussion and changing of ideas between students and teachers.

Further more, system must give a lot of pertinent additive functions such as bulletin, self-exam for students and other functions. In order to manage these functions, corresponding management functions should be offered. Above all, a powerful authoring tool is very important to supply.

3. Design and Implement

Considering the characteristics of classroom teaching of EM, we select the images of PowerPoint files and sound of teacher's to be main part of the content for review after class. It is necessary to keep the synchronization of images and sound when they compose the primary sect of the web page. In order to complement the instructional materials, we add a region of text beside the image region which is used to display the script of the speech of teacher. At the same time, the resource which are quoted by teacher in classroom such as video, animation and other format files are all included in one relevant web page. Thus, all of the images, sound, text and resource come into being a template web page which could be the foundation of all the instructional materials and the authoring tool is also developed in conformity to this template.

template web page

Besides, a professional BBS- Discussion Area and Asking and Answering system are developed for EM course to content the communication requirement. In the other hand, every function also hold a corresponding management function for teacher. For example, the management for user system and information release and discussion is indispensable. The management for self-exam also provide the statistical tool that teachers could find out the problem of students. All functions are developed for web and provide by web and use through web.

management function interface

4. The Application Procedure and Effect Analysis

4.1: The application procedure of the system is as follows:

1. When development completed, the system is handed over to the teacher, who will take the full responsibility of content management as a webmaster.

2. At the beginning of semester, the teacher determined the qualification of registered students with the User Administration function and gave them the corresponding permission.

3. Relevant information could be delivered on web before class, such as introduction to the course and teacher, suggestion on learning, and notification, etc.

4. In class the teacher could adjust the time for instruction and discussion.

5. After class, the teacher could publish today's could deliver the instructional materials, and students could review the essence of course content after class, do

instructional material on web through the authoring tool and keep the teaching pages dynamic by editing at any time. The post-test is also delivered on web through the management tool.

6. To get feedback from students, the teacher could organize discussion on the taught contents as webmaster of the Discussion Area.

7. Students could communicate with teacher via email for questions.

8. Student could examine themselves by post-tests provided.

9. The teacher could track students learning and adjust the method of teaching on the basis of information collected from the Discussion Area, Question Answering Area and statistics of post-tests

4.2: Effect Analysis

The system provides a platform, on which teacher some post-tests, and exchange ideas in the Discussion Area with teacher and each other. The medium of network

854

creates free space for participants, thus arousing their enthusiasm for communication. The combination of a variety of interactions also helps increase the actual efficiency and student involvement in communication. In this sense, the network acts as the extension of classroom, which has diversified the roles of both teacher and students, and given the teacher more control over the instructional process. It can be concluded that the web assistance system has improved the effect of classroom instruction.

5. Proposal for Improvement

There still leave much work to do for the improvement of the instructional system established. For instance, the efficiency and accuracy of the user management module within the system could be greatly improved by sharing data with the well-developed University EMIS. Besides, though developed for course Engineering Mechanics originally, the authoring tool is applicable as well to similar courses, which are noted for the teachers' full utilization of electronic presentation together with excellent verbal skill. For courses of other types, however, the tool may not serve well.

We have developed course-targeted small-size system in preference to universal large-size platform for the reason that it is the best choice at present. On the other hand, we'll continue analyzing features of various courses and developing correspondent web-based instructional system. Only when the works accumulated are ample enough, could we have a deep understanding on the generality and peculiarity of these small-size systems, and even go further to the construction of a large-size platform. A universal platform developed this way, we believe, may be more accessible and usable to the teachers.

A Study of the Vocational Teachers' Knowledge Management Platform

Dr. Rong-Jui Fong,, Dr. Hung-Jen Yang & Cheng-fu Chiang
Department of Industrial Technology Education
National Kaohsiung Normal University
Taiwan, R.O.C.

Abstract

The basis of the research is Ikujiro Nonaka and Hirotaka Takeuchi's knowledge management theory so as to develop junior high vocational teachers' knowledge management platform and to provide the practical training community the mechanism for the dialogue space and knowledge sharing. Therefore, it could assist the vocational teachers to make good use of the critical knowledge of teaching, administration, preceptors' practice and on-the-job learning activities, which is expected to promote the acquirement, application, dissemination and creation of knowledge for the sake of practice teachers' professional growth. The method of the research adopts systematical research. The researcher deals with the need analysis by the knowledge chain of the practical training community, including the practical guidance professors, practical guidance teachers and practice teachers. The researcher also collects the documents and individual experiences of the practical training community's critical knowledge, which is built and managed by the platform.

Introduction

The research purpose was to probe into the need for junior high vocational teachers' knowledge management platform system development; the research method adopts systematic one; the research analyzed the needs for the platform system development by one knowledge chain formed by practical training community, then, proved the need by applying Ikujiro Nonaka and Hirotaka Takeuchi's knowledge management theory and finally, established the conclusion.

The research structure was firstly, to proceed the inference and conception of the systematic need by the critical knowledge related the outer environment, the knowledge management platform and to prove it by Hirotaka Takeuchi and Takeuchi's knowledge management theory. The research subject was the junior high vocational teachersl..

The 21st century is the age of knowledge economy. Peter Drucker indicates in the book of Post-Capital Society that the future will be the society of knowledge economy, and the knowledge capital will replace the traditional productive elements: capital, land and labor. If we can code, disseminate and share the professional knowledge and experiences, it's more efficient to assist the practice teachers and progress the educational quality. (Woodell, 2001)[1]

The check-up standard

The researcher uses Nonaka and Tajeuchi's knowledge management theory as the check-up standard of this research.

1. The models of knowledge conversion's knowledge is created by socialization, externalization, combination and internalization. Its knowledge is resonance, conception, system and operation.
2. Knowledge spiral means the alternation and results of continuous interaction between tacit and explicit knowledge and knowledge transformation.

The process analysis of the platform system

The structure of the process is as follows:

1. Decide the topic of knowledge chain: Find out the critical knowledge and flow path in the knowledge chain.
2. Draw the process graph of knowledge chain: The purpose is to create the most valuable knowledge, information and data for the practice teachers from the knowledge chain.
3. Draw the internet graph of knowledge chain: Find out the location of knowledge and the people who have the knowledge.
4. Decide the structure of knowledge: The structure is divided into employees, knowledge content and technology.
   a. Employees : The school is the non-profit organization that promotes the teaching quality and innovation mainly, and uses the existed practical community to make teachers cooperate.
   b. Knowledge content: This discusses how to collect, make up, save, send and create knowledge and how to build the common resource categories and knowledge contents to share knowledge..

c. Technology: About the application of information technology, we pay attention to the on-location equipments in school.

The need for systematic function

1. Entrance website: The platform is the web interface. The user can access information quickly by the browser. Offer personal entrance website, inclusive of personal workshop, community workshop and knowledge database.
2. Document knowledge database management: Mostly, knowledge is expressed by documents so the document management is the center of knowledge management. This can offer consultant, information, knowledge, discussing single document window with more convenient knowledge sharing environment.
3. Subject knowledge database management: This can offer teachers to collect, save, apply and create knowledge.
4. Building the community : Create and accumulate knowledge organization by the practical community.
5. Sharing knowledge: Offer the operation environment of critical flow path, critical knowledge resource categories, the blank structuralized files of knowledge in each step, practical files and knowledge sharing.
6. Interaction: This is one channel to send information and consult. The members of the community can offer information, share experiences, discuss and communicate with emails.

7. Systematic management : Offer users to access websites and limit the right of released documents. Make proper information security control according to different users.

The research found the knowledge content has 7 categories and four attributes.

Conclusions

According to the research result, the researcher offers the conclusions as follows.

1. The result after proving fits in with the theory knowledge spiral and the model of knowledge conversion by Nonaka and Takeuchi's the knowledge management.
2. The result of the platform need: the need for systematic content has nine flow paths, seven categories and four attributes. The need for systematic function offers seven functions.
3. The concrete structure of the need of junior high vocational teachers' knowledge management platform is as follows:

References

[1]Woodell, J. (2001). Knowledge Networks in the Education Enterprise. *Multimedia Schools*, 8(2), pp. 48-51.

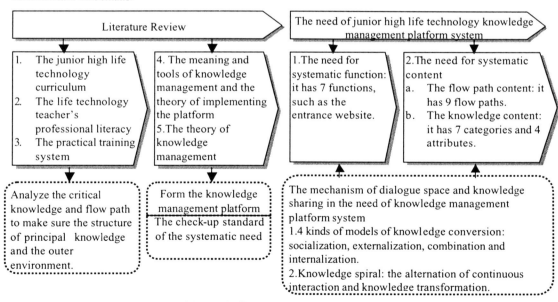

Figure 1: The concrete structure of the need of junior high vocational teachers' knowledge management platform

Remote Lecture Based on Instruction with Blackboard Using High-Quality Media Systems

Toshihiro Hayashi   Kenzi Watanabe   Yukuo Hayashida   Hiroki Kodo
Faculty of Science and Engineering, Saga University
E-mail Address: {hayashi, hayasida, watanabe, h_kondo}@is.saga-u.ac.jp

Abstract

Recently, various kinds of high-quality media systems have been developed. It is expected that these systems can be used to remote lectures. We are adopting these systems including high-speed network to construct a remote lecture based on "Instruction with Blackboard", which provides old-fashioned but very common style of lecture. This instruction style has been often avoided in remote lecture so far, because it requires high-quality data transmission. However, it is no doubt that this style of instruction is very popular teaching way still now. Therefore, it is educationally meaningful that this teaching way is realized on remote lecture. This paper describes a construction method of the remote lecture based on Instruction with Blackboard and the experiment on the remote lecture using high-quality media systems.

1: Introduction

Recently, information network has been rapidly developed so that there have been a lot of academic research and activities about remote lecture[1]. In the remote lecture environment, teachers generally tend to use computer-based presentation tools because of the use of narrow bandwidth networks. As for the traditional lecture style, use of blackboard is very popular. In the style, instructors construct their lecture with writing educational contents on the blackboard. We call this style "IB2: Instruction with BlackBoard" hereafter. It is no doubt that IB2 is very popular way for teaching still now. Therefore, it is educationally meaningful that IB2 is realized on remote lecture.

More recently, several high-quality media systems have been developed in both domains of hardware and software. In addition, we can now use high-speed network such as gigabit networks which can transmit high-quality image data. These technical advantages can suggest that IB2 can be adopted in remote lecture. However these systems and high-speed network are not originally oriented to constructing remote lecture. This is our main motivation to investigate how to construct remote lecture based on IB2 using high-quality media systems, and we have proposed the construction model of remote lecture

based on IB2 and done the preliminary experiments using DVTS[2] on LAN environment[3, 4].

As for the latest our experiment, we have realized a remote lecture based on IB2 using Digital Video devices with IEEE1394 interface[5], notebook computers installed DVTS and JGN(Japan Gigabit Network)[6] between Saga University and Tokushima University in Japan. In this paper, we describe the method of remote lecture based on IB2 and the latest experiment on the remote lecture using high-quality media systems including high-speed network.

2: Outline of our remote lecture

We experimented on remote lecture base on IB2 between Tokushima University and Saga University in Japan. The instructor was in a studio of Tokushima University and gave 90 minute lecture to students in a lecture room of Saga University via JGN.

Figure 1 shows the total system configuration of the remote lecture. Saga University and Tokushima University are connected through JGN. We can use 135Mbps network at Saga University and 50Mbps network at Tokushima University. We used DVTS for transmitting voice and image data. DVTS can transmit DV frames (including voice and image data) encapsulated into UDP packets via Internet. DVTS does not compress data so that the data transmission requires approximately 32Mbps bandwidth. In this experiment, huge data transmission could be realized by using mainly DVTS and JGN.

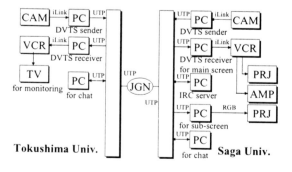

Figure 1: system configuration of remote lecture

3: Circumstances of the remote lecture

Figure 2 shows a snapshot of the circumstances of the lecture room. The remote lecture successfully progressed as same as normal lecture. Our experiment staffs tried to compare the atmosphere of the remote lecture with that of normal lecture, but they could not fined obvious differences between two lectures in the level of subjective evaluation.

Figure 2. Circumstances of lecture room

4: Evaluation

After our experiment on the remote lecture, we sent out questionnaires in order to investigate students' impression to our remote lecture. Main items of the questionnaires are about quality of image and sound (voice), and necessity of the Sub-screen. We did normal lectures before this remote lecture. As for the quality of image and sound (voice), we had them to compare these two lectures. **Table 1** shows the results of our questionnaires.

From the questionnaire results of the item 1, 2, and 3, it is found that many students did not feel the quality of image and sound was different between two types of lectures. We think high-quality data transmission by DVTS has influence on the evaluation result. We can also suggest that DVTS can provide high-quality dada transmission enough to construct remote lecture based on IB2. From the questionnaire results of the item 4, we can strongly argue that the Sub-screen is necessary for remote lecture based on IB2. From these results, we can say this remote lecture was well-designed in this experiment and high-quality media systems worked well in the remote lecture.

Table 1: Results of questionnaires

	Bad	Not so good	Same	Good	Very good
1. Easy to watch written characters ?	1	10	13	4	7
2. Easy to identify colors ?	2	10	10	4	9
3. Easy to listen the instructor's voice ?	1	4	11	6	13
	Strongly no	No	Fair	Yes	Strongly yes
4. Need sub-screen ?	1	0	3	8	23

5: Summary

In this paper, we described the experiment using high-quality media systems including high-speed network. In this experiment, we have confirmed remote lecture based on IB2 can be constructed using high-quality media systems and our lecture construction design could provide similar lecture environment with normal lecture. However, this remote lecture does not put emphasis on the rich interaction between the instructor and students. As for our future work, we must improve the remote lecture style focusing on enhancing rich interactions and we also consider how to adopt high-quality media systems for satisfying this requirement.

References

[1] Engineering Outreach at the University of Idaho, "*Distance Education at a Glance*", http://www.uidaho.edu/evo/distglan.html

[2] Hayashi, T., Watanabe, K., Hayashida, Y. and Kondo, H.: "Distance lecture based on instruction with blackboard", *ITHET01: International Conference on Information Technology Based Higher Education and Training, published as CD-ROM*(2001).

[3] Hayashi, T., Watanabe, K., Hayashida, Y. and Kondo, H.: "Remote Lecture Based on Instruction with Blackboard Using High-Quality Audio/Video Stream", *ICCE2001: International Conference on Computers in education*, pp.910-913 (2001).

[4] Wide Project: "DVTS", http://www.sfc.wide.ad.jp/DVTS/

[5] Apple Computer inc.: "FireWire", http//www.apple.co.jp/firewire

[6] Telecommunications Advancement Organization: "JGN: Japan Gigabit Network": http://www.jgn.tao.go.jp/english/index_E.html

Remote Meteorological Observation System and Interactive Data Publishing on Web with XML for Science Education

Masato SOGA, Kengo NIINOBE, Yoshiharu MORIMOTO, Motoharu FUJIGAKI, Atsushi NAKAJIMA, Hiroki TANIKAWA, Masahumi MIWA, Hiroshi YAMADA, Koji KATO

Faculty of Systems Engineering, Wakayama University,
930 Sakaedani, Wakayama, 640-8510 Japan
E-mail: soga@sys.wakayama-u.ac.jp

Abstract

We developed a remote meteorological observation system and interactive data publishing system on web. Meteorological sensors collect data and send it to DBMS. When students retrieve past data on the web, the data are brought with XML. Therefore the data can be transformed by XSLT with XSL style format in accordance with students' demand. The system has flexible GUI by using XML. Also the system can generate some pairs of problem and answer automatically to learn meteorology. This system will contribute to science education.

1. Introduction

Traditionally meteorological data was observed by meteorological observatory and satellites. People can get the data by weather forecast on TV or Web. However, those data is macro data, so that people cannot know detail data where they live. Especially Japan has a lot of mountains, lakes, rivers and the sea. Every climate differs from each other. Weathers in some small areas are much different from weather in macro area which includes the small areas.

In this background, we developed a remote meteorological observation system using Internet. The system collects meteorological data by sensors, such as air temperature, humidity, air pressure, wind direction and wind force, etc. Also the system publishes them on the web automatically.

Similar systems were developed in the past [1]-[5], but those systems publish the data by static form on the web. They had less flexibility for the interaction between students. Students could not demand the style of display such as graph and tables. Our system can change the style format of display in accordance with the demand from students. The system is enough flexible to show the data in a various forms.

This system is applicable to science education in elementary or high schools. Students can get the meteorological data in every one hour on the web. For instance, they can learn the relationship between weather and temperature or humidity, comparing the weather they saw from the window and data on the web from the sensor. They can study change of wind direction and wind force while low pressure is passing around their region. If we install the system in the high density in a small area such as one city, students can collect the data as micrometeorology. For example, students can study the difference of temperature between a park and top of a building in the same city.

Since the data are published on web, students can observe many data in various places simultaneously. Students can compare data between different places. Moreover the data are stored into database. Students can look up past data, not only the data in the day time, but also during nights. Students can use 24 hours data in different places.

Moreover, our system can generate some pairs of problem and answer to learn or study meteorology. This point also distinguishes the system from others.

2. System composition

We designed the system to realize two demands simultaneously. The two demands are as follows.

(1) Meteorological sensor collects a lot of data everyday that it is necessary to manage the huge amount of data.

(2) Students demand various retrieval and display style of result to the system. Therefore the system must be able to reply the demands flexibly.

To solve the demand (1), it is necessary to use database management system (DBMS). DBMS enables to manage huge amount of data easily. Also DBMS enables to retrieve necessary data very quickly. However, DBMS does not have flexibility for user interface. Moreover Students have to learn SQL to retrieve something from DBMS. SQL is not easy for users who do not know the computer system well. Also, DBMS cannot satisfy with the demand (2).

By this reason, we used CGI and XML for the interface between users and DBMS. Figure 1 shows the system composition. The system prepares menu for retrieval. The examples of retrieval or demands are as follows.

(a) Retrieve specific data on a certain day and time

(b) Demand a graph of temperature in a day

(c) Demand a graph of amount of rainfall in a month

(d) Retrieve days which had over 20 degrees temperature

These retrieval or demands are sent to database by Java Server Pages (JSP) in a database server. The JSP translates the demands into appropriate SQL commands. We used PostgreSQL as the DBMS. JSP translates the result from the DBMS into XML data. Then the XML data is displayed by transformed by XSLT with XSL style sheet. Appropriate XSL style sheet is selected in accordance with students' demand. The system prepares various XSL style sheets such as graphs and tables. Therefore the system can reply students' demand and retrieval flexibly.

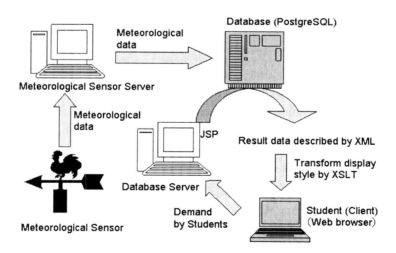

Figure 1. System composition

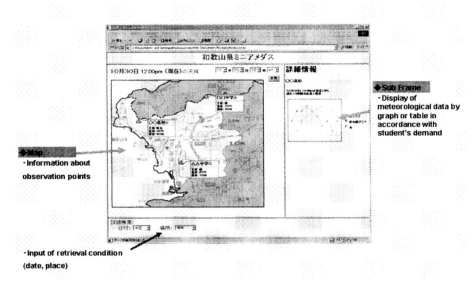

Figure 2. Graphical User Interface

3. Graphical user interface

Figure 2 shows graphical user interface (GUI) for the system. The GUI consists of three frames. Main frame has a map of the region where meteorological sensors are installed. Students can easily know the place of the observation points, and understand the environment, such as river side, city center, or country side. The map helps the students to understand relationship between meteorological data and environment of the observation points from the view point of micrometeorology.

Sub frame shows meteorological data in accordance with students' demand such as graph or table. This frame is necessary for students to answer the questions generated by the system.

4. Understanding of meteorology and problem generation

What is necessary for understanding meteorology? Figure 3 is a chart of learning plan in meteorology. Meteorology is classified into two large parts, they are global meteorology and micrometeorology. Our system assists students to observe and understand micrometeorology. Students can observe meteorological data by our system. Then they can analyze the relationship between the meteorological data and land data. Land data are the data which affects climate in micrometeorology. For instance, they are land shape or environment, such as northern slope of hill, top of the hill, top of a building, river side, sea side, on the farm, etc.

Meteorological data are described with XML, so it is possible for the system to understand what every datum is. Therefore the system can generate problems for exercise. Problem examples for elementary school students are as follows.

(1) Answer highest temperature yesterday.

(2) Answer the day which rained most last month.

These two problems are solved by looking up past data. Students need abilities to read graph. Reading graph ability is one of most necessary ability for science learning.

(3) Answer hottest place yesterday.

This problem is solved by looking up past data. Students need abilities to compare graphs. The system can generate automatically these (1)-(3) problem and answer. If the students are smart enough, the problem (3) give a chance for them to analyze the relationship between meteorological data and land data in figure 3.

Problem examples for high school students are as follows.

(4) Built a micro atmospheric circulation model

This problem is concerning to (3). Unfortunately the answer of this problem is so complicated that the system cannot generate it automatically, however, this problem is interesting enough for students with good science teacher.

(5) Answer the trajectory on which a low pressure or typhoon went by analyzing wind direction.

(6) Answer the date and time when a cold front passed.

These two problems are rather for global meteorology. Strong low pressure and typhoon have always a rule that they have counterclockwise wind into their center in the northern hemisphere. Using

the rule, it is possible for the system to generate answer of problem (5). The answer of problem (6) is also possible to generate by the rule of temperature difference between before and after the cold front.

5. Conclusion

In this paper, we described remote meteorological observation system and interactive data publishing on web with XML for science education. We suggested how to use database and XML simultaneously. The system can have flexible user interface with XML. Also we described the problem generation by the system for learning meteorology. XML enables the system to generate some pairs of problems and answers automatically.

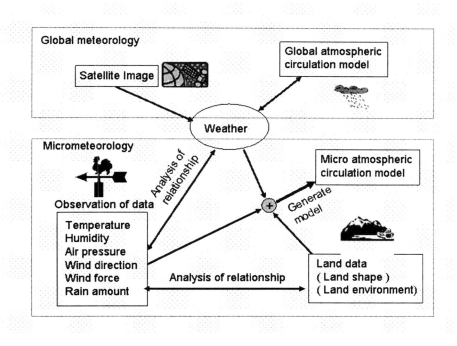

Figure 3. Learning plan in meteorology

References

[1]   Project   Wind   home   page
http://walkone.hus.osaka-u.ac.jp/wroot/wind/   (in
Japanese)

[2] Takanezawa today   http://www.tochigi.com/cam/
(in Japanese)

[3]   Lumcon   current   weather
http://weather.lumcon.edu/

[4]   Les   Condition   Presentes
http://cafe.rapidus.net/raymagny/raymagny/newpage1
.htm (in French)

[5]Weather   conditions   at   West   Auckland
http://snoopy.falkor.gen.nz/weathercgi/weather.cgi

A Development of Classroom Design Simulator for Interactive Video Teleconference

Satoshi YAMAZAKI   Naoto NAKAMURA

yamazaki@nao.net.it-chiba.ac.jp nakamura@nao.net.it-chiba.ac.jp

Chiba Institute of Technology
Department of Network Science
Narashino, Chiba, Japan 275-0016

Youzou MIYADERA   Setsuo YOKOYAMA

miyadera@u-gakugei.ac.jp   yokoyama@u-gakugei.ac.jp

Tokyo Gakugei University
Department of Information Science
Koganei, Tokyo, Japan 184-8501

Abstract

"Visual Field Record System" is aim to support participant's behavior analysis in distance education using interactive video teleconference system. An examination of the eye camera position is important to use the system effectively. Because the camera's angle and zoom rate is considered participant's behavior in this system. Actually, there are some problems that it originates in the camera position at the system. We approached these problems by developing the eye camera install-simulator including arrangement of the classroom equipments. This simulator is called Classroom Design Simulator.

In this paper, it describe about functions and operations of the simulator. After that, the system is evaluated by the application to a case. It was shown that this system was useful for a distance education planner as a result.

1. Introduction

In the broadband network age, participants such as students or teachers are able to join in a distance classroom by interactive video teleconference system individually. The system is usually composed from video monitor and eye camera that is remote controlled via network.

On the evaluation of the educational effectiveness using these educational systems, participant's behavior is important. The evaluation can be analyzed from records of the participant's behavior.

In Figure 1, Participant's visual field is equivalent to the eye camera's view. In other words, the visual field is the combination with the two functions. One of the functions is recording eye camera's status such as current zoom rate, pan, and tilt. Another function is recording eye camera's linear video image.

On above philosophy, "Visual Field Record System" has already proposed and developed [1]. The system has following functions.

- Display change of the visual field graphically.
- Enumerate watching time of each visual field.
- Calculate total watching time at the selected visual field range.
- Automatic pick-out visual fields by pattern such as a change of pan, tilt, and zoom.
- Search and show a video image corresponding to visual field from recorded linear image.

Using this VFR system, some problems are pointed out. One of the problems is relationship between classroom equipment's location and a camera's position. For example, a participant such as a teacher who has to look at student's expression will want to take a close-up of their faces. Only when the relationship is appropriate, the participant is able to start the action.

Therefore, a simulator that is able to install a camera in consideration of the classroom equipment's location is necessary. It is called Classroom Design Simulator. Using this simulator, the relationship between equipments and eye camera can be confirmed in advance.

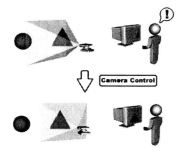

Figure 1. Relationship between camera view and participant's view

2. Classroom Design Simulator

Classroom Design Simulator is composed by the following two sub-systems. A relationship between two sub-systems is shown in Figure 2.

Classroom authoring sub-system is able to arrange classroom equipments including eye camera in the 3D virtual space. Screenshot is shown in the figure 3. A designer (distance education planner) has to arrange a distance classroom with this system firstly. A designer is able to install an eye camera with confirming its view range at this stage. In the same way, multiple cameras can be installed in one classroom.

Secondly, The designer evaluates a camera position by using the camera control simulator sub-system. By evaluation from camera view, we can discover problems such as objects out of range, objects override at same range, and etc. The designer arrange again back to the classroom authoring sub-system if necessary. Though this system is usually controlled by the control device, it has the function which inputs recorded camera's status data by Visual Field Record System, too. That is, a problem can be discovered quickly in the design of the classroom which in distance education has already been done.

Outline of each sub-system's function is following.

Classroom authoring sub-system
- An arrangement of the classroom equipments such as deck, chair, laboratory table and etc.
- Building of the wall, the ceiling, and etc.
- A setting of the camera position.
- Viewpoint is freedom.
- Load presetting class style such as Japanese hi-school, hi-school laboratory, and etc. And customize it.
- Import 3D Model data by Other Modeling tools.

Camera control simulator sub-system
- Authoring classroom can be evaluated from camera view, by calling the view change function of classroom authoring sub-system.
- Loading and setup performance information of the eye camera such as maximum zoom rate, move range, controlled latency and etc.
- Camera control with a controller to use in Visual Field Record System
- Camera control from recorded eye camera's status data by Visual Field Record System

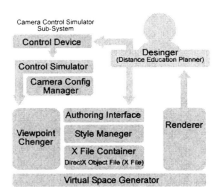

Figure 2. Classroom Authoring Sub-System

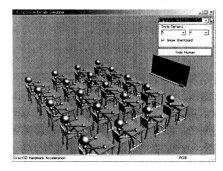

Figure 3. Classroom Authoring Sub-System

3. Conclusion

We have already been analyzed pre-service teacher training using Visual Field Record System at the distance hi-school science laboratory. There were some problems that it originated from the eye camera's position. For example, a part of the chemical apparatus couldn't be watched by a limit of the eye camera range.

Using Classroom Design Simulator at this classroom, it is discovered that a camera's direction is not suitable for analysis aim. In addition, an improvement plan that is able to watch a detail of the apparatus could be re-designed.

From the above result, this system is effective in the design of the distance classroom. It was more effective with the case that many cameras were installed in the distance classroom.

References

[1] Satoshi YAMAZAKI, Ken HIRAGA Naoto NAKAMURA, Youzou MIYADERA, Setsuo YOKOYAMA, "Visual Field Record System for the Purpose of the Behavior Analysis in Distance Education", *ITHET2001 CD-ROM p.No 132*

Internet-based Japanese Language Learning System for Handwriting Kanji Characters Beautifully

Kazuaki Ando, Toshinori Yamasaki
Faculty of Engineering, Kagawa University
2217-20 Hayashi, Takamatsu 761-0396, JAPAN
{ando, yamasaki}@eng.kagawa-u.ac.jp

Naoko Yamashita
Faculty of Education, Kagawa University
1-1 Saiwai, Takamatsu 760-8522 JAPAN
nyamash@ed.kagawa-u.ac.jp

Abstract

Japanese character consists of several kinds of characters such as Hiragana, Katakana, and Kanji. It is difficult to read and write Japanese characters for foreigners from the alphabetical culture area because the structure of them is more complicated than that of alphabetic character. This paper describes a training system for handwriting Japanese characters beautifully in the Internet environment. The learner can acquire the stroke order that is the fundamental handwriting skills of Japanese character. Everybody practices how to write beautiful Kanji repeatedly according to the suitable guidance from a Web server, and always uses this system from anywhere, since our system uses the information communication technology.

1. Introduction

The several interesting education systems which use Internet technology are proposed with the spread of the network society. In the geography learning through web reference, we can compare the world wide geography and meteorology with the local one where we live in, and can learn the characteristic of the weather. The real time observation science learning is interesting in the advanced science subject, where the remote control of the expensive equipment and the star observation by telephoto lens located the remote place. The new style social subject learning is reported using the electronic distinct contents including the historical and cultural resources. As the learning by internet tools enables us to learn always, anyone, anywhere, the learning person can grapple more actively with the problem which it should solve. In the learning by the internet tools, we can interchange easily with the students who have the similar learning subjects. Also, in the internet learning, we can do empirical learning compared with the old style learning which was limited only to the classroom because

of spreading the unknown experienced field. Consequently, these new learning systems promote learning opportunity and the life long learning oriented society.

The foreigners who stay in Japan and who want to learn Japanese have been steadily increasing according to remarkable internationalization of Japan. However, the aliens using alphabet languages, such as English, French and so on, are difficult to master how to write Japanese characters correctly, since the structure of them is more complicated than that of alphabetic letter. For example, in order to write beautiful Japanese characters correctly by hand, it is important to write characters according to the suitable writing stroke order. The stroke order is one of the fundamental skills to write a beautiful and suitable character. The correct stroke order is useful for memorizing kanji. However, there is no default rule for the stroke order. The stroke order originated from the empirical writing skill which is devised by a forefather for handwriting beautifully. Therefore, it is hard to master the stroke order for the alien who learns Japanese for the first time. Moreover, the kanji shows the meaning in one character, we raise and create the handwriting to the brush handwriting calligraphy art. Also from this point, we can say that it is important to write kanji beautifully. To acquire the reading and writing of such Japanese characters, it is effective to practice through handwriting Japanese character actually.

From the above described, we are developing internet-based Japanese learning system on using an on-line character recognition technique[3]. We can learn how to write Japanese Kanji characters correctly through handwriting. The learner inputs the practice character by hand. After sending the input data to the Web server, the system compares an input character with a model character in a reference database. Finally, the system gives the learner the suitable guidance how to write characters correctly via Internet. The system has another function. The learner can ask the system about how to write Japanese character suitably, the meaning of Japanese characters, and so on. It is called Question-Answering(QA) module. The learner can practice

867

the way of beautiful handwriting Japanese Kanji characters repeatedly according to the instruction by the system, and get useful information about Japanese characters from anywhere.

2. Internet-based Language Learning System

2.1. The outline of the system

We use the character recognition technique for the language learning system. The purpose, however, is different. The purpose of the character recognition system is to recognize unknown input character. On the other hand, the language learning system knows a kind of the input character beforehand. The language learning system estimates the way of writing Japanese Kanji characters and gives how to write the Kanji characters beautifully.

The figure 1 shows the outline of online character recognition system and our system. In the character recognition, the system does pre-processing such as the noise removal, the normalization of the size and position to the inputted unknown character. Next, the system classifies the input character by feature extractions such as the stroke shape, the cross and contact point of the stroke through comparing the input character with the reference character in the dictionary. On the other hand, the language learning system also does pre-processing and a feature extraction for the inputted known character same as the character recognition system. After that, the system compares an input character and the model character in the reference database. Finally, the system estimates an improper handwriting way and gives the learner the suitable guidance how to write Japanese characters correctly.

Figure 2 shows the outline of our system. The learner inputs a practice character using the tablet or mouse from the Web client. The data of the input character is sent to the Web server through the input/output interface after pre-processing. The system generates the guidance for writing beautiful Kanji character after evaluating a stroke order by comparing the input character and the model one in the reference database. The learner can learn how to write characters correctly according to the guidance from the server. The learner can also ask the system about how to write Japanese character, the meaning of Japanese characters, and so on. It is called Question-Answering(QA) module. The module analyzes the query written by natural language from the user and generates appropriate answers based on the template and query analysis. This paper reports the stroke evaluation module only, because the QA module is not yet completed.

We develop the stroke evaluation part by dividing into 4 modules from the input of the practice character to the stroke order evaluation and the guidance shown in figure 3. The procedure of the processing outline is described below:

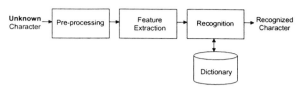

(a) On line character recognition system

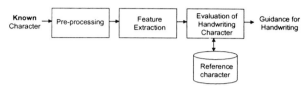

(b) Japanese learning system

Figure 1. Online character recognition system and our system

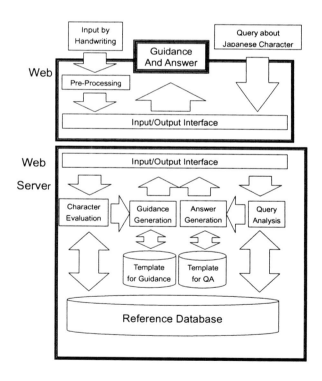

Figure 2. The outline of internet-based language learning system

Client

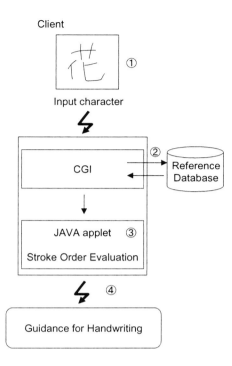

Input character

CGI ②

Reference Database

JAVA applet ③

Stroke Order Evaluation

④

Guidance for Handwriting

Figure 3. The outline of evaluation process

1) The learner inputs a practice Kanji character using the mouse and sends it to the Web server.

2) In the server, the system prepares a model character from the reference database by the CGI program.

3) The system evaluates the stroke order of the input character according to matching the input character and the model one with Java applet.

4) The system gives writing guidance to the client based on the evaluation result for the stroke order.

2.2. On-line input of the practice character and the pre-processing

The learner inputs the handwriting character in the frame by the mouse. The input practice character is a time serious data which consist of the position coordinates ranging written sequence of the character, the system can evaluate the dynamic features such as the stroke order and the writing pen speed, too. Figure 5 shows the Input frame. The size of frame is 30×30[mm]. In the input process, the system displays a sequence of stroke coordinate dynamically. The system normalizes the input character and the reference one to adjust the size and the stroke shape distortion. The system normalizes the characters to 256×256[Dot]. After that, the overlap of the pen point coordinate is excluded(4).

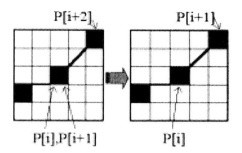

Figure 4. Excluding the overlap of the pen point coordinate

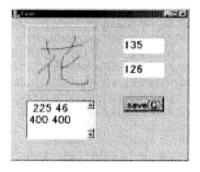

Figure 5. input frame

In this system, we adopt the letter size normalization and the position normalization according to the gravity center of the letter for matching processing of the stroke order evaluation, which is described later. Finally, the data of an input character includes stroke features, such as a termination code of the stroke and an end code of the input character in addition to the position coordinate of the handwriting.

2.3. Reference database

In order to evaluate the stroke order of the practice character, the system refers to a reference database consisting of model characters in the Web server. The reference character database is formed by on-line input of the block style character of the Japanese textbook according to the suitable stroke order. The reference database in this system includes 2000 typical characters of the daily-use Kanji. It contains the stroke order which is based on literature[2] about 2000 daily-use standard character species in Japan. An input character data has 120 bytes, the total size of the reference database is 240KB. Figure 6 shows some Kanji in

Figure 6. Example of Kanji character in the reference database

Figure 7. Character shape

the database.

2.4. Stroke order evaluation

In Japanese language, the stroke order is essential because the number of strokes of a Kanji is greater than that of alphabet. For writing beautiful characters, we must write characters in the proper stroke order. The stroke order can easily be extracted, because the input practice character in this system is a time serious data which consist of the position coordinates ranging written sequence of the character. A proper stroke order is not decided in the rule. The stroke order is taught from the forefather as a traditional writing rule for writing a beautiful handwriting at the moderate speed. For example, the character shape of the handwriting depends on the each stroke order as shown Figure 7.

The stroke order is evaluated in comparison with that of the model character in the database. That is, the input

Model Character j

	1	2	3	4
1	d_{11}	d_{12}	d_{13}	d_{14}
2	d_{21}	d_{22}	d_{23}	d_{24}
3	d_{31}	d_{32}	d_{33}	d_{34}
4	d_{41}	d_{42}	d_{43}	d_{44}

Input character i

Figure 8. Interstroke distance matrix D

character is matched to the model character by using the interstroke distance matrix D. A stroke is represented by three points: start, middle and end points of the stroke data. This method is called the three point stroke approximation. It is effective in case Kanji that has a lot of straight line elements[1].

Suppose that i and j denotes a stroke number of input and reference character, respectively. The element d_{ij} of the interstroke distance matrix D is calculated as follows:

where p_1 and p_2 are the position coordinates of the input and the model character respectively.

Figure 8 shows the example of the interstroke distance matrix D. The i-th stroke of the input character correspond to j-th stroke of the model in which interstroke distance d_{ij} is minimum. In case the proper stroke order, the diagonal elements $d_{11}, d_{22}, \cdots d_{44}$ have the minimum values in each stroke number. For example, the element d_{22} is the minimum among the stroke distance d_{2j} (j=1$\cdots$4) for the 2nd stroke. From the above results, the 2nd stroke of the input character is the proper order. The element d_{34} is the minimum among d_{3j} (j=1$\cdots$4) for the 3rd stroke. In this case, it becomes evident that the 3rd stroke of the input character was improper sequence in writing. This means that the 3rd stroke of the input character must be written at 4th.

3. Experimental Results

The learner inputs a practice character into the frame(figure 5) from the mouse by hand. After inputting a character, the system sends the character data to the Web server (figure 2). The 2000 daily-use kanji are stored in the reference database. The system extracts the model character from the database by CGI, and it compares the stroke order of the input character with that of the model character. The guidance is generated based on the template and the result.

Figure 9. Example of Kanji Learning -Proper Stroke-

Figure 10. Example of Kanji Learning - Improper Stroke-

The system gives evaluation and guidance when the learner inputs a file name and pushes "an execution" button. A learning example is shown in figure 9. In figure 9, the upper and middle part shows the model character, its stroke order, and the practice character, its stroke order, respectively. The lower part in figure 9 shows a distance matrix D among the strokes, evaluation results of the stroke order, and guidance for fair handwriting. The figure 9 shows the proper stroke order in practice handwriting. On the other hand, the figure 10 is the improper stroke order, which is different from the model one. The system points out the mistake of the stroke order. In the 20 times input experiment, the system mistake two examples in the stroke order evaluation.

4. Conclusion

This paper described a internet-based instruction system for writing Japanese characters correctly and beautifully. Our system is focused on learning of the stroke order of Japanese Kanji, which is one of the fundamental skills for writing beautiful Japanese characters. First, the learner inputs a handwriting character by a mouse on the side of the client. The server system evaluates the stroke order of the input character after comparing the input character and the model one in the reference database. The learner can practice how to write character beautifully according to the suitable guidance from the system. Because this system is implemented on the Internet, the learner can practice how to

write Japanese character correctly from everywhere when the need arises.

In this system, learner inputs a handwriting character with a mouse. For the more natural input interface, the tablet-type input device is desirable in this system. Also, the system needs more than one step from the input of the practice character to the output of the evaluation and the guidance. We must revise these problems in the future. Finally, we have to design the question-answering module, also.

Acknowledgement

This research was partially supported by the Ministry of Education, Science, Sports and Culture, Grant-in-Aid for Scientific Research(B)(2), 13558018, Scientific Research(C)(2), 13680242, and Young Scientists Research(B), 14780292.

References

[1] T. K.Odaka and I.Masuda. Stroke order free on-line handwritten character recognition algorithm. *Trans. of IEICE Japan*, J65-D(6):679–686, 1982.

[2] Kume. *Shin-Kanji-Hyou niyoru hitujyun-shidousouran.* Mitsuru Tosho Syuppan, Japan, 1977.

[3] S. T.Yamasaki and Y.Sakurai. Training system for handwriting chinese characters using on-line character recognition. *Trans. of IEICE Japan*, J65-D(10):1211–1218, 1982.

A Web-based Collaborative Enabled Multimedia Content Authoring and Management System for Interactive and Personalized Online Learning

S.N. CHEONG   H.S.KAM   AZHAR K.M.   M. HANMANDLU
Multimedia University, Jalan Multimedia, 63100, Cyberjaya, Selangor, Malaysia
{ sncheong, hskam, azhar.mustapha, madasu.hanmandlu }@mmu.edu.my
http://www.mmu.edu.my

Abstract

This paper describes the design and implementation of a web-based Collaborative enabled Multimedia Content Authoring and Management System (CMCAMS) for organizing, integrating and composing personalized and interactive course notes for online education. A 5-layered architecture is proposed for the CMCAMS and is implemented using the Java 2 Enterprise Edition (J2EE). A Web-based distance education system has been developed over this framework to test its effectiveness. This system enables educators to manage personalized learning materials that are structured, profiled and streamed to students. It will examine the user's profile to identify what level of difficulty to incorporate and what kind of presentation style to adopt based on the bandwidth available to students. The CMCAMS uses XML and XSLT techniques to generates SMIL documents, which form the backbone for educational online materials. The CMCAMS has several essential features: (1) Remote Access (2) Easy to use and (3) Support for Multi-Style.

1: Introduction

In recent years, Information and Communication Technology (ICT) and multimedia technology have increasingly altered the landscape of the educational field particularly in higher education. The revolution in the ICT arena has produced a new age of digitalism, which uses digital media as a way to learn and communicate with each other through a method known as online learning. The use of multimedia or multiple digital media elements in online education is becoming an emerging trend in the communication of educational information. Multimedia "provides a means to supplement a presenter's efforts to garner attention, increase retention, improve comprehension, and to bring an audience into agreement" [1].

Nevertheless, streaming multimedia elements in an online learning environment across the Internet poses great challenges to academicians. First, the bandwidth availability to different students may vary tremendously. Students with a powerful Multimedia PC and a high bandwidth Internet connection will find multimedia an effective instructional medium for delivering information. On the other hand, students with a slow Internet connection will experience a lot of problems in accessing multimedia packed online educational materials. Student's attention span is another main issue. For instance, a student who has had a previous course in Object Oriented Programming might want to skip the introductory concepts and jump straight into APIs, while a beginner would be better off going through the basics. Thus, the current trend of one-size-fits-all online education materials is inadequate. With the flexibility allowed to the digital form of media presentation, an online learning system should try to accommodate the needs of as many different students as possible through personalization. Most people would agree that such a personalization of educational online notes is desirable.

Thus, in this paper we present a "Web-based Collaborative Multimedia Content Authoring and Management System (CMCAMS) for effective interactive and personalized material in online education" that provides a novel approach for organizing, integrating and composing personalized course notes for online education.

2: Design Issues and framework for CMCAMS

Online learning materials, from a student's viewpoint, can be treated as a sequence of webpages. A webpage, of course can contains multimedia elements, hyperlinks and animation. In our methodology, we address three issues that we consider central to producing a flexible and easy to use multimedia content management system:

1. *Remote Access-* It must provide an effective collaboration interface to academicians within an university or between universities in the content production process.

2. *Easy to Use*- It should be relatively straightforward to produce interactive and personalized educational online notes from the digital archive of educational materials.

3. *Support for Multi-Style*- There should exist a method for quickly producing multi-style educational online notes to meet the needs of different students.

We deal with the first issue by developing a web application on top of the J2EE platform [5] that provides a robust scalable system to academic personnel to manage and deliver personalized education materials. It helps organize content from inception through deployment and eventually, to archiving and deletion of education online notes notwithstanding time and location challenges. Instructors from different universities can collaborate by contributing to our centralized database system via an Internet connection. At the same time, they can retrieve and filter content elements from the central database to compose online notes from wherever they are located. It is built using a multi-tier architecture that consists of the following layers: presentation layer, application logic layer, persistence layer, database layer and streaming platform.

Regarding the second issue, educational resource elements are stored in a multimedia database. Individual educational element in the multimedia database is represented by an XML-based conceptual model that consists of different types of information such as subject name, object ID, metadata, date, hyperlinks, version and so on. Our approach treats each of them as a building block Extensive Markup Language (XML) that can be combined together to form a Synchronized Multimedia Integration Language (SMIL) document by using Extensive Markup Language (XSLT) techniques. SMIL is a language for describing interactive synchronized multimedia distributed on the Web [3, 4]. The personalized educational material (SMIL files) is logically divided into two sections: the layout section and the body section. Template designers will work on the layout section by specifying the type and position of content in the SMIL file. The academicians will focus on producing content for the body section without bothering about its presentation. The composition process is accomplished by putting together the edited content into pre-designed templates done by the layout designer and storing it back into the database for final review. Once the content item is completed, the coordinator will publish it to the web for the students. Presentation style that is personalized is achieved by using XSLT stylesheets that convert multiple XML documents into SMIL files by selecting, more or less automatically, the set of suitable presentations according to the student needs. Fig. 1 shows a sample of online multimedia educational material composed with a pre-defined layout using our CMCAMS.

Concerning the third issue, we note that the system should accommodate students of different levels, interests, background and the availability of bandwidth. In our approach, we provide an easy way to generate multi-style content items with the same resource elements. This means that different users may encounter the same content with different multimedia design and level of detail. The deciding factors are based on the student profile. A Web-based educational application for distance education has been developed to test the effectiveness of the proposed CMCAMS framework.

Fig. 1: Sample page created by CMCAMS that arranges content based on a predefined layout chosen according to user needs.

3: Conclusion

In this paper, we have presented the design of a 5-layered web application, built using J2EE i.e. a collaborative enabled multimedia content authoring and management system (CMCAMS). The framework has several novel features when compared to conventional approaches. These include a collaborative environment, a set of management tools for easy content authoring and user profiling and a method for quickly producing multi-style educational online notes to achieve personalization in online learning. The application can be remotely used by relevant personnel without any need of additional hardware or software.

4: References:

[1]   R. Lindstrom, The Business Week Guide to Multimedia Presentations: Create Dynamic Presentations That Inspire, New York: McGraw-Hill 1994, ch2, pp 33-46.

[2]   Lloyd Rutledge, SMIL 2.0 XML for Web Multimedia, *IEEE INTERNET COMPUTING*, Vol. 5, No. 5, 2001, pp.78-84.

[3]   Synchronized Multimedia, *the World-Wide-Web Consortium*, http://www.w3.org/AudioVideo/

[4]   Java™ 2 Enterprise Edition Developer's Guide, *Sun Microsystems Incs.*, http://java.sun.com/j2ee/j2sdkee/techdocs/guides/ejb/html/Dev GuideTOC.html

E-Learning Initiative Based on a WEB-Data-Based University Information Management System

Isidor Kamrat, Franz Haselbacher
Computing and Information Services Center
Technical University of Graz, Austria

Abstract

The Technical University of Graz has started an e-learning initiative to support multimedia methods in Engineering Education. Our first target was to provide all of our courses' documents on the web. Moreover, the use of interactive tools as well as monitoring features and tests will be used. A major factor is internal transparency of our courses' contents, which will result in a better adaptation and demarcation of all courses. Furthermore an improved level of interactions between instructors and students, especially during courses, is aimed for. For this an other purposes our university decided to create an overall information management system which is used as the e-learning portal. So we have designed a data-model from scratch that incorporates all resources of our university. As user-interface we have implemented a WEB-database application, that includes all features of a state-of-the-art intranet-portal.

The E-learning Initiative
1. At the Beginning

The Technical University of Graz has started an e-learning initiative to support multimedia methods in Engineering Education. Our target is to provide all of our courses' documents (scripts, exercises and certain exams) on the world wide web. Moreover, the use of interactive tools (animations, simulations) as well as monitoring features and tests in order to prove your own knowledge, will be used. A major factor is internal transparency of our courses' contents, which will result in a better adaptation and demarcation of all courses. Furthermore an improved level of interactions between instructors and students, especially during courses, is aimed for.

During this starting-phase 12 different projects were subsidised. Those subsidies were only given for personnel costs that resulted from developing contents for existing courses in the web.

For all these projects, there were different goals, as well as methods:

- online course-scripts, developing a didactically appropriate screen-layout
- flash-animation, electronic communication
- java-applets for multiple choice tests
- virtual laboratories

- generic module for online tests ("TUGtor")
- interactive use and adjusting standard software (Matlab)

An eLS-server was installed as the central "learning platform", the TU Graz's central information management system (TUGonline) is used as a portal. At the end of December 2001, 40% of the approximately 3,200 courses had links to electronic scripts, about 5% had links to exercises and certain exams for practising. A central web site was established, primarily used as information and communication-system for instructors, as well as for documentation purposes. Current developments and links to other activities are also provided (http://MML.TUGraz.at).

In order to manage these projects, a co-ordination team and three working groups (AGs) were established. The co-ordination team was responsible for choosing projects, the distribution of resources and had a co-ordinating function. AG1 chose the correct use of IT-tools, AG3 the right didactically methods, and AG2 had to find incentives for instructors – AG2 has not been activated yet.

What are the first experiences with that project? According to an evaluation made by students, there's a good acceptance of the project, especially the possibilities for interaction, the actuality of information, the high level of communication and the innovation itself were rated best, followed by virtual laboratories, tests and self-evaluation programs. The problem, that has to be faced, is the slow transfer-rate of modems at home, as well as the fact that students do not want read and thus learn in front of computer-screens; more printing facilities are required. The wide variety of projects during this phase was very useful, in order to show up the different initial conditions, views and keys. Especially the factor of time was underestimated in the beginning. All experiences were considered and discussed in the AGs.

2. Two projects in detail
Lecture „Fundamentals of Electric Networks"

The lecture „Fundamentals of Electric Networks" was implemented as a Web-Based lecture in the frame of eLS. The aim was to cover topics like network elements, network characteristics, network graph theory, analysis of linear networks including sinusoidal steady-state analysis, resonance circuits, transfer functions and

874

transient analysis. After a short introduction explaining the goals each chapter was divided into a theoretical part with definitions and derivations and into a "virtual lab", where students can get a deeper insight into complex processes, apply their knowledge to simple examples or verify solutions obtained by different methods of solution. For instance, a nodal analysis package, solving both AC and DC networks with independent and dependent sources is available. Students have to transfer the network into a certain form and they get the respective nodal voltage and some additional information as a result All virtual labs were implemented as JAVA applets to make this course as independent of plug-ins as possible. Each chapter concludes with a summary and some questions, which help the student to assess her or his achieved knowledge. Parallel to this course a number of examples corresponding to the individual chapters was developed and converted into HTML format and will be added to the course.

Web-based Education in Bioinformatics: Computer Supported Collaborative Learning Project

Bioinformatics is a new interdisciplinary research area at the interface of biology, medicine, mathematics and computer science. Bioinformatics is concerned with the gathering, analysis, and exploitation of data. Biological data is not only generated in overwhelming amounts today, it is also of a widely disparate nature. The challenge when teaching bioinformatics and other interdisciplinary subjects is to find ways of integrating, correlating and unifying these disparate sources of data. Additionally, the students are faced with an ever-increasing mass of information, which is rapidly updated or even replaced.

In order to overcome these difficulties, i.e. to teach a subject in information intensive, highly dynamic area, we have initiated a Web-based Education in Bioinformatics, a computer supported collaborative learning project at the Graz University of Technology in collaboration with the University in Uppsala (http://www.linnaeus.bmc.uu.se/). The basic concept of the Bioinformatics project is reciprocal, evaluation-based collaborative learning and teaching. We create modularized and linked learning units and assemble these in a web-based learning resource for bioinformatics. We examine how the learning condition is improved by giving the students the opportunity to actively participate in redesigning the web-book based on comments given in daily on-line evaluations. We believe that the concept of using a theory-anchored evaluation approach in a highly dynamic and integrative web-based learning environment that is jointly assembled and evaluated by students and teachers is likely to show its versatility in many other interdisciplinary and rapidly expanding sciences and disciplines in the near future.

3. The next steps

As all projects were a success, not only the results are further used, but they are going to be improved and used in other fields. All instructors are still motivated and they are planning further, improving activities. The central co-ordination and central support of the projects, as well as the web portal were a success. For the further improvement of multimedia-learning at the TUG, clearer goals and main-topics have to be defined.

- Establishment of a centre of competence for co-ordination of all activities and for better technical and didactical support
- New professional didactic concepts
- Creating incentives for instructors
- structural adjustments of study-plans
- who are our "customers"(students at TUG, other education institutions, alumni,...)
- discussion and evaluation of goals, including students' thoughts
- internationalisation
- building an e-learning portal for all education and teaching activities

The WEB-databased university-information-management-system

1. The pushing facts

The major problems concerning the cooperation between the administrational staff and the research- and education-departments:

Lack of an all-enclosing data model

Resources were stored in different databases with no relations between them, therefore it was not possible to get a combined view of resources and their relationships. The main reason for that was the lack of an all enclosing data-model (an entity-relationship-model that includes all the resources of the university). Such a model is needed as the basis for tools maintaining resources and their relations and tools delivering combined views of them.

Collection and manipulation of data by paper

The administration staff has to collect or manipulate data on different resources (personnel, lectures,..) for different reasons (statistics for the head of university or the ministry, printing a curriculum,...). This was done mainly by paper that often lead to incorrect or unsatisfying results. Checking constraints on data collected or manipulated by paper forces immense additional work.

Hands out

Hands out of the lectures were made in different ways. Although they were produced on a computer, no electronic version was offered to the students. A major factor is internal transparency of the courses' contents, which will result in a better adaptation and demarcation of all courses.

These facts lead to the start of a project for setting up a system that should allow a smooth management of resources of our university by different groups.

2. The project

The project started in January 1997. It was driven by some basic rules:
- data should be collected or manipulated electronically at the responsible organization
- each data-item should exist only once in the system, no duplicates, no transfers
- each person on the university should have a personal identification in the system
- the persons privileges in the system should depend on its functions on the university
- only one central database should be used (for maintenance- and support-reasons)

2.1 Decisions on principle questions
The question of „how to start"
There are several alternative answers to that question:
(1) you can outsource the design and the implementation to a company
(2) you can buy a commercial product
(3) you can wait for better products and lower prices
(4) you can do it inhouse
We did an evaluation on the alternatives and came to the conclusion that the costs for outsourcing (alternative one and two) were - and are still - immense high. There are a only a few companies in Europe that offer commercial   university-information-management-systems. In May 1998 the Austrian Universities made an evaluation on these systems and came to the conclusion that there are many constraints typical for austrian universities that cannot be parameterized by default in the systems and therefore have to be programmed additionally. Alternative three was not taken into consideration, because at that time there was a real demand for such a system from the whole university. At the end we decided in cooperation with the leadership of the university that the design and the implementation should be done inhouse by a group of our computing and information services center.

The question of database technology
At that time we had good experience with relational databases of type ORACLE and we decided to use it as database for our system.

The question of the user-interface
We decided the interface to be a standard internet browser, because it's already implemented on nearly every PC.

The question of the programming technology
We decided to use Oracle's PL/SQL as the language to access the database combined with an HTML-library and Java-Scripts. This combination runs very stable and supports nearly every browser-version.

2.2 The entity-relationship(E/R)-model
The design of the E/R-model started from scratch and is the result of many interviews made with the different groups. The whole E/R-model consists mainly of six sub-E/R-models with base-entities representing the base-resources, and the relations between them (see grafic).

The E/R-model has now the size of about 500 entities and is still growing because new applications force the addition of new entities, attributes in existing entities or relations. Despite the size of the model there were only minor changes necessary in the past. This leads us to the conclusion that applications, user-interfaces and programming-technologies change in time but the E/R-model once build, only undergoes minor changes, it is just growing. The full knowledge on the E/R-model gives us the opportunity to act and react very flexible to requirements from the university by changing or adding entities, relations and their proper applications. This is one of the problems with commercial products, where you don't get any information about their E/R-model, you just get access on a meta-level. For us the knowledge on the E/R-model is the most important value for the establishment and maintenance of our system.

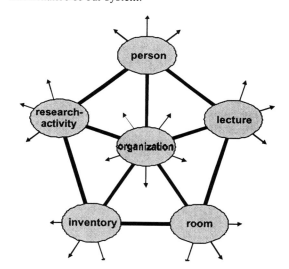

2.3 The application-model
The application-model is designed in a very generic way. It consists of five embedded layers (see grafic). The whole model with its layers is fully integrated in the E/R-model, with each layer as an entity and relations between adjacent layers.

876

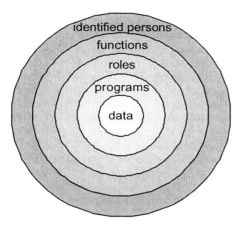

data: are the entities and their relations representing the different resources.

programs: are applications that have access to the data. New applications are planned and invented only in accordance with the leadership of the university. This is very important, because it ensures that the application will be used by concerned groups.

roles: define privileges for programs. Each program is connected to one ore more roles that are unique to it. For example: the role „edit-room" defines the privilege for the program „room-management" to edit the attributes of the „room"-entity in the database.

functions: are the interface between identified persons and roles and therefore define the way for an identified person to access data: identified person -> function -> role -> program -> data.

The relation between function and role, as well as function and identified person is a many to many. This gives us a maximum of flexibility. The attachment of functions to roles is done by the leadership of the university in accordance with our service center.

A function is always connected to an organization, that means a person gets a function only in relation to an organization. Therefore the attachment of functions to identified persons is done by the proper organizations. For example:

- the identified person „John Smith" is connected to
- the function „lecture-manager", that is connected to
- the role „edit-lecture" of
- the program „lecture-management", that operates on
- the data „lectures" of the organization „computing department", to which the function belongs.

The function „lecture-manager" is also defined in any other department.

2.4 The identification-model

One goal designing the identification-model was to allow a very decentralized access-management of the system. The access is given by the function-manager of the organization where a person is working or has a function. Each person as a member of our university has the right to get an access to the system. All students also get a personal access to the system by default.

The identification takes place by simply using the username/password in a login procedure. This procedure stores both values in a so called "realm" of the browser. The realm is sent to the system and checked there each time a transaction takes place. The user is logged in as long as the browser is running. Another way of logging out is by entering an invalid username, for example „anonymous". For the future we are thinking of identification- and access-technology using digital signature. We have already started a project with smartcards using chip-technology.

3. The motivating facts

What the system mainly does is

- to partitionate the maintenance of resource-information between departments and the administration group. That means, that each single resource-item has to be attached to a responsible group.
- to incorporate the major rules and constraints that are needed for maintaining resource-data.

This needs a lot of interviews and discussions with the groups. When you want the system to become accepted by the groups you have to find the motivating facts for each group to use the system. We have listed some of the facts for each group below:

The administration group

In the past each administration subgroup maintained her own database for her resource with no relations to other resources. In our system the relations themselves have to be maintained too, which means additional work for the administration group and the departments. But there are also some benefits the administration group gets out of the system:

- Many data-items are now maintained by departments, that had to be maintained by the administration group in the past
- The WEB-based presentation of the resources and their relations to the whole university leads to an immense feedback concerning the integrity and actuality of data. This helps to keep the data up to date.
- The system allows to integrate administrational constraints in evaluation-masks that was not possible by using paper. Therefore no more controlling of data is needed afterwards.

The other support centers

They cooperate with the departments in a very similar way the administrational group does. Therefore they also can use the system for better management and maintenance of their resources, that are

- books and other multimedia-items like CDs and videos (Library center)
- hardware-configuration, software-licences, network-addresses, etc. (Computing and Information Services Center)
- research-activities and publications (Research & Technology Information Unit)

- statistical information for the leadership of the university, the ministry or other organizations (Rector's staff)

The departments

The system transfers the maintenance of parts of information on all major resources to the departments, which means additional administrational work for them but there are also some benefits:
- They can maintain their resource-data in one single system
- They can do it with tools that offer one „look and feel"-interface
- They can do it independently of time and space, because it is WEB-based.
- They can now manipulate information they always wanted to
- They are maintaining *t h e i r* resource-information and they are not transferring data about resources to the administration staff anymore.
- They get a lot of views on their resources, depending on the relations. One very successful application is the „business-card" of a person. It contains a lot of related resources, some of them can be manipulated and some are maintained by the administration staff and are generated in the view:
    - The name and title (is generated)
    - The organization, the persons belongs to (is generated)
    - The persons telephone-number (is generated)
    - The persons working room (is generated)
    - The persons lectures (is generated)
    - The persons research-activities (is generated)
    - The persons email-address (can be manipulated dynamically)
    - The persons home-page (can be manipulated dynamically)

The leadership

Having a system that offers relations between all resources of the university the leadership can be supported with all kind of views including any select-criteria it wants. These results can be very helpful in the process of making plans, strategies or decisions.

The students

Most of the systems benefits are for students. They can get online up-to-date information on many items:
- lectures and all the resources related to them (person, time, room, ...)
- a view of their curriculum and the actual lectures attached to it
- the relations between resources offer integrated views, where they can navigate to any related information (for example: curriculum -> lecture -> lecturer -> „business card" of the lecturer)
- The system offers browse- and search-applications within each resource, that makes it very easy to find a specific information
- The system is WEB-based, so the students can get the information anywhere and anytime

Using the personal identification in the system the student can take personal actions or get personal information such as:
- Maintain his work- and home-address
- Subscribe/Unsubscribe to a lecture
- Register/Unregister for an examination
- Getting information about his marks
- Getting information about his status quo in the curriculum
- Getting information about his examination dates
- Getting access to the e-learning modules

4. Experiences after four years of operation

The system went into operation in January 1998. Over the years we added a lot of applications offering access to the following resources:
- lectures
- curriculum
- research-activities
- inventory
- rooms
- organizations
- persons „Business card" and functions
- event-calendar
- hostname

The impact of the system to the different groups can be categorised in the following manner:

Acceptance

The system was first accepted by the different groups with some precaution. But over the years the groups began to recognize, that this system really fits their needs for information-management.

One of the most accepted features in the system is the business card of a person, where the person gets all the related resources (lectures, research-activities, organization, address, telephone-number, functions, …) automatically generated from the system.

Ideas

Many people came up with ideas concerning existing applications which lead to a long list of additional features to be implemented. All groups that are managing information in cooperation with departments recognized the benefits of the system and came up with new ideas for future applications. Together with the leadership of the university we had to set up a priority-list of new applications to be integrated in the system.

5. The next steps

The following items are part of the new version:
- A user-definable view on the system
- A navigation-system that is clear and easy
- Enough space on the screen for the information the user selects
- Full integration of all e-learning activities on the Campus

Case Retrieval in CBR-Tutor

Rhodora L. Reyes and Raymund C. Sison
College of Computer Studies, De La Salle University- Professional Schools Inc.
rhoda@ccs.dlsu.edu.ph, raymund@ccs.dlsu.edu.ph

Abstract

CBR-Tutor is an Internet agent-based tutoring system that uses case-based reasoning approach in providing adaptive instruction to its learners [5]. Cases can quickly recognize whether a teaching strategy is relevant to apply in a given situation. It is composed of four types of agents. These are the System Agent (SA), Case Facilitator Agent (CFA), Case-Based Information Agent (CIA) and Case-Based Tutor Agent (CTA). The CTAs interact directly with the learner. It has a set of local cases, which are commonly used. If the local cases are not useful for the new situation, the CTA will request retrieval from the global set of cases. The CIAs are responsible for storing and retrieving cases from the global case libraries. These cases contain situations experienced by the CTAs in the system. This paper presents how cases are retrieved in CBR-Tutor.

1.0 Introduction

CBR-Tutor is an Internet agent-based tutoring system that uses case-based reasoning approach in providing adaptive instruction [5]. It is composed of agents that retrieve useful teaching cases, reuse, adapt, repair and learn these cases. The first process in a CBR-cycle is the retrieval of useful and similar cases. [6] discussed how a case is indexed and organized, which are important factors in the retrieval process. The indexes and the organization of indexes help the case retrieval find in the case library (or memory) the experience closest to the new case. Once the most appropriate case is selected, the case is reused and whenever an old situation is not exactly the same as the new situation, adaptation is done.

This paper discusses how cases are retrieved in CBR-Tutor. Section 2 discusses the case retrieval methods of CBR-Tutor. An illustration on how similar cases are retrieved is also presented. We conclude in Section 3 with a the summary and discussion of the retrieved cases and ongoing research.

2.0 Case Retrieval

Case retrieval does not only focus on the similarity among cases, it must be able to find useful cases that are similar to the new problem that will help the reasoner (Case-based Tutor Agent) performs its given tasks. Before retrieving, a reasoner must be able to anticipate problems so that the reasoner can retrieve cases that avoid them [4].

In CBR-Tutor, the CIAs are mainly responsible for retrieving useful cases. However, CTAs can also retrieve from its local case-based library[1] and only requests for retrieval of cases to the CFA if it doesn't have an appropriate case[2]. For the CIA to be able to achieve its main tasks, it has to evaluate and filter cases. As all other case retrievals, case retrieval in CBR-Tutor has a combination of searching and matching. The algorithm for retrieving cases is described in Listing 1.

2.1 Assessing Situation

Situation assessment is the process of analyzing and elaborating the current case (or situation) for retrieval and organizing cases for learning. In case retrieval, the first step is to assess the situation. The *feature attributes* (or slot[3]) of a case are fixed but it is possible that some of the attributes don't have values. The purpose of the situation assessment is to identify what possible indexes will be used.

---

[1] The local case-based library contains the most recently used cases by the Case-based Tutor Agent (CTA).

[2] The retrieval method used by the CTA is different and simpler than the method used by the CIA because it stores only few cases. It uses the *serial-search-partial-match* retrieval method.

[3] The term *attribute* and *slot* are used interchangeably in this paper.

```
     For each of the CIA assigned to retrieve:
1.   The new case is analyzed, elaborated and indexed
     (situation assessment procedure)
2.   The indexes for the new situation and the anticipators
     (both output of step 1) are used to search the case library;
     while searching:
          a.   Matching procedure is called to assess the
               degree of match between the new situation and
               cases in the case library
          b.   Degree of match is assessed in each dimension
          c.   Partially-match cases are returned
3.   CIA analyzes returned case(s) by ranking the cases from
     highest to lowest, to determine useful cases.
4.   If several cases are returned, the  case with the highest
     rank is selected and  prepared for adaptation
```

Listing 1. CBR-Tutor's case retrieval algorithm.

Elaboration is done by identifying the observable and predictive features (features that have values) in the new case. It is possible that several elaborations will be suggested and it will be expensive if all suggested elaboration would be done. Since the organizational structure of the cases is designed as *prioritized redundant discrimination network* [7], elaboration is generally suggested by priority. One important task of the *situation assessment procedure* is that it tells the retriever of *potential problems* so that the retriever can try to find plans that avoid these problems during *adaptation*. This procedure uses the information determined by CTA (particularly the *evaluation module*) to predict problems when new goals or situations come in. The information contains the *goal* and the *feedback, failed_feature and new_feature_value attributes* that states if the plan succeeds or is modified. This information is stored in the *situation assessment list of anticipators*. Listing 2 shows how situation assessment is done.

For example, given the current case's index and anticipators as follows,

Current case's index	**Anticipator's features**
(event <Tutor initiate>)	event=(<Tutor Initiate>)
(goal< Introduce New Concept>)	topic = (<Classes, Objects>)
(topic <Classes, Objects >)	learner_goal= (<nil>)
(learner_goal <nil>)	student_level= (<Average>)
(learning_style < nil >)	error_per_topic=(<nil>)
(student_level <Average >)	failed_feature = (<learning style = nil>)
(error per topic <nil >)	new_feature_value = (<visual>)

The *failure anticipator* in the example is the *learning style* attribute. The value of the *new_feature_value* indicates the value that should be substituted to avoid failure. The anticipator is the result of evaluation of the previous cases (cases stored in the case library). It is taken from the *outcome* part of a case. Given the new situation and the anticipator, the situation assessment algorithm states that the values of the corresponding feature should be compared to the value of the failed feature. If they are the same then it means that there is a great possibility that the plan that will be retrieved having these values will cause a problem (based on experience of the reasoner). Thus, the situation assessment procedure will replace the values of the feature attributes with the suggested values (*new_feature_value*) to avoid future problems. This is also true in real world experience. Whenever a teacher anticipates that the student will be asking for more examples, the teacher will include in its plan that an additional example will be given to the student.

```
1.   If the request type is to retrieve a case then
     1.1.   Identify the goal of the new case
     1.2.   Given the goal,
            1.2.1.   Search the list of, look for the attribute that has the same goal and attributes
            1.2.2.   Identify the features that are possible anticipators (failed feature)
            1.2.3.   Compare the values of the failed feature and values of the corresponding feature in the current case
            1.2.4.   If the same then
                     1.2.4.1.If the request is to add a case then remove the value failed_feature  in the list of indexes
                     1.2.4.2. If the request is to retrieve a case then replace the values of the features with the suggested values
                     1.2.4.3. Otherwise, do not consider anticipators
     1.3.   Index the case including the anticipators
            1.3.1.   Identify features (attributes) in the situation description that have values (i.e., value is not nil)
            1.3.2.   Forward to the retriever as indexes (including the anticipators)
```

Listing 2. Algorithm for situation assessment.

Given the example above, the new set of indexes including the anticipator is as follows:

```
(event              <student request>)
(goal               <Introduce New Concept>)
(topic              <Classes, Objects >)
(learner_goal       <new example>)
(learning_style     < Visual  >)
        (student_level      <Average>)
(error_per_topic    <nil >)
```

Given the indexes and anticipators, the next step in case retrieval is to *search* the case library and perform the matching and ranking procedure. Since the cases are organized as *prioritized redundant discrimination network*, the network is traversed to search for the appropriate case. In some cases, searching is done parallel. This happens when more than one CIAs handle the same type of cases, that is, cases having the same reasoning goals. Listing 3 shows the algorithm on how the network is traversed.

2.2 Traversing Case Network

Traversal of the case organization is done in depth-first search manner. Each of the indexes identified during the situation assessment procedure is compared to the first level indexes of the network (or tree). For every first level node that corresponds to the indexes of the new case, a depth-first search is done. See Figure 1. The degree of similarity and match is computed until a case is found. The aggregate match score of the old case to the new case is computed. The algorithm does not check anymore if the root GE (i.e., generalized episode containing the reasoning goal) because the new case will not be given to the CIA if it doesn't have the same reasoning goal.

2.3 Matching and Ranking Cases

Matching and ranking is a procedure in case retrieval that selects which cases are appropriate among the cases in the case library. As the process of searching the library is done, the search process asks the matching function to compute for the degree of match among indexes. Based on the result of the matches, the search function collects a set of cases that partially matches the new situation. The result is then ranked to identify which best address the requirements of the new situation.

The algorithm for checking correspondence, computing the degree of similarity and degree of matching that is used while traversing the network is shown in Listing 3. The *nearest-neighbor matching* approach is used. Since the numeric evaluation function can only rank cases but cannot recognize cases that are not useful, an exclusion step is included to look for difference between cases that are known to predict if the cases are not useful (i.e., difference in reasoning goal). Since only cases having the same goal as the new case are matched against the new case, cases that are not useful are automatically eliminated. This is based on the belief that the teaching goal is an important factor in deciding what instructional strategy to use. This belief is also shown in the result of the survey among teachers regarding the factors that they use in planning for instructional activities.

In checking the similarity between cases, the first step is to identify the *correspondence* among features. Finding correspondences is done to determine which

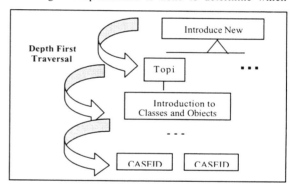

Figure 1. Depth-First Traversal of the Case Organization.

features in the new situation should be matched to which features in a stored case [3]. One way to check the correspondence is to check if the two values fill the same attribute. Once the correspondence has been found, the degree of similarity is computed quantitatively or qualitatively. Table 1 shows the values for the similarity function for each feature and the weight of each feature. Those values that are not compared with a value means that the degree of similarity is zero (0) by default.

```
1.  Checking the correspondence:
    1.1.  Check the corresponding feature in the cases stored in
          the case library using the following rules
          1.1.1.    Values filling the same attribute correspond to
                    each other.
          1.1.2.    Values filling the same role in two predicate
                    clauses correspond to each other
2.  Computing the degree of similarity:
    2.1.  Compute the degree of similarity of corresponding
          features by:
          2.1.1.    Computation of distance on a qualitative and
                    quantitative scale
3.  Computing the degree of match:
    3.1.  Compute the degree of match using the following
```

$$
\text{function:} \quad \frac{\sum_{i=1}^{n} w_i (sim \ (f_i^l, f_i^r))}{\sum_{i-1}^{n} w_i}
$$

```
    3.2.  Add the results for all features to derive an aggregate
          match score.
    3.3.  Rank cases from highest to lowest
```

Listing 3. Algorithm for checking correspondence and computing the degree of similarity and match.

Where,
w_i = the weight of the importance of dimension i,
sim = the similarity function for primitives, and

$f_i^l \, and f_i^r$ = Values for the feature f_i in the input

A *combination of heuristic and numerical evaluation function* is used to compute for the matching and ranking of cases. The *heuristic function* filters cases that had mismatches in important features before comparing cases for their degree of similarity. To measure the degree of match of each pair, the Cognitive System's (1992), evaluation function is adapted [3] (as shown in Listing 3).

The assignment of importance value (or weight) to the dimension is done manually as the case library is being built. The similarity is computed by checking if the values belong to the same quantitative scale (e.g., grade of 94-100 is excellent) and qualitative scale (e.g., error belongs to same classification). For the *goal, topic, learner error per topic attributes* the degree of similarity is 1 if the values of the old and new case are exactly the same. Otherwise, the degree of similarity is computed by computing ratio of similarity . If there is only one topic to be taught and they are not similar then the degree of similarity is zero. However, for the *goal attribute*, the value will never be zero because only CIAs having at least one of the goals similar to the current case are asked by the CFA to retrieve cases.

In the presented retrieval method, whenever a candidate set or partial matches have been collected and better matching cases need to be extracted from the set, aggregate matching is required. Aggregate match is computed using the numeric evaluation function that combines that degree of match along each dimension with a value representing the importance of the dimension. After all the related cases with their aggregate match score are retrieved, the cases are ranked from highest to lowest. If more than one case have the highest rank, then all of those cases are returned. Otherwise, only the highest case is given to the requesting tutor agent (or CTA).

2.4 Illustration

Given the cases in the Case Organization example and the current case index. The most similar case is CaseID_2. Figure 2 shows the partial case organization and the current case index.

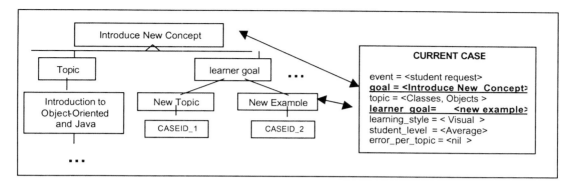

Figure 2. Example Partial Case Organization and Current Case Index.

Since the *topic* is different, the path from the *topic* feature is not traversed, the *request* feature is then compared. Only caseid_2 matches the value of the *request* feature of the current case. The degree of match is then computed.

The degree of match is still needed to be computed even if there is only one case that is considered most similar to the current case. The reason behind this is that it is possible for other *Case Information Agents* (CIAs) to have the cases having the same goal as the current case (or having the current case's goal as a subset of its goal, e.g., goal = <Introduce New Concept, Assess>). In such cases, the CIAs will also retrieve the most similar case in their case library. The Case Facilitator Agent will be responsible for ranking all the cases returned by the CIAs.

In the example, the degree of match of the current case and CaseID_2 is computed using the function for computing the degree of match shown in Equation 1. The cases degree of match is 0.75.

3.0 Summary and Conclusion

This paper presented how CBR-Tutor retrieves cases. The feature weights and value similarity weights used in computing for the degree of similarity among cases are based on the survey made to programming teachers in the College of Computer Studies, De La Salle University, Manila. Each of the respondents was asked to identify and rate their criteria for planning their course activities. The cases in CBR-Tutor are organized as prioritized redundant discrimination network [7]. This affects how cases are retrieved and re-indexed (or learned). Currently, more cases are being collected to be able to test and analyze the results of the application of CBR approach in a tutoring system. Students who will

be taking up the Java programming course will also be asked to use the system to be able to evaluate the performance of CBR-Tutor.

References:

1. Aamodt, A., Plaza, E. (1994). Case-Based Reasoning: Foundational Issues, Methodological Variations, and System Approaches. *AI Communications.* IOS Press, Vol. 7:1, pp. 39-59

2. Jona, Menachem (1998). Representing and Applying Teaching Strategies in Computer-Based Learning-by-Doing Tutors. In Schank, R. (Ed). *Inside Multi-Media Case-Based Instruction.* Lawrence Erlbaum Associates, Publishers. Mahwah, New Jersey.

3. Kolodner, J. (1993). *Case-Based Reasoning.* Morgan Kaufmann Publishers, Inc.

4. Reisbeck, C. and Schank, R. (1989). *Inside Case-based Reasoning.* Hillsdale, New Jersey: Lawrence Erlbaum Associates, Publishers.

5. Reyes, R. and Sison, R.(2000). CBR-Tutor: A Case-Based Reasoning Approach to an Internet Agent-Based Tutoring System. *International Conference on Computers In Education/ International Conference on Computer –Assisted Instruction 2000.* Taipei, Taiwan. November 21-24, 2000

6. Reyes,R. and Sison R. (2001) . Using Case-Based Reasoning in an Internet-based Tutoring Systems. *International Conference in Artificial Intelligence in Education 2001 (AIED 2001).* San Antonio, Texas. May 2001.

7. Reyes, R. and Sison, R. (2001b). Representing and Organizing Cases in CBR-Tutor. *International Conference on Computers In Education/ International Conference on Computer –Assisted Instruction 2000.* South Korea. November 2001

8. Sison, R . (2000). Multistrategy Discovery and Detection of Novice Programmer Errors. Machine Learning, 38, 157-180. Kluwer Academic Publishers, Netherlands.

Using Role Theory in Monitoring Web Group Learning Systems

Gwo-Dong Chen, Chin-Yeh Wang, Kuo-Liang Ou , *Baw-Jhiune Liu

Department of Computer Science and Information Engineering

National Central University, Chung-Li TAIWAN 32054

{chen,chinyea,klou}@db.csie.ncu.edu.tw

*Department of Computer Science and Information Engineering

Yuan-Ze University, Chung-li, TAIWAN, 320

bjliu@saturn.yzu.edu.tw

ABSTRACT

Role theory has been proposed to explain group teamwork. Thus, it may also be valid to explain group learning performance. However, teachers in both conventional classrooms and web learning systems are difficult to figure out what role a student played in a group and what relationship between existence of roles and group performance. In a web learning system, interactions among group members can be recorded in a database. Computer tools can be developed to do the tasks for teachers. In this paper we develop a tool to capture the roles that a student plays in her/his learning group. Then, tools using machine learning techniques are built to find the relationship between existence of roles and group performance. A tool then built to predict the group performance based on the relationship captured. Experiment result is shown that demonstrates that role theory is effective to predict group performance.

Keywords: Group member roles analysis, web-based collaborative learning, group's social interaction

INTRODUCTION

To explore how the behavior of members in a group affects the group performance, many social science researches focused on roles investigation in groups. For example, Robbins indicated that a role is "a set of expected behavior patterns attributed to someone occupying a given position in a social unit" [16]. Chesler and Fox [6] indicated that a role is "a patterned sequence of feelings, words, and actions". Most researches

emphasize on the effect of group *leaderships* to group performance [13] [15]. However, the existence of *member-roles* is also an effective indicator for group performance and less discussed [3]. Some researches have investigated on the member-roles on group performance. The Belbins' role theory[2][4], Benne and Sheats ' [3] and Heap's researches [8] indicated the functionality of member-roles that affects the group performance. Henry and Stevens [9], Sommerville and Dalziel [20] provided experiences on exploring the effect of member-roles on team building and group works. These researchers provide valuable experience for teachers to monitoring learning groups by detecting the existence of certain roles in a group.

However, to detect the existence of roles in a group is not easy. In a conventional classroom, teachers need to keep their eyes and ears on all groups' interaction. If there are many groups in a class, the teachers are not able to do the task for all groups. A teacher may capture the information by asking students or using a questionnaire [4]. Teachers will need quite a lot of effort to monitor groups by using role theory.

In a web-based group learning environment, teachers are difficult to figure out the roles of a group member by watching interaction in the discussion board. Although the interaction contents of groups can be recorded in a database, teachers need to detect the *roles* that a group member plays and explore the relationship between existences of roles and group learning performance. Since the member-roles are developed from social interactions and can become a part of one's social identity [4], extracting and analyzing the social interactive patterns is required when extracting the member-roles. After the member-roles extracted, relationship between existences of member-roles and learning performance can be

884

captured so that teachers can monitor the group leaning based on the findings.

However, in accomplishing the above works, teachers face the following issues: (1)students' social interaction are always large in quantity and unorganized, teachers must spend lots of efforts to identify the roles that a student played from students' social interaction, and (2)the relationship between member-roles and group learning performance needed to be captured so that teachers can monitor group learning. It also requires a lot of efforts.

In this paper we develop a tool to capture the roles that a student plays in her/his learning group. Then, machine

relationship captured. We also show an experiment result that demonstrates that role theory is effective to predict group performance.

METHODOLOGY OVERVIEW

To extract the social interaction patterns from group interactions on a web learning system, we employ Information Retrieval techniques to assist teachers in analyzing the large quantity of textual group interaction in a database. The *IBM Intelligent Miner* is a commercial product that extracts the topics and abstract of documents

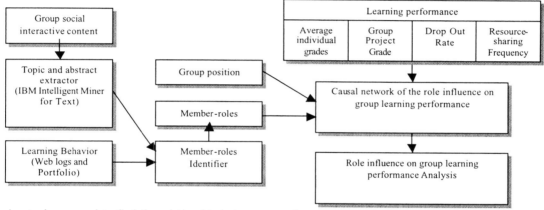

learning tools are used to find the relationship between existence of roles and group performance. A tool then built to predict the group performance based on the

that support teachers to extract the roles that a student plays in a group according to Role theory.

Figure 1. The methodology to extract and apply the relationship between the existence of roles and group performance

Figure 1 illustrated the process flow for teachers to detect the member-roles and discover their influence on group learning performance. A role identifying tool is built for capturing the roles that a student plays in a group. Three learning performance indicators are discussed for the influence of the existence of the roles on: (1) individual grades, (2)group project grades, and (3)drop out rate. The average individual grades are obtained from individual examination outcomes in groups. These outcomes represent the individuals' learning performance and members' assistance to individuals. The groups' project grades are obtained from groups' project outcomes. These outcomes represent the groups' learning performance and the individuals' assistance to groups. The

following will explore the relationship between member-roles and both individual and group learning outcomes.

Finally, a good group should also encourage all members to participate [14]. Many teachers in CMC learning environment are concerning about avoiding the students giving up learning and dropping out. Thus, this paper explores the relationship between existence of the roles and drop out rate of a group.

DETECTING THE EXISTENCE OF ROLES IN A WEB GROUP LEARNING ENVIRONMENT

In this section, Benne and Sheats' categories of member-roles are described. All the definitions of member-roles are employed in the web group learning environment. Teachers can detect the existence of a role manually by investigating the learning behaviors, the members' interactive patterns, and questionnaire answer by students. IBM text miner is used to extract the topic and keywords of each post that a student issued in his/her group discussion board. A machine learning tool then extract the rules that represent the relationship between the topics and keywords of a student interaction and the roles that the student played. A role identification tool is built based on the rules. There are 60 students that are divided into 2 classes. Each class has 30 students. Both classes use the same questionnaire to ask students how other group peers behave based on the functionalities proposed in Benne Role theory. Together with learning behavior, the teachers then identify the roles that a student played. One class is used to derive the rules. The other class then is used to validate the rules. The accuracy rate of the validation is above 90%[10].

The functional roles of group members

Benne and Sheats identified 27 member-roles in their research 'Functional roles of group members"[3], and classified into three broad groupings. They are *Group task roles; Group building and maintenance roles; Individual roles.*

The definitions of above member-roles [3] are employed. Following section will describe the criteria of detecting the member-roles by observing the interactive patterns and individual learning behaviors that corresponding to above member-roles definitions.

Criteria of detecting the member-roles by observing the interactive patterns and individual learning behaviors

There are 11 member-roles detected in our experiment class by observing the interactive patterns and individual learning behaviors. Researchers have defined the member-roles criteria [3][5]. The member-roles names are listed as below: *Initiator-contributors, Information givers, Opinion givers, Coordinators, Energizer; Procedural technician and recorder, Encourager, Follower, Playboy, Dominator,* and *Fellow-traveller.*

In this research, teachers detect above 11 member-roles by observing the group interactive patterns, login frequency and work on project frequency. A student who is in accordance to the above criteria of a role represents she/he plays the member-roles in a group. A student may play several roles at the same time. A group may also have several members play the same role concurrently.

RESULT AND EXPERIENCE

The experimental of our method includes 7 teachers, 5 teaching assistants and 706 students. The students are teachers of elementary schools and middle schools. They are not majored in computer science and lived widespread all over Taiwan Island. The best way for them to communicate is through the computer network. The subject students studied the "Introduction of Computer Network" course on a web-based group learning environment. The course period is two months, January-March 2000. The class adopted a group learning strategy with a web interface for performing and recording group projects and inter and intra group discussions. The curriculum included some fundamental concepts of computer networks and the programming language/application for constructing WWW pages such as TCP/IP, Network security, HTML, JavaScript, FrontPage. Teachers captured the interactions in the groups from the web logs.

To analyze the relationship between the existence of member-roles and the three indicators of group performance: average individual grades, group project grades and drop out rate. The statistical T-test evaluation is employed to examine the significant range of periodicity $(P<0.01)$ on these three indicators. Meanwhile, data mining tool – BKD[21] was employed to explore the relationships between the existence of member-roles and group performance. This information helps teachers understand the member-roles influence on the learning performance. A tool is built based on the information to monitor the groups for teachers.

The evaluation of relationship between the existence of member-roles and group learning performance

To evaluate the significant of member-roles on group learning performance, the t-test are employed at first to estimate each significant value on four indicators of learning performance: individual grades, group project grade and drop out rate. The results are showed as below:

Detected Member-roles	Individual grades	Group project grade	Drop out rate
Initiator - contributor	0.000*	0.000*	0.000*
Information - giver	0.000*	0.000*	0.000*
Opinion - giver	0.000*	0.185	0.063
coordinator	0.000*	0.000*	0.000*
energizer	0.000*	0.000*	0.000*
Procedural technician	0.000*	0.011	0.000
encourager	0.000*	0.000*	0.000*
harmonizer	0.000*	0.018	0.046
Playboy	0.000*	0.008*	0.008*
dominator	0.000*	0.000*	0.000*
Fellow-traveler	0.122	0.003*	0.003*

$p < 0.01$

Table 1. The significant of influence of detected member-roles on individual grades, group project grades, and group drop rate

Table 1 shows that a student who plays each roles or not has significant different on individual grades except the *fellow-traveler* role. In third column shows that the number of members who play each roles in a group has significant different on group project grades except the *opinion-giver* role, *procedural technician* and *harmonizer*. In the last column shows that the number of members who play each roles or not in a group has significant different on group project grades except the *opinion-giver, procedural technician* and *harmonizer*.

The relationship network between member-roles and individual learning performance

Because the data of 706 individual play the 11 member-roles are log data, the Bayesian Belief Network analysis is employed to extract the relationship between member-roles and individual grade.

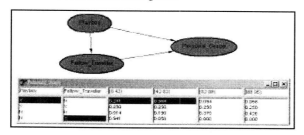

Figure 2 The causal network of influence of member-roles on individual grades

Figure 2 illustrates that *playboy* and *fellow* have a partial influence on individual grade.

If a member who is not a *playboy* and plays the *follower*, there are high probability (94.1%) that this member will get low individual grade (0-42, grade D).

The other rules devised by BKD are as listed as follows.

If a group has both *initiator* and *dominator*, the group grade will have 61.8% probability above other 75% groups in classroom.

If a group lack *coordinator*, the project grade of the group will have 84.1% probability in the lowest 25%.

Fellow travelers have 99.2% will drop out the class, and *playboy* have 69.7% will drop out the class.

If student neither a *playboy* nor a *fellow traveler*, he will not drop out in 94.2%.

In resource share aspect, *fellow traveler* have 99.9% that he/she will not share resource with other group members and *procedural technician* have 84.9% of sharing resource with other group members.

CONCLUSION

To assist teaches detecting the member-roles and extracting the relationship between member-roles and group learning performance, this paper presented the methodology for identifying member-roles that a student plays in a group. Three primary group performance indicators are considered: (1)individual grades, (2)group project grade, and (3)group drop out rate. The analysis shows that most of the member-roles have significant influence on group learning performance.

The regression analysis shows that the *dominator, encourager, opinion, playboy, initiator-contributor, coordinator,* and *opinion giver* have positive influence on group project grade. However, the *fellow-traveller, follower, procedural technician* and *recorder,* and *energizer* have stronger negative influence on group project grade. All of the member-roles do not have significant influence on group drop out rate. With the assisting of member-roles detecting and influence extracting tools, teaches can monitor the group learning by monitoring the existence of member-roles in a group.

References

[1] L. Argote, *Organizational learning: creating, retaining, and transferring knowledge*. Kluwer Academic Publishers Group, MA, USA, 1999.

[2] R.M. Belbin, *Management Teams*. Wiley, New York, USA, 1981

[3] K.D. Benne, and P. Sheats, Functional roles of group members. *Journal of Social Issues*, 4:2, 41-49, 1948.

[4] B.J. Biddle, *Role Theory: Expectations, Identities and Behaviors*. Academic Press, New York, 1979

[5] G.D. Chen, K.L. Ou, C.C. Liu and BJ. Liu, *Intervention and strategy analysis for web group-learning*. Journal of Computer Assisted Learning (JCAL), Vol. 17(1), 58-71, 2001.

[6] M. Chesler and R. Fox, *Role-playing methods in the classroom*. Chicago:Science Research Associates, 1966.

[7] L. Harasom, S.R. Hiltz, L. Teles, and M. Turoff, *Learning Networks*. MIT press, Cambridge, Massachusett, USA, 1995.

[8] K. Heap, *Group theory for social workers: an introduction*. Oxford: Pergamon Press, 1977.

[9] S.M. Henry and K.T. Stevens, Using Belbins' leadership role to improve team effectiveness: An empirical investigation. *The journal of systems and software*, 44 241-250, 1999

[10] H.W. Hsiao and G.D. Chen, A group monitoring system by role analysis of web group works and activities. Master Thesis of Computer Science Information Engineering, National Central University, Taiwan, 2001

[11] D.W. Johnson, and R.T. Johnson, *Cooperation and Competition: Theroy and Research*. Interaction Book Company. Minnesota, USA, 1989.

[12] H.F. Kaiser, The varimax criterion for analytic retation in analysis. *Psychometrika*, 23, pp.187-200, 1958.

[13] J.L. Keedy, Examining teacher instructional leadership within the small group dynamics of collegial groups, *Teaching and Teacher Education*, 15:7,pp.785-799, 1999

[14] J. Rabow, M.A. Charness, J. Kipperman, and S. Radcliffe-Vasile, William Fawcett Hill's *Learning through discussion*, (3rd) pp.1-7. Sage Pub. CA. U.S.A., 1994.

[15] T. Reponen, Is leaderships possible at loosely coupled organization such as university? *Higher Education Policy*, 12, pp.237-244, 1999

[16] S. Robbins, *Organizational behavior: concepts, controversies and applications*, Prentice Hall: Englewood Cliffs, NJ, USA, 1991.

[17] SPSS developed by SPSS Inc., URL is http://www.spss.com/

[18] G. Stasser, Pooling of Unshared Information During Group Discussion, *Group Process and Productivity*, (Worchel, S., Wood, W., and Simpson, J.A. editors), Sage publications, USA, 1992.

[19] G. Stasser, and W. Titus, Effects of information load and percentage of shared information on the dissemination of unshared information during group discussion. *Journal of Personality and Social Psychology*, 53, pp.81-93, 1987.

[20] J. Sommerville, and S. Dalziel, Project teambuilding – the applicability of Belbin's team-role self-perception inventory. *International Journal of Project Management*, 16:3. 165-171, 1998.

[21] P. Spirtes, and C. Meek, Learning Bayesian Networks with Discrete Variables from Data. *Proceeding of Knowledge Discovery and Data Mining*, pp.294-299, 1995.

The War-Gaming Training System Based on HLA Distributed Architecture

Tainchi Lu and Guanchi Wu
Institute of Computer Science and Information Engineering,
National Chiayi University, Chiayi, Taiwan, R.O.C.
E-mail: tclu@mail.ncyu.edu.tw

Abstract

This paper describes the design of HLA distributed architecture to support an interactive, interoperable, and collaborative war-gaming simulation using Java technology and IEEE standard 1516 – High Level Architecture (HLA). Based on the Run-Time Infrastructure (RTI) services which are specified in HLA and Java application programming interface (API) of the RTI, the proposed distributed virtual environment (DVE) provides a practical foundation to enhance interactivity, portability, and interoperability for distributed simulation. Moreover, we build up a 3D synthetic virtual world for aircraft simulator by means of Java 3D API in which Java 3D technology could support a simple, portable, and flexible programming model for 3D scene construction. From the system implementation and experimental results, we show that the proposed HLA distributed architecture is a practical and scalable design that is applicable for a wide variety of moderate DVEs.

Keywords: Distributed Virtual Environment (DVE); High Level Architecture (HLA); Java 3D API

1. Introduction

Nowadays, distributed virtual environment (DVE) [1, 2, 3, 4, 5] is a grand-challenging research paradigm, sophisticated scientists aim to model a real-life virtual world and develop a large-scale distributed architecture. Moreover, DVE has become increasingly important for military training, in entertainment, educational, medical, industrial, and academic sectors. To date, numerous common technical frameworks for distributed modeling and simulation (M&S) have been identified successfully to facilitate the development of the DVE. The U.S. Department of Defense (DOD) M&S master plan has completely specified a common technical framework for M&S and high level architecture (HLA) [6] is one of sub-objectives within this master plan. The HLA was approved as an open standard through the IEEE organization as IEEE 1516 in September 2000 and it consists of three primary components, namely federation rules [7], the HLA interface specification [8], and the object model template (OMT) [9].

DVE tends to exchange a variety of mixed information, such as audio, video, graphical objects, and so on. It is obviously that DVE server must support clients with low response time and high throughputs. As far as a generic central server environment is concerned,

we suppose that it suffers low efficiency and high overload for the sake of the permanent computing power of a single server and for lack of load-balancing mechanism. However, it provides a versatile model for developing a wide range of networked platform due to a simple design, an easy programming, a comprehensive usage, etc. In this paper, we propose the HLA distributed architecture to support a 3D war-gaming simulation that is built upon the infrastructure of HLA. Referring to a common HLA federation first, it can be viewed as an integrated architecture to facilitate interoperability among the individual simulators (i.e. federates). In other words, it can be regarded as a distributed system with multiple heterogeneous servers to specify the exchange of data and coordinate among participating members of a federation. Consequently, we also suppose that the common HLA federation can distribute the computation loads to each federate and gain the lower network latency than the central server environment. Notice that, given the model of the common HLA federation, we are concerned with the question of how to extend an HLA federation to support a client-server mechanism over the Internet. As a result, we combine the Java RMI with the HLA RTI to not only support the distributed multi-server environment but also provide multi-player implementation with client-server architecture. Furthermore, a simple 3D aircraft simulator is developed by Java 3D API [10] to execute within client sites. Relying on the Java RMI and the HLA RTI, client players that are dominated by different federate agents could communicate and interact with each other towards the specific autonomous 3D objects throughout the virtual world [11].

2. Background

2.1 IEEE 1516: High Level Architecture

High Level Architecture (HLA) is an integrated and general-purpose architecture, which is developed to provide a common interoperable and reusable architecture for distributed modeling and simulation. The HLA consists of three core components, including federation rules, interface specification, and the object model template (OMT). A federate is defined as a member of an HLA federation, so all applications (i.e. simulators) participated in a federation are specified as federates. Hence, an HLA federation is a set of interacting federates to aim at a specific objective.

The federation rules describe the responsibilities of federates and their mutual relationships with the run-time infrastructure (RTI). The interface specification identifies how federates will interact with the federation through the RTI. The HLA OMT provides a common framework for all objects and interactions managed by a federate. Its components consist of object model identification table, object class structure table, interaction class structure table, attributed table, routing space table, and FOM/SOM lexicon. On the other hand, all data types for each of these object attributes need to be defined according to the OMT format and syntax. The RTI provides sufficient services for simulation systems and specifies the federate interface using the following languages: CORBA IDL, C, C++, Ada 95, and Java. It is available to support Solaris, IRIX, AIX, HP-UX, Windows NT and Linux operating systems. Moreover, the RTI services are classified into six categories that describe the interface between federates and the RTI. For more detailed description of HLA, you can refer to [7, 8, 9].

2.3 Java 3D API

Java is explicitly a sophisticated programming language that is appropriate for designing a wide range of platform-independent distributed systems. In addition, the Sun Microsystems Java 3D [10] facilitates system software developers to design their visualization simulations [12] and to make it possible to show 3D graphical contents on the Web. By leveraging the inherent strengths of the Java language, Java 3D API extends the Java conventional concept of "Write Once, Run Anywhere" to 3D graphics applications. Programmers can easily incorporate high-quality, scalable, platform-independent 3D graphics with Java technology-based applications and applets. This assists developers to build, render, and control the behaviors of 3D objects for visual systems. Figure 1 shows the Java

3D object hierarchy laid out by Java 3D API. Java 3D API supports a scene graph structure using object hierarchy for constructing individual graphics element as separate objects, it enables users to manipulate a scene graph and to control viewing and rendering.

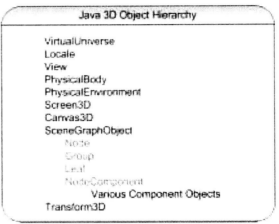

Figure 1. The Java 3D object hierarchy

3. Federation and Federate

We show our proposed HLA distributed architecture in Figure 2. Each simulation is referred to as a federate. The collection of federates interconnecting through the run time infrastructure (RTI) is referred to as an HLA federation. There are three federates, named HLA federate 1, federate 2, and federate 3, to participate in an HLA federation. The RTI provides the means for each federate agent to coordinate the execution and exchange of shared information.

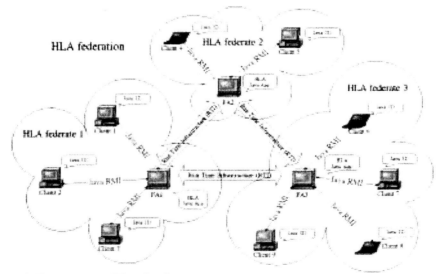

Figure 2. The proposed HLA distributed architecture, which consists of an HLA federation and three HLA federates

Therefore, the attributes and interactions of object instants that are specified in the HLA OMT can be declared, created, deleted, subscribed, published, and updated by the authorized federate agents via the RTI. Accordingly, clients can optionally connect to any arbitrary FA to be a member of this federate, because each federate is an individual simulator and has different customized functionalities. The 3D synthetic world for war game is built up by means of Java 3D API, Java applications, and external authoring tool of graphical objects. Clients connect to FAs and download Java applications from the FAs. Therefore, these clients can be invoked RMI stubs by the FA to communicate with one another whether it is located in the local or remote federate.

4. Experimental Results

Figure 3 illustrates three experimental simulation environments, one is a traditional central server environment, another is a common HLA federation, and the other is the proposed HLA distributed architecture. Throughout the experimental simulation, we compare the central server environment with the HLA distributed architecture in terms of estimating their mean response time. The discrete Poisson process with mean task arrival rate λ is adopted to serve as the task arriving model for a single server. The requesting tasks requested by the clients are queued in FCFS order at the server site.

In Table 1, we list the pre-defined parameters in comparison with the central server environment and the proposed HLA distributed architecture. Figure 4 shows our preliminary experimental results. The horizontal axis is the number of clients and the vertical axis is the mean response time measured in millisecond. Due to the communication and computation loads are distributed to three federate agents, we can see that the central server environment gains the more response time than the HLA distributed architecture as increasing the number of clients.

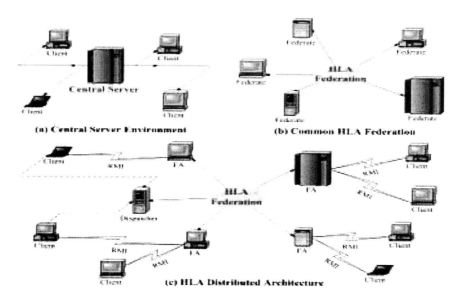

Figure 3. The experimental simulation environment in comparison with (a) a central server environment, (b) a common HLA federation, and (c) the HLA distributed architecture

Table 1. Parameters for the experimental simulation

	The central server environment	The HLA distributed architecture
Number of hosts	1	3
Number of clients	10	10
Client connection rate	1 client per 30 seconds	1 client per 30 seconds
Task arrival rate	E(X)=13	E(X)=13

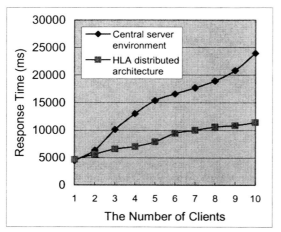

Figure 4. The mean response time compared with the central server environment and the HLA distributed architecture

5. System Overview

Based on the HLA object model Template (OMT) specification, we adopt object class structure table to declare three object instances, namely aircraft, projectile, and obstacle, to be used to present a simple 3D aircraft simulator. Three basic capabilities are specified with respect to a given object instance: publishable (P), 7subscribable (S), and neither publishable nor subscribable (N). An object instance (e.g. aircraft) should be declared the capability of P, S or N first before it begins to simulate in the virtual world. The system refers to the declared volume size of each object instance to encapsulate the object instance within a well-defined 3D spatial space. During the period of simulation, client players can change position of an object instance by the keyboard's arrow keys and the positional updates are sent to the connected federate agent (FA) immediately. The FA broadcasts the positional and information updates of this object instance to all other FAs via RTI and multicasts these updates to the local specific client players, which subscribe the object and have the spatial space overlap with it. Similarly, players can fire a projectile to damage an obstacle and create an explosion in the period of simulation. We show our graphical user interface of the 3D aircraft simulator in Figure 5. Figure 6 illustrates the underlying flowchart for client players simulated in this aircraft war game.

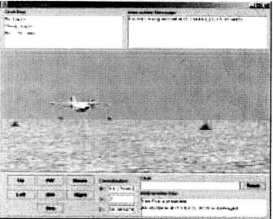

Figure 5. The graphical user interface of the 3D aircraft simulator

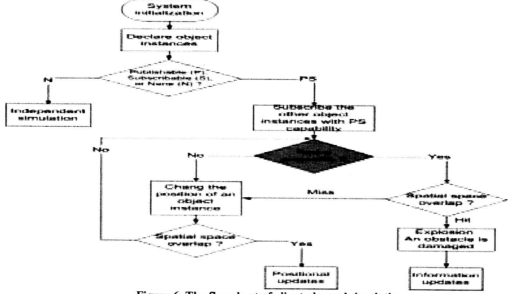

Figure 6. The flowchart of client players' simulation

892

6. Future Work

In our future work, adaptive visibility culling for 3D locales is the on-going research issue to reduce the computation costs and accelerate the rendering time. Moreover, the HLA time management is intended to integrate with our current HLA distributed architecture to deal with both soft and hard real-time simulations.

References

1.   Shervin Shirmohammadi and Nicolas D. Georganas, "An end-to-end communication architecture for collaborative virtual environments," Computer Networks, Vol. 35, pp. 351-367 (2001).

2.   Chong-Wei Xu and Bo He, "PCB – A Distributed System in CORBA," Journal of Parallel and Distributed Computing, Vol. 60, pp. 1293-1310 (2000).

3.   Shivakant Mishra, Lan Fei, Xiao Lin, and Guming Xing, "On Group Communication Support in CORBA," IEEE Transactions on Parallel and Distributed Systems, Vol. 12, No. 2, pp. 193-208 (2001).

4.   C. Bouras, A. Philopoulos, and Th. Tsiatsos, "E-Learning through Distributed Virtual Environments," Journal of Network and Computer Applications, Vol. 24, pp. 175-199 (2001).

5.   H. Afsarmanesh et al., "A Reference Architecture for Scientific Virtual Laboratories," Future Generation Computer Systems, Vol. 17, pp. 999-1008 (2001).

6.   Tainchi Lu, Chungnan Lee, Ming-tang Lin, and Wenyang Hsia, "Supporting Large-Scale Distributed Simulation Using HLA," ACM Transactions on Modeling and Computer Simulation, Vol. 10, No. 3, pp. 268-294 (2000).

7.   U.S. Department of Defense Modeling and Simulation Office (DMSO). February (1998). *High Level Architecture Rules*. Version 1.3. Available through the Internet: http://www.dmso.mil/.

8.   U.S. Department of Defense Modeling and Simulation Office (DMSO). April (1998). *High Level Architecture Interface Specification*. Version 1.3. Available through the Internet: http://www.dmso.mil/.

9.   U.S. Department of Defense Modeling and Simulation Office (DMSO). February (1998). *High Level Architecture Object Model Template Specification*. Version 1.3. Available through the Internet: http://www.dmso.mil/.

10. Sun Microsystems, Inc. Java 3D API Specification, Version 1.2. Available through the Internet: http://java.sun.com/products/java-media/3D/

11. Soraia Raupp Musse and Daniel Thalmann, "Hierarchical Model for Real Time Simulation of Virtual Human Crowds," IEEE Transactions on Visualization and Computer Graphics, Vol. 7, No. 2, pp. 152-164 (2001).

12. Chad F. Salisbury, Steven D. Farr, and Jason A. Moore, "Web-based Simulation Visualization using Java 3D," In Proceeding of the 1999 Winter Simulation Conference, pp. 1425-1429 (1999).

Learning Control Systems on the Web

CC Chan, Reggie Kwan and SF Chan
School of Science and Technology
The Open University of Hong Kong SAR, China

Abstract

Recent advances in Internet technology and computing processing power have driven the distance education institutions to offer courses with increasingly use of Web technology. Through the Web, needless to say all, for example, discussion forum or alike is made available for learners to share their learning experiences and the efficient mode on course delivery allows them to access course related material with a lot of convenience and at their own pace. In line with this environment, a research project has been taken out to build a Web-based learning module in control systems on which this paper will focus to address the learning effectiveness of control system principles in this way. The authors will draw special attention to the hypermedia features designed in this module. Some of the limitations of the module are also discussed.

Introduction

One of the major issues in control systems course will be the study of first and second order systems' behaviours. Their performances with impulse and step inputs will often be investigated and the stability analysis of systems is also a key topic in the course. With respect to these the main features of this module are introduced. Several programming languages with windows application such as C++, Java, Visual Basic and ToolBook are considered. Visual Basic which features user friendly, easy to manage under Web environment, and the most importantly simple to use, as well as HTML, is thus chosen for the project.

Features for enhancing effective learning

When the system starts, learners will see the main page of the learning module that introduces basic concepts of 'open loop control system' and 'closed loop control system'. This introduction page outlines the main content of the module via hypertext links, namely, 'First Order System', 'Second Order System', 'Higher Order System', 'Root locus Techniques' and 'Quiz'. With these learners are free to choose which part of the content that they are interested to study. A number of special features of the module that have been designed are highlighted as follows :

* *Using Buttons to Navigate*

In this learning system, the buttons are clearly named which help users to travel around and navigate to different pages of the learning module.

* *Viewing diagrams and animations*

Sometimes, learners will come across some content containing 'coloured' words. When they click on these words, they will be brought to another page containing the figure and animations.

Creating animations in diagrams or figures are very important as these help explain some ideas and actions clearly. For instance, when the 'second order open loop response plot' is triggered, an input form of time response plot pops up. Then the learners can enter the input parameters of the control system such as damping ratio and coefficients of transfer function. Having entered these values, learners can click on 'Open Loop Pulse Time Response' button and the time response plot will pop up. They can also compare this impulse time response with step time response by clicking on 'Open Loop Step Time Response' button. The diagram will show the two different plots on the same screen for learners to compare their different system behaviours. Click on 'Redraw button' will clear the plots. Similarly, click on 'Higher order system ' or 'Root-locus Techniques' will bring them to the relevant pages for other plots.

* *Running of the Interactive Self-test*

When learners have finished their study, they may want to have a test for themselves by visiting 'Quiz page' which shows 20 self-assessment questions along side with Yes/No option buttons. After check on these and then press 'score' button, learner's score will pop up showing the performance of the test. Press on 'Reset' button will reset the answers and learners can then re-enter the test.

Evaluation

For the research findings, this experimental project has been undertaken an evaluation exercise to determine the effectiveness of this Web-based learning module and to provide us valuable comments which are useful for future development of using Web.

Overview of evaluation result: -

* Most learners find this module being helpful to their study of control system and is user friendly.

* Best features are its capability of showing dynamic system responses. Use of animation arouses learners' interest and help understanding abstract concepts. Self-test questions are useful

in assessing learners' learning outcomes.

* The module is rather short, and expect to see more detailed presentation of subject matter.

* Web-based learning is very convenient as learners can access to the material at their own pace and at any time; OUHK should develop more this type of hypermedia course material.

* Part of the material appears to be computerized page turning with which learners quickly become bored and no Index and Help menus.

* Prefer hard copy of course material as it is more comfortable to read; access to the Web is just an add-on features though it is sometimes helpful.

To sum up students who took part in the evaluation exercise generally provided favorable comments on using emerging technology in course development and would like to see more courses featuring this Web-based learning approach to enhance the effectiveness of their study.

Conclusion

It is clear that web-based learning material has become increasingly important in distance learning environment. From the learners' point of view, those who took part in the evaluation of the module were aware of its weaknesses and deficiencies. However, they also recognised the potential strengths of the system for the teaching and learning of courses. They were keen to see OUHK build on this experience, and produce more sophisticated learning resources, which should rely less on pages of text and more on the available features of hypermedia. This project provides encouragement to OUHK in its efforts to use new and emerging technologies in course development and delivery for the benefit of distance learners.

A Web-Based Information-Learning-Passport System Using the ARCS Model

* Chih-Hung Lai, Jie-Chi Yang, Bau-Lo Jheng, Tak-Wai Chan, Chin-Wen Ho, ** Jing-San Liang
* Department of Computer Science and Information Engineering, National Central University, Taiwan
e-mail: {laich, yang, guava, chan, hocw }@src.ncu.edu.tw
** Taipei Yeng Chow Elementary School, Taiwan
rebecca@mail.yces.tp.edu.tw

Abstract: The purpose of this study is to develop a passport system based on ARCS model for Internet users to learn basic information technology skills. The system is designed to increase learners' motivation and use it actively. Due to an assistant learning mechanism, it can improve learners' information literacy. The learning contents are about information technologies. The styles of the test include multi-choices and practical manipulation tasks. The system automatically evaluates the results, records the process and outcome of the test. The system adopts a role-play strategy, so that users can proceed to the test in the form of games. When a user encounters problems in the test, he/she can find relevant information to assist his/her learning. The main users of the system are teachers and students of junior high schools and elementary schools at Taoyuan County in Taiwan. From December 1999 to June 2001, 1,273,783 users have already used the system.

1: Introduction

The learning motivation is a crucial factor. It may influence how learning gets started and continued, and how students' motivation can be arisen or maintained. Therefore, if an online test can engage students to use it actively and have high motivation for using it, the achievements will be greatly improved. On the other hand, the common online tests only concern if students can pass the test. They don't offer the function of learning. But when students encounter problems in the test, they may need instant help. If they can get assistance at once, it's opportunity for them to learn effectively. This is the first motivation of this study.

The most places which learning take place are schools. However, common online testing systems do not support school operating system. So we will provide functions for teachers to teach and manage their classes easily. This is the second motivation of this study.

Most of the online tests adopt multi-choices, practical tests are seldom used. Although there are many advantages in multi-choices [1], there are many limitations when adopting it as a method to test users. Developing a system that can provide practical manipulation on line is the third motivation of this study.

According to these motivations, the purpose of this study is to develop an information-learning-passport system. The system includes three functions.
1. Increase learners' learning motivation and improve their learning achievement
2. Combine the operation of classes to understand individual and global information literacy.
3. Provide a practical manipulation test on line

2: Methodology

Learners stand a main role in learning activities. Learning achievements are influenced by learner's motivation and ability. And learning motivation is a key point in learning. Many scholars' researches are about motivation. Keller presents ARCS model, which emphasizes how to motivate one's internal and external factors. In the model, the four factors extend into some practical strategies as follows:
1. Attention: arise learners' interest and curiosity.
2. Relevance: meet learners' individual needs and goals, and develop one's positive learning attitude.
3. Confidence: help learners build confidence and capacity to accomplish the task.
4. Satisfaction: learners can gain internal and external encouragement and rewards by achieving it.

According to the ARCS model, we probe into the model to apply in the information-learning-passport system, show as table 1.

Component	Definition	Information-learning-passport design
Attention	draw learners' interest and arise his curiosity	Game-oriented interface, role play
Relevance	meet learners' individual needs and goals, and develop one's positive learning attitude	The content is basic skill in the modern computerized society
Confidence	help learners build confidence and capacity to accomplish the task	Divide the learning targets and provide relevant information
Satisfaction	learners can gain internal and external encouragement and rewards by achieving it	Awards and Honor Boards

Table 1 the information-learning-passport system mapping to the ARCS model

3: Implementation

The information-learning-passport system is a test system, which is set up on the global information system. The contents of its test are the technique and knowledge for information technologies. The system utilizes stories to play games. The user plays a role to challenge monsters in the game. The testing program is running while users play. When users have problems or questions, they can find online relevant information to help them learn easily.

The database is the core of the system. Its operation depends on the eight modules, as showed in Figure 1.

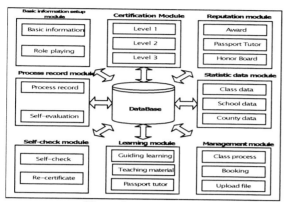

Figure 1 system structure

The certification module provides user interfaces for users to certificate. The contents of certification are the knowledge and technique of information technologies. If they focus on knowledge, the certification will be multi-choices, which are randomly chosen from database. If they focus on skills, the questions will be the styles of practical manipulation tasks. The system will automatically score after users take the online test.

The reputation module provides the design for awards, Honor Board and Passport Tutors. After passing certification, users can get award and print it out to increase their self-confidence. Those who overcome the challenge and success will be listed on Honor Board once per week. It will encourage users to upgrade and satisfy their own achievement. Those who face difficulty can also get assistance from those who are listed on the Honor Board.

All the processes of the challenge will be recorded when a user proceeds to get certification. It will indicate his outcome in detail about time consuming for getting some sublevels. It also gives some feedback about why the user does not complete his challenge and let users learn from his errors according to the recorded process.

In order to help users get certification easily, the learning module designs three assistant functions. First, it adopts interactive method to provide learning information guidance for users. Secondly, before users go into this system, it will list the requirement of fundamental capability or what kind of knowledge should be understood, the difficulty for every certification item in advance, other average testing frequency, testing time as well. Third, it provides the learning channel. When users encounter problems in the way of certification, in addition to get assistant from "learning file area", they also get help from Passport Tutors and people who are on the Honor Board.

In statistic data module, there are four kinds of perspectives to show certification result. They are student viewpoint, teacher viewpoint, school viewpoint

and local education bureau viewpoint. A student can check his own certification result and understand which place his result is in his grade. A teacher can know every student's certification status and detail well. For the school viewpoint, it is clear that school official can clearly understand the information skill degree of teachers and students. For the Education Bureau, it can show the data to realize the performance of every school while they promote it as well.

4: Result

The main users of the system are teachers and students of junior high schools and elementary schools at Taoyuan County in Taiwan. From December 1999 to June 2001, 1,273,783 users in total have already used the system, including 15427 teachers and 108356 students. The number of passed users in every level is showed as table 2.

pass	Teacher number	Teacher pass rate	Student number	Student pass rate
level 1	10983	71.19%	34432	31.78%
level 2	9769	63.32%	23845	22.01%
level 3	8748	56.71%	24193	22.33%
All	7833	50.77%	15438	14.25%

Table 2 using result of information- learning -passport

Based on the statistic analysis above and interview some teachers and students, we come to the conclusion:
(1) Most students just use computer in their computer class. And few students can surf on the Internet when they go back home.
(2) Most students got into certification program in the computer class. It made the system loading heavy. So it toke longer time to make certification.
(3) A few teachers are not aggressive to learn information skill. It may prevent students from participating this program.

Acknowledgment

This project was funded by the Ministry of Education (January 2000, to December, 2003): Program for Promoting Academic Excellence of Universities. (Project No. 89-H-FA07-1-4)

References

[1] Tamir, P (1997), Justifying the selection of answers in multiple choice items, *International Journal of Science Education*, 12(5), 563-573

[2] Keller, J.M. (1987). Development and use of the ARCS model of instructional design. *Journal of Instructional Development*, 10(3), 2-10.

[3] Malone, T. W. (1981). Toward a theory of intrinsically motivating instruction. *Cognitive Science*, 5, 333-369.

Uses of learning objects in a wireless Internet based learning system

Young-Kyun Baek, skytop@chollian.net
Hyun-Jung Cho, jcamsi@chollian.net
Bo-Kyeong Kim, bokangs@hanmail.net
Korea National University of Education

Abstract

The scope and characteristics of wireless Internet have been explored to serve as a basis for the building of a wireless Internet based learning system. Technically, the concept of learning objects is introduced; the concept of LCMS is introduced in terms of learning management, delivery, and authoring; finally the map of a learning system is presented. Those concepts and the map presented are expected to support students' learning in wireless Internet based learning.

1. Introduction

E-learning has been enriched by securing learning spaces and a variety of interaction between content providers and learners. However, very recently mLearning which combines e-learning with mobile devices such as cellular phones and PDA (Personal Digital Assistant) has emerged. Those devices are characterized by mobile computing and mobile communication. In this article, components of a wireless Internet based learning system are to be explored. Those components in all are considered to contribute to giving students more individualized learning information and providing a learning environment with no spacious limitations. And a method for building the system will be suggested.

2. Definitions and Characteristics of wireless Internet

Wireless Internet, as the name suggests, means that the Internet is accessed through wireless devices such as PDA's, wireless modems or wireless LAN cards. The scope of wireless Internet is very wide depending on the types of platform and network. Wireless Internet can be figured out as follows:

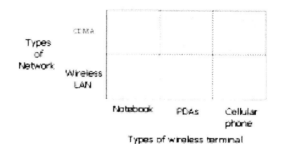

[Picture 1] Definition of wireless Internet

This article focuses on a narrow definition of wireless learning systems. Thus, it focuses on cellular phones. In this discussion of adopting learning objects for wireless Internet based learning, a very narrow definition is more suitable for building up a combined system.

When wireless Internet is conceived as cellular phones or PDA's accessing Internet services, it has its own characteristics. They are as follows:

Mobility. Users carry cellular phones or PDA's. They can get access to the Internet at any place whenever they want to connect to the Internet.

Timeliness. Wireless Internet devices are always on line, so it is possible to send any information or content to users even though they are in unwanted or unconscious situations.

Individualization/Privacy. Information to be sent

is individualized and private so far as users' location information. They can be variable according to users' demand.

Simplicity. Due to limited speed and interface, operations to connect to the Internet are very simplified and the contents are very specific and simple.

3. Learning Objects

In programming terminology, an object is a minimal unit or module of a program, standing by itself and including codes plus data. In the field of computer programming, objects' reusability contributes to increasing the productivity of software development.

Learning objects are productive in that they are used as many times as they are needed even in other programs. Learning objects, according to LTSC (Learning Technology Standards Committee) of the IEEE, are defined as follows (Wiley, 2000):

any entity, digital or non-digital, which can be used, re-used or referenced during technology-supported learning. Examples of technology-supported learning include computer-based training systems, interactive learning environments, intelligent computer-aided instruction systems, distance learning systems, and collaborative learning environments. Examples of Learning Objects include multimedia content, instructional content, learning objectives, instructional software and software tools, and persons, organizations, or events referenced during technology supported learning

But learning objects seem to be defined in so many ways by people employing them. In this article, Wiley's definition is adopted, because it is very useful for instructors and learners as well as for instructional designers. According to Wiley (In Press), a "Learning Object is a reusable digital resource to support technology-supported learning." When this type of definition is introduced in a wireless Internet based

learning system, the reusability and small size of learning objects can be very efficient in composing and delivering learning contents. They are also in good harmony with wireless Internet and mobile devices.

4. LCMS

Mobile devices have the shortcomings of small screens, low processing speed, and limited storage while they can provide very specific learning materials for an individual learner with mobility at any time. To guarantee effective learning with mobile devices to happen, Quinn (2000) pointed out that "learners need to access all materials and exchange information that is independent of system preferences and to link a Learning Management System. "

LCMS is an integrated system functionally combining LMS (Learning Management System) with CMS (Content Management System). That is, it has the contents development and management functions of CMS as well as the learning management functions of LMS. LCMS is a platform on which contents are developed, stored, and managed with learning objects. It is used in repetition and helps organize adaptive contents for individual learners and provide templates for instructional design. Thus, it supports a speedy instructional system development. Several functions of LCMS are as follows (Brennan, 2001):

First, automated authoring functions - utilizing templates for adaptive learning for each learner.

Second, various delivery functions – LCMS adopts various teaching strategies in delivering learning objects.

Third, database functions – LCMS has a database management system for structuring, storing, and searching learning objects with reference to metadata.

Last, management functions – LCMS has basic administrative functions of managing student records and learning history, etc.

Those functions of LCMS can contribute to building

an effective learning system with wireless Internet and mobile devices.

5. Map of a Wireless Internet Based Learning System

Based on the above discussion, four aspects of a wireless Internet based learning system are presented as follows:

Aspects	Functions
Learning contents	Making very small units of learning objects applicable for specific and detailed knowledge buildup
Management of learning	Recording background data, learning styles, and progress of learners
Delivery of learning	Adopting teaching strategies for individual learners through various templates
Authoring of learning objects	Carrying a wired authoring system for selecting and organizing learning objects

A final concept map for wireless internet based learning system with four aspects is presented as following:

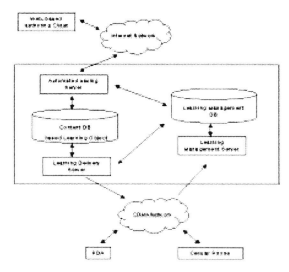

[Picture 2] Basic concept map of WIBLS

6. Conclusion

Mobility, timeliness, individuality in a wireless Internet environment, simplicity, and limited storage and speed of mobile devices cannot be disregarded in building a new learning system. Also learning objects and LCMS are variables that should be included in this learning system. This article just presented a basic concept map of WIBLS. Further discussions on learning object design, instructional design strategy, and delivery methods are needed for WIBLS.

REFERENCES

[1] ShotsBerger , Paul G.and Ronald Vetter. (2000. SEP-OCT). The Handheld Web: How Mobile Wireless Technologies Will Change Web-Based Instruction and Training. Educational Technology, 49-51.

[2] Wiley, D. (2000). Learning Ojbect design and sequencing theory. Brigham Young University.

[3] Wiley, D. (In Press). Connecting learning objects to instructional design theory: A definition, a metaphor, and a taxonomy. In David Wiley (Ed.), *The Instructional Use of Learning Objects*, Association for Educational Communications and Technology.

[4] Brennan, M., Funke, S., & Anderson, C. (2001), The learning content management system: A new eLearning Market Segment Emerges, White Paper, International Data Corporationl

[5] Clark Quinn, (2000), "mLearning : Mobile, Wireless, In-Your-Pocket Learning", [On-line]http://www.linezine.com

Development of a Dynamic Web-Based Information System for Parents and Pupils to Enhance Decision-Making by School Personnel A Case Study of Jurong Primary School, Singapore

WEE Toon Huey   Takanori MAESAKO*

Ministry of Education, Singapore   *Graduate School of Human Sciences, Osaka University

Abstract

A dynamic web-based information system was developed, tested and evaluated at Jurong Primary School in Singapore from August to December 2001. The various questionnaires for the stakeholders prepared by the school staff and the author were successfully administered through the system. The system supports a consultative style of decision-making that enables the stakeholders to contribute their views. The server can compile the responses, and then present the results to all. Hence, the school leaders can make timely and informed decisions that improve the school's programmes. In addition, the system facilitates communication between the school and the home, and encourages collaboration. Finally, it supports the teachers in analysing the students, and performs both formative and summative evaluation of lessons or other academic programmes. This paper provides an insight as to how such a system supports curricular and non-curricular decision-making incorporating the stakeholders' involvement.

1. Background

Learning is no longer encapsulated by time, place, and age, but has become a pervasive activity and attitude that continues throughout one's lifetime, and is supported by all segments of society. Furthermore, education is no longer the exclusive responsibility of teachers, but actively involves the participation and collaboration of stakeholders such as parents and experts in the community in preparing the students intellectually and morally [1]. The challenge for schools is to effectively involve all the stakeholders inside and outside the school in maximising the potential of the students' learning. Vygotsky points out the importance of our social community in the development of cognition. When children enter school, they bring with

them the cultural heritage of their home. In the school they find another culture to which they must adapt. Hence, the school needs to collaborate and join in partnership with the parents and the community to fully develop the educational potential of their children [2]. In Vygotsky's brand of constructivism called social constructivism, one's constructs of knowledge or meanings are bound by one's social cultural influence or bearings. Such views are also rooted in recent notions of situated cognition, where social, historical, and cultural contexts are intricately linked to the interpretations of meanings and knowledge. Each person living in his own society has developed a point of view that is in line with the mainstream perspectives of that society. The interpretation of knowledge is inevitably influenced by one's worldview acquired through social interactions within one's culture. Hence, by exchanging and sharing notions with others such as other children, parents and teachers, ideas are formed and thinking occurs. For example, the Internet can be used to enhance communication between the students and the teachers, or among the stakeholders so as to socially construct knowledge [3]. The Internet is connecting schools with one another and with homes, businesses, libraries, museums and other community resources. This connection between schools and homes will help students extend their academic day, allow teachers to draw on significant experiences from students' everyday lives, and enable parents to become more involved with the education of their children and to find extended educational opportunities for themselves.

All these connections will enable students to relate what is happening in the world outside to what is happening in the school, allow teachers to coordinate formal education with informal learning, and the community to reintegrate education into daily life [1, 4]. Hence, the school should take advantage of the non-formal instructional experiences that already exist in the homes, workplaces, and community and tie them with the formal curriculum of the school. In doing so, the teachers develop a greater sense of control and ability to influence their work environment, thus creating ownership [5]. Sustainable communities hold a long-term perspective and understand their interdependence with education. Community members understand as individuals that the evolution of each young child depends on the individual attention that he or she receives [4]. All these connections will result in a change from traditional paradigm to an emerging paradigm [6]. Learners in the emerging paradigm are more active in their learning through asking questions and seeking answers. Furthermore, they learn better by getting involved in teamwork both inside and outside school. The schools are well integrated into the community and information about them is openly available to all the stakeholders. Parents work with schools to co-steer instruction and provide a life-long learning model also play a crucial role in the children's learning process.

An organisation is a dynamic and complex ecological system. It needs an information system that deals with all the stakeholders inside and outside the organisation [7]. A learning or self-renewing organisation can only maintain its fluidity and stability if it has continuing access to new information on external factors and internal resources. A good information system enables all members of an organisation to monitor the effect of their actions and decisions. Without good information, an organisation is blind to its past achievements and failures, and to its future

an information system that can provide information to and feedback from the various stakeholders. They can then tailor immediate services to improve instructional programmes that enhance the students' achievement based on the feedback [8].

2. Dynamic Web-Based Information System

A dynamic web-based information system, *Community and Parents in Support of Schools Online* (eCOMP@SS), is a unique system where a critical mass of students, teachers, parents, experts, entrepreneurs and community stakeholders can congregate virtually to contribute views, ideas and make choices through the online questionnaires posted by the school leader(s) (*See figure*). The school's leadership system can address values, focus on students' learning and track performance excellence through quality questionnaires. The school can also execute its own responsibilities towards society by incorporating the stakeholders' involvement in activities both inside and outside the school. The web-based information system also enables the school to set clear stakeholder-focused strategic directions based on timely needs and to track the performance of the programmes. It allows the school to know and to utilise the full potential of its staff in order to create an excellent school. The full potential of the teachers can be developed through shared values or a common vision, and a school culture that inspires trust and practises empowerment such as providing opportunities for

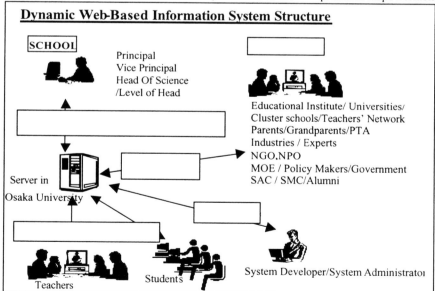

Dynamic Web-Based Information System Structure

SCHOOL

Principal
Vice Principal
Head Of Science
/Level of Head

Educational Institute/ Universities/
Cluster schools/Teachers' Network
Parents/Grandparents/PTA
Industries / Experts
NGO,NPO
MOE / Policy Makers/Government
SAC / SMC/Alumni

Server in
Osaka University

Teachers

Students

System Developer/System Administrator

involvement. The eCOMP@SS allows the school and the community stakeholders to design, implement and improve the key processes collectively in order to provide holistic education and to work towards enhancing the students' well-being. To sum up, a school can manage its internal resources and its external partnerships effectively and efficiently, in order to support the strategic planning and operation of its processes with the help of timely and accurate information [9]. People are the source of new ideas, improvements and

potential [1]. A school is an organisation in which until the school leaders understand what is going on, judgments and decisions based on intuition and experience will be flawed, distorted, incomplete, or inaccurate. School leaders need

innovations that sustained achievement is built upon, and the dynamic web-based information system can facilitate this aspect. The school will be able to discern clearly its strengths and areas for improvement, and hence it is an invaluable learning experience for both the school and its stakeholders.

3. A Case Study of Jurong Primary School

The eCOMP@SS was developed by the Microsoft's Active Server Pages (ASP), and was tested and evaluated at Jurong Primary School (JPS) in Singapore from August to December 2001. Online questionnaires for the stakeholders prepared by the school leaders and the author were successfully administered through the system. They have provided some useful insight as to how such web-based information system aids school personnel in adopting a consultative style of decision-making in both curricular and non-curricular matters with the stakeholders' involvement.

The questionnaire 'Parent Involvement' was created by the Vice-Principal to determine how the parents of class 5A students viewed the school activities, and in what ways they could effectively volunteer their services to the school based on their ability, interest, time, commitment and motivation. However, only one parent participated in this first survey after about one week. This is despite the fact that 60% of the parents had Internet access from their homes or offices. Some of the reasons for the poor response were later given at the evaluation of the eCOMP@SS by the school staff, students and parents who participated. Firstly, the school has never requested that these parents volunteer their services, and they were not mentally and physically ready to volunteer. Believing that the school shouldered the full responsibility of the education of their children was the mindset of some parents. Secondly, according to some students' feedback, their parents did not understand English, and their hope was for the questionnaires to be in their respective mother tongue languages. Thirdly, as gathered from the interview with the form teacher, the parents of the students in her class were busy with work, with some working overseas, and some were single parents, or some neither understood how to access the Internet nor English. In addition, some parents preferred meeting personally, receiving contact through the mail and telephone rather than making use of a new unfamiliar system. They did not feel secure with the system unless it was ensured that their identities remain absolutely confidential.

The questionnaire 'Getting To Know More About Your Child' was created by the form teacher to determine how her students spend their time outside school, and what kind of informal educational experience outside the school they have. 12 parents (31.6%) participated, and the questionnaire provides many interesting results for the

form teacher to consider ways to maximise the children's potential. Firstly, the teacher and parents need to work together to ensure that the pupils plan and manage their time faithfully. Secondly, JPS can consider organising workshops related to parenting matters for the mothers, so that they can play a more active role in educating their children at home. Moreover, parents can network among themselves by arranging to take turns in guiding the children who are staying in the same neighbourhood and are of similar academic level as their own children. Similarly, the school and the parents, or the parents themselves can work together to further develop pupils with similar special talents. The teachers should also give extra support to the children whose parents are not available to guide them in their project work. Thirdly, the school can further develop or improve non-academic skills such as swimming, music and art. From the feedback given, the school is required to organise more enrichment activities for the pupils to take part in with their parents during the school holidays. Fourthly, the form teacher manages to find out from the parents what television programmes her students watch and the time they spend watching these programmes. This enables her to provide proper guidance to her pupils. Next, the questionnaire also helps to determine if her students are getting along well with their peers in school. In fact, one parent said he was not sure about the above matter, and the teacher can actually find out the identity of this parent from the system administrator and then do a follow-up with the pupil concerned. Lastly, the survey suggests that the school should coordinate more with the various community groups that organise the Internet awareness programmes that help the parents to supervise their children. Furthermore, it is necessary for the school to provide multi-media learning resources in the school library for those parents who do not have access to these resources at home.

The Principal prepared the questionnaire 'To Improve School Organisation, Administration and Facilities' to determine the status of the organisation and administration of the school over the past 3 years. Furthermore, under the Programme for Rebuilding and IMproving Existing schools (PRIME) project, he would like to find out from the parents what the facilities that they like to see in the new school campus. Moreover, the survey includes an investigation of the extent of the parents' interest in forming a Parent Support Group (PSG) in the school, which is part of the school's long-term strategic objective. 12 parents and a former student in Canada participated in the online survey. Questions 1 to 13 are related to the school organisation, questions 14 to 19, the school administration, and questions 20 to 26, the school facilities. The first section provides useful information on the school organisation such as the school vision, parents' involvement in the school's decision-making through PSG's representatives, volunteering in PSG, 'Meet the Parents' session, and communication between the school and the parents. The school should also continue with the monthly newsletter (JPS Link) as most parents receive updated information from here. Nevertheless, the homepage and online JPS Link shows potential for those parents or former pupils who are now working overseas. The second section provides more positive feedback on the school administration such as the management of the school by the Principal and the working attitude of other administrative staff. As a matter of fact, there is more positive feedback in this section, and it indeed serves as a motivation and morale booster for the administrative staff. Nevertheless, a few negative comments should be taken positively to improve the school's services. The third section provides valuable information on the school facilities and the preferred enrolment for the school leaders to consider in the PRIME project.

The questionnaires 'Science Practical Test' targeted at class 5A pupils and the science teachers were created by the Level Head to evaluate the new science practical test. The feedback will be used to consider ways to improve the science practical test the following year. 38 pupils and 5 science teachers participated in the online evaluation. Majority of the teachers agreed that the school should conduct the science practical test, and they believed that the science practical test was a good learning experience for the pupils. Majority of the teachers agreed with the pupils that the amount of time given to complete the questions was sufficient, and that having 2 questions was quite appropriate although one teacher suggested that one question was enough, and it be set at a more difficult level. The students also evaluated whether Q1 and Q2 were interesting, easy, confusing, tedious or tricky. More than 90% of the pupils enjoyed the new science practical test, and many of them felt that the test was easy and useful. Lastly, about half of the students looked forward to another science practical test next year.

The questionnaire 'Living Together (Before)' created by the science teacher, was conducted before instruction to determine class 5A pupils' pre-knowledge and misconceptions. It is a short online quiz comprising of 10 questions on the science topic. Based on the feedback, the teachers can customise the instructions to cater to her students' needs. In addition, the questionnaire 'Living Together (After)' prepared by the author was conducted after the science teacher came back from a long medical leave. The purpose is to determine the students' knowledge of the topic taught by the relief teacher, and then the science teacher would conduct a follow-up lesson based on the results to clarify the students' misconceptions before the final examination in late October 2001. Various types of questions such as yes-no choice questions, multiple-choice questions, more-than-one-answer questions and fill-in-the blank questions were prepared in both the online quizzes. Based on the feedback given, majority of the students enjoyed learning science, and they found the science lessons interesting. In addition, almost all the students enjoyed the experiments and the IT-related lessons. Hence, the science teacher can consider using these modes to deliver the lessons more often.

4. Evaluation of the eCOMP@SS System

The questionnaires to evaluate the eCOMP@SS system were prepared by the author and a summary of the results is shown in the table below.

	Questions	Pupils	Parents	Staff
1.	The eCOMP@SS is easy to use.	84.1%	100%	100%
2.	The questions are easy to understand.	70.4%	100%	-
3.	The results presented are easy to understand.	59.0%	50.0%	100%
4.	The eCOMP@SS is accessible from anywhere.	77.3%	100%	100%
5.	I like to provide feedback to the school.	36.4%	75.0%	-
6.	The eCOMP@SS is the best channel to contribute feedback.	72.7%	75.0%	-
7.	I want to be more involved in the school programmes.	49.1%	8.3%	-

All the staff who participated agreed that the results were useful to them, and they could use the eCOMP@SS to determine the students' pre-knowledge and misconceptions before lessons. Similarly, they could use the eCOMP@SS to understand the students better, for instance, regarding what the students do at home. This will help them to evaluate lessons and allow the stakeholders such as experts and parents to contribute opinions or suggestions on academic content, thus creating diversity in instruction. Moreover, the school leaders can adopt a consultative decision-making style with the system. On the contrary, they also agreed that there were situations where an autocratic decision-making style was more appropriate. Nevertheless, they agreed that after analysing the responses from the stakeholders through the eCOMP@SS, they might change their initial decision or modify their approach in an earlier decision. They all agreed that the eCOMP@SS supported them in making informed and timely decisions. Besides, the staff agreed that the eCOMP@SS supported decisions in curricular and non-curricular matters based on the formative and summative evaluation they conducted. Despite the poor initial response, 3 out of 5 staff agreed that the stakeholders were motivated to provide views, feedback and suggestions to the school through the eCOMP@SS. Most importantly, the staff all agreed that there was more positive and constructive feedback from the stakeholders via the eCOMP@SS. Finally, there is the view that the eCOMP@SS allows the school leaders to adopt a strategic decision-making approach.

5. Conclusion

The various curricular and non-curricular questionnaires prepared by the various school staff in the eCOMP@SS, have enabled the various stakeholders inside and outside the school to support the school's decision-making. As a result, all the school staff agreed that such a system enabled them to adopt a consultative form of decision-making style. Besides, the server compiled all the responses of the online questionnaires, and then presented them to all the stakeholders and decision-makers. As such, all the school staff agreed that they could make timely and informed decisions that could benefit students in both the short and the long term, and that such forms of participation led to the commitment of some parents in supporting the school. Naturally, the ecological harmony among all the stakeholders can be achieved in the long term. In addition, the eCOMP@SS shows positive signs that it can facilitate good communication between the school and the homes, promote volunteering, stimulate home support for learning, help to represent other parents and encourage collaborating. Most significant is the finding that the eCOMP@SS supports the teachers in analysing the students and enables evaluation on lessons or academic programmes. The eCOMP@SS is indeed a feasible system and is critically important in monitoring, evaluating, and adjusting the implementation of action plans or programmes. Unfortunately, due to time constraints, a comprehensive study that extends to other community stakeholders, the school leaders' decision-making styles in various other situations are not possible yet. There was also not enough time for the teachers to use the eCOMP@SS to obtain diverse opinions and suggestions on academic content and to create diversity in instruction based on these experts' feedback. Nevertheless, the development of IT in education and community-home-school partnerships shows that the eCOMP@SS has the potential for further research that may benefit schools. Without doubt, the eCOMP@SS serves as an excellent 'online compass' in providing vital information about the direction the school should head towards in improving education for students with parents' involvement.

6. References

1. Razik, T.A. and Swanson, A.D. 2001. Fundamental Concepts of Educational Leadership (2nd Ed.) Merrill Prentice Hall. Chapters 10 and 15.

2. Gage and Berliner 1992. Educational Psychology (5th Edition): Houghton Mifflin Company. pp. 122-127.

3. William, M.D. et al. 2000. Integrating Technology into Teaching and Learning – Concepts and Applications (2nd Edition). Prentice Hall. Chapters 7, 9 and 10.

4. Senge, Peter et al. 2000. Schools That Learn: A Fifth Discipline Fieldbook for Educators, Parents, and Everyone Who Cares About Education. pp. 459 - 553

5. Ackerman, R.H. et al. 1996 Making Sense as a School Leader: Persisting Questions, Creative opportunities. Jossey Bass Inc. pp. 105 - 151.

6. Pelgrum, W.J. and Anderson, R.E. 1999. ICT and The Emerging Paradigm for Life Long Learning: a Worldwide Educational Assessment of Infrastructure, Goals and Practices. International Association for the Evaluation of Educational Achievement. pp. 1-18, 89-116 & 119-153.

7. Covey, S.R. 1999. Principle-Centred Leadership: Using Stakeholder Information System. Simon & Schuster UK Ltd. Chapter 22 pp. 224 - 235.

8. Snowden, P.E. & Gorton R.A. 1998. School Leadership & Administration: Important Concepts, Case Studies & Simulation – Chapter 1 Decision Making. McGraw Hill, 1998. pp.1 - 29.

9. Nahavandi, Afsaneh 2000. The Art and Sciences of Leadership – Using Resources Effectively. Prentice Hall. pp. 99-127.

A Software Design Process to Facilitate the Teaching of Mathematics

Janelle Pollard and Roger Duke, University of Queensland, ITEE.

Abstract

Despite the existence of a large range of software to support the teaching of mathematics, most mathematical educational software makes only limited use of the potential user interfaces. In particular, students are typically restricted in how they can express their working and solutions. This paper looks at the issue of how to design mathematical educational software to help students solve problems in a natural unrestricted manner. The focus is on describing, through a case study, a process for designing software that mirrors the pencil and paper way students traditionally solve mathematical problems.

1: Introduction

Despite the existence of a large range of software to support the teaching of mathematics, most mathematical educational software makes use of very limited user interfaces. For example, many programs simply require students to input their answers to specific problems or present students little more than pre-prepared solutions.

The focus of this paper is to demonstrate one process for extracting possible interfaces that enables students to input their working in a natural format similar to what they would do with pencil and paper. The ultimate aim is to design software that adds to what a student can do with pencil and paper but without forcing upon the student a particular solution strategy and without taking from the student the need to be individualistically creative and inventive.

2: The case study

Students were asked to attempt to solve the following problem [3].

These counters show the digits 1 - 9 and two addition signs. They have been arranged to make a total of 1,368.

In what different ways can you arrange the counters make a total of 1,188?

There are three main reasons this problem was chosen. Firstly, the problem is conceptually simple and does not require particular mathematical skills or techniques. Secondly, it is open ended with a number of solutions possible. Thirdly, it can be approached in a number of valid ways.

3: Data collection

Seven students, each with different mathematical skill levels (from final year high school to honours degree) were asked to solve this problem with pencil and paper. They were allowed as much time as they needed, though all stopped working inside ten minutes. Six of the seven found at least one solution; four found more than one solution; none were able to say how many solutions existed.

Afterwards, each student was asked to explain their strategy; notes about their strategy were recorded, along with notes on any distinctive approaches or techniques.

4: Data analysis

Analysis of the students' work can explain strategies used to solve the task and detect any errors in thinking [1][2]. Five common strategies for solving this particular task were identified:

☑ Swap two numbers of the original sum
☑ Find combinations for the ones or hundred columns
☑ Trial and error
☒ Subtract the answer from the example.
☒ Algebraic substitution for the number 1 to 9

(The first three strategies led to correct solutions, whereas the last two always seemed to end in dead ends.) The next step was to design an interface which allowed students to use as many of these problem solving strategies as possible. To do this, closer analysis of their working was required. Each worked solution was translated into a flow chart designed to capture the main steps in solving the problem, as performed by the student.

From the analysis of each student's flowchart, common aspects were identified and five main interface components were identified. With these five components it is possible to capture the working of each of the students. The components were:

* **the problem statement component** *where the original sum as presented in the problem was copied (this was usually the first step),*
* **a template component** *consisting of a 3 by 3 grid into which number could be inserted when searching for a solution,*
* **a combination/workspace component** *in which various combinations and sums of digits could be tested,*
* **a list of the numbers** *to keep track of which of the numbers 1 to 9 have been used so far,*
* **a summary component** *to record the attempts at a solution.*

5: The combination/workspace component

Taking just the combination/workspace component as an example, three interfaces were designed. The first interface enabled students to input a number; the computer then returns a list of combinations of numbers summing to the supplied number. The second interface used a standard text area enables students to type in any numbers, letters and symbols found on a standard keyboard, starting in the top left-hand corner and working from left to right. Neither of these two designs allows for the way students actual used pencil and paper. Students often wrote downwards and even left to right when summing numbers. The third interface was created to facilitate this by enabling the user to click and type anywhere in the editor; if 'enter' is pressed the curser moves down one line, relative to where they started typing.

6: Combining the various software interface components

We wish to combine the five main interface components in different ways so as to facilitate different learning strategies. One approach to help us overcome the common problem of discounting designs simply because they do not fit in with our implicit design beliefs is to insist we design at least one interface for each of the major categorise of software. There are several categorization systems for different types of programs [4][5][7][8]. In this case study we use the following categorization developed by Pollard [6]:

1. **Resource** electronic book
2. **Tool** computer as a (sophisticated) calculator
3. **Drill** given a question, input an answer and receive feedback
4. **Worksheet** given several questions, input answers and receive feedback
5. **Simulation** given a puzzle or virtual experiment, solve on the screen
6. **Discovery** presented with a scenario, manipulate the environment, check solutions or request more information

Interfaces for each of these categories were designed. The design which facilitates most of the five different components used by students is the *discovery* design. However, it is also the design which adds little to what is already facilitated by the humble pencil and paper. The *tool* design removes the tediousness of performing the addition and allows the student to focus solely on developing a strategy for solving the problem. The *simulation* design on the other hand provides guidance as to where errors have occurred by having numbers which add up to the wrong value turn a different colour. Hence a combination of some of these features and compromises between the extremes may develop a more educationally beneficial piece of software.

Having created these designs there remains one thing to do before considering implementing, and that is to ask the following two questions:

1. **Am I adding anything to the solving of the task by using a computer?** (What benefit is there for using a computer instead of any other resource?)
2. **Can I capture in the program at least the most common methods used to solve the task?** (It may not be possible to allow students to, say, draw a diagram on the screen. If so, is it still worthwhile designing software?)

7: Conclusions

Through the design process described, a series of interface designs were created which each look at the problem from different directions. The designs ranged from allowing the student to input no working through to facilitating all working expressed on paper by the students. The simple collection of students' work suggested several diverse interfaces and suggested various strategies for solving the problem.

More important than the actual interfaces designed, is the design process itself. The system for defining the task, collecting student solutions, analysing the flow of student working, grouping like methods and components, designing main components and finally designing interfaces from all existing categories of software, is a design process which we believe can be used to design and justify educational software that facilitates natural, unforced solving of tasks on computers.

References

[1] **Hoffer, A** (1978) *Didactics and mathematics : the art and science of learning and teaching mathematics.* Palo Alto, Cal: Creative Publications pp 127-142

[2] **Baker, A.** and **Baker, J. (1990)** *Mathematics in Process.* Eleanor Curtain Publishing, Australia.

[3] **Baker, J.** (2002) *The Naturally Mathematical Challenge 2001: Level 2.* Natural Maths, Australia.

[4] **Mawata, C.** (1998) *Uses of Java Applets in Mathematics Education.* University of Tennessee at Chattanooga. Proceedings of the Third Asia Technology Conference in Mathematics.

[5] **Pollard, J.** and **Duke, R.** (2001a) Effective Mathematics Education Software in the Primary School: A Teachers' Perspective. University of Queensland. Proceedings of the Sixth Asia Technology Conference in Mathematics

[6] **Pollard, J.** and **Duke, R.** (2001b) From Maths Problem to Program: *What's the best path?* 'Rethinking Structures and Practices' Conference, 19-20 October 2001, University of Queensland. (To appear)

[7] **Sims, R.** (1991) *Computer Based Training: a Handbook for Training Professionals,* Knowledge craft pg 135-139

[8] **Wills, S.** (1994). *Beyond Browsing: Making Interactive Multimedia Interactive,* in Rethinking the Role of Education in the Technological Age, EdTech94 Conference, Singapore May 1994, 54-68.

Soft Project Management Toward Socio Faculty Development

Akira Takemura
Seiryo Women's Junior College

Abstract

Activation in management of societal projects seems still difficult. Especially, in the case of projects that include various stakeholders, it is necessary for project leaders to adopt transparent process-explanation. As a methodology for their willing participation, we can expect the problem solving by a soft-approach, which is clearly different from the conventional plant-typed one. The soft-approach is the creative problem solving which is mainly based on the activity of improvement and review of socio faculty development. In this paper, as a study on the guideline for soft project management toward socio faculty development, the approach coordinator for segmental committee-typed problem solving is advocated. The roles and concrete activities of the approach coordinator including the working groups are mentioned.
Keywords: Socio Faculty Model, Approach Coordinator, Transparency and Relativity, Substantial Value of Critical Awareness, Approach Evaluating

1. Socio Faculty Model

As the normative characteristics for the socio faculty development, there are three-typed properties, which are subjective property of self-esteem, restrictive property of accountability and active one of continuous learning as shown in Fig.1. Self-esteem is a normative subjective property. The project member should perceive various problem situations keenly and break through initiatively. Especially he should have responsibility on his decision and skill to esteem himself independently. Accountability is a normative restrictive property. Until now, Japanese people have not lessoned to externalize his idea generation in school days consciously. Further they don't have recognition to have accountability to their idea in public. The accountability seems to be restriction for us to overcome. Actually in socio framework, all of the project member have to think; "which idea is desirable and feasible?" "What effects are expected?" from the viewpoint of "Cost to Satisfaction". Accordingly he must think to have accountability to his original opinion through conversations. These conversations mean not only verbal dialogue to the other but also self-conversation by using externalizing tools. Society is an endless open system. It is a knotty and rapid changing problem situation. It has been

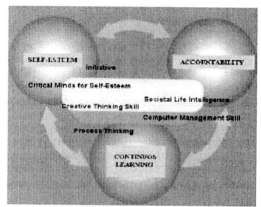

Fig.1 Socio Faculty Model

producing both effects and next causes. In this system, project members have to collaborate to learn their problem situation continuously with accumulative process thinking.

Visions for socio faculty development

As feasible self-esteem members, new typed project leader [Takemura2000a] and delegated working groups are advocated. For self-reproductive continuous learning, collaborative-arbitration feedback typed workflow is adopted. For accountability, the transparent process and relativity for group decision making are discussed. To promote accountability, some externalizing tool, for example AT-Method [Takemura2001], can be utilized.

2. Faculty development typed project

Characteristics of three projects are shown in Table 1.
The plant development typed project in which a project manager leads the other member corresponds to the activity of the decision making type of 'Attendance-Judgment'. For the consensus building, it would be most desirable for all the participants to commit to negotiate each other. In this 'commitment-negotiation' type, a group member can dialogue thorough all the process of learning activity. The most important role of a project leader: facilitator is to activate their dialogue. He has no necessity to explain the objectivity or well-grounded reason of their decision. He has no right to

Table 1 Characteristics of faculty developed typed project

Project Type	Self Learning	Faculty Development	Plant Development
Project Leader	Facilitator	Approach Coordinator	Project Manager (Supervisor)
Participation type & Decision Making Type	Commitment-Negotiation	Collaboration-Arbitration	Attendance-Judgment
Accountability Authority Responsibility	big small dispersion	⟷	small big concentration

obtain the participant's decision. They must charge themselves with all the responsibility.

However, except small group cases, there are a lot of fetters to realize 'commitment-negotiation' typed consensus building. Those may be caused by the old typed Japanese education and its cultural climate. Therefore, the bereaved project: 'collaboration-arbitration' type is expected for practical consensus building. Now it is important to prepare the workflow of this typed project. And on this project management, a project leader of a working group has special characteristics. His authority is not bigger than the project manager (or supervisor). His accountability is bigger than the project manager, and his responsibility is dispersed in stakeholders. It is necessary for him to equip dialogue ability to stain participant's satisfactory relationship of mutual trusts as well as facilitator. And he must give account of transparent approach process

→ Problem situation(P.S.)
- Organizing the 1st working group by A.C.
- Questionnaire gathering from stakeholder
- Arranging a problem situation
  - Considering the consequences of each problem
- Problem filtering
  - Cause analysis of filtered problems
- Breaking up the 1st working group by A.C.

1st contact to stakeholder

Pointing each filtered problem
- Critical awareness value of the 1st problem
- Critical awareness value of the 2nd problem

SUM= substantial value of critical awareness

- Organizing the 2nd working group by A.C. (for example by using Questionnaire Content Matrix)
- Set up the threshold of consciousness on the critical awareness values
- Discussing the policy for faculty development
  - Idea generation for solving points and theme
  - Prototyping scenario from theme
- Breaking up the 2nd working group by A.C.

2nd contact to stakeholder
Adoption of a theme and scenario

- Organizing the project by A.C.
  - Project actions
    - Planning
    - Quantitative evaluation of Proposal: Quality, Cost, Appointed date vs. Effect
    - Come into existence of stainable maintenance problem
    - Supply
  - End of project action
- Breaking up the project by A.C

Approach evaluating
← 3rd contact to stakeholder

Fig.2 Collaboration-arbitration Typed Workflow

and relativity to all the participant-stakeholders. This typed leader is named 'approach coordinator (A.C.)'.

3 Collaboration-arbitration typed workflow

The workflow for continuous learning activity is described as shown in Fig.2.

Some characteristics of the workflow

1) Substantial value of critical awareness

An awareness of the issues means the gap between one's target and present situation. His critical mind always changes and repeats endless self-awareness. The person has been dealt with this as no value. However there must be a man who is willing to pay some money if his problem may be resolved. Therefore critical mind is valuable. Problem situation is an entity derived from stakeholders' critical minds. The substantial value of critical awareness shows a value of this entity. The objectifying as a value can trigger off a resolving action.

2) Approach evaluating

a) Evaluation of approach documentation

b) Satisfaction check by using a thinking backward sheet

c) Change of critical awareness value

The change of critical awareness value is lastly calculated from following formulation.

$$\text{ChangeofCriticalAwarenessValue} = \frac{\text{NextCriticalAwarenessValue}}{\text{PreviousCriticalAwarenessValue}} \quad (1)$$

If the calculated value of problem environment is no more than 1, it is recognized that A.C. and stakeholders can success in their project. If more than 1, some stainable problems may come into existence.

References

Takemura, A., 2000a, Approach-Coordinators Inside of Organization as to be for Committee Typed Problem Solving, *Memoirs of Seiryo Women's Junior College*, No.29, 17-36 (in Japanese).

Takemura, A., 2000b, *Some Thoughts on System Analysis and Creative Thinking*, Tokyo: KIBUNDO (in Japanese).

Takemura, A., 2001, A Prototyping of AT-Method: Assembling Tools for Convergent Thinking Method, Proc. of International Conference on Computers in Education 2001 Seoul Korea, 1002-1009.

The Method to Visualize the Domain-oriented-explanation of Program's Behaviors

Fumihiko Anma, Taketoshi Ando, Ryoji Itoh, Tatsuhiro Konishi, Yukihiro Itoh
Faculty of Information, Shizuoka University.
E-mail: anma@cs.inf.shizuoka.ac.jp

Abstract

In this paper, we discuss the method of visualization of the explanations generated by our educational system. The system gives domain-oriented-explanations of programs. Our system can help learners to understand model programs and to find bugs in their programs by themselves. It generates explanations of the program's behaviors. Our previous system can output verbal explanations. However it is not easy for novice learners to get a concrete image of behavior of the program. Therefore we are trying to add a facility of generating explanations by visualizing the state of the world.

1 Introduction

The purpose of our research is to construct an educational system that helps novice-programming learners by explaining domain-oriented-functions of programs. Our previous system outputs explanations using vocabularies on the world where the problem is present. We call such a world 'the domain world' of the program. However, some learners cannot get a concrete image of behavior of the program from verbal explanations. Visual explanations are more effective to understand algorithms. Many algorithm animation systems have been developed [3]. In most of such systems that generate animations including concrete objects, teachers have to embody commands for drawing objects to the programs. On the other hand, our system can generate a visual explanation without such commands. In this paper, we discuss the method to generate visual explanations.

2 Our previous work

2.1 Domain world models

Our system has a domain world model and simulates a target program on the model, to understand behavior of the program. By using the result of understanding, it generates an explanation of the program's behaviors. However it is difficult to simulate behavior of all types of program on the only one domain world model. Then we examine programming exercises and classify them into 15 types. We have to design individual domain world model for each type of exercises [1][2]. In previous work, we constructed the *'greater and lesser world model'* for the exercises solved by paying attention to numerical order such as an exercise of sorting and the *'two dimensional space world model'* that is used for some numerical analyzing methods such as

'Newton method' or 'Simpson method'.

2.2 Generation of a verbal explanation

Our system generates verbal explanations of target programs written in PASCAL language. In order to make a familiar explanation, our system likens values in an array to cards or balls. Figure 1 shows an example of verbal explanations generated by our system. It illustrates the verbal explanation of behavior of a sorting program on the *'greater and lesser world'*.

Figure1: an example of the system's outputs

3 Visualization of explanations of programs

3.1 Drawing procedure

When the system outputs visual explanations, they are desirable to correspond to verbal explanations. Therefore, our system generates one picture per each statement. Each picture shows the state after execution of each statement. In accordance with the order of execution of the program, the system shows each picture with a verbal explanation. In each picture, entities constructing a world model are drawn. The variations of entities are different by the domain world. For example, the *'greater and lesser world'* can be constructed from various sizes of balls. We prepare procedures that draw entities for each domain world. We call the procedures 'drawing procedure'.

3.2 Generation of drawing data

Each picture represents the state of the domain world. In order to draw each picture, it is necessary that the system know information on the world after execution of the statement, such as number of entities, positions of them, size of them and so on. We call the information the 'drawing data'. We define the initial drawing data by each exercise. The drawing data can be generated by modifying the previous drawing data according to execution of a statement. The modification is done in the following way: First, the system identifies the operation corresponding to the statement. Next, it identifies the entities operated by the statement. Then it modifies the drawing data by a procedure defined for each operation. As long as the system draws pictures of the *'greater and lesser world'*, it can identify an entity and an operation from the syntactic pattern of the statement. For example, the pattern "variable_1 := value_1" means that the operation "movement" is applied to "value_1" in order to move the value to the position "variable_1" regardless of context. Therefore, we define procedures to update a drawing data for every syntactic pattern of statement, i.e. for assignment statement, read statement, for statement, and if statement.

3.3 Example of the visualization system of the *'greater and lesser world'*

For example, when a learner inputs the program shown in Figure 2, our system outputs verbal explanations (a), (b) and (c). The Figure 3 shows the output of the prototype system that visualizes the behavior of the program in the *'greater and lesser world'*.

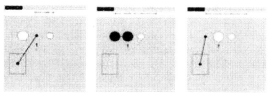

Figure 2: a verbal explanation

(a) x:=a[2]; (b) a[2]:=a[1]; (c) a[1]:=x;
Figure 3: an explanation of sorting

4 Extension of the visualization

4.1 The problem of extension

In order to handle general domain worlds, we have to resolve a problem concerning to simulation. In the general world such as *'two dimensional world'*, it is usual that the same syntactic pattern of sentences have different roles in a general domain world. For example, in the *'two dimensional space'*, an assignment statement may have a role to define the intersection point of two lines, or a role to define the middle point of two points. Accordingly it is difficult to recognize the role of the statement by syntactic pattern of the sentence. As a result the problem of ambiguity of the role of the values in the statements is caused.

4.2 The drawing procedure and the drawing data in the world of the *'two dimensional space'*

When we think extension of the visualization method, we can apply the following framework.
1 We define the drawing procedure of each entity.
2 We define the updating functions for each data.
3 The system draws the initial state of the world.
4 The system calculates the drawing data after executing

a certain statement.
5 The system draws the following states by executing drawing procedure with the new drawing data.
In the *'greater and lesser world'*, the system can update drawing data by using the syntactic pattern of the sentence in the step 4. Instead, the system updates drawing data by referring the domain world model. In the simulation process, all entities in the domain world are discovered and each attribute of them is clarified. Moreover, each variable manipulated in each statement is connected with corresponding attribute of a certain entity. So, the system can update drawing data in the following way:
(1) The system identifies a variable the value of which is changed by executing the targeted statement.
(2) It identifies the entity operated by the statement by checking the connection between the variable and an attribute of the entity.
(3) It arranges the drawing data for the entity, and adds the data to previous drawing data.

4.3 An Example of the visualization system of the *'two dimensional space'* world

Figure 4 shows the output of the behavior of the Newton Method program.

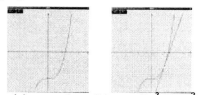

(a) x := x1; (b) x := ((x^3-2)/3x^2)+x1;
Figure 4: an explanation of the Newton Method

5 Conclusion

In this paper, we discuss the method to visualize the behavior of the program. The method are applied to the domain world of the *'greater and lesser'* and the *'two dimensional space'*. We have to extend the system that can output the visualization of the buggy program in future work.

References

[1] Itoh, R., Nishizawa, M., Konishi, T., Itoh, Y.: "A programming learning system which makes Domain – Oriented - Explanations", Proc. of ICCE'98, Beijing, China, Vol.1, pp.432-440, (1998).
[2] Ando, T., Itoh, R., Konishi, T., Itoh, Y.: "Extension of the Educational System that Generates Domain-Oriented-Explanations of Programs -On Methods for Designing Domain World Models and for Simulation-", Proc. of ICCE'99, Chiba, Japan, Vol.1, pp.856-860, (1999).
[3] Brown, M. H.: "Zeus: A system for algorithm animation and multi-view editing (research report No.75)", DEC systems research center, (1992).

Interpretation of Ungrammatical Sentences in a Language Education System for Nonnative Speakers

Masahiro Suzuki, Toshihiko Itoh, Tatsuhiro Konishi, Makoto Kondo, Yukihiro Itoh
Faculty of Information, Shizuoka University, Japan
E-mail : cs7047@cs.inf.shizuoka.ac.jp

Abstract

In learning foreign languages, especially when the learners want to polish their conversation skills, they need to put themselves in a variety of situations where they perform various tasks in their target languages. Conventional language education systems offer exercises for fixed phrases or conversation practice using predetermined dialog patterns. Ideally, the learners should participate in a dialog that dynamically changes in accordance with the utterances of the participants, and they should decide what to say by themselves according to the changing environment. Such a learning environment needs a teacher to participate in the dialog and help the learners continue the conversation even if their utterances are ungrammatical. This research aims to construct a system that plays a teacher's role of this kind. This paper is concerned with how to develop a system that accepts and interprets both grammatical and ungrammatical inputs.

1. Introduction

This paper deals with how to achieve the interpretation of ungrammatical sentences in a language education system based on the communicative approach (henceforth, CA). Based on the technique to be proposed in this paper, a Japanese education system for nonnative speakers is currently under development. The system is outlined later in this paper.

The number of non-Japanese studying the Japanese language keeps increasing both in and outside Japan. On the other hand, those learners do not have good chances of using their language skills freely in a practical environment, and the need for a practical Japanese education system has been increasing.

Methodologically, language teaching has two aspects: (1) teaching knowledge about the target languages (grammar, constructions, etc.) and (2) improving the learners' communicative ability. Conventional language education systems mostly focus on the former aspect. The exceptions include [1] and a consumer product called "Native World" (Oki Software). However, they employ formulaic dialog patterns and the learners engage in repetitive practice of the patterns. Actual conversation, however, involves much more sentence styles and its content varies widely. In addition, the topic of conversation often switches from one to another, and the interruption of the conversational flow by a new topic is not rare, either. In such changeable conversation, the participants must understand each other's utterances and convey their intention in order to achieve successful communication. The CA gives the highest priority to the improvement of learners' communicative ability in this sense.

Taking these into consideration, we are developing a practical Japanese education system that engages in conversation with a learner and accepts whatever input the learner thinks is appropriate. Such a system significantly improves learning environment for language learners because a conversation partner (i.e. the system) is available for the learners anytime and anywhere as far as the system is prepared for them.

2. Learning Environment

Several teaching methods have been proposed in the CA. One of them includes role playing associated with a practical function/objective like asking the way to a destination. Let us call such a function/objective a task. When a teacher and a student are playing their roles, the teacher tries his/her best to continue the conversation. When the student makes grammatical errors, the teacher does not stop the conversation for correcting the errors; rather, the teacher continues to play the role by inferring what the student has tried to convey from the content of the student's task and the preceding conversational flow. This is because error correction often discourages the learners from using their language skills. According to the CA, grammatical correctness is of less importance than conveying one's intention.

Our prototype system is employing this type of teaching method as shown in Figure 1. One of the biggest advantages of this approach is that careful setting of a task enables us to control what to teach through the task. In fact, we have confirmed that certain tasks, if properly set up, prompt the learners' utterances involving particular grammatical constructions. It opens a way to a future system that will detect the learner's errors and automatically offer tasks that encourage the learner to produce sentences involving grammatical constructions that the learner does not have a good command of.

Task {
Make a hotel reservation
Conditions: (a) location = Hamamatsu (b) rate = less than 7,000 yen
}

U: Hotel. I want reserve.
S: Do you want to make a hotel reservation ?
U: Hamamatsu is good.
S: Are you looking for a hotel in Hamamatsu ?
U: Yes.
S: A Hotel and B Hotel are available.

Figure 1: Role Playing Using the System

3. Fundamental Considerations
3.1. Prerequisites for a Dialog System

A dialog system generally needs to identify problems to be solved and conditions for the problem solving. This should be achieved by using the input sentences, the context of the dialog and the system's knowledge. The diversity of input sentences makes it very difficult for the system to carry out the above jobs. This is mainly because input sentences with different styles are mapped onto semantic representations with different forms, which we cannot formally evaluate. Stating it specifically, when two words combine into a phrase (i.e. a dependency structure), the semantics of the words, however precisely defined, does not tell us the meaning of the whole phrase. Consequently, the following problems arise.

(a) The variety of surface dependency structures is carried over to the diversity of the corresponding semantic representations without interpreting the dependency structures.

(b) The variety of semantic representations leads to the variety of relations between semantic structures and their meanings; hence, it becomes very difficult to formally evaluate the meaning of a given semantic representation.

A Japanese dialog system being developed in the JDT project [2] circumvents the problems; however, it is not implemented so as to accept ungrammatical sentences. We have extended the JDT system to build our prototype system that accepts ungrammatical sentences.

3.2. Generation of Semantic Representations from Ungrammatical Sentences

As mentioned in section 2, the CA gives the highest priority to the improvement of learners' communicative ability. Accordingly, as far as a teacher understands the intention of a student's utterance, the teacher continues the conversation, ignoring whatever errors the student has made. Unfortunately, however, there are no established methods for (1) distinguishing ungrammatical inputs from grammatical ones and (2) inferring the intention of ungrammatical inputs by subtracting meaningful expressions from the inputs. This is mainly because current syntactic parsers store rules for parsing grammatical sentences correctly. Therefore, ungrammatical inputs are not presupposed in current syntactic parsers. To circumvent this problem, let us take the following steps.

(1) to identify grammaticality of inputs by adding restrictive grammatical rules to a current parser

(2) to subtract content words from ungrammatical inputs and infer the intention through matching the content words with the system's knowledge about a given task

As for grammatical inputs, the semantic representations are generated based on the outputs of a syntactic parser.

3.3. Learners' Misunderstanding of Tasks

Within our teaching method, learners should correctly understand the content of a given task. If they misunderstand a task, they will make utterances irrelevant to the task. The system, therefore, should recognize the relevance of an utterance to the task.

3.4. Feedback to Learners

In the CA, a teacher should give appropriate feedback like error correction to learners at some point in their activity; otherwise, the learners might acquire incorrect knowledge about their target languages. The JDT dialog system is well capable of embodying such educational tactics within its dialog management. It is because the JDT system is controlled by a set of rules and its knowledge for problem solving. The system cyclically compares conditionals of the rules with semantic representations accumulated in the context and follows the rule that matches to the current context. Although the system is capable of embodying educational tactics, no such tactics is implemented in the current prototype system.

4. Implementations
4.1. Semantic Representations in the JDT System

The relation between a predicate and its case elements/adverbials can always be translated into a set of ordered pairs of an attribute of the event denoted by the predicate and its value: <event attribute, value>. Semantic representations in the JDT system embed such pairs within themselves as basic units, which is shown in Figure 2. Such semantic representations make it possible to translate a variety of surface predicates into a single identifying predicate. Consequently, various surface dependencies are reduced to one type of dependency held between a nominal case element and its complement. This enables us to overcome the problem discussed in section 3.1. In addition, semantics of attribute nouns can be defined if we properly delimit a target domain. In such a well-delimited domain, the semantics of attribute nouns enables us to define the universal set of possible meanings. Interpretation of a given sentence is realized as matching between attributes and mapping from attributes to the universal set.

Figure 2: Partial Semantic Representation

4.2. Task Knowledge

As mentioned in section 3.2, a dialog system for foreign language education should accept ungrammatical inputs. In actual conversation between a teacher and a student, the teacher presupposes a set of possible utterances of the student from the context including the content of their task, what the students has said so far, etc. The presupposition helps the teacher interpret the student's ungrammatical utterances. Our system realizes such presupposition as *task knowledge*, which is a set of JDT-style semantic representations for possible utterances in a particular task. The system interprets ungrammatical inputs referring to the task knowledge. Figure 3 shows how semantic representations are

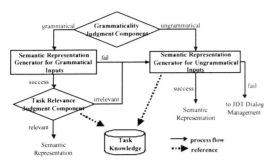

Figure 3: Process Flow of the System

generated in our system.

4.3. Grammaticality Judgment Component

The Grammaticality Judgment Component judges whether an input sentence is grammatical or not. Syntactic parsing is carried out by the CSK parser (CSK), which has a set of parsing rules based on the grammar of the Japanese language. The parser infers and complements a possible dependency as much as possible and, therefore, often 'succeeds' in parsing ungrammatical inputs, and outputs incorrect dependency structures. On the other hand, we can register semantic features compliant to the parser's concept hierarchy into its lexicon. We can also define a set of rules for undesirable dependency. These rules are defined in terms of words, parts of speech, semantic features and combinations of these. These features of the CSK parser enable us to define a set of grammatical rules for identifying ungrammatical sentences independently from tasks. We have adjusted the parser so that it rejects sentences that involve typical errors made by Japanese learners. The adjustment has been based on an error analysis reported in [3]. The Grammaticality Judgment Component regards sentences parsed successfully by the parser as grammatical and those rejected by the parser as ungrammatical.

4.4. Semantic Representation Generator for Grammatical Inputs

Input sentences judged as grammatical go to the Semantic Representation Generator for Grammatical Inputs and the corresponding semantic representations with the form discussed in section 4.1 are generated. In generating semantic representations from grammatical inputs, the system employs the framework reported in [2].

4.5. Semantic Representation Generator for Ungrammatical Inputs

When an input is judged as ungrammatical, the system generates a list of concepts representing content words contained in the input. The system then tries to generate a semantic representation from this list. When a content word is ambiguous, it is difficult to identify the concept associated with it. Specifically, if an ungrammatical input is something like "hoteru-no onsen-ga aru ga yoi (hotel-GEN [1] hot spring-NOM [2] be/exist NOM good)," we cannot determine whether *aru* in this example corresponds to English *be* or *exist*. Thus, when an input contains a word that is ambiguous in *n*-ways, the system generates *n*-numbered lists each of which is associated with one of the possible concepts representing the ambiguous word.

In actual conversation, we can understand the intention of the speaker even though the utterances often involve word order change and omission of words. This is because we are put in a particular context that delimits the topics in the conversation, and the limitation on the topics enables us to determine the relations between the concepts in an utterance to some reliable degree. In order to determine the relations among the concepts in the list mentioned above, the system takes advantage of the task knowledge discussed in section 4.2. Each concept appearing in the task knowledge is associated with pairs of an event attribute and its value. All the attribute-value pairs are listed in a table that we call an attribute-value table. When the system generates a semantic representation from the list of concepts appearing in an ungrammatical input, the system refers to the attribute-value table and recursively searches for a concept that can be associated with an attribute of a given concept. Figure 4 shows the generation of a semantic representation for the ungrammatical sentence "chikaku Hamanako-wa hoteru-wa ii (neighboring spot Lake Hamana-TOP[3] hotel-TOP good).

4.6. Task Relevance Judgment Component

The Grammaticality Judgment Component only distinguishes grammatical inputs from ungrammatical ones. Therefore, if a learner does not understand the task and makes an input irrelevant to it, the system cannot properly respond to the learner. If the system can determine the relevance of a given semantic representation to the task, the system is able to properly respond to the learner even if the input is irrelevant to the task.

Within the current framework, we can describe the system's task knowledge with a certain degree of generality. Consequently, the relevance of a given semantic representation can be determined by examining its synonimity to (a part of) the task knowledge. Since the semantic interpretation in our system is achieved

---

[1] genitive case marker
[2] nominative case marker
[3] topic marker

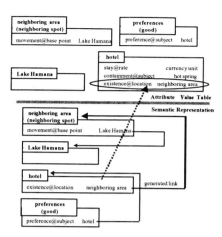

Figure 4: Semantic Representation of Ungrammatical Inputs

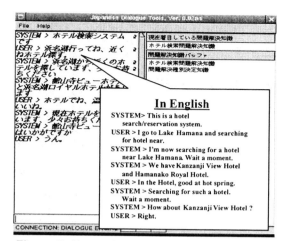

Figure 5: Example Dialog of the System

through the accumulation of semantic representations involving attribute-value pairs, synonymity judgment can be realized as matching between attribute-value pairs. Currently, this component is yet to be implemented.

5. Example

We have extended the JDT system so as to embody the Semantic Representation Generators for Grammatical/Ungrammatical Inputs. Figure 5 shows how it works. In this example, the first and the second utterances of the user are ungrammatical. The system's responses to those ungrammatical inputs clearly show that it successfully interprets them and continues the conversation. At present, the system cannot recognize inputs irrelevant to a given task, since the Task Relevance Judgment Component has not been implemented.

6. Evaluation
6.1. Evaluation of Grammaticality Judgment Component

We have evaluated the Grammaticality Judgment Component by comparing the outputs of the component with the corresponding human judgments. We have collected ungrammatical examples from [3], and divided them into two groups: one is for a closed test (437 sentences) and the other is for an open test (429 sentences). The grammaticality of each sentence has been judged by human subjects. Table 1 shows the result of the evaluation before adjusting the system as described in section 4.3. The positive/negative columns indicate whether the system has judged the sentences as grammatical or not. The true/false rows indicate whether the human subjects have judged them as grammatical or not. Within our framework for the generation of semantic representations discussed in sections 4.4 and 4.5, the grammatical sentences that the

system incorrectly judges as ungrammatical (the true-negative section in Table 1) do not cause serious problems. This is because if the system succeeds in morphological parsing of those examples, the Semantic Representation Generator for Ungrammatical Inputs generates their semantic representations.

Serious problems may arise if the system incorrectly judges ungrammatical sentences as grammatical because the Semantic Representation Generator for Grammatical Inputs cannot generate appropriate semantic representations from such ungrammatical sentences. Taking these into account, we have added grammatical rules based on learners' typical errors. In adding the rules, their generality has also been considered. After the adjustment, the result has changed as shown in Table2. The ratio of correct judgments (i.e. the true-positive and false-negative sections) was 83.7% before the adjustment and the adjustment has raised it to 91.3%. The sentences in the true-negative section have decreased from 54 sentences (12.3%) to 17 sentences (3.8%).

In order to determine the validity of the added grammatical rules, the open test using 429 sentences has been conducted. The result is shown in Table 3. The result shows no significant differences from the result in Table 2. It means that the added grammatical rules are general enough to be useful for other sets of data, indicating that their validity is not restricted to a particular kind of task.

6.2. Evaluation of Semantic Representation Generator for Ungrammatical Inputs

The Semantic Representation Generator for Ungrammatical Inputs has been evaluated in the following manner. Before the evaluation, we have created 53 ungrammatical sentences that would appear in the following task.

		System	
		Positive	Negative
Hu-man	True	331	17
	False	54	35

Table1: Closed Test Result (before adjustment)

		System	
		Positive	Negative
Hu-man	True	327	21
	False	17	72

Table2: Closed Test Result (after adjustment)

		System	
		Positive	Negative
Hu-man	True	317	32
	False	20	60

Table3: Open Test Result

Task: Search for a hotel that satisfies the following conditions:

(1) the hotel is located near Hamamatsu Station;

(2) the hotel is located near a hospital;

(3) the hotel has a hot spring bath;

(4) the rate of the hotel is lower than 7,000 yen.

Typical errors found in [3] have been taken into account in creating the examples.

The output semantic representations from these examples have been compared with the interpretations of these examples by human subjects. The subjects are three students at the Faculty of Information, Shizuoka University. After the explanation of our teaching method, the subjects have been given a list of the ungrammatical examples and asked to infer the intention of each sentence and describe it in a grammatical sentence. Note that the evaluation result may be biased by the seriousness of the errors. In order to circumvent the potential problem, we have classified the examples into the following two groups.

(A) ungrammatical sentences that all the subjects interpret synonymously
(B) ungrammatical sentences that all the subjects do not interpret synonymously

46 sentences have been classified into the group A and 7 examples have been classified into the group B. The criterion for the group B amounts to saying that even the human subjects cannot reproduce the intention of those examples uniformly.

In our system, continuation of conversation does not depend on the identity of an output with the corresponding human interpretation. Note that the system's response is controlled by a set of rules. Consequently, if an output from an ungrammatical input triggers the same rule as the one that is triggered by the corresponding grammatical input, then the system successfully continues the conversation irrespective of whether the output is identical with the corresponding human interpretation. This means that even if the system's output is not exactly identical to the human interpretation, we may reasonably regard them as virtually identical with each other since the system's behaviors triggered by them are exactly identical. Accordingly, we have examined whether the system's outputs from the examples in the group A trigger the same rules as the ones that would be trigged by the corresponding human interpretations (i.e. the semantic representations generated from the subjects' answers).

As a result, all the 46 examples have been confirmed to trigger the same rules as the corresponding human interpretations would.

In addition, all the subjects have uniformly reproduced the intention of 17 sentences out of the 46 examples in the group A; that is, as for these 17 sentences, the subjects' answers would result in the identical semantic representations. Among the 17 examples, the system has generated 14 semantic representations that are identical with those generated from the subjects' answers. As for the other 3 sentences, all the subjects have described the intentions by relative clauses as in "a hotel that is located near Hamamatsu Station" whereas the system has the corresponding expressions with an adnominal phrase as in "a hotel near Hamamatsu Station". This difference has resulted in the different semantic representations. Recall that the difference of those semantic representations has not prompted the different behavior of the system.

7. Summary and Further Problems

This paper has proposed a Japanese education system for non-native speakers based on the CA. The technique to achieve the interpretation of ungrammatical sentences has been examined in detail. We have extended an existing parser so that the system determines the grammaticality of input sentences. Semantic Representation Generators for Grammatical/ Ungrammatical Inputs have also been implemented. The Grammaticality Judgment Component and the Semantic Representation Generators for Ungrammatical Inputs have been evaluated and their validity has been confirmed. Improvement of the Grammaticality Judgment Component and implementation of the Task Relevance Judgment Component remain as further topics of the research. Embodying educational tactics into our system should also be considered in the future research.

References

[1] Sagou, N., Takeda, N.: "The CAL System for English Conversation using Role Playing Game" (in Japanese), IPSG SIGnotes Computers in Education, No.58, pp.13-20, (2000)
[2] Noguchi, Y., Ikegaya, Y., Takagi, A., Nakashima, H., Konishi, T., Itoh, T., Kondoh, M., Itoh, Y.: "A Framework for Semantic Representation for Natural Language Dialog system", SNLP-O-COCOSDA, pp.231-236, (2002)
[3] Ichikawa, Y.: "*Nihongo goyou reibun shou jiten*". Bonjinsha, Tokyo. (1997)

From the communication situation and intention to the linguistic form: design approach of the PILÉFACE system

Ruddy Lelouche

Département d'Informatique, UNIVERSITÉ LAVAL, Québec G1K 7P4, CANADA

Tel.: (+1-418) 656 2131 (2597)   Fax: (+1-418) 656 2324   E-mail: Ruddy.Lelouche@ift.ulaval.ca

Abstract

In language learning, the communicative competence implies that the language learner master certain pragmatic usage rules, which are mastered by the native speaker, but unspoken and unwritten, and therefore implicit. The PILÉFACE system (for "Programme Intelligent pour les Langues Étrangères Favorisant l'Approche Communicative de l'Enseignement") is aimed at establishing the relationships, in a given communicative setting, between the communicative situation description and communication intention on the one hand, and the linguistic form(s) adequately expressing that intention in that context on the other hand. In this paper, we present the design method of PILÉFACE and the resulting system architecture, and finally a complete example of how the system operates.

Keywords: Intelligent tutoring systems, language learning, pragmatics, communicative situation, communication intention, linguistic realization, representation and simulation of implicit knowledge, architecture, system design.

Introduction

In language learning, the learner is expected not only to acquire a linguistic competence, i.e. to assimilate lexical and grammatical knowledge and correctly use that knowledge, but also to acquire a communicative competence, i.e. to adequately express her communicative goal in a given communicative setting (for a change, we use the feminine as our generic gender). To do so, she must be aware of the relevant parameters describing a given situation and to choose accordingly which linguistic production to use in order to express her goal. This can be done by using certain pragmatic usage rules. Indeed, the pragmatic aspect of language, i.e. by definition "those linguistic investigations that make necessary reference to aspects of the context, where the term *context* is understood to cover the identities of participants, the temporal and spatial parameters of the speech event, and ... the beliefs, knowledge and intentions of the participants in that speech event, and no doubt much besides" [Levinson, 1983, p. 5], refers widely to implicit knowledge. And making implicit knowledge explicit is one of the difficult

and challenging problems of artificial intelligence, in particular in conjunction with common sense representation and reasoning [Jackson, 1990, p. 13]. Certainly pragmatics had been tackled in computational linguistics long before our research started [Allen & Perrault, 1980], but not (to our knowledge) its incorporation into a program aimed at second language acquisition.

Most pragmatic usage rules used in everyday communication are mastered by the native speaker, but unspoken and unwritten, and therefore implicit. Because of the importance of these usage rules in the communicative approach [Hymes, 1984], we were interested in a computer program that could take them into account in foreign language teaching, in our case French as a second language. This endeavor to define implicit and explicit knowledge progressively led us to more fundamental research questions [Huot & Lelouche, 1991]. The purpose of this article is to point to the problems we encountered and to explain the design methodology we used in our attempt to solve them, i.e. in designing the PILÉFACE language learning system (an acronym for "Programme Intelligent pour les Langues Étrangères Favorisant l'Approche Communicative de l'Enseignement").

The paper by Lelouche [1994] describes what making something explicit means; here, we concentrate mainly on the PILÉFACE foundations and architecture. First, section 1 recalls its objectives. Then section 2 defines its complete albeit informal specifications. Section 3 describes the reasoning mechanisms used and the resulting system architecture. Finally, section 4 presents a complete example of how the system operates.

1. Objectives of PILÉFACE

The PILÉFACE system establishes the relationships between, on the one hand, the *situation description* and the *communication intention* and, on the other hand, the *linguistic production(s)* adequately expressing that intention in that context. It was designed with three goals in mind, presented in [Lelouche & Huot, 1985]. Here, we limit our discussion to the linguistic goal of PILÉFACE, namely taking into account the pragmatic aspects of speech acts.

The system is to operate under one of three modes, as shown on figure 1. In *generation mode*, the system is to produce *utterances* consistent with the communication situation and the communication intention. In *analysis mode*, the system should determine whether, how and why an utterance, proposed by a student for instance, is or is not consistent with the predefined communication situation and intention. A third mode links conceptually our research to the future tutoring module of the system: the *tutoring mode* will exhibit the capabilities of the above two, but also some additional dialogue and feedback capabilities. Note that the third mode is outside the scope of this paper.

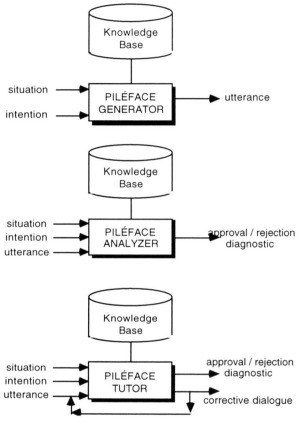

Figure 1. - The three modes of the PILÉFACE system

2. Data organization: problem specification

The first difficulty we had to address was to organize and specify the problem data, i.e. completely describe the communication intention (2.1), the communication situation (2.2), and the corresponding linguistic production or form, here an utterance (2.3).

2.1 Communication intention

The *communication intention* or goal [Austin, 1962; Searle, 1969, 1979] is the simplest, since it is clearly specified. In fact, we had to restrict the expertise domain of our system [Hayes-Roth & al., 1983] and, in order to abide by the communicative approach principles, we chose the

communication intention as the criterion used to do so. In its first version, our system thus only deals with the intention of *greeting someone* in a face-to-face setting, since it is one of the first communication intentions expressed by an individual. Other possible intentions to communicate are: excusing oneself, saying goodbye, or making a request.

2.2 Communication situation

The *communication situation* was the most complex problem data to formalize. To describe it, we developed a model [Lelouche, 1986] that:
- *separates* the situation parameters describing the situation, from the social, cultural, affective, psychological, and economic elements associated with it;
- *is adaptable* to various kinds of situation descriptions, with various levels of precision or of insight;
- distinguishes *background parameters* (only one instance for a given particular situation), that are mostly spacio-temporal indications, from *individual parameters* (one instance per actor or character), that determine the character's identification, social status and behaviors, as well as the various roles (real or fictitious) she might play; in particular, our model accounts for situations involving loaned roles (*X* believes that *Y* thinks that ...) or borrowed roles (*X* wants *Y* to believe that ...) ;
- takes into account the fact that *role parameters are directed* in general.

The main interest of the proposed model is the first one, namely the separation between the *situation parameters*, used to describe a situation and fed into the system for each problem-solving session, and the *general knowledge* associated with them, independent from any particular situation and stored in permanent external knowledge bases. This knowledge is necessary to fully interpret the implications of the situation parameters and to make proper inferences from them. The interested reader is refered to [Lelouche, 1994], that presents in detail the groups of parameters we have identified so far, as well as the general external knowledge associated with each group.

2.3 Linguistic form or utterance

The last component of the problem data is the linguistic form or *utterance* used to express the communication intention, here greeting someone. Utterances are described by a formal BNF-type grammar and by sets of rules of different kinds: *syntactic* (agreement rules for instance), *semantic* (only certain adjectives may be used to address the interlocutor), and naturally *pragmatic* (to make the utterance components appropriate to the situation). Our grammar specifies three main components for a greeting utterance: a *greeting formula* like "good morning", "hello", "hi", etc. (only mandatory component), a *term of address* like "Sir", "Professor", a first name, "honey", "you", etc., and an *inquiry* like "how are you?", "OK?", etc. This knowledge is also stored in an external problem-independent base. Finally, we also have a dictionary to describe and store the various terms that may appear in a target-language utterance; its structure is not described here.

3. Reasoning mechanisms and system architecture of PILÉFACE

The reasoning mechanisms of the PILÉFACE system result from two fundamental decisions about the flow of knowledge from the communication situation and intention to the corresponding utterance(s) to be generated or analysed. These decisions allow us to define the exchange style (3.1) and the summarized context (3.2), which can then lead us to define the system architecture (3.3).

3.1 Exchange style

The first decision is *theoretic*. It consists of separating the linguistic aspects of the problem, that characterize the utterance (see 2.3), from the other aspects (sociological, cultural, geographical, and psychological) identified earlier, that characterize the situation (see 2.2). We thus defined an arbitrary border, called the *exchange style*, as a compulsory intermediate step of the system cognitive process. Its definition is based on the following criterion: if we were interested in teaching English or Spanish rather than French as a target language, the rules deriving the exchange style from the given communication situation description would be left unchanged (in a given culture), whereas the rules using the exchange style to derive and generate or analyse possible utterances would have to be modified according to the selected target language. Incidentally, that separation led us to realize that some communicative situation parameters influence the exchange style, while some others, used only in the utterance generation or analysis (like the adressee's name or the time of day) do not.

At present, the exchange style (still evolving) is made of five ordinal parameters containing the global characteristics of the linguistic realization to be generated (for each one, the possible values are given in parentheses, and the default value is underlined): the exchange style *level* (respectful, polite, and/or familiar), the *personalization index* (impersonal, nominative, affective, and/or intimate), the realization *tonality* (serious, casual, and/or folksy), the realization *insistance* (stressed, normal, and/or reduced), and the retained *addressing style* (use of "tu", and/or use of "vous"). Every one of these parameters may take a single value or a sequence of consecutive values; thus the system can accept several possible forms of linguistic realizations compatible with the given situation, when the context allows it.

3.2 Summarized context

The second decision has an *empirical* basis. It consists of extracting from the description of the communication situation (complete and possibly complex) some information that is perceived to be necessary and sufficient to derive the utterance(s), or the exchange style. Indeed, this complete description can be quite complex; for example, Preston [1986], by comparing and comparing the

classifications of variables made by various authors, showed us that about 50 factors may influence the linguistic form (in our case, the final utterance). The main reasons underlying this decision are to circumvent the combinatorial explosion, by describing the current situation with a higher, more general abstraction level [Lenat & al., 1979]. That extracted information constitutes the *summarized context*. It is presently made of five variables (same parenthesized information): the *degree of mutual acquaintance* between the speaker and the addressee (none, simple, companionship, friendship, or intimacy), the *degree of freedom* of the exchange (formal, neutral, or informal), the *relative social level* of the speaker (inferior, equal or unknown, or superior), the *degree of intensity* of the exchange (negative, null, or positive), and the locutor's *psychological state* (reserved, normal, or expansive). Contrary to the exchange style parameters, each summarized context parameter should normally take a single value: the one adequately summarizing the input communication situation parameters.

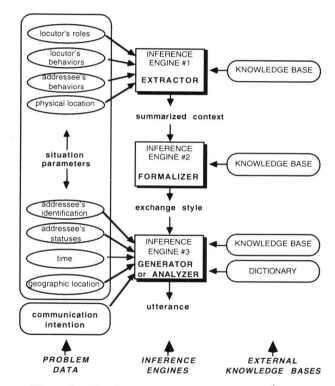

Figure 2. - The three inference engines of PILÉFACE.

3.3 System architecture: three serial modules

Thus, on the reasoning chain going from the given situation description (and communication intention) to the linguistic form (or utterance) to be produced or analyzed, we defined at least two compulsory intermediate passage points, i.e. the summarized context and the exchange style. In a divide-and-conquer way, these two passage points led us to model the cognitive process of PILÉFACE as a serial set of three different *inference engines* as shown in figure 2, each one having its own permanent knowledge base.

At present, we have only implemented the formalizer, the generator, and the analyzer. A fundamental and extensive theoretic study in linguistics is in progress to define and model the various situation parameters and their interrelationships, so that we could, starting with a (possibly very complex) situation description, (almost) automatically build the summarized context.

4. A complete example as processed by PILÉFACE

In order to illustrate our approach, we now discuss a complete generation example, in which the computer program acts as the addressee and the student plays the speaker's role.

4.1 Problem statement (situation description)

In this example, the program presents the following situation description to the student (recall that, in North-American universities, the academic year begins in September):

I am Ruddy Lelouche, your professor, French, male, strict, and distant. You are a freshman, quite shy, and you meet me in a hallway of the Computer Science Department building at Laval University, at the end of September, on a recess afternoon. You are with friends whom you want to impress; you would like to greet me in order to show your friends that you already know me well, and that I also already know you. What do you say?

The situation parameters corresponding to that situation are presented in [Lelouche, 1994], but not detailed here. At present, this correspondence is planned to be made manually, i.e. the situation will be simultaneously expressed to the student using the natural language description above, and to the extractor using the equivalent parameters.

4.2 Description of the summarized context

According to our model, the corresponding summarized context (see 3.2) is the following:

degree of mutual acquaintance:	simple acquaintance
degree of freedom:	formal (no freedom)
relative social level:	inferior (to the addressee)
degree of intensity:	positive
locutor's psychological state:	reserved

This summarized context will have to be generated by the extractor, when it is automated, from the complete formal situation parameters. As can be seen, the summarized context is made of the minimal information needed, either in generation mode to guarantee the semantic and pragmatic adequacy of the generated utterances with the situation, or in analysis mode to diagnose whether the input proposed utterance is appropriate in the given situation.

4.3 Description of the exchange style

The summarized context stated above leads to the following exchange style (see 3.1):

exchange style level:	respectful
personalization index:	nominative (some familiarity is possible)
realization tonality:	casual
realization insistence:	stressed
addressing style:	use of "vous"

This exchange style is generated from the summarized context by our formalizer (see details in [Lelouche, 1994]).

4.4 Possible utterances

In this exchange style, one might find an apparent contradiction between the exchange style level and the personalization index, both derived from the problem statement. It is the responsibility of the generator or analyzer (depending on the mode used) to solve this inconsistency. The reasoning mechanism implemented in PILÉFACE is the following. First, the exchange style level *requires* the use of a relatively sophisticated language, as well as a respectful term of address. The possible familiarity (personalization index and utterance tonality) *may* therefore only be taken into account by an adequate inquiry (which then becomes compulsory) or by a sufficiently personalized term of address. Consequently, the generator will only generate, and the analyzer will only accept, utterances that meet these two conditions. Possible utterances could thus be:

Bonjour Monsieur le professeur! Comment allez-vous?
Good afternoon, professor! How are you?

or, a little bit more risky and less adequate (guess why!):

Bonjour mon cher Monsieur Lelouche!
Good afternoon my dear Mr. Lelouche!

5. Implementation considerations

5.1 Two prototypes

So far, we have developed two prototypes in BNR Prolog on Macintosh. In both, the input situation is given as a summarized context. The *PILÉFACE-Generation* prototype and the *PILÉFACE-Analysis* prototype correspond to the first two modes shown on figure 1. The first results obtained with these two prototypes are promising, in spite of the incompleteness of the knowledge bases.

5.2 Strong points of our model

In spite of the partial character of our present implementation, we believe that our design approach has definitely a few strong points.

A first one is the introduction of the *exchange style*, that separates the knowledge about the world from the one truly concerning the language used. As a result, the tasks to be performed by two engines out of three, namely the extractor and the formalizer, are independent of both the selected processing mode (generation or analysis) and the language to be acquired (here French).

Secondly, by introducing the *summarized context*, the pragmatic usage rules were confined to the knowledge base of the extractor. Thus we thus able to obtain some results without having to wait for their being totally identified, structured and implemented.

Thirdly, by considering a *three-engine architecture*, we may easily adopt a distinct representation language (and a different tool) for each engine as well as for its associated external knowledge base. Such a choice could be justified by the different nature of the knowledge used by each of the processes and of the types of inferences to be made.

5.3 Further work

At present, the formalizer, the generator and the analyzer are implemented in the operational version of PILÉFACE. The extractor is only partly designed, and thus most of the usage rules are not implemented. However, this is not by accident: these usage rules, which are probably the ones in greater number, are the most difficult to be made explicit, and that probably explains why making them explicit is still a fundamental research problem in linguistics. As a result, designing the extractor will be the most difficult part of the system, but also the most rewarding.

Conclusion

Making explicit the implicit usage rules governing the various language mechanisms is a large and difficult problem, to the resolution of which we attempted to contribute. On the complex reasoning path going from the input situation description and communication intention at one end to the corresponding output linguistic form(s) at the other, our divide-and-conquer design approach defined two markers, namely the the summarized context and the exchange style. We then presented the resulting architecture of that system as three infrence engines, and we illustrated its operation with a complete example at work. In this research endeavour, we were greatly supported by our team's interdisciplinarity: computer science and language teaching specialists.

The reasoning processes these usage rules permit are brought into play "spontaneously and intuitively" by any native speaker. However, making them explicit is not simple. Certainly, our approach also opens the way to a mechanisation of the usage rules and to a simulation of the native speaker's intuitive "reasoning" process, and both are partially implemented in the PILÉFACE system. But is the native speaker's reasoning the same as PILÉFACE's? Very unlikely! PILÉFACE is too complex! This problem is indeed a particular case of common-sense modelling and the associated reasoning mechanisms: their computer implementation has long been — and to a great extent it still is— a stumbling block of artificial intelligence research. The difficulty comes from the fact that, in spite

of their apparent simplicity, there are so many rules and so many interconnected parameters that attempting to make them all explicit is probably an illusion: as soon as a rule or a parameter is dug out, another one comes up which is still missing to complete the expected inference chain.

Acknowledgements

The author wants to deeply thank his colleague Diane Huot, our expert in linguistics and language teaching, for her collaboration and implication in the PILÉFACE team.

References

Allen J. F. & Perreault C. R. (1980) "Analyzing intention in utterances". *Artificial Intelligence*, Vol. 15, pp. 143-178. Reprinted in *Readings in Natural Language Processing* (B. Grosz, K. Jones, B. Webber, eds.). Morgan Kaufmann (Los Altos, California, U.S.A.), 1986, pp. 441-458.

Austin J.L. (1962) *How to do Things with Words.* Clarendon Press (Oxford, England).

Hayes-Roth F., Waterman D. A. & Lenat D. B., eds. (1983) *Building Expert Systems.* Addison-Wesley (Reading, Mass., U.S.A.).

Huot D. & Lelouche R. (1991) "Les variables de la situation de communication dans l'enseignement du français langue seconde ou étrangère : quelques difficultés de définition". *Revue de l'ACLA - Journal of the CAAL*, Vol. 13, N° 2 (Automne 1991), p. 85-94.

Hymes D. H. (1984) *Vers la Compétence de Communication* (Towards Communication Competence). Hatier (Paris, France), November.

Jackson P. (1990) *Introduction to Expert Systems, 2nd edition.* Addison-Wesley (Reading, Mass., U.S.A.).

Lelouche R. (1994) "Dealing with pragmatic and implicit information in an ICALL system: the PILÉFACE example". *Journal of Artificial Intelligence and Education*, Vol. 5, No. 4, p. 501-532.

Lelouche R. (1986) "Quelques aperçus sur la modélisation de la description statique d'une scène". Proc. of the *Second International Conf. on Artificial Intelligence (CIIAM 86)*, Marseille (France), 2-5 December 1986. Hermès (Paris), pp. 121-139.

Lelouche R. & Huot D. (1985) *Fondements et objectifs d'un système intelligent pour l'apprentissage des langues* (Bases and Objectives of an Intelligent System for Language Learning). Research report DIUL-RR-8506, Computer Science Department, Laval University (Québec, Canada), May 85, 42 p.

Lenat D., Hayes-Roth F. & Klahr P. (1979) *Cognitive Economy.* Working paper HPP-79-15, Stanford Heuristic Programming Project, Stanford University (Stanford, California), June 1979, 46 p.

Levinson S. C. (1983) *Pragmatics.* Cambridge University Press (Cambridge, G.-B. and New-York, N.-Y.).

Preston D. R. (1986) "Fifty some-odd categories of language variation". *International Journal of the Sociology of Language*, Vol. 57, p. 9-47.

Searle, J. (1979). *Expression and Meaning: Studies in the Theory of Speech Acts.* Cambridge University Press (Oxford, England).

Searle J. (1969) *Speech Acts.* Cambridge University Press (Oxford, England).

VR-based Interactive Learning Environment for Power Plant Operator

Yukihiro Matsubara and Toshinori Yamasaki
Faculty of Engineering, Kagawa University
Hayashi, Takamatsu, Kagawa 761-0396 Japan
Email: {matsubar, yamasaki}@eng.kagawa-u.ac.jp

Abstract

This paper presents a VR-based ILE, which integrates virtual reality (VR) technology into interactive learning environment (ILE). It is said that ILE is composed of Intelligent Tutoring System (ITS) and micro world. ILE supports a student's discovery learning activity and fosters his/her creativity and adaptability. Moreover, we integrate VR technology into ILE and build discovery learning environments with reality. Using VR-based ILE, it is possible for a student to relate knowledge to skills and to acquire both of them. Student can get confidence and experience with reality. We apply the VR-based ILE to a training system for power plant operators.

1 Introduction

The aim of Intelligent Tutoring System (ITS) is to design the behavior of intelligent human teachers on computers. ITS[1] has a student model and an individual tutoring model, and realizes the individualized instruction of all students. However, students often become passive, because ITS takes the initiative in their learning process. In general, it is said that ILE integrates the advantage of micro world with that of ITS. Micro world does not have the function of positive teaching but encourages students to take spontaneous and discovery activities. On the other hand, because of the progress of hardware, various kinds of media are developed. Especially, it is virtual reality (VR) technology that has the potential to be applied to educational systems [2].

In this paper, we propose a VR-based ILE which integrates VR technology into ILE. The aim of our research is to develop VR-based ILE. Particularly, the learning target is operator training on a power plant control room. The demand for safety measures is increased from year to year, and we focus on educational curriculums not only to give knowledge but also to relate knowledge to skills and to acquire both of them.

2 VR-based ILE

ILE unites the advantage of ITS which can teach the knowledge systematically and the advantage of micro world which can support individual discovery learning, and it supports two types of tutoring methods, system oriented and learner oriented ones. The VR-based ILE is tutoring systems that incorporates VR into micro world, which can instruct with immerse viewing.

We focused on the subjects as sub-operators (novice operators) who don't have experience to control a power plant. And the goal is to acquire knowledge on emergency procedures. At first we produced a prototype system, which can teach "Loss of Coolant Accident" (one of actually occurring accidents). The configuration of the system is shown in Figure 1. The system is composed of a VR module and ITS module. The ITS module gives the domain knowledge, and catches the student's level of understanding, and it can teach individually. The VR module simulates a power generating system and a central control room. It deepens learners' understanding about the internal structure of a power plant, and how to operate a plant in case of an accident.

3 VR Module

The VR module is composed of two sub-modules as follows: One, which is called Walk-through sub-module, enables students to explore freely in VR environments which show the structure of a power plant. The other, which is called VR-simulation sub-module, enables them to learn skills/operations. The system configurations of both sub-modules are oriented to that of micro world, and both sub-modules encourage students to take spontaneous and discovery activities. The VR module has four kinds of interface, namely Head Mounted Display (HMD), magnetic track, 2D-mouse and space-ball.

3.1 Walk-through sub-module

One of the effective ways in which people can understand the target knowledge is to allow for different approaches to the target, based on the student's abilities/desires. It is more effective for them to get visual instructions too. By the way, it is difficult for human to approach the power plant because of its dangerous structure. Accordingly, the operator and sub-operator used to get knowledge about the power plant structure with models, 2D-pictures, photographs and so on. That is the reasons why it is not possible for them to acquire knowledge with reality, and it is difficult for elementary operators to understand knowledge about the power plant structure. Therefore, the walk-through sub-module shows students more real 3D-pictures with VR technology and gives the environment to support spontaneous learning by themselves.

3.2 VR-simulation sub-module

The aim of VR-simulation sub-module is to support discovery learning by students themselves. This sub-module provides them learning environments, which support the acquisition and simulation of skills/operations by using their knowledge and to set up situation freely. The roles of the plant operator are mainly "Watching", "Judgment" and "Operation". Therefore we build the functions of the power plant with VR technology. This sub-module enables sub-operators to learn how to operate with reality which they can't get on the traditional CAI for operator training.

4   Example

We show system examples concerned with the operator training system along the learning process. Particularly, examples give the learning process from the applied questions on ITS module to the simulation on VR-simulation sub-module as shown in Figure 2.

[Step 1] On the ITS module, a student learns the plant operational procedure and knowledge related it by using text knowledge and fundamental/applied questions oriented actual situation on the plant control room. In the case of applied questions, if a student has errors (miss conception), this module retrieves some related questions, namely fundamental questions, and gives the low understanding level questions. Also, if the current question is the question about operation, this module enables a student to make sure of the plant transitional process based on the correct answer with a simple control panel as shown in Figure 2(a).

[Step 2] After the learning on the ITS module, the student model is transferred from the ITS module to the VR module. The VR module gives the student messages about the procedural knowledge of the low level understanding based on the student model as shown Figure 2(b). Then, the student simulates and practices skills, paying attention to those messages.

[Step 3] The student simulates by using the virtual power plant control system as shown Figure 2(c) and (d). He/She relates skills to procedural and declarative knowledge and acquires them. At the same time, the VR module creates the operations history during simulation.

[Step 4] After the VR-simulation, it is possible for the student to examine his/her right and wrong information

5   Conclusions

This paper proposed a framework of the VR-based ILE. VR-based ILE supports discovery learning with reality. It is possible for students to relate skills to knowledge and to acquire both of them. And we described prototype system for power plant sub-operator.

This research has been made possible through Grant-in Aid for Scientific Research (B)(13558018), (C)(13680242) and on Priority Areas (A)(13020234) from The Ministry of Education, Culture, Sports, Science and Technology of Japan.

References

[1]   E. Wenger, Artificial Intelligence and Tutoring Systems, Morgan Kaufmann Publishers, 1987.

[2]   S. Benford, and et.al, Managing mutual awareness in collaborative virtual environments, Proceedings of the Virtual Reality Software and Technology Conference,

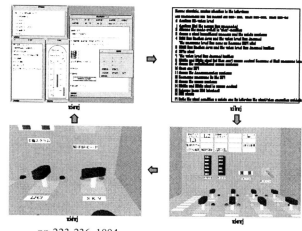

pp.223-236, 1994.

Fig. 2 Example of Operator Training

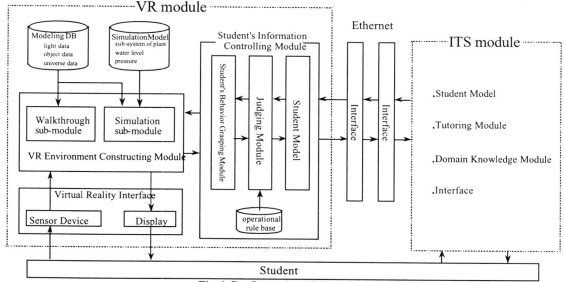

Fig. 1 Configuration of the system

Computer-Based Learning Units for Many Languages and Cultures

Alfred Bork
Information and Computer Science
University of California, Irvine
(bork@ uci.edu)

Rika Yoshii
Department of Computer Science
California State University, San Marcos
(ryoshii@csusm.edu)

Abstract

As we begin to address the global problems of learning, we note that there are many different languages and cultures in the world. If learning material is to be usable with many students in the world, we need to be concerned with the cultural and language differences among students. We need global materials that meet individual cultural needs. This paper discusses the Irvine-Geneva development strategy and how it supports, and can be made to support further, development of global materials.

1: Type of learning material

We must first ask what learning material is needed for universal global education. There will not be a unique answer to this question; however, we would argue that the following ingredients are essential:

1. Individualization: The material must adapt to each user. If we are to pursue global education, we will have a great many different types of users. Each user will have unique abilities and learning problems. The learning material must recognize these, and so must treat each person as an individual.

2. Affordability: The material must be affordable, both by individuals and by countries. In making this calculation, we must take into account all expenses for development and delivery of the learning materials, including profit if the materials are developed by a for-profit organization.

3. Collaborative Learning: The material must allow collaborative learning. We imagine a group of two to three students sitting around a computer. This is especially important for students who are not familiar with computers.

4. Mastery: The learning material should strive for success for all users. Failure is not acceptable.

5. Languages: The material must be available in many different languages of the world with many different writing systems. This cannot simply use direct translations since each culture has its own ways of expressing the same concept or feeling.

6. Culture: Learning units should match and respect the culture of each group. This includes not just the types of materials to be used but also how the materials will be presented.

7. Motivating: The learning units must be intrinsically motivating. Many of the usual student "threats", such as grades, may not be available. Again, what is motivating may depend on the user's culture. This goal is especially important for the countries in which only certain types of students will get attention from a human instructor.

8. Delivery: Delivery mechanisms must be available for reaching everyone, even very poor students. This must include environments without schools.

Some of these goals require distance learning with computers. The development strategy developed at the University of California, Irvine, in cooperation with the University of Geneva, is capable of meeting all the requirements just stated. In the next two sections we will briefly discuss the Irvine-Geneva development strategy in relation to the above requirements.

2: Interaction and individualization go hand in hand

Interaction is a spectrum. Most learning material available might be called "slightly interactive." Our development strategy strives toward learning material that is interactive in the sense that an individual human tutor, working with one or several students, is interactive. Several factors are critical.

Quality: First, each interaction should be of high quality, meaning that it should allow us to collect as much information on how the student is doing as possible so the material can adapt to her needs. In our materials, a typical interaction consists of a question from the computer, and a free-form student reply, in the student's native language. The program analyzes the reply in deciding how to respond to the student. A free-form answer allows the program to gather more useful information than a multiple choice question.

Frequency: We also require very frequent interactions, where the time between interactions is no more than 20 seconds. With frequent interactions we can 1) gather more useful information, leading to individualization, and 2) keep the student focused on the material and motivated.

When the learning material incorporates many learning strategies (for example, a variety of exercises for learning the same concept), individualization makes learning material suitable for a student of any culture. The level of interaction is a function of the design process, discussed in the next section.

3: Affordable development strategy

The Irvine-Geneva development system was begun over 30 years ago. The development system might historically be thought of as having several stages. In the first, we developed the methodology and programming tools to be used in producing highly interactive learning units. This was done primarily at the University of California, Irvine [1][3][4]. Then in the second stage we developed software tools to support this methodology for producing interactive learning materials. This was done primarily at the University of Geneva, in Switzerland [2]. Currently, support tools in Java are being developed at California State University, San Marcos [5] to make the learning materials available via the web.

There are four important aspects of the development process - management, design (including translation), implementation, and evaluation. Here, we discuss the latter three.

3.1: Design: supporting interaction, individualization, collaborative learning, and mastery

Design is the most important step in determining the quality of the final learning material. The designers will be groups of teachers experienced in the subject matter. That is, for designing material to learn arithmetic, we want experienced teachers of arithmetic who are conscious of student learning problems.

The designers describe all pedagogical details of the final program. This includes the messages to be presented to the student, either in voice or on the screen, the analysis of student input, and how to proceed next. Analysis of student input requires the designers to list all anticipated answer categories and answer patterns for each category. For each answer category, the next action to be taken by the program is indicated.

The designers must make the material intrinsically motivating to a wide variety of students.

- The designers must make sure high quality frequent interactions are used throughout the material.
- They must decide what information about student performance is to be recorded and how that information is used in the program to make the material individualized.
- They must make sure a group of two to three students can use the material together.
- They make the determination of what constitutes mastery.

The designers need a mechanism for recording all these decisions, easy to use by those not familiar with computers. We developed over thirty years ago a visual document, a "script". A script shows all the decisions we have described. See Figure 1 for an example of a scripted exercise. Teachers of many countries, such as Japan, Switzerland, and Italy, learned the notation by observing others for a few minutes.

3.2: International design groups for multi-cultural designs

To produce global materials, the design groups should have strong international composition. There are differences in how a given subject is taught in different countries. There are differences in the ways students are complimented or given help. There are visual aids to which certain cultures respond better than the others. Our goal is to produce learning materials that can supply a variety of techniques borrowed from many different countries and provide interactions comfortable to any culture.

In a large project there will be many design groups each with three to five teachers, so there are many opportunities to bring in people from different cultures. However, it must be noted that the design groups must have a common language in which a script is written. This language is normally the language of the target students. The international groups, however, should make an effort to list answer categories which are not restricted to the culture of the target students.

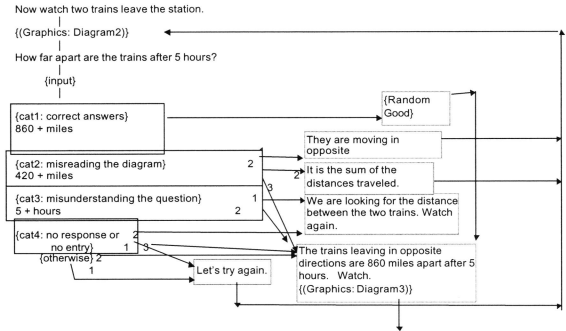

Now watch two trains leave the station.
|
{(Graphics: Diagram2)}
|
How far apart are the trains after 5 hours?
|
{input}
|

{cat1: correct answers}
860 + miles

{cat2: misreading the diagram}   2
420 + miles

{cat3: misunderstanding the question}   1
5 + hours   2

{cat4: no response or   2
        no entry}   1   3
{otherwise} 2
            1

Let's try again.

{Random Good}

They are moving in opposite

It is the sum of the distances traveled.

We are looking for the distance between the two trains. Watch again.

The trains leaving in opposite directions are 860 miles apart after 5 hours. Watch.
{(Graphics: Diagram3)}

Figure 1. Sample script

3.3: Translation to new languages and making cultural adjustments

Let us suppose that the design was done in English. Then let us further imagine that the new language is to be Japanese. There are at least two aspects to the translation of the script. The first is to translate messages that the student is to receive. These may be messages on the screen, or they may be voice messages, or both. The translator has to be sufficiently familiar with students learning the subject matter to be able to choose the common phrases for that field.

The most difficult part comes in handling student responses. In the initial language, English in this case, the answer patterns are for answers that are expected for students working in English. The translation is not a direct translation of answers. The translator must be familiar with students in this subject area in English and in Japanese since these students may express the same concept differently. For example, in listening to badly spoken French, an American student may answer that the accent was bad. The word "accent" is "ku-choo" or "namari" in Japanese. However, it should be translated into "hatsuon" (pronunciation) since Japanese students would not think of "namari" when listening to a non-native speaker.

There may be differences due to the student's culture that the translator may catch during the translation process. We give a minor example of cultural differences from work at the University of California, Irvine. In a program to discover the concept of heat, we began with thermometers. Early questions concerned how students measure their body temperature. We assumed, as is common in English speaking countries, that the student will put a thermometer in the mouth. But in some cultures, including Japanese, this is not appropriate. If there are responses unique to the target culture and the international group of designers could not anticipate such responses, the script must be modified to include handling of these cases. Design sessions with a small group of teachers of the target culture may be necessary. With proper software, script modifications are easy.

3.4: Script editing made easier

Initially our designs were paper documents. Often now the design is entered directly into the computer. This is made possible by an interactive script editor. If the script is done on paper, we can move it to the computer later. The script is stored in the computer, and can be updated easily. The script editor was written by Bertrand Ibraham, of the University of Geneva. Another script editor is being developed in Java at California State University, San Marcos [5].

Currently, these editors use the Roman alphabet. Even for Japanese, normally using non-Roman characters, transliteration into Roomaji can be used for scripting purposes. The San Marcos editor, written in Java, assumes double-byte codes for character representation, making it easier to support Chinese and Japanese characters. Discussion on non-Roman character representation is beyond the scope of this paper.

To aid the translation effort, the messages can appear in one window in the initial language, and in another window the translator can suggest the translated material.

3.5: Affordable implementation: minimizing the need for programmers

At this stage we move from design to a program running on a computer. We need to prepare the program and all associated visual materials. The running program must undergo beta testing to remove errors.

The Geneva script editor can produce much of the code from the stored script. The developer can choose the programming language. The code uses the tools (i.e. pre-defined routines) developed at the University of California, Irvine [3]. These tools were extended to handle non-English European languages when some of our learning units were translated into French.

The San Marcos script editor comes with a script interpreter which executes the stored script. No programmer is necessary. However, the learning material is limited to the features allowed by the script interpreter. The script interpreter is written in Java which supports double-byte codes for characters.

3.6: Full evaluation in each language

No matter how skilled the designers and translators are, several stages of formal evaluation are important. We normally do this for the design language, but in a multiple language project it must be done with each new language. Sizable numbers of students in each of the languages must run the program, and it must save the data to determine where changes should be made. Students in each culture must learn effectively. After evaluation, corrections are made in the program. With the script editor, most changes can be made directly in the stored script, and new code is generated quickly.

4: Maintenance in many languages

Even after delivery, changes are possible. If the units are available in seventeen languages, and we need to make a change, that change will initially be made in one language. Then we need to identify what changes are necessary in the other sixteen languages. A variation of the duel window strategy used for translation will help. The Geneva script editor also synchronizes different language versions of a script. The editor knows where to find each piece of text in different language versions.

5: Affordable delivery

An important factor leading to low costs for a student learning hour is an affordable delivery system. Initially we expect a variety of delivery methods, including Internet and CD ROM. Eventually it appears that two-way satellite connections will be an inexpensive delivery method for large numbers. A World Bank study suggests this possibility. We also can use, particularly for poor parts of the world, a less expensive learning appliance than current personal computers, to provide just learning. A much simpler operating system will be sufficient. Such a machine can be built in volume for less than $100, we believe.

6: Conclusion

We have discussed a strategy for developing learning materials for many languages and cultures:

- Design sessions and design scripting tools which support interaction, individualization, collaborative learning and mastery.
- International groups of designers for multi-cultural designs.
- Support software tools for multiple languages.
- Script editors and interpreters minimizing the need for programmers.
- Evaluation and maintenance for multiple languages and cultures.

The existence of extensive materials in several languages, with different cultures, allows extensive research with large numbers of students on the issues of cultural differences. For example, how do students in different cultures differ in the way they learn arithmetic? What are the differences in learning styles in different cultures? (e.g. What were the effects of peer learning; what sequence of exercises they needed; what common errors they made; what help sequences helped them, etc.) Much of the student performance records can be kept on the computer and be analyzed later for these purposes. These ideas are expanded further in [6] and in papers at www.ics.uci.edu/~bork.

7: References

[1] A. Bork, *Interaction: Lessons from Computer-based Learning. Interactive Media: Working Methods and Practical*

Applications, Diana Laurillard ed., Ellis Horwood Limited, Chichester, England, 1987.

[2] A. Bork, et al., "The Irvine-Geneva Course Development System", *Proceedings of IFIP*, Madrid, Spain, September 1992, pp. 253-261.

[3] S. Franklin, et al., *StringAnalysis Unit Reference Guide, Ports Unit Reference Guide, Keyed Files Reference Guide*, Educational Technology Center, University of California, Irvine, 1985.

[4] R. Yoshii, et al., "Strategies for Interaction: Programs with Video for Learning Languages", *Journal of Interactive Instruction Development*, 1992, 5, (2), pp. 3-9.

[5] R. Yoshii, X. Wu, and Y. Miao, *Tools in Java for Conversational Tutoring : Script Editor and Script Interpreter*, California State University San Marcos, 2001.

[6] A. Bork, and S. Gunnarsdottir, *Tutorial Distance Learning - Rebuilding Our Educational System*, Kluwer Academic Systems, New York, 2001.

ICT in Japanese University Language Education: A case study.

Malcolm H Field, Waseda University

Abstract

This paper reports part of a study conducted at a university in Japan. The belief that ICT provides students with more opportunities to negotiate target forms has been used to justify its use in language education. This study could not substantiate that ICT will change the way language is used in Japan or that CALL is providing new ways for learning and acquiring a new language. Students were experiencing difficulties in prioritising their learning repertoire between the acquisition of computer skills and language proficiency. Individuals experienced positive and negative coding and de-coding filters when communicating in ICT and this was related to the validity and reliability applied to the text. The value attached to the ICT interaction may influence the degree to which the ICT event influences face-to-face communicative acts.

1. Introduction

The use of Information and Communication Technologies (ICT)[1] for teaching purposes is transforming many of the processes of educational delivery. Education is immersed within the ICT phenomenon and therefore studies need to consider whether education, pedagogy and learning are being positively or adversely affected.

This paper reports part of a study that was conducted at a mid-sized private university in central Japan. The author was not the teacher of the ICT-based classes and the students did not meet him until the end of the study. The research sought to address the influence of ICT on language use and language education. Several sub-questions were also considered and two of these included: *Are interactions and communication changing through ICT usage,* and *what is the impact and effectiveness of ICT in language learning?* These are discussed in this paper.

2. Literature

The majority of the research on classroom computer-mediated-communication has usually begun with the assumption that minimal teacher control and input is beneficial for the acquisition of the target language and culture (Chapelle, 2001). The focus of ICT on teaching and learning has been on a means for communication: between learners and teachers, learners

and learners and between different groups of learners. The role of the teacher and learner in the ICT process depends much upon the educational and pedagogical philosophies of the teacher (Levy, 1997).

The belief that ICT can provide students with more opportunities to negotiate target forms, as interaction can be extended to out-of-class situations, has particularly been used to justify the use of ICT in language education. It has been argued that ICT-based communication provides many benefits for learning (Warschauer & Meskill, 2000, Warschauer, 1999a, 1996, Chen & Looi, 1999, Sernak & Wolfe, 1998, St. John & Cash, 1995, Kern, 1995, Sakamoto, 1992). The author believes that the introduction of ICT alone into the classroom will not bring about the social transformation in education and will not enable students to make effective use of the tools. In other words, there will be a tendency to utilize previously learned methods and practices (Warschauer & Meskill, 2000, Field, 1999).

For Japanese students specifically, Holmes (1999) argues that Japanese ESL students often reach university lacking effective meta-cognitive strategies for understanding how to learn. In Japan, most first year students entering each April have little technical knowledge about ICT (Pellowe, 1999). Carroll (1998) found that the concept of 'circular communication' promoted as a benefit of the use of ICT did not work well with students that came from hierarchical structured societies. Japan continues to favour a hierarchical society and this may negate the communicative benefits that ICT provides.

The average Japanese language student must complete compulsory units of study for which they generally find boring. They are, therefore, not motivated and rote learn material to pass requisite grammar tests. Recent theoretical and pedagogical trends in second language acquisition favour sociolinguistic or sociocognitive pedagogy over the drilling, testing, and language appreciation activities that once dominated. The social and cultural contexts are considered as the starting point for all language learning (Gardner, 1985, Kress, 1988). Both cultural and social learning contexts produce outcomes on bilingual proficiency that cyclically influence attitudes and cultural values. For the Japanese, difficulties in foreign language learning may lie in the social and cultural spheres rather than in the grammatical forms (Field, 1998, DeMente, 1993, Suzuki, 1986). For the Japanese, this may equate to the learning of languages that are not culturally compatible with the Japanese language and culture. ICT, therefore, may in fact only

---

[1] The acronym ICT is preferred to IT as it implies that the use of the new technologies involve communication and interaction rather than tools merely for the provision of information alone.

perpetuate previously acquired (language) learning habits if new ones are not introduced and provided.

Research that addresses the influence of ICT on language is an important step in further understanding ICTs in education, and needs to be examined across cultures and across learning strategies and preferences. What is required is an examination of ICT and language learning through new paradigms that are built upon the research traditions that are devoted to understanding language, culture, and other aspects of the social setting (Koschmann, 1996). The research from which this paper stems used a holistic approach to examine ICT, language, education and culture in Japan.

3. Methodology

The data for this paper were generated from written protocols (essays), a bulletin board (BBS) discussion and e-mail interaction. The written protocols provided open-ended questions around the theme of language use, cultural understanding, and IT knowledge. The students were encouraged to reply in either Japanese or English and their responses were cross-referenced if a response in both languages was forthcoming. Two distinct approaches were used for BBS interactions to enable the students to develop their skills, competence and confidence with the tool. These approaches involved, firstly, a structured method, where students responded to set questions on the BBS, and secondly, a semi-structured exercise, where the students responded to themes and to each other. Both were in-class activities. The e-mail interaction with the author was not an in-class activity and the interaction sought to examine both the students' theoretical beliefs about their language use, and provide text-based communicative examples that could be analysed. The researcher was granted access to the students through one of the ICT-class teachers and although he interacted with the students electronically, he did not meet them until an focus-group interview at the end of the research.

4. Population

A total of 130 first year students participated in the 18-month study at a university in Nagoya, Japan. All students were enrolled within the Faculty of Foreign Languages and Asian Studies and CALL was a component of their academic program. Forty-one percent were male and fifty-nine percent were female. 70% stated that they used a computer at home and more than two-thirds acknowledged using e-mail and the Internet. The female students had a higher frequency of using the computer both at home (74%) and at university (88%) than the male students (66% - 83% respectively). The

reason for this result was hypothesised by one of the CALL teachers:

> I think that the better boys are going to the better universities and there are not as many girls in those better universities. So we get a very high level girl – the type of girl that should be in the better universities but hasn't applied and they haven't applied or social reasons – they are not encouraged to go further – to their full potential.

5. Results

Several repeating concepts were identified through the analysis of the theoretical (student opinions) and empirical evidence (BBS and e-mail text) generated throughout the study.[2]

5.1 Impact of ICT on language and language education

The positive impact of ICT on language acquisition was not conclusive. On the contrary, there was strong evidence to suggest that many students were having difficulties reconciling the ICT skills and EFL acquisition components of the course. This was attributed to conflicting demands being placed upon the student's learning repertoire, as many had never experienced an all-English class that covered new material. Simultaneous and in some cases competing demands were being made upon the students' cognitive skills and repertoire of learning strategies from three distinct, though related, objects of study: (i) the curriculum, English as a foreign language; (ii) the practice environment of the computer; and (iii) the use as ICT as the information resource.

If ICT based language classes are to have the positive impact on language learning, and provide the advantages that some research has claimed, students will need to be organised according to their language and ICT skills proficiency. Two separate though inter-related courses need to be offered to the students. The objectives for these courses need to be clearly specified. The first of these courses is an ICT skills' course that should be conducted in L1. The second course should be an all-English EFL (L2) course with the foci on general L2 proficiency. Objectives of the courses need to be made clear and educators should also be aware of the nature and objectives of ICT based language education. Once the students have attained the requisite L2 proficiency and ICT skills, they should be given the option of continuing their university L2 studies in either classes that utilise ICT (CALL) or in classes that do not utilise ICT. Students choosing not to enrol in an L2 CALL class can, therefore, continue their L2 studies using the traditional language teaching pedagogies and learning tools. Students choosing to enrol in classes that employ a CALL curriculum would then be able to draw on schemata developed from their previous two distinct, though related, courses. Two models are proposed that would be useful platforms from which an ICT pedagogy and further research into ICT L2 education in Japan could be based. The first model is The Theory of Curriculum Development (attached), which highlights the need to develop ICT skills in the Japanese language and improve L2 proficiency before participating in ICT based L2 classes (above). The second model is the Theory of Learner Development, which focuses on the interactive processes of these courses, such as timing, sequential learning, error recognition, extension, communication.

The provision of opportunities to learn and produce language through ICT alone, however, may not produce language or communicative proficiency. Learners need to be made aware of the language required in the interaction and deviations (from these 'correct' language forms) need to be addressed. Language educators must decide whether there is a need to develop 'standard' English grammar and syntax for L2 ICT communication. If ICT based language instruction demands correct grammatical forms that can be transferred to face-to-face speech acts, then research is needed to determine and support the assumption that there will be language transference from ICT (text based) communication to a face-to-face (oral) event.

5.2 Reliability and Validity

The degree and speed of any influence from ICT on either L1 or L2 use in face-to-face events and on the first culture (C1) may be related to the degree of reliability and validity the user has with ICT text coding and decoding filters. That is, the degree of transference from ICT-based communication to a face-to-face event may depend on the extent the user attributes reliability and

validity to the ICT event. It is hypothesised that the perceived reliability and validity of the text in the ICT communicative act will influence the degree and speed of the affect on C1 and L1. Fifty percent of the student group believed that they were able to express themselves through ICT; therefore, half the study group do not experience problems encoding the text. Up to 66% were shown to have, however, a negative experience when decoding the text. The negative experience is considered a lack of confidence in the reliability and validity of the text. The decoding reliability and validity of the text is influenced by various filters including; the anonymity of the other, the act of writing or communicating in a non face-to-face situation, the nature of the Internet, and the inability to trust the other in the ICT communicative act. When encoding or decoding filters are negative, reliability and validity of the text is perceived as low. Reciprocally, when encoding or decoding filters are positive, reliability and validity of the text will be perceived as high (Diagram 1).

A communicative interaction in ICT may, therefore, have several outcomes. It may be negative-negative, negative-positive, positive-negative or positive-positive. These outcomes are not static but dynamic and case specific. If ICT communication is considered akin to face-to-face communication, then implications need to be considered. It is hypothesised that the positive-positive ICT experience will have a greater and faster influence on face-to-face C1 and L1 communication and interaction. Unless the ICT text-based communication is perceived positively, the influence on face-to-face synchronous events is believed to be minimal.

The ability to express personal beliefs and opinions, C1/L1 expectations and L1 style determine the encoding and decoding filters (positive or negative) and the degree of validity and reliability attached to the text and event. A positive-positive engagement has greater potential to affect L1/C1 ICT-based communication and

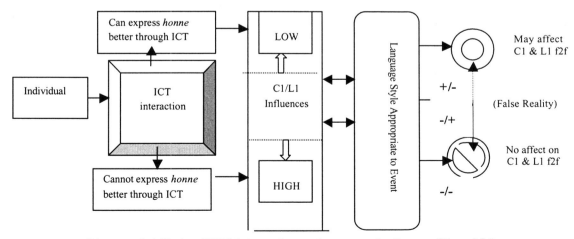

Diagram 1 Affects of ICT interaction and communication on C1 and L1

interaction, and potentially a face-to-face event, than a negative-negative or negative-positive engagement. A false reality is created in a positive-negative engagement or negative-positive engagement. False-reality communication and interaction is when an individual has a perception of release from L1 and C1 expectations through the ICT event but continues to communicate and interact in the expected C1 manner in ICT unaware that there has not been change. It is hypothesised that a false reality scenario has only a low potential to affect face-to-face L1 and C1 communication and interaction.

6. Summary and Conclusion

This study could not substantiate that ICT is changing or will change the way language is used in Japan or that CALL was providing new ways for learning and acquiring a new language. Individuals experienced positive and negative coding and de-coding filters when communicating in ICT and this is hypothesised as a high or low belief in the validity and reliability of the text. The value attached to the ICT communicative interaction may, therefore, influence the degree to which the ICT event has an effect on face-to-face communicative acts. Students also were experiencing difficulties in prioritising their learning repertoire between the acquisition of computer skills and language proficiency. The need to provide alternative and/or simultaneous ICT and L2 courses has been shown to be necessary.

ICT-based L2 education needs to recognise that students may not be utilising the opportunities to use, evaluate and extend their target language through CALL classes. Teachers need to recognise that students must attain pre-requisite ICT and L2 skills before they will be able to adequately make use of the opportunities the new teaching tools provide. Finally, from the results of this study, educators need to recognise that students may not readily adjust to the new teaching paradigms, or that ICT-based education is allowing the students to practice language that will enhance their face-to-face communicative strategies. What may be required, on the other hand, is a process of bringing the students to appreciate the new tools and learning paradigms, which may correspond to the learning strategies they have acquired up to their university education life. It may be that educators in Japan will need to wait until the current primary school students reach tertiary education before the benefits of an ICT-based curriculum can be fully appreciated, as this future generation of students are more likely to be exposed to both the new and traditional learning and teaching paradigms and will, therefore, be more flexible to the utilise the opportunities through the alternative methods. Notwithstanding, research needs to continually consider the effectiveness of an ICT-based

approach so teachers can adopt practices that most optimally suit their students.

References

1. Carroll, (1998). Academic discussion list, http://zeus.gmd.de/ifets/, sited October, 1998
2. Chapelle, C.A. (2001). *Computer Applications in Second Language Acquisition.* Cambridge, England, Cambridge University Press
3. DeMente, B.L. (1993). *Behind the Japanese Bow: An Indepth Guide to Understanding and Predicting Japanese Behavior.* Chicago, Ill: Passport Books
4. Field, M.H. (1999). New Wine and Old Wineskins: Call and Language. In Paul Lewis (Ed.), *CALLING ASIA: The Proceedings of the 4th Annual JALT CALL SIG Conference,* Kyoto, Japan, May 1999, (149-152), Nagoya: JALT
5. Gardner, R. (1985). *Social Psychology and Second Language Learning,* London: Edward Arnold
6. Holmes, B. (1999). ESL VLES: Self-Reflexive Constructionism by Japanese Students. In Paul Lewis (Ed.), *CALLING ASIA: The Proceedings of the 4th Annual JALT CALL SIG Conference,* Kyoto, Japan, May 1999, (189-192), Nagoya: JALT
7. Kern, R. (1995). Restructuring classroom interaction with networked computers: Effects on quantity and quality of language production. *Modern Language Journal,* 79/4, (457-476).
8. Koschmann, T. (1996). Paradigm shifts and instructional technology. In T. Koschmann (Ed.), *CSCL: Theory and Practice of an Emerging Paradigm,* Mahwah, New Jersey, Lawrence Erlbaum Associates, (1-23), cited in Chapelle, C. (2001).
9. Kress, G. (1988). Language as social practice. In G. Kress (Ed.), *Communication and culture,* Kensington: University of New South Wales Press
10. Levy, M. (1997). *Computer-Assisted Language learning: Context and Conceptualization,* Oxford, England, Clarendon Press
11. Pellowe, B. (1999). Designing WebPages to Introduce EFL students to the Internet. In Paul Lewis (Ed.), *CALLING ASIA: The Proceedings of the 4th Annual JALT CALL SIG Conference,* Kyoto, Japan, May 1999, (203-206), Nagoya: JALT
12. Sakamoto, T. (1992). Impact of informatics on school education systems: National strategies for the introduction of Informatics into schools - Nonsystematic but still systematic, *Education and Computing,* Vol.8, (129-135)
13. Sernak, K.S. & Wolfe, C.S. (1998). Creating Multicultural Understanding and Community in Pre-service Education Classes via E-mail, *J.I. of Technology & Teacher Education,* 6/4, (303-329)
14. St. John, E. & Cash, D. (1995). Language learning via e-mail: Demonstrable success with German. In M. Warschauer (Ed.), *Virtual connections: Online activities and projects for networking language learners.* Honolulu: Hawaii, University of Hawaii, Second Language Teaching Curriculum Center
15. Suzuki, T. (1986). Language and Behavior in Japan: The Conceptualization of Personal Relations. In Takie

Sugiyama Lebra & William P. Lebra (Eds.), *Japanese Culture and Behavior: Selected Readings*, Honolulu, Hawaii: Honolulu University Press (201-246)

16. Warschauer, M. & Meskill, C. (2000). Technology and second language learning. In J. Rosenthal (Ed.), *Handbook of undergraduate second language education*. Mahwah: New Jersey, Lawrence Erlbaum, (303-318)

17. Warschauer, M. (1999a). *Electronic Literacies: Language, culture, and power in online education*. Mahwah: New Jersey, Erlbaum Associates and www.gse.uci.edu/markw/elec-intro.html, sited September 2000

18. Warschauer, M. (1996). Comparing face-to-face and electronic discussion in the second language classroom. *CALICO Journal* 13/2, (7-26)

A Theory of Curriculum Development

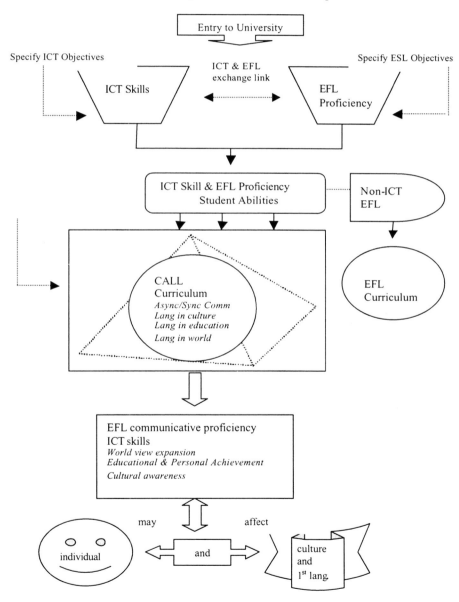

A Reading Contract System Based on Mission-Based Learning

Jie Chi Yang[*], Chih Hung Chen[**], Yu Bin Chen[*], Chih Hung Lai[*], Tak Wai Chan[*], Tzu Chien Liu[***]

[*] Dept. of Computer Science and Information Engineering, National Central University, Taiwan
E-mail: {yang, aahhh, laich, chan}@src.ncu.edu.tw
[**] Dept. of Mechanical Engineering, National Central University, Taiwan
E-mail: spooky@mail2000.com.tw
[***] Center for Teacher Education, National Central University, Taiwan
E-mail: ltc@cc.ncu.edu.tw

Abstract

This paper describes a system, called reading contract system, based on the concept of mission-based learning. The system is developed in order to foster children's reading habits and active learning attitudes under the design of mission-based learning. Activities in a reading contract are designed to include the steps of dealing with a contract. During the process, children must take risks to fail and try to develop responsibility for accomplishing the task in limited time. The spirit conforms to the most critical characteristic of mission-based learning. The reading contract system is built on a reading website. In this learning environment, some aids and tools are provided to help children setting and achieving their learning goals on reading. The role of parents and teachers is to assist children facing their tasks and collaborate with them in the learning communities.

Keywords: web-based learning environment, mission-based learning, goal setting theory, reading contract

1. Introduction

The development of information and communication technology (ICT) changes traditional learning environments. The advances of ICT have also provided new contexts for teaching and learning. Many new learning and teaching styles emerge and integrate with traditional styles. ICT provides interactive and multimedia learning and communicating environments for learning. Teachers can use more and more new teaching styles during normal class periods even during after class activities. The emergence of new learning styles also makes learners have more choices to have suitable learning processes. Learners can get more on knowledge or experiences through these learning processes.

Mission-based learning is one space of complex problem learning that intends to promote students to accomplish a task and is designed to encourage students to integrate and to use the information in a creative way to solve problems [1]. Today, schools always evaluate students by their performances, but not their attitudes. In other words, one's schools mark may not correlate with one's achievement. Commitment, persistence, and willingness to take risks are perhaps more important than learning ability to succeed in one's career. Mission-based learning intends to help students develop a healthy attitude while facing stress and to foster their ability of accomplishing tasks at risk of failing. By taking missions, students undergo a series of actions in order to achieve their missions. During the processes, students will learn how to apply their knowledge and use limited resources to solve problems. With mission-based learning, students can learn how to turn obstacles into opportunities [7]. The missions may fail. Students should take the risks and insist on overcoming all obstacles. This is the most important conception of mission-based learning. The four characteristics of mission-based learning are listed as follows:

(1) It provides chances for students to learn how to deal something with;
(2) It makes students insist on accomplishing the task;
(3) It lets students apply knowledge what they learnt;
(4) It teaches students to contribute themselves to society.

Reading is the base of learning. People always learn and get experiences by reading. Therefore, fostering children's reading habits and active learning attitudes is an important issue of educational policy. The children reading campaign proposed by the Ministry of Education in Taiwan is an example [6]. Not only the reading contents, but also the reading behavior, namely, how to form a good reading habit, are emphasized in elementary schools in Taiwan. A reading website is developed to provide reading information for children, parents and teachers, and assist them in cultivating children's reading habits. The reading website provides a lot of tools and aids to help children setting and achieving their learning goals on forming good reading habits [8, 9].

The aim of this study is to develop a reading contract system based on the concept of mission-based learning. The system is built on the reading website and is designed to help children making their reading plan as schedule, developing active learning attitudes, and increasing their reading interests. With the assistances of the system, it helps children to get not only knowledge but also learn to achieve a task under stress. The following sections describe the design principles, implementation and evaluation of the reading contract system.

2. Design principles of the system

This section describes the design principles of the reading contract system. First of all, the motivation of why the term 'contract' is used is described.

'Contract' is a social activity and usually represents a social standard in the adult society. In general, people think it is not appropriate to let children contact with contract activities early. However, fostering correct concepts from one's childhood like money management will have assistance in their future. This is why the concept of contract is considered in the design of the system.

'Reading contract' combined the concepts of reading and contract. Activities in a reading contract are designed to include the steps of making contract contents, concluding reading contract, executing the contract, like the steps of dealing with a contract in our real life. With these steps, children exactly make their reading plans themselves and literally execute their contracts. During the process, children must take risks to fail and try to develop responsibility for accomplishing the task in limited time. After the task, the children should reflect why they succeeded or failed and what they learnt. The spirit conforms to the most critical characteristic of mission-based learning.

The reading contract system is designed as a game-based style because target users of the system are children. There are seven stages in the system. Every stage is given the meaning for a task. Children must pass these stages to accomplish the whole tasks during a reading contract activity. After finishing every stage, children can get badges as rewards that prove their performances. Some stages are designed that children should collaborate with their parents and teachers, that is, children should get some helps from their parents and teachers. This design is under considerations that the importance and promotion of the 'parent-children reading' and 'teacher-student reading'. Parents and teachers can take the opportunity to help their children

or students to read and foster correct learning attitudes.

The main page of the reading contract system is shown in Figure 1, which indicates every entrance for the seven stages. The meanings and functions of the seven stages are described as the following:

Stage 1: named Courage Stage, children should first register to the reading contract system and login to the system. The first stage is relatively easy since the authors tried to motivate children to use the system. Another reason is that login to a system is also a good start for children.

Stage 2: named Honest Stage, children should choose some books and make their reading schedules honestly. The system provides a database of recommended books for children by some reliable organizations. When children chose books for reading, they should make a reading contract with their parents or teachers in order to ensure that they will accomplish their reading schedules, that is, achieve the learning goals as scheduled. The role of parents and teachers is to assist children facing their tasks and collaborate with them.

Stage 3: named United Stage, children should recommend their friends to take part in the reading contract activity. This is designed for collaborative learning with peers.

Stage 4: named Wisdom Stage, children should post some reports on the discussion board about what they have learned on their reading activities. This is designed for sharing their experiences and thoughts to others.

Stage 5: named Justice Stage, children should recommend their friends some books that they have already read or they think they are also good for others. The recommend books are then added into the database for others use.

Stage 6: named Persistence Stage, children accomplish their reading schedules with determination and willpower. It means that children insist on achieving their learning goals as scheduled. Parents and teachers will help to confirm their achievement in this stage.

Stage 7: named Angel Stage, children are hoped to contribute their books that they have already read to class libraries. Children shared their books with other classmates; they also gained the opportunity to read other books from others.

7.Angel Stage

2.Honest Stage

4.Wisdom Stage

1.Courage Stage

6.Persistence Stage

5.Justice Stage

3.United Stage

Figure 1. The main page of the reading contract system.

3. Implementation of the system

This section describes the system diagram and implementation of the reading contract system. The reading contract system is built on the reading website which is one of an item of the children reading campaign proposed by the Ministry of Education in Taiwan. The reading website is developed to provide reading information for children. Parents and teachers can use the system to assist children in cultivating their reading habits. For forming a learning community based on community-based learning, the system is integrated with a famous educational portal site in Taiwan, called EduCities [1], in the beginning of the year 2002.

The reading website aims to develop a web-based learning environment based on the concept of goal setting theory [4, 5]. In this learning environment, some aids and tools are provided to help learners setting and achieving their learning goals on reading. To help learners setting their learning goals, the system provides the functions of setting precise goals, adapting to learners' individual characteristics, setting goals by instructors' help, quantifying goals, and making learning goals. To help learners achieving their learning goals, the system is designed as learner-centered and personalized environment. With regard to the set goals, the system provides tools for monitoring the schedule, tracing the progress, and viewing the status of these goals. The system provides rewards as feedbacks to learners for their achievements.

Figure 2 shows the system diagram of the reading website. The system consists of five main modules, that is, User Function Module, Goal Function Module, Learning History Module, Evaluation Function Module,

and Interactive Function Module.

- **User Function Module**: This module includes login, user interface management, personal information management center, and personalization.
- **Goal Function Module**: This module is the core module of the system. The module provides some tools for supporting goal setting, goal planning, goal monitoring, and goal management.
- **Learning History Module**: This module records personal learning behavior history and goal setting history of reading activities on the web-based learning environment.
- **Evaluation Function Module**: In order to judge the degree of learners' efforts, to diagnose learners' difficult on learning, the Evaluation Function Module provides functions for evaluating learners' learning performance. Parents or teachers can immediately send messages to their children or students. This kind of formative evaluation can encourage learners and help them to modify their learning goals timely. There are two kinds of evaluations to help learners evaluate their performances, namely, learners could evaluate themselves or be evaluated by others.
- **Interactive Function Module**: Learners interact with others in the Interactive Function Module. Parents and teachers can use this module to interact with children to know their learning situations. Learners can learn more and achieve better learning effects by interacting with others, especially their parents, teachers, and peers.

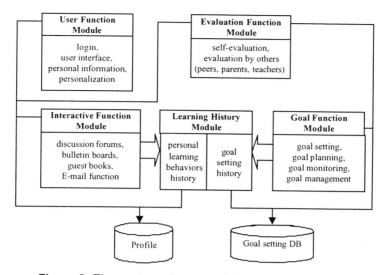

Figure 2. The system diagram of the reading website.

The reading contract system integrated with all the basic modules in the reading website. The system is developed using the concept of mission-based learning that is designed under the seven stages described in Section 2.

Children use the User Function Module to register and login to the reading contract system. The Goal Function Module helps children to make their reading schedules on their reading contracts. Children choose some books from a database of recommended books for children by some reliable organizations. Some useful information is provided to help children achieving their learning goals. For example, the system provides the progress charts to show the status of schedule. The system monitors children's goals and reminds them when necessary. The system also automatically provides some recommended books according to children's interest. Figure 3 illustrates these functions. The

Interactive Function Module provides discussion forums, bulletin boards, voting system, E-mail function, recommendation system, and notification function. Children can share their thoughts, feelings, or ideas by using these functions. Especially for discussion forums, the system provides one discussion forum for each one book. Children can discuss any book with others who have the same interest in that book. Children also may recommend their friends about their favorite books by using these interactive functions. According to these interactions, parents and teachers may check to understand the learning situations, aptitudes, and interests of their children or students. Parents and teachers can guide children with these interactions in the Evaluation Function Module by giving some messages. Children also may be evaluated by peers or themselves. The Learning History Module records all operations of children on the reading website.

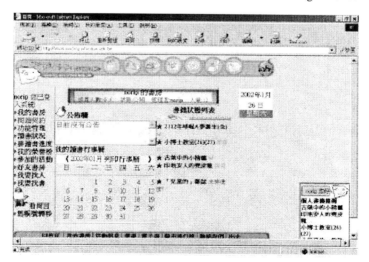

Figure 3. The system displays the status of schedule and recommended books.

4. Evaluation

The reading contract system is released to the Internet in the beginning of the year 2002. In a short period of three months passed, there are 125 schools, which are distributed over all counties in Taiwan, asked for participating in the reading contract activity. The requests are divided into three types. First, students request to participate in the reading contract activity for individual use. Second, teachers request to participate for use in their class. Third, principals request to participate for use in their school, that is, they promote the reading contract activity to their school. This result shows that teachers have great interests in the system.

There are 2,740 users have already registered to the reading website. Among them, there are 2,602 users are using the reading contract system. They totally made their reading plans to read 9,795 books in their reading schedules. In average, one user made plan to read 3.76 books. Among these reading plans, there are 5,701 books have been read on time. Although some books are still having not read before the expiration dates, few books have not read after the expiration dates.

5. Conclusion

This paper described the reading contract system based on the concept of mission-based learning. With the design of mission-based learning in the system, children learn how to turn obstacles into opportunities and accomplish the tasks at risk of failing. The integration of the concept of contract makes children foster commitment, persistence, and willingness in their daily life. Activities in a reading contract are designed to include the steps of dealing with a contract. In the system, some aids and tools are provided to help children setting and achieving their learning goals on reading. The role of parents and teachers is also considered to assist children facing their tasks and collaborate with them in the learning communities.

Evaluation on the situation of the reading contract activity shows that teachers have great interests in the system. The analysis of system usage also shows that children use the system in a good way. The authors plan to conduct an empirical study to evaluate the effectiveness of the system in the near future.

Acknowledgements

This study was supported by grants from the National Science Council (Project No. 90-2511-S-008-012, from December 1, 2001 to July 31, 2002) and the Ministry of Education (from September 1, 2000 to December 31, 2000) in Taiwan.

References

[1] Chan, T.W., Hue, C.W., Chou, C.Y., & Tzeng, O.J.L. (2001). Four spaces of network learning models. *International Journal of Computers & Education,* 37(2), 141-161.
[2] Keller, J.M., "Development and use of the ARCS model of instructional design". *Journal of Instructional Development,* 10, 3, 1987, 2-10.
[3] Keller, J.M., & Suzuki, K., "Use of the ARCS Motivation Model in Courseware design", In: D.H. Jonassen, *Instructional Design for Microcomputer Courseware,* Hillsdale, New Jersey: Lawrence Erlbaum Associates, 1988, 401-434
[4] Locke, E.A., "Toward a theory of task performance and incentives", *Organizational Behavior and Human Performance,* 3, 1968, 157-189.
[5] Locke, E.A., & Latham, G.P. (1990). *A theory of goal setting and task performance.* Englewood Cliffes, NJ: Prentice-Hall.
[6] Ministry of Education (2000). *Action plan for children reading campaign.* Taiwan.
[7] Stoltz, P.G. & Pulatie, D. (1997). *Adversity quotient: turning obstacles into opportunities*, John Wiley & Sons.
[8] Wang, S.H., Yang, J.C., Ho, C.W., & Chan, T.W. (2001). Development of a web-based learning environment using goal setting theory - an example of reading website. In *Proceedings of the 5th Global Chinese Conference on Computers in Education* (GCCCE 2001). Chung-Li, Taiwan. pp.748-755.
[9] Yang, J.C. (2002). Development of a web-based learning environment based on the concept of goal setting theory, International Conference on Engineering Education. (accepted)

Learning through Question and Answer Interactions on the Web.

Dr Sandra Schuck,
Faculty of Education, University of Technology, Sydney

Abstract

The paper discusses the use of a Question and Answer section of a Discussion Board on a computer-mediated web conferencing tool, and the way in which this facility fits with ideas of social learning. A description will be provided of how learning was developed through questions and answers in this subject and insights will be shared regarding the various uses of this facility by the students. Issues related to participation, peer misconceptions and teacher intervention are raised and discussed.

1 Introduction

Over the last two decades, education has been undergoing major paradigm shifts. These shifts include changes in theories of learning from transmission to constructivism and moves from teacher-centred to student-centred control of learning situations [1]. In our mathematics education subjects we employ computer-mediated conferencing as one of the means of challenging student beliefs about learning, teaching and mathematics education [6]. This paper focuses on the pedagogical value of using a Question and Answer facility in computer-mediated conferencing.

It is becoming increasingly common for teacher educators to base their teaching philosophies on principles of social learning [4]. Social learning situations involve learners in actively constructing meaning, not in isolation, but in collaboration with others. Salomon and Perkins [5] suggest that learning usually entails some social mediation. They elaborate on the concept of social mediation as participatory knowledge construction, whereby learning is seen as "a matter of participation in a social process of knowledge construction" p 4. This paper focuses on this form of learning and discusses how a question and answer forum can contribute to shared knowledge construction.

1.1 How question and answer forums fit in a view of social learning.

This paper discusses the use of a Question and Answer discussion forum created in a web-based conferencing tool. For me, the introduction of a Q&A section fitted well with my socio-cultural theoretical framework for teaching. I believe in the importance of communities of learners and in opportunities to create rich questions or to encourage students to pose their own questions for investigation. In

what follows I discuss this use of the Q&A facility and also raise issues about participation and teacher roles.

2 The Study

First year primary teacher education students at an Australian university are enrolled in a mathematics education subject in their second semester. The subject is primarily offered in face-to-face mode on campus, but also involves the use of a computer mediated discussion tool. A Question and Answer forum has been placed on the discussion board and students are encouraged to post questions about the use of the technology or about the content of the subject, the study of measurement. Students are also encouraged to respond to any of the questions or statements made in this section. In this way students act as advisers for each other, or share ideas on any of the issues raised in class.

The Q&A activity reflected the shifts in teaching advocated by the reform movement in school mathematics. These reforms encourage students to work as mathematical communities and to use logic and mathematical evidence as verification, rather than accepting the teacher as sole authority [3].

In the study, I considered the experiences of the students over two offerings of the subject, in consecutive years. I evaluated the Questions and Answers section by monitoring the content that appeared in this section of the Discussion Board. We also had a mid-semester evaluation in which students were asked to evaluate aspects of the subject and in particular, the Question and Answer section. These evaluations were anonymous. For this paper, I will discuss some of the issues raised and also outline some examples of powerful learning that took place through the Q&A facility.

2.1 Findings from the Question and Answer section of the discussion

About 40% of the 150 students used the Q&A forum. Of those who did, 66% found it interesting and worthwhile. Those who were critical of its use expressed a number of views: some felt that they had nothing to say and were being coerced into using the discussion as it would give the lecturers a good impression of them, others were concerned that their peers' answers to questions might be incorrect and they did not feel able to assess whether this was the case.

As a result, usually a core of students would participate in the online discussion. For these students, there were benefits. However, those who did not visit the discussion site at any point did not view such interactions as meeting their needs. This point matches the findings of Selwyn [7] who had similar experiences in a network of special education teachers. It supports the view that electronic learning environments do not suit all learners [2] and the opportunity to learn in different ways, using different tools and approaches should be offered to all learners.

For those who did participate in the Q&A section, their interactions appeared to be useful and resulted in some powerful learning for some of the students. An example of such an interaction follows.

A question had been posed in class as to how the area of an irregular shape could be measured. A student (George) responded by suggesting a solution in which the area and perimeter were seen as in directly related, thus suggesting that finding one would lead to the solution of the other. I asked students to think about George's solution and respond with their thoughts in the Q&A forum. The first response in the forum was along the lines suggested by George, arguing for finding the perimeter to find the area. In response to this posting a number of other responses appeared, each with a very clear explanation of why the area could not be found using the perimeter. A very convincing explanation by George who had reflected on his earlier suggestion and was able to show its flaws, ended the discussion, as all reading it acknowledged that it was compelling and clear. To me, this discussion demonstrated the strength of the tool for developing collaborative learning and for promoting deeper thinking.

It is worth noting that the 13-day long discussion terminated after George's clear response. Students' concerns about not recognising whether a solution to a question was valid or not were dispelled when they read George's response. So his response in fact cleared up two misconceptions for the students, one regarding the area of irregular shapes and one regarding students' abilities to discern when an argument made sense.

2.2 Other examples

Some of the questions were about use of the technology, for example, questions about how to change passwords or how to print. Students were quick to respond to their peers and seemed to take some pride in knowing how to help.

Other examples enabled students to share teaching ideas when they were on the practicum in schools. One student asked for ideas on teaching a particular topic and was answered by a number of students all offering ideas and suggestions and reporting on their experiences. The discussion was useful in developing students' ideas for teaching. The students appeared to be eager to support one another in the suggestions they offered.

The above are only a few of the examples of the diverse way the Q&A forum was used. In the next section the benefits of such a forum and the issues arising from its use are discussed.

3 Discussion

The Q&A forum had much to offer in the way of collaborative knowledge construction. Students valued their peers' opinions and learnt from each other, both about mathematical concepts and about teaching these concepts. It was clear to students when input was authoritative. So the Q&A forum was instrumental in developing a community of learners. The role of the teacher here was to set up some of the problems, to ensure that conceptual understanding of content was being developed, and to act as an observer of the activities, only stepping in when absolutely required.

However, an issue regarding participation needs to be considered. Although the forum was used regularly and was found to be extremely useful to many of the students, there was also a large number of students who did not access the forum at all. These students gave reasons for not accessing the forum as not enjoying using this technology, not having time or not seeing the need for it. These reasons need to be respected and I believe that unless students can see value in using a particular approach to learning, that they should not have to use that approach. This suggests that those students who prefer to interact in other ways should be encouraged to do so and alternative ways of learning should be provided in all subjects. A respect for individual differences is central to ideas of effective education.

4 References

1 Barker, P (1999) Using intranets to support teaching and learning, *Innovations in Education and Training International, 36*, 1, 3-10.
2 Hartley, K., & Bendixen, L. (2001) Educational research in the internet age: Examining the role of individual characteristics. *Educational Researcher, 30* (9), 22-26
3 National Council of Teachers of Mathematics (NCTM) (2000). *Principles and Standards for School Mathematics*. Reston, VA: NCTM
4 Putnam, R., & Borko, H. (2000). What do new views of knowledge and thinking have to say about research on teaching? *Educational Researcher, 29* (1), 4-15
5 Salomon, G and Perkins, D (1998) Individual and social aspects of learning. In Pearson, P D and Ashgar, I (eds) *Review of Research in Education, American Educational Research Association*, Washington.
6 Schuck, S. & Foley, G. (1999) Viewing mathematics in new ways: Can electronic learning communities assist? *Mathematics Teacher Education and Development*, 1, 22-37.
7 Selwyn, N. (2000) 'Creating a 'Connected' Community? Teachers' Use of an Electronic Discussion Group' *Teachers College Record 101*(4), 750-778

The Museum Network and On Demand Systems for School Education Based on XML

Kumiko IWAZAKI*, Takami YASUDA**, Shigeki YOKOI***, Toshio OKAMOTO*

Graduate School of Information Systems, University of Electro-Communications *

School of Informatics and Science, Nagoya University **

Graduate School of Human Informatics, Nagoya University ***

Abstract

In recent years, much attention has been given worldwide to practical use of museum resources for school education through the Internet. We have developed a web-based system using XML (eXtensible Markup Language). The system helps us to use digital museum resources effectively among museums, schools, and research organizations on networks. The Museum Network, which we have defined, is a model to indicate how to deal with digital museum or school resources using metadata standards such as Dublin Core (DC)/XML. We used this model and developed several kinds of systems: "Online Teaching Material", "School Trip Guide", and "Museum Search System", and made clear the effects of the Museum Network. In this system, once we enter museum resources into a database, we can deal with these resources in each of our systems. Moreover, when a user selects his own interest or purpose, the system chooses the exact resources from the database by using metadata and makes personalized pages automatically. For that reason, the system offers the appropriate materials to schools; consequently we expect strong collaboration between museums and schools on the web through the Museum Network.

1 Background of Our Work

Nowadays, we have many chances to use superior museum resources in museum search systems, teaching materials or museum information pages on the Internet. However, these web pages were developed using unique data formats, so each museum resource is incompatible with another museum's resources. By the way, in recent years, it has become necessary to retrieve museum resources, not so much from each museum's individual database as all museums' databases and to give users full access to resource information according to their demands, especially for schools. In our approach, we defined common metadata for resources and put each resources prescribed metadata by using XML for exchange of resources. For example, we describe <TITLE> as name of an exhibit item. We developed the "Online Teaching Material" and so on, with the idea. Furthermore, if a curator enters museum resources in the database once, it is possible to use them in the each of systems. In such instances, we can store museum resources efficiently and retrieve them efficiently, since

they utilize the same resources.

2 Museum Network

2.1 Outline of Museum Network

"Museum Network", as we have defined it, is a network for offering museum or educational resources according to user's "interests", "levels", "experiences", "purposes", or "situations" using standardized resources. The unique aspect is the way standardized resources provide description. We describe every resource with metadata such as name, explanation, priority, or creator instead of each web page or packaged software. Because detailed descriptive metadata is used, varieties of resource combinations are realized and it is possible to offer exact materials to users.

The following systems were developed with this concept in mind.

1. integrate museum resources and textbook : "Online Teaching Material"
2. search resources from separate museum databases: "Museum Search System"
3. get the big picture view of a museum, suggest a personalized route map: "School Trip Guide"

We prepared for many kinds of situations and usages in school settings. This then enables strong collaboration between museums and schools.

2.2 Management of Metadata

In our network, all the digital resources are controlled with standardized metadata. We decided to base these metadata on DC, which is used in many online libraries and museum organizations. In this system, we utilize <TITLE> for the name of an exhibit item, <DESCRIPTION> for explanation of the exhibition item, etc., using DC. For example, an exhibition of "Toyoda Wooden Hand Loom" can be described as follows.

```
<EXHIBITION id=324232>
  <TITLE>TOYODA WOODEN HAND LOOM</TITLE>
  <SUBJECT>TOYODA SAKICHI</SUBJECT>
  <TYPE>phisicalobject</TYPE>
</EXHIBITION>
```

However, if users want to use the system for schools, museum resources have to be described by grade, difficulty, and educational information. Consequently, we use the "Learning Object Metadata (LOM)" for educational terms in our systems. Having been standardized by the IEEE, remarkable developments are expected. In addition, because the Japanese language uses "kanji" and "hiragana" expressions as well as difficult words and idiomatic phrases, we defined metadata for children using DC extensions which are described easily by writing by them in "hiragana". Moreover, we prescribe our original metadata such as <PRIORITY> which indicates priority of the exhibit item.

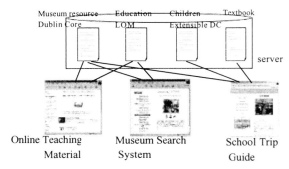

Figure1: the Museum Network

3 Functions and Features of Each System

In our system, we combine museum resources using DC/XML with educational information using LOM/XML etc., Then, using XSLT and CGI we create web pages by using museum resources on the web through JavaScript or XSL. We developed several kinds of systems .

3.1 Online Teaching Material

We developed a learning tool that inserts related museum resources into a seventh grade science textbook . In January 2001, we experimented with it at a Junior High School in collaboration with Nagoya City Science Museum over fiber optic lines. In this system, we implemented a personalized function to change museum resources flexibly to adapt to the user's position, whether teacher or student. Moreover, after learning about diurnal motion and the waxing and waning of Mars by using "Online Teaching Material", students went to the museum to study these topics in more detail. According to questionnaire data, 70% of students said that system is useful for study, especially pre-study for museums. As a consequence of the experiment, we confirmed the effectiveness of this as a learning tool with museum and school collaboration. Museums have a lot of invaluable collections, so it is a very important system for schools.

3.2 School Trip Guide

In partnership with the Toyota Commemorative Museum of Industry and Technology, we developed a system that automatically produces individual route maps in accordance with <SUBJECT> etc. [Fig.2]. In the museum, they have many kinds of moving exhibitions, so we entered many videos with curator's comments instead of images of the exhibition. Moreover,

we added a personalized function that adapts the explanation for children or adults accordingly. This function is realized by specifying which XML file the system reads, DC/XML or CHILDREN/XML. In addition, on the assumption that school groups have limited time to look around in a museum, we added a function of make a short list of route guide according to exhibition's priority.

Before going to a museum, it is important to learn about collections and prepare the way to see important resources within a limited amount of time . We think the system will be a good tool for producing school trip guides.

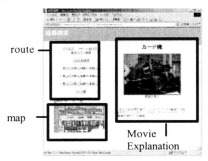

Figure2: School Trip Guide

4 Conclusion

The Museum Network has an important part to play in "Collaboration" among museums or between museums and schools, and "Personalization" offers museums resources according to user's demands. To effectively realize these roles of the museum network, we organized museum resources by entering standardized metadata by XML. We adopted DC for museum and LOM for education to describe resources and this enables different museums to exchange resources. Moreover, we developed several systems such as "Online Teaching Materials" which take advantage of metadata and XML features. These systems can make individual pages according to user's personalization (knowledge level, interests) or learning time and situation automatically. These are very important functions when a teacher uses this system in school settings. Through this study, it has been made clear that the system has great benefits for schools and museums. It is imperative that we promote museum network infrastructure .

Mission-Based Learning Model and Its Instructional Activity Design

Yueh-Chun Shih*   Nian-Shing Chen**
Department of Information Management
National Sun Yat-sen University
stone@cc.nsysu.edu.tw*   nschen@cc.nsysu.edu.tw**

Abstract

A task-based learning model defines the process whereby students organize teams to accomplish some tasks by using and integrating what they have learnt in a creative way through access to the resources available on network. The task-based learning model can be further broken down into sub-divisions to address different perspectives. The mission-based learning model is one of those. The mission-based learning model particularly helps students develop attitude and ability to accomplish some special task accepting the risk that they may fail. The main characteristics of a mission-based learning model are commitment, risk-taking, persistence and learning by error.

In this study, we develop a typical instructional activity, named "Telling Story about Paper Bill", as mission-based learning model. The activity we propose is intended to help students integrate knowledge such as history, geography, environment, animal-care and computer skill. During this process of integration, students should develop attitudes of commitment, risk-taking and persistence, and the ability to accomplish tasks collaboratively.

Keywords: *Mission-based Learning Model, Instructional Activity Design, Task-based learning model.*

1. Introduction

The goal of education is to intend to help students solve different kind problems autonomously. The purpose of developing task-based learning is to provide students with integrated knowledge and prepare them for attaining the problem-solving abilities. Chan et al. have identified four spaces of emerging network-based collaborative learning models. A mission-based learning model is one of them [2].

Like the task-based learning model, the mission-based learning model consist of the following five core capabilities:

(1). Knowledge integration.
(2). Teamwork and cooperative learning.
(3). Critical thinking.
(4). Complex problem solving.
(5). Creativity.

The mission-based model also emphasizes commitment, risk-taking and persistence.

2. Mission-based Learning

Mission

A mission here means a goal-oriented, real-life, and motivated activity under time pressure and limited resources, which is designed for students to engage themselves during their learning process. When assigned one, students will take responsibilities to accomplish it. Then a series of activities will be taking place and learning will occur during the process.

Mission-based Learning (MBL)

Simply put, mission-based learning model intends to help students develop attitude and ability of accomplishing some special task under the risk that they may fail. Students also learn to be responsible, willing to take risk, and persistent in completing the task under time and limited resources pressure.

The following section will draw the main characteristics of mission-based learning model from previous researches.

Commitment

Commitment reflects the extent to which an individual is involved in whatever he or she is doing. Committed people have a sense of purpose and do not give up under pressure because they tend to invest themselves in the situation. Usually, the difficulty of the appointed goal will affect his goal commitment and in turn affect the work performance [3,4]. Thus, "goal commitment" plays an important role in goal setting.

Persistence

Persistence here means the effort expended on a task over an extended period of time. Many entrepreneurs eventually succeed because their internal locus of control helps them overcome setbacks and keep persistence [1,6].

Persistent people tend to see obstacles as challenges to be overcome rather than as reasons to fail. A difficult goal that is important to an individual is a constant reminder to keep exerting effort in the appropriate direction.

Risk-taking

McClenlland proposed that high achievement-motivated people share three common characteristics. Simple put, high achievement-motivated people prefer challenge and risk-taking. Challenge is represented by the belief that change is a normal part of life [5].

Thus the main characteristics of mission-based learning model are *commitment, persistence* and *risk-taking.*

3. Instructional Activity of MBL Model

According to above three main characteristics, we proposed a typical instructional activity, named "Telling Story about Paper Bill", for mission-based learning model.

Mission Goal

Paper bills play an important role in our life. Pictures or characters on paper bill reflect our history, culture and environment (see figure 1). Design a Website that documents and showcases pictures and characters on the current paper bill. All work has to be done in 4 hours at school.

The benefits of proposed activity are shown as follows:

- Students learned more about the WWW and how to create web pages.
- Supervisors/teachers understood the value of the Internet in classroom curriculum.
- Students learned about their history and culture.
- Students learned to work with each other.
- Students and teachers within same team were motivated to share and collaborate.

Figure 1. Samples of some NT Paper Bill.

Eligibility

Participative students must be between the ages of ten and sixteen years. Each participating team needs to form 5-person team with same grade.

Mission Narrative

Observe and record the following elements of your team's work and include that information in the required Mission Narrative. You may want to act as activity historians to observe and describe these processes.

- Describe how the activities conducted by your team processed.
- Describe how the workload distributed by your team processed.
- Describe how the creative problem solving proposed by your team processed.
- Describe how the obstacles overcame by your team processed.
- Describe what you have learned from the activity.

Peer Review and Final Judging

We suggest that Web works will be evaluated in a two-stage process: peer review and expert judges. All decisions of the judges will be final and are not subject to review or revision.

Evaluation Rubric

Final judges and Peer Review will be suggested using the same evaluation rubric (see Table 1).

Table 1. Evaluation Rubric

Evaluation Items	Scores
The rate of mission achievement	10
Strategy and Methodology	8
The time of mission achievement	5
The completeness of Mission Narrative	5
The completeness of Web pages	5

In order to balance the weight of each item, final scores of each entry obtained from each reviewer will do multiplication for these five items. Thus, the highest scores of entry will be 10000 (10 X 8 X 5 X 5 X 5).

4. Conclusion

There is a best annotation for mission-based learning, that is, "Education is that which remains, if one has forgotten everything he learned in school."said by Albert Einstein. Even though we do not believe that educators must apply any learning model to their instructional activities. But we hope that the typical MBL instructional activity we proposed could help educators to adopt and integrate to their curriculum.

We will hold a contest of the mission-based learning. We will observe two aspects of the learning results from that activity: 1) review of the contest activities, 2) analysis of student's character of problem solving. In addition, we will try to identify the difficulty and cause of give-up that the teams have encountered. Eventually, we will try to find out the framework of MBL by using qualitative and quantitative methodology.

Acknowledgement

The study is supported by National Science Council of R.O.C. (Project No. NSC91-2511-S-110-004).

Reference

[1] Bluen, S.D., Barling, J., and Burns, W., "Predicting Sales Performance, Job, Satisfaction, and Depression by Using the Achievement Strivings and Impatience-Irritability Dimensions of Type A Behavior," *Journal of Applied Psychology*, April 1990, pp. 212-216.

[2] Chan, T.W., Hue, C.W., Chou, C.Y., and Tzeng, Ovid J.L., "Four Spaces of Network Learning Models", Computer & Education, 2001.

[3] Hollenbeck, J.R., O 'Leary, A.M., Klein, H.J., & Patrick,M.W., "Investigation of the Construct Validity of a Self-Report Measure of Goal Commitment," *Journal of Applied Psychology,* (74:6), 1989, pp. 951-956.

[4] Locke, E.A., Shaw, N.R., Saari, L.M., & Latham, G.P., "Goal Setting and Task Performance . 1969-1980." *Psychologyical Bulletin*, 90(1), 1981, pp. 125-152.

[5] McClenlland, D.C., *The Achieving Society*, New York: Free Press, 1961.

[6] Shaver, K.G., "The Entrepreneurial Personality Myth," *Business and Economic Review*, April/June 1995, pp. 20-23.

Multilayer Educational Services Platforms and Its Implementation

Li-Jie Chang, Jie-Chi Yang, Tak-Wai Chan
Department of Computer Science and Information Engineering,
National Central University, Chungli, 320, Taiwan
Tel: + 886-3-4227151-4843   Fax: +886-3-4261931
Email: {jie, yang, chan}@src.ncu.edu.tw

Abstract

How apply the online social learning communities into physical social learning communities is an important research issue. This work describes the design and implementation of multilayer educational services platforms for learners to construct their own online social learning communities and to integrate their online environments into a large public learning portal site – EduCities. In order to integrate different kinds of learning environments, multilayer framework were designed. An architecture called EduX is proposed and implemented to integrate with K-12 learning communities. One year after the EduX system was released on the Internet, 1,802 schools, 13,023 classes, and 96,222 individuals in Taiwan had registered to use the system to construct their own online learning communities. Evaluation results indicate that the system is satisfied with teachers and students in building K-12 learning communities.

Keywords: *online learning communities; K-12 education; distributed learning environments; architectures for educational technology system*

1: Introduction

Online learning communities have been successful over recent years [2] [4] [5]. However, physical social learning communities cannot be neglected in the formation of online social learning communities. The evolving of online social learning communities is strongly impacted by physical social learning communities. Moreover, physical social learning communities should be combined with online social learning communities.

The "EduCities" [1] website is a popular educational portal in Taiwan, and supports the construction of online learning communities. The main users of the EduCities are teachers, students, and parents. One year after the EduCities released on the

Internet, users in the EduCities continue to present many challenges. One challenge is that teachers and students spend most of their time in schools and families. They pay much attention to their daily environments in which they have their own identity and feel belonging. The EduCities learning portal site must be reorganized to suit school-based and class-based learning styles, especially in K-12 learning environment. In sun, a physical learning environment has distinct organization and ecology, and educational portals must be restructured. Accordingly, the EduCities is being modified to meet users' expectations.

This study aims to develop multilayer educational services platforms on which learners can construct their own online social learning communities, integrate their learning communities with other such communities and interact with others in different layers. The multilayer educational services platforms are mapped onto physical social learning environments according to users' expectation. Section 2 describes the concept of multilayer educational services platforms, called "EduX". Section 3 describes the implementation of the "EduX system". The system was evaluated to verify its design as described in Section 4.

2: The EduX Concept

Similar to other social groups, educational groups owns their organizations [3]. Social organization should be considered by an educational portal site. EduX attempts to extend physical social learning groups to online multilayer educational services platforms that allow participants to establish easily and organize online learning communities while interacting with others.

2.1: The EduCities

EduCities is a portal site for learning. At the EduCities website, all activities take place in the conceptual central area. The EduCities website has fruitful organized online learning communities. One year later after the EduCities was released, users have provided many feedbacks. One valuable comment is that users have many social relationships in physical learning environments, and they expect that online learning communities are similar to their physical learning environments. Participants own their identifications in physical learning communities, and users expect the identifications are extending from physical to online. Accordingly, the EduCities website is re-organized so that users can more easily perform their learning activities. The rights, interactions, and relationships that exist in physical social learning communities can be implemented online. Members of both online and physical communities have common views, value systems, and visions. Online learning communities can support a physical group by increasing the frequency and quality of interactions. Consequently, the EduCites website was re-organized in response to users' strong requests. Under the structure of the modified EduCities, many schools are constructing their "small EduCities", called EduTowns. An EduTown is a school-based learning environment that represents a school. All inter-schools activities occur in the

EduCities, whereas all intra-school activities occur in EduTown. In an EduTown, there are many EduVillages each of which is a class-based learning environment that represents a class. A mayor of EduVillage could be a teacher or a student. In the EduVillage are many EduCitizens. An EduCitizen is a personal learning environment. An EduCitizen controlled by a teacher, a student, or a member of staff. Now, "physical social learning communities" are forming in online EduCities.

2.2: Definition of the EduX

The concept of EduX is used to describe the re-organized platforms. EduXs are multilayer educational services platforms which consist of EduX layers and EduX relations. The definition of the EduX is shown in Figure 1, and the EduX concept is shown in Figure 2. The EduXs provide multilayer structure to support learners to construct their online learning environments. Participants interact with other via platforms. On each EduX layer are many service items that are developed by third-party developers provided to participants to enable them to construct their own online social learning environments.

EduX = (EduX layers, EduX relations)
EduX layer = (Social identification, Services, Protocols, Participants)
EduX relations = (R^v, R^h)
R_v : vertical relations of EduX layers, $R^v \geq 0$
R_h : horizontal relations of EduX layers, $R^h \geq 0$
Social identification $\in$ { SI^1, SI^2, … …, SI^m }
The name of SI^1, SI^2, … …, SI^m are defined by system developers.
Services = ? Service items
Service item = (Software applications, Content)
Protocols: interactive mechanizes among service items, EduX layers, and participants.
Participant = (Participant identification, Participant relations)
Participant identification = { PI^1, PI^2, … …, PI^m }
　　The name of PI^1, PI^2, … …, PI^m are defined by system developers.
Participant relations = (PR^v, PR^h)
PR_v : vertical relations of participant, $R^v \geq 0$
PR_h : horizontal relations of participant, $R^h \geq 0$

Figure 1. Definition of the EduX.

2.2.1: EduX layers

An EduX consists of several EduX layers. An EduX layer consists of social identification, services, protocols, and participants. Each EduX layer is managed by at least one participant.

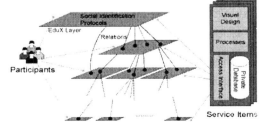

Figure 2. The EduX concept

Social identification: The EduX layers are named according to a set of social identifications. For example, a set of social identifications could be defined as inter-schools, school, class, or personal. The system developers define the social identifies. Participants sense their position by these social identifications.

Service items: Services in EduX include software applications and contents, which are provided by third-party. Service items are plugged into an EduX layer. Mayors who manage the EduX layer have the right to determine which service items are accessible or hidden in their EduX layers.

Protocols: Activities protocols are the interactive mechanism among service items, EduX layers, and participants.

Participants: In the EduX model, different participants have different roles. These roles are specified by the participant's identity and relationships. For example, one of the participants' identification sets could be as president, member of staff, teacher, student, parent, volunteer.

2.2.2: Relations

EduX involves two basic vector relations, the vertical relations R^v, and the horizontal relationship R^h. R^v represents the vertical relationship between the current EduX layer and another EduX layer. R^h represents the horizontal relationship between two EduX layers.

2.3: SDA circle on EduX

The EduX is a multilayer educational services platforms concept. Researchers can release their systems to participants via the platforms. The Supply-Deliver-Analyze (SDA) circle describes the relationship between system developers and participants of EduX.

Supply: In EduX, system suppliers provide service items to participants. The suppliers could be researchers, teachers, educational volunteers, and so on. Those service items are plugged into suitable EduX layers via a service items management interface, which is managed maintainers of the EduX system.

Deliver: Service items, which plugged into EduX service items management interface, are delivered to participants through the EduX layer.

Analyze: Participants who use the service items will

produce many activities logs. The technologies applied to analyze such data depend on analysts' requests. Data mining technology is one kind of technologies to analyze these data. There are a lot of steps to analyze the data, including data collecting, cleaning, selection, transformation, mining, and so on. Those data will feedback to system developers to modify their system.

3: Implementation

The EduX system is implemented to study with the EduX concept. Metaphorical cities, towns, villages, and citizens are used to help participants to understand the concept of layers.

3.1: EduX layer of EduX system

■ Social identification

The EduX system includes four EduX layers, called EduCity, EduTown, EduVillage, and EduCitizen. Their features are described as follows:

(1) EduCity: An EduCity represents as a learning portal site. Inter-schools activities occur in this layer.

(2) EduTown: An EduTown represents a school-based learning environment. Many EduTowns are present in an EduCity. All intra-school and inter-classes activities occur in their EduTown. An EduTown is managed by a "mayor" who is a teacher with computer background.

(3) EduVillage: An EduVillage represents as a class-based learning environment. Man EduVillages are present in an EduTown. All intra-class activities occur in EduVillages. An EduVillage is also managed by a "mayor", who is a teacher or a student in a class.

(4) EduCitizens: An EduCitizen is a participant's personal website. All personal learning environments are built in this layer. An EduCitizen is managed by the learner him/herself.

■ Services

As the Figure 1 shown, services are combined with many service items. Different EduX layers require different services. The services are categorized into three types. They are service items for schools (SIFSs), service items for classes (SIFCs), and service items for participants (SIFPs). The service items in each EduX layer are further classified into content services, community building services, application services, and other services.

SIFS: SIFSs are suitable to school-based learning environment. Such as calendar records, notice boards, bulletin boards, chat rooms, FAQ boards, school timetables, and other items are involved.

SIFC: SIFCs are suitable to class-based learning environment. Such as notice boards, meeting rooms, announcements, class albums, class calendars, and other items are involved.

SIFP: SIFPs are suitable for individual-based learning environments. Such as daily records, web mails, announcements, notes, personal games, and other items are involved.

■ Participants

A participant in an EduX system has one of four different roles as follows:

P1 = Mayor of EduCity who manages all mayors of EduTowns

P2 = Mayor of EduTown who manages all mayors of EduVillages in the EduTown

P3 = Mayor of EduVillage who manages all participants in the EduVillage

P4 = Participants who manage his or her own learning environment

3.2: SDA circle of EduX system

The SDA circle, implemented in the EduX system, is described as follows.

Supply: All service items include application service items, content service items, community building service items, SIFSs, SIFCs, SIFPs, and others, are designed by the suppliers of the service items.

Deliver: the EduX system maintains channels which connect to all schools, classes, and individual learners who use the EduX system.

Analyze: Three pieces of basic system data are collected: web logs, activities logs, and questionnaire logs. More data can be logged if needed. The results of the data analysis are feedback to system developers.

4: System Evaluation

The EduX system was released on the Internet (http://edutowns.educities.edu.tw/) on January 5, 2001. The system is designed for schools and classes, the main users of the system are elementary, junior and senior high school students and teachers in Taiwan. The website is in the traditional Chinese language. Teachers can applied their school as an EduTown, and establish their EduVillages and EduCitizens. Teachers and students can use the system either in school or at home.

■ Statistics of schools, classes, and individuals

Up to and including March 2002, more than 1,802 EduTowns, 13,023 EduVillages and 96,222 EduCitizens had registered to use the EduX system. Figure 3 shows the growth of the EduX system.

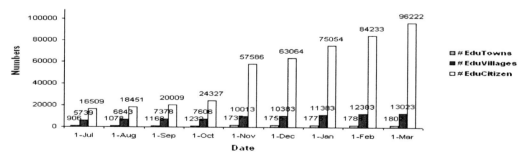

Figure 3. Growth of the EduX system.

■ Statistics of daily hit rates

Online data logs and their analysis can be used directly to elucidate the status of the system. The hit rates of the EduX system were analyzed to determine the users' behavior. The hit rates records were collected daily during August 25 to October 25, 2001. As Figure 4 shown, three peaks occurred in each day. The first peak is from 8 a.m. to 12 a.m.; the second peak is from 1 p.m. to 4 p.m. Thus, students use the system at school. The third peak is from 5 p.m. to 11 p.m., indicates students use the system even when at home. Users also use the system at weekends is observed. These results show that many users use the system in and out of school, on weekdays and weekends.

948

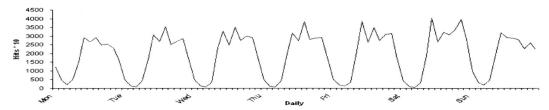

Figure 4. Daily hits rates.

5: Conclusions

Like physical social learning communities, online social learning communities have their structure, logic, and value system. Online social learning communities are combining with physical social learning communities. This paper proposed the EduX concept of multilayer educational services platforms to integrate online social learning communities and physical social learning communities. The EduX system has been implemented and released on the Internet for use by schools, classes, and individuals. Growth of the system indicated that multilayer educational services platforms are suited to schools in Taiwan. The system daily hit rates revealed that users accept the system. More detailed evaluations are required in the near future to clarify the system's performance, as judged by teachers, and students.

Acknowledgement

This project is supported by a grant from the Ministry of Education in Taiwan, No. 89-H-FA07-1-4.

References

[1] Chan, T. W., Hue, C. W., Chou, C. Y. & Tzeng, Ovid J. L. (2001). Four spaces of network learning models. *International Journal of Computers & Education,* 37(2), 141-161.

[2] Oren, A., Nachmias, R., Mioduser, D. & Lahav, O. (2000). Learnet – A model for virtual learning communities in the world wide web. *International Journal of Educational Telecommunications.* 6(2), 141 – 157.

[3] Owens, R. G. (1998). *Organizational Behavior in Education (sixth edition).* Boston: Allyn and Bacon Publishers.

[4] Preece, J. (2000). *Online Communities, Designing Usability, Supporting Sociability.* NY: Wiley Publisher.

[5] Wachter, R. M., Gupta, J. N.D. & Quaddus, M. A. (2000). IT takes a village: Virtual communities in support of education. *International Journal of Information Management.* 20, 473-489.

The Sharable Content Object Reference Model (SCORM) – A Critical Review

Oliver Bohl, Dr. Jörg Schellhase, Ruth Sengler, Prof. Dr. Udo Winand
University of Kassel

Abstract

Learning technology standards are increasingly gaining in importance in the field of Web-based teaching. At present, two standards dominating the market are taking shape. These are the SCORM standard of the ADL initiative and the AICC standard of the AICC organization. Based on the AICC and LOM meta data standards, the SCORM standard stands the chance to become the standard dominating the market. A number of restrictions are involved with the SCORM standard, though. The article shows general deficiencies of the SCORM standard that are critical concerning the market value of SCOs, the process of producing WBTs on the basis of different SCO providers, the maintenance of SCOs and WBTs (consisting of several SCOs), and the quality of WBTs based on SCOs of different providers.

1: Introduction

Over the past few years several initiatives developed, at first in the USA, aiming at the standardization of computer based teaching components. This article focuses on the SCORM (Sharable Content Object Reference Model) standard of the ADL (Advanced Distributed Learning, http://www.adlnet.org) initiative. Why are standards like SCORM important for Web-based learning environments and technologies? Considering the increasing number of virtual learning environments, it is obvious that the same contents are processed several times for multimedia use because they cannot be discovered or used straight away. This is where standardization efforts start from.

2: Analysis of the SCORM

Fundamental objectives of the SCORM standard are the easy portability of learning content from one Learning Management System (LMS) to another as well as the reusability of learning objects. The easy portability of WBTs creates an additional benefit for vendors of learning content and LMSs because the high costs for portation are reduced. WBTs can exchange data with the LMS via standardized interfaces. Above all, the metadata model of the LOM standard integrated in the SCORM supports the retrieval of learning objects in varying constellations. SCORM denominates the smallest unit which can be administered by an LMS as a Sharable Content Object (SCO). A Sharable Content Object (SCO) represents one or more assets which use the SCORM run-time environment to communicate with different LMSs. An SCO represents the lowest level of content granularity which can be tracked by an LMS. An SCO should be independent of learning context to be reusable in different learning situations. Moreover, several SCOs can be assembled to form learning or exercise units on a super ordinate level. To make a potential reuse practicable, SCOs should be small units. They can be the basis for sharable content repositories which facilitate their exchange. Only an LMS may launch an SCO, an SCO must not launch other SCOs. [2]

2.1: Potentials of the SCORM

An important advantage of SCORM compliant WBTs is that they are basically interoperable with all SCORM compliant LMSs. In addition, they can exchange important user data, metadata on SCOs, and a variety of interaction data (e.g. choice of path, current position in the SCO, comments and annotations, duration, scores) in a standardized way with SCORM compliant LMSs. The basic metadata of a SCORM compliant SCO are transferred to the LMS in the form of files when the SCO is delivered, so that many metadata do not have to be fed to the LMS separately.

When using SCORM compliant SCOs, an LMS can offer learners a learning account. Learner scores can be managed course comprehensively in a standardized way via this learning account. Furthermore, the learner can take a look at a table of his or her learning status relating to single SCOs at any time. SCO-specific comments a lecturer has left for a certain learner can be displayed when the SCO is started. The administration of the current position in an individual SCO can be done by the LMS, so that this information can be transferred when the SCO is launched. Annotations transferred from the SCOs to the LMS can be managed by the LMS and be presented to the lecturer in a well-structured form. The data, which according to SCORM can be transferred to the LMS, facilitates a comfortable supervision of the learning progress. The LMS could offer aggregated representations of test results and an overview about SCOs that learners have already been worked with. Learning histories of the learners could be managed. Tracking data, transferred from the SCOs to the LMS, could be presented to the tutors in different views, so that they receive valuable indications concerning the further design of content.

2.2: Deficits of the SCORM

It is the vision of the SCORM to collect SCOs in comprehensive repositories and to open them for reuse, while aspects of didactic adjustments of SCOs by tutors, possibly even to the learner, or copyright aspects are left out of consideration. The extensive cataloguing by means of metadata is an obstacle for developers and vendors because existing content has to be provided with metadata to be SCORM compliant. Further aspects are left out of consideration. For example, it is not intended that a SCO can signal to the LMS how it wants to behave in a specific learner context. Therefore, it is impossible to repeat parts of a SCO because of a negative test result. Using SCORM it is also impossible for a tutor to adapt content learner-specific. [1]

The following observations are based on the premise that there is a market for small SCOs which are independent of learning context. The offered SCOs were developed with different authoring tools. Possibly, some SCOs have their own navigation and sequencing elements. It is to be assumed that the style of language, the semantics of words, the way of presenting content, the processing of media, and further important contents of the individual SCOs differ. With authoring tools conforming to SCORM, different SCOs could be assembled to form complex SCOs by the mechanism of content aggregation. First of all, this presupposes a costly inspection and evaluation of suitable SCOs. Possibly, SCOs not yet existing on the market have to be developed separately. The functionality and comfortability of an SCO assembled in this way now decisively depends on the possibilities of the LMS the SCO is supposed to work with. The usefulness of this SCO therefore depends on the LMS. In addition, the SCORM currently only offers limited sequencing and navigation possibilities [2] which again limits the possible support of LMSs. The content pages of the SCO neither offer additional information depending on the learning context nor orientation help because this would contradict the SCORM's paradigma. Furthermore, the SCO does not have any, respectively has only few additional learning context-specific functionalities, which exceed the metadata descriptions of the individual SCOs and polished access structures (with the exception of a table of contents) cannot be supported, either.

From a learner's point of view, the SCO presents itself as a hotchpotch of ill-matched content. The learner has to work out contextual relations for himself because SCO comprehensive contexts are explained only partially. Parallel to a global navigation provided by the LMS, the learner has to adapt to different SCO-specific local navigation elements. Apart from such a SCO hardly being able to impart complex facts adequately, such a SCO appears to be hardly attractive and suitable for everyday use. Some of the described difficulties could be circumvented, if a SCO was designed completely anew and all SCOs were developed in a standardized way. But strictly speaking, even in this case information dependent of learning context would not be allowed to be integrated in the SCOs because then a substantial argument for using the SCORM standard would no longer apply. The whole range of problems described above still applies to other vendors who use the SCOs developed in this way.

At least it is debatable whether the approach propagated by the SCORM promotes the development of high-quality SCOs. Even if it were possible to buy SCOs and adjust their "Look & Feel", it is uncertain whether that does make sense or is even practicable. It would require a lot of additional work and would have the consequence, that when buying newer versions of the SCOs, the same work has to be done again. These statements suggest that as a rule SCOs will be difficult to commercialise as long as they are not high-quality animations or videos. In this case, a market for SCOs is only of slight interest to potential SCO developers. It is astonishing, that up to now there is no market for high-quality animations and videos, especially as such a market could quite easily be realized by simple means even without approaches for standardization.

3: Conclusion

This article has explained potential benefits of SCORM. The main advantages are in the field of portability of learning content, the standardized communication interface between the LMS and WBTs as well as in supporting the reusability of learning objects. Nevertheless the article has shown problems that are critical concerning the market value of SCOs, the process of producing WBTs on the basis of different SCO providers, the maintenance of SCOs and WBTs (consisting of several SCOs), and the quality of WBTs based on SCOs of different providers.

The SCORM should not rashly be viewed negatively. The development of standards is a continuous process. But in the framework of further developments, the criticized aspects mentioned should be taken into consideration.

4: References

[1] Cohen, E. J.: The Emerging Standards Effort in E-Learning. Will SCORM lead the way? e-learning Magazine. http://www.elearningmag.com, 2002-03-18.
[2] Dodds, P.: Advanced Distributed Learning, Sharable Content Object Reference Model Version 1.2, Release 2001. http://www.adlnet.org, 2002-03-25.

E-learning and the Status of Knowledge in the Information Age

Pithamber R. Polsani
Assistant Professor
Department of Spanish & Portuguese
&
Faculty Specialist
The Virtual Adaptive Learning Architecture
The University of Arizona

ABSTRACT

This paper advocates the constitution of E-learning as an independent field of knowledge production and circulation. Such an event should start first by identifying the space of its function: the network organized as a rhizome. The second important step in this direction is delineating clearly the object of E-learning: the production and circulation of performative knowledge that can be rapidly generated and circulated as the market configurations change. The third critical step in establishing the E-learning field is recognizing the uniqueness of information and communication technologies and the optimal use of technology's potential. The forth crucial element in this directions is creating E-learning as a vibrant learning environments wherein a user goes through life like an interactive experience that is customizable for individuals or groups of individuals. In order to achieve the finer level of customization, the architecture of E-learning should be conceptualized with two guiding principles: modularity and the linkage system.

Introduction

Every stage of societal development requires an educational system that can adequately reflect its needs and demands. Consequently, modern institutions of higher learning are designed to bring about appropriate changes in administrative organization, curriculum, and learning methodologies in order to shape learners into active participants and productive members of a society.

Currently we are witnessing in education global shifts that reflect changes brought about by computers and communication technology. This shift may be called Electronic Learning, or E-learning. E-learning is a mode of knowledge production and circulation wherein information technologies play a decisive role.

With the emergence of the Internet as the prime form of global communication and information exchange, E-learning has been brought to the forefront. Many universities and private companies specializing in corporate personnel training worldwide are embracing web delivered instruction enthusiastically. In recent years, new public and private universities have been established to offer full-fledged degree programs delivered exclusively online. Despite its many advocates and large number of course offerings, E-learning has yet to emerge as a viable alternative to traditional classroom oriented instruction[1]. E-learning's inability to take a decisive step in this direction is due to a failure in sketching out a well thought out ground plan and a sound strategy towards achieving it. The lack of solid foundations is reflected in the current practices of E-learning: web pages with course syllabus and bulletin boards; instructor's class notes online; digital replication of traditional course content. In its current form, E-learning is nothing but one more course delivery mechanism for distance education.

E-learning can establish itself as a critical form of knowledge production and circulation only when it is constituted as an independent field by opening up its own space of operation, developing a coherent methodology and logical procedures for creating and delivering knowledge objects.

The first step towards instituting E-learning should begin by evolving a reasoned set of answers to the following questions:
- What does E-learning produce?
- What is the nature of the product?
- How is it exchanged and circulated?

---

[1] According to the Sloan Consortium Catalog of Alfred P. Sloan Foundation, the Sloan consortium members to date have offered well over 100,000 course units online. The website list contains 369 degree programs offered by one hundred institutions in the United States. http://www.sloan-c.org/catalog/

- Who participates in this exchange?
- What are the benefits of E-learning?

This paper is an attempt to formulate, albeit in a theoretical fashion, responses to these questions.

Open Space: The Rhizome

Every field requires an open space in which to operate. For example, nature is science's space of operation, as is human culture for the humanities. E-learning's open space is the network. One major consequence of information and communication technologies is the formation of a network, the web of interconnected devices through which all data is transmitted, transactions are conducted, and human interactions take place. Human beings not only use the network for various purposes, but they also facilitate its connections. In this regard we should view individuals as instances of this network.

The network of E-learning can be characterized fundamentally as a rhizome. A rhizome is defined by French philosophers Deleuze and Guattari in their work, *A Thousand Plateaus: Capitalism and Schizophrenia* is "an acentered, nonhierarchical, non-signifying system without a general and without an organizing memory or central automation, defined solely by a circulation of states [21]." There are six basic features of a rhizome: connection, heterogeneity, multiplicity, a-signifying rupture, cartography, and decalcomania. The first two features characterize the rhizome as a nonhierarchical space of connections wherein all nodes are interconnected without any one node assuming a central position. According to the multiplicity principle, there are many connections that link one point to another; however, it is the multiple connections instead of the points themselves that have importance. The a-signifying rupture gives the rhizome its indestructible character. If the network ruptures at a given point it will not collapse but will continue through another line since the rhizome is a multiplicity of connections. The last two principles define the rhizome as a map, and like a map the rhizome exists independently of whatever it is a map of. Also like a map, the rhizome has multiple points of entry and can be read in any way.

Deleuze and Guattari use rhizome, a biological term that refers to a root-like stem emitting roots and usually producing leaves at its apex, as a metaphor for describing social formation in advanced capitalist societies. The Internet, with its rapid growth and acceptance worldwide, is emerging as the form of sociality connecting institutions, governments, businesses, social groups and individuals in an irrevocable bond of interdependency. Education as an important component for the well-being

and growth of societies is permanently drawn into it. Educators have to urgently rethink questions such as what is education? How is it produced? And how is it transmitted?

Since the open space of E-learning is the network as rhizome, it cannot rely on the narrative framework that describes other forms of traditional education. Traditional classroom instructional dynamics may be described by a sender-receiver-referent model. According to this model, the teacher is a sender who stands before a class for sixty minutes and transmits information; the student is a receiver who patiently awaits the sixty minutes to pass; and the textbook, a bound volume of knowledge, is the referent. In this model all three participants—sender, receiver, and referent— occupy predetermined positions in a hierarchically organized space. Because the very foundation of E-learning is a nonhierarchical and decentered rhizome, the content development, instructional design, and mechanisms of assessment have to be thought anew.

Status of knowledge in the Post-Industrial Society

What is produced and circulated by E-learning in the rhizomatic space of the network is knowledge. In the last 50 years advances in industrial technology, informatics, communications, cybernetics, computer hardware, programming languages, biotechnology, information storage and retrieval devices, and audio-visual media have had a profound impact on knowledge, altering its status and utility. Today knowledge no longer receives its legitimacy thorough the grand narratives of human emancipation and speculative spirit, but is judged by performative criteria instead. The institutions of higher learning have yet to incorporate fully into their administrative and curricular policy this altered definition of knowledge. Consequently, the two contradictory notions of knowledge exist simultaneously in today's universities, resulting in a constant—but ultimately confused and ineffective—redefinition of their role and function in the society.

Before the advent of the post-industrial age in the 1960s, Enlightenment and post-Enlightenment ideas determined the purpose and use of knowledge. The European Enlightenment defined the human being as a subject whose destiny is the realization of its full potentialities through reason. Philosophers argued that the scientific knowledge needed for cultivation of reason was denied to subjects by religious institutions and despotic regimes. Therefore the public policy reforms during the eighteenth century focused mainly on school education resulting in constitutional guarantees of primary education to all its citizens. On the university level, knowledge was seen as an end in itself. The goal of acquiring learning was the realization of spirit, life, and emancipation of humanity and the purpose of production of knowledge was the moral and spiritual guidance of a nation. In this regard the mission of the universities was to lay "open the whole body of learning and expound both the principles and foundation of all knowledge [33]." Therefore the liberal arts, the theoretical sciences, and mathematics became the preferred subjects, and philosophy—as the discipline that unifies both the sciences and humanities—acquired a privileged status. Owing to this conceptualization of knowledge, universities were not expected to be responsive to society's needs. As a result, institutions of higher learning acquired the image of ivory towers, and professors, the inhabitants of those towers, became distinguished individuals.

In the contemporary conceptualization of knowledge, its purpose is no longer to realize spirit or emancipate humanity but to add value to human abilities expressed as labor. Since learning has value, its valuation is determined by its utility and exchange. Thus the criterion for judging knowledge is its performance.

The legitimacy of performative knowledge is no longer granted by the grand narratives of emancipation, but by the market. The market should be understood as a grouping of various forces such as public policy, industrial complexes, the financial sector, technology, business modeling, and so on. The character of the market at any given time is determined by the configuration of dominant forces that participate in it. For example, throughout the 1990s technology[2] was the dominant force that defined the nature of the market, but with the collapse of Dotcom bubble, technology is now giving way to the business model as a leading force. The market, unlike the narratives of emancipation and speculative spirit, which are valid for long durations, is in a constant flux shifting rapidly from one configuration to the other. As a result the knowledge requirements imposed by the market are also altering expeditiously. The only thing that is constant with the market is the change. Therefore education should be defined as preparedness for change, and the knowledge acquired through education should be performative.

Performative knowledge no longer asks the questions, is it true? Is it just? Is it moral? It asks instead: Is it useful? Is it efficient? Is it marketable? With preparedness for change as a fundamental principle, performative knowledge can be grouped into two categories, functional knowledge and optimal knowledge[3]. Functional knowledge is the ability to access correct information in the right way at the right moment to perform tasks. Optimal knowledge on the other hand is the capacity to arrange previously independent data into a new series of arrangements to generate new projects or optimize the existing projects. As the market requirements of learning are changing constantly, performative knowledge cannot be transmitted en block; instead it should be arranged into up-to-date knowledge banks that can be accessed by individual learners. Similarly, knowledge modules should be appropriately customized to the requirements of individual participants. The traditional educational system, which is established in a geographical space with physical assets and which relies on the transportation of its participants, will not be able to live up to these new tasks. E-learning that is driven by information and communication technologies, which are inherently flexible and effective, is the appropriate from of knowledge production and circulation for the new reality of the market.

Technology and E-learning

The operational space of E-learning is the network organized as a rhizome, and its objective is the production of performative knowledge that responds to the changing configurations of the market. The means of producing and circulating this knowledge is computer technology. Recent advances in multimedia software and programming language have established computers as unique and radically different technological devices from other technologies that aided the production and circulation of knowledge.

The first major technological invention offered to knowledge was writing. With the invention of writing, learning could be transferred from individuals to stone, copper and paper. As recorded knowledge was now mobile, it became independent of the individual or group who produced it. Additionally writing enabled the preservation of learning, thereby enabling others to access it. The Greeks called writing a mnemotechnic, memory-enhancing technique. Interestingly, Socrates, in Plato's dialogue *Pheadrus*, denounces writing, calling it a poison that endangered the human capacity for memory[4].

---

[2] The technology in 90's replaced the labor as one of the driving forces of the market.

[3] Here I am borrowing Lyotard's types of knowledge in post-industrial society and developing it further to adequately suit my theory about market configurations. See Jean-François Lyotard [6].

[4] Socrates recounts the following myth about the invention of writing and its effects on people. "At the Egyptian city of Naucratis, there was a famous old god, whose name was Theuth; ...he was the inventor of many arts, such as arithmetic and calculation and geometry and astronomy and draughts and dice, but his great discovery was the use of letters. Now in those days the god Thamus was the king of the whole country of Egypt; To him came Theuth and showed his inventions, desiring that the other Egyptians might be allowed to have the benefit of

954

The second important technological breakthrough that ensured the preservation and circulation of knowledge was the printing press. The printing press overcame the limitations of writing by making it possible to produce rapidly hundreds and thousands of identical copies of a piece of writing. With the advent of the printing press, there was an explosion of production and circulation of knowledge.

The third crucial invention was audio-visual devices like photography, the phonograph, cinema, video, and the like. These new mechanisms of recording and exchanging information developed their own language and rules of production.

Although technological innovation accelerated the creation and transmission of knowledge, these devices possess an inherent limitation—their materiality. Their use in education is limited owing to the fact that several equipments were needed and that the experience they offered to the learner was sequential.

Computers have overcome the inherent limitations of all other technological innovations so far used in the propagation of learning. A computer is at once a writing, recording, printing and circulation device. Additionally, multimedia computers enable a simultaneous experience of textual and audio-visual elements bring it closer to how we experience reality. Furthermore, this technology adds an important dimension to the simultaneity of user interaction and real-time transmission.

As the possibilities offered by computers and multimedia software are radically different and innovative E-learning should not reduce them into simple distance education delivery mechanisms. The full potential of these technologies can be realized and appropriately used in the service of learning only when E-learning establishes itself as an independent field with a comprehensible ground plan, a rational methodology, and a clear strategy for achieving it.

Objectives and Procedures for E-learning

I have argued so far for the constitution of E-learning as an independent field of knowledge production and circulation. Such an event should start first by identifying the space of its function: the network organized as a rhizome. The second important step in this direction is delineating clearly the object of E-learning: the production and circulation of performative knowledge that can be rapidly generated and circulated as the market configurations change. The third critical step in establishing the E-learning field is recognizing the uniqueness of information and communication technologies and the optimal use of technology's potential. In this section, I would like to put forward very briefly some objectives for E-learning and practical procedures for achieving these goals.

Like other fields, E-learning should clearly articulate objectives and establish procedures for accomplishing its goals. The objective of E-learning should be to create vibrant learning environments wherein a user goes through life like an interactive experience. Environment and Experience are two fundamental concepts that guide the E-learning field.

The idea of environment is akin to an ecological system that is characterized by the diversity of species and their unity in interdependency. Similarly, E-learning should offer a great variety of elements, all joined together to generate unforgettable experiences in the user.

Likewise, Experience is a mechanism for engaging learners, committing them in a personal and memorable way to the subject matter. Experiences in general are personal: they occur within an individual, and they engage each individual in an emotional, physical and spiritual level. Consequently, no two experiences are identical. Given the nature of experience, E-learning therefore should be customizable for individuals or groups of individuals. In order to achieve the finer level of customization, the architecture of E-learning should be conceptualized with two guiding principles: modularity and the linkage system.

The fundamental requirement for modular architecture and the linkage system is the separation of content from the instructional use of the content. The content should be created as discreet, self-standing modules that are predisposed for reuse in multiple

them he enumerated them, and Thamus enquired about their several uses, and praised some of them and censured others.... when they came to letters, this, said Theuth, will make the Egyptians wiser and give them better memories; it is a specific both for the memory and for the wit. Thamus replied: O most ingenious Theuth, ... in this instance, you who are the father of letters, from a paternal love of your own children have been led to attribute to them a quality which they cannot have; for this discovery of yours will create forgetfulness in the learners' souls, because they will not use their memories; they will trust to the external written characters and not remember of themselves. The specific which you have discovered is an aid not to memory, but to reminiscence, and you give your disciples not truth, but only the semblance of truth; they will be hearers of many things and will have learned nothing; they will appear to be omniscient and will generally know nothing; they will be tiresome company, having the show of wisdom without the reality." [274d-275d].

contexts[5]. In this regard, we should borrow the notion of object and its architecture from object oriented programming and adapt it creatively to the educational content. With the modular approach we can bring great efficiency into content development. The ideational value of the content should well thought out to adequately fulfill the requirements of performative knowledge, especially rapid adaptability to the changing configurations of market.

The instructional design should concentrate on using existing content objects to generate learning environments and memorable experiences that are unique to individual needs. In this regard, we should creatively emulate product design principles and methods from commercial advertising, computer gaming, theatre, stage performances and visual media. As Brenda Laurel argues in her book *Computers as Theatre* human-computer interaction should be a "designed experience." According to Laurel, "thinking about interfaces is thinking too small. Designing human-computer experience isn't about building a better desktop. It's about creating imaginary worlds that have a special relationship to reality—worlds in which we can extend, amplify, and enrich our own capabilities to think, feel and act [32-33]." As the operational space of E-learning is the network organized as a rhizome, the customized environments and experiences also should be rhizome-like: without hierarchies, depths, or separations. The reader and the writer should come together in the network for an interminable experience.

Similarly, the modular architecture and the linkage mechanism should be an open, but a standards based system. The standards should focus on areas like technology, modularity of learning objects, and visual layout etc. Like in the object oriented programming commonly agreed upon specification will make the learning modules independent of system allowing a greater participation of educators for furthering the acceptability of E-learning.

Conclusion

In this paper I have argued for a clear articulation of the future direction of E-learning. It may be too early to talk about the future since E-learning is still in its infancy. However, one lesson taught by the Dotcom bubble is that the infant mortality is very high among ideas for employing new technologies. I do not believe that the fate of E-learning will be similar to the short life of Dotcoms because E-learning is a structural necessity for the new social formation in which the network is the form of sociality. Nevertheless, E-learning should recognize its vital role in the emergent global society and institute itself as an independent field of knowledge production and circulation.

References

1. Deleuze, Gilles and Felix Guattari. (Translation: Brian Massumi) *A Thousand Plateaus: Capitalism and Schizophrenia.* Minneapolis: University of Minnesota Press, 1987.
2. Jean-François Lyotard. (Translation Geoff Bennington and Brian Massumi) *The Postmodern Condition: A Report on Knowledge.* Minneapolis: University of Minnesota Press, 1984.
3. Plato. (Edited: Edith Hamilton and Huntington Cairns) *The Collected Dialogues.* New York: Pantheon Books, 1961.
4. Brenda Laurel. *Computers as Theater.* Reading, Mass.: Addison-Wesley, 1993

---

[5] The Virtual Adaptive Learning Architecture being developed at Faculty Center for Instructional Innovation, University of Arizona, has taken this approach for creating content. The team is implementing a modular architecture and linkage system known as Reusable Learning Objects and Reusable Instructional Objects developed by this author.

An Approach for Automatic Learning and Inference by Knowledge Map

Chang-Kai Hsu, Jyh-Cheng Chang, Maiga Chang, Jihn-Chang Jehng and Jia-Sheng Heh

ken@mcsl.ice.cycu.edu.tw, eoda@mcsl.ice.cycu.edu.tw, maiga@ms2.hinet.net,

jehng@src.ncu.edu.tw, jsheh@ice.cycu.edu.tw

Dept. of Information Computer and Engineering,

Chung-Yuan Christian Univ., Chung-Li, 320, Taiwan

Abstract

Knowledge is represented by graph or map is simpler than represented by proposition logics. Students who use the knowledge representation of knowledge map quickly learn to read a graph as *IF-THEN* and do all their reasoning directly on the graphs without translating them to rules or propositions. Instead, many graphic notations have been developed. Knowledge Map (KM) is a graphic system of logic that is as general as proposition logics.

Keywords: knowledge representation, conceptual graph, knowledge map.

1. Introduction

Knowledge representations that use some notations or expressions, such as text, table or graph, to represent knowledge had been researched many years by researchers. According to these representations, the graph is more readable and realizable by human than others because it more simper and more intension to represent. [CHO93]

Knowledge Map were designed to have a direct mapping to and from structured documents; in addition, to use the knowledge map be knowledge representation for problem solving can also be an application in computer system. [HaF94]

2. Knowledge Formulation

Content structures are used to determine the sequence and content of instructions to promote understanding of the author's perspective on the content area. Content structures are constructed from the sentences, denoted by p_m, which always have some topic or subtopics as Figure 1 shown below.[Nict99]

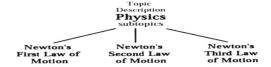

Figure 1. Content structure

Concept θ_i is the basic unit of knowledge used to represent something. The *concept space*, $\underline{\theta 0} = \{\theta_i\}$, represents the discourse of all the concepts, such as all students in this school or all keywords in Physics. A *concept set*, denoted as $\underline{\theta} = \{\theta_i\} \subseteq \underline{\theta 0}$, is one subset of concepts.

A *concept relation*, represented as $\rho_k(\theta_{i1}, \theta_{i2}, \ldots)$, is an aggregation (relation) of knowledge pieces (concepts $\theta_{i1}, \theta_{i2}, \ldots$) with some specific relation style $\rho_k(\cdot)$. The *concept relation space*, symbolized as $\underline{\rho 0} = \{\rho_k\}$, is the discourse of all the concept relation.

Formally, a *proposition* can be represented as $\phi_k(\rho_j(\theta_{i1}, \theta_{i2}, \ldots))$, mapping a concept relation $\rho_j(\theta_{i1}, \theta_{i2}, \ldots)$ into a value $\phi(\cdot) \in V_\phi$. The *value set* V_ϕ adopts usually true-false logic, and can be other data types such as fuzzy sets or continuous values. The *proposition space*, $\underline{\phi 0} = \{\phi_k\}$, represents the discourse of all the proposition, such as all statements or valus in Physics. A *proposition set*, denoted as $\underline{\phi} = \{\phi_k\}$

$\subseteq \underline{\phi 0}$, is one set of propositions.

3. Analysis of Knowledge Hierarchical

The general *knowledge unit*, denoted as $KU_p(\theta_i, \underline{\phi})$, that includes the concept and all its propositions (*knowledge schemas*). And each proposition maps a concept relation and its concepts. For instance, the concept relations in the propositions about bird are

"BIRD can FLY"= $\rho_{CAN}(\theta_{BIRD}, \theta_{MAMMAL})$, and

"BIRD has WINGS"=$\rho_{HAS\_A}(\theta_{BIRD}, \theta_{WINGS})$ etc.

The relations of concepts inside a knowledge unit, $\rho_{INTERPRETATION}(\theta_{SIGNIFIER}, \theta_{SIGNIFIED})$. The propositions of those knowledge units' concept relations can also express:

- production rule,

    $\rho_{iF\_THEN}(\rho_{IF}(\theta_1, \theta_2, ...), \rho_{THEN}(\theta_1, \theta_2, ...))$

- concept schema

    $\rho_{SCHEMA}(\theta_{OBJ}, \theta_{ATTR1}, \theta_{ATTR2}, ...) =$

    $\rho_{SCHEMA}(\theta_{OBJ}, \rho_{LINK}(\theta_{OBJ}, \theta_{ATTR1}),$

    $\rho_{LINK}(\theta_{OBJ}, \theta_{ATTR2}), ...)$

- formula,

    $\rho_{FORMULA}(\theta_{X1}, \theta_{X2}, \theta_Y, ...)$

- concept hierarchy, syntagm,

    $\rho_{IS\_A}(\theta_1, \theta_2), \rho_{HAS\_A}(\theta_1, \theta_2)$ ...etc.

If $CG(\underline{\theta}, \rho_{CLUSTER} \cup \rho_{LINKAGE})$ is a lattice, then it is called $KH(\underline{\theta}, \rho_{KIND} \cup \rho_{PART})$.

- Concept intension, specify(θ_i)

    specify(θ_i) = {θ_j: level(θ_j)=level(θ_i) +1 and

    $\rho_k(\theta_i, \theta_j), \rho_k \in \rho_{CLUSTER}$ }

- Concept extension, generalize(θ_i)

    generalize(θ_i) = {θ_j: level(θ_j)=level(θ_i) - 1 and

    $\rho_k(\theta_j, \theta_i), \rho_k \in \rho_{CLUSTER}$}

4. 3-stage learning algorithm for constructing knowledge map

The knowledge map is learning from sentences that got from text/html, if some concepts, relations and propositions are defined.

Algorithm 1: Learning algorithm

Step 1: Select the main topic for the knowledge map and store it in the root knowledge units.

Step 2: Decomposition proposition to a number of relations.

Step 3: Categorize the concepts, grouping similar concepts and labeling the groups.

Composition or decomposition of two knowledge maps:

Algorithm 2: (De)Composition algorithm

Step 1: Union the concept space.

Step 2: Removing the redundant concepts if they exist.

Step 3: Removing the transitive relation and multi-relation if they exist.

5. Discussion and Conclusion

In this paper, one knowledge representation method is discussed, especially for structured document. Many problems in other fields, which are procedural problem in the mathematics, may also be solved by Knowledge Map (KM). Figure 5. A Knowledge Map from website.

References

[CHO93] Gary Chartrand and Ortrud R. Oellermann, Applied and Algorithmic Graph Theory, McGraw-Hill, Inc., pp. 58-60, 1993

[HaF94] Jiawei Han and Yongjian Fu, "Dynamic Generation and Refinement of concept Hierarchies for Knowledge Discovery in Databases", Proc. AAAI'94 Workshop on Knowledge in Databases, 1994

[Nict99] *Physics and Chemical Textbook for Junior High School*, National Institute for Compilation and Translation, Taipei, Vol.2, Section 8-1, pp.20-25, 1999 (in Chinese)

Using Data Mining for Improving Web-Based Course Design

Niko Myller [*] <niko.myller@cs.joensuu.fi>
Jarkko Suhonen [*] <jarkko.suhonen@cs.joensuu.fi>
Erkki Sutinen [*] <erkki.sutinen@cs.joensuu.fi>

[*]Department of Computer Science
University of Joensuu, Finland

Abstract

The distance education field offers several potential data sources for data mining applications. These applications can help both instructors and students in the web-based learning setting. One of the interesting aspects of data mining in education is to collect and interpret the information from several courses. This information can be used for example to assign heterogeneous groups in programming courses or projects and to evaluate the actual learning.

1. Introduction

Distance education settings offer interesting challenges for data mining methods. The need for interpreting scattered information from diverse sources of data is obvious. There are several challenges when utilizing this information in distance education courses like how to identify an individual student's difficulties or, predict his future performance, or build collaborative groups of students with complementary expertise profiles. One solution is to make use of available data mining techniques.

The Virtual Approbatur is an ongoing distance education project at the Department of Computer, University of Joensuu. The objective of the project is to offer high school students an opportunity to take 15 credits of Computer Science studies in one and a half years via the Internet [4], [5].

The Virtual Approbatur program offers a diverse and various sources for collecting interesting data. At this far in two years time we have had over 200 students participating in 20 different courses. In this paper we will concentrate only on a particular example from a set of diverse possible applications.

We have information about students' backgrounds, opinions about the program, their success in exercises and exams. This data can be used to enhance the quality of the program in many aspects. Furthermore, the data mining

applications and techniques have raised the interest in the educational domain. For example in the National University of Singapore the data mining application have been used for classifying and selecting those students who need extra classes in a given subject. With the help of data mining they are able to select the targeted students much more precisely than by traditional methods [8]. There are also some other examples of applying data mining and related method of Bayesian modeling in education and educational research [2], [6].

However, in this paper we will present our findings of applying data mining in the context of Virtual Approbatur for improving the course design. The examples covered in the paper are related to making assumptions and clustering the students by their performance in the exercises at the programming courses. Our method is to tag the exercises according to the particular knowledge or concept of programming needed to solve the given problem. Furthermore, we have collected the marks that students have received during the courses. In this way we have a solid base of data about the performance of the students related to concepts and knowledge taught during the courses.

2. Collection of the Data

In order to apply the data mining techniques to data collected from programming courses we needed to make some preparations. The First step was to assign both the students and the exercises with proper metadata information. This information can then be directly used by the mining application.

2.1 Metadata of Exercises

In our context the metadata of exercises includes both standard metadata elements and elements that are specific for our application. The standard metadata elements includes; identifier of an exercise, creation date, author, etc. In this paper we include only identifier element, because no other is relevant. The domain specific elements are presented in Table 1. The first thirteen elements are all weights and the value of each element is in range from zero to one. The weight means that in courses like programming there are exercises with more emphasis on variables than on methods or data structures whereas other exercise can test the understanding of different loop structures. The weights describe the need of the skill or understanding of the concept in order to complete the exercise.

A couple of examples from our database can be found in Table 2. Observe that an instance presented in Table 2 expresses the values for a group of exercises. At the Virtual Approbatur courses there are 4-5 exercises in each week and students receive points according to their performance in all the exercises for each week. Because of the limitations in WebCT technical platform, we cannot at the moment store values of individual exercises. Hence, we must make a compromise that the value of each instance presents the weight of one week exercises. However, the exam exercises can be covered in more detail.

2.2 Performance Data

Metadata of students includes information about the students' performance in the programming courses during Virtual Approbatur studies. Students' metadata was formed from the exercise metadata and the data collected from the student's success in the exercises. The exercise points were collected from each exercise and each student from the learning environment. The information was brought to the database software with the exercise metadata and a view from students' metadata was formed. The view consisted of the students' UID, total number of exercise points from all exercises and the same elements as in the exercise metadata description but now in a sense of students' skills. Hence, the data in Table 3 presents the students performance in different concepts and skills. Currently our database includes 102 instances.

To get a view of the student's metadata description the student's points from each exercise were multiplied with the weight that describe how much each skill was needed in the exercise as presented in the exercise metadata. All the skill points for each skill from the submitted exercises were summed up. Furthermore, the maximum skill points for each skill were calculated from the exercise metadata description and the students' skills points were divided with maximum skill points for each skill. The resulted skill values describe the percentage of the skill points student has received compared to the maximum points possible to receive for each skill. The formula of the skill value is presented in Figure 1.

Element	Explanation	Includes
ID	Identifies each exercise	Id-Code for exercises at programming course and exam.
Bas	All the basic concepts related to programming	Notion of algorithm, symbols, comments.
Var	Notion of variables.	Variable declarations, basic types, constants literals.
Oper	Operators, basic arithmetic expressions.	E.g. IO-statements belongs to this class.
IF	IF, IF-THEN, ELSE-IF, CASE-structures.	What is the meaning of IF-structures?
Rep	WHILE, DO-WHILE, FOR-structures.	Meaning of repetition.
Arr	Vectors, basic array operations.	What is an array? How it can be used?
Met	Methods, functions, parameters.	What is the meaning of methods? Concept of modularity.
App	Applets and basic graphics.	Applets vs. applications.
OO	Object-oriented structures	Classes, objects, inheritance, constructors.
Ani	Animations, threads.	Notion of making animations.
Even	Event handling	Keyboard and mouse programming.
Data	Basic data structures and files.	N-dimensional arrays, stacks, queues.
Java	Structures that a related to Java.	Exceptions.
Points	Maximum number of points	

Table 1: Metadata Elements of Exercises

3. Applying the Data Mining Methods

3.1 Using Clustering to Form Heterogeneous Groups

The database can be used to identify *heterogeneous groups* in terms of programming skills to form groups for programming projects. There are students that are better in loops or others that are good at event-driven programming. It is important that different kinds of skills are equally distributed in each group that students could learn from each other and use those skills at which they are good.

In order to form heterogeneous groups clustering could be used to construct homogeneous groups according to the students' skills. Next, the students in each homogeneous group could be distributed equally to form new heterogeneous groups.
We have used the EM (Expectation-Maximization) – algorithm for clustering the students. EM algorithm is based on a *k-means* clustering algorithm. It adapts the procedure used for k-means algorithm and then iterates it. The initial parameters for algorithm are guessed and used then to calculate the cluster probabilities for each instance. EM uses these probabilities to re-estimate the parameters and repeat this procedure until the parameters do not change [1], [3]. In this way the algorithm finds

only the local maxima, so the algorithm must be repeated with different kinds of initial parameters.

The data set described in Sections 2.1 and 2.2 can be used with clustering method EM. We could use the identified centre points and distribution of the classes for dividing the students in each cluster and then divide the clusters equally in as many groups as needed in projects.

3.2 Predicting Exam Results According to the Skills Shown in Exercises

Other application of the data mining techniques is to find out whether *the skills shown in the exercises also are valid and at the same level in exams*. If we have a student who has shown in exercises that she handles the loop structures very well does that mean that she performs in exam also very well? In general, which skills are the most significant ones for the exam result? In other words, which skills should we consider most significant for the student when she tries to learn programming?

This can be done with the data set shown in Chapter 2 except that we calculate the skill values shown in exercises just for one course or courses before the exam considered and we add the exam mark as a new attribute field. Then we try to find simple predicting rules that could predict the exam mark with some skill values. If we can find some simple rules that would help us to find the fields of improvement.

ID	Bas	Var	Oper	IF	Rep	Arr	Met	App	OO	Ani	Even	Data	Java	Points
prog101ex1	0.72	0.1	0.08	0.11	0.04	0.00	0.1	0.14	0.00	0.00	0.00	0.00	0.00	5
prog101ex2	0.23	0.58	0.61	0.00	0.00	0.00	0.00	0.00	0.00	0.00	0.00	0.00	0.00	4
...	...	...	...	...	...	...	...	...	...	...	...	...	...	...
prog201ex1	0	0	0	0.15	0	0.04	0.44	0.44	0.67	0	0.24	0	0.14	5

Table 2: Example of Exercise Instances

StudentID	Points	Bas	Var	Oper	..	Data	Java
student1	76	0.501	0.506	0.494	..	0.466	0.783
student2	93	0.528	0.603	0.604	..	0.864	0.964
student3	35	0.197	0.227	0.216	..	0.133	0.250

Table 3: Metadata Description of the Students.

$$Skill\_Value = \frac{\sum_{i=0}^{n} W_i * EP_i}{\sum_{i=0}^{n} W_i * MP_i},$$

where W_i is the weight of the certain concept or skill in the exercise i, EP_i is the points that student has received from the exercise i and MP_i is the maximum points possible to receive from the exercise i.

Figure 1: Formula for calculating the values of exercise skills

In the second case we could make a data set that consists of the attributes described in Chapter 2. But we do not consider the exam question weights and marks when counting the skill values. Furthermore, we make new attributes for the skills that are calculated by multiplying the points received from the exam questions and exam question weights. Then we try to find correlation between the skills shown in exercises and the skills shown in the exam. In these two cases classification rules finding or associative methods would be most useful. In first case C4.5 method [9] and in second case linear regression [7] is used. In linear regression the strength of correlation is measured with the correlation coefficient. In classification rules the coverage and accuracy of the rules are considered.

4. Results

4.1 Assigning Heterogeneous Groups

We processed the database presented in Chapter 2 with EM-clustering algorithm. We received the results found at Table 4. The probability column stands for the probability that a instance taken from the data set belongs to that cluster.

After the first try out we changed the properties of the algorithm. The results of second processing can be found at Table 5. The information presented in the Tables 4 and 5 give us a 4-5 possible homogeneous groups. The group with low total skills includes students that have received relatively low marks on each attribute. Two average groups can be formed so that attribute values of each student are between 0.12 and 0.54. These students present the average level of skills and as one can see from the probabilities of the average groups the largest amount of students belong to these groups. The next two groups consist of students with relatively high attribute values in all elements. These students can be classified as high performers.

In order to form heterogeneous groups we divide the student population according to the clusters found with EM-algorithm. After the homogenous groups have been assigned we pick a student from each group to form a heterogeneous group of 4-5 students.

No.	Characteristics/Description	Total Skills	Probability
0	All the means of the attributes are above 0.5. No difference between easy and difficult subjects	Very good	0.193
1	The means of the attributes are between 0.3 and 0.6. No significant difference between easy and difficult subjects.	Good	0.142
2	The means are between 0.5 and 0.08. Clear distinction between easy and difficult skills.	Low	0.258
3	The means are between 0.53 and 0.17. Minor difference between different skills.	Average	0.205
4	The means are between 0.52 and 0.25. Minor differences between different skills,	Average	0.201

Table 4: Results of first EM-clustering

No.	Characteristics/Description	Total Skills	Probability
0	Attribute values of clustering are between 0.52 and 0.12. Clear distinction between easy and difficult subjects	Average	0.2355
1	The means of the attributes are between 0.54 and 0.25. Minor difference between easy and difficult subjects.	Average	0.3881
2	All attributes between 0.57 and 0.72. No major differences.	Very Good	0.1183
3	All attributes between 0.57 and 0.89. Mostly very high values. No major differences.	Excellent	0.0968
4	Attributes between 0.03 and 0.487. Clear distinction between easy and difficult subjects	Low	0.1613

Table 5: Results of EM-clustering with altered properties

Predicted attribute	Linear Model	Correlation coefficient
Loop skills shown in exam	Loops_in_exam = 0.6569 * Operators_exercises + 0.1206	0.5756
Applet skills shown in exam	Applets_in_exam = 0.3674 * Basics_exercises - 0.3578 * Variables_exercises + 0.4479 * If-statements_exercises + 0.5013	0.347

Table 6: Few examples of the results of linear regression model

4.2 Predicting the Exam Results

We processed the database presented in Chapter 2 and Section 3.2 with linear regression finding method. We received the results shown in the Table 6.

When making a linear model for one skill in exam from the skills shown in exercises in easy topic like loops the correlation is moderate and the linear model is understandable and easily interpreted. It is quite obvious that operators and loops relate strongly with each other so if student has learned operators well she is able to understand loops easily and use the loop structures in exam. But when interpreting the linear model of applets skills shown in exam the model gets obscure. It is understandable that basic concepts like understanding of variables and if-statements are related to applets but the way in which the variable skills relate to applets is not easily interpreted because if student is strong with variables it means that she cannot handle applets and it seems that this does not make any sense. Moreover, the correlation of this model is only weak. In general, the results of this kind of prediction are not very reliable and more detailed models are probably needed to solve this kind of problems.

5. Conclusion

The methods described in this paper are the first data mining steps on the way towards an environment targeted for assisting students in project assignments. We acknowledge that the data collected from the students could be expanded. We could ask the students about their prior experience in programming, their preferences in the project topic or their opinions about the preferred working methods to assign the groups or topic of the project [10].

To expand the information received from students we could use for example the twelve factors model presented by Shrock and Wilson [11]. The model included twelve possible predictive factors in an introductory computer science course. The factors included math background, attribution of success/failure, domain specific self-efficacy, encouragement, and comfort level in the course, work style preference, previous programming experience, previous non-programming computer experience, and gender. These factors, when utilized by data mining schemes, would give us a wide range of interesting and challenging ways to predict students' behavior.

The development of data mining methods and the use of collected data are still underway. The preliminary results presented in this paper give us a first indication on how, when and why the information received from data mining application can be used to enhance the Virtual Approbatur studies.

References

[1] Cheeseman, P., Stutz, J., Bayesian Classification (AutoClass): Theory and Results, In. Fayyad, U.M., Piatetsky-Shapiro, G., Smyth, P., Uthurusamy, R., (eds.), Advances in Knowledge Discovery and Data Mining, Menlo Park, CA:AAAI Press, 1995, 153-180.

[2] Chen, C.-F., Lin, M.-H., Tzeng, T.-S., Yeh, C.-J., Wang T.-P., The application of Data Mining to On-line Education and Training, Proceedings of ICCE/Schoolnet 2001, Seoul, Korea, November 12-15, 2001, 1350-1353.

[3] Frank, E., Witten, I.H., Data Mining – Practical Machine Learning Tools and Techniques with Java Implementations, Morgan Kaufman Publishers, 2000.

[4] Haataja, A., Suhonen J., Sutinen, E., How to Learn Introductory Programming over Web, Informatica 25(2):165-171, July 2001

[5] Haataja, A., Suhonen, J., Sutinen, E., Torvinen, S., High School Students Learning Computer Science over the Web, Interactive Multimedia Electronic Journal of Computer-Enhanced Learning (IMEJ), 3(2), October 2001.

[6] Kurhila, J., Miettinen, M., Niemivirta, M., Nokelainen, P., Silander, T., Tirri, H., Bayesian Modeling in an Adaptive On-Line Questionnaire for Edcation and Educational Research, Proceedings of PEG2001, Tampere, Finland, June 23-26, 2001.

[7] Lawson, C.L., Hanson, R.J., Solving Least Squares Problems, Philadelphia, SIAM Publications, 1995.

[8] Ma, Y., Lee, S.M., Liu, B., Yu, P.S., Wong, C.K., Targeting the Right Students Using Data Mining, Proceedings of the Sixth ACM SIGKDD International Conference on Knowledge Discovery and Data Mining, Boston, Massachusetts, United States, 2000, 457-464.

[9] Quinlan, J.R., C4.5: Programs for Machine Learning, San Fransisco, Morgan Kaufmann, 1993.

[10] Redmond, M.A, A Computer Program to Aid Assignment of Student Project Groups, Proceedings of the 32nd SIGCSE Technical Symposium on Computer Science Education, Charlotte, North Carolina, USA, February 21-25, 2001, 134-138.

[11] Shrock, S., Wilson, B.C., Contributing to Success in an Introductory Computer Science Course: A Study of Twelve Factors, Proceedings of the 32nd SIGCSE Technical Symposium on Computer Science Education, Charlotte, North Carolina, USA, February 21-25, 2001, 184-188.

Student Resistance to ICT in Education

L. M. Hunt, M. J. W. Thomas & L. Eagle
College of Business, Massey University

Abstract

The polarisation of views on the introduction of ICT in education makes it hard to get a clear perspective on student attitudes to ICT, particularly in relation to other more traditional teaching modes. While the decision to use ICT may be pedagogically sound, resistance to its acceptance may discourage enthusiastic staff, sour student learning experiences and ultimately reduce institutions' ability to produce graduates who are computer-literate life long learners. This paper reports on a large scale study (n = 1,279) that compared student attitudes to a range of teaching modes, identified differences in attitude associated with demographic variables and examined the effect of student characteristics on such attitudes. Traditional teaching modes were found to be strongly preferred above all others. Technology and student-based teaching modes were the least preferred. Implications for developing collaborative learning communities on-line to promote greater learning autonomy and independent learners are discussed.

Introduction

The appeal of information and communication technology-based teaching modes is that they seem to have something for everyone. Institutions are excited by the potential to penetrate new markets, particularly in the distance education field, and perhaps reduce the cost of education [1]. Teachers are seduced by the promise of being able to implement truly collaborative learning through learning communities, create authentic tasks and develop cognitive apprenticeships [2, 3], and students of course will have greater flexibility and independence in their study [4]. However, successful implementation of new information and communication technologies (ICT) in education also depends on acceptance by students. Such acceptance may depend on a range of factors such as managing the change process [5]; student characteristics such as learning styles [6]; previous experience and demographic factors [7]. The evidence to date points to a greater enthusiasm by staff than students [8].

Teaching Modes Preferences

The debate on the value of ICT in education has clearly drawn battle lines. The advocates claim positive student attitudes and experiences as part of their support for technology. For example, Morss and Fleming [9] found most students reported high levels of satisfaction with the on-line tools, did not feel that on-line learning placed an undue time burden on them and strongly supported its continued use. However, some students (about 20%) also expressed reservations about its effectiveness in learning. Kendall [10] did not find the same reservations about learning effectiveness, but she did report similar levels of student satisfaction with the tools and experience of on-line learning. An enthographic study by Wegerif [11] also reported positive student experiences in an Asynchronous Learning Network environment learning community.

Opponents of technology-based teaching argue that students generally "want the genuine face-to-face education they paid for, not a cyber-counterfeit." [12 p.10]. Noble states that administrators at educational institutions frequently make cynical claims of student demand for technology-based education driving the adoption of new technology, when in reality they have rejected its introduction on every occasion they have been given a genuine choice. Others, alarmed by the wholesale adoption of new technology, claim the literature is dominated by overly enthusiastic supporters who minimize the problems experienced by students; studies that are more anecdotal than systematically empirical and research that has an uncritical acceptance of assumptions about the educational benefits of technology [13-15]. These studies often find high levels of student dissatisfaction with technology, emphasizing the frustration of learning in a technology-based environment, high levels of anxiety and confusion associated with ambiguous instructions [11, 14, 16].

Others have tried to understand the basis of student attitudes to teaching modes, including ICT, by examining the relationship between student characteristics such as learning styles and preference for teaching modes [6, 17, 18]. Shaw and Marlow [6], for example found that students with a "theorist" learning style held negative views of ICT delivery. Smith [18] found that technology students with a high preference for structure preferred collaborative learning modes. Smith (2001) also found preference variations based on age and gender. An earlier study by Sadler-Smith and Riding (1999) found an overall preference for traditional teaching modes such as lecturers, but students with a wholist-analyst style preferred a collaborative mode. They too, found gender effects. In a variation on this theme, Owen and Straton [19] were able to show similar preferences to Sadler-Smith and Riding [17], which they called co-operative (students working together to achieve a learning goal), competitive (student works alone to compete with other students), and individualistic (students work to achieve their own goals) modes.

Differences in attitudes to teaching modes based on demographic variables can also be found. Shaw and Marlow [6] reported no gender differences in attitudes to the use of information and communications technology (ICT), but marked differences in age, with younger, first-year students displaying a more positive attitude than second and third year students. Overall, however, students in the study preferred traditional, teacher-led learning modes. Hart [20], using hypertext documents, reported a generally favourable attitude to the use of computers for teaching but found a large number of students also printed the materials to create their own print-based workbook, partially negating the intent of using computers. The students most likely to do this were female, had less experience of computers and were full-time rather than part-time students.

Many studies on student attitudes are limited because they measure only attitude to the new technologies, and ignore comparisons with other teaching modes [9] or make comparisons between traditional and technology teaching modes using very small samples, often a single course [21] [10]. There are few large scale, cross-modal studies that also identify the causes or influences on student attitudes to teaching modes. This paper reports on a large scale study (n = 1,279) that compared student attitudes to a range of teaching modes, identified differences in attitude associated with demographic variables and examined the effect of student characteristics on such attitudes.

Method

Participants in the study were 1279 students enrolled in the College of Business at a New Zealand university. They were recruited on a voluntary basis from a pool of students, using a stratified sampling technique to ensure a broad representation of the different student groups and year levels. To summarise the major demographic characteristics of the participants, 45 percent were male, and 55 percent female. The sample contained a broad spread of ages from under 20 to over 40. Seventeen percent were Asian, seven percent Polynesian and 75 percent Caucasian. These proportions within the sample reflect well the current student population. The sample also contained a balanced representation of the major student groups in relation to the level of award in which students were enrolled, and the their mode of study (distance education or internal).

Results

The teaching modes preferences measure was subject to a principal component analysis. This procedure was useful in reducing the data. The components from this procedure were then subjected to further examination along demographic lines using ANOVA and t-tests (see [22] for full results of this analysis). In a third stage, student characteristics were regressed onto teaching modes to see if these were influential in determining students' preferences for particular modes. The results are briefly described below.

The teaching mode scale produced four components accounting for 59% of the variance (see table 1). The first component was labeled technology-based modes, and included a range of technologies from email, to video-conferencing, to web-based courses. Component two comprised those modes related to close personal interaction with instructing staff, such as one-on-one teaching. Student-based modes, such as student presentations and group-work, made up the third component, and the last component included traditional teaching modes such as lectures, study guides and tutorials. Overall students showed the greatest preference for those teaching modes with which they were most familiar, that is, traditional modes. This is consistent with the findings of Saddler-Smith (1999). Personalised and technology-based modes received much lower preference ratings, while student-based modes, with which students were familiar, generally received very low ratings.

Modes	Loadings	Eigenvalues	% of vairance	Reliabilities	Means	S.D.
Technology-based	.48 - .84	6.49	34	.92	2.82	.96
Personalised	.38 - .82	2.2	11.6	.59	2.95	.97
Student-based	.75 - .81	1.34	7.07	.56	2.58	1.05
Traditional	.52 - .77	1.2	6.07	.72	3.76	.72

Table 1: Principal Components Analyses of Preferences for Teaching Modes

Student Characteristics and Teaching Modes

Standard multiple regression was performed to determine the influence of a range of student characteristics on preference for teaching modes [see 22 for selection of student characteristics]. Multiple regression was chosen as an appropriate measure for predicting the influence of several independent variables on a dependent variable. Standard multiple regression in which all of the independent variables were entered in a single block was used as there was no strong theoretical basis for ordering their entry into the equation [23].

Student characteristics accounted for between 9 and 32% of the variance. In each regression, intrinsic motivation was one of the strongest predictors of a high preference rating.

For traditional modes of teaching the strongest predictor was dependent learning, followed very closely by intrinsic motivation. A listening style was the third predictor, followed by goal-focus, effort and preference for structure respectively. There was a negative correlation with independent learning and anxiety. The same negative correlation was found between anxiety and student-based modes of teaching, but not with the other two teaching modes. In the case of student-based teaching modes it seems likely that the public-speaking aspect of the mode may be a significant contributor to the anxiety, while in the traditional mode, the lack of control over the pace of learning may be a factor. The lowest contribution to the preference for a traditional mode was made by ambition. Overall, these student characteristics accounted for 13.2% of the variance.

Student Characteristics	Traditional		Personalised		Technology-based		Student based	
	Beta	T Ratio	Beta	T Ratio	Beta	T Ratio	Beta	T Ratio
Positive attitude to IT	-.039	-1.14	.032	.869	.467**	14.81	.028	.901
Anxiety	-.088*	-2.75	.021	.612	.017	.573	-.088*	-3.020
Negative attitude to IT	.004	.119	.054	1.48	-.011	-.34	-.018	-.563
Visual style	-.005	-.175	.068*	2.16	.086*	3.159	.067*	2.53
Collaborative style	.011	.370	.086*	2.79	-.015	-.554	.511**	19.41
Intrinsic motivation	.132**	3.94	.191**	5.38	.131**	4.24	.163**	5.33
Effort	.098*	2.69	.092*	2.40	.047	1.39	.012	.367
Extrinsic motivation	-.063	-1.92	-.040	-1.146	-.005	-.161	.029	.975
Listening style	.115**	3.97	.042	1.55	.017	.636	.027	1.03
Ambition	.070*	2.22	-.034	-1.01	-.018	-.625	.026	.909
Strategic focus	.110**	3.64	.066	2.08	-.032	-1.15	.006	.213
Dependent learning	.134**	4.43	-.047	-1.46	.037	1.31	-.012	-.418
Need for structure	.092*	2.91	.041	1.20	-.016	-.552	.007	.228
Busyness	-.007	-.209	-.009	-.259	.060*	1.97	.042	1.43
Factual course preference	-.026	-.89	-/011	-.339	.002	.068	-.042	-.1.56
Independent learning	-.082*	-2.79	-.033	-1.05	.048	1.76	.009	.342
R^2	.144		.102		.304		.322	
Adjusted R^2	.132		.089		.294		.312	
F	12.39		7.78		30.18		33.54	
F Sign	.0000		.0000		.0000		.0000	

** $p < .01$ * $p < .05$

Table 2: Standard Multiple Regression of learning orientation components on preference for teaching modes

The largest predictor of technology-based modes, unsurprisingly, was a positive attitude to computers and IT. This was followed by intrinsic motivation in second place. A visual style was the third predictor followed by a small contribution from busyness (too much time pressure to think about ideas from class or reading. Altogether 29.4% of the variance was accounted for.

A collaborative learning style made a very strong predictor of student-based teaching modes, followed by intrinsic motivation. As mentioned previously, anxiety also had a negative correlation with this mode. These three variables accounted for 31.2% of the variance. Only 8.9% of the variance of a preference for personalized teaching modes was accounted for by student characteristics. The most important of these was intrinsic motivation. Smaller contributions were made by effort and a visual style.

A collaborative learning style made a very strong predictor of student-based teaching modes, followed by intrinsic motivation. As mentioned previously, anxiety also had a negative correlation with this mode. These three variables accounted for 31.2% of the variance.
Only 8.9% of the variance of a preference for personalized teaching modes was accounted for by student characteristics. The most important of these was intrinsic motivation. Smaller contributions were made by effort and a visual style.

Discussion

Students' preference for traditional modes of teaching at a time when Universities seek to introduce new technology based modes on a large scale should give pause for thought. Saddler-Smith & Riding (1999) explained similar preferences with reference to Knowles' distinction between pedagogy and andragogy. Students were seen as teacher-dependent (pedagogical), rather than self-directed and motivated (andragogical), and thus were more comfortable with a teacher-controlled learning environment. Such an interpretation is supported by the regression results above, which found dependent learning to be the largest predictor of a preference for traditional modes with a contribution from a need for structure. The negative correlation with independent learning confirms the view. If traditional modes foster or sustain learning dependency then this may support the case made by Davidson [24] for weaning students off comfortable preferences rather than matching them with their preferences as advocated by others [for example, see 25].

The new technology-based modes were favoured by students who had a positive attitude to and experience with computers. A visual style was also associated with this preference. A feature of the visual style scale was the suggestion of an anti-reading bias. Perhaps what is being detected here is a social movement away from densely written text to a higher use of graphics and images to convey information. Certainly since Macintosh introduction icon-based menus, the use of icons has pervaded computer screen design. Further evidence of a social trend towards the use of images is apparent in the emergence of the graphic novel. This is a cross between a comic and a novel, with the story told in a sophisticated combination of text and pictures. The target market for these novels is the adolescent and young adult market.

Technology-based teaching modes overall were placed third after traditional and personalized modes. The comments made by students in the open-ended questions provided some insight into its low rating. A large group of students made strongly-worded and scathing comments regarding the frequent and frustrating failures of the technology to perform. Such experiences would certainly foster student resistance to change. Other comments came from students who had very limited experience with computers and felt intimidated by them. They strongly opposed their introduction as a teaching mode.

Student-based modes, overall, were the most disliked. This is partly explained by the relatively small number of students who have a collaborative learning style, many of whom were Asian or Polynesian. This finding is supported by other studies that found Caucasians had a lower preference for working collaboratively and cooperatively than other ethnic groups. For example, Mexican-Americans and African-Americans were found to be more group-oriented than white students [Remirez, 1982 cited in 24]. Further support is given by Anderson and Adams [25] who concluded that women and non-Caucasian males had a higher preference for peer cooperation than Caucasian males.

The implications of this general dislike for student-based teaching modes for on-line learning should be of concern. Educational research has long identified interaction between students as a key variable in learning [26]; [27]. Much of the current interest in on-line learning has been driven by its potential to harvest the benefits of collaborative learning through the establishment of learning communities. Group work is thought to facilitate learning in a number of ways. Cohen [28] found that working with others reduced uncertainty when faced with new, complex tasks and increased engagement with the task. Others have shown how the nature of the interaction between students provides alternative models of thinking and clarification of concepts as they are forced to defend or explain their own views [29-31]. If large groups of students feel uncomfortable with collaborative learning modes this may provide a significant obstacle to implementing some of the most beneficial aspects of on-line learning.

Conclusions

In the current transition from traditional to newer modes of teaching, consideration needs to be given to the interaction between students and mode preference. While institutions can take comfort in the result that the most powerful predictor of teaching mode overall was intrinsic motivation, suggesting that students who are strongly motivated to learn will feel reasonably comfortable and able to adapt whatever the mode, they must also recognize that large portions of their students may be feel strongly about being made to learn in unfamiliar modes. Akerlind and Trevitt [5] argues that resistance to change is likely to be greatest when it conflicts with the students' past learning experiences, particularly when it also involves using the technology to foster a more active, self-directed style of learning.

Universities tend to identify graduate qualities as including: being able to work independently and collaboratively, becoming life long learners (independent learning) and being proficient communicators [see for example, 32]. An integration of technology-based modes with student-based modes would seem to offer the best opportunity to develop these qualities. However, as the two least popular teaching modes, managing a change that will bring them into much more prominent and pervasive roles requires careful consideration. The result of mismanaging this process is clearly evident in the staff and student rebellions at York University and UCLA [12]. Change is stressful and has the potential to impinge on the learning process. Failing to recognize and manage this aspect of the process proactively can cause staff and students to become disillusioned with the technology, preventing them from realizing its educational potential.

References

1. Feenberg, A., *Distance learning: Promise or threat?* 1999.
2. Shaffer, D.W. and M. Resnick, *"Thick" authenticity: New media and authentic learning.* Journal of Interactive Learning Research, 1999. **10**(2): p. 195-215.
3. Hung, D.W.L. and D.-T. Chen, *Appropriating and negotiating knowledge: Technologies for a community of learners.* Educational Technology, 2000. May-June: p. 29-32.
4. MacDonald, J., N. Heap, and r. Mason, *"Have I learnt it?" Evaluating skills for resource-based study using electronic resources.* British Journal of Educational Technology, 2001. **32**(4): p. 419-433.
5. Akerlind, G. and C. Trevitt, *Enhancing learning through technology: when students resist the change.* 1995, Ascilite.
6. Shaw, G. and N. Marlow, *The role of student learning styles, gender, attitudes and perceptions on information and communication technology assisted learning.* Computers & Education, 1999. **33**: p. 223-234.
7. Spennemann, D.H.R., *Gender imbalances in computer access among environmental students.* Journal of Instructional Science and Technology, 1996. **1**(2).
8. Hara, N. and R. Kling, *Students' frustrations with a web-based distance education course.* First Monday, 1999. **4**(12).
9. Morss, D.A. and P.A. Fleming, *WebCT in the classroom: A student view.* 1998, North american Web Developers conference.
10. Kendall, M., *Teaching online to campus-based students: The experience of using WebCT for the community information module at Manchester Metropolitan University.* Education for Information, 2001. **19**: p. 325-346.
11. Wegerif, R., *The social dimension of asynchronous learning networks.* Journal of Asynchronous Learning Networks, 1998. **2**(1).
12. Noble, D.F., *Digital diploma mills: The automation of higher education.* firstmonday, 1997(3).
13. Windschitl, M., *The WWW and classroom research: What path should we take?* Educational Researcher, 1998. **27**: p.28-33.
14. Hara, N. and R. Kling, *Students' distress with a web-based distance education course.* Information, Communication & Society, 2000. **3**(4): p. 557-579.
15. Oppenheimer, T., *The computer delusion*, in *The Atlantic Monthly.* 1997. p. 45-62.
16. Burge, E.J., *Learning in computer conferenced contexts: The learners' perspective.* Journal of distance Education, 1994. **9**(1): p. 19-43.
17. Sadler-Smith, E. and R. Riding, *Cognitive style and instructional preferences.* Instructional Science, 1999. **27**: p. 355-371.
18. Smith, P., *Technology students learning preferences and the design of flexible learning programmes.* Instructional Science, 2001. **29**: p. 237-254.
19. Owens, L. and R.G. Straton, *The development of a co-operative, competitive, and individualised learning preference scale for students.* British Journal of Educational Psychology, 1980. **50**: p. 147-161.
20. Hart, G., *Learning styles and hypertext: exploring user attitudes.* 1995: http://www.ascilite.org.au/conferences/melbourne95/stmu/papers/hart.pdf.
21. Sosabowski, M.H., K. Herson, and A.W. Lloyd, *Enhancing Learning and Teaching Quality: Integration of Networked Learning Technologies into Undergraduate Modules.* Active Learning, 1998: p. 1-6.
22. Hunt, L.M., M. Thomas, and L. Eagle, *Professional learners: Students as informed and informing partners in the learning transaction.* Research and Development in higher Education, 2001. **24**: p. 62-70.
23. Tabachnick, B.G. and L.S. Fidell, *Using Multivariate Statistics.* 3rd ed. 1989, New York, USA: Harper and Collins College Publishers.
24. Swanson, L.J., *Learning styles: A review of the literature*, in *The Claremont Graduate School.* 1995, U.S. Department of Education.
25. Anderson, J.A. and M. Adams, *Acknowledging the learning styles of diverse student populations: Implications for instructional design*, in *Teaching for diversity*, N.V. Chism, Editor. 1992, Jossey-Bass Publishers: San Francisco. p. 19-34.
26. Slavin, R.E., *Cooperative learning.* 1983, New York: Longman.
27. Brookfield, S.D., *Understanding and facilitating adult learning.* 1986, San Francisco: Jossey-Bass.
28. Cohen, E.G., *Talking and working together: Status, interaction and learning.*, in *The social context of instruction*, M. Hallinan, Editor. 1984, Academic Press: New York.
29. Sharan, S., *Cooperative learning in small groups: Recent methods and effects on achievment, attitudes and ethnic relations.* Review of Educational Research, 1980. **50**(2): p. 241-71.
30. Slavin, R.E., *Cooperative learning.* Review of Educational Research, 1980. **50**(2): p. 315-42.
31. Webb, N.M., *Group process: The key to learning in groups.* New Directions for Methodology of Social and Behavioural Sciences, 1980. **6**: p. 77-87.
32. Fraser, G.S., *Learning and Teaching Plan.* 1998, Massey University: Palmerston North.

Using Neural Networks to Predict Student's Performance

Timothy Wang and Antonija Mitrovic
Intelligent Computer Tutoring Group
Department of Computer Science, University of Canterbury
Private Bag 4800, Christchurch, New Zealand
tanja@cosc.canterbury.ac.nz

Abstract

This paper presents a first step towards an intelligent problem selection agent for the SQL-Tutor [6,7] Intelligent Tutoring system. Currently SQL-Tutor uses an overly simple problem selection strategy, which selects a problem based on a single construct the student has most problems with. This strategy very often results in problems that are too easy/difficult for the student. Here we propose an intelligent problem-selection agent, which identifies the appropriate problem for a student in two stages. It firstly predicts the number of errors the student will make on a set of problems, and then in the second stage decides on a suitable problem for the student. In order to develop such an agent, we trained a feed-forward, backpropagation neural network to predict the number of errors a student will make. The achieved prediction accuracy is high, showing that a neural network is capable of making such predictions. However, the developed network cannot be used on-line, as it requires values that are not readily available. We present the plan for developing a modified network and for completing the problem selection agent.

1. Introduction

In order to be truly adaptive, Intelligent Tutoring Systems (ITS) need to use the information in the student model to guide all instructional decision making. There has been much research in the field of student modeling, and student models that can reasonably accurately predict student post-test performance have been developed. One of possible usages of such predictions is to select problems at the appropriate level for a student at any time during instruction.

We have developed SQL-Tutor [7], an ITS that teaches the SQL database language to university students. SQL-Tutor uses Constraint-Based Modeling (CBM) [11] to model the domain knowledge and the knowledge of its students. The basic unit of knowledge in CBM is a constraint, which specifies the conditions a student's solution must satisfy in order to be correct. SQL-Tutor uses a very simple problem selection strategy: it identifies the constraint the student has violated most often, and then picks an unsolved problem at the appropriate level of difficulty that uses the focus constraint. This strategy may results in a problem that introduces novel constructs or emphasizes a completely different part of the domain, and therefore the student may find the problem too simple or too difficult.

In past work, we used Bayesian networks to predict student's performance, and used the prediction to select an appropriate problem to present to the student [3]. For each problem, simple Bayesian networks were used to make predictions about student performance on constraints. These multiple predictions were then combined heuristically to give an overall measure of the value of each candidate problem. An evaluation study performed in 1999 showed that problems selected on the basis of such probabilistic student models were better suited to students' needs and abilities that the ones selected by the original strategy presented earlier [3]. However, the approach was sensitive to a number of prior probabilities, and heuristics used to estimate probabilities and select a problem from a set of candidates.

This paper presents a new approach to developing an intelligent problem selection agent, based on artificial neural networks. We plan to develop an agent that predicts the number of errors the student will make on problems, and then uses the predictions to select the next problem. Since knowledge necessary for problem selection is not readily available, we will train a neural network on data from previous studies, and that adapt the network online during each individual session. Before we embark on the agent development, we decided to test the predictive capabilities of neural networks in a simplified setting. This paper presents the results of this preliminary experiment.

In the next section, we briefly present the SQL-Tutor system by highlighting itw most important features. Section 3 presents our approach to developing the problem-selection agent, and is followed by the description of how a neural network was trained to predict students' performance in section 4. We present prediction accuracy in section 5, and then discuss related work in the next section. The final section presents conclusions and plans for future work.

2. SQL-Tutor

SQL-Tutor is an ITS that helps university-level students to learn SQL. The architecture of the stand-alone version of the system is illustrated in Figure 1. For a detailed

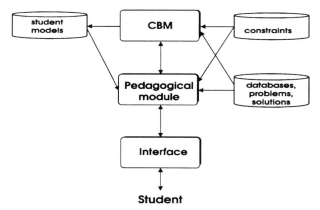

Fig. 1. Architecture of SQL-Tutor

discussion of the system and the Web-enabled version of it, see [5]; here we present only some of its most important features. SQL-Tutor consists of an interface, a pedagogical module, which determines the timing and content of pedagogical actions, and a student modeller (CBM), which analyses student answers. The system contains definitions of several databases, and a set of problems and the ideal solutions to them. Each problem is assigned a complexity level, ranging from one (easiest) to nine (hardest). SQL-Tutor contains no domain module. In order to check the correctness of the student's solution, SQL-Tutor compares it to the correct solution, using domain knowledge represented in the form of more than 550 constraints. It uses Constraint-Based Modeling [11] to model knowledge of its students. When the student submits a solution, the student modeller analyses it and identifies any violated constraint. If the solution is correct, the student is given a congratulatory message. In the opposite case, the pedagogical module provides a feedback message, whose level determines how much information is provided to the student. Currently, there are six levels of feedback in SQL-Tutor: positive/negative feedback, error flag, hint, detailed hint, partial solution and complete solution. At the lowest level (positive/negative feedback), the message simply informs the student whether the solution is correct or not and, in the later case, how many errors there are. An error flag message informs the student about the clause (part of the solution) in which the error occurred. A hint-type

message gives more information about the type of error, in the form of a general description of the error. This description is directly taken from the definition of constraint. A detailed hint provides additional information about the error, giving a hint as to how to correct the solution. Partial solution feedback displays the correct content of the incorrect clause, while the complete solution simply displays the correct solution of the current problem. The last two levels are only available on request, and would not be offered to the student automatically. The student is also assigned a level, which increases as a student successfully completes problems indicating proficiency and mastery of SQL.

Students have two ways of selecting problems in SQL-Tutor. They may work their way through a series of problems for each database, in the increasing order of complexity. The other option is a system-selected problem, when the system selects an appropriate problem for the student on the basis of his/her student model. SQL-Tutor has been evaluated in five studies since 1998, which all provided evidence for the sound foundation of CBM, and showed that students significantly improve their knowledge by using the system [6].

3. An Intelligent Problem-Selection Agent

The agent we propose here will have knowledge about each student, which will enable it to select a problem at the appropriate level of complexity at any time during instruction. The knowledge base of SQL-Tutor is quite large, and therefore symbolic approaches would require a lot of reasoning to come up with a satisfactory decision. Furthermore, we have previously encountered problems with a probabilistic student model, due to a large number of prior probabilities needed, and the heuristics necessary to select the problem out of a set of candidates. Therefore, we decided to explore the capabilities of artificial neural networks (ANN) for this kind of instructional decision-making.

The agent will be developed in two phases. The first phase includes the development of a neural network of suitable architecture and training the network to produce satisfactory predictions of student's behaviour. The second phase will include the development of a mechanism for deciding upon the best problem to present to the student next, based on predictions generated by the neural network. In the next section, we present our experiences during a preliminary investigation of predictive capabilities of ANNs in educational settings.

4. Training a Neural Network

As stated earlier, the purpose of the preliminary experiment was to determine whether predictive abilities

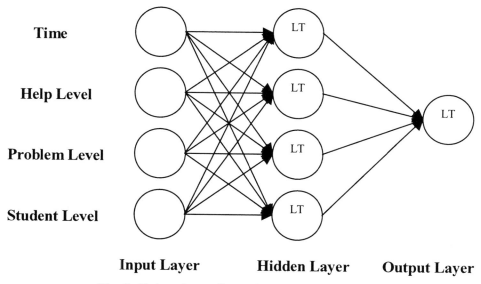

Time

Help Level

Problem Level

Student Level

Input Layer   **Hidden Layer**   **Output Layer**

Fig. 2. Network configuration for error prediction

of ANNs are satisfactory for usage in instructional decision-making. To experiment with neural networks, we used NeuroDimension's NeuroSolutions 4.1 workbench [9], which provides the tools to implement and test various configurations of neural networks and learning algorithms. Our neural network is a feed-forward network, with four inputs, a single hidden layer, and a single output, illustrated in Figure 2. We used delta-bar-delta backpropagation and a linear tanh (LT) transfer function.

The training data was collected in the evaluation study performed on SQL-Tutor in 2001. The goal of this study was to evaluate the effects of an open student model on student's learning and self-assessment skills [8]. Although the goal of the study was very specific, and not related to problem selection, the data collected the study included all the necessary information for training the neural network.

In the study, all actions a student performed were recorded in a log. For each action (such as submitting a solution, asking for help etc), we recorded the action itself, the student's level and the timestamp. When the student submitted a solution, we additionally stored the id of the problem, the student's solution, and the lists of violated and satisfied constraints. If a student asked for a new problem, we recorded the problem's id and level of complexity.

The inputs to the network correspond to four values extracted from students' logs: the time (in seconds) needed to solve the problem, the level of help requested by the student, the complexity level of the problem and the current level of the student. On the basis of these inputs, the network predicts the number of errors the student will make (i.e., the number of violated constraints). The

prediction is considered to be incorrect if the predicted number of errors differs from the actual number of errors by more than 0.5. The network was trained with all the data from 2001 study, to produce a population student model. 57 epochs with MSE of 0.000107 were needed to achieve 98.06% accuracy. The correlation r for the network was 0.99.

5. Prediction Accuracy

Starting with the population student model discussed in the previous section, we individualized the network by using the data for a single student only. From all the available data, we selected 244 individual sessions. These sessions ranged in their lengths, with shortest containing just one submitted solution, to 153 submissions. When processing a single session, we propagated each submission through the network, and compared the predicted outcome with the actual one. The number of incorrect predictions per session ranged from 0 to 40, with an average of 2.17%. The average prediction accuracy for all individual sessions was 98.41%. The network produced the total of 72 incorrect predictions, out of 4541 submissions. Table 1 categorizes the outcomes as *No errors* (all predictions were correct), *one error* (there was one incorrect prediction in the whole session), *two errors* and *greater than two errors* per student sessions.

A further investigation of incorrect predictions reveals that the most frequent ones cover the situation when the network predicts the student's solution will be correct. 52 incorrect predictions (out of the total of 72 incorrect predictions) belong to this category. 40 of these predictions could be excluded if the upper and lower bound was extended to ±0.55. When retraining the network with the modified threshold, the network accuracy improved from 98.41% to 99.41%.

	Freq.	%	Cum. Freq.	Cum. %
No errors	186	76.23	186	76.23
1 error	47	19.26	233	95.49
2 errors	9	3.69	242	99.18
> 2 errors	2	0.82	244	100.00

Table 1: Categorisation of incorrect predictions

We were also interested in how quickly the network adapts to the individual student. Figure 3 shows how the number of incorrect predictions varies over time. It displays the number of incorrect predictions that occur on the first submission up to the sixth submission for each individual session, thus illustrating the capabilities of the network to adapt to each individual student. It can be seen that the corrected threshold (±0.55) enables the network to predict student's behaviour much better, at the same time reducing the *One error* entry in Table 1 from 47 to 17 and increasing the *No error* percentage from 76% to 83%.

6. Related Work

Artificial neural networks have been extensively studied and applied in many areas of artificial intelligence (AI), such as pattern recognition, speech understanding and robotics. However, in the area of ITS, there are surprisingly few projects using ANNs. Two projects [4,10] involved using ANNs to generate student models. Mengel and Lively [4] used a feed-forward backpropagation network to predict student's solution for a subtraction problem. Subtraction was chosen because an extensive bug library containing 110 typical student errors was readily available [2]. Although the network achieved high prediction accuracy (96%), this particular approach is not feasible if the bug library is not available. Bug libraries are very expensive to acquire, and do not transfer well between different student populations [7]. Therefore, this approach has a very serious limitation.

Posey and Hawkes [10] also discuss how neural networks can be used to generate student models. They describe an ANN used in TAPS, an arithmetic tutor, which models students using fuzzy logic. The topology of the network is determined by the domain structure in TAPS, where each skill is decomposed into a number of subskills. There is a node for each skill/subskill in the network, and therefore each node has symbolic meaning. Students'

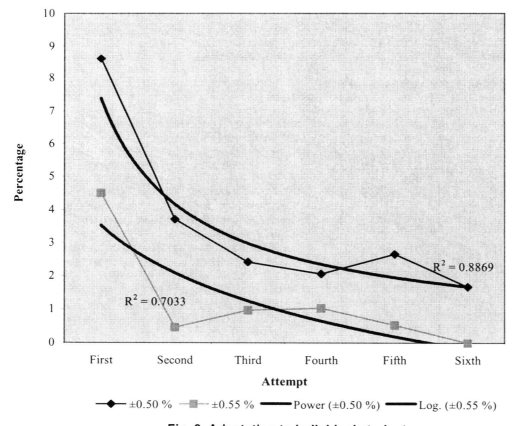

Fig. 3. Adaptation to individual students

performance on each subskill can be observed, and the network then learns the skill-subskill importance measures, represented as connection weights. The network starts from incomplete knowledge provided by a human expert, and refines it into a more complete and accurate student model. The same network can also be used to derive the domain model, based on an approximation of it provided by the human expert.

Beck and Woolf [1] describe a project that is in many respects similar to the one we performed. An ANN is used to predict the time the student will need to solve a problem within a MFD (mixed numbers, fractions and decimals) tutor. The structure of the network they use is similar to the one we propose, a feed-forward network with a single hidden layer consisting of 4 neurons. The inputs (25 of them) include the student's proficiency, problem type, time necessary to solve the last problem of this type, problem difficulty and the student's estimate of his/her ability. The authors developed a population student model first, and then tested its behaviour on individual sessions. The network proposed in this paper requires 5-10 problems to converge. In our case, the network converges after six submissions on average, but the submissions may all be for the same problem. Also, our network requires only four inputs to achieve high prediction accuracy. The authors say that predicting the time is used by the tutor to control problem complexity, but they do not elaborate on how that is done.

7. Conclusions and Further Work

In this paper, we discussed the possibility of using neural networks to predict student's behaviour in intelligent educational systems. We trained a simple feed-forward network using the data collected in the 2001 study of SQL-Tutor. The network predicts the number of errors the student will make in the next submission, given four inputs: the time (in seconds) needed by the student to generate the solution, the level of help requested by the student, the complexity level of the problem and the current level of the student. The population student model was firstly produced using all the data, with the prediction accuracy of 98.06%. This network was then used to predict the behaviour of each individual student. The population student model can be adapted with the data from an individual session, and it learns to predict accurately after only six submissions. It was shown that the prediction accuracy is high, and can be further improved by tailoring the parameters used. The network performs better is a student submits more than one solution in a session, as that provides the data for the network to adapt to the individual student over time.

This paper presents the results of the preliminary investigation of ANNs in the context of SQL-Tutor. Although the discussed network predicts student's behaviour very reliably, it is not possible to use this network to select problems, as one of the inputs is the time needed by the student to solve the problem. This information is not readily available when selecting problems in an on-line situation. Therefore, we are now developing a new network, which will take into consideration the content of the student model instead of the time. Based on our experiences presented in this paper, we believe that the new network would behave equally well. The new network will predict the number of errors for a set of candidate problems, and that will enable us to select the next problem for the student to work on. We plan to have the new network ready to perform a new evaluation study in September 2002.

References

1. J. Beck, B.P. Woolf, Using a Learning Agent with a Student Model. In: B. Goettl, H. Halff, C. Redfield, V. Shute (eds), *Proc. ITS'98*, Springer-Verlag Berlin, 1998, 6-15.
2. J.E. Friend, R.R. Burton, *Teacher's Guide for Diagnostic Testing in Arithmetic: Subtraction*. Palo Alto, CA: Cognitive and Instructional Sciences, 1980.
3. M. Mayo, A. Mitrovic, Using a probabilistic student model to control problem difficulty. In: G. Gauthier, C. Frasson and K. VanLehn (eds), *Proc. ITS'2000*, Springer-Verlag Berlin, 2000 524-533.
4. S. Mengel, W. Lively, Using a Neural Network to Predict Student Responses. *Proc. 1992 ACM/SIGAPP Symp. on Applied Computing*, 2, 1992, 669-676.
5. A. Mitrovic, K. Hausler, Porting SQL-Tutor to the Web. *Proc. ITS'2000 workshop on Adaptive and Intelligent Web-based Education Systems*, 2000, 37-44.
6. A. Mitrovic, B. Martin, M. Mayo, Using Evaluation to Shape ITS Design: Results and Experiences with SQL-Tutor. *Int. J. User Modeling and User-Adapted Interaction*, vol. 12, no. 203, 2002, 243-279.
7. A. Mitrovic, S. Ohlsson, Evaluation of a Constraint-based Tutor for a Database Language. *Int. J. Artificial Intelligence in Education,* 10(3-4), 1999, 238-256.
8. A. Mitrovic, B. Martin. Evaluating the effects of open student models on learning. In: P. de Bra, P. Brusilovsky and R. Conejo (eds) *Proc. 2nd Int. Conf on Adaptive Hypermedia and Adaptive Web-based Systems AH 2002*, Malaga Spain, LCNS 2347, 2002, 296-305.
9. NeuroDimension Inc., NeuroSoilutions, http://www.nd.com
10. C.L. Posey, L.W. Hawkes, Neural Networks Applied to Knowledge Acquisition in the Student Model. *Information Sciences*, 88, 1996, 275-298.
11. S. Ohlsson, Constraint-based student modeling. In: Greer, J.E., McCalla, G (eds): *Student modeling: the key to individualized knowledge-based instruction*, 1994, 167-189.

Malaysian In-Service Teachers: An assessment of their IT Preparedness

*Wong Su Luan, Kamariah Abu Bakar, Ramlah Hamzah and Rohani Ahmad Tarmizi.
Universiti Putra Malaysia, *suluan@educ.upm.edu.my

ABSTRACT

This paper aims to describe Malaysian in-service teachers' IT preparedness. IT preparedness is measured in terms of their actual IT skills, and knowledge as well as their attitudes toward IT. The study revealed that the teachers are IT skilled. However, they are only proficient in several types of productivity tools. The results also showed that two extreme groups existed, those who are highly proficient in certain productivity tools and those who are not. The teachers, however, are knowledgeable about IT and have very positive attitudes toward IT.

Introduction

Even though IT is relatively new in Malaysia, several studies have been conducted recently by Malaysian researchers about teachers and IT in our country. It is heartening to note that this trend of research is fast catching up among our academicians and researchers. For example, Jusoh (2000) found that in-service teachers enjoyed using computers. They indicated that they are aware of the positive influence of computers on education. Most importantly, the teachers felt that they were ready to learn computers. Pihie and Elias (2000) concurred with this view when their study showed that the teachers perceive themselves as knowledgeable about IT and are aware that IT can enhance the teaching and learning process. While these studies centred around teachers in West Malaysia, studies conducted in East Malaysia are scarce. One pertinent case study on a residential science school in Sabah by Pang (2000), reported that teachers perceived themselves as skilled in word processing, electronic presentation and spreadsheet software. They were, however, not skilled in dBase, web publishing, local area network and programming.

Statement of the Problem

With the implementation of Smart Schools nation-wide, approximately 450,000 teachers in the country must be fully IT prepared. The pressure on teachers to become IT literate as well as to understand the education implications of the new technology has, therefore, become urgent. However, before they can integrate this new technology, these teachers must be trained to be skilled and knowledgeable about IT with the right attitudes. No studies have been conducted in this country to find out the level of teachers' IT preparedness. For this reason, this study is timely. We feel that it is of paramount importance to assess in-service teachers' actual IT skills and knowledge as well as their attitudes toward IT rather than just studying their perceptions.

Objectives of the Study

The objectives of the study were to
1. determine the demographic characteristics of teachers;
2. assess the in-service teachers' actual IT skills, knowledge about IT and attitudes toward IT;
3. assess the in-service teachers' IT preparedness.

Instrumentation

The instrument was developed by Wong (2002) and was constructed in the Malay language. Part A was paper based while Parts B and C were web based. Part A measured the teachers' actual IT skills. The skills were measured in terms of the teachers' ability to execute a series of 74 tasks. The tasks were measured in two dimensions based on the table of content specification. The first dimension comprised content categories pertaining to productivity tools (word processing, spreadsheet, database and presentation), World Wide Web (WWW) and electronic mail while the second dimension comprised task categories (basic operation, management and design). All skills measured did not require direct observation. Each item was a task that the participant was required to perform. For that reason, the tasks could be categorised into 'able to' and 'unable to'.

Part B measured their knowledge about IT based on the table of content specification. It was measured in terms of 25 multiple-choice questions. The first dimension of the table comprised system hardware, system software, WWW and electronic mail while the second dimension comprised the three lower levels of Bloom's Taxonomy (knowledge, comprehension and application). Four alternatives were constructed for each item.

Lastly, Part C measured the teachers' attitudes toward IT based on the table of content specification and consisted of two dimensions. The first dimension comprised specific software applications, software applications in general, computer and IT in general. The second dimension consisted of confidence, usefulness, anxiety and aversion. This part comprised 34 five-point Likert's scale statements. The five choice Likert scale was used, hence the scale in Part C ranged from strongly "agree=5, slightly agree=4, not sure=3, slightly disagree=2, strongly disagree=1" for positive items and vice versa for negative items.

A pilot test was conducted with 49 teacher trainees from Universiti Putra Malaysia prior to the actual study. The reliability of scores for Parts A, B and C were .94, .85 and .92 respectively. The reliability of scores for the actual study were .98, .84 and .94.

Sample Selection and Data Collection

Sixty in-service teachers who were selected by the state education department to attend the in-service teachers' IT/computer training courses, participated in the study. The teachers were assessed after they finished the course. The tests were conducted in the computer laboratories in three teacher training colleges. Each participant was given a desktop to work on, access to the Internet and a piece of diskette to save their work into.

Demographic characteristics

Fifty female and 10 male participants were involved in this stage. Their ages ranged between 25 and 42 years. Data from seven participants were discarded because they could not complete any part of the instrument due to technical fault. The majority of the teachers were primary school teachers (73.6%) and the rest were secondary school teachers (26.4%). Forty-seven of the participants indicated that they had prior computer experience ranging from 1 to 13 years before enrolling in the computer course. Only six had never used a computer before.

Actual IT Skills

The results in Table 1 show that the majority of the participants had high level of IT skills (39.6%) with 11.3% in the below average category. The lowest score recorded was 16.0 and the highest score was 97.0. The mean score for IT skills was 58.7 (SD= 24.7). Table 2 shows the participants had the highest level of skills in using word processing (88.7%) followed by presentation (66.0%) and spreadsheet (50.9%). They had the lowest level of skills in Internet (18.9%).

Table 1: Levels of Actual IT skills

IT skills level						
None	Below average	Average	Above average	High	Mean	SD
(%)	(%)	(%)	(%)	(%)		
0.0	11.3	28.3	20.8	39.6	58.7	24.7

Table 2: Levels of actual IT skills for selected productivity tools

PT	None	Below average	Average	Above average	High	Mean	SD
WP	0.0	0.0	0.0	11.3	88.7	17.6	2.6
SS	15.1	18.9	7.5	7.5	50.9	17.8	12.2
DB	50.9	0.0	5.7	11.3	32.1	7.6	8.3
PR	22.6	0.0	7.5	3.8	66.0	12.0	7.1
I	60.4	3.8	5.7	11.3	18.9	3.6	5.0

PT=Productivity tools; WP=Word Processing; SS= Spreadsheet; DB=Database; PR=Presentation; I=Internet

Knowledge about IT

As shown in Table 3, the majority of the participants had only average (30.2%) and above average (58.5%) knowledge about IT. The scores ranged from 4.0 to 22.0. The mean of correct responses was 15.1 (SD=4.2).

Table 3: Levels of knowledge about IT

IT knowledge level						
None	Below average	Average	Above average	High	Mean	SD
(%)	(%)	(%)	(%)	(%)		
0.0	1.9	30.2	58.5	9.4	15.1	4.2

Objective 4: Attitudes toward IT

Most of the participants' attitudes toward IT were highly positive (Table 5). The scores ranged from a low of 94.0 to a high of 169.0. The mean score of knowledge about IT was 140.3 (SD= 16.2). The dimensions measured were usefulness, confidence, anxiety and aversion. Based on the results in Table 6, the majority of the participants found IT to be useful. They had confidence with low aversion towards IT. Only a handful had high level of anxiety.

Table 5: Levels of Attitudes toward IT

Attitudes toward IT				
Negative (%)	Positive (%)	Highly positive (%)	Mean	SD
0.0	18.9	81.1	140.3	16.2

Table 6: Levels of Attitudes toward IT according to sub-domains

	Low	Moderate	High	Mean	SD
Useful	0.0	5.7	94.3	43.8	4.0
Confidence	1.9	50.9	47.2	25.6	4.5
Anxiety	35.8	60.4	3.8	36.6	6.3
Aversion	86.8	13.2	0.0	26.4	3.0

Objective 6: IT Preparedness

Scores of the three constructs (skills, knowledge and attitudes) were summed up to arrive at the composite measure of IT preparedness. The highest composite score was 127.0 and the lowest score was 274.0. The mean score of IT preparedness was 214.10 (SD=36.10). The percentage of students was almost equally distributed between moderate (47.2%) and highly (52.8%) IT prepared (Table 7).

Table 7: Levels of IT preparedness toward IT

IT preparedness level				
Poor (%)	Moderate (%)	Highly (%)	Mean	SD
0.0	47.2	52.8	214.0	36.1

Objectives 7: Relationship between variables

Using the descriptors suggested by Guildford (1956), the correlations between IT preparedness and age, teaching experience and prior computer experience range from low to moderate (Table 7). The correlations between IT preparedness and age, teaching experience were however negative.

Table 7: Correlations of IT Preparedness with Selected Demographic Variables

	IT preparedness 1	Age 2	Teaching experience 3	Computer experience 4
1	-	-.147	-.091	.622*
2		-	.842*	-.095
3			-	-.050
4				-

*. Correlation is significant at the .05 (2-tailed)

Discussion

On the whole, the participants were found to possess a reasonable level of IT skills where they scored highest in word processing. They, however, scored the lowest in database. This finding is consistent with the case study by Pang (2001). This problem seems to be an international one as Cuckle, Clarke and Jenkins (2000) revealed that Postgraduate Certificate of Education teachers in England were most competent in word processing and least competent in database and programming. Based on the results in Table 3, it was concluded that the majority of them have average and above average knowledge of IT. The participants reported positively high attitudes toward IT. Most of the participants found IT to be useful but they had only moderate confidence. They, however, had low aversion toward IT. What is worrying is that there were participants with moderate level of anxiety. It is important to reduce students' computer anxiety level (Presno, 1998) because computer anxiety can reduce students' effectiveness in the utilisation of computers (Rozell and Gardner, 1999).

With the scores of three constructs (skills, knowledge and attitudes) summed up to represent IT preparedness, the data showed that the majority of participants were higly IT prepared. None of the participants were poorly IT prepared.

There is a moderate negative relationship between IT preparedness and the following two variables: age and teaching experience. The older participants with more teaching experience were less IT prepared compared to the younger ones with less teaching experience. Perhaps, the younger participants were exposed to computers during their schooling days. There is also a moderate relationship but in positive direction, between IT preparedness and prior computer experience. The more experience they had with computers, the more IT prepared they were. This result concurred with the findings of findings of Wild (1995) that IT attitudes and skills were influenced by prior computer experience. The study also found that males were better IT prepared than females. This hypothesis concurred with the research findings by Liao (1997) who found that males were more positive about IT than females.

Conclusion

The results of this study have thrown light on how IT prepared in-service Malaysian teachers are. We are concerned that there are teachers who have poor skills in several productivity tools tested despite undergoing formal training before they were assessed. It appears that most of them used the computers mostly for word processing. The results seem to indicate that there are two extreme groups, those who are highly proficient in using the productivity tools and those who are not proficient. This strongly signals that the IT training provided must be relooked into to find out its effectiveness. Overall, the level of teachers' IT skills is high but the same cannot be said when the skills level is seen according to the types of productivity tools. Most of them are knowledgeable about IT and have very positive overall attitudes toward IT. With such attitudes, they will most likely be more motivated to use IT in the classrooms.

References:

Cuckle, P., Clarke, S. and Jenkins, I. (2000). Students' information and communications technology skills and their use during teacher training. *Journal of Information Technology for Teacher Education*, 9(1), 9-22.

Guildford, J. P. (1956). *Fundamental statistics in psychology and education*. New York: McGraw Hill.

Jusoh, R. (2000). Persepsi guru-guru sekolah menengah terhadap penggunaan komputer dalam pendidikan. . In Pihie, Z.A.L. et al. (Eds), Proceedings of the International Conference: Education and ICT in the new millennium (pp. 495-504). Serdang: Universiti Putra Malaysia.

Liao, Y.K. (1997). The comparison of inservice and preservice teachers' attitudes toward educational computing in Taiwan. In SITE Conference held in Orlando, Florida, 10-14 March 1998: online proceedings edited by J. Willis and P.William. Va: AACTE. Retrieved May 10 1999 from the World Wide Web: http://www.coe.uh.edu/insite/elec_pub/HTML1997/re_liao.htm

Presno, C. (1998). Taking the byte out of Internet anxiety: Instructional techniques that reduce computer/Internet anxiety in the classroom. *Journal of Educational Computing Research*, 18(2), 147-161.

Pang, V. (2000). The antecedents of an ICT-enriched curriculum. In Pihie, Z.A.L. et al. (Eds), Proceedings of the International Conference: Education and ICT in the new millennium (pp.444-466). Serdang: Universiti Putra Malaysia.

Pihie, Z.A.L. & Elias, H. (2000). Secondary school teachers' perceptions on the usage of ICT in enhancing teaching. In Pihie, Z.A.L. et al. (Eds), Proceedings of the International Conference: Education and ICT in the new millennium (pp.343-349). Serdang: Universiti Putra Malaysia.

Rozell, E, J., and Gardner, W. L. III (1999). Computer-related success and failure: A longitudinal field study of the factors influencing computer-related performance. *Computers in Human Behaviour*, 15(1), 1-10.

Wild, M. (1995). Pre-Service teacher education programs for information technology: An effective education? *Journal of Information Technology in Teacher Education,* 4(1), 7-20.

Wong, S.L. (2002). Development and validation of an Information Technology (IT) based instrument to measure teachers' IT preparedness. Published doctoral thesis, Universiti Putra Malaysia, Serdang, Selangor, Malaysia.

Towards an understanding of the use of digital images in teaching and learning

Grainne Conole
Research and Graduate School of Education,
University of Southampton
Email: g.c.conole@soton.ac.uk

Jill Evans and Ellen Sims
Institute for Learning and Research Technology
8-10 Berkeley Square
University of Bristol

Abstract

Visual images proliferate within educational contexts and are accessible across a range of media: in print, via the Web, as part of learning resources and in multimedia software. The increased ease of access to images has been mirrored by an increase in their use by academics. However, it is evident from the literature that there is a need for more research into how to make the best use of images within learning and teaching resources. The word 'image' is, in a sense, deceptive. A little thought illustrates that there are a significant number of different types of 'images' or pictorial/graphical representations. This paper distils out the key features that emerge from the research findings and map these to relevant pedagogical theories. The presentation will attempt to define different image types in order to make the ways in which they can be used to support learning and teaching more transparent. Furthermore, a better understanding and categorisation of digital images will help to facilitate the integration of image resources with pedagogical practice.

Introduction

Visual images proliferate within educational contexts and are accessible across a range of media: in print, via the Web, in learning resources and multimedia software. The increased ease of access to images has been mirrored by an increase in their use by academics. However, it is evident from recent research [1-3] that there is a need for documentation on how to make the best use of images within learning and teaching resources.

The word 'image' is, in a sense, deceptive. A little thought illustrates that there are a significant number of different types of 'images' or pictorial/graphical representations. This paper will outline key research work in this area and map this to related pedagogical

theories. A fuller description of this work is described elsewhere [4].

Various initiatives within the educational sector are enabling the creation of digital image resources. The resource must be evaluated against a set of criteria including: need, potential uptake and usage and value for money. The success of these initiatives depends on a number of factors. Adequate and production of high quality image collections is one, as is an understanding of the use of images to support learning and teaching processes.

When focusing on possible reasons for the current under use of images in an educational context, three main issues arise [5]:

- There is no clear picture of the different categories/types of images that exist, and how they inter-relate.

- There is little systematic documentation of the ways in which different image categories can be used appropriately, particularly within an educational context. For example, when might it be more appropriate to use a two-dimensional schematic map as opposed to a digital 'photo-realistic' image? When is a real-time representation more informative than a series of stills? How much difference does a full colour image make as opposed to a simple grey-scale version? Decisions such as these are currently made intuitively, rather than against a set of clear criteria. Furthermore, appropriate use may be a simple decision for an "imaging expert," but as images become more widely used by a larger percentage of the teaching population, clearer guidelines may be needed. It is also important to note that in some subject areas images and their related taxonomies are clear aspects of scholarly practice. In others this sense of categorisation and taxonomy is less well developed.

- There is a need for documentation of the ways in which images are being and can be used to

978

support learning and teaching mapped against the different categories of images.

Image-related initiatives

A number of recent image research and related initiatives are highlighted here. Categorisation and mapping of images is especially timely given the imminent delivery of large image resources via data centres, e.g. the JISC Image Digitisation Initiative (JIDI) images (http://www.ilrt.bristol.ac.uk/jidi/) being delivered to the community through the Visual Arts Data Service (VADS) (http://vads.ahds.ac.uk/). Other collections are being made available by other data delivery mechanisms and these resources comprise the JISC's range of online resources and service to support learning and teaching. The Support Initiative for Multimedia Applications (SIMA) covered the use and capture of images for learning [6]. These findings supported the view that illustrations can, when used appropriately, enhance learning:

"Images are generally more evocative than words and more precise in triggering a wide range of associations, enhance creative thinking and memory."

Guidelines and examples of best practice on the use of digital images are available online from the JISC-funded Technical Advisory Service for Images (TASI) http://www.tasi.ac.uk/advice/using/using.html which shows how to use images in different types of electronic resources. Research indicates that images can be used to enhance learning [7-9]. In particular that the capacity for recognition memory for images is limitless, and that images will remain in long-term memory as long as they are meaningful [10]. This reinforces the importance of understanding which type of image would provide the most benefit to a particular learning experience.

Several recent initiatives have attempted to increase the use of existing resources and collections, by providing advice and exemplars of good practice. The Promoting the use of On-line Image Collections in Learning and Teaching In the Visual Arts (PICTIVA) project aims to promote image collections by developing generic tools to support access to the images, producing supporting materials, advising on evaluation of tools and materials, and producing a series of case studies [3]. Similarly, the Enhancing the Bristol BioMed for Learning and Teaching project (BB-LT) has developed a series of 'How to' guides, case studies and tutorials to promote the use of images in the biomedical community [1]. Finally, the FILTER project (Focusing Images for Learning and Teaching – an Enriched Resource) is extending this framework to provide exemplars of effective image use across subject areas, and both generic and subject-specific learning and teaching resources [2].

Pedagogic theory and images

Pedagogical theory can be considered across a spectrum from behavioural and cognitive theories through to more socio-cultural and constructivist theories. This section will outline some of the key issues in image research and map these to points along the spectrum.

For decades, image research was largely based on cognitive theory. For example, Croft [11] suggested that a cognitive science approach leads to the two theories of visual processing; dual coding theory [12, 13] and cue summation theory [14, 15]. Dual coding theory proposes that although verbal and visual information are encoded separately by the brain, they are interconnected, so that a concept represented as an image in the visual system can also be converted to a verbal label in the other system, or vice versa. Cue summation predicts that learning is increased as the number of available cues or stimuli is increased. These theories also map to Bruner's more general concept attainment theory of knowledge, which acknowledges that given it is impossible to know everything about a subject, it is more important to have a rich conceptual framework of understanding [16]. This has been suggested as a potential theoretical basis for image selection and use [11, 17, 18].

Dwyer used text with images containing differing degrees of detail and realism (ranging from simple black and white drawings to colour photographs) to test and measure achievement of specific learning objectives [19]. This behaviourist approach has been criticised, however, recent work confirmed that *"visualization is an important instructional variable"* and that *"not all types of visuals are equally effective in facilitating achievement of different educational objectives"* [20].

This is corroborated by recent research, which adds to the body of evidence demonstrating that appropriate images *"reliably improve the reading-to-learn process"* [17]. The converse of this is that images will not facilitate learning when information contained in the images is not required for attainment, or when the information is insufficiently related to the text or task [20].

Instructional development and design theory may suggest a further approach to image selection and use. The theoretical underpinning for these models and methods [21] [22] [23] [24] can be viewed as on a continuum from teacher and outcome-centred (behaviourist, cognitive) to learner and process-centred (constructivist, conversational). However they have in common analysis/evaluation processes relevant and adaptable to the process of image selection and use.

In the broader educational arena there is a move from a focus on a learner- and/or content-centred perspective to a wider socio-cultural approach. Martinez argues that cognitive approaches are inadequate as they focus on how individuals think and ignore the emotional and environmental dimensions of the *whole-person perspective*' [25]. Martinez further argues that personalisation of learning will promote success. The implications for image use are that images may be selected or adapted based on learner needs and preferences, and visual content increased or reduced accordingly. Shah and Hoeffner suggest the need for 'graphical literacy' to improve comprehension and interpretation of graphical data [26]. Whilst, Avgerinou and Ericson have identified a range of acquirable visual competencies and skills [27]. This suggests that it may be appropriate to afford degrees of learner control in image selection, giving rise to a need for both learners and teachers to acquire relevant competencies and skills in visual communication.

Image use in practice

Image use is culturally situated: some subject domains, for example, are intrinsically visual and the use of images reflects 'traditional' practice and supports learning in those areas, whilst others have not extensively used images. However, the increased access to a variety of images afforded by online environments and the availability of accessible image software means that images may now be placed in new contexts to replace or reconstruct traditional mediation or relationships between tutor and learner. Research shows that people do not read from the screen so much as scan [28]. In computer-mediated instruction images play an increased role in gaining and holding interest, and in delivering messages efficiently. However this increase in the potential use of images across different subject domains means that there is a greater requirement to provide support, advice and guidance on appropriate uses and integration within learning and teaching.

A number of sources offering advice for image selection and use are emerging from several domains. Carney and Levin suggest ten rules for effective use of images with text, including use in computer-based materials [17]. Lowe offers advice for selection and placement of illustrations in distance learning materials. Shah and Hoeffner make nine recommendations regarding the graphical display of data to promote effective use and presentation [26]. Tufte offers guidance for displaying quantitative, evidential and narrative information [29].

However, this is still a relatively nascent area and further research into image use across a range of media and identification of any implications for learning and teaching is required. Clark argues that there is no intrinsic benefit from the use of media; it is the content and design of instruction that influence learning [30]. He further states that any instruction can be designed for a variety of media. Implication for images is that the more formats in which an image can be made available the more flexibly and widely it can be used. The choice of media decision may be down to external limitations, e.g. cost, accessibility, availability, etc., rather than anything intrinsic to a medium.

An exploration of image use raises a range of questions and debates around the notion of visual and media literacy, and around the types of new skills that teachers and students will need in order to effectively use and communicate with images. There is a need for generic, image-type and subject-specific guidelines for image use and evaluation.

References

1. BB-LT, *BB-LT - Using images for learning and teaching*. 2000, Institute for Learning and Research Technology.
2. FILTER, *FILTER - Focusing Images for Learning and Teaching - an enriched resource*. 2000, Institute for Learning and Research Technology.
3. PICTIVA, *Promoting the use of On-line Image Collections in Learning and Teaching In the Visual Arts*. 2000, VADS.
4. Conole, G., J. Evans, and E. Simms, *Use and reuse of digital images in learning and teaching*, in *Reuse of Educational Resources for Networked Learning*, A. Littlejohn, Editor. 2002, Routledge: London.
5. Evans, J., G. Conole, and K. Young. *Focusing Images for Learning and Teaching*. in *ASCILITE*. 2001. Melbourne, Australia.
6. Williams, J., Lock, A., Crisp, J. and Longstaffe, A., *The Use and Capture of Images for Computer-Based Learning II*. 1995, University of Bristol: Bristol.
7. Levie, W.H. and R. Lentz, *Effects of text illustrations: A review of research*. 1982. **Educational Communication and Technology Journal**(30 (4)): p. 195-232.
8. Paivio, A., T.B. Rogers, and P.C. Smythe, *Why are pictures easier to recall than words?* Psychonomic Science, 1968. **11**(4): p. 137-138.
9. Paivio, A.L.J.W.S., *Imagery and long-term memory*, in *Studies in long term memory*, A. Kennedy and A. Wilkes, Editors. 1975, John Wiley: London. p. 57-85.
10. Freedman, J. and R.N. Haber, *One reason why we rarely forget a face*. Bulletin of the Psychonomic Society, 1974. **3**: p. 107-109.
11. Croft, R.S. and J.K. Burton, *Toward a new theory for selecting instructional visuals*, in *Imagery and visual lliteracy*., B.R.A.a.G.R.E. Beauchamp D G, Editor. 1995, Blacksburg, VA: The International Visual Literacy Association. p. 145-154.

12.   Paivio, A., *Imagery and Verbal Processes*. 1971, New York: Holt, Rinehart & Winston.

13.   Paivio, A., *Mental Representations*. 1986, New York: Oxford University Press.

14.   Severin, W.J., *Another look at cue summation*. Audio Visual Communications Review, 1967. **15**: p. 233-245.

15.   Miller, N.E., *Graphic communication and the crisis in education*. AV Communication Review, 1957. **5**: p. 1-120.

16.   Bruner, J., *Beyond the information given*. 1974, London: George Allen & Unwin Ltd.

17.   Carney, R.N. and J.R. Levin, *Pictorial illustrations still improve students' learning from text*. Educational Psychology Review, 2002. **14**(1): p. 5-26.

18.   Croft, R.S., *Digital enhancement of photographic illustrations for concept learning in nature*, in *Exploring the visual future: art design, science and technology*, W.V.S.a.L.J. Griffiin R E, Editor. 2001, Blacksburg, VA: The International Visual Literacy Association. p. 69/74.

19.   Dwyer, F.M., *Strategies for imrpoving visual learning*. 1978: State College. PA: Learning Services.

20.   Dwyer, F. and R. Baker, *A systemic meta-analytic assessment of the instructional effects of varied visuals on different types of educational objectives*, in *Exploring the visual future: art design, science and technology*, W.V.S.a.L.J. Griffiin R E, Editor. 2001, Blacksburg, VA: The International Visual Literacy Association. p. 129-134.

21.   Gagne, R.M., L.J. Briggs, and W.W. Wager, *Principles of instructional design (4th edition)*. 1992: Fort Worth: Harcourt, Brace, Jovanovich College Publishers.

22.   Morrison, G.R., S.M. Ross, and J.E. Kemp, *Design Effective Instruction (3rd edition)*. 2001, New York: Wiley.

23.   Diamond, R.M., *Designing and improving courses and curricula in higher education: a systematic approach*. 1989, San Francisco, CA: Jossey-Bass.

24.   Laurillard, d., *Rethinking university tecahing - a framework for the effective use of educational technology*. 2nd ed. 2001, London: Routledge.

25.   Martinez, M., *Designing learning objects to personalize learning*, in *The instructional use of learning objects*, D. Wiley, Editor. 2001, Association for Instructional Technology and the Association for Educational Communications and Technology.

26.   Shah, P. and J. Hoeffner, *Review of graph comprehension research: implicatons for instruction*. Educational Psychology Review, 2001. **14**(1): p. 47-69.

27.   Avgerinou, M. and J. Ericson, *A review of the concept of visual literacy*. British Journal of Educational Technology, 1997. **28**(4).

28.   Neilson, J., *How Users Read on the Web - Jakob Nielsen's Alertbox for October 1*. 1996.

29.   Tufte, E.R., *Visual explanations: images and quantitites, evidence and narrative*. 1997: Graphics Press. 156.

30.   Clark, R.E., *Media will never influence learning*. Education, Technology, Research and Development, 1994. **42**(2): p. 21-29.

Developing On-line Tools to Support Learners in Problem-Solving Activities

Gwyn Brickell, Barry Harper, Brian Ferry.

Research Centre for Interactive Learning Environments

Faculty of Education, University of Wollongong
Wollongong, Australia.
Gwyn_Brickell@uow.edu.au

ABSTRACT

In recent years, research has focused on understanding how learners can benefit from tools that can assist in the development of informal reasoning skills when constructing arguments in collaborative learning with web-based learning environments. A common approach taken by each of these systems is to use support mechanisms (scaffolding) to facilitate student learning through the development of improved reasoning and argumentation skills. The authors of this paper have been developing computer-based learning environments for the past ten years, and have developed several award winning CD-ROM packages that feature a range of cognitive tools designed to assist learning. The development of these products has provided a rich source of information about learner use of cognitive tools. Our research has shown that two recurring issues keep emerging:

1.   There is a need to develop generic cognitive tools that assist learners to understand and solve problems that relate to different knowledge domains

2.   There is a need to help learners to analyse and structure information gathered, when they use cognitive tools.

This paper reports on the outcomes of a study into the reasoning and argumentation skills of pre-service education students engaged in problem solving within a computer-based learning environment. The implications for the design of a support framework to assist in this process will also be discussed.

KEYWORDS

Cognitive tools, scaffolding, problem solving, argumentation

BACKGROUND TO THE PROJECT

As prevailing learning theory has moved from an information processing approach in examining problems to a constructivist approach, the importance of the structure of the learning task and how learners are supported in its achievement becomes more critical. David Jonassen (2000) has organized the work of several designers into a classification framework based on the different types of cognitive demands that the problem tasks place on learners. His framework schema identifies the type of problem and the degree of structure and abstract nature of the problem. In this paper we explore the world of 'trouble-shooting problems' and 'diagnosis-solution problems' (Jonassen, 2000) and the methods that can be used to create a range of possible solution strategies for them.

The research team has been developing effective technology to support collaborative forms of teaching and learning for the past ten years. The outcomes of this research resulted in the development of the International award winning educational CD-ROM packages, *Investigating Lake Iluka* (1993), *Exploring the Nardoo* (1996) and *Stagestruck* (1999). Each of these products encourage learners to be actively involved in knowledge construction through the use of cognitive tools (Jonassen, 1996) that support them in thinking, problem solving and learning.

The development of these products has provided the research team with experimental environments in which to explore the development and use of a range of cognitive tools by learners. However, research on their use has demonstrated that some tools did not support learners as well as intended. In particular, research showed that:

1.   The existing cognitive tools needed to be refined so that learners could use the tools more effectively to solve problem with varying degrees of complexity.

2.   Learners needed better support to analyse and structure the information generated when they used the cognitive tools in creating effective arguments to support their solutions.

ASSOCIATED RESEARCH PROJECT

Constructivist learning theory shifts the focus for organising knowledge construction from the teacher to the learner. Learners therefore need to develop a range of information processing skills to cope with this change. When faced with the responsibility for knowledge construction, they are thrown on their own management resources. While some may have the metacognitive skills to cope, many fend poorly in the increased complexity of such a learning environment. Many see the task as daunting and complex and feel ill-prepared for such creative freedom and choice of direction. Such learners need tools to support them to represent the knowledge they are acquiring and to facilitate higher-order thinking.

This research used the findings from previous studies as a foundation to investigate cognitive frameworks that support learners' problem-solving skills. The research for the framework has focused on the three main areas: *problem clarification* (identifying the nature of the task and what information was required or provided); *solution formulation* including data collection and the solution process (sorting out the resources and generating new information as required); and *presentation of argument* for the solution (identifying propositions and the appropriate evidence for support or refuting the argument).

Using *Exploring the Nardoo* (1995) as the investigative tool, the current investigation sought to develop a better understanding of how learners identify problems in computer-based learning environments. This information would then be used to help guide the development of a cognitive tool (or tools) to assist learners with their reasoning and problem solving skills.

Research Questions

The study's objective was to gain a better understanding how learners identify, organise and present information when problem solving in computer-based learning environments. To support this objective the following questions were used in guiding the research:What cognitive strategies do learners use in problem clarification and problem resolution, when attempting ill-structured problems within a technology-supported learning environment?

2.   What strategies support problem clarification and assist learners in accessing and making effective use of information when completing a specific task?

For research questions 1 and 2, the exploratory study (Yin, 1994) focused on the strategies employed by learners as they investigate the problem space to develop understanding. The primary data gathering strategies adopted for this focussed on individual student written work, audiotape transcripts, participant observation and student interviews.

Data Collection Process

Problem solving involves the application of a range of skills, which enable the learner to recognise and identify the problem, form hypotheses, search for and collate information through observation and measurement, and to interpret and analyse the data in proposing a solution(s) to the problem. Many of the steps in the problem solving process are quite simple manipulative skills but others involve complex thinking ability and some structural knowledge. Structural knowledge is knowledge of how the relationships within a domain are integrated and interrelated (Diekhoff, 1983; Beissner et al, 1993). In an attempt to support the structural knowledge of each participant during the problem solving process four specific support frameworks were identified for use in this study. Each of these support frameworks, Concept Mapping (Novak, 1990), Venn Diagrams (Gunstone & White, 1986), Critical Thinking (Ennis, 1991) and Six Thinking Hats (De Bono, 1992) have been identified as alternative learning strategies that assist learners in processing and analysing information. It was thought that the support framework would provide cognitive support for problem solving and the development of higher order thinking skills that would facilitate more efficient problem clarification, together with better reasoning and argumentation outcomes.

Participants. Volunteers were called from a cohort of 250 students (200 female, 50 male) enrolled in Information Technology for Learning, a first year undergraduate information technology class in the Faculty of Education at the University of Wollongong. Of this group of students a sample of 32 participants (27 female, 5 male) agreed to participate in the study. Participants were randomly assigned to one of four tutorial groups for the purpose of training in their allocated strategy and in the use of the CD-ROM.
The researcher, as participant observer, attributed meaning to the participants' words and actions following transcription of audio recordings.

The Study. The study was carried out over a period of twelve weeks and conducted in two phases, a training phase and a problem-solving phase. The training phase was conducted with four groups of eight students, each group being assigned to one of the four problem solving strategies. Group membership was fixed during this phase. Components of the training phase were:

problem solving strategy tutorial: each group was issued with and instructed on the theoretical principles of their designated support strategy. Designed by the researcher, this booklet provided a theoretical outline of the strategy and a series of non-domain specific problems to work through using the designated strategy. The researcher modelled the problem solving process using the strategy assigned to each group. All group members were provided with the strategy outline in written form and given time to work on example problems using their assigned strategy. Participants were encouraged to work collaboratively and present their solutions to the group for reinforcement of the strategy concepts.

CD-ROM tutorial: all groups were instructed on the use of the investigating tool and given an opportunity to develop their skills, with both the software tools and their designated strategy, using alternative problems to those investigated in the study.

The problem-solving phase was conducted on an individual basis as it was considered that a deeper understanding of the individual problem solving strategies of each participant could be obtained. Components of the problem-solving phase were:

Apple iMac computer and software: Each participant was seated in front of the computer containing the interactive computer program, *Exploring the Nardoo*. This software possesses many of the attributes of a constructivist learning environment (Jonassen et al, 1999) providing learners with opportunities to actively manipulate a range of information sources and knowledge construction tools while engaged in problem solving. Time was allowed for all subjects to reacquaint themselves with the software and ensure they were comfortable with the setting before commencing the assigned problem. The researcher only intervened or answered questions if participants had difficulties with the equipment or expressed confusion with navigational aspects of the CD-ROM.

electronic notebook (PDA): *Exploring the Nardoo* provides the learner with a flexible set of cognitive tools made available through the metaphor of a personal digital assistant (PDA). This device provides access to navigation and measurement tools. It also affords the opportunity to record data, write notes, collect source material (images, text, video, audio) to support the problem before reflecting upon or reworking their ideas.

participant workbook: For both problem-solving sessions participants were provided with a booklet to record their developmental strategies (plans, predictions, summaries, ideas, causal links, solution outlines) in helping them develop their solution to the problem(s).

audio-recorder: Participants were asked to verbalise their thought processes during their problem solving strategies. The audio-tapes were transcribed verbatum, coded appropriately and set aside for later analysis to note the incidences of higher order skills associated with reasoning and argumentation.

researcher's observations booklet: This artefact, designed by the researcher, was used to record each participant's progress through his or her individual information gathering process. This allowed the researcher to accurately record a chronological sequence of events as each participant attempted to solve the problem(s). Also, hand-written notes were taken of any thoughts and actions each participant verbalised during the process.

problem solving support framework: The specific support framework used in the initial training session was available for each participant as a reference source if required. Designed by the researcher, this booklet provided a theoretical outline of the framework together with a series of non-domain specific problems for the participants to work through.

participant survey: Following the completion of both experiments, participants were asked to complete a questionnaire based on their framework use during the experimental phase. The questionnaire consisted of a combination of both open-ended questions (participants were required to generate their own responses) and closed questions (participants were restricted to a choice of specified alternatives).

INDICATIONS FROM THE STUDY

Even though many of the participants gathered a number of pieces of evidence to support their solution, it appeared that in constructing their responses they preferentially consider only one or two pieces of information rather than discriminating between a variety of issues. However, not all of the supporting evidence was accessed by a number of participants with essential articles being 'missed' in the information gathering process, resulting in the formation of 'weak' responses when developing an argument to support the solving of the problem. Participants used a combination of their individual strategies and their assigned framework. Many participants demonstrated a fragmentary approach to both information gathering and in the analysis and comparing of supporting information for the problem under investigation. Both these skills tended to be more systematic with the investigation of the second problem. In general, for both problems under investigation, a variety of strategies were used in accessing information, in the pattern of exploration in developing mental representations of the problem, in the use of the media elements and in the use of the 'guides' in helping direct the focus of investigation.

Based on the four problem solving frameworks used in the study, the following generalisations are made: the two frameworks Six Hats and Critical Thinking provide stimulus for students to seek out data and make some preliminary analysis of the suitability of the data in addressing a possible solution to the problem. Participants using these frameworks presented clearer representations and better argued solutions to the problem. The other two frameworks, Venn Diagram and Concept Mapping, focussed more on the organization of ideas once they were identified. In either case, students, when taught one framework and then asked to use it for problem solving, did so with greater allegiance for the first two frameworks than the second two. It is conjectured that this was due to the focus of the framework on data identification.

IMPLICATIONS FOR DESIGN OF AN ON-LINE SUPPORT FRAMEWORK

Problem solving requires a range of skills and background knowledge from the learner. David Jonassen (2000) suggested that the skills required of the learner involved a combination of recognizing variations in the type of problem (degree of structure, complexity and abstraction), the form of representation of the problem (context, cues/clues, and modality), and the individual's knowledge (both in terms of the domain of the problem and the strategies for operating and persevering within the problem domain). This suggests that the strategies in this study would have specific applications to aspects of the solution framework design depending on what aspect of problem solving is highlighted, particularly if learners concentrate on the generation of ideas rather then suggest a mechanism through which a solution might be found. In short they provide not only an idea-generating framework but also ways of organising the ideas to ensure that a solution can be produced. This study has provided agreement for the design elements that Jonassen proposes.

This exploratory investigation indicated that learners engaged in interactive computer-based learning need additional support to represent the knowledge and information they have acquired in the process. This could be achieved through helping learners identify patterns, links and similarities in these complex learning environments. The application of the frameworks in this study supports that contention that there are several processes at work in the development of a problem solution. A series of frameworks each with its own strength is preferable for learners with different processing needs. The concept mapping approach does

generate a range of ideas but it requires an additional support to turn the range of ideas into a supported argument. Tools like 'Inspiration'™ assist with the task by enabling the initial map to be re-represented into a different mode to assist with the structured of the argument. However, the nature of the argumentation requires an additional manipulation of the content and hence even this tool cannot help with the final presentation of the ideas. However, the tool exists outside the information collection and where resources are being accessed and directly manipulated the tool is not accessible. Thus if one requirement in the design of a cognitive framework structure is that it be available in conjunction with the problem space, this tool will not be suitable. Further it can be argued that such tools do not support domain-specific reasoning should that be required. The context of this study sought to overcome this issue by linking the tools directly into the problem space.

For this study the importance of domain knowledge has been underscored in that those learners who could operate within the knowledge domain scored a solution framework more expeditiously and their strategies that contributed to the final solution were more direct and focused, although no participants in the study had a specific and strong background in the knowledge domain. Even though each participant was presented with a cognitive support framework, those with less relevant frameworks found that the sequences they followed did not lead to well-reasoned solutions. Thus if the approach does not match the task a solution is not easily achieved and supported. In all cases the results supported the contention that the investigation of a solution(s), and the reporting and support for that solution were two quite different processes.

REFERENCES

Beissner, K. L., Jonassen, D. H., Grabowski, B. L. (1993). Using & Selecting Graphic Techniques to Acquire Structural Knowledge. In 15th Annual Proceedings of the *Association for Educational Communications & Technology*. 155-176.

De Bono, (1992). Six Thinking Hats. Victoria, Australia. Hawker Brownlow Education.

Diekhoff, G. M. (1983) Relationship judgements in the evaluation of structural understanding. *Journal of Educational Psychology*, vol.75, 227-233.

Ennis, R.H. (1991). Critical Thinking. Columbus, OH: Prentice Hall

Gunstone,R.F. & White, R.T. (1986). Assessing Understanding by Means of Venn Diagrams. *Science Education*, Vol. 70(2), p.151-158

Interactive Multimedia Learning Laboratory. (1993). *Investigating Lake Iluka* [Computer Software]. Belconnen, Australia. Interactive Multimedia Pty, Ltd. http://www.emlab.uow.edu.au/iluka.htm

Interactive Multimedia Learning Laboratory. (1996). *Exploring the Nardoo.* [Computer Software]. Belconnen, Australia. Interactive Multimedia Pty, Ltd. http://www.emlab.uow.edu.au/Nardoo/nardoo.htm

Interactive Multimedia Learning Laboratory. (1999). *Stagestruck* [Computer Software]. Belconnen, Australia. Interactive Multimedia Pty, Ltd. http://www.emlab.uow.edu.au/stagestruck.htm

Jonassen, D. H. (2000). Towards a Design Theory of Problem Solving. In ETR&D, Vol.48. pp.63-85

Jonassen, D. H. (1996) Computers in the Classroom: Mindtools for Critical Thinking. Englewood Cliffs, New Jersey: Prentice-Hall Inc.

Novak, J.D. (1990). Concept maps and Vee Diagrams: two metacognitive tools to facilitate meaningful learning. *Instructional Science* 19: 29-52.

Yin, R. K. (1994). Case Study Research: Design & Methods (2nd Ed.). Thousand Oaks, CA: Sage.

ACKNOWLEDGMENT

This research was conducted with financial assistance from an Australian Research Council Grant #A10012013, *An interactive multimedia solution framework for problem identification, solution formation and argumentation*. The chief investigators were Professor John Hedberg and Professor Barry Harper.

Jonassen, D.H., Peck K.L. & Wilson, B.G. (1999). *Learning with technology: A constructivist perspective*. New Jersey: Prentice-Hall, Inc.

Dialogue in Learning: Implications for the Design of Computer-Based Educational Systems

John Cook
Learning Technology Research Institute
University of North London, 166-220 Holloway Road, London, N7 8DB, UK
Email: j.cook@unl.ac.uk

Abstract

This paper surveys the literature on the role of dialogue in learning, with an emphasis on implications for the design of computer-based educational systems. In order to structure the survey we will look at dialogue by viewing it as potentially belonging to one of three levels: (i) rote-learning, question and answer, (ii) adaptive dialogue, which mediates between learner and resource and (iii) responsive dialogue, i.e. dialogue about the aim and structure of the educational experience.

Keywords: literature survey, learning through dialogue, teaching/learning strategies, design principles

1. Introduction

This paper examines the issues related to learning from dialogue, with an emphasis on implications for the design of computer-based educational systems. Given the current interest in networked, online and mobile learning, which rely heavily on asynchronous and synchronous dialogues, such an review would seem timely.

2. How and why does one learn from dialogue?

Dialogue between teachers and students may be important in promoting learning (e.g. Vygotsky [22]; Leontiev [13]; Lipman [14]; Jones and Mercer [11]; Freire [6]; Pilkington and Mallen [19]; Mercer [15]). In order to structure this survey we will look at dialogue by viewing it as potentially belonging to one of three levels: (i) rote-learning, question and answer, (ii) adaptive dialogue, which mediates between learner and resource and (iii) responsive dialogue, i.e. dialogue about the aim and structure of the educational

experience. The major focus of this paper is the adaptive dialogue layer.

3. Rote-learning dialogue layer

Computers can support dialogue at the lowest of our layers, although this is an area that is often ignored. Freire [6] introduces, and dislikes, the 'Banking' concept, which is conceived as a teacher full of knowledge depositing knowledge in the students through a process of transmission. Banking is similar to the concept of knowledge communication [23], where knowledge is seen as being transmitted to the learner in a pre-determined format, to be absorbed by the learner. An example of the rote-learning dialogue layer would be drill-and-practice software. These systems perform a useful role in that they can automate assessment in memory recall quizzes. This layer is not the focus of our paper.

4. Adaptive dialogue layer

In this section we describe the way that a teacher mediates between learner and learning resource, i.e. the adaptive dialogue layer. The adaptive dialogue layer is somewhat akin to the "interaction paradigm", which is one concern of research into cooperative learning (Dillenbourg, Baker et al., [5]). The interaction paradigm aims to understand and model the relationship between different types of learning and types of communicative interactions involving learners.

Students who are placed in a learning environment will usually need to interact with a teacher or learning facilitator at some point, in order to receive guidance [7], feedback and explanations. The adaptive role of a teacher is of central importance to learning [12] because learning resources and media, such as books, journals, CD-ROMS, online databases or World Wide Web resources, etc., are rarely able to adapt to a particular group or individual's learning requirement. Students bring different histories of learning with them to a particular situation and therefore have different learning needs [12]. Furthermore, these resources and media, typically, do not provide guidance on how they should be integrated and embedded in a coherent fashion so that learning can occur. For example, the tutor may be required to mediate between the learner and their understanding of the way in which they should use learning resources in order to meet the assessed learning outcomes of a particular programme of study. Consequently, in a learning environment, we get a complex set of relationships between how a learner thinks, i.e. cognition, how the learner interacts with teachers and peers, and the various media and resources that are available to support learning. The institution and society in which the learning takes place will also exert an influence on learning in more subtle ways (this is a concern of the responsive layer).

The teacher can also help the learner to become more autonomous, to learn how to learn, and to reflect on his or her own problem-solving. The way that such explanation and guidance is provided by a teacher is usually through dialogue, either face-to-face, written or virtual, since this enables the teacher's help to be adapted and individualised to a particular student's needs. Dialogue also enables the student to verbalise and articulate his or her needs and understanding. This latter process of making knowledge explicit, and reflecting on it may itself be an interactive learning mechanism [4]. Providing computer-based learning support that is able to acquire aspects of the role of 'teacher as mediator' is a growing area of research and development.

In contrast, Constructivism (described by [24]) sees the major goal of education as the creation of rich sets of cognitive tools to help learners explore and interact with their environment and is closely associated with Piaget's [18] genetic epistemology theory of cognitive development. Papert's [17] Turtle Logo is a classic example of a learning environment that attempts to embody cognitively relevant tools in the environment. In the case of Logo, the cognitive tools, or cognitive hooks as Papert called them, are claimed to be the graphical immediacy of geometry drawn in real-time. These cognitive hooks are intended for the young learner to use as a tool to enhance the motor skills which they have acquired from birth. Cognitive tools are generalisable tools used to engage learners in meaningful cognitive processing, knowledge construction and facilitation. For example, computer-based cognitive tools are in effect cognitive amplification tools that are part of the environment. Environments that employ cognitive tools are described as distributing cognition; they are constructivist because they actively engage learners in the creation of knowledge that reflects their comprehension and conception of the information rather than focusing on the presentation or transmission of objective knowledge. It is this last item that contrasts with the behavioural approach (see, [9], for a description) which would focus on content selection, sequencing, structuring and presentation. However, this approach (providing cognitive tools or amplifiers) has various drawbacks. Firstly, the gap between a novice learner and the environment may be too large to 'hang on to' (Elsom-Cook, [7], p. 67). Secondly, to facilitate the learning of reflective skills a microworld like Logo would need to somehow store information in the interface about a set of goals to achieve these skills and to make directly accessible the deep semantics of such skills ([7], p. 6). We could call this the over amplification problem. To overcome this over amplification problem some systems [e.g. MetaMuse [2], see below) attempt to provide structured interactions in the form of scaffolding and cognitive apprenticeship support.

Taking a different perspective, Jones and Mercer [11] have argued that a theory of learning, e.g. Behaviourism or Constructivism, is not the best framework for analysing what goes on in understanding the use of media like computers in education, rather a theory and analysis of teaching-and-learning is needed. Jones and Mercer are in favour of approaches to understanding teaching and learning that have been based on Vygotsky's *cultural-historical theory* of human activity. For Vygotsky [22], human mental functions appear first as inter-individual and then intra-individual, that is, by the use of socially developed tools, both technological and psychological ones. For Vygotsky, however, the unit of analysis was still the mediated action of an individual and how that individual developed. Vygotsky also put forward the concept of the zone of proximal development (ZPD), which is the difference between a learner's real level of development and their potential level of development. It is for the previously stated reasons that we place Vygotsky in our adaptive layer, although there may be an argument for also placing him in the responsive dialogue layer (such a discussion is, however, beyond the scope of this paper).

Recent work with computer-based simulations (e.g. [21]), which are used to help students acquire explanatory accounts of the real world, shows that students may fail to generate deep causal models of the behaviour under simulation because they concentrate on manipulating the simulation objects. With respect to the previously stated finding, Pilkington and Mallen [19] make a strong case for a more Vygotskian [22] perspective in interaction, i.e. where the teacher mediates knowledge about the society and culture so that it can be internalised by the learner. Interestingly this raises the following question: is this knowledge already formed and finding its way into the learner? If so, this would suggest Freire's Banking model of education. In fact we do not mean to suggest this interpretation. In our interpretation, interaction is seen as an important component of the learning environment, helping students to recognise and resolve inconsistency, i.e. it has an adaptive mediating role. Furthermore, Pilkington and Mallen have also point out that:

"...if we are to improve the quality of the interaction, then we need to understand the mechanisms by which dialogues work ... We need to know how and why, some kinds of dialogue ... seem able to trigger reflective engagement and conceptual change." ([19], p. 213–4)

Indeed, recently, Hartley and Ravenscroft [10] have suggested that dialogue with a teacher may be required if the goal is to promote reflection and conceptual change:

"... self-reflection, or even reflective discussion between students may not be effective in changing beliefs and their 'organisation' into conception. This requires dialogue with a teacher. But ... can a computer system be improved/designed to assist the reflective process, and if so, what are the requirements of its improvements?" ([10], p. 3).

Ravenscroft has followed up this work by showing how work on dialogue games (e.g. [20]) can be used to systematically investigate and design or animate communicative interactions and online conversations. In a related area, Baker and Lund [1] have described a model of task-oriented dialogue that forms the basis of design and implementation of tools for computer-mediated communication between learners and teachers in a computer-supported collaborative learning environment.

Lipman [14] has proposed an approach to learning through dialogue and has suggested that we must stipulate that education should include reasoning and judgement about knowledge. Education in the Lipman sense of the word is not 'simply' learning, it is a Vygotskian-like teacher-guided community of inquiry that places an emphasis on social interaction and cooperative learning. Lipman calls this the reflective model of education practice. Lipman's work has been influential on the author's own work in the area of promoting learning through dialogue. MetaMuse [2] is a system that attempts to promote a Lipman-like community of inquiry [14] in the context of undergraduate musical composition. MetaMuse is based on a theoretical and dialogue analysis approach [3] that makes used of higher-level, goal-based interaction analysis and communicative act theory. A screenshot from MetaMuse is shown in Figure 1.

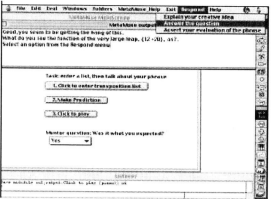

Figure 1. Example of MetaMuse interface

Mercer [15] has recently extended the work of Vygotsky and Lipman by suggesting a breaking down of dialogue in a different way: disputational, cumulative, and exploratory, which begins to suggest the useful features of each to learners (though there is still a long way to go). Mercer also talks about ways dialogue can fail as well as be successful, which seems critical to furthering our understanding of the area. Furthermore, the Vicarious Learning project attempts to suggest what dialogue contributes to learning that may be quite difficult to achieve in other ways, see for example http://kn.cilt.org/cscl99/A43/A43.HTM.

5. Responsive dialogue layer

To be truly equal and transformative, dialogue should not just be about content or about making appropriate use of a learning environment; it has to extend to the choice of what is to be learned, decisions about how it is to be learned and even institutional questions [16]. This relates to the way that some distance learning writers talk about transactional distance: the perceived degree of separation during interaction between and among students and teachers. Moore and Kearsley [16] describe transactional distance as having two components: dialogue and structure. Dialogue refers to communication between students and their teacher, i.e. our adaptive dialogue layer, and structure refers to the "responsiveness" of the educational plan to the individual student. By educational plan we refer to an orchestrated learning environment, e.g. a module that draws upon problem-based learning or an institution that is based on a particular educational school of thought. The educational plan can thus include theory and models of learning and interaction.

Work is currently being done with the applications of Bakhtin's model of dialogic discourse to computer-mediated communication [8]. While not really concerned with design, these early attempts at introducing Bakhtinian theory into the analysis of the uses of educational technology problematise the concept of dialogue and see it as a broad and complex activity, which is inscribed by struggles of power and authority. While it is beyond the scope of this paper to discuss any of this work in detail, it is, nevertheless, useful to acknowledge that such work is ongoing, albeit in early stages.

Leontiev [22] expanded Vygotsky's cultural-historical theory to an *activity theory* approach to human interaction where reality consists of mediated, social, hierarchically organised, developing, internal and external, object-oriented activities. For Leontiev the unit of analysis was extended to include the collective activity, something done by the community with a motive (which need not be consciously recognised), which is composed of individual actions directed towards a goal. The individual's mediated actions could still be analysed, but there was now a social dimension which could be used to understand the individual's actions. It is for this reason, and the recognition of a motive, that we place Leontiev in the responsive dialogue layer.

6. Conclusions

In this paper we have examined the role of dialogue in computer-based learning. It would appear that certain types of learning may not occur unless dialogue takes place between a tutor and learner(s). Interaction has an adaptive mediating role, helping students to recognise and resolve inconsistency. To be truly equal and transformative, dialogue has to be responsive to institutional questions and educational plans. A critique of the breakdown into rote, adaptive and responsive dialogues is that it gives no indication of what the relevant features of dialogues are, and how these can be helpful or unhelpful to learning. Any of these layers for a dialogue could be useful at a given time, but we need to know which constitutes an effective one. This paper has only touched on such issues. Our main concern has been to map out the problem space in a structured way. This will, we hope, lay the foundations for further fruitful debate on how to use computer-based systems to promote educationally productive dialogues.

Acknowledgements

Thanks to Alan Mclean, Jean McKendree & the reviewers for helpful comments on this paper.

References

[1] Baker, M. J. and Lund, K. (1997). Promoting Reflective Interactions in a CSCL Environment. *Journal of Computer Assisted Learning,* 13, 175–193.

[2] Cook, J. (2001). Bridging the Gap Between Empirical Data on Open-Ended Tutorial Interactions and Computational Models. *International Journal of Artificial Intelligence in Education.* 12 (1), 85–99. < http://cbl.leeds.ac.uk/ijaied/>

[3] Cook, J. (1998). Mentoring, Metacognition and Music: Interaction Analyses and Implications for Intelligent Learning Environments. *International Journal of Artificial Intelligence in Education,* 9, 45–87. < http://cbl.leeds.ac.uk/ijaied/>

[4] Chi, M. T. H., Bassok, M., Lewis, M., Reimann, P. and Glaser, R. (1989). Self-Explanation: How Students Study and Use Examples in Learning to Solve Problems. *Cognitive Science,* 13, 145–182.

[5] Dillenbourg, P., Baker, M. J., Blaye, A. and O'Malley, C. (1995). The evolution of research on collaborative learning. In Spada, H. and Reimann, P. (Eds.) *Learning in Humans and Machines,* pp. 189-205, London: Pergamon.

[6] Freire , P. (1993). *Pedagogy of the Oppressed.* London: Penguin Books.

[7] Elsom-Cook, M. (1990). Guided Discovery Tutoring. In Elsom-Cook, M. (Ed.) *Guided Discovery Tutoring for ICAI research* (pp. 3–23). London: Paul Chapman Publishing.

[8] Galin, J. and Latchaw, J. (1998). *The Dialogic Classroom: Teachers Integrating Computer Technology, Pedagogy, and Research.* NCTE.

[9] Hartley, R. (1998). New Technologies and Learning. In Shorrocks-Taylor, D. (Ed.), *Directions in Educational Psychology* (pp. 19–38). London: Whurr Publishers Ltd.

[10] Hartley, R. and Ravenscroft, A. (1993). Computer Aided Reflection: An Overview of SCILAB. *Paper presented at the SMILE Workshop, September 29th - October 1st,* Computer Based Learning Unit, University of Leeds, UK.

[11] Jones, A. and Mercer, N. (1993). Theories of learning and information technology. In Scrimshaw, P. (Ed.) *Language, Classroom and Computers* (pp. 11–26). London: Routledge.

[12] Laurillard, D. (1993). *Rethinking University Teaching: A framework for the effective use of educational technology.* London: Routledge.

[13] Leontiev, A. N. (1975). *Activity, Consciousness, Personality.* Moscow.

[14] Lipman, M. (1991). *Thinking in Education.* New York: Cambridge University Press.

[15] Mercer, N. (2000). *Words and Minds: How we use language to think together.* London: Routledge.

[16] Moore, M. G. and Kearsley, G. (1996). *Distance education: a systems view.* Wadsworth.

[17] Papert, S. (1980). *Mindstorms.* Brighton: Harvester.

[18] Piaget, J. (1971). *Biology and Knowledge.* Edinburgh University Press.

[19] Pilkington, R. and Mallen, C. (1996). Dialogue games to support reasoning and reflection in diagnostic tasks. In Brna, P., Paiva, A. and Self, J. (Eds.) *European Conference on Artificial Intelligence in Education (EuroAIED)* (pp. 213–219), held at Fundacao Caloustre Gulbenkian, Lisbon, Portugal, September 30–October 2, 1996. Edicoes Colibri.

[20] Ravenscroft, A. and Matheson, M.P. (2002). Developing and evaluating dialogue games for collaborative e-learning interaction. *Journal of Computer Assisted Learning: Special Issue: Context, collaboration, computers and learning,* 18 (1), 93–102.

[21] Twigger, D., Byard, M., Draper, S., Driver, R., Hartley, J. R., Hennessy, S., Mallen, C., Mohammed, R., O'Malley, C., O'Shea, T. and Scanlon, E. (1991). The conceptual change in science project. *Journal of Computer Assisted Learning,* 7, 144–155.

[22] Vygotsky, L. S. (1978). *Mind in Society. The Development of Higher Psychological Processes.* Edited by Cole, M., John-Steiner, V., Scribner, S. and Souberman, E. Cambridge, Mass.: Harvard University Press.

[23] Wenger, E. (1987). *Artificial Intelligence and Tutoring System.* Los Altos, California: Morgan Kaufmann.

[24] Wasson, B. (1996). Instructional Planning and Contemporary Theories of Learning: Is this a Self-Contradiction? In Brna, P., Paiva, A. and Self, J. (Eds.), *European Conference on Artificial Intelligence in Education (EuroAIED)* (pp. 23–30), held at Fundacao Caloustre Gulbenkian, Lisbon, Portugal, September 30–October 2, 1996. Edicoes Colibri.

Learner's Response Analysis for The Lesson Improvement

Eiichi TSUKAMOTO* and Kanji AKAHORI**

* Department of Human Sciences, Toyo Eiwa University, 32 Miho-cho, Midori-ku,
Yokohama-shi, 226-0015 Japan

**Graduate School of Decision Science and Technology, Tokyo Institute of Technology,
2-12-1, O-okayama, Meguro-ku, Tokyo, 152-8552 Japan

Abstract

In a lesson improvement, it is very important to grasp a student's understanding change. Previously, by analyzing the "study chart" freely described by the student, Tsukamoto and others performed response analysis of a student's understanding change, and showed one direction to the lesson improvement. However, since analyzing a student response had many required time and labors for the teacher or the researcher, it was difficult to apply to an everyday lesson improvement. This research shows the method of the collection and analysis of the student response for a lesson improvement by studying the meaning of a student response. The effect was evaluated in the informational lesson and clarified. Four categories of a student response existed on the rational and the irrational mental function, and the researcher was able to make the lesson improvement by looking down at this balance. In addition, it became clear that collecting student responses itself leads to the lesson improvement by the student.

Key word: Lesson Improvement, Understanding Change, and Response Analysis

1: Background

If we hope to improve our lesson, we have to use a student's response. Tsukamoto (1999) reported the recording method of the student response card for his lesson improvement. And Tsukamoto and others (2001) reported the analyzing method of this card for the lesson improvement. However it took long time for the teacher, because a teacher must read many response cards. Therefore, it is difficult to use at the usual lesson in many schools.

The purpose of this research is to investigate the analysis method of the student response cards which are written by the students in a classroom. In this research the web based collection system of the student response was made and used. And the analysis method of the collected information with a personal computer was reported. This collection and analyzing system was evaluated at the information science education at a university.

The main subject of this research is contained in the following two points. The first point is how to collect the student's real response. The second point is the how to find out the meaningful information, that is a useful information for the lesson improvement.

This paper shows that there are four categories in a student response. That is feeling, evaluation, understanding, and relative. And in this research, the real lesson improvement is reported using these four categories balances.

2: Learner's response

In advance of this investigation, we have started gathering the learner's response carefully. And the keywords that considered related to the learner's comprehension change have been fended out from the learner's response.

There were so many words in the learner's response and they look like meaningless. We researcher the meaning of those keywords and finally applied them into four categories as shown in the Table 1.

fourth is the relative impression about the learning object.

So the keywords were distributed to four categories of (A) from (D), and they were further divided into two classifications, so finally were classified into eight and the code of 1-8 was assigned to each.

Because such categorization and classification is a trial one for this research, we investigated the meaning and usefulness of this keywords classification for the final target of this research, that is the lesson improvement..

Table 1. Sample Keywords

Category Code	(A) Feeling of the study		(B) Standard of self-valuation		(C) Understanding of the study		(D) Relation with the subject to learn	
	1	2	3	4	5	6	7	8
Classification	Affirmation	Negation	Themselves	Comparison with others	Affirmation	Negation	Considering in the learner	Reasoning in an subject
Meaning and Intention	Joy, surprise, expectation, etc.	Fatigue, dislike, uneasiness, etc.	The intention to study, volition, etc.	Teacher, classmate, etc.	Knowledge, memory, understanding, etc.	Same as the left (not necessarily negative)	Usage, possibility, convenience, etc.	Contents assumption, personification, metaphor etc.
Example	pleasant	difficult	do my best	cannot follow	understand	not understand	convenient	should become liked c
Sample Keywords	pleasant, became pleasant; substantial; glad; was glad; exciting has been felt pleasant; felt relieved; good; felt easy; impressed interesting, becoming interesting; fresh	got tired; uneasy; be tired somewhat uneasy; disagreeable; become tense got tired although interesting.	want to do; do my best advance study more; want to be able to do; want to practice want to carry out	not able to follow; will be behind; can follow?; want to follow firmly sometimes cannot follow	understand have to memorize; not forget knowledge increases; beneficial; understand well	difficult; was difficult; complicated; puzzling; not understand. not yet understand; considers carefully	want to master comfort, able to do; can use now; done well; convenient; use personally; found how to use; be able to treat; utilize a machine	machine is wise should become like this, butð c; have pushed twice it must be two sheets that I printed many things are not yet known.

The four categories are as follows.

The first is the student's interest and the second is the standard of self-evaluation. The third is understanding of the contents of the lesson and the

A to D four categories are as follows.

(A) Comment of feeling to study

   1 Affirmation (surprise, expectation, etc.)

   2 Negative (fatigue, dislike, uneasiness, etc.)

(B) Comment in connection with the standard of self-valuation

    3 The standard of evaluations is in self (the intention to study, volition, etc.).

    4 The standard of evaluations is in the comparison with others (lesson progress, classmate, etc.).

(C) Comment in connection with understanding of the contents of study

    5 Affirmation (knowledge, memory, understanding, etc.)

    6 Negative (it is not necessarily present negative.)

(D) Comment in connection with the relation with the subject to learn

    7 Cognition by the learner (use, possibility of, convenience, etc.)

    8 Reasoning in the objects (contents assumption, personification, etc.)

First of all the many student's responses ware gathered in many lessons and divided into four categories. And final categorization referred to the system of analysis psychology created by Carl Gustav Jung and was performed carefully. Finally they are divided into four categories that are feeling, evaluation, understanding, and relative.

In the Web based collection system, the student responses were collected by some questions in each category. In this system, so many sample keywords were shown in the web screen that the students could choose the keyword that is they want say. However in order to guarantee a student's flexibility, when they need a new expression, they can describe freely. The example of the web design is shown in figure 1.

In order to get the student's responses in a kind of sentence as showed in the figer1 that is for example "A is B, so I feel C" the web is designed.

The students were permitted to input freely in A part and B part. But they were requested to select the

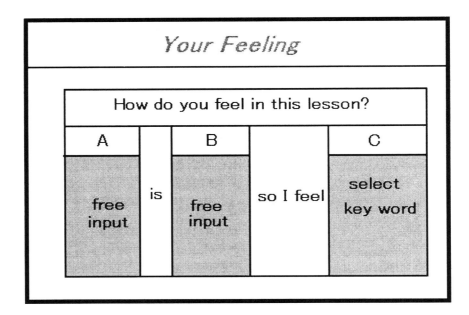

Fig. 1. Web design

3: Web based design

key word from the sample they were shown on a screen. And for each four categories the Web are designed in the same way.

We call A part Object, B part Description and C part Thinking.

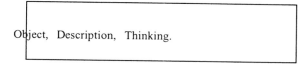

Object, Description, Thinking.

Fig. 2. Input sentence

In this research, the portion of object and description are thought as an introductory part for description of the "thinking". That is because research was focused on the portion of "thinking" which students shows their understanding reference.

In the part of thinking by showing the input keyword we could guide the students to know the meaning of they are expected. The sample of the input in the "feeling" is shown in table 2.

Table 2. Sample key words of "feeling"

Object	Situation	Thinking
File.	convenient	impressed
Computer setup	difficult	become tense
Usage of a file	understand well	substantial
Explanation	intelligible	substantial
First experience	be able to do	be satisfied
Operation	able to do smoothly	be satisfied
Explanation	intelligible	be satisfied
File arrangement	done	be satisfied
Lesson	difficult	got tired
Today's lesson	fine work	be tired
Contents	be puzzling	be tired
Progress of study	falls behind	be tired

We can know how the contents of a lesson were accepted in the student by seeing this result. Furthermore, we can find out how the student itself

considered the lesson and how the student is observing it and grasped the situation. Since every student's response is raw information in this stage, it is helpful as a material for the individual instruction for each student.

However the purpose of this research is not analyzing each student's situation but is making a lesson improvement system based on the web based student's response, we an lazed the frequency of the keyword appearance in each four categories

By this method, student's responses were collected for every lesson and the keyword appearance was investigated.

4. Lesson Analysis

Four student response A) feeling, B) evaluation, C) understanding, and D) relative can be applied to four mental situation in the system of analysis psychology created by Carl Gustav Jung. A) Feeling can be regarded as Jung's "feeling" Jung says. B) Evaluation is considered as same as Jung's "sensation" because the student evaluate the content of the lesson sensuously.

And C) understanding is the understanding based on a student's thinking, it is applied to Jung's "thinking". The last D) relative is same as Jung's "intuition" because the students just guesses at their heart something by their intuition.

By considering as mentioned above, the student response was classified into four categories of A) feeling, B) evaluation, C) understanding, and D) relative. And by seeing the balance of this four category's positive and negative responses, we can get the information, which is useful to a lesson improvement in like a bird's-eye view.

995

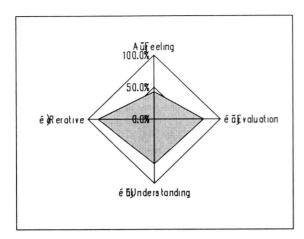

Figure 3. Balance of keywords

Fig. 3 shows the balance of the whole student response in a lesson by expressing an affirmation and negation ratio to a radar chart, respectively about four categories of a student response. By seeing this, this lesson can be considered as the thinking lesson rather than a pleasant lesson.

It is difficult to fill all students' needs in a lesson, but we can plan to do the what kind of lesson beforehand. And we can grasp the carried-out result from a student response chart and can reflected to the next lesson. In such a case, this system is very effective.

5. System Evaluation

This system was evaluated in the information science education of the freshman in T women's university. It experimented in two classes of 40 students, and the contents of the lesson improved actually. It is big progress that the result has been visually grasped from the balance of Fig. 3 in those lessons.

Thus, by grasping the state of a student response in this system, it can be done to look down at the state of bird's view at each time. Consequently, the feature of a lesson of each time can be expected beforehand the lesson, and the lesson improvement can be done finally.

6. Conclusion

In this research, the following point is clarified.
(1) The student response in a lesson is collectable by the Web system.
(2) The lesson improvement can be done in the balance of the four categories.

References

1. Adrian F. Ashman & Robert N. F. Conway (1997) An Introduction to Cognitive Education, Routledge

2. Kawai H. (1967) Jung's psychology. Baifukan Co., Ltd., Japanese

3. Sakamoto T. (2001) An educational media science. Ohm-Sha Ltd. , in Japanese

4. Tsukamoto, E. (1999) Instructional Design for Information Sciences, Advanced Research in Computers and Communications in Education pp.703. 706

5. Tsukamoto, E., Akahori, K.., (2001) Protocol Analysis of Learner's Comprehension, Advanced Research in Computers and Communications in Education pp.543. 546

Concept Gaming

Pasi J. Eronen[1], Jussi Nuutinen[1], Erkki Rautama[2], Erkki Sutinen[1], Jorma Tarhio[3]

[1] Department of Computer Science, University of Joensuu, P.O. Box 111, FIN–80101 Joensuu, Finland, {peronen, jussian, sutinen}@cs.joensuu.fi

[2] Department of Computer Science, University of Helsinki, P.O. Box 26, FIN–00014 University of Helsinki, Finland, erkki.rautama@cs.helsinki.fi

[3] Department of Computer Science and Engineering, Helsinki University of Technology, P.O. Box 5400, FIN–02015 HUT, Finland, jorma.tarhio@hut.fi

Abstract

Concept learning belongs to the fundamental challenges of educational technology. Contrary to the current trend of designing and implementing contents for various web–based virtual courses, concept learning requires cognitive tools rather than digital materials. We introduce a novel scheme to generate computer games from concept maps made by a teacher or a learner herself. Concept gaming exceeds the potential of previous software packages for concept mapping in a significant feature: it adds excitement and tension to the process of building a meaningful composition of concepts related to each other. In addition, concept gaming supports learning at various levels, from memorizing up to open problem solving.

1 Introduction

Concept maps are widely discussed means of visualizing one's inner cognitive structures. It is argued that with the help of preparing those structures, one has got a possibility to reflect own conceptions and correct potential misconceptions, thus building a new corrected structure into one's mind. This all has its roots in David Ausubel's learning theory of meaningful learning [2], which Joseph D. Novak later turned into a method now known as concept maps [7]. Concept mapping is widely used to assist learning [6], planning, and problem solving.

With the emergent discussion about concept maps in general, it is natural to extend them by the power of technology. With the new software implementations users have been able to construct a static map of their concepts to help them to clarify their thinking and learning. As an example of such formalisms, the genetic graphs [5] are intended to present processes with static images. This static approach is however quite limited for general use. Gaines [4] and Rautama et al. [8] present a method for dynamic presentation of concept maps as scripts, showing the construction process. There are also techniques, with which the concept maps can be shown through the web interface [4, 9].

These conceptualizing tools have been of great value to teachers and advanced, self–guided learners. In this paper, we propose the idea of concept gaming, which combines the powerful learning tool, concept maps, with a motivating factor—excitement.

In our opinion, the designers of learning environments have got many things to learn from the computer games. Computer gaming is inherently exciting, which creates intrinsic motivation for the youth and also the adults to acquire skills —i.e. to learn—in order to be successful in the game [1]. We argue, that this should be also the case with learning.

Therefore, adding the elements of excitement and success from computer games into a learning tool should serve as means to make using those tools attractive and worth bothering. In concept gaming, the contextually bound concept map building is connected with typical gaming ideas—competition, fight against time, growing challenges, winning oneself, scoring and development of one's skills as a player and simultaneously as a learner.

2 Concept Gaming

A concept map is a graphical representation of interrelated concepts. Concepts are shown as labeled nodes and their relationships as arcs, which may be labeled or unlabeled, directed or undirected. The basis of concept gaming is a selection of game schemes. A game consists of a game scheme run with a certain concept map. Here the concept map and its subject area can be arbitrary, and the map can be made by a teacher or a learner herself or it can be copied from a textbook.

To clarify and concretize our ideas, we introduce some features of a prototype CMG we implemented to test our approach. CMG (short for Concept Map Games) contains currently five game schemes:

1. **Removed concept names:** At first the map is shown without the names of concepts. The correct names are given in a list. The player moves one name at a time from the list to its proper place.

2. **Removed relation names:** This is analogous to the first one, but now the map is shown without the names of relations.

3. **Shuffled concepts:** The names of the concepts have been shuffled. The player tries to correct the map by repeatedly exchanging the names of two concepts.

4. **Shuffled relations:** The start and end concepts of each relation have been randomly reselected. The player should move the relations back to their correct positions.

5. **Trivia:** The player is given a concept and a relation starting from that concept. The player should infer which concept the relation leads to.

These five schemes are only examples of the game types that can be included in CMG. It is possible e.g. to design games that are focused on some certain subject area. In that case the concept maps may have to be constructed according to some guidelines but the game scheme itself can be more detailed and complex.

The concept map is loaded in the beginning of each game. In the end CMG shows the score and the correct answer. Scoring is based on correctness and speed. For example in game scheme 1 each correct concept name gives a certain amount of points. CMG also contains an editor with which the user can create new concept maps. The editor includes tools for constructing a concept map as well as adjusting the visual parameters such as color and appearance of the map elements. After a map is saved, it can be applied to any game scheme.

3 From Closed to Open Gaming

Generative nature is a major difference between a conventional learning game and the idea of concept gaming. A conventional game is typically connected with a single subject area whereas a concept game is a scheme, which generates games on various subjects. A concept map given as input to the generator determines the subject area of the game. Note that this concept map can be a ready-made map or a map made by the user—student or teacher—herself. Generative nature is also present in another respect. The user is able to generate several different games from the same concept map.

The game schemes presented so far require that each game has a fixed target map. In a more general approach, the target map is not necessarily completely specified. The reason for supporting relaxed ways of gaming is to support various learning methods. These methods start from primitive mechanized memorizing ending up to open problem solving (Fig. 1).

The simplest game type is called closed gaming, where the result map of the game is known before the game ends. Closed gaming is considered to help learning methods like repetition and memorizing. Examples of games that belong to these themes vary from basic connectivity problems between concepts to jigsaw puzzle, where concepts should be placed to their correct places.

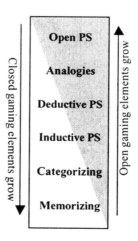

Figure 1. Concept gaming supports variety of learning methods

The most versatile type is open gaming, because of its main idea of being constructive and open-ended. This kind of gaming serves especially the needs of higher learning methods, namely open problem solving skills. The gaming here is not necessarily gaming in the traditional sense, but its idea is to allow a learner to construct new ideas on the basis of one's old concepts. This can be helped by offering the learner new randomized edges or concept nodes to be added into existing concept map. These randomized events are called distant thought models and are considered to help a learner to find novel sights into her work, much like they are utilized in a creativity enhancing software found on the market.

One must note, however, that there is a continuum from closed type of concept gaming to open gaming. Rather than tightly categorizing games, it is more useful to identify the aspects of a certain game that could be expanded or extended towards the targeted educational need. In addition, one game session might consist of several features, some more closed than others. This means that a game can support different learning methods at the same time. For example, a game for ecology education might consist of two-faced nodes, one side representing a natural phenomenon and the other a concrete example of it. The player is supposed to organize the nodes into a map that represents the interplay between different phenomena. Learning the two faces of the nodes helps one to memorize ecological factors, whereas constructing the interplay supports higher–level learning goals. This essentially takes a concept gamer from a fuzzy, blurred image of conceptual reality towards a more formal and stringent conceptual construct.

4 SWOT Analysis

We have also done a preliminary SWOT analysis from the learner's (Table 1) and teacher's (Table 2) points of view to find out the strengths, weaknesses, opportunities, and threats of our ideas. From the learner's point of view the important strengths of concept gaming are based on its support for variety of learning methods and help for cognitive processes. Cognitive processes are helped in two ways; first concept gaming helps a learner to construct her inner cognitive structures; secondly it helps the learner to make her implicit structures explicit, thus helping in self–re–evaluation of those.

As being a computerized tool, one of the weaknesses of the system is the computer usage skills that are needed for utilization of it. Another weakness is that the learner needs thinking skills that help her to conceptualize and abstract things and phenomena, which on the other hand are developed by using the system. This development as a learner is also one the opportunities that we see this system offers to the learner.

Concept gaming helps a learner to acquire new learning strategies, which helps her to achieve her goals as a learner more efficiently. We also argue that concept gaming brings the tension and excitement of computer games to learning. Threats are in our opinion bound with the physical limitations of the computers and the oppressive nature of the opinions by the ready–made solutions and teachers' unresponsive attitude towards alternative solutions. The display of the computer can be too small and place–bound surrounding to apply our system seamlessly to normal teaching. It is also worth thinking whether the learner can hold up to her thoughts, even when being correct, if she is made to play with the authority's vision of the same matter.

Strengths:	**Weaknesses:**
<ul><li>Supports learners with different learning skills and methods</li><li>Helps to construct new inner cognitive structures out of the information</li><li>Helps to visualize the learner's implicit structures</li></ul>	<ul><li>Computer usage skills are needed</li><li>Learner needs abstract, conceptualized thinking skills</li></ul>
Opportunities:	**Threats:**
<ul><li>Helps learners to acquire new learning strategies</li><li>Brings tension and excitement to learning</li></ul>	<ul><li>Learning space is limited to size of the computer's display</li><li>The original own ideas might be abolished after seeing the version done by authority, namely the teacher</li></ul>

Table 1. SWOT analysis from the learner's point of view

From the teacher's point of view our system's strengths are especially concentrated on helping the learner–teacher interaction. Concept mapping equips the teacher with a novel medium of evaluating the learning process of her student [7, 3]. The different game types support the teacher to acknowledge the differences between the ways learners learn and build their knowledge structures. The results that learners achieve by using the system help the teacher to understand the level of knowledge acquired by learners. In addition, they concretely visualize the differences of comprehension between the learner and teacher. The achieved results serve also the teacher when self–assessing her own work.

The weaknesses include, as in the learner's case, the need for computer usage skills. It is also worth mentioning that a new tool brings in the need for constructing the concept maps for the concept game system, which can be time consuming. The opportunity, which we considered to be especially interesting, is the excitement and tension of brought to learning experience by concept gaming, which helps creating good learning situation atmosphere.

The threats that we discovered in our analysis include concern over predetermined, closed gaming and the role of the computerization in this setting. We wondered, whether closed gaming would serve too much of rote learning goals. After taking this under closer examination, we discovered that it is possible to include also a support for higher learning elements into simpler game schemes as was introduced earlier in this paper. Another threat is the potential needlessness of the computer to produce this kind of game. We argue that especially game schemes supporting higher learning might be too complicated to realize with a reasonable amount of work and time with only pieces of paper and a pen.

Strengths:	Weaknesses:
• Helps to understand the learners' ways of learning • Helps to see the amount of knowledge adopted by learners • Helps to understand the differences between own and the learners' comprehension • Helps to meet the needs of the different kinds of learning strategies	• Work needed for constructing the new maps for different contexts • Computer usage skills are needed • Computers are needed in the learning situation
Opportunities:	**Threats:**
• Learning experience can be exciting, thus creating good atmosphere in the learning situation • Sharing and exchanging the concept maps • Tool to study the learning process	• Closed game schemes tend to be mechanized, encouraging learner to think in a too straightforward and prepared way, abolishing their own ideas • Some ideas might be realized with pieces of paper and a pen

Table 2. SWOT analysis from the teacher's point of view

5 Concluding Remarks

We feel that concept gaming has potential to become an important learning aid. It has several advantages. A game can be automatically generated from any topic. With concept gaming the learner is able to analyze her comprehension and to learn new contents. Concept gaming supports various, more advanced learning methods in addition to memorizing.

Open gaming helps to develop higher learning methods, especially open problem–solving skills of the learner. As a side effect, we expect that concept gaming will not only make learners more familiar with concept mapping, but they start to apply concept mapping in analyzing and memorizing. After tuning and improving our prototype, we will later on run extensive tests in order to measure the effect of concept gaming on learning outcomes among various student groups.

The concept gaming serves also the teacher in her evaluation process of learner, in her self–evaluation, and comparison of her and her learners' comprehension. We also argue that the data gathered from usage of the concept gaming system, helps both the teachers and researchers in their research of cognitive aspects of learning.

The built–in randomness of concept gaming compels the learner to think of unconventional and even surprising connections. This helps her to better recognize wrong structures and to create novel ideas. Randomness guarantees that the exactly same game occurs very seldom, if the input map is nontrivial.

The design of the user interface is important for this type of game in order to attract students of different ages and backgrounds. We have started a project to test our prototype in a real learning situation in an elementary school in order to improve its usability. Later on we plan to offer an adjustable user interface so that besides the default look and feel, the user is able to change several details according to her liking.

The benefit of concept gaming depends partly on number of the ready–made concept maps available in the format of the system. A web–based database would give additional value and reduce the amount of work that the teacher must do in order to start using the proposed system.

References

[1] Alessi, S., & Trollip, S. 1985. *Computer–Based Instruction: Methods and Development*. Prentice–Hall, Englewood Cliffs.

[2] Ausubel, David P. 1963. *The Psychology of Meaningful Verbal Learning*. New York: Grune & Stratton.

[3] Bykov, V., & Dovgiallo, A. 1997. *Concept mapping towards a tool for active learning.* In: New Media and Telematic Technologies for Education in Eastern European Countries (ed. Kommers, P., et.al.), Twente University Press, the Netherlands, 193–202.

[4] Gaines, B. R., & Shaw, M. L. G. 1995. Concept maps as hypermedia components. *International Journal of Human–Computer Studies*, 43, 3, 323–361.

[5] Goldstein, I. P. 1982. *The genetic graph: a representation for the evolution of procedural knowledge.* In: Sleeman, D., Brown, J. S. Eds. Intelligent Tutoring Systems. Academic Press, London 51–77.

[6] Jonassen, D. H. et al. 1997. Concept maps as cognitive learning and assessment tools. *Journal of Interactive Learning Research 8*, 3/4.

[7] Novak, J. D. & Gowin, D. B. 1984. *Learning How to Learn.* Cambridge, England: Cambridge University Press.

[8] Rautama, E., Sutinen, E., Tarhio, J. 1997. Supporting learning process with concept map scripts. *Journal of Interactive Learning Research 8*, 3/4, 407–420.

[9] Rautama, E., Karvonen, A., Tarhio, J., Turkia, J. *Versatile concept map viewing on the Web.* In: Proc. ITiCSE '01, Innovation and Technology in Computer Science Education, ACM, 2001, 105–108.

Representational Versatility and Linear Algebraic Equations

Ye Yoon Hong & Mike Thomas
The University of Auckland
<hong@math.auckland.ac.nz>, <m.thomas@math.auckland.ac.nz>

Abstract

The value of encouraging students to form rich links between different rep-resentations of mathematical concepts has been recognised for some time. However, in practice this is often not done in teaching. This paper describes an attempt to use computer algebra system (CAS) calculators to assist 14/15 year old students to build links between the algebra and graphs, tables and ordered pairs for solutions to linear algebraic equations. The results show that these students found the CAS calculators difficult to use and, although they did better at solving the equations they did not improve very much in their representational versatility.

Key words: **CAS calculator, algebra, representation, function, concepts, equation**

Background

Although we may not always be aware of it, what we learn in mathematics is often dependent on the representation in which we interact with the mathematical ideas. For example we may have constructed the belief, or we may have been taught, that we can recognise even numbers because they end in zero or a digit divisible by two, eg 12, 34, 56, etc. However later on we may realise that while this can be a very useful test, it does depend on the base that we represent the numbers in. For example, 12_3, 34_5, and 56_7 are all odd numbers, while 22_3, 24_5 and 46_7 are all even.

This may cause us to have to reconstruct our mental schemas [1], which is a primary way we make progress in our understanding of mathematics. Since concepts in mathematics, such as the numbers above, can be represented in a number of different ways, it makes sense to consider the representations of mathematical constructs that students are exposed to in their learning and the ways in which they are interacting with them [2].

If we take the idea of function for example, then we can represent a simple function such as squaring a value in an algebraic manner, as $y=x^2$, $f(x) = x^2$ or as $f:x \rightarrow x^2$, geometrically on cartesian axes as a parabola, in a table of values, as an ordered pair (x, x^2), by Venn diagrams with arrows linking the elements, or with two vertically placed real number lines linked by horizontal arrows, etc. Thurston [3] discusses a similar list for the concept of derivative, although without talking about representations, and calls them "different ways of *thinking about* or *conceiving of* the derivative" [original italics] and then comments on how he remembers "spending a good deal of mental time and effort digesting and practicing with each, reconciling it with the others." (p. 30). It is increasingly being recognised that it is this time in the learning process, the forming and cementing of cognitive links between different representations of the same concept that is essential for the construction of rich concept images [4] in any area. One reason for this is that each representation can emphasise, or de-emphasise, different characteristics of the construct presented [5]. In the example of function above, the idea of 1-1 may be more easily seen in one representation, while that of being onto may be better in another. Thus, if each representational form captures a special aspect of the concept, equivalence of meaning between any two representational forms must be established. This ability to establish meaningful links between and among representational forms and to translate from one representation to another has been referred to as *representational fluency* [6], or as *representational competence* [7]. Thomas [8, 9] has introduced the concept of *representational versatility* to include both fluency of translation between representations, and the ability to interact procedurally and conceptually with individual representations.

The integration of graphic and CAS calculators in learning schemes holds promise of encouraging students' *representational versatility* since these calculators not only employ a number of linked mathematical representation systems, such as tables, algebraic symbols, graphs and ordered pairs, but provide a dynamic environment with instant feedback. The graphic calculator (GC), has for some time been suggested as capable of supporting the construction of mathematical meanings across representations [10]. Ruthven [11], for example, demonstrated that this could be the case by using GCs to help students link graphic and algebraic representations. They were assisted to recognise when a given graph came from a family of curves, and the multi-representational features of the GC were shown to enrich problem solving strategies. Similarly, the GC study of Asp, Dowsey, and Stacey [12] reported a significant improvement on interpretation of graphs and on the matching of their shape with symbolic algebraic forms. Another by Harskamp, Suhre, & Van Streun [13] showed that access to GCs improved students function graphing approaches. However the research of Gray and Thomas [14] reported mixed results on their efforts to employ GCs to help students link different representational forms. More recently the CAS calculator has been shown to be of some value in learning the concepts of parameter [15], and function [16].

One area of learning where students have often not been able to make links between representations has been in the study of linear algebraic equations in secondary school. Graphical solutions are considered but links made are often few, and many students a do not consider solutions from tables. It was against this background that this study looked at using CAS calculators to encourage students' *representational versatility* with regard to linear equations.

Method

This study involved 18 students (10 male, 8 female) aged 14-15 years from single class of lower achieving students from a school in Auckland, New Zealand. The students spent one week working from an algebra module integrating the TI–92 CAS calculator. It contained a description of the basic facilities of the TI–92 and then showed how, using a 'Press', 'See', and 'Explanation' format, linear equations can be solved in three different ways: algebraically, graphically, and numerically from a table of values.

Two algebraic methods were given, using the TI–92 to solve the equation directly and also using a standard balancing algorithm. An illustrative section from the module showing the four methods for the equation $2x - 5 = 3x - 9$ are given in Figure 1 (note the section is incomplete and some formatting has been changed). The fact that the solution is the same in each case was emphasised. Two parallel tests, divided into sections A and B and comprising different numerical values, were constructed as pre– and post–tests. Section A of these

tests comprised standard textbooks questions such as solving: $5x-8=3x+2$; $m=8-3m$; and $6-8n = -3+n$. In contrast, section B addressed the students' conceptual thinking in solving equations, both within and across different representations. The concept of equivalent equations having the same solution is also important and we wanted to know whether the students were able to conserve solutions of equations and thus could recognise equivalence without having to calculate solutions. In order to test their ability to link equations within the symbolic representation we asked questions such as:

B1. Do the following pairs of two equations have the same solution? Give reasons for your answer.
a) $6x - 2 = 4x + 4$ c) $2 - 6x = 2x - 6$
    $6x - 2 - 4 = 4x + 4 - 4$ $2 - 3x = 5x - 6$
f) $9 - 4x = 6 - x$
    $9 - x = 6 - 4x$

We have previously described how there is a difference a *legitimate transformation* of an equation, and a *productive transformation*, one which moves more rapidly towards the solution [17]. However, a student who has constructed the concept of conservation of equation solution under a *legitimate transformation* such as adding $\pm k$ or $\pm kx$ to both sides or multiplying throughout by $\pm k$, should be able to see that the second equation in each case above will have the same solution as the first equation because they have been transformed in a legitimate way.

The module was initially given to the class teacher, who familiarised herself with the content. The first named researcher met with her to answer questions and to make sure that she was comfortable with the calculator and the material. The teacher then taught the class for four one hour lessons, two covering basic facilities of the calculators including introducing graphs and tables, the other two describing how to solve equations in different ways on the TI–92. The students only previous experience was in solving equations algebraically, and they were weak at this.

Method 1 a)		$2x - 5 = 3x - 9$ is solved by an algebraic method.
⬥ [HOME] F2 1 $2x$ ⊟ 5 [=] $3x$ ⊟ 9 , x ⟩ [ENTER]	▪ solve($2 \cdot x - 5 = 3 \cdot x - 9, x$) $x = 4$ solve(2x=5=3x-9,x)	The ⟨ , ⟩ x tells the calculator to solve with respect to x. $x = 4$ is the value which makes both sides equal in value.
Method 1 b)		To find the value of x, we need to simplify the given expression step by step:
$2x$ ⊟ 5 [=] $3x$ ⊟ 9 [ENTER] $2x$ ⊟ 5 ⊞ 5 [=] $3x$ ⊟ 9 ⊞ 5 [ENTER] $2x$ ⊟ $3x$ [=] $3x$ ⊟ 4 ⊟ $3x$ [ENTER] (-) x ÷ (-) 1 [=] (-) 4 ÷ (-) 1 [ENTER]	▪ $2 \cdot x - 5 = 3 \cdot x - 9$ $2 \cdot x - 5 = 3 \cdot x - 9$ ▪ $2 \cdot x - 5 + 5 = 3 \cdot x - 9 + 5$ $2 \cdot x = 3 \cdot x - 4$ ▪ $2 \cdot x - 3 \cdot x = 3 \cdot x - 4 - 3 \cdot x$ $-x = -4$ ▪ $\frac{-x}{-1} = 4/1$ $x = 4$ -x/-1=-4/-1	If we add 5 to both sides, the expression is simplified to $2x=3x-4$. If we subtract $3x$, the expression is simplified to $-x = -4$. If we divide by -1, finally we get $x=4$

1003

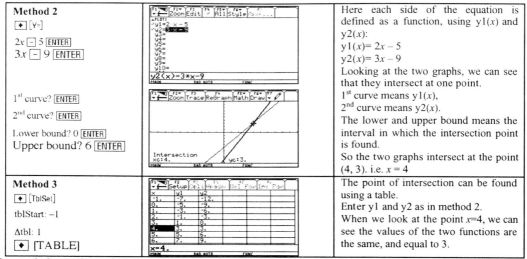

Method 2		Here each side of the equation is defined as a function, using y1(x) and y2(x): y1(x)= 2x − 5 y2(x)= 3x − 9 Looking at the two graphs, we can see that they intersect at one point. 1st curve means y1(x), 2nd curve means y2(x). The lower and upper bound means the interval in which the intersection point is found. So the two graphs intersect at the point (4, 3). i.e. $x = 4$
◆ [Y=] 2x − 5 ENTER 3x − 9 ENTER 1st curve? ENTER 2nd curve? ENTER Lower bound? 0 ENTER Upper bound? 6 ENTER		
Method 3		The point of intersection can be found using a table. Enter y1 and y2 as in method 2. When we look at the point $x=4$, we can see the values of the two functions are the same, and equal to 3.
◆ [TblSet] tblStart: −1 Δtbl: 1 ◆ [TABLE]		

Figure 1. A section of the module showing the layout and calculator screens for solving linear equations.

Each student had access to their own TI–92 CAS calculator, which they kept with them for the whole of the time of the study in school, although they were not able to take them home. During lessons the teacher stood at the front of the class, who sat in the traditional rows of desks, demonstrating each step while the students followed in the module and copied her working onto their own calculator. She employed a calculator viewscreen and projected the image using an overhead projector. After the teacher's explanation, the students spent the rest of the hour practising while the teacher circulated and assisted with any problems. At the end of fourth lesson the students were given an attitude test and a questionnaire, followed the next day by the post-test.

Results and Discussion

Overall the students did significantly better on the section A questions after the calculator work than they did before (max score=7; m_{pre}=3.06, m_{post}=4.86, t=3.03, p<.005). Furthermore there was also a significant increase in performance on the section B questions (max score=33; m_{pre}=0.88, m_{post}=4.72, t=4.55, p<.0001). Although there were relatively few examples of clear progress on improvement to inter-representational fluency a few instances emerged. There was some weak evidence of an improvement on performance in question B7 (max score=2; m_{pre}= 0.17, m_{post}=0.67, t=1.34, p<.1), which checked whether students could make links between the algebraic, tabular and graphical representations by asking them to solve an algebraically presented equation using a

given function table or graph.

In the questionnaire students were asked "Is there a relationship between A, B, C in following diagrams? If so then, what is it?" Figure 2 shows the three diagrams given and the responses of two of the students. These students have made some of the key the links between the representations and have seen that they can be used to show an equivalent function equality. Student A shows the "equal point[s]" on the tables of the functions and has marked the point of intersection (2, 4) on the graph, stating that "2 & 4 are the intersection point." Student B has shown clearly the relationship between the expressions on either side of the algebraic equation and the graphs of these taken as functions, stating "is representing the parts of the equation." She has also made the link to the solution in the tables of values of the functions. Neither student was able to see these links on the pre-test, both of them producing no response on the corresponding question. When asked on the questionnaire "How many different ways can an equation be represented?" 7 of the 18 students indicated that they understood that there are 3 or more ways of doing so, and 4 specifically mentioned 'graph, table and equation'. It is interesting to note that they have no other way of describing the algebraic form than to call it an equation. This at least a small step on the road to linking them. The students also did better, although not strikingly so, on question B2 where they had to match diagrams showing graphs and tables similar to those shown in Figure 2, to corresponding algebraic equations (max score=6; m_{pre}=0.17, m_{post}=0.61, t=2.00, p<.05).

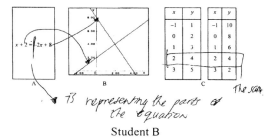

Student A   Student B

Figure 2. *Two examples of students who have made the inter-representational links for linear equations.*

In contrast, the results of question B1 show that the students do not yet have the concept of conservation of equation solutions under a legitimate transformation. While there was a significant improvement in the answering of this question (max score=6; m_{pre}=0.28, m_{post}=3.11, t=4.36, p<.0005), most students were not able to apply the transformational reasoning to obtain their answer. Instead they interacted procedurally with the equations [9], solving both of them separately and then comparing the answers. Figure 3 shows some examples of student working on this question, and we note that student D has not solved the first equation in part a) correctly.

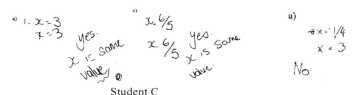

Student C   Student D

Figure 3. *Procedural working of two students solving equivalent linear equations.*

In addition, because they had access to the CAS calculators in the tests, some of the students used these to solve the equations (see Figure 4). Thus they were still interacting with the equations in a procedural rather than a conceptual way, simply using the technology to mediate the procedure. In this way students run the added risk of an entry slip causing an error, and student E in Figure 4 has done just this, failing to enter the left hand side of the second equation correctly. Clearly more work is needed to build a good understanding of the use of legitimate and productive transformations of equations.

On the negative side, the students in the research study commented that they had some problems using the complex calculators. "It takes too long to find the keys", "It took a long time typing things", and "Frustrating, lots of buttons to push", were typical comments. Apart from four students who got on well, the others remarked that they found the calculator too complicated, confusing, hard to understand, and difficult to use.

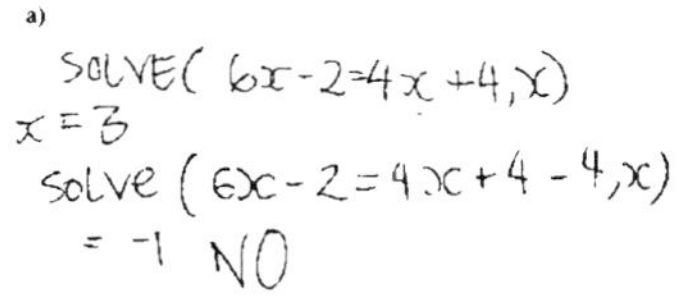

a)
SOLVE(6x-2=4x+4,x)
x=3
solve (6x-2=4x+4-4,x)
= -1 NO

a)
x = 3
x = 3
Solve(6·x-2=4x+4,x)=x=3
Solve 6x-2-4=4x+4-4,x)
= 3
yes they do

Student E 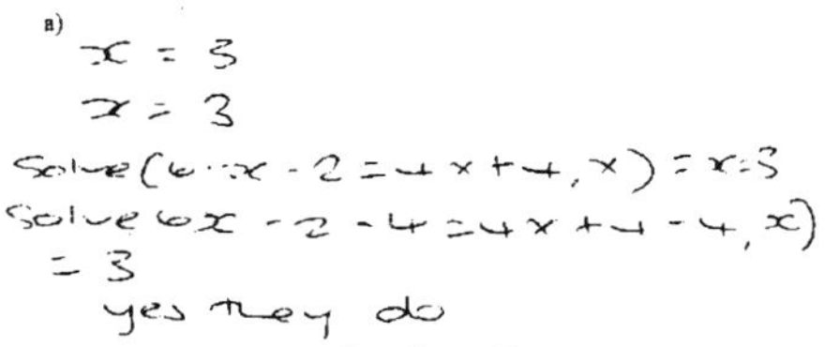   Student F

Figure 4. *Procedural working of two students using CAS calculators to solve equivalent linear equations.*

There is certainly a steep learning curve with the use of technology such as these CAS calculators, and this is a major drawback in gaining the most from promised learning benefits. We are still confident that CAS calculators can be useful for building representational versatility of linear equations, but this will clearly involve longer than a single week working with the calculators. It takes students a while to come to grips with the steep learning curve required to become proficient basic users of this technology, and this has to be allowed for [18]. The concept of equation is not an easy one for students to grasp, but we were encouraged by one students' answer to the question "What is an equation?". He said "A mathematical statement that two expressions are equal.", which is quite an insight for these weak students. Further, understanding the links between methods of solving equations in different representations takes time. However, as Moshkovitch, Schoenfeld, and Arcavi [19] rightly suggest we should ask, first of our students' understanding "Can the student move flexibly across representations and perspectives when the task warrants it?", and second of our curriculum development, "Does any curriculum we propose make adequate connections across representations and perspectives? If not it had better be revised". We believe that these are crucial questions to which we should add "Can our students interact conceptually with various representations of a concept?" [9]. Obtaining positive answers to these questions will take time, but will be worth the effort.

References

[1] Skemp, R. R. (1979). *Intelligence, Learning and Action – A Foundation For Theory and Practice in Education*, Chichester, UK: Wiley.

[2] Kaput, J. J. (1998). Representations, inscriptions, descriptions and learning: A kaleidoscope of windows, *Journal of Mathematical Behavior, 17*(2), 265–281.

[3] Thurston, W. P. (1995). On proof and progress in mathematics, *For the Learning of Mathematics, 15*(1), 29–37.

[4] Tall D. O., & Vinner S. (1981). Concept image and concept definition in mathematics with particular reference to limits and continuity, *Educational Studies in Mathematics, 81*, 151-169.

[5] Lesh, R. (1999). The development of representational abilities in middle school mathematics. In I. E. Sigel (Ed.), *Development of Mental Representation: Theories and Application* (pp. 323-350). New Jersey: Lawrence Erlbaum.

[6] Lesh, R. (2000). What mathematical abilities are most needed for success beyond school in a technology based *Age of Information?*, In M. O. J. Thomas (Ed.) *Proceedings of TIME 2000 an International Conference on Technology in Mathematics Education*, (pp. 73–83). Auckland, New Zealand.

[7] Shafrir, U. (1999). Representational competence. In I. E. Sigel (Ed.), *Development of Mental Representation: Theories and Applications* (pp. 371-390). New Jersey: Lawrence Erlbaum.

[8] Thomas, M. O. J. (2001). Building a conceptual algebra curriculum: The role of technological tools, *Proceedings of the International Congress of Mathematical Instruction (ICMI) The Future of the Teaching and Learning of Algebra*, Melbourne, 582–589.

[9] Thomas, M. O. J., & Hong, Y. Y. (2001). Representations as conceptual tools: Process and structural perspectives. *Proceedings of the 25th international Conference of the International Group for the Psychology of Mathematics Education*, Utrecht, The Netherlands, *4*, 257–264. [11] Ruthven, K. (1990). The influence of graphic calculator use on translation from graphic to symbolic forms. *Educational Studies in Mathematics, 21*, 143–50.

[10] Kaput, J. J. (1989). Linking representations in the symbol systems of algebra, In S. Wagner and C. Kieran (Eds.), *Research Issues in the learning and Teaching of Algebra* (pp. 167-194). Reston, Virginia. The National Council of Teachers of Mathematics.

[12] Asp, G., Dowsey, J., & Stacey, K. (1993). Linear and quadratic graphs with the aid of technology, In B. Atweh, C. Kanes, M. Carss, & G. Booker (Eds.) Contexts in Mathematics Education (Proceedings of the 16th Conference of the Mathematics Education Research Group of Australasia, pp. 51–56). Brisbane: MERGA.

[13] Harskamp, E., Suhre, C., & Van Streun, A. (2000). The graphics calculator and students' solution strategies, *Mathematics Education Research Journal, 12*, 37–52.

[14] Gray, R. & Thomas, M. O. J. (2001). Quadratic equation representations and graphic calculators: Procedural and conceptual interactions, *Proceedings of the 24th Mathematics Education Research Group of Australasia Conference*, Sydney, 257–264.

[15] Drijvers, P. (2001). The concept of parameter in a computer algebra environment, *Proceedings of the International Congress of Mathematical Instruction (ICMI) The Future of the Teaching and Learning of Algebra*, Melbourne, 221–227.

[16] Zbiek, R. M., & Heid, M. K. (2001). Dynamic aspects of function representations, *Proceedings of the International Congress of Mathematical Instruction (ICMI) The Future of the Teaching and Learning of Algebra*, Melbourne, 682–689.

[17] Hong, Y. Y, Thomas, M. O. J. & Kwon, O. (2000). Understanding linear algebraic equations via super-calculator representations, *Proceedings of the 24th Conference of the International Group for the Psychology of Mathematics Education*, Hiroshima, Japan, *3*, 57–64.

[18] Kissane, B, & Thomas, M. O. J. (in preparation). Algebra and the CAS calculator, In H. Chick & K. Stacey (Eds.) *The Future of the Teaching and Learning of Algebra*, ICMI.

[19] Moschkovich, J, Schoenfeld, A. H., & Arcavi, A. (1993). Aspects of understanding: On multiple perspectives and representations of linear relations and connections among them, In T. A Romberg, E. Fennema, & T. P. Carpenter (Eds.), *Integrating research on the graphical representations of functions* (pp. 69–100), Hillsdale, N J: Lawrence Erlbaum.

Effective Facilitation of Virtual Dialogues:
Tested Strategies and Practical Guidelines

By Maureen Brown Yoder
Lesley University,
Cambridge, MA USA

Online discussions can enhance Internet-based as well as traditional format classes. Course topics can be expanded and explored and students can express their opinions and debate controversial issues. When online discussions are not skillfully facilitated, however, they can become confusing and chaotic, with some people dominating the interactions and others hesitant to participate.

Skillful facilitation can increase participation, focus the dialogue if it has drifted from the topic, and promote and support thoughtful, meaningful responses. Writing effective group and individual interventions can be the key to successful facilitation.

If you are faced with the challenge of facilitating online interactions and fostering online collaboration, there are tested strategies that can be learned, then modified for individual use. The following observations and suggestions are the result of five years of teaching in and observing an Internet-based, online Master's degree program. Classes averaged 15 students each and more than 2,000 students were observed. Student course evaluations and unsolicited comments reinforced the findings of online instructors.

The unique phenomena of online communication

There are important similarities as well as significant differences between face to face and online communication. Understanding them will inform the monitoring of online discussions.

In traditional classrooms, efforts are made to encourage a distribution of participation, to acknowledge contributions without being judgmental, and to avoid people interrupting other people. This can be done by calling on students with raised hands and encouraging non-contributors to participate. In online discussions contributions are made asynchronously so taking turns is built into the system.

Unless someone is taking notes, there is no written record of what has been said in a face to face discussion. With online interaction, both participants and facilitators have a written record of previous contributions that can be referred back to, organized, and analyzed.

No special skills are required to participate in a traditional discussion. For online discussions, participants must be comfortable with the technology and be able to navigate to and from the conference area. They also need guidelines on writing descriptive subjects for their postings and knowing when to begin a new thread. Training is usually required to master the mechanics of the process.

Some people participate in face to face discussions with confidence and are outspoken, opinionated, loud, and effective. In an online discussion, those same people may not be coherent writers and may lack patience when they have to plan out and write up their thoughts.

In face to face classes, some people may be introverted or shy, and do not contribute to a discussion. Those same people can shine in an online environment when they can plan out what they are going to say and carefully construct an online entry.

Face to face discussion contributions are often spur of the moment, spontaneous reactions. Online discussion contributions tend to include well-constructed entries that are more formal than email communication. Participants usually pay more attention to spelling, grammar, and punctuation.

In a traditional discussion, tone of voice, accents, and body language help convey a message. In online discussions, emotion is conveyed with words and sometimes emoticons. Capital letters and punctuation can be used for emphasis.

Effective strategies for online discussion facilitation

The ideal is to have online conference participants so motivated and involved that the online discussion remains lively and productive until it reaches its natural conclusion. Unfortunately, without facilitation, most online discussions become confusing or inactive.

Increasing participation

Good planning by the facilitator involves creating a topic for the discussion that reflects the goals of the class and presents a compelling topic or controversial issue. Guidelines should include expectations about the frequency and content of student postings. Participants are usually expected to reflect on previous contributions, think about their own beliefs on the topic, gather additional supporting information if necessary, then write a thoughtful, articulate contribution to the discussion.

Discussions are most effective when there is some sort of incentive for participants to contribute. Often, a high interest topic about which students have strong opinions and a desire

to voice them will usually lead to active involvement. In a credit bearing course the incentive is usually a grade, or points toward a grade. Discussion involvement is often part of the class participation portion of the syllabus. Some instructors require a specific amount of postings per week, and ask that a certain percentage are responses to existing postings, and a certain percentage are initiations of a new topic.

Strategies for deepening and focusing dialogue

Fewer, but carefully constructed, instructor interventions can be effective in promoting thoughtful and thought provoking contributions by students. Collison et.al describe the roles that instructors can use when discussion participation wanes or uncomfortable situations arise. An instructor should be aware of all postings and the depth of involvement by participants. When the discussion becomes unfocussed or off-track, the instructor must carefully intervene, asking questions and making suggestions in a way that encourages the participants to dig deeper and think harder but does not discourage them from participating.

When a discussion becomes heated

Sometimes a highly charged conflict emerges and a discussion becomes emotional or argumentative. A participant may write something inappropriate to the group or to another individual. For a facilitator to intervene effectively, they must be sensitive to the reaction their postings might have. Often, a private email to a student about a concern will prevent the embarrassment that a public posting might cause. Less common are phone calls to online students but in some circumstances when an issue has escalated to an uncomfortable level, a voice conversation can clarify misunderstandings, calm an angry student or ease hurt feelings.

Dos and Don'ts – Specific Guidelines

Don't launch right into a serious discussion without first allowing an online community to develop. Do generate ice breaking activities where there is no right or wrong answer, where humor is welcome and personal information is encouraged. Share your own background and outside interests as an example. Activities that encourage imagination and creative writing sometimes work well. An area of the class Web page can be set aside for student introductions and can remain up for the duration of the semester.

Don't assume that students will know what is expected of them. Do make sure all class requirements are very clear, including the expectations around contributions to discussions. Stating the number and frequency of discussion contributions in not enough. The type of contribution should be described. "I agree", "Me, too." or "No way!" should be sufficient or acceptable. Opinions should be spelled out with a rationale. Postings that pose challenging questions should be encouraged. Responses that answer other participant's questions should provide clear explanations and examples. Participants should be taught how to include Web links for further reading, images for enhancing a thought, and multi-colored and bold text for emphasis.

Don't publicly praise an individual participant or use their posting as a good example. Other students may be discouraged; thinking their contributions was not adequate. Do privately acknowledge a good contribution, how appropriate it was, how it helped to move the dialog into a more thoughtful direction, or how it prompted others to participate that had not previously contributed. BlackBoard has an area where you can have a discussion with an individual student that can be password protected.

Don't take sides or voice your personal opinion on an issue. Students may begin to frame their postings to reflect your view. Do acknowledge the many perspectives that have been voiced.

Don't analyze contributions, as it is impossible to not infuse your slant on opinions and incorporate your own interpretation of student postings. Those who don't agree could feel defeated and discouraged. Do acknowledge that there are a variety of views and encourage further exploration of the issue. State the importance of respecting other people's opinions and urge everyone to support their views with additional information. Sarah Haavind refers to this as setting a "landscape", rather than summarizing.

Fostering an online learning community

Participants in an online course discussion will participate more freely when there is familiarity and trust among the participants. A comfortable online learning community is formed when informal interaction is supported along with academic activity.

In a face to face class, there are opportunities for informal relationships to develop when students talk before and after class. In an online format social interaction is more deliberative, but can be promoted and encouraged by the instructor with a separate conference area devoted to non course related discussion. Students may focus on sports, current events, or their social lives. They are there to share good news such as babies being born and they often provide support for classmates going through difficult times. When light hearted, friendly interchanges take place the students experience the online equivalent to the face to face class coffee break. Students who form informal relationships are more comfortable working with each other in more serious aspects of a course.

Technology supports the facilitation of online discussions

Commercial tools for course development provide features to help instructors monitor discussion and guide collaboration. These include the ability to search, sort, and analyze student participation in threaded discussion. Available data can increase the level of understanding of the class as a whole. Additionally, the ability to create both public and private discussion areas allows the instructor to support groups of students as well as individual students.

Conclusion

Skillful facilitation of an online discussion can be the key to effective interaction between students. Knowledge of the unique aspects of online interaction is useful when attempting to understand the phenomena of online communication. Facilitators can foster informal online communication so that students feel comfortable in more serious environments. When facilitators employ strategies for deepening and focusing discussions then effective debate and exploration of course concepts will enrich the learning experience for students

Collison, G., Elbaum, B., Haavind, S., & Tinker, R. (2000). Facilitating online learning: Effective strategies for moderators. Madison, WI: Atwood Publishing.

Implementing generic learning designs based upon quality ICT exemplars

John Hedberg,
University of Wollongong
with Ron Oliver, Edith Cowan University
Barry Harper, Sandra Wills, Shirley Agostinho,
University of Wollongong

Abstract

Within the context of an AUTC funded Project: Information and Communication Technologies and Their Role in Flexible Learning, this paper presents an analysis of learning designs using ICTs and how this grounded approach might be a more useful structure to design effective learning environments. The project has developed generic or reusable frameworks for technology-enhanced high quality learning experiences in higher education and this paper will present several examples of the original design and how the key elements were selected and developed for use by others. As this project is currently developing these generic exemplars of learning designs, the final presentation will demonstrate how the designs might be reengineered to become useful templates for other instructors and other knowledge domains.

Introduction

There is growing awareness today of the value of learning environments in higher education that foster knowledge construction. This awareness has coincided with the development and increased uptake of information and communication technologies as supports for learning and increasingly we are seeing examples and instances of the learning settings based on constructivist principles (Harper & Hedberg, 1997). These principles posit that learning is achieved by the active construction of knowledge supported by multiple perspectives within meaningful contexts. In constructivist theories, social interactions among learners are seen to play a critical role in the processes of learning and cognition (eg. Vygotsky, 1978).

In the past, the conventional process of teaching, and that of instructional design, has typically revolved around a teacher planning and leading students through a series of instructional sequences and events to achieve a desired learning outcome (eg. Gagné & Briggs, 1974). Typically these forms of teaching focus upon organised transmission of a body of knowledge followed by some forms of interaction with the material to consolidate the knowledge acquisition. Contemporary learning theory is based upon the notion that learning is an active process of constructing knowledge rather than acquiring knowledge and that instruction is the process by which

this knowledge construction is supported rather than a process of knowledge transmission (Duffy & Cunningham, 1996).

Instructional Design

In learning settings that support knowledge construction, the emphasis is placed on learning as a process of personal understanding and the development of meaning in ways which are active and interpretative. In this domain, learning is viewed as the construction of meaning rather than as the memorisation of facts (eg. Lebow, 1993). Technology-based approaches to learning provide many opportunities for constructivist learning through their provision and support for resource-based, student-centred settings and by enabling learning to be related to context and to practice (eg. Berge, 1998; Barron, 1998).

In contemporary learning, we use the concept of a learning environment to describe the setting in which learning takes place. A learning environment typically contains the learner and a space where the learner acts with tools and devices to collect and interpret information through a process of interaction with others. The concept of a learning environment is that of a flexible learning space and quite different to the instructional sequence which has previously characterised instructional design strategies.

The conventional art of instructional design has previously been very well defined and many guidelines and models have been developed to guide instructional designers in the process of developing instructional sequences (eg. Gagné, Briggs & Wager, 1992). Instructional design for learning settings that promote knowledge construction is a far more complex process. There is a distinct shortage of models and explicit frameworks for instructional designers. Jonassen (1994) argues that there cannot really be any firm models guiding the design of constructivist settings since knowledge construction is so context-specific. Lefoe (1998) argues that learning design theory today serves to provide principles and general concepts by which learning environments can be planned. The process is far less rigid and has fewer guidelines than previously and is a very difficult process for many.

Describing learning environments that support knowledge construction

Many writers have, however, attempted to provide guidance for the design of constructivist learning settings by articulating the underpinning characteristics. For example, Cunningham, Duffy & Knuth (1993) argue that constructivist learning environments are characterised by seven pedagogical goals in that constructivist learning settings are those which concurrently:

- provide experience in the knowledge construction process;
- provide experience in and appreciation for, multiple perspectives;
- embed learning in realistic and relevant contexts;
- encourage ownership and voice in the learning process;
- embed learning in social experience;
- encourage the use of multiple modes of representation; and
- encourage self-awareness in the knowledge construction process.

Others have added extra detail to these goals by suggesting that support and resources should embed the reasons for engagement into the learning activity itself. This approach ensures that the learner can explore options and, in particular, examine errors and failures to ensure they can understand the relatedness and the limits to their conceptual understandings (Lebow, 1993). In particular to support the translation into online forms we have the guidance from Jonassen and Tessmer (1996/7) who have proposed that we need to develop strategies that support:-

- Active learners to engage in interaction with and manipulation of the exploration environments that we construct.
- Learners to explore and strategically search through these environments
- Intentional learners willingly trying to achieve cognitive objectives
- Conversational learners engaged in dialogue with other learners and with instructional systems
- Reflective learners articulating what they have learned and reflecting on the processes and decisions that were included in the process
- Ampliative learners who generate assumptions, attributes and implications of what they learn

The descriptions that writers have provided of the elements required for constructivist learning settings can help designers to understand the forms of learning activity which are required but often fail to provide adequate guidance for the actual learning designs that can encapsulate such principles in cohesive and supportive ways. Hannafin, Hall, Land, and Hill (1994) suggested that appropriate forms of learning settings are open-ended and characterised by learner engagement in cognitively complex tasks involving such activities as problem solving, critical thinking, collaboration and self-regulation.

There is currently little empirical work that can guide the design of learning settings that support knowledge construction. Different authors and different projects have described a range of distinct forms of learning settings that have been designed to encourage learner activities that support knowledge construction. The following examples are presented.

Ip and Naidu (2001) outline a range of experienced-based pedagogical designs suitable for online learning. They argue that one characteristic feature of such experienced-based learning designs is the nature of the learning experience. They distinguish between first-person- experience-based designs and third-person-experienced-based designs. The distinction is based on whether the learning occurs through first-hand experience, for example in a simulation or role play setting, or from a third person information source through such means as resources and content forms.

Jonassen (2000) describes learning designs that support knowledge construction as problem-based learning settings and describes eleven problem-types in a form that suggests a continuum from problem solving based on the application of rules; activities based on incidents and events; through to solutions that require strategic planning and activity; and problem solutions based on learners' performances.

Oliver (1999) and Oliver and Herrington (2001) have synthesised the range of learning designs by developing a framework that identifies the critical elements required in a learning design, particularly when ICT mediated. The critical elements comprise the content or resources learners interact with, the tasks or activities learners are required to perform, and the support mechanisms provided to assist learners to engage with the tasks and resources. This is illustrated in Figure 1.

A Framework for describing learning designs

In our research associated with the AUTC Project: *Information and Communication Technologies and Their Role in Flexible Learning*, we have been exploring strategies by which the nature and scope of the forms of learning designs described above can be formalised. Having formal descriptions will provide the means to more easily guide the instructional design process and will also provide some means for institutions to provide supports and structures for teachers wishing to employ them.

As part of the project the researchers and other project members analysed a wide range of technology-based learning designs to identify its underpinning pedagogies. These designs were collated from a variety of sources including CAUT and CUTSD funded ICT-based projects. The analysis of the learning designs was based on the identification of the three critical elements: learning tasks, learning resources and learning supports (Oliver, 1999). The analysis was conducted by examining the descriptions of all the learning design exemplars to determine emergent clusters. The work by Ip and Naidu (2001) informed this process and the various problem types described by Jonassen (2000) were used as a means to develop a framework by which learning designs might be classified and described.

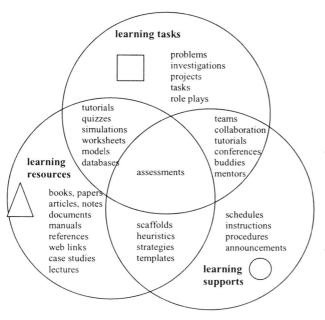

Figure 1: Elements of a learning design. Based on Oliver and Herrington (2001).

Based on the project team's grounded analysis plus further exploration of the Jonassen (2000) problem types, there appear three discrete forms of learning design within the eleven. These discrete forms each encompass a number of the problem types and appear capable of being used to further categorise potential learning designs. The problems encompassed within Jonassen's descriptions are typically either of a rule-focused, an incident-focused, or a strategy-focused form. Our inquiry suggests a fourth type of learning design, that of role-focused and devised two additional problem types that are characteristic of this form. The four types of learning designs that emerge from this form of analysis and development are shown in Table 1. The learning designs are discrete and follow what might be seen as a continuum describing the scope of their complexity and open-ness. Table 1 shows these forms and provides descriptions of each learning activity focus and the forms of learning outcome that are associated with each.

The nature of the various learning designs described in Table 1 can be further demonstrated and exemplified by considering the forms of tasks, supports and learning resources that each would require in a learning setting (Oliver, 1999).

Learning design Focus	Description	Learning Outcomes
Rule focus	The learning task requires learners to apply standard procedures and rules in the solution. Eg the application of given procedures and rules in defined ways to effect a solution.	A capacity to meaningfully and reflectively apply procedures and processes.
Incident focus	The learning activities require learners to reflect and take decisions based on the authentic actions and events.	Disambiguate scenario using an understanding of procedures, roles and the ability to apply knowledge and processes.
Strategy focus	Learning is focussed around the strategies employed to achieve the task goals. Often the strategy options are generated as part of the solution.	A capacity to apply knowledge in meaningful ways in real-life settings often with time and performance constraints.
Role focus	The learning is achieved through learners' participation as a player and participant in a setting that models a real world application.	An understanding of issues, processes and interactions of multi-variable situations with outcomes based on the multiple perspectives of roles taken.

Table 1: A framework for a learning design typology

Describing learning designs in generic forms

In our project, we have a need to be able to articulate clearly the nature and scope of different forms of learning design in ways that will enable that design to be applied across a variety of settings and disciplines. We clearly have a need for some strategy by which the various learning designs can be described and variations and instances can be accommodated. To achieve this goal, we have proposed the use of a temporal sequencing strategy based on the three critical elements of learning environments proposed by Oliver (1999). In the following section, we propose a series of potential generic categorisations based on the four main forms of learning designs using a temporal representation describing the interactions of the tasks, resources and supports. It is our intention to work with the generic descriptions and to refine their elements and components through their application to the various forms of learning design that emerge from our investigations and inquiries.

1. Rule-focused learning designs

Figure 2 shows a temporal sequence for the form of learning design we have designated rule-focused. Rule-focused designs are those that are primarily comprised of closed tasks whose completion requires the application of some form of rules, procedures or algorithms. In rule-focused learning designs, the resources which learners use include the procedural and system descriptions needed for the application and the learning environment, together with the necessary supports to enable learners to achieve success in their efforts. The learning is achieved through learners applying standard procedures and rules in developing a solution. For example, algorithmic approaches involve the application of given procedures and rules in defined ways to effect a solution. The task designs need to provide learners with opportunities to meaningfully and reflectively apply procedures and processes to specific closed, logical and bounded tasks.

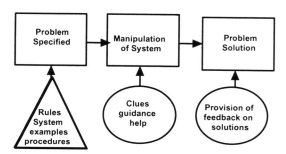

Figure 2: Temporal sequence describing a rule-focused learning design

2. Incident-focused learning designs

In an incident-focused learning design, the learning activity is based around learners' exposure to, and participation in, events or incidents of an authentic and real nature. The learning is focused around activities that require learners to reflect and take decisions about the actions and events. The temporal sequence shows learning processes which begin with a description of the incident, elaboration of that incident through reflection, a group or individual process to find a solution or to come to a decision, declaration of a solution or decision, and provision of feedback on solution or decision.

Incident-focused learning designs can be supported through learner collaboration and through opportunities to articulate and reflect on the learning provided by a teacher acting as a mentor. The learning centres around activities that require learners to reflect and take decisions focused on the incidents and events that are represented. The setting requires a range of resources to

provide rich descriptions and information about the incident.

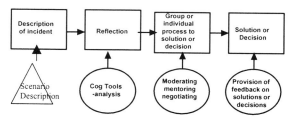

Figure 3: Temporal sequence describing an incident-focused learning design

3. Strategy-focused learning designs

Strategy-focused learning designs are characterised by such activities as complex and ill-defined tasks, decision-making tasks, some trouble shooting tasks, diagnosis solutions and strategic performance tasks. The temporal sequence shown in the example (Figure 5) later in this paper suggests a learning design where learners undertake a series of activities and at the same time interact with a variety of resources and learning supports. The process involves specification of the strategic problem, elaboration of that problem through reflection, a group or individual process to carry out the task, declaration of a solution or outcome from the tasks and reflection on the learning process.

In strategy-focused learning designs, learning is focused around tasks that require strategic planning and activity. The environment requires authentic resources that support multiple perspectives, provide such elaborations as expert judgements and which also provide descriptions of theoretical underpinnings. Typically learners are also provided with sample tasks and solutions, cases, tactics, strategies and treatments. Support is provided through a teacher acting as a coach and facilitator, and often through collaborative learning tasks involving such strategies as peer assessments and the provision of meaningful opportunities and contexts for articulation and reflection.

4. Role-focused learning design

In role-focused learning, learners acquire skills, knowledge and understanding through the assumption of roles within real-life settings. The design typically involves some purposeful and directed preparation and role-playing in scenarios that have been developed to provide the forms of learning opportunities sought in the objectives. The temporal sequence shown in Figure 4 involves the declaration of learner role, on-line dialogue to clarify this role, presentation of a dilemma to resolve, on-line dialogue to resolve the dilemma within the perspective of a role, a possible negotiated resolution to the dilemma and reflection on the process.

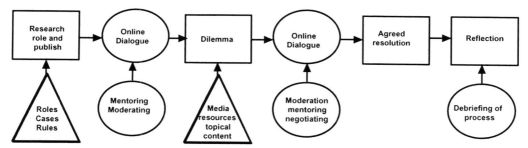

Figure 4: Sequence describing a role-focused learning design

In role-focused settings, learning is achieved through learners' participation as a player and participant in a setting, which models a real world application. Learners apply judgements and make decisions focused on understanding of the setting in real time scenarios. The settings require an array of resources to support the learners' role including procedural descriptions, role definitions, resources to define and guide roles, scenarios, topical content and cases. Typically the role of the teacher is that of a moderator and mentor, who creates opportunities for the learners to articulate and reflect on their learning experiences.

An exemplar — "Interactive Multimedia Design" a strategy-focused learning design

Many of the learning designs evaluated have clever implementations of a pedagogical framework. Many have used standard tools available in learning management systems such as discussion forums or email listservers to establish links and share resources or ideas. Some such as the following design have used the technology to support simple problem solving and reflection. This example is a whole course in which there are a series of learning tasks which build to create the learning experience. The subject aims to:

1. prepare participants to design and develop interactive multimedia in collaborative teams.
2. experience the team design process and reflect on this experience

3. review the process of interactive multimedia development
4. develop specific skills to fulfil their role in the team

The sequence begins with an analysis of a case, moves to a comparison with a second case to identify nuances in design approaches, students then red a set of informational tasks following a textbook structure, which contributes background for the major task. The final project for the course is based around an interactive multimedia design problem which runs parallel to the textbook learning tasks and the whole learning experience is consolidated with a reflective task which compares both cases, the personal experience of design and the theoretical issues raised through the standard textbook. The choice of the cases was to support the transfer of learning of a set of ideas which are loosely transferred from the theory. In design problems, the rules are creatively applied and the strategy might vary considerably from particular one design brief to another.

This design is in fact a compendium of learning designs. Each might be chosen individually but together they make a powerful set of tasks that mutually support the transfer of learning in an ill-structured knowledge domain. The first two tasks are case-study problems, the third is the major design problem and the other tasks are informational and strategic to ensure that the learning outcomes are the focus of the experience rather than these elements being seen as discrete and unrelated pieces (See Figure 5).

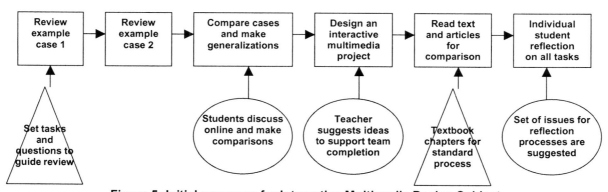

Figure 5: Initial sequence for Interactive Multimedia Design Subject

While the design task includes scaffolds and comparisons with other examples, there are many

elements in this particular instance, which might be separated into smaller learning designs to achieve similar outcomes in less time with fewer resources. The CD-ROM examples are very complex and were created by a team of experts. Thus the degree of complexity needs to be made explicit and the sets of resources included in each example needs to be constrained to focus upon the main learning outcomes. In the evaluation it was felt that if this is not made explicit in the course it may cause students to have unrealistic expectations of their own individual performance, their team's performance within the course, and what to expect in the field of multimedia development in general, outside the course.

Summary and Conclusions

The project is currently attempting to use these various forms of generic learning design to extend the range of problem-types described by Jonassen (2000) and to create linkages to some additional problem designs which have arisen from the grounded review and re-development of projects. At the same time the project team has been using the generic descriptions to create a comprehensive set of examples of best practice in technology-based learning and to explore the effective pedagogies underpinning these examples.

As the project progresses, it aims to document in very detailed ways, the forms of the learning designs and to provide templates and frameworks that will enable teachers wishing to implement such designs to have some firm guidance and support in the process. The project has developed a Web site that is being used to inform people of the progress and ultimately to provide access to the resources and materials that are developed. (http://www.learningdesigns.uow.edu.au)

Acknowledgements

The authors would like to acknowledge that this publication was made possible through participation in the 2000-2002 Australian Universities Teaching Committee project titled: *Information and Communication Technologies and Their Role in Flexible Learning* funded through the Higher Education Innovation Programme (HEIP) via the Commonwealth Department of Education, Science and Training. For information about this project contact: Project Manager, Dr Shirley Agostinho (University of Wollongong).

The Interactive Multimedia Design exemplar was derived from a case study research project by Sue Bennett and was based around a course taught on campus and in Hong Kong by Drs Lori Lockyer and John Hedberg at the University of Wollongong.

Address for Correspondence

John G Hedberg PhD, Professor of Education, Faculty of Education, University of Wollongong, Wollongong, NSW 2522 Australia. E-mail: jhedberg@uow.edu.au

References

1. Barron, A. (1998). Designing Web-based training. *British Journal of Educational Technology, 29*(4), 355-371.
2. Berge, Z. (1998). Guiding principles in Web-based instructional design. *Education Media International, 35*(2), 72-76.
3. Duffy, T., & Cunningham, D. (1996). Constructivism: Implications for the design and delivery of instruction, *Handbook of research for educational telecommunications and technology* (pp. 170-198). New York: MacMillan.
4. Cunningham, D., Duffy, T. & Knuth, R. (1993). Textbook of the Future. In C, McKnight (Ed.) *Hypertext: A psychological perspective*. London: Ellis, Horwood Publications.
5. Gagne, R. & Briggs, L. (1974). *Principles of instructional design*. New York: Holt, Rinehart and Winston.
6. Gagne, R. Briggs, L. & Wager, W (1992). *Principles of instructional design*. 4th ed. New York: Holt, Rinehart and Winston.
7. Harper, B., & Hedberg, J. (1997). *Creating motivating interactive learning environments: a constructivist view*. Paper presented at the ASCILITE'97, Perth: Curtin University. Available: http://www.curtin.edu.au/conference/ASCILITE97/papers/Harper/Harper.html [Accessed March 2002]
8. Hannafin, M.J., Hall, C., Land, S., & Hill, J. (1994). Learning in open-ended environments: Assumptions, methods, and implications. *Educational Technology, 34*(8), 48-55.
9. Ip, A., & Naidu, S. (2001). Experienced-based pedagogical designs for elearning. *Educational Technology: The Magazine for Managers of Change in Education. 41*(5) September-October Special Issue on "Knowing the Web". (pp. 53-58). Englewood Cliffs, NJ: Educational Technology Publications.
10. Jonassen, D. (1994). Thinking technology: Toward a constructivist design model. *Educational Technology, 34*(3), 34-37.
11. Jonassen, D. H. (2000). Toward a design theory of problem solving. *Educational Technology Research and Development*, 48(4), pp. 63-85.
12. Jonassen, D. H., & Tessmer, M.(1996/7). An Outcomes-Based Taxonomy for Instructional Systems Design, Evaluation, and Research. *Training Research Journal*, 2, 11-46.
13. Lebow, D. (1993). Constructivist values for instructional systems design: Five principles toward a new mindset. *Educational Technology, Research and Development, 41*(3), 4-16.
14. Lefoe, G. (1998). *Creating constructivist learning environments on the Web: The challenge in higher education*. Paper presented at the ASCILITE 1998, University of Wollongong
15. Oliver, R. (1999). Exploring strategies for on-line teaching and learning. *Distance Education, 20*(2), 240-254.
16. Oliver, R. & Herrington, J. (2001). *Teaching and learning online: A beginner's guide to e-learning and e-teaching in higher education*. Edith Cowan University: Western Australia.
17. Vygotsky, L. (1978). *Mind in society*. Cambridge, Massachusetts: Harvard University Press.

Using Pedagogical Advisement in Technology-Based Environments

John V. Dempsey, Brenda C. Litchfield, University of South Alabama
and Richard Van Eck, University of Memphis

Abstract

Education graduate students completed a technology-based instructional module on introductory statistics with a solicited guidance mechanism. Randomly assigned subjects used on-screen digitized video of a human advisor, on-screen text-based advisor, pull-down digitized video of a human advisor, or pull-down text-based advisor. Results indicated the on-screen video-based advisor condition resulted in higher advisor use than both the text-based and video-based pull-down advisor conditions. Advisor use was significantly correlated with performance during instruction, to time spent during instruction, and to television hours watched per week, but not with retention scores

Introduction

One of the more interesting practical questions involving the use of the Internet or multimedia for instructional purposes concerns the best way to "coach" a student who needs additional help in understanding complex concepts. It is suggested by some researchers [3] that this coaching (or advisement) acts as an intermediate point between generative and supplantive instruction. This study investigated the use of video pedagogical advisor to assist students in learning statistical concepts via computer-based instruction. Ease of use of the advisor is an important concern, particularly with more passive learners [2].who makes suggestions or asks questions about specific content domains.

The use of advisement in computer-mediated lessons has been well supported since microcomputers first came into use. Studies by Tennyson [4] found that designing computer-based lessons using learner control with advisement increased performance when compared to lessons designed with either adaptive (program) control or learner control without advisement. In most cases, performance increase was accompanied by a decrease in total instructional time compared to adaptive control methods [4, 5]. Although some advisement strategies have been shown to be effective, getting

The purpose of this study was to explore the use of advisement and the modality of the advisement mechanism in a technology-based module. Independent variables were placement of the advisor (pull-down menu access to the advisor vs. an on-screen access) and the modality of the advisor (digitized video of a human advisor vs. a text-based advisor).

Method

Subjects were 43 females and 15 males aged 21 through 57 years, with an average age of 35. Subjects were drawn from three graduate educational research survey courses and one graduate psychological principles of learning course at a southeastern university. Subjects had attended an average of 3.2 computer-related classes, had 4.9 years of computer experience, and watched television 11.3 hours per week.

Materials and Instruments

A 40-minute instructional module on statistics was developed using Macromedia Authorware. The computer program tracked student performance, time, and advisor use during instruction. An 18-item delayed posttest was constructed based on the content objectives for the statistical module.

Procedure

Subjects were randomly assigned to one of two levels of each independent variable: on-screen video, pull-down video, on-screen text, and pull-down text. Immediately after subjects completed the instructional module, they completed the ARCS-based attitude-toward-instruction instrument. One week later, the PALS instrument and the posttest were administered to the subjects prior to in-class study of the material covered in the instructional module.

Results

A one-way ANOVA indicated significant differences in advisor use between groups (F=3.385, p = .025). The video-based on-screen advisor condition resulted in higher advisor use (EMM=5.25) than both the text-based (EMM=.866) and video-based (EMM=1) pull-down advisor conditions, but not the text-based on-screen condition, although it was used on average almost twice as much (EMM=2.384).

A one-way ANCOVA indicated significant differences in advisor use between groups when controlling for anxiety (F=3.352, p = .026). Results were similar to the ANOVA, in which the video-based on-screen advisor condition resulted in higher advisor use (EMM=5.26) than both the text-based (EMM=.862) and video-based (EMM=.949) pull-down advisor conditions, but not the text-based on-screen condition (EMM=2.431).

One-way ANOVAs and ANCOVAs failed to yield significant differences between groups for any other measures, including PALS scores.

Pearson Product Moment Correlations indicated that advisor use was significantly related to performance during instruction (.407, p<.01) to time spent during instruction (.432, p < .01), and to television hours watched per week (.292, p < .05). Anxiety and computer classes were significantly related (.341, p < .05), as were performance during instruction and time spent during instruction (.427, p < .01) and performance during instruction and motivation (.462, p < .01). Performance during instruction was significantly related to posttest scores (.402, p < .01) and to motivation (.27, p< .05). Television hours watched was significantly related to computer experience (.283, p < .05). PALS scores were not significantly related to advisor use. Correlations performed between advisor use and PALS scores by condition indicated no significant relationship. A similar analysis of advisor use and television hours watched indicated that the significant correlation found earlier was located specifically in the text obvious condition.

Discussion

Our first expectation, that the on-screen conditions would result in more frequent advisor use than the pull-down conditions, was partially supported. Subjects who had on-screen access to an advisor used advisement more than four times as often on average than those who had pull-down access to an advisor (3.965 vs. .931). The on-screen video condition was statistically different from both pulldown conditions. The on-screen text condition, although higher than both pulldown conditions, was not statistically different. This data may indicate the modality bias against a text-based advisor which Gay, et al., [1] found can be overcome by placement of the advisor.

Our second expectation, that the video advisor would be used more frequently than the text advisor was not supported. Although the mean advisor use for the video

conditions was higher than those for the text conditions, the differences were not statistically significant.

Our third expectation, that the use of an advisor will lead to higher motivation indices in general and that video advisement in particular will result in higher motivation indices than text, was not supported. Subjects' motivation scores were in no way associated with their advisor use.

Our fourth expectation, that advisor use would be significantly correlated with performance during instruction and for the delayed posttest was partially supported. Advisor use was significantly correlated with performance during instruction but not with delayed posttest scores. Because posttest scores and performance during instruction were significantly correlated, the researchers concluded that the tests are reliable. The failure of advisor use to make a difference in delayed posttest scores may say something about the long-term effects of advisement. A more likely explanation might be that the advisement was not effective enough to make long-term gains significant. Also, because subjects were aware that their performance was not graded and that their professor would not know their performance results, subjects may not have engaged in any outside rehearsal or practice of the relevant information.

Our fifth expectation, that passive learners would use advisement less than active learners, and that this difference would be reduced or eliminated in the on-screen advisement conditions, was not supported.

References

1. Gay, G., & Mazur, J. (1993) The utility of computer tracking tools for user-centered design. *Educational Technology (Research Section), 33*(4), 45-59.
2. Lee, Y.B., & Lehman, J.D. (1993). Instructional cueing in hypermedia: A study with active and passive learners. Journal of Educational Multimedia and Hypermedia, 2 (10), 25-37
3. Smith, P.L. (1992, April). *A Model for Selecting from Supplantive and Generative Instructional Strategies for Problem-Solving Instruction.* Paper presented at the annual meeting of the American Educational Research Association, San Francisco, CA.
4. Tennyson, R.D. (1980). Instructional control strategies and content structure as design variables in concept acquisition using computer-based instruction. *Journal of Educational Psychology, 72*(4), 525-532.
5. Tennyson, R.D. (1981). Use of adaptive information for advisement in learning concepts and rules using computer-assisted instruction. American Educational Research Journal, 4, 425-438.

A Study on the Agent-based Word-recognition Learning System for Pupils with Moderate Mental Retardation

Yun-Lung Lin*, Tien-Yu Li, & Ming-Chung, Chen

National Taiwan Normal University, Taiwan

*E-mail: harrison@ice.ntnu.edu.tw

ABSTRACT

The purpose of this study is to explore the influence on the learning effectiveness for mental retardation students by using the Agent-based Word-recognition learning system. The system applied the teaching agent to increase learner's motivation and used stimulus fading strategy to enhance the learning effectiveness. A multiple probes of single-subject design was adopted. A nine-year-old pupil with moderate mental retardation participated in the study. The experiment shows that the subject can identify the target words correctly without the presence of known pictorial cues. The learning system combining teaching agent and stimulus-fading strategy is efficient in teaching word recognition for pupils with moderate retardation.

Keywords

moderate retardation, teaching agent, stimulus fading strategy

1. Introduction

Web-based learning is the trend of Computer Assisted Learning (CAL). However, very few of them are especially designed for mentally retarded students. Despite the retarded pupils have lower ability and deficiencies in abstract thinking, remembrance and concentration. However, if the content of the system could be presented in concrete ways and combined with their experience, it should be able to improve their learning performance.

Previous research had shown the effectiveness by using stimulus fading strategies in word-recognition teaching. Nevertheless, many teachers do not incline to use them because it involves labor-consuming work for preparing materials. For the purpose of removing the barriers of what are mentioned above, using computerized learning system may be more effective and efficient.

The use of agents within computer mediated learning environments is currently an important issue of the development in CAL. Pedagogical agents must support individualized learning by its rich user interface, multimodal dialog, and proper guiding[1]. This study is to find out the effect on the learning efficiency of moderate mental-retarded pupil receiving a training session of agent-based learning system, which applies the stimulus fading strategy.

2. Method
2.1 System Design
We created the teaching agent by using Microsoft Agent to provide adaptive instruction and illustration. The system embedded IBM Via Voice to support Text-to-Speech Engine(TTS). The teaching agent plays several roles, including motivating, demonstrating, guiding, questioning, and testing. To evaluate learners' learning outcomes, we use a database to collect the data that the user clicks.

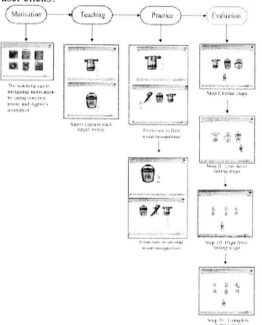

Figure 1. The System Architecture

2.2 Content
As shown in Figure 1, the system supports four phrases, including intriguing motivation, teaching activities, practicing and evaluation. The selection of the contents is based on the rules of functionality and practicability. Four functional Chinese words (towel[..], bucket[..], cloth[..], and scuffs[..]) were selected and served as target words. The system is integrated with the techniques of Agent, Text-to-Speech Engine (TTS) and some learning strategies (e.g., Multi-Hint Strategy, Situated Learning Strategy, and Read-aloud Strategy).

2.3 Stimulus Fading Strategy
Two types of stimulus fading strategies were shown as in Figure 2 and Figure 3. In terms of external stimulus-fading, a picture is presented separately in space from the word, and the picture is systematically and

gradually faded out.

Figure 2: A sample of external stimulus-fading

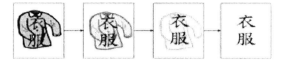

Figure 3: A sample of internal stimulus-fading

Because of concentration ability deficiency, the literature is considered that pictorial cues could interfere with pupils' attempts to deal with written words since they are likely to pay attentions to the picture instead of the words [2]. For the internal stimulus fading strategy, a picture is superimposed directly on the word and then the picture was systematically and gradually faded out. The learner could focus on the same point. The system adopted the internal stimulus-fading strategy.

3.1 Subject
A nine-year-old pupil with moderate mental retardation participated in the study. The subject was selected according to the following three criteria. First, it is on record that she was unable to recognize words taught in class. Secondly, she could follow her teacher's directions. Thirdly, she could identify pictures of familiar items.

3.2 Procedure
3.2.1 Baseline
The subject's familiarity with the target word was tested. The pupil was asked to point out the target words without cues. Each target word was assessed five times. During the baseline assessments, the researchers just recorded pupils' responses and no feedback was given.

3.2.2 Instruction
The subject had a fifteen-minute learning session in the morning five times a week. The procedures included demonstration, practice, and evaluation. The subject could not enter to the next fading step until she reached the master criteria, 80% of correct responses for each word in three consecutive sessions. Then the instruction procedure was repeated during Step II (the pictures with 45% fade out) and Step III (the pictures with 75% fade out) and final step instruction (words only).

3.2.3 Maintenance
To examine whether the subject could recognize the targets words which have been taught, maintenance tests were administered after the instruction period. No instruction was delivered during the maintenance stage.

4. Results
Figure 4 presents the date that the correct responses of the four target words during the baseline, instruction, and

maintenance sessions. The subject showed his reluctance to participate in some sessions, but this result implied that the subject could still shift his attention from the picture into the target word without much difficulty. The result also indicated that the subject could maintain his correct responses above the master level for each target word. In other words, the teaching agent learning system embedding stimulus-fading strategy was efficient in teaching word recognition to the pupil.

It is discovered that the system will equip the users with better learning effectiveness for the learning activities.

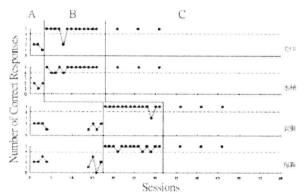

Figure 4: The number of correct responses during baseline and instruction for the subject
*A: Baseline B: Instruction C: Maintenance

5. Conclusions
In this study we examined the effects of picture fading technique on agent-based learning system for pupil with moderate disabilities. The result of this study showed that the learning system can be an effective and efficient teaching tool for teaching pupils with moderate mental retardation.

Based on this study, major findings were:
1. For pupils with mental retardation, using stimulus fading strategies on word-recognition instruction can be an effective method.
2. The learning system embedded teaching agent can arouse learners' motivation.
3. Fading strategy can be adopted to fade pictures and text, and to develop software packages with a view to reduce teachers' pain when preparing teaching materials.

6. Reference

[1] Dowling, C. (November, 2000), *Educational agents and social construction of knowledge: some issues and implications*, Paper presented at the conference of International Conference on Computer-Assisted Instruction 2000.

[2] Sue, W. R. (written in Chinese), (1992), *A comparison of two stimulus fading procedures in teaching functional academic skills to students with moderate mental retardation*, Unpublished master thesis, National Changhua Normal University.

Computer anxiety and skill-based class organization in computer literacy education

Akira Harada, Torii Minoru, Michio Nakanishi, Hideo Masuda, Tsuyoshi Sugano

Osaka University, Japan

(harada@hus.osaka-u.ac.jp, naka@ime.cmc.osaka-u.ac.jp)

Abstract

The relationship of computer anxiety and skill-based class organization was investigated in a sample of 277 individuals who were attending the computer literacy course in Osaka University. The "operation anxiety" is defined by four questions in the questionnaire survey, and the scores are analyzed using three major factors: class, faculty and time. Results indicate that the average scores of the operation anxiety in the less experienced class significantly decreased by the half of the semester, which proves the effectiveness of the class organization method. In contrast to it, the anxiety scores of the experienced class students increased. The authors believe the increase came from a kind of intrinsic motivation and is no problem for those students to learn more challenging tasks.

1. Introduction

There has been a great deal of research on computer anxiety from many aspects. For example, the relationship of computer anxiety and computer experience was presented in [1][2][3]. The authors have been teaching a computer literacy course for freshmen in Faculty of Human Science, Osaka University, since 1995. While many students do have a certain exposure to computers in high school, it is difficult to assume that all students are computer literate upon graduation of high school. The authors have adopted the class re-organization method for four years based on the mid-term exam which requires hands-on computer operations [4]. This paper examines whether skill-based class organization would be effective in reducing computer anxiety in individuals in computer literacy education.

2. Method

2.1 Participants and instrumentation

The sample was comprised of 277 first year undergraduate students in Human Sciences and in Letters, who took the computer literacy course at Osaka University in 2001.

There were three questionnaire surveys; prior to beginning class in April, at mid-term in June, and at term end in September. The questions were printed on a sheet of paper, and students were asked to express how they feel at each point in time: 1="not at all (strongly disagree)", 2="a little", 3="a fair amount", 4="much" and 5="strongly agree". A survey instrument consisted of 79 questions, whose answers were options on a 5-point Likert scale as written above, and was designed to measure the experience of computer use, computer skill level, attitude toward computer and computer anxiety. The number of three questions were 12, 12, 16 and 39, respectively.

In this paper, the authors will consider "operation anxiety" to be closely related to computer operations. Scores of the following four questions are evaluated as the operation anxiety:

(1) It scares me to think that I could destroy the computer by hitting the wrong key.

(2) I feel insecure whenever I think of being assigned a job which requires computer operation after graduation.

(3) I feel at ease when I see someone is struggling with his/her computer.

(4) I feel apprehensive about using computers in front of others.

2.2 Class organization

In 2001, the authors planned to find out the effect of class organization. Students majoring in Human Sciences were physically organized into three groups according to the skill level scores which were calculated from the pre-class questionnaire survey except the anxiety scores. The authors assume that skill level is in proportion to the computer experience. The students who obtained high scores were grouped into class A. The second high students were into class B and the most un-experienced students were into class C.

On the other hand, students majoring Letters were also asked to answer the same questionnaire survey. Though the scores of the questions were not used for physical class organization, the authors organized three "virtual" classes based on the scores of the pre-class questions (again, except the anxiety scores). As in the case of Human Sciences, the authors call this virtual three classes as A, B and C, respectively.

After the seven-week class hours, the authors set a mid-term examination that demands 1-hour hands on work, because there were differences between students

Table 1. Significant transitions

	Faculty	Class	Time period	Score transition
*1	Letters	C	mid-term to term end	Declining
*2	Human Sciences	C	pre-term to mid-term	Inclining
*3	Human Sciences	C	pre-term to term end	Declining
*4	Letters	A	pre-term to term end	Inclining
*5	Human Sciences	A	pre-term to mid-term	Inclining

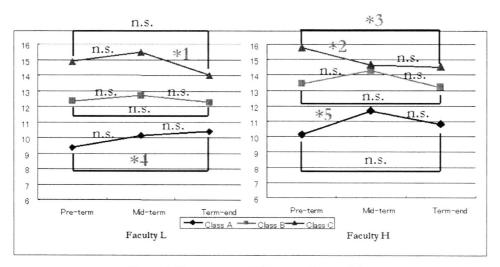

Figure 1. Mean scores of the operation anxiety

how fast they got accustomed to computer operations in class. The exam scores of class A was the highest and C was the lowest in Human Sciences classes, which means the class organization based on the pre-class questionnaire survey was adequate.

3. Result

To determine factors that affected the "operation anxiety", the authors used three-way ANOVA. There were three factors: *faculty* (two levels: Human Sciences and Letters), *class* based on pre-class computer experience (three levels: class A, B and C), and *time* (three levels: pre-class, mid-term and term end). The result of the multiple comparisons between three main factors using Tukey-Kramer procedure is shown in Figure 1. In Figure 1, the asterisk (*) above a straight line shows that the transition of the mean anxiety scores is significant. Table 1 summarizes the significant transitions.

The findings are twofold. First, the anxiety scores of class A students in Human Sciences and Letters increased as shown by *4 and *5. The authors believe this anxiety is not the kind of interference but intrinsic motivation. Second, there exists time delay of the decrease as shown by *1, *2 and *3. The score decreased earlier in Human

Sciences than in Letters because students who have had less computer experience began to feel at ease in the first half of the course.

4. Conclusion

The relationship of computer anxiety and skill-based class organization was investigated in the computer literacy education. The mean score of the operation anxiety in the class of experienced students increased, whereas it decreased in the class of less experienced students.

References

[1] J.Beckers and H.G.Schmidt : "The structure of computer anxiety: a six-factor model", Computers in Human Behavior, 17, 35-49 (2001).

[2] N.Bozionelos : "Computer anxiety: relationship with computer experience and prevalence", Computers in Human Behavior, 17, 213-224 (2001).

[3] D.McIlroy, B.Bunting, K.Tierney and M. Gordon : "The relation of gender and background experience to self-reported computing anxieties and cognitions", Computers in Human Behavior, 17, 21-23 (2001).

[4] A.Harada, M.Nakanishi and M. Komori : "Evaluation of class organization in computer literacy classes", ICCE, 460-466 (2000)

When Technology is Mandatory - Factors Influencing Users Satisfaction

Julia S. J. Yeo, Aybüke Aurum, Meliha Handzic, Peter Parkin
School of Information Systems, Technology and Management
University of New South Wales, Sydney, NSW, Australia 2052
{julia.yeo; aybuke; m.handzic; p.parkin}@unsw.edu.au

Abstract

One commonly acknowledged factor in the successful implementation of any application or information system is user satisfaction. This paper studied users' judgments on a new technology in an educational context. This study found that, while perceived usefulness and perceived ease of use each had a positive correlation with user satisfaction, there are likely to be additional factors that contribute to user satisfaction.

1: Introduction and Prior Research

Significant progress has been made over the last decade in predicting user acceptance of information systems and software applications. In particular, substantial theoretical and empirical support has accumulated in favour of the technology acceptance model (TAM) [1,5,8]. TAM theorises that an individual's behaviour intention to use a system is determined by his or her perceived usefulness in that system and his or her perceived ease of use of that system. Perceived usefulness is the degree to which an individual believes that a particular information system would enhance his or her job performance. Perceived ease of use is the degree to which a person believes that using a particular system would be free of effort [5]. Other studies have since extended TAM to include other variables such as attitude towards the technology, information quality, system quality, individual impact such as users experience, and organisational impact to be drivers of user acceptance [6,7,8].

One of the findings reported in a recent study by Bhattacherjee [4, p.1] was that *user satisfaction is influenced by perceived usefulness and users' confirmation of expectation from prior IS use.* Results of Baroudi *et al*'s study [3] indicate that high user satisfaction with a system leads to greater system usage. Most of the above-mentioned studies have researched user satisfaction and acceptance in situations where users have options in choosing their tools and systems. However in many industrial and educational environments only particular technology is available to users. This raises questions as to whether the user satisfaction/acceptance influences of TAM apply in these mandatory

environments. This paper attempts to address some of these questions by investigating the end users' perception of usefulness and ease of use of the MS Access application and their satisfaction with the application in a mandatory situation.

2: Method

This study applied a quasi-experimental research design with user satisfaction, perceived usefulness and perceived ease of use as the variables. The participants were undergraduate students attending an introductory database course at the University of New South Wales. Majority of the participants were first year undergraduate students from Information Systems (IS) and Software Engineering with a small proportion of students in their second year of studies from the School of Computer Science. Students were required to implement their database using MS Access as part of a course assignment. They had to learn how to operate MS Access on their own to complete their assignment. There was no training provided although trivial "how-to" support was available from computer laboratory supervisors. The assignment required students to design/create forms, tables, specific queries, and specific reports.

The research was conducted using a short questionnaire by drawing from a number of existing surveys that have been shown to have validity [2,5]. The questions were modified to suit the task environment and survey population. The subjects' responses were captured on five point Likert scales with one being strongly disagree and five being strongly agree. The questionnaires were distributed during tutorial class sessions, one week before the end of the semester. A total of 250 subjects voluntarily participated in the study and 215 usable responses were obtained.

3: Data Analysis, Results and Discussion

In this paper, a descriptive and analytical statistical approach was taken to examine the positive direct relationship between perceived usefulness, perceived ease of use and satisfaction. This analysis was undertaken primarily by applying a least-squares linear regression approach using satisfaction as the dependant variable. In addition, ANOVA tests were used to examine some of the potentially confounding factors.

The averages of user satisfaction, perceived usefulness and perceived ease of use were 3.45, 3.77, and 3.43 respectively. High levels of satisfaction were evident with 83% of subjects strongly agreeing or agreeing with positive satisfaction-related questions.

Software Engineering and Computer Science student subjects had on average slightly more technology experience (5.7 years) compared to their IS counterparts (5.61 years) and 34% of the subjects were female. There was no significant difference in satisfaction levels between the different groups of students by degree or gender.

The correlation between perceived usefulness and perceived ease of use is 0.392. The correlation between each of these variables and satisfaction was 0.405 and 0.410 respectively. Thus, there is moderate support for our hypothesis that perceived usefulness and perceived ease of use are associated with and are perhaps drivers of satisfaction. Figure 1 presents a graphical overview that is also consistent with our hypothesis.

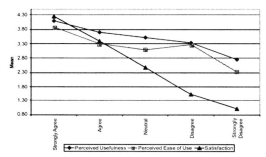

Figure 1. Perceived Usefulness, Perceived Ease of Use and User Satisfaction

The linear regression coefficients of perceived usefulness (0.38) and perceived ease of use (0.34) were both significant ($P<0.001$). Although this supports the contention that these variables contribute to satisfaction, there are certainly other factors involved as together the variables account for only 24% of the variation in satisfaction.

4: Conclusions

The main findings of this study indicate that both perceived usefulness and perceived ease of use have a positive correlation with user satisfaction in the situation when users are given no other choice but to accept application software. This suggests that, in a mandatory environment, potential user assessments of the perceived usefulness and perceived ease of use of a new or proposed system may provide useful insights into later user satisfaction with an ensuing system as well as system usage and the success of an implementation project. The tertiary educational sector in particular seems rich in these mandatory software environments where students are increasingly being expected to use both web-enabled enrolment and administrative software as well as university course-related software.

These findings are tempered by the nature of the subjects in that they are quite likely to have pre-conceived positive attitudes toward technology. Attitude may well proved to be a major additional driver of satisfaction in a mandatory setting. In order to examine these issues in a general manner, further research is required involving other tasks, context and user groups.

Future work may also examine whether the linear model of the relationship between our experimental variables used herein is the most suitable.

5: Acknowledgments

The authors would like to acknowledge Robert Booth and Irem Sevinç, Business Information Technology students, from School of Information Systems, Technology and Management, University of New South Wales for their valuable contribution to this paper.

6: References

[1] Adams, D., Nelson, R., Todd, P., Perceived usefulness, ease of use, and usage of information technology: a replication. *MIS Quarterly*, June 1992, 227-274

[2] Bailey, J. and Pearson, W. Development of a Tool for Measuring and Analysing Computer User Satisfaction. *Management Science*. 1983. 29(5), 530-545

[3] Baroudi, J.J., Olson, M.H., Ives, B. An Empirical Study of the Impact of User Involvement on System Usage and Information Satisfaction. *Communications of the ACM*, 29(3), March 1986, 232-238

[4] Bhattacherjee, A. Understanding Information Systems Continuance: An expectation-confirmation model. *MIS Quarterly*. 25(3), Sept 2001. 351-370

[5] Davis, F.D. Perceived Usefulness, perceived ease of use, and user acceptance of information technology. *MIS Quarterly*. 13(3), 1989. 319 339

[6] DeLone, W. and McLean, E. Information Systems Success: The Quest for the Dependent Variable, *Information Systems Research*. 1(3), March 1999 60-93

[7] Lederer, A.L., Maupin, D.J., Sena, M.P., Zhuang, Y. The technology acceptance model and the World Wide Web, *Decision Support Systems*, 29, 2000, 269-282

[8] Venkatesh, V. and Davis, F.D. A Theoretical Extension of the Technology Acceptance Model: Four Longitudinal Field Studies. *Management Science*, 46(2), 2000, 186-204

Learning attitudes decisive to students' cognitive and knowledge development

Dr. Anders Jakobsson
Malmö/Lund University, Sweden
Teacher Education
205 06 Malmö
anders.jakobsson@lut.mah.se

Abstract

This study gives an account of a teaching situation with 20 student's aged 14-15. The students have worked with a problem focussed on the greenhouse effect, based on a problem solving way of working. They have worked in groups and have had access to ICT, books, articles and a special resource page on the Internet. The purpose has been to account for the ways in which the students' knowledge develops during the problem solving process and what the factors are that influence learning. In order to explain the causes I have constructed five different "learning attitudes". These are: Creators of meaning, Constructors of knowledge, Ethical evaluators, Reproducers and Maintainers of relationships. When these learning attitudes are related to the students' knowledge development it becomes evident that the creators of meaning, constructors of knowledge and ethical evaluators have a predominantly stronger cognitive and knowledge development that the reproducers and maintainers of relationships.

Introduction

Having access to ICT is often described as a prerequisite in order that students can develop new knowledge and acquire a deeper understanding of a subject. However studies about teaching and learning have not been able to unequivocally demonstrate the fact that students learn better, in-depth or more extensively with the help of computers (Pedersen 1998, SITE 1998, CSCL 1999, et al). The question of whether students learn better through the use of computers is wrongly formulated due to the fact that it is grounded in an unreflective technical-optimistic approach which in turn risks to overlook any critical analysis of the actual possibilities of the use of information technology. From a historical perspective Cuban (1989) describes how every new technological improvement during the twentieth century has resulted in expectations of new ways of working and a more efficient learning environment within various educational organisations. Technology when assimilated has resulted in certain changes, but not to the extent that has been expected. Most of the basic structures of teaching, organisational forms and theories of knowledge have remained unaffected. Cuban contends that there is a risk that this new technology will be no exception. During recent years educational researchers have instead turned their focus from technology to ways in which different forms of collaboration and interaction between students enhance learning. This interest is based on the growing concordance among teachers and researchers about the positive effects of collaboration for student performances within, for example, the area of problem solving (Hertz-Lazarowitz & Miller, 1992, Slavin 1992, Johnsson & Johnsson 1994). O'Donnel and King (1999) contend that research involving "peer learning" above all strives to describe and understand how interaction between students influences learning perspectives in a theoretical as well as practical way. Palincsar and Herrenkohl (1999) contend that effective collaborative learning implies that the students need to be involved in a socialisation process intent on creating a common linguistic and social world in the classroom. Teaching needs to train students to publicise their experiences and thoughts about the content of teaching. In their study (Palincsar & Herrenkohl 1999) concerning the problem solving capacity of students in groups, those who attained the highest results were students who had had this specific training.

It is however important to be aware of the fact that these studies have not, in any distinct way, been able to describe what the factors are that influence student learning when a problem solving and information seeking way of working is applied. Studies still lack descriptions of the ways in which students' learning develops when they collaborate in groups as well as studies which, much more thoroughly, can describe the factors that influence students' learning during different forms of collaboration.

The study

This study comprises 20 students (14-15 years old) who, during a period of seven weeks, worked with a problem focussing on the greenhouse effect and the future climate on earth. The exercise was constructed so as to encourage a problem solving and explorative way of working. The problem is concerned with earth's global climate, the ensuing greenhouse effect and the ways in which mankind's activities may influence the balance between them. The students have been presented with an actual dilemma in the form of two completely contradictory descriptions of the earth's future climate. The first suggests that the Northern Hemisphere is moving towards a new ice age, the second that the earth's global temperature is slowly increasing. The challenge for the students has been to describe the basic phenomena and factors that influence the earth's global temperature in various ways, decide on the relevance of the accumulated information and subsequently how this information can be used in order to try to solve the problem. During the information-seeking phase of the problem solving process the students have had access to ICT, books, articles and a website with resources (databases).

The students have worked with the problem in groups of four. The teacher has functioned more as a mentor, when compared to the traditional teacher role. During the problem solving process the groups have to a great extent worked independently and there have been no regular teaching situations. The purpose of this has been to study the factors that motivate the students' cognitive and knowledge development as well as to determine how collaboration and access to ICT has enhanced learning. It has been imperative to carefully observe situations in which particular students develop a usage of scientific concepts and change their understanding of the problem in a qualitative way. Each student's understanding has been determined by tests before and after the process, and has also been analysed during the course of the process. In order to be able to analyse and describe the students' cognitive and knowledge development during the problem solving process it has been necessary to conduct a quantitative study based on video recordings in the classroom.

The aims of the study have been formulated as follows:

- To account for what the factors and situations are that enhance students' learning and understanding of scientific concepts and theories during different phases of the problem solving process.

- To account for ways in which interaction and collaboration between students enhance their learning and understanding of scientific concepts and theories during problem solving in groups.

Developmental categories – one way of describing students' development of knowledge

In order to describe students' cognitive and knowledge it has been necessary to construct relatively detailed *developmental categories*. The purpose has been to create an implement with which to describe the students' successive development and expansion of knowledge and understanding during the problem solving process. The *developmental categories* have created the possibility of being able to interpret the students' cognitive and knowledge development during different phases throughout the process, not just before and after. The goal has been to create clear and concise differences between the different categories as well as being able to describe a qualitative ascension regarding knowledge and understanding of the problem. The six developmental categories can, in general terms, be described as follows:

The six developmental categories

I. The greenhouse effect – what is it?
II. The greenhouse effect has to do with the ozone layer and acidification.
III. The earth can be compared to a greenhouse.
IV. The greenhouse effect has to do with gases in the atmosphere.
V. The greenhouse effect has always existed, but the combustion of fossilised fuel enhances the effect.
VI. The greenhouse effect is a balance between incoming solar radiation and outgoing heat radiation.

Examples of cognitive and knowledge development during the problem solving process

In the following section a few examples will be given of the placement of some of the students in developmental categories during separate working shifts throughout the project. This makes it possible to trace the way in which each student develops his/her knowledge and understanding throughout the process. In Figure 1 it is possible to determine four of the students' points of departure in regard to knowledge at the outset of the study as well as accumulated knowledge at the completion of the study. By a thorough and time-consuming analysis of approx. 50 hours of video recordings it has also been possible to ascertain a number of *quantitative developmental situations* during the problem solving process. These can be considered to be clear indications of the fact that a student has developed knowledge and understanding of the problem on a new and higher level than before and can thereby be placed in a higher *developmental category.*

	Prior to work shifts V 5-7	4/3 shift 1	5/3 shift 2	11/3 shift 3	12/3 shift 4	16/3 shift 5	23/3 shift 6	25/3 shift 7	After the work shifts V12-13
Carl	DC IV			DC V			DC VI		DC VI
Tova	DC II		DC III+IV	0	0		DC V		DC V
Evert	DC I		0				DC II	0	DC II
Agnes	DC I	0	0	0	0	DC II	DC III	0	DC III

Figure 1. Placement of four students in developmental categories (DC) during the problem solving process. (0 implies that the student has been absent).

What are the influences to students' cognitive and knowledge development during the process?

If one compares all the students' knowledge and understanding prior to and after the work process it becomes evident that the students have gone through a total of 51 *developmental steps*. During analysis of the video recordings it has been possible to identify 39 *developmental situations*. The video recordings have made it possible to study in detail that which has motivated the students to take these *qualitative developmental steps*. This was done by mapping each student's development during analysis and studying what occurred prior to the acquisition of a *qualitative developmental step*. The results of the analysis indicate that the following factors have the greatest influence:

a. Learning attitudes
b. The ability to collaborate.
c. Using computers as a means to enhance critical thinking.

Learning attitudes

The study has thus shown that there is a connection between students' different learning attitudes and their cognitive and knowledge development. The students' varying success can however not be solely related to the different learning strategies they use. The students' fundamental approach to science, ways of working, collaboration, information seeking, learning and theories of knowledge all influence their attitudes to this specific teaching situation. I have observed and constructed five different approaches that I have chosen to call "learning attitudes". These five learning attitudes are:

• Creators of meaning
• Constructors of knowledge
• Ethical evaluators
• Reproducers
• Maintainers of relationships

Creators of meaning

Creators of meaning attempt to place the content of what is taught into an understandable and meaningful context. He/she strives to understand how this content relates to everyday living, the outside world and what it implies in relation to his/her own life. Meaning created in this way thus becomes a process whereby content is continuously set in relation to as well as compared to one's own life and world-view. Collaboration, discussions and reasoning with other students become a driving force and an important part of the creator of meaning's learning process. He/she is given the opportunity of communicating, conversing, questioning, formulating hypotheses and experiencing how others react to different assumptions.

Constructors of knowledge

Constructors of knowledge strive towards independently building and constructing a comprehensive structure and understanding of the subject matter. Scientific concepts and theories are compared and related to one other in such a way that a successively increasing knowledge and understanding develops. If constructors of knowledge find that their own structure of knowledge is weak or lacks substance, he/she proceeds further in order to seek new information. Here the construction of knowledge has to do mainly with an inner process of thought that to a great extent is independent of one's surroundings. Collaboration and discussions with other students are not decisive for constructors of knowledge to succeed in building or constructing an understanding of their own.

Ethical evaluators

A prerequisite for ethical evaluators to develop knowledge of Science is for the teaching situation to include discussions on questions of value and ethical standpoints. When this is focused on in teaching, ethical evaluators become interested and absorbed which in turn motivates them towards an understanding of scientific concepts and theories. Collaboration and discussions are important elements in the learning process of ethical evaluators. In such situations he/she is given the opportunity of sharing views with others, developing new ideas and discussing hypotheses. By listening to the ideas and perspectives of others they enhance their own understanding and learning.

Reproducers

Reproducers regard Science as a subject concerned with facts and isolated sections that do not need to be fitted into any context to be understood. This type of student does not search for meaning nor try to relate that which he/she reads into any meaningful whole. He/she normally looks for complete and reproductive answers and has difficulties relating questions, discovering contradictions and making comparisons. Connections and patterns between scientific concepts and theories are thus not clear and the subject matter becomes difficult to understand. If the teaching situation does not include elements

that clarify various connections or elements that help develop the students' metacognition, there is a risk that the reproducer retains his/her learning attitude and only develops surface knowledge. Collaboration gives the reproducer the opportunity of experiencing how other students work, the strategies they use as well as how they reason and discuss.

Maintainers of relationships

Maintainers of relationships do not have any specific interest in Science. Often, he/she has not understood the value or significance of the subject and experiences it as meaningless and uninteresting. School however plays an important part in the daily life of a maintainer of relationships in that it offers opportunities for meeting friends and creating a network of social contacts. As a substantial part of the school day is used to maintain and develop this social network this gradually develops into the main task at school. To maintainers of relationships, collaboration and group discussions are an important and exciting part of their school experience. During these situations he/she is given additional opportunities to develop that which he/she considers most important and a large part of the time is spent discussing issues of little relevance to the school subject.

Learning attitudes and cognitive and knowledge development

If one relates the students' cognitive and knowledge development to the learning attitude they adhere to, a clear pattern can be ascertained. This pattern becomes clear when related to the level of knowledge attained by the pupil or related to the number of developmental categories the student undergoes. The 12 students who attained some of the two highest developmental categories can be classed as being either creators of meaning, constructors of knowledge or ethical evaluators. A statistical calculation of the mean related to the progress of these students showed the value to be 5.3 of a possible 6.0. The same pattern becomes evident when one considers the students whose cognitive and knowledge development is intense during the problem solving process. Among the ten students who have undergone three or four developmental stages, nine can be classed as being either creators of meaning, constructors of knowledge or ethical evaluators. This study shows an evident connection between a positive development of cognition and knowledge during the problem solving process and the learning attitude the student posits.

If one instead focuses on the six students who only pass through one or two developmental stages and who do not have any of the two highest developmental categories, the picture changes. Of these students, four can be classed as reproducers and two as maintainers of relationships. A statistical calculation of the mean related to the progress of these students showed the value to be 3.3 of a possible 6.0. There are marked differences in the results between the students in the successful learning attitude group and the students in the less successful group. The students' learning attitudes seem to be of crucial importance to the development of knowledge during the problem solving process.

Collaboration influences students' cognitive and knowledge development

Analysis of the students' cognitive and knowledge development clearly shows that the ways in which the students make use of collaborative ways of working is one of the factors that has the clearest connection to a positive cognitive and knowledge development. In this study it has been possible to deduce the cognitive and knowledge development of specific students from different collaborative situations during the problem solving process. This possibility has, to my knowledge, not been evident in other studies. I have been able to identify some types of collaboration that seem to me to be more productive than others. These are:

Productive types of collaboration
a. Asymmetric collaboration
b. Collaboration that results in a change of perspective
c. Collaboration that develops the student's theory of knowledge

Asymmetric collaboration implies that two students with relatively big differences in levels of knowledge and understanding collaborate in such a way that it is of benefit to them both. For one of the students collaboration can imply a reappraisal of previous assumptions leading to understanding on a new level. For the other student collaboration implies that he/she needs to restructure and reorganise his/her own knowledge in order to convince a fellow student. Collaboration resulting in a change of perspective also leads to a qualitative development of knowledge and understanding for the students involved. Collaboration leads them to discover new perspectives and to develop new understanding on a higher level. Collaboration that develops the student's theory of knowledge does not, in effect, result in an exchange of information or knowledge. Rather, it results in the student being able to develop his/her own way of relating to knowledge and learning.

The study indicates that there are relatively large individual differences in the ability of being able to utilise collaboration for one's own development of knowledge. 14 of the study's 20 students use collaboration as their most frequent way of working, four of the students collaborate as easily as they work independently and two of the students seldom collaborate. Girls in general are better at taking advantage of opportunities for collaboration and are also able to utilise these instances more productively. The study also indicates that collaboration should not be forced; instead it should exist as a free choice and a possible resource during the work process. It is also evident that students need training in order to develop an effective and progressive capacity for collaboration.

References

CSCL (1999). Computer Support for Collaborative learning. Conference in Palo Alto, Califonia 1999.

Hertz-Lazarowitz, R. och Miller, N. (1992) (Ed). *Interaction in cooperative groups.* Cambridge University Press. Cambridge.

Johnsson, D & Johnsson R (1994). Learning *Together and Alone,* Allyn and Bacon, Boston.

O'Donell, A. & King, A. (1999). Cognitive Perspectives on Peer Learning, A. In A. O'Donell & A. King (Eds.), *Cognitive Perspectives on Peer Learning.* London: Lawrence Erlbaum.

Palincsar, S. & Herrenkohl, L. (1999). Designing Collaborative Contexts, In A. O'Donell & A. King (Eds.), *Cognitive Perspectives on Peer Learning.* London: Lawrence Erlbaum.

Pedersen. J. (1998). *Informationstekniken i skolan: En forskningsöversikt.* Skolverket. Liber distribution. Stockholm.

SITE (1998) *Society for Information Technology & Teacher Education.* 9 th International Conferece in Washington 1998.

Slavin; R (1992). When and Why Does Cooperative Learning Increase Achievement. I Hertz-Lazarowitz och Miller (Ed) 1992. Interaction in cooperative groups. Cambridge University Press. Cambridge.

A Breath of Fresh Air:
Reflecting on the Changing Practices of Assessment Online

Meg O'Reilly
Teaching and Learning Centre
Southern Cross University, NSW 2480
AUSTRALIA

Abstract

"Prior to a flight we are reminded that in an emergency we are to place the oxygen mask on our own faces before we place them on a child to ensure we can assist the child. Unfortunately, with regard to teacher learning... we spend a great deal of time placing oxygen masks on other people's faces while we ourselves are suffocating" (Zederayko & Ward, 1999: 36 [28]).

To breathe in some new ideas on assessment for learners in the changing online world, academic staff need to have time, energy and will for fresh reflections and collective dialogue upon their innovations. This paper sets out the backdrop for an action research project which is proposed to investigate how we might improve our strategies for assessing student learning in the computer-mediated context of higher education.

Introduction

Action research has credibility and currency as a research tool within educational contexts. As such this method has been chosen as the basis for a research project in an Australian university which aims to:

- focus staff on their own adaptations to the changing situation of teaching and learning in the context offered by the online environment
- raise awareness of assessment possibilities offered by online approaches to teaching and learning
- assist staff to reconceptualise and improve assessment practices for the online context
- support staff in authoring and publishing their own action learning activities in journal articles and conference papers.

The paper describes a range of issues preliminary to the research project, and thereby drops the oxygen mask down within reach of academic staff.

Traditional notions of assessment

A traditional notion of assessment is that it is an event that is separate from and follows the teaching activities. In this case, assessment is considered to provide a measure of learning, and thus enables accreditation. Furthermore, this notion advocates a scientific approach in that efficiency, reliability, and technical defensibility must be evident in all assessments. Such a notion of assessment also implies a view of the general processes of teaching and learning – that knowledge is relatively stable and defined, and that learning occurs through the transmission of such knowledge. In this model, testing is required to confirm any evidence of learning, and the locus of control resides with the teacher.

There is now an increasing awareness that the purposes and roles of assessment are much broader than previously appreciated (Dochy and McDowell, 1997 [10]; Biggs, 1999 [4]). Far from being a post hoc activity, assessment is now clearly moving into the centre of our teaching and learning considerations (Morgan and O'Reilly, 1999 [20]) with student learning as its core priority. Research into student learning has consistently found assessment to be **the** focus of students' attention, determining how they prioritise their study time, what they regard as relevant to their goals, and the kinds of learning approaches they bring to bear (Dekkers et al, 1992 [9]; Lockwood, 1992 [16]; Ramsden, 1997 [25]; Rowntree, 1977 [26]). Assessment is now commonly seen as the primary mechanism through which several agendas are impacted – i.e. how learning opportunities are created, feedback is provided and learners are motivated – rather than simply being an end-of-term event that grades, sorts and reports on performance.

At the same time, developing effective assessment practices is a process considered integral to course design. While on the one hand the process of assessment needs to be efficient, reliable, valid and technically supported, it also needs to be internally consistent i.e. the learning objectives need to be clearly conveyed in measurable terms, and the learning activities must be both developmental in nature and in keeping with the final assessment task. Constructive alignment (Biggs, 1999 [4]) is a term which describes such an internal consistency within a subject between its learning objectives, student activities and the assessment tasks.

Now that constructive alignment is reasonably common currency in higher education, all the take-off and landing gear of our assessment practices can be said to be in working order, and there has been little need for emergency measures except in isolated cases within institutions.

Moving assessment online

Throughout this period of telecommunications innovation in higher education, now in its fourth decade,

a significant level of exploration has been occurring within universities regarding the ways in which to make full use of emerging opportunities. However, a good understanding of how can we improve the strategies for assessing student learning in the computer-mediated context of higher education is yet to develop (Alexander and McKenzie, 1998 [1]). From a more optimistic standpoint McDowell (1996) declares:
"The possibility that innovative assessment encourages students to take a deep approach to their learning and foster intrinsic interest in their studies is widely welcomed" (in McAlpine and Higgison, 2000: 4.1 [18]).

Clearly we are challenged by this new medium which offers opportunities for dynamic and integrated presentation methods, high levels of activity and interactivity, as well as affording more and improved support for students as they progress through their studies (Peters, 2000 [24]). In terms of bringing assessment to life in an online context, our task as educators is to actively engage learners in assessment for learning.

The important thing will be to obtain assurances that the constructive alignment of our teaching is evident to our students, ourselves and to other stakeholders. While this principle of constructive alignment (Biggs, 1999 [4]) applies to all modes of teaching and learning, it is of special significance in the online environment since not all assessment tasks or methods might translate to the new medium. Alternatively the existing methods of assessment may not suffice to address the new skills and approaches to learning which might be the result of learning online. Assessment for learning online therefore also requires that the tasks we are asking students to undertake are authentic and relevant to the full list of learning outcomes we are hoping students achieve.

An abundance of anecdotal wisdom

From reading the current literature on teaching, learning and assessment online it seems that academic staff who have experimented and reflected upon their innovations, have yet to express their insights in a coherent way which adds to an appropriate theoretical framework. A framework for online assessment as it supports teacher-directed, student-directed or peer-directed approaches is available in O'Reilly (2002 [22]) and it is hoped to further develop this through research.

In general, the literature reveals assessment methods which cover both individual and group approaches e.g. the quizzes and tests which can be taken online by individual learners, as well as the interactive forms of dialogue, debate and presentation which require the joint engagement of more than one person. A recent publication of international case studies by Murphy, Walker and Webb (2001 [21]) provides four well articulated cases under the heading 'Teaching and Assessment Issues'. While the academic staff who have shared their experiences in these cases have provided exemplary critical reflection upon their own practices,

once again reference to sustained research does not go beyond the evaluative format which examines one's practices in isolation from peers.

More critical research and that which provides a broader or more longitudinal perspective than "what we've done at our place, and how it worked" is urgently being sought (Mason, 2001 [17]). Educators now need to take some deep abdominal breaths rather than embark upon another trial and error style implementation of online assessment. For academics to deeply reflect upon the suitability of their assessment approaches for the online context there needs to be a focus of support through a process of practitioner based collaborative and self-review.

Quality assurance, benchmarking our teaching

While it is commonly assumed that academic staff who have been appointed to undertake assessment of student learning must be by definition competent and capable of doing so, this may be rather a shaky assumption, given that staff are usually appointed for their contributions to disciplinary research and scholarship. In order to enhance the capability of our staff in both teaching and assessment, the benchmarks of quality need to be made explicit and the achievement of these must be supported by staff development programs aimed at exploring the established institutional guidelines for assessment, marking and grading.

Workshops, 'clinics' and collaborative attention to the details of the art of assessment can often occur as a result of institutional strategy or as components of accredited courses e.g. Graduate Certificate in Teaching and Learning. In some cases in Australian universities such scholarship in teaching is mandatory and this effectively supports moves to enhance the nexus between teaching and research (Melrose, 2001 [19]).

In the online context, a coordinated and scholarly approach to assessment is even more critical, since staff are often simultaneously coming to terms with the technical demands of the environment while also concerning themselves with the substance of an assessment activity. The need for strategic support has been specified by Stephens, Bull and Wade (1998 [27]) who reported on collaborative developments across several institutions in the UK in the design and implementation of Computer Assisted Assessment packages. In their recommendations to structure support for pedagogically sound assessment approaches in the online context Stephens, Bull and Wade (1998 [27]) suggest coordination strategies at institutional and departmental levels, the establishment of liaison committees between schools/faculties and service units, the allocation of innovations and development funds, staff development programs, evaluation procedures and the establishment of standards (pedagogic, operational and technical).

To measure oneself and one's practice against such institutional benchmarks as reported by Stephens, Bull and Wade (1998 [27]) requires conscious attention by academic staff and is best achieved through collaboration with a critical friend (Brockbank and McGill, 1998 [6]), and as a focus for research.

Strategies for professional development

Lifelong learning

How many University teachers are in a constant search for understanding and continuous improvement of their professional practices? Without fully searching the literature, I would hazard a guess from my experiences in working with a whole host of staff across the tertiary sector, that **most** academic staff endeavour to have consideration for their own effectiveness as teachers. At times this may be called 'the will to survive' and might relate to either the need for securing a job within the current context of casualisation of employment, or the need to survive an allocation of some challenging teaching duties.

In some cases, this desire for effectiveness is driven by a sincere wish to support student learning, to share knowledge and its construction. In other cases, the imperative for reflection and improvement can become overshadowed over time by contentment with a familiar and workable status quo. If you feel you know how to use the oxygen mask, do you bother to pay attention with each and every presentation on take-off?

Academic staff development

Whatever constraints or affordances accompany each of our situations, as educators, we have responsibilities to our students to be active in our ongoing pursuit of understanding and continuous improvement of our professional practice. But how do we do this? Where do we turn for some non-punitive assistance with improving our teaching? Reflections on our own teaching and learning approaches can be supported through a number of avenues such as – regular collection of feedback sheets from students, internal or external peer review of our teaching resources and lesson plans, collegial review of our performance by staff in the Academic Staff Development Unit (or similar), and the more formal processes and documentation involved in subject and course review.

Even with the support of professional development and quality review systems within our own institutions, how do we keep abreast of the changing dimensions of higher education as it seeks to incorporate technological advances into its mainstream activities? Studies have revealed that academic staff development practices in Australian Universities either lag behind the pace of innovative teaching activities (Ellis, O'Reilly and Debreceny, 1998 [11]), or the details of such programs are closely guarded behind firewalls. Each institution which does not work on the principle of open access to staff development information, seeks to reinvent resources and staff development activities for their own context. This conveys an impression that professional development is a key to the organisation's competitive edge rather than a fundamental and ubiquitous obligation to our students (O'Reilly, Ellis and Newton, 2000 [23]).

Critical reflection and action research

As well as institutional professional development programs and accredited courses, self-reflection is also a powerful mechanism by which to develop a deeper understanding of one's own familiarity with current educational theories, as well as one's competence and confidence with the teaching and learning process. Using a professional journal in the course of one's practice is a commonly suggested strategy for staying with the immediate concerns and working them through using critical reflection (Holly, 1984 [13]).

Critical self-reflection is, however, easier said than done (Fisher, unpub [12]). The difficulties in critical self-reflection as described by Fisher are not insurmountable when finer grained elements of the reflective process are made explicit, these being one's values, beliefs, assumptions and biases. Through a reflective action learning cycle, such elements can be noted as the lenses through which our decisions and actions are implemented. When considering our approaches to teaching, learning and assessment, a clear process of questioning and challenging ourselves can help to inform regular revisions and justify adjustments as appropriate to improving student learning.

In some action research literature, distinctions between 'innovation focused' and 'action learning focused' professional development highlight the differences between learning from respected others versus learning through our own problem-solving in context (Brooker et al, 1998 [8]). At Southern Cross University, innovations in teaching, learning and assessment have been centrally supported and encouraged from 1998. More recently, the University has established a Key Research Area in action research. It therefore seems both timely and relevant to be preparing for an action research project which investigates how we can improve the strategies for assessing student learning in the computer-mediated context of higher education.

Action research for conceptualising reflection in professional development

"Action research points in the direction of a Copernican revolution in professional development and school improvement by placing teacher learning, rather than teacher training, in a prominent position in the teacher-education sky" (Auger and Wideman, 2000: 124 [3])

Both the literature on pre-service teacher education and that of academic professional development in the university sector touches on the usefulness of action research. In a context of educational change, action research can assist teachers to reflect upon their role as change agents (Lock, 2001 [15]). Furthermore, the action research process is one in which it is possible to investigate situations or practices occuring in reality in order to change them.

Participatory action research (Kemmis and Wilkinson, 1998 [14]) can be readily applied to the kind of professional development, problem solving in curriculum development and improvement of practices which is being proposed by this author. By nature, participatory action research is both participatory and a social activity involving mutual observations and discussions in the context of the principle thematic concerns of the project. It is practical and collaborative, providing opportunities for engaging in examinations and interactions over issues of mutual interest. It is emancipatory, giving rise to insights which enable attention to constraints and solutions to frustrations which have accumulated in the ordinary momentum of work. Finally it is critical and reflexive, providing a framework by which to question and challenge one's own ways of working and to move beyond unproductive or alienating practices to find ways to change and improve.

Reflection on practice: Case study

In anticipation of the action research project mentioned in this paper, a 4-week intensive staff development workshop was carried out online. The main aim of the workshop was to immerse staff in the online environment for a hands-on experience of online interactivity through a series of individual and group, synchronous and asynchronous activities. The second principal aim of the workshop was to promote ongoing reflection on practice.

13 participants took part over the month-long series of readings, discussions, group work and reflections. It is beyond the scope of this paper to describe in detail the events of the online workshop and the responses of both participants and facilitator. However, it may be useful to consider the feedback received from participants on conclusion of the workshop. While the focus topics were principally about questions of interaction and facilitation, respondents also provided some ideas to inform future staff development projects on the questions of online assessment.

7 participants returned their evaluation comments (54% response rate). The majority of respondents commented on the value of experiencing online interaction from a student's perspective, together with all its concomitant challenges of time and technology. Several key ideas were reported as intended innovations for the future teaching e.g. incorporation of online interaction for both on-campus and off-campus learning tasks; use of the synchronous virtual classroom to replace teletutorials; the use of discussion archives for assessable tasks requiring analysis and synthesis of the

work of peers; inclusion of an online librarian to assist in assignment completion.

Using an online reflective journal

Ideas on future innovations were generated not only from participants' experiences but also from reflections they recorded during the workshop. Ideas appeared in the evaluation comments and were also evident throughout forum areas as well as in personal reflective journals that were trialed by 6 of the 13 participants. 2 of these 6 staff who used the reflective online journal, explicitly appreciated its effectiveness for noting their thoughts within an unstructured area. Their enthusiasm translated to plans for inclusion of such a reflective learning task in their teaching. One respondent, who in the privacy of the personal journal mused that she might not be "suited to discussing online", said in the evaluation that she gained most benefit from considering students experiences including the use of an online personal journal. Another commented that even though she sets the journal activity as one of her assessment tasks, she planned to review her expectations of students after personally experiencing the effect of the journal task in the workshop context.

The project ahead

Given that the workshop experience was an engaging and collegial trial of experiential and reflective activities, it seems that productive academic reflection on the practices of assessment could also benefit from participatory action research. For the promises of participatory action research to be fulfilled, the outcomes of each evaluation cycle can be used to inform staff development, and to foster the energy and willpower to question and proceed beyond existing limitations.

In the forthcoming project, reflection will be stimulated and reinforced by the keeping of journals pertaining to critical events in the design and development of assessment tasks, marking criteria and grade descriptors, and the interactions occurring around the assessment events. Fortnightly meetings with staff in action learning sets will provide additional data on their approaches to assessment and their critical reflections on these. Peer involvement in these meetings will represent the critical friend relationship for most, though some staff may also choose to discuss details of their work with other peers. Publications by academic staff will be encouraged on completion of each cycle of planning, action, observation and reflection.

Concluding comments

Together with the defined approaches of participatory action research, questions of how learning opportunities can be created online, how feedback might best be provided to sustain students' progress and how learners can be motivated and supported, will all inform the picture of improvements to assessment practices online. We must now reach for the oxygen mask, take another deep breath and proceed into a series of reflective cycles in order to achieve a dialectic of studying the online assessment practices in order to change them.

Initial data from this action research project about online assessment will be presented at the conference.

References

1. Alexander and McKenzie, 1998 *An Evaluation of Information Technology Projects for University Learning* Canberra: AGPS, CUTSD
2. Atweh, B, Kemmis, S and Weeks, P (Eds) *Action Research in Practice* London: Routledge
3. Auger, W and Wideman, R 2000 ' Using Action Research to Open the Door to Life-Long Professional Learning' *Education* Fall 2000 v121, i1
4. Biggs, J 1999 'What the Student Does' *Higher Education and Research* Vol 18, No 1, pp. 57–75
5. Booth, R, Hartcher, R and Hyde, P (in press) 'Creating quality online assessment – the experience to date' paper presented at AVETRA 2002
6. Brockbank, A and McGill, I 1998 *Facilitating Reflective Learning in Higher Education* Buckingham: Society for Research in Higher Education and Open University Press
7. Brown, S, Race P, and Bull J (Eds) 1999 *Computer-Assisted Assessment in Higher Education* London: Kogan Page
8. Brooker, R, Smeal, G, Ehrich, L, Daws, L and Brannock, J 1998 'Action Research for Professional Development on Gender Issues' in B Atweh, S Kemmis, and P Weeks, (Eds) *Action Research in Practice* London: Routledge pp. 189–211
9. Dekkers, J, Cuskelly, E Kemp, N and Phillips, J 1992 'Use of instructional materials by distance education students: Patterns and student perceptions' in B Scriven, R Lundin and Y Ryan (Eds) *Distance Education for the Twenty First Century: Selected Papers from the 16th World Conference of the International Council for Distance Education* Oslo:ICDE pp. 378–386
10. Dochy, F and McDowell, L 1997 'Assessment as a tool for learning', *Studies in Educational Evaluation* , 23 (4), pp. 279–298
11. Ellis, A, O'Reilly, M & Debreceny, R 1998 'Staff development responses to the demand for online teaching and learning' *ASCILITE98 Proceedings from 15th Annual Conference of the Australasian Society for Computers in Learning in Tertiary Education,* Woolongong: UoW Press, pp.191—201 **http://www.ascilite.org.au/conferences/wollongong98/asc98-pdf/ellis0005.pdf**
12. Fisher, K (unpub) 'Can Critical Thinking be Taught?' draft paper being prepared for publication in 2002
13. Holly, M 1984 *Keeping a personal-professional journal* Geelong: Deakin University Press
14. Kemmis, S and Wilkinson, M 1998 'Participatory action research and the study of practice' in Atweh, B, Kemmis, S and Weeks, P (Eds) *Action Research in Practice* London: Routledge, pp. 21–36
15. Lock, R 2001 'The Framing of Teacher's Work for Change Through Action Research' *Research Quarterly for Exercise and Sport*, March 2001, v72, i1, pA–54
16. Lockwood, F 1992 *Activities in Self-Instructional Texts* London: Kogan Page
17. Mason, R 2001 Keynote Presentation at *Improving Student Learning Symposium*, Heriot-Watt University, Edinburgh, September 2001
18. McAlpine, M and Higgison, C 2000 The OTiS Online Tutoring e-book **http://otis.scotcit.ac.uk/onlinebook/otis-T402.htm**
19. Melrose, M 2001 'Academic Work in the Engaged University: What is the Research/Teaching/Community Service Nexus and how can it be encouraged?' *HERDSA News* December 2001, pp.9–12
20. Morgan, C and O'Reilly, M 1999 *Assessing Open and Distance Learners* London: Kogan Page
21. Murphy, D, Walker, R and Webb, G 2001 *Online Learning and Teaching with Technology* London: Kogan Page
22. O'Reilly, M 2002 'Improving Student Learning via Online Assessment' in *Improving Student Learning 9 Improving Student Learning Using Learning Technologies* Chris Rust (Ed), Oxford: Oxford Centre for Staff and Learning Development (OCSLD), pp. 269–280
23. O'Reilly, M, Ellis, A & Newton, D 2000 'The role of university web pages in staff development: supporting teaching and learning online' *AusWeb2000 Conference*, Cairns, 12—17 June, pp.222—237 **http://ausweb.scu.edu.au/aw2k/papers/o_reilly/index.html**
24. Peters, O 2000 'Digital Learning Environments: New Possibilities and Opportunities' *Instructional Review of Research in Open and Distance Learning* Vol 1 No 1 **http://www.icaap.org/iuicode/149.1.1.7**
25. Ramsden, P 1997 'The context of learning in academic departments' *The Experience of Learning* 2nd edn Edinburgh: Scottish Academic Press
26. Rowntree, D 1977 *Assessing Students: How shall we know them?* London: Kogan Page
27. Stephens, D, Bull, J and Wade, W 1998 'Computer-assisted Assessment: Suggested Guidelines for an institutional strategy' in *Assessment & Evaluation in Higher Education 23 (3)* pp283–293
28. Zederayko, G and Ward, K 1999 'Schools as Learning Organisations: How can the work of teachers be both teaching and learning?' *National Association of Secondary School Principals Bulletin* 83 (604): pp35–45

Helping Students to Help Themselves: Case Studies from a Metacognitive Approach to Computer Learning and Teaching

Renata Phelps
Lecturer
School of Education
Southern Cross University
PO Box 157, Lismore 2480, Australia
rphelps@scu.edu.au

Allan Ellis
Associate Professor
School of Social and Workplace Development
Southern Cross University
PO Box 157, Lismore 2480, Australia
aellis@scu.edu.au

Abstract

End-user training in the use of computer software and hardware has become a significant area of professional development in a range of educational, organisational and community contexts. However, technology is developing at such a rapid rate that, if an individual undertakes training in how to use a particular piece of software, that knowledge is likely to be inadequate or out-of-date in a very short period of time. Training contexts that emphasise the centrality of the 'trainer' or teacher inevitably foster learner dependency. Although such learning contexts may be 'comfortable' and 'familiar' for some students they do not accord with the learning patterns of many 'capable' computer users. Computer education, which fosters learner independence, holds greater potential for developing life-long, capable computer users in rapidly evolving technology contexts. Three case studies are presented which illustrate the potential of a metacognitive approach to computer learning in 'helping students to help themselves'.

Introduction

'Within many vocations, technology is changing at such a rate that one's occupational preparation can become obsolete in a matter of years. One of the specific implications of such rapid technological developments is the heightening of the need for learning throughout life' [1]. This statement is no more relevant than in the context of computer education and training. End-user training in the use of computer software and hardware has become a significant area of professional development in a range of educational, organisational and community contexts. Yet, technology is developing at such a rapid rate that, if an individual undertakes training in how to use a particular piece of software, that knowledge and skill set is likely to be inadequate or out-of-date in a very short period of time. This rate of change, which can often be measured in terms of months not years, particularly for individual software products and hardware components, places immense strain on everyone involved with technology and can produced adverse cognitive, affective and motivational consequences [2]. Relevant professional development

programs for computing require more than skills training. They require a focus on attitudes, values and beliefs that develop confidence for ongoing learning. Learning to use computers involves learning to adapt to change, to be flexible, intuitive and above all persistent. Learning through independent hands-on experience and regular practice is vital. Learners who know how to be self-directed and independent will be more successful than those dependent on structured routines or guidelines [3, 4]. Successful computer learning thus requires learning approaches closer to those implicit in the contemporary adult education literature.

The research described in this paper addresses two of the conference's key questions, namely that *'tutors' culture leads them to expect to teach; why should they change that role?'*; and that *'learners' culture leads them to expect to be taught; why should they have to work more?'* The first of these two questions is answered through the argument above. Technology is developing so quickly that it makes no sense for teachers to try to hold on to a central directive role in 'training'. The direction of computer learning cannot rest solely in the hands of teachers for purely pragmatic reasons. The pace of change itself makes such a centrality impractical and certainly not cost effective.

It is from just this basis, a perceived necessity to emancipate computer learners from a reliance on the role of the tutor, that this research arose. This presentation reports on an action research project which has been focusing on developing teaching approaches which foster 'capable' computer users [5-7]. It will be demonstrated that while *some* students certainly do 'expect to be taught' and do find the transition to a more active role in the learning process difficult, for others this is a liberating experience. It will also be argued that an approach to computer learning which is experiential, exploratory, reflective and directed *by* learners is an approach which comes naturally to many, particularly once they are given 'permission' and flexibility to legitimise their already innate learning modes.

The research discussed in this presentation focussed upon the development and delivery of a computer unit offered as a core to pre-service teacher education students in both the Bachelor of Education (Primary) and Diploma of Education (Secondary) degrees at Southern Cross University, NSW, Australia. The conference presentation of this paper will present a series of case studies, drawn from the action research undertaking, to illustrate how a metacognitive approach to computer learning can 'help students to help themselves'.

The Metacognitive Approach

The term 'metacognition' refers to knowledge concerning one's own cognitive processes and products or anything related to them [8]. Informed by the literature surrounding metacognition and metalearning [9-11] and Ertmer and Newby's [12] notion of 'expert learners', this research has entailed the development and refinement of a metacognitive approach to computer education. The resultant model will be demonstrated in the presentation. In the context of the research, metacognitive teaching approaches were defined as those which assist the student to become more aware of their current attitudes towards computers (metacognitive knowledge) and their past and current learning approaches with regard computer skills (metacognitive experience and strategies).

Theory surrounding aspects of metacognition, and its relevance to computer use, was shared with students. The Unit provided a range of prompts for learners to relate prior experiences to new learning tasks through active processes of inquiry and reflection. Student were required to keep a journal which documented their reflections, although the journal task remained quite open and flexible, allowing students the opportunity to demonstrate their experiences and understandings in multiple and varied ways. The students were thus provided with maximum flexibility in the content and assessment and were encouraged to 'experiment' with a range of learning approaches, including self-directed and small group approaches.

To illustrate how this research can enhance understanding of the two conference questions, three contrasting case studies will be presented. These case studies tell us quite a lot about the two conference questions, particularly in the computer learning context. Firstly, not all students necessarily prefer to be taught in a teacher directed context. Many students assume, and come to prefer, self-directed computer learning approaches. These students are inevitably the 'capable' ones. Many aspects of this research support the notion that the flexible learning context is confronting and surprising for many students and does require changes in expectation. However for many students, being given the support structures and frameworks, and more importantly, the validation to learn independently, can be an empowering and liberating experience. Some students will inevitably be

confronted by non-teacher directed learning. However, wrapping such an approach in a metacognitive framework can assist students to engage in both cognitive self-appraisal and cognitive self-management [13]. In this framework computer teaching fosters independent and capable computer users and 'helps students to help themselves'.

References

1. Candy, P., G. Crebert, and J. O'Leary, Developing Lifelong Learners through Undergraduate Education. 1994, Canberra: Australian Government Publishing Service.
2. Rozell, E.J. and W.L. Gardner, Computer friend or foe? The influence of optimistic versus pessimistic attributional styles and gender on user reactions and performance, in Attribution Theory: An Organizational Perspective, M.J. Martinko, Editor. 1995, St Lucie Press: Delray Beach, Florida. p. 125-145.
3. Ropp, M.M., Exploring individual characteristics associated with learning to use computers and their use as pedagogical tools in preservice teacher preparation, in Department of Counseling, Educational Psychology and Special Education. 1997, Michigan State University.
4. Ropp, M.M. A new approach to supporting reflective, self-regulated computer learning. in Society for Information Technology and Teacher Education 98. 1998.
5. Phelps, R., Mapping the Complexity of Computer Learning: Journeying Beyond Teaching for Computer Competence to Facilitating Computer Capability. 2002, Southern Cross University: Lismore.
6. Phelps, R. Capability versus competency in information technology education: Challenging the learning context for lifelong technological literacy. in Eighth International Literacy & Education Research Network Conference on Learning. 2001. Spetses, Greece.
7. Phelps, R., A. Ellis, and S. Hase. The role of metacognitive and reflective learning processes in developing capable computer users. in Meeting at the Crossroads: Proceedings of the Australian Society for Computers in Learning in Tertiary Education (ASCILITE). 2001. Melbourne: University of Melbourne.
8. Flavell, J.H., Metacognitive aspects of problem solving, in The Nature of Intelligence, L.B. Resnick, Editor. 1976, Erlbaum: Hillsdale, NJ. p. 231-235.
9. Biggs, J., The role of metalearning in study processes. British Journal of Educational Psychology, 1985. 55: p. 185-212.
10. Bandura, A., Cultivating competence, self-efficacy and intrinsic interest through proximal self-motivation. Journal of Personality and Social Psychology, 1981. 41(3): p. 586-598.
11. Zimmerman, B.J., S. Bonner, and R. Kovach, Developing Self-regulated Learners: Beyond Achievement to Self-efficacy. 1996, Washington, DC: American Psychological Association.
12. Ertmer, P.A. and T.J. Newby, The expert learner: Strategic, self-regulated and reflective. Instructional Science, 1996. 24: p. 1-24.
13. Paris, S.G. and P. Winograd, How metacognition can promote academic learning and instruction, in Dimensions of Thinking and Cognitive Instruction, B. Jones and L. Idol, Editors. 1990, Lawrence Erlbaum: Hillsdale, NJ. p. 15-51.

Learning to Teach Elementary Mathematics and Science: A Global Learning Dimension

Mara Alagic   Kay Gibson   Connie Haack
Department of Curriculum and Instruction
Wichita State University, Wichita, Kansas, USA

Abstract

Research and experience suggest that structured reflections and metacognitive thinking positively influence prospective teachers' pedagogical content knowledge (PCK), and beliefs and attitudes (dispositions) about mathematics and science learning and teaching. To provide a motivating learning environment for such activities, prospective teachers from different educational cultures will be paired in a global learning project. They will (1) engage in interactive (online) reflective journaling based on experiences that combine content and pedagogy and (2) have an opportunity to design a sequence of activities to teach a mathematics and science concept that will be displayed on joint web pages. The project is guided by a series of questions about the effects of cross-cultural shared experiences on the development of specific PCK and on prospective teachers' dispositions?

Introduction

There is a need to develop a greater self-efficacy related to mathematics and science learning and teaching in elementary teachers. Many have negative beliefs, attitudes and anxieties about learning mathematics and science that constitute a significant barrier to teaching these subjects in a meaningful way. They developed their beliefs over time before entering the university. Changing these undesirable dispositions takes time ([5]) and teacher educators in the USA and Australia are making efforts to overcome this barrier ([7], [8], [9], [10]).

Reflective teacher educators positively affect the education experiences of their students both in the development of positive dispositions and PCK ([2], [3], [4], [5]). Abell and Bryan ([1]) designed their elementary science methods course around "(t)he reflection orientation ... grounded in the belief that learning to teach science, like learning science itself, is a process of re-evaluating and reforming one's existing theories in light of perturbing evidence (p.154)."

The aim of this project ([6]) is to enrich the diversity of cultural perspectives to which students of elementary education are exposed by teaming them with their counterparts in sister classes at collaborating overseas institutions. Students at Wichita State University (WSU) In the USA are sharing learning experiences with their counterparts at Queensland University of Technology (QUT) in Australia.

Learning Environment

At WSU, students of elementary education take an integrated mathematics and science methods class in the first semester of their senior year, just prior to their student teaching semester. Reflective practice is nurtured to ensure a supportive environment that addresses the barrier of teachers' negative beliefs, attitudes and anxieties. Student responses to weekly online reflective questions focus attention on a number of issues related to teacher dispositions and topics arising from classroom activities. Reflections allow faculty to gain insight into the thinking of students, and these insights guide their efforts to cultivate effective mathematics and science teaching. In addition, students have increased opportunities to form the habit of reflective journaling. Anecdotal evidence suggests that students are particularly motivated to examine their thoughts in relation to those of their classmates. Online synopses of their responses often raise the level of interest and result in further discussions about students' positive growth in PCK and dispositions.

Reflective thinking is fostered in lesson preparation and teaching assignments. Lesson planning and peer teaching requires a reflection on the process and product. The course culminates in a five-week field experience with opportunities that demand reflection on teaching in the elementary classroom. For most of the students, the primary concern expressed in the latter reflections is about classroom management, but there are always some who recognize the need to reflect more directly on their mathematics and science related PCK.

To encourage more students to recognize this need, Teacher's Inquiry into Children's Knowledge and Learning Evolvement (TICKLE) was designed as a set of assignments to make the connection between content learning and teaching practice more apparent to the students. Each student works with a child between the ages of four and twelve and explores the child's thinking about concepts within a broader topic such as volume, light and fractions. Before each TICKLE assignment, a collection of activities is introduced to provide the background needed to design activities that they deem developmentally appropriate for the child with whom they are working. Class discussions about TICKLE findings result in the development of students' new PCK and a deeper understanding of the sequence necessary to teach a given concept. As a result they also begin to answer for themselves the question: What is appropriate for the grade level that I'll be teaching?

A New Dimension: Global Learning

Global learning is more than merely distance learning, more than just the application of communication technology. It is concerned with learning at a distance plus diverse cultural perspectives, language differences, time zone differences and making the best use of innovative pedagogical strategies along with appropriate enabling communication technologies. The students achieve global awareness for the topic being studied moving from the number and nature of perspectives encountered on one campus or in one region or country to the global arena.

Diversity of learners, even within a single classroom, demands a diversity of teaching approaches. As expected in the presence of student diversity, multiple strategies have met with mixed success. Some students respond to a given strategy and others respond to significantly different ones. However, the common thread among successful strategies has been an emphasis on reflective thinking about learning, and learning to teach mathematics and science. With this in mind, this project is attempting to extend the reflective, metacognitive environment by pairing students at WSU with their counterparts at QUT to determine how cross-cultural reflection and communication affect students' learning and dispositions.

To become acquainted with each other's dispositions, paired students co-reflect via email. They engage in guided reflections centered on questions related to their personal beliefs about teaching and learning mathematics and science. This ongoing reflective practice provides a supportive learning environment to encourage the changing of undesirable dispositions and the development of mathematics and science activities for teaching with understanding ([3]). The project is an integral part of the course throughout the semester in the form of discussion groups and specific assignments in content and pedagogy.

Students at both universities have an opportunity to work with the same mathematics and science curriculum. Based on this curriculum, pairs of students develop and may publish on the web a collection of activities. In the process of designing these activities, students are exchanging guided reflections on their individual learning as well as the collaborative, creative process in order to support meta-cognitive thinking and learning in the development of PCK and positive dispositions.

Expectations

For WSU and QUT faculty and students, a global learning environment designed in this manner provides reflective opportunities through content-specific dialogue. These cross-cultural shared experiences should positively effect students' development of PCK and bring about positive changes in their evolving dispositions. Through reflective dialogue the self-efficacy of students and their appreciation of learning in other cultures should be enhanced. It is also expected that students will gain an appreciation that some elements of mathematics/science anxiety are universal across cultures while others are dependent on the cultural context. This supports a major goal of the teacher education program to prepare students to teach in a multicultural, global community.

References

[1] Abell, S.K. & Bryan, L.A. (1997). Reconceptualizing the elementary science methods course using a reflection orientation. *Journal of Science Teacher Education, 8*(3), 153-166.

[2] Clarke, B. (2000). Supporting Teachers in Understanding, Assessing and Developing Children's Mathematics through Sharing Children's Thinking. Paper presented at The 9th International Congress of Mathematics Education.

[3] Fennema, E. & Romberg T. A. (Eds.). (1998) *Mathematics classrooms that promote understanding.* Mahwah, NJ: Erlbaum, Lawrence

[4] Francis, A., Tyson, L., & Wilder, M. (1999). An analysis of the efficacy of a reflective thinking instructional module on the reflective thinking demonstrated in the field experience logs of early elementary preservice teachers. *Action in Teacher Education, 21*(3), 38-44.

[5] Hart, L.C. (2002). Preservice teachers' beliefs and practices after participating in an integrated content/methods course. *School Science and Mathematics, 102*(1), 4-11.

[6] Haack, C., Alagic, M. & Gibson, K. (2002). Instructional strategies in mathematics and science for elementary teachers. Wichita State University. Grant proposal.

[7] Mulholland, J. & Wallace, J. (2001). Teacher induction and elementary science teaching: Enhancing self-efficacy. *Teaching and Education, 17,* 243-261.

[8] Ramey-Gassert, L. & Shroyer, M.G. (1992). Enhancing science teaching efficacy in preservice elementary teachers. *Journal of Elementary Science Education, 4*(1), 26-34.

[9] Schoon, K.J. & Boone, W.J. (1998). Self-efficacy and alternative conceptions of science of preservice elementary teachers. *Science Education, 82,* 553-568.

[10] Watters, J. & Ginns, I.S. (1995). Origins of, and changes in preservice teachers' science teaching self-efficacy. Paper presented at the annual meeting of the National Association for Research in Science Teaching.

A Study of Developing Reflective Practices for Preservice Teachers through a Web-based Electronic Teaching Portfolio and Video-on-demand Assessment Program

Hitoshi Miyata
Center for Educational Research and Practice
Faculty of Education, Shiga University
Japan
miyata@sue.shiga-u.ac.jp

Abstract

Web-based electronic teaching portfolios and videoclipped teaching episodes using by Video-On-Demand(VOD) System can serve as devices for reflective inquiry and self-assessment by preservice teachers during the student teaching semester. Carefully structured procedures in a web-based electronic teaching portfolio and VOD Assessment Program can assist preservice teachers in developing the pedagogical knowledge and skills necessary to effectively plan, implement, evaluate, and manage instruction. Adequate orientation and training in the program will enable preservice teachers to engage in the reflective processes of observing, analyzing, and evaluating their teaching performance. Carefully designed procedures can result in the videoclipped teaching episodes being utilized as effective tools for the improvement of instruction rather than simply a souvenir or memento from the student teaching semester. This paper presents the web-based electronic teaching portfolio and VOD Assessment Program employed in the Center for Educational Research and Practice of Shiga University in Japan. The Program has been a valuable tool for helping education majors make the transition from student to teacher.

1. Introduction

The importance of developing in new teachers the ability to reflect on their practice of teaching has been well-established (Posner, 1989; O'Donoghue, 1996). Several studies (Freiberg, Waxman & Houston, 1987; Freiberg & Waxman, 1988) indicate that reflecting upon teaching during student teaching can enhance the repertoire of pedagogical knowledge. Koorland, Tuckman, Wallat, Long, Thomson & Silverman (1985) state that self-assessment may be the key to creating better student teachers. Teacher education programs need to encourage preservice teachers to initiate self-assessment that will develop the type of reflection necessary for a prospective teacher to continually evaluate and modify instruction within the classroom. Most preservice teachers rely on cooperating teachers and university supervisors for constructive feedback on their teaching. Observations and evaluations conducted by cooperating teachers and university supervisors are the most common sources of data during the student teaching experience. Unfortunately, due to the limited number of observations and conference sessions generally conducted, depending solely on outside sources for feedback on instruction may inhibit professional growth. Student teaching is the capstone event of the education program and it is extremely important for preservice teachers to receive as much feedback as possible during this experience. The data provided preservice teachers should be drawn from a variety of sources to complement the feedback provided by college supervisors and cooperating teachers (Freiberg & Jerome, 1988). Encouraging preservice teachers to effectively assess their own teaching will help them overcome weaknesses and maintain strengths. Preservice teachers are capable of analyzing their own teaching, want to improve their teaching skills, and would be willing to evaluate their own instruction if they had the resources (Oliva, 1988). Preservice teachers will be in a position to critique their own classroom instruction if they are provided appropriate background and experience. In order for preservice teachers to effectively assess their own teaching, accurate data must be gathered. This data can be acquired through journals, logs, portfolios, audiotapes, and videotapes. Research supports the use of videotaped teaching episodes to foster self-assessment and enhance teaching performance (Sparks-Langer & Colton, 1991; Struyk, 1991). Simply videotaping preservice teachers and having them analyze their teaching without a systematic set of procedures or background and training in the process will be ineffective. Carefully structured procedures need to be established that can assist preservice teachers in developing the pedagogical knowledge and skills necessary to effectively plan, implement, evaluate, and manage instruction.

2. A Web-based Electronic Teaching Portfolio and Video-on-demand Assessment Program at Shiga University

The following information summarizes the process established at Shiga University to utilize a web-based electronic teaching portfolio and video-on-demand assessment program in order to encourage reflection and self-assessment by preservice teachers. It has been developed to enable preservice teachers to engage in the reflective processes of observing, analyzing, and evaluating their teaching performance.

2.1 Course-Embedded Instruction on Reflection, Self-Assessment, and Videoclipping

The research supports methods course-embedded instruction for self-assessment. A study by Jensen, Shepston, Connor, and Kilmer (1994) indicated that preservice teachers could benefit from more instructional experience with videotaping, self-assessment, and reflection in general. The more familiar students are with assessment measures and the more exposure they have to both self-assessment and assessment by supervising teachers, the more competent they will

become (Thomson, 1992). The use of videotaped teaching episodes as an instructional tool in teacher education methods classes prior to student teaching enables preservice teachers to be more self-confident and effective teachers (Thomson, 1992). Although elements of effective instruction are reviewed and discussed in all education classes at Shiga University, a more intense study of effective teaching and appraisal systems is undertaken in methods classes. Carefully developed inventories that are based on behaviors associated with effective instruction are examined. This information is linked with assessment activities conducted in the methods classes. Former students have granted the Education Department permission to use their videoclips on the web in education classes for instructional purposes. Methods class students view and analyze videoclipped teaching episodes to compare with known principles of effective instruction. They are taught to assess procedures and consider alternatives, identify and offer changes for nonproductive routines, and think about ways to improve on the lesson. Once students have become familiar with assessment terminology, the next logical step should be the implementation of the terminology in real class situations that are videotaped for self-assessment (Thomson, 1992). Education methods classes are sequenced and clustered in order to block time for team teaching and field-based experiences. Coordinated with methods classes (currently Language, Arts, Social Studies, Mathematics, and Science) are field experiences that provide students with an opportunity to relate principles and theories learned in class with actual practice in schools and allow students to present lessons to students in elementary classrooms. During this field-based assignment, students (assigned in pairs) are videoclipped at least once for each subject area and are required to complete reflection questionnaires for each episode. Methods class instructors view the videoclip on the web with the students and guide them in methods of self-assessment. Although this process is time consuming for the instructor and students, early feedback on teaching skills during methods classes results in better preparation and success for student teaching (Rogers & Tucker, 1993). Students believe this instruction prepared them to effectively monitor their practices and make adjustments to them during the professional semester.

2.2 Student Teaching Semester

Preservice teachers participate in a eight-week, full-time student teaching semester in the Shiga University attached school district. They are generally assigned to one cooperating teacher who has completed workshops or classes in supervision provided by Shiga University. A full time college supervisor is also assigned for the entire experience. The first week of the professional semester are spent on campus for orientation activities. As a part of orientation, guidelines associated with effective instruction and self-assessment techniques that were examined and applied in methods classes are reviewed to encourage preservice teachers to make critical decisions regarding their instructional effectiveness. Preservice teachers also review the procedures and expectations of the Video-on-demand Assessment Program.

2.3 Videoclipping Procedures

Attached school districts that accept Shiga University preservice teachers support the videotaping of instruction. The districts' only requirement is for permission slips to be sent home to parents/guardians prior to the taping. Students that did not return permission slips are kept out of camera view. Availability of cameras is not an issue since the Education Department has three cameras, most schools have at least one, and many students have their own cameras. The cooperating teacher, another student teacher in the building, or the college supervisor, can conduct videotaping. Preservice teachers are required to videotape a minimum of three lessons over the eight-week period. The first videoclip is to be completed by week two, the second by week four, and the final by week six. This timing and number of videoclipping allow for early interventions and opportunities to assess growth and determine areas that need improvement. Preservice teachers are advised to videoclip a lesson that will give them an opportunity to analyze and reflect on the effects of their teaching, see [Figure 1]. The length of time for the videoclipping varies with the type of activity and grade level but normally runs from thirty to forty minutes.

2.4 Reflection Instrument

Preservice teachers complete the same reflection instrument used in methods classes. This instrument incorporates generally agreed upon language derived from the effective teaching literature that clearly describe observable teacher behaviors. The reflection instrument focuses on three major areas of instruction: (1) Classroom Environment; (2) Communication Skills; and, (3) Teaching Procedures. The instrument contains specific items to be rated and open-ended questions that enable the individual to analyze and reflect on their practice, assess the effects of their teaching, and improve and refine their instruction. Preservice teachers rate specific behaviors as either Proficient (Effectively demonstrated the skill well above the required level), Satisfactory (Demonstrated a steady performance and effectively met the standard requirements), or Improvement Needed (Demonstrated some competencies but improvement

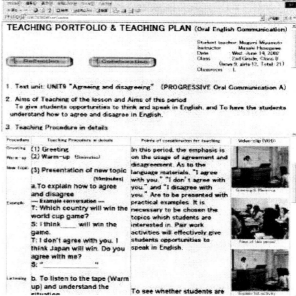

Figure 1: A Web-based Electronic Teaching Portfolio with Videoclips

required). An example of an item would be: "Activated students' prior knowledge and linked this to new information." Open-ended questions for each area (Classroom Environment, Communication Skills, and Teaching Procedures) include, "What do you perceive as the most positive aspects of your teaching procedures?" and, "In the area of classroom environment you are not satisfied with, briefly describe strategies you will consider for improvement." Two additional open-ended questions focus on growth and considerations for additional improvement: "In what specific areas of instructional skills or classroom techniques assessed in previous videoclipped teaching episodes or observations have you shown improvement? Briefly describe how you accomplished this." And, "What specific areas of instructional skills or classroom techniques will you focus on for the next videoclipped teaching episode or observation?" Preservice teachers are directed to view the videoclip at least three times to focus separately on each area when completing the instrument. The completed instrument is reviewed in conferences held with the college supervisor or cooperating teacher and serves as a guide for areas to focus on in the next videoclip or observation, see [Figure 2].

2.5 VOD (Video on Demand) Conferences

Preservice teachers have indicated that optimum learning from the videoclip occurred when the student and college supervisor viewed the videoclip together and discussed the assessment in the context of the lesson being watched. This dialogue between the student and supervisor provided a smoother transition between methods classes and student teaching, resulting in better understanding of the evaluation process and a more positive attitude toward the student teaching experience (Thomson, 1992). Moore (1988) found it imperative that the videotaped lesson is cooperatively analyzed by the preservice teacher and college supervisor. The main purpose of the preservice teacher/ college supervisor VOD conference is to promote the preservice teacher's ability to reflect upon his or her own teaching and guide them in considering their own methods for improving instruction. This conference gives preservice teachers time with the supervisor to verbally analyze their own practice and effects on

students, generate alternative strategies to use, and commit to self-examination and self-improvement. A college supervisor/ preservice teacher conference always follows the first and second videoclipped teaching episode. The progress and ability of the preservice teacher determine a conference for the final videoclip. Most of the cooperating teachers that have been assigned Shiga University student teachers have completed a five credit, tuition-free graduate course, Supervision of Preservice Teachers. In this course they become familiar with the Video-on-demand Assessment program and are encouraged to view the videoclips with the preservice teachers, see [Figure 2]. Through video-on-demand conferences with the college supervisor and cooperating teacher, preservice teachers receive guidance and direction for reflecting on his or her practice. This is also a time for everyone to consider areas to be focused on in the next videoclipping or observation.

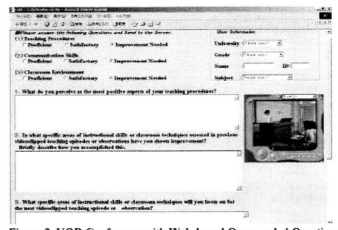

Figure 2 VOD Conference with Web-based Open-ended Questions

3. Conclusion

It is clearly evident the time required by all individuals involved in this process is extensive. However, preservice teachers and college faculty consider the experience worth the time (Blake, Foster & Hurley, 1996; Holodick, Scappaticci, & Drazdowski, 1999). Although the primary purpose of videoclipping preservice teachers is for the improvement of instruction, the practice is also encouraged by some organizations. Not only the National Board for Professional Teaching Standards in USA (1997) but also some Prefectural Board of Education in Japan requires candidates to submit a portfolio as part of the application process for the certification. It is suggested that candidates include in the portfolio four or five classroom-based exercises (may include videoclip of classroom interaction or discussion) and written analysis of the teaching reflected in the videoclip. If colleges of teacher education are going to prepare highly effective teachers who are capable of evaluating their teaching in the light of student learning, the time must be taken to provide education majors with the necessary training and experience in this process. Shiga University places a high priority on developing a preservice teacher's ability to become a reflective practitioner. Time is committed to learning, experimentation, critical analysis, and practice of skills necessary to effectively reflect. The videoclipped teaching episodes are utilized as effective tools for the improvement of instruction rather than simply a souvenir or memento from the student teaching semester. The Web-based Electronic Teaching Portfolio and Video-on-demand Assessment Program in Shiga University has been a valuable vehicle for helping education majors acquire the knowledge and skills required for professional development and a successful transition from student to teacher.

References

[1] Blake, S., Foster, D., & Hurley, S. (1996). Polyphonic presentation of first teaching experiences with reflective observations. *Technology and Teacher Education Annual, 1996*, Association for the Advancement of Computing in Education, Charlottesville, VA. 341-344.

[2] Freiberg, H.J., & Waxman, H.C. (1988). Alternative feedback approaches for improving student teachers' classroom instruction. *Journal of Teacher Education*, 39(4), 8-14.

[3] Freiberg, H.J., Waxman, H.C., & Houston, W.R. (1987). Enriching feedback to student teachers through small group discussion. *Teacher Education Quarterly*, 14(3), 71-82.

[4] Holodick, N.A., Scappaticci, F.T. & Drazdowski, T. (1999). Developing Reflective Practices of Preservice Teachers through a Video Assessment Program. *Proceedings of SITE99*, San Antonio, TX USA.

[5] Jensen, R.A., Shepston, T.J., Connor, K., & Kilmer, N. (1994). Fear of the known: Using audio-visual technology as a tool for reflection in teacher education. (ERIC Reproduction Service No. ED387482).

[6] Koorland, M., Tuckman, B., Wallat, C., Long, B., Thomson, S. & Silverman, M. (1985). A pilot evaluation of the pre-ed program: An innovative student-teacher supervision model. *Educational Technology*, 25 (10), 45-47.

[7] Moore, S. (1988). Seeing is believing: Supervision of teaching by means of videotape. *Action in Teacher Education*, 10 (2), 47-49.

[8] National Board for Professional Teaching Standards in USA. (1997). [On-line]. Available: http://www.nbpts.org/nbpts/standards/intro.html

[9] O'Donoghue, T.A., & Brooker, R. (1996). The rhetoric and the reality of the promotion of reflection during practice teaching: An Australian case study. *Journal of Teacher Education*, 47(2), 99-109.

[10] Oliva, P.F. (1989). *Supervision for today's schools*. 3 rd Ed. New York: Longman.

[11] Posner, G.J. (1989). *Field experience: Methods of reflective teaching. 2 nd E*d. New York: Longman.

[12] Rogers, S.F. & Tucker, B.H. (1993). *Video portfolios: Collaboration in literacy teaching assessment.* (ERIC document Reproduction Service No. 364879)

[13] Sparks-Langer, G.M. & Colton, A.B. (1991). Synthesis of research on teachers' reflectivity. *Educational Leadership*, 48(6), 37-44.

[14] Struyk, L.R. (1991). *Self-evaluation procedures for teachers.* (ERIC Document Reproduction Service No. 336361).

[15] Thomson, W.S. (1992). *Using videotape as a supplement to traditional student teacher supervision.* (ERIC Document Reproduction Service No. ED 357014).

Shaping Teacher Preparation Content
According to Emerging Pedagogical Paradigms

Giuliana Dettori (*), Paola Forcheri(#), Maria Teresa Molfino(#), Stefano Moretti(#), Alfonso Quarati(#)
(#) IMATI CNR– (*) ITD CNR
Via De Marini, 6 - 16149 Genova, Italy
e-mail {forcheri, molfino, moretti, quarati}@ima.ge.cnr.it, dettori@itd.ge.cnr.it

Abstract

We describe the main lines of a teacher preparation model aiming to help teachers experience the opportunities and difficulties of using ICT (Information and Communication Technology) as a means for encouraging students to learn from and with peers. Based on our experience with in-service and pre-service teachers, we firstly discuss the levels of competence to be achieved by trainee teachers, putting them in relation with the training objectives. Then we introduce our model, and discuss the results of an experiment on the practical applicability of our ideas. With our work we intend to contribute to define innovations to be introduced in ICT training to support teachers in understanding how, and under what conditions, technology can support the emerging pedagogical practices that emphasise learner-controlled learning.

1: Introduction

The current social and cultural context calls for continuous education. This need for learning throughout one's whole life requires the school system to modify its objectives and guide students to developing approaches to learning adjustable according to the requirements of a globalised and changing context. Traditional education processes constitute only a partial response to this need. This situation, and the diffusion of technology, are at the base of the growing interest in the study of the conditions that give impulse to collaborative and self-regulated learning [4], as well as in the analysis of the problems related to the introduction of ICT in the school world as a means to autonomously access resources and develop social interaction [6].

However, to transform people's attention toward these issues into school innovation, the education system has to reshape the role of the teachers, and devise new models for teacher preparation on ICT which are suitable for helping them to: 1) lead students to turn into learning occasions the opportunities of interaction and autonomous access to information offered by ICT; 2) become aware of the problems to be solved in order to realise an educational scenery apt to support the emerging pedagogical practices centred on learner-controlled learning. In fact,

though computers are spread in the school world, their role in education is still not clearly defined nor widely accepted, and the interest for their potential as a learning resource is still marginal with respect to the attention paid to the development of ICT competence [10].

Limited technological and pedagogical knowledge of teachers [7] is one of the main causes of this situation. To overcome this problem, educators should be trained to effectively use the new technologies in their work [1], [9], underlining that computational environments can be useful tools in the educational process, but learning to use them takes time and may involve specific pedagogical and epistemological decisions [8]. Educators should experiment the variety of possibilities offered by ICT for encouraging the acquisition of learning abilities [5].

Based on these considerations, we sketch a model for designing teacher preparation on introductory ICT, aiming to encourage trainees to acquire knowledge on ICT and, contextually, experience its use to support learner-controlled learning. A preliminary experiment of our proposal was carried out in the academic year 2001-02 in the course 'Multimedia in education' of the Teacher Specialisation post-graduate school (SSIS) of the University of Genoa (Italy).

2: Our model for teacher preparation

We worked out a model for teacher preparation courses apt to support the development of new approaches to learning, based on the objective to guide trainees to develop various kinds competence, i.e. 1) to use ICT as a commodity; 2) to evaluate if, and to what extent, it can be useful in teaching; 3) to understand the problems connected to the spread of ICT; and also: 4) to overcome the view of ICT just as a commodity; 5) to recognise it as a means to increase the opportunities of learning by selecting, evaluating and sharing information; 6) to frame its introduction in the context of the pedagogical decisions. These objectives allow the integration of a vision of ICT as a learning topic with that of ICT as a means to learning, and give an opportunity to make trainees experiment with peer-to-peer and autonomous learning. They can then be summarized in two main points:

- Acquiring *knowledge* on ICT and its relationship with the socio-economic evolution.
- Building *awareness* of the opportunities offered by ICT's most common tools for encouraging new forms of learning, and of the related problems.

In turn, these objectives entail different levels of competence, which raise from considering them from different points of views and at different levels of depth: acquisition of concepts and tools; realisation of practical experiences; development of critical reflections. *Concepts and tools* to be introduced should be chosen to build a common knowledge on the topic aimed to constitute a pedagogical and technical basis for future collaboration and further deepening, taking into account the different backgrounds and interests of the participants. *Practical experiences* should lead participants to: 1) experience opportunities and personal difficulties with autonomous and peer-to-peer learning; 2) operatively analyse the opportunity of integrating ICT in school in the light of already stated pedagogical objectives. *Critical reflections* should be aimed to encourage participants 1) to understand the impact of ICT on society; 2) to acquire methods and tools to critically analyse the conditions needed to turn ICT opportunities for social interaction and autonomous access to knowledge into a means for building knowledge about ICT itself; 3) to acquire elements for generalising these methods and tools for possible application in the area of professional interest.

These considerations, which are based on our experience with teacher training, led us to design the model for teacher preparation summarised in Fig. 1. This figure illustrates the content that should be introduced based on the different levels of competence related to the objectives, keeping into consideration the actors of the training process and what kinds of interactions should occur in order to enable teachers to contribute to re-elaborate the educational framework of the current school system.

Due to the range of training aspects to be considered, the full model is hardly realisable within one course. Nevertheless, in order to concretely experience the difficulties of a training including all these aspects, we partially experimented our approach in the course 'Multimedia in education' of the Teacher Specialisation postgraduate school (SSIS) of the University of Genoa (Italy), during the academic years 2001-02. This model follows, and complements, a previous model of learning to learn as problem solving, worked out during the two previous academic years of the same specialisation school [3].

3: An experimentation of our model

Context. The SSIS has currently an experimental character, since only from the school year 1999-2000 the Italian school system provides a specific (and obligatory) educational path for teachers-to-be. The SSIS accepts a limited number of participants per year, lasts 4 semesters

and includes institutional activities (classes, laboratories, training) for a total of 120 credits (according to the rules of the ECTS system, decision CEE 87/327 of 15.6.1987) and a total of class hours between 1000 and 1500 per year. The course 'Multimedia in education' (25 hours, 3 credits) aims to give all participants methodological and operational basic competence on ICT, as necessary for a conscious use of multimedia and network tools within the school practice (operating system; word processor; spreadsheet; databases; multimedia; Internet to communicate, co-operate and find information). The number of participants (trainee teachers) who take regularly part into the course are around 100 per year, divided into three teaching specialisation, Humanities (about two thirds), Foreign languages (about one sixth), Scientific disciplines (about one sixth). The participants enrolled have different backgrounds and different levels of knowledge of basic technology concepts. Some of them have never used a computer before, many have used some tools (mostly word processors or e-mail programs) but do not have a good command of them, some have a good mastering of one or more tools but limited knowledge on computer functioning or theoretical foundations, few have a more complete ICT formation. Some tools are well known to some participants, some others to other ones.

Organisation of the work. The course included theoretical lessons, lab activities to be carried out partly autonomously partly in groups, and a final educational project. According to the model of Fig. 1, the theoretical lessons aimed to introduce concepts and tool as well as to stimulate reflection, the assigned activities constituted the core of the learning experience and offered a practical basis to deepen critical thinking, the final educational project aimed to exploit the results of the overall work and to express personal ideas and knowledge. We explained to the participants at the very beginning that the course's objectives were not limited to knowledge on concepts and tools, and what kind of work was consequently required of them. In spite of the limited number of hours of the course, we proposed a high number of activities, divided in groups according to their objectives, and asked participants to choose, among them, what to develop for the final exam. The activities were to be carried out during the computer labs or in individual extra hours of work. Some examples of activities, with an indication of the kind of competence to be achieved, are shown in Table 1.

Results. The reaction of the participants was analysed based on the observation of their behaviour in the lab, the outcome of the activities, the final educational project and an end-of-course questionnaire. The questionnaire included both technical questions (aiming to verify the knowledge acquired or the level of awareness achieved), and evaluation ones (aiming to detect the student's perception of the impact of the various activities and learning experiences carried out during the course). For lack of space, we briefly overview only qualitative results. Quantitative data can be found in [3].

In spite of the problems due to the variety of backgrounds of the participants, the outcomes of the observation, confirmed by the questionnaire and the results of both the final projects and the activities, are quite positive as concerns the learning of the topic, the climate of collaboration among peers, the stimulus received to propose autonomous solutions to problems and to deepen topics. Another positive aspect was the feeling of satisfaction shown by the participants with non-scientific background: the variety of work proposed, in fact, gave them the opportunity of carrying out activities requiring a moderate level of technical knowledge but a high level of ability of written communication, negotiation, etc.

However, as concerns the degree of acceptance by the participants of this kind of approach to learning, several difficulties have been highlighted, mainly regarding the time and effort required, the work with other participants and the discrepancy between the nature of the course and trainee's expectations about it. Difficulties in the collaboration with peers were strictly linked, in our case, to the expectations, since participants were used to regard the trainer more as a controller of their activity than as a supervisor and mentor of peer-to-peer co-operation. Such a situation is rather difficult to modify, since a climate of reciprocal trust has to be created, so that trainees are encouraged to keep control of their own learning (with the help of the trainer), and the work has to be organised so that both trainer and trainees are facilitated in changing pre-existing attitudes. As concerns the difficulties in carrying out peer-to-peer interaction via network, in our case they were mainly due to lack of previous experience, to the limited knowledge participants had of each other, to differences in backgrounds, study habits and interests, to the problem of finding a common (written) language for communication; to the need to practically organise the work. These obstacles made most participants perceive distance collaboration as a loss of time rather than as a useful learning occasion.

4: Discussion

An experience like the one described above requires a considerable investment of both trainers and trainees as concerns time and effort. In fact, the majority of participants found that the time initially planned for the course was not enough to carry out the work. On the other hand,

Competence	Example of activity
Individual work	
Reflection on the effects of ICT on society.	Give examples of: newspaper's articles you read about the web; situations in which you have seen a web address, reviews of web sites, etc.
Analysis of one's own knowledge and capabilities to learn from a variety of sources.	Illustrate the web aspects you know (socio-economic, historical, technical etc.), commenting your level of mastering and giving examples of means and occasions which led you to acquire knowledge about the Web.
Exam of the capability and problems of formulating a personal learning path about an ICT aspect.	Indicate some aspects of multimedia you would like to deepen and explain why. Sketch what line you would like to follow to this aim, what kinds of source you intend to rely on, starting from your initial knowledge and from the difficulties you expect to find.
Practice with ICT as a tool for self-regulated learning.	Build an index of Web sites including material suitable to understand what the European Computer Driving Licence (ECDL) is, and to prepare the exams to get it. Information on ECDL can be found at http://www.ecdl.com/.
Group work	
Reflect on ICT as a tool for knowledge transfer and sharing	Negotiate within your group some topic of common interest. Build in collaboration an index of Web sites on this topic and make a brief review of each site as concerns objective, content and validity.
Practice with ICT as a tool for co-operating with peers.	Make agreements with a colleague (or a group of colleagues) and, by communicating via e-mail, prepare a joint letter summarising your opinions about the course. At the end, send the letter to the course teacher (by e-mail).
Practice with ICT as a tool for reciprocal teaching/ Reflect on the ability to learn from peers.	Write a short paper about e-mail. Send it to a number of your colleagues asking for their comments. Analyse their answer and, based on the suggestions you agree with, prepare a revised version of your paper.
Shared analysis of the problems to be faced when using a same tool for professional development or classroom practice.	Choose one of the tools introduced. Discuss with a group of colleagues aspects of your own activity that could take advantage from it. Analyse the educational potential and drawbacks, giving examples of possible uses in the classroom, and specifying with what kind of students.

Table 1. Examples of activities proposed, and correspondent kind of competence to be achieved

the influence of such an experience on learning abilities can be fully appreciated only when the learners have the opportunity to apply the acquired competence on a variety of different situations and tasks. The difficulty to appreciate immediately the importance of the achieved results with respect to the time and effort spent is, likely, a relevant factor which discourages many trainees to commit on this kind of investment. In our opinion, this is one of the main obstacles that prevent learners from changing their traditional educational view. Hence, we think that learning with peers should be explicitly included among course's institutional objectives, so to be taken into consideration in the evaluation phase, thus constraining learners to consciously work in this direction.

Problems related to expectations derive from the existence of stereotypes on the educational process. Working on a topic where there is not a long-established school tradition, like ICT, helps overcome this problem only as concerns the way content knowledge is approached, but has very limited influence regarding the general attitude toward teaching and learning: the teacher/trainer is still seen as knowledge transmitter, while the learners/trainees consider themselves as receivers of the teaching rather than subjects of the learning process. Changing these roles entails establishing a new kind of educational contract. This is a difficult task to accomplish, since changing the perception of role is more difficult than changing topic-related conceptions, in that role perception is rooted in the social system of beliefs [2], and there is no teaching topic so new and unusual to easily overwrite them. Hence, to really make the educational system evolve towards different learning paradigms, a change in educational contract should be supported and fostered by the whole school system.

We can derive from our experience some suggestions to help realise the conditions improving teacher preparation so to meet the needs of the current socio-cultural context. Trainers should explain explicitly their educational philosophy and the different levels of preparation that the trainees need to achieve; activities should be articulated so to gradually reduce the trainer's intervention; peer-to-peer learning activities should be based on applications which call at play some competence of the students not necessarily shared by all group members, so to emphasise the need and advantages of peer collaboration; projects should be devised so the trainees must find by themselves the tools necessary to solve the problems involved, in relation to their competence and to the project's requirements.

Moreover, concerning collaborative activities, the problems we experienced in our work suggest us: to start this kind of activity once some reciprocal acquaintance and trust has started establishing; possibly to make some face-to-face group work precede the activity via network; to take into consideration the influence of pre-conceptions on interactions and, if necessary, explicitly address them;

to monitor group behaviour carefully so to opportunely adjust possible mis-functionings; to assist participants in the organisation of the first activities that involve net communication; to propose assignments which favour the exploitation of the competence of all; to propose highly articulated and complex projects only when people start identifying themselves with the team; to make sure that the time dedicated to group work via network is enough to allow participants avail themselves of other's experience. This number of difficulties to overcome indicates that setting up the right conditions to orient teacher preparation towards peer-to-peer learning is a long and complex task. It is very difficult to achieve a good level of ability in peer co-operation in the short time of a teacher preparation program, let alone within a single course. Hence, we think that it should be fostered over the whole school period, so it can become a consolidated ability to relay on, and a help to successfully carry out life-long learning.

References

[1] Carr-Chellman A.A. & Dyer D. (2000). The Pain and Ecstasy: Pre-service Teacher Perceptions On Changing Teacher Roles and Technology, Educational Technology & Society 3(2), http://ifets.ieee.org/periodical/.

[2] Dettori, G. (2002). Introducing IT in Mathematics Education: Prospects for Curriculum Revision and Teacher Training; in Subject Teaching and Teacher Education in the New Century: Research and Innovation, Yin Cheong Cheng et al eds., Kluwer Academic Publishers. 141-165.

[3] Dettori, G., Forcheri, P., Molfino, M.T., Quarati, A (2002), Learning to learn as a problem solving process:a role for ICT in teacher training, IMA-CNR Tech. Rep. N.1 2002.

[4] Dillenbourg, P. (ed.). (1999). *Collaborative Learning - Cognitive and Computational Approaches*, Elsevier Science Ltd, Oxford U.K..

[5] Forcheri P., Molfino M.T. & Quarati A. (2000). The influence of technology on educational interactions, *Proc. of Open Classrooms in the Digital Age*, N.Kastis ed., pp. 66-71.

[6] Mc Laurin C. & Olivier R. (1999). Pedagogic roles and dynamics in telematics environments, in *Telematics in education*, Selinger R. & Pearson J. (eds.), Elsevier Science Ltd, Oxford U.K., 32-50.

[7] Pelgrum W.J. (2001) *Obstacles to the integration of ICT in education: results from a worldwide educational assessment*, Computers & Education 37, 163-178.

[8] Salomon, G. (2000). It's not just the tool, but the educational rationale that counts, Proceeding sof ED-Media 2000, http://www.aace.org/conf/edmedia/00/salomonkeynote.htm

[9] Vrasidas C. & McIsaac M.S. (2001). Integrating Technology in Teaching and Teacher Education: Implications for Policy and Curriculum Reform, Educational Media International (EMI), Vol.38, Nos. 2/3, 127-132.

[10] Watson D.M.,(2001) Pedagogy before Technology: Rethinking the Relationship between ICT and Teaching, *Education and Information Technologies*, 4, Dec. 01, 251-266.

Knowledge   Teacher trainer   Awareness

Concepts and tools
- Technological model underlying the computing technology.
- Most diffused kinds of applications for individual work and different tools for its realisation.
- Technological concept of networked computer system.
- Most diffused internet services and examples of tools for their use.
- Models and approaches to knowledge representation brought about by the computing technology: Multimedia and hypermedia.

Direct experience
- Practice with technological tools and models and figure out examples of practical applications.
- Experience benefits/problems in the use of the tools introduced.
- Verify one's own knowledge and competence by means of knowledge transfer activities and autonomus reflection.

Critical reflection
- Evolution of the computer technology and relationships between technical changes and socio-economic situation: influence on the organization of the work; new jobs; new approaches to existing jobs.
- Evaluation of the applications introduced w.r.t. to the socio-economic context, in particular the school.
- From stand-alone to networked computing. Impact of the net on the organization of work, models of communications, knowledge sharing and information distribution.

Concepts and tools
- Pedagogical, epistemological and operative problems related to the introduction of ICT tools in school.
- Impact of basic ICT tools for information management; technical difficulties, cognitive problems in their use, problems perceived with respect to standard tools.
- Impact of basic ICT tools for autonomous access to knowledge: technical aspects, guidelines in the choice of the resources.

Direct experience
- Produce some example of educational material, clearly explain the pedagogical context of use and objectives, and analyse possible difficulties in the practical application.
- Practice with ICT as a tool for learning from peers by means of reciprocal teaching; negotiation; organization of a distance group-discussions; preparation of a FAQ service, distance cooperation to work out a common document or project, request information.
- Practise with ICT as a tool for self-regulated learning: analyse how to search for information and evaluate the sources; perform a critical analysis of the operative problems to be faced.

Critical reflection
- Cognitive and operative problems to be faced when using a same tool for professional development or classroom practice.
- Reflection on the difficulties met while carrying out the activities assigned.
- Reflection on possible changes brought about by the use of technological tools in the interaction with peers and teacher.
- Reflection on personal abilities to learn from peers.
- Impact on education of the hypermedia model for knowledge representation and acquisition.

School system

Trainee teachers

Figure 1 - The variety of aspects of ICT competence to be considered in teacher education in order to give trainee teachers a preparation responding to the current educational needs

A Classification Schema of Online Tutor Competencies

Doug Reid, Edith Cowan University

Abstract

There are many ways to classify the competencies of online tutors. This paper will investigate an innovative classification schema of online tutor competency based on an analysis of the current literature, with particular reference to the work of several selected authors. This schema has been developed to investigate the role these competencies play within the online learning environment. The study is focussing on the instructional and guidance roles of online tutors rather than the roles of course coordinators or developers of instructional material.

Competencies is a term used throughout the literature to describe many different descriptors of tutors and their actions. Berge (1995) calls them behavioural recommendations, while Cyrs (1997) calls them skills and strategies. Furst-Bowe (1996) use competencies to describe knowledge, skills, and abilities, which is opposed to Schoenfeld-Tacher & Persichette (2000) who separate skills from competencies that include knowledge, character traits, abilities and strategies.

Introduction

After examining many of the methods of classification and the individual competencies presented throughout the literature, the author had a list of over 500 individual competencies. This led to a decision to focus his effort on a limited number of sources (Berge, 1995; Cyrs, 1997; Goodyear, Salmon, Spector, Steeples & Tickner, 2001; Salmon, 2000), as each additional source added both individual competencies and a new organizational schema for the competencies.

A number of categories may be identified which are a mix of what is constant in the literature and what is scattered throughout the literature. The author created a list of the competencies organized by creator and creator-labelled category. There were a large number of competencies and categories that were equivalent in various articles. Each individual competency was examined and sorted with other competencies which appeared to the author to fit together. After

the competencies from the literature were combined and sorted, the author labelled the categorized groups of competencies based on categories used in the literature. This resulted in 5 categories, which are:

1. Technical Knowledge

The literature used general terms, like Berge's (1995) use of "technical", to Goodyear et al. (2001) use of "technologist", to Salmon's (2000) use of "technical skills". Throughout the literature, the themes include attitude toward technology, choice of technology, resources, technological pedagogy, technical support and use of technology.

2. Content Expertise

As the literature was examined there were skills and traits which fitted together from different authors. This category encapsulates numerous themes from the literature. In this schema, these themes have been labelled content expertise, finding & providing resources, question analysis, relevant tasks and enriching interactions.

3. Process Facilitation

Process facilitation is by far the largest category in this organizational schema. The literature is filled with examples of aspects of process facilitation. This category is diffused throughout Berge (1995) having items in many of his categories. Goodyear et al. (2001) have designer and process facilitator roles with similarities to this category. Salmon (2000) has similar categories including understanding of online process, personal characteristics and online communication skills.

4. Evaluation

Authors have divided this category into very different schemas. Goodyear et al. (2001) divides this category into its assessor, researcher and designer roles. Cyrs (1997) does not even have it as a separate category but includes bits of it throughout his schema. Berge (1995) includes this category in his pedagogical facilitation. In this case, the category of Evaluation includes themes such as: assessment, course evolution, feedback and monitoring. The category is about the evaluation of the entire offering, providing assessment for students as well as evaluating the course and planning changes, modifications or corrections to improve the entire online experience.

5. Course Management

Course Management is a category which accumulates competencies that deal with offering an online educational experience, but do not fit in any of the other categories I have examined. Administrator / Manager from Goodyear et al. (2001) and Berge's (1995) Managerial Facilitation are quite close to Course Management. Being the institutional contact, performing administrative functions and keeping the course organization running smoothly are the type of themes covered by this category.

Conclusion

This classification schema has been created as part of a study exploring what competencies are needed to be an online tutor. The actual research question is "What are the relationships between the factors that affect the competencies required by online tutors in tertiary education and the competencies displayed?" This study will employ ethnographic approaches such as participant observation and interviewing to gather data in regard to the competencies required to be an online tutor.

References

[1] Berge, Z. (1995). The role of the online instructor/facilitator. *Educational Technology, 35*(1), 22-30.

[2] Cyrs, T. (1997). Competence in teaching at a distance. *New Directions for Teaching and Learning, 71,* 15-18.

[3] Furst-Bowe, J. (1996). An analysis of the competencies needed by trainers to use computer-based technologies and distance learning systems. *Performance Improvement Quarterly, 9*(4), 57-78.

[4] Goodyear, P., Salmon, G., Spector, J., Steeples, C., & Tickner, S. (2001). Competencies for online teaching: a special report. *Educational Technology Research and Development, 1,* 65-72.

[5] Salmon, G. (2000). *E-Moderating: The key to teaching and learning online.* London: Kogan Page Limited.

[6] Schoenfeld-Tacher, R., & Persichette, K. (2000, July). *Differential skills and competencies required of faculty teaching distance education courses* (1),. International Journal of Educational Technology. Available: http://www.ecel.uwa.edu.au/ijet/v2n1/schoenfeld-tacher/index.html [2001, August 7, 2001].

Enhancing pre-service teachers' learning about on-line learning through use of a Self-managed On-line Learning Environment

Kai-ming LI*, Yiu-sing LAM, Pak-hung LI, Kwok-leung WU
Department of Information and Applied Technology, Hong Kong Institute of Education
10, Lo Ping Road, Tai Po, N.T. Hong Kong SAR, China
*kmli@ied.edu.hk

Abstract

This paper describes the development of a web-based Self-managed On-line Learning Environment (SOLE) and its feedback from pre-service teachers participated in a pilot project. The main purpose of this project was to enhance the understanding about on-line learning through the actual use of SOLE while pre-service teachers were doing their Teaching Practice in schools. Preliminary results showed that participants in the pilot study expressed positive attitudes and reported better understanding about using on-line learning in their future teaching. However, the unsolved technical problems in the trial process affected their confidence in attempting student-centred learning strategy with the use the system.

Keywords: Teaching/Learning Strategies, Internet based Systems

Introduction

This paper describes a pilot project[1] on pre-service teachers' learning about on-line learning. In the project, a Self-managed On-line Learning Environment (SOLE) was developed for a group of pre-service teachers who were doing an "Information Technology in Education" module in Hong Kong Institute of Education. The main purpose of this project was to enhance the understanding about on-line learning through the actual use of SOLE while pre-service teachers were doing their Teaching Practice in schools.

Background

Internet as a tool for learning has been widely used in all school levels recently. From the constructivist view of learning, it is believed that Internet as an information delivery and access platform, a gateway to the outside world, a resources warehouse, a communication centre and a learning partner can enhance learning e.g. [1] [2] [3] [4]. Therefore, helping pre-service teachers to master the technologies and concepts of on-line or web-based learning becomes an inevitable objective in most of the technology in education related module in a teacher education programme. It is evident that future teaching is influenced by the learning experiences that pre-service teachers gained in their tertiary education [5]. Abdal-Haqq (1995) [6] also suggested that the best way for effective technology in education programme is to provide the opportunities for pre-service teachers to apply and integrate technology in the actual teaching situation. Recent studies also point out that the provision of instructional models for classroom implementations of technology is far more significant than the reception of knowledge and skills of technology if teacher education programmes are to be successful [7] [8]. Furthermore, effective learning in a teacher education programme arrives only when pre-service teachers are able to test out the principles and theories in particular teaching contexts and to build their own knowledge through active reflection [9] [10]. In the present project, the application of on-line learning environment was modelled through the use of the institute's teaching and learning platform by the authors. The use of SOLE in Teaching Practice provided authentic experiences and tools for the pre-service teachers. Such experiences then formed the basis for reflection.

SOLE system overview

SOLE is a web-based system that simulates the operation of a teaching and learning platform. It allows the teaching staff or system administrator (first level users) of a teaching organisation to disseminate the different rights of the system applications to designated users, for instance, the pre-service teachers (second level users) in the present project. The designated users can then use the system and further disseminate the rights to other users, students of the pre-service teachers (third level users) in this case. Such feature enables users of different levels who own the administration right to create and manage a number of independent SOLEs. Therefore, each pre-service teacher in the project becomes a SOLE

---
[1] This project titled "Teaching with Information Technology via use of a Self-managed On-line Learning Environment" was supported by the Information Technology Strategy Committee Grant 2001-02 of the Hong Kong Institute of Education.

administrator and has the chance to manage and develop on-line learning activities for his/her students.

In the SOLE, the resources building application allows the upper level users to establish a filing structure and to upload files of various formats to the system. A tool for creating Internet hyperlinks is also built in this application. The discussion forum-building tool enables the upper level users to create more than one forum. They can create different discussion topics and to assign specific "Forum Managers" to look after the forums. Apart from written messages for communication in the forum, users can choose to use the specifically designed tool for sound recording. The purpose of such design is to encourage communication among the low level users who were primary students in Hong Kong and were incompetent in keyboarding or Chinese input skill. SOLE also provides a web server function for users to upload their own homepages. The form tool in SOLE allows the upper level users to create online exercises or tests and survey for their sub-level users. The system also provides an online marking tool for the upper level users. Result is sent to the sub-level users directly from the system and is stored in the system for later retrieval. Another survey form tool enables the upper level users to develop an on-line survey form. Feedback from sub-level users in response type or short essay can be retrieved from the report and statistics tool of the system.

Pilot Study

SOLE was introduced in a topic about on-line learning in a group of seven pre-service teachers taking the "Information Technology in Education" related module. These teachers were brought into the context of "on-line learning" via studying research and exemplars in the literature with an on-line teaching and learning platform modelled by the authors. The pre-service teachers showed positive attitudes and reported better understanding about using on-line learning in their future teaching in an interview after the project. However, the unsolved technical problems in the trial process affected their confidence in attempting student-centred learning strategy with the use of the system. Nevertheless, the feedbacks from the experiences of these participants helped the continuous development of the SOLE.

Conclusions and Suggestions

This paper has described the development of SOLE. Pilot study showed positive effect on the mastery of learning about web learning. This paper also suggests that further in-depth study on the effectiveness of the application of SOLE in actual school teaching with more pre-service teachers should be conducted after the identified problems have been fixed.

It is believed that SOLE will be a powerful tool for pre-service teachers to experience and master the knowledge and skills of on-line learning. It is also addressed that the "learning use of technologies through actual using technologies" strategy employed in this project was also crucial to enhance learning. However, more evidence should be collected through more similar studies before conclusions can be drawn. It is also suggested that SOLE can be a powerful tool for the professional development about on-line learning for in-service teachers when it is well developed. It is expected that when a teacher is granted the administration right in SOLE, he/she can try out as many teaching strategies as he/she can without interfering with the existing school intranet system or learning platform. Through such self-managed activities, the educational use of Information Technology can then be promoted.

References

[1]   Andres Y.M. (1996). *Advantages to Telecomputing: Reasons to use the Internet in your classroom.* http://www.gsn/teach/articles/advan.html.

[2]   Kearsley, G. (1996). *The World Wide Web: Global access to education.* USA: American Association for the Advancement of Science.

[3]   Harris, J. (1998). Curriculum-based telecollaboration: using activity structures to design student projects. *Learning & Leading with Technololgy*, 26(1), 7-15.

[4]   Stephenson, J. (2001). *Teaching & learning online: pedagogies for new technologies*. London: Kogan Page.

[5]   Adams, P.E. & Krockover, G.H. (1997), Beginning science teacher cognition and its origins in the pre service secondary science teacher program. *Journal of Research in Science Teaching*, 34, 633-653.

[6]   Abdal-Haqq, I. (1995). *Infusing technology into perservice teacher education. ERIC digest.* (ERIC Document Reproduction Service Number: ED 389 699)

[7]   Novak, D. & Knowles, J. (1991). Beginning elementary teachers' use of computers in classroom instruction. *Action in Teacher Education.* 8(2), 43-51.

[8]   Faison, C.L. (1996). Modeling instructional technology use in teacher preparation: Why we can't wait. *Educational Technology*, 36(5), 57-59.

[9]   Korthagen, F.A.J. and Wubbels, Th. (1995). Characteristics of reflective practitioners: Towards an operationalisation of the concept of reflection. *Teachers and Teaching: Theory and Practice,* 1(1), 51-72.

[10]   Shulman, L. (1987). Knowledge and teaching: Foundations of the new reforms. *Harvard Educational Review*, 57, 1-22.

The Learning of Plans in Programming: A Program Completion Approach

Stuart Garner
Edith Cowan University, Perth, Western Australia

Abstract

Programming plans are stereotyped sequences of computer instructions, that form a hierarchy of generalised programming knowledge. They can be thought of as the building blocks of computer programs. In the learning of programming, it is necessary for students to build knowledge of a variety of plans that they can then make use of during the development of larger programs.

This paper discusses two methods by which students can learn such plans, the "conventional" method that has been used by instructors for many years, and the "completion" method. The completion method requires students to complete part-complete solutions to given programming problems.

As part of a research project, some students were observed using the completion method in conjunction with a software tool, CORT (code restructuring tool). The paper reports on one particular observation in which a student was required to build a programming plan. It concludes that the student gained a deep understanding of how the plan worked during the knowledge construction process.

1. Introduction

Learning to write computer programs is not easy (du Boulay, 1986; Scholtz & Wiedenbeck, 1992) and this is reflected in the low levels of achievement experienced by many students in first programming courses. For example Lisack (Lisack, 1998) states that:

> *Students have difficulty learning programming as they are trying to develop skills in three areas at the same time, these being: using the program development environment; learning the programming language syntax; and developing logic design.*

In the area of logic design, it is necessary for students to learn the fundamental programming plans, or building blocks, that are used to create programs. There are several pedagogical approaches to the teaching and learning of

programming, however they these approaches have changed little over the years.

This paper will discuss a "conventional" approach to learning to program with the "completion" method of learning to program, particularly in the area of programming plans. It will also describe how one particular student used the completion method approach for a programming problem that required an "array loading" plan.

2. What is a Programming Plan?

Expert programmers have the necessary cognitive schemata to easily perform familiar programming tasks and also to interpret unfamiliar situations in terms of their generalised knowledge (Van Merrienboer & Paas, 1990). In the domain of programming these specific schemata are known as programming plans and they are learned programming language templates, or stereotyped sequences of computer instructions, that form a hierarchy of generalised knowledge.

An example of a program with its plans identified is

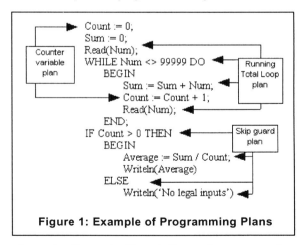

Figure 1: Example of Programming Plans

shown in figure 1. The challenge for programming instructors is how to facilitate student learning so that students can learn such plans and then apply them to new problem situations.

3. The Conventional Method of Learning Programming

Probably the most common pedagogical approach to the teaching and learning of programming that is used in schools, colleges and universities today is still the following (Linn & Dalbey, 1985):

- Learn the syntax and semantics of one language feature at a time.
- Learn to combine the language feature with known design skills to develop programs to solve problems (this expands the students' design skills and includes patterns and procedural skills such as planning, testing and reformulating).
- Develop general problem solving skills.

With respect to the above, good pedagogy therefore requires the instructor to keep initial facts, models, and rules simple and only expand and refine them as students gain experience (Winslow, 1996). Winslow also makes a very valid point when he states:

> One wonders, for example, about teaching sophisticated material to CS1 (an introductory programming course) students when study after study has shown that they do not understand basic loops.

This comment by Winslow is very appropriate in the context of this paper as a "basic loop" is one example of a programming plan. The case that follows later in the paper concerns how a student attempted to learn and understand a programming plan that included a basic loop.

3.1 An Example

Let us consider the teaching and learning of simple array processing in programming. Using the conventional approach to the teaching and learning of programming, the following would most probably have happened:

- The teacher would have introduced and explained loop processing, arrays, and counting to the students.
- The teacher would have shown example programs to the students. Such programs would have included various programming plans as described earlier.
- The students would have been given problems to solve that required the use of certain programming plans. An example of such a problem that students might be given to attempt in an introductory programming course that utilises the Visual BASIC programming language, is as follows:

Write a program which inputs 8 numbers contained in the file **numbers.txt** into an array. This should be done in the **Form_Load** event procedure.

Then, when a button is clicked, the program should display three columns, the first column containing the original 8 numbers, the second column containing the 8 numbers in reverse order, and the third column containing the sum of the corresponding numbers in columns 1 and 2.

Part of the solution to this programming problem would require the following programming code which can be considered to be an "array loading" plan.

```
Let index = 1
Do While Not EOF(1)
    Input #1, Numbers(index)
    Let index = index + 1
Loop
```

In this conventional method of teaching and learning programming, most students would search for and find a similar example of such an "array loading" plan. They would then copy and paste the appropriate code into their solution and amend it where necessary.

The students may well appear to have been successful in solving the problem. The question however arises as to whether the student actually **understands** the way the plan is being executed by the computer including the changes to the values of the variables. Often this is not the case and is one reason why many students have difficulty with more complex problems.

4. The Completion Method

The completion method of learning programming uses incomplete, well-structured and understandable program examples that require students to generate the missing code or "complete" the examples. This forces students to study the incomplete examples as it would not be possible for their completion without a thorough understanding of the examples' workings. An important aspect is that the incomplete examples are carefully designed as they have to contain enough "clues" in the code to guide the students in their completion. It is suggested that this method facilitates both automation, students having programming plans available for mapping to new problem situations, and schemata acquisition as they are forced to mindfully abstract these from the incomplete programs (Van Merrienboer & Paas, 1990).

A software tool has been built to support this completion method (Garner, 2000; Garner, 2001) and is utilised in introductory programming courses at Edith Cowan University, Australia. The tool is named CORT (Code Restructuring Tool) and the interface comprises two windows as shown in figure 2. The right-hand window contains the part-complete solution to a given programming problem, and the left-hand window contains possible lines of code that can be used to complete the program. A CORT problem may have more lines in the

5. CORT in Practice

As part of a research study into the completion method and CORT, some students were observed attempting to

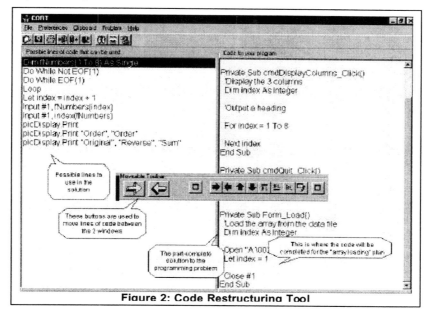

Figure 2: Code Restructuring Tool

left-hand window than are necessary, some lines acting as distracters to force students to think more carefully about the lines to choose.

Lines can be moved between the windows by clicking on the large arrows on the toolbar. Other buttons on the toolbar can be used to rearrange lines in the right-hand window. When a student wishes to test the code, the contents of the right-hand window are copied to the windows clipboard and then pasted into Visual BASIC. The program can then be run.

Let us consider the teaching and learning of simple array processing in programming using this completion method. The following would most probably happen:

- The teacher would have introduced and explained loop processing, arrays, and counting to the students.
- The teacher would have shown example programs to the students. Such programs would have included various programming plans as described earlier.
- The students would have been given problems to solve that required the use of certain programming plans. Such problems would be attempted within the CORT environment.
- A student does **not** copy and paste the lines of code from an example as in the conventional method, but builds, test, and refines the code that makes up the plan within CORT.
-

solve a variety of programming problems using CORT. One of the questions that they attempted was that shown in section 3.1 above and some of these observations will now be described for one particular student. This description concerns only the "array loading" plan shown earlier.

In CORT, the **only** line of code that was displayed for students in the right-hand window for this plan was:

```
Let index = 1
```

The lines displayed in the left-hand window of CORT that were relevant to this plan were:

```
Do While Not EOF(1)
Do While EOF(1)
Loop
Let index = index + 1
Input #1, Numbers(index)
Input #1, index(Numbers)
```

The actions that the student took are shown in table 1.

The total time taken by the student to complete the program correctly was approximately 20 minutes

6. Conclusions

The use of CORT in conjunction with the program completion method enables the student learning to be focussed on the key programming plans which students have to learn. As can be seen in the above example, the student's learning was scaffolded so that it was almost had gained a deep understanding of how the programming plan worked.

With the conventional method of learning programming, students usually do not make mistakes during the plan construction as they normally copy the code from a similar example. Student understanding of how the particular plan works is consequently low.

A possible future research area would be to compare

Student Action	Code in "Array loading" plan
1. He moved four lines from the left-hand window to the right-hand window. He tested the program in Visual BASIC and received an error message indicating the first two lines were the wrong way round.	**Loop** **Do While Not EOF(1)** Let index = 1 **Input #1, Numbers(index)** **Let index = index + 1**
2. He swapped the first two lines and retested in Visual BASIC. He got an "endless loop" as there was no code between the first two lines. He used Visual BASIC's tracing mechanism to step through the code to help him reach this conclusion.	**Do While Not EOF(1)** **Loop** Let index = 1 Input #1, Numbers(index) Let index = index + 1
3. He rearranged the lines of code within CORT and retested in Visual BASIC. The program ran, however the output (produced from code in another part of the program) was incorrect. He recognised that there was something wrong with the contents of the array, Numbers().	Do While Not EOF(1) **Let index = 1** **Input #1, Numbers(index)** **Let index = index + 1** Loop
4. He swapped the Input statement within CORT for the other (incorrect) input statement. This gave an error message indicating that an array was expected (note that the array name is Numbers).	Do While Not EOF(1) Let index = 1 **Input #1, index(Numbers)** Let index = index + 1 Loop
5. He swapped the lines around again so that the code was again the same as in 3 above. This time he traced and stepped through the code using Visual BASIC's tracing mechanism. He saw that the value of the variable **index** was changing in value between 1 and 2 and recognised that this was wrong.	Do While Not EOF(1) Let index = 1 Input #1, Numbers(index) Let index = index + 1 Loop

6. He moved the line:
    Let index = 1
to before the loop and retested the program. It was now correct.
	Let index = 1
	Do While Not EOF(1)
	   Input #1, Numbers(index)
	   Let index = index + 1
	Loop

Table 1: Actions of a Student who was Observed using CORT

inevitable that he would finally create the "correct" plan.

During this process, the student's internal schemata had been amended as he obtained feedback during his program testing. The important point is that he had constructed the knowledge himself and felt a great sense of achievement when the program worked correctly. He how different students, who have learned programming by either conventional or completion methods, perform in the generation of larger programs.

7. References

du Boulay, B. (1986). "Some Difficulties in Learning to Program." Journal of Educational Computing Research 2(1): 57-73.

Garner, S. (2000). A Code Restructuring Tool to help Scaffold Novice Programmers. International Conference in Computer Education, ICCE2000, Taipei, Taiwan, National Tsing Hua University, Taiwan.

Garner, S. K. (2001). A tool to support the use of part-complete solutions in the learning of programming. Informing Science 2001, Cracow University of Economics, Krakow, Poland.

Linn, M. and J. Dalbey (1985). "Cognitive Consequences of Programming Instruction." Educational Psychologist 20(4): 191-206.

Lisack, S. K. (1998). Helping Students Succeed in a First programming Course: A Way to Correct Background Deficiencies. International Association for Computer Information Systems Conference, Cancun, Mexico.

Scholtz, J. and S. Wiedenbeck (1992). "The role of planning in learning a new programming language." International journal of man-machine studies 37: 191-214.

Van Merrienboer, J. J. G. (1990). "Strategies for Programming Instruction in High School: Program Completion vs. Program Generation." Journal of educational computing research. 6(3): 265-270.

Winslow, L. (1996). "Programming Pedagogy-- A Psychological Overview." SIGCSE Bulletin 28(3 (September 1996)).

Using On-Line Discussion to Develop Preservice Teacher Understanding of Classroom Management.

By Brian Ferry, Julie Kiggins and Garry Hoban
Faculty of Education
University of Wollongong
Email: bferry@uow.edu.au

ABSTRACT

This paper describes how a knowledge building community (KBC) of preservice teachers used an on-line discussion forum to develop knowledge about the role of the teacher in modern schools. It traces their initial use of the technology and follows the evolution of its use over a three-year period describing the role of the students and university lecturers in facilitating discussion. The paper then focuses on how members of the KBC used an on-line discussion forum to reflect on and share learning experiences as they developed classroom management strategies.

INTRODUCTION

Studies of learning in schools and universities show that knowledge is often presented in a fragmented and decontextualised way (Entwhistle, Entwhistle & Tait, 1993). As a result the knowledge is not retrievable in real-life situations because there is no link to the situation in which it applies. Teacher education courses have been criticised for the same reasons (Ramsey, 2000) explaining why many researchers report that beginning teachers are unable to relate what they have studied at university to how it can be translated into effective classroom practice (MACQT, 1998).

Moreover, reviews of beginning teacher competencies over the past 80 years continually identify a number of key management skills that are inadequately developed. These include: student discipline, motivating students, dealing with individual differences, insufficient and/or inadequate resources, organisation of classwork, assessing student work, and relationships with parents (Koetsier & Wubbels, 1995). The Ramsey (2000) review of teacher education in NSW supported these findings and asserted that preservice teachers do not understand how to manage the classroom so that it becomes an effective learning environment.

One way to address this deficiency is to re-think school-based practice teaching programs. Since 1999, Ferry, Cambourne and Kiggins have coordinated a team of researchers who have re-conceptualised the school-based practice teaching by planning, implementing and evaluating an alternative approach known as the 'Knowledge Building Community' or KBC (Ferry,

Kiggins, Hoban & Lockyer, 2000.). The KBC consisted of a group of peers, lecturers and school-based teachers, who all play a role in supporting decisions and encouraging reflection.

Research about the KBC program has shown that a focus on the development of knowledge and skills in contexts that reflect the way that they are used in real life is an effective and powerful approach to teacher education. A critical aspect is the notion of the apprentice (or neophyte) observing a 'community of practice' (Lave & Wagner, 1991). This process allows the neophyte to progressively piece together the culture of the group and to understand what it means to be a member. To facilitate the process we made use of an on-line discussion forum to create a dynamic learning community whose task was to build knowledge about the teaching profession.

This study emphasised sustained conversations and activities that were grounded in real life experience. Thus, the research focus is on how KBC members used an on-line discussion forum to reflect on and share learning experiences as they developed understandings of effective classroom management strategies.

BACKGROUND

When information comes to people via the Internet there are many benefits such as: direct access to a broader range of information; access to learning environments outside normal lecture and tutorial times; greater opportunity for experiencing a variety of instructional strategies including small group discussion and collaborative projects; and exposure to a forum for expressing and sharing ideas (Lockyer, Patterson & Harper, 1999). Some researchers claim that education that is entirely based on such technology contributes to a loss of community (Besser and Bonn, 1996), but Romiszowski and Mason (1996) showed that technology does allow for genuine conveyance of human communication. This study contributes to this debate by focusing on the use used an on-line discussion forum to foster preservice teacher understanding of the role teachers take in managing the classroom.

A KNOWLEDGE BUILDING COMMUNITY (KBC) IN TEACHER EDUCATION

A 'knowledge building community' (KBC) is described by Berieter and Scardamalia (1993) as a group of people who investigate problems. Members work as groups and are engaged in progressive discourse in an iterative process of knowledge building. The Faculty of Education at the University of Wollongong wanted to use a KBC approach to respond to recurrent themes emerging from studies that sought to follow-up graduates of teacher education courses. One was that often students reported that they left university feeling under-prepared for life in classrooms and confused by what confronted them when they arrived at schools and became part of a team that managed the school (Ramsey, 2000). Schools reported that a majority of recent graduates were unaware of how school and classroom cultures operated – particularly how teachers worked in small problem-solving teams to manage the school (MACQT, 1998; Ramsey 2000).

The on-line discussion forum was designed to provide students with a communication tool to engage in informal processes of knowledge sharing and construction. We believed that such a forum supplements face-to-face teaching by providing discussion forums that are non-threatening. The forum also allows individuals to maintain links with their community of practice and to take advantage of the scaffolding that is provided by a dynamic social context - allowing for legitimate peripheral participation (Lave & Wegner, 1991).

The literature claims that "professional socialisation is a complex and variable form of learning, highly collaborative in nature"(Weedman, 1998, p.1) and involves the transmission of social constructs, language, belief systems and symbolic lives that are unique to the profession (Schon, 1983). Brown and Duguid (1993) argue that this type of learning makes use of knowledge that must be 'stolen'. They contend that the most important knowledge is that which cannot be taught and students must find ways to 'steal' it from their educational environment.

The initial KBC course had two parts. The first part ran for five weeks and was designed to prepare students to work in a learning community and to understand how people work in teams to solve problems. During the second part of the KBC course students attended their host school for two days per week and attended university for one or two days per week. Whilst in schools they had two main roles. One was to be an effective teaching associate and the other was to be what we called 'an educational anthropologist'.

An educational anthropologist 'lives' within the school community and 'steals knowledge' (Brown & Duguid, 1993) that helps them to understanding of the culture of their schools and of the actions of the children and teachers that they observe. Thus, they work with a number of teachers, school executive and allied professionals (e.g. counsellors, teacher aides, school executive, special support staff) who act as 'informants' about their profession and the culture of the school.

This study focuses on the second year of the KBC. These students completed the Year 1 KBC program in 1999 and were developing many of the skills needed to be a successful teaching associate and educational anthropologist. Also they had developed basic planning skills and had some understanding of how teachers work with a team of professionals to manage safe, secure and productive learning environments.

The goal of the second year of KBC was for preservice teachers to develop the knowledge and skills needed to begin to effectively manage a safe, secure and productive learning environment. To help achieve this they spent 2 days per week in schools and 2 days at university focusing on problem-based tasks that are jointly constructed by the host school, university and the preservice teachers.

PURPOSE OF STUDY

The purposes of the study were:
1. To understand how members of the knowledge building community made use of an on-line discussion forum to developed their understanding of the role of primary school teachers- in particular effectively managing a safe, secure and productive learning environments;
2. To describe the role that the lecturers took in mediating on-line discussion among members of the knowledge-building community.

The following research questions were posed:
1. How did student use of an on-line discussion forum help them to develop an understanding of the role of primary teachers in effectively managing safe, secure and productive learning environments?
2. What were some of the limitations associated with the use of an on-line discussion forum?
3. What role did the lecturers play in mediating the on-line discussions?

PARTICIPANTS

This study, conducted in (2000), was limited to a group of 24 Year 2 primary education students enrolled in a KBC course in teacher education. The age of the students ranged from 18 years to 45 years and gender composition was three males and 21 females.

During the second week of the session all participants were taught to use an on-line discussion forum embedded in WebCT. Although WebCT could be accessed from home computers, we also allowed access to a group of five computers located in their university home-room or from any of the computers within the university computing laboratories. The purpose of the WebCT site was to create the discussion forum and data from the 945 entries made over a 12 week period that is used in this study.

LIMITATIONS

Knowledge building for the KBC involved three sources: the community of learners (i.e. preservice teachers, lecturers and teachers), school based learning and problem-based learning. The scope of this study is focused on how an asynchronous discussion forum is used as a means of synthesizing these sources of learning.

METHODS

The purpose of the first part of the study was to understand how members of the KBC made use of an on-line discussion forum to develop an understanding of the role of teachers in effectively managing safe, secure and productive learning environments. Data were gathered from two sources: text downloaded from the asynchronous forum and interviews with lecturers. Students gave us permission to download their messages and were aware that others would be able to read their messages. They wished to be identified as they wanted to show others how they used the discussion space. Data pertaining to the lecturers' role in mediating on-line discussion and verification came from post-session interviews with lecturers and analysis of downloaded text from the forum.

RESULTS AND DISCUSSION

The results are organised under the headings of lecturer input, classroom experience, reflecting and connecting to illustrate how the inputs from various sources helped in building community knowledge about classroom management. The ways in which the on-line discussion forum was used and the roles the lecturers played in facilitating on-line discussion are also described in this section.

Lecturer input

KBC students had the option of attending lecturers that were relevant to their school experiences during the session. And they attend a total of 6 from the 80 available to mainstream students. They were careful to select only those that would add to their current needs, as illustrated by the entries below.

Article No. 65 posted by *J* on Wed, Mar. 22, 2000, 14:14

> I also learnt a lot from the lecture this week on difficult behaviours. I thought it was fantastic to hear the real life experiences of the lecturer.

Article No. 93: posted by *L* on Sun, Mar. 26, 2000, 07:53

> For myself, this lecture was one of the best and most useful, if not THE best...

Later L reflected on the readings she had done and made following comments:

Glasser's points of psychological needs of children (us all): Love/belonging, Power Control (power to, rather than power over), Freedom Independence, Fun/Excitement. We have to do something to meet these needs in the classroom to decreased behaviour problems.

Later the lecturer provided KBC students with the opportunity to view a video on classroom management produced by Bill Rogers, a world-renown expert. Their comments follow:

Article No. 172: posted by *K* on Tue, Apr. 4, 2000, 11:48

> ...I must agree with J that although he seemed a bit of a clown.. the underlying meaning was quite beneficial to my learning... It reminded me of last year's teaching.. there was one boy who I'm sure always mucked up just to test my management strategies. Which back then were non existent. Having, listened to D's lectures and from watching this video, I have thought of some things I could have tried on this young man.

At this stage the KBC students were starting to focus in on their school experience. They were making connections to past experiences and planning for their next experience in schools which was about to commence. Also one of lecturers, Julie was encouraging to follow up and apply what they had learnt at university.

Classroom Experience

This section looks at how the classroom experience linked to their university experience. The discussion shows how the students looked for connections to their university work but at the same time they made use of other sources of learning such as their mentor teachers, peers and facilitators. It shows that many were naïve about how teachers managed classrooms but at the same time they were prepared to question and challenge some of the strategies they observed.

Article No. 197: posted by *F* on Wed, Apr. 5, 2000, 20:22

I watch a lesson today by a male teacher and he used a lot of Bill Roger's ideas and guess what...they worked. ...It all made sense.

Article No. 203: posted by *L* on Wed, April. 5, 2000, 21:24

I thought you might like to know about what my mentor teacher told us about "classroom rules" she explained that children in her class, have sometimes not been able to effectively use the rules up on the wall as they cannot read them yet! She suggests using picture clues on the walls.

Facilitator input- Article No. 214: posted by J on Thursday, April 6th, 2000, 17:04

Lisa, Thanks for sharing that advice about the rules that is a really great management strategy, ie using pictures as clues to reinforce the class rules. Did any one else pick up anything different? Julie

Article No. 405: posted by *K* on Tue, Apr. 18, 2000, 12:02

I actually have found it interesting in the K/1 classroom I'm in, that there doesn't seem to be ANY sign of class rules....The teacher seems to just discipline right then and there as she teaches...

Article No. 292: posted by *JT* on Tue, Apr. 11, 2000, 12:45

Hi Everyone! One thing I noticed after my first day at school was the amount of bribing the teachers do to get the students to behave. My teacher has a points system. The students are rewarded for good behaviour by receiving 10 points. At the end of the term the students with the most points receive a prize.

Anyway the following day I had to take a music lesson. I couldn't believe how disruptive the students actually were.. . That's when I realised that bribery works....

Sure prizes and stickers may get the students to be quiet, but it doesn't mean they will learn anything. Just because the students are silent does not mean they are hearing what you are saying.

Facilitator input - Article No. 330: posted by *Br* on Fri, Apr. 14, 2000, 17:11

J do believe that classroom management it isn't as simple as bribery. Do would others like to comment?. Brian

There were 195 entries relating to classroom management and coding of these data showed that as time in the classroom increased student discussion move from a focus more on daily class-based experiences to the more difficult cases that times appeared to be intractable. Management problems were shared and successful outcomes celebrated on line and those problems that were not solved were shared so at least their learning community could be supportive.

Reflecting and connecting

This section provides examples of student reflection and it also illustrates how they were connecting the various source of knowledge together to generate their own understanding of classroom management. They have used a wide variety of sources including recommended texts, mentor teachers and peers.

Article No. 425: posted by *M* on Tue, Apr. 18, 2000, 12:40

My mentor told me to remember two important C's-they are consistency and compassion. Consistency in your expectations from the students/what you expect from them. Compassion in that you care about them as individuals -it's not just a job.

Article No. 556: posted by *R* on Sat, May. 20, 2000, 10:50

I have found that to be able to implement good behaviour management strategies, it is very important to provide a safe welcoming environment for the students.... When the students enter the room, there is a warm friendly feeling which is non-threatening for the students..

Article No. 614:posted by *K* on Wed, May. 24, 2000, 19:07

I have come to the conclusion that one of the best methods of managing secondary behaviour is by "tactically ignoring" it...Sometimes, the best method to use to curb their behaviour is simply to ignore that they exist. Then they no longer have a reason to misbehave.

Article No. 679: posted by *H* on Tue, May. 30, 2000, 12:28

Prac teaching is a great opportunity to practice different management strategies. While I have been teaching kindergarten, I have realised that you need an array of management strategies. With the younger students quickly losing their motivation and concentration to learn the teacher must be prepared to steer the students back on track...

Article No. 692: posted by *RY* on Tue, May. 30, 2000, 17:03

My prac session this year has helped me immensely to improve my strategies and techniques in order to gain classroom control. Being placed in one of the wildest classes in the school has also helped me to understand why children behave like this... such as the very

clever, but extremely naughty children, and the children with no desire for learning at all.
Article No. 706: posted by *Ko* on Fri, Jun. 2, 2000, 00:51
My mentor teacher has also been encouraging me to use my teacher's voice. At first I felt too timid to be firm with and get cross at the students. But I have learnt that without using your teacher's voice, students will not respect and respond to you. If students do misbehave, I have found that it pays to 'act' very cross and displeased.

Other entries followed similar themes. In most cases students adjusted to the routine of the mentor teacher's class and often followed similar strategies. They were prepared to question these strategies and to look for alternatives from peers, suggested readings and university facilitators.

DISCUSSION AND CONCLUSION

The discussion space was an effective tool for the sharing of knowledge and experiences. Over time the entries demonstrated a growth in knowledge and understanding that appeared to lead to improved management in the classroom. Also the student entries from later in the session support the assertion that they developed greater understanding of strategies related to the management of safe, and productive learning environments.

One advantage of the discussion space is accessibility. Students could add entries at any time and at any place that had an Internet connection. It appeared that they liked the opportunity to share experiences and knowledge with peers and the collegial tone of the entries is an indicator of this. However, a word of caution needs to be raised. This group was experienced in using discussion spaces and had worked together in various problem-solving groups for more than a year. As a result their face-to-face discussion skills as well as their on-line skills were highly developed. Further, they were engaged in teaching experiences that were relevant to their current and future needs. Facilitators need to be aware that just adding a chat space to a subject is not enough. There needs to a process that helps student engage with each other and other participants. Also the chat space has to fulfill a purpose that is relevant to the needs of students.

However, there were some limitations as two students were reluctant to share knowledge on-line and they did not enjoy using the discussion space. This indicates that it is dangerous to assume that ALL students will find this means of learning effective and comfortable. Another limitation is the size of the group - 24 students generated over 950 entries and these were read and responded to.

The task is time consuming, taking 10 to 15 minutes per day. If the group were larger the task of responding would be too onerous.

At this stage we can confidently report that our experience with on-line discussion spaces to support a knowledge building community of beginning teachers has been mostly positive. Many of our colleagues have used this technology with mixed success and we speculate that they may have under-estimated the prior preparation need to turn the technology from an add-on to a useful learning tool.

REFERENCES

Bereiter, C. & Scardamalia, M. (1993). *Surpassing ourselves.* Open Court. Illinois.

Besser, H. & Bonn, M. (1996). Impact of distance independent education. *Journal of the American Society of Information Science* 47, 817-883.

Brown, J. S. & Duguid, P. (1993) Stolen knowledge. *Educational Technology.* 33, 10-15.

Darling-Hammond, L. (1999).Teacher Education: Rethinking Practice and Policy. *Unicorn* 25(1), 31-48.

Entwhistle, N., Entwhistle A., & Tait H.(1993*).* Academic Understanding and the Contexts to Enhance It: A perspective from research on student learning. In T.M. Duffy, J.Lowyck & D.H. Jonassen (Eds*.) Design Environments for Constructive Learning*. Heidelberg: Springer-Verlag, 331-357.

Ferry, B., Kiggins, J., Hoban, G. & Lockyer, L. (2000). Using computer-mediated-communication to form a knowledge-building community with beginning teachers. *Educational Technology and Society,* 3(3), 496-505.

Koetsier, C.P. & Wubbels, J. T. (1995). Bridging the Gap Between Initial Teacher Training and Teacher Induction. Journal of Education for Teaching 21(3), 333-345.

Lave, J. & Wenger, E. (1991). *Situated learning: Legitimate peripheral participation.* Cambridge: Cambridge University Press.

Lockyer, L., Patterson, J., & Harper, B. (1999). Measuring effectiveness of health education in a Web-based learning environment: a preliminary report. *Higher Education Research & Development.* 18(2), 233-246.

MACQT, (1998). Teacher preparation for student management: Responses and directions. *Report by Ministerial Advisory Council on the Quality of Teaching, October, 1998.* Sydney: NSW Department of Education and Training.

Ramsey, G. (2000). *Quality Matters: Revitalising teaching: critical times, critical choices.* Report on the Review of Teacher Education, NSW. Sydney: Department of Education and Training.

Romiszowski, A. J., & Mason, R. (1996). Computer-mediated communication. In D. H. Jonassen (Ed.), *Handbook of Research for Educational Communications and Technology.* (pp. 438-456). New York: Macmillian LIBRARY Reference USA.

Scardamalia, M. &. Bereiter,C. (1996). Engaging Students in a Knowledge Society. Educational Leadership. 54 (3), 6-10

Weedman, J. (1998*) Burglar's tools: the use of collaborative technology in professional socialisation.* Paper presented at ASIS Midyear'98 Proceedings. Available at URL

The Pedagogy and Practice of Role-Play:
Using a Negotiation Simulation to Teach Social Science Theory

Dr. David Humphreys

Senior Lecturer in Environmental Policy, Open University, United Kingdom

Abstract

Audio-visual conferencing software enables students to participate in role-play simulations from remote sites. This paper details the teaching methodology for Open University Masters course D833 'Environmental Practice: Negotiating Policy in a Global Society'. The course includes a negotiation role-play simulation that aims to simulate multilateral negotiations at the United Nations. The simulation provides a 'laboratory' for students to experiment with and enhance their understanding of theories of negotiation, international cooperation and international environmental law. Students are guided in using theory (i) to participate in the simulation as interested participants with a vested stake in the simulation, and (ii) to explain the process and outcome of the simulation as disinterested objective scholars. Students thus gain experience in working with theory in two different though interrelated roles – those of the practitioner and the social scientist.

The Open University

The Open University (OU) has 150,000+ students and is committed to providing high quality courses for part-time students studying from a distance. For most courses assessment is 50% by continuous assessment and 50% by final examination. Continuous assessment takes the form of Tutor Marked Assignments (TMAs) which are sent – and returned with grade, comment and feedback – by post or electronically (e-TMAs).

A central component of the OU's strategy for the use of IT in course delivery is the development of a real time audio-visual conferencing system, *Lyceum*. Computer conferencing can fill various teaching needs: moderated tutorials can be held using shared applications with which students collaboratively work on ideas; student 'self help' groups can be formed. The technology also allows students to participate in live role-play simulations. It is this last area with which we are concerned here.

Three *Lyceum* modules have been developed. Concept Map enables students collaboratively to chart concepts and their relationships by posting, labelling and linking nodes (boxes). Whiteboard is a shared canvas which students can use to draw simple diagrams and to import electronic images from outside *Lyceum*. The third module – Document – enables the collaborative writing and editing of text. As well as working online, students can work offline with each *Lyceum* module at home.

D833

D833 aims to teach students the theory and practice of negotiating. Students are introduced to negotiating theory, theories of international cooperation and international environmental law. Six tutorials are held during the course using *Lyceum*. Additionally, each student is given a role as a government delegate. They are provided with a 'country profile', and guided in researching their role through selected web pages available on the D833 home page. They work with their role in nine 2-hour negotiation sessions in a simulation designed around the procedures used in UN environmental negotiations. The objective of the negotiations is to agree an International Convention on Forests. Delegates elect a chair from amongst themselves for each 2-hour session. The negotiations are serviced by the 'Secretariat' (a trained OU tutor). There is no face-to-face interaction on the course.

Research for the course included a visit to the 4th session of the Intergovernmental Forum on Forests at the UN in New York in February 2000. This visit revealed some important informal (often hidden) dynamics of multilateral negotiation that the course team have incorporated into the simulation. See Table 1 below.

Figure 1 below illustrates the online D833 interface. There is a Plenary room where the master text is kept. Smaller pieces of text may be assigned to Working Group rooms for negotiation. Students change rooms by clicking on the room they wish to enter.

Informal dynamics of multilateral negotiation	How these dynamics have been incorporated in the D833 simulation
Many important deals are brokered informally in 'the corridors'.	The D833 Corridor (Figure 1) is a public space where any delegate can participate in informal discussion.
Private whispered discussion frequently occurs during multilateral negotiations.	There are two Whisper Spaces. These are best conceptualised as private spaces at the back of the Plenary. Delegates can converse privately while continuing to observe modifications made to the *Lyceum* Plenary modules.
'Who is talking to who' is an often hidden dynamic of multilateral negotiations. Keeping track of this can provide clues to the sort of deals being brokered.	At the bottom of every room (except the Plenary, where occupants are listed separately, and the Corridor) is an 'eye' (Figure 1). When a student clicks on the 'eye' a drop-down list appears of all the occupants in the room.

Table 1   Informal dynamics of negotiation incorporated in the D833 simulation

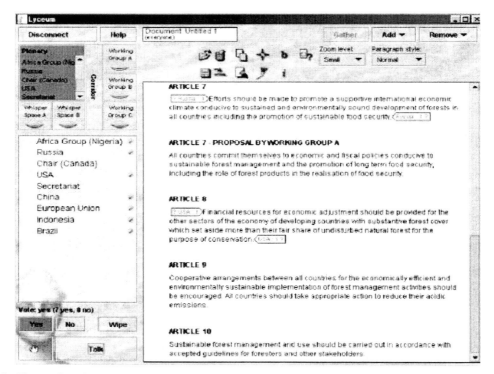

Figure 1   The online *Lyceum* interface using the Document module. The Plenary is greyed, indicating that this is the room in which the user is currently located. The 'Yes' button is greyed, indicating that the user has voted 'Yes'. The ticks indicate users who have voted 'Yes'. Note the vote tally.

The *Lyceum* Document module in D833

When negotiating text at the UN any delegate can propose a new formulation and any delegate can dispute text. Text is disputed at the UN by inserting square brackets, with an open [sign at the start of the offending word(s) and a close] sign at the end. Where x pieces of text have been disputed there will be x sets of square brackets. Clearly this system would not work electronically, as the software would be unable to determine which open [sign relates to which close] sign. The *Lyceum* team have therefore developed a system of dispute tags. Each tag is uniquely numbered and carries the name of the disputing 'country'. In Figure 1 above it can be seen that Russia has disputed Article 7. As the Plenary could not agree on a new formulation of Article 7, further negotiations on this article took place in Working Group A, where a new proposal was agreed. This was *copied* in Working Group A and then *pasted* into the Plenary text for further deliberation. (*Lyceum* has also developed a tags system that denotes who has inserted text. This system has not been adopted for D833, as it is not consistent with UN procedures.)

The pedagogic strategy of D833

The D833 course team drew upon the OU's accumulated expertise in using the *Lyceum* synchronous conferencing system and asynchronous conferencing such as FirstClass for other courses. The OU has found that in order to be effective:

- Computer conferencing should have a clearly defined place within the course (and should not be a 'bolt on' feature).

- The learning objectives of computer conferencing should be clearly defined in advance.

- Computer conferencing should be effectively moderated.

- There should be opportunity for individual reflection and/or group debriefing and/or tutor feedback of what has been learned from computer conferencing.

D833, which aims to be policy relevant, sets out to teach negotiation as an essentially social activity. The simulation enables students to understand the interactive dynamics of negotiating. It is impossible to capture and represent this using conventional print resources. The simulation also provides a framework for situated learning, and embodies the idea that learning is a progression.

The use of the simulation emphasises that negotiation is a *mutual learning process*. At the start of the simulation the collective knowledge of the participants is unevenly distributed and dispersed amongst delegates. This will change as the simulation progresses: if there is to be a negotiated settlement some coordination between delegates is needed, and this can only take place through interaction and mutual discovery.

Learning requires active engagement and practice. As Knight and Trowler argue, deep learning requires not only a thorough comprehension of theoretical and conceptual ideas; it also requires application. If skills are to be learned there must be opportunity for feedback, reflection and fine tuning.[1] The D833 simulation gives students the opportunity to understand theory through the provision of a focused collection of readings and an accompanying Study Guide, including interactive exercises.

The course teaches social science theory from two perspectives: that of the academic; and that of the practitioner. First, students are taught to relate theory to practice as social scientists, that is to explain and analyse the process and (at the end of the course) the outcome of the simulation. Students are required to disengage from their role, viewing their performance in the simulation objectively and disinterestedly as an object of study.

Second, D833 makes explicit the iterative relationship between theory and practice. Students are guided to use their theoretical and conceptual understanding of negotiation in the 'laboratory' of the simulation. Reflexive thinking on the use of theory in the simulation will reinforce students' understanding both of negotiation and of using theory as a practitioner. Students thus gain a first hand understanding of the iterative relationship between theory and practice (Figure 2).

Following on from this, all TMA and examination questions focus directly on the simulation and require students either to use theory to analyse the negotiations as an academic observer or to explain their negotiation aims, strategy and tactics in the simulation using course theory. An example of a question that assesses student ability to analyse the negotiations as an observer is:

'Judging from events so far in the simulation, future negotiations will involve delegates negotiating alone, rather than forming themselves into coalitions.' Discuss this statement with reference to the simulation.

This question assesses students' understanding of coalition theory, and their ability to use such theory to interrogate and evaluate the processes observed in the

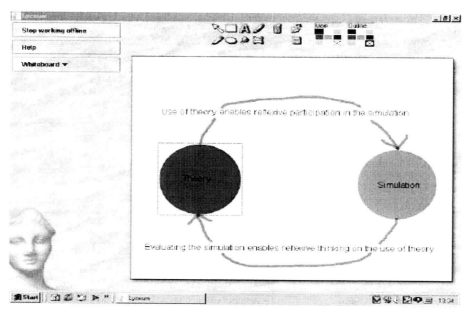

Figure 2   A combination of tools has been used in the *Lyceum* Whiteboard to chart the iterative relationship between theory and practice in an online negotiation simulation.

simulation. The relationship between the theory of the course and the negotiation simulation is thus central to the D833 assessment strategy. It cannot be neglected if students are to be successful on the course. Note that the assessment strategy is not separate from the pedagogic strategy. Students are advised that in thinking through their TMA answers they may gain useful insights that they can employ as a delegate later in the simulation.

It is clear that the relationship between the role of 'delegate' and that of student is central to the pedagogic strategy of the course. We now consider this relationship in more detail.

Working with two roles

Students work with two roles on D833: as a Masters-level student pursuing an academic course of study; and as a 'government delegate' pursuing negotiating objectives in a simulation. To a large extent they must practice keeping these two roles separate by practising 'taking off one hat' and 'putting on another' during the course. But when should they change hats? There is no simple answer to this, but it is likely that at any time a student sits down to study the course they will find themselves thinking

alternately as a student and as a negotiator. For example, a student may realise that a part of the Study Guide has reinforced their understanding of a particular theory. In the next moment the student may realise that this theory can be utilised to make a particular negotiating move in the simulation.

However, while students must 'wear different hats' there is an interaction between these roles throughout the course. To illustrate this the Study Guide of the course presents students with the thinking of the financial speculator George Soros. Soros emphasises that he has two roles. First, he seeks to understand the market dispassionately and objectively. He observes market movements and analyses his observations to see if any general trends are discernible. This will tell him which way the market is moving, and whether he should buy or sell.

But by buying and selling Soros has ceased to be entirely objective. He has entered the market, and by doing so he has moved from being a disinterested analyst to a participant with a financial stake in future market movements. Furthermore, by participating in the market he may alter the behaviours of other actors, and so change the trends he earlier observed. Soros is very aware of these

Course component	Student role	Delegate role
Computer conferencing	e-tutorials moderated by a trained tutor	Negotiation simulation moderated by the 'Secretariat' (trained OU tutor)
Guided use of theory	To analyse the simulation as an objective observer	To inform negotiation aims, strategy and tactics
Interacting with peers	In tutorials or using email: debate the course material with other students as scholars	In the simulation or using email: Pursue the 'national interest' while also working with other delegates to solve a common interest problem
Feedback	From tutor (TMA marking) and from other students in e-tutorials.	From other delegates: informally by email and in formal negotiating exchanges in the simulation.

Table 2   D833 learning methodology

two separate roles. As a participant he wants to make as large a profit as possible, in much the same way that students seek to realise their interests as a 'government delegate' in the D833 simulation. But at no time does Soros cease being an analyst. He accepts his interventions may alter the trends he earlier observed, and that they may lead to new trends. But, first, Soros is aware of why he acts as he does. He tries to explain his own subjective behaviour by wearing his objective analyst's hat. Second, he will not just accept that his behaviour may change trends. He will try to explain how and in what ways his actions affect the market. If, and again wearing his analyst's hat, he can explain why people react to his interventions in a certain way, then he will be 'one step ahead of the game' when he next makes a market intervention. [2]

Concluding thoughts

D833 offers a learning methodology that encompasses moderated computer conferencing, the guided use of theory, interaction with peers and feedback (Table 2). In addition students are encouraged to reflect on their progress by keeping a negotiation journal (which is not assessed).

D833 aims to provide a rounded teaching and learning strategy by approaching the use of social sciences theory from the perspective of the scholar and from that of the practitioner. It is intended that students will gain a deep appreciation of the practical and professional relevance of scholarly research.

The D833 online interface and the *Lyceum* Document module were extensively tested by some 25 participants including an external assessor between June 2001 and February 2002. Some minor initial inefficiencies were identified that required reprogramming. The software has passed the OU's quality assurance procedures. With all design and development work successfully completed D833 is now ready for its first presentation commencing November 2002.

While it is clear that the technology works, it is not, at this writing, clear how successful the learning methodology will be. A thorough assessment of this methodology will take place at the end of the first presentation. This will be based on the first presentation and will include the findings of course team members who attend a sample of negotiation sessions and e-tutorials, scrutiny of TMAs and examination scripts, the results of a questionnaire survey sent to all students, and a debriefing of all tutors and 'Secretariat' staff.

References

1   Knight, P. and Trowler, P. (2001) *Departmental Leadership in Higher Education*, Buckingham: SRHE/Open University Press.

2   Soros, G. (1998) *The Crisis of Global Capitalism*, London: Little Brown and Co.

Collaborative Learning and Other Successful Strategies for On-line Homework

P. M. Kotas and J. E. Finck

Physics Department, Central Michigan University, Mt. Pleasant, Michigan 48859

Abstract

Central Michigan University has utilized the Internet and the Computer-Assisted Personalized Approach (CAPA) for homework in physics classes. Student activity on CAPA is automatically recorded and logged into the system's files. These log files have been examined to determine when students worked on their assignments. Additional information about the students and their habits were obtained through surveys and institutional data. An analysis of this data indicates that collaborative learning flourishes in an asynchronous environment, and significant relationships exist between study behavior and achievement.

Most physics teachers would agree that problem solving is an integral part of the leaning process [1-5]. It is certainly reasonable, therefore, to expect that the manner in which students engage themselves with their homework is important. However, relatively little attention has been paid specifically to the mechanics of how students actually do homework outside the classroom.

Recent integration of the Internet in physics classes has opened the door to directly observing students' homework behavior. At Central Michigan University (CMU), the Computer-Assisted Personalized Approach (CAPA) has been used in introductory physics courses to conduct homework over the Internet [3, 6, 7]. This system allows instructors to create problem sets with variables that can be randomized and modified for each student. Thus problem sets are individualized.

As a result of using CAPA in several introductory physics courses at CMU, it was possible to examine the system's log files to gain insight into when students were doing their homework. General homework patterns are identified and analyzed with respect to student achievement, as well as other measured behaviors and demographic and academic factors.

The data collected in this study was taken from three introductory, algebra-based college physics courses. Each course had enrollments of about 100. Some demographic and academic information about the students was available through the Registrar's office, while additional data was procured by surveying the students directly.

Students were required to submit answers to their assignments using CAPA. Each time an answer to a problem was submitted the student was identified, the time and date of submission were recorded. Each submission was logged and recorded to as a "hit.

Several parameters regarding the course structure have important implications for this study and should be kept in mind: (1) The class met Monday through Thursday; (2) A help room staffed by undergraduate physics majors was available during these evenings; (3) Homework was always due at 3:00 AM on Sunday.

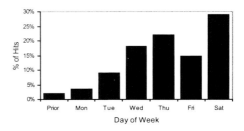

Figure 1. Normalized distribution of total hits.

In Figure 1, the total hits for a class are distributed by day of the week, revealing an overall picture of when students did their work. The total hit distribution indicates that there was a steady rise in activity through Thursday, the last day that class was in session. The drop in activity on Friday was then followed by a surge on the final day available to complete assignments.

The CAPA data permits an analysis of student achievement with respect to various measures of homework behavior. Figure 2 displays the hit distributions for five groups that are based on final grade. The 1st quarter group consists of the top 25% of the students who completed the class, while the bottom 25% constitutes the fourth quarter group. The students who, at some point in the semester, withdrew from the class make up the fifth group labeled "W."

Distinct differences in the hit distributions between groups are seen. Students in the top half of the class submitted seventy-five percent of their total hits by Thursday. Forty-one percent of the hits from the students in the bottom quarter occurred on Saturday, and students who ended up withdrawing did nearly 60% of their work on the last day. In addition, students who did their homework earlier in the week were more likely to be engaged in their physics homework on a daily basis. Students in the top 25% of the class worked on homework an average of 2.6 days per week while the students in the bottom fourth of the class worked an average of 1.7 days per week.

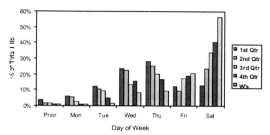

Figure 2. Hit distributions based on final grades.

With the use of CAPA data and survey results, it was possible to make general observations with regard to other behaviors. For example, one survey item asked the students the extent to which they collaborated. Eighty-four percent of the students indicated that they collaborated with other students to some degree. This certainly presents evidence that an asynchronous learning tool does not inhibit collaborative learning. Furthermore, the data shows that students who regularly worked with others completed their assignments earlier and did well in the class.

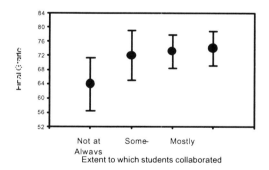

Figure 3. Final grades compared to collaboration.

Figure 3 displays student performance based on the extent to which they collaborated on homework. A significant difference in final grades exists between students who reported never having collaborated and those who reported having worked with other students at least some of the time. Students who generally worked in study groups tended to do their problems one at a time and appeared to be more dependent on the immediate feedback from CAPA.

The results presented in this study may have significant implications concerning future studies within the educational realm, especially in light of recent findings [5, 8]. First, it has

clearly been demonstrated that significant relationships exist between homework behavior and achievement in college physics courses. It has also been demonstrated that the presence of certain behavioral factors can have significant effects on relationships between performance and other commonly investigated factors. These findings support the claim [8] that such relevant information about students cannot be excluded from educational studies, such as those purporting to compare instructional methods and those that attempt to measure learning effectiveness. Second, there is an evident movement in academia (particularly in physics) toward the integration of online homework systems. This study has demonstrated that such systems have an inherent capability of providing researchers valuable information about students' study habits. Third, it has been argued that asynchronous learning environments are more effective for collaborative learning, and in this study collaboration was found to be a significant factor related to achievement

For future study it would be fruitful to examine such behaviors in relation to other factors associated with learning, such as learning styles, attitudes, environmental variables, and learning strategies and methods. Additional contextual factors should be considered, to include students' extra-curricular activities. Such inquiries could prove to be beneficial for research involved with learning effectiveness.

References

1. E. Kashy, S.J. Gaff, N.H. Pawley, "Conceptual questions in computer-assisted assignments," Am. J. Phys. **63**(11), 1000-1005 (1995).

2. E. Redish and R.N. Steinberg, "Teaching physics: figuring out what works," Physics Today. **52**(1), 1124-1130 (1999).

3. E. Kashy, B.M. Sherrill, and Y. Tsai, "CAPA, an integrated computer assisted personalized assignment system," Am. J. Phys. **61**(12), 1124-1130 (1993).

4. An extensive review of the problem solving literature can be found in D.P. Maloney, in *Handbook of Research on Science Teaching and Learning*, D. Gabel, ed., Macmillan, New York (1993), p. 327.

5. S. Ziegler, "Homework," *Encyclopedia of Educational Research*, 6th Ed.

6. E. Kashy, D.J. Morrissey, and Y. Tsai, "An introduction to CAPA, a versatile tool for science education," MSU-NSCL Report 971, September 1995.

7. M. Thoennessen and M. J. Harrison, "Computer-assisted assignments in a large physics class," Computers Educ. **27**, 141 (1996).

8. E.H. Joy II and F.E. Garcia, "Measuring learning effectiveness: a new look at no-significant-difference findings," JALN. **4**(1), 33-39 (2000).

Three Pedagogical C's of Internet Learning Communities

Jan McNeil, Lecturer, Centre for English Language
Communication (CELC), National University of Singapore and
Malkeet Singh, Biological Science and Mathematics Teacher,
Canberra Secondary School, Singapore Ministry of Education

Abstract

On today's Knowledge Age fast track, the only constant
change seems to be change itself. This paper presents and
discusses how learning communities on the Internet can
provide enriching creative, cognitive and collaborative
learning environments for exploring knowledge and
solving problems. Specific examples are also given of
simulated environments for practicing transferable skills
and WWW-based learning resources and tools, which are
currently being used in Singapore. The conclusion is that
the three C's of creativity, cognition and collaboration are
especially important aspects of teaching and learning
pedagogies in today's global village.

Introduction

The work of Lev Vygotsky, a theorist and researcher
in the 1920's and early 1930's whose developmental
theories on the role of cultural learning and schooling have
significantly influenced education today, provides a
research base for this paper. Vygotsky's principal premise
was that human beings are products of their human
cultures as well as of biology. Moreover, intellectual
functioning is the product of social history; and language is
the key mode by which cultures are learned and through
which verbal thinking is organized and actions are
regulated. People learn such higher functioning from
interacting with others around them. There is also a need
for creative, cognitive and collaborative communications
[4].

Creative

First, creatively, there is a need to align technology
with instructional goals by integrating the World Wide
Web into teaching and learning practices. Three levels of
difficulties and stages need to be addressed. The first stage
involves linking learning to the world of work and moving
from using knowledge in one discipline to applying
knowledge within disciplines. The second stage deals with
applying knowledge between disciplines to real world,

predictable problems. Finally, the third stage involves
applying knowledge to real world, unpredictable problems.

A model, which is currently being used in Singapore,
exemplifies the concepts discussed in this paper. In this
example, process skills are effectively woven into subject
content, enabling both to be concurrently internalized.
Additionally, related WWW lessons and activities have
been designed and can be supplemented, transferred and
tailor made to fit individual learning environments.
Learners can, therefore, have access to a plethora of
information, including investigative research, and be
provided with a virtual environment that effectively
mimics real world conditions.

Cognitive

Secondly, the paradigm shift, which is occurring in
many educational systems throughout the world today,
compels educators to prepare students to be net savvy and
info savvy individuals who are able to function effectively
in cognitive areas by using the 5 A's of: (1) Asking key
questions, (2) Accessing relevant information, (3)
Analyzing acquired information, (4) Applying information
to tasks and (5) Assessing processes and results [2].

Moreover, in addition to the positive impact of
learning through using computers in traditional ways for
drill and practice and tutorial instruction, a greater
potential exists for engaging learners in problem-solving
activities and higher order thinking (HOT) skills [5]. These
HOT skills require manipulation of ideas and information
in ways that change implications and meaning [3].
Learners can thus use WWW-based learning resources and
tools to discover rewarding, new meanings and solve
problems through such processes as combining ideas and
facts to hypothesize, generalize, synthesize, explain and
arrive at interpretations or conclusions.

To further develop cognitive abilities, the Internet can
also be used to help students examine and learn from
authentic, real-life situations in their content areas. To
enhance the development of thinking skills, educators need
to provide a plethora of application opportunities during
lessons and assignments. Doing so not only broadens

horizons but also simultaneously helps to develop multiple perspectives.

Examples of these processes include activities from web-based lessons currently being used in Singapore, which have been designed to encourage learners to explore various conditions associated with heart diseases and to relate these findings to the importance of having a healthy lifestyle. Such activities enable learners to go beyond the written objectives by exploring real life situations. Students can also learn more about the importance of circulatory system functions and have opportunities to role-play. For example, they can imagine that they are nutritionists who create a special diet program to be marketed to investors.

Collaborative

Thirdly, proponents argue that collaborative learning in schools provides opportunities for students in large classes to interact on a smaller scale and prepares students for the "real world." Effective, collaborative communications are also essential components of successful learning processes; and because " . . . no one knows it all; collaborative learning is not just nice, but (also) necessary . . . " [1]. The predominant philosophical underpinnings of collaboration are for teachers to use a "coach approach" and function as a "guide on the side" as opposed to being a "sage on stage."

The website http://studyhit.tripod.com/studyhit1.htm was created in Singapore in October 2000 to provide topic links as well as sample lesson plans to help teachers plan web-based lessons. This website is constantly being updated. In February 2001, 56 students at Canberra Secondary School in Singapore, who were taught using web-based lessons, were surveyed.

Results revealed that all of these students preferred WWW-based lessons more than traditional chalk and talk. Questions asked included whether websites were useful for online instruction, quizzes, self check work, e-conferencing, discussion forums and projects. Respondents reported that they found the web-based lessons to be stimulating and that their levels of concentration on the concepts presented were definitely increased because of the learning resources and tools, which were used. They also commented that they enjoyed these educational experiences and wanted to have more, which were similar.

Ongoing surveys are also being conducted at Canberra Secondary School at individual levels, each of which has 320 students, who are divided into express, normal academic and normal technical streams. Findings can be used to tailor-make lessons based on student preferences.

Conclusion

In conclusion, learning communities on the Internet can effectively implement pedagogical paradigm shifts by using creative, cognitive and collaborative teaching and learning strategies.

References

1. Brown, A. L. (1994).'The advancement of learning.' Educational Researcher, 23(8), 4-12.

2. Jukes, I., Dosaj, A., Matheson, J., McKay, B., McKay, W., Holmes, L., and Armstrong S., (1998). *NetSavvy: Information Literacy for the Communication Age*. Printed in USA.

3. Newmann, J. and Wehlage, G.G. (1993). 'Five standards of authentic instruction.' *Educational Leadership,* 50 (7), 8-12.

4. Tinzmann, M.B., Jones, B.F. Fennimore, T.F., Bakker, J., Fine, C. and Pierce, J. (1990). [Internet], 'What is the collaborative classroom?' Oak Brook: North Central Regional Educational Library. http://www.ncrel.org/sdrs.areas/rpl_esys/collab.htm. November 12, 2001.

5. Wager, W. (1997). Instructional Technology and The Teacher Educator. *Teacher Education and Special Education,* 20 (4): 378-388.

Jan McNeil has taught speech and English communications courses at colleges and universities in Singapore, Hawaii, Florida, Tennessee and Mississippi and secondary schools in Louisiana and Taiwan. Research interests include the use of computers in education, collaboration, constructivism, creativity, critical thinking, multicultural education, multiple intelligences, teacher education and the creation and delivery of mutually beneficial and enjoyable student-centered learning experiences.

Malkeet Singh, B.Sc (Hons), PGDE(Sec), is currently involved in ongoing distance education courses and has taught life sciences and mathematics courses at secondary schools in Singapore. His research interests include IT savvy education, cognitive coaching, collaboration, creativity, critical thinking, multiple intelligences, teacher education and the creation and delivery of enriching student-centered learning. He is also an avid research mentor and guide to students in hands-on life sciences projects.

An Electronic Performance Support System for the eLearner

Diane Ruelland

druellan@licef.teluq.uquebec.ca

Anne Brisebois

abrisebo@licef.teluq.uquebec.ca

LICEF research centre, Tele-universite, Quebec, Canada

Abstract

A longitudinal research aimed at identifying the eLearner's needs for support showed the importance of self-management processes on-line and the difficulties they represent for the adult who does not have access to relevant support in a Web-based Learning Environment (WBLE). This paper will present the conceptual model of tasks, objects and resources that served as a guide to build a cluster of tools to support self-management on-line. The framework guiding this work at LICEF research center borrows from theory and practice of distance learning as well as findings from metacognitive studies.

Key words. Self-directed learning, web-based learning, eLearning skills, metacognition, self-management.

1. New role for the eLearner

The distance in space and time among peers and between the learner and the trainer/tutor, the freedom in processing web information and the team networking are among the eLearning features, which create flexible and open-ended learning environments [1]. These conditions provide the adult learner with a greater amount of flexibility and control over the learning process than in a traditional classroom setting. eLearning conditions have the effect of transferring parts of the instructional design tasks to the learner such as defining his/her own learning needs and choosing relevant information to learn [2]. WBLE is more than a learner-centered approach. It puts the learner in a proactive position in order to progress and succeed. This situation addresses self-directed learning tasks with high level skills related to metacognitive strategies such as planning, self-monitoring and self-evaluation [3].

The managerial tasks sorted out in our study are not new but the objects, which are to be taken into account while applying these processes in eLearning, have new components [4]. For example, to manage one's rhythm of learning in an asynchronous and collaborative setting is different than in a classroom setting. It is also different to control one's comprehension while reading a print book

than while searching and consulting web pages on a specific topic.

Furthermore, our study showed that due to the combination of distance, multimedia information and network collaboration in the same environment, control opportunities are multiplied, decision-making is more complex and difficulties are just amplified. To adopt a proactive role represents a new attitude and it proved to be confusing and unfamiliar with most people [4] [5].

2. To learn about this new role

To understand better this new position of the eLearner, we applied a research-development method, which includes three main steps as illustrated in Figure 1: modeling the process, creating support tools and using tools with learners.

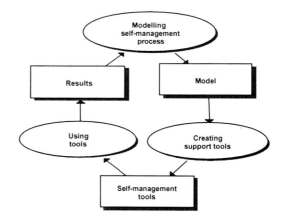

Figure 1 - Research method

The first step was to model the objects, the tasks and the resources involved in the eControl process. The sources of information used to build this model come from the fields of research related to eLearning (distance education, network collaboration, multimedia information processing) and self-management (adult learning, metacognition, autonomy and motivation), and from data collected during the pilot testing.

The second step was to design and develop interactive prototypes of tools with functionalities that can support the managerial tasks defined in the model.

The third step was to use the prototypes in eLearning settings, to observe students in action and to collect data in order to validate the model and to improve our understanding of the processes. The results allowed us to obtain relevant new knowledge about eLearning, to organize the model in coherent clusters of tasks and to establish priorities for the subsequent cycle of research.

These three steps were conducted over three cycles, each one addressing a specific aspect of the eLearning problem: self-management at distance, in multimedia environment and in network collaboration.

The added value of our work is two-fold. It yields an integrated vision of the distance, multimedia and collaborative features of eLearning as well as an operational definition of the metacognitive skills involved in self-management. It is limited to the knowledge of researchers and users of the eLearning and to the

technologies, which are in a continuous state of development.

3. eLearning Self-management model

Resulting from the R-D method is a model of the self-management process in an eLearning setting [6]. It contains three types of knowledge: procedural, conceptual and strategic as illustrated in Figure 2.

The procedural knowledge (how) is represented by oval shapes in the graphic and it describes the three metacognitive processes of control to be performed by the eLearner [7]:

- planning is the control applied before learning;
- self-monitoring is the control applied while learning;
- self-evaluation is the control applied after a lesson.

Each one of these processes is broken down into three procedures to loop the complete metacognitive process over learning [8]:

- awareness;
- judgment
- decision making

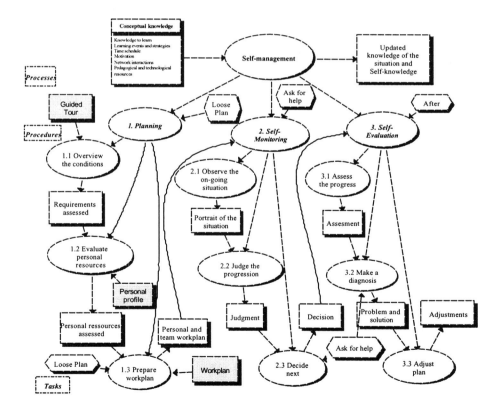

Figure 2 - Overview of the self-management model

Each procedure is, in turn, detailed into a sequence of tasks and operations, which will guide the design of interactive tools: this is the purpose of the modeling process. Because of space limitation we do not expose the tasks level in the graphic below.

The conceptual knowledge (what) describes the information to process and the products to deliver with each metacognitive procedure and is represented by rectangular shapes in the graphic. It is organized around the six major conditions influencing eLearning [9]: knowledge to acquire; learning activities to complete; learning time schedule; motivation; network interaction among peers; technological and pedagogical resources. For example, the procedure "to overview the conditions" includes six tasks which are: "to overview the knowledge to acquire", "to overview the learning activities to complete", " to overview…" etc… These six concepts apply to the eLearning context as well as to the eLearner's resources. They are also detailed at the task level to specify the information the eLearner needs to know to complete the task as illustrated below with the personal profile tool.

The strategic knowledge (why) states a suggestion to guide efficient applications of a task and is represented in the graphic by hexagonal shapes. Examples of strategic knowledge are:

- A planning suggestion is "to set up a loose plan of actions in order to be able to adapt the time schedule more easily to unexpected events". These events are frequent in adult life and they often are a source of delay because it is not possible to catch up with a tight workplan [10].
- A self-monitoring suggestion is to "ask for help when one's limitations prevent the progress in learning" [11].

The strategic knowledge of self-management was partly inspired by the learning difficulties identified throughout the study and it aims at alleviating them with proper interactive support.

4. Self-management Electronic Performance Support System (EPSS)

The self-management procedures, their inputs and outputs identified in the model above allowed specifying some interactive tools and guiding their design. In this context, an EPSS is seen as a set of tools supporting the activation and realization of self-management tasks within the eLearning space. In Figure 2 we locate three tools (in gray scale) designed to support the planning process in a WBLE. Each tool is linked to a procedure and its attributes come from the conceptual knowledge related to this procedure. Its interactive functionalities are related to the tasks and operations included in the procedure. Each tool gives shape to a self-management technique: to explore the eLearning conditions, to self-assess learning needs, to plan the eLearning process, to locate a problem, etc. The guided tour tool is linked to the procedure "Overview the conditions of learning". It is related to the awareness procedure of the planning process. It shows what and how to explore in order to get a clear understanding of the six learning conditions (conceptual knowledge), prior to preparing a workplan. The guided tour is a PowerPoint demo of the syllabus that informs the learner not only about the interactive resources available in a WBLE but also about the following items: learning objectives and knowledge to acquire; learning events; time schedule of the course; peers to contact on the network; choices offered to the learner.

The personal profile tool showed in Figure 3 is linked to

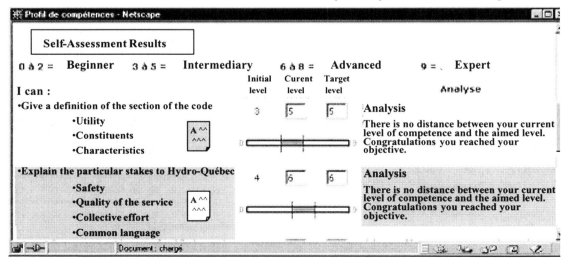

Figure 3 - Personal profile tool

the procedure "Evaluate personal resources" which is the judgment procedure of the planning process. It shows what and how to self-assess personal resources in relation with the knowledge to acquire. It serves to prepare a relevant workplan: strengths and weaknesses related to the content; strengths and weaknesses related to the eLearning strategies; prerequisites; personal goal.

For each skill listed (column on the left side), the learner enters a number from 0 to 9 representing his estimate of the level of knowledge mastered (in left box) and of his goal (in right box). A legend of the evaluation scale and extracts of documents exemplifying various cases of application of the competence are guiding the judgment. The tool can be used as often as desired during the learning process. The first evaluation of the knowledge mastered (current level) sets the initial level. A scale bar gives a schematic representation of this information. The two vertical lines on the scale bar indicate the entry level and the goal set by the learner and the dark section shows the progression of the learner in the knowledge acquisition. Each time the learner estimates his current

level, the scale bar is updated according to his new estimate.

The system applies a group of rules to analyze the data supplied by the learner and gives the results (column on the right side) by stating the learning events most suitable to the personal learning needs and the level of effort one should render in order to complete these events. By using this tool the learner becomes aware of his/her state of comprehension, self-evaluates and is ready to take planning decisions about his learning process based on relevant criteria.

The workplan tool shown in Figure 4 is linked to the procedure "Prepare a workplan". It is related to the decision-making procedure of the planning process. It allows the learner to set priorities among the learning events, adjust the duration time to complete homework and organize a team workplan. These tasks are performed within the limits set by the course designer and the personal resources available.

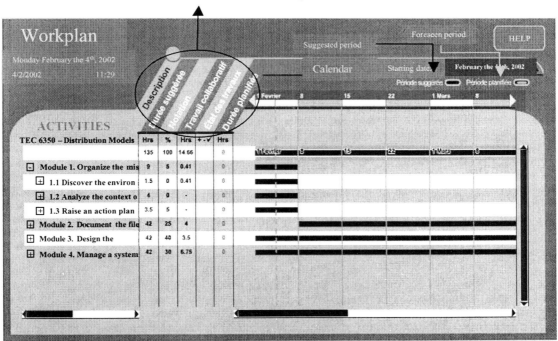

Figure 4 - Workplan tool

It contains the following items whose data are color-coded in the workplan according to the agent providing the information. : the learner (green) or the designer (black).

- Activities (list of learning events);
- calendar (start-up and deadline dates, holidays, tests, trainer feedback);
- recall of the learning features (suggested duration time of events, score obtained, suggested duration time of collaborative work);
- status of the personal learning process: (status of an event: delayed; on time; ahead of time; foreseen duration time of an event).

The tools share a common database and this main characteristic allows for a systemic approach of the self-management process, which gives complete power to the learner over the self-management tasks. For example, input from the learner through the use of the personal profile tool, is deposited into the database so the information can be retrieved by the workplan to recall previous estimate of personal resources: strengths and weaknesses of personal learning needs. This connection between the personal profile tool and the workplan tool allows the learner to choose learning events, set priorities and time schedule according to personal needs estimated previously. The self-management model gives an integrated and interrelated vision of the metacognitive tasks and objects to design tools that should improve the metacognitive performance of the learner in the following manner. At the conceptual level, the EPSS steers the learner's attention toward metacognitive objects, which is an essential condition to the efficient execution of the tasks. It also makes this targeted information available to the learner, alleviating his/her cognitive load. At the procedural level, the system offers an integrated set of tools, prompting the learner to carry out efforts on basic operations required to accomplish metacognitive tasks. Actually, 4 actors support the learner's metacognitive performance by supplying strategic information (Paquette, Brisebois & Ruelland, 2002):

- trainers or tutors through their feedback and evaluation,
- peers through collaborative work,
- computer agents through direct advice
- the learner him/herself, through his/her own believes.

Still under development, the body of rules and heuristics hidden behind the interventions of these actors and regulating the metacognitive process needs to be addressed.

5. Conclusion

Through our research we have addressed self-management as an essential skill in an eLearning situation and the results produced a conceptual model of tasks with tools to support them in a WBLE. The study pointed out a list of difficulties, which this skill brings about for the adult learner. These difficulties are mainly related to a low awareness and a poor mastery of knowledge comprehension and time management skills [11]. They are also related to the absence of relevant support in the environment, which can lead the eLearner to dropping out [12]. To improve the cognitive accessibility of eLearning, it is crucial to address this problem with efficient strategies. Our work is a step toward supporting both time and comprehension control in a WBLE. Our model can also serve to renew other support strategies like e-facilitating models to support self-management skills.

[1] Harasim, L. M. (1995). *TeleLearning Network Centers of Excellence, Building a Knowledge Society, Strategic Plan*, C1-C22.
[2] Mayes, T. (1996). *Distance Learning and the New Technology; A Learner-Centered View*. Institute for Computer-Based Learning, Heriot-Watt University, Edinburg. http://www.icbl.hw.ac.uk/ctl/mayes/paper10.html
[3] Jones, M.G., Farquhar, J.D. & Surry, D.W. (1995). Using metacognitive theories to design user interfaces for computer-based learning, *Educational Technology*, July-Aug, 12-22.
[4] Belisle, C. & Linard, M. (1996). Quelles nouvelles competences des acteurs de la formation dans le contexte des TIC?, *Éducation permanente*, 127(2), 19-47.
[5] Burge, E.J. (1994). Learning in computer conference contexts:The learners' perspective, *Journal of Distance Education*, 9(1), 19-43.
[6] Ruelland, D. (2000). *Vers un modele d'autogestion en situation de tele-apprentissage*, These de doctorat Ph.D., Faculte des etudes superieures, Universite de Montreal, Montreal, Canada
[7] Brown, A. (1987), Metacognition, Executive control, Self-regulation and more mysterious mechanisms, in *Metacognition, Motivation and Understanding*, Weinert, F.E. & Kluwe, R.H. (Eds), Lawrence Erlbaum, Hillsdale, N.J., 65-116.
[8] Noel, B. (1990). *La metacognition*, De Boeck-Wesmael, Bruxelles.
[9] Flavell, J.H. (1979). Metacognition and Cognitive Monitoring, A new Area of Cognitive-Developmental Inquiry, *American Psychologist*, 34(10), 906-911.
[10] Paquette, G., Brisebois, A., Ruelland, D. (2002). Combining cognitive, affective, social and metacognitive learner attributes for assistance in distributed learning environment, eLearn 2002, Montreal.
[11] Ruelland, D. (2002). *Self-Directed Learning +, a model of supports for the workplace*. 16ᵉ Symposium on Self-Directed Learning, Motorola University, Feb. 5-9, Boynton Beach, Fl.
[12] Garland, M. (1993). Ethnography Penetrates the « I didn't Have Time » Rationale to Elucidate Higher Order *Reasons for Distance Education Withdrawal, Research in Distance Education*, 5(1-2), 6-10.

Comparative Study on Trouble Recognition in the Process of Information Education between Teachers and Children

Takeshi KITAZAWA
Tokyo Institute of Technology,
2-12-1 O-okayama, Meguro-ku, Tokyo
152-8552. Japan
kitazawa@ak.cradle.titech.ac.jp

Hiroshi KATO
National Institute
of Multimedia Education
2-12, Wakaba, Mihama-ku, Chiba
261-0014. Japan
hkato@nime.ac.jp

Kanji AKAHORI
Tokyo Institute of Technology,
2-12-1 O-okayama, Meguro-ku, Tokyo
152-8552. Japan
akahori@ak.cradle.titech.ac.jp

Abstract

This paper describes teachers' recognition about children's trouble and children's recognition about trouble in the class of information education. We found that teachers tend to recognize that children's trouble is about the computer system and function or process of using the software, on the other hand, children tend to recognize that it is the situation they are stopped by something during their work. We also found children become aware of the trouble only of the present. Teachers should pay attention to a child's stages of development, and suggest the way to find the meta-recognition which children fall short of in the future.

1. Introductions

Recently, information education has been getting popular rapidly in the Japanese primary schools due to Japanese political program. However, Curriculum of information education has not yet been established at primary schools. On the other hand, many Japanese researches have proposed curriculums of the information education, and have argued from the various aspects. However, Sato (1999) claimed that issues on teacher's practice are more essential than those on curriculum. Therefore, promoting teacher's skills of information education is necessary at primary school. Although there are researches such as an analysis on the computer attitudes for education and the computer anxiety of in-service teachers (TAKAYAMA, 1993), the issue of increasing teacher's skills of information education is still in controversy.

The objectives of this paper are to improve contents of information education by suggesting the differences in what teachers and children recognize as a problem when using computers. This paper describes results of the comparative study between teachers and children's recognition on the trouble in the information education classes.

2. Method

The primary school investigated this time is a private elementary school in Tokyo. First, we carried out

questionnaire survey to 6 teachers (from the 3rd grade to the 5th grade) committing the information education on January 23, 2002. Second, we carried out the interview of 39 children (15 in the 3rd grade, 17 in the 4th grade, and 7 in the 5th grade) on February through March, 2002. We did video recording and analyzed children's answer in an interview. Third, we compared the answers of the teachers with those of the children, classifying them into categories.

The following questions were asked to the subjects:

To teacher: What kind of question did your children ask to you at class of information education?

To children: What kind of question did you have at class of information education this year?

3. Results

The following results were obtained by analyzing teachers' and children's answer (Table 1). In the first place, we summarized teachers' answer such as "An unexpected screen was shown with proper procedure at starting or finishing the machine. (A strange message was indicated)" as the category "Error indication" to clarify the meaning of their comments. We also summarized children's answer such as "I didn't know English of the keyboard." as "The arrangement of the keyboard". In the second place, we grouped the category into six groups; "Computer system and function", "Typing", "Sentence composition", "Drawing", "File operation", "The Internet".

As the result of analysis, we found "Computer system and function" was almost recognized by both teachers and children as trouble. Teachers less recognized "Typing", "Sentence composition", and "File operation" as trouble. But teacher hardly answered "Drawing" and "The Internet", although children answered.

4. Discussion

Judging from the above, the relations of teacher's and child's trouble recognition are as follows (Figure 1). For instance, when children was using search engine of internet, since all of the children accessed simultaneously, they could not see web pages successfully the trouble is

Table1. Teachers and children's trouble recognition in information education

Troubles	Answer	Teachers	Children
Computer system and function	Printing	2	5
	Freeze of computer system	4	4
	The time to access	1	1
	Monitor's contact defect	1	1
	Error indication	1	1
	Start and finish error of computer system	0	2
Typing	Double consonants and contracted sounds	2	2
	Using "Cube paint" application	1	0
	The operation of the character change	1	5
	Form position	1	0
	The understanding of the Roman alphabet	0	4
	Arrangement of keyboard	0	1
	The operation of typing	0	1
Sentence composition	The decoration of the character	1	1
	Insert of the figure	1	0
	Indication	1	0
	Movement of the line	0	1
Drawing	Invisible characters because the color is the same as that of the background	1	0
	Mouse control	0	1
	Daubing	0	5
File operation	The general idea of the directory structure	1	1
	File load	2	0
	Work extinction in the middle of the work	0	3
The Internet	About input of key words	0	2
	Failure in search Web	0	5
	Others	0	2

Figure1. The relations of teacher's and child's

trouble recognition

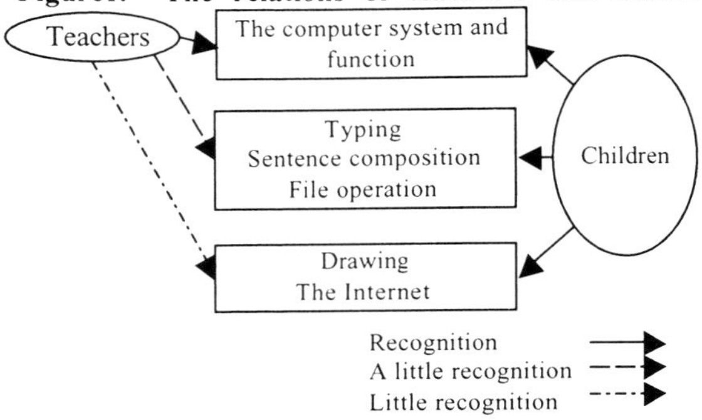

categorized as "The time to access". Both teachers and children recognized it as a trouble. On the other hand, when children get stuck in typing, they recognized it as a trouble, while teachers hardly not. At the moment, teachers barely recognized the children's trouble. About "Typing", "Sentence composition", "File operation", teachers viewed them as rather easy trouble. Therefore, it can be said that these troubles are hard for teacher to recognize as child's troubles.

However, in terms of the way of search (shown as "The Internet"), there was a big difference between teachers view and children one, that is, teachers did not recognize it as a children's trouble. Many teachers assume that children can use the Internet very well only if they teach how to use the Internet (KIKUCHI & AKAHORI, 2001). The differences in recognition were

also reported by Givvin et al. (2001). They found a considerable gap between teacher's evaluation of children's motivation toward the class and children's self-evaluation.

Thus, a teacher should teach information education recognizing the gap. The gap was seen especially in "Drawing" and "The Internet". Unlike "Sentence composition" and "File operation", these have a variety of ways to do, so they are potentially fallible. Therefore, the teacher could not foresee what children do with a computer and how to use it for learning. This can be why the teacher could not find limit of children's computer operation base on children's stages of development. As a future subject, we will research what kind of trouble children of each grade recognize. We also need to research teachers' recognition of children's trouble about information education considering contents of guidance and the computer skill.

References

Manabu, SATO. (1999). "Curriculum research and teacher research", Tadahiko, ABIKO. (ed.), *New edition curriculum research initiation*, Keisoshobo, Japan, pp157-179.

Soji, TAKAYAMA. (1993). "An analysis on the computer attitudes for education and the computer anxiety of in-service teachers", *Japanese Journal of Educational Psychology*, vol.41, pp313-323.

Hidefumi, KIKUCHI & Kanji, AKAHORI. (2001). "Ethnomethodlogical Case Study of ICT Education in Elementary School", Proceedings of ICCE, Vol.3, pp.1354-1361

Givvin K.B., Stipek DJ., Salmon J.M., MacGyvers V.L. (2001)."In the Eyes of the Beholder: Students' and Teachers' Judgments of Students' Motivation", Teaching and Teacher Education (An International Journal of Research and Studies), Vol.17, No.3, pp.321-331.

Telementoring in Surgery in East Coast

Dr U Kyaw Tin Hla* , Dr Ma Soe Soe Nwe**
Associate Professor / Consultant Surgeon*, Resident Medical Officer**
*Department of Surgery , ** Dept of Community Health and Family Medicine, Kulliyyah of Medicine,
International Islamic University Malaysia IIUM, Email ukyaw@iiu.edu.my,* kthla@hotmail.com,* ,
Jeruntut Hospital, Jeruntut, Pahang Darul Makmur**, MALAYSIA, Email masoe@iiu.edu.my**,
snsoe62@hotmail.com,**

Abstract

Telementoring in surgical operations in remote areas of Malaysia as i inaccessible parts of rest of the world could be made a reality making use of existing hardware/ software solutions and facilities over the WWW in a cost effective way . The project making use of MSN Community and My Web was found to be viable even with the available facilities. at a reasonable cost. An acceptable teaching-learning mechanism could be achieved for −clinical use for surgical trainees

This is a continuation of a pilot project in the new educational pedagogy with promising future expansion, allowing real-time supervision of students of surgery. The teaching -learning process, takes place in a environment shared by the learner and facilitators;the teacher being at a remote site. Learning could be achieved at a minimum cost especially in training of surgeons in districts like East coast of Malaysia

1.Introduction

Mentoring or **supervision** in surgical operation is very labour –intensive. Hand on learning needs to be achieved in teaching–learning process in operation theatre. This requires one to one learning in the presence of an instructor, expensive and time consuming. **Telementoring** in surgical operations in remote areas of Malaysia like the inaccessible parts of rest of the world could be made a reality making use of existing hardware/ software solutions and facilities over the WWW in a cost- effective way.

This is a continuation of a pilot project in the effective use of new educational pedagogy, with a future. Instead of presence of the teacher on–site, he is at a remote site, but still has the advantage of letting the trainee see through a series of slides, take through the operative steps as if in real-time but still manage to guide the necessary important steps to achieve better end therapeutic results; with more lives being saved.

2.Hypotheses and Rationales

Telementoring in surgical operations in remote of the world could be made a reality making use of existing hardwares/ software and facilities over the WWW in a cost effective way at the same time achieving an acceptable end result. The protocol must lead to improved clinical care for decision making before and during surgical undertaking .

3.Objectives of Project

Step1.a. To try out clinically acceptable quality recordings of surgical operations while the author operate in Operation Theatre during emergency surgery in Kuantan General Hospital (HTAA)and digitize them .
a.To try to transfer images over the internet using easily available existing hardware and software solutions .
b.Evaluate the acceptability of output, results for clinical decision making after use of this new facilities.

3.Materials and Methods

Step (1) Archival of operative steps and setting up teaching protocol for major life saving under-taking like emergency surgery as in acute abdomen example liver injury.All put into a series of power-point slides.
1. Recordings were done using a Sony TRV 301E Digital camera on Sony Hi 8digital tape while surgery was carried out by theauthor. The video recordings were turned into digital clips (of 100 Megabytes ,AVI approximately) on a Sony VAIO Laptop Personal Computer , PCG-F360 using video-capturing software DV Gate Motion / DV Gatestill from Sony bundled together in the laptop and Firewire Link IEE 1394 for fast transfer at 200MB/ sec rate in real time. Firstly the clips of approximately 100 Meg were converted into raw avi uncompressed using software MainActor. The resulting avi produced were turned

	Before	After MSN Chat and seeing the PowerPoint slides over the web
Understanding of pathogenetic mechanism	+	+++
Improved patient manbagement before transfer	++	++++
Confidence gained by the trainee	++	+++++
Happy with clarity of clinical digitized picture resolution	++	++++

into media file compatible with Microsoft Media Player using on Demand Producer , a Window 2000 Professional product.From each of these digitized clips good clinical operative pictures were put into series of powerpoints slides.

2 These series of teaching -learning slides with vivid operative steps were up-loaded onto the shared document files in My Picture/ My Web Document files of MSN community which is usually shared by my trainees in the district like Jeruntut (and and my students of surgery in the IIUM alike).The trainee would look into these before he or she go in for the emergency surgery or manage such a case before transfer to our tertiary center for further management. This protocol can reduce the possible mortality and morbidity.This is in the pipeline to study the effectiveness of such a use of this newer teaching – learning facility for the benefit of the community..

4.Results

4.1.Findings -.The evaluations as shown in the table for the available digital capture and powerpoint teaching slides made from them were used over the WWW MSN chat and MSN Community My group(MY WEB),showed favorable results on all test-runs Same Powerpoint slides containing archived digital clips of operation on repair of Liver lacerations / acute abdomen surgery were used for standard comparison.It was tested in 9 occasions involving two to four trainees/ students..

5.Conclusion

The pilot project was successful even wit the available facilities.Transfer of knowledge and teaching–learning was achieved with acceptable resolutions, clarity and definitions for clinical use and supervision prior to surgical undertaking, at the remote site.This is a pilot project with a view to future expansion in the use of new educational pedagogy allowing the real-time supervision of teaching -learning process of students .One site in IIUM Kuantan and satellite site in Jeruntut where junior medical officer are stationed.

6.Inference

This is an interim results report of our encouraging on-going research.It is cost effective too. Using

relatively less costly, easily available hardware software solutions and Internet which could be used to enhance the teaching -learning process where the mentor the senior surgeon or the instructor can allow the teaching-learning to take place and the quality of patient care in a remote area can be effectively enhanced making possible telementoring of surgical undertakings/ operations over the internet; a very cost-effective solutions in this part of the world where rough terrain and problems of access into inner parts of Pahang make immediate transfer of patients impossible. This could also be used in other parts of Malaysia or rest of the world .

Bibliography

Alex Krassel, Steve Robinson, (1998). *Microsoft's NetMeeting 2.1 COM Interfaces: Understanding How They Work*.URL:http://www.panthersoft.com

Dena S. Puskin, Carole L. Mintzer, and CathyWasem,(1997).Telemedicine : Buiding Rural System For Today and Tomorrow.URL: http://www.nal.usda.gov/orhp/chapter.htm

Kristine M. Scannell, Douglas A. Perednia, Henry M. Kissman, (1995). *Telemedicine: Past, Present, and Future* URL: http://www.nlm.nih.gov/pubs/cbm/telembib.html

Hla, Kyaw Tin, New Paradigm of Facilitating Problem - Based Learning (PBL) over the World WideWeb in University Malaysia Sarawak, Presented at ICCE 99, Chiba, Japan; Advanced Research in Computers and Communications in Education,G. Cumming et al (Eds), IOS Press, , Amsterdam,The Netherlands pp819-820, 1999

Hla, Kyaw Tin, PBL over the Internet, Presented at ICCE97, Kuching, Sarawak

Hla, Kyaw Tin (1999-2000). Personal communications *l: Personal communications with Khairuddin FIT*.University Malaysia Sarawak, Malaysia.

Hla, Kyaw Tin , Nwe SS (2000). Telementoring in Surgery,ICCE 2000,Tiape, Tiawan

Hla, Kyaw Tin,Nwe SS (2001) Archival of Clinical Material, Interactivity and Discussion over Chat and MSN Explorer , a Prelude to Telementoring in Surgery ICCE 2001,Seoul, Korea

Leigh Anne Rettinger, (1995). *Desktop Videoconferencing: Technology and Use for Remote SeminarDelivery*.URL:http://www2.nscu.edu/eos/ser vice/ece/project/succeed_info/larettin/thesis

M.Vadivale,(1998).*Telemedicine*URL: http://www.geocities.com/HotSprings/2188/internet6.html

Narayanan Kulathuramaiyer, (1999). *Personal communication: Project Requirement Analysis*. University Malaysia Sarawak, Malaysia.

Paul MacLaren, C J Ball, (1995). *Telemedicine :Lesson remain unheeded*.URL http://www.bmj.com/archive/6991ed3.htm

Yale University of Medicine (1999). *Telemedicine* URL: http://info.med.yale.edu/yfp/about.html

Identifying Critical Needs for Student Success in Online Learning

Scot Headley and Mary Ann Brewer
George Fox University

Abstract

As a first step in developing a resource system for students enrolled in graduate education courses at George Fox University, School of Education personnel surveyed students regarding their competence and perceived importance of a number of skills determined to be important for success in online learning. A review of the literature revealed a number of needed skills and characteristics. A web-based questionnaire was employed for data collection. Critical needs were determined by comparing the areas of low initial competence with those skills perceived by the students to be of high importance. Areas of critical need included skills in accessing internet sites and browser usage, research activities and competence, and communication skills for online learning. Faculty members intend to use the findings to prioritize the selection of elements to be included in a student resource system.

Educators consistently look for ways to maximize student achievement. Learning strategies utilized in traditional school settings are well defined and clearly understood. Students are guided to develop a personalized repertoire of skills that bring academic success. But do these same strategies transfer successfully to the new environment of online learning? Do students utilize the most effective strategies? What perceptions do they have regarding the advantages and disadvantages of online learning? Is there a model for the most effective resources for an online program?

The nature of online learning calls for students to be highly motivated, independent, and self-regulated. To be academically successful, they must be active learners with good organizational and time management skills, capable of adapting to a new learning environment. Understanding these characteristics, the educator's task is to determine which strategies will enhance student learning.

Zariski and Styles (2000) interviewed undergraduate students in a Legal Studies and Law unit at Murdoch University. They studied learning strategies of rehearsal, elaboration, organization, completing activities, time management and volitional strategies, environment for study, adaptive strategies – help seeking and use of resources, and metacognitive strategies – planning, monitoring, evaluating. Technical demands overshadowed a focus on cognitive strategies for many

students, especially new to the online environment. There was a request for tutorials to be available throughout the unit. Students recognized the need for effective time management and self- regulating strategies.

Shih, Ingebritsen, Pleasants, Flickinger, and Brown (1998) examined the relationship of learning styles, learning strategies, and patterns of learning in an online environment. They drew a distinction between learning styles that may be difficult for a student to change and learning strategies over which the student has a great deal of control. They found that a student's overall achievement was directly related to the use of a wide range of learning strategies which supported the earlier findings of Pintrich and Johnson (1990), and Weinstein and Underwood (1985).

In an examination of the online graduate program at Drexel University, Hislop (1999) included in the observations on teaching and learning a look at student participation in the online environment. Hislop noted that student participation is a key learning strategy.

In order to maximize learning, it is important for teachers to provide students with the necessary resources in a timely and effective manner. But what are the priorities for those resources? No one knows better than the students themselves. Personnel in the School of Education at George Fox University seek to address the needs of students in online courses through the development of an internet-based resource center that would allow students and prospective students the opportunity to explore and learn in the online environment. Student exploration and learning through this center would occur prior to or while enrolled in graduate courses in the School of Education.

A first step in identifying the needs of online students at George Fox University was to survey the students using a web-based questionnaire. Through an analysis of the findings and a review of other institutions' efforts, we seek to improve our students' success in internet-based learning.

George Fox University is an independent university located in Newberg, Oregon, USA. Students in graduate programs in education have been participating in online courses for about five years. The web-based teaching and learning environment was developed and is maintained by faculty members in the School of Education. This system makes use of asynchronous and real-time interaction through discussion forums, email, and chat rooms.

Individual and group learning activities are conducted through a web-based interactive environment.

The goal of this study was to discover the critical preparation needs of students in online courses. Twenty-seven students enrolled in courses in the School's M.Ed. and Doctor of Education programs in the spring Semester, 2002, completed a questionnaire that was constructed using Test Pilot, a test authoring application. Items on the questionnaire were devised which allowed students to describe their initial competence in a number of skills required for successful online learning. Students were also asked to state the perceived importance of each of the skills. Critical need was determined by discovering those skills that were both areas of low initial competence and high-perceived importance.

Preliminary findings indicate that areas of critical need are of three general types; a) skills related to using web browsers generally and in accessing the university web site, b) skills related to carrying out research related to course activities, and c) communication skills. Figure 1 presents the types of need and specific skills in each of the three areas.

Type of Need	Specific Skills and Activities
Access	1. Using web browsers 2. Accessing and navigating the university website
Research	1. Using search engines 2. Evaluating credibility of information on WWW 3. Using library databases 4. Requesting library resources
Communication	1. Composing and posting in course discussion areas 2. Developing an online communicative presence

Figure 1. Critical Needs

We intend to use the information from this study to target our development efforts at building tutorials and resource helps for online students. Students come to our courses at all stages of familiarity and skill in working in an internet-based environment. The goal is to build a resource system that will address the critical needs of students. Potentially, this could include an online resource center, linked to the GFU website. It would be composed of an orientation to online learning, assessment instrument to identify student strengths and weaknesses in the online environment, tutorials addressing the specific skills and activities noted in figure 1, and a comprehensive FAQ sheet. Additionally, the survey findings would give direction in preparation of an Online Orientation Handbook sent to students enrolling for the first time in an online class. Available in hard copy form, this would serve as a transition tool from the traditional class to the online learning format.

Further plans include using the survey with students in the Master of Arts in Teaching (MAT) program in fall Semester, 2002. These students represent two groups in the MAT program: the first cohort started in January 2002 and will have partially completed the program with a mix of online and face-to-face classes, and the second, has a start date of January 2003. The goal is to gather information that will be of substantial assistance at the beginning of the program, as well as meeting ongoing needs of all online students.

This project is enabling us to make decisions on investing our limited resources into areas of greatest need. Faculty and staff time can then be used to begin constructing the key elements of the student resource system.

References:
(1) Hislop, Gregory (1999). Working Professionals as Part-time On-line Learners. [Online]. Available http://www.aln.org/alnweb/journal/Vol4_issue2/le/hislop/LE-hislop.htm.
(2) Pintrich, P. R. & Johnson, G. R. (1990). Assessing and improving students' learning strategies. New Directions for Teaching and Learning, 42, 83-92.
(3) Shih, Ching-Chun; Ingebritsen, Tom; Pleasants, John; Flickinger, Kathleen; & Brown, George. (1998). Learning Strategies and Other Factors Influencing Achievement via Web Courses. Distance Learning '98, Proceedings of the Annual Conference on Distance teaching & Learning (14th, Madison, WI, August 5-7, 1998).
(4) Weinstein, C. E. & Underwood, V. (1985). Learning Strategies: The how of learning. In Judith W. Segal, Susan F. Chipman and Robert Glaser (Eds.) Thinking and Learning Skills. Hillsdale, NJ: Erlbaum.
(5) Zariski A. and Styles, I. (2000). Enhancing student strategies for online learning. In A. Herrmann and M.M. Kulski (Eds.), Flexible Futures in Tertiary Teaching. Proceedings of the 9th Annual Teaching Learning Forum, 2-4 February 2000. Perth: Curtin University of Technology. http://cleo.murdoch.edu.au/confs/tlf/tlf2000/zariski.html

Providing Assistance for Proofs in the Teaching of Theory of Computation

Padmanabhan Krishnan
School of Information Technology
Bond University
Gold Coast, Queensland 4229, Australia
E-mail: pkrishna@bond.edu.au

Abstract

In this article we present a technique which helps students in understanding proofs in the context of automata theory. The main conclusion is that student understanding can be improved by using a collection of lemmas and trying to automate the proof in a mechanical theorem prover.

1. Introduction

It is fair to say that a typical undergraduate student in Computer Science finds the classical course on automata theory very hard. This has the effect that more practical courses that depend on automata theory are avoided. For instance, students who have found the course on automata theory hard do not study applications of model checking as it depends on automata theory. However, the automata theory used in such a course on model checking is not very deep. Furthermore, in the advanced course the students are not expected to construct proofs by hand. Rather they have to use a model checker as a tool to prove the required properties.

One of the key reasons for this is the difficulty in understanding and writing proofs. Permitting students to collaborate does not necessarily overcome this problem. Common mistakes made by a majority students are only amplified. Providing a fixed number of hints is also not always appropriate. The students have to be encouraged to construct their own proof (and not be constrained to any fixed proof).

Hence a rigorous tool which can find a variety of errors is required. The tool must be also able to accept a variety of arguments as input. Existing tools such as those described in [3, 6] focus more on "mechanical concepts" such as determinisation and minimisation of finite automata, derivation of strings using context free grammars etc. However, they do not assist in the more "theoretical concepts" such as pumping lemma for regular languages or proving elementary properties about languages [4, 2].

In this paper we argue for the benefits of using a mechanical theorem prover in the teaching of automata theory. However, as theorem provers are not easy to use, we do not expect students to use them. In fact, students are not aware about the existence of the tool. The role of the instructor is to act as the interpreter between the student and the tool. We suggest that our approach helps the student to understand proofs with the assistance of a tool and an instructor.

Owing to the generality of theorem provers, they can be used in a variety of ways. Apart from encoding the various student arguments, the instructor can also provide some of the lemmas needed to automate the proof. The student can then choose from these lemmas to attempt the proof. If a wrong lemma is chosen, the prover is unlikely to make progress. One can then undo the various commands, and proceed by choosing another lemma. The details necessary to complete a proof provide the student with the necessary practice. Once the proof process is complete, the axioms used in the process can be examined. This can also be used by the students to learn about the proof process and how to structure proofs. This is obtained by the lecturer examining the proof trees (similar to those shown in Figure 1). For instance, the sub-tree shown in the figure indicates selection of the counter-example agenAnBn(n!1) and then using two lemmas, viz, agenEQ followed by EQABAX. The other steps are just theorem prover commands used to complete the proof.

There has been some research on better ways to structure proofs [5] and ways to generate student interest in proofs [1]. However, the first report is more concerned about structuring large proofs while the second report is on a better way to introduce logic and other aspects to an uninterested student. Here the aim is to be assist the student in getting a better understanding of the proof process.

The author has been involved in this course for the past nine years. Initially, collaboration on assignments was permitted. However this did not translate to better understanding. But after the process was adopted, there has been a noticeable improvement in the understanding of the topics

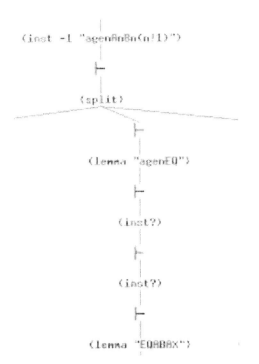

Figure 1. Proof Tree

(in terms of the questions asked in class, attempts at solving homework problems etc.) The author's teaching evaluation also increased.

2. Costs

In this article we have presented the details of a technique to aid students to overcome bottlenecks in the process of constructing proofs. We now comment on the cost to the teacher. The first cost of adopting this approach is the need to code up all the simple definitions in the theorem prover. We use the theorem prover PVS [7] to code the relevant models and prove the required theorems. Completing the basic definitions for the various examples used in a typical course took the author about two days. But the author was already familiar with PVS and its various features. One of the key issues will be to identify a set of definitions that can be used for a variety of issues thereby reducing the coding effort. Another significant cost is the need to carry out the proofs and encode the lemmas that will aid learning. These lemmas are used to provide hints when a student is stuck. Here it is harder to estimate the time spent as the lemmas used were identified over 2-3 years. These were based on the questions asked by the students and the mistakes made in their home-works. However, we estimate that it is not

longer than 4 weeks of work.

A more time consuming aspect is the translation of the student's reasoning into PVS input. Trying to do this online is not satisfactory. The main problem is the time required to incorporate the current state of the proof tree into the reasoning presented by the student. Most of the time was actually spent in examining the proof trees and generating the feedback which characterises potential problems. In some cases, the only valid answer appears to be 'you are way off target, try something else'.

3. Conclusion and Future Work

In principle, a theorem prover can be used to provide assistance for a student to understand the proof process. Given the current state of the art in theorem provers, this cannot be done without instructor intervention. However, by not restricting the tool to provide fixed hints, the learning can be tailored to particular students. The generality of theorem provers can be used to cater to variety of students; but this generality is also a limitation. The next phase of the research is to build a tool that translates between the formal language of PVS and the informal but precise language that students should use.

References

[1] D. Gries and F. B. Schneider. A New Discrete-Math Course. Technical report, Cornell University, April 1994.

[2] J. E. Hopcroft, R. Motwani, and J. D. Ullman. *Introduction to Automata Theory, Languages and Computation.* Addison Wesley, 2001.

[3] T. Hung and S. H. Rodger. Increasing visualization and interaction in an automata theory course. In *Proceedings of the ACM SIGCSE Technical Symposium on Computer Science Education*, pages 6–10, 2000.

[4] D. Kozen. *Automata and Computability.* Springer, 1997.

[5] L. Lamport. How to Write a Proof. Technical report, DEC SRC Report, 1993.

[6] M. B. Robinson, J. A. Hamshar, J. E. Novillo, and A. T. Duchowski. A java based tool for reasoning about models of computation through simulating finite automata and turing machines. In *Proceedings of the ACM SIGCSE Technical Symposium on Computer Science Education*, pages 105–109, 1999.

[7] J. Rushby. Specification, proof checking, and model checking for protocols and distributed systems with PVS. In *Tutorial presented at FORTE X/PSTV XVII '97: Formal Description Techniques and Protocol Specification, Testing and Verification*, Nov. 1997.

Virtual Learning Experiences Outside Of The Classroom: Connecting Educationally Oriented Organisations And Classrooms Using Online Projects

Ann Trewern, University of Otago. ann.trewern@stonebow.otago.ac.nz
Monika Fry Megabright. monika@megabright.co.nz

Abstract
*Two online projects are described in this paper. **Wara Blong Life** and **Sniff, Swing and Swipe** were ten-week, online activity-based projects offered in 2001 to elementary, middle and junior secondary school classes from all over New Zealand.*

Keywords: teaching and learning strategies, design principles.

Introduction

Many organisations such as city councils, zoos, museums and theme parks have a strongly educative mission as part of their overall function. These organisations frequently develop rich and educationally relevant resources as part of their core work, yet for a number of reasons these resources remain inaccessible or are infrequently utilised by teachers and schools.

During 2001 and 2002 the two online projects described were designed and developed in close association with two quite different organisations with an educative mission. The aim of these projects was to set a problem requiring the design and development of a product that would assist in solving the problem given a certain real-world constraints. The projects described were set within the particular curriculum context of technology education. The projects provided links between organisations and classrooms by offering a workable instructional framework or a process by which the two groups can usefully work together. A wide range of technology tools including project webpages, email, online forms and computer conferencing software were used to link resources from each organisation and the students.

Wara Blong Life

http://education.otago.ac.nz/NZLNet/WaraBlongLife/home.html is pidgin for Water for Survival. This organisation were keen to raise the awareness of New Zealand children about the difficulties encountered in accessing clean water by their peers in the Eastern Highland areas of Papua and New Guinea. It was decided to ask New Zealand students to help with an authentic sanitation and health education situation in primary and community schools in the Eastern Highlands of Papua New Guinea. A current self-help sanitation project that is providing water tanks to Eastern Highlands schools can only provide enough clean drinking water for half a litre per student per day (2 cups), making water too precious to use for washing hands after going to the toilet. The problem task set for project participants was to design an effective method of hand washing for children that required very little water. Participating groups were required to design an effective solution to the problem that was durable, user-friendly and effective, and could be made from found materials.

Sanitation can be a difficult content area for teachers and there are very few suitable child relevant resources available for classroom use. Information kits, and games resources, were provided by the Water for Survival organisation and these were made available for teachers to download. Computer conferencing software was utilised to set up a question and answer area where students posted questions to the 'Ask An Engineer' discussion area. Water, waste, civil engineers and a microbiologist were available to answer student questions. Designing and making their solutions required students to extend and deepen their understanding and to consider the beliefs, values and ethics of the Papua New Guinea highlanders as well as consideration of the impact on the people of such a technological development.

The experts were also involved in judging the students' designs and evaluating the level of student research. Feedback was provided to all entrants based on the initial design brief.

Sniff Swing and Swipe
http://education.otago.ac.nz/nzlnet/candoatakzoo/home.html

For this project students were required to gather background information, and design and develop behavioural enrichment activities for four zoo animals that included the ring-tailed lemur, meerkat, zebra and kea (a parrot native to New Zealand). Students needed to gather information about the animal's movement capability and behaviours when designing a behavioural enrichment prototype which would encourage physical exercise and mental stimulation by their selected animal.

The involvement of Zoo Keepers and Auckland Zoo Educators was a central aspect of the **Sniff, Swing and Swipe** project. The narrow focus and specificity of the content area was difficult for teachers to manage using generally available information resources. Computer conferencing was not used in this project as a means of group communication as the experts were not extensive users of technology. Instead, students could email questions directly to the project moderator who sent them off to the zoo educators if the answer could not be found easily by any other means. This was also the easiest way to handle requests for information from experts. However, considerable emphasis was placed on the experts in this project. Each individual keeper was featured on a webpage which provided background details about them, their job, the animals they were responsible for, existing behavioural enrichment the keepers had developed for their animals and helpful hints for future designs. This encouraged children to identify closely with their particular keeper and at the end of the project several children sent Christmas messages.

Implementation stages for these projects and points of involvement by experts

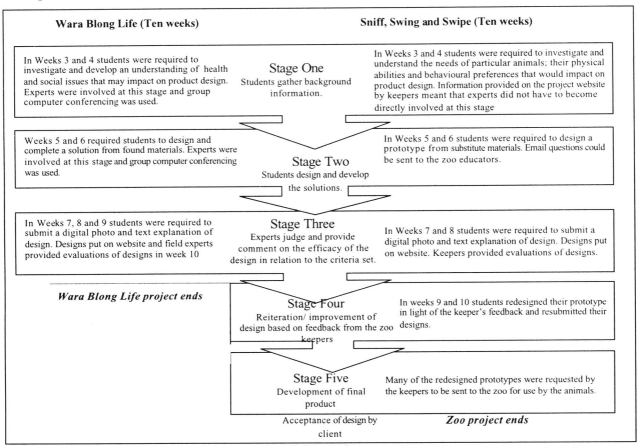

Figure 1: Shows the instructional phases of the project

Conclusion

We believe there is considerable merit in examining the close relationship between knowing and acting or doing. In each of the projects described in this paper inquiry has been driven by the need to make an artefact and for students to provide an explanation or to demonstrate their outcome. When motivated and challenged by finding real solutions students need to make answers. "Learning is an outcome that occurs because the making requires the student to extend his or her understanding in action – whether the article constructed is a material object, an explanatory demonstration or a theoretical formulation" ([1]. When students are required to extend their understanding in action there is invariably the need to ask questions and seek solutions beyond the classroom. Easy access to field experts has been of paramount importance to the success of these online projects. So too has the role of field experts as evaluators of student presentations.

References
[1] Wells, G. (1997). Dialogic Inquiry in education: Building on the legacy of Vygotsky. [Online] http://www.oise.utoronto.ca/~gwells/NCTE.html File retrieved 27.10.01

Optional Strategies for Developing Teacher Technological Competencies

Dennis B. Sharpe
Memorial University of Newfoundland, Canada

Abstract

The escalating developments in computer related technology have profound implications for the teaching profession, yet research continues to reveal a lack of appropriate competencies among groups of in-service teachers. This paper examines a number of factors that need to be addressed when considering appropriate professional development options. A number of strategies are then examined that can potentially provide and support teacher development in this area and also encourage the future continued upgrading of computer competencies for use in teaching and learning situations.

1: Introduction

The rapid and escalating pace of the development of technology, and in particular, computer-based technology, is undeniable, and permeates all facets of our lives, including education. Information and communications technology growth and application is particularly dominant and developing not only as an important facet of the teaching and learning process, but as a way to find, control, manipulate information and communicate with others within a multitude of educational contexts. Implications for teaching and learning are profound as schools become networked and more and more computer-based technology is introduced at increasingly sophisticated levels. Teachers need to be technologically literate and able to adapt readily and easily to changes if they are to successfully implement technology in the classroom [1] [2] [3]. A recent Statistics Canada report, *Education Indicators in Canada* [4] describes the current status of information and communications technology in schools and states that "in most provinces, lack of knowledge or skills in using computers for instructional purposes was cited (by respondents) as a major obstacle in schools" (p. 72). It is also evident that the attitudes and capabilities of teachers with respect to technology impact directly on their use of technology: that is, there is a positive correlation between attitude and capability, and between attitude/capability and level of use in the classroom and for other professional purposes.

In order for teachers to become familiar with, develop positive attitudes toward, and be confident with, for example, new technologies, it takes time, resources,

willingness to learn and on-going support systems. Change is often slow, but needs to be guided by a clear mission, set of goals and an appropriate plan of action. Most, if not all Provinces and States in North America have developed strategies for the implementation of computer, information and communications technology into schools; and have identified specific student competencies/outcomes through both particular courses or through the integration of technology across the curriculum. It is therefore logical to assume that we need competent qualified teachers to deal with this.

The purpose of this paper is to first of all present a summary of the results of a recent survey that examined levels of teacher competence and attitudes toward computer-based technology. Given the implications of this in terms of facilitating teacher development, a number of factors to consider are then reviewed along with examples of possible strategies to follow.

2: Research Results

What then is the current state of teacher attitudes and competencies in technology? Recent research based on a comprehensive survey of the current levels of competency (as identified by the International Society for Technology in Education [5] foundation standards for teachers) and attitudes toward computers of a sample of 380 primary, elementary and high school teachers in Newfoundland, Canada [6] revealed a number of factors:

- Overall, teachers rated their computer and information technologies competencies fairly low. Mean scores (based on a scale of 1 to 9 where 1 = not yet ready to learn, and 9 = could teach it to others) ranged from 4.15 in professional productivity to 3.32 in computer use for student inquiry and assessment. The mean score on the integrating technology scale was 3.27.

- A breakdown of these competency score means based on demographic variables revealed several differences within the group. Females rated themselves significantly lower than males (3.67 compared to 4.69); younger teachers (20-30 year age group) rated themselves significantly higher than those in the over 40 category (4.98 compared to 3.68); and high school teachers rated themselves significantly higher than primary/elementary teachers (4.39 compared to 3.18).

- Attitudes toward computer and information technologies were generally positive. Mean scores on the six scales of the instrument were enthusiasm/enjoyment 1.90, computer anxiety 2.26, computer avoidance 1.52, attitude toward email 2.39, negative impact 2.22, and productivity 1.77 (based on a five- point Likert scale).

- There were no significant differences based on gender or school type (primary, elementary, etc.) for any of the attitude scales. However, the over 40 age category of teachers were significantly less positive than those under 40 on the enthusiasm/enjoyment, computer avoidance, and productivity scales.

- There was a significant correlation between positive attitudes and higher technology competence levels with correlation coefficients ranging from -0.162 to -0.687 between the various attitude and competency scales. The highest correlation was between professional productivity and computer anxiety: as anxiety decreased, productivity increased.

These survey findings suggest, overall, that although attitudes of the teachers were positive, their computer technology competency levels were low, with differences within the group based mainly on gender and age.

Results of this and other research across North America [7] [8] [9] [10] suggest low levels of competency and use of computer technology and thus affirm the commonly held belief that fairly extensive opportunities for in-service are required within the school system. Variations in competencies and attitudes based on age were also evident in the research literature [11] [12] [13]. Similarly, gender differences have been evidenced in a number of reports [14] [15] [16]. In-service would therefore need to address individual teacher differences based on these demographics and other factors. Given this, what options and approaches are available to address the discrepancy between current and desired levels of competency and attitudes?

3: Some Considerations

Before we examine possible in-service options, there are a number of factors that should be taken into consideration. These include, among other things, the actual competencies to be attained, the planning process, and teachers as adult learners.

3.1: Levels of Competency

One of the basic considerations when providing in-service is the appropriate minimum level of competency that teachers need to attain in computer-based technology. The International Society for Technology in Education recommended foundation standards are frequently cited as a baseline [17]. These standards encompass basic computer/technology operations and concepts, personal and professional use of technology, and applications of technology in instruction. The Society also publishes *Standards for Advanced Programs in Educational Computing and Technology Leadership* and other guides that might appeal to teachers who wish to proceed to higher levels of competence. In fact, having these or other such options available for in-service programming would potentially provide a continuum of competencies and experiences. This would also enable planners to address the needs of a much more diverse group of teachers and start individuals at an appropriate level. It has further suggested [18] that these more advanced standards be defined and developed within the subject and grade levels that teachers are involved with. Such a "real world" or authentic approach is likely to appeal to a larger group of educators and to the successful acquisition of competencies that teachers can more easily relate to classroom applications.

3.2: Planning

Time and resources need to be allocated to the careful planning of any in-service activities. For example, a number of authors [19] [20] advocate a needs assessment process in conjunction with setting up a mission statement, set of goals, objectives, content identification, delivery system and an evaluation scheme to help establish a viable program. Within such a structure, content and delivery systems can be designed that would address the specific needs for a school, school district, or State/Province wide program. A properly conducted needs assessment would not only provide current levels of teacher competencies and attitudes toward technology, but also enable planners to collect data on possible resources. For example, it is important to know the kinds and types of hardware and software currently available and in use in schools, in resource centres, or in personal use by the target group, and thus establish what additional resources and supports might be needed for in-service delivery.

The change process is also important to consider in planning, particularly with respect to individuals or groups who are somewhat reluctant to embrace new technologies. Whilst the research of King [6] revealed positive attitudes toward computer-based technology, this may not always be the case; and given the strong correlation between attitudes (motivation) and computer competency attainment and use, it is important to diagnose resistance to change and plan accordingly. Many studies have confirmed that anxiety and negative feelings toward computers tend to disperse as competence and knowledge are established [12] [21] [22].

Another part of the planning process should address the needs of new entrants into the teaching profession, particularly as greater numbers of pre-service programs establish minimum exit levels of computer competencies for graduates. This in turn will likely diminish the need for basic competency development, but increase the demand for advanced and emerging skills and applications. A consequence of this for in-service program planning is to have in place a continuous improvement process that enables appropriate new technology to be incorporated into professional development activities.

3.3: Teachers as Adult Learners

While it is not the intent of this paper to delve into adult learning theory in great depth, it is pertinent to mention a few related considerations. For example, adults like to feel comfortable and at ease in the learning situation, especially when developing skills and competencies in an area that is relatively new or challenging to them. As MacKeracher [23] puts it: "Learning is facilitated in learning environments which are free from threats and which provide support for personal change. Learning activities need to include opportunities for testing new behaviours in relative safety, developing mutually trusting relationships, encouraging descriptive feedback, and reducing fear of failure" (p. 41). She also affirms the need, where ever possible, for adult learners to be involved in selecting their own goals, and that past experiences be used as a resource or starting point and connected to new experiences through reflective learning activities.

Encouraging adults to learn, retain and use new information and competencies can be further enhanced by the application of several other basic principles. These might include:

- The use of lots of "hands-on" examples and realistic problems in keeping with their professional interests and needs. It would be particularly important to discuss the relevance, meaningfulness and application (of new skills, etc.) to their immediate and future situations.
- Diagnosing any resistance to new information and taking appropriate action.
- Building confidence in new material through the active participation, discussion and involvement of learners within a "threat free" environment that allows for both short term and long term feedback and positive reinforcement.
- Allowing for a variety of learning styles through optional activities and teaching techniques.

Many of the above adult learner principles would be relatively easy to apply to teachers engaged in the development of computer-based competencies through planned in-service activities; and the resultant positive experiences would almost certainly, in turn, build positive attitudes. Successful experiences also have the potential to create the confidence required for the learner (the teacher) to be more self-directed in similar future activities, resulting in decreased reliance on planned workshops and other professional development. In fact, self-directedness could be a direct intended goal of the initial in-service activities.

4: Possible Strategies

The literature is replete with examples of in-service professional development related activities and opportunities, many of which could easily be adjusted to incorporate the above considerations. It is also evident that there are typically no "quick fixes". In-service type activities need to be well planned, but more importantly, be part of a sustained effort with quality follow-up support and resources on an on-going basis [24] [25] [26]. Such supports can take many forms, but on-site or on-line help, easily accessed, is a key success factor.

Maddin [27] reported on a pilot program that focused on teachers using technology on-the-job (school) site. Some of the processes employed in this in-service included: (a) teachers shadowing other teachers to observe successful technology applications; (b) one-on-one coaching of one teacher by another, with a focus on a particular teacher's needs; (c) a "rotating topics" approach with three coaches working with a small group of teachers, each focusing on a different aspect of technology in meaningful classroom contexts; and (d) a walk-in clinic that enabled teachers to simply voluntarily drop by for help or advice. Both Maddin and Holzberg [28] also describe processes that involve using students who are proficient in a technology as a teacher. This might be less attractive to some teachers as adult learners, but should be considered as a useful option.

Other authors [29] describe a "summer camp" approach where participants are immersed in a rich technology environment that focuses on constructivism and student-based learning applications. Embedded in this approach is a process to help teachers develop their own learning and technology plans, thus following a basic tenet of adult learning.

A process of developing "mentors" [30] or "lead teachers" is a method of providing an on-site resource in schools. This approach can work well provided that: (a) time and resources are available to initially develop the expertise of the lead teacher; and (b) that that teacher is then allocated sufficient time and resources to work with others. An extension of the mentoring approach would be the creation of communities of learners (teachers) who work and support each other in developing computer-based competencies and applications. Given current internet access and communications technology, group members could be widely dispersed yet be able to work effectively together. In fact, on-line discussion and interest groups are becoming common-place.

On-line, CD-based tutorials and other digital forms of information applicable to learning about technology are available from numerous sources (see for example, the Microsoft [31] teacher training web page), or are relatively easy to develop. Many existing software programs also contain teaching tutorials. This group of resources not only address specific computer-based issues and competencies, but are usually easily accessed, are typically formatted for individual learning, and have associated "help" programs. Once teachers, for example, are past the basics, such technological resources help ease the burden on specifically planned in-service and can be accessed virtually at any time by individuals. Such approaches and resources have the added advantage of helping to inculcate some of the fundamental technology concepts available for educational purposes. The initial challenge though, is to bring the teachers as learners to a level at which they can comfortably work productively with computer technology with some degree of confidence.

There is also a proposed "hybrid" model [32] that combines the best of the more traditional face-to-face traditional professional development practices with on-line activities. This combination has obvious advantages in terms of facilitating initial learning and competency development, and then utilizing a potentially efficient and effective means of additional teacher development. It should be further emphasized that online activity based training and development encourages content exploration, refection, and increased participation and collaboration.

Overall, there are numerous options available for in-service programming aimed at helping teachers develop computer-based technology competencies and applications. The local (school) context, needs of teachers, opportunities and available expertise are likely to guide the processes involved and approaches used. However, regardless of the chosen method, feedback and evaluation procedures should be considered an important component of any planned in-service, especially when long term commitments are in place. It is also important to embed follow-up activities into professional development endeavours that will not only help reinforce new concepts and procedures, but also encourage continued involvement in upgrading and thus foster and promote lifelong learning opportunity [32] [33].

5: Conclusion

The need for teacher development in this area is evident and critical for both pre- and in-service teachers and other educators. A recent survey of competencies and attitudes toward technology (computer-based) technology in Newfoundland confirmed this. Teacher development is a challenge in terms of the gap between the varying levels of current competence and use of technology, motivation and attitudes of educators, and what might be considered minimum required competencies. An examination of some current professional development practices in this area reveals many apparently successful yet different approaches by schools and school districts across North America. Approaches chosen should address the "local" situation and take into account a variety considerations, including the nature of adult learning.

The issue of developing competencies is further exacerbated by the changing developmental nature of technology and the virtual flood of software products, computer hardware, internet sites and other resources that are flowing into the market place. The overall challenge is to put into effect a systematic process that educators are comfortable working with, that is supportive, and that encourages learner independence and attitudes that result in a continuous developmental perspective within an authentic educational environment.

6: References

[1]   Panel on Educational Technology. (1995). *Report to the president on the use of technology to strengthen K-12 education in the United States.* Washington, DC: U.S. Department of Education.

[2]   Province of Alberta. (1998). *Information and communications technology, kindergarten to grade 12: An interim program of studies.* Edmonton: Alberta Education Curriculum Branch.

[3]   State of Arizona. (1997). *Technology standards.* Phoenix: Arizona Department of Education.

[4]   Statistics Canada (2000). Education indicators in Canada. Report on the pan-Canadian education indicators program 1999. Ottawa: Statistics Canada & the Council of Ministers of Education Canada

[5]   International Society for Technology in Education. (1998). *ISTE recommended foundations in technology for all teachers.* International Society for Technology in Education. http://www.iste.org/Resources/Prpjects/TechStandards/found.html

[6]   King, B. N. K. (1999). *The current state of technology competencies of teachers in Newfoundland schools.* Memorial University of Newfoundland, St. John's, Newfoundland, Canada.

[7]   Ely, D. P. (1995). *Technology is the answer! But what is the question?* The James P. Curtis Distinguished Lecture, Capstone College of Education Society, University of Alabama.

[8]   Mathews, J. D. (1998). *Predicting teacher perceived technology use: Needs assessment model for small rural schools.* (ED418828). Springfield, VA: ERIC Document Reproduction Service.

[9]   Schofield, J. W. (1995). *Computers and classroom culture.* Cambridge, NY: Cambridge University Press.

[10]   U.S. Congress Office of Technology Assessment. (1995). *Teachers and technology: Making the connection.* (OTA-EHR-616). Washington, DC: U.S. Government Printing Office.

[11]   Cambrie, M. A. $ Cook, D. L. (1997). Measurement and remediation of computer anxiety. *Educational Computing,* 27 (120, 15-20.

[12]   Dyck, J. L. & Smither, J. A. (1994). Age differences in computer anxiety: The role of computer experience, gender and education. *Journal of Educational Computing Research,* 10(3), 239-248

[13]   Meskill, C. & Melendez, J. (1997). Training adults in computers: A case study of Egyptian professional educators. *Journal of Technology and Teacher Education,* 5(1), 79-100.

[14]   Coley, R. J., Cradler, J. & Engel, P. K. (1997). *Computers and classrooms. The status of technology in U.S. schools.* (Policy Information Report.) Princeton, New Jersey: Policy Information Center.

[15]   Shashaani, L. (1993). Gender-based differences in attitudes toward computers. *Computers Educ.,* 20(2), 169-181.

[16]   Zoller, U. & Ben-Chaim, D. (1996). Computer inclination of students and their teachers in the context of computer literacy education. *Journal of Computers in Mathematics and Science Teaching,* 15(4), 401-422.

[17]   Weibe, J. H. & Taylor, H. G. (1997). What should teachers know about technology? A revised look at the ISTE foundations. *Journal of Computing in Teacher Education,* 13(4), 5-9.

[18]   Peck, K. L. (1998). Ready, aim, fire. Toward meaningful technology standards for educators and students. *TecTrends,* 43(2), 47-53.

[19]   Rothwell, W. J. & Kazanas, H. C. (1998). *Mastering the instructional design process: A systematic approach.* San Francisco: Jossey-Bass

[20]   Shambaugh, R. N. & Magliaro, S. G. (1997). *Mastering the possibilities: A process approach to instructional design.* Toronto: Allyn & Bacon.

[21]   Lloyd, B. H. & Gressard, C. P. (1996). Gender and amount of computer experience of teachers in staff development programs: Effects on computer attitudes and perceptions of usefulness. *AEDS Journal, Summer,* 302-311.

[22]   Sacks, C. H., Bellisimo, Y. & Mergendoller, J. (1994). Attitudes toward computers and computer use: The gender issue. *Journal of Research on Computing in Education,* 26(2), 256-269.

[23]   MacKeracher, D. (1996). *Making sense of adult learning.* Toronto: Coltmore Concepts.

[24]   Clifford, W. (1998). Updating teachers' technology skills. *Momentum,* 29(3), 34-36.

[25]   Clouse, R. W. & Alexander, E. (1997). Classrooms of the 21st century: Teacher competence, confidence and collaboration. *Journal of Educational Technology Systems,* 26(2), 97-111.

[26]   Zweir, J. (1998). Successful staff development. Microsoft=s K-12 Connection. [Available on-line] http://www.microsoft.com/education/k12articles/ccjun98.asp

[27]   Maddin, E. A. (1997). The real learning begins back in the classroom: On-the-job training and support for teachers using technology. *Educational Technology,* Sept.-Oct., 56-61.

[28]   Holzberg, C. S. (1997). Teach your teachers well: Successful strategies for staff development. *Technology and Learning,* 17(6), 34-40.

[29]   DeWert, M. H. & Cory, S. L. (1998). Educators go to SCOUT camp for technology-enhanced learning. *Journal of Staff Development,* 19(Winter), 32-38.

[30]   Milone, M. N. (1998). Staff development success stories. *Technology and Learning,* 18(7), 44-52.

[31]   Microsoft. (2000). *Microsoft professional development initiatives for K-12 teachers.* [Available on-line] http://www.microsoft.com/education/teachertraining/

[32]   Barkley, S & Bianco, T. (2002). Part digital training, part human touch. *Journal of Staff Development,* 23 (1), 42-45.

[33]   Brand, G. A. (1997). Training teachers for using technology. *Journal of Staff Development,* 19 (1), 15-20.

[34]   Cambrie, M. A. & Cook, D. L. (1997). Measurement and remediation of computer anxiety. *Educational Technology,* 27(12). 15-20.

Design and Implementation of the Self-test Module in Web Courses[*]

Yu-Jin ZHANG, Fan JIANG, Hao-Ji HU, Dan XU
Department of Electronic Engineering, Tsinghua University, Beijing 100084, China
zhangyj@ee.tsinghua.edu.cn

Abstract

This paper is focused on the design, development and implementation of self-test module and its question units. First, several general considerations in designing the self-test module for web course are introduced and discussed. The factors should be considered include the interface, the exercise problem as well as the hint and explanatory answer. Then, multiple real techniques in implementing such a module for a special web course about image processing and analysis are presented. The functions realized contain multiple selection of response code, practical hint or cue, explanatory answer, as well as statistic of score. Finally, some examples of resulted modules are illustrated to provide an overview of the module and several bright points of design strategy. The generalization of the approach is also discussed.

Key Words: E-learning, Web course, Self-test, Interface design, Interactive Learning Environment.

1. Introduction

The Global Information Infrastructure (GII) program started several years ago has offered a number of possibilities to apply information technology over a broad range of applications benefiting our society. With the rapid progresses of computer and communication technology as well as fast evolution of profession, continuous education and distance learning become the must and their deployment is always on the rise. Continuous education offers to people who are facing new challenge the way for capturing the novel trend in the discipline and busyness. Distance learning consists of the conducting of education and training at a long distance by using modern telecommunication technology, which enables people to learn what, where, when and how they want [1]. In reality, distance learning is no longer viewed as magic legend of advanced technology. It is but an indispensable part of modern life [2].

Distance learning as a new mode of education is particularly suitable for working people who in many cases should conduct self-learning or independent learning. For such a purpose, many online web courses have been developed which offer learners some novel learning styles. Examination/test is often considered as an effective way to evaluate the learning results, but in addition, it is also one style and procedure of learning. It has shown that using all learning styles would greatly strengthen the learning outcome [3]. In web course, test is frequently implemented as a self-reliant module (self-test module) in counting the difference between learning in the class and in remote place with/without teacher/coaches and in corresponding to the distance learner's requirements. Appropriate design of the test module would yield twice the result with half the effort in learning procedure.

In this paper, some general designing considerations in developing the self-test module for web courses are first discussed in the next section. According to these consideration guidelines, an actual self-test module for a new web course "Fundamentals of Image Processing and Analysis" is developed [4]. The practical developments are described, and some examples of this module are given in section 3. Finally, several concluding remarks are provided in section 4.

2. Designing Considerations

Counting the factors of self-study, the running form of self-test module should be such that the computer provides exercise problems according to the course contents, then students make the exercises and give the solutions to the problems, and finally computer check the correctness of solutions. This form provides an environment that learners could check their learning effects at time to fully understanding the principles and rises learner's ability to solve real problems. One advantage of this form is that even such a course is conducted in class, the time and efforts for teacher to correct the exercises and/or answer the questions.

The suitable design of self-test module is an indispensable part for web course design. In fact, except the contents of course, the following considerations should also be made.

---

[*] : This work has been supported by Ministry of Education (NENC-2000-29).

2.1 Interface

The interface in web course provides a way for communication between the computer and users. In general, the interface of different self-test units should be concise (such as the interface layout), uniform (such as the window locations) and easily operable (such as the keys for interaction). Thus users could quickly be familiar with the various functions provided by the interface and be concentrated on the test itself instead of spending time to learn how to use the interface.

2.2 Exercise problems

For a remote study, the interaction / connection between teachers and students could be less frequent, so the representation of exercise problem should be directly perceived through the senses.

Due to the limitations of computer in understanding natural language, the types of exercises are somehow bounded. The basic presentation forms of problems should be to provide clear explanation of some concepts and ask user to select from them. Yet, different variations are still needed and possible. For example, for filling blank exercises, instead of just leave a blank, the problem can provide a number of words or phrases as candidate and ask user to select the answer from them. Question-answer exercises can be realized by giving a question and assign one of the possible answers from the candidate list similar to filling blank. Calculating exercises can be transformed to provide a list of computing results and ask user to select from them.

2.3 Hint and explanatory answer

In simple cases, as the answers are marked with different choice, the computer can only provide the brief answer by indicating the code for corresponding selection. However, hint and explanatory answer are useful to help learners for further studying. Hint is important as user can get more insight from it for better understanding the problem and find the way to give the solution. In addition, this can split a test into two levels, so it would be more efficient and flexible. Explanatory answer is also important as learner can deeply capture the principle of problems. It helps learner to learn more things from making exercises. Reading the explanation is also an education phase.

3. Practical Implementation and Examples

Following the above designing considerations, a self-test module for a web course "Fundamentals of Image Processing and Analysis" is developed. This course is mainly concerned with different principles and techniques for manipulating (processing and/or analysis) digital images [4]. This course is targeted for continuous education and/or distance learning at the graduate level and is mainly for people with different background than signal and information processing.

At the current moment, this course consists of 60 study sections, and the self-test module provides a number of self-test units for each study sections. On basis of a special study of different Web course developmental tools, these self-test units are finally developed by using Flash [5]. Totally 219 self-test units are designed [6]. Some of them are taken as examples in the following.

Figure 1 gives the representative screen layout of a unit. On the top line is the title of the unit. Under the title line, the left half is for problem/question, which includes the text, drawing, picture, table, formula, etc. for explaining the problem and for the four choices to make reply. Also under the title line, the superior part of right half is for solution/answer. It includes 4 selection keys for answering the question, and three function icons for actions of answering, finding hint and displaying correct answer, respectively (more detailed discussion will be given in the end of this section). The lowest right part of the layout is for selecting exercise label as for each study unit several exercises are provided. It also serves to show the statistic of test results. The label corresponding to correctly answered exercise will be marked with a red "√", while the label corresponding to incorrectly answered exercise will be marked with a black "•".

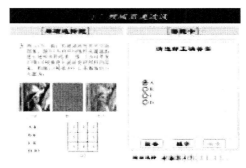

Figure 1   A typical layout of self-test unit

Sometimes, a long exercise problem may be encountered. In such a case, the free space in the right part of screen can be used. Figure 2 gives an example of this situation; the figure for the problem is located inside the answering square.

The course contents are related to image manipulation. Occasionally, not only the problem part is illustrated with drawing and/or picture, the answer to the problem is also illustrated with drawing and/or picture to give a concise and clear result. One example is shown in Figure 3.

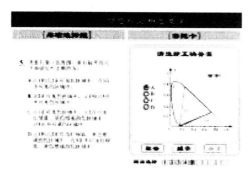

Figure 2　An example of long exercise problem

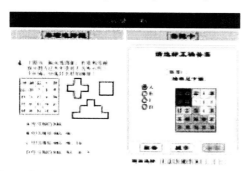

Figure 3　An example of unit with drawing in both sides

All the above examples are to select single correct response, that is, only one of four choices is the answer. However, multiple responses are also permitted in certain problems as for one question several answers can be produced. One example is shown in Figure 4, not only the running head at the problem part indicates that this is a multi-choice problem, but also the 4 selection keys become square (instead of circle) to awake the learner.

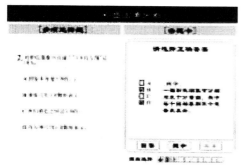

Figure 4　An example of multi-response interface

Finally, different functions of answering block are illustrated in Figure 5. Figure 5(a) shows the function of

answer; the judgement result is shown in the middle of window. Figure 5(b) shows the function of hint provides some cue for make correct answer. This function can be activated before answering to get some cues to solve the problem, and can be activated after one/more trying of answering to get some cues to correct the answer. Figure 5(c) shows the function of displaying correct answer, excerpt correct code, some explanations are provided to give learner more reasons.

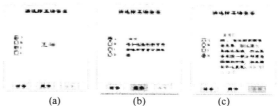

　　(a)　　　　　　　(b)　　　　　　　(c)

Figure 5　Different functions of answering block

4.　Concluding Remarks

(1)　Several general considerations for self-test module design and development are introduced and discussed in this paper.

(2)　A real self-test module for the web course "Fundamentals of Image Processing and Analysis" is implemented. It has a uniform configuration for all self-test units and provides sufficient functions to make the self-test suitable for web course use.

(3)　The principles for designing self-test module are general ones; they set a base line for development of self-test modules of web courses.

(4)　The develop procedure and the implementation techniques used for realizing the self-test module presented in this paper would also be usable for self-test modules of other web course.

References

[1]　Zhang Y J. "A tele-teaching practice using 'Tsinghua WebSchool'", Proc. ICCE'01, 173-176, 2001.

[2]　http://www.webc.com.cn/a22.htm

[3]　Feldman L J, Hofinger R J. Active participation by sophomore students in the design of experiments, ASEE/IEEE Frontiers in Education Conference, 1526-1527, 1997.

[4]　Zhu X Q, Zhang Y J, Liu W J. IP&A-Web: an online course of image processing and analysis, Proc. ICCE'01, 729-734, 2001.

[5]　Zhu X Q, Zhang Y J, Liu W J. Evaluation and comparison of web course developmental tools and technology: a case study, Proc. ICCE'01, 610-615, 2001.

[6]　Zhang Y J, Liu W J. A new web course ---- 'Fundamentals of Image Processing and Analysis'", Proc. 6th Global Chinese Conference on Computer in Education, 1: 597-602, 2002.

Strategies for Improving a Java-based, First Year Programming Course

Michael Blumenstein
School of Information Technology, Griffith University-Gold Coast
PMB 50, Gold Coast Mail Centre, QLD 9726, Australia
E-mail: m.blumenstein@mailbox.gu.edu.au

Abstract

This paper describes the evolution of a first year Java course at Griffith University - Gold Coast since Semester 1, 2000 to the present day. The course was updated to emphasise program design and to implement and evaluate an "objects-as-needed" approach to first year programming. A number of strategies were tested to increase consistency amongst teaching staff, improve delivery of course resources, successfully cater to a wide variety of students and to enhance the learning experience in general. The success of the revised course has been measured by evaluating student feedback and performance. Currently, a focus group-based strategy of evaluation is being adopted to determine students' attitudes to the most recently implemented changes.

1. Introduction

In the last few years, the literature has been inundated with papers describing the difficult transition from the use of procedural to object-oriented languages in the teaching curriculum [3]. Many institutions have favoured the adoption of Java as their language of choice for their first year programming course. At this stage, some universities are still pre-occupied with the question: "Not whether Java but how Java" [14]. There are a number of contentious, and some say unresolved issues that have plagued the minds of educators across the globe when dealing with the above question. Some of these issues have been tackled in the last two years whilst revising the first year Java course at Griffith University.

In particular, one of the major issues that presented itself during the revision of the Programming 1 course was the choice of methodology for teaching object-oriented programming. This paper discusses the dramatic changes and resulting experience obtained in revising the Programming 1 course. Particular attention is paid to the areas of: 1) Teaching resources, 2) Delivery of teaching materials, 3) Teaching methodology and 4) Assessment.

The remainder of this paper is divided into 4 Sections. Section 2 addresses the challenges that were considered whilst evaluating the Programming 1 course. Section 3 deals with the various strategies that were used to modify the course and Section 4 gives a description of the effectiveness of the newly revised curriculum. Finally, Section 5 offers conclusions and discusses future developments relating to Programming 1.

2. Background of the Course and Challenges Faced

This section addresses challenges that were tackled whilst revising the Programming 1 curriculum. In particular, factors that were specific to the Gold Coast campus will be addressed as well as general issues that are faced by all educators dealing with Java as a first language.

2.1 Campus Demographics

The first year programming course at the Gold Coast campus attracts a wide variety of students from different disciplines and backgrounds. For Multimedia and Information Technology students, Programming 1 is a core course in the first year of their degree. In Semester 1, the majority of students (80-90%) are Information Technology students. However, in Semester 2, the Multimedia students dominate the Programming 1 course's demographics. In both semesters the remainder of students enrolled are from other disciplines.

Whilst reviewing the course, the previous convenor indicated that there was a peculiar trend with regards to the performance of students over the two semesters. Specifically, the students enrolled in Semester 1 usually outperformed the students in Semester 2 in terms of academic achievement. It seemed that this trend might have correlated with the fact that the majority of students enrolled in Semester 2 were Multimedia students. Through their own experiences Allen and Bluff [1] note that disparities between these two groups arise due to the different expectations that each has. Specifically they mention that many Multimedia students are led to believe that their degree will be centred on more visual aspects of interface and application design rather than the more technical aspects of application development.

2.2 General Challenges

A more common issue that was addressed included whether to teach Java "objects first" or to continue along the lines that it had been taught in 1999 i.e. "structured programming-first" in a console-based environment.

Finally, an on-going challenge faced by the previous course convenor was to determine the best assessment strategies for the Java course. There were many problems with the assessment pieces that were set in 1999 including the sheer number of deliverables and a lack of individual assessment under "exam conditions".

3. Revision of the P1 Course

This section details the evolution of the Programming 1 course with particular attention to four areas: 1) Teaching Resources, 2) Delivery of Teaching Materials, 3) Tutor Support and Communication and finally 4) Assessment.

3.1 Teaching Resources

3.1.1 Objects "gently" and Textbook Choice. Prior to revising the Java course, a brand-new textbook [8] was considered as a replacement for the one used previously. Upon reviewing the text, it seemed that the question of objects was handled in a "gentle" and hence favourable manner. More specifically, it did not take the stance of either of the radical methods i.e. "objects-first" [6] or "structured programming-first" [4]. Instead, the text took the approach of introducing object-oriented concepts "as needed" [8].

The textbook was also attractive for another reason. It facilitated a shift away from entirely console-based applications and presented an opportunity to embrace GUI ones. However, rather than plaguing the students with the complexities of AWT, they were able to make use of the BreezyGUI package that was included with the textbook. The authors of the textbook, along with a number of other educators, are convinced that students are far keener to learn programming when they are able to produce applications with easy to build interfaces [7], [10]. It was also hypothesized that it would be appropriate for teaching the Multimedia students in Semester 2, as they would be able to develop applications more relevant to their field of interest.

3.1.2 Console-based Applications. Although BreezyGUI provided an excellent strategy for motivating students from most disciplines to commence and enjoy programming, it was felt that students would benefit from obtaining a more balanced view of programming in Java. It was therefore decided that students be introduced to console-based programs in the first few weeks of the course. The problems associated with Java and its

complicated I/O operations are well known [2], [11]. The solutions to teaching these difficulties vary, however the method chosen for Programming 1 was to share resources from Griffith University's Nathan campus. Specifically, custom-built classes for input and output were adopted: SimpleReader() and SimpleWriter() [13]. Classes of this nature have been adopted by a number of educators [2], and have allowed students to focus on the task of performing input and output rather than dealing with the complexities of Java's stream classes.

3.1.3 Design Paradigm. Upon commencing the course evaluation process, it was evident that emphasis on application design had not been prevalent between 1998 and 1999. This was an area of concern and would need to be investigated. As the proposed course structure would at times follow the textbook closely, the design paradigm would have to match this structure. It was therefore decided to adopt the Structured Design Chart (SDC) paradigm for teaching design. SDCs are based on Nassi-Schneiderman diagrams [12] and have one distinct advantage over other design techniques: not only do they provide the student with the final algorithm, but they also display the steps that were taken to get it.

3.2 Delivery of Teaching Materials

The method of material delivery chosen went along similar lines to previous semesters. There were four hours of contact time per week including one two-hour lecture and a single two-hour computer laboratory. It was felt that the class size, although reasonably large, could still benefit from material delivery in a lecture situation. Outside of these times, students were able to attend consultation times with their tutors or the course convenor.

To complement the contact time described above, the Programming 1 webpage and the School network became the centre pieces of "after-hours" material delivery. In previous years, little or no emphasis was placed on the webpage as a teaching aid. It was the task of the convenor to alter this state of affairs so that the focus could be reassigned towards that of "flexible delivery". All lecture material, tutorial exercises, assessment items, hints, course outline, staff contact details and announcements were hence placed on an easy to navigate, rapidly accessible page.

3.3 Tutor Support and Communication

Tutor instruction and communication was of particular importance with regards to the student numbers. It is for this reason that a close rapport was maintained (in the form of fortnightly meetings) between the convenor and each tutor to ensure consistency and quality with regards to delivery of weekly teaching material in computer laboratory time.

3.4 Assessment

Student assessment prior to 2000 was in the form of 11 short, take home laboratory modules and one major project. Upon reviewing the nature of these assessment items more closely, it was clear that this method of student performance evaluation had many disadvantages. Firstly, the shear number of assessment items that needed to be collected from students over the course of a semester was overwhelming. As a result of this excessive assessment load, many were lost, and it was then difficult to track them down at a later time. The assessment load also increased the marking load for the convenor and the tutors. Finally, due to the fact that the assessment items were not to be completed under "exam conditions", students had the benefit of working with others, using code from the textbook or notes and finally the possibility of plagiarism.

Due to the problems discussed above, the assessment methodology for the course was investigated. Although it was agreed that the concept of frequently assessing the students was beneficial, it was necessary to incorporate assessment pieces that could evaluate students' individual performance. This necessity led to the introduction of a mid-semester exam and a final exam into the course in addition to practical assessment such as laboratory assessments and a project. It was later found that this assessment structure was challenging for the students and seemed to evaluate their performance well on all topics in the course. However as will be seen in later sections, it would not remain static throughout 2000 and 2001.

4. Outcomes and Discussion

The following sections will relate some of the experience obtained from teaching students at the School of Information Technology over four semesters. The subsections presented below testify to the fact that the course structure agreed with certain student groups but was substantially more difficult for others. To dynamically address the needs of students with different backgrounds, minor changes to the course and assessment structure were made to increase student learning and to evaluate student performance more effectively.

4.1 Programming 1: Semester 1 & 2, 2000

Initially, the delivery of the course in Semester 1 proved to be quite challenging due to the added novelty and embellishments already discussed. Regardless, the new course structure proved to be reasonably successful. The main evidence for the course's success was sourced from student performance and student feedback. Both

were satisfactory in Semester 1 as may be seen in Table 1 & Figure 1.

Table 1. Profile of Grades (Gr.) for Programming 1 from Semester 1, 2000 up to and including Semester 2, 2001. The failure rate in brackets includes those students that did not submit the majority of assessment items.

Semester 1, 2000		Semester 2, 2000		Semester 1, 2001		Semester 2, 2001	
Gr.	%	Gr.	%	Gr.	%	Gr.	%
HD	11.8	HD	8.11	HD	18.1	HD	5.5
D	12.2	D	8.11	D	13.2	D	15.1
C	15.1	C	10.4	C	20.6	C	12.4
P	20.4	P	16.7	P	13.2	P	21.1
F	14.7 (28.2)	F	26.6 (37.8)	F	12.8 (23.5)	F	12.39 (26.1)

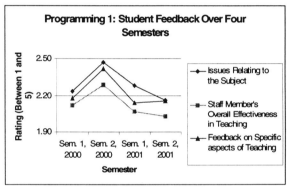

Figure 1. Programming 1: Student Feedback. The y-axis represents average student ratings on a scale between 1 and 5 (1 signifies 'Outstanding' and 5 signifies 'Very Poor')

4.1.1 Student Performance in Semester 1. It might be useful to look at the profile of grades obtained by students at the end of Semester 1. Nearly 40% of students obtained a grade of a Credit or above. The failure rate obtained (whilst including only those students that submitted a majority/all of the assessment items) was an acceptable level: 14.69%. Unfortunately, the failure rate for students that only submitted 1-3 pieces of assessment out of a possible 6 was higher: 28.2%. This demonstrates the fact that some students did not withdraw from the course at the appropriate time and did not complete their studies. Others simply did not attend lectures and laboratories or had fee problems.

4.1.2 Student Feedback: Implications for Semester 2. At the conclusion of Semester 1, there were a number of issues brought up by students in their written feedback that was helpful for the upcoming semester. The main issues were with regards to assessment. It was generally felt that the number of assessment items was excessive. It was for this reason that the curriculum was altered in Semester 2, 2000 so that one set of lab assessments (practical programming problems) was removed to enable students to focus on their end of semester projects.

4.1.3 Evaluation of Student Performance in Semester 2.
The minor improvements in the organisation of the course, and many positive written statements and feedback from students and tutors in Semester 1 attested to the general level of satisfaction from students with respect to teaching and learning in the course. To a large extent, the profiles of student grades in Semester 2 seemed to be similar to those in the previous semester (aside from a small increase in the number of failures).

An investigation of student demographics and performance found that a high proportion of students that did not perform well in the course were undertaking a Multimedia or Commercial computing (Business) degree. Aside from the above evidence, written student feedback correlated well with the poor performance of the groups mentioned. Specifically, a number of comments from Multimedia students were evaluated and reflected upon. The comments were all along the same lines, focussing on the fact that "...we (Multimedia students) will not need programming for our prospective jobs and therefore do not see the point of doing it". This particular view seems odd as many Multimedia students will be required to develop webpages that will in turn require knowledge of Java and applets. Nevertheless, it seems that this attitude is not an isolated view and it may be the reason for a lack of effort and enthusiasm on the part of certain student groups undertaking first year programming.

4.2 Programming 1: Semester 1 & 2, 2001

4.2.1 Student Motivation and the Importance of Practicing Programming.
With regards to motivation, most tutors, found that in Semester 2, 2000 students were not attending laboratories frequently and in many cases were not completing their assigned programming exercises. As an initiative to tackle the above problems, it was decided that students would be asked to submit their weekly exercises for marks. Students would therefore be "obliged" to, at the very least, attempt the weekly exercises and could work at a constant pace throughout the semester. This is supported by Duke *et al* [3] who agree that "...it is only through practice that a computer language, like any language, can be mastered". As may be seen in Table 1, the use of these exercises seemed to have a positive affect on student performance in Semesters 1 & 2, 2001. To complement the above evidence, Figure 1 displays all time highs in positive student feedback for both Semesters 1 and 2, 2001.

4.2.2 Issues Relating to Semester 2, 2001.
In Semester 2, a different approach for assessing students' practical programming performance was tested. Rather than completing the lab assessments as a solely take-home exercise, it was decided that they be divided into two parts. Part one would be an in-class assessment to take place in laboratory time and the second part would remain a take-home component to complement the former. This assessment piece was executed very successfully with little or no difficulties across all labs.

4.3 Programming 1: Semester 1, 2002

4.3.1 Teaching Objects Early.
As may be seen from the student performance and subject evaluations from 2000 and 2001, the newly instituted Programming 1 curriculum proved to be quite successful. However, upon reflection and a thorough evaluation of students' work, it was noted that there were a large number of students who were still finding the concepts of object-orientation difficult to master. The objects-gently approach, although successful, had its drawbacks. Specifically, students seemed to struggle at project time whilst attempting to master user-defined classes.

It was due to this observation that the Programming 1 course was guided through an extra evolutionary step. In Semester 1 2002, the approach to teaching objects became less "gentle" and slightly more inclined to the "objects-first" approach [6]. At approximately the same time, the 2nd edition of the Lambert & Osborne text [9] was released. It provided good support for this approach and hence it was adopted for Semester 1, 2002.

With the advent of this less "gentle" approach to teaching objects, the following were the main changes that were implemented: 1) Basic concepts and terminology of Object-Oriented programming were dealt with in lecture 1, 2) Object instantiation and message passing were cursively covered in lecture 3, 3) The application object and other O-O issues were covered in more detail in lecture 4.

4.3.2 Focus Groups and Programming 1.
With the advent of the course modifications described in Section 4.3.1, one of the initiatives considered important was to undertake an evaluation of student opinions and attitudes towards the course. The feedback obtained, would provide a reasonable idea of how the new, less "gentle" approach to teaching objects was being received by students.

The methodology chosen for evaluating the students' attitudes was: The "focus group" approach [5]. In this approach, groups of students representative of the population are chosen to respond (in written form) and reflect on issues pertaining to the course at various intervals throughout the semester. The first set of focus group "meetings" were convened during laboratory time in week 6 of the semester. This coincided with the completion of lectures dealing with the more assertive object-related material. Three labs consisting of 20 students each were randomly chosen. The second "meeting" is to take place in Week 12 to determine how students are coping with advanced O-O concepts after being exposed to objects early on in the semester.

The student demographics in each lab suggested an even spread of IT students and those from other disciplines. The following questions were given to students:

1. What are your current feelings towards the course?
2. What do you like about the course so far?
3. What do you dislike about the course?
4. What would you change about the course?

From the preliminary study, the feedback is very positive. As would be expected, students that are not undertaking an IT program have been finding it difficult, however they have expressed their enjoyment. On the other hand nearly all IT-based students are finding the course challenging and informative.

As this is only the preliminary stage of the focus group study, conclusions will be deferred until the end of the course. However, from the evidence sourced, it may be observed that in general, students find the less "gentle" approach to learning objects challenging in the first few weeks.

5. Conclusions and the Future of P1

This paper has described various challenges that were faced prior to and during the re-design of the Programming 1 course at Griffith University. Following the implementation of various changes to the course, the learning outcomes of students along with student feedback were measured over four semesters. It was shown that the learning outcomes for Semester 2, 2001 were the highest of all four semesters. This may be attributed to initiatives that were adopted to continually monitor student progress by encouraging the completion of weekly exercises. The amount of positive student feedback was at its highest in Semesters 1 and 2, 2001 and had increased significantly from the earlier semesters of the course.

Another adjustment to the course curriculum has been implemented in Semester 1, 2002. In a preliminary focus group study, written feedback suggests that students are coping well with the new "objects early" approach to programming. Further focus group meetings will be held again at the conclusion of the semester. In future, it may also be necessary to further investigate the applicability of Programming 1 to Multimedia students. Student feedback

and performance (based solely on Semester 2, 2000 and 2001) suggests that the course might benefit from further modifications to incorporate topics that are relevant to Multimedia students as well as those of other disciplines.

6. References

[1] Allen, R. K. and Bluff, K., Jumping into Java: Object-Oriented Software Development for the Masses, ACSE '98, (1998), 165-172.

[2] Clark, D. and MacNish, C., Java as a teaching language-opportunities, pitfalls and solutions, ACSE '98, (1998), 173-179.

[3] Duke, R., Salzman, E., Burmeister, J., Poon, J., Murray, L., Teaching Programming to Beginners-choosing the language is just the first step, ACSE '00, (2000), 79-86.

[4] Gibbons, J., Structured programming in Java, CTI Computing - Monitor 9, Java in the Computing Curriculum II, (Spring 1998), http://www.ulst.ac.uk/cticomp/gibbons.html (downloaded 22/10/01).

[5] Goodrum, D., Hackling, M. and Rennie, L., The status and quality of teaching and learning of science in Australian schools, A Research Report prepared for the Department of Education, Training and Youth Affairs, (2001).

[6] Kölling, M. and Rosenburg, J., Guidelines for Teaching Object Orientation with Java, ITiCSE 2001, (2001), 33-36.

[7] Lambert, K., and Osborne, M., Easy GUIs with Java in the Computer Science Curriculum, 30th Annual SIGCSE Technical Symposium, New Orleans, (March 1999).

[8] Lambert, K. A., Osborne, M., JAVA: A Framework for Programming and Problem Solving (1st Edition), Brooks/Cole Publishing Company, Pacific Grove CA, 1999.

[9] Lambert, K. A., Osborne, M., JAVA: A Framework for Programming and Problem Solving (2nd Edition), Brooks/Cole Publishing Company, Pacific Grove CA, 2002.

[10] Martin, F. and Williams, P., Java: teaching and learning in large classes within a modular scheme, CTI Computing - Monitor 9, Java in the Computing Curriculum II, (Spring 1998), http://www.ulst.ac.uk/cticomp/fmartin.html (downloaded 22/10/01).

[11] Martin, P., Java, the good, the bad and the ugly, CTI Computing - Monitor 9, Java in the Computing Curriculum II, (Spring 1998), http://www.ulst.ac.uk/cticomp/pmartin.html (downloaded 22/10/01).

[12] Robertson, L. A., Simple Program Design (2nd Edition), Thomas Nelson, Australia, 1993.

[13] Rock, A., SimpleReader and SimpleWriter I/O package (abr.srw), (2001), http://www.cit.gu.edu.au/~arock/p1.01.2/ (downloaded 29/04/02).

[14] Wallace, C., Martin, P. and Lang, B., Not Whether Java but how Java, CTI Computing - Monitor 8, Java in the Computing Curriculum, (1997), http://www.ulst.ac.uk/cticomp/not.html (downloaded 22/10/01).

A Research and Development on Curriculum Framework around ICT Literacies for Teachers

Wakio OYANAGI

(Center for Research and Development, Nara University of Education, Japan)

This paper will present a curriculum framework aimed at developing ICT literacies for teachers. The framework originates from a theoretical perspective that sees ICT literacies in terms of social practice and a changing discourse about communication. Specifically, the paper will report how the framework has been applied to the Information and Communication Technologies (ICT) curriculum in Japan. The goal is to fully integrate ICT into a program of ICT literacies across the curriculum. The framework represents a perspective for doing so, recognizing that many teachers are not consciously aware of ICT literacies, or even if they are aware of it, they cannot conceptualize how it might be integrated meaningfully into the curriculum. To illustrate how the framework might be applied, data from some instances at Japanese school will be presented. The teacher who is the focus of the instances is an expert teacher who at the time of data collection had begun to use multi-media but had little awareness of or commitment to ICT literacies. The teacher's shift toward an awareness of ICT literacies will be presented in light of the framework presented at the outset of the paper

1: Introduction

Why was "Curriculum Framework around ICT Literacies for Teachers" set as the topic of this paper?

We have already had some excellent ideas of the standard qualification around ICT literacies for teachers and the preceding researches to integrate ICT into subject matters. For example, we can find some ideas easily in ISTE (International Society for Technology in Education), ITEA (International Technology Education Association), the various trials of other universities, and the rubric around ICT in the various countries etc. Also referring to them, we have attempted to educate university students at the coursework we call "operation of ICT" and "instruction method and technology" in Japan

However the integration hasn't always succeeded. The course teachers often tend to teach university students the instruction technology based on subject contents from the operational and functional aspects, not from critical and social aspects. Though the university students might learn the competences to operate ICT in the subject teaching, they don't have any opportunities to analyze the subject contents using ICT from critical and social aspects and to reflect their own activity using ICT from critical and social aspects.

The problem is that university teachers often read the current policy and plan around ICT for teacher education from narrow aspects. So the classroom teachers feel the difficulty to design the classes from wide and deep aspects as results of coursework in university.

In summary, university teachers should reconsider the content of their coursework around ICT, by collecting and analyzing the data about teacher's practical trouble and the unexpected effects. Also it is necessary for prospective teachers and in-service teachers to have some opportunities to reflect their images of the class using ICT from wide aspects as much as possible. So I took this topic because we need a frame of reference for university and school teachers to get wide aspects from a sound ICT pedagogy.

From the above mentioned, the topic of this paper is decided.

As a procedure to explore this topic, this paper sets the following key question. And I try to answer the key question from the some instances and the references to various research papers and books around ICT literacies.

2: A key question

How can "Curriculum Framework around ICT Literacies for Teachers" be constructed from wide aspects?

3: What are ICT Literacies?

As I told at "Introduction", recently the term of "ICT" is popular at teacher education in Japan. The university teachers, who have the responsibility of educational method etc., often use this term. But the images of ICT often depend on computer science and technology without communication. So if we attempt to look at ICT from wide aspects, we should rethink the meaning and range of ICT in teacher education. Also, if we draw on ICT from not only the physical aspects and functional aspects, but also the knowledge and ability to be requested the school teachers, we should think "ICT as literacies", which express both the abilities and their social meaning. Thereupon, I chose the term of ICT "Literacies". Of course, we have many terms to express the similar meaning, for example, computer literacy, media literacy, technological literacy etc. However in case of thinking of the teacher's capacity around ICT, we can't avoid referring to ICT Literacies.

So, in this paper, I attempt to use the term of "ICT Literacies" from wide aspect rather than narrow aspect, which only operate ICT. Also I try to define the ICT Literacies by referring to the definition of other similar literacy here.

For example, Technology for all Americans projects (2000) defines the Technological literacy as following. "Technological literacy is the ability to use, manage, access, and understand technology. A technologically literate person understands, in increasingly sophisticated ways that evolve over time, what technology is, how it is created, and how it shapes society, and in turn is shaped by society. He or she will be able to hear a story about technology on television or read it in the newspaper and evaluate the information in the story intelligently, put that information in context, and form an opinion based on that information. A technologically literate person will be comfortable with and objective about technology, neither scared of it nor infatuated with it."[4]

Spitzer, Eisenberg, and Lowe (1998) show the features of literacy of visual, media, computer, network, and information as following. "Visual literacy is defined as the ability to understand and use images, including the ability to think, learn, and express oneself in terms of images". "Media literacy is defined as the ability of a citizen to access, analyze, and produce information for specific outcomes". "Computer literacy is generally thought of as familiarity with the personal computer and the ability to create and manipulate documents and data via word processing, spreadsheets, databases, and other software tools". "Closely related to computer literacy is network literacy a term that is still evolving. In order to locate, access, and use information in a networked environment such as the World Wide Web, users must be network literate". "To be information literate, a person must be able to recognize when information is needed and have the ability to locate, evaluate, and use effectively the needed information".[8]

Gilster(1997), wrote the book of title "Digital literacy", defines the Digital literacy as following. "Digital literacy is the

ability to understand and use information in multiple formats from a wide range of sources when it is presented via computers."[2]

Warschauer (1999) defines the Electronic literacy as following. "Electronic literacy involves not only adapting our eyes to read from the screen instead of the page but also adapting our vision of the nature of literacy and the purposes of reading and writing."[9]

Potter (1998) defines the Media literacy as following. "Media literacy is a perspective from which we expose ourselves to the media and interpret the meaning of the messages we encounter. We build this perspective from knowledge structures. To build our knowledge structures, we need tools and raw material. The tools are our skills; the raw material is information from the media and from the real world. " [7]

Knobel, and Healy (1998) define the critical literacy as following. "we define critical literacy as the analysis and critique of the relationships among language, power, social groups and social practices".[5]

The various literacies, which I cited at the above, have common points and different points. Though the relationship among them is complicated, you might find the character of skill-technology base, representation base, or sociocultural base, etc. in each definition.

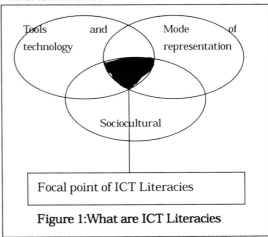

Figure 1:What are ICT Literacies

As a result, referring to the above preceding studies, I attempted to understand ICT Literacies as figure1. In short, ICT literacies relate to "the literacies based on tools and technology's conception", "the literacies based on mode of representation", and "the literacies based on sociocultural conception". However ICT literacies take notice of interaction among them. In other words, ICT Literacies include the all of literacies cited at the above as relative area. I think ICT literate person draws on "the literacies based on tools and technology's conception", "the literacies based on mode of representation", and "the literacies based on sociocultural conception".

4: Exploring the key aspects of curriculum framework

To answer the above key question, at first, I tried to analyze the some instances of 20 teachers at primary school in Japan. I focused on what kinds of ICT literacies were requested each teacher, through typical 3 instances. Then I attempted to define the key aspects of curriculum framework to be able to give the perspective as next step to the teacher.

In what follows, I try to show a model around teacher's shift toward an awareness of ICT literacies by using the typical 3 instances at primary school in Japan. Figure2 shows this model.

Figure2 expresses the wall, which the teacher often faces in her/his practice using ICT. First wall appears when the teacher tries to acquire the knowledge about ICT and the operational /functional skills.

Second wall appears when teacher tries to acquire the knowledge, ability and perspective to integrate ICT into subject matters.

Third wall appears when teacher tries to construct the class using ICT from wide aspects.

4.1: Instance 1 : Math in Grade 5 at primary school

This teacher has the 20 year's experience as primary school teacher. She has much knowledge and rich experience about instruction skill about math.

An aim of this class is to use ICT to prompt the understanding how to calculate an area of a parallelogram. As method and media, she used traditional lecture method, computer, and touch screen projector.

What she emphasizes in this class was to make students understand how to calculate an area of a parallelogram using ICT. However, during the class, she often had troubles around the operation of ICT. When she couldn't use the ICT according to her aims, she returned to traditional method. She wanted to teach students math using ICT. But students wanted to learn how to operate the material on computer. At first, students were very interested in ICT. She often limited student's utilization of ICT freely. Gradually, students weren't interested in the class. As she had attention to do the math class using ICT effectively, she wasn't conscious of the differences between her aims and students' needs. She faced the first wall. As she has rich experience as teacher, she can talk the perspective to integrate ICT into math and can plan the class from wide aspect. However, the nervousness of ICT operation gave her the uneasy judgment of instruction. At that time, what was requested her was the systematic knowledge around ICT and operational/functional skill around ICT.

	Operational/functional		
Knowledge about ICT			
Skill about ICT			

4.2: Instance 2: History in Grade 6 at primary school

This teacher has the 13 year's experience as primary school teacher. He has much knowledge and rich experience around ICT.

An aim of this class is to make students construct the story of historical events and give the presentation of the research. As method and media, he used cooperative learning method by groups, books, TV, VTR, Computer, Audio CD and Internet.

What he emphasizes in this class was to make students clear their own interests and investigate the historical events critically and practically using the various media. (He was interested in media literacy and information literacy). If students requested to learn how to use media and understand the functionality, according to necessity, he led students to the media and ICT world.

Both teacher and students started from a topic of history textbook. Both tried to inquire into historical events from

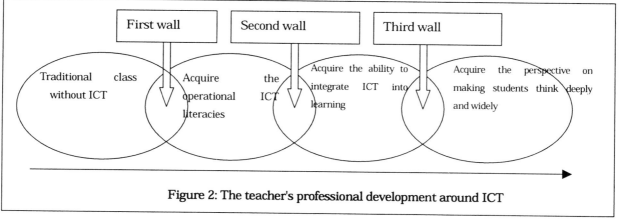

Figure 2: The teacher's professional development around ICT

multiple aspects. Some students became the active users of ICT as results.

As he had rich experience around ICT, he was already beyond the first wall. However he faced the second wall. He paid attention to critical reading about the materials to integrate ICT into history. However he didn't have the concrete strategy about how he should guide the students to critical reading of the historical events. He needed to brush up "the literacies based on mode of representation".

Especially, in this case, what is requested him was the systematic knowledge around critical thinking and to pay attention to the critical aspects around the utilization of ICT in his class.

	Operational/functional	Critical	
Literacy through ICT			

4.3: Instance 3: Reading in Grade 6 at primary school

This teacher has the 23 year's experience as primary school teacher. She has much knowledge and rich experience around both reading and ICT.

An aim of this class was to make students read the life history of "Mother Teresa" deeply through communicating with the prospective teachers (from the different age stances). As method and media, she used collaborate learning method, teleconference system and BBS.

What she emphasizes was to make students read the literature beyond classroom discussion by using ICT.

Students, teacher, and preservice teacher students worked together about reading the life history of "Mother Teresa". Then they told their feeling and thinking from each stance, compared with their own stance, and discussed their life from now on by using teleconference system (real time and different place)and BBS (different time and different place). Also teacher set the opportunity for her students and preservice teacher students to meet face to face after the end of classes.

As she had rich experience around both reading and ICT, she was already beyond the first wall and second wall. However she faced the third wall. She paid attention to social practice. She tried to make students look at the differrent thinking at different stance and in social practice. However she was worried about how she should guide her students to social practice. She needed to integrate "the literacies based on sociocultural conception" into "the literacies based on tools and technology's conception" and "the literacies based on mode of representation", which she had already acquired, in order to construct the reading class by using ICT from wide aspects.

What is requested her was the systematic knowledge around

scaffolding the students toward the social practice and was to pay attention to the other instances of practice from the social aspects, relating to the utilization of ICT in her class.

	Operational/functional	Critical	Social
Multiple views			
Perspectives			

From the above mention, I could extract some key aspects here, as the ideas to construct the curriculum framework around ICT literacies from wide aspects.

5: Constructing a taxonomy of curricular goals for ICT Literacies

Up to this point, I could extract the some key aspects for the curriculum framework. By making the table, which expresses their aspects meaningfully, we can proceed to the next step. That is to make clear the curricular goals for ICT Literacies.

At first, I decided to set the area of influence or effect as the horizontal line. This has a range from local to global. This is composed of functional, critical, sociocultural as aspects.

Functional aspect means that teachers can access and operate ICT fluently, according to the aims.

Critical aspect means that teachers can analyze, interpret, and evaluate the meaning of information on ICT, relating to actual social praxis.

Sociocultural aspect means that teachers can pay attention to the socio-historical relationship between human and ICT from wide aspects and can participate in social praxis positively.

Next, as well, I decided to set the relation between literacy and ICT as the vertical line. This has a range from "the literacy to be able to use ICT as tool" to "the literacy to have the meta-cognition about the own activity". This is composed of literacy through ICT, literacy about ICT, and literacy as ICT, as each aspect.

"Literacy through ICT" means that teachers can use ICT flexibly as tool in subject teaching, and can deal with the digital information by using ICT practically.

"Literacy about ICT" means that teachers can understand the

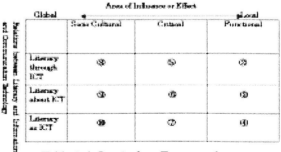

Table 1. A Curriculum Framework

structure, function, and character of ICT.

"Literacy as ICT" means that teachers can reflect their own activity to use ICT and can communicate the best way to accomplish their goals with collaborators.

Table 1 expresses curriculum framework based on 3×3 aspects. Each element (from ② to ⑩) is the goal which teachers should aim at in each practice.

① To challenge the class by using ICT from now on.

② To make students acquire the ability to use ICT flexibly when they learn subject's contents and explore a topic.

③ To make students acquire the knowledge to use ICT flexibly when the students learn the domain of ICT by using ICT.

④ To make students acquire the disposition and thinking method to monitor and control their own activity when the students use ICT to learn subject's contents and the domain of ICT.

⑤ To make students acquire the ability to read the various information in the social praxis analytically and critically when they learn subject's contents and explore a topic by using ICT.

⑥ To make students acquire the knowledge to read the various information in the social praxis analytically and critically when the students learn the domain of ICT by using ICT.

⑦ To make students acquire the disposition and thinking method to monitor and control their own activity when they read the various information in the social praxis analytically and critically by using ICT

⑧ To make students acquire the ability to evaluate the cultural inheritances and their own experiences socially and historically and acquire the attitude to participate in social praxis positively when the students learn subject's contents and explore topics by using ICT.

⑨ To make students acquire the knowledge to evaluate the cultural inheritances and their own experiences socially and historically and to participate in social praxis positively when the students learn the domain of ICT by using ICT.

⑩ To make students acquire the disposition and thinking method to monitor and control their own activity when they evaluate the cultural inheritances and their own experiences socially and historically and to participate in social praxis positively by using ICT.

6: Conclusion

Up to this point, I presented an idea to produce " A Curriculum Framework around ICT Literacies for Teachers " from wide aspects. This is the conclusion of this paper.

By the way, for whom is the above framework useful? Here,

I attempt to make it clear as another conclusion of this paper.

The first, this framework is very useful for the teacher, who explores the practice around ICT, because the teacher can reflect their stance in practice by using this framework.

The second, this framework is very useful for the researcher, who explores the practical findings around ICT practice, because the researcher can analyze the ICT practice systematically, widely and deeply by using this framework.

Finally, this framework is very useful for the teacher educator, who explores how to instruct ICT practice to preservice teacher students and inservice teachers in the coursework and workshop, because the teacher educator can have the holistic and systematic aspects around ICT practice by using this framework.

I expect this suggestion will be to answer the key question.

References

1.Bigum,C. and Green,B.(1993). Technologizing literacy: or, interrupting the dream of reason. In Luke,A. and Gilbert,P. (Ed.).*Literacy on Contexts. Australian Perspectives and Isuues.* NSW, Australia. Allen& Unwin.

2.Gilster, P. (1997). *Digital literacy.* New York. Wiley Computer Publishing. p.1.

3.International Society for Technology in Education, (1998). *National educational technology standards for students: Essential Conditions to make it happen..*

4.International Technology Education Association. (2000). Technology for all Americans projects. *Standards for Technological Literacy: Content for the study of Technology.* Virginia. p.9.

5.Knobel, M. and Healy, A. (Ed.). (1998).*Critical literacies in the primary classroom.* NSW, Australia. PETA. p.127.

6.Lankshear,C. and Snyder, I., with Green,B. (2000). *Teachers and technoliteracy. Managing literacy, technology and learning in schools.* NSW, Australia. Allen& Unwin.

7..Potter, W. J. (1998).*Media Literacy..* Thousand Oaks, California. Sage. p.5.

8.Spitzer, K.L., Eisenberg, M.B. and Lowe, C.A. (1998). *Information literacy: Essential skills for the information age.* Syracuse, New York. Eric Clearinghouse on Information & Technology Syracuse University. pp.22-29.

9.Warschauer, M. (1999). *Electronic literacy: Language, culture, and power in online education.* Mahwah, New Jersey. LEA. p.13.

Acknowledgements

I would like to thank David Reinking for their comments on earlier draft of this article. He gave me some ideas to make the ICT literacies clear.

Multimedia Planning Method and Mutual Evaluation System on the Web in Computer Literacy Education

Masayoshi YANAGISAWA,

Eiichi TSUKAMOTO

Faculty of Human Sciences, Toyo Eiwa University, JAPAN

my@toyoeiwa.ac.jp

tukamoto@toyoeiwa.ac.jp

Abstract

Due to the lack of available time within university curriculums it is often very difficult to adequately teach the concept and functions of most programming languages or multimedia environments. Moreover the teaching of these subjects to students from non science/technology backgrounds require further additional time and is not often suited to students who wish to pursue a career as a concept developer or website designer. For these reasons the Multimedia Planning Method was developed in order for students to learn the important issues surrounding software development without becoming involved in the actual learning of programming languages or multimedia environments. In this method students devise plans to market a multimedia product and produce a pamphlet for advertisement purposes. Through this assignment it is felt that students acquire computer skills and gain an understanding of the concept of multimedia. The mutual evaluation system was developed in order for students to evaluate and comment on each others work and to learn the processes involved in software development and design.

Keywords

Multimedia, Mutual Evaluation, Peer Assessment, Individual Learning, Web Based Learning (WBL), Bulletin Board System (BBS)

Background and Objectives

We believe that one of the biggest problems facing the teaching of computing based subjects in higher education centers upon the lack of available time in the curriculum to dedicate to these lessons. For example at our university taught computer programming classes are typically limited only one hour a week. As a result, many universities students are now being taught only how to use COTS (commercially-off-the-shelf) computer software as opposed to learning how to program.. To make matters worse, the lack of time dedicated to teaching students

how to use the often user friendly but highly specialized functions within a multimedia package means that many users are unable to become confident and proficient users.

It is often difficult to teach any computer based subject to students who are not majors from either a computer science or technology based discipline. In the case of the university named above, students are not typically from a mathematics or computer science background. To teach a computer based subject to students from a different discipline is often a challenging activity for the teachers concerned. Within this paper a method was developed and termed, the Multimedia Planning Method [1][2], the central principle within this method is that it allows students to become familiar with the essence of multimedia development without having to master the software.

An additional problem that has been noted at many universities concerns the evaluation and marking of students work. Students often put a considerable amount of time and effort into their finished work or report and therefore should receive a full evaluation and assessment of their work. It is often the case that the professors in charge of assessing the work do not have enough time to examine each report fully or fully evaluate the design and contents of the deliverable. This results in students receiving a series of brief comments but not a comprehensive analysis and critique of their work.

With these problems in mind, it was decided to develop a mutual assessment method that would not only enable students to evaluate each others work on the web but would also allow professional designers or programmers to evaluate and comment on students work.

The Multimedia Planning Method

For students who are not majors in computer science and technology based subjects it is often noted that they require a longer period of time to learn either how to program or how to use a multimedia package.

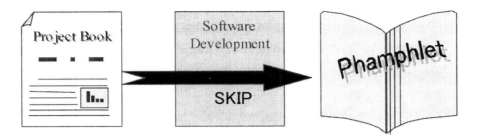

Figure 1: Concept of Multimedia Planning Method

Without actually implementing actual multimedia software, it is difficult to understand the concept of multimedia. Therefore a method was developed to understand the concept of multimedia software without the implementation of actual multimedia, "The Multimedia Planning Method".

Central to this method is the idea that students have to plan the production of a pamphlet which will be designed in a computer based environment (See Figure 1).

Initially students are introduced to a variety of products that were developed using multimedia packages. After this point they begin to consider the issues surrounding the development of a new product using a multimedia package. They are only required to conceptualize the product, its main functions etc, but there is no need for them to actually develop it. Instead students skip the actual development phase and move straight onto the advertising phase where they then think about exactly how they wish to advertise their product in a pamphlet. The benefit of using this approach is that students are not required to develop the software but do instead focus on the planning aspects of software development. They are also required to use their knowledge of the various types of multimedia software available at present, its suitability to various tasks and the issues surrounding the advertising of new piece of software.

Concrete Method in Classroom

This method was used for an "Information Planning" class. The students were sophomore and senior female university students who were not majoring in a science or technology based subject. They had acquired basic computer literacy skills such as typing and were proficient users of the internet, word processing and spread sheet packages and had basic information science knowledge. None of the students had any experience with computer programming. The objectives of this class were to familiarize themselves with the main functions of multimedia software and to acquire a basic knowledge of the subject area that would in turn allow them to compete with other graduates for jobs in the information industry sector.

Students first experience with a piece of multimedia software was a package designed to help learners of English. With each class students were shown a number of different multimedia packages. After this introduction they are asked to set about making project book that should contain details of their own original multimedia deliverable. The project books were also evaluated students can begin to make the pamphlet to advertise their own software.

The pamphlet must contain four pages and must bind like real one. Students are allowed to use any software to make the pamphlet. Although almost all students have only a basic knowledge of Microsoft Word and Windows, they have access to many tools/equipments such as graphic tools, a digital camera, image scanner etc. Traditionally when students wish to learn how to use a new piece of equipment they often find a teacher or an assistant to show them how to use the equipment. But in this situation they are not permitted to ask questions but are instead encouraged to teach themselves. The rationale behind making them learn by themselves is that if teachers/assistants demonstrate the equipment students have a tendency to only learn the procedure and do not gain a well rounded knowledge of the piece of equipment in question.

Results of Multimedia Planning Method

In our university, the Multimedia Planning Method has been in use for four years. And almost all pamphlets made by students have been impressive in terms of ideas, design and technology. This result was not foreseen at the beginning of this project. The pamphlets are produced using a variety of software and tools e.g. Microsoft Word, Front Page, Power

Point, Photo Editor, Adobe Photoshop, digital cameras, laptops, image scanner, color printers etc, in spite of most students only having basic computer skills. Figure 2 shows an example of a pamphlet. This sample advertises a piece of software that enables users to see many pictures with music and takes them on a tour of relaxing places such as parks and woodland and the idea of aroma therapy is also introduced. The cover page contains a title and images (the title of this software is FOREST). The contents of this software are explained on pages 2-3. And in the scoop page, there is specified information about the system requirements needed to run this piece of software, the price and the virtual company name and address. To make this pamphlet this student learned Adobe Photoshop by herself.

In this case study, the following data was used to analyze.

1) Comments from the students after each class.
2) A questionnaire about computer skills before the introduction of this method.
3) A questionnaire about their progress during the course of this assignment.
4) A questionnaire about their computer skills after this assignment.
5) Observations and remarks about using this method.

Figure 3 shows a summary of the 5 point scale questionnaire after this method was compared with a normal class where the teacher teaches traditional computer studies. Although satisfaction is rated quite low, other items achieved good scores. Students were highly motivated in terms of their involvement in this assignment and they wanted to produce good work. A possible reason as to why satisfaction was rated so lowly arises from the lack of time that students felt they had to produce the pamphlet.

Each pamphlet was evaluated and marked by students. Using these marks students pamphlets were divided into two groups for further analysis. Table 1 displays two typical kinds of comments from either students whose work was well evaluated or students whose work was evaluated as being poor. It should be noted that the level of computer skills held by both of these students was the same prior to this assignment. When analyzing the methods used in the production of these pamphlets, there have been a number of differences between high-scoring students and low-scoring students that have been found. For example, high-scoring students always appear to ask for someone else's advice like classmates, other friends or their parent. The results of this questionnaire revealed that high scoring students typically looked to either compete or co-operate with other students. On the other hand, low-scoring students rarely ask questions or consult anyone. They always aim to work and produce the pamphlet on their own. This finding suggests that in order to encourage low scoring students group based projects would be extremely beneficial.

Cover

two-page spread

Scroop

Figure 2: An Example of Pamphlet

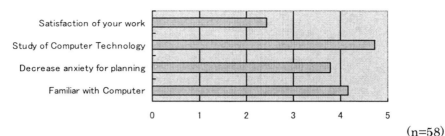

(n=58)

Figure 3: Result of questionnaire after this method

Table 1: Two typical comments from two different students

Comments from students who were evaluated well	Comment from students who were not evaluated well
Although I had an extremely hard time because I didn't have any technical skills before this assignment, I am very satisfied with this assignment. Through this assignment, I think I have gained a lot of new knowledge and skills.	*In this assignment, the result was only evaluated. Even if we struggled to make it and took enormous time, only the last design and concept were only evaluated. I am very frustrated and I really wanted them to evaluate my effort and time.*
In our usual class the teacher or assistant helps us. But in this assignment, we had to do all of it by ourselves. I think that why we got so many new skills.	*Although I was actually quite excited by this assignment and class, I could not make my work well because there ware big gap between my ideal pamphlet and my skills.*

Method 2: Mutual Evaluation System

There are many students that take this particular class. Therefore, it is too difficult to evaluate all the pamphlets properly in detail and to write good comments as time is often limited. Furthermore, multimedia software and the designed pamphlets have to be evaluated on many points such as concept, design and technology and so on. The mutual evaluation system on the web was especially developed for the task of pamphlet evaluation. This method was used our previous Problem Based Learning System and students could receive fair-minded evaluation each other [3]. Therefore, the mutual evaluation was implemented in this system. The system could also be used by the teacher prior to the assignment being issued to students as a means of illustrating the nature of the task and using previous students work as examples of what has been produced, the differences between high scoring and low scoring students work Although this method was developed for this project, it can be generalized and used in other classes to assess other styles of report or assignments. Figure 4 shows the web image of the Mutual Evaluation System.

Ranking Page

Evaluation Page

Figure 4: Mutual Evaluation System

This system has the following functions/pages.

1) Logon: each student has to use their own account because students are required evaluate other students' pamphlets independently and these evaluations should be secret.

2) List of pamphlets: Almost 70 pamphlets' their names, thumbnails, current score, and short PR comments are listed.

3) Evaluation: All four pages of pamphlet thumbnails are shown and each has its own BBS (bulletin board system) where students can post comments. Furthermore, students can evaluate the pamphlet using 5 point scale on points such as concept, design, technology (making the pamphlet) and total evaluation (whether student would want to buy the product or not) (See Figure 4 Left). When students click the thumbnails a larger image is displayed.

4) Ranking of pamphlets: Based upon the result of the ranking exercise by students, all pamphlets are ranked (See Figure 4 Right). The total points and the average of summation are calculated on the background when every rank is posted and the ranking of pamphlets are changed using this average point automatically in real time. The site only lists the top 20 pamphlets.

This system was developed under the Microsoft Internet Information Server and Active Sever Pages Technology. Microsoft Access was used as the database. All pamphlets' page images were input as JPEG format in this system. Depending on the access speed in students' home internet environment three different compression rate of images could be selected in order to aid students' evaluation of the pamphlets from home.

Results of Mutual Evaluation System

All students are required to comment and evaluate at least 10 pamphlets. And in order to evaluate from a professional viewpoint, 4 professionals (designers and programmers) were requested to issue their comments and rate each pamphlet.

This mutual evaluation system was appreciated by both students and professionals. Many comments and rating were posted using this system. The results generated by the questionnaire revealed that many students felt that this mutual evaluation was good system, that their assignments and efforts were well evaluated and that the comments from other students were helpful.

Discussion

Using this Multimedia Planning Method, students were not only able to learn multimedia software concept but also gained many computer skills through the production of pamphlets. Although current practices usually dictate that lessons should be teacher orientated, the implementation of this method has shown that students could and did learn by themselves. The successful factors identified in this self learning environment are as follows. 1) Role Playing (A student is a producer or designer in a virtual company and they have to propose their own plan to their virtual boss.) 2) An examination genuine software and the issues underlying the production of a pamphlet 3) The teacher never teaches a procedure. 4) Environment (Students could freely use the computer rooms, laptops, personal computers, digital cameras and image scanners) 5) Evaluation from other students.

In this Multimedia Planning method students are not required to learn how to code. The results of this study suggest that students do not necessarily need to be able to program in order to conceptualize the processes required to produce a working piece of software. It is not suggested that this method be adopted in classes or programs whose primary goal is to produce computer programmer. Instead the implementation of this method should be for students who wish to pursue a career in the areas of concept planning or website design. This method was successfully implemented in a University and it is felt that it could be adapted to suit the needs and facilities of high schools and junior high schools.

References

[1] Yanagisawa,M. & Tsukamoto,E. (2000) Development of Information Literacy by Multi Media Planning Method and Peer Assessment, The Sixth Joint Conference on Educational Technology, pp.387-388.

[2] Yanagisawa,M., Tsukamoto,E. (2000) Changing the Students' Learning Attitude Through Designing the Multimedia Software Pamphlets, Proceedings of the 24th Annual Meeting, Japan Society for Science Education, pp.221-222.

[3] Madhumita,B., Yanagisawa,M., Akahori,K.(1999) Internet Based Collaborative Evaluation of Learning in a PBL Environment, Advanced Research in Computers and Communications in Education, G.Cumming et al.(Eds.), IOS Press, Vol.2, pp.181-184.

Teaching-Learning Interchange:
An Online Support Community for New Teachers

Pamela Redmond
University of San Francisco
2130 Fulton Street
San Francisco, California 94117
Redmond@usfca.edu

David Georgi
California State University, Bakersfield
9001 Stockdale Highway
Bakersfield, California 93311
dgeorgi@csub.edu

Abstract

The Teaching-Learning Interchange (TLI), a federal Preparing Tomorrow's Teachers to Use Technologies project, will be in its second year of developing an online support community for "pre-intern teachers," a designation in California for new teachers who are not credentialed and have not passed subject matter competency. The intent of the pre-intern program is to provide a way for those wishing to enter the teaching profession to attain subject matter competency and a credential while they are working in the classroom. The program originated because of a severe teacher shortage in California; 30,000 new teachers are needed each year for the coming ten years. TLI has partnered with 15 county offices to have access to pre-interns and corporate partners who are developing emerging technologies that are being piloted with select mentor and pre-intern teachers. This paper will describe how new technologies are being applied to the needs of pre-interns.

Introduction

The Teaching-Learning Interchange (TLI) is piloting a study to determine the effectiveness of several emerging technologies in an online community to support the neediest of new teachers, California's "pre-intern" teachers, a designation in California for new teachers who are not credentialed and have not passed subject matter competency. The study asks the following questions:

- What are the essential requirements for a successful online support community for new teachers?
- Can new teacher mentoring be effectively augmented through the use of electronic communication tools?
- What are the detractors to the technology enhanced mentoring experience?
- What were the unexpected outcomes from the technology augmented experience?

- What are the perceived benefits of the various communications tools to the program and to the mentoring process?

Description of Technologies for Pre-intern Needs

The TLI includes several corporate partners who are developing emerging technologies that have potential to address the needs of new teachers Lesson Lab provides online video of classroom practice that is particularly useful in helping pre-interns understand and plan for the complexities of classroom management and lesson delivery. LessonLab has a unique software package that allows instructors and pre-interns to time index a video of classroom practice while online. For example, an instructor can create an assignment to demonstrate a particular teaching practice, like responding to the efforts of learners. The assignment can provide a link to where an example, say at 12 minutes 32 seconds of a 60 minute video. The assignment can then require pre-interns to view all or some of the entire video and mark where they see examples of effective or ineffective practice and write narrative descriptions of their perceptions. When the assignment is completed by all the pre-interns, a chart showing all the examples marked by pre-interns can be displayed, forming the basis of a dialog on examples marked by many and those marked by only one or two. Both instructors and pre-interns can create annotated notebooks with time codes, allowing easy access to examples of classroom practice by all concerned. Threaded discussions can also incorporate this time code feature, adding richness to dialog. The advantage of this approach is that teaching is shown within a realistic context including both effective and ineffective teaching practice. Pre-interns can explore practice via synchronous and asynchronous online discussions to obtain deep levels of understanding of the complexities of teaching. Both instructors and pre-interns are expected to report that this technology is very helpful in improving their classroom management, lesson planning and delivery. Barriers might include difficulties learning the interface.

Apple Computer recently redesigned its Apple Learning Interchange (ALI) to include video cases along with Units of Practice for particular lessons and links to related resources. A search engine is included on this portal that links Units of Practice to state and/or subject standards. Pre-interns will be given structured access to the ALI. They are expected to report that the ALI is useful in obtaining and adapting lesson plans, viewing examples of successful practice and accessing resources and standards. Barriers may be information overload.

ClearPhone provides software for conducting video conferences among small groups anytime/anywhere via Internet access. TLI identified a number of subject matter science specialists (the area of greatest need) from the Exploratorium. They are being connected with pre-interns who need to attain subject matter competence. Each participant will be given a net cam, whiteboard and software. Online meetings will be conducted in which several pre-interns can meet with a specialist and discuss topics covered on the Praxis science test. The whiteboard allows participants to share lesson plans and student work samples. Expectations are that both the specialists and pre-interns will give ClearPhone high marks in the ability to meet from distant locations. Those in rural areas with long distances are expected to have similar benefits to those in congested urban areas, notably the efficiency of meeting without the disadvantages of travel to a common location. The pre-interns in the project are expected to score higher on subject matter exams than pre-interns in general.

InRessonance is a contracted service that is experienced in supporting web-based communities. It will provide technology-integrated model lesson plan training and online conferencing services.

Conclusion

The experiments of the TLI in providing such state-of-the-art technology to new teachers is expected to produce a wealth of useful applications that have great potential in future teacher preparation programs, as well as identifying a number of potential problems that go along with such innovations.

The Development of a Course to Prepare E-Moderators to Run an International On-Line Teacher Training Course.

Phil Riding[1] and Chris Daw[2]

[1]*Interactive Technologies in Assessment and Learning Unit*
[2]*Curriculum and Teacher Support Group, Cambridge International Examinations*
University of Cambridge Local Examinations Syndicate
1 Hills Road, Cambridge, CB1 2EU, UK

p.riding@ucles-red.cam.ac.uk

Abstract

In this paper we describe the development of a course designed to prepare on-line teacher trainers (e-moderators) to deliver an on-line teacher training course. The e-moderators were to deliver the courses to teachers world-wide using a simple 'home-grown' virtual learning environment consisting of ordinary e-mail and e-mail-based discussion lists, coupled with a dedicated web-based environment for document sharing. We describe the training issues we identified, the training provided, and how the lessons learnt have informed subsequent phases and design of the moderator-training.

1. Introduction

The University of Cambridge Local Examinations Syndicate (UCLES) is a major provider of examinations both within the UK and internationally. UCLES is committed to providing high quality support and training to teachers of its syllabuses and has an extensive programme of in-service training. UCLES' International Division (Cambridge International Examinations) provides assessments for schools in more than 150 countries. Providing training at reasonable cost and useful intervals for a community so disparate and geographically widespread is a continuous challenge.

The Interactive Technologies in Assessment and Learning (ITAL) unit is a research group tasked with investigating the use of internet-based technologies in UCLES' business. One area of investigation has been the use of Internet–based technologies as a way of bringing together geographically isolated teachers.

Strands of recent thought about effective learning and professional development stress the primacy of peer interaction, continuing reflection, the importance of experience and the grounding of theory in practice [1, 7].

The building of teacher networks or communities is increasingly seen as a way of fostering the conditions in which this type of development can take place, allowing teachers to share experience, information and good practice [2]. We have already shown how email-based discussion list technology can be used to build lively, syllabus-focussed, on-line teacher communities and how these communities can contribute to effective teacher development [4]. We therefore decided to use such lists as the technological basis of the course. We supplemented these lists with web-based repositories of documents and Frequently Asked Questions to create a low-cost and easy to use 'virtual learning environment' [3].

The facilitation of such communities demands new roles and skills of those charged with the task. Successful face-to-face teachers do not necessarily make successful on-line moderators. We agree with Salmon [5] that:

> *Any significant initiative aimed at changing teaching methods or the introduction of technology into teaching and learning should include effective e-moderator support and training, otherwise its outcomes are likely to be meagre and unsuccessful.*

Our task was to devise a course that would convert good face-to-face teachers into good on-line moderators.

The experiential view of learning also informed the way we, as staff and potential moderators, designed and modified the course itself. We were relatively new to on-line learning and understood that however much we read in the literature and talked to practitioners, there could be no substitute for our own experience. We needed to make sure that we provided ourselves with opportunities and time to reflect on the courses and the research and to allow that reflection and learning to feed into subsequent stages of course design.

2. The Course

The potential e-moderators were all experienced face-to-face teachers, but they had varying degrees of knowledge and experience of internet-based technologies and of on-line teaching and learning. All had reasonable keyboard skills and were comfortable with e-mail and web technologies.

The initial structure of the course to be run by the e-tutors consisted of three separate modules, each of two weeks, making a six-week course. Each module would consist of stimulus materials, reading materials and a research activity. Finally, e-tutors would set a formative assessment assignment. The assignments would all involve some aspect of teaching practice. This structure was open to revision and development based on our own and the moderators' experiences.

Initially the course was entirely email based, with assignments distributed and returned as attachments. The moderators were to use person-to-person e-mail messages to communicate with individual participants and to give personal instructions, encouragement and feedback on assignments. Running in parallel to this was a many-to-many e-mail discussion group that would enable the moderator and participants to discuss matters of common interest and concern, as a group. Later, as will be seen, we developed a web-based system for document sharing.

2.1. Course aims

We took Salmon's five-stage model of e-moderating as the basis of the course design [6]. This model provided a useful 'scaffold' on which to base the first iteration of the moderator training course. It describes five levels of competence ranging from simple access to the technology, to autonomous learning and critical thinking.

Our aims roughly mirror these five stages. We wanted to give the prospective moderators:
- An understanding of the technology to be used (stage 1: Access and motivation)

- an understanding of the concepts surrounding the use of email discussion lists and how the different methods of communication would facilitate conversations person-to-person and person-to-group (stage 2: Socialisation)
- The conceptual information necessary to set suitable on-line tasks, to enable them to write effective content materials and to produce useful formative assessment. (stage 3: Information exchange)
- an understanding of the issues arising from and the techniques required for the effective moderation of on-line discussion and the creation and fostering of on-line communities (stage 4: Knowledge construction)
- Opportunities to reflect on their on-line experiences and to begin to think about how they would approach their own teaching on-line. (stage 5: Development)

3. Iteration 1

This first e-tutor course was initiated by a face-to-face meeting with the four e-tutors. During this day-long meeting we demonstrated the mechanics of using the discussion list technology, including the moderation process. We also discussed issues relating to the management of on-line groups, and also made decisions about the range and content of assignments.

Following the face-to-face meeting the e-moderators remained in contact with each other and with the trainers through the medium of an email discussion list. This, we hoped, would allow them to continue discussion of issues raised during the day, and provide ongoing support during the running of their courses. By using the same technology as they would use to deliver their training, it also provided 'hands on' experience.

3.1. Feedback and reflections on iteration 1

There were x e-moderators in the first cohort and following the training they guided most of their participants to a successful outcome in all but a handful of cases. All of them reported that they would be happy to be involved in future on-line training courses. All of them felt that they had been 'well' or 'very well' supported during the training and the delivery of the courses, and

1113

they all reported that they felt 'more confident' with the use of the technology after the training and after running their courses.

The amount of time they reported having spent in learning to use the technology varied from 20 hours in the case of the least experienced tutor to only 2.5 hours in the case of the most. This suggested that there was probably a need for more exposure to the technology during the initial training.

We were disappointed with the lack of on-line discussion that occurred between the moderators during their training and it was obvious to us that we needed to be much more active in encouraging discussion and reflection.

It was clear that some moderators were much better at facilitating discussion and a sense of community among the participants. It was also clear that the amount of reflection that the moderators elicited from participants varied widely – on some courses the discussion was dominated by 'procedural' messages while on others the discussion was more involved. This led us to conclude that we needed to work with the prospective moderators in alerting them to the techniques and skills needed to encourage such interaction.

When asked what would be the ideal preparation for e-tutors, given their own experience, they were unanimous in saying 'doing it!' This was as strong an endorsement of the experiential methodology as we could have hoped for!

There were therefore a number of issues that we would need to address before embarking on the second course.

- More 'hands on' experience of the technology and the on-line environment before starting their courses.
- They need more training in the moderation of discussion lists. If we are to engage teachers in on-line reflective discussion, the tutors need to be better at promoting and maintaining such discussion
- Tutors also needed help with dealing with the process of on-line 'classroom management' (e.g. dealing with 'difficult' or disruptive students)
- We need to use e-moderating skills ourselves to more effectively creating a community of e-tutors who will support each other during the training and afterwards

In order to address these issues we made a number of changes to the course structure.

4. Iteration 2

The main difference between the first and second course was that the second was conducted entirely on-line, with no face-to-face meeting. Apart from our feeling that the more experience the moderators got on-line the better, one of the trainees was based in Switzerland and therefore unable to attend a face-to-face session.

For the first phase of the training, we had the new tutors 'observe' (take part but not actively participate) on the on-line courses run by the tutors from the first courses. For half of this time we asked them to observe the process from the viewpoint of a participant, for the second half as a tutor. For both halves we asked them to identify two 'critical incidents' which illuminate the differences between face-to-face and on-line training.

The second phase was based around a two-week on-line discussion forum. During this phase the main focus was the critical incidents identified during the first phase. We aimed to use these as jumping off points for discussion. We wanted the moderators to relate them to their previous experiences as face-to-face teachers. We would pull out general principles and relate them to the literature and other people's experiences. We would provide various inputs – documents, website and book references, but we saw these as background reference and summary information and not essential to the course itself. We did not expect the moderators to read them all. We expected them to spend a minimum of nine hours reading and responding to discussions over the two-week period.

We invited the more experienced e-moderators who had already run on-line training courses would join the discussions.

We had no fixed content for the discussion in phase two; we wanted to respond to the concerns and interests of the trainees as much as possible. Having said that, we aimed to cover some if not all, of the following topics:

On-line teaching and learning
- The technology
- The vocabulary
- Advantages
- Disadvantages

Roles of the on-line tutor
- Social – creating an on-line community

- Pedagogical – promoting effective learning, types of interaction, feedback
- Managerial – dealing with and managing on-line discussions, motivation, facilitation
- Technical – dealing with email discussion lists

During the third phase, the on-line discussion facility would continue to be available after the course and into the moderators' time as on-line tutors, to provide continuing support from peers and from us, and as a forum for continued reflection.

Being members of these two lists gave the tutors more experience of the on-line environment and the issues facing both them as tutors and those facing the on-line students.

In this way we hoped to provide prospective tutors with examples of good practice (either on the observed courses or on the training course) and we will be able to concentrate on issues such as the creation and maintenance of an on-line community where discussion flows.

4.1. Feedback and Reflections on iteration 2

Again, feedback from the 5 e-moderators who took the course was very favourable, all of them reporting that they felt 'well' or 'very well' prepared for the on-line experience, and all expressed an interest in undertaking more work along these lines.

The amount of time they reported having spent in learning to use the technology was generally less than that reported in the first cohort, ranging from 1 to a maximum of 8 hours, suggesting that the increased exposure to the technology had been useful. However, this cohort was perhaps slightly more familiar with technology than the first one.

The observation exercise in phase 1 was seen as particularly useful. Certainly their experiences during this phase provided useful foci of discussion even before the start of the 'formal' part of the training. The 'task' (identifying critical incidents for future discussion) were found useful in that they 'made you look even deeper and not want to miss anything' but 'didn't distract from the job in hand of watching what was going on'.

Although we did not expect many messages or discussion during this six week period there were 61 messages to the list, with discussion covering a wide range of topics, from basic issues like the mechanics of dealing with a lot of emails and technical issues, to more 'advanced' topics like the advantages and disadvantages of asynchronous communication and the effect of the lack of visual cues in on-line discussion. Despite this, many of the e-moderators would have welcomed even more discussion, and for the third iteration we intend to lift the (informal) embargo on discussion during the observation phase. An important part of this phase was the participation of the more experienced e-moderators (who actually ran the observed courses).

The activity during Phase 1 compared very favourably with the discussion that took place during Phase 2, the 'formal' two-week period. Here we saw 31 messages to the list. These fell into two categories – those, which were elicited by our (planned) activities, and those that arose 'naturally' and informally from contributions by the moderators. As mentioned above, we intended to cover a range of issues, using moderators' 'critical incidents' as stimuli, and although we tried to do this, we found that time constraints, and the interests of the moderators tended to preclude this. Discussion that followed 'our' agenda included:

- How to prepare students for the technology
- Advantages/disadvantages of on-line learning
- Pedagogical issues)how best to encourage reflection and discussion)

While discussion that followed the e-moderators' agenda included:

- Classroom management issues (how best to organise workgroups, etc.)
- Advantages and disadvantages of having a synchronous option
- The nature of discussion – the balance between 'nitty gritty' administration messages and 'real' professional discussion, the value of 'socialising' messages,

Discussion during the third phase (during the actual running of the teacher training courses) saw a brief initial burst of activity as the moderators got to grips with the reality of being in charge of a course and the technology. Issues raised were chiefly technical (how to work the moderation, how to deal with assignment download problems). After this discussion died down as the moderators got on with the task of running their courses. One or two issues did arise (e.g. the ethics of sharing email addresses among participants) but these did not elicit much discussion.

So, how did this group get on with their courses? Post course feedback from the e-moderators did express some dissatisfaction with the level and intensity of discussion on their courses, although we felt that the quality of discussion had been better than during the first course. This lack of engagement was often put down to either the nature of the exercises they gave the students (which involved them working in small groups 'away' from the main discussion list) or to the fact that the teachers were unused to or unwilling to engage in this form of teacher training for cultural or other reasons.

This does at least show some awareness among the moderators of the difficulties that on-line students have in participating in such courses. Iteration 3 of the training will include time to reconsider the types of activities to be used on the teacher training courses. In addition we will address the cultural issues raised and discuss ways of addressing this.

5. Conclusions

Although we set out with an experiential learning agenda, we initially fell into the trap of trying to create a traditional course with a face-to-face meeting and with a well-defined beginning and end. However, we found that no matter how much we tried to describe or provide a semblance of the experience of being an on-line tutor, there was simply no substitute for actually experiencing it from a student and from a tutor's perspective. Although our e-moderators were experienced face-to-face tutors, with well developed teaching skills, they needed to see and feel for themselves what on-line training means in reality, and relate that experience to their own.

An important lesson we learnt was that it was important to be flexible and responsive to the group's own agenda and to allow time for this to be addressed. Our (rather ambitious) plans to cover a long list of 'issues' was subverted by the group, who, understandably, had their own borne out of their experience.

For that reason we are moving away from a 'one-off' event with a well-defined beginning and end and toward a more diffuse model that starts to build what Wenger [8] calls a 'Community of Practice'. This type of community is characterised by the common purpose of its members, by its own self-defined agenda, by its ongoing nature, and by its membership, which includes experienced as well as novice practitioners. New e-moderators join this larger community during their 'formal' training and receive the ongoing benefit of having access to more experienced moderators.

It looks like a community of e-moderators has started to grow which will develop over the future iterations of the course, raising and addressing its own issues, sharing expertise and providing its own training programme in parallel to ours. Future research will investigate to what extent this is true.

6. References

[1]   Kolb D. (1984) *Experiential Learning. Experience as the Source of Learning and Development.* Englewood Cliffs, Prentice-Hall, New Jersey USA.

[2]   Lieberman, A. (2000) Networks as Learning Communities: Shaping the Future of Teacher Development. *Journal of Teacher Education* 51(3), 221-227

[3]   Riding, P. and Allington, D. *The Development of a Low Cost, Easy-to-Maintain Platform for the Building and Support of On-line Teacher Communities.* In preparation

[4]   Riding, P. (2001) On-Line Teacher Communities and Continuing Professional Development. *Teacher Development* 5 (3)

[5]   Salmon, G. (2000) *E-Moderating: The Key to Teaching and Learning On-line.* Kogan Page, London, UK. p.55

[6]   Ibid. p.26

[7]   Schön, D (1990) *Educating the Reflective Practitioner*: Jossey-Bass Wiley, San Francisco, USA.

[8]   Wenger, E. (1998) *Communities of Practice: Learning, Meaning and Identity.* Cambridge University Press: Cambridge.

7. Acknowledgements

We would like to thank colleagues in Cambridge International Examinations (CIE), in particular Melanie Baker of the Curriculum and Teacher Support Group, without whose help this work would not have been possible.

An earlier version of this paper was presented at the European Distance Education Network (EDEN) Conference in Granada, Spain, in June 2002.

All Work and No Play?
The Design and Development of a Virtual Social Space (VSS) to Support Distance Learning Students

Miguel Baptista Nunes
Department of Information Studies
University of Sheffield
Regent Court, Sheffield, S1 4DP
j.m.nunes@sheffield.ac.uk
tel: +44 114 22 22645

Maggie McPherson
Department of Information Studies
University of Sheffield
Regent Court, Sheffield, S1 4DP
m.a.mcpherson@sheffield.ac.uk
tel: +44 114 22 22696

Chris Firth
Learning Media Unit
University of Sheffield
5 Favell Road, Sheffield, S3 7QX c.d.firth@shef.ac.uk
tel: +44 114 22 20411

David Gilchrist
Logica (UK) Ltd
United Kingdom House (5th Floor)
180 Oxford Street, London, W1D 1NN.
gilchristd@logica.com
tel: +44 20744664859

Abstract

The disappearance of physical social spaces from today's society is seen by some scholars to be a modern phenomenon, resulting in increasing isolation and lack of socialisation. In fact, this is always the case in distance education, due to geographical dispersion and disparate time schedules of learners. Very often, peer-to-peer socialisation in distance education only occurs as part of formal learning activities, or is just left to the student's own initiative. This situation is then compounded by the modularity of VLEs, forcing students to jump from one module space to another as they progress through a course. All discussion threads, conversations or record of previous dialogues are then lost. This paper describes the design and development of a Virtual Social Space (VSS) to resolve this predicament and support the creation of a learning community for a Continuing Professional Distance Education (CPDE) Masters in IT Management programme.

Introduction

Distance Education (DE) is an exciting and rapidly growing phenomenon that schools, universities, education boards, and governments are actively exploring. The major trigger for this renewed interest in a well tested, but never really widespread mode of delivery, has been the recent inclusion of eLearning concepts and technologies. In its purest form, it is an educational arrangement where tutors and learners interact and engage in learning activities apart from one another, away from the regular place of learning, for part or all of the regular learning period.

Therefore, and as pointed out by Galusha (1997), while distance education has been in existence for at least 100 years, the delivery medium has changed from pencil and paper correspondence courses to real-time Internet courses. But, regardless of the medium, distance courses have common and inherent characteristics that will result in similar benefits and problems.

Traditionally, problems and barriers encountered by students fall into several distinct categories (Galusha, 1997): costs and motivators, feedback and teacher contact, student support and services, alienation and isolation, lack of experience, and training. From these, student support may be the most critical factor for the success of DE. Isolation, which results from the physical separation, different time schedules and diverse learning paces, is inherent in the distance learning model. Thus, support for distance learners should not be overlooked when designing and planning distance programs, i.e. academic, pastoral, subject matter and technical assistance. The inclusion of eLearning approaches and technologies is perceived to be able to resolve most of these support and communication problems.

In fact, as part of most Virtual Learning Environments (VLEs), online communication has been seen to open up several new possibilities for enabling interactions among peers, tutors and academic staff. Communication in these VLEs are enabled by a range of simply implemented but powerful online capabilities such as email, bulletin boards, chat rooms and discussion groups. Lake (1999) proposes several modes of communication: one-way (tutor $\prod$ students) communication through course notes and explicit knowledge web pages; two-way discussions (tutor $\sqrt{}$ students) through tutorial learning activities and unstructured communication (tutor $\sqrt{}$ student $\sqrt{}$ student) either in informal asynchronous communication areas (the 'Cafeteria') or in private chat rooms.

DE programme syllabi are usually arranged around a series of modules that have to be completed by students in order to attain the necessary number of credits.

1117

When translated into a VLE design, DE courses often have a modular architecture. Each module has its own individual web based learning course environment and assigned tutors. Students jump from one course module to the next until they acquire the necessary credits. These module spaces are usually separate subject areas, with no direct connection between them. Consequently, students lose a holistic view of the programme and the building of a course/learning community is made extremely difficult. This modular approach provides an ideal support for the first two types of communication described above, but a "module Cafeteria" is adequate to support informal and social communication only while undertaking a particular module.

In fact, since students are regularly transferred from one module environment to the next, the socialising and study mechanisms (e.g. non-module specific topics, discussion threads, well known environments, link facilities) are constantly disrupted. Furthermore, students lack an overall anchoring space that binds the different modules, cohorts and tutors together.

This situation was identified as a crucial area for research by the academic team in charge of a part-time DE MA in Information Technology Management (MA ITM) at the Department of Information Studies, University of Sheffield, UK. Through action research, the team identified the need to provide a persistent overall course area for administrative support, general course and university information, as well as online peer-to-peer communication and socialising in a familiar setting. This resulted in the Virtual Social Space (VSS) presented in this paper.

What is social space?

The research team's initial ideas as to what constituted a "social space" centred on a number of assumptions. It is, on most occasions, an area limited by its physical boundaries. It is a place where individuals can meet face-to-face (f2f) with one another and interact in an informal manner. Usually, these areas are clearly demarcated from areas of work, however, participants do bring in elements of work if they want to. If the social space is a physical area, it might be decorated in a way that reflects the unique identity of the group of individuals who use it. This perception of a social space is not easily transposed into a web-based virtual space.

Lefebvre (1991) quoted by Wise (1999) presents three ways of thinking about space: spatial practice, representations of space, and representational space.

- Spatial practice "embraces production and reproduction, and the particular locations and spatial sets characteristic of each social formation, in this case a DE learning community. Spatial practice ensures continuity and some degree of cohesion, and in this case a sense of belonging to a DE course and cohesion as members of the cohort of that course;
- Representations of space are abstract and conceptualised constructs, that in this case is a virtual environment supported by web technology;
- Representational space (or, better and more literally, spaces of representation) is "space as directly lived through its associated images and symbols, and hence the space of inhabitants and 'users'".

Therefore, and as noted by Wise (1999), a social space is perceived, conceived, and lived by a community. In the case of this research, the need for this space was *perceived* by both staff and students, designed and *conceived* by the research team according to the *perceived* needs of students, and is now currently being *lived* by the present cohort of ITM students and tutors.

Design and Development of the VSS

The early design and structure of the VSS resulted from an MSc research project undertaken by Gilchrist (2000). The initial set of requirements was identified through a questionnaire sent to students. The questionnaire was split into four sections: "Getting to know you", "Social Scenes", "Comfort and Advice", and "Logging On". The first section acted as a gentle introduction to the questionnaire and consisted of background and demographic questions. The second section asked the respondents to think about the ways in which they had socially interacted with each other and to consider their attitudes towards their learning environment and their fellow students. The third section focussed on their use of the existing student support system within the Department. The final section asked them about their use of the University computer system and introduced them to the modus operandi of the research project.

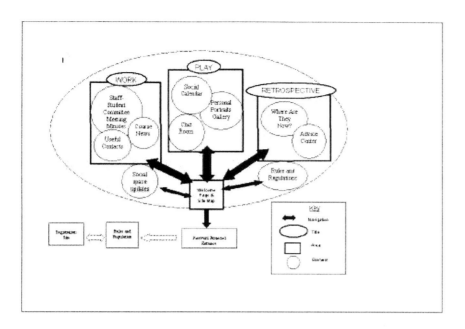

Fig. 1 - VSS architecture.

Through this questionnaire Gilchrist (2000) identified the need for a number of elements of perceived by the students to be important components of a VSS, namely: a *Personal Portraits Gallery*, a *Chat Room*, a *Social Calendar*, a *Course News* section, a *Useful Contacts* section and an *Alumni* section. These elements were then grouped into three major VSS areas: *Work* related area, leisure *(Play)* area and a *Retrospective* look into course advice and alumni area.

The VSS for the MA in ITM course was then developed using a prototyping approach. Prototyping can be defined as, *"building a physical working model of the proposed system, and using it to identify weaknesses in our understanding of the real requirements"* (Crinnion 1991: 17). The initial VSS prototype was a working model and a first attempt to incorporate the elements outlined above into a web site. The prototype was built using WebCT (the VLE adopted by the University of Sheffield) and aimed at providing a representational space in which the students could socialise. The feedback obtained from testing this prototype was then used to develop it further. The architecture of this prototype is illustrated in Fig. 1.

This initial work was then further developed with the help of the Learning Media Unit and evolved to the final VSS implementation as illustrated in Fig 2. The home page provides entry points into three main areas: the *Work Zone*, the *Social Circle* and the *History Channel*.

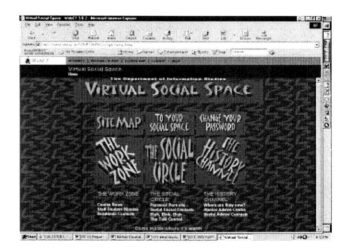

Fig. 2 – The VSS Home Page

The Work Zone

This area comprises the following main areas: *Useful Academic Contacts*, *Course News*, *Course Information* and the *Staff-Student Committee Meeting Minutes*.

The intention for this area is to allow students to obtain practical and administrative information relating to their studies. This area should also provide students useful contact details related to academic, social and other matters of interest to their academic lives.

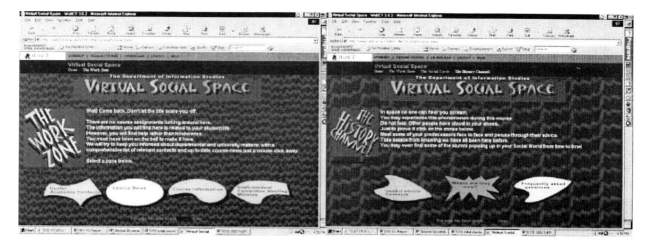

Fig. 3 – The Work Zone   Fig. 4 – The History Channel

The Social Circle Zone

The Social Circle includes the *Chat Room, Social Calendar, Useful Social Contacts* and the *Personal Portrait Gallery.*

The Personal Portraits Gallery is supported by a student home page tool provided by WebCT. Students can personalise their own space within this area. This facility allows students to establish their own identities within the social area as well as enabling them to actively contribute and be involved with the VSS.

The perceived need for a Chat Room was actually implemented by using the asynchronous WebCT Bulletin Board. The choice for an asynchronous solution was based on practical evidence that DE students tend to prefer this type of communication method. It is an area for the informal exchange of personal, social and course related information. Similarly, the Social Calendar was also implemented using a WebCT tool that facilitates the exchange of social event information amongst all of the students involved. Its functionality means that students can post their own social events up in the calendar. It is another area that will allow the students to contribute and interact with the site.

The History Channel

The *Advice Centre* included in this area takes the form of a "Frequently Asked Questions" (FAQ) area in which students can ask questions and leave advice for future years. This serves two purposes. Firstly, it is a facility that enables the reification of experiences across cohorts of students and secondly it will encourage new visitors to get involved with to the site as it is already inhabited (Chen, 1999).

Finally the *Where are they Now?* area is basically set of Alumni's pages. Alumni are graduates of previous courses who provide information about their current positions and often report of the impact of the MA n ITM in their careers.

Conclusions and Future Work

Designing the VSS for the MA in ITM was an excellent challenge to both tutors and students involved. The process encouraged the team to think broadly and research laterally about DE student experience, as well as to question and mature a number of theoretical assumptions about student interaction and the process of learning.

Early evaluation has shown that despite a very high initial interest by the students, the VSS is currently underused. Students do visit the site at regular intervals, but only a small group of first year students have really used it as a social space. Further investigation has shown that other students, that did not have the VSS available from the start of their courses, had already created parallel communication channels (e.g. email list and Yahoo Clubs), which they kept as their favourite socialisation vehicle. In fact, although they expressed appreciation of having such a site, they have continued using their familiar CMC environments. Thus, results of these early evaluation results are not absolutely conclusive. The research team will carry out a full investigation by the end of the first year of usage and will also follow closely the small community already being formed.

Bibliography

Chen, C. (1999) *Information Visualisation and Virtual Environments.* London: Springer-Verlag.

Crinnion, J. (1991). *Evolutionary Systems Development: a practical guide to the use of prototyping within a structured systems methodology.* London: Pitman Publishing.

Galusha Jill M (1997) *Barriers to Learning in Distance Education,* University of Southern Mississippi http://www.infrastruction.com/barriers.htm.

Gilchrist, D (2000) "All Work and No Play? The Design and Development of a Social Student Support System for the MSc Information Systems Students", MSc in Information Systems Dissertation, Sheffield, University of Sheffield

Lake, D. (1999). Reducing isolation for distance students: An online initiative. In K. Martin, N. Stanley and N. Davison (Eds), Teaching in the Disciplines/ Learning in Context, 210-214. In Proceedings of the 8th Annual Teaching Learning Forum, The University of Western Australia, February 1999. Perth: UWA. http://cea.curtin.edu.au/tlf/tlf1999/lake.html

Lefebvre, Henri (1991). *The production of space.* Trans. D. Nicholson-Smith. Cambridge, MA: Blackwell.

Wise, J.M. (1999) "*Culture and* Technology" *CULTSTUD-L Columns,* http://www.cas.usf.edu/ communication/rodman/cultstud/columns/jw-24-10-99.html

Building an International On-line Teacher Community to Support Continuing Professional Development

Matthew Parrott[1] and Phil Riding[2]
[1]Cambridge International Examinations
[2]Interactive Technologies in Assessment and Learning Unit
University of Cambridge Local Examinations Syndicate, Hills Road, Cambridge UK
E-mail: parrott.m@ucles.org.uk

Abstract

The following paper describes the initial experience of a major international examination board in setting up and running an email discussion group for teachers of a syllabus taught in more than 80 countries. In it we describe how the group was established, how its members used it, and contrast this with our experience of similar teacher groups in the UK.

1. Introduction

Cambridge International Examinations (CIE) is part of the University of Cambridge Local Examinations Syndicate (UCLES), a major provider of examinations both within the UK and internationally. CIE has an extensive programme of in-service training. Since CIE provides assessments for schools in more than 150 countries, providing support and training at reasonable cost and useful intervals is a continuous challenge.

UCLES, through the Interactive Technologies in Assessment and Learning (ITAL) unit, has been investigating the use of asynchronous e-mail based discussion groups to address this issue. Such groups offer a way of bringing geographically widespread teachers together to engage in the sort of reflective, collegiate and experiential interaction that is increasingly seen as the basis of effective professional development [2]. ITAL has used e-mail based discussion groups to support the creation of on-line communities of teachers in the UK, and shown how these communities can contribute to effective informal teacher development [3]. We were therefore interested in bringing this experience to bear in an international context.

2. Creating the Group

A pilot project was set up to create and grow an email discussion group for one of a range of new modular qualifications offered by CIE. We felt that this would be a good starting point for the sort of community that we wished to develop, since it is new to teachers, in terms of its subject content, structure and assessment methods.

The group was restricted to teachers at centres offering the syllabus, and was 'lightly' moderated. We advertised the groups in a number of ways; sending a letter to all registered Centres; posting information and joining details on CIE's public website; e-mailing Centres (who often correspond with us by e-mail) encouraging them to join; and including the group details in the signature of all relevant e-mail messages.

3. Evolution of the Group

The group grew in membership quite quickly. In the first 12 months, it had grown to almost 80 members. The membership consisted of a wide range of nationalities, living and teaching in a wide spread of countries, including Argentina, Peru, India, Pakistan, Hong Kong, China, Singapore, Taiwan, Thailand, Malaysia, Brunei, Cyprus, Greece, South Africa, Zambia.

4. Message Analysis
4.1. Method

To get an overview as to how the teachers used the discussion groups, we analysed the messages sent to the ICT Career Awards group over a twelve month period (April 2001 to March 2002), a total of 181 messages. We followed a similar methodology that we had used in analysing the UK teacher groups [3]; i.e. individual messages were retrieved from the archives and coded according to their content and to their function.

5. Results
5.1. Message Content

Figure 1 summarises the results of the content analysis. The majority of messages (55%) were exam related, but a substantial proportion (35%) were concerned with more general teaching issues. Smaller percentages were introductions (7%) and messages relating to the administration of the group itself (2%).

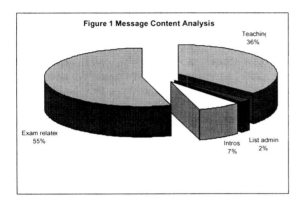

Figure 1 Message Content Analysis

5.2. Message Function

Figure 2 shows the breakdown of the messages by function. It is clear that the majority of messages are queries (31%) and responses to those queries (49% of the messages). Smaller percentages of the messages were unsolicited items of information (9%), messages designed to initiate discussion (4%) and messages whose function seemed to be to foster a sense of community among the group members.

6. Analysis

The proportion of examination related messages (messages directly related to what was expected of students in the examination rather than how to teach it) contrasts with our experience in the UK, where this proportion was somewhat lower (at between 14 and 23%). This reflects the fact that this group was supporting a new qualification, and that many of the messages were queries directed at CIE asking for clarification and information about the examination. We expect the proportion of examination-related messages to decrease once the teachers become more comfortable with its demands. Despite this, it is interesting to see that some 36% of messages related to the teaching in a more general sense.

7. Facilitating the Group

Facilitator training is an area we are interested in developing, and we have already started a program to address this [1]. We hope to take a similar experiential and reflective approach to this as we have done with the teacher support itself, and create an internal 'meta-group' for facilitators to discuss and share best practice based on their experiences.

8. Issues/Conclusions

The fact that this was a newly established syllabus had a significant impact. Messages tended to concentrate on examination-related issues rather than more general pedagogical ones. Experience of our UK-based groups has shown that those with established syllabuses tend to grow more quickly with discussion focusing more quickly on pedagogical issues.

There was some evidence that cultural differences between members, and also, to some extent, their confidence and ability to write in English did impact on the contributions received to the group. Some teachers were clearly used to using English in their email communications, whereas many wanted to join the groups and observe the discussion without contributing.

There are a number of questions that this work has raised, but not yet answered. What are the facilitation issues that multi-cultural groups raise? Can we expect the same level of participation in such a group as we get in a more culturally homogeneous group? What will the effect of differing philosophies of education in different countries be? Only if the group moves beyond its present focus on the examination will we start to gather evidence to answer these questions.

9. References

[1] Daw, C. and Riding, P. (2002) Preparing and Supporting E-tutors in the Running of an International On-line Teacher Training Course: An Experiential Approach. *Proceedings of the 2002 European Distance Education Network Annual Conference: Open and Distance Learning in Europe and Beyond.* Wagner, E. and Szücs, A. (eds.)
[2] Marx, R.W., Blumenfrld, P.C., Krajcik, J.S. and Soloway, E. (1998) New Technologies for Teacher Professional Development. *Teaching and Teacher Education*, 14 (1) pp. 33 – 52
[3] Riding, P. (2001) On-Line Teacher Communities and Continuing Professional Development. *Teacher Development* 5 (3) pp. 283 - 295

A Computational Scheme for Monitoring Online Learning Progress

Isaac Pak-Wah Fung
Institute of Information Sciences & Technology
Massey University
Palmerston North, New Zealand
P.W.Fung@massey.ac.nz

Abstract

This paper describes a scheme of adaptive advising students on how much time they should spend on traversing the course network. The scheme is based on the notion of critical path embodied in the network. While web-based online learning emphases student's initiative in managing his own learning, experiences tell us that some students are always at the risk of being lost in the cyber campus. If they are not monitored closely, their successful completion of the course on time would be in jeopardy. The novelty of the scheme is on its time-based feature. Developers specify the expected time to be spent on each unit and thereby the study patterns of individual students can be closely monitoring. In events of 'abnormality' such as a topic is still not yet browsed after a specified time, the system would alert the student and instructor accordingly.

'What', 'How' and 'When' - A trilogy of Online Learning

Among education providers, the foremost matter of concern is on the content of the subject domain, i.e. '*what*' is included in the course. Since online learning became an acceptable alternative to the traditional classroom based learning, tremendous resources from all sectors have been poured into the development of flexible platforms for hosting learning materials. One notably characteristic of online learning is its emphasis on learning, i.e. students are expected to learn, not to be taught, the subject domain themselves by studying the materials posted on the web. Described and extensively cited in [1], it is now widely agreed that the notion of topic nodes and the directed graphs formalism are versatile representational tools of modelling course structures. By representing the learning primitives as nodes and their interrelationship, such as prerequisite, as directed graphs, courses can be adaptively presented to the students according to their learning styles. In other words, the issue of '*how*' has been extensively investigated and addressed. In [2] and in this paper, the author aims to push the envelope further to another dimension of online learning – '*when*'. In most cases, online learners are expected to complete a course within a pre-specified time frame, say one semester. Under such circumstances, could the course provider give some sort of guidance to the students to ensure the course is completed on time? What is the implication of some topics which were repeatedly and protractedly browsed? If there is still no record of logging in to the system from some students after half of the semester has elapsed, say, should the system (or instructor) take some actions? Suppose a student wants to take a break at the middle of semester, say to have a holiday or visit his sick relative, would the break affect the progress of his study? Could the system advise the students accordingly? These are typical scenarios pertinent to the temporal features of the course network. In [1] and [2], a hybrid representational formalism, namely Timed Course Chart, has been proposed to capture both the ontological and temporal characteristics of a course. The scheme described in this paper basically examines the course structure and determine the *critical path* of the network. The nodes on the critical path have no room for any delayed study. Students have to adhere to their timing requirements because any delay would result in the delay of the entire course. For the non-critical nodes, however, leeway exists and a little holdup would not affect the progress of the whole course.

An Algorithm for Finding the Critical Path

The algorithm [3] consists of two phases and works on course networks that contains no cycles. This is a sensible assumption as we would not expect a course is designed on cyclical repetition of different topics.

Phase 1: Forward Scanning. Scanned forwardly, the nodes is consecutively labelled with two weights p and e.

- Assign $p_0 = 0$ and $e_0 = 0$ to the START node.
- Compute, for each arc$_{ij}$ incident to node j, the sum $e_i + c_{ij}$
- Choose the maximum value of these sums for all such arcs ij, and set e_j equal to this value.

Set p_j equal to the value of i for which this sum is largest; in the case of a tie, choose any of the values.

Phase 2: Backward Scanning.

- Start with the FINISH node $n+1$ and mark the arc joining this node to the preceding node p_{n+1}.
- Consider the node j from which the last marked arc is incident. Mark the arc joining this node to the preceding node p_j. Repeat until the START node is reached.

The marked arcs form the critical path of the network. Shown in Figure 1 is an example of a timed course network which has its critical path marked.

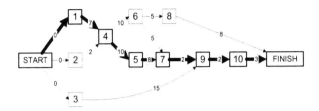

Figure 1: Critical path of a course network.

The Four Timing Parameters – EST, LST, EFT and LFT.

Upon constructing the critical path, four timing parameters associated with each node can be computed:

- **Earliest Starting Time (EST)** – the node cannot be started earlier than the EST until its preceding nodes have been completed.
- **Latest Starting Time (LST)** – the latest time of starting to study the node without delaying the whole study plan.
- **Earliest Finishing Time (EFT)** – the earliest possible time of completion of the node.
- **Latest Finishing Time (LFT)** – This node needs to be finished on or earlier than its LFT otherwise other nodes might be delayed.

A Scheme of Time-based Advising

The scope of the applicability of the timing parameters is potentially very wide. Not only they can be used for advising students on making learning progress, to the course developers, on the other hand, some of the features are very useful in course evaluation. Reported in Table 1 is a partial list of actions of the scheme that can be taken. The table should be read with the following conventions:

- Time is represented as a continuous time line with an arbitrary starting time

- t – a point-based timer which starts clocking when the course is officially started
- t_s – the actual starting time of any course node
- t_f – the actual finish time of any course node

Events	Alerting the student	Alerting the instructor
$t < EST_i$	Earlier browsing of material is subjected to the instructor's approval.	Advise the student on the appropriateness of starting a topic earlier.
$EST_i \leq t \leq LST_i$	NIL	NIL
Node i is activated at $t > LST_i$	Work harder to ensure the node is finished on or before LFT_i	Give attention to the student as s/he might delay the entire study plan
$(t_{fi} - t_{si}) < D_i$	Advise him/her not to overlook some crucial concepts	Was the topic not challenging enough? Should extra materials be included? Was D_i overestimated?

Table 1: Action List of Time-based Advising

Concluding Summary

This paper introduces the dimension of time management into online learning advising in the hope of enhancing the effectiveness and efficacy of learning. By specifying the time requirements on a course network, the system can exploit the course structure and provides sensible adaptive time-based advice to both the students and instructors. There are still outstanding issues, however. The granularity of the time specification has been limited to a monolithic form which might be too rigid. Smarter students definitely would spend less time on the topics and less smart students could need extra time but both groups could still finish the course on time. The current version of the idea is incapable of handling this variety of student abilities. The assumption of non-cyclical networks might also be annoying to some instructors as their courses could really need some sort of repetition.

References

[1] Fung, I.P.W. (2000) *A Hybrid Approach for Representing and Delivery Curriculum Contents*. In Proceedings of International Workshop on Advanced Learning Technology, Palmerston North, New Zealand, IEEE Computer Press.

[2] Fung, I.P.W. (2001) *On Monitoring Study Progress with Time-base Course Planning*. In Proceedings of International Conference on Advanced Learning Technology, Madison, Wisconsin, USA, IEEE Computer Press.

[3] Fung, I.P.W. (in press) *On computing the critical path of a course network*.

[4] Stern, M.K. & Woolf, B.P. (1998) *Curriculum Sequencing in a Web-based Tutor*. In Proceedings of Intelligent Tutoring Systems '98, 4th International Conference, San Antonio, Texas, USA, Springer Verlag.

The factors related to learning outcome in Web-based lifelong learning program

HyeJeon Suh[1], YoungSook Suh[2]
[1]Visiting Scholar, Purdue University, USA
[2]Professor, Sookmyung Women's University, Korea

ABSTRACT

The purpose of this study was to identify factors' direct and indirect influence on learning outcome and to examine relationship among learning outcomes. In this study, all independent variables were categorized into four main factors and under these factors, 16 sub-factors were grouped. Regression and path analysis between these factors and three aspects of learning outcome (participation, satisfaction, and achievement) as dependent variables indicated that instructional design-related factors were the most influential. In addition, learning environment-related factors were also the more important factors than learner and online facilitator-related factors. To maximize learners' educational outcomes, a strategy to maintain learner's motivation and to interact with learners must be established under well-harmonized learner's environment. This paper also presents some important suggestions to faculty, administrators and instructor who develop web-base lifelong course.

I. Introduction

The web-based education has various educational benefits, but its benefits cannot be achieved without an appropriate design and program development. To maximize the benefits the best strategies must be well established based on the consideration of factors that affect learning outcome.

Numerous studies have examined factors related to the successful implementation of web-based (e.g. [1]) and distance education (e.g. [3]). Based on previous studies, the factors can be classified into four categories: learner-related, online facilitator-related, instructional design-related and learning environment-related factors. Although previous studies have provided useful information, it is difficult to integrate results from the studies to make a holistic picture of the factors because the studies have examined factors individually. The holistic picture can be achieved after considering factors of four categories together and comprehensively as the factors do not always work independently.

Therefore, the purpose of this study was to identify factors' direct and indirect influences on learning outcome when four categories were considered together as independent variables, and the relationship between learning outcomes was examined through path analysis

II. Method

For this study, 124 adult learners were selected. They were taking a Web-based lifelong education course consisted of contents about child counseling and psychology for ten weeks organized by Sookmyung Women's University in Korea. The reasons of selecting these participants were because that all learning were provided via only online and this course had appropriate conditions to identify whether online facilitator, who manages and directs this course, affects learning outcome or not.

The independent variables of this study were sixteen factors in four categories: learner factors (self-regulated learning strategies, Internet ability, intrinsic control, learning motivation, attitude toward cyber education, and previous knowledge), online facilitator factors (pedagogical, social, and managerial roles), instructional design factors (interactive design, motivation design, interface design, and content organization), learning environment factors (physical environment, psychological environment, and technical support). For measuring these independent variables, survey was conducted. After survey items were developed by researcher on the basis of review of literature and previous survey work [4], factor analysis was conducted to identify sub-factors and validity of questionnaire. The reliability was a=.93. Participation, satisfaction and achievement as dependent variables were investigated through survey and server database. Collected data was analyzed through regression and path analysis by using SAS program.

III. Result

By extracting only sub-factors whose ß value revealed statistical significance after hierarchical regression with all variables, simultaneous regression was conducted. The results were schematically described in Figure 1. First of all, of these sub-factors, physical environment showed the greatest influence on participation. The five sub-factors including physical environment affecting participation explained 31 percentage of participation in web-based lifelong education (F=11.68, p<.001). Second, it was revealed that motivation design factor was the most influential factor on satisfaction. Also, of five factors affecting satisfaction, three factors included in instructional design-related factor explained almost 58 percentage of satisfaction (F=176.04, p<.001). Third, motivation design had the greatest influence on achievement and three sub-factors affecting achievement explained 37 percentage of achievement (F=14.56, p<.001).

Path analysis to see indirect influence of independent variables on learning outcomes (participation, satisfaction and achievement) and relationships between learning outcomes showed that physical environment, motivation design, and psychological environment affected achievement indirectly via participation (Data not shown). Particularly, influence of physical and psychological environments liable to be ignored in regression analysis was estimated by using path analysis in this study. In overall, the result indicated that motivation design was the most powerful factor affecting learners' achievement both indirectly and directly. However, there was no factor that indirectly affected satisfaction via participation.

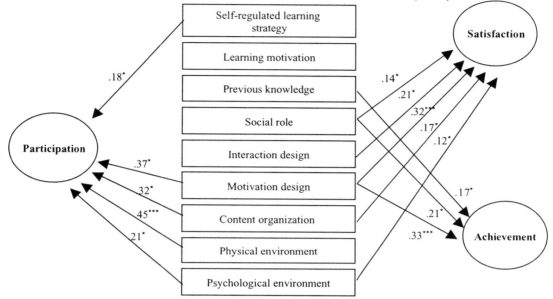

Figure 1. The result of regression

IV. Discussion

Results of this study provide some important suggestions to faculty, administrators, designers and instructors who develop curriculums for web-based lifelong education. First of all, instructors and designers have to focus on systematic instructional design because this study showed that instructional design-related factors including motivation design were the most influential factors on learning outcomes. In particular, strategies to maintain learner's motivation during learning need to be well established because adult learners who have to work and learn simultaneously tend to lose their motivation due to a variety of changes in their circumstance and stress from their personal and social lives. Second, results of this study suggest that it is important that adult learner's personal environment is well harmonized and integrated with their learning. Therefore, a well-established system to facilitate communication and to check learner's progress is required because instructors in web-based course can understand and support learners' learning environment by checking their progress and communicating with them continuously. Third, in general online facilitator in web-based education does not perceive the importance of their social role [2]. However, the results of this study revealed that their social role and support have important influence for learners to implement successful achievement. This suggests that facilitators have to support the online course focusing on their social roles to promote learners to participate in learning activities and to make learners familiar with other course-mates.

V. Reference

[1] Gunawardena, C.N., & Zittle, F.J. (1997). Social presence as a predictor of satisfaction within a computer-mediated conferencing environment. *The American Journal of Distance Education, 111(3)*, 8-26.

[2] Oh, I. (1998). The facilitator's role of web-based learning. *Corporate Education Research, 1(1)*, 125-142.

[3] Riddle, J. F. (1994). *Factors which contribute to grade achievement and course satisfaction of distance education students*. Unpublished doctoral dissertation. University of Northern Colorado, Greeley.

[4] Suh, Y., & Suh, H. (2001). Evaluation of management and analysis of satisfaction of web-based training for early childhood teacher. *The Korea Journal of Child Studies, 22(2)*, 219-235.

Common Framework Design for Development of 3D Learning Materials in Virtual Space

Hitoshi Sasaki, Shoichi Iwasaki and Makoto Takeya

Faculty of Engineering, Takushoku University, 815-1 Tatemachi, Hachioji-shi, Tokyo, 193-0985 Japan

1. Introduction

In recent years, a great number of educational environments and learning materials utilizing virtual space with 3D CG have been developed by actively making use of the processing ability and drawing ability of the computer[1-3]. However, a unified method of design and use that takes advantage of the present concept of virtual space educational systems and educational materials does not exist, thus making it necessary to create the contents of learning materials as well as design the interface for each. An authoring system that supports the development of contents utilizing virtual space does exist; however because these are general-purpose instruments, there are times when it is not feasible to use them for education purposes. It then becomes necessary to construct an environment, etc. specifically for learning materials. To create learning materials, therefore, one must be in control of every aspect of the system being used, and this puts a great burden on the creator of the learning materials. In addition, learning materials using virtual space are not created on the assumption that they will be recycled or used again. Thus it is generally very difficult to use learning materials developed for one system on another system, which means that only a few learning materials can be recycled. Because the operation methods and packaging functions are vastly different, it is almost impossible for educators to use a variety of learning Materials at the same time, and it also becomes necessary to learn how to use each of the various learning Materials. Thus both the authors of learning Materials and educators must expend a great deal of effort and cost to areas other than development and learning.

We are, therefore, working to develop a framework to construct a learning environme nt using virtual space, with a format utilizing this virtual space to create learning Materials for which a standardized interface can be used. By utilizing this framework, the creator of learning Materials will be freed from the burden of dealing with ele ments that do not directly relate to the learning Materials such as the interface, and the learners will be able to study different learning materials utilizing the same environment.

In this paper, we will first discuss problems the authors discovered as they tested a multi-user distance learning system (Virtual School[4]) using virtual space that they developed. Based on the problems, we will conduct an examination of the interface and methods for developing learning materials. Next we will suggest a framework to be used to construct a learning environment utilizing virtual space with this comprehensive system. As a model for developing learning materials utilizing this framework, we will report on its effectiveness from the point of view of how much it costs to create the learning materials.

2. Framework Design Principle

Thinking about an educational support system that uses networks, a learning environment based on a web browser exists, and because of that, an environment where moveable learning materials can be easily created is readily available. However, because it is necessary to have individual environments for each learning material that uses virtual space, the authoring of learning materials requires a certain amount of specialized knowledge, and this is not a simple task. In the past, these authors have developed and implemented a virtual school for distance learning using virtual space and through this experience have found the following problem areas.

2.1 Simplification of development the 3D learning material

Because a knowledge of 3D graphics and API that are used within a program is necessary to create 3D learning materials, the only people who can create such learning materials at the present time are researchers and a certain number of people who possess this type of specialized knowledge. When wanting to actually apply these materials in an educational setting, it is necessary to have educators and learners who have such knowledge to create and use such materials.

2.2 Supply of unified interface

It costs as much to re-use parts of learning materials that were used in the past as it does to create new learning materials, thus making it very difficult to change or add to existing materials. In addition, the use of learning materials utilizing virtual space that are available on the Internet is different depending on whether they were created using VRML and JavaScript or Java Applet. Because some of these possess a specialized interface, it is extremely difficult to make use of them to create new

1128

learning materials.

2.3 Sharing materials on the network

Learning materials are designed and packaged to correspond with their intended use, and the interface used to call up and control them is not standardized. No preparations have been made to interface between learning materials, which makes it necessary for the authors of learning materials to work independently. Because of this, it is very difficult to set up a variety of already existing learning materials within the classroom of the virtual school and use them together.

2.4 Continuous usage of teaching tools

Virtual space is largely used for 3D learning materials and communication that shares virtual space. The consultation of textbooks or reference books and the taking of notes must be carried on outside of virtual space. Because of this, it is necessary to move back and forth between virtual space and real space, and this hinders smooth and harmonious learning. In addition, while a student is taking notes or reading a textbook, movement in virtual space must come to a halt, and s/he cannot deal with other students and teachers, thus making study activities and communication incompatible. In order for students to actively participate in learning while using learning materials involving virtual space, these problems must be solved. As a first step to finding solutions, we are developing a framework for the authoring of learning materials with the following characteristics.

3. The framework for developing learning materials

A framework where multiple numbers of learning materials can be operated within the same virtual space was developed; while using certain learning materials, this makes it possible to call up learning materials used in the past for review; and multiple numbers of learning materials can be connected for instruction and study. Because the virtual school, which serves as the base, is a distance learning system, it was assumed that it would be conducted over a network, and an environment where multiple numbers of learners would be able to study within the same virtual space was provided. Thus the learning materials created using this framework could be shared by multiple numbers of users on their PCs. This system is made up of a server program and a client program. The server controls the virtual space where learning takes place, handles data for each individual learner, and manages the learning materials, and the client provides the interface where operations take place. By connecting a multiple number of clients, it is possible for more than one client to utilize the virtual space at the same time. Because only Java and Java3D API are used, they can be operated on a variety of operating systems.

With this framework, the user interface for utilizing these learning materials provides a virtual space browser that offers the virtual space where learning activities are carried out and the avatar controller used to operate the learning materials. Also the avatar who will act for the user is provided as an object within the virtual space. These are managed through a user management function and a database for each user. The virtual space constructed using this framework utilizes the class interface created from the following shared format. As the users share the conditions of this instance, a shared virtual space comes into being.

In the framework used for developing learning materials, the format is described using Java language and is defined as a class file. The functions necessary for the movement of objects within the virtual space are defined by the basic class VS_Object. The VS_Object class contains the methods to carry out communication with other objects, a description of its own movements, the construction of scene graphs, the re-use of animation graphics, and the movement controls for the learning materials. Learning materials are created by the use and overriding of methods needed to create learning material classes that succeed the VS_Object class. The data needed to construct scene graphs from data for shape/form and animation are also defined as a class. This makes it possible to freely add to the VS_Object class.

In order to enable communication between learning materials, it is necessary to define the messages sent from one learning material to another as data. These are defined as VS_Message class. By defining messages between learning materials as a class, the classes succeeding the VS_Message class can also be sent and received, thus making it possible to exchange data freely. Communication can thus take place between learning materials that are developed independently, and a number of different learning materials can be combined to create new learning materials.

4. An example of learning material development and verification of the efficiency of this development

In this chapter a cost comparison is made between an example created to verify the effectiveness of this framework and one created using a different method. By the visual use of LAN construction and shapes, a LAN traffic learning material is displayed in a form that is very close to reality. They were created to support visual understanding. LAN construction utilizes 3D graphics, which allows visualization from all angles where a situation is connected via 3D graphics. The 3D animation, which uses an input/output packet for traffic and a delete packet, is displayed visually. As a visualization method to show a situation concretely, connections are shown as ON and OFF, and the input/output packet passes through transparent wiring which can be shown by expanding and contracting the radius of the cylinder. When the delete packet comes into being, the animated figure of a ball dropping from a node appears. In order to observe the traffic and conditions of this network, the network information, input/output packet and delete packet for the IP is acquired through the use of the SNMP management protocol. Connection information is received in real time by use of the connection condition confirmation command. When the first set-up is completed, information is received from the server, changing condition-animation appears, and it becomes possible to view the construction and condition of the newly built network from any angle by using the changing viewpoint function.

4.1 Packaging of learning materials that study LAN traffic

The display object that handles the display of information, the computer object that handles packet data, the cable object that forwards packets within objects, and the hub object that breaks up the sources of output of a packet are being created as objects used to manage the input/output packet, the delete packet, and the information about connection condition. To carry out simulations on the network, a manager PC object has been created to manage all of the traffic. The use of this makes it possible to move traffic information. The created object has the same function as the actual object, and by simulating each function, it becomes possible to re-use parts when creating full-scale learning materials to study LAN.

Fig.1 Our system by using our framework

Because it is necessary to arrange computer and hub objects in virtual space, the layout of rooms for object arrangement and construction of LAN has been done. In the virtual space browser for the framework, objects can be added within the virtual space through the use of the avatar controller, and this function is used to create object functions. In avatar controller's object menu, there is an add function that allows objects to be added to virtual space. From this file dialogue, you can add the node to virtual space. Fig. 1 illustrates the virtual space built by using these functions to create a LAN.

4.2 Traffic information simulation function

From the SNMP server that functions as a manager PC object, it is possible to set up traffic that combines the simulation with the whole. By having avatar approach the manager PC, the amount being transmitted can be compared to the maximum amount transmittable for the network card within the program. By using the simulation function, the manager PC is capable of sending a packet to each object, and based on a set ratio, the traffic information for the network can be changed by altering the packet amount. Also, the condition of the input/output packet is shown by the thickness and color of the cable object, and the delete packet is illustrated by showing a ball dropping from a node.

4.3 Cost comparison

To compare costs, a LAN traffic learning material and one similar to it are developed, one with C++ language and the other with OpenGL. In Table 1, the number of lines in each program of learning material developed by the existing method and the learning material developed using this framework were compared function by function. The virtual space construction area includes the calculation of coordinates for building a 3D environment and the GUI part of the main screen. Because the main

Table 1. The comparison of the number of program lines

	C++ and OpenGL	Our system
Building of virtual space	787	88
Animate cartoon	605	310
Display of data	64	45
Save / Load data	560	-
Others	230	-
Total	2,246	453

class that handles these on the framework is provided, this amounts to a display of only the lines needed to read the shape/form data and those displaying the movements peculiar to the object. The traffic animation relationship involves the handling of the calculation of the coordinates that connect the two node by cables, the handling of the changes in value of the input/output packet as shown by the thickness of the cable, and the program that describes the display of the delete packet. In addition to these, a display of the building of an interface using the system and a display of how these are handled. Because the function of preserving and reading an object's data and other functions are provided for in the framework, they are marked " -" in the Table 1.

The results of the above comparison show that when using the existing development method, the program required 2,246 lines where as that using the framework was completed using only 453 lines thus reducing the burden of the program lines using C++ and OpenGL by approximately 80%. An examination of individual results shows that the number of lines related to the building of virtual space is significantly lower, and by using this framework for virtual space it is easily possible to build virtual space. Also, by using the class library provided on the platform, less lines related to information such as the display of animation and text data are needed. Therefore it is thought that from the point of view of the ease of developing learning materials using this framework, this method is very effective.

5. Conclusion

In this paper, we have proposed a framework to support the development of 3D virtual space. We have also provided one example of our development of learning materials using this framework. In a comparison with existing learning materials, we confirmed the efficiency of the framework. In the future, we plan to investigate and evaluate all aspects of usage including the interface. While abstracting a variety of important and necessary issues discovered when the materials are actually used in an educational setting, we plan to work on packaging these.

Reference

[1] L. R. Porter, "Creating the virtual classroom –Distance learning with the Internet-", Wiley computer Publishing, 1997.

[2] O. Ui, M Nakayama and Y. Shimizu: "Relation between transmission configuration and evaluation of learning in satellite communication learning," 12th Nat. Conv. Japan Soc Educ. Eng.K1p2B5, pp.205-206, 1996(in Japanese).

[3] S. Fujiki, H. Itose and K. Itoyama: "Learning using a TV conference system and trial class learnig", Tech. Rep. IEICEJ, ET97-33, 1997(in Japanese).

[4] K. Shirato, H. Sasaki and M. Takeya: "Development and application of a distance learning system by using virtual reality technology", Trans. IEICE Vol.J83-D-I, No.6, pp.619-626, 2000(in Japanese).

Knowledge Repository Oriented e-Learning System and its Evaluation for a Cooperative Linkage between University and Industry

Toshio OKAMOTO[1], Mizue KAYAMA[2] and Hisayoshi INOUE[3]

[1] University of Electro- Communications Graduate School of Information Systems
[2] Senshu University, School of Network and Information
[3] Jyoetsu University of Education, Center for Educational Research and Development

Abstract

This paper presents a web-based distance education system that contains synchronous (live) video lectures, asynchronous learning materials with video-on-demand (VOD) archive data, and question & answer functions through digital reporting between a lecturer and students. It is intended to provide a collaborative workplace to encourage interactions among a lecturer/learners. As such, this environment enables learners to exchange their knowledge and their way of thinking, furthermore, to refine/build the knowledge acquired via lectures. One of the main purposes in our research is to build a flexible e-Learning environment by embedding self/collaborative support functions for the digitized live lectures in order to reinforce much more meaningful knowledge and skills. Moreover, we propose an innovative educational method of a cooperative link between a university and an industry for the higher education. The knowledge repository means a kind of data-warehouse with the computational mechanism to handle/manage various data occurred in e-Learning process. The knowledge repository may be utilized for any information referencing, diagnosing/evaluating of learners' activities, consulting and so on. We also tackle problems of knowledge sharing, knowledge-retrieval and various types of collaboration in the learning environment. The heart of our project is the exploration of how we can effectively make use of this knowledge repository to support learners who have a range of different needs, though we don't mention its technical details here.

1. Introduction

The Industry and University cooperation program is a project of the Japanese Ministry of Education(JME) [2]. The objective of this program is not only the completion of an environment where upstanding members of the society with business, industry or university background can learn, but also to the connection and harmonization of university educational research and society practice and practical business. Specifically, the program aims at offering the university student access to the practical, business point of view and practical knowledge on one hand, and the industry and company employee an opportunity to improve oneself and an access to higher knowledge and education [4]. In this way, we are promoting an educational collaboration program that binds university and industry [8].

The JME appointed the University of Electro-Communications (UEC) with the enacting of this cooperation program between Industry and University. The target learners are industry people as well as regular students of the university, who wish to learn about the new Information Technology (IT) issues. The actual putting into practice involves the extension of the existing curriculum towards more flexibility [5, 6].

In this paper we report about our experiences with the introducing of this program, about the framework, settings, actual implementation and first results. We analyze these results and the problems we encountered, as well as offer constructive solutions. Furthermore, we have developed the knowledge repository in e-Learning environment such as an analyzer/summarizer by the statistical natural language processing for data log of discussion/communication process between learners and a teacher, though we can't introduce its details here

2. The Program

The subject of career development involving acquiring of high experience and knowledge in the field of information communication technology is an important subject for the future information communication society. The starting courses of the program involve this discipline. The lectures were focused on high information technology, large-scale information system planning and application, and network technology.

For the first year period, the courses involved the following topics:

- Multimedia Communication Technology
- Information Security

Moreover, the appointed lecturers for the industry and university cooperation program are not only researchers and professors from our graduate school, but also company researchers and implementers as well. This is due to the fact that it is important for students to acquire knowledge about not only the theoretical side related to information systems, but also about the practical side.

The lectures are held as collaborative lectures of the type called *"omnibus"* (each lecturer presents only one lecture). Although this new curriculum is of a flexible nature, with many evening hours (to ensure easy participation from far sites) and a relatively concentrated information contents given over a short time period (again, to ensure that company workers loose not too many hours with this program), the UEC graduate school has established a regular credit system for certification purposes. The level of certification is Master level.

3. Experimental Situation

Here we report an example situation of a lecture entitled "multimedia communication science/ technology and application". The syllabus of this lecture includes: multimedia and distributed cooperation, CSCL (collaborative system collaborative learning) and collaborative memory, multimedia communication technology, ATM networks, new Internet technology, media representation form and application, data mining, multimedia and distributed cooperation learning support systems, knowledge management, standardization and new business models. The total number of learners attending the lecture was 63, among who only 13 were curriculum students. This time, the distance company sites that cooperated were located near Tokyo, in Kanagawa prefecture. The distance companies were linked via Internet and ISDN circuit, therefore establishing a real time bi-directional information transmitting and receiving environment. Figure 1 displays the geographical distribution of the distance company sites.

From the distance company sites to the UEC, the needed round trip time of the closest site is of 2 hours by public transportation, and for the furthermost the round trip is of about 6 hours. Therefore, considering the hours of time saved and the convenience of the distance education method, the system presents evident merit for both learners from far company sites as well as company managers.

4. Distance Education System Configuration

It is necessary to provide a lecture environment that guarantees both the lecture movie, sound and lecture materials presentation distribution for attending students, as well as a dialogue function supporting the communication between lecturer and students. We have implemented these functions by using a VOD (Video On Demand)[3,7] server and a WWW (World Wide Web) server. Figure 2 shows the system configuration of the distance learning system.

Each site has to configure the transmission server and the viewer. Each distance lecture site establishes two dedicated channels: one for receiving only and one for sending only. By connecting respectively the lecture classroom transmission with the distance site reception and the distance site transmission with the lecture classroom reception, bi-directional communication is implemented. Below, each function is outlined.

1) Transmission function of lecture's movie and sound : the

Figure 1. Distribution of distant company sites

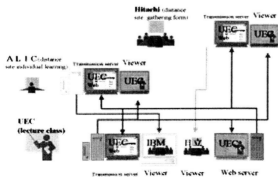

Figure 2. Distance learning system configuration

movie and sound of the lecture is distributed to the attending sites with the help of the VOD server real time transmission function[10]. Moreover, in the case of some companies, their Internet access and therefore, the transmission/ reception of lecture movie and sound is not free. To cope with such a network environment, we had to ensure a dedicated Proxy server that relays the distribution of lecture movie and sound between Internet sites, to ensure the data reception. Students at far sites attend lectures by viewing the lecture movie and sound data distributed by the VOD server.

2) Lecture material presentation function : the lecture materials are formatted as HTML (Hyper Text Markup Language) sources and offered to students via the WWW server. Students use the WWW browser to access the lecture materials and to follow the lecture progress by referring the appropriate page.

3) Dialogue (chat) function : the communication tool between lecturer and student: Is ensured by a CGI (Common Gateway Interface) program written in Perl (Practical Extraction and Report Language). Lecturer and students access the CGI program via the WWW browser and perform a questions and answers session via the chat terminal screen.

One problem appearing is that the lecture movie and sound data sending and reception conditions depend on the network traffic conditions. Namely, if the reception data has a delay, far site students have difficulty in viewing the lecture, therefore failing to understand the lecture contents. Therefore we have setup a bi-directional communication channel between lecture site and far sites. In this way the communication channel between lecturer and students is guaranteed, independent of the Internet network conditions. Figure 3 shows the distance lecture environment structure (lecture site -> far sites) as well as the interface of both lecturer and students. As can be seen in the figure, the lecture manager transforms the lecture materials into HTML form and performs the registration into the lecture materials database.

Figure 4 displays the main menu lecture site and attending sites registration window. Concretely, data recorded are machine name (organization name), VOD server IP address and port number and VOD contents stream identifier. Students attend lectures (Figure 4) via our distance lecture environment interface. Firstly, they select the lecture movie "reception" button from the main menu. The system than enquires for the movie to display.

4.1 The Environment for Distributed e-Learning Contents

We have developed Web-based learning materials "Multimedia Communication Technology" by HTML, PERL, CGI, Java and

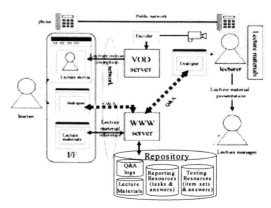

Figure 3. Hybrid e-Learning environment system

Figure 4. Lecture / distance learner site registration

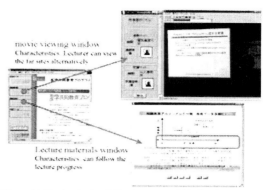

Figure 5. Movie playback/ lecture material indication

VOD materials by Stream Authorware tool. The VOD materials consist of the archive data of movies / sounds from the live lectures in remote areas. According to the stream of movies, PowerPoint manuscript for each lecture is inserted with a synchronous signal in an appropriate position. This environment has three pull-down menus (i.e., a learning objective, a learning mode, and a contents-catalog) to enable learners to select and retrieve whatever they need. This distributing function has been implemented in our original Learning Management System (LMS) named RAPSODY [9].

4.2 The Collaborative Workplace for Question & Answer

We built a collaborative workplace to encourage interactions among lecturer/learners. In such a case, learners can exchange their knowledge and their way of thinking, furthermore they can refine/build the knowledge acquired via lectures. By a collaborative workplace, we mean a kind of BBS, nevertheless, in addition to Chat function, this workplace enables data/information sharing transmitted from different sites. Each student can drug/drop any data whatever they need from personal (individual) workplace to collaborative workplace and vice versa. In addition, s/he can transmit with attaching some annotations for arbitrary objects in the collaborative workplace. Those data are saved in the log-repository with the standardized record format through the collaborative memory. If somebody wants to refer/analyze those data for any purpose such as knowledge mining/management and so on, s/he would reuse this repository under the lecturer's admission.

4.3 The Assessment Module for Learners

After lecture/web-learning, a test or reporting for learners as a summative evaluation is needed. In this environment, we have provided the repository of a set of test items and reporting tasks according to subjects (course-unit) matched with each learning objective. Students can pick up certain amount of test items or reporting tasks designated by a lecturer, and then reply/send back their answers to *the digital pigeon box*. As such, a lecturer can score and evaluate their achievements online. The simultaneous test is carried out in order to avoid a student's copying behavior from others. Moreover, the *text analyzer* was implemented to check the similarity of the reporting contents from the students automatically. This analyzer was built on the statistical natural language processing method, performing the following functions: picking up important keywords, its occurrence frequency, and co-occurrence of the related word for a certain word.

After pressing the button "lecture site ->lecture movie", the

system pops up the "lecture movie playback" window and starts the playback (figure 5). Moreover, when clicking the main menu's "lecture materials presentation" button, the system presents the lecture materials, too. Students can browse the lecture material via the buttons "advance" and "return". To enable the questions and answers session, the lecturer has to select from the main menu the dialogue tool "startup", action that will generate a "chat" window.

Lecturers attend lectures via a similar procedure to the students. Firstly, they select the lecture movie "reception" button from the main menu (figure 4). If the students' far sites are equipped with VOD server, video camera, microphone and movie encoder, it is possible for lecturers to receive the image (and sound) of the students attending the lectures. Similarly to the students, the lecturer can view the movie and sound and use the playback function. Moreover, in the case of multiple far sites, the lecturer can switch between them. Questions and answers sessions are possible as full movie and sound exchange, as chat (in text format) or via the regular telephone line.

5. Evaluation of the Industry and University Education Cooperation Program

The evaluation of the program focuses on how many of the objectives stated in the introduction were actually achieved, and was performed from the 2 points of view enumerated below:

1) *Science and technology aspect:* Here we analyze the operations, functions and the lecture movie and sound data transmission and reception.

2) *Educational aspect:* Here we examine the meaning and significance of the distance education lecture in the frame of the industry and university collaboration project, via questionnaires filled in by the students.

The analysis of the lectures from the above-mentioned points of view is a continuous process.

(1a) Science and technology aspects; evaluation 1: movie and sound data transmission and reception aspect

We have measured the delays, time-lapses and evolution of the lecture movie and sound data transmission. For this purpose, we have analyzed a situation with 3 sites exchanging VOD data. Each site was respectively connected to the Internet via either a high speed -, low speed dedicated circuit (maximum rate 128 kbps), or via a business provider dial up IP link. For the analysis of the transmission, we have collected data from each site on the movie bit rate (figure 6), movie frame rate (figure 7) and sound bit rate (figure 8). As can be seen in the figures, the maximum real transmission values are, respectively, 48 kbps for the maximum real movie bit rate, 10 fps for the greatest real movie frame rate and 13.2 kbps for the highest real sound bit rate.

We will firstly discuss the movie transmission. For movie bit rates of 40 kbps and above, the lecture transmission is stable, with little interruptions, and the frame transmission is of about 5 frames per second. However, we have experienced that for the dial up connections, reception at the students' far sites is is of about 1 frame per 10 to 20 seconds. At this rate, the lecture movie playback window often freezes into a still image for several seconds. Students attending lectures from such sites complained therefore that movie and sound reception is often asynchronous. Compared with the movie data reception, the sound reception was relatively stable for all participating sites. The above experimental result shows clearly that for such distance lectures the limitation is given by the movie reception, and that it is recommended to implement distance lecture environments on network circuits allowing maximum transmission capacity of 128 kbps or above. If a provider IP connection cannot be avoided, the distance lecture environment can be improved with a number of adjustments, as follows.

The first adjustment is related to the lecturer's actions. The VOD system used in our distance lecture environment complies with the H.261 standard, which bases the movie distribution on information compression via a frame prediction mechanism. Namely, the

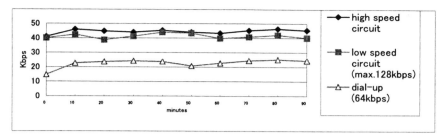

Figure 6. Movie bit rate time series

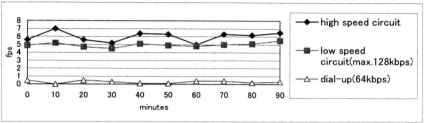

Figure 7. Movie frame rate time series

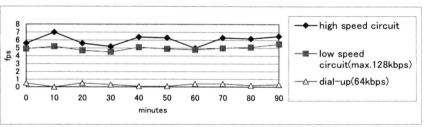

Figure 8. Sound bit rate time series

transmitted/ received information weight changes according to the movie data, movie complexity and details, movement intensity, etc. If the lecturer's actions are various, the transmission data weight grows. However, if the lecturer's actions during the lecture are moderate, the movie changes are reduced and therefore the lecture movie distribution can become a little more stable. As another adjustment, the creation of a dedicated low speed circuit for the VOD server is necessary.

If these adjustments are made, all sites can reach similar bit rate, and the distribution occurs according to the different frame rates. I.e., according to the network bandwidth of the access points, the distribution to high speed circuit students' far sites should be high rate, whereas the low speed circuit far sites should receive low rate movie and sound data.

(1b) Science and technology aspects; evaluation 2: distance education system operatively and functions

We have identified a few possible improvement points concerning lecturing via a distance education system, with focus on application result, operatively and function. Table 1 shows the recommended improvements for the distance lecture environment. Some items in the table point to proposed solutions, others to counter-measures, and again others just present situational examinations.

(2) Educational aspects evaluation: questionnaire survey

After each industry and university cooperation program lecture we have asked the learners to fill in a questionnaire. The questionnaire contains 21 questions that are a combination of both

Table 1: Problems and solutions of the distance learning environment implementation

Encountered problems	Solutions/Results
Web lecture materials are not synchronous with the lecturer indications. If the lecturer is browsing quickly through the material (as often in the second half of the lecture), the distance learners cannot keep up with the current page.	By using applications with share function, the synchronous display in both lecture room and far sites is possible. One drawback is that the lecturer's personal browsing through the material is not possible anymore.
The circuit speeds of the distance lecture sites differ. Reception is therefore difficult for some sites.	Multiple preparations are necessary for correct movie & sound transmission. The server setup should follow the various requirements of the distance sites.
During the Q&A session, the communication quality is reduced by the existent delay between lecture room and far sites.	There is no fundamental replacement scheme at present. New infrastructure and communication hardware is necessary. Rehearsal prior to the actual Q&A session is useful (or guidance of session by a chair person).
The phone line Q&A sound problems: 1) Noise, hauling; 2) Speaker volume & receiver volume differ.	1) Noise, hauling are caused by the using of a large combination of equipment 2) The volume difference can be cancelled by the circuit resistance value.

1135

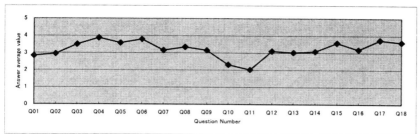

Figure 9. Curriculum questionnaire result average (first lecture in series)

free description form questions and questions with a 5 steps assessment scale. For the latter, the students should choose the most appropriate of the 5 steps (5: I strongly think so, 4:I incline to think so, 3: Neither Nor, 2: I incline not to think so, 1: I definitely don't think so).

As the industry and university cooperation program lectures cycle is not yet finished, we couldn't aggregate all the questionnaire results yet, and therefore cannot establish conclusive results yet. However, as at present we have finished the first round of lectures, it is possible to derive some suggestions and hints. Figure 9 shows the average answers of the first lecture. Questionnaires were anonymous and 38 questionnaires were returned from the 63 distributed. As the questionnaire (table 2) average is in general around 3-4, the result can be called satisfactory. Especially, questions Q4-6 (about students interest in the subject, the motivating effect of the lecture and about the knowledge they acquired) showed a high score.

Students had an average of 2.8 preliminary knowledge on the subject (Question Q1). This result possibly points to the fact that learners with no prior knowledge, up to learners with some prior specialty knowledge all were interested in the lecture. As the acquisition of high-level specialty knowledge is the main object of the industry and university cooperation program, this is an extremely important pointer. A low result was noticeable especially for questions Q10 and Q11 (regarding the far site transmission situation). Therefore, an important sub-goal and improvement point for the next lectures is the harmonization of the transmission with the far sites. As these were the results of the first lesson in the series, such problems were perhaps unavoidable, and the management and synchronization of lecturer, lecture manager, technical supporters, and teaching assistants was difficult to establish. Some of these problems have already been solved in the following lectures of the

same cycle, but as the results were not yet analyzed, we present here our first experiences only, to be of use and serve to guide other educators worldwide.

6. Conclusion

In this paper we have presented our experience with the introducing of the industry and university education cooperation project at our graduate school to promote the future high level information communication society based on life-long education. Especially, we have highlighted the following points.

1) The implementation method as well as possible problems of the distance lecture environment offering synchronous study possibility at the lecture site as well as far sites, based on bi-directional communication.

2) The issue of curriculum integration and certification/recognition of both on-site and far-site learners. Whole learners achieve credits according to the Master course credit system.

3) We have discussed and presented our efforts in the direction of building the infra-structure necessary to support the lecturing within the industry and university education cooperation program. Specifically, we referred to the prior collecting of information, which is to be sent together with the lecture movie and sound transmission.

We hope to support and respond to the forecasted growing future learning demand, especially on advanced IT topics, and to create the chance and environment for a wide area high-level education.

Acknowledgements

Special thanks to Mr. Kiyoshi Hara (Japan UNISYS), Mr. Akihiko Koga (HITACHI), Mr. Yuji Tokiwa (IBM) and Mr. Kenji Ito(ALIC) for their cooperation during this program.

References

[1] B. Collis, : Design, Development and Implementation of a WWW-Based Course-Support System, In Proc. of *7th International Conference on Computer and Education*, pp.11-18, 1999.

[2] Japanese Minatory of Education, Culture Sports Science and Technology : http://www.mext.go.jp

[3] J. Peltoniemi, "Video-on-Demand Overview", http://www.cs.tut.fi/tlt/stuff/vod/ VoDOverview/vod1.html ,1995

[4] L.G. Salvador, : Continuing Education Through Distance Training, In Proc. of *7th International Conference on Computer and Education*, pp.512-515, 1999.

[5] M.J.Rosenberg, : E-Learning –strategies for delivering knowledge in the digital age-, McGraw-Hill Companies, Inc., USA, 2001.

[6] M. Slomen, : The e-learning revolution – from propositions to action-, Chartered Institute of Personnel and Development, London, 2001.

[7] S. Hui, "Video-On-Demand in Education", http://www.cityu.edu.hk/~ccncom/net14/vod2.htm

[8] T. Okamoto, (research representative/delegate) : Advanced Information Society; synthetic research on the contents, system and form of teachers' education - final report, 3 year research grant of the Ministry of Education, (A)(1)09308004 stage report. 2000.

[9] T. Okamoto, A.I.Cristea and M. Kayama, Towards Intelligent Media-Oriented Distance learning and Education Environments, Proceedings of *8th International Conference on Computer in Education*, pp.61-72, 2000.

[10] T. Okamoto, T. Matsui, H. Inoue and A. Cristea, A Distance-Education Self-Learning Support System based on a VOD Server, Proceedings of *International Workshop on Advanced Learning Technologies*, pp.71-78, 2000.

Table 2 Question items

Q1. Did you have previous knowledge on the contents of this lecture?

Q2. Is there an important connection between today's lecture and your research/study field?

Q3. Do you think you will be able to use today's lecture contents in your future research/job?

Q4. Are you interested in the topics presented by today's lecture?

Q5. Do you feel that today's lecture has opened new perspectives?

Q6. Did today's lecture deepen your knowledge?

Q7. Was today's lecture according to your expectations?

Q8. Was today's lecture level appropriate?

Q9. Was today's presented subject of expertise of importance?

Q10. Was the cooperation with the far sites smooth?

Q11. Could you consider the far sites part integrated in the lecture environment?

Q12. Did the lecture materials offered with the lecture help you in understanding the lecture?

Q13. Did lecturing and lecture material presentation run smoothly?

Q14. Was question asking made easy by the offered environment?

Q15. Were today's sound and movie transmission clear?

Q16. Was today's lecture complete and sufficient for you, although designed as a distance education lecture?

Q17. Was the time distribution appropriate for today's lecture?

Q18. Was the time distribution appropriate for far sites, with regard to the Q&A session?

Design and Implementation of a Web-Based Classroom Management Support System for Elementary School Classroom Management

Chul Kim · Oh-Soo Jung · Dai-sung Ma

Department of Computer Science Education,

Gwangju National University of Education, Korea

Abstract

One of the changes that the "Information Age" has brought to classrooms is that a Web-Based Classroom Management Support System (WBC) is now required for more efficient classroom management in elementary schools. This research aims at finding desirable Internet uses for more efficient classroom management through designing and implementing a web-based classroom support system. It has been possible to support classroom management beyond the limits of time and space with content found on the web and through guiding learners' internet usage in educational directions utilizing the resources on the web in more academic ways, and developing each learners' own special abilities and aptitudes. A WBC system is expected to offer upgraded classroom management when applied in classrooms to help direct learners' active participation.

1. The objects of the research

The ability to use computers by elementary school students in South Korea has made remarkable progress. To follow up with this change of the teaching environment, teachers need to diversify their teaching abilities and methods as well as understand each student's interests and needs and cope with them properly so that the students can implement self-directed learning. These changes in the educational environment also require diverse methods of classroom management. Students are asking for advice and answers to their inquiries without any limit of time and space. Under these circumstances, where it is impossible to ignore the cyber world in managing a class, a Web-Based Classroom Management Support System(WBC) is necessary as a cyber environment where outside-class study guidance and counseling can be taken care of at the same time for more efficient classroom management. This research aims at designing and implementing a WBC to discover desirable Internet uses and to lead to more efficient classroom management.

2. Designing and Implementation of the WBC

The WBC has its basic aim in supporting classroom management by substituting educational activities that are difficult to realize with classroom management principles. This research institutes basic directions in designing the WBC for the efficient management of a cyber classroom. First, the construction of the WBC should reduce time and space limits in managing a classroom. Second, the WBC should strengthen classroom management by supporting teaching and learning operations, discretional activities, character education and creativity development. Third, the WBC should provide learners with various menus, so that the learners can take an active part in the learning process. Fourth, the WBC should intensify its educational content, so that the learners can implement self-directed learning and take on responsibility for their own study. Fifth, the WBC should limit the one-directional transmission mode of "html" documents, and strengthen interactional elements. The following states the points to be concerned with in designing the menu in accordance with these basic directions. First, the menu for the WBC should be constituted with items that can be found on the web and it should support classroom management. Second, for smooth connection, the WBC should be constructed mainly with texts and with essential graphics. Third, the WBC should attach great importance to interactional exchanges between the teacher and the students, and between the students themselves, as well have space for the students' diverse activities. Fourth, the WBC should break from the teacher's one-directional presentation of materials, and lead to the interaction of teaching and learning activities. Fifth, the WBC should minimize its access process by simplifying its structure, so that the users can access the page they want easily.

The areas of WBC that can be operated on the web amongst various methods of class management can be grouped as the Class Introduction Area, the Teaching and Learning Area, the Discretional Activity Area, the Extra Culicular Activity Area, the Character Education Area, and Study Contents Area. Items applicable to each area constitute the following WBC, as shown below.

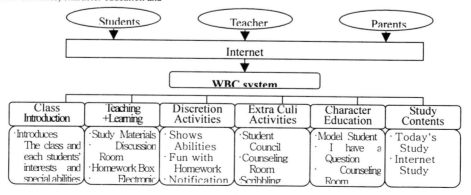

3. Application of the WBC

The application experiment of the WBC for this research was conducted for eight months, from March 1, 2001 to October 30, 2001, with 72 sixth-grade students at Naju Nampyeong Elementary School in South Korea

3.1. Changes in the students' understanding of computer use and in their Internet use

As the table shows, the frequency of using Internet resources has remarkably increased with the WBC system applied to the teaching and learning process. This indicates that correct guidance of Internet use can lead to very encouraging effects. The more the students used the Internet for studying, the less time they spent using the net for games or entertainment. As appears on the table, the number of students who used the net as a study resource increased by 55.6%. In addition, the 70% increase in the students' understanding that the computer is a tool for information acquirement indicates that this research contributed to changing the children's understanding in a positive direction.

<Table #2> Changes in the students' understanding of computer use and in their Internet use (N=72)

		Before		After		Incre ase Rate
		N	%	N	%	
Internet uses	Computer games	46	63.9	16	22.2	-41.7
	Chatting	13	18.1	7	9.7	-8.3
	Studying	1	1.4	41	56.9	55.6
	Movies, music	2	2.8	1	1.4	-1.4
	E-mailing	11	15.3	7	9.7	-5.6
Under-standing of computer use	A tool for information	1	1.4	52	72.2	70.8
	A complex machinery for calculation	1	1.4	0	0.0	-1.4
	A tool for data saving	17	23.6	12	16.7	-6.9
	A tool for entertainment	53	73.6	8	11.1	-62.5

3.2. Changes in the frequency of educational use of the Internet, and in the students' ability to solve homework

<Table #3> Changes in the frequency of educational use of the Internet, and in the students' ability to work on homework (N=72)

		Before		After		Rate of Increase
		N	%	N	%	
Hours of Internet use for studying (per week)	0 hour	38	52.8	0	0.0	-52.8
	1-2 hours	22	30.6	5	6.9	-23.6
	3-4 hours	7	9.7	37	51.4	41.7
	5-6 hours	4	5.6	16	22.2	16.7
	More than 6 hours	1	1.4	14	19.4	18.1
Hours of Internet use for gaming, entertainmen t and chatting (per week)	0 hour	6	8.3	8	11.1	2.8
	1-2 hours	17	23.6	16	22.2	-1.4
	3-4 hours	20	27.8	19	26.4	-1.4
	5-6 hours	5	6.9	9	12.5	5.6
	More than 6 hours	24	33.3	20	27.8	-5.6
Working on homework using the Internet	Self-directed work	2	2.8	53	73.6	70.8
	Possible with others' help	22	30.6	14	19.4	-11.1
	Not confident	48	66.7	5	6.9	-59.7

After the WBC application, the number of the students who used the Internet for studying for more than 3 hours per week increased by 90%. This indicates that the experiment contributed to encouraging the students to use the net as an educational tool. When the WBC was applied to the teaching and learning process, the students not only did their homework, but also developed their cooperative spirit and responsibility through working on projects with others. Though the hours using the Internet for study increased, there was no change in the hours spent for computer games or entertainment. This can be understood as an indicator that the upper-grade students have already formed the habit of playing computer games, and that the teacher's guidance for educational Internet use should be provided to the lower-grade students before they develop an addictive attitude toward games. In terms of working on homework, students who had shown a lack of confidence in doing homework by themselves increased their ability to solve problems using the net, as well as increased their self-confidence.

4. Conclusion

It is very important to construct a menu for the WBC in which teaching and learning operations, values education, and creativity education are included. Operating the WBC to make up for the weak points of classroom management has led the researcher to the following conclusions: First, the application of the WBC re-directed the students' Internet use, and encouraged their ability to use the net as study material. It also increased their confidence in working on homework. It, however, also brought up the necessity of correct Internet-use guidance for lower-grade students, and showed no decline in the hours that the students spent in using computers for non-educational purposes, such as gaming. Second, the students appeared to want a group to which they could belong in the cyber world. Those who belonged to a cyber group also showed high participation in a positive way in the actual classroom. The easy and convenient mobility and production capabilities of the WBC helped the students submit their reports and homework instantly. It also encouraged the habit of reading along, thus having an effect on reading education. The students further had the opportunity of reflection, as they could see the results of their study on the spot. Third, as they were more interested in the cyber class, the students who had taken active part in the activities to develop their interests and special abilities became a great support for classroom management beyond the limits of time and space. Fourth, the Discussion Room, which was operated in a closed-door way, drew a positive reaction from the students. Frequent counseling and exchange of opinions between the teacher and the students, or between the students themselves, helped the students to develop their characters, and prevented any conflict between groups in the class, building up a classroom atmosphere where the students actually praised each other. Finally, though on-line classroom management can result in more work for the teacher, this problem can be solved with an Internet system that provides a homepage. Too much dependence on on-line classroom management, however, might cause a lack of direct contact between the teacher and the students. The WBC can offer an opportunity to upgrade education only when it leads to the students' own active participation in the class.

7. References

[1] Gyeng-Tek Kim, Chul Kim, The Design and Implementation of Class Management System for Character Education, Journal of The KAIE, 4(2), 147-158

[2] Youngyun Bak(1999), The Design of Web-Based Learning, Yangsuwon, Korea.

[3] Badrul H Khan(1997) Web-Based Instruction Educational Technology Publications, Englewood Cliffs, New Jersey.

[4] David Mioduser(1999).Web_BasedLearning Environments(WBLE): Current State and Emerging Trends, Tel-Aviv University, Israel.

[5] http://home.opentown.net/~chamdali

[6] http://heoju.new21.org

[7] http://kamang.woorizip.com

[8] http://myhome.netsgo.com/PSYMLOVE

[9] http://saem4u.new21.org

Development of Internet Virtual Butterfly Museum

Wernhuar Tarng
Department of Mathematics and Science Education
National Hsin-Chu Teachers College
Hsin-Chu, Taiwan, R.O.C.

Abstract

The butterfly is a valuable nature resource from the viewpoint of education and tourism. In recent years, the over-exploitation of mountainous areas and overuse of pesticide results in dramatic decrease of butterfly species and populations. This paper studies the related network and virtual reality technologies for developing a virtual butterfly museum, and the objective is to provide students and the general public with a web-learning environment for studying butterfly ecology. The virtual museum exhibits several species of butterflies, including Pieridae, Papilionidae, Danaidae, Satyridae, Nymphalidae, as well as insects often seen in Taiwan. We can visit it through network at any time and from anywhere to proceed with observation and learning activities, and discuss with others on the website. Therefore, it can help people understand butterfly ecology and promote the protection of natural environments.

1. Introduction

Butterflies and moths belong to the order Lepidoptera, class Insecta and have been on earth for more than 200 million years. Like beetles, bees and ants, they undergo complete metamorphosis [1]. Since butterflies are found commonly in the wild, they are excellent teaching materials for natural science education. Observation of insects' life cycle is an important part of life education. An insect's life cycle includes the egg, larva, pupa, imago, and finally producing offspring before the end of its life journey [2]. Through the observation, we can see how the circle of life continues to gain numerous inspirations. In the ecosystem, butterflies pollinate flowers as they gather nectar, which helps plants to reproduce. They are also indispensable in the food chain of ecosystems in that larvae feed on plants while butterflies serve as food for predators. Butterflies are beautiful insects with light and graceful bodies, and their dazzling colors and elegant dances instill vigor and vitality into the natural world. Large numbers of butterflies can always attract droves of visitors and are thereby of great value to tourism.

Normally, butterflies have a life cycle from 2 or 3 months to half year, and imagos have an even shorter lifespan. For example, *Pieris Rapae* can only live for 5 to 6 days. Butterfly eggs and larvae can usually be found on their host plants. Larvae feed on leaves of host plants and shed skin several times before turning into pupae. Mature larvae will find secretive places, safe from predators such as birds and lizards, to turn into pupae. Normally, imagos emerge from pupae and develop wings after a period of 5 to 10 days. Butterflies absorb nectar from all kinds of plant with mouthparts and help distribute pollen at the same time. Breeding and observing the growth of butterflies is a very important activity in nature science education. We can collect butterfly eggs or larvae to observe their life cycles, and use newly emerged butterflies to make specimens.

Suitable natural environments are vital to the survival of butterflies. Because many schools cannot provide appropriate environments for butterflies as they are situated in city areas, only few butterfly species can thrive on campus. For the purpose of education and recreation, insect museums or artificial butterfly gardens are widely set up in many countries, which exhibit real butterflies and specimens, provide multi-media information, and offer resources for related researches. A butterfly museum must grow host plants for eggs and larvae as well as nectar plants for imagos. Besides, it requires careful control of temperature and humidity to create a suitable environment for butterflies. Nevertheless, it is still very hard to maintain the diversity and populations, and is even harder when the sources for collection become scarcer. To avoid the shortage of butterflies in the museum, replenishing the butterfly population through breeding is a feasible approach.

Recently, virtual reality technology has been widely applied in science, engineering, education, entertainment, national defense [3], because a virtual and close-to-real environment can avoid danger and reduce the cost in real world while satisfying most of the requirements [4]. Since virtual reality is very suitable for applications in science education [5], we can use it to develop virtual websites for the purpose of course learning [6,7]. As a matter of fact, if we can develop a virtual butterfly museum on the website by incorporating real situation into learning activities, we can solve the above problems and achieve the goal of natural science education at the same time. In this way, we don't have to capture butterflies for making specimens, and many rare species can also be seen in the virtual butterfly museum.

The advance in computer and network technologies facilitates the access of information, and learning through network has become an important and efficient way to obtain knowledge. In traditional teaching models, it's very difficult for a teacher to satisfy the need of most students. By using modern distance-learning systems, students can control their learning speeds according to individual ability and interest, and the learning activities can proceed at any time and from anywhere [8]. For most students, network learning is more independent and active, and it provides an open environment to the general public while satisfies the need of students with different levels and backgrounds [9]. Therefore, applying computer and network technologies to remedy the insufficiency in traditional teaching activities has become a new trend in school teaching.

This paper studies how to develop a virtual butterfly museum using virtual reality and network technologies, and the objective is to provide students and the general public with a network learning environment where they can visit and obtain the related knowledge. We use computer graphic techniques to create the 3D dynamic models of butterflies, of which the behavior and motion are simulated by the control of random state-transition mechanism [10]. In the design of virtual butterfly museum, we develop a green house with transparent hemispheric roof, surrounded by lush grass and tall trees with clear stream and white fence aside. We grow many kinds of host plants and nectar plants inside the green house to provide a suitable ecological environment for butterflies. The museum exhibits several species of butterflies, including *Pieridae*, *Papilionidae*, *Danaidae*, *Satyridae*, *Nymphalidae*, as well as insects often seen in Taiwan. When visitors enter the museum, they can see a lot of butterflies flying around beautiful flowers.

The design of virtual butterfly museum requires the participation of researchers in the fields of virtual reality and network technologies, butterfly ecology, and natural science education. With their cooperation, information on the website can be organized and applied efficiently in natural science education. To achieve this goal, butterfly ecologists have to decide the contents of exhibition in the virtual butterfly museum, and collect the related data, which are then analyzed, selected, and compiled into teaching materials. The natural science teachers have to decide the contents and forms of course materials for displaying on the website to satisfy the requirement of school teaching. Computer engineers and programmers are responsible for the design of better visual effects and user-friendly interfaces to provide easy access to the courseware. In the designing process, experts from the related fields collaborate, exchange ideas, and learn from one another to create a specialized virtual butterfly museum to meet the needs of education.

Unlike real butterfly museums, the construction of virtual butterfly museums is not restricted by topography or weather, and it is not necessary to catch or to breed butterflies, or even to kill them for making specimens. Besides, a lot of rare species can be created easily and therefore most of the problems against real butterfly museums can be solved easily. The application of virtual butterfly museum is not limited by time, space or the age of users, and it can save the efforts and costs of traveling and visiting a real butterfly museum. The stereo visual effects and interactive interfaces have converted pure media into immersion of real ecological environments. Therefore, it is a useful teaching aid for natural science education. The remaining of this paper is organized as following. Section 2 describes the construction of 3D butterfly model and the simulation of its flying motion. Section 3 shows the development of virtual butterfly museum and the species of butterflies displayed inside. Section 4 is the conclusion of this paper.

2. Constructing 3D Butterfly Model

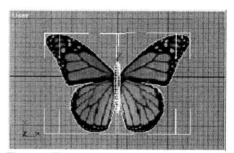

Figure 1. The scanned image as texture material

The major part for the design of virtual butterfly museum is the displaying of dynamic butterfly models, which can be achieved by computer graphic techniques [11]. We first obtain the scanned images of butterflies, and remove their background to produce the required texture materials. Then, we draw the outlines from different elevations to determine the shapes of butterfly models. We can select points along the outlines and use them as vertices to form the surface of butterfly models. The rendering software will determine the hidden surfaces according to the view position of observers [12], and calculate the illumination based on the light source and its incident angle [13]. Finally, we paste texture image (Figure 1) onto the surface [14], and the completed model can fly and change direction randomly in the 3D virtual scene under the control of program.

To simulate the motion of butterflies in virtual 3D space, we create the model of movement and rotation according to the behavior of butterflies. We use state transition mechanism to imitate the behavior of a butterfly, of which the time intervals for state transition are

1140

exponentially distributed. After the probabilities of state transition are determined, a Markov model is used to simulate the motion of a butterfly. By using stochastic models, even the same kind of butterflies will generate different paths in flying motion. For different kinds of butterflies, we can adjust the probabilities of state transition to imitate different behaviors.

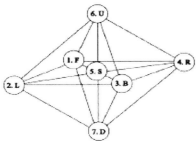

Figure 2. The state-transition diagram to simulate the movement in 3D space

Figure 2 shows the state-transition diagram of horizontal and vertical movement. We define seven states: 1.forwards (F), 2.left (L), 3.backwards (B), 4.right (R), 5.stop (S), 6.up (U), and 7.down (D), and every state can be transformed into any other states randomly. In Figure 3, we define the wing angles in flying motion by the following five states: 1.angle A, 2.angle B, 3.angle C, 4.angle D, and 5.angle E, but only neighboring states can be transformed mutually. The state-transition matrixes can be created after the probabilities for each pair of state transition are determined. The control program uses a random number generator to produce the direction and duration for the next movement. When a butterfly approaches nectar sources, it has a higher probability to enter the state "stop", and the control program will use a larger number as the time constant in the distribution function for flying motion. In that case, the flying motion will become relatively slow or even stop.

angle A   angle B   angle C   angle D   angle E
Figure3. The wing angles to simulate flying motion

The motion defined by the state transition diagram requires the movement and rotation related to the current state of butterfly model. Since the movement of butterfly model is equivalent to the movement of all polygons and points composing the model, we have to calculate the new positions for all points after movement such that the butterfly model can be redrawn. In 3D space, a point $P=[x \ y \ z]$ moves by the vector of $\vec{V}=[\lambda \ m \ n]$ to reach the new position $P=[x' \ y' \ z']$, which is computed as

$P'=[x' \ y' \ z']=P+\vec{V}=[x+\lambda \ y+m \ z+n]$. Since we consider the case of rigid movement, the new positions for the remaining points of the butterfly model can also be computed by the addition of vector $\vec{V}$.

The rotation of butterfly model requires the rotation of all polygons and points composing the model, so we must calculate the new positions of all points after rotation and then the butterfly model can be redrawn. In 3D space, a point $P=[x \ y \ z]$ rotates about the X-axis for a degree of θ, and the new position $P'=[x' \ y' \ z']$ is computed by the equation $P'=[x \ y\cos\theta-z\sin\theta \ y\sin\theta+z\cos\theta]$. Similarly, we can also rotate the butterfly model about the Y-axis or Z-axis, and their transformation equations are $P'=[x\cos\theta+z\sin\theta \ y \ -x\sin\theta+z\cos\theta]$ and $P'=[x\cos\theta-y\sin\theta \ x\cos\theta+y\sin\theta \ z]$, respectively.

Because the rotation of butterfly model requires the rotation of all points composing the model, we have to perform the above transformations for every point. Then, we map the model onto the visual plane and redraw the projected polygons by pasting texture. We put the completed butterfly model and the decorative objects such as flowers and host plants into the virtual butterfly museum. Besides, we must add the setting of collision detection to prevent the butterflies from penetrating the green house and flying away.

3. Developing Virtual Butterfly Museum

Figure 4. The development of virtual butterfly museum

Virtual butterfly museum is a network-learning system developed by virtual reality and network technologies. We first create 3D dynamic butterfly models using computer graphic techniques, and their flying motions are simulated by the control of state-transition mechanism. The virtual scene of butterfly museum is designed as a green house with transparent hemispheric roof (Figure 4), surrounded by lush grass and tall trees with clear stream and white fence aside. In the green house, we grow many kinds of host plants and nectar plants to provide a suitable ecological environment for butterflies. The design of flowers, trees and other insects in the virtual scene is similar to that of butterflies. We obtain the images of these objects, and then use computer graphic techniques to construction their 3D models. For the insects such as bees and beetles, we also need to simulate their motion by state-transition mechanism. The museum exhibits several species of butterflies (Figure 5), including *Pieridae*, *Papilionidae*, *Danaidae*, *Satyridae*, *Nymphalidae*, as described in the following:

Pieridae   *Papilionidae*   *Danaidae*   *Satyridae*   *Nymphalidae*

Figure 5. Species exhibited in virtual butterfly museum

- *Pieridae*

This family is characterized by colorful species of bright yellow and white. Some have markings of bright red, orange, peach and green. There are approximately 1,000 *Pieridae* species in the world, among which 33 are unique to Taiwan. Some species are known for group migration. For example, *Colias Croceus* crosses the English Channel each year from Europe to England, and a number of group migrations of *Catopsilia Pomona* have been recorded in Asia. The host plants of *Pieridae* are mostly from the families *Leguminosae* and *Cruciferae*. However, *Eurema Hecabe* has been observed in recent years to consume *Breynia Officinalis Hemsi* of the *Euphorbiaceae* family.

- *Papilionidae*

This family is characterized by a wide variety of attractive species. Generally speaking, they are large in size and bright in color. They have triangular forewings, and hind wings that have waved margins, often with protuberances. The wings have markings in red, yellow, blue, green or white, often with a brilliant metallic shine. Black butterflies often have markings of blue, green or red. There are more than 660 known *Papilionidae* species in the world, among which 32 species can be found in Taiwan. Most South American species are black with bright-colored markings. Asian, Indian and Australian species are mostly *Graphium Sarpedon Connectens*, *Papilio Paris Hermosanus* and *Troides Aeacus*. *Papilionidae* larvae feed on plants belonging to the families *Aristolochia*, *Lauraceae* and *Rutaceae*.

- *Danaidae*

Species of this family are found only in tropical areas, mostly in India and Australia. *Danaus Plexippus*, the most renowned member of the family, migrates from North America each year to spend the winter in Mexico. Liu-Kuei, situated in southern Taiwan, is famous for the *Euploea Tulliolus* that spend the winter there. They fly and glide slowly along the forests. Many species of this family are poisonous because of the plants consumed at their larva stage. As a result, even birds that prey on butterflies stay away from them. The male *Euploea Tulliolus* has a hidden scented hair pencil at the rear of its abdomen, which protrudes and contracts during flight to court females. *Danaidae* larvae feed on poisonous grass of the family *Asclepiadaceae*, and they have bright and warning colors of yellow and black.

- *Satyridae*

This family is found all over the world. The majority of the species have eye-shaped markings. This family is characterized by at least one forewing vein, enlarged at the base. Normally, *Satyridae* species prefer dim places and fly under bushes in an undulatory manner. Unlike the common belief that butterflies prefer nectar, members of this family favor rotten fruits, even animal droppings. They are most active in dim light. *Satyridae* larvae mainly feed on host plants from the families *Gramineae* and *Cyperaceae*, and sometimes even ferns.

- *Nymphalidae*

This family is characterized by its excellent flying capacities and likings for sunshine. Imagoes prefer animal body fluids, sap, and rotten fruits to nectar. Although species of this family can be found all over the world, they are mostly in tropical areas where a variety of beautiful flowers flourish, such as *Agrias* in South America. This family also thrives in Asia, for example, *Polyura Eudamippus*, *Kallima Inachis*, and *Euthalia Irrubescens*. *Nymphalidae* larvae feed on *dicotyledonous* plants and some of them have interesting feeding habits.

To enhance the understanding of butterfly's life cycle, we have designed the function of breeding box in our virtual butterfly museum Visitors can obtain their own breeding boxes to observe the growing process of butterflies. They have to register for an account and then start by selecting desired species and reading related information on the website to become familiar with the host plants. They can observe the life cycle of butterflies from the egg, larva and pupa to imago through network. The breeding box is designed with video streams to record the life cycle of butterflies. Thus, the system can determine the growing stage according to the time when the box is opened, and play the corresponding video streams for observation. For instance, users might discover that the larvae have emerged from eggs a few days later and started to feed on leaves. They can write down their observations to realize the changes that take place in each stage.

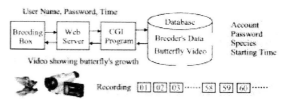

Figure 6. The design of on-line breeding box

We record the life cycle of butterflies by fixed time intervals, e.g. one minute per day, to save the disk space and the time for downloading. For the stages of egg and pupa, we use static images instead of video data to save more disk space since the object is not in motion. The compressed format (MPEG) of video files is used and set to auto-playback mode to reduce the amount of data (less than 500 KB) in each breeding box. In that case, it takes no more than 10 seconds to download the data under a common network environment (e.g., ADSL 512K/64K bps). The total amount of data, including texts, images, and video streams, for each butterfly species is about 10 MB. However, the critical section such as emerging from pupa to become imago is completely recorded. Besides, users are notified in advance by e-mail so that they can open the breeding box just in time to see the whole process to take place. By adding the function of breeding box, we wish to increase the interest of visitors and enhance their understanding of butterfly's life cycle and host plants. We have also added network resources and discussion areas related to the topics of ecological and environmental protection, hoping to provide teachers with the best assistance in natural science education.

4. Conclusions

The development of Internet virtual butterfly museum includes the design of dynamic butterfly models, virtual scenes of butterfly museum, online breeding box, and the virtual website. Also, the functions of active exploration and interactive learning can be enhanced by the addition of network resources and discussion groups related to the topics of ecological and environmental protection. People can learn about many species of butterflies and exchange their ideas by forming discussion groups on the website. They can also raise butterflies in breeding box to acquire more knowledge about their life cycles and host plants. The breeding process is interesting, which incorporates real situation into learning activities, and is a natural way of learning at minimum costs. Therefore, we encourage researchers in the related fields to work together for developing more network resources.

The virtual butterfly museum serves both educational and recreational functions. It can raise the interest and learning effects of students since the way of its design is very close to a real ecological environment. Besides, it is a recreational website for the general public where people can visit to spend their leisure time while obtaining the related knowledge. Constructing and maintaining a real butterfly museum costs a lot of money and manpower, and we must travel to the museum and purchase tickets in order to visit it. On the other hand, a virtual butterfly museum is developed by virtual reality and network technologies, so people can visit it through network to see different species of butterflies flying around beautiful flowers, and they can learn more about their life cycles and host plants through breeding activities.

The application of virtual butterfly museum is not limited by time or space, and visitors can save the time and cost of traveling to real butterfly museums. Besides, it provides an alternative learning environment, which serves educational purpose via network, offers new style of learning with computer technology, and increases interest and efficiency with virtual reality technology. Students can visit it through network at any time and from anywhere, and control the speeds of learning according to their interest and abilities It is highly interactive, providing 3D visual effects, and allowing for distance learning, and thus can serve as a useful teaching aid in natural science education. Therefore, it can help us understand butterfly species and promote the protection of their ecological environments.

Acknowledgement

The author wishes to thank for the financial support of the National Science Council of the Republic of China under the contract number NSC 91-2520-S-134-004.

References

[1] Wang, S. Y. (1987) Introduction to Butterflies, Taipei: *Taiwan Provincial Museum.*

[2] Lee, C. Y. and Wang, S. Y. (1996) The Observation and Breeding of Butterflies, Taipei: *Taiwan Provincial Museum.*

[3] Earnshaw, R. A., Vince, J. A. and Jones, H. (1995) Virtual Reality Applications San Diego, *Academic Press.*

[4] Burdea, G. and Goiffet, P. (1994) Virtual Reality Technology, New York, *John Wiley & Sons.*

[5] Tarng, W. (1998) "The Development of Internet Virtual Classroom for Application in Elementary Schools", *Distance Education, Taiwan,* 5, 5-18.

[6] Tarng, W. (2000) "Internet Virtual Astronomical Museum", *Information and Education, Taiwan,* 79, 63-77.

[7] Tarng, W. (2001) "Internet Virtual Marine Ecological Museum", *Instructional Technology and Media, Taiwan,* 57, 58-68.

[8] Porter, Lynnette R. (1997) Creating the Virtual Classroom - Distance Learning with the Internet, New York, *John Wiley & Sons.*

[9] Muhlhauser, M. (1992) "Hypermedia and Navigation as a Basis for Authoring Learning Environments". *Journal of Educational Multimedia and Hypermedia,* 1(3), 287-294.

[10] Cinlar, Erhan (1975) Introduction to Stochastic Processes, Englewood Cliffs: *Prentice-Hall.*

[11] Rogers, D. F. and Adams, J. A. (1985) Mathematical Elements for Computer Graphics, *Mc Graw Hill.*

[12] Weiler, K. and Atherton, P. (1977) "Hidden Surface Removal Using Polygon Area Sorting", *Computer Graphics*, 11, 214-222.

[13] Warn, D. R. (1983) "Lighting Controls for Synthetic Images", *Computer Graphics,* 17, 13-21.

[14] Blinn, James F. and Newell, Martin, E. (1976) "Texture and Reflection in Computer Generated Images", *CACM,* 19, 542-547.

Jump-starting Learning Communities in the Philippines Using Available Online Tools: Educational Outcomes and Student Feedback

Mariano Ramirez Jr, PhD
The University of New South Wales

Abstract

This paper describes the pioneering trials in using widely available and accessible online tools to build a course-based learning community in a higher education institution in the Philippines. A quasi-experiment was devised using two intact groups to determine cognitive learning outcomes for an online course on Ecological Product Design, and focus group discussions and survey questionnaires gathered student feedback on their online experiences. The study found that the achievement scores of the online and face-to-face students during both the pre-test and post-test examinations were not significantly different. In general, the online participants appreciated the convenience, flexibility, appropriate pace, and increased freedom and self-responsibility that the "new way to learn" afforded in their off-campus learning communities. In the end, this project was able to demonstrate that the online tools of information technology can be ingenuously harnessed to allow peers to study and work together in spite of separation and relatively simple resources.

Background

In recent years, Filipino students found themselves facing increased difficulty in safely accessing the physical campuses of their schools, resulting in a significant loss in contact time with their teachers and in a greatly diminished lesson coverage and learning experience. Parents naturally feel uneasy about letting their children leave home for school, in the light of such precarious situations as flooded streets, political protest rallies, bomb explosions, incidents of rape and kidnapping, as well as the bumper-to-bumper traffic has become a daily routine for commuters in Metro Manila.

Lesson delivery via information and communication technologies is one way to mitigate the impacts of the above impediments to safe educational access, as it allows the learning experience to continue in the security of each other's domiciles. Various evaluative studies [6,8] draw attention to the possibility of "no significant difference" in student achievements between the face-to-face tradition and Internet-based distance learning models.

Nevertheless, some authorities maintain that online education will never be equal to conventional classroom instruction [4], and one critic has branded virtual universities as "digital diploma mills" [3].

The dozens of web-based educational delivery applications commercially available now in the technologically advanced economies are generally unaffordable and incompatible with the somewhat simpler needs of learning communities in the Philippines. A different strategy must obviously be formulated for realistically harnessing the power of the Internet for improving educational access in a developing country.

Trial online modules for a course in Ecological Product Design (EcoDesign) were developed at the De La Salle University College of Saint Benilde (CSB) in Manila in 1998 by the author of this paper.

In 1999, CSB became the first Philippine institution to acquire the WebCT™ course management software for supplementing traditional classes with programmed lessons on the Internet. Despite the software's many promises, it fell short of many teachers' expectations, as the early version that the College acquired was still largely in its developmental stages. Various programming imperfections and errors were perceptibly impeding the smooth flow of the conduct of the trial lessons, and a significant amount of time was spent by teachers, students and network administrators trying to resolve software-related lesson delivery and interaction issues. The WebCT platform was regarded by many as not being "transparent", as it was expected to be working silently behind the scenes and allowing the learning experience to take place without the participants being bothered by it. Moreover, the College network was disappointingly slow and home-based users couldn't effectively connect to it without suffering frequent disconnection events. CSB's initially limited WebCT licenses also meant that not everybody in the College community would have access to this online experience.

The Study

A quasi-experimental research was devised to examine the hypothesis that instruction in an online learning community can result in cognitive and affective outcomes comparable to that in a face-to-face classroom.

Two intact classes of third-year Industrial Design students enrolled in an EcoDesign course were chosen to unknowingly participate in a trial examining the learning effects of Internet-based educational tools.

The EcoDesign course is a technology-intensive subject that focuses on the creation and patronization of products that promote ecological balance and a healthy living environment. The usual pedagogy in this course involves a mix of environmental science theories and application of sustainable strategies in industrial design. Teaching methods conventionally used are PowerPoint presentations, blackboard lectures, paper-based quizzes, group brainstorming exercises, studio conceptualisation leading to the formulation of ecological product solutions, and personal consultations with the teacher in class.

The research was conducted over a period of seven weeks. In one block (the control group) students attended classes on-campus with the teacher physically present. In the other (experimental) block, students formed off-campus learning communities and "met" and interacted with their teacher and classmates via online tools.

Both blocks were quizzed for prior knowledge before the start of the experiment: the two groups did not differ significantly in mean pre-test scores [Table 2]. At the end of the course, both blocks took the same paper-based final examination on-campus. This test was the determinant for assessing the equivalence of learning under the two educational delivery systems.

Instructional Innovation Methodology

Participants in the online learning experiment were given three weeks to secure Internet access and to obtain an email account. During this preparatory period students were also expected to practice themselves with such online technologies as chatrooms and web browsing. Most have claimed prior competence with these Internet-based tools. Those who lacked the experience were encouraged to seek tutelage from their peers.

The following pedagogical strategies and activities were used on the online learning communities.

CD-ROM Lectures. The teacher's PowerPoint presentations were saved on compact discs and distributed to the off-campus students. As the lectures included a fair amount of video clips and animations – plus a demo version of the EcoDesign analysis software EcoScan (from www.pre.nl) and other utilities – the CD-ROM was considered far more cost effective than requiring the students to download or view the material while connected to the Internet.

Quizzes. At a designated time every week the teacher "handed out" quizzes in Excel format to the online students via email, and expected the answers back in 30 minutes. The Excel software compares every response with the answer key using a logical function, returning a

point for every correct match. Students receive emailed feedback on their scores about half an hour after the quiz receiving time closes, a feature which was much appreciated.

Discussions. Before the quizzes were emailed out, all students were expected to log into the global chatroom where the teacher opens up a live forum about the day's topic which was on the CD-ROM. Other issues about online class tasks are also raised during the live chat.

Group Brainstorming. The online students were divided into clusters of threes; these clusters became mini learning communities with their own chatrooms. Under time pressure, students attempted to accomplish the task of the hour by actively brainstorming within their chatrooms, on such topics as reuse possibilities for glass, paper or plastic waste. The teacher was considered a "guest" in every group's chatroom and had free access to each room, but students were not allowed to enter and eavesdrop into others' chatrooms. The teacher routinely checked on each group's progress in the chatroom and ensured that discussions are kept on track. At the end of every timed session, students were required to submit a transcript of the chat. The free public domain software mIRC (from www.mirc.com) was used for chatting.

Design Projects. Students submitted concepts and final solutions to individual design projects via email. Most did their technical drawings and pictorial renderings using CAD (computer-aided design) software such as AutoCAD and 3D Studio Max, and these students found that submitting CAD files online saved them money which would have gone to paying a large-format color printing service.

Consultations. Student inquiries about the tasks were answered by the teacher via email and broadcasted to all participants, to avoid having to answer the same question repetitively. Students who were rather shy in asking questions found such email broadcasting useful. Replies to project-specific inquiries were emailed to the relevant students only.

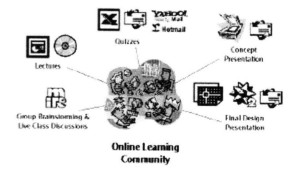

Figure 1. Structure of the Online Classroom using Available Online Tools

Cognitive Learning Results

The cognitive effects from learning EcoDesign in an online community were quantitatively measured from pre-test and post-test score differentials.

Mean post-test comparison of the two groups show a marginal arithmetic difference in favour of the online class [Table 1]. Mann-Whitney U calculations show that this is not statistically significant, and one can accept equivalence of the two groups in terms of test achievements [Table 2]. This similarity in examination outcomes indicates that students can learn the same amount in the EcoDesign course whether they attend classes on-campus or online.

F2F Student	F2F Pre-test Score	F2F Post-test Score	F2F Post-test less Pre-test	OL Student	OL Pre-test Score	OL Post-test Score	OL Post-test less Pre-test
Mean	38.7	69.8	31.1	Mean	38.9	70.5	31.6
SD	10.1	14.9		SD	6.2	15.8	
Min	13.4	45.8	3.5	Min	25.4	37.4	-4.4
Max	51.7	96.5	60.1	Max	47.7	98.9	51.3
Range	38.3	50.6	56.6	Range	22.2	61.5	55.7

Table 1. Summary of Pre-Test and Post-test Results of Face-to-Face (F2F) and Online (OL) Classes

Array 1: F2F Array 2: OL	Pre-test Scores	Post-test Scores
Value of the U statistic	223	218.5
Expectation	234	234
Variance	1754.753	1752.774
Normalized statistic used for the Wilcoxon-Mann-Whitney test	-0.26259	-0.37023
Critical value under normality assumption with a 0.05 significance level	-1.9600	-1.9600
p-value corresponding to the U value under normality assumption	0.7929	0.7112
Conclusion: With a confidence range of 95%,	Accept arrays 1 & 2 as identical	Accept arrays 1 & 2 as identical

Table 2. Summary of XLSTAT comparisons of the pretest and posttest scores, using 2-tailed Mann-Whitney U Test $\alpha=0.05$

Participant Feedback: Appreciation and Discontent

The behavioural and emotional effects of participating in the online learning community were gathered using two instruments: a Likert-style questionnaire which produced quantitative indicators of the opinions; and qualitative discussions in focus groups to elucidate on the numerical results. Responses to the 57-item attitudinal questionnaire were interpreted using the following scale: 1.00 to 1.49 strong disagreement; 1.50 to 2.49 disagreement; 2.50 to 3.49 neutral; 3.50 to 4.49 agreement; and 4.50 to 5.00 strong agreement.

The act of learning via Internet tools was generally looked upon in a positive way. Many considered the networked learning community a "success", and a number expressed willingness to continue learning the online way for certain subjects where the method proves practical. In general, the students appreciated the convenience, flexibility, and appropriate pace that the "new way to learn" afforded in the networked learning communities. Several welcomed the innovative strategy as a challenging opportunity for themselves, and as a break from the "teacher talks, students listen" pedagogical tradition that they have been subjected to since grade school. Participants were amused that they can communicate and collaborate on group projects even without their physical togetherness (mean=4.0, sd=0.98).

Many felt liberated from the controls implicit in the arbitrary power of the face-to-face teacher. Suddenly they were free from the usual rules of the physical classroom, and they appreciated the absence of such repressions as no talking, no eating, no walking around, no going out, etc. They found ease of movement and felt unconfined, contrary to the traditional classroom settings.

They took pleasure in experiencing the lessons in the comfort of their own homes, without having to travel and being stressed by traffic congestion. They did not have to be up so early to bathe or dress up or to take a rushed breakfast in preparation for school; they can even wake up late or just in time for the online session. Another stress-removing factor was the fact that students can learn the materials at their own pace, without having to keep up with fast lectures or fast-learning classmates.

Posting questions or messages to the teacher via the email list made students feel more at ease than questioning face to face. This is probably explained by the Filipino student's trait of deference for their mentors while inside the classroom. It is not customary for Filipino teachers and pupils to carry on conversation or contact outside of class hours. Students agreed that email offered them an informal off-campus, off-classroom contact with their teacher and peers, thereby opening more channels for communication (mean=3.6, sd=1.02).

Many valued the chance that online learning allows them to discover on their own, instead of having a teacher instructing them step by step (mean=3.5, sd=0.95). Putting them in charge of their own learning has pushed them towards developing discipline in their study habits, and instilled in them a greater sense of responsibility, independence from the instructor, and interdependence with their peers in their learning communities.

Students appreciated the fact that the chatroom discussions can be recorded so that they did not have to take down notes. Those who missed a particular session can review the saved transcript to get a feel of what transpired during their absence. Knowing that their chat transcripts would be submitted also kept the discussions on track: some admitted that without these transcripts they would probably have just talked about other things.

While participants appreciated the innovative features of the online community, they expressed various frustrations and disinclinations about their experience. Most dissatisfaction sprang from network problems, centring on difficulties with initiating connections with Internet service providers, with reconnection after disengagement, and with logging into the chatrooms. Whenever participants get disconnected from the network, they miss part of the discussion.

A good number expressed feelings that the online method seemed to be "an expensive way to learn", because they had to pay for Internet time, although they failed to consider the cost of the time, effort and money saved by not travelling to campus.

Remarks about sluggish links to the participants' ISP servers were abundant, and emails sometimes took more time than necessary to send and receive. On several instances, the Hotmail website (which many used as for their web-based email address) wasn't functional, so students could neither check nor send mails.

Hassles surfaced with the use of chat when the whole class overcrowded the global chatroom: it was chaotic, with too many people trying to ask questions all at once. There was a deluge of nonsensical and repetitive postings.

Students who were used to having a classmate physically beside them argued that the virtual learning community could curtail the close relationships and bonding between students. Many however reasoned that the online methods actually allowed them to have a discussion with peers whom they normally do not converse with in the physical classroom.

Participants valued the fact that email messaging reduced the urgency of responding, but disliked it when message recipients delayed their responses markedly. Problems with email bordered on non-receipt by the other party of email attachments such as quizzes and sketches, either due to Internet server inefficiency, or to file size limitations imposed by the email server, resulting in messages bouncing back to the sender.

Students detested the time spent in having to image-scan concept drawings, then emailing the scanned file to the teacher or group mates, waiting for the other party to successfully retrieve the message, and waiting for the response, which could take some time if the other party does not act on the inquiry with immediacy. (A whiteboard feature via Microsoft Netmeeting and a digitising tablet could have been used to combat this inconvenience.) They tended to compare the graphics incapability and text-based limitations of the online tools to the straightforward manner in the traditional classroom in which they could sketch on a pad, show their teacher or group mates, and instantaneously receive comments. Many found it limiting to explain their visual concepts with words. Those who did not have scanning equipment also had to pay for bureau services.

Participants unanimously admitted that there is a great temptation to cheat in the online quizzes because of the absence of a proctor. A sizeable number confessed that they "looked back" at the lesson materials while they took the online quizzes.

Current technologies for holding automated examinations are only able to engage the learner with fixed-response questions. While the advantages of speed in assessing correctness and the complete absence of checker subjectivity are obvious, students' higher-order thinking capacities could be little challenged by such question types.

Participants strongly recommended that the online learning community method be fully or partially replicated in some of their other courses within the Industrial Design curriculum. It appears that the medium renders itself most practicable in such "general education" courses as Communication Skills, Psychology, History, and Sociology. Participants had widespread agreement that subjects like these do not necessitate a high degree of personal student-teacher contact, and can be easily learned off-campus using good self-instructional materials, online consultation with the teacher, self-tests, and some online collaboration activities with other students whenever applicable.

Many creative subjects which have a large lecture component for the presentation of theories, practical examples and animated demonstrations – such as Furniture, Packaging, and Ergonomics – can benefit considerably from supplementation with multimedia-integrative lessons for off-campus delivery. However, the idea creation components of these courses, which are visually demanding, should probably still be done via face-to-face sessions.

It is apparent that the application of the Internet in education will intensify in the near future. Computers will also continue to increase in power while dropping in cost and escalating in speed and reliability [1], and the price tag for sending information will keep plummeting, to the point where communication charges will be too cheap to meter [7]. Indeed these are very good signals for the growth of online learning communities as the logical next step towards arriving at an effective alternative pedagogy for the very near future.

Conclusions

The study allows us to reach the following generalization with confidence: that instruction via an online learning community can result in educational outcomes comparable to that of face-to-face teaching in a physical classroom. Furthermore:

Conclusion 1: Cognitive learning outcomes among online and face-to-face learning communities are statistically very similar. In some instances students using Internet tools were able to post gains slightly larger than the face-to-face students, but in general the pre-test and post-test results could not show appreciable differences in learning achievements. The study results imply that students in online communities have the potential of learning just as well and attaining the same academic levels as their on-campus counterparts.

Conclusion 2: Students derive about the same amount of satisfaction in the virtual learning community as they do in the traditional classroom. The qualitative portion of the study point to the insight that student satisfaction can be reasonably derived from online means of teaching EcoDesign. While some online students might not have liked certain aspects of teaching design subjects via electronic means as much as they have liked it done face-to-face, the experiment participants nevertheless echoed their positive attitude towards the other benefits that the new learning mode offers. Travel time economy, personal security, and "all the comforts of home" are consistently the best-rated bonuses of the networked learning community. By being selective with the courses where Internet tools are highly appropriate, student satisfaction with their educational experience is more likely to be achieved.

Conclusion 3: The absence of face-to-face contact does not necessarily result in a substantially inferior learning. The study demonstrates that achievement in a learning community can be independent of the location or setting where the teaching takes place. Collaborating students appeared to perform equally well whether their teacher was physically in front of them or was only manifesting his/her presence in a virtual sense.

The absent attributes of the traditional teaching method were clearly yearned for in the virtual class: eye contact, speech intonation and modulation, verbal humour, on-the-spot sketches and diagrams, and verbal interaction with no time delay.

It is imperative to assert that academics need to recognize the difference that the online experience has

with the face-to-face classroom, and given the right stimulus it is possible for networked learners to outperform their traditional counterparts, or at least be as good in spite of the transactional distance and asynchronicity of interactions.

The conclusions support the familiar philosophy that educational media and educational technologies are mere vehicles for delivering instruction, and that they have no intrinsic effect on the amount of learning gained. The messages contained in the educational media, the overall instructional designs, and the interactions with peers are the crucial elements for learning effectiveness, not the media by themselves. This supports Pogrow's [5] assertion that "the sophistication of the learning produced by technology depends on the sophistication of the conversation surrounding its use, not the sophistication of the technology."

Lastly, this study of online learning communities upholds the theory by Moore & Kearsley [2] that "what makes any course good or poor is a consequence of how well it is designed, delivered and conducted, not whether the students are face-to-face or at a distance".

Author Information

Mariano Ramirez Jr, PhD, was former Academic Chair for Industrial Design at the De La Salle University College of Saint Benilde in Manila, Philippines, and is now a lecturer at the University of New South Wales in Sydney, Australia.

References

1. Bourne, J.R. (1998). "Net learning: strategies for on campus and off campus network enabled learning" in Journal of Asynchronous Learning Networks Sep 98.
2. Moore, M. and Kearsley, G. (1996). Distance Education: A Systems View. Belmont: Wadsworth.
3. Noble, D.F. (1997). "Digital diploma mills: The automation of higher education" in First Monday Peer Reviewed Journal on the Internet Vol 3 No 1
4. Phipps, R., & Merisotis, J. (2000). Quality on the line: benchmarks for success in Internet-based distance education. Washington DC: Institute for Higher Education Policy
5. Pogrow, S. (1997). "Using technology to combine process and content" in Costa A & Liebmann R (eds). Supporting the spirit of learning: when process is content. Thousand Oaks CA: Corwin Press.
6. Russell, T. (2000). The No Significant Difference Phenomenon 5ed. Chapel Hill NC: North Carolina State University Office of Instructional Telecommunications.
7. Thornburg, D.D. (1997). 2020 Visions for the Future of Education. Washington DC: Congressional Institute for the Future.
8. Wegner, S.B., Holloway, K.C., & Garton, E.M. (1999). "The effects of Internet-based instruction on student learning" in Journal of Asynchronous Learning Networks Nov 99.

Mobile Learning: Cell Phones and PDAs for Education

Chris Houser, Patricia Thornton, David Kluge *Kinjo Gakuin University, Japan*

Abstract

We introduce m-learning – learning with mobile devices, such as cell phones and pocket computers. We review the hardware and research on m-learning, and discuss our future work with mobile foreign-language study.

1: Introduction

Web-based learning, embraced by many educators, extends study beyond physical classrooms. M-learning - learning with mobile devices - promises continued extension towards "anywhere, anytime" learning. This paper introduces m-learning, summarizing the limits of current mobile hardware, examining its use in education around the world, and proposing a roadmap for creating and evaluating materials for m-learning foreign languages.

2: Background: Mobile Devices

This section analyzes two mobile devices: PDAs and cell phones.

PDAs (Personal Digital Assistants) are pocket-sized computers. PDAs are extensible, with optional hardware (e.g., keyboards and wireless networks) and software (e.g., word processors, databases, bilingual dictionaries, flash-cards). PDAs cost US$100-500, but most programs are free, so running costs are zero.

Cell phones use the wireless Internet to exchange voice messages, email, and small web pages, anywhere and anytime. While they lack the flexibility of PDAs, cell phones compensate using the web: Students study foreign-language vocabulary using a PDA's custom flash-card program or hangman game; Students study using a cell phone's similar website. Cell phones are initially cheaper than PDAs: Japanese carriers subsidize hardware by bundling expensive service plans, so cell phones enjoy low initial cost (often zero), but high running costs (averaging US$700/year; the wireless web costs US$6-$70/hour). Since most students already carry phones, most classes are already equipped.

Mobile devices perform many of the functions of desktop computers, with the advantages of simplicity (being easier to learn and use) and improved **access** (being usable anywhere, anytime). But three limitations prevent mobile devices from replacing desktop PCs: bandwidth, running costs, and text input speed. The low **bandwidth** (data transfer rate) of most cell phones and wireless PDA modems prohibits quality video and sound (as needed for studying foreign-language pronunciation). A few new phones can stream media, but **cost** US$3-15/minute. Further, mobile **text input speed** is slow (10 words per minute on cell phones, 15-

25 on PDAs; cf. 60 on desktop PCs). So m-learners need to limit their media to reading and multiple-choice questions.

3: Previous Work: Review of Educational Projects using Mobile Devices

Projects using mobile devices in various learning environments have begun to appear. We found nine such projects in Europe, Asia, North America and South America. These projects were set in universities, elementary schools, corporate training programs, and distance learning programs. The projects experimented with a wide range of educational activities on PDAs and cell phones: foreign-language vocabulary lessons via cell phone email; collaborative simulations using the infrared network ('beaming') capabilities of PDAs; 'just-in-time' administration (scheduling, study prompts, and reminders) via cell phones; business-oriented problem-based learning modules on PDAs; and recorded foreign-language listening materials accessed on cell phones. These projects all use mobile devices as one part of a *blended* educational program that may combine face-to-face, Web, and mobile components. They show that the unique combination of features in mobile devices - **portability, connectivity, and low cost** - makes them valuable educational tools.

Three projects are particularly notable. One, *Learning on the Move* [1], researches the educational use of mobile phone email at Japanese universities, where spaced (repeated, interval) practice of foreign language vocabulary is difficult to facilitate, since classes meet only once a week. But most Japanese university students constantly carry cell phones. This project emailed short, daily lessons to students, providing spaced practice of foreign-language vocabulary. The researchers observed few usability problems, and found cell-phone email produced learning superior to desktop email, mobile web, and paper.

Researchers in the United States have developed several educational programs for PDAs [2]. Designed for elementary schools, these programs allow educators to freely experiment with m-learning. These programs include the game-like quiz *Bubble Blasters,* the science simulation *Cooties,* and the concept map editor *PiCoMap.*

One of the earliest blended (Web + mobile phone) courses was offered for business training in Singapore. *eBusiness on the Move* [3] sent textual course content, quizzes, reminders, and human prompts to students' cell phones. Participants highly evaluated the convenience of mobile study, and appreciated the fine factoring of information enforced by the tiny size of their mobile phones' memory and screen, but were skeptical about the idea of offering an entire distance course using only mobile phones.

3: Future Work: Research Proposal

Our proposed research examines both cell phones and PDAs in a blended environment for studying English as a foreign language at a Japanese university. One focus is pedagogy: therefore, a major part of our research is developing, evaluating, and analysing language learning activities, and then composing activities into a curriculum. We use Brown's [4] framework to design and maintain language curricula, which advocates continuously evaluating needs, objectives, tests, materials, and teaching (see Figure 1). We focus on evaluation, teaching, and materials, including mobile hardware and software.

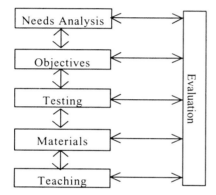

Figure 1. Systematic approach to designing and maintaining language curricula [4, p. 20, Fig. 1.2]

Brown describes teaching as comprising approaches, syllabuses, techniques, and activities. After analysing mobile hardware and software materials, we work bottom-up, first creating *activities* that are easily learned, easily used, and pedagogically appropriate. We combine them into *techniques* and *syllabi*, creating an *approach* for using mobile technology in language education.

Finally we *evaluate* the activities in Brown's three dimensions: process-product continuum, formative-summative dichotomy, and quantitative-qualitative continuum.

We brainstormed 31 activities for class administration (e.g., announcing homework assignments) and for study (e.g., emailing intermediate products of group work between members). (Although most of these activities could be used in any class, some apply only to the study of foreign-language speaking, listening, writing, and reading.) We analyze how well each of these activities exploit both the general concept of mobility, and specific mobile technologies such as infrared networks. In our future research, we will experiment with these activities in college classes, quantifying their advantages over non-mobile implementations. Our desired research outcomes include the following:

- a *taxonomy* of the relevant characteristics and educational uses of mobile technology
- a suite of classroom-tested mobile educational *software* and internet services
- a collection of technologically and pedagogically appropriate *activities*
- an *evaluation* of those activities
- a *curriculum* comprising well-evaluated activities
- a *method* or guideline for selecting or creating further m-learning activities.

4: Conclusion

Several studies have demonstrated the great promise of mobile learning. Conscious of the limitations of mobile hardware, we propose designing software for educational activities, and collecting these into a coherent method for m-learning. We feel that this research will help popularize and quantify the effects of m-learning.

References

[1] P. Thornton & C. Houser, "Learning on the Move: Foreign language vocabulary via SMS." *ED-Media 2001 Proceedings*, pp. 1846-1847. Norfolk, Virginia: Association for the Advancement of Computing in Education, 2001.

[2] E. Soloway, C. Norris, P. Blumenfeld, B. Fishman, J. Krajcik, & B. Marx. "Handheld devices are ready-at-hand." *Communications of the ACM,* Vol. 44, No. 6, pp. 15-20, 2001.

[3] G. Ring, "Case study: Combining Web and WAP to deliver e-learning." *Learning Circuits,* 2001. www.learningcircuits.org/2001/jun2001/ring.html

[4] J. D. Brown, *The elements of language curriculum: A systematic approach to program development.* Boston, MA: Newbury House, 1995.

The Development of a Method of Cyber Learning with Conceptual Models of Knowledge Construction

Jeong-rang Kim · Yong-ju Ki · Dai-Sung Ma

Gwangju National University of Education, Dept's of Computer Science Education

ABSTRACT

In this knowledge-based society, a person should be possessed of abilities to create new knowledge while selecting, acquiring, and processing knowledge and information in line with his or her own purpose and communicating this new knowledge to other people.

With the emergence of the world wide web, cyber learning, in the form of web-based instruction has been brought to the fore. The established way of cyber learning, however, is based on a system where learners should proceed with their study on their own, instead of relying on interaction between teachers and learners. The established way of cyber learning leaves much to be desired in terms of its application to a class, and is often bereft of a system capable of recreating knowledge as a result of study.

Accordingly, this study is designed to develop a cyber learning system using models with the concepts of knowledge construction. This system enabled students to cultivate their abilities to analyze materials and to improve their creativity. When applied to the teaching-learning process of social studies, the system was capable of being applied to a process from a stage of grasping problems, to a stage of learning completion. The system also enabled teachers and students to produce study results, and enabled students to recreate knowledge, in the form of homepages, from constructed learning resources, instead of producing only fragmental knowledge.

1. Introduction

The 21st Century needs the raising of creative human beings capable of diverse thinking. An education is now required to raise human beings with minds open to new experiences, with the creativity for continuously generating new ideas, and with a spirit of inquiry and cognitive curiosity. Web-based instruction is a new teaching and learning method that has evolved with the appearance of the world wide web[1]. One of the most influential instruction forms of this web-based instruction is cyber learning. This new form of learning has the aim of providing learners, more than teachers or educational institutions, with instruction, at more convenient times and spaces[2]. The recent cyber learning websites, however, have a tendency to exhibit one-directional study material while ignoring each individual's own learning inclinations[3]. These sites seem to be unable to serve the purpose of raising a creative human being, as they are used in fragments during a class and require the users to submit a report in the form of a file made with their application programs.

This thesis aims to extend students' creative learning abilities through developing a system capable of recreating knowledge. This system is to be applied to a class from its introduction stage to its arrangement stage, not in the form of a simple report with fragmentary study information, but in the form of a homepage and through applying a study unit prepared by reconstructing the curriculum to this cyber system.

2. Conceptual Model of Knowledge Construction

2.1 The concept of knowledge

Knowledge can be defined as verified truth. It is formed in the process of human cognitive activities under certain circumstances, and is thought to enhance added value through improving and developing a new working process, or carrying out an innovation to change the existing framework[4].

2.2 The process of knowledge construction

Nonaka(1995) defines knowledge construction as the

development of knowledge in both quantity and quality through an interaction and circulation process between tacit knowledge and explicit knowledge, and proposes that the process of knowledge construction is a spiral process. From this spiral process of knowledge construction are derived four patterns of knowledge transformation: socialization, externalization, internalization, and combination. The repetitive transformations between individual knowledge and organizational knowledge, through the constant circulation process of these four patterns, create added value[5]. The process of knowledge construction is advanced with both individual and collaborative activities. To construct the knowledge that is useful for both individuals and the society, the individual and collaborative activities should proceed like toothed-wheels in gear, and should produce the knowledge of the four patterns. The activities executed in the process of knowledge construction can thus be divided into individual knowledge construction(IKC) activities and collaborative knowledge construction(CKC) activities[6].

2.3 The conceptual model of knowledge construction

2.3.1 The Individual Knowledge Construction(IKC) function

In the process of individual knowledge construction, the knowledge that is expressed and materialized outward becomes assimilated with, and adjusts itself to, an individual and subjective knowledge structure through an individual's cognitive activities of recognition, interpretation, analysis and understanding[6].

- Notes: Taking notes, regardless of their form, of learners' own ideas or important information during the learning process functions as a rehearsal strategy that helps learners activate the process of handling short-term memories, and retaining them for a long time.
- Concept Map: A concept map shows and presents an individual's concepts in a diagram to help the individual form knowledge and form concepts, understanding the relations, structures and systems of concepts through individual cognitive activities.
- Goal Management: Goal management functions to help learners concretize the goals they wish to achieve at the beginning of their

learning processes, and presents them on the screen to remind each learner of these goals while their learning proceeds.
- Self-monitoring: Self-monitoring functions to build metacognitive learning strategies which control and manage learners' cognitive processes.
- Rumination: Rumination functions to help learners reflect on their own learning process and keep a record of this reflection.
- Learning Record Analysis: Through analyzing a learning record, learners can have an opportunity to look back on their learning procedures and strategies, and to get a wider view of and reflect on their learning process.

2.3.2 The Collaborative Knowledge Construction(CKC) function

In the process of the collaborative knowledge construction, individuals recognize the necessity of a common object of a group, and construct new knowledge through interaction between individuals for knowledge sharing[6].
- Monitoring: Monitoring provides learners with an opportunity to detect problems in the process of knowledge sharing and correct them.
- Learning Guidance: Learning guidance provides learners with guidance to correct the problems detected while monitoring a sharing process such as group constitution or collaborative learning.
- Collaboration History: Collaboration history is the most extensive database and includes every message exchanged through the communication channel, all the records of the learners' collaborative working processes, as well as interaction patterns.

3. Knowledge Construction System

3.1 The structural map of the knowledge construction system

The knowledge construction system is composed to help learners cope with preparatory work for the next class and as an introduction to learning activities on their own<Picture 1>. Learners construct knowledge using

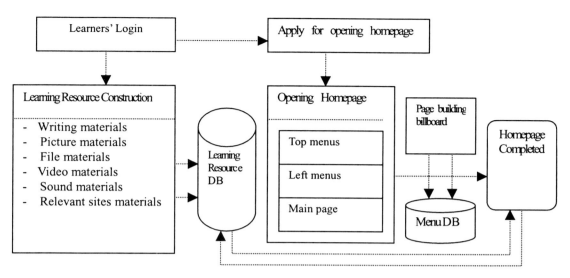

<Picture 1> The structural map of knowledge construction system

study materials that the teacher registered, "Q&A", "Conversation Room", or "Discussion Room". On the basis of the knowledge acquired in the process of knowledge construction individual or group reports and web reports in the form of homepages are prepared. These reports later have a role as supplementary materials for feed-back and achievement evaluation. Learners use study notes to put their study into shape and to solve questions that the teacher presents, so that the results of these activities can be recorded and used as reference materials for student counseling and achievement evaluation.

3.2 The composition of menus

To construct a cyber learning system using the knowledge construction model, so that it can carry a series of learning processes from the stage of understanding problems to the stage of arranging learning, menus need to be composed as shown in <Table #1>.

Menu	Description	Knowledge Construction Model
I Studied This Way	Keeps a record on the learning process.	Learning record analysis
Bulletin Board	The official announcement related to learning	Learning guidance

Preparatory Work	Registers preview homework before the class	Learning guidance/ Goal
Activity Introduction	Activities performed during the class	
Helpful Materials	Teacher's material	Learning guidance
Q & A	Questions coming up during the class	
E-mail	E-mailing between the teacher and learners, and between learners	Learning assistance
Conversation Room	Leads each learners' group to converse about their learning	
Discussion Room	Writes learner's opinion on a subject in the form of statement or in the form of Yes/No voting	
Homework Give-in	Learners upload the materials acquired from their learning.	Knowledge construction
Homepage	Learners apply to open a homepage and construct the screen	
Teacher's Material	Web materials for motivation involving and learning	Learning guidance

1153

	arrangement	
Reflection	Writes opinions about the class afterwards	Rumination
Evaluation	Saves results of evaluation	Self-monitoring
Presentation	Selects necessary materials from the uploaded study material	
Study Notes	Writes results of learning	Note

<Table 1> The composition of menus with the conceptual model of knowledge construction applied

3.3 The learning process map of the knowledge construction system

Learners log onto the site as students and examine the motivation-involving materials and the preparatory homework presented in "Helpful Materials" to decide what subject to study. After that, they open "Study Notes" to input the subject of study, and prepare to take notes. Learners should work on the study subject with guidance, presented by the teacher beforehand, and should build their own homepage. On the basis of each individual homepage, they eventually build a group homepage. Each group leader presents their group homepage to the class. The teacher and learners arrange their study content using the "Study Notes", on the basis of the presentation. After learning, learners check their achievement, working on evaluation questions, and write their opinions about the study. This process of leaning can be configured as in <Picture 2>.

4. Application of the system

4.1 The duration and the object of application

This system was applied to the teaching and learning process of social studies for 36 fourth-grade students in "S" elementary school, North District, Gwangju City, for a period of 6 months from May to October, 2001. After the application, a survey was conducted to ascertain the degree of the students' using the system, and their ability to use computers.

4.2 The applied content

Two units from the social studies textbook for the fourth grade were selected to be applied in the system: "Cultural Heritages and Museums", and "Domestic Life and Leisure Activities". The cyber learning system introduced in this thesis was applied to the teaching and learning process.

4.3 The result of the survey on the degree of usage

The survey was conducted on the composition and efficiency of the system. 89.9% of the students showed a preference to cyber learning, while 75% answered that it was convenient to work on assignments using the knowledge construction system. The result of the survey appears in <Table #2>.

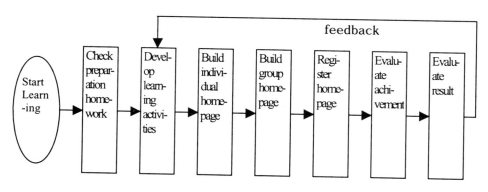

<Picture 2> The learning process map

1154

Items	Questions	SA	A	SS	DA	SDA
Composition of the system	Is the screen composition easy for cyber learning?	55.6	25.0	16.7	2.8	0
	Is the screen design easy for learning?	41.7	25.0	27.8	5.6	0
	Is it easy to select menus?	55.6	19.4	16.7	5.6	2.8
	Is it convenient to submit reports?	55.6	22.2	19.4	0	2.8
Efficiency of the system	Preference to cyber learning	72.2	16.7	2.8	8.3	0
	Is the system helpful for the social studies class?	61.1	30.6	5.6	2.8	0
	Is it convenient to construct resources?	50.0	25.0	22.2	2.8	0
	Is it convenient to answer a question?	63.9	11.1	19.4	2.8	2.8
	Preference to the report in the form of a homepage	55.6	30.6	11.1	2.8	0

SA : Strongly agree   A : Agree   SS : So-so   DA : Disagree   SDA : Strongly Disagree

\<Table 2\> The result of the survey

5. Conclusion

In this research, a cyber learning system was constructed which was capable of proceeding a series of learning processes from the stage of grasping problems to the stage of learning completion. The system was able to help recreate knowledge, not simply construct fragmentary knowledge. Applied to the teaching and learning process of a social studies class, the system showed the following educational effects:

- With the system, which can be applied to each step of the learning process, from grasping problems to learning completion, it was possible to conduct a cyber class.
- The system expanded the learning space from school to home, resulting in the effect of allowing students to experience home study.
- With the "Q & A" and "Conversation Room" sections, it was possible to have a two-way conversational class.
- The system, in which teacher and learners work together to produce a result of learning, and not one in which the teacher provides materials one-directionally, helped to bring about greater educational effects.
- Building an individual homepage on the basis of materials from the web enabled the learners to enjoy self-learning and self-directed study.

- The system, with which the learners could reconstruct knowledge in the form of a homepage on the basis of learning resources, helped the students develop material-analyzing abilities and more creativity.
- With the "Discussion Room" and "Conversation Room", the learners were able to develop their abilities to assert their points and the system helped to foster tolerance and consideration for others.

References

[1] Na, Il-ju. Web-Based Education, Education Science, 1999.

[2] Park, Jong-seon. 'Study on Search Support Technique for Designing a Web-Based Adaptive Courseware.' Education Technology, Vol. 15, No. 1, 1998.

[3] Son Jeong-ah et al. 'Developing Program Training Courseware for Interactional Distant Education.' Education Technology, Vol. 14, No. 2, 1998.

[4] Drucker, P.F. The Theory of Business. Havard Business Review, September-October, p.95-104, 1994.

[5] Nonaka, I. & Hiroaka, T. The Knowledge Creating Company-How Japanese Companies Create the Dynamics of Innovation. Oxford University Press, 1995.

[6] Kang, Myeong-hee et al. 'Web-Based Knowledge Construction System.' BK21, 2000

A Virtual Reality Application for Distance Learning of Taiwan Stream Erosion in Geosciences

LI Fung-Chun*, Jacques ANGELIER**, Benoît DEFFONTAINES**, Hu Jyr-Ching***,Hsu Shih-Hao*, LEE Chin-Hui*, Huang Chia-Hui*, Chen Cheng-Hung*

*Department of Nature Science Education, National Tainan Teachers College, Tainan, Taiwan R.O.C. li@ipx.ntntc.edu.tw Tel +886-6-2133111ext 668 Fax +886-6-2144409

**Tectonique Quantitative, Dept. of Geotectonique, T26-E1, Case 129, Universite Pierre et Marie Curie, 4, pl. Jussieu, 75252 Paris Cedex 05, France jacques.angelier@lgs.jussieu.fr benoit.deffontaines@lgs.jussieu.fr

***Dept of Geology, National Taiwan University, Taipei, Taiwan jchu@gl.ntu.edu.tw

ABSTRACT

The purpose of this study is to develop a distance learning program based on virtual reality (hereafter: VR). The stream erosion (hereafter: SE) in Taiwan is chosen as a case study of interactive VR distance learning (hereafter: DL). This study integrates various sources to develop an interactive VR distance learning program. Taiwan is one of the areas with a high stream erosion rate in the world. This high erosion rate has attracted worldwide attention and is regarded as a good example for geosciences education. This research is aimed to help motivate learners with concrete information that is perceptually easy to process. Also, in the VR distance learning environment unlike the traditional classroom, each student can learn individually with the computer according to his/her own time, location, and pace.

Keywords: Virtual Reality (VR), Distance Learning (DL), Stream Erosion (SE), Discharge, Sediment Content, Suspended Load

1 Purpose of Study

The purpose of this study is to develop a distance learning (DL) program on Taiwan stream erosion

(SE) based on virtual reality (VR). Taiwan is one of the areas in the world with the highest stream erosion rate (Yuan-Hui Li, 1976). For this reason, the SE in Taiwan is chosen as a case study for the interactive VR distance learning in geosciences. Three of the rivers in Taiwan: Tsengwen Chi, Liwu Chi and Tanshui are selected as examples of SE and VR. This system is set up in the National Tainan Teachers College (NTNTC) in Taiwan.

Figure 1. one of the virtual reality systems at NTNTC.
http://nature.ntntc.edu.tw/center/earth/vr.htm

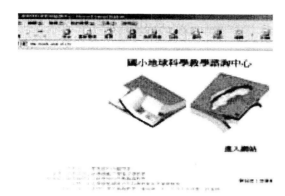

Figure 2   another virtual reality system at NTNTC.

http://nature.ntntc.edu.tw/center/

2 Backgrounds

2.1 Geographic background

Taiwan's growing population and specific natural phenomena -- unstable geology, typhoons, heavy rainfalls, and over-developments on landform – contribute to the daily safety pressure of the natural environment. Because of this, it becomes urgent to prevent the natural environmental disasters in Taiwan.

2.2 Geologic background

Taiwan, one of the areas with a high erosion rate in the world, is located on the active orogenic belt. Its high erosion rate has received global attention and is regarded as a good example for homeland education. In terms of education, the goals and objectives of environmental education, the importance of providing students with basic geologic knowledge, awareness and concern about environmental interactions within SE systems, and a variety of experiences in the environment are clearly described.

2.3 Virtual reality technology and tools

The underlying technologies and principles have evolved over the last 30 years. Ivan Sutherland, who first wrote about a computer-generated illusion, points out: "The screen is a window through which one sees a virtual world. The challenge is to make that world look real, act real, sound real, feel real." It takes over 25 years for computer graphics and display technologies to become an effective means of creating virtual reality. Today's tools with   a variety of functions work for different purposes as they address several human sensorial channels. Our lab has 3-D position sensors, trackballs, 3-D probes, sensing gloves, stereo viewing devices, etc. Taiwan's National Council for Science and Ministry of Education support all those virtual reality tools.

3 Procedure and Method

3.1 Collecting the original data of the erosive rates

There are 124 stream-flow gauging stations around the island: 39   in the north, 33 in the center, 26 in the south, 26 in the east. The focus of the   raw data collected is on the discharge, sediment content and suspended load. "Denudation of Taiwan Island since the Pliocene Epoch"(Yuan-Hui Li, 1976) is adopted as the method of the erosion rates. Each basin corresponds with the data of the rainfalls and typhoons collected at the same spot during the same period.

3.2 Field investigation of stream

(1)   Using Karng-Hsing Maps and GIS for Positioning (Exactness about 50 – 100 m), we

1157

try to find out the exact locations and routes of these 124 stations for promoting the statistical process of the field investigation and related records of suspended load.

(2) We then take these exact data to construct the database containing the discharge, sediment content, and suspended load of each basin.

3.3 Integrating GIS and Remote Sensing (RS)

(1) GIS: attribute maps digitized

(a) We use ARC Digitizing System (ADS) of ARC\INFO digitized tablet to control digitizer.

(b) We use the scanner only for complicated lines such as contour. We manually create the drawing which is then processed as an image with Microstation 2000 for Windows 2000. After that, we convert these images into the lineament, rectors into exact coordinates containing the longitude and latitude for ARC/INFO to recognize.

(2) Processing, interpreting, analyzing on the annual SPOT satellite image, we explore source erosion changing of each basin.

3.4 Analyzing the erosion rates by statistical analysis

(1) (Ergodic method): With the spatial samplings as the principles of the interval samplings, we calculate peak cut and valley cut, and explore the pale geography in the past as well as the potential landform changing model in the future.

(2) Fractal Geometry inquiry landforms in Taiwan: Erosion action increases the drastic roughness of landform. Expansive and sedimentary actions make the original landform flatter. It is understood how the climate and the structure lead to the change of the landform. Through the analysis of Fractal Geometry, we might interpret the factors of how the climate and structure change the landform (Chase, 1992). Inquiring the relationships residing in the block shape, sediment content, and suspended load of each basin, we hope to simulate the landscape in Taiwan in the years to come.

3.5 Creating the Objectives of VR and integrating didactic concepts and interactive VR

A river like an animal or a plant has a life cycle. In its initial stage, it flows quickly in a narrow, steep-side valley whose floor is broken by potholes and waterfalls. As time passes, erosion widens the valley and lowers its floor. Now that the gradient is reduced, the river flows more slowly. Its initial bends become more pronounced because of the nature of its valley floor. It reaches the stage of maturity now. As erosion continues the valley is opened out more and more. The gradient is further reduced, and deposition now becomes active. The river drops layers of sediments and these ultimately extend over the entire floor of its valley where they build up a gently sloping plain called a flood plain. The river valleys such as Tsengwen Chi, Liwu Chi and Tanshui River contain many beautifully narrow, steep-sided valleys in upper course.

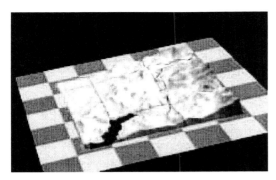

The Virtual Reality of Tsengwen Chi

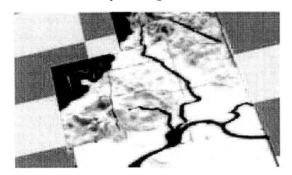

The Virtual Reality of Tanshui River

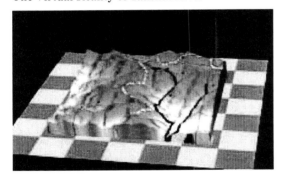

The Virtual Reality of Liwu Chi

This is a steep-sides valley of Liwu Chi whose valley is broken by potholes.

3.6 Creating a distance learning system

It is based on WWW for querying and displaying the erosive processes. A part of this study is now on-line to be used through the Internet (http://210.59.93.196) and is collecting the experiment data for the future research.

(1) We will use ActiveX control component to embed Active VRML with Home page, and to

develop 3-D interactive images based on ArcView IMS (Internet Map Server) (via Internet) for querying processes.

(2) With the presentation of visualization, we intend to cope with humanization style towards spatial analysis processes (Rober, 1995; Stanley, 1989) by displaying the interactive model interpersonally.

4 Results and Implications

In this study, we create a virtual reality application program for distance learning of Taiwan stream erosion in geosciences. . All of our VR visualize the effects of related earth science concepts or phenomena. The technical devices used in this study are especially adopted for VR purposes. In our lab, we use a lot of hardware. Please hyperlink 2002ICCE-Hardware.doc here for details. The group of our students in this study has made some comparative learning experiments on both the traditional method (control group) and the DL of VR (experimental group) in education. Pre-test scores are used as covariates to understand the potential differences of student's knowledge. The test of homogeneity of regression shows that the homogeneity of regression of the two groups is not significantly different (F=. 01, P>.01). In contrast, the posttest scores of one experimental group and one control group (by the traditional method -- paper-and-pencil without VR) are significantly different (F=4.12, p<. 01). The experimental group, who obviously benefit from 3D vision, recognize the situation more rapidly. That makes them more self-reliant and willing to accept any challenging material. They also show more curiosity and interest. According to the result of this study, it is predictable that VR will have a great effect on education in the future.

The traditional teaching method of earth science depends on "pen and paper sketches", map, OHP, slices, photos and verbal explanation. If one drawing may be worth many hundreds of word, visualization aids for complicated three-dimensional (3-D) solid objects are greatly helpful for both the teacher and students (Ki-Sang Song, 2000). The test results between the traditional teaching method of SE and the virtual reality method of SE show that the virtual reality of SE may enhance students' learning in geosciences. Through this VR of SE, the students can understand Taiwan stream erosion even better. The manipulation of virtual objects can allow the students to explore freely and integrate the objects into a new method to solve their problems.

One of the strengths of interactivity in VR is the capability to provide the students with rapid, compelling interaction as well as feedback to the learner. Moreover, Interactive VR technology can help motivate learners with the concrete information that is perceptually easy to process. As well, in the VR distance learning environment unlike the traditional classroom, each student can do individual learning with the computer according to his/her own time, location, and pace.

We would like to thank Taiwan's Ministry of Education and National Council for Science for their grants. Without these two grants, we could not have completed this study. We were awarded a three-year research grant from Taiwan's Ministry of Education for this study -- 1,500,000 NT$ in 1999, 800,000 NT$ in 2000, and 1,100,000 NT$ in 2001. With the grant, we purchased the needed hardware and hired ten research assistants. We also received a research grant from Taiwan's National Council for Science (under Grant no. NSC 89-2515-S-024-002, NSC 89-2515-S-024-003, NSC 89-2511-S-024-008, NSC 90-2520-S-024-001, NSC 90-2515-S-024-001, NSC 90-2116-M-024-001), with which we could afford to hire six research assistants each year.

5 References

[1] Song, K., Han, B. and Lee, W. "A Virtual Reality Application for Middle School Geometry Class", ICCE/ICCAI 2000 , Vol 2, 1369-1375, (2002).

[2]Wang, H. and Hu, J. "Using virtual reality courseware to enhance secondary school student learning in geosciences", ICCE/ICCAI 2000 , Vol 2,1376-1382, (2000).

[3] Yang, R., Tsai,Y. and Lin, S. "Web-Based Subject-Oriented Learning on Geophysics For Senior High School", ICCE/ICCAI 2000, Vol 2,1354-1355, (2002).

[4] Hwang, F. "A Constructivist Virtual Physics Laboratory", ICCE/ICCAI 2000, Vol 2,1289-1294, (2000).

[5] Chen,W. and Siong, T. "An Affordable Virtual Reality Technology for Constructivist Learning Environments,. GCCCE 2000", p414~421, (2000).

[6]. Tsai, C., Tseng S.S., and Su, G. "⓵ ⓸ ▢▢ ⯏▰▢ ◍ ⋛◕⯈◯ ⬥◕⌖▢◐",. GCCCE 2000, pp320~327, (2000).

[7] Li, Y. "Denudation of Taiwan Island since the Pliocene Epoch", Geology vol4 no2 Feb 1976, pp105~107, (1976).

Model for a European, Networked University

Harald Haugen
Stord/Haugesund University College
N-5409 Stord
Norway

Bodil Ask
Agder University College
N-4876 Grimstad
Norway

Thorleif Hjeltnes
Sør-Trøndelag University College
N7418 Trondheim
Norway

Abstract

The idea of developing a model for a European Networked University (MENU) originates from an initiative taken by the European Commission in 2001 aiming at mobilising existing resources for designing tomorrows education. As part of this programme, a group of eleven European universities are testing the MENU model, based on experiences and results from previous projects and R&D work.

The partners are defining models for collaboration (partnership agreement), for joint study plans, organization and economic strategy, to be tested and evaluated through user trials. Based on these models, the goal is to establish a sustainable ENU - a European Networked University.

Key words: International WBE, Online Degree Programs, Collaboration

1 Background

New technology and global networks give students opportunities to study where and when they want. E-learning indicates a paradigm shift in higher education, where the days of one provider of knowledge and once-in-a-lifetime education are obsolete. The shift forces traditional, higher educational institutions to re think their methods, pedagogy and organisational systems. This requires new approaches to higher education, where collaboration, networks and joint efforts are crucial. Internet is the backbone for practical solutions. This in turn, invites for collaboration and exchange of knowledge, expertise, material - and study programmes.

Buzz words like *e-learning, academic mobility, student flexibility* and *life-long learning* represent complex areas of organisational, economic, technical and pedagogical changes. Previously changes have been enforced and accepted gradually as educators and learners have adapted to the new ideas. The new challenge now is the speed and the multiplicity at which the new strategies are being introduced and spread around the world.

1.1 The European situation

Obstacles like language barriers, strong national traditions and regulations and complex routines for exchange of academic credits and grades between institutions re present extra challenges to joint international prospects. Mass education and joint study programs across boarders is still at an early stage.

Direct exchange of cours es and course ma terial, acceptance of credits and exams are complex matters. Since the production of net-based learning material is rather time and resource consuming, much effort can be saved by close collaboration between institutions and staff members with common interests. Former projects have shown rather promising results here, proving that it is really possible to collaborate in this field. There is more to gain by collaboration than by competition.

Through different projects over the past 6 -8 years there has been a gradual evolvement of goals and results. More details may be found by visiting web sites indicated in the references.

1.1.1 European projects. The DELTA programme (1988-94) funded several larger projects, among them **JITOL** - Just In Time Open Learning (1992-94). 12 partners challenged existing technology and software to test new ideas about net based open learning. This gave rise to new projects and further development.

MECPOL[1] – Models for European Collaboration and Pedagogy in Open Learning (1995-98) pioneered the ODL strand (Open and Distance Learning) that was funded by the Socrates programme. 8 partner institutions surveyed existing models, and designed new models for ODL.

DoODL[2] - Dissemination of Open and Distance Learning (1996-98) was a follow-up of the MECPOL, where focus was set on dissemination and implementation of the models for ODL – both inside and between institutions.

SHARP[3] - SHArable Representation of Practice (1997-99) focused on the use of video/multimedia in ODL material. A common database was established for sharing of video re sources with annotations.

EuroCompetence[4] - A university / workplace model for development and sharing of knowledge on European

Collaboration (1998 –2000) also contributes to experiences. Main objectives here were methods and tools for international, professional collaboration over Internet.

1.1.2 National projects. Several national ODL projects around Europe are producing valuable contributions to the total development of ODL or e-learning. Relevant examples are

NITOL [5] - Norway-net with IT for Open Learning (1994 – 99) started as a national version of the JITOL project, involving 4 Norwegian institutions. The project grew rapidly from a limited R&D project to a national provider of net based, higher education, with more than 5000 student entries in 1999. It was decided to split the organisation. R&D activities remain in NITOL, while student- and course activities now are organised in -

NVU [6] - Norwegian Networked University (1999 -), extended from the initial four NITOL institutions to nine Norwegian universities, at present with more than 200 courses on-line.

FVU - Finnish Virtual University [7] involves 21 Finnish universities in a joint network, providing higher education to students all over Finland.

1.2 The e-learning initiative

Several initiatives are taken during the past decades to improve education and the level of competence among it's citizens. The application of new information and communication technology (ICT) is more focused as the technology develops and spreads in the society. Based on different political manifests, new programmes and funding systems have been initiated.

The e-Learning Initiative taken by the European Commission in Brussels, has led to The eLearning Action Plan[8] and the allocation of funding. This is an action to boost the change from traditional education to systematic applications of ICT for the provision of flexible learning and competence building - *Designing tomorrow's education,* as the Commission says.

In its resolution of July 2001 the Council of the EU invites the member states to 16 different actions, among these an invitation[9]

- to foster the European dimension of joint development of ICT-mediated and ICT-complimented curricula in higher education, by encouraging common approaches in higher education certification models and quality assurance

- to promote collaboration and exchange of experiences in the area of e-Learning and pedagogical development, especially with a view to:

- *supporting trans-national virtual meeting places,*
- *stimulate European networking at all levels and in this context establish and provide networks for the benefit of teacher training,*

On the basis of these documents a the Commission issued the Call for proposals[10] in June 2001, for preparatory and innovative actions. Particular areas are identified, among these

- virtual European universities, based on partnerships and cooperation with other universities - - - - - for European degrees combining courses and materials from different universities; - - -

2 The MENU project[11]

Most of the 11 partners in the project have long experience from net based learning activities at university level, as well as from national and international collaboration. Some of the partners represent already existing networks of academic institutions, e.g. The Finnish Virtual University[7] (FVU, 21 member institutions) and the Norwegian NettWorkUniversity[6] (NVU, 9 institutions)..

From previous projects the partners knew that net-based collaboration and joint ventures between traditional universities are possible at national and at limited international levels. The current project aims at extending these activities to a Pan-European level, establishing it with a true European dimension. Concentration of the content to ICT-related studies implies an implicit contribution to the ICT literacy and exploitation of technology in education and amongst the general public.

The project focuses on joint efforts and collaboration to create a international consortium or a network for higher education, applying experiences and findings from previous work.

2.1 Activities

1. Organise a network of institutions, or a 'European Networked University' (ENU), consisting of
   a. Partnership agreement
   b. Operational objectives and practices of ENU
   c. Structure for sustainability for a permanent e-learning activity
2. Establish) European Master Degree programmes as a demonstrator, showing
   a. Specification of structure and content, with preliminary study plans
   b. Establish academic and political acceptance and agreements

3. Establish a system for quality assurance (QAS) for content, level, methods, services etc. in e-learning

4. A seminar for dissemination of findings

2.2 Anticipated results

1. The model for a sustainable ENU with an array of study programmes, available throughout Europe

2. A common QAS for general acceptance of credits and degrees obtained through ENU

3. Operational study plans for European Master De gree programmes, based on contributions from several countries and institutions, a model showing

4. Publication of experiences, results and guidelines for the establishment of a permanent ENU

2.3 Pedagogical and didactical approaches

The project is not primarily aimed at development of new didactical models, it will rely on existing systems and models, and direct its actions more towards the organisation dynamics that apply previously obtained results. State of the art methods and systems will be applied, in line with experiences at the partner institutions.

2.4 Objectives

The authors of the proposal had some definite objectives in mind, adapted to the principles laid out in the call. Among the central ideas:

– Operationalizing the political principles stated in the e-learning action plan, by establishing a strategic and business plan for an ENU, accepted and integrated into national educational programmes

– Demonstrating development of joint study programmes across institutional and national borders

– Establishing a model for management and services for a virtual university. Options for scalability (up/down) for ENU as an independent organisation *or* as a virtual network

2.5 Target groups

– National authorities, decision-makers and administrators (Ministries of Education etc.)

– University teaching staff , leaders and administrative personnel

– Curriculum developers and administrators

– Learners (students, adults, teachers)

By involving these target groups, the intention is that institutions will be more European, flexible and ICT-

minded, making e-learning an important part of university policies. A central obstacle in this process is often the incompatibility of assessment and quality assurance systems between institutions and countries in Europe. Joint efforts towards a common QAS will be of great value in an international education market. Findings from the project are intended to help decision makers in their process of planning future educational systems, exploiting the potential of e-learning. Learners will have easier access to a variety of study programmes, with international acceptance and accreditation.

2.6 Establishing the project organisation

There are four main stages in the project
1. Establishing the partnership and agreeing on principles, goals and methods
2. Analysing existing institutional strategies and systems in order to create the necessary documents / plans for the joint model
3. Testing the model by running real courses on the net; quality assurance
4. Finalising the model, based on plans and experiences; dissemination of results

Parallel to these stages there is an evaluation process for the whole project going on, as well as the management of project activities.

The organisation of 11 partners in a collaborative project offers a relevant test bed for the intended networked university that is expected to be the dynamic outcome.

The technical and pedagogical methods applied in the project are based on previous projects and experiences among partners. A further exchange of know-how and competence is the basis for project development. This includes exchange of educational resources (research results, learning material, access to expertise etc.), virtual mobility of students (taking courses across the network, international/European degrees etc.), virtual mobility of staff (providing material and guidance across institutional and national borders), and the synergy of combining already existing administrative systems.

The organisational method for the project is based particularly on the experiences from the Norwegian NVU and the MECPOL project, where models for collaboration and organisation have been prescribed and tested at a smaller scale (4 – 10 institutions). Partners in these projects strongly believe that this method is scalable and can constitute the core of the MENU organisation. It is also believed that this organisational model makes it possible not only for large institutions to offer e-learning programmes, but also for smaller institutions, through collaboration. A major task in the project is to develop this into sustainable model for larger networks and international student bodies.

A quality assurance system (QAS) is a central task in the project. To survive the international hype of e-learning, universities must make the most out of their tradition on professionalism and research based guarantees for quality and relevance of their courses and study programmes. This task is approached by surveying existing QAS at the partner institutions and other available material on the topic, forming a synergetic product that is taking the new learning environments and methods of assessment into account[12].

2.6.1 Technological systems. Through previous national and international projects the policy has been to stick to general, open systems instead of committing the group to proprietary systems. This may cause some delays and extra difficulties in production and distribution. But on the other hand, it will avoid compatibility problems, extra costs and installation procedures for the users.

2.6.2 Learning environment. The first attempts to create Open and Distance learning (ODL), were clearly coloured by traditions from paper based distance education and by lectures in classrooms. Expressions like *virtual classrooms*, fixed *schedules* with *lessons* and *assignments* are clear reminiscences of classical universities and correspondence schools. Nothing wrong with building on solid traditions, but this might not exploit the full potential of the technology, the possibilities for improving the learning environment. MENU hopes to combine well established principles with innovative and visionary methods.

The learning environment tool should provide 4 main arenas:

1. **Presentation-/lecture area** for text files, web-sites, overheads, video, animation etc.
2. **Working area** with software tools, word processor, group-ware, workbook/portfolio etc.
3. **Knowledge-area** with oracles & help services, a FAQ-base, library services via Internet etc.
4. **Private area** for private files, a database, workbook, personal work-/study plan etc.

On top of this, there has to be a communication environment.

The project will stick to the principle of open, general tools for implementation of the learning environment.

3 Outcomes

The project is still at an early stage and outcomes can be predicted mainly on the basis of plans and visions. The main output of the project is the model for a European Networked University, ENU. It will be made available to interested parties through different methods of dissemination. Means for evaluating the model and its functionality are the 'user trials', i.e. the Demonstrator. Dissemination will be done at an international conference that is planned in April 2003. Feed-back from partners and outside institutions will judge the quality and relevance of the products.

Other outputs are parts of this main product, the ENU model. The demonstrator will prove - or disapprove - that the model really works.

Dissemination material, both as informal publications and as more scientific reports will be made available. Publications and reports will be made available on the Internet, at a particular web site for the project[10], and as links from more general information sites (e.g. ISOC).

Working in surroundings of multimedia, it is natural that parts of the material will be published through video and graphic recordings. It is the intention to produce video sequences of lectures, demonstrations etc., and to make this available over the Internet. The technology of digital video and 'streaming video' will be tested as part of the demonstrator as well as at the international conference.

3.1 Organisation

The model will outline how a future European Networked University, ENU, can be established. This will include

- a strategic plan of ENU, development and expansion
- a business plan; how funding and economy can be sound enough for a sustainable consortium
- study programmes and study plans, including exchange of modules and courses, mutually acceptable assessment systems, grading systems etc.
- a quality assurance system across institutional and national borders
-

3.2 User trials

The project group has promised to run part of at least one master degree study programme as a demonstrator of the functionality of the model. Initially 2 alternative master programmes are being tested: *ICT in Education* and *ICT Engineering*, both hosted by Norwegian institutions. Both of these are in close agreement with the EU Council resolution, where both studies are aiming at education and training of teachers (ICT in Education) and study programmes to increase the skills within ICT (ICT Engineering) are central goals. The demonstrators start in September 2002, and preliminary reports will be made out in April - June 2003. The trials will certainly include national students, but will hopefully also attract an international group of students.

3.3 Collaboration

How can two or more institutions collaborate so that each one of them promote their own competitive potential to recruit new students? Taking it for granted that there is only a fixed number of students to compete for, this may be hard to see. Our experience, however, is that through collaboration and sharing of expertise and exchange of products between partners in order to offer better and more flexible study opportunities, a larger total number of students may be recruited, thus improving the results for all partners involved. The movement towards lifelong learning for all, provides the extra potential by involving adult professionals of many trades. These future 'students' are often restricted by daily work, families, geographic location and available funding, and will see e-learning as a natural solution to their needs.

Moreover, both young and adult students will gain by the collaborative venture, at least in two ways:

1) Study material and learning environment provided by joint efforts, have a higher quality and usability than if each individual institution, with limited resources, should develop it all alone

2) Access and availability is improved by offering the studies from multiple locations, thus closer to a larger part of the population, e.g. for marketing, local support and physical meetings of regional groups

Thus the principle of collaboration leads to a win-win situation, for both institutions and learners. This is also relevant for on-campus students who are offered the same on-line learning material as a basis or as a supplement to regular lectures and paper based material.

3.3.1 Obstacles.
It seems to be a basic mistrust between institutions that are traditionally competing in the same market. Our past projects indicate that binding contracts and signed documents are necessary as a basis for collaboration, committing both professional staff and administration to accept the terms of joint ventures. Some of the critical points are

- mutual acceptance of student qualifications
- exchange of material and know-how / expertise
- agreements on strategies for programmes involved
- common or mutually accepted evaluation systems
- economic terms for students and staff (fees and compensations systems)
- marketing of studies and registration of students

All these items will be settled and agreed upon in a partner contract for MENU, before conflicts appear and spoil the positive attitude for collaboration.

4 Vision

Revised documents of strategic plan, business plan, study plans and the experiences from the model trials, the demonstrators and its evaluation, will be the basis for a more permanent ENU organisation. The 11 partners will be the core institutions of the consortium, but will also invite others to join. Some of the plans will be disseminated at the dedicated MENU dissemination conference in Valencia, Spain, April 2003.

The organisational model of MENU will be the most important outcome of the project. This model will, however, be based on accumulated experiences and previous models that have been tested in limited environments.

If successful, this organisation will promote virtual mobility of students, academic staff and highly skilled experts. This will also prepare the grounds for mutual and international recognition of academic standards, credits and competence. Hopefully it will help overcoming barriers of language, cultural and political differences, and academic pride related to availability and acceptance of higher education. This is in accordance with the EU educational policy, but may also have effects far beyond Europe.

5 References

[1] MECPOL –
http://www.aitel.hist.no/prosjekter/ekstern/mecpol/
[2] DoODL - http://www.aitel.hist.no/prosjekter/ekstern/doodl/
[3] SHARP - http://www.softlab.ntua.gr/sharp/start.html
[4] EuroCompetence - http://www.tisip.no/ec/
[5] Haugen, H. & Ask, B.:'From R&D Project to a Networked University -The Story of NITOL', in Telecommunications for Education and Training, 1999, or http://www.nitol.no
[6] NVU - http://www.nvu.no
[7] FVU, Finnish Virutal University, http://www.virtualuniversity.fi
[8] COM(2001)172 final, Brussels, 28.3.2001 - http://europa.eu.int/comm/education/elearning/doc_en.html
[9] Official Journal of the European Communities, 20.7.2001; C 204/3 - http://europa.eu.int/comm/education/elearning/doc_en.html
[10] Official Journal of the European Communities, 9.6.2001; C 166/38 - http://europa.eu.int/comm/education/elearning/doc_en.html
[11] MENU: Models of a European Networked University for e-learning (NO001E-LEARN01-1) http://www.hsh.no/menu
[12] http://elm.wi-inf.uni-essen.de/en/standard/quality.html

UK Models of Virtual Universities

Robin Mason and Frank Rennie

BACKGROUND

Recently the British Council sponsored a workshop on UK approaches to virtual teaching. Four different applications of online delivery of courses were explored through presentations from expert practitioners at each of the universities. A partnership model was represented by The University of the Highlands and Islands (UHI); an evolutionary model by the UK Open University (OU); a brokerage model by the eUniversity (eU) and a local study centre model by the University for Industry (Ufi). By studying these different models in turn, insights into common problems were gained which this paper aims to outline. These issues are:

- How to maintain or improve quality of teaching in the online environment.

- How to blend online and traditional media for the optimum mix.

- How to support students studying online courses.

Details of the original workshop are available on the British Council website at: http://www.britishcouncil.org/networkevents/education.htm

THE MODELS

There are any number of ways of categorising the burgeoning examples of virtual universities. See for example Stephenson, 2001; Tschang and Della Senta, 2001; Slater, 2002. These categories focus either on what services the virtual university provides or on the organisational model it represents. In reality, most current applications are a mixture of elements and do not fit neatly into categories. That applies to the four examples described here and so the categories provided are descriptors indicating distinguishing features rather than exclusive determiners.

1. The University of the Highlands and Islands Millennium Institute (UHI)

The UHI is a partnership of 13 existing campus-based colleges and research centres, forming a single Institute for Higher Education, with a strategic plan for the establishment of a university for the region by 2006 (see www.uhi.ac.uk) . A primary aim of the UHI is to enable a streamlined access to both Further Education (vocational) and Higher Education (academic) throughout the Highlands and Islands of Scotland. This requires a new approach to distributed learning using the facilities of the Academic Partners, plus a network of Local Learning Centres to provide access for hundreds of island communities and remote villages in a region with the second-lowest population density in Europe. A second objective is to retain and attract new students to the region by the provision of high quality education, careers, and quality of lfe opportunities. Around 10,000 FE and 4,000 HE students currently access undergraduate and post graduate tuition through a range of media, including face-to-face, video-conferences, audio-conferences, web-based resources, e-mail, NetMeeting, and other online resources. HE learning modules are delivered across the network, and students are hosted in one of the Academic Partners or their local centres, which provides an interesting comparison of the relationship between online communities and physical geographical learning communities.

2. The Open University

The OU is an adult distance teaching university which is slowly evolving into a virtual university. While most courses continue to be taught through printed material sent to students' homes, the tutoring support of students is increasingly provided online. Currently 170,000 students have online accounts to send in their assignments, access electronic resource materials, register and carry out other administrative tasks, and primarily to interact with their tutor and fellow students.

Through extensive surveying of its existing and potential students, the OU keeps in close touch with the study habits, access to ICT, and aspirations (or otherwise) of its target study body regarding e-learning. Early indications of courses with online content were that students printed out the material in order to study away from the computer screen. As this practice changes, so the University will develop content for the Web, just as it has gradually increased the level of services and amount of tutoring offered online as home access to the Internet reaches 75% of the target population.

3.   The eUniversity

The idea of the eU is that a single organisational framework will allow all UK higher education institutions to compete on an international scale by pooling key resources and using the private sector when appropriate. The eU will provide a platform which integrates pedagogical facilities for online course delivery and interaction with all the administrative facilities of a university – registering, recording, assessing, marketing. It will establish partnerships with institutions abroad to offer the programmes through local facilities, including face-to-face contact. The UK university which provides the course content will accredit, tutor and quality assure the materials and the processes.

The aims of the eU are to arrest the decline in the UK market share of a rapidly expanding global HE learning market as well as to help with the planned increase in the UK higher education participation rate to 50% of school leavers.

4.   The University for Industry

Learndirect is Ufi's network of over 1500 local e-learning centres located throughout the UK. The majority of these e-learning centres are operated by local and national organisations known as Ufi hubs. The hubs are working in partnership with Ufi to create the **learndirect** network and develop its services. Over 600 organisations are working in partnership with Ufi as part of local, employer and sector-based hubs. Partners involved with Ufi hubs and operating **learndirect** centres are typically employers, business organisations, colleges, universities and private training providers, Learning and Skills Councils, local authorities, libraries, trades unions, and sports and community organisations.

There are currently 594 **learndirect** courses on offer in IT skills; business skills; the basics of reading, writing and number; retail and distribution; environmental services; automotive components; and multimedia. Despite its name, most Ufi courses are at pre-university level and many address basic literacy skills. More than 75 per cent of these courses are online and delivered through the **learndirect** website at www.learndirect.co.uk. As one of Ufi's priorities is meeting the training needs of small and medium-sized enterprises, nearly 300 of the courses available so far are written with SMEs in mind. There are free course tasters on the website.

ISSUES OF VIRTUAL TEACHING

Each of these four virtual teaching institutions has a slightly different mission and target student body. Yet each faces many of the same issues in teaching online.

Quality versus cost

Unofficially it is acknowledged amongst academics and administrators that technology adds to the cost of course delivery – though very few institutions are able (or willing!) to say by how much. If well implemented, technology can improve the quality of courses, both by giving students the skills they need to work in an increasingly networked society, but also by providing rich resources, opportunities for team work and interaction with peers and tutors, and multimedia learning experiences. Economies of scale contribute to the OU's ability to use graphics, animations and other costly resources where courses are delivered to large numbers of students over several years. UHI benefits from a network of videoconferencing systems installed in local centres throughout the Highlands and Islands. This provides high quality contact for very remote learners. The eU, like Ufi, is aiming to develop local centres in addition to providing online support.

It is very clear from the evidence of online practitioners that the support of a tutor, whether online, face-to-face or by videoconferencing, is one of the key elements of a quality learning experience from the learner's point of view. This conclusion is clear from the MIT Open Courseware initiative whereby content can be made available freely on the web. What counts is the personal support to help learners study the material (and of course the accreditation system to validate the learning).

The OU has the longest track record of supporting students online of any of the four institutions. One experienced OU tutor on the British Council workshop reported that she had, over the years, moved increasingly away from teaching content to facilitating learning, and increasingly to facilitating learning how to learn.

Blended learning

All four institutions had adopted a blended approach to course delivery, based on the separation of content and support. The content is prepared by a team of course designers, subject experts and technical support staff – either for the web or for print. Students are assigned to a tutor group which meets either synchronously or asynchronously and either face-to-face or online. Many variations of these elements are practiced. The context of the course and of the student population determines the optimum mix. There is considerable evidence that the more disadvantaged the learner, the more they require face-to-face support. Consequently the Ufi relies heavily on its learning hubs to provide local support. The OU provides face-to-face tutorials for most of its entry level courses, but increasingly online-only tutoring for more advanced and postgraduate courses. The eU is beginning its portfolio of programmes with Masters level courses, although it intends to follow the

initial launch with undergraduate courses. Students may be more mature learners, but another difficulty faces the eU: many students will be studying in their second language and this is notoriously problematic in trying to activate online discussions. Consequently local, face-to-face tutoring outside the UK is considered desirable.

Supporting online courses

A number of key lessons about facilitating online learning emerged from the analysis of these four UK models:

- Context: The context within which online learning is offered must be appropriate in the first place. The advantages of the media must be made obvious to both staff and students through exploiting the unique features (access for remote learners, using the resources of the web, online interaction with peers and tutors) and minimizing the disadvantages (overload of information, complicated software).

- Course design. Uses of online technologies need to be well structured to avoid overload and assist navigation through resources. The assessment strategy should be integrated with the course activities and reflect the aims and objectives of the course.

- Tutor role. Tutors need to develop their facilitation skills to be successful online. Ways of limiting the demands on their time need to be sought, otherwise 'interaction fatigue' leads to early burn out.

- Extended resources. The more extensive the online facilities offered by the institution (for example, library, registration and payment, counselling, course information), the more effectively learners can take advantage of what networking offers.

CONCLUSIONS

Two issues stand out most strongly from this analysis of different models of virtual provision of education. The first of these is the nature of tutorial support provided by the institution – whether totally online or combined with face-to-face meetings. This raises the issue of local study centres and telecentres. At the conference in December, we hope to be able to report the outcomes of our study relating online tutoring with the use of local centres, and to comment on the contribution of local centres to the learning outcomes of online courses.

The second issue arising from our discussion relates to the way in which virtual institutions position themselves on the quality/access/cost triangle. Finding a balance between increasing access, improving quality and reducing costs is always challenging and each institution settles for a different solution, emphasising one aspect more than the other two. This helps to orient each to a slightly different student market, which in the end should grow the market for all providers.

REFERENCES

Slater, J (2002). Transformational Brokerage: the eUniversity.

Stephenson, J. (ed.)(2001) *Teaching and Learning Online Pedagogies for New Technologies*. Kogan Page, London.

Tschang, F and Della Senta, T (eds) (2001). *Access to Knowledge. New Information Technologies and the Emergence of the Virtual University*. Elsevier Science, London.

Virtual Universities: a Critical Approach.

Panagiotes S. Anastasiades
Assistant Professor
University of Crete, Department of Education
GR-74100 Rethymno Crete, Greece
e-mail: panas@panteion.gr   URL: www.cs.ucy.ac.cy/~panas/
Vice- President of the Permanent Scientific Committee on Social Issues of the Greek Computer

Abstract

The rapid development of educational technologies, combined with the Internet boom at a worldwide level, gives rise to favorable conditions for the establishment of a new model of university training. The first part of this work will give a description of the major components of the new virtual university. The second part will attempt a critical approach of the sense of virtual university from a social and a philosophical point of view. Focal point of this work will be the danger of having a sweeping uniformity among university departments all over the world, together with the necessity to prevent university institutes from becoming units of providing distance learning material in package form.

1. Introduction

The rapid development of the new information and communications technologies [1], in conjunction with the massive use of computers and the Internet boom [2], create new data at an international level. The transfer of capitals in the new technological environment, released a huge power on the part of international capital market.

The very rapid and secure flow of vast amounts of funds towards every direction created the conditions for the consolidation of the phenomenon of globalized economy [3]. The educational systems are called upon to serve the new dogma, the new vision, and the new reality. This is the dogma of the free, according to many [4] or wild, according to others [5], market.

Conventional educational systems are unable to keep pace with the demands of a world where the universal spiritual values show signs of weariness compared to the respective material ones [6]. The conventional educational environment [7] or, in other words, the first category of teaching activities [8], served quite successfully the social and financial needs of an era, which seems to fade away with time. The new technologies of communications and information make possible the development of a totally different educational environment, by means of the "educational technologies", as they are called [9] One of the

characteristics of the new technological age in the area of education will be the transition from a student-centered education to the concept of independent studies [10].

2. The Virtual University – A Critical Approach

The development and establishment of a supranational homogenized teaching and administrative environment in the area of higher education creates the conditions for the formation of a new individualized virtual learning model at a planetary level [11]. There's no doubt that the University should be in direct and constant interaction with the area of businesses and the labor market. At the same time, however, it should remain firm and unalterable in relation to the philosophy that ought to govern a university institute and distinguish it from a training center. This is not so easy in our times, since reality itself often becomes oppressive enough to enforce violent changes and put forward the idea of adjustability as the only weapon towards survival and competitiveness.

At this point, a crucial question comes into sight: will the virtual universities of the future be able to maintain the basic philosophy behind university education or are they going to drift into providing modern knowledge in the form of information packages to their distant students?

What is the dividing line between information and knowledge in these days of informational cataclysm?

In an age when everything changes at an incredibly high speed, perhaps we cannot afford the luxury of going deeper into the sea of knowledge. Thus, our interest is probably concentrated on how to teach students to manage in the best possible way the vast volume of information they can now access.

Actually, the following dilemma is brought up from several directions: will the new model of virtual university give priority to the necessity of the times or is it going to remain adhered to the dogma of an era which seems to go out of sight as the time goes by?

As part of this work, it would be expedient to reword the question as follows: in what way will the virtual university manage to combine the overwhelming pressure for modern and uniform learning with the cultural and pedagogic need for pluralism and deeper knowledge?

According to the model of virtual university we have described, the student will be free to choose his professor regardless of the geographic distance that might exist between them.

Studying in a virtual university like that enables the student to acquaint himself with different educational and learning systems. This way, he improves his adjustability to different levels of culture and philosophy in the area of the university, which is now virtual.

This will help him a lot in being receptive to the continuous changes that will take place throughout his professional life.

Therefore, the maintenance of the philosophy, viewpoint and culture in general, which is peculiar to each university department, is a crucial factor in the training of students in a constantly changing environment. Thus, the virtual university does not impose absolute uniformity and the leveling of everything – quite the contrary.

The model of virtual university that we described guarantees diversity and pluralism, together with the students' access to different levels of culture and philosophic systems.

But how is the issue of deeper knowledge going to be guaranteed? This question, in the context of the virtual model of university training, becomes much more difficult to answer.

The difficulty lies in the fact that the virtual university professors will have a greater degree of independence than they would have in the traditional model.

As a matter of fact, the curricula and the professors who will undertake to teach the courses will be the mirror of a department in this new virtual university.

However, a very important role in the evaluation of each professor in the virtual university plays the level and the number of students that will select him. So in order to prevent the student from getting caught, in making his choice, in the vortex of modern but superficial knowledge, it is necessary to take preventive measures at three levels.

On the first level, a complete system of orienting students in relation to the university's role and character in modern times should be developed.

This endeavor aims at building people who are aware and who are able to choose curricula and courses that promote a combination of modern and also scientifically structured and deeper knowledge.

On the second level, this combinational rationale should pervade not only the curriculum but also the content of the courses and, most importantly, the way they are taught. This way, the students will be encouraged to choose from a great variety of courses, which will be based on the combinational rationale of modern and at the same time deeper knowledge.

On the third level, there should be a consolidation of the rationale that the new form of virtual university will also accompany the student after he graduates, throughout his professional life.

The development of reliable systems of lifetime learning as part of the virtual university, in cooperation with people of recognized merit and experience who are in the labor market, is one of the most important priorities in the new era of education.

3. Conclusions

The new form of virtual university incorporates in a workable way all the modern educational technologies, and especially the unlimited possibilities offered by open and distance learning via the Internet. The danger of a sweeping uniformity can be avoided, if we accept that the diversity provided by the virtual university helps its students adjust themselves faster to a world which his constantly changing. The precise organization of flexible curricula, teaching methodologies and systems of orientation and lifetime learning are some of the components of the new virtual model of university education. If these requirements are met, virtual universities will be able to combine in the best possible way the provision of modern and at the same time scientifically substantiated knowledge.

4. References

[1] Dutton, William (ed) *Information and Communication Technologies*. Oxford University Press, 1996

[2] Morneau Jill and Anderson Kim (2000). Caution: Internet Revolution Ahead. *TechWeb News*, [http://www.teledotcom.com/article/TEL20001026S0002].

[3] Eichengreen,B. (1996). *Globalization Capital. A History of the International Monetary System*. Princeton University Press.

[4] Friedman Thomas. (2000). *The Lexus and the Olive Tree: Understanding Globalization*. Anchor Books.

[5] Deppe,F. (1995). *The New International Status*. Athens, A.A Libani.

[6] Anastasiades, P. (2000). *The Information Age*. Athens, A.A Libani.

[7] Kaye, A. & Rumble,G. (1979). *An analysis of distance teaching systems*. Open University.

[8] Moore (1977) *On a theory of independent study*. Hagen:Fernunivrsiat(ZIFF).

[9] Hawkridge, D. 1976. Next year jerusalem! The rise of educational technology. *British Journal of Educational Technology*, 7(1)7-30.

[10] Wedemeyer, (1971). *Independent study - The Encyclopedia of education Vol. 4,* New York: Macmillan

[11] Anastasiades, P. (2001). The Vision of an Interplanetary Individualized Virtual University in the Age of Globalization». Proceedings of the Webnet 2001 World Conference on the WWW and the Internet. October 23-27, 2001 Orlando, Florida, USA.

Building Synchronous Voice-based 3D Learning Spaces

Philip Marriott and Dr Jane Hiscock
School of Communication, Information and New Media
University of South Australia

Abstract

This paper introduces a project at the University of South Australia to develop purpose-built 3D online learning spaces for synchronous voice-based small group teaching and learning. Justification for the project is given in terms of existing deficiencies with 'space-less' text-based synchronous communication methods and tools. Initial survey results of a large class of students who have used a variety of synchronous tools for small group learning are presented, these show a student preference for synchronous voice over text. It is argued that this preference will increase with increasing student familiarity with synchronous voice. A project timeline is presented stating intended progress by December 2002.

Introduction

The online learning environment at the University of South Australia concentrates on asynchronous methods of delivery and interaction [1]; such as email, web documents, and voice/text-based discussion forums. The lesser synchronous component of the online environment is addressed with the provision of text-based chat, real-time video conferencing using Netmeeting, and of course, the telephone. These synchronous tools are mostly adequate for one-to-one communication, however we believe they are often less suited for small group teaching and learning as would typically occur in a face-to-face tutorial class. As a School we value the learning interactions that occur in our tutorials and would like online learners to share in these experiences. We are therefore exploring options for online equivalents that promote active learning [2]. One such option is the development of synchronous voice-based communication in purpose-built 3D online learning spaces. The intention is to create and manage an online learning environment that is conducive to small group synchronous chat.

This paper introduces a project at the School of Communication, Information, and New Media at the University of South Australia to develop purpose-built 3D online learning spaces for voice-based small group teaching and learning. This project is special in that it combines the concepts of voice and space to create online learning environments. Presented here is work in progress and there are many questions to be answered in the following months.

Voice and Space

The concept of 'space' as applied to online learning is important [3] though often overlooked. Architecture is a crucial defining feature of society and we go to great efforts to create and modify physical spaces for our real-world activities. Some spaces are clearly more conducive to certain types of talk than others. The design of physical education spaces is a common interest of staff and students. Yet, in most implementations of online teaching and learning, space is ignored.

Text, or literacy, and voice, or orality, require different forms of thinking and not interchangeable [4]. To simply substitute text for what is usually done with voice is not valid. However this is what has been commonly done with synchronous online communication, which has been dominated by text, regardless of the context or purpose. Synchronous text has a number of disadvantages and is dependent on written language skills, typing speed, and experience with the technology. While many shortcuts or abbreviations are used by experienced chatters (for example SMS messages) these must be understood by all parties and present a significant learning curve for beginners. Text chat is inherently slow when compared to spoken language. It can be argued that these real-time text-based conversations are not our natural or preferred means of communication and text chat 'rarely allows for productive discussion or participation and frequently disintegrates into simple one-line contributions of minimal depth' [5]. With the lifting of technical limitations perhaps voice now has a greater part to play [6].

A readily available solution to the marriage of voice and space is the Traveler software. Traveler is a server and client software system that allows multiple users to become Avatars and navigate 3D VRML worlds and conduct realistic real-time lip-synced conversations in groups. Traveler was developed in 1995 by Onlive Technologies. It was very advanced for its time and often exceeded the performance and bandwidth of the available computers. Consequently Traveler had a very small user base [7]. Today, with advances in hardware and networking, Traveler is now viable. A single Traveler server has been setup in our University and students use Traveler clients installed on either University computers or their home computers – the whole system working seamlessly from within a web browser. Unfortunately Traveler is no longer under development. The present owners of Traveler, Digital Space Inc [http://www.digitalspace.com], are working with Adobe on their new Atmosphere product (3D world builder) [http://www.adobe.com/products/atmosphere/] and the future looks promising for a successor to Traveler in the near future.

Traveler allows users to move into different spaces (moving to different 3D worlds) and to easily move to form differing groups that make some physical sense. Traveler worlds can be created using 3D modeling software that outputs VRML (Virtual Reality Modeling Language). Most Traveler worlds have been created for their aesthetic or entertainment value and while it is possible to hold classes in an underground cavern, or Bar, or on the moon (and we are presently doing this). These spaces may serve as a distraction and are unrelated to the task. What we are exploring is the creation of purpose-built educational VRML spaces. How these will look will depend on what activities we want to occur in these spaces. For example, we may want a space that has a central meeting place with clearly identifiable breakout spaces that can be easily visited by the tutor. We may want to give access to certain online resources in certain positions in certain spaces and so on.

Initial Survey Results

600 students from the course "Computers, Communication, and Society", an introductory course in electronic communication, used a variety of synchronous and asynchronous online tools to complete group related tasks over a 10 week period. Synchronous tools used were: a web-based Java text chat system; The Palace - a 2D Avatar and text chat system, Netmeeting – a video conferencing system (one-to-one in our implementation), and Traveler – a 3D lip sync voice based Avatar system.

As part of the evaluation of the course, students were asked which method of synchronous communication they preferred for small group work. 19% preferred Netmeeting, 38% text chat, 33% Traveler, and 10% The Palace. Overall, 71% preferred synchronous voice over synchronous text. Those who chose synchronous text stated that familiarity with the technology was the most significant factor in their preference for text while those who chose synchronous voice commonly referred to the 'efficiency' and 'naturalness' of voice.

Ongoing research into asynchronous text vs voice conducted with the same course [8] suggests that students may change their preference for asynchronous text-based discussion given sufficient practice and success with voice. This trend may also be evident with synchronous text vs voice and further practice with synchronous voice (in the context of Traveler) has been scheduled for the remainder of the

semester. Later evaluations will possibly show a swing to voice as a consequence. We believe that there is sufficient evidence from these early indicators to continue our project.

Timeline

Our current task is to clearly define the anticipated activities that will occur in these 3D spaces. Concurrently we are developing expertise in building 3D worlds and Avatars. Next we will build a range of spaces that can be trialed with our students. Based on results of staff and student surveys and interviews we intend to build a final set of rooms that can be made available to the wider university.

In December we will be in a position to report on the process of building, testing, and evaluating these spaces. We will be able to demonstrate and discuss the application of purpose-built 3D educational spaces with synchronous voice as a part of our University online learning environment.

References

1. Reid, I.C., *Beyond Models: Developing a University Strategy for Online Instruction.* Journal of Asynchronous Learning Networks, 1999. **3**(1).
2. Brooks, D.W., *Web-teaching : a guide to designing interactive teaching for the World Wide Web.* Innovations in science education and technology. 1997, New York: Plenum Press. xix, 214.
3. Damer, B., S. Gold, and J.d. Bruin. *Steps toward Learning in Virtual World Cyberspace:TheU Virtual University and BOWorld.* in *Interactions in Virtual Worlds: Proceedings Twente Workshop on Language Technology (TWLT) 15.* 1999. Universiteit Twente: Faculteit Informatica.
4. Ong, W.J., *Orality and literacy: the technologizing of the word.* 1982, New York: Methuen.
5. Palloff, R.M. and K. Pratt, *Building learning communities in cyberspace : effective strategies for the online classroom.* 1st ed. The Jossey-Bass higher and adult education series. 1999, San Francisco: Jossey-Bass Publishers. xxiv, 206.
6. Kouki, R. and D. Wright, *Telelearning via the Internet.* 1999, Hershey, PA: Idea Group Pub. 197.
7. Knight, R., *Traveller History.* 1999.
8. Marriott, P., *Asynchronous Voice: Some Design Issues.* Journal of Information Technology Theory and Application, 2001. **3**(3): p. 33-43.

Acknowledgements

Thankyou to Bruce Damer and Steve Turner for their supply and setup of Traveler client and server software.

Cross-Cultural Internet Based Resource for Teaching Democracy

Ilia Goldfarb, Creative Director/Web Developer
The Spirit of Democracy Project, Faculty of Education
University of New Brunswick, Canada
and
Irina Kondratova, Research Officer, National Research Council
Institute for Information Technology e-Business, Canada

Abstract

The Spirit of Democracy Project was initiated in 2000 by the Citizenship Education Group at UNB, Canada, in partnership with the Russian Association for Civic Education. The goal of this project is to help Russian educators to develop a new dynamic approach to citizenship education in public schools. The focus of the Project is the development of online curriculum resources for use by teachers in Russia and Canada. The Canadian and Russian project teams are developing materials for similar topics based on local content. Researchers create learning opportunities using situations and springboards. The situations present democratic issues and concepts, for example the value of loyalty, or the meaning of privacy. An important role in the Project is assigned to visual materials and creative use of hypermedia. The project site brought together a community of practice in cyberspace – a community of social studies researchers and teachers from Russia and Canada.

Introduction

The Spirit of Democracy Project began in the summer of 2000. The project was initiated by the University of New Brunswick, Canada, Faculty of Education, Citizenship Education Research and Development Group, in partnership with the Russian Association for Civic Education and Uchitelskaya Gazeta, and was made possible through financial contribution from the Canadian International Development Agency.

The goal of the project is to help Russian educators to develop a new dynamic approach to citizenship education in public schools. The main focus of the Project is on the development of online citizenship education resources for use by teachers in Russia and Canada. The approaches used to convey "the spirit of democracy" include blended learning, situated learning, and creative use of Web media to effectively teach democracy. A lot of effort has been put into making the Project site a truly democratic learning environment, including links to national and international democratic sources.

After two years we can already call this project a success – the Russian team, participating in the project, have developed and posted on the Project Web site more than 50 different topics related to citizenship and democracy, and the Canadian team posted 27 such topics [1]. Researchers and schoolteachers develop these topics collaboratively. Project materials posted on the Web have already been successfully used by Canadian and Russian teachers in a classroom environment and received positive responses.

Project description

Learning approach used

The Spirit of Democracy project is using the Web to deliver online resources: content, instructions, along with a discussion environment for teachers and students. These curriculum resources can be used as a complete set of materials or as individual lesson topics for different subjects such as Social Studies, History, Citizenship Education, etc. The Canadian and Russian project teams are developing project materials for similar topics based on local content. As a result, the information presented on the Canadian site is relevant to the lives of young Canadians, and the content on the Russian site may differ and is relevant to the lives of Russian students.

Combined with the creative use of multimedia and hypermedia Web based learning offers unique opportunities for educators. The Spirit of Democracy Project's learning approach is based on the ideas of Lev Semenovich Vygotsky who is widely known as "The Mozart of Psychology". Vygotsky, along with Piaget and Bruner developed the foundation for the concepts of Situated Learning and Anchored Instruction [2].

The Situated Learning approach is based on Situated Cognition Theory that suggests that learning is tied to authentic activity, context and culture [3]. As mentioned by Hughes [4]: "An authentic context for citizenship learning must be a situation in which 'real' citizens might be required to think and to act. It can be current, historical, or both; it can be near or far in both time and place". The Spirit of Democracy Project provides teachers and students with a wide range of such "real life" situations. The Project is using a "blended learning" approach in which teachers use online materials in combination with conventional classroom training.

Web media by its nature is the most democratic type of media and is ideally suited for conveying the "spirit of democracy" idea. In this paper authors are using the Web media definition from Huss [5], where the Web media is defined as the use of the text, images, animations, sounds and video on the Web, supported by Hypertext Markup Language (HTML).

Web-based studies allow students to access all original materials, even those provided for teachers. The Web also serves as a unique source of "live" information. By providing hypertext links to government organizations, international organizations, educational Web sites, and online magazines, The Spirit of Democracy learning materials are always up-to date and offer information on recent important developments in the area of Citizenship and Social Studies in Canada, Russia and all over the world.

Creative use of Web media

Within The Spirit of Democracy Project, developers, on both sides, create learning opportunities using situations and springboards (anchors). The situations present democratic issues and concepts, for example the value of loyalty, or the meaning of privacy. The uniqueness of the approach taken by the Spirit of

Democracy project is that researchers use authentic materials to involve students in learning and discovery. A very important role is assigned to visual materials. The situation is usually presented to students by showing a sequence of 8-10 pictures. The pictures should be descriptive enough to tell the story and appealing enough to draw the students in to a discussion about a particular topic. To achieve these results, the project illustrator has to work closely with researchers to portray the situations they want to use.

The topic of "Privacy" is a good example of such joint work between a researcher and an illustrator. One of the scenarios dealing with the topic of "Legal Aspects of Privacy" involves a discussion on the case of unreasonable search and seizure (Mr. Bagnell's case). In the learning activity "You Be the Judge" students need to learn all the details of the case and make a legal judgment [6]. The factual materials of the case are presented as a series of illustrations that lead students through the sequence of events of the actual case (Figure 1). One of the important conditions of this activity is to create an illusion of the court environment and help students experience the process of rendering a fair judgment. The use of visuals here is much more appropriate than the use of newspaper or magazine articles. Such articles usually contain judgmental opinions that may influence students' decisions one way or another. The researcher needed to spend a considerable amount of time working with the illustrator on the details of each scene, making sure that it properly presents all the facts of the case without any additional visual information that might influence students' opinion.

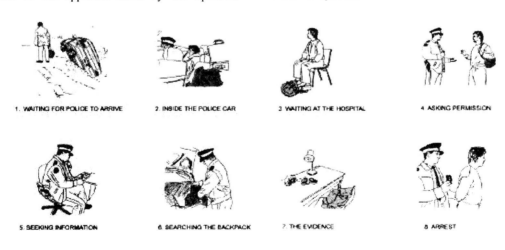

1. WAITING FOR POLICE TO ARRIVE   2. INSIDE THE POLICE CAR   3. WAITING AT THE HOSPITAL   4. ASKING PERMISSION

5. SEEKING INFORMATION   6. SEARCHING THE BACKPACK   7. THE EVIDENCE   8. ARREST

Figure 1. Mr. Bagnell's case

1175

Along with the visual story presented through illustrations, the hypertext links allow students to learn the facts of the case and get additional supportive information, such as, excerpts from the Canadian Charter of Rights and Freedoms, the Controlled drugs and Substances Act, excerpts from precedents that deal with search and seizure cases and from the Privacy Act of New Brunswick, and a discussion of reasonable grounds. It is interesting to mention that our Russian colleagues are having a difficult time translating the word "privacy" as there is no equivalent in the Russian language. Currently in Russia people are using the English word "privacy" to convey the correct meaning of the concept. The idea of having a Privacy Commissioner is also something unheard of in Russian society.

One more example of using images, creatively, to engage students in discussion about democratic issues, like "Freedom of religion", is an interactive presentation of the famous Russian painting "Boyarynya Morozova" by Surikov [7]. In this painting the artist depicts Feodosiya Morozova, who was an active supporter of the old-believer movement in the Russian church, and a crowd made up of vivid individuals. The image map of the painting is hyperlinked to the close-ups of the individual characters portrayed by the painter. During the class discussion the teacher can, using this interactive image, focus student's attention on different human faces in this complex masterpiece portraying a whole range of attitudes towards religion. This helps to initiate a class discussion about a real historical event and how different people with their own beliefs and values view this event.

Unfortunately, the use of multimedia in this international project is heavily restricted by bandwidth limitations on the Russian partners' side. Russian schools, especially in rural areas, have very slow Internet connections. Due to these bandwidth limitations, in some cases video clips on springboards had to be substituted by a sequence of compressed images and songs were replaced by text.

Cultural issues

Because of the international nature of The Spirit of Democracy Project, it presented an opportunity for both teams to develop inter-cultural awareness and understanding. Most of the cultural issues were related to the Web site design and project logo. The process of logo design is an illustration of the complex issues that can arise between two teams working together in different countries with different histories and cultures.

At the beginning of the project it was decided that both teams, Russian and Canadian, would develop their own content. In the first three moths of the project a question was raised about designing a logo. The process of logo design is a good illustration of the complex relationship between the two teams. The Project asked a Canadian graphic artist to design a logo for the Spirit of Democracy project. The artist created the first logo based on the existing Russian interpretation of democratic symbols (Figure 2, a). This logo was discussed during the meetings of the Canadian team and was rejected as being not a "true North American democratic symbol" and also having nothing to do with Russia. A second attempt produced a logo that used an image of the Russian "White House" (former Russian Parliament building) as a symbol of democracy (Figure 2,b). This logo was accepted by Canadian team, but strongly rejected by Russian team members. Russians argued that government buildings in Russian culture are not associated with symbols of democracy. Finally, the artist created the third version of

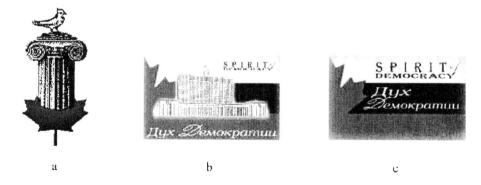

a   b   c

Figure 2. The project logo

the Project logo by removing all imagery and blending two national flags in one image with typography as a main graphic element (Figure 2, c). Both teams accepted this logo as a working draft.

Interface design and translation tools

It is important to mention a creative approach in interface design utilized by The Spirit of Democracy Project. The majority of graphic navigation elements are intentionally designed as hypertext links and not as images. This approach allows the use of automatic translation tools to translate not only the content of individual web pages, but also the navigational elements, thus allowing international users access to the entire content of the Canadian Web site. In the future, with the development of the automatic translation technology, the content of the entire Project site, including Russian web pages, will be available for international users. However, even today, using the Web based automatic translation engine, we provide an option to translate Canadian pages into four languages such as French, Spanish, German and Italian.

The quality of the automatic translation is reasonable, for example the French translation was evaluated and found to be of acceptable quality. However, this is not the case with all languages. For example, when using the service in Spanish, the word "Spirit" in the phrase "Spirit of Democracy" gets translated to the word "alcohol". We believe that, in the future, with the development of better translation tools, these problems will be solved.

It is worthwhile to mention collaborative idea, used in the design of a site map, for the Project Web site. In fact, there are two different site maps, for Russian and Canadian sections. Each navigational map provides hyperlinks not only to local pages, but also allows users to navigate the counterpart site, e.g. Canadian site map provides links not only to Canadian pages, but also helps Canadian users navigate the Russian content, and vice versa. This setup allows users with limited knowledge of a foreign language to explore content on the "foreign" Web site.

Project and the community of practice

The project site brought together a community of practice in cyberspace – a community of social studies researchers and teachers from Russia and Canada. We found that sharing experiences is a valuable part of the virtual community. The virtual community can form within a single school district, province, country and, in our case, between two countries, thus fading the boundaries between counties and continents. International virtual communities can provide teachers, and, in turn, students with the opportunities to develop relationships with people from diverse cultures and backgrounds and

provide an environment that will transform participants into more tolerant and respectful citizens [8].

The concept of community of practice is well known in education and also widely used in knowledge management literature. As broadly defined by Wender and Snyder [9], community of practice is "a group of people informally bound together by shared expertise and passion for a joint enterprise". As emphasized by Duek [10], another essential part of the community of practice is a social dimension: "Emphasis is on sharing of knowledge between people, building communities of knowledge workers, sharing personal experiences, building effective and socially satisfying network of people…"

The educators engaged in the network-based learning can benefit from the experience of the business world where support of information technologies is combined with the knowledge and understanding of knowledge management methods, and the organization of communities of practice engaged in collaborative learning [11]. In order for a community of practice to continue to exist and develop, it needs to be supported by a comprehensive knowledge management framework. This framework shall include several essential components such as supportive environmental factors, effective management system and some incentives for sharing [12]. Thus, in order for the existing Spirit of Democracy's virtual community to continue to exist and function successfully, we believe it would be necessary to create a supporting management framework for the project.

One of the models of the supportive framework for the virtual community of practice that is well developed is the Web portal model [13]. We believe that a logical extension of the Spirit of Democracy Project into the second phase would be to create a "Spirit of Democracy" portal that will accommodate resources to support the work of the Spirit of Democracy's community members and also will create an online collaborative work and learning environment.

A possible model for this type of collaborative work environment would be a model where the Project Portal provides free access to the repository of resource materials, search and retrieval tools, and a discussion forum for scholars, teachers and students. The participating universities and organizations, schools, and teachers submit raw materials (ideas, papers, pictures, lesson plans, springboards, etc.) in to the repository where they are classified according to topics. A peer review process of submissions, by content experts from the social sciences and education community, is undertaken to assure the quality of submissions. This proposed Project Portal will provide an environment of a "live" and dynamic forum, where educators exchange information, get peer reviews and comments on their work, and get valuable feedback from other educators and from students.

A good example of a successful e-Democracy forum is Politalk [14] – a forum that facilitates democratic deliberation. On this forum citizens debate important democratic issues such as campaign finance reform, globalization, transportation, etc. So far the forum was very successful in presenting a diverse set of opinions. According to Bearse [15] it also "...managed to avoid the 'flaming', ideological fixations and personality colorings that have afflicted other e-mail interchanges" due to the following main features:

1. Recruitment of a cross-section of resource people that post background information, including government officials and experts. They also participate in discussions;
2. Having a good forum moderator who sets rules, monitor debates and archives the proceedings.

To assure successful functioning of the proposed Spirit of Democracy Portal we believe it would be crucial to use similar strategies for building the Project's support team.

Conclusions

The organizing idea for this project was born several years ago when two Canadian researchers, Andrew Hughes and Alan Sears witnessed a compelling appeal from colleagues from Argentina at a civic education conference. Argentinean educators, working to foster an emerging democratic culture in their country said "Don't teach us about the structures of democracy - we know all about the structures of democracy; teach us the spirit of democracy" [16].

In the summer of 2000 Russian and Canadian teams for the Spirit of Democracy project met for the first time in Canada to discuss how they are going to teach "the spirit of democracy". Today, after two years of successful collaboration, numerous project materials posted on the Web have already been successfully tried by Canadian and Russian teachers in a classroom environment and received positive responses. Today many participating Canadian and Russian schools are Spirit of Democracy online resources to conduct classes and educate youngsters on democratic values and the spirit of democracy.

Acknowledgements

The authors would like to acknowledge the financial support provided for the project by the Canadian International Development Agency and the University of New Brunswick.

References

1. The Spirit of Democracy Project (2002a). Splash Page. http://www.unb.ca/democracy
2. The Spirit of Democracy Project (2002b). The Spirit of Democracy Learning Approach. http://www.unb.ca/democracy/Project/IdeasInDemocracy/SituatedLearning/SituatedLearning1.html
3. Brown, J.S., Collings, A., & Duguid, P. (1989). Situated Cognition and the Culture of Learning. Educational Researcher, 18 (1), 32-41.
4. Hughes, A.S., Long, N., & Perry, M. (2000). Learning the Spirit of Democracy: The Project's Background and an Illustration. Proceedings of the Citizenship 2020 Conference: Assuming Responsibility for Our Future, McGill Institute for the Study of Canada, Montreal.
5. Huss D. (1999). Corel Photo-Paint 9: The Official Guide. The McGraw-Hill Companies.
6. The Spirit of Democracy Project. (2002c). You Be the Judge. http://www.unb.ca/democracy/Project/IdeasInDemocracy/privacy/LegalPrivacy/LegalPrivacy2.html
7. The Spirit of Democracy Project. (2002d). Boyarynya Morozova. http://www.unb.ca/democracy/Project/IncludeIdeas/RecentExamples/workshopFreedoms/FundamentalFreedoms.htm
8. Cifuentes, L. & Murphy, K.L. (2000). Promoting Multicultural Understanding and Positive Self-Concept Through a Distance Learning Community: Cultural Connections, Educational Technology Research and Development, Vol.48, No. 1, 69-83.
9. Wender, E.C. & Snyder, W.M. (2000). Communities of Practice: The Organizational Frontier, Harvard Business Review 78, No. 1, 139-145.
10. Duek, G. (2001). Views of Knowledge are Human Views, IBM Systems Journal, Vol.40, No. 4, 885-888.
11. Trentin, G. (2001). From Formal Training to Communities of Practice via Network-Based Learning, Educational Technology, March-April 2001.
12. Gongla, P. & Rizzuto, C.R. (2001). Evolving Communities of Practice: IBM Global Services Experience, IBM Systems Journal, Vol.40, No. 4, 842-862.
13. Bressler, S. E. & Grantham, C.E. (2000). Communities of Commerce. McGraw-Hill.
14. Politalk. (2002). Civil Discussion on Controversial Topics, http://www.politalk.com/
15. Bearse, P. (2002, to be published). Laboring in the Vineyards or The People, Yes: How "Ordinary" People Can Make a Difference – Through Politics, http://www.politalk.com/topics/election/posts/bearse.html
16. The Spirit of Democracy Project. (2002e). Home Page, http://www.unb.ca/democracy/Project/Project2.html

Web-Based Learning and Teacher Preparation:
Lessons Learned

Patricia E. Ragan, Ph.D.
Arthur Lacey, M.S.
Robert Nagy, Ph.D.
University of Wisconsin-Green Bay

Abstract

Data was collected on technology-related issues involved in the conversion of a teacher preparation program into an online, competency, and field-based model. Faculty issues involving instructional design, workload, and merit/tenure were examined, as well as the effects of web-based course delivery on student and faculty interaction, competency acquisition, technology proficiency, and learning outcomes. Results support significant improvement in technology proficiency, comfort level, and perceptions of competence for faculty and students. In addition, competency acquisition remained constant or improved across all courses in the program sequence. Future research is needed using a larger population sample and an experimental/control group paradigm.

Introduction

Distance learning can provide students with the accessibility and flexibility needed to participate in individual and group experiences from their homes, job sites, and/or field placements. While critics (Cornell, 1999; Mergendoller, 2000) maintain that distance learning depersonalizes the teacher/student relationship and limits the interpersonal interaction, research shows that online courses can be designed to promote higher order learning such as analysis, synthesis, and evaluation (Fulton, 1998). Dusick (1998) believes that web-based instruction fosters teamwork and cooperative effort. McKenzie (1998) reports positively on the ability to monitor student hits, time in specific areas, and to generate histograms of student progress. Additionally, Odasz (2000) claims that one of the biggest advantages is being able to set time allowed for online quizzes and the number of times students can take each quiz.

Many conditions support the need for distance learning in teacher preparation. Increased numbers of nontraditional students, longer commuting distances for students, and the federal mandate to provide intensive and extensive field-based experiences all equate to decreased available seat-time and issues of accessibility. Despite growing support (Maddux, et.al, 1999; Zhao, 1998), little data is available on the effectiveness of online instruction in teacher preparation and it remains controversial (Goldworthy, 2000).

Project Overview

With funding from a 3-year FIPSE grant, this project examined the effectiveness of web-based strategies to enhance and supplement teaching and learning in a small teacher preparation program. A standards-based curriculum with clearly defined competencies was first designed to ensure pre-service teacher proficiency in all applicable standards, an outside consultant was brought in to provide training in online instructional design, and course content was converted to the web-based environment. Pre-service teachers were placed in classroom settings with mentoring support from master teachers and accessed course content through online core modules and campus-based seminars for reflection and discussion. Information was gathered on the technology-related problems and obstacles encountered by faculty and students in converting and using web-based software. The study additionally examined the positive and negative outcomes of web-based course delivery, including issues of instructional design, workload, competency-acquisition, interaction, and student learning outcomes.

Results

Significant increases in student learning in the area of technology are reported. Chi-square analyses of pre and post data on technology knowledge, skills, and attitudes over the 3-years of the grant, yielded significant gains for students across all areas and for all courses at a significance level of .02 or better. Student comfort levels with technology, as well as their perceptions of success, as measured by course evaluations, also increased for all course offerings across the 3-years of the grant.

Exams were taken online by students three times during each course offering, with three opportunities to reach 93% criteria. Changes in average scores and changes in the average number of times taken were examined using 2-way ANOVA's. Results were statistically significant ($p < .02$) with average scores increasing and number of times taken decreasing each year of the project. Tukey-t's indicated significance could be attributed to a dramatic increase in second year average scores and a dramatic decrease in times taken in the third year.

Survey responses asked pre-service students in the online program and alumni teachers in the field to indicate their agreement or disagreement on a 4-point scale. Responses were coded and chi-square analyses done to determine if there were differences in perceptions of program competence. There were no significant differences ($p < .325$) in the two group's perceptions of the overall quality of their preparation, but significant differences in perceptions of competency acquisition were found in eight areas: (a) knowledge of cultural and linguistic diversity; (b) cross-cultural learning; (c) collaboration with diverse families; (d) knowledge of resources and services for families; (e) assessment strategies; (f) collaboration with colleagues; (g) knowledge of major issues; and (h) use of technology. Significantly more pre-service teachers rated learning in these areas as good or excellent than did alumni teachers in the field, suggesting that performance-based learning in relevant classroom settings was supported and enhanced using online course delivery.

Conclusions

Concerns expressed by faculty over the 3-years of the project have important implications for the future success of online learning and teacher preparation. Faculty reported limited institutional support for online teaching and an absence of adequate training in instructional design and interactive strategies. The rigidity of traditional faculty roles created excessive workloads within the existing "course-for-credit" structure of higher education and was not recognized within the merit/tenure process. Mentoring support in the field, for example, was considered to be a critical component by students and faculty alike, and there was a lack of institutional support for mentoring as part of faculty load.

Despite recurring obstacles, the long-term positive outcomes far outweighed initial concerns, and project results support online/distance learning as a viable option for the delivery of instruction in teacher preparation. Students and instructors alike reported flexibility in delivery and access as a strength, and competency acquisition was not negatively affected and, in fact, improved in several areas. Instructor feedback reported that distance learning encourages students to take personal responsibility for their learning, supports the development of time management skills, facilitates high-levels of quality interaction with all students, and provides opportunities for regular and frequent feedback and review based on ongoing student processing. Equally relevant, was the flexibility it provided in delivery and

access, thus supporting more extensive course related field placements and performance-based learning.

The results of this study suggest strong benefits from the use of distance learning in teacher preparation and contribute to a growing collection of data on learning outcomes using online instruction in teacher preparation programs. However, replication is needed using a larger sample and an experimental design methodology. A cross-sectional design and stratified sampling would be able to address socioeconomic, gender, and ethnic differences, as well. Furthermore, future research needs to address the differences between rural and urban students in relation to technological literacy, and longitudinal data needs to be gathered on the long-term effects on faculty roles and perceptions of learning success, as well as changes in workload and merit/tenure policies on campuses using distance learning.

The move to introduce technology into teacher preparation served as a major catalyst for change in the use of technology in the education unit and other units across campus, in the level of support provided by the university, in the student's level of technological proficiency, and most importantly, in student's performance-based learning and competency acquisition. It is hoped that this study will serve as a impetus and resource for the future development of distance learning in teacher preparation.

References

Cornell, R. (1999). The onrush of technology in education: The professor's new dilemma. *Educational Technology, 39* (3), 60-64.

Dusick, D. M. (1998). What social cognitive factors influence faculty members' use of computers for teaching? A literature review. *Journal of Research on Computing in Education, 31*(2), 123-136.

Fulton, K. (1998). Learning in a digital age: Insights into the issues. *T.H.E. Journal, 25*(7), 60-63.

Goldworthy, R. (2000). Collaborative classrooms. *Learning and Leading with Technology, 27*(4), 6-9.

McKenzie, J. (1998). Grazing the net. *Phi Delta Kappan*, 26-31.

Mergendoller, J. R. (2000). Technology and learning: A critical assessment. *Principal, 79*(3), 5-9.

Odasz, F. (2000). Collaborative internet tools. *Learning and Leading with Technology, 27*(4), 10-15.

Development of generator for lesson plan making support systems

Shinya KOUNO[1], Setsuo YOKOYAMA[1], Naoto NAKAMURA[2], Nobuyoshi YONEZAWA[3] and Youzou MIYADERA[1]

1) Tokyo Gakugei Univ., 4-1-1, Nukuikita, Koganei, Tokyo JAPAN, Email {shinya, yokoyama, miyadera}@u-gakugei.ac.jp
2) Chiba Institute of Technology, 2-17-1 Tsudanuma, Narashino, Chiba, JAPAN, Email nakamura@nao.net.it-chiba.ac.jp
3) Kogakuin University, 1-24-2 Nishi-Shinjuku, Shinjuku-ku, Tokyo JAPAN, Email ct72058@ns.kogakuin.ac.jp

Abstract

This study has developed a generator system that generates various type of lesson plan making support systems automatically. The framework and items that each teacher needs are defined, and the generator automatically generates a lesson plan making support system according to the definition.

First, this have developed the formal definition of description format for describing lesson plans using the extended BNF notation. It becomes possible for the users to input ant edit whatever they need according to the description format. The user can write a grammatically correct lesson plan and edit it without grammatical errors (Healthness).

Second, this developed a generator that automatically generates the Java source code of a system corresponding to the description format. The generator can deal with the frameworks and input items that various teachers want to have in their lesson plans (Completeness). It can also generate a system according to each user's purpose (Generality).

1. Introduction

Educators typically use similar frameworks to create lesson plans. However, the forms and the items used in lesson plans vary depending on the teacher. Thus, it is difficult to make those lesson plans a data base automatically while keeping the correspondence of the form and the item of the lesson plan which each teacher wrote. In the current systems, the framework, input items, and form are already defined in the systems, or lesson plans written on paper are transferred into an image-file, and then registered in the database [1][2][3][4]. These methods lack reusability. Many lesson plan support systems have emerged from past studies. These systems support the lesson plan process by preparing the model of the class, and then selecting the content of the class from the model. Using these systems as training systems allows users to make a consistent lesson plan. Therefore, these systems are useful. However, only one kind of lesson plan can be realized. Hence, it is impossible to deal with the myriad framework, form, and items that each teacher needs. The supported system has to demonstrate the following two points:

1. Make a lesson plan that is consistent.
2. Output a unique lesson plan that is based on each form, items, and framework.

It is also difficult to develop the systems that are compatible for use with each planner and subject. The cause is that each system has a peculiar frame. This problem can be solved by providing the system a constant rule. That is, it is a grammar by which the form and the frame of the lesson plan are defined. The generator which analyzes the description according to the rule and generates the lesson plan making support system solves the problem.

The purpose of this research is as follow: First, formally defining the lesson plan description method. Second, the development of the generator (The user can freely set the item, the element, and the input method etc., based on the definition.) which automatically generates the lesson plan making support system (This system is called LPSS).

This paper is organized as follows. Section 2 describes the outline of the generator used to generate the LPSS, formally defines the Lesson Plan description method and the System created by using the generator. Section 3 describes the development of the generator. Section 4 describes the features, functions, and structure of the LPSS created by using the generator. Section 5 presents the summary and discusses the anticipated future problems.

2. Generator
2.1 Necessity

Most of the developed LPSSs have structures comprised of a only form, framework, and item. In these systems the user only inputs the required content where the system demands. As a result, a relevant lesson plan is produced [5][6][7][8][9]. However, it corresponds to the form only of one. In these ideas, it can not be compatible to various lesson plans.

Thus, we thought that having the proper generator would solve the problem. The generator automatically generates the LPSS based on the description of the given lesson-plan rule.

Consequently, it is possible to easily construct a LPSS by using the various input forms used to create lesson plans that are based on what the user inputs.

2.2 Overview

This generator is operated by inputting the description format of a lesson plan that was written in accord with certain rules. This generator automatically generates a LPSS that corresponds to a given user and subject by rewriting the description format if necessary. The generator was mounted using a CGI described using the Perl language. In addition, the generated LPSS is a JAVA program because it has to be usable on the Internet (Figure 1).

The target users of this system are student teachers and guidance counselors. The guidance teacher inputs to the generator the description form that records the items, elements, and the framework. Then, the generator creates the LPSS, which automatically presents the necessary input fields for the student teacher. The student teacher can make a lesson plan that conforms to the guidance teacher's format by using the created system.

If each teacher describes a rule, then this generator can generate a customized lesson plan that is based on each teacher's idea. Hence, this system can be used not only by probationary teachers, but by veteran teachers as well. LPSSs made by the generator is compatible, that is, the lesson plans made by the LPSSs is compatible.

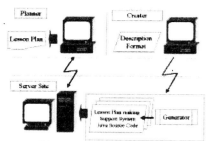

Figure 1: System Diagram

2.3 Input

2.3.1 Input information

We analyzed a group of lesson plans to clarify their current state and components [10]. The lesson plans are those actually made by a guidance counselor or student teacher. Most lesson plans are composed of the content & method of instruction, student reactions & activities, and points to keep in mind.

The first step was to extract the words and the actions in the lesson plans. The second step involved rewriting the time series to clarify the time flow of the instructional design.

The following features were found.

• In the lesson plans, there are different kinds of input elements that make up each item.

• The input element is not described in the place of a correct item. (For instance, the description concerning method of instruction is written in the place of student reactions.)

• It is difficult to understand the relation of the input element.

We think that it is necessary to define the component that belongs to the item that composes the lesson plan and to support the user to be able to input the component to an appropriate item.

The input to the generator has two parts. One is "Item Part"(IP) and another is "Description Convention Part"(DCP). IP is set of items, which compose the lesson plan. The rules, position of the cell that inputs a word and action, Edit command and Class form etc., are described in the description convention part. The lesson plan description format (DF) is defined by DCP and IP.

Figure 2 shows the interface of the LPSS. The IP defines the composition of the row and the DCP provides the types of inputs described in the row. The DCP defines the commands and system messages, which can be used at each stage and Form of table.

Editing by using the correspondence as a lesson plan enabled the editor command to be built into the DCP. It is effective to introduce the formal language used by developing a language processor for the automatic generation of the LPSS. To deal with the DF formally, the DCP was written by extending the BNF notation. Table 1 shows an example of a DF.

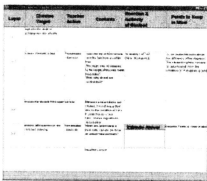

Figure 2: Interface

2.3.2 Description Format

The DF is composed of the IP where a set of items that compose a lesson plan are described and the DCP where the grammar was defined by extending the BNF notation.

Item Part

The IP is described at the head of the description format. Each item is corresponds to each column in the interface of the table form. Each item is separated by a comma.
Column = (item1, item2, item3, …)

Description Convention Part

The DCP is composed of the terminal nodes, non-terminal nodes, editor commands, and the selection items. It writes using the extended BNF notation. Each notation is shown as follows.

Terminal node = [element: num: command "Message "]

. Element: Minimum unit in the lesson plan. Element is a kind of input data in terminal node.

. Num The numerical value means the column number of the table formats.

. Command: "/INPUT" is a command that enables user to input and edit text directly. "/DEF" is a command to setup messages that user can select only by pop-up menu.

. Messages: the message text telling the user

Non-Terminal node = <terminal node, …>.

Non-terminal node is composed of some terminal nodes and non-terminal nodes.

Omit-able node = encloses with "{ }".

Command - executable commands be delimited by "/ /"

Selection_item - [select: position: "message": selections]

. Position: position where the pop-up menu is displayed.

. Messages: the message displayed in the pop-up menu

. Choices

-The choices are presented and marked off the delimitation "|".

-The words in the quotation marks are displayed in the pop-up menu

-A command in < > is an element of DCP

1182

Repetition of 0 times or more - [ ]* or <>*
Repetition of one time or more - [ ]+ or <>+

It is also possible to describe the description convention by using two or more lines and describes ";" at the end of line. The character string enclosed with "" in the DF shows the message displayed on the LPSS.

2.3.3 Significance of formalization

The formalization of the lesson plan is significant in two ways. One is soundness. The user can write a grammatically correct lesson plan as well as edit a lesson plan without introducing grammatically errors. Another is completeness; this generator and DF can deal with various frameworks and items in lesson plans according to the teachers' needs.

2.4 Output

The lesson plan making system created by the generator assumes use on the Internet, and it was programmed using Java source code. Figure 2 shows an interface of this system created with the generator, which input the description form shown in Table 1. The created LPSS has the table-type interface composed of an item defined by IP and Column, which displays the layered structure of the lesson plan. This column is located on the left side of the table. An item defined in IP queues up sequentially on the right side, and composes the table. A column conforming to the numerical value described in the item of the terminal node recorded with the DF is a place that can be input. In that case, the message that presses the input is displayed on the cell that needs inputting.

By this method, the system is maintaining the elements of the cell and information on the coordinates, i.e., the selection item which the system presents is judged.

The system prepares the editing commands for the structure of the lesson plan beforehand. The commands for insertion, deletion, copy, etc. can be selected by using the pop-up menu. The processing that corresponds to these commands while maintaining the structure described by the command is necessary when the DF is done. As a result, insertion and the deletion to a different structure can be prevented.

3. Development of generator

3.1 Requirement specification

consideration of the variety of users environments. So, I thought of the following specifications.

- The generator interface is a Web browser.
- The generated system is a platform-independent one..
- The language used in the database is used to develop the LPSS so that there is intimacy.

3.2 System configuration

The generator inputs the DF of the lesson plan. As a result, the generator generates the Java source code of the LPSS which can execute the operation and the input according to the DF automatically. This generator is composed of two subsystems; a parsing part and a code generation part. The generator does the parsing of the DF described by the text. And the JAVA source code of the LPSS is created (Figure 3).

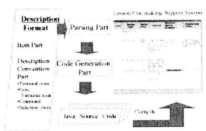

Figure 3: Generator Diagram

Parsing part

The parsing part analyzes the description format and makes a table of the terminal nodes and a parsing table. This part extracts the kind, attribute, message of the terminal node, and message and choice which compose the selection item by using the table.

Code generation part

The code generation part generates the Java source code of the LPSS based on the data obtained in the parsing part. This subsystem is mounted by using PERL, and it compiles the output JAVA source code and outputs the LPSS.

The generated LPSS have the table-form interface. It is composed of the item defined in the IP and column, for which layered structure of lesson plan is displayed The

---

Column = (Layer, Division-Target, Teacher-Action, Contents, Reaction & Activity of Student, The Points to Keep in Mind);
<Instruction-Design>::=[/SELECT "Command": "CUT"/CUT/| "COPY"/ COPY / | " PASTE" / PASTE / |"CREATE" / CREATE/ |"DELETE"
/ DELETE / | " RANK" / RANK /] [Division-Target : 1 : /INPUT " Input the Target] [/ SELECT " Select from makes the class and
    progresses the class" : "makes the class" <Lesson-Form> | "progresses the class" <Division>+] ;
<Lesson-Form>::= [/SELECT "Select the Lesson-Form" : "Lecture-Form"<Lecture-Form> | "Presentation-Exercises-Form" <
    Presentation-Exercises-Form >];
<Lecture-Form>::= [Lesson-Form : 2 : /DEF "Lecture-Form"][Explanation: 3: /INPUT "Input the explanation"] [GreenBoard-Design: 3:
    /INPUT "Input the GreenBoard-Design"];
< Presentation-Exercises -Form >::= [Lesson-Form : 2 : /DEF "Presentation-Exercises -Form"] <Presentation-Exercises>[Estimate-Answer: 4:
    /INPUT "Input the Estimate-Answer"][Explanation: 3: /INPUT "Input the explanation"][GreenBoard-Design: 3: /INPUT "Input the
    GreenBoard-Design"];
< Presentation-Exercises >::= [Question: 3: /INPUT "Input the Question"][/SELECT "Method of setting questions": "Writing-GreenBoard"
    [Method: 2: /DEF "Writing-GreenBoard"] | "Print" [Method: 2: /DEF "Print"]] | "Word-of-Mouth"[Method: 2: /DEF "Word-of-Mouth"]]:

Table1: Example of description format

The generator in this research and the LPSS generated based on the assumption of Internet use and making to the data base. For this case, it is necessary to develop in tables of the necessary number of columns are generated based on the names and number of items as defined by the IP.

Each item is allocated in the column in described order.

The subsystem makes the pop-up menu which displays "Message described in the selection item" and "Optional element" for the editor command and the select sentence. This subsystem makes the class that corresponds to each selection item. The processing is analyzed from the description format, and the processing system is built into the LPSS. Figure 4 is a program described to display the selection items of the class form in Table 1. The LPSS is the one that the JAVA program group generated by using these processes was compiled

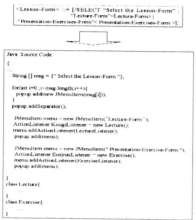

```
<Lesson-Form> ::= [/SELECT "Select the Lesson-Form" ;
           "Lecture-Form"<Lecture-Form> |
 "Presentation-Exercises-Form"< Presentation-Exercises-Form >];
```

```
Java Source Code
{
  ...
  String [] msg = (" Select the Lesson-Form ");

  for(int i=0 ;i<msg.length; i++){
    popup.add(new JMenuItem(msg[i]));
  }
  popup.addSeparator();

  JMenuItem menu = new JMenuItem("Lecture-Form ");
  ActionListener KougiListener = new Lecture();
  menu.addActionListener(LectureListener);
  popup.add(menu);

  JMenuItem menu = new JMenuItem(" Presentation-Exercise-Form ");
  ActionListener EnsyuuListener = new Exercise();
  menu.addActionListener(ExerciseListener);
  popup.add(menu);
}
class Lecture{
  ...
}
class Exercise{
  ...
}
```

Figure 4: Generated program example

4. Lesson Plan making Support System
4.1 The system generation
The description format is input from the input screen using text.On the input screen, the user selects the sample of the description format, and has it presented. If they need to edit the sample, they edit it, and make the description format for each lesson plan.Moreover, they can prepare the edit command and the selection item beforehand in the DF. They transmit the description format to the system, and generate the lesson plan making support system.

4.2 Operation example
Table 1 shows an example of a LPSS generated with the description format. Figure 5 shows the initial screen when LPSS is started. The interface is a table form composed of columns by which the layered structure is shown along with columns of five items, because it is defined in the IP that Column = (Division-Target, Teacher-Action, Contents, Reaction & Activity of Student, The Points to Keep in Mind).

The column on the left shows the layered structure of the lesson plan Initial state is assumed to be 0, and the layered structure of "1, 2, 3, ..." and the item is shown by the numerical value sequentially. The user makes the lesson plan by operating the input and the selection according to the system message.

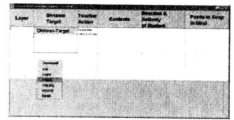

Figure 5: Initial screen

In Table 1, <Instructional-Design> is composed by sets of <Division> as defined in the DCP. The system presents the message that presses the input of [Division-Target] at column corresponding to figure described as item that [Division-Target] belongs.

In this case, because the purpose is defined as 1, the system presents the message in column 2 from the left.

The user can edit it by double-clicking the cell in which the message is presented. Next, the system displays the message defined on the cell by the selection item, and presents the selection of <Lesson-Form> or new [Division-Target], that composes origin [Division-Target], by the pop-up menu. In right-clicking on the cell, an optional element is displayed by the pop-up menu. The user selects the menu, and advances the operation.

There are three kinds of operations.

1. User makes the content of the class intended for the <Division>.
2. User progresses the <Division>.
3. User reserves the input and the operation of the <Division>, and makes new <Division>.

In the case of 1: selects <Lesson-Form> from the menu of the selection item. As a result, the message which selects the class form is presented. Then, selects the class form. Next, the message that presses the input to the element that composes the selected class form is presented. The planner inputs content in accordance with the message.

In the case of 2: selects <Division> from the menu of the selection item. New <Division> is made, and the planner repeats the current work. <Division> means development from edited <Division>. It means the layer of new <Division> falls, and "1-2" is displayed in the left-most cell that shows the structure.

In the case of 3: The input and the operation of edited <Division> are reserved, and the planner makes renewing <Division>. In that case, the planner makes a new <Division> by using the "CREATE" edit command. The system maintains the composition information and input information of each <Division>, thus making possible renewing <Division>. Therefore, the planner comes to be able to make a Lesson Plan by using both the top-down and the bottom-up methods (Figure 6, 7). This introduces variety to the making of the lesson plan. In the operation of these two methods, hierarchically expressing the class structure is thought to allow various the realization of structures possible.

Figure 6: Top Down Method

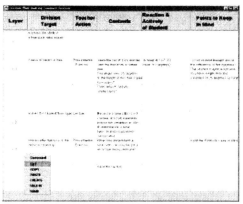

Figure 7: Bottom-Up Method

Additionally, the command to edit the class structure includes the command by which to copy, paste, delete, and operate the hierarchy. When the planner edits the class structure, the menu of an executable editor command is displayed to the planner by right-clicking on the cell that the edit targets. The planner selects a necessary command and edits the class structure from among that. These edit commands define the function beforehand in the system. As a result, the editing of a compatible class structure becomes possible. The resulting Lesson Plan is restructured in the format of TeX and output. As a result, using a PostScript file and a PDF file made from the source file of the TeX of the Lesson Plan becomes possible.

4.3 Feature

The generator uses the DF (defined the description conventions of the item and the input needed to make the Lesson Plan formal) to generate the LPSS. As a result, the LPSS became a system with the following features.

(1) Making of Sound Lesson Plan: The input and the operation according to the format are done by building in the command. Therefore, the made Lesson Plan is sound.

(2) Diversification of making method: The planner can make the Lesson Plan bottom-up or top down. As a result, the planner is not limited by the input procedure of the system, and they can do the instructional plan flexibly. Moreover, the LPSS that is produced matches the edited screen. Therefore, when the planner makes the Lesson

Plan, easy confirmation of the state of the Lesson Plan becomes possible.

(3) Easy operation: The LPSS is an interface that uses the Java table. The LPSS became a system able to operate the class structure and be easily edited because it used the function of an existing table.

4.4 Possibility of making a database

Doing automatic extracting of the key items of the different elements that comprise a Lesson Plan from the DF becomes easy. As a result, it is thought that registration will be made easier by using the database and the automatic generation of the search engine. It will present problems to attempt to add the database function in the future.

5. Conclusion

We reported on a study were the development a system for the automatic preparation of lesson plans was investigated. A generator, was created to create a LPSS that conforms to the requirements of the individual user. By building a database that is based information such as the item name, the editor command, and the presentation message, and inputting the DF that defines the form of the Lesson Plan, which is necessary in the description convention step of automatic lesson plan generation. This generator is a system that generates automatically in accordance with manufacturer's DF, as for the LPSS.

Furthermore, making the support system resulted in our being able to make a Lesson Plan that was characterized by soundness and integrity, and we demonstrated that generality is possible.

The Lesson Plan made by using the LPSS is constructed a database. The development of the authoring system, which can easily make the DF is necessary, because the DF inputs with the text, making of the DF of the Lesson Plan is not easy.

References
[1] http://www.fes.miyazaki-u.ac.jp/HomePage/gakyu/clas4-1/zuko/botan/sidouan/sidouan.html
[2] http://jcultra.cc.osaka-kyoiku.ac.jp/LPIW/
[3] http://www.lessonplanspage.com/
[4] http://teachers.net/
[5] Nakadake, O., "Studies on the Development of System Concerned with Teaching", JET95-2, pp.47-54 (1994).
[6] Okamoto, T., Matsuda, N.,: "Development of Expert System for Instructional Design", JET94-2, pp.29-32 (1994).
[7] Okamoto, T., Matsuda, N.,: "Development of a Learning Support System on the Distributed Cooperative Environment", JET94-2, pp.33-36 (1996).
[8] Matsuda, T., et al.: "Development and Evaluation of Training System for Instructional design", Japan Educational Technology, Vol22, No4, pp263-278 (1999)
[9] Matsuda, T., Nomura, T., and Enoki, T., : "Development of a High School Math Textbook Database and Its Application in an Instructional Design System", Japan Educational Technology, Vol22, No1, pp.13-27 (1998).
[10] Souma, T., Kouno, S.,: "Development and Evaluation of a Computer Supported System to draw up Teaching Plan", Tec. Rep. IEICE.ET2000-55,pp.71-78 (2000).

Taking Benefit of the Structure to Improve the Retrieval of Pedagogical Resources

Bich-Liên Doan and Yolaine Bourda
SUPELEC,
Plateau de Moulon, 3 rue Joliot Curie, 92192 Gif/Yvette.
E-mail : (Bich-Lien.Doan , Yolaine.Bourda)@supelec.fr
France

Abstract

This paper describes a new Information Retrieval System for pedagogical content. Each pedagogical resource is explicit thanks to metadata and structure. We explain how to manipulate the structure of these multimedia resources at an appropriate level of granularity (resources, set of resources). Finally we propose combining the structural and the textual analysis of the resources to improve the performance of the system.

1. Building pedagogical resources

The World Wide Web has become a well-known medium for teachers to publish and for learners to access educational material. The WWW is a hypertext graph where the nodes are HTML pages and the links are text anchors which point to another page. But educational resources on the WWW lack explicit semantics and structure. This can be improved by the use of metadata to describe the semantic content [4] and by the use of typed links to represent the structure of the resources. Standardized metadata such as Dublin Core Education [1], LOM [2] bring better understanding of the educational resources content and aim, but there is a little description of the structure of these resources. By structure we mean the logical structure, ie the logical organization of a resource or a document.

Links between resources are often chosen by the author during the conception stage, but the types of links are not explicit with the Hypertextual Markup Language (HTML). To mitigate these problems, we consider that a pedagogical resource is either an atomic unit of information such as an image, a passage, a title..., or a composition of other resources. A resource can be defined as a semantic unit of information, autonomous in the sense that it can be given as a response to a user request. From there, we can consider different levels of resources. A global resource can be structured in a hierarchy of several resources, it is composed of structured elements representing either section, paragraph, image, sound, graph called resources too. Each level in the hierarchy corresponds to a different level of granularity. We

choose a tree structure of nodes for our example to be understandable, but in fact, we can have a Directed Acyclic Graph (DAG) structure. For example we can have a first organization level, composed of several domains, sub-domains and so on. Each hierarchical level represents a level of granularity, the lowest level of granularity is that of the components of the atomic resources (not decomposable). This concept of granularity is significant because it intervenes in all the stages of our new information retrieval system. Indeed, during the description of the resources, our formalism makes it possible to describe resources, to express the structural or semantic relations between the resources, to adapt this description to structured pages with the HTML format (META tags) or XML (the tags are defined by the author of the pages according to a particular DTD). Thus, it is possible to explicit the various types of relations between resources, between components of various natures (multi-media like its, image, video) or of various types like paragraphs, references, summaries...

The semantics and the structure of resources as we specified previously may be done by the author of the pages, manually, thanks to metadata. A classical hierarchical clustering algorithm can determine the hierarchy of resources and provide the summary of each cluster. The first solution enables a precise control and the labeling of each represent of clusters by the author, but it requires human help. The second solution is completely automatic but the drawback is that the labels are a list of keywords extracted from the resources and maybe some concepts are omitted. For a quality reason and to enable the author to control the indexing stage, we build the structured resources with the help of the author of resources.

At the building stage of the educational resources, we propose to describe the resources using the IEEE LOM[2] semantics and to apply the RDF serialization[3] with the XML syntax[4].
This is a first example of a learning resource described thanks to LOM metadata:

```
<?xml version="1.0" encoding="iso-8859-1" ?>
```

```
<educational_resources>
<General>
<title><langstring
xml:lang="en">"Computer science history,
image of the Cray CDC
6600"</langstring></title>
<identifier><entry>"http://www.bld.fr/eduResources
/"</entry></identifier>
<keyword>"course, computer science,
history, Cray"</Keyword>
</General>
<LifeCycle>
        <contribute><entity>Bich-Liên
Doan</entity><date>"2000
september"</date>
        </contribute>
</LifeCycle>
<Educational>
<intendeduserrole>" 1rst year Paris XII
university's students"</intenteduserrole>
</Educational>
<Technical><format>img/bmp</format>
</Technical>
</educational_resources>
```

In the following sections, we take the example of an E-learning Web course delivered at SUPELEC's school. In this example, there is one "computer science course" resource which is composed of other resources. The educational resource material has been created by Yolaine Bourda. The domain of the resource is the database management systems (DBMS), including the SQL language. The courses are currently used by students both in Paris and in different geographical places of the SUPELEC's school: Metz and Rennes. Firstly, the audience is the SUPELEC's students but it can also be extended to any e-learner who can access the http://wwwlsi.supelec.fr/www/yb/poly_bd/ site.

This is an example of the LOM metadata describing three resources:

```
<?xml version="1.0" encoding="iso-8859-1"
?>
<educational_resources>
<General>
<title><langstring
xml:lang="en">"Learning
databases"</langstring></title>
<identifier><entry>"http://wwwlsi.supelec.fr/www/y
b/poly_bd/"</entry></identifier>
<keyword>"course, computer
science"</Keyword>
</General>
<LifeCycle>
        <contribute><entity>"Yolaine
Bourda"</entity><date>"1997
september"</date></contribute>
</LifeCycle>
<Educational>
<intendeduserrole>"2nd year Supelec's
students"</intenteduserrole>
</Educational></educational_resources>
<educational_resources>
```

```
<General>
<title><langstring xml:lang="en">What
is a DBMS?</langstring></titel>
<identifier><entry>"http://wwwlsi.supelec.fr/ww
w/yb/poly_bd/tdm"</entry></identifier>
<keyword>"DBMS"</Keyword>
</General>
<Relation>
    <kind>"isPartOf"</kind>
    <resource><identifier>"http://wwwlsi.supele
c.fr/www/yb/poly_bd/"</identifier></resource>
</Relation>
</General>
</educational_resources>
<educational resources>
<General>
<title><langstring xml:lang="en">
"Learning SQL"</langstring></titel>
<identifier><entry>"http://wwwlsi.supelec.fr/ww
w/yb/poly_bd/tdm_sql"</entry></identifier>
<keyword>"SQL"</Keyword>
</General>
<Relation>
    <kind>"isPartOf"</kind>
    <resource><identifier>"http://wwwlsi.supele
c.fr/www/yb/poly_bd/"</identifier></resource>
</Relation>
</General>
</educational_resources>
```

Through this example, we know that the same author is responsible for the publication of the three documents, and that the date of creation is the same too; nevertheless, this piece of information has been omitted when the resources composing the root document have been described. We show in the following section that this omitted information may be deduced thanks to the structural links. The e-learning resources and their organization are partially illustrated in figure 1.

The first resource d represents the Web site as a collection of E-learning resources. Each resource is described thanks to the LOM metadata. d is composed of the two resources $d1$ and $d2$. The "isPartOf" and "requires" attributes represent structural links. Why is it important to use these structural links? Let's take an example (figure 2) without using the structure. Each resource is described with the local LOM attributes. At the indexing stage, the hierarchical structure of these resources is lost, so is the hypertextual structure of Web pages when the pages are indexed by classical search tools. Each of the resources $d,d2,d21,d22$ is indexed as an atomic resource, unlinked to other resources. Querying a resource published in 1997 and dealing with SQL will not be retrieved by such an information retrieval system. Querying a resource concerning both the terms "query" from $d21$ and "update" from $d22$ will provide no answer, whereas the response should be $d2$. To solve these problems, we propose to take into account the structural links.

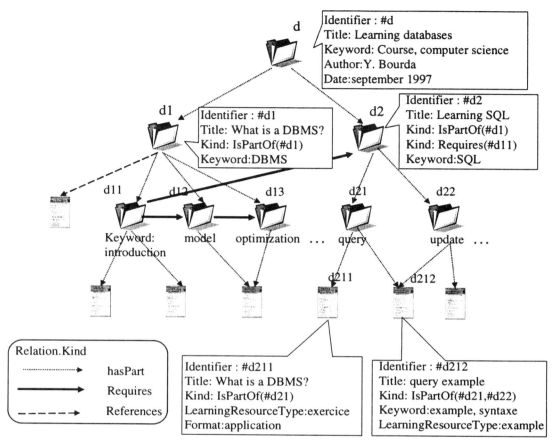

Figure 1

2. Indexing pedagogical resources

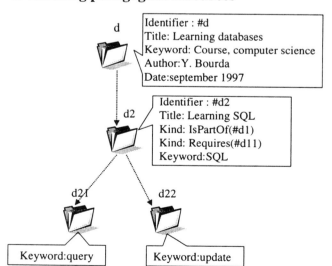

Figure 2

The structure has been previously defined as the structural links -isPartOf and prerequisites attributes-, and the whole attributes follow the LOM standard. Because each resource is associated to some metadata, the hierarchy of resources (in fact it is a directed acyclic graph) induces a hierarchy of metadata. Labeling each level of resource with a keyword attribute builds a hierarchy of keywords by the way of the structure. Each attribute can be static or dynamic. Static means that the attributes are local to the resource and that they can't be propagated along the hierarchy of the metadata. For example, the "kind" and "identifier" attributes are static. "Dynamic ascending" and "dynamic descending" respectively mean that the attributes can be propagated along the hierarchy towards the root or towards the leaves. For example, in figure 3, "author" is a dynamic descending attribute, therefore every resources composing *d* inherit from the value of author. "Keyword" is both a ascending and descending attribute, so *d211* and *d212* are indexed by keyword = course + computer science + SQL + query.

We define the context of a resource as its metadata, including content, structure and attributes of its ancestors. Each resource belongs to a context. Let's go back to the

1188

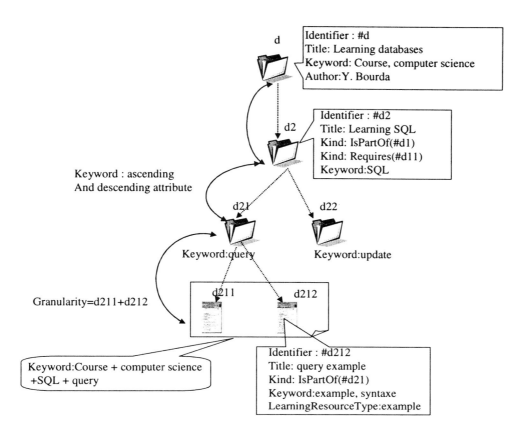

Figure 3

library example, and consider a page of a book. This page takes place in a section, within a page, within the book itself. Each level of organization of the book gives a context, from the highest level (root is the book) to the next level in the hierarchy up to the page level.

Besides the metadata, we choose to index the whole textual content of the resources, to enable the end-user to query this content in natural language. Each resource is associated with an index composed of attributes, content and structure.

From our model of resources, the indices of resources can be built a priori, i.e. all the values are propagated in the building of the index or a posteriori, i.e. the values are propagated at the request time. There is a balance between the two solutions in terms of index access time and volume storage optimization. For efficiency reasons the indices are built a priori.

3. Requesting pedagogical resources

Let's assume that DB is the corpus of the resources. We suppose that the modifications structure-induced have been taken into account at the creation, indexing and evaluation stages. In order to support the new functionalities we introduced in our paper, we defined a new query language

that supports:

- dynamic granularity of the response, i.e. the granularity of the resource (a chapter, a section, an image) is not expressed in the query but determined by the information retrieval system with the evaluation function at the request time,
- querying on metadata attributes of each resource,
- contextual requests, i.e. it is possible to specify in which context (referring to the definition of the context) the matter of request is required,
- combination of multi-typed requests allowing the system to manage requests against resources of various types,
- Prerequisites for one educational resource.

We opt for an OQL-like syntax defined by the ODMG[5].

We give several examples showing the power of expressiveness of the query using both metadata and structure.

Query 1: find courses whose author is Yolaine Bourda
```
Select      d     from     DB      where
d.lifeCycle.contributor="Yolaine
Bourda"
```

Thanks to the propagation of the "contributor" attribute, the result is all the resources identified by: *d, d1, d2, d11...*

Query 2: find all resources that are prerequisites in the context of a SQL course

```
Select d.requires from DB where d in
(select d from DB where d->context()
about 'SQL' and 'course')
```

First, the system chose only the resources belonging to the course and SQL domain, then it retrieves the prerequisites thanks to the "requires" attribute : *d11.*

Query 3: find an application illustrating "select" in an SQL course.

```
Select d from DB where
d.technical.format= "application" and
d.keyword='SQL' and d.keyword='course'
```

The system will return *d211*, notice that there is no notion of context in the request, the context is implicitly created at the indexing stage and used at the requesting stage. Now we give an example of a complex query, combining both multi-type, context (explicitly in the query), and structure :

image_input: a photo of the Cray CDC 6600.

Query: find resources containing images like "image_input" dealing with history in the context of computer science.

```
Select d from DB where d->keyword() =
'history' AND d -> context() about
`computer science' AND image_input
approx (select i from DB where i.type =
image AND i in d ->descendants() AND i
~~ image_input)
```

4. Conclusion

Classical information retrieval systems provide static responses (fixed by the pre-defined granularity of resources), without taking into account neither the structure of a resource nor its semantics. Here we explain how to explicit the structure and the context of educational resources, and we suggest a new information retrieval system that can index and search educational resources organized into multi-typed resources. This will enable end-users to request in a powerful semantic query language and to provide more suitable and contextual responses at several levels of granularity.

5. References

[1]http://www.dublincore.org/documents/education-namespace/

[2] http://ltsc.ieee.org/wg12/index.html

[3] http://www.w3c.org/XML

[4] Walid Kekhia and Yolaine Bourda. Implementing Learning Object Metadata using RDF. Ed-Media, Tampere, 2001

[5] http://www.odmg.org/

Replicating Reality - a better way to understanding

Robert Craig and Chris Messom

Institute of Information and Mathematical Sciences,
Massey University,
New Zealand
{R.G.Craig,C.H.Messom}@massey.ac.nz

Abstract

This paper proposes replication as an approach to conducting online experiments. Replication indicates the use of previously stored 'real-world' data as opposed to using the results of a simulated experiment. It is argued that real data is more meaningful than simulated data since it is grounded in real experimentation rather than generated artificially. A learning management system that uses replication of reality for online experiments is introduced. The online experiment system is discussed, as is the approach of replication and some possible data management strategies.

1: Introduction

Resource limitations imposed on engineering schools during the past two decades have forced them to seek more cost effective methods of preparing their students for industry with the result that hands-on laboratory experimentation is now frequently replaced by demonstrations and computer simulation [1]. Early simulation pioneers emphasised simulation as complementary to and not a substitute for hands-on experimentation [1,2], so although simulation affords significant cost advantages over hardware experiments, its effectiveness and appropriateness in the education process needs to be considered.

Remote experiment systems range from custom made hardware and interfaces to commercial interfaces provided by companies such as LabView, MatLab and EmWare [3-5]. A standard communication interface is advantageous since it allows a single standard server to interface with the equipment allowing rapid development of remote laboratory modules.

Several authors [6-9] have pioneered work in online experiments for higher education. Their systems use video to provide the user with a realistic experience of the experiment system. The experiment discussed in this paper uses an alternate approach, 3D photo-realistic animation, giving improved performance in situations where the communication bandwidth is limited and when data storage is limited. This is the case when users access the equipment remotely over the internet using commodity modems and low end PCs.

Enloe et al [10] identify a problem with online experiment systems that do not provide a rich user experience. If the online view of the experiment is little more than that which can be provided by a sophisticated simulator then there will be little educational benefit from the use of the system. Enloe et al [10] even propose that potential users of the online system be exposed to the real equipment so that they can ground their online experience of the system in reality. The system discussed here aims to provide a user experience that is rich and an educational experience that is at least as good as and perhaps in some circumstances even better than using the real equipment.

Many of the technical challenges of remote experimentation are being solved, but integrating such systems into a student management system using pedagogically sounds principles are still in the early stages of development. Colwell et al [11] discuss the Instructional Management System (IMS) specification for interoperability, but do not show how the relevant guidelines are to be applied to remote laboratory experiments.

2: Current educational process using simulation

Thomas & Hooper [12] provide a comprehensive survey of the use of simulation and has identified that the benefits of their use are observed when testing for transfer and application rather than testing for knowledge. Some experiments are more suitable for simulation, particularly those in which a procedural skill is being transferred.

Complex circuit design and integrated circuit (IC) design are examples where simulators, in this case logic simulators, are essentially the only option in an educational setting. Manual testing and assessment becomes impracticable as the number of input permutations increases exponentially [13]. Not only does the logic simulator permit the circuit to be designed and tested, it also represents a standard industrial design and development process i.e. initial circuit design - simulated testing and modification cycle - hardware production - hardware testing. Consequently the use of simulators appropriately familiarises students with the industrial function of simulators themselves as well as enabling them to experiment with the components.

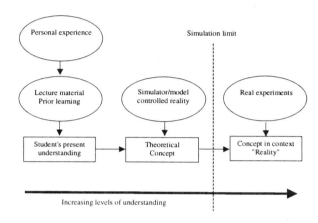

Fig. 1. Educational process using simulation

Industrial control or circuit design using discrete components are examples where simulation is not appropriate. 'Real world' situations such as broken wiring, dry solder joints, electromagnetic interference, variable friction, and component failure are avoided by the use of simulators, resulting in students who believe that successful simulation invariably leads to functioning hardware. Figure 1 illustrates this process. The students' personal experience, prior learning, lecture material and simulator experiments can only take the learning so far, a limit in understanding is reached.

Hessami & Sillitoe [14] discuss the necessity for students to reconcile the difference between theory and experiment. Tawney [15] found students unaware that simulation was essentially a representation of theory and that a real experiment may not behave entirely as predicted, and Magin & Kanapathipillai [1] complement Tawney's work[15] by reporting that most students were aware of how experimentation improved their appreciation of the limitations of theory.

The findings of Tawney [15], Magin and Kanapathipillai [1], and Hessami and Sillitoe [14] suggest that something more real than simulation is required if we are to adequately prepare our students for industry.

3: Replication as an improvement on simulation

Hands-on experimentation is the in-context application of theory, offering a student the greatest opportunity for understanding how an object functions in the real world. Online education precludes hands-on experimentation. Hence, in the absence of such an option, experiencing the results from a previous reality, *replication*, is identical from the perspective of the student to conducting the online experiment in the present. Additionally, the ability to upload multiple experiments has significant advantages over observing a single 'real' experiment.

Replication is a process that delivers previously recorded experimental data, enabling the student to experience a previous reality. Experimental data is retrieved from a database where the experiment results have been grouped according to input parameters and/or component failure. When an experiment is requested an appropriate experimental result data set is randomly assigned to the student. Consequently, should the student run the experiment again with the same input parameters, the data received will be similar but not necessarily identical to the previous experimental data. Which is what would be expected from the real, uncontrolled, world.

4: Proposed educational process using replication

Web-mediated access allows student connections to be controlled by a web server that can keep track of the students' state during a particular experiment session. The web server can ensure only authorised access to the experiment is allowed. A big advantage of the web-mediated approach is that the remote experiment system can be integrated into web based curriculum management systems. The system allows past experimental data to be stored in a database so that it can be retrieved and returned to the student system.

Figure 2 compared with figure 1 illustrates the difference between a system based on simulation and one based on real experiments and replicated reality. A simulated system essentially provides prescribed results, the results are safe, that is to say they support the theoretical concept that is being learned. Real systems start to behave in ways that are not predicted by the concept that is being learned when the system is working on and beyond the limits of application. A student is expected to identify these boundaries as understanding increases. Finally the experiment results are not predicted by the concept under study whenever there is a component failure in the system. In order to identify a component failure the student must understand that the unpredictable behaviour is not from the system working on or beyond the limits of applicability but is due to a component failure. To identify the fault and identify the cause represents a high level of understanding that is grounded in reality.

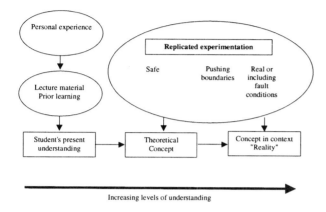

Fig. 2. Educational process using replication

4.1: Student and data management

Given that real-world experimentation is open to an array of confusing performances as a result of component failure or pushing the limits of the system, previously recorded results could be categorised prior to general release. In this manner a replicated reality system can control the type of results that are returned to the student in order to enhance the educational experience.

The ability to supply either real-time or replicate previously stored results presents the opportunity to tailor an experimental environment to suit those involved. Confronting students with a situation for which they are ill-equipped may result in misunderstanding and demotivation. Supplying experimental data of an appropriate educational level will protect students from unnecessary confusion thus maximising their understanding and intellectual growth. As the student's understanding improves the data restrictions may be released, permitting exposure to more advanced information and

The proposed experiment data categories are;

Safe:	Well within system limits, nothing unexpected.
Onlimits:	May produce unexpected, frequently unrepeatable, results.
Failure:	Unanticipated and frequently unrepeatable results.

The proposed student categories are;

Novice:	Weak understanding of concept.
Proficient:	Concept at the limit of their understanding.
Advanced:	Clear grasp of concept, ready to absorb more.

Having categorised student ability and type of data gathered from the experiment the data could then be presented to students in a manner that enhances the learning of the concept that is being investigated. A matrix of the categories of data that can be presented to different types of students is given in table 1. The table shows that to scaffold the development of understanding for novice students they should be presented with only safe data. This would help them develop an understanding of the ideal application of the concept.

Data type Proficiency level	Safe	OnLimits	Failure
Novice	X		
Proficient	X	X	
Advanced	X	X	X

Table 1. Matrix of student proficiency vs experiment types

Students that have demonstrated an understanding of the ideal application of the concept (the proficient students) could then be exposed to the experiments on the limits of predictable performance. They should learn to identify the results that are inconsistent with the concept and identify that indeed the experiment is working with parameters that are on or beyond the limits of applicability. Having demonstrated both the understanding of the ideal application and limits of applicability of the concept, students (the advanced students) could be exposed to failure mode data. The students should be able to learn to identify the failures and explain the possible causes of the failure.

4.2: The Internet based laboratory system

The experimental platform being used is a robot soccer system consisting of remotely controlled two-wheeled robots and a video camera mounted vertically above a wooden soccer pitch. Feedback is provided by an NTSC video signal from the camera of the soccer pitch. The signal is captured and processed identifying the robot position (X, Y) and orientation ($\emptyset$). The positional information is then transmitted over the network to the robot controller program, which uses the current error in the control variable to calculate and wirelessly transmit the required control signals back to the robot. This is the extent of the stand-alone experimental platform.

Experiments were conducted in real time, developing superior control algorithms for the robot. Making the position and orientation information (X, Y, ∅) available to the web server allows the experiment to be run online. Positional data can be transmitted to any client programs that request the information. See figure 3 below for a schematic overview of the mobile robot system. Additional details of the system have been reported in Messom & Craig [16].

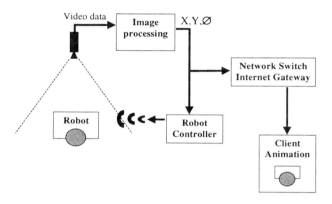

Fig. 3. Overall experimental system

Students conducting experiments are connected to the system as web clients. The client receives the robot positional information (X, Y, ∅) and reconstructs the video image. A 3D view of the robot motion is reconstructed so that the detailed movement of the robot can be seen. As bandwidth and storage capacity of systems increase, it is envisaged that using animation approaches for displaying experimental results can be reduced in favour of using full frame video. However experimental data will still be transmitted for plotting graphs, analysing experimental results and augmenting reality by rerunning results from multiple experiments using different parameters in parallel. The high bandwidth and high storage capacity systems of the future will still make use of many of the student and experiment management features discussed in this paper.

Piguet & Gillet [17] discuss the role of network delay in remote tele-operated equipment. The average network delay is too large for most mechatronic systems to be controlled remotely. The controller must reside at the server side while, a supervisory controller remotely updates the controller parameter values. Piguet & Gillet [17] also discuss a communication system that adapts to the available bandwidth for a system that has limited and

variable bandwidth. The system varies the quality (resolution) of the video streams as the available bandwidth varies and also makes use of augmented reality (2D animations) to display the state of the experiment when the video image degrades too much.

4.3: Developing the replication environment

The replication environment consists of three major components, the student client system, the instructional management system based on a web server and the experiment data that is stored in a database, illustrated in figure 4. The three components make use of standard development technologies, the database is mySQL and the web server is apache but can be any commercial or open source system. The client is written in Java but can be developed with any technology that supports the http protocol for interfacing to the web server.

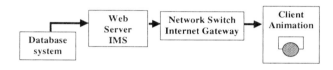

Fig. 4. Replicated reality system

The replicated reality system relies on having a large database of experimental data. The robot control experiments generate approximately 400 bytes of data per second, so the storage space required is within currently available systems. This data can be gathered from experiments run by students online, in which experiment results are tagged with the system parameters. This approach allows multiple sets of data to be stored for a particular set of parameters. The experiments that are on the limits of predicted behaviour and experiments with component faults are identified by the instructors so that they can be used by the instructional management system in a manner that optimises learning experiences of the students.

5: Discussion

The replicated reality system not only tries to emulate the advantages of a real experiment, but by its nature can improve on a real experiment in several ways. Replicated reality extends the single data single student (SDSS) format of a real experimental platform by allowing multiple data multiple student (MDMS), single data multiple student (SDMS) and multiple data single student (MDSS) modes. The ability to have multiple students apparently simultaneously working on the experiment represents significant cost savings for experiment platforms that are expensive. For cheaper experiments, the student management and flexible access afforded by the replicated reality system might also make the necessary network and server infrastructure investments cost effective.

MDMS is the standard real experiment format when the students are experimenting individually on their own equipment. To model this scenario the replicated reality system would send different, randomly assigned data to students that are online. The advantage of the replicated reality system is that the real equipment is effectively being shared.

SDMS is the situation where all students receive the same data, that is as though all the students are gathered around the same experiment receiving a demonstration. In this mode the students' experience of the experiment is extremely controlled.

MDSS allows multiple experiments to be run simultaneously on the same equipment, that is, data generated at different times by the same equipment can be run and displayed simultaneously on a split screen, or even animated in situ allowing comparative performances to be investigated. This can be used to observe the difference between the performance with varying parameters. The technique can also be used to compare real results with simulated results allowing the student to observe the differences between them.

The MDSS mode essentially gives the student access to tools that are not available in the real system, the ability to run different experiments concurrently and make comparative analysis of the results. In this mode, the replicated reality work-bench is 'better' than the real experiment system.

6: Conclusions

This paper has introduced replicating reality as an approach to managing student learning using online experimentation with real equipment and devices. It shows that replicated reality not only emulates real experimentation but also improves upon it by managing the student interaction with the system. It is expected that having experienced the replicated reality systems, students will be able to transfer their experience to real systems since their understanding has been based on data that has been taken directly from real experiments.

References

[1] D. Magin and S. Kanapathipillai, (2000), "Engineering Students' Understanding of the Role of Experimentation", Dec 2000, European Journal of Engineering Education, Vol 25, pp 351-358, Abingdon.

[2] R. Barnard (1985), "Experience with low cost laboratory data", Int Journal of Mechanical Engineering Education, Vol 78, pp 95-99.

[3] Labview available http://www.labview.com/

[4] Matlab available http://www.mathworks.com/

[5] EmWare available http://www.emware.com/

[6] C.D. Cheng, P. Vadekkepat, C.C. Ko, B.M. Chen and X. Xiang, (2001) "Robot motion Control and Image Reconstruction over the Internet", Proceedings of CIRAS 2001, Singapore, 423-428.

[7] C.C. Ko, B.M. Chen, J. Chen. Y.Zhuang and K.C. Tan, (2001), "Development of a Web-based Laboratory for control experiments on a coupled tank apparatus", IEEE Transactions on Education, Vol 44, No 1, pp. 76-86, February 2001.

[8] H. Shen, Z. Xu, B. Dalager, V. Kristiansen, O. Strom, M.S. Shur, T.A. Fjeldly, J.Q. Lu, & T. Ytterdal (1999), "Conducting Laboratory Experiments over the Internet", IEEE Transactions on Education, 42(3), 180-185.

[9] K. Yeung and J. Huang, (2001), "Development of A Remote-Access Laboratory: A DC Motor Control Experiment", Proc. of the IASTED Applied Informatics Conference, AI2001, Innsbruck, Austria, pp.444-449.

[10] C.L. Enloe, W.A. Pakula, G.A. Finney & R.K. Haarland (1999), "Teleoperation in the undergraduate physics laboratory-teaching an old dog new tricks", IEEE Transactions on Education, 42(3), 174-179.

[11] C. Colwell, E. Scanlon, M. Cooper, (2002), "Using remote laboratories to extend access to science and engineering", Computers & Education, Vol 38, pp 65-76.

[12] R. Thomas and E. Hooper, (1991), "Simulations: An opportunity we are missing", Journal of Research on Computing in Education, Summer 91, Vol. 23, Issue 4, pp 497 - 514.

[13] M.J. Johnson and R.G. Craig, in press, "Computer Systems Pedagogy using Digital Logic Simulation", Proceedings of ICCE 2002, Auckland, NZ.

[14] M. Hessami and J. Sillitoe (1992), "The role of laboratory experiments and the impact of high-tech equipment on engineering education", Australasian Journal of Engineering Education, Vol 3, 119-126.

[15] D. Tawney, (1976), "Simulation and modeling in science computer assisted learning", Tech report no 11, National Development project in Computer Assisted Learning, London.

[16] C.H. Messom and R.G. Craig, (2002), "Web Based Laboratory for Controlling Real Robot Systems", Proceedings of DEANZ 2002, Wellington, New Zealand.

[17] Y. Piguet and D Gillet (1999), "Java-Based Remote Experimentation for Control Algorithms Prototyping", American Control Conference, San Diego, USA, 1465-1469

WebCT: A Tool for Proselytism!

Ruddy LELOUCHE
E-mail: Ruddy.Lelouche@ift.ulaval.cag
Phone: + 1 (418) 656 2131 ext. 25973

Martin PAGÉ
E-mail: Martin.Page@acm.or
Phone: + 33 (0) 1 64 57 38.03

Computer Science Department, UNIVERSITÉ LAVAL, Québec, G1K 7P4   CANADA
Note: Under a study abroad program, M. Pagé is currently based at Université d'Évry – Val d'Essonne, near Paris, France

Abstract

This short paper presents arguments to use TIC for teaching and learning. It starts with an overview of the environment that the education sector is currently facing, and then describes an experimentation with an actual Internet-based learning environment: WebCT. This research offers theoretical and practical foundations to promote this use.

Keywords: Internet-based learning environment, society, education, learning, WebCT, Technologies of information and communication (TIC).

1. Introduction

For quite some time, people in education have been tremendously interested in using the facilities provided by the *technologies of information and communication* (TIC). However, many teachers, as well as education and political leaders, do not seem completely convinced that software solutions may help them to meet their educational goals. On the other hand, we happen to have conducted a research experimentation with an actual *Internet-based learning environment* (IBLE): WebCT. This research tried to offer theoretical and practical foundations to promote the use of the TIC for educational purposes.

As a partial result of this research, this paper present arguments to use TIC for learning. It starts with a presentation of the sicio-economic and technological contexts in which the education sector is presently immersed. Then, it presents some existing links between education and TIC, and identifies tools and functionalities which, when present, should strengthen the capacity of an IBLE to meet educational expectations. Finally, this paper present a broad outline of an experimentation with WebCT that we have conducted to identify its most important characteristics regarding key education-related needs.

2. Context in using the TIC

Many factors have an effect upon the use of TIC for education and training. Educational, social, economic, and technologic contexts form the changing environment in which decisions about computerization of learning are made. The various aspects of this environment have been known and discussed for some time now, and we do not present them further in this short paper. Let us simply

conclude that the new educational and most broadly social situation, but also economic imperatives and technological breakthroughs are major aspects of the present context for using the TIC in education. These aspects build an environment, which, we believe, is more than encouraging for experimenting with TIC as a part of the solution to education's challenges.

3. Evolution of Education vs. the TIC

Many models were constructed to describe, explain, and understand teaching and learning. Among them, the *exploratory approach*, based on *constructivism* [1], can be adopted. In this model, the teacher is a *facilitator*, helping the student in his learning. Training is then developed in small groups, where students and the teacher are determining together the teaching content and rhythm, as well as the classroom procedures and the evaluation modes. Exchange and discussion are key notions in this model.

In this context, the TIC, particularly with innovations brought in by Internet, offer medias consistent with this approach. Now, to benefit from the characteristics and advantages of TIC, and mostly of the Internet, education and training must review their teaching styles. Indeed, learners now have access to other knowledge sources, and they want more interactions with their teachers. The latter must then adapt to this new pedagogy integrating TIC everyday [2].

However, this adaptation can stumble over many obstacles. To avoid this risk, teachers should be enticed to learn new Internet tools, to overcome resistance to technological changes, and to put an added value on their changing roles.

4. Tools and capabilities supporting the education process

To promote the use of IBLEs, human factors in software are as important as tools and technological functionalities or characteristics. Basically, we need the following tools and functionalities, reported by the French Education Ministry, depending on each wide user category.

To *the teacher*, the product should give ways to:
- develop pedagogic content and stream;
- individualize his or her teaching;
- incorporate pedagogic multimedia resources;
- monitor the students' learning activities.

To *the students*, the software should provide:

- on-line or off-line (by download) access to contents;
- ways to organize and visualize their work progress;
- self-paced exercises, auto-evaluation and transmission of their work to be corrected.

To *the teacher and students*, the product should give interactive exchange capabilities via:
- student-to-student and student-to-teacher communication;
- the creation of discussion forums (e.g. theme-based);
- collaboration between students to common projects.

The software should also account for the needs of the *technological administrator*:
- ease of installation and maintenance;
- management of access rights;
- communication with the institution information systems: registrar, libraries, etc.

At last, three musts of this technology are of use to *all*:
- to be based on Internet technologies;
- to be accessed through the standard telephone network;
- to avoid the installation of any specific software on the student's workstation.

Many commercial softwares abide by these characteristics [3]. *WebCT*, a leading software on the market, is our preferred choice. It allows teachers, with or without technological know-how, *to create courses* using Internet functionalities and protocols. It takes in charge various *roles* (a role is a set of functionalities that a user can access), like: teacher-conceptor, student, guest, tutor, and technological administrator. Depending on to these people's respective responsibilities, WebCT can offer functionalities related to: content development, pedagogy, supervision of learner's participation and progress, learning, planning, and student–student and teacher–student(s) interactions.

The teacher-designer of the course uses a Web browser-like interface to connect to a *WebCT server*, on which his or her course is thus made available. This course content can make use of all medias supported by Internet standard protocols, and its visualization is made using existing Web browsers. Once a course has been developed and made available on the WebCT server, students can access it using their preferred Web browser.

According to WebCT Inc., the software was used by more than 3.6 millions students in September 1999, for 97000 courses offered by more than 800 colleges and universities spread in more than 40 countries.

5. Outline of our experiments with WebCT

In our research work, we have conducted a few experiments with WebCT. In order to do so, we installed the software on a Linux workstation, and we created a first typical training set of about ten Web pages.

Results

This first experiment showed us that:
- reusing existing digital educational material is easy;
- *directive* and *explorative* pedagogical approaches can be tried, in line with students' and teachers' expectations;

- the student's responsibility toward his or her learning is increased, because (s)he must be effectively involved to exploit the WebCT capabilities;
- the teacher can become a guide, thus escaping from the traditional *master to students* relationship.

These advantages do not cost too much! It took us:
- for software installation: one hour and a half;
- for the creation of a typical training set (10 Web pages) from artefacts existing as HTML pages: three hours;
- for the WebCT creation of accounts for three test students: half an hour.

Discussion

For the teacher-designer, the pedagogical utility of WebCT, in our opinion, is multiple.
- Experimentation with different modes for preparing typical training sets (alone, in a team of teachers, etc.) is facilitated by the digitalisation of pedagogic contents.
- Easy browsing, by fellow teachers, of the content made available on WebCT facilitates professional exchanges.
- A product like WebCT contributes in developing the students' capacity for autonomous learning.

For the learner, we think the didactic pertinence of this software is of utmost importance.
- The student's personal development is effected not only with knowledge (knowledge acquisition), but also with know-how (application of that knowledge, in particular to problem solving) and with know-how-to-be (via interactions with other students and with teacher) using appropriate WebCT tools or functionalities.
- The learner develops his/her capacity to use *adequately and efficiently* the available computerized research tools.

6. Conclusion

Still today, many teachers, education and politic leaders, do not seem to be fully convinced about the educational advantages of TIC. That is why our intent was to present arguments to promote using these technologies for educational purposes. To do so, we covered theoretical and practical arguments. Besides, the first results of our experiments with WebCT have revealed many advantages that teachers and learners could grasp from using TIC for learning. By its installation like by its operation, WebCT could contribute to lower the reluctance sometimes encountered in the education domain.

6. References

[1] Bruner, J. S. (1966). *Towards a Theory of Instruction.* Harvard University Press (Cambridge, MA., USA), 176 p.

[2] Hazari, S. I. (1998). *Evaluation and Selection of Web Course Management Tools.* Web Page accessed on 2 fév. 2000 http://sunil.umd.edu/webct

[3] Pagé, M. (2000). *WebCT: État de la situation et Rapport d'analyse.* Rapport du cours Ingénierie documentaire et multimédia. DESS, Univ. d'Évry – Val d'Essonne (France), 40 pages.

Development of an ECB on Computer Networks Based on WWW Technologies, Resources and Usability Criteria

Pilu Crescenzi   Gaia Innocenti
Università degli Studi di Firenze
Dipartimento di Sistemi e Informatica
Via C. Lombroso 6/17, 50134 Firenze, Italy
{piluc, innocent}@dsi.unifi.it

Abstract

According to Baas, van den Eijnde, and Junger (2001) an electronic course book (in short, ECB) is a learning module consisting of menu-driven hyperdocuments with a functional use of interactivity and multimedia, presented on the WWW and/or CDROM. The main purpose of this paper is to propose a model for the development of a computer network ECB based on (a) the integration of several tools, which are dispersed in the WWW as university course materials and that for their multimedia nature could not be inserted in a paper book, and (b) on WWW usability criteria, which make the design of the book very different from that of a printed book. The ECB will turn out to be useful both to teachers (while giving their lectures) since they will take advantage of the slide-based presentation of the text and of the several simulation tools included in the ECB, and to students (while studying the material) since they will be able to learn by reading, by doing and by answering.

1. Introduction

An electronic course book (in short, ECB) is usually conceived in order to give students an alternative mean of study compared with static classical textbooks. As a matter of fact, an ECB provides information that are not restricted to just text materials, but may include audio and video resources as well as applications, thus extending the capabilities of traditional textbooks.

Several studies have focused on the new opportunities given by the use of these new technologies (see, for example, the special issue of *IEEE Transactions on Education* on the application of information technologies to engineering and science education [6]): Indeed, even before computers became so popular, the psychologist Skinner suggested using mechanical devices in order to support the learning process [12]. As a result, virtually any academic and commercial organization interested in the utilization of technology in learning (also called e-learning) has put some effort in the development of ECBs. More recently, the huge expansion of the World Wide Web (in short, WWW) has strongly motivated the design and development of hypertext for engineering and science education (although the concept of hypertext is much older [3, 4]): Hypertext learning material have become more and more sophisticated and the concept of an active learning hypertextbook (either for the WWW [2] or for CDROM [5]) is currently gaining ground.

In this paper we will refer to the following definition of ECB which is taken from [1] and includes, in our opinion, the concept of an active learning hypertextbook: an ECB is a complete or partial module on screen, consisting of a collection of menu-driven hyperdocuments with a functional use of interactivity and multimedia, presented on the WWW and/or CDROM. Several features have to be taken into consideration in developing ECBs. For example, in [2] the authors considered downloading, installation, and maintenance issues, platform dependence, and single concept animations versus integrated learning resources as the main concerns to be addressed by WWW based ECB. In [1], instead, several problems mainly related to WWW usability criteria [9] are described and some corresponding solutions to these problems are proposed.

The goal of this paper is to propose a model for the development of an ECB for teaching computer network concepts to undergraduate students, who are guided through these concepts with useful aids such as videos, applets and interactive exercises. To this aim, we will make use of WWW technologies (such as HTML, JavaScript and Java) and of WWW resources (such as applets, images and videos, which will be mainly collected from the huge amount of information dispersed in the Internet) in order to take into account all the observations discussed in [2]. Moreover, we will follow several WWW usability criteria while design-

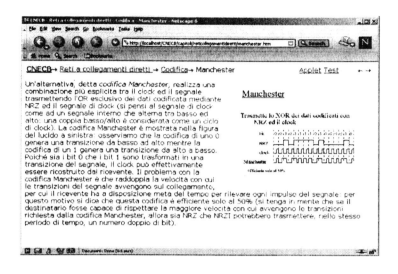

Figure 1. An example of slide-based WWW page of the ECB

ing the ECB: For example, since the WWW is well suited for short documents with many links, we will organize the learning material into small units which correspond to the content accompanying one or two slides of a teacher's presentation.

An ECB can be viewed as an aspect of the emerging e-learning technology, which proposes many other tools such as live tutorials, chatting facilities, and so on. In particular, the online learning courseware that companies produce (see for example, CISCO or Dell e-learning courses) are generally made ex-novo, thus following a different philosophy from ours (that is, collecting already published multimedial resources). Moreover, the online material provided usually does not consider usability criteria, thus presenting appealing graphics and animations which can be displayed only via downloadable additional software (such as plug-ins). Last but not least, the ECBs which are produced by commercial organizations are mainly presented as finished products: companies are not interested in providing the model employed for the development of the courseware unless under payment, while the main purpose of this paper is to present a model to be used for the creation of ECBs respecting WWW usability criteria.

The idea of creating an ECB was born as a requirement for a computer network course held at the University of Florence. We had a collection of materials such as textbooks, applets and videoclips that had to be organized in some way in order to be effectively used. Our first idea was to make an ECB to be first used during the laboratory lessons and then delivered to the students, with the purpose to give them all the materials introduced during the course. From this initial requirement, we found out the usefulness of such a tool both

for students and for teachers. The first ones could enjoy the multimedia instruments provided, they could play an active role in their understanding of the subject, and, above all, they could be able to learn by reading, by doing and by answering. On the other hand, teachers could take advantage of the slide-based presentation of the text and of the several simulation tools included in the ECB itself.

The paper is organized as follows. In Section 2 we briefly describe the design process used in developing the computer network ECB by referring to the conceptual model presented in [8]. In Section 3 we show some examples of how the WWW usability criteria guided the development of the ECB, while in Section 4 we describe the WWW resources that are integrated into the ECB in order to form a comprehensive and cohesive package to be used for both teaching and learning. Finally, in Section 5 we propose some future research directions starting from the project described in this paper.

2. The ECB Design

The computer network ECB has been designed by assuming that the *target users* are undergraduate students with a basic mathematical and computer background: In particular, in the case of our University, these are students at the second year of the Computer Science degree program. The *goal/objectives* of the ECB is to provide a tool for an independent study of computer network concepts and the *pedagogical model* chosen is a slide-based presentation of the contents with reinforcement using animations, applications and exercises. For what concerns the *user interface*, we will discuss about it in the next section since its design has been

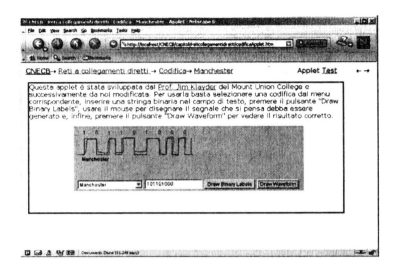

Figure 2. An example of applet integrated into the ECB

mainly based on WWW usability criteria. The *structure* and the *content* of the ECB has been designed on the ground of the textbook which has been adopted in the last three years for the Computer Network class within the Computer Science degree program at the University of Florence [10]. Finally, the *format*, that is the type of media that is used to deliver the content, consists of text, audio, video, graphics and applications.

3. WWW Usability Criteria Application

Web Usability has become more and more important in the last few years due to the peculiar characteristics of the WWW users: This is also true in the case of WWW-based training [7]. For this reason we have chosen to apply some WWW usability criteria while developing our computer network ECB: In this section, we will give three examples of this approach.

First, "as a rule of thumb content should account for at least half of a page's design, and preferably closer to 80 percent. Navigation should be kept below 20 percent of the space" [9]. For this reason, we have decided to organize each single page as shown in Figure 1: As it can be easily computed, the content occupies more than 75 percent of the page (including the browser bars). Clearly, the navigation bar has had to be reduced and to this aim we have organized it into three components. The component on the left shows the current position of the user within the ECB according to a book-chapter-section-slide hierarchy; the central component indicates whether there are additional materials associated with the slide such as animations, applets or questions; the component on the right, finally, allows the user to navi-

gate through the sequence of slides.

Secondly, another well-known WWW usability criterion consists of limiting the size of each page both because of the request time and because of the fact that WWW users do not like to read long documents. This is consistent with Skinner's opinion that "a very large number of very small steps and reinforcement must be contingent upon the accomplishment of each step" [11]. For this reason, we have decided to organize the material into learning small units addressing a more or less self-contained learning atoms: In particular, we found natural to associate each of these learning atoms with one or at most two slides used during a teacher's presentation. For example, Figure 1 shows the learning atom corresponding to the slide explaining the Manchester encoding used on Ethernet local area networks.

Finally, one more WWW usability criterion we have adopted is the one establishing that the response time should be predictable: Indeed, each page included in the ECB requires the download of at most 60 Kilobytes so that the response time should never be longer than 10 seconds which is considered the maximum time interval the user can tolerate without diverting his attention away from the content.

4. WWW Resources Integration

One of the main goals of the ECB is to allow students to learn not only by reading but also by viewing, listening, doing and answering. For this reason we looked on the WWW for resources of different types such as animations, audio and video files, applets and javascript applications, and tests. Indeed, it is huge the amount of such a material which is publicly available: We have chosen a selection of

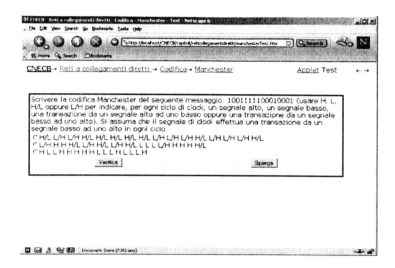

Figure 3. An example of question integrated into the ECB

this material and we have integrated it into the ECB in a consistent way (we have already seen how these resources are integrated into the slide-based organization of the ECB).

A classical textbook can contain text and figures, but neither one nor the other ones enable the readers to actively interact with the subject. An ECB fills this lack thanks to the ability of embedding interactive applications which can present the same subject from a new point of view. An application can be a Java applet, a videoclip or whatever provides a tool that the reader may use when needed. The user himself is then responsible for the interaction (executing the applet or viewing the videoclip) and he is able to guide his personal phase of understanding, according to his speed of comprehension and his needs. For what concerns the choice of the applets and of the javascript applications, we have systematically preferred the ones which allow us to create an exploratory learning environment in which the student composes the response rather than just looking at the automatic execution of the application. For example, several applets are available which explain different ways of encoding digital data into signals: Among these applets, we have chosen the one shown in Figure 2 which forces the user to first draw the response before checking its correctness (by clicking the `Draw Waveform` button).

Tests are further instruments of active interaction. This kind of multiple choice examination is embedded along the text throughout the ECB and it gives the reader the chance to evaluate his level of understanding. Each question presents at least three answers but only one is correct (see Figure 3). The user is helped in his assignment by some hints, that can be required when needed (by clicking the `Spiega` button). The choice of integrating questions along the presented sub-

ject is due to our idea of gathering and storing information in a tied environment, where everything is organized around the subject. The reader does not have to bother where the evaluation tests are located and, at the same time, he is invited to verify his understanding just after having read the lesson.

5. Conclusions

In this paper we have described the design and the development of an ECB for computer networks based on WWW technologies, resources, and usability criteria. According to the definition of an ECB, all the material can be either browsed on the WWW or included in a CDROM. This latter solution has the clear advantage that students do not have to be on line all the time, but on the other hand it does not allow us to completely exploit the potential of WWW.

The ECB model presented in this paper can obviously be applied to other subjects: It is our intention to start developing a similar ECB for Java programming. Moreover, this slide-based model should also allow us to easily integrate the ECB with a video presentation of the material: It is just a matter of reading the text while showing (in a synchronized way) the content of the slides.

More interestingly, our model naturally leads to the development of an *ECB production application* which should support the producer to integrate slides, text, exercises, applets and animations by means of a graphical user interface: It is our main objective to develop such an application within the next year.

References

[1] K. Baas, J. van den Eijnde, and J. Junger. A Practical Model for the Development of Web Based Interactive Courses. In *Proc. of the 31st ASEE/IEEE Frontiers in Education Conference*. Reno, Oct 2001.

[2] C. Boroni, F. Goosey, M. Grinder, and R. Ross. Engaging Students with Active Learning Resources: Hypertextbooks for the Web. *Proc. of the 32nd SIGCSE Technical Symposium on Computer Science Education (SIGCSE Bulletin)*, 33(1):65–69, 2001.

[3] V. Bush. As We May Think. *Atlantic Monthly*, 176(1):101–108, 1945.

[4] J. Conklin. Hypertext: An Introduction and Survey. *IEEE Computer*, 20(9):17–41, 1987.

[5] D. Gries, P. Gries, and P. Hall. *ProgramLive CD*. John Wiley, 2001.

[6] M. Hagler, J. Yeargan, and W. Marcy. Preface to Special Issue on the Application of Information Technologies to Engineering and Science Education. *IEEE Transactions on Education*, 39(3):285–286, 1996.

[7] B. Khan. *Web-Based Training*. Educational Technology Publications, 2000.

[8] J. Morariu. Hypermedia in Instruction and Training: The Power and the Promise. *Educational Technology*, 28(11):17–20, 1988.

[9] J. Nielsen. *Designing Web Usability: The Practice of Simplicity*. New Riders Publishing, 2000.

[10] L. Peterson and B. Davie. *Computer Networks: A Systems Approach*. Morgan Kaufmann, 2000.

[11] B. Skinner. The Science of Learning and the Art of Teaching. *Harvard Educational Review*, 24(2):86–97, 1954.

[12] B. Skinner. *The Technology of Teaching*. Appleton-Century-Crofts, 1968.

Intercultural Web Communication with Haiku and Haiga

between America and Japan through the Internet

Kenichi YAMAMOTO: Gifu City Women's College
Yukuo ISOMOTO: Graduate School of Nagoya City University
Yoshihisa YAMADA: Gifu Keizai University

Jeanne EMRICH: American Poet
Yasuo TAKEDA: Ichimura Gakuen Junior College
Mayumi OHASHI: Gifu City Women's College

Abstract

In the recent information age, we have a big world, so called, "the Internet" or "the cyber space", which has become an important medium for international communication year by year. In order to improve students' communication ability, the authors have been teaching intercultural communication and systematizing its method by using e-mail and web pages on the Internet. In the class, our students communicate with foreign students by using *haiku* (traditional Japanese short poems) and *haiga* (Chinese ink paintings). Students increase their ability to express their intentions and feelings through short poems and computer graphics. In this paper, the authors discuss the method and the effect of the intercultural communication training with haiku and haiga through the Internet.

Key Words: Intercultural Communication, Communication Tool, Internet, Computer Graphics, Digital Contents

1. Introduction

Since October 1997, the authors have opened a web site called "Haiku & Haiga"[1] for the purpose of intercultural communication. At the site, a haiga can be chosen from many works composed by our students and be inserted in e-mail as a CG (Computer Graphics) image (see Fig.1). In the United States, J. Emrich, a poet, has also opened a web site called "HAIGA Online"[2]. The authors and J. Emrich have cooperated to promote intercultural communication with haiku and haiga by applying computer technology. In this paper, we discuss our educational collaboration for intercultural communication by haiku and haiga between America and Japan through the Internet.

Fig.1 Haiga composed by a student

2. "Haiku" and "Haiga" as teaching materials

Haiku is a traditional Japanese poem. It is also the shortest form of poetry all over the world and has the following characteristics:

- three lines
- 5-7-5 syllables (but not strictly)
- seasonal word
- simple and objective description
- insight into the essence of being

Haiga is both a visual and literary art form. An appreciation and knowledge of philosophy, poetry, fine art, films, music, computer graphics, and photography all contribute, whether directly or indirectly, to haiga works. When you try to paint and compose haiga, you must become a haiku lover at once.

By using new computer software for graphic design and image manipulation, haiga can be created on computers going beyond the traditional ink brush painting. Some are afraid that the form is no longer recognizable as haiga, but others accept this new form. At our school, students have been making haiku in English classes for over ten years. Now the personal computer is used to make haiga with computer graphics. This is not traditional Japanese haiga such as Basho and Buson drawn with Chinese ink and brush, called "Suibokuga". Yet, we try to represent the lifestyle of modern young people. It has given rise to a new Internet generation, through "Haiga Communication".

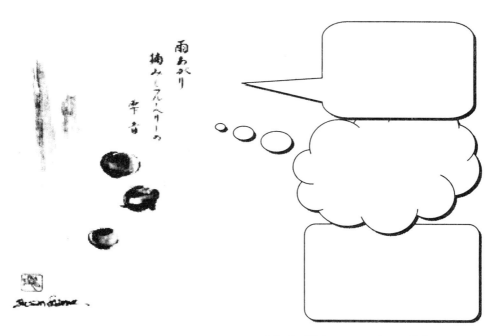

Fig.2　Haiga created in collaboration

Haiga consist of haiku and a haiku image.　These are the fundamental elements of haiga (see Fig.2).　We think that haiga will spread to the world through the Internet because of its simplicity and compactness. We can put haiku on haiga and simply take it all in with our eyes and our heart.

3. Computer and Web Site for haiga

Computer networks and multimedia computers make up the infra-structure of an information oriented society. The Internet in computer network systems makes our world-wide communication possible.　Through network servers, we can send/accept e-mails, and have access to web pages.　Actually, in our classes, the Internet plays an essential role in the educational environment.

Multimedia computers and other information technology, contribute to information processing and information retrieval.　For instance, with the use of a multimedia computer, you can compose haiku or create haiga. Moreover, you can have access to educational information and works of haiga through the Internet (via computer networks or local area networks).

4. Discussion and Conclusion

One of our key words in modern society is "global communication" through the Internet.　When we want to communicate with others all over the world, the Internet is one of the best communication tools today.

Our students communicate with the students of Thomas More College (our sister college in the suburbs of Cincinnati Ohio, USA) by sharing haiku and haiga in English via e-mail and our web site.　We met each other on the Internet and continued communicating by e-mail for more than one year.　We have exchanged our ideas, opinions, feelings, and knowledge about haiku and haiga. Through our communication, we have come to understand that haiku and haiga can lead us to a higher level of intercultural communication between countries. We can further our mutual understanding between American and Japanese students with haiku and haiga in English by collaborating through the global network toward the future.

In the information age, education should be executed in a suitable style.　In this paper, the authors discussed how the Internet and multimedia computers are useful and practical tools for intercultural communication which should be implemented in universities and colleges.

References
1)　http://www02.so-net.ne.jp/~yamamok/index.html
2)　http://members.aol.com/HAIGA/HAIGAOnline.in dex.html

Who Moved my Chalk? A Toolbox for Language Teachers

Barry Natusch, Nihon University, Tokyo

Abstract

Technology, media and the Internet are major agents of change in the language teaching profession. This presentation introduces skills and tools language teachers need to do their job more effectively and how they can embark on a strategy of self-development seeking assistance from institutional and organizational programs, peers and other sources. The following topics are addressed:
(a) Changes in learning patterns and educational activities brought about by the development of information technology
(b) Skills teachers personally need to develop in response to these changes particularly in the use of computers, media, and digital devices
(c) A toolbox of hardware, software and manuals tailored to the needs of language teachers
(d) Specific information technology-related initiatives taken by governments, institutions and organizations in Japan, China, Taiwan and Korea
(e)   Strategies for personal development among language teachers

Technology, media and the Internet are major agents of change in language teaching. Bates [1] notes that " Although technology infrastructure plans are essential, they are not sufficient. It is equally important to develop academic or teaching plans that specify the ways in which technologies will be incorporated into teaching learning activities."

In responding to these changes affecting the process of second or foreign language learning, teachers need to upgrade their information literacy and computer literacy since changes are occurring in the way we select, capture, prepare and present information. In the past, a language teacher needed only a textbook, some chalk and a well thought-out talk. Traditional teaching skills included choosing appropriate materials, planning lessons, explaining clearly, and using a blackboard or OHP effectively.   Nowadays, teachers also need to know where to find useful materials on the Internet or on e-media, to be able to capture, modify and save text, graphics, sound and video files by handling tools such as computers, digital cameras, video cameras, video machines, and scanners. Table 1 highlights the difference between traditional and contemporary teacher skills.

A teacher needs tools as much as a plumber or an electrician. In the past, a teacher's toolbox contained only a textbook, worksheets, a grade-book, chalk and a red pen, now more tools are needed. Tools and resources which help teachers do a better job are listed in Table 2.

Just as individuals are sensing the need to respond to changes brought about by information technology, so too are governments, institutions and organizations mounting initiatives such as promoting online materials. As academic organizations become larger, they often split into smaller, more focused groups serving as forums for discussion and exchanges of online resources. Language teachers themselves can upgrade their skills from organizations, peers, and students.

In the end, the information technology revolution is about both institutional and personal responsibility. Organizations need to initiate training programs and teachers themselves need to take steps to position themselves close to IT initiatives, learn new skills, and seek out assistants to act as instructors or trainers.

References

[1]   Bates, A.W. 1999. Managing Change Technological Change: Strategies for College and University Leaders. Jossey-Bass.

Traditional Language Teaching Skills	New Language Teaching Skills
plans lessons	plans using organizing software
uses library for texts and magazines	uses Internet to get resources: texts, digital images and videoclips, sophisticated word and phrase searches
chooses appropriate teaching materials	uses e-tools to search for language samples, still and moving images, use concordancing software etc
designs worksheets, uses charts etc	authors materials on a CALL system has ability to visualize info in 2D and 3D
has proficiency in target and learner's languages	uses computer in > target and learner's language uses MT programs such as Babel Fish appropriately
uses blackboard, OHP	technical ability includes use of computer, scanner, digital camera, videocamera presents using media such as CALL, computer, projector, video, etc uses a variety of graphics maintains own website of materials
gives clear explanations	gives clear explanations, enhanced by appropriate media support
formulates questions, quizzes and tests	uses CALL software for routine learning tasks
evaluates students	uses CALL software to gather quantitative data on Ss uses OCR forms for testing uses CBT scores of TOEFL etc uses plagiarizing software to identify questionable work
communicates with students in and out of class	communicates with students by weekly emails, has students establish their own usergroups (MLs) can direct students to appropriate chat sessions
communicates with colleagues via telephone, meetings, memos, etc	communicates via meetings, emails, videoconferencing, subscribes to usergroups
keeps up with developments in the field by reading journals, attending conferences	mixes reading, conference attending, emailing and videoconferencing

Table 1

Traditional vs new language teaching skills

Hardware	Hardware operating software and utilities	Applications	Manuals
Base computer **Image** digicam handicam webcam scanner **Communication** modem ADSL etc networking equipment peripheral hubs **Output** printer **External storage** CD-R, CD-RW, DVD, hard drive for video clips flash memory port for Smart media, memory stick	**Operating System** recovery disks patches **Computer Management** partitioning utility remote access **Security** antivirus software firewall **Peripherals** updated versions of printer, scanner, monitor drivers	**Internet Access** browser IE email Express, Eudora updated versions of Acrobat Reader, Flash, Shockwave, RealPlayer, etc **Text editing** Word Translation bilingual OCR Concordancing Athelstan **Reference** encyclopedias Britannica **Sound analysis** WAV files MP3 **Charting** spreadsheet Excel **Graphics** Filing: My Pictures image editing: Photoshop video editing: Premiere **Presentation** PowerPoint webpaging: Dreamweaver **CALL** Hot Potatoes Crossword Maker **Authoring** Director Flash Authorware	**Introductory** Ten Minutes SAMS guides Dummies IDG **Comprehensive** The Bible series Pogue

Table 2

Contents of a language teacher's toolbox

Web based Self-directed Learning Environment Using Learner's Annotation

Youji Ochi[1], Riko Wakita[2] and Yoneo Yano[1]

[1] Faculty of Engineering, Tokushima University
[2] Faculty of Education and Regional Studies, Fukui University
2-1 Minamijosanjima, Tokushima, Japan

E-mail: {ochi, yano}@is.tokushima-u.ac.jp

Abstract

In this paper, we introduce a Web based self-directed learning environment using a student's Web-annotation and describe the evaluation of our system. SDL (Self-Directed-Learning) is one of the teaching methods that supports the autonomous learning of the learner. However, it is difficult for the learners to choose a web page suitable for their learning purpose as the learning resource in the web based SDL. We developed a prototype system that is called "Retracer". Our environment recommends the web pages and information that it is useful for the learner using the learner's annotation. This method analyzes the feature of a Web page, and extracts the learning resource suitable for a student need using a Web-annotation. Finally, we got the good result in a trial use.

Keywords: Self-directed Learning, Web Based Learning, Annotation Environment, Recommender System

1. Introduction

Recently, the people who demand any learning after graduation have increased rapidly. The learning approach is called "Life Long Learning". Since WWW realizes a hyper-text environment and has come into wide use recently, the research about Life Long Learning using WWW becomes popular. It is important to deal with the change and diversification of the learning needs in order to practice the learning style. SDL (Self-Directed-Learning) is one of the teaching methods that supports the autonomous learning of the learner, which corresponds the learner's diversification. SDL has three following features.

(1) The self-setting of the goal by a learner
(2) The self-selection of the teaching material based on the goal by a learner

(3) The self-evaluation and monitor of the achievement by a learner.

We focus on the learning method using a Web page as her/his teaching material in order to practice SDL. In SDL, the learner controls her/his learning by her/himself, and her/his learning is positively advanced using the opportunity. The basis of the autonomy of her/his learning is the responsibility of her/his learning. The processes in which the learner experiences her/his independent activity are important. However, there is richly information with the possibility as a learning resource in Internet. Therefore, it is difficult to practice the Web based SDL effectively without providing the appropriate information. Moreover, it is difficult for the learners to choose a web page suitable for their learning purpose as the learning resource in the method.

We have developed Web Annotation environment "Web-Retracer" in order to solve the above-mentioned problem.

Annotation systems are meant to give electronic documents some of the same note-taking possibilities as paper documents. There have been many attempts to build such systems[1][2][3], whereby people could easily mark-up documents on the World-Wide Web. However, there is nowadays few annotation framework as a educational supporting System. Our environment recommends the web pages and information that it is useful for the learner using the learner's annotation.

2. Our approach

2.1 Problem of Web based SDL

The SDL is very effective approach to deal with the diversification of the learning needs. However, it is necessary to describe in the following in order to effectively advance the learning.
(1) The necessity of providing the appropriate

information: In the SDL, providing appropriate information is necessary in order to choose the more appropriate teaching material that is suitable for her/himself. By providing appropriate information, it is possible that the learner evaluates learning process and learning method of the self.

(2) The necessity of supporting the autonomous activity: The learner has the responsibility to her/his learning on the autonomous learning. the autonomous learning is not successful by itself, but must be produced by the process in which the learner experiences the autonomous activity. Moreover, it is important to critically do the introspection of learning style and learning method in the process [7].

It is difficult for the learner to promote to controlling the own learning by her/himself without the appropriate information. Therefore, the learner must be supported to retrieve a web resource in order to realize the learner's autonomous activity. A keyword-based retrieval technique is considered in order to provide the web resource web (page) suitable for the user's demand. However, retrieval by keyword has the tendency to show an unnecessary reference result. [5].

2.2 Supporting method in learning condition

We considered the learning condition in SDL to provide the suitable supporting method for the learner. We classified the conditions under (A) The goal of the self has not been decided and (B) The knowledge for the learning goal is insufficient. Then we propose supporting methods of the system from the viewpoint of the learner's object and interest in the conditions.

(A-1) Providing information for setting the goal: We think that a learning goal which other learner has set can also be the new goal for the learner. For example, a goal set by many learners is said a notable learning item. This information supports the learner to set the appropriate goal widely for the learner.

(A-2) Providing information for evaluating the learning achievement: The question of another learner is an opportunity for a learner in order to evaluate her/his condition of learning objectively. The learner is able to judge her/his own intelligibility in proportion to whether s/he can understand for the question. It also becomes a chance for the learner to set the next learning goal.

(B-1) Providing information on the teaching material concerning the learning goal: It is difficult for the learner to discover the appropriate resource from Internet. If a learner can be found the resource related to her/his goal from the rich resource, it is necessary to provide information for choosing the teaching material to solve the learning goal.

(B-2) Providing information on the specialist on the learning goal: It is sometimes difficult for a learner to solve her/his question by her/himself even if s/he can retrieve many web resources. We think the specialist who can solve a learner's goal exist on Internet. They can be human resource for the learning.

3. Web based SDL Environment

3.1 Outline of Web-Retracer

We are developing web based self-directed learning environment that is called "Web-Retracer". Web-Retracer allows the learner to annotate the existing web content. Web-Retracer has the following three environments in order to solve the problem stated for the foregoing paragraph.

(1) Annotation environment
A student can embed notes information at arbitrary Web pages. This realizes the resource improvement due to the student. Especially, Web-Retracer has "Q and A System" as Annotation environment. The annotation is linked to the Web contents dynamically. This framework is called "Adaptive Link Generation", which supports an environment suitable for users [4]. We have implemented it in Dynamic HTML. Web-Retracer has an annotation layer over the Web contents to embed the annotation on the WWW.

(2) Knowledge resource sharing environment
A student's annotations are treated as "Knowledge Resource". Web-Retracer records the knowledge resource from all students. Web-Retracer embedded the "Question Icon" that is hyper-link to the student's question. Clicking the icon, the students can accumulate Annotation information embedded in Annotation environment, and own jointly among students. By this approach, the learning purpose clarifies and the limit of individual learning is canceled.

(3) Web resource sharing environment
Web-Retracer accumulates as Web pages that the student had treated. The system treats the pages as "Web resource" and shows them in Web Resource List. By sharing accumulated Web resource among students, a system supports reuse of Web resource.

Web-Retracer supports self-directed learning of a student according to these three environments.

3.2 User Interface

The system's interface has been designed in such a way as to be as user-friendly as possible, even for people who are not expert computer users. Fig.1 depicts a user-interface of Web-Retracer. It is based on HTML

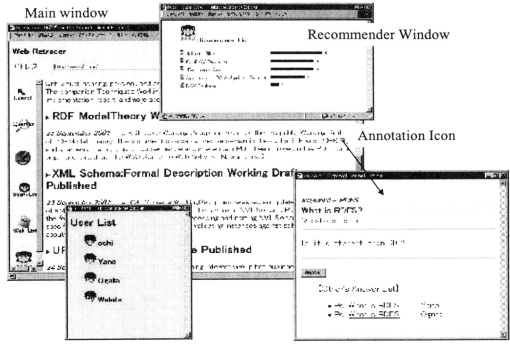

Main window

Recommender Window

Annotation Icon

User List

Annotation window

Figure 1. User interface

and JavaScript technology on Microsoft Internet Explore. Main window consists of an HTML page with three frames. The address-frame contains the address-input-field for the student to input a URL. The menu-frame contains the controls icon to manage the user interaction for system function. The main-frame shows the Web pages that the student select to learn different services and it changes depending on the service selected. It can also display the information of any of the links contained in those pages, such as the lessons registered in the network.

3.3 Functions of Supporting SDL

Web-Retracer recommends learning resource suitable for the learning condition using the annotation in order to realize the effective SDL. We implemented the following functions.

(1) Answer request
We define a learner who embedded a answer on a web page as a expert about the web. The system calculates the possibility in which the answer of each learner for question information is possible from the embedding frequency of question and answer of the learner. Finally, when the corresponding learner login the system, our

system displays the question with the high possibility of replying for her/him.

(2)Relational resource recommendation
Our system recommends the Web resource of which relate to the learner's question as a learning teaching material in order to support her/him to acquire her/his necessary knowledge. To begin with, the system analyzes the morphological of her/his question and pick up the noun. The system calculates TF (Term of Frequency) value and IDF (Inverse Document Frequency) value [6][7] of each noun to define the weight of the noun. We define the gathering of this noun as an interest of the learner. In the same way, our system calculates TF value and IDF value of each noun of the Web resource. We define the gathering of this noun as content in the Web resource. In the tables, it is assumed that it is similar so that cosine value is close to 1 [6]. Then, the system recommends the Web resource whose related-degree is high, when the system displays question information to the learner.

(3)Web resource recommendation
This function shows the following information for the learner to set her/his objective by her/himself.
(3-1) The web pages which many users read: We define the page with many reading learners as learning item that

attracts the attention. Using all learners' reading history, our system presents them.

(3-2) The pages that embedded many questions: We define the page where many question have embedded as the resource which contains the many learning theme. Using all learners' question history, our system presents them.

(3-3) The pages that embedded many answers: We define it as the resource in which the learner notices the page where answer information has mainly been embedded especially. Using all learners' question history, our system presents them.

(4) Function of annotation recommendation

Showing the other's question that is related to the learner's one, s/he can know a new viewpoint or approach that are different from her/his ones. We think that it supports her/his discovery of the new learning item and evaluation of her/his learning achievement. This function takes out the gathering of the noun from the question that the learner embedded. The system calculates TF value and IDF value of each noun to define the weight of the noun. We define the gathering of this noun as an interest of the learner. Using the table of TF and IDF, this system compares question content of each learner. when the learner accessed a page, our system displays the other's question that is related highly to the learner's question in the page.

4. Evaluation

In this chapter, we report the trial result in the experimental operation of Web-Retracer.

4.1 Method

We divided the examinee into group with the support and group without the support. Then, we investigated the effectiveness of the learning item recommendation according to the questionnaire, and compared the estimated result. We prepared university students of 8 and graduate students of 12 persons on this trial as an examinee. We divided them into one group with the learning resource recommendation support and one group without the learning resource recommendation support. The trial period was for one week. The learner of both groups learned a knowledge concerning the information technology. Under the trial, the learner judged the following.

(1) The evaluation on the answer request function

We investigated whether the learners have the ability of answer for all questions that have not got the answer and whether they are interested in the questions.

(2) The evaluation on relational resource recommendation.

We investigated whether the learner sensed with beneficial for read Web.

After the trial period, we prepared 5 questionnaire items in order to investigate effectiveness of the each function for SDL. The learners score the evaluation point from 1 to 5 with their comment.

(3) The evaluation on the Web resource recommendation.

We prepared the following three-questionnaire items.
(Q1) Was it necessary to show the page which many users read?
(Q2) Was it necessary to show the page embedded many questions?
(Q3) Was it necessary to show the page embedded many answers?

(4) The evaluation on the annotation recommendation

We prepared the following three-questionnaire items.
(Q4) Was it necessary to show other's question related your question?
(Q5) Were the recommended questions suitable for you?

4.2 Result

(1) The evaluation on the answer request

A figure of 5.1 shows the result when the system asked the question to the learners in the trial-use, whether they had an ability to answer it and were interest in it. The proportion which the learner could answer the question was 51.5%, but the proportion which the learner was interested it was 80.3%. The system seldom prevented their learning, and it was possible to make the new chance of their learning rather (Fig.2).

(2) The evaluation on relational resource recommendation.

The evaluation of supported group was high when it was compared with the non-supported group (Fig.3).

(3) The evaluation on the Web resource recommendation

In all evaluation items, the value of the supported group was more than no-supported group. And, there were more favorable comments on the supported group. From this fact, the recommendation of the learning resource is indispensable in order to perform SDL effectively. We think that the Web resource recommendation of this system functioned effectively (Fig.4).

(4)The evaluation on the annotation recommendation

In Q.3, the value of the supported group was more than no-supported group. We are get a the following affirmative comment, "The other's viewpoint and different approach was necessary in order to advance the learning. We consider that the annotation recommendation functioned effectively, because the value of Q.5 was 4.3 (Fig.5).

5. Conclusion

In this paper, we propose web based self-directed learning environment, which has recommending methods of the resource united with a student's needs on the basis of a student's learning and Web browsing history. Our system can set not only by her/his interest but also by her/his understanding state, and can recommend the resources suitable for her/his learning. In this paper, we reported the trial result in the experimental operation of Web-Retracer. We got the good result for supporting SDL.

[1]José Kahan, Marja-Riitta Koivunen, Eric Prud' Hommeaux, Ralph R. Swick:Annotea: An Open RDF Infrastructure for Shared Web Annotations, Proceedings of Tenth International World Wide Web Conference, pp.623-632, 2001

[2]Martin Röscheisen, Christian Mogensen, Terry Winograd: Beyond Browsing: Shared Comments, SOAPs, Trails, and On-line Communities, Proceedings of The Third International World-Wide Web Conference, 1995

[3]Davis, J.R. and Huttenlocher, Shared Annotation for Cooperative Learning" Proceedings of Computer Support for Cooperative Learning Conference,1995

[4] L. David: Learning as dialogue: The dependence of learner autonomy on teacher autonomy SYSTEM VOL.23 NO.2 pp175-181,1995

[5] Brusilovsky, P.: "Adaptive Hypermedia", User Modeling and User-Adapted Interaction 11, pp.87-110, 2001

[6] Masahiro Morita, Information filtering system, IPSJ Magazine, vol. 37, no.8, pp.751-757, 1996

[7] Salton,G and Buckley, C: Term-weighting approaches in automatic text retrieval, Information Processing and Management, Nol.24,No.5,pp513-523,1988

[8] Sparck Jones, K: A statistical interpretation of term specify and its application in retrieval, Journal of Documentation, Vol.28, No.1.pp.11-21, 1972

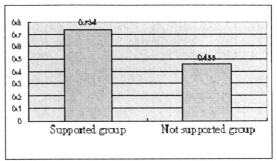

Figure 2. Answer request

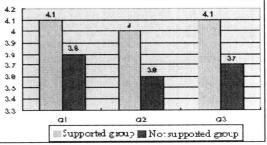

Figure.3 Relational resource recommendation

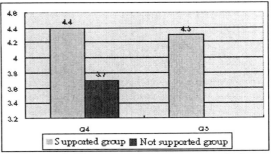

Figure.4 Web resource recommendation

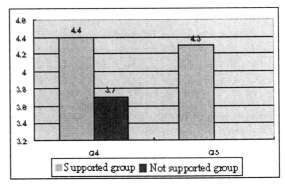

Figure.5 Annotation recommendation

Design of Online Basketball Course Based on WWW

Zhang Yingjie, Zhang Bin, Li Bo
Department of Physical Education,
Tsinghua University, Beijing, 100084 China
E-mail: zhyingjie@sina.com

Han Xibin
The Center for Educational Software,
Tsinghua University, Beijing, 100084 China
E-mail: hanxb@tsinghua.edu.cn

Abstract

Online physical courses based on WWW have special features. In this paper, taking the online basketball course as an example, we present the principles for design of online physical courses. The whole structures is established according to the course objectives, contents and media materials. Methods to design instructional contents, multimedia materials and user interface of online courses is discussed for physical education based on WWW.

1. Introduction

The main feature of physical education courses like basketball is practice out of door. With traditional instructional methods, teachers face some problems. For examples, they have not enough time to explain systematically the theories and methods about a course and not all teachers can exactly demonstrate actions of techniques about the course, etc. The WWW-based instructional technologies supply a solution.

With WWW-based instructional technologies, the theories and methods of physical education can be explained systematically in online courses, the actions of techniques can be demonstrated with multimedia materials, such as video clips which can be replayed by students in Internet, the learning materials can be updated conveniently by teachers, much more references in Internet can be linked into online courses to enlarge the learning space of students[1].

In this paper, taking the online basketball course as an example, we discuss the design principles, whole structures, and methods to design instructional contents, multimedia materials and user interface of online courses for physical education based on WWW.

2. Design Principles

Constructivism [2] promotes the view that learning is an active process in which learners construct meaning, going beyond the information given and discovering principles for themselves. Based the learning theory of Constructivism, we present the principles to design online courses for physical education based on WWW as follows.

? The students are main roles in instructional activities.

? Learning circumstances is more important for students to construct meaning than teaching circumstances.

? Collaborative learning activities are able to help students get more knowledge than single learning activities.

? Supporting students learning is more important by using all kinds of information resources than supporting teachers instructing.

? Teachers should play more active roles in guiding students learning www-based instructional enviro nment.

3. Design of Whole Structure

The whole structure of online basketball course is designed according to the course objectives, content and media materials. The online basketball course includes six parts: history, basic skills, elementary tactics, body quality, game rules, sport Injure, basketball sport websites.

4. Design of Instructional Content

4.1. Extension of Learning Content

In the online basketball course, a large of extensive learning materials are supplied to students who can learn the basketball theories and techniques by themselves with these materials based on Web. These materials include not only the contents which are necessary to be understood by all students, but also almost all basketball theories and techniques which are very useful to the students who are interested in basketball sport. In addition, many basketball sport websites are linked to the relative learning context in the online course.

4.2. Update of Learning Content

The learning materials need to be modified and enlarged dynamically by teachers according to the opinions which are presented by students in their learning process.

4.3. Concise Structure of Learning Material Units

The learning materials need to be organized with a concise structure to meet students to learn by themselves based on Web.

4.4. Multimedia Materials

The learning materials not only include traditional texts, but also involve a large of multimedia elements, such as images, animations, audio and video clips.

5. Design of Multimedia Materials

Different instructional media can encourage learning process in which students construct the meaning in terms they personally understand. In addition to design of each kind of media element, we pay more attention to hyperlinked multimedia incorporating a variety of media, which can facilitate students understanding process [3].

5.1. Design of texts

The texts are used not only to explain instructional content in the online basketball course, but also to show the process of explaining content clearly. For an example, to introduce a technique action we divided the texts into six parts, i.e. the method of action, the key point of action, difficulty of action, common mistakes, correcting methods of the mistakes and the methods of exercise. Some marking characters are edited in the above content scripts to show the hypertext points which will be used by programmers. The scripts are edited with MS-word. The words of the scripts are usually 3-5 times more than traditional teaching materials.

5.2. Design of images

The images are classified into two kinds. One is called photo which is scanned into a computer to show real technique action. Another is called graph which is drawn on computer to show scheme of action's process.

5.3. Design of animations

The animations are very useful to illustrate many movement processes. In online basketball course, elementary tactics are explained through animations with

voice. The animations are able to show the methods and lines of co-operations among players.

5.4. Design of audio materials

Because of the bandwidth limit of Internet, using too many audio materials could cause bad performance of online courses. So, audio is usually used in the place where it is especially needed, such as the voice explanation in a clip of animation and video.

5.5. Design of video materials

Video clips are used to exactly show technique actions and tactic processes. In these video clips slow movements are designed to help students see high speed actions more clear. Many clips of real games is cut and edited to show how these techniques and tactics are applied by basketball player.

6. Design of User Interface

The user interface controls how the user interacts with the online course. Multimedia with hyperlinks can produce an interactive interface, which let the user to be more active than traditional media such as books and television. The graphical users interface of the online basketball course is developed based on the MS Windows operating system.

According to the whole structure of the online basketball course, the user interfaces are divided into three layers. The first layer is home page of the online course. The second layer is content selecting menu. The third layer is content explaining interface.

7. Conclusion

Online physical courses based on WWW have special features. In the paper, taking the online basketball course as an example, we suggest that the design of online physical courses are based on the learning theory of Constructivism. The whole structures is established according to the course objectives, contents and media materials. Methods to design instructional contents, multimedia materials and user interfaces of online courses is discussed for physical education based on WWW.

[1]Zhang Yingjie, el. Designing Online Instructional Environment for Physical Education Based on Web, Proceeding of 2001 ICCE, Seoul, Korea

[2] Alan Staley, Niall MacKenzie, Enabling Curriculum Re-design Through Asynchronous Learning Networks, JALN Volume 4, Issue 1 - June 2000

[3] Don Lehman ,Designing Hypertext Multimedia Educational Software, ALN Magazine Volume 4, Issue 2 - December 2000

A Study on the Development of Multimedia Contents for Preservice Teacher Education Focused on Early Childhood Language Arts Courses

Kim, Jeong Hee

Professor, Department of Early Childhood Education, Kyungnam College of Information & Technology

kimjh@kit.ac.kr

Abstract

A multimedia instruction that integrates different types of media is a way to maximize learning effectiveness, and three-dimensional lessons through a variety of multimedia will be able to offer a more realistic education as an innovative alternative to one-sided, lecture-oriented instruction. The growth of computer engineering has an extremely positive effect on early childhood education as well as prospective teacher education for young children. In order to meet the demands of the times and keep up with the changing educational environment, this studies intent is to develop multimedia contents for early childhood language arts courses, to suggest how it could be developed, and finally suggest its practical use.

1. The need for the development of multimedia contents

The advance of computer technology plays an instrumental role in impacting not only preservice teacher education in early childhood education department but early childhood education as well. Universities need to develop teaching and learning methods utilizing multimedia to its fullest as a means to replace traditional face-to-face education. The purpose of this study is, therefore, to develop multimedia content for early childhood language arts courses to keep up with the changing educational environment. By early childhood, nearly 90 percent of all language skills are developed, therefore it is a critical period for language development. Consequently, language education is one of the primary early childhood education areas. So, it is very meaningful to develop multimedia contents for early childhood language arts courses which educators in the field of Early childhood education and parents would be interested in. The educational benefits of multimedia contents can be listed as below: Multimedia contents can raise learner achievement. The contents developed in this study were designed to teach theories through text and movies, pictures, sound and animation and were employed for practical lessons. It also provides both the theory and practical knowledge of early childhood language arts, empowering learners to learn in an easier and more motivated manner through both the internet or with a CD-ROM title, without being restricted by time and space.

2. Multimedia Contents Development for early childhood language arts courses

Out of multimedia contents for early childhood language art courses, a listening chapter can be presented as follows:The listening chapter consists of two portions, as opposed to a single text-centered one, a document portion and lecture-type movie portion. The former includes text about the entire course, and the latter gives a summarized explanation about the same. In the second part, theoretical explanations are provided through movies, and sound, images, animation are all put to use for additional explanation in such a way to help learners fully comprehend the lecture. The following software programs were utilized for the contents:

Authoring tools: Director, Namo Webeditor, Flash, etc. Image production: Photoshop, Illustrate, 3DCool, etc. Sound and image production: Real Video, Premiere, etc. Others: Word processor, HTML. Operating system: Hangul , Windows98/NT

The listening chapter is composed of six sections. The first section describes the concept of listening. The second one offers the general principles of listening education. The third section explains listening instruction strategies. The fourth section provides an activity to listen to fairy tales. The fifth section includes listening activity materials, and the sixth discusses the practical listening activities. Every section is made up of text and movies that give an explanation about what learners should learn. When additional explanation is required, pictures, animation, images and additional movies are utilized to facilitate learning effectiveness and help the learners comprehend the lesson better. Each section has a subscreen, which consists of movies and documents. The documents provide text about each section, and the movie portion offers lecture-type movies and additional explanation for each sector. The main screen includes the Table of Contents as seen in Figure 1.

(Figure 1)

Once the main screen has popped up, if the learner clicks the " Listening Chapter", the chapter's Table of contents will appear. See Figure 2.

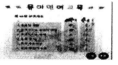

(Figure 2)

By clicking on the forth section, " Listening to Fairy Tales", Figure 3 will pop up.

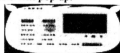

(Figure 3)

On this screen, the learner can watch and listen to the lecturer' explantion and instructions and click on the icons on the screen By clicking various icons, they can have access to an orally narrated fairy tale(Figure 4), picture tales(Figure 5) or puppet tales(Figure 6). Through this they can learn and enjoy various types of fairy tales. movies, sound, and animations that were utilized by learners in experiencing various methods to convey fairy tales.

If learners click on the "orally narrated fairy tales" icon in Figure 3, they can view " Little Cat's Hiccough" as seen in Figure 4 The storyteller on the screen is a prospective teacher.

(Figure 4)

If learners click on one of the various "picture fairy tales"in Figure 5 They can view picturebook type fairy tales through animation and audio. All "picture fairy tales"were produced by students of the early childhood education department.

(Figure 5)

In Figure 3, If learners click on the "puppet tales" icon, They can view a puppet show, as seen in Figure 6.

(Figure 6)

If learners click on the fifth section-"listening activity materials" as in Figure 7, the movie of the lecturer appears. After listening to the lecture, if the learner clicks on the " listening activity materials" icons, they can view a photo of each material.

(Figure 7)

If learners click on the sixth section, they can listen to an explanation of a practical listening activity for use in a kindergarten classroom. After the explanation(Figure 8), the learner can view a realistic listening activity as seen in Figure 9.

(Figure 8)

(Figure 9)

3. Expected Results and Future Challenges

The above-mentioned type of multimedia contents for early childhood language art courses are expected to make the following contributions:

The use of multimedia for education could produce best results in both theory and practice, as an excellent alternative to traditional lessons. Secondly, if supplied on the Internet or on CD-ROM, it will offer relevant information or free learning opportunities, without being restricted by time and space. Finally, the adoption of an animation program could encourage students to be more interactive in class. The Web-based contents could be designed to further interaction between learners and instructors. This will provide higher motivation and learner-centered instruction to students. There are neither sufficient authentic guidelines for the development of multimedia contents [1], nor enough relevant theoretical studies. In the future, more research efforts are required to address such problems.

<References>

Barnard. J.(1992) *Multimedia and the Future of Distance Learning Technology.* EMI, 29(3)

Bibicom(1999) *Director7 and Lingo*, Bibicom

Bibicom(1999) *What's New Photoshop 5*, Bibicom

Bibicom(1999) *Premiere 5*, Bibicom

Hansen, E.(1989) "Interective Video for Reflection: Learning Theory and New Use of the Medium." *Educational Technology,*29(7), 7-15

Kim In-seok, et al.(2001) *Multimedia-Assisted English Teaching and Learning*, Hakmoon Co, 44.

[1] Kim Yeoung-hwan(1997) *Educational Technology for 21C*, Keoyukkeohak Co, 310-313.

Kim Hyeong-Jae(2002) *Digital Contents Production for Multimedia Experts*, Doseosaneup Co, 24-25.

Mary Renck Jalongo(2000) *Early Childhood Language Arts*, Allyn & Bacon

Park Seong-ik, et al.(998*) Recent Research of Educational Technology*, Keoyukkeohak Co, 49.

Yang Yeoung-seon, et. al.(1998) "Research of Teaching-Learning Method using Multimedia," *Multimedia Surpport Center* 1,6.

Reusing Web Learning Portfolios by Case-Based Reasoning Technology to Scaffold Problem Solving

Chen-Chung Liu, Ping-Hsing Don, Kun-Lin Chen, Baw-Jhiune Liu
Department of Computer Engineering and Science
Yuan Ze University, Chung-Li, Taiwan
Email: christia@saturn.yzu.edu.tw

Abstract

This study attempted to reuse the web learning portfolios to scaffold problem solving for activating students' Zone of Proximal Development. First, we analyzed cases from students' learning portfolios for getting case knowledge and student ability, and then used Case Based Reasoning technology for recommending cases to students. After students referred these cases, we adopted Data Mining technology and Issue-Based Information System to analyze the match model between students and cases. Finally, we constructed an online Case Based Learning System, which could retrieve and reuse the fitting cases to effectively scaffold problem solving on student learning process.

I. Introduction

Vygotsky's theorem indicates experts' supports can help students activate their Zone of Proximal Development (ZPD). Whether peer support can lift up student's learning ability or not, there were some educators attempting to develop peer support [1] with a view to activating the ZPD [2] and extending student's independent learning zone in a learning environment. Therefore, providing peer support in a student's learning process will certainly activate the student's ZPD. Some researchers [3] utilized past case experience to enhance learning, they all emphasized that reusing cases after classification and collection would help the learning process in the future.

It is not true that every expert support can help students extend their knowledge, so we have to find out the fitting peers based on their abilities from accumulated cases, and then recommend these cases to students, that is to say, we use peer case as peer support. Therefore, we analyze accumulated cases firstly for getting cases' knowledge and students' abilities and then use Case Based Reasoning (CBR) technology to recommend cases to students. Further, we adopt Data Mining technology and Issue-Based Information System (IBIS) [4] to obtain

a best match model between students and cases for case retrieval and provision.

II. CBR and IBIS

Because CBR is an open way to deal with problems, which based on the concepts of accumulated experiences will be better than Rule-Based Reasoning (RBR) [5] in handling an unknown circumstance. A past case represents a past experience in CBR. Accordingly, if you need to solve this same kind of problem, you can use the same experience for reference. Therefore, we can use the CBR tool to recommend peers' cases to students for reference.

IBIS provided a simple and formal structure to help a group of people who had no confidence get a better answer from discussions, conflicts and repetition opinions. So using IBIS is for the result that people can use discussions and communications to make their different concepts get the agreement through the three opinion quantities of issues, positions and arguments. The three quantities can be regarded as the *information exchange quantity*, which is more that means effectiveness in a discussion. Besides, the *concept utility quantity* using the issue concept from Q&A is the ability of extracting concepts and program segments from recommended cases. Therefore, after students get recommended cases, we can use the quantification of students' Q&A in IBIS to analyze the achievement of recommended cases.

III. Research Methodology

There were 53 students taking the *Java Programming Language* course, so we used the JAVA concepts for analyzing students' cases. Because each student's case had different concepts, which were his knowledge representations could be referred by others, we would induce the classification of case characteristic, and have the unity description of the teacher's reviewed content. After an online database accumulated these cases, we would use each curriculum concept for observing and

analyzing these cases, which were described as below:
1) First, we used the compiler to separate every student's case (or production) from wrong or correct case for analyzing and inducing curriculum concepts.
2) We got the correct and wrong concept model from above correct and wrong cases.
3) We put the correct and wrong concept model into student case concept model and revised the teacher's reviews of student's cases to be the descriptions of concepts, which were the annotation of student case concepts and were saved into case database.
4) Aiming on the representations of students' cases, we would describe the each student ability with concept description which was saved into student ability database.

Therefore, we could establish the match model from each classified concept type. Because we hoped to recommend cases to students immediately, we used the CBR-Works [6] to be the tool of recommendation. When CBR-Works got a student's concept ability from his past cases, the CBR-Works would use the upper match model to retrieve peers' cases, and then actively recommend them to the student.

Because we used a teacher's viewpoint to make up the match model, this was not sure that the match model could satisfy the student's need. After a student had referenced recommended cases and answered the Q&A, we would analyze IBIS information exchange quantity and concept utility quantity to diagnose these recommended cases. We adopted Data Mining's Classification method to analysis the different quantity of special concepts between students and cases.

IV. Experiment

Every student's cases such as practices in curriculum were collected for the source of cases. Figure 1 was the framework of Case Base Learning (CBL) System including CBR, match model, and student case analysis model.

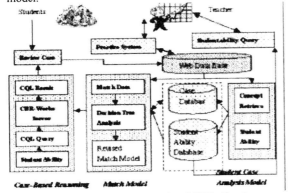

Figure 1: The framework of CBL System

We used C5.0 [7] as Decision Tree analysis software and set a threshold related to the case number and confidence in C5.0 to filter out new match rules. The decision achievement was IBIS information exchange quantity and concept utility quantity. We extracted each rule conformed to that the case number should exceeded 5 (Cover>=5) and the Confidence should exceeded 0.6. Therefore, we could get new rules from above results to revise the prior match model.

We used the questionnaire of user's acceptance of information technology from Davis [9] to understand the perceived usefulness and perceived easiness of students when using CBL system. After our statistic analysis of the perceived usefulness of the system from questionnaire, 69.3% students thought the system was useful, and of the perceived easiness of the system, 72.4% students thought the system was easy to use, so almost 70% students accepted the system.

V. Conclusion

The experimental achievement showed the system could reuse the accumulated cases and support effective leaning. Students not only just got the difficult cases from teachers but also got the fitting cases developed by peers for problem solving, that is, these recommended cases would effectively activate their ZPD. On the other side, the burden of teachers would be reduced when the accumulated cases had grown up.

References

[1] J. Baker and G. Dillon (1999) Peer Support on The Web Innovations in Education and Training International, 36:1, pp. 65-79.
[2] De Guerrero, M. C. M., & Villamil, O. S. (2000) Activating the ZPD: Mutual scaffolding in L2 peer revision. Modern Language Journal, 84 (1), p51-68.
[3] I. Becerra-Fernandez, D. Aha (1999) "Case-Based Problem Solving for Knowledge Management Systems" Twelfth International Florida Artificial Intelligence Research Symposium Conference, Orlando, Florida.
[4] J. Conklin, M. L. Begeman (1988) "IBIS: A Hypertext Tool for Exploratory Policy Discussion." TOIS : ACM Transactions on Office Information Systems 6(4), pp.303-331.
[5] Lifeng, Liu; Zengqiang, Mi; Zhe, Zhang; Baizhen, Liu (1998) "Research on case organization and retrieval of case and rule based reasoning approaches for electric power engineering design," Power System Technology, 1998. International Conference on, Vol.2, pp. 1082-1085.
[6] WWW URL for CBR-Works : http://www.tecinno.com/start.htm
[7] WWW URL for C5.0/See5.0: http://www.rulequest.com/
[8] Davis, F.D. (1989) "Perceived usefulness, perceived ease of use, and user, and user acceptance of information technology, " MIS Quarterly, 13(3), 319-339.

A Web Retrieval Support System with a Comment Sharing Environment: Toward an Adaptive Web-based IR System

Hiroyuki Mitsuhara[1], Youji Ochi[1], Kazuhide Kanenishi[2] and Yoneo Yano[1]
[1] Faculty of Engineering, Tokushima University
[2] Center for Advanced Information Technology, Tokushima University
2-1 Minamijosanjima, Tokushima, Japan
E-mail: {mituhara, ochi, marukin, yano}@is.tokushima-u.ac.jp

Abstract

A search engine is frequently used to look up interesting/unknown topics in web-based exploratory learning, but occasionally it returns meaningless pages (hyperlinks), which can interrupt finding suitable pages. This paper describes a web retrieval support system with a comment sharing environment, which aims at reducing loads in search activity. The effectiveness of this system has been shown through an experiment. This system is not currently adaptive but can be extended to a web-based adaptive IR (Information Retrieval) system.

Keywords: Comment sharing environment, search engine, adaptive web-based IR system, loads in search activity, exploratory learning.

1. Introduction

The web can be regarded as vast teaching material since it has numerous informative pages. Nowadays, learners actively learn through exploring the web. Such a learning method is called exploratory learning and practiced in not only school education but also life long learning. At the beginning of exploration or during exploration, learners frequently try to find suitable pages for fulfilling their needs, goals, or interests by using a search engine. A search engine is very powerful tool but occasionally it returns meaningless pages (hyperlinks), which can interrupt finding suitable pages. This is caused by an insufficient search query. In particular, novice learners who are unfamiliar with a learning topic can have difficulty in designating a sufficient search query to narrow down a search focus. Even if meaningless pages are eliminated with a sufficient search query, it is hard for learners to select a suitable page quickly from similar pages. Although search results generally consist of page title, URL, summary text, and statistic, these are not useful enough to select a suitable page. In this situation, learners have to visit a page and estimate its value repeatedly. Thus, learners are excessively given loads in search activity and consequently lose learning volition.

Recent search engines are equipped with functionalities of supporting search activity. For example, Alexa Web Search presents users with information for clarifying retrieved pages such as ratings, comments, related pages, etc, which are offered by users [1]. Lycos analyzes search query logs with the technique of agglomerative clustering and suggests alternative search queries for rephrasing users' needs [2]. SearchPad recalls users to successful search by presenting individual users' histories of search queries and visited pages [3]. In addition, many adaptive web-based IR (Information Retrieval) systems have been developed that function as a meta-search engine [4]. Syskill&Webert suggests suitable search queries and annotates pages (hyperlinks) of a search result on the basis of individual users' interests [5]. A system developed by Marinilli et al. sorts pages on the basis of individual users' preferences [6]. A mechanism proposed by Huang et al. suggests additional search queries on the basis of individual users' needs [7]. GOOSE elicits suitable search queries from natural language that articulates individual users' goals [8].

A web search retrieval support system WebCOBALT (Web Contents Observable System) has been developed in order to reduce loads in search activity. This system enables learners to write comments on pages retrieved by an existing search engine and share the comments. Learners can find a suitable page without excessive loads, referring to the comments. This system, which adopts Alexa Web Search's approach, is not currently adaptive but can be extended to a web-based adaptive IR system.

The remainder of this paper is organized as follows. Section 2 describes the outline of WebCOBALT, focusing on its fundamental idea and functions. Section 3 illustrates its user interface. Section 4 reports the results of a small-scale experiment. Section 5 considers prospective adaptivity of WebCOBALT.

2. WebCOBALT

WebCOBALT reduces loads in search activity by supplementing drawback in search engines with a comment sharing environment, which enables users to write comments (e.g. complementary explanations, questions, and personal remarks) on information (e.g. web pages) and share the comments. This environment can heighten learning effectiveness. For example, SharlokII facilitates problem solving by enabling learners to share various kinds of information such as questions, answers, comments, and hyperlinks [9]. ReCoNote facilitates knowledge construction by enabling learners to share web notes structured with mutual links with comments [10]. Annotea, which enables users to extend shared comments (annotations) based on XML technologies, may facilitate long-term discussion resulting from the comments [11].

In WebCOBALT, learners can write comments on pages retrieved by an existing search engine and share the comments attached to the search result. Each comment has one of three attributes, "informative", "neutral", "useless", which is designated by a learner. The comments may indicate informative pages, which are not shown in summary text generated by a search engine. For example, "This page is easy to understand thanks to useful diagrams" and "This page is proper for review because there are many quizzes", which have the "informative" attribute, can be clues used to find a suitable page. Conversely, "This page does not describe truth" and "This page is filled with harmful information", which have the "useless" attribute, can be clues not to visit unsuitable pages. Learners refer to the comments and efficiently find a suitable page without actually visiting the pages. Thus, enabling learners to share the comments leads to reduction of loads in search activity. Figure 1 shows the framework of WebCOBALT. As shown in Fig.1, this system is similar to a meta-search engine[1]; there are advantages from the viewpoint of system developers: no intricate retrieval algorithms and no huge databases. WebCOBALT has the following functions in addition to comment sharing.

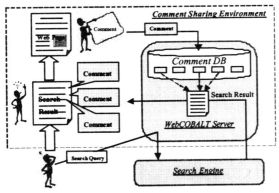

Figure 1. Framework of WebCOBALT

Bookmark: When finding an informative page during exploration, learners usually record the page as bookmarks, which are subsequently used to reflect on learning. WebCOBALT automatically builds a personal bookmark including pages with informative comments (i.e. comments with the "informative" attribute) written by a learner. This function facilitates not only reflection but also the increase of comments.

Sorting: The informative contained in a page will be clarified as the comments on the page increase. WebCOBALT simplifies finding a suitable page by sorting pages retrieved in descending order of the number of comments on each page.

3. User Interface

Learners can use this system on a web browser without plug-in software.

Main Frame: In this frame (Fig. 2(A)), the search result retrieved by goo[2] is displayed using stretch-text, which reduces information overload by hiding comments in the initial state; page titles and the number of comments are displayed. In order for a learner to notice pages with comments written by him/herself, a red circular icon is embedded in the titles of such pages. As soon as he/she clicks on a page title, its comment area is expanded/closed under the title. The comment area describes URL, summary text generated by goo, comment, commentator's e-mail address, etc. If a page has some comments, the learner can choose one from a commentator list (pull-down menu). By clicking on the "Read this page" button, the page is presented in this frame.

Retrieval Frame: In this frame (Fig. 2(B)), components for designating a search query are displayed. In addition, the learner can invoke his/her bookmark by clicking on the anchor text of "My Bookmark".

Bookmark Window: In this window, a personal bookmark is displayed in the same design of the search result. The learner can effectively reflect on learning, referring to comments attached to his/her bookmark. He/she can delete a page from his/her bookmark.

Comment Window: In this window (Fig. 2(C)), components for writing comments are displayed. This window disappears immediately after the learner clicks on the "Submit" button.

4. Experiment

---

[1] Strictly, a meta-search engine may utilize several existing search engines.
[2] A commercial Japanese search engine (robot search service). http://www.goo.ne.jp/

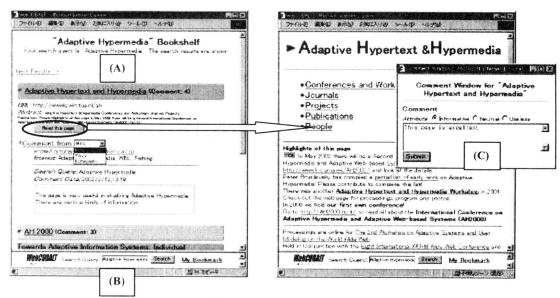

Figure 2. User interface

A comparison experiment between WebCOBALT and an existing search engine was done on a small scale in order to evaluate the effectiveness of comment sharing. Subjects of this experiment were graduate and undergraduate students who belonged to the department of computer science at Tokushima University. Twenty subjects were randomly divided into the following groups and were given the same task.

Group A (10 persons): They used goo.

Group B (10 persons): They used WebCOBALT without a bookmark function or a comment window.

Task: They had to look up nine items of three topics shown in Table 1 by using an allocated system (goo or WebCOBALT) and record answers to each item in a DOC file by copy & paste.

Specific evaluating points were the number of pages that were visited in each topic and the time needed to complete each topic. In this experiment, search queries and search options were fixed to ensure that all the subjects always received the same search result. Experiment time was not restricted and the subjects were allowed to abandon the items when they were not able to find suitable pages. WebCOBALT had attached the following types of comments to the search result in advance.

Comment type 1: It is clear that the page satisfies an item (e.g. "This page has a photomicrograph of bacteria that are the origin of puffer's poison").

Comment type 2: It is clear that the page does not satisfy an item (e.g. "This page describes how to cook Afghan foods").

Comment type 3: It is unknown whether or not the page

satisfies an item (e.g. "This page is good to study copyright law superficially").

Topic A: Puffer's poison (Tetrodotoxin)	
Traits of this topic in search activity: The subjects have to find suitable pages from many pages that include similar information.	
A-1	Find a photomicrograph of bacteria that make puffer's poison.
A-2	Does a horseshoe crab have puffer's poison?
A-3	What are symptoms of puffer poisoning and measures against it?
Topic B: Afghanistan	
Traits of this topic in search activity: The subjects have to find suitable pages from many pages unrelated with the task (e.g. pages concerning fund raising).	
B-1	Enumerate races, languages, religions, and the government of Afghanistan.
B-2	How many Afghan refugees exist?
B-3	Look up recent medical treatment and humanitarian supports in Afghanistan.
Topic C: Copyright law	
Traits of this topic in search activity: The subjects will have difficulty in finding suitable pages directly from the search result. They have to find suitable pages by traversing a few layers.	
C-1	What kinds of computer programs are protected by copyright law?
C-2	Under what conditions can we quote information with copyright?
C-3	Look up copyright law in education.

Table 1. Tasks in the experiment

4.1 Results

DOC files collected indicated that one subject in group A abandoned two items and one subject in group B abandoned one item. The others completed all the items.

Time: Figure 3 shows the mean time (min.) needed for the subjects to complete each topic. Figure 4 shows the subjective time needed to complete the task (all the items), which was asked with a questionnaire (five degrees) "Did you complete this task earlier than you predicted?"

For the two topics, actual time consumption by group B exceeds that of group A. On the other hand, subjective time consumption by group B is fairly superior to that of group A.

Visit: Figure 5 shows the mean number of pages that the subjects visited in each topic. In topic A and B, the mean number of group B is notably lower than that of group A.

4.2 Considerations

Although the effectiveness of comment sharing is doubtful according to Fig. 3, Fig. 4 indicates that group B completed the task without excessive loads. Actual time consumption of group B was increased by thorough reference to comments. This ground appears as the results of questionnaires shown in Table 2. Group B noticed the importance of comments and made active use of the comments to select suitable pages from the search results. Furthermore, several of them took interest in the topics by referring to comments.

Figure 5 indicates that group B found suitable pages efficiently by referring to comments. It is clearly conceivable that comments attached to the search result reduced a load in search activity. Group A had to infer to the content of a page from summary texts generated by goo and actually visit the page to confirm whether it satisfied an item. Repetition of this activity increased the number of pages visited and subjective time consumption of group A. Overall from the above considerations, it may be concluded that comment sharing reduced loads in search activity.

The fact that there is no notable difference between two groups in Topic C may be caused by its trait in search activity that both groups had to traverse a few layers to find suitable pages. In other words, almost all comments in Topic C were superficial (i.e. Comment type 3) and did not describe paths to those suitable pages. Therefore the same traverse was imposed on both groups however the number of pages visited by group B was unexpectedly increased. From this situation, WebCOBALT was recognized to be effective under the condition that the trait of comments corresponds to that of a task.

5. Prospective Adaptivity

WebCOBALT is not currently an adaptive system. Does it

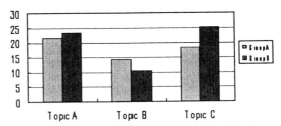

Figure 3. The mean time (min.) needed by the

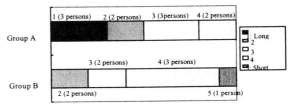

Figure 4. Subjective time needed to complete the task

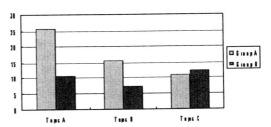

Figure 5. The mean number of pages that the subjects visited in each topic

Question	Answer
Q1: How many comments did you refer to?	All comments: 5 persons
	Almost all comments: 3persons
	Half comments: 2 persons
Q2: Did you take interests in the topics by referring to comments?	Definitely yes: 1 person
	Yes: 3 persons
	No: 6 persons
Q3: Are comments helpful for your search activity?	Definitely yes: 2 persons
	Yes: 8 persons

Table 2. Results of questionnaires

need to have adaptivity? What does it adapt? How does it build a learner model? To expand this system to a web-based adaptive IR system, these questions need to be considered.

The increase of comments causes information overload. As described above, the current system displays meaningless comments unrelated with a task. To make matters worse, it may rank pages with many meaningless comments higher. This situation disrupts the search and consequently lowers learning effectiveness. Adaptivity can be applied to remedy this problem. A significant issue is how the system identifies learners' tasks. Our intuition is that a task may be revealed as a search query. For example, a learner who is interested in Adaptive Hypermedia (AH for short) will designate "Adaptive Hypermedia" as a search query in order to find pages with comprehensive contents. A learner who understands AH roughly but is unfamiliar with AI technology used in AH will designate "Adaptive Hypermedia AI technology" in order to find pages with detailed contents. The following assumptions are therefore derived.

- *Similarity between tasks can be replaced with similarity between learners.*
- *Similarity between learners can be replaced with similarity between search queries.*
- *A learner prefers pages that similar learners estimated to be informative.*

The current system already stores search queries, URLs, and attributes of page estimation. These data can be used as a learner model. Similarity between search queries can be calculated by means of simple keyword matching, the Pearson's correlation coefficient or other methods. A principal element to be adapted in the current system is comments. Meaningless comments unrelated to the learner's current task should be eliminated. If that happens, pages related with the task will be ranked higher and the learner may find a suitable page smoothly. The prospective adaptivity will be actualized using the following adaptation technologies.

Adaptive Link Sorting: To sort pages (hyperlinks) in order of high similarity between tasks (specifically, the current task of a learner and the past tasks of other learners) is very profitable for learners. WebCOBALT first calculates the similarity between search queries from search queries of comments on pages retrieved. Comments with low similarity are eliminated. Secondly, it picks up pages with informative comments from pages with high similarity. The pages picked up will be suitable for the current task. Thirdly, it sorts these pages in order of useful information.

Adaptive Link Generation: Numerous web pages are created daily and search results are frequently renewed. In this situation, pages that similar learners estimated to be informative are not always retrieved. WebCOBALT copes with this problem by generating hyperlinks that connect to suitable pages independently of the search result. After performing the above adaptive link sorting, it first picks up pages that do not exist in the current search result but were previously evaluated to be informative by similar learners. Secondly, it sorts these pages in order of useful information. Thirdly, it generates hyperlinks that connect to these pages.

6. Conclusions

This paper has described the web retrieval support system with a comment sharing environment and indicated that this system can be extended to a web-based adaptive IR system. To combine collaborativity with adaptivity will enhance the quality of search engines. However it is true that this research is currently insufficient. We recognize that further considerations, surveys, and experiments are required in order to prove soundness of our idea for the adaptivity.

Acknowledgements
This research was supported in part by the grant-in-aid for Scientific Research (B)(2) No.13480047 from Japan Society for the Promotion of Science.
This research was supported by a grant to RCAST at Doshisha University from the Ministry of Education, Science, Sports and Culture, Japan.

References
1. Alexa Web Search. http://www.alexa.com/
2. Beeferman, D., and Berger, A.: Agglomerative clustering of a search engine query log, Proc. of the Sixth ACM SIGKDD International Conference on Knowledge Discovery and Data Mining, pp.407-415 (2000).
3. Bharat, K.: SearchPad: Explicit Capture of Search Context to Support Web Search, Proc. of WWW9 International Conference (2000). http://www9.org/w9cdrom/173/173.html
4. Brusilovsky, P.: Adaptive Hypermedia, User Models and User-Adapted Interaction 11, pp87-110 (2001).
5. Pazzani, M., Muramatsu, J., Billsus, D.: Syskill & Webert: Identifying interesting web sites, Proc. of the Thirteenth National Conference on Artificial Intelligence (AAAI'96), pp.54-61 (1996). http://www.ics.uci.edu/~pazzani/Syskill.html
6. Marinilli, M., Micarelli, A., Sciarrone, F.: A Case-Based Approach to Adaptive Information Filtering for the WWW, Proc. of the Second Workshop on Adaptive Systems and User Modeling on the World Wide Web, pp.81-87 (1999).
7. Huang, C. K., Oyang, Y. J., and Chien L. F.: A Contextual Term Suggestion Mechanism for Interactive Web Search, Proc. of the First Asia-Pacific Conference on Web Intelligence: Research and Development (WI2001), pp.272-281 (2001).
8. Liu, H., Lieberman, H., and Selker T.: GOOSE: A Goal-Oriented Search Engine with Commonsense, Proc. of the Second International Conference on Adaptive Hypermedia and Adaptive Web-Based Systems (AH2002), pp.253-263 (2002).
9. Ogata, H., Imai, K., Matsuura, K., and Yano, Y.: Knowledge Awareness Map for Open-ended and Collaborative Learning on the World Wide Web, Proc. of the 9th International Conference on Computers in Education (ICCE'99), pp.319-326 (1999).
10. Miyake, N. and Masukawa, H.: Relation-Making to Sense-Making: Supporting College Students' Constructive Understanding with an Enriched Collaborative Note-Sharing System, Proc. of the 4th International Conference of the Learning Science, pp.41-47 (2000).
11. Kahan, J., Koivunen, M.R., Prud'Hommeaux, E., and Swick, R.R.: Annotea: An Open RDF Infrastructure for Shared Web Annotations, Proc. of the WWW10 International Conference (2001). Available online at http://www10.org/cdrom/papers/488/

Developing Web-based On-demand Learning System

Hiroyuki MURAKOSHI†   Mikio KISHI†   Koichiro OCHIMIZU†
†School of Information Science
Japan Advanced Institute of Science and Technology

Email: murakosi@jaist.ac.jp, mkishi@jaist.ac.jp, ochimizu@jaist.ac.jp

Abstract

Web-based distance learning system supports distributed and asynchronous learning. Web-based learning approach became more popular, and many Web-based learning systems have been developed. In this paper, we describe new functions to support on-demand learning in our Web-based learning system. We also report the results of an experiment to confirm the effectiveness of the new functions

1 Introduction

Web-based distance learning system supports distributed and asynchronous learning. Web-based learning approach became more popular, and many Web-based learning systems have been developed. For example, WebCT is a well-known Web-based learning system[1]. However, these systems have been designed and developed for the purpose of courseware learning, and it will be difficult to find the appropriate learning contents which users demand to study. We think that it will be especially difficult to search the multimedia contents which are composed of the video or animation images.

We have a research object of developing a method to provide the learners with the appropriate contents in the Web-based learning system which has multimedia contents such video and animation image. In this paper, we describe a prototype of Web-based on-demand learning system we developed. Our Web-based learning system is composed of the video image viewer of teacher, teaching material viewer, text viewer. We developed a preliminary version of two kinds of Web-based learning systems. In order to solve the problems concerned with this system, we developed three new functions, a retrieval function to search for the demanded contents, a bookmark function to record the points they were not able to understand or thought important, and a function to select media. From the results of the experiment to confirm the effectiveness of the new functions, we assumed that they would be more effective in on-demand learning. This result will show a preliminary clue to successful Web-based on-demand learning.

2 Preliminary Web-based Learning System

We have developed two kinds of Web-based learning systems in JAIST Virtual University Project. In this section, we describe these systems in detail.

2.1 First Version: "Artificial Intelligence"

Figure 1 shows the snapshot of our preliminary Web-based learning system designed for learning "Artificial Intelligence" which is opened by Professor Tojo in JAIST. This course is composed of 15 lessons. One lesson takes about 50 minutes. Note that one usual classroom lesson takes about 90 minutes. Our system is composed of the video image viewer of teacher, teaching material viewer, text viewer, movie slider function tool boxes, indexes, a FAQ function tool and a bulletin board. In the video viewer of teacher, the video image of the RealVideo format taken a picture by focusing on the teacher is displayed. In teaching materials viewer, the presentation slides are displayed synchronizing with the video image. They can be also displayed the marking to explaining point by using Macromedia Flash[2]. In the text viewer, the content that the teacher spoke is displayed as it is. So learners can confirm the part they missed hearing, and take a note. They can also study the meaning of the term of texts because there is a link to the glossary. Synchronization of the video image, teaching materials and text contents is realized by SMIL[3]. Indexes in the left area are linked to learning components. In addition, learners can interact with not only the teacher but also the other learners by using the FAQ tool and the bulletin board. This system requires a personal computer with Windows OS.

We have experimented on the effectiveness of learning with our Web-based learning system[4]. The following problems have become clear.

- It tended to be difficult for the learners to concentrate to study.

- The learners tended to feel eyestrain.

2.2 Second Version: "Software Design Methodology"

We have improved our Web-based learning system described in Section 2.1. Figure 2 shows the snapshot of our improved Web-based learning system designed for learning "Software Design Methodology" which is opened by Professor Katayama in JAIST. The following points are improved. They may be effective in the concentration on learning and easing eyestrain.

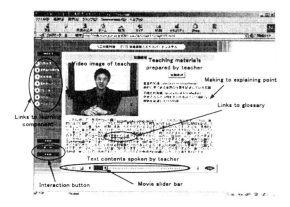

Figure 1: Web-based Learning System (Artificial Intelligence)

- We made the video image of the teacher smaller and teaching materials play a central role in learning. We think the smaller video image would be effective in the presence and atmosphere in the lecture. Learners will mainly pay attention to the teaching materials.

- We added the system to on/off function of the text contents spoken by the teacher. The function make it possible for users to show the text and put it out of sight.

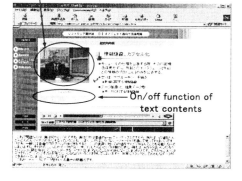

Figure 2: Web-based Learning System (Software Design Methodology)

2.3 The Problem

We obtained information by means of questionnaires from the learners using two kinds of Web-based learning systems described in Section 2 to examine the problem of them. We also analyzed access logs to confirm the effectiveness of retrieval function, that is, the indexed information of contents and the slider bar to move multimedia contents which were equipped with the systems. As a result, the following problems became clear.

- The learners can not find the appropriate contents demanded to learn with the exception of the divided lesson.

- The learners can not apply their past learning record.

- The systems are not equipped to print out teaching materials or text contents.

- The learners tended to come and go in front and behind using the slider bar because it was necessary to appoint the place for learning intuitively.

3 Development of New Functions

We improved our Web-based learning system to solve the problems described in Section 2.3. Figure 3 show a snapshot of the screen where the learners can acquire indexed information. The learners can use retrieval function and bookmark function by using the function select button in the upper left area. In this section, we explain the retrieval function and the bookmark function in detail.

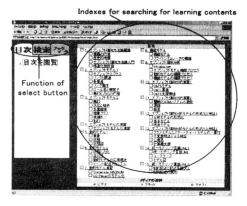

Figure 3: Screen of Indexed Information

3.1 Retrieval Function

It will be useful for learners to use indexed information for searching for contents demanded to learn. However, the contents found by the information are learning components which were divided a lesson into, and the learners can not search for the contents with the exception of the learning components. So we developed the retrieval function to search for demanded contents. The teaching material is composed of many slide sheets. The function is executed by keyword matching with text data in the multimedia contents and provide the learners with the point of a specific slide sheet. There are text contents spoken by the teacher and described in the teaching materials in

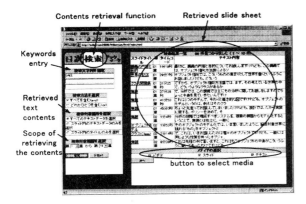

Figure 4: Screen of Retrieval Function

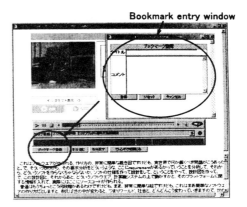

Figure 5: Screen of Bookmark Function

this multimedia contents. There are also title data of the teaching materials.

Figure 4 show a snapshot of the retrieval function. Users can choose the kinds of the retrieved text contents, all text data or text data in teaching materials, title data in teaching materials. They can also choose the scope of retrieving the contents.

3.2 Bookmark Function

Learners will often want to repeatedly study the points they were not able to understand or thought important. However, it is difficult to search multimedia contents such as our Web-based learning system for the demanded points because the learners must intuitively use the slider bar to appoint the place for learning. We think that it will be necessary the computer support to resolve such a problem. We developed a bookmark function in our Web-based learning system. The function make it possible for the learners to record the points they were not able to understand or thought important. Recorded data are stored in their own bookmark files. This function helps the learners to study repeatedly. Figure 5 show a snapshot of the screen of the bookmark function.

3.3 Function to Select Media

Our Web-based learning system described in Section 2 is composed of the video image of teacher, presentation material viewer and text viewer spoken by the teacher. Learner study their media synchronously. However they would not necessarily like to need their media at the same time. For example, they may want to print out presentation materials or text data spoken by the teacher to review the lessons. So we developed the function to select media in our Web-based learning system. The learners can get only necessary media by using the function to select media when they study learning contents in our Web-based learning system. Figure 6 show a snapshot of the screen of the selected media (text + slide sheet). The example of the button to select media is shown in the lower right area of Figure 4.

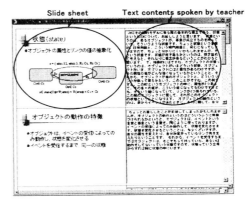

Figure 6: Example of Screen of Selected Media(Text + Slide Sheet)

4 Evaluation

In order to confirm the effectiveness of the new functions we developed, we set up an experiment where twelve graduate students reviewed six lessons of "Software Design Methodology" in JAIST using our improved Web-based learning system. They already have studied the above lessons in real class room or using our old Web-based learning system. Note that they have been attending the lecture of "Software Design Methodology" during the experiment.

4.1 Evaluation using AHP

AHP [5] helps us choose one of several alternatives effectively based on some criteria. We have focused the scores of each alternative and developed a method for extracting important parameters as clues to improve the Web-based learning system using AHP [4][6]. Using this method, we evaluated effectiveness of our improved Web-based learning system compared with our old Web-based learning system.

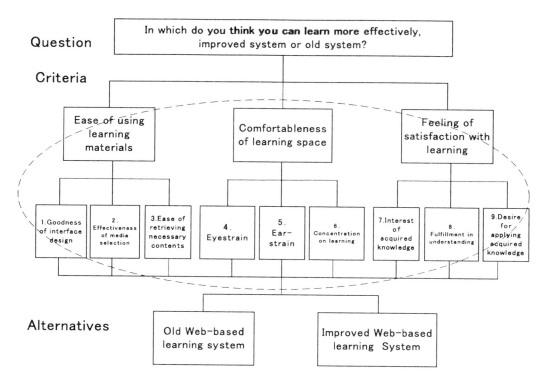

Figure 7: AHP Hierarchical Diagram

The AHP hierarchical diagram to compare the effectiveness of our improved Web-based learning system with that of our old system is shown in Figure 7. Dotted circles show enumerated criteria. We call our Web-based learning system described Section 3 improved Web-based learning system. We also call two kinds of Web-based learning systems described in Section 2 old Web-based learning system. We applied criteria extracted to compare the effectiveness of Web-based learning with that of classroom learning [7] to the criteria selected to evaluate the effectiveness of Web-based learning.

We made two kinds of questionnaire sheets for the calculation by the AHP diagram shown in Figure 7. One is a sheet to give a weight to every pairs of criteria. Another is a sheet to give a weight to our improved Web-based learning and our old system to each criterion. After their learning we collected sheets answered by 12 students who attended empirical lectures. We excluded two students because the value of his/her AHP adjustment (C.I.) exceeded the permitted value. The C.I. is a criterion for measuring consistency when subjects evaluate a weight.

Table 1 shows the score of our old system and our improved system of every criterion. The third row shows the order of precedence by the results of T-test (a statistical significant level is 5%). Note that the blank space shows no significant difference. We think

that statistical significant difference between scores of the improved system and the old system will characterize the style of learning. We also think that the levels of scores will show the effectiveness of learning. Table 2 shows 9 criteria classified into four categories (characteristic table). We regarded the average score of criteria as the threshold of the high and low. In Table 2, the threshold value is 11.1 and a statistical significant level is 5%. The italic font numbers mean that the score of our improved Web-based system is lower than our old system. The results of Table 1 and Table 2 will show the following findings.

- "3.Ease of retrieving necessary contents", "6. Concentration on learning" and "9. Desire for applying acquired knowledge" will be important parameters that characterize difference between the effectiveness of our improved Web-based learning system and that of our old system.

- The new functions described in Section 3, retrieval function, bookmark function, and function to select media will be more effective in on-demand learning.

4.2 Evaluation using Questionnaire
We collected the questionnaire about the retrieval and bookmark function to confirm the effectiveness of

Table 1: Comparison of Improved System with Old System

Criteria	Old	T-test	Improved	Score
3	6.789	<	15.744	22.53
9	4.396	<	8.330	12.73
6	2.603	<	9.910	12.51
1	3.129		8.653	11.7
4	3.941		7.741	11.68
8	3.670	<	6.811	10.48
7	3.808	<	5.772	9.58
2	1.287	<	3.283	4.57
5	1.533		2.607	4.14
total	31.155	<	68.849	100

Table 2: Result of Questionnaire

	Statistical Significant Difference	No Statistical Significant Difference
Score is High ($\geq$ 11.1)	3,6,9	1,4
Score is Low (< 11.1)	2,7,8	5

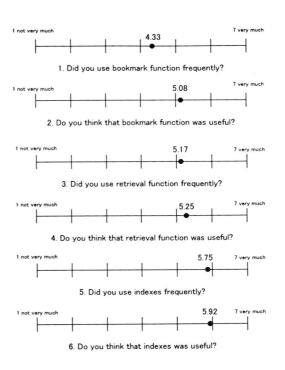

Figure 8: Results

them in detail. The results of the questionnaire are shown in Figure 8. The total number of answers for the questionnaire is 12. The round marks show the average. The results will show the following findings.

- The retrieval and bookmark function will be as useful as the indexed information. In this experiment, the subjects learned the contents which they already have studied in classroom. So the indexed information would be useful.

- The bookmark function was not used as frequently as the retrieval function and the indexed information. We think that it will be necessary to examine our method of storing in the bookmark files.

5 Conclusion

In this paper, we described the new functions to support on-demand learning in our Web-based learning system to learn "Software Design Methodology". From the results of the experiment to confirm the effectiveness of the new functions we also assumed that they would be more effective in on-demand learning. This result will show a preliminary clue to successful Web-based on-demand learning. We plan to evaluate the effectiveness of the new functions when the learners prepare lessons and study by themselves. we also plan to improve our method of storing in the bookmark files using the bookmark function.

References

[1] http://www.webct.com/.

[2] http://www.macromedia.com/.

[3] http://www.w3.org/AudioVideo/.

[4] Atsuo Inomata, Mikio Kishi, Hiroyuki Murakoshi, Satoshi Tojo, and Koichiro Ochimizu. Evaluation Method of Web-based Learning System. In *International Conference on Information Technology Based Higher Education and Training(ITHET01)*, July 2001.

[5] Thomas L. Saaty. *The Analytic Hierarchy Process.* McGraw Hill, 1980.

[6] Hiroyuki Murakoshi, Tsuyoshi Kawarasaki, and Koichiro Ochimizu. Comparison using AHP of Web-based Learning with Classroom Learning. In *First International Workshop on Internet-Supported Education(WISE2001)*, pp. 67–73. IEEE Computer Society Press, Jan. 2001.

[7] Atsuo Inomata, Hiroyuki Murakoshi, Satoshi Tojo, and Koichiro Ochimizu. Extracting Parameters to measure the effectiveness of Distance Learning Materials. *TECHNICAL REPORT OF IEICE ET2001-56*, Vol. 101, No. 433, pp. 5–12, Nov. 2001(in Japanese).

Design of Web-based Support System of Educational Programs for Museum of Science and Innovation

Satoru Fujitani
Mejiro University College
4-31-1, Naka-ochiai, Shinjuku,
Tokyo 161-8539, Japan
fujitani@mejiro.ac.jp

Shoko Mitsuishi   Masaki Makihara
National Museum of Emerging Science and Innovation
2-41-3, Aomi, Koto, Tokyo 135-0064, Japan

Abstract

This paper describes ongoing research of design of web-based support system for educational program held in a science museum. We are now going to develop the system at National Museum of Emerging Science and Innovation in Tokyo, Japan. Educators and learners can access to the web site for making learning activity plan, searching learning resources, carrying out their researches, and discussing with people involved in the museum. The system will aim at offering the science museum as learning environment which explains the importance of science and technology, and the pleasure of research.

1. Research Backgrounds

Educational program in a museum [1][2][3] is a popular way to offer learning resources for deeper understandings of exhibits more effective. Meanwhile, many educators hope that museums will offer not only educational program, but also the consecutive and comprehensive learning support from the museum. In Japan, although there are some noteworthy activities in science museums that hold comprehensive learning [4], many school children have few chances to participate such activities until these days. Students who are just browsing around in the museum are not uncommon.

For consecutive learning support from the museum, one of the answers is in the network. From the viewpoint of network-based support for education, so-called "virtual museum" technology enables to provide additional opportunities for information access [5][6]. Offering web-based curriculum for science education also gives favorable results that learners will find them exciting and engaging [7]. Moreover, many recent researches argue that communication over the net affects learning. Computers are also defined as tools for communication on educational

settings [8][9][10][11]. With the network-based activities, more fulfilling educational program should be promoted.

2. Educational Program and Design of Web-based Support System

Thereinbefore, we conduct research project that sets a final target on developing a new way of management of the educational program in science museum for stimulating learning activities for school learners and educators. In this chapter, we will describe the outline of the educational program, and the web-based support system in detail.

2.1 Outline of the Educational Program

The educational program research has carried out at National Museum of Emerging Science and Innovation (MeSci) in Tokyo, Japan [12]. MeSci, opened in July 2001, is the place for encountering and learning about cutting edge science and technology.

Figure 1 shows outline of the educational program. The program is consisted of three major items: "Activities for Guests" which are pre-established programs for visitors to explore and learn from exhibits, "Supplementary Readers" which is the writings in terms of pedagogical issues around the exhibits, and "Cyberspace for Guests" which is a web site used for preparation and follow-ups of educational program. All items are integrated so that visitors can carry out project-based or problem-based learning activities in the museum.

2.2 Cyberspace for Guests

"Cyberspace for Guests" is a web site for supporting the educational program. This site is mainly for both educators and learners, and they can access to learning resources for the program. The web site is specialized for following three functions. We will describe them in detail.

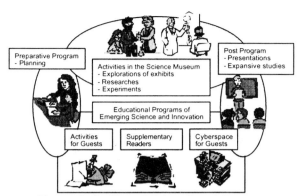

Figure 1: Outline of Educational Programs

2.2.1 Support Tools for Program Planning. For educators who are not familiar with educational program at the museum, we are planning tutorial programs and planning support tools for the educational program. With the tutorial, educators will learn what kind of learning activities can the program provide. Using planning support tools, educators can select workshop topics for the learners, and it helps them to make learning activity plan for school. It makes expected outcome and evaluation measure clear. Moreover, negotiation with educators and the museum staff about program schedule is necessary, because the period of the program is limited though interests of educators and learners are widely spread.

2.2.2 Supplementary Readers Database. Especially in our museum MeSci, up-to-date topics of cutting edge technology and science are dealt with. In order to supply such lively and helpful information to learners, network-based document distribution method should be adopted. Moreover, we can set several topics even from one exhibit for educational program. It is convenient for learners to get brochure without more than necessary. Thus, we are planning to use on-demand PDF (Portable Document Format) file generating software [13] to supply supplementary readers related to exhibits at the museum. This system enables to output PDF files from contents database, e.g. articles, figures, pictures etc., and layout information of PDF written by XML. Curators and interpreters need not to generate PDF file manually. Indeed, we shall pay attention to copyright issues for providing the information.

2.2.3 Discussion Area for Guests. Some learners should associate their experiences with another learning activities or classroom studies. "Discussion area for guests" supports post-program activities such as further discussion and continuing study for educators and learners. Learners explore discussion bulletin boards and additional information web pages for expansive studies. People involved to museum, e.g., curators, interpreters, and volunteers, as specialists of the certain science and

technology areas, also appear in the discussion area and support the learners to be audience and to offer helpful information. Participants of the discussion area are limited to the learners and people involved to museum. By limiting the participants, learners can control their situation trustworthy. Under these conditions, we expect they can share joy of discussion and discovery in the program as seen in previous research [10].

3. Conclusions

The web-based educational program support system will aim at offering the science museum as learning environment which explains the importance of science and technology, and the pleasure of research. We hope it stimulates creativity and originality of children. We will investigate about the learning contents, guidance method, and teaching-materials development of the educational program from the viewpoint of science education and educational technology.

References

[1] Timothy Ambrose, Managing New Museums, (Satoshi Ohori & Eiji Mizushima, Trans. in Japanese) Tokyo: Tokyodo Book Publishing, 1997. (Original work published U.K.: The Stationery Office Books, 1993.)

[2] Philadelphia Museum of Art, Education, [On-line], Available: http://www.philamuseum.org/education/

[3] Education, Cité des Sciences et de lindustrie, [On-line, written in French], Available: http://www.cite-sciences.fr/francais/ala_cite/act_educ/global_fs.htm

[4] Tetsuichi Hamaguchi, Welcome to "After-school museum" (in Japanese), Tokyo: Chijinshokan Publishing, 2000.

[5] Elliott Ostler, et al., Art and Technology Integration Project: Year 1 Status Report, (ERIC Document Reproduction Service No. ED 398 906)

[6] The Community Discovered, [On-line], Available: http://communitydisc.wst.esu3.k12.ne.us/

[7] The Web-based Inquiry Science Environment, [On-line], Available: http://wise.berkeley.edu/

[8] Satoru Fujitani & Kanji Akahori, An Effectiveness Study of Web-based Application for Mailing List Summary and Review, Proceedings of ICCE/ICCAI 2000, Vol.1, pp.215-221, 2000.

[9] Satoru Fujitani & Kanji Akahori, A Summary Extraction Method of E-mail Discussion and Its Web-based Application to Mailing List Review, Educational Technology Research, Vol.23, No.1-2, pp.1-12, 2000.

[10] Noyuri Mima, Children in the "Wonder-Box Network" (in Japanese), Tokyo: Justsystem, January, 1997.

[11] Rena M. Palloff & Keith Pratt, Building Learning Communities in Cyberspace, CA: Jossey-Bass Publishers, 1999.

[12] National Museum of Emerging Science and Innovation, [On-line], Available: http://www.miraikan.jst.go.jp/

[13] "biz-Stream"-On-demand PDF Generator, Brainsellers.com Corp., [On-line], Available: http://www.brainsellers.com/

A Web-based Training System for Evaluating Online Educational Resources

Gyo Sik Moon

Dept. of Computer Education, Taegu National University of Education, Taegu, Korea

Abstract

As the World Wide Web gains influence in teaching and learning, the role of teachers shifts from didactic to facilitative. This new role emphasizes the use of Web materials as a cognitive tool as well as learning resources, which necessitates skills to search, evaluate, and select suitable contents for educational needs out of a vast reservoir of information of the Web. To address this issue a Web-based project was developed to train participants to search and evaluate Web-based educational resources. Participants were asked to report the result of evaluating online materials and to consider how online resources can be integrated into classroom-based education. The main objective of the project was to promote the awareness of online resources and their educational values through a systematic training procedure. The paper shows that the project improved the participants' awareness of educational Web sites and the significance of their utilization in the classroom.

Keywords: Teacher training, Web-based training system, Evaluation of Web-based education materials

1. INTRODUCTION

Utilizing Web sites in classroom is getting much attention from educators as an effective tool to allow students to use information technology in their learning. Everyday lots of newly published Web sites are emerged on a wide range of interest areas. And many are suitable enough to be used in the classroom education. The Web is considered as a new educational media effectively delivering instructional materials. However, the integration of Web technologies into the classroom education is at an incipient stage. We hope to increase the utilization of educational sites on the Web for supporting learning activities. We believe that teacher's ability and willingness to apply the new educational media is crucial to modernize schools so that teaching and learning activities can be done in an environment agreeable with the social context of information age.

Because of the above-mentioned reason, teachers' colleges need to put a special emphasis on ICT (Information and Communication Technology) in their curricula [1]. For instance, teachers' colleges in Korea are now equipped with Internet-based learning environments, funded by the government. However, we have not yet seen what we wanted to see as the result of investment of expensive information facilities. The quality of education improved by the technology is not significant enough to be cost-effective, which is stated in recent works [2].

According to the statistics gathered from 154 students at a local teachers' college in Korea last year, educational sites are the least favored Web sites, accounting only for 11% of the total use. Table 1 shows that students use the World Wide Web for their personal needs such as hobby and entertainment (38%), socialization (36%), shopping and banking (15%). Most of the educational use is due to information search on the Web to do their homework assignments (57%), suggesting that homework assignments requiring information out of the Web may be an effective tool to make students use the Web for learning. Also, the survey indicates that ICT-based learning activities need to be developed and conducted to promote students' awareness of educational resources on the Web.

Hobby, Entertainment	38%
Socialization	36%
Shopping, Banking	15%
Education	11%

Table 1: Students' Usage of Web Sites by Type

As the World Wide Web plays an important role of a cognitive tool for teaching and learning teachers are supposed to be capable of doing the role of facilitators and guides [3]. Using the World Wide Web as learning resources demands that teachers' role should be facilitative rather than didactic.

This new role requires teachers to learn new skills to utilize Web sites for pedagogical needs. Teachers should be able to find out what they are looking for from Web sites and utilize the resources for their instructional purposes. The process involves selecting right information compatible with instructional objectives. This selection process requires formative evaluation of Web resources. Teachers as facilitators in networked learning environment need to be trained as evaluators who are knowledgeable about factors affecting the effectiveness of Web-based instruction materials. And the skill can be acquired through actual evaluations of a variety of Web sites with the help of a predefined set of criteria to assess the quality of online resources.

To do that a Web-based evaluation procedure was designed and developed to allow students at a local teachers' college in Korea to participate in the evaluation project. Participants were asked to report the result of evaluating online materials as a term project during a regular semester. Next, they were asked to consider how the online resources could be integrated into a course.

A Web-based evaluation system was developed so that participants were able to perform every activity via the Web. We observe that, firstly, the evaluation project improved the students' awareness of educational Web sites and the significance of their utilization for classroom education. Secondly, the Web-based evaluation system provided a practical supportive tool for the project because of its interactivity, efficiency, flexibility, and economy.

2. THE EVALUATION PROCEDURE

The main objective of the project lies in building up students' ability to assess Web materials and utilize them in the classroom by promoting the awareness of online resources and their educational values through a systematic training procedure. To this end each participant is asked to find any five educational sites that may be supportive of classroom-based education and report evaluation results on each site to the system on the Web. However, school homepages are excluded because of their similar objectives and contents. The overall procedure is shown in Figure 1.

The procedure consists of the following steps;

(1) Pre-evaluation Training: This preliminary session introduces basic concepts of Web-based instruction materials and the evaluation process. Participants understand essential aspects of educational sites through the session that shows carefully selected exemplary sites domestic and international to demonstrate pedagogical values of high quality educational sites. The necessary techniques to perform the evaluation project are presented concerning how to search Web sites that meet their needs, how to evaluate the sites they found, and how to use the Web-based evaluation system to report evaluation results.

(2) Registration and Validation: User validation is required to use the evaluation system for writing/updating information. But the system is open to anyone for browsing.

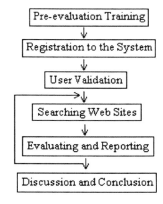

Figure 1: Overall Evaluation Procedure

(3) Searching: Participants are allowed to search as many Web sites as they want, but they can only select five

sites for evaluation.

(4) Evaluating and Reporting: Each participant conducts evaluation of five educational sites. However, the maximum number of evaluations allowed for a site is limited to ten, which is to avoid overcrowding at a handful of popular sites and to encourage them to experience as many Web sites as possible. Evaluators are asked to write an online review to share opinions with peers and to fill in online evaluation form, an 8-item Likert-type questionnaire measuring a site's educational quality.

(5) Discussion and Conclusion: Upon completion of evaluation, evaluation results are summarized and presented to the participants. Some of the prominent sites are selected to study features conducive to learning and discuss issues concerning utilization of them in the classroom.

3. WEB-BASED EVALUATION SYSTEM

The system consists of a set of programs written in Microsoft ASP (Active Server Pages) on a Web server running on the Windows NT operating system. The system works with Microsoft SQL database to maintain evaluation results reported by the participants. And it has shown fairly stable condition experiencing no noticeable problems such as communication delay. Evaluation was conducted via the Web for three weeks in September 2001 during a regular semester. Six major features of the system are shown as the following.

3.1 THE MAIN WINDOW

The Web site visitor can browse the sorted listing of sites evaluated, each of which links to the result of evaluations for the site. From this, visitors can go to an individual site by clicking the site's URL. One can enter a unique site number to go directly to the record if it is known. The search button links to the search menu from which different types of searches can be performed. Both adding new evaluations to existing sites and adding new sites for evaluation to the current list can be performed from the main window.

3.2 SITE REGISTRATION

The evaluator can enter the site URL and its title to add new site information. The information is stored into

the database only when the site is found to be new to the database to avoid having duplicate sites in the database. Then the evaluator is ready to enter the site-specific information stated in the following section.

3.3 SITE INFORMATION

The evaluator is asked to register a site by reporting its external data such as organizational type, and service type for classification. Organizational type is broken down into university/college, primary school, secondary school, non-profit organization, private organization, and government organization. The contents of a site can be a determinant of its service type – learning material, news, organization/association, broadcasting, counseling, research, etc.

3.4 EVALUATION FORM

The evaluation form contains a 8-item Likert-type questionnaire to measure essential qualities of an educational site and a review form to type in evaluators' opinion. The items are: accuracy, authenticity, effectiveness, usability, legibility, interactivity, communicativeness, and aesthetic integrity. Many different sets of measuring criteria have been reported in the community [4][5]. So, we can pick up a model that meets the requirements. Experiences tell us that too many evaluation items could overburden students and 8 items are appropriate to achieve the training purpose.

In addition to the formal evaluation, participants are asked to express their own opinion including prominent features, merits and demerits, and so on. Reviews would greatly help visitors decide whether or not the site fits for their needs. To provide objective views multiple reviews are allowed for a site.

The overall structure of the system is depicted in Figure 2.

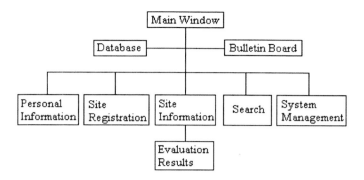

Figure 2: Overall Structure

4. RESULTS OF THE EVALUATION PROJECT

The Web-based evaluation project was conducted for three weeks and 154 students of a teachers' college in Korea were participated in the project. Each participant was asked to report evaluation results of five Web-based educational sites. After finishing the project, we can summarize the results of the project as the following;

(1) The average time spent per student for the project was 6 hours and 40 minutes.

(2) The average number of sites searched per student was 20.

(3) 72% of the participants realized the richness of Web resources and expressed the possibility of the utilization of them for the classroom-based education. They also expressed willingness to integrate Web resources into the classroom.

Furthermore, they thought they should learn more about computer education for their career. Many students expressed a strong desire to create their own Web sites for educational use.

(4) Issues of integrating Web resources into a course were discussed in class. Existing methods for integration were introduced and discussed how to adapt them to the Web materials.

5. CONCLUSION

A Web-based project for the evaluation of Web-based education materials was conducted for students of a teachers' college in Korea to promote the awareness of online resources and their educational values through a systematic training procedure. As the result of this project

the students' ability to assess Web materials and the students' awareness of educational Web sites were improved considerably. Also, the students' attitude toward the Web-based project was positive because of its interactivity, efficiency, flexibility, and economy.

REFERENCES

[1] Kim, Y. G. (1999). The direction of information technology in education for pre-service teachers training. Journal of The Korean Association of Information Education, 3(2), 54-71.

[2] Lee, C. H., Shin, S. B., Yoo, I. H., & Lee, T. W. (2000). Model of ICT utilization curriculum for pre-service teachers. The Journal of Korean Association of Computer Education, 3(1), 87-96.

[3] Sherry, L., & Wilson, B. Transformative communication as a stimulus to Web innovations, In: Web-Based Instruction, Khan, B. H. (Editor), Educational Technology Publications. 1997. 67-73.

[4] Kim, J. R., Ma, D. S., Hong, S. J. (2001) A study on evaluation Internet Web sites for education, ICCE-2001. Vol.1. 126-133.

[5] Khan, B. H., Vega, R. Factors to consider when evaluating Web-based instruction course: A Survey, In: Web-Based Instruction, Khan, B. H. (Editor), Educational Technology Publications. 1997. 375-378.

A Study on the Design and Evaluation of an Adaptive Web Browser for Students with Reading Difficulties

Chi Nung Chu [1], Ming Chung Chen [2], Tien Yu Li [3]

[1] Chung Kuo institute of Technology, 56, Sec. 3, Shinglung Rd., Taipei, 116 Taiwan
nung@mail.ckitc.edy.tw

[2] National Chiayi University, 300, Shiuefu Rd., Chiayi, 600 Taiwan
ming@chen.twmail.cc

[3] National Taiwan Normal University, 162, Sec. 1, Hoping East Rd., Taipei, 106 Taiwan
tienyu@ice.ntnu.edu.tw

Abstract

The web-based learning has been becoming an important channel for the education renovation. However, the children with reading difficulties, including the mental retardation and learning disabilities, have difficulties with word decoding and comprehension. To learn from the Internet, they are facing two challenges in manipulating browser to read through the web and comprehending the contents on the web pages. The Adaptive Web Browser (AWB) in our design, integrating the technologies of HTML interpreter, text-to-speech engine and picture communication symbols (PCS), facilitates comprehending the contents on web pages with auxiliary speaking sound or picture produced automatically as needed. In examining its usability, the result indicates that the Adaptive Web Browser can help the students with reading difficulties facilitate access to the web and increase comprehension of contents on the web pages.

1 Introduction

Accessing the Internet has been becoming one of the basic skills for all students. They should learn to use the browser, such as Internet Explorer, to surf the Internet. In order to use the functions provided by browsers, students must have a good conceptual model of the system. They must also recognize the words shown on the web pages to understand the meaning of the contents. However, students with reading difficulties, including mental retardation and learning disabilities, cause problems in developing well conceptual models of the interface and in developing word recognition abilities of the meaning of written language [2].

By means of auxiliary voice and pictures, learners could understand the words shown on the web pages that they could not recognize [1][3]. Thus, the purposes of this research are to design an AWB with the PCS and synthesized Chinese text-to-speech engine, and to evaluate the usability of the AWB.

2 Design of AWB

2.1 The Framework of AWB System

AWB is developed on the basis of the Microsoft Internet Explorer engine running on the Windows platform. The AWB system includes two major components; one is the Chinese text-to-speech engine used as a voice output producer, the other is the PCS database acting as the source of pop-up images to assist the children in reading on the Internet. The integrated AWB software is installed at the client side.

2.2 The Features of AWB System

2.2.1 Simplified Interface. Considering the users' cognition abilities, we modify the toolbar of AWB with functions used most frequently in IE. With voice description for the functions on the toolbar, users could easily learn to interact with the AWB.

2.2.2 Voice and Picture Assistance. The AWB could read out the word or sentences highlighted by the users in synthesized voice output. Users could listen to the contents of the web page instead of reading. And by connecting to the database with about 3,000 pictures, the AWB can automatically pop-up the corresponding PCS near the target word or phrase as the user move the mouse over it. In the same time, the AWB can speak the target word out by clicking the right button.

3 Evaluation of AWB

3.1 Method of Evaluation

We conducted an experiment to evaluate the usability of the AWB. The items for evaluation include the simplicity of the interface operation, and the effectiveness of assisting reading comprehension of the AWB. In order to avoid the sequence effect of the experimental materials and browsers, we arrange the sequence of reading browsers and interchange the articles for the browsers randomly. The test score will be computed and analyzed in repeat measurement T-test.

3.2 Result

There are 10 7th to 9th grade students with moderate mental retardation selected to participate the evaluation. Three of them are female and seven ones are male.

3.2.1 The Simplicity of The Interface Operation. The mean of correct response is shown on Table 1. As Table 1 indicates that the interface of the AWB is very simple and easy for the learners with moderate mental

retardation to learn to operate correctly in a short period.

	For-ward	Back-ward	Re-fresh	Stop	Go Home	Speak Out	Picture assistance
Mean	4	4	4	4	4	4	3.9

Table 1 the mean of correct response on each function button and picture assistance (n=10)

3.3.2 The Effectiveness of Assisting Reading Comprehension. The subjects' performance of reading comprehension by utilizing IE and AWB was shown on Table 2. The result indicates the mean scores of using these two browsers are significantly different based on the result of the t-test ($t=3.14$, $P<.05$).

	IE	AWB
Mean	3.10	4.90
SD	1.97	.32
T		3.14 *

Note: * presented P < .05

Table 2 the subjects' performance on two browser (n=10)

Reference

1. Anglin, G. J., "Effect of pictures on recall of written prose: How durable are picture effects?", Educational Communication and Technology,35(1) 25-31,.1987.

2. Mann, V. (1994). Phonological skills and the prediction of early reading problems. In N. C. Jordan & J. Goldsmithmm-Phillips (Eds.), Learning disabilities: New directions for assessment and intervention (pp. 67-84). Boston, MA: Allyn and Bacon.

3. Pufpaff, L. A., Blischak, D. M., & Lloyd, L. L., "Effects of modified orthography on the identification of printed words", American Journal on Mental Retardation, No. 105, pp. 14-24,(2000).

Mathematical Education Technology Based on the Theory of Cognitive Constructivism and Concept Map

Pao-Ta Yu* and Chung-Ming Own
Department of Computer Science and Information Engineering
National Chung Cheng University
160, San-Hsing, Ming-Hsiung
Chiayi, Taiwan 62107, R.O.C
csipty@cs.ccu.edu.tw*

Abstract

The World Wide Web has been seen more and more as an effective and above all in expensive means of delivering courses. In the search for an effective approach for Web learning, a self-reliance learning environment is required. This paper examines the "symbol pad" learning environment in cognitive constructivism. Hence, through XML-based equation technology for mathematical learning, we can provide the learner to arrange their learning sequences and construct their deep thinking and knowledge.

1. Introduction

The growth of the internet and the World Wide Web, in particular, are attracting the attention of most of the educational institutions, government agencies, commercial companies, and other organizations around the world. This is manifest in the increasing number of distance education [1]. For the good of saving cost and easily updating materials, learning via Web is seen as an effective alternative to traditional face to face modes of education.

On the other hand, learning would be exceedingly laborious, not to mention risky, if people had to rely solely on the effects of their own actions. Fortunately, most human behavior is learned observationally through the following method: by observing others one forms an idea of how new behaviors are performed, and this information provides as a guide for the action on later occasions [2]. Hence, the learning performance says that our knowledge is actively constructed by the learner, not passively received from the environment [3].

Permanently, teachers tend to put most of their effort on designing the content in their classes, and what effort is left is put on measuring what learners have been learned [4]. It is significant that in most course descriptions what teachers do in class make the focus in attention. Most recently, paying more attention to what students do is getting more and more attention. Hence, education become as student-centred, students have to construct knowledge by themselves. It's a Constructivism.

Constructivism is building on knowledge known by the student. It is a theory, a tool, a methodology for examining educational practices. There are, however, two major strands of the constructivism perspective. These two strands, cognitive constructivism and social constructivism, are different in emphasis, but they also share many common perspectives about teaching and learning. To our knowledge, cognitive constructivism is based on that humans must "construct" their own

*This work is supported by the NSC 90-2520-S-194-001.

knowledge through experience. It means students cannot be "given" information before they understand and use [5]. On the contrary, social constructivism treats learning as a process of enculturation through social interaction [5].

As we know, there are at least five facets of learning environment to realize the concept of constructivism [6]:

1) Information Banks,
2) Symbol Pads,
3) Constructions Kits,
4) Phenomenaria, and
5) Task Managers.

In this research, we try to apply the learning environment of "symbol pad" to specify how to realize the teaching and learning concept into the technology domain.

2. Symbol Pads

Symbol pads is the basic function in educational environments, it provide surfaces for the construction and manipulation of symbols and language for a long time [6]. Examples include student notebooks, index cards, word processors, drawing programs, and database programs. A basic function of educational environments for a long time has been to provide surfaces for the construction and manipulation of symbols. From the hand-held slate to the student's notebook to laptop computer, diverse resources have served to support learners' short term memories as they record ideas, develop outlines, formulate and manipulate equations, and so on. Technology expands the power of such symbol pads in a number of ways. Devices such as word processors allow the easy editing and rearranging of large chunks of text. Drawing programs permit carefully controlled composition of drawings with flexible editing (Perkins, 1991).

Actually, the main concept of symbol pad can be classified into two points due to the new idea developed in the past decade (Jonassen, 1999):

1) To provide a symbolic surface to let the learners progress their learning sequences.
2) To provide a thinking mechanism or memory mechanism to let the learners construct their deep thinking and knowledge.

The above two points incline to concept domain and then need some methodologies to realize those two concepts.

3. The Platform on WWW

In our research, we implement the web page technology (server programming) to realize the concept of symbol pad for mathematical education. This system is used in the lecture of probability in 2001 spring semester for 49 students to construct their deep thinking and understanding about some specified topics of probability. We proposed the mathematic editor which is an equation editor designed by Java and based in the standard of MathXML to realize the "symbol surface". On the other hand, we used concept map to realize the "thinking mechanism" designed by editor tools, such as MS Word and FrontPage. Finally, all the students' portfolios can be stored in a database via the front-tier of web page. Then, we introduce the specification of our system as follows.

Concept Map Builder

Concept map was proposed by Novak and Gowin in 1984, and it is based on the meaningful learning [8]. It is a visible graph of an individual's knowledge structure on a special subject as constructed by the individual. Concept map is a hierarchical graph, which the general concepts are higher than the particular concepts. In the concept map, there are some concepts and links. Concepts are enclosed with circles or ovals and links are straight line. Two concepts and one link compose a proposition. A concept can link to several concepts, but one link only connects with two concepts.

Figure 1 is the interface of our concept map builder. This builder is a "what you see what you get" editor. In the project tab, it represents the name of a series of concept maps. Each editing pages is represented as a page of concept map. For the purpose to apply our concept map as a quiz, the designer will leave some nodes as blank. Figure 2 is the control bar of this builder. According to priority of icons, the designer can add an editing page, add a node, draw a link between two nodes, choice a node, adjust the scaffold and close this page. Figure 3 is the mathematic editor for each concept map node in out builder.

The web-based testing system

The concept map which was made in the builder is shown in the left down in our web-based testing system. The right up of this system is the scope of the test, user name, user number, current state, and score. When students are ready for accepting the quiz, they can choice the blank node of this concept map, and fill the answer in the answer area. The mathematic editor is the same in Figure 3. After their finishing their quizzing, the system will prompt the correct answer and evaluate their grades.

4. Experiment

Our population is used in the lecture of probability in 2001 spring semester for 49 students. Our system supports concept map about the course contents of Bernoulli distribution, Poisson distribution and Normal distribution. These students are separated into two groups, experiment group and contrast group. The former includes 23 students those who take the

lecture with system support. The latter includes 26 students those who take the lecture with traditional learning.

Case 1: Compare the performances about the students with system support.

During our system supporting, we collect the variety of students' performances. We classify them into two groups: group1 is an unrestrained group with lower performance, the other is the opposite. Table 1 is the ratio of these two group students in Bernoulli, Poisson and Summary tests. The ratio is calculated with following Eq. (1).

Table1. Ratio of the students who make progressed with the system support

(The summary test includes the course content about Bernoulli distribution, Poisson distribution and Normal distribution)

	Bernoulli	Poisson	Summary
Group1	75%	41.67%	50%
Group2	94.74%	83.33%	100%

In this case, the students in group1 use the system with unrestrained attitude, on the contrary, the students in group2 use the system with cautious. Hence, the rations of progress in group2 outperform then group1 in each test.

Case 2: Compare the performances about the students in experiment group and contrast group

For the purpose to compare the effective of our system, we collect the information in two groups. The students in experiment group take the test with the system support. The students in contrast group take the test with traditional learning strategy. Table 2 shows the ratio of these two groups in Bernoulli,

Poisson and Summary tests. The ratio is calculated with following Eq. (2).

In each test, if a student's score in post-test is larger than the score in pre-test, we say that this student makes progress in this test.

Table 2. Ratio of the students who make progress in contrast group and experiment group

	Bernoulli	Poisson	Summary
Contrast group	65.38%	42.31%	46.15%
Experiment group	80.77%	57.69%	50%

From Table 2, we can obviously observe that the ratio in experiment group is larger than the ratio in contrast group. This indicated that this system had a better learning impact on students than the traditional learning strategy.

5. Conclusion

It has been argued that students do not like to learn at a distance (Simonsen, 1995), but the convenience and flexibility of an external mode of delivery is making distance education an attractive proposition for students. Hence, self-reliance is required to ensure that students can arrange their own learning environment. The Cognitive Constructivism is a brilliant solution. Applying the learning environment of symbol pads, we can realize the teaching and learning concept into the technology domain. In our system, we can let students progress their learning sequences by equation editor, and construct their knowledge by concept map. In essence, the results of experiment shows that student can make more progress at a distance with Cognitive Constructivism learning environment.

6. Reference

[1]. Pagram, J. & McMahon, M. Web-cD: an interactive learning experience for distance education students studying interactive multimedia, International conference on computer in education, Kuching, Malaysia, 2-6 Dec. 1997.

[2]. Bandura, A. Social learning theory, New York: Prentice Hall, 1977.

[3]. Piaget, J. Henriques, G. and Ascher, A. Morphisms and categories, Hillsdale, NJ: Erlbaum Associates, 1992.

[4]. Stark, J. S. Lattuca, L. R. Shaping the college curriculum: academic plans in action, Boston: Alyn and Bacon, 1997.

[5]. Piaget, J. The development of thought: equilibration of cognitive structures, New Yourk: Viking.

[6]. Perkins, D. N. Technology meets constructivism: do they make a marriage?, Educational technology, May 1991.

[7]. Simonsen, M. Does anyone really want to learn at a distance?, Techtrends, 40(50), Dec. 1995.

[8]. Novak, J.D. & Gowin, D.B. Learning How to Learnm, Cambridge University Press. Cambridge.

$$\frac{\text{the amount of students who make progress between pre and post test in each group}}{\text{total students in each group}} \times 100\% \quad (1)$$

$$\frac{\text{the amount of students who make progress in each group}}{\text{the total students in each group}} \times 100\% \quad (2)$$

Project Tab   Link   Node

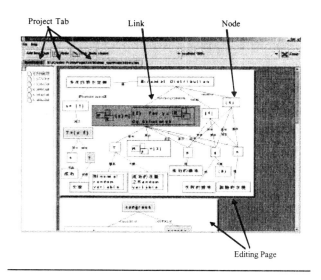

Editing Page

Figure 1 The interface of concept map builder

Figure 2

The control bar of concept map builder

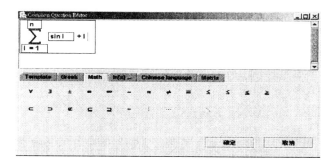

Figure 3 The mathematic editor for concept map node

The Role of Discussion Rooms
in Developing e-Learning Community:
The Experience of University of Bahrain

Fatima Mohamed Al-Balooshi
Chairman, Educational Technology Department,
Assistant Professor of Educational Technology,
College of Education, University of Bahrain.

Abstract

This study will discuss the role of discussion rooms in developing and maintaining communities of e-learning as well as promoting students' learning skills. It was based on an on-line course at University of Bahrain. The course was delivered using discussion rooms as a major communication tool. A survey assessing students' attitudes toward discussion rooms was conducted. The results showed a positive attitude toward discussion rooms and their role in enhancing students study skills. The study proposes strategies for implementing successful discussion rooms.

Introduction

Since the mid-1990s, observers have been identifying various phenomena in cyber space that have swept the world. One of the most important phenomena is the emergence of e-communities that developed with the advent of the Internet. It was noted that e-communities were forming rapidly one after another, with certain rules to follow, creating human-oriented social interaction that is accumulated into a special type of symbolic space.

Recent studies have indicated that the creation of successful, harmonious, and sustainable e-community is considered a crucial element in the success of the teaching-learning process through the internet (Kun-je, 1999; Gilroy, 2001). Therefore, e-Communities play a major role in establishing e-learning.

This paper will look at many of the elements that must be managed to create e-learning programs where real knowledge is gained, communities of e-learning are developed, and high levels of student satisfaction are generated. It will present a case-study at the University of Bahrain on creating and managing e-learning communities based on enhancing student interaction and collaboration through discussion rooms in an on-line course.

The purpose of the study

Based on the assumption that for e-learning to be successful the development of its e-community has to be successful as well, this study examines the effects of discussion rooms in developing and maintaining e-learning communities. Its purpose is to examine student attitudes towards using discussion rooms compared to the various elements of communication and interaction in e-learning such as e-mail, student homepages, whiteboard, and chat rooms. The study will also explore the types of student learning skills and the roles of the instructor that were developed through this process.

The research questions

This study will address the following questions:
- How effective are discussion rooms in developing e-community in an online course?
- How effective are discussion rooms, from the point of view of students, in promoting student learning skills?
- How do discussion rooms affect the role of the instructor?
- What are good strategies to implement discussion rooms successfully in the e-learning process?

Terms used in the study

e-Community

A term used in this paper synonymously with cyber community. It is the place where human relations are made through the media of electronic networks. It knows no restrictions or conditions, such as time, space, sex, age, class, or race. It is a center formed by multiple individuals' interests and understanding (Kun-je, 1999). Members of these communities tend to create their own e-personalities. According to Pallof & Pratt (1999, pp 22), for this e-personality to exist it must be able to: 1) carry on an internal dialogue in order to formulate responses; 2) create an internal sense of privacy; 3) deal with emotional issues in textual form; 4) create a mental picture of the partner on the other side of the line; and 5) create a sense of presence online

e-Learning

Dong (2001) defines e-learning as asynchronous, computer-based courses comprised of faculty and students in the pursuit of knowledge where the members of the class are physically separated and not constrained by time or place. e-Learning takes learning and teaching into a new frontier of a socially-intertwined process. It is considered the third generation of distance learning as it adds human support through on-line tutors, thereby extending the scope of what can effectively be taught into many new subject areas. e-Learning provides a new set of tools that can add value to all of the traditional learning modes -- from classroom experiences to learning from books (Horton, 2001).

Discussion rooms

A term used synonymously with discussion groups and discussion lists. According to Horton (2000), discussion groups provide an opportunity for ongoing electronic conversations among a group of people. Threaded discussion groups allow time to compose responses, maintain separate threads for ongoing subjects, let everyone talk at the same time, and can manage discussions among hundreds of participants. They offer some important advantages over chat and e-mail. Chat is usually restricted to hectic exchange of small ideas, immediate reactions, and emotional responses among only a few individuals. While discussions in e-mail lists lack continuity and organization.

Literature review

According to Jay Cross (2001), research on online pedagogy, design, and facilitation demonstrates that learning is a social process, and the internet is a social place. Therefore, discussion groups and online moderators are a necessary ingredient of improving e-learning. Gilroy (2001) supports this notion as she sees that the creation of learning communities in the e-learning arena is of enormous importance. Nonetheless, she believes that this is not an easy task and requires resources such as time and/or money matched with deep social and structural understanding. Therefore, for any e-learning experience to develop or emerge it must fulfill the key elements of a successful e-community. Pallof & Pratt (1999, pp 24) indicate some of these elements as follows: clearly define the purpose of the group; create a distinctive virtual gathering place for the group; promote effective leadership from within; define norms and a clear code of conduct; allow and facilitate subgroups; promote a range of member roles; and allow members to resolve their own disputes.

There are several indicators of a successful e-learning experience. A clear indicator of such experience is the ability of members in an e-learning community to collaborate and create knowledge. Other indicators according to Pallof & Pratt (1999, pp 32), are as follows: 1) active interaction involving both course content and personal communication; 2) collaborative learning indicated by comments directed primarily student to student rather than student to instructor; 3) socially constructed meaning through agreement or questioning on certain issues; 4) sharing of resources among students; and 5) expressions of support and encouragement exchanged between students, as well as willingness to critically evaluate the work of others.

An environment with the attributes mentioned above can certainly foster strong social relationships but probably with very little learning. This shows the importance of the instructor role who needs to remain actively engaged in the process in order to guide students back to the learning goals. It is the development of a strong learning community and not just social community that is the distinguishing feature e-learning.

Method of the study

Subjects

This study was conducted at University of Bahrain through an on-line course titled "Instructional Computing EDTC 321". It was offered to third year undergraduates at the college of Education in the second semester of the academic year 2001/2002. This course was delivered and administered by the author. The total number of students was 72 and they were divided into two sections (35, 37). All the students had previous experience with using the internet, but none had taken any on-line courses before.

Description of the course

Based on the university of Bahrain's initiative to introduce e-learning to their students, a pilot project was carried out using one of the courses offered by the university. The author was given the task to undertake this project. Certain criteria was set for choosing a course for this project such as that the course is mainly theoretical and the students taking it should have some experience in using the internet. Based on these criteria, EDTC 321 was the most suitable course for this project and which was taught in Arabic.

The course was completely delivered over the internet using a commercially available software for course design and management WebCT (see Figure 1). The course was based on an asynchronous interactive e-learning model.

The instructor allocated the first two weeks of the course for training the students on the course software in a traditional face-to-face setup. After that, the instructor met the students only online using the various communication tools provided by the course software.

Figure 1. "Computer Assisted Learning " on-line course main page

The communication tools included discussion rooms, e-mail, calendar announcements, chat rooms, and a whiteboard. Throughout the course, students were introduced to a new lecture every week. They had to read assigned material dealing with that lecture and discuss it later with their instructor and peers in a designated discussion room. Each lecture had it's own discussion room (see Figure 2). Communication in the discussion rooms was text-based; therefore students writing skills had a direct impact on their communications with their teacher and peers.

Figure 2. Organization of discussion rooms in the on-line course

In addition, specific projects were assigned to teams of students and extra private discussion rooms were allocated for each team. Occasionally, students used e-mail for their inquiries with the instructor and other students. They used chat rooms and white boards less frequently. The course evaluation included exams (in classroom), projects, and participation in discussion rooms.

Instruments and Procedure

The study was conducted using a survey to assess student attitude towards discussion rooms. The scale rated seven items on a 2-point scale, with 1 equaling *yes* and 0 equaling *no*. The survey was conducted at the end of the semester. In addition data on student activities were collected from the *"track student"* feature of the WebCT.

Findings

Results of the student survey are shown in Table 1. The data on student activity in the course was collected from the course administration program WebCT. The instructor of the course outlines additional information on student activity in discussion rooms.

No.	Questions	Yes %	No %
1.	Do you think that participating in class discussion made you write more coherently?	95.9	4.1
2.	Did you participate in class discussion more in this course than in face-to-face classroom?	87.8	12.2
3.	Do you think more carefully before responding to questions in the discussion room?	95.9	4.1
4.	Do you think that participating in class discussion helped you better understand the lecture as compared to face-to-face classroom?	67.3	32.7
5.	Did you have a well-connected relationship with your instructor compared to face-to-face classroom?	44.9	55.1
6.	Did you feel close to your peers in this course compared to face-to-face courses?	36.7	63.3
7.	Would you rather have online class discussion in all your courses?	83.7	16.3

Table 1. The effectiveness of discussion rooms from the point of view of students

Discussion

Overall, discussion rooms had great impact on student learning more than any other tool. Observing student activity in the course showed that such communication tool allowed students to:
• Interact with each other asynchronously most of the time.

• Answer each other's questions and help each other in explaining certain concepts
• Continue discussions on the same topics as long as they are allowed to or as it necessary.
• Express their ideas and join in discussions without hesitation even for those students who seemed not willing to contribute in face-to-face classroom discussions.
• Take time to read questions and compose well-thought and coherent replies.

Table 1 shows that most students agree that discussion rooms had improved their skills in reading, writing, and comprehension. In addition, the questionnaire indicated that students preferred online discussion over face-to-face as it had no social constraints. Furthermore, students felt strong social relationships with their instructors more than with their peers. In addition, more then half of the students indicated that they have stronger social relationships with their teachers and peers in face-to-face courses compared to the on-line course.

Finally, from the instructor's point of view, the e-learning experience as opposed to the face-to-face learning had many advantages such as:
• It automatically changed the role of the instructor into a facilitator, administrator, and organizer of the learning process rather than the center of the learning process as experienced in most face-to-face classrooms.
• It allowed the instructor to build stronger and friendlier relationships with students through discussion and e-mail.

Still e-learning requires greater effort and more time to be spent by the instructor to manage the course, follow up students' participation and reply to enquiries of every single student in the class.

Recommendations

From this experience one can outline strategies for effective discussion rooms and to be implemented as follows:
• Participation in discussion rooms must be an important part of course requirements. In this course a 20% of the total course mark seemed to be appropriate for effective discussion participation.
• Designate a discussion room for each lecture in the course in order to make sure that all students follow up and discuss each lecture and not overlook or miss anyone of them.
• Allocate a specific period of time for discussing each lecture (for example one week for each). Although one might not prefer time constraints on discussion, from a practical point of view it is better to impose such time constraint in order to keep students on schedule. In addition, to insure compliance and participation within the assigned timeframe, one might even lock the discussion room after the time expires.

• Start each discussion with some brain storming questions or activities. Later, at the end of the discussion period post some concluding remarks of student discussions.
• The instructor should have a continuous presence in the discussion room in order to regulate student discussion and to guide them to the objectives of the discussion of each lecture.
• Assign special interest discussion rooms for other purposes such as sharing internet resources or assignment discussion or team discussion, etc.

Conclusion

Opportunities to educate and train are tremendous with e-learning. A successful e-learning program should provide both support and challenge to the students. It should focus on creating a safe and comfortable learning community alongside stimulating and challenging learners intellectually. Discussion is an integral element of a successful e-community in the e-learning environment. With good strategies for implementing discussion rooms, students can feel the effectiveness of participation and therefore become more connected to their e-learning community.

Bibliography

1. Cross, Jay. (2001). "Frontline: eLearningForum". [http://www.learningcircuits.org/2001/feb2001/cross.html].
2. Dong, F. (2001). "*Can You Succeed as a Cyberstudent? How to develop communication skills on the Web*". E-learning Magazine, Sept. [http://www.elearningmag.com/Sept01/cyberstudent.asp].
3. Etzioni, A. (2000). "*Creating good communities and good societies*". Contemporary Sociology, Vol. 29, Issue 1, January , pp. 188-195. [http://www.gwu.edu/~ccps/etzioni/A276.html].
4. Gilroy, K. (2001). "*Collaborative E-learning: The Right Approach*". Otter Group Report. Cambridge, Massachusetts, March 28, 2001. [http://www.ottergroup.com/otter-with comments/right_approach.html].
5. Horton, W. (2000). "*Designing Web-based Training*". John Wiley & Sons, Inc., N.Y.
6. Khan, B. (1997). "*Web-Based Instruction*". Educational technology publications, N.Y.
7. Kun-je, C. (1999). "*Building Cyber-Learning Communities*". [http://home.donga.ac.kr/~daudh/ magazine/116/bitb.htm]
8. Pallof, R. & Pratt, K. (1999). "*Building Learning Communities in Cyberspace*". Jossey-Bass Publishers, San Francisco.
9. Smith, J. (2001). "*How to Teach Online: Migrating terrestrial teaching talents to the virtual classroom*". The OTTER Group. [http://www.ottergroup.com/otter-with comments/right_approach.html

Categorizing Questions According To A Navigation List For A Web-Based Self-Teaching System : AEGIS

Tsunenori Mine, Akira Suganuma, and Takayoshi Shoudai
Faculty of Information Science and Electrical Engineering, Kyushu University
6-1 Kasuga-kouen, Kasuga, Fukuoka 816-8580, Japan
{mine,suga}@is.kyushu-u.ac.jp, shoudai@i.kyushu-u.ac.jp

Abstract

With increasing access to the Internet and the wealth of material online, a Web-based self-teaching system has considerable educational value. Accordingly, we developed AEGIS (Automatic Exercise Generator based on the Intelligence of Students), which automatically generates questions whose difficulty level fits the achievement level of a student. However, it was implicitly assumed that all the questions were already categorized according to their subjects. In practice, this is not the case, but it is unreasonable (because of time and cost) to expect teachers to categorize each question into a suitable subject domain. Therefore, we need a method for categorizing questions automatically according to specified teaching concepts.

This paper presents an automatic question categorization mechanism according to both a list of teaching concepts, called a Navigation List (NaviList for short), and the meaning of questions. We define an XML tag called a CONCEPT tag, which indicates a concept in a question, and an ontology, which is a hierarchical cluster of concepts. The method uses the tags and the ontology to categorize questions, based on the similarity between each category in a NaviList pre-composed by a teacher and an ontological concept specified by a CONCEPT tag in a question.

1 Introduction

The World Wide Web is a widely accessible public source of information, which encourages exploration and self-help in the pursuit of knowledge, and provides a wide variety of multi-media contents and added-value services. In an educational domain, many teachers hold lectures using Web contents as a teaching material and even develop new lecture methods based on Web technologies. A Web-based self-teaching system, which enables a student to study something at his/her own pace, anytime and any-where, has considerable educational benefits, not only for students who take part in a lecture, but also for other people who do not directly take it.

We have developed several kinds of Web-based self-teaching systems[1, 2, 3]. Through our experiences of teaching in classes and developing such systems, we recognized the necessity of methods both for evaluating students' achievement levels and for generating questions suitable for the students automatically.

We have consequently designed and developed an automatic evaluator of a student's achievement level called AEGIS(Automatic Exercise Generator based on the Intelligence of Students)[4]. AEGIS generates questions from tagged documents, presents them to students and marks their answers automatically. AEGIS however expects that the source documents for generating questions have already been categorized into a particular domain according to their subjects. So, AEGIS presents questions to students according to their achievement level, but not to the domain where the questions belong.

From the point of view of an educational policy, these questions should be tailored according to a concept or an aim of a lecture because each teacher teaches his/her students based on these concepts and aims. The questions should also be given to students in a suitable order for his/her lecture. For example, in the case of teaching a programming language, we may want to present the questions classified under the category of 'programming language specification' when focusing on the grammar of the language. On the other hand, we may want to give the questions classified under 'programming patterns' when focusing on program design. In both cases, the same questions can be given although the order of presentation may be different. However, it requires a long time and high cost for a teacher to categorize questions one by one into their suitable domains. It is therefore important to develop a method for categorizing questions automatically according to the teaching concept of a lecture.

This paper presents an automatic question categorization mechanism according to both a list of teacher's teaching concepts, called Navigation List (**NaviList** for short), and the meaning of questions. We define both an XML tag called a CONCEPT tag, which indicates a concept in a question, and a method, which categorizes questions based on the similarity between each category in a NaviList precomposed by a teacher and one or more keywords surrounded by the CONCEPT tags in a question. Such keywords give a context-sensitive representation of the conceptual meaning of a question. The similarity calculation is performed with an ontology, which is a hierarchical cluster of questions' concepts. Each question is categorized into its most similar category in a NaviList, provided that its similarity is over a predetermined threshold.

After a student selects a category, AEGIS can then choose the most suitable questions from the category for him/her, according to both his/her achievement level and the difficulty level of the question, just as before.

2 A Method for Mapping Questions with a Category in a NaviList

Our method maps a question onto a category item in a NaviList if the similarity between them is over a threshold, which is determined empirically. The similarity is calculated based on the concepts of a question and those of the category. The easiest way to calculate the similarity between them would be matching concept labels attached to a question with those to the category. Unfortunately, this method sometimes fails because it requires consistency in choosing and attaching concept labels to questions and categories. This is difficult to realize, especially when different people are making the associations. In any case, concept labels are not always the same although they may be connected with some relationship such as a-kind-of, synonym, a-part-of, and so forth. Concepts of a category in a NaviList usually subsume those of questions. Therefore the similarity calculation between concepts of both a NaviList category and a question requires an ontology related to them (Fig.1).

Our method defines an ontology as a hierarchical cluster that consists of common concepts of its sub clusters, recursively. The cluster is constructed by a simple linkage clustering method[7, 8]. The cluster's primitive cluster, called the base cluster, consists of both a main concept and its related concepts of questions and NaviList categories. The main concept can be regarded as a class and its related concepts as its instances. Although a created cluster has at most a few hierarchies, it is enough for our purpose because the purpose is not to calculate the exact or precise similarity between them, but just to find a connection between a question and a NaviList category.

When we construct the ontology, first, we apply a mor-

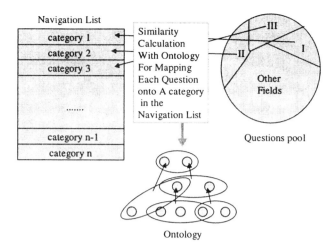

Figure 1. Mapping a concept of a question onto that of a category in a NaviList

phological analyzer[6] to teaching documents. Then, concept labels of a question are attached to the words of specific parts of speech such as a common noun, proper noun or undefined, for example an operator or a reserved word of a programming language.

The concept labels of a NaviList category are mostly chosen by NaviList creators (e.g. teachers) from the representative concepts in superior level sub-clusters. The representative concepts are selected by calculating the weight of their frequency in a question text, which is referred to as TF(text frequency), and inverse question text frequency, referred to as IDF(inverse document frequency).

A procedure to create an ontology is as follows:

1. Transform teaching documents(e.g. MS Power Point slides) into Web(XML or HTML) format documents.

2. Eliminate XML and HTML tags from the Web format documents to give plain text documents.

3. Apply a morphological analyzer to the plain text documents.

4. Reconnect keywords that have been segmented too much, with hand-written rules.

5. Extract salient keywords according to their TF.IDF weight.

6. Cluster the keywords by a simple linkage clustering method[7, 8].

Table 1 depicts a part of ontology automatically generated from lecture slides about the introduction to C programming.

Table 1. A part of an ontology created automatically from Power Point lecture slides about the introduction to C programming

A part of Ontology related to Text File	
Main Concept	Related Concepts
text file	character, line, unit, fprintf, random access, sequential, fgetc
fgetc	character, processing, text file, lecture, fgets, input, line, sscanf, unit, output, fprintf
fprintf	character, processing, text file, fgets, line, unit, fgetc
line	character, processing, text file, fgets, fprintf, fgetc
unit	text file, fprintf, fgetc
character	raw, text file, string, line, float, numerical value, concatenation, output, order, fprintf, comparison, letter, for, creating date, author, error level, fgetc, abcde, World

3 A Concept Tag and a Category of a NaviList

This section, first, gives explanations about a new tag, called a *CONCEPT* tag ⟨CONCEPT⟩. Categories in a NaviList are constructed with keywords in a teaching document. Such keywords are surrounded by concept tags and represent the conceptual meaning of the document. As mentioned in Section 2, we map these keywords onto categories in a NaviList.

The tag ⟨CONCEPT⟩ is defined by a DTD of XML (Fig.2). Tagging a teaching document is partially automated. First a morphological analyzer[6] is applied to the teaching document, and then tags are automatically attached to the document in a simple way based on past attachment processes. After that, using an authoring tool for XML, the system asks the user to confirm whether or not newly tagged areas are correct. The authoring tool can automatically attach concept tags to the areas with the same keyword to which the concept tag has been attached in the past.

We specify a question in teaching documents by tags which were formally defined by a DTD of XML[4]. These tags are also described in Fig.2, which include a tag ⟨QUESTION⟩ for specifying an area of a question, a tag ⟨DEL⟩ for specifying a solution, and a tag ⟨LABEL⟩ for a hint of some questions. The tag ⟨DEL⟩ has an attribute LEVEL for specifying a pair of initial minimum and maximum difficulties of the question's solution. For more de-

```
⟨!DOCTYPE EXERCISE [
⟨!ELEMENT QUESTION (#PCDATA | DEL | CONCEPT
                                    | LABEL )*⟩
⟨!ELEMENT DEL        (#PCDATA)⟩
⟨!ELEMENT CONCEPT    (#PCDATA)⟩
⟨!ELEMENT LABEL      (#PCDATA)⟩
⟨!ATTLIST QUESTION SUBJECT CDATA #IMPLIED⟩
⟨!ATTLIST DEL        CAND   CDATA #IMPLIED
                     LEVEL  NMTOKENS #REQUIRED
                     GROUP NMTOKEN #IMPLIED
                     REF    IDREF #IMPLIED⟩
⟨!ATTLIST LABEL      NAME   ID #IMPLIED⟩
] ⟩
```

Figure 2. DTD of the tags defined for AEGIS

tailed definitions and explanations, please see [4].

An example of a teaching document with ⟨CONCEPT⟩ tags, is described in Fig.3. The example has some words which are surrounded by ⟨CONCEPT⟩ tags. These ⟨CONCEPT⟩ tags specify important concepts for teaching the subject. The concepts are used to construct categories of a NaviList and an ontology, and also to map a question onto a category of the NaviList. The question specified by a tag ⟨QUESTION⟩ has to contain several keywords surrounded by a tag ⟨CONCEPT⟩, otherwise it is meaningless. Each question is classified into a category in a NaviList. Each category represents one of the important subjects in a teaching document.

Since we believe that the difficulty of categories' concepts in a NaviList should depend on the order of the categories in the NaviList, a question will be categorized into such a category any of whose concepts' difficulty is more than or equal to that of any concepts of a question.

4 The Construction and Functions of AEGIS

Once categorizing questions has been finished, AEGIS chooses questions from one of the categories. AEGIS is implemented in Java. It runs under JDK (ver. 1.3) and Tomcat (ver. 3.2). The system is based on the MVC (Model, View, Controller) model. The MVC model is an application architecture, which was firstly introduced at a Smalltalk programming environment. This model divides an application into three parts which are called Model (or logic), View (or presentation), and Controller (or communication, control). These three parts can be developed separately because they are functionally independent from each other. This model supports modular system development and ease of maintenance.

Our system AEGIS consists of two subsystems: the *Manager System* and the *User System*. The Manager System is used for teachers to manage questions. This system

In the previous section, we learned a ⟨CONCEPT⟩ program ⟨/CONCEPT⟩ for adding two integers and showing the answer on the display. In the similar way, for all basic ⟨CONCEPT⟩ arithmetic operations ⟨/CONCEPT⟩ including ⟨CONCEPT⟩ addition ⟨/CONCEPT⟩, ⟨CONCEPT⟩ subtraction ⟨/CONCEPT⟩, ⟨CONCEPT⟩ multiplication ⟨/CONCEPT⟩ , and ⟨CONCEPT⟩ division ⟨/CONCEPT⟩, we can make a Pascal program in the following way.
⟨QUESTIONSUBJECT = "arithmeticoperations"⟩
This program computes the multiplication and division for two input integers and shows the answer.

```
program enzan;
var x,y:integer;
    seki,shou:integer;
begin
    ⟨CONCEPT⟩write ⟨/CONCEPT⟩('Input two integers : ');
    ⟨CONCEPT⟩readln ⟨/CONCEPT⟩(x,y);
    seki:=⟨DEL CAND="x,xy,x×y,x mul y" LEVEL="1 5"⟩x*y⟨/DEL⟩;
    shou:=⟨DEL CAND="x/y,x÷y,xdivy,x mod y" LEVEL="1 5"⟩x div y⟨/DEL⟩;
    ⟨CONCEPT⟩writeln ⟨/CONCEPT⟩('Seki:',seki);
    ⟨CONCEPT⟩writeln ⟨/CONCEPT⟩('Shou:',shou)
end.
```

⟨/QUESTION⟩
The 7th statement multiplies x by y, and the 8th statement divides x by y. We note that the answer of "div" is an integer.

Figure 3. Example of teaching documents with the tags

also supports teachers in creating a NaviList with an ontology generated from concepts of their teaching documents.

The other system, the User System, helps students to learn a subject. It has two function modes: *Learning Mode* and *Test Mode*. In Learning Mode, AEGIS shows part of a teaching text in its normal form (e.g. Power Point slide, Web pages, etc.), which is utilized for generating questions. It is useful for students to learn its contents and to confirm their understanding of those contents. Furthermore, from the point of view of teaching materials creator (e.g. a teacher), Learning Mode can be used for checking how many students understand the materials and then the appropriateness of the slides to describe questions suitable for the students. In Test Mode, AEGIS generates questions to let students try to answer. The questions AEGIS generates have various levels according to each student's achievement level. After submitting their answers, AEGIS marks those answers and returns the marked results to the student. The types of a question AEGIS generates are a multiple-choice question, fill-the-gap question, and error-correcting question. The difficulty of a question is strongly related to the type of the question. The marked results of a series of questions are stored into each student's profile, and it is used to evaluate the new achievement level of the student. At the same time, AEGIS evaluates the new difficulty level of questions. These two evaluations are dynamically computed at some predetermined intervals. We have evaluated the effectiveness of the updating mechanism of both levels by computer simulations [5, 9], and showed that the estimated difficulty level of a question gradually approaches the inherent one of the question and the estimated achievement

level of a student does also his/her inherent one, provided that we assumed there are such inherent levels.

Fig.4 and Fig.5 depict a snapshot of Learning Mode and that of Test Mode, respectively, both of which generate a fill-the-gap question.

5 Concluding Remarks

AEGIS[4] is a Web-based self-teaching system, which searches teaching documents described in XML and generates three types of questions automatically. A question to be generated is based on both its difficulty level and the achievement level of a student who tries the question. In order to generate the questions automatically, the questions in a teaching document are specified by an XML tag, called a QUESTION tag. The user profiles of AEGIS keep his/her marked results and are utilized to make AEGIS generate a next question. This generating a question is managed by one of AEGIS's subsystems, called the *User System*. The effectiveness of this User System was reported by computer simulations[5, 9].

However, it had been implicitly assumed that all the questions were already categorized according to their subjects. This paper presented a new subsystem of AEGIS, called the *Manager System*, and a method for categorizing questions which AEGIS generates automatically, using a new XML tag called a CONCEPT tag. The Manager System categorizes these questions into the categories of a NaviList created by teachers, and assists the students in mastering their subject by navigating them through a lecture

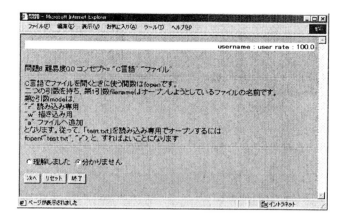

Figure 4. Learning Mode

course's contents, with continual assessment and feedback by asking and marking appropriate questions.

Teaching materials for AEGIS are intended for text documents written in XML or HTML. Recently many teachers use a presentation software for their lectures, for example Microsoft Power Point. The files of Power Point can be transformed into Web documents without any difficulties. They are good materials to generate questions. Although AEGIS can deal with the documents to create an ontology and to map a question onto a category in a NaviList, it does not surround appropriate keywords by ⟨CONCEPT⟩ tags yet automatically. We need to continuously investigate a method to solve the problem. We also have to evaluate the created ontology and our presented method to map a question onto a category in a NaviList.

AEGIS is implemented as a Java application. The modular design supported by the MVC model has made it straightforward to extend AEGIS with the new subsystem reported here. The same modularity should support extension to AEGIS in its implementation as a multi-agent system using the KODAMA framework[10].

Acknowledgment

This research was partly supported by a Grant-in-Aid for Scientific Research on Priority Areas (2) from the Ministry of Education, Culture, Sports, Science and Technology, No. 14022239, 2002, and by a Grant for Special Academic Research P&P from Kyushu University, type C, 2001-2002.

References

[1] H. Sato, T. Mine, T. Shoudai, H. Arimura, and S. Hirokawa. On web visualizing how programs run for teaching 2300 students. In *ICCE(International Conference on Computers in Education)97 in Malaysia*, pages 952–954, 1997.

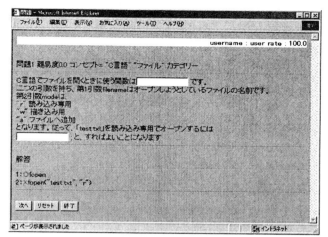

Figure 5. Test Mode

[2] T. Mine, D. Nagano, K. Baba, T. Shoudai, and S. Hirokawa. On-web visualizing a mechanism of a single chip computer for computer literacy courses. In *ICCE(International Conference on Computers in Education)98*, volume 2, pages 496–499, 1998.

[3] A. Suganuma, R. Fujimoto, and Y. Tsutsumi. An WWW-based supporting system realizing cooperative environment for classroom teaching. In *World Conference on the WWW and Internet*, pages 830–831, 2000.

[4] T. Mine, A. Suganuma, and T. Shoudai. The design and implementation of automatic exercise generator with tagged documents based on the intelligence of students:AEGIS. In *the ICCE/ICCAI 2000*, pages 651–658, 2000.

[5] A. Suganuma, T. Mine, and T. Shoudai. Automatic generating appropriate exercises based on dynamic evaluating both students' and questions' levels. In *ED-MEDIA 2002–World Conference on Educational Multimedia, Hypermedia & Telecommunications*, pages 1898–1903, 2002.

[6] Y. Matsumoto, A. Kitauchi, T. Yamashita, Y. Hirano, H. Matsuda, K. Takaoka, and M. Asahara. Morphological analysis system CHASEN version 2.2.8 manual. In *Technical report, Nara Institute of Science and Technology*, 2001.

[7] T. Mine, S. Lu, and M. Amamiya. Discovering relationships between topics of conferences by filtering, extracting and clustering. In *the 3rd International Workshop on Natural Language and Information Systems(NLIS2002)*, to appear, 2002.

[8] O. Zamir and O. Etzioni. Web document clustering:a feasibility demonstration. In *the 21th Intl. ACM SIGIR Conference*, pages 46–54, 1998.

[9] A. Suganuma, T. Mine, and T. Shoudai. AEGIS : Automatic exercise generator based on the intelligence of students with tagged documents. In *5th Joint Conference on Knowledge-Based Software Engineering(JCKBSE2002)*, to appear, 2002.

[10] G. Zhong, S. Amamiya, K. Takahashi, T. Mine, and M. Amamiya. The design and application of KODAMA system. In *IEICE Transactions on Information and Systems*, E85-D(4), pages 637–646, 2002.

A Support for Navigation Path Planning with Adaptive Previewing for Web-based Learning

Shinobu Hasegawa
Center for Information Science, JAIST
1-1, Asahidai, Tatsunokuchi, Ishikawa 923-1292, Japan
hasegawa@jaist.ac.jp

Akihiro Kashihara, Jun'ichi Toyoca
I.S.I.R., Osaka University
8-1, Mihogaoka, Ibaraki, Osaka, 567-0047, Japan
{kasihara,toyoda}@ai.sanken.osaka-u.ac.jp

Abstract

How to help learners plan a navigation path on the Web is an important issue in web-based learning/education. Our approach to this issue is to allow the learners to preview a sequence of web pages as navigation path plan. In this paper, we introduce an assistant system that enables learners to plan the navigation path in a self-directed way before navigating hyperspace provided by web-based learning resources. It also realizes an adaptive previewing in accordance with their planning context. Since the adaptive previewing gives the learners in advance an overview of the contents to be learned, their learning in the hyperspace can be improved.

1. Introduction

Existing web-based learning resources generally provide learners with hyperspace where they can navigate the web pages in a self-directed way to learn the domain concepts/knowledge. The self-directed navigation involves making a sequence of the pages navigated, which is called navigation path [2]. Making a navigation path is an important process of the self-directed learning in hyperspace [4].

On the other hand, learners often fail in making a navigation path due to a cognitive overload, which is caused by diverse cognitive efforts not only at planning a navigation path but also at setting up global/local learning goals, comprehending the contents navigated, and so on [2, 5]. Although such navigation problem has been a major issue addressed in educational hypermedia/ hypertext systems [1], the important point towards resolving the problem in the context of self-directed learning is how to help learners monitor their own navigation process [4]. In this paper, we address the issue of how to help learners navigate in existing web-based learning resources [4]. Our approach to this issue is to provide them with a navigation path planning environment apart from hyperspace. The key point of this idea is to allow learners to preview a sequence of web pages as navigation path plan. The previewing enables them to plan the navigation path in a self-directed way before navigating the hyperspace. It is accordingly expected to call their attention to making a navigation path.

The important point of this approach is how to provide learners with a proper previewing of the web pages on the navigation path plan. In general, web page often has several topics. Which topic should be principally previewed depends on the context of planning the navigation path. The main issue addressed here is accordingly how to adapt the previewing to the context of planning a navigation path, which we call adaptive previewing of navigation path [3]. The adaptive previewing identifies the focal topic that learners intend to focus on in the web page, and generates the page preview with hierarchical structure of the HTML document. Such adaptive previewing enables learners to plan a navigation path in a proper way.

2. Navigation Path Planning

2.1 Difficulty in Navigation

On the Web, learners can navigate web pages in a self-directed way by following links among the pages to learn domain concepts/knowledge embedded in the navigated pages. However, learners often fail in making the navigation path and reach an impasse. There are two main causes as follows [5].
- The learners cannot foresee what they should navigate next from the current page for achieving their learning goal due to the complexity of hyperspace.
- The learners need to concurrently make diverse cognitive efforts not only at planning a navigation path but also at setting up global/local learning goals, comprehending the contents navigated, and so on.

2.2 Framework

The important points towards the problem are how to give learners a transparent overview of hyperspace and how to call their attention to planning a navigation path [4].

The main point of this idea is to divide learning process into planning and navigation phases. In the planning phase, learners decide a sequence of pages to navigate. In the navigation phase, on the other hand, they are expected to navigate hyperspace according to the path planned. These phases are repeated during learning in hyperspace. Our approach is accordingly to provide planning and navigation environments for each phase and to support cognitive efforts on each phase.

Following the idea of path previewing, we have developed Path

Planning Assistant. Figure 1 User Interface ce of Planning Assistant, which consists of Page Previewer, Path Previewer, Hyperspace Map, and Navigation Controller. Page Previewer displays an overview of a web page, which learners select in

Hyperspace Map. Path Previewer makes a sequence of previewed pages with a link list which includes anchors of the links that the current page contains. The learners can select any one from the list to have a preview of the page, and displays it as navigation path preview. These facilities help them plan which pages to navigate without navigating real web pages. Navigation Controller, on the other hand, enables learners to navigate along their navigation path plan in a simply way.

3. Adaptive Previewing

3.1 Problem Addressed

Although web page generally includes several topics, every topic does not always need to be previewed when learners plan a navigation path. Which topic should be principally previewed depends on the topic learners intend to focus on in Path Previewer. We call it focal topic. The problem addressed in the adaptive previewing of path planning is to generate a proper page preview in consideration of the focal topic that is regarded as the contextual information of planning the navigation path [3].

3.2 Adaptive Preview Generation

In the adaptive previewing, the preview generation consists of the following two steps that are executed in Path Previewer:
(1) To identify the focal topic of learners, and
(2) To identify the focal section, that is information to be previewed according to the focal topic.
Path Previewer first identifies the focal topic with keywords included in the anchor that learners select from the link list of the current page for previewing the next page.
By using Heading elements in the HTML document of the page, Path Previewer next divides the document into several sections. The Heading elements represent hierarchical structure of the document. Following the hierarchy, Path Previewer identifies the focal section whose Heading element includes the focal topic, as the sections to be previewed. If no Heading element includes the focal topic, it finds in which section keywords representing the focal topic appear most frequently and selects this as the focal section to be previewed.
Path Previewer next extracts information to be previewed to generate the adaptive preview. It first extracts not only the Heading element of the identified section but also Title element and the ancestor/descendant Heading elements. This enables the path preview to preserve the hierarchical structure of topics embedded in the page. Path Previewer then extracts key information from the identified section. Path Previewer also generates the link list including anchors of all links in the page, in which the anchors included in the section previewed take precedence.

3.3 Case Study

We have had a case study whose purpose was to ascertain how proper the section that the adaptive previewing identified is compared to the section that each subject identified after navigation according to some navigation path plans.
We prepared four navigation path plans from two web-based learning resources. Each navigation path was planned with its own learning goal, and was composed of four pages. Subjects were five graduate students in technology.
The procedure of this study with each subject was as follows:
(1) He/she was provided with each path plan, in which he/she was given the explanation about the learning goal embedded.

Table 2. Results of Case Study

	Cases
Correspondence	32 (53%)
Partial Match	21 (35%)
Difference	7 (12%)

(2) He/she was required to use web browser to navigate and learn the four web pages according to the path plan and the learning goal. He/she was also required to copy and paste part in each page, on which he/she focused in navigation.
In this study, the suitability of path previewing was measured as how section previewed by the adaptive previewing was included in the contents subjects copied and pasted.
Table 1 shows the results of this study. Correspondence means that the section, which is identified in both, agreed completely. Partial Match means that the section that the subject identified includes the section that the adaptive previewing identified. Difference also means that the section disagreed. These results show that the system-identified sections agreed with the subject-identified sections approximately about 88% of their total composition.
Although these results were limited to two resources used in this study, we believe that the adaptive previewing enables learners to provide a better preview in accordance with their planning context.

4. Conclusion

This paper has described a navigation path planning aid for self-directed learning in hyperspace provided by web-based learning resources. The key idea is to provide learners with adaptive preview of navigation path plan to help them plan their navigation process, which is an important process of the self-directed learning. The adaptive previewing enables them to plan the navigation path in a proper way before navigating hyperspace.
In the future, we need a more detailed evaluation of the adaptive navigation path previewing with the system. We would also like to improve it according to the results.

References

[1] Brusilovsky, P. Methods and Techniques of Adaptive Hypermedia, Journal of User Modeling and User-Adapted Interaction, 6, 87-129 (1996).
[2] Hammond, N. Learning with Hypertext: Problems, Principles and Prospects, in McKnight, C., Dillon, A., and Richardson, J. (eds): HYPERTEXT A Psychological Perspective, Ellis Horwood Limited, 51-69 (1993).
[3] Kashihara, A., Hasegawa, S., and Toyoda, J.: How to Facilitate Navigation Planning in Self-directed Learning on the Web, Proc. of AH2002 Workshop on Adaptive Systems for Web-based Education, 117-124 (2002).
[4] Suzuki, R., Hasegawa, S., Kashihara, A., and Toyoda, J. A Navigation Path Planning Assistant for Web-based Learning, Proc. of ED-MEDIA 2001, 851-1856 (2001).
[5] Thuering, M., Hannemann, J., and Haake, J.M. Hypermedia and Cognition: Designing for Comprehension. Communication of the ACM, 38, 8, ACM Press, 57-66 (1995).

The Art of Intro — Developing Digital Genres for Learning

Gunnar Liestøl
Dept. of Media & Communication
University of Oslo
gunnar.liestol@media.uio.no

Abstract

This paper argues that in order to further improve the quality of digital learning environments one must also invest in the invention and development of digital genres. Quality and complexity at the level of document genres, messages and meaning will be defining criteria for superior digital learning environments. The paper suggests that perspectives from genre theory should be applied to the understanding and development of learning objects. Based on a survey of various genres, in both traditional learning environments and digital formats, such as computer games, a prototype genre — the Intro — is presented for application in educational project work.

Introduction

In societies where information and knowledge are the primary object of communication and exchange, diversity and complexity increasingly emerge at the level of signification and meaning. Objects and artefacts, which store information and generate meaning and knowledge in interaction with its users, are key commodities in the knowledge society. There is no reason to believe that this is not also the case regarding the development of digital learning environments. This paper reports on a project where invention and development of digital genres is the central concern. Before describing the prototype genre under construction it briefly contextualizes this endeavor by relating the current conception of learning objects to the traditional concept of genre. Further, it presents some of the background and motivation for selecting this particular kind of prototype/genre. The paper concludes with suggestions for further work in this field, particularly the challenges related to interdisciplinarity and methodological integration and compatibility.

Learning Objects and Genre

Over the last couple of years, the broad field of 'computers in education' seems to have been dominated by a hype surrounding 'e-learning' and a bend towards instructional design predominantly targeted at corporate training rather than universities and higher education. Key software solutions related to these achievements are Learning Management Systems (LMS) or Learning and Content Management Systems (LCMS). A central concept here is the *Learning Object*. What is a Learning Object? According to one definition Learning Objects are "... any entity, digital or non-digital, which can be used, re-used or referenced during technology supported learning. [...] Examples of Learning

Objects include multimedia content, instructional content, learning objectives, instructional software and software tools, and persons, organizations, or events referenced during technology supported learning." (LOM 2000) This definition is wide, most probably too wide, because any object, resource, action or event loosely linked to a learning activity seems to be a Learning Object. Consequently this definition has met criticism. Wiley (2000: 4) suggests a more narrow description of a Learning Object: "Any digital resource that can be reused to support learning." Further, Wiley suggests the atom-metaphor rather than the extensively used LEGO-metaphor to describe the selection—combination process of learning objects for the purpose of instructional course design, because, contrary to the combination of LEGO-bricks there are certain constraints for how atoms may be combined in order to build molecules. Finally, Wiley suggest a taxonomy of Learning Objects, depending on how they are combined and generated (2000, 11-15). The concept of learning objects has its origin in object-oriented programming where the creation of components that can be reused are highly evaluated (Dahl & Nygaard, 1966). Although Learning Objects can be understood both from the point of view of informatics as well as within the constrained paradigm of LMSs and instructional design, I believe it is important to understand Learning Objects (or its equivalents) beyond these perspectives: as objects or artefacts that mediate and generate *meaning* in interaction with users. If we ignore the digital for a moment and look at traditional, analog 'learning objects' from traditional learning environments, resources that can be reused to support

learning could be a lecture, a presentation, a textbook (or parts of it), an essay, a thesis etc., that is any oral or written *genre* practiced in educational institutions (in addition to hardware such as paper, pencil, blackboard and other physical tools relevant to activities of learning). 'Learning objects' of the past constitute genres, and there is no reason to believe that the same should not be the case with learning objects in the digital age. However, if kinds of learning objects are to be conceived as genres, it is necessary to briefly re-examine the way we traditionally contextualize digital media both in learning and other contexts.

Beyond Hardware and Software
Traditionally one divides the computer (and thus digital media) into hardware and software. The digital medium achieves its multi-functionality because of the dynamics between these levels. While depending on basically the same physical hardware platform a computer can take on being different 'machines' conditioned only by the software activated. The level of software may again be divided into operating systems and applications, for example the Linux OS and a text editor running under that OS. Software applications, however, are used as means for other ends, for example the messages one writes and reads inside text editors. We might say that applications, such as a text or image editors, mediate *actions*, while the documents or messages they create mediate *meaning*. Applications as tools are certainly important learning objects, but also the documents these tools produce and make possible. This level of documents, messages and meaning used in communication and exchange — e-mail messages, web pages, streamed

video sequences — I call *Meaningware* (Liestøl, 1995 & 2002). Learning objects may be found at the levels of hardware, software and meaningware; but if digital learning objects are to become a substantial part of any digital or blended learning environment, they must to a larger extent be conceived and designed as *meaningware*. In traditional learning environments (as mentioned above) the dominant learning objects constitute and are divided into genres (lectures, essays, textbooks, assignments, project presentations etc.). How do we divide digital learning objects into genres? Today, this hardly makes sense. While genres are useful categories in other digital domains, such as computer games, little progress has so far been made in digital learning when it comes to innovative and inventive genre development. Attempts at presenting taxonomies have been put forward (for example Wiley above), but these are technology dependent rather than categorizations of digital documents shaped and harnessed by meaningful communication and exchange in actual learning environments. One may argue that the stored, streamed and annotated lecture or the Powerpoint presentations are new digital genres. To some extent that is correct, but on the other hand, let us hope genre development in digital media is not limited to those forms and tools. However, if we give more priority to the genre perspective and its focus on messages and meaning we may be better able to exploit the vast potential of digital media for the purpose of learning.

Formats in Project Work and Means for Making Genres

How does one go about making a digital genre? For the sake of time and argument some fast decisions must be made. For this project the educational setting of project work was selected. All project work starts with some kind of introduction to the assignment: the teacher presents the task and the topic, and hopefully at the same time motivates the student to conduct further research and work on her own. In the beginning/opening such an introduction is linear. As a genre, an introduction to a project is akin to the lecture and the encyclopedia article: it present and problematize a topic and at the same time introduce resources for further exploration and research. The purpose of our research was to invent a digital genre, which, independent of topic, could serve this function in the introductory phase of students' project work. Based in previous research (Liestøl, 1999) and extensive surveys of computer game structures short video sequences was selected as the basic format. Many computer games, particularly in the adventure genre, have temporal introductions, that is short movies that present the task or the problem to be solved in the game. Problem solving in computer games has certain affinities with problem solving in project work, and the linear movie-like introduction moves the player from a state of passive consumption (broadcast mode) to a state of active participation and problem solving. Our purpose was then to invent a genre that exploited all these different genres or genre elements: the lecture, the project introduction, the encyclopedia essay and the computer game introduction. This 'new' genre, is just called, the *Intro*, and the vehicle for its delivery the *IntroPlayer* (1).

The *IntroPlayer* prototype

In the case described below the IntroPlayer presents a general introduction to the Norwegian dramatist Henrik Ibsen. The Intro is activated from a web page, the *IntroIndex*. During the general presentation six links are introduced, three of them point to other Intros (with subtopics detailing information about three of Ibsen's best known plays), while the other three recommend and introduce relevant web sites for further research.

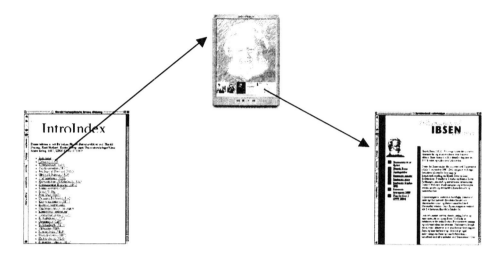

After accessing the IntroIndex the user selects an Intro of her own choice, in this case the Intro on Henrik Ibsen, and after viewing the Ibsen Intro she selects one of the suggested web sites for further study.

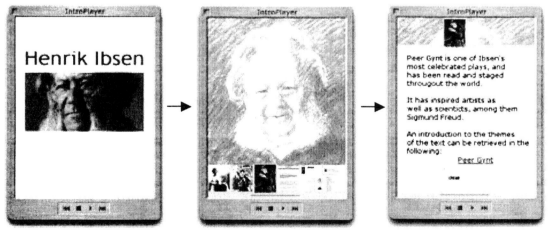

1. The opening frame of the Henrik Ibsen intro. It starts to play automatically when accessed from the IntroIndex page (or elsewhere).

2. A link icon that has been presented by the intro is selected by the user while the Intro continues to play until its end.

3. When the link icon is activated the temporal sequence is paused and a text field emerges with information about the link destination.

The Intro structure is a temporal sequence that moves from linearity to multilinearity.

Conclusion

The Intro format has been tested applying various topics, for example in Media Studies at University level (introduction to the history of hypertext, and introduction to the history of the computer as a medium). The results from these tests are encouraging and the IntroPlayer will be tested with students in the fall of 2002. So far the greatest challenge lies in design methodologies. Since the invention and design of the Intro format strongly encourage focus on the genre and meaning level (meaningware) cross-disciplinary negotiations are necessary. This is particularly the case concerning the relationship between models for system development, such as the Spiral model (Boehm 1997), on the one side and methods of interpretation, such as hermeneutics (Gadamer 1997) on the other. The methods of ancient rhetoric, however, might constitute a middle ground between the two.

Notes:

(1) The *IntroPlayer* is developed in QuickTime 6.0. With its skin-features one may customize the shape of the presentation window. With an editor such as LiveStage Pro 3.1 one gets easy access to the interactive and programmable features of the QuickTime architecture. The *IntroPlayer* in its current version applies the MPEG4 compression codec, plays at 15 fps in a frame measuring 240x320, and has a steady data stream of about 35 Kbytes ps.

References:

Boehm, B. (et. al) (1997) 'Developing Multimedia Applications with the WinWin Spiral model.' in *Proceedings, ESEC/FSE 97* and ACM Software Engineering Notes, November 1997.

Dahl, O. J. & Nygaard, K. (1966). 'SIMULA - An algol based simulation language.' *Communications of the ACM*, 9 (9), p. 671-678.

Gadamer, H. G. (1997) *Truth and Method. Second revised edition.* New York: Continuum

Liestøl, G. (1995) 'Fra retorikk til teknikk' in *As Time Goes By. Festskrift til Bjørn Sørenssen*, Trondheim: Tapir Forlag.

Liestøl, G. (1999) *Essays in Rhetorics of Hypermedia Design*, Dept. of Media & Communication, University of Oslo, 265 pp.

Liestøl, G (2002) 'Gameplay — from Synthesis to Analysis (and vice versa). Topics of Conceptualization in Digital Media' in *Digital Media Revisited* (eds. Liestøl, Morrison & Rasmussen), Cambridge: MIT Press.

Wiley, D. A. (2000). 'Connecting learning objects to instructional design theory: A definition, a metaphor, and a taxonomy'. In D. A. Wiley (Ed.), *The Instructional Use of Learning Objects: Online Version.* Retrieved 04. 18. 2002, from the World Wide Web: http://reusability.org/read/chapters/wiley.doc

LOM (2000). LOM working draft v4.1 [Online]. Available: http://ltsc.ieee.org/doc/wg12/LOMv4.1.htm

Development and Evaluation of "FATHeRS" as a Portal Site for Japanese School ICT Education Practices

Tatsuya HORITA*, Jun TAKAHASHI**, Mamoru MURAKAMI***, Norihiro MIYAZAKI****

* Faculty of Information, SHIZUOKA University <horita@horitan.net>
** Faculty of Education, TOYAMA University <jun@yokosuka.com>
*** Graduate School of Informatics, SHIZUOKA University <alt@mx2.sala.or.jp>
**** Graduate School of Informatics, SHIZUOKA University <noriweb@d3.dion.ne.jp>

Abstract

Schoolteachers are still confused with ICT education in Japan. Teachers who have already practiced ICT education and have practical know-how should be delivered to assist ordinary teachers. We developed and distributed the useful materials for practice of Japanese ICT education through the website "FATHeRS". We had run it as a pavilion in Japanese Internet Fair 2001. Consequently, the website obtained a lot of accesses of about 9,000 page views per a day. The mainly used contents were "Everyday Digital Camera Map" and "ICT quiz" for students. In the materials for teachers, "the Collection of Practical Illustrations," "One Point Advice" and "Let's Try ICT Education" were often accessed. "FATHeRS" is the only website distributes such materials systematically for schools in Japan. So, "FATHeRS" was thought advisable and won many prizes in ICT education area.

1. Problem

The dramatic advances in Information Communication Technology (ICT) in recent years have made widespread ICT education essential. To this end, the Japanese MEXT (the Ministry of Education, Culture, Sports, Science and Technology) allocated funds from the national budget to popularize ICT education and enrich the infrastructure. All schools (including elementary, junior high, high school and school for special education needs) became part of the Internet infrastructure by the fiscal year 2001. By the fiscal year 2005, two computers will be installed in every classroom of all schools, and connected to the broadband Internet.

However, schoolteachers are still confused with ICT education. Neither the definition of ICT education nor its positioning in the new educational course has been fully understood by ordinary teachers. Most of the teacher training is about computer operation yet; training about instructional design of ICT education is still neglected. Therefore there is still a major obstacle in the smooth distribution of ICT Education.

To address this problem, teachers who have already practiced ICT education and have practical know-how should be delivered to assist ordinary teachers.

2. Objective of the Project and Viewpoint of Evaluation

(1) The Objective of this Project

Figure 1: Top Page of "FATHeRS" for students

The objective of this project was to develop useful materials, to distribute them systematically by Internet website and to concurrently organize a community for teachers (Horita et al. 2001). In this project, we ran the website "FATHeRS" that we developed with FUJITSU Limited as one of the exhibits in the Internet Fair 2001 (INPAKU) that Japanese government sponsors in year 2001 (http://www.inpaku-FATHeRS.com) [Figure 1].

In the website, we suggest a concrete form of instructional information, and distribute by Internet to develop and enhance ICT education practices.

(2) The Viewpoints of Evaluation
In order to evaluate the efficacy of the project, we considered the following points.

Table 1: The Topics of Monthly Contests

Month	Title	Summary
January	I wish there could be such personal computers!	Students draw future PCs in the picture, take photographs of them with the digital camera, and send them.
February	Let's make the homepages of the schools that you have never been to.	Students exchange information for companion's school with the various means, by making the page of the school that they have never been to.
March	Let's make cooking map!	Students make cooking with the specialty that they live or cooking with the characteristics, and take photographs of them with the digital camera, and send them.
April	Please teach us, about your school and your friends!	Students introduce the state of the new grade and the class by the photographs and the sentences.
May	Quiz: What is this?	Students think about pleasant quizzes, by using the image of two sheets of digital cameras
June	To expedition teams, gather!	Students go to the factories and stores around school, and put the results examined about the factories and stores together in the web page.
July	Let's learn with FATHeRS!	Each student puts the results that did inquiry learning together in the web pages, by using link collections in FATHeRS.
August	Various Contest in Summer Vacation	Each student applies one of various contests, like "picture dairy in summer," "research with parents and children," "Founds in the mountains and at the sea," and "Dr. insect collector."
September	Let's examine, create, play with your self-made game data	Each student decides theme to examine, arrange and create game data in simple format, and play together with networking friends.
October	Look for the scoop of your town!	Each student makes web page to advertise about the characteristics, boast, festival and events of the area which one lives in.
November	Let's try to raise plants, and compare them!	Each student raises and observes the plants from the sowing to the harvest, and completes growth diary on the web page.

1258

- 1: The Frequency of access to the website
- 2: The questionnaire to the teachers

- 3: The social evaluation of the website

3. Materials, Community, and the Management of the Website

(1) Materials

The developed website "FATHeRS" consists of two sections "Room for Kids" and "Room for Teachers". "Room for Kids" has about 3,200 pages, and "Room for Teachers" has about 1,100 pages.

In "Room for Kids," we have established a contest for students every month. We have designed it so that students can easily try and challenge new study subject one after another. This section proved to be quite easy to use in actual classroom situations. [Table 1] shows the topic of each monthly contest. We also established an "Everyday Digital Camera Map" (EDCM) as a major learning content. Students that belong to other schools share digital pictures using EDCM concerning a selected topic twice a week. For example, when the topic is "school lunch," students take digital pictures of their school lunch menu of the day, and send it to the website management staff. Browsing pictures on the web page, they find regional differences in the menu and dishes [Figure 2].

On the other hand, "Room for Teachers" has some suggestions for instruction designing and making images of ICT class concrete. For example, a section called "One Point Advice" shares every school's practical know-how using digital camera. And in the section "Let's Try ICT Education," there are the practical points communicated through interviews with some pioneers as well as FAQs about ICT Education. We selected a number of typical ICT learning activities for which we provided concrete illustrations [Figure 3]. Teachers will pay more attention to ICT education using these illustrations in the designing process of their instructional plan..

(2) Community

At present, the community consists of the website management staff and 200 teachers.

The members used a mailing list to exchange opinions and ideas. 3,800 emails were exchanged in the past year. At the beginning of the community, the management staff's opinions occupied most of the correspondence, but gradually, teacher's opinions have increased.

Also, the management staff published an email magazine. Over 300 teachers read the magazine, which has been published 40 times in a year.

4. Evaluation

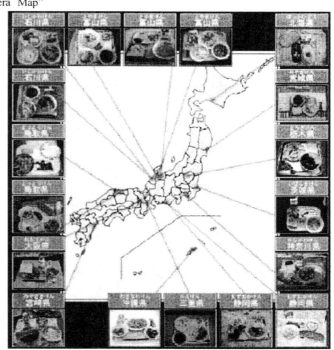

Figure 2: "Everyday Digital Camera Map"

(1) The Frequency of Access to the Website

We analyzed the total 2,895,499 records from the year January

1st, 2001 to December 31st, 2001. The number of accesses to the "FATHeRS" has increased continuously since the time of establishment. The average is 9,000 page views per a day.

Although access to the top page is decreasing gradually, access to the individual links is not decreasing. It seems that the users access the links directly.

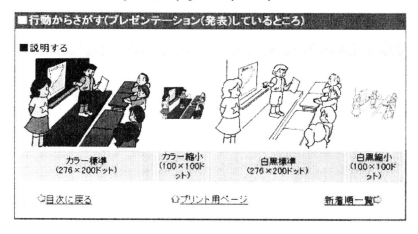

Figure 3: "Practical Illustrations (For Teachers)"

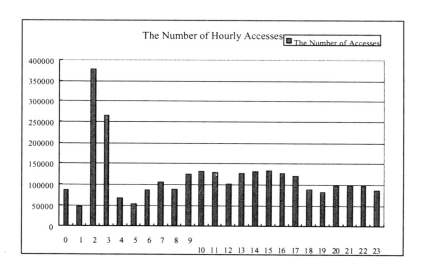

Figure 4: The Number of Accesses Classified by Time

[Figure 4] shows the number of accesses classified by time. There are many accesses at 2:00 and 3:00 by robot agents of Search Engines. There is much access on Tuesday and Thursday; in 10-11 o'clock and 13-14 o'clock. It shows that center of the access is use in the schools because Japanese schools are active in these days and times.

(2) The Questionnaire to the Teachers

In this project, we managed teachers' community in addition to website development. The teachers who participate in the mailing list have more than doubled from the beginning. According to amount of email circulation (more than 3,800 copies), the list functioned actively. It is because the teachers who felt friendly to "FATHeRS" took part in the planning positively.

On the other hand, we also administered a questionnaire to the teachers who were opposed to "FATHeRS" The subjects of this questionnaire are 70 teachers who belong to the questionnaire reply group called "iMi-net" which is managed by FUJITSU Limited. Questionnaires were collected by the e-mail for the period of a week from November 26th, 2001 to December 2nd, 2001, that is the final stage of "FATHeRS". As a result, the teachers thought advisable of "FATHeRS", and

For the students, the most frequently accessed link was the "Everyday Digital Camera Map", the next most frequently accessed link being the "ICT Quiz." For teachers, there was much access to "the Collection of Illustrations" which can be used in actual, classroom practice. The number of accesses for "One Point Advice," and "Let's Try ICT Education" remained constant.

wanted to join the events. The examples of their opinions are following: want to entry the contest (About 95%); want to join EDCM (About 92%) and so on. We received many opinions imaging to use the website in the class actually, for example, EDCM for junior high students and some illustrations imaging volunteerism and international understanding learning are needed.

(3) The Social Evaluation

The prizes for each department were taken vote on by the viewers who accessed 300 or more pavilions, in the Internet exposition. "FATHeRS" won the Grand-Prix of the Year (14 websites won the prize among 300 or so pavilions), because "FATHeRS" had been continuously located in the 2nd or 3rd place in the "Contributed to Society" department. "FATHeRS" also won the Idea Prize from the Government.

In addition, 10 practices including "FATHeRS" are nominated for "the 2nd Educational Practice Using the Internet Contest" sponsored by MEXT among 91 practices. Furthermore, in "the 9th My Townmap Contest" sponsored by Information Processing Support Foundation, "FATHeRS" is one of the 31 finalists now.

As a result, we judge that contribution to popularizing ICT education was highly recognized in the society.

5. Conclusion

We developed and distributed the useful materials for practice of Japanese ICT education through the website "FATHeRS". We had run it as a pavilion in Japanese Internet Fair 2001. Consequently, the website obtained a lot of accesses of about 9,000 page views per a day. The mainly used contents were "Everyday Digital Camera Map" and "ICT quiz" for students. In the materials for teachers, "the Collection of Practical Illustrations," "One Point Advice" and "Let's Try ICT Education" were often accessed.

"FATHeRS" is the only website distributes such materials systematically for schools in Japan. So, "FATHeRS" was thought advisable and won many prizes in ICT education area.

We thank to External Affairs Group, FUJITSU Limited for cooperating us to design and develop "FATHeRS".

6. Reference

[1] Tatsuya HORITA, Jun TAKAHASHI, Toshinori TAKAHASHI, "Development of Portal Site for Japanese Schools to Popularize ICT Education Practices", *Proceedings of ICCE2001, ICCE, pp.1665-1666*

XLX – A Platform for Graduate-Level Exercises

Bodo Hüsemann, Jens Lechtenbörger, Gottfried Vossen, Peter Westerkamp
Dept. of Information Systems, University of Muenster
Leonardo-Campus 3, D-48149 Muenster, Germany, April 2002

Abstract

E-learning has become an important topic these days, both in academia and industry. This paper reports on a newly created Web-based platform, called eXtreme e-Learning eXperience (XLX), to perform exercise work of technically oriented graduate-level university courses, in support of blended learning. In addition to providing a course portal with traditional teaching material, an email list, and a discussion forum, XLX's main contribution lies in a personalized training section that allows transparent access to underlying (possibly commercial) third-party systems such as database systems, XSLT processors, or workflow management systems for hands-on experience and increased students' motivation.

1   Introduction

E-learning has become an important topic these days, both in academia and industry. The basic premise is the increased exploitation of computers, the Internet, and the Web for educational purposes, and the belief that this exploitation has many benefits. The application scenarios for e-learning vary considerably, from company-internal training of new employees to virtual universities offering complete study programs over the Web. In this paper, we report on a newly created platform for graduate-level exercise work which represents our approach to blended learning.

Our platform generally follows the decomposition of a learning platform into *authoring system* for content creation and exchange, *run-time system* for learners to work on learning units, and *learning management system* for managing and configuring content, for keeping track of learners as well as for other administrative tasks, as established in [9] and shown in Figure 1.

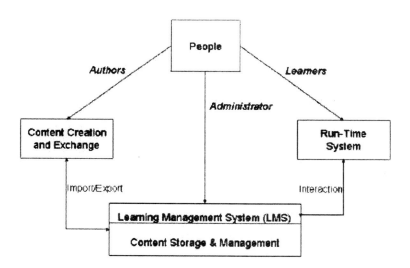

Figure 1: Organization of a Learning Platform.

In this paper we report on an ongoing project involving the development of an e-learning system called „eXtreme eLearning eXperience" (XLX), which is used in support of the exercise portions of technically oriented university courses (e.g., database systems, database implementation, computer networks, workflow management). XLX is part of our "blended learning strategy" that consists of regular classroom teaching and electronic exercise work. We are convinced that classroom teaching in the mentioned courses is necessary and leads to better learning results than complete web-courses.

In the Section 2 we discuss basic considerations and assumptions which have guided the design and implementation of the XLX platform. The platform itself is briefly described in Section 3. A discussion of related work and some conclusions are summarized in Section 4.

2   Basic Considerations for XLX

Our motivation for the development of XLX is based on the following observations:

1. Current university classes (and embedded exercises) typically take place in strictly periodic meetings, are bound to certain teaching-environments, mostly ignoring the progress, needs, and time constraints of individual students.
2. The above mentioned target courses for our system, in particular databases and information systems, offer lots of potential for computer-based, interactive, often visualized or animated, training and testing.
3. Students need to practice and train their skills with full-scale Software-Systems (e.g. DBMS) which are often available at the university only. Moreover, if the software is also allowed to be used at home, they don't have the knowledge to install and administer it or their hardware doesn't comply to the installation-requirements.
4. Students spend less and less time and efforts to work up courses and exercises continuously. Reasons for this trend are manifold and shall not be discussed here.

The XLX platform allows us to address the above observations as follows. Students can work on their exercises anytime and anyplace if Internet access and a standard web browser are available. Students may determine their own pace when solving exercises; however, a didactically meaningful sequencing of exercises is enforced by the system (as is a time limit per assignment). Moreover, students may ask for additional exercises either if they have difficulties with the presented material or if they would like to work on more challenging problems. Finally, learning modules based on realistic problems and transparent access to underlying commercial systems raise hopes in more fun and better learning

success while solving the exercises accompanying a course.

XLX embodies a personalized learning platform that offers hands-on experience in terms of practical exercises covering a wide range of conceptual, language specific, or algorithmic aspects of a particular field. XLX gives transparent access to underlying (commercial) systems (e.g., database or workflow management systems), which are administrated centrally in our group. As explained above, the XLX platform is designed as a supplement to traditional lectures, not a replacement for them. XLX supports web-based exercise solving, where exercises include "arithmetical" tasks, e.g., in the context of the relational algebra, formulation of queries or programs, e.g., in SQL or XSLT, or practical projects based on real-world systems.

The XLX platform organizes exercise solving in terms of closed user groups, where every member has his or her own password-protected account. Each account provides access to a course portal that offers traditional material such as slides, lecture notes, and further links as well as an email list, a discussion forum, and, most importantly, a personalized training section. This training section is divided into two parts:

1. **Test section**: In this section students are enabled to train their skills concerning course relevant techniques (e.g., SQL queries, object-relational features of SQL:1999, transformation of XML documents with XSLT), and they can deepen their understanding of covered algorithmic techniques (e.g., database system algorithms such as algebraic query optimization, two-phase-locking protocol for transaction synchronization, redo-winners protocols for restarts after system crashes [19]).

2. **Submit section**: This section contains the exercises that have to be solved during the term and ahead of predefined deadlines. New exercises show up in this section as the necessary background is covered in class. Solutions can be prepared and sometimes tested in the above mentioned test section. Once submitted, solutions cannot be changed any more by students, and they appear on the worklist of a teaching assistant by whom they are corrected and annotated. So far, the XLX platform knows four types of exercises: free-text, multiple choice, SQL queries, and XSLT transformations. While the first two of these exercise types are standard ingredients of e-learning systems, the latter two are unique to our system, as they are coupled with transparently integrated underlying systems, in our case a relational database for SQL (IBM DB2 UDB V7) and an XSLT processor (Sablotron). The integration of different systems avoids technological and administrative barriers as students do not have to install these systems at home; instead, these systems are accessed

via standard web browsers. Finally, we note that exercises for the last three of the above types are stored along with solutions inside the XLX platform, which allows for automatic prechecking of solutions and makes life of teaching assistants easier.

3   Architecture of the XLX Platform

The XLX platform was designed with several technical requirements in mind. On the client side, it should be independent of hardware, location, or operating systems used; on the server side, it should be able to generate web pages dynamically, provide security as far as personal data is concerned, and deliver 24/7 availability. XLX is based on open source software (except for integrated third-party systems) and is implemented in three-tier client-server architecture as shown in Figure 2. Web clients form the outermost layer can access the platform via a web browser. A web server builds the second layer and processes client requests. A database server represents the core of the innermost layer which also is the integration layer for different third party systems (like, e.g., IBM DB2). Internet-based client access allows for platform

independence on the client side and enables continuous availability. The HTML pages of the XLX system can be rendered by all current browsers, and session cookies are used to identify students and to track their actions; besides, extended browser functionalities such as plugins or Java are not needed.

The XLX platform is implemented on top of an Apache web server and a mySQL database running under Linux, i.e., based on open source software. The mySQL database contains student data, exercises and solutions. Communication between clients and XLX platform is secured by SSL (HTTPS), which provides basic security of confidential student data (passwords, solutions, students' grading). All web pages are generated dynamically by PHP4 scripts (ordinary pages) and Java Servlets (database connections via JDBC). The database server IBM DB2 UDB V7 is used for database related exercises (SQL:1999, object-relational features, DB2 extenders). Thanks to the IBM DB2 scholar's program there are no costs involved using DB2 at universities. Finally, PHP is used for calls to the Sablotron XSLT command-line processor from Ginger Alliance.

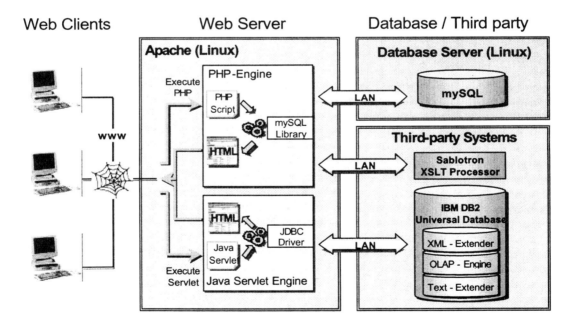

Figure 2: Three-tier Client-Server-Architecture of XLX.

1264

4   Discussion and Conclusions

XLX has been successfully used during the last year in four different courses having more than three-hundred students working on exercises. The curricula of these courses were about databases, XML and computer networks. Each student had to solve an average number of 40 exercises throughout the term. The XML-course was a teleteaching-cooperation with the University of Augsburg (Germany) where XLX was used by the students in Muenster and Augsburg to solve the corresponding exercises. From Mai to August 2002 XLX was used by the University of Essen (Germany) to train students in their virtual program VAWi [16].

We recognized a high acceptance of the system and especially of the test section. There was a frequent usage of the third-party systems, for example hundred students of one course generated 50.000 SQL-statements to query the integrated DB2 database. Students accessed the XLX-platform from all over the world and all around the clock. Some of them, who stayed abroad, for example in Finland and Australia, used the system to work on the exercises to manage their examination after their return.

XLX is not the only system that has been developed over the years for supporting classroom-based teaching and learning. Indeed, there are many others, like e.g., the Webassign-Hagen [17] project of the University Hagen or the equally named System Webassign-Carolina [18] of the North Carolina State University. These Systems also focus on supporting web-based tests and exercises. One of the main intentions of the XLX-platform is the natural integration of third party modules to allow hands on experience with real-world enterprise application-systems.

Moreover, XLX competes with a number of commercial platforms for e-learning inside or outside universities, colleges, and other institutions as well as platforms employed in organizations and companies. Indeed, organizational learning is of increasing importance these days, as many companies have discovered two sides of the coin: On the one hand, an e-learning system can be used for continued, on-the-job training of new and also of experienced employees. On the other, a carefully designed e-learning system can at the same be used for knowledge management, since experienced learners can be motivated to feed their knowledge back into the system, in order to preserve it, to develop it, and to share it with others.

To achieve the goal of combining organizational learning with knowledge management, various tasks need to be tackled, among them the definition, specification, and creation of *learning objects* as content units that from the basis of a learning platform, see [3], [5], and others, and the proper exchangeability of learning objects through metadata specifications and XML Schemas, see [1], [9], or [10]. We plan to extend the XLX platform in this direction, thereby making its inner structure more amenable to a component structure as we have shown in Figure 1.

The XLX platform can be found on the web under URL https://dbms.uni-muenster.de/xlx. Its frontend is entirely designed in English so that even foreign learners can use it. A demo access can be obtained over the Web.

References

[1]   ADL (2001). *The SCORM Content Aggregation Model*, Version 1.2. Advanced Distributed Learning Initiative, October 2001.

[2]   Anido-Rifon, L., et al. (2001). *A Component Model for Standardized Web-Basd Education*. ACM Journal of Educational Resources in Computing, 1(2), Summer 2001.

[3]   Barritt, C. (2001). *CISCO Systems Reusable Learning Object Strategy – Designing Information and Learning Objects Through Concept, Fact, Procedure, Process, and Principle Templates*, Version 4.0. White Paper, CISCO Systems, Inc., November 2001.

[4]   Constantini, F., C. Toinard (2001). *Collaborative Learning with the Distributed Building Site Metaphor*. IEEE Multimedia, Issue 3, 21-29.

[5]   Downes, S. (2001). *Learning Objects: Resources for Distances Education Worldwide*. International Review of Research in Open and Distance Learning 2 (1).

[6]   El Saddik, A., S. Fischer, R. Steinmetz (2001). *Reusability and Adaptability of Interactive Resources in Web-Based Educational Systems*. ACM Journal of Educational Resources in Computing 1 (1).

[7]   Fischer, S. (2001). *Course and Exercise Sequencing Using Metadata in Adaptive Hypermedia Learning Systems*. ACM Journal of Educational Resources in Computing, 1(1), Spring 2001.

[8]   Harasim, L. (1999). *A Framework for Online Learning: The Virtual-U*. IEEE Computer, September, 44-49.

[9]   IMS Global Learning Consortium, Inc. (2001). *IMS Content Packaging Best Practice Guide*, Version 1.1.2. August 2001.

[10]   Kooper, R. (2001). *Modeling units of study from a pedagogical perspective – the pedagogical meta-model behind EML*. Open University o the Netherlands, Heerlen, The Netherlands, June 2001.

[11]   Leidig, T. (2001). L^3 – Towards an Open Learning Environment. ACM Journal of Educational Resources in Computing, 1(1), Spring 2001.

[12]   Pfahl, D. et al. (2001) *CORONET-Train: A Methodology for Web-Based Collaborative Learning*

in Software Organizations. Techn. Report, Fraunhofer IESE.

[13]   Salmon, G. (2000). *E-Moderating – The Key to Teaching and Learning Online*. Stylus Publishing, Sterling, Virginia.

[14]   Shang, Y., H. Shi, S.-S. Chen (2001). *An Intelligent Distributed Environment for Active Learning. ACM* Journal of Educational Resources in Computing, 1(2), Summer 2001.

[15]   Shotsberger, P.G., R. Vetter (2001). *Teaching and Learning in the Wireless Classroom*. IEEE Computer, March 2001, 110-111.

[16]   VAWi, "Virtuelle Aus- und Weiterbildung Wirtschaftsinformatik", Universität Essen, Prof. Dr. H. H. Adelsberger, http://www.vawi.de/, 2002

[17]   Webassign (2002). Fernuniversität Hagen, Prof. Dr. H.-W. Six, Lehrgebiet Praktische Informatik III, Software Engineering, http://niobe.fernuni-hagen.de/WebAssign/, 26.04.2002.

[18]   Webassign-Carolina (2002). North Carolina State University, http://www.webassign.net/, 26.04.2002.

[19]   Weikum, G., G. Vossen (2002). Transactional Information Systems – Theory, Algorithms, and The Practice of Concurrency Control and Recovery. Morgan Kaufmann Publishers, San Francisco, CA.

Multimedia Online Quiz System in Collaboration with Specialists

Kyoko Umeda, Takami Yasuda*, and Shigeki Yokoi**
Aichi University of Education, School of Informatics and Sciences Nagoya University*, Graduate
School of Human Informatics Nagoya University**, Japan

Abstract

The purpose of this research is to create a comprehensive multimedia online quiz system on the Web that makes it easy to create and administer a "rich" online quiz, and to reuse and exchange it efficiency with collaboration from specialists such as teachers or curators. For the first phase, we proposed a method of packaging of multimedia online quiz, and developed the Online Quiz system. Also, an experiment was conducted under a high speed network environment. Based on the results of first phase, we are developing the authoring tool of multimedia online quiz for reuse and exchange it efficiency.

1. Introduction

In recent years, multimedia learning resources available on the Web have been increasing. Moreover, opportunities for the use of multimedia learning resources will increase because broadband computer networks will grow enabling people to access those resources with ease and high speed, even from remote places. Under these circumstances, we should consider the quality of learning resources [1]. In this paper, we define a "rich" learning resource as follows:

(1) It consists of various types of media, such as text, sound, animation, and video as appropriate.

(2) It is made not only by companies, but also by individuals in collaboration with specialists such as teachers or curators.

(3) It is constructed so that it is easy to exchange parts of the resource with other "rich" learning resources, and to reuse parts of itself easily.

The purpose of this research is to create a comprehensive multimedia online quiz system on the Web that makes it easy to create and administer a "rich" online quiz, and to reuse and exchange it efficiency with collaboration from

specialists such as teachers or curators. We also intend to use this system at the Nagoya Science Museum (Nagoya, Japan) and make it available on the Web to improve the system from feedback from users.

2. Progress of the Research

2.1 Method of the creation of the multimedia online quiz system

We developed the multimedia online quiz system in cooperation with the Nagoya Science Museum curator in late 2000, and an experiment was conducted with 1,000 households under a high speed network environment until the first half of 2001[2].

This system was developed to fulfill the following points:

(A) The procedure of including various multimedia materials into the online quiz is simple.

(B) Collaboration with the curator, the designer, and engineer is easily possible.

The reason we targeted quizzes is that we thought a quiz can maintain a motivation to learning because it can be done with enjoyment. Consequently, quizzes have been shown through actual results at the Nagoya Science Museum to be an effective educational activity targeting general citizens. This system is not limited only to simple quizzes, but can be adapted to multiple-choice type learning resources.

To accomplish the above (A) and (B), we proposed a new method for packaging the multimedia learning resources by using XML (Extensible Markup Language). This method is composed of four steps:

1) Defining an XML template for arrangement of various types of materials.

2) Making a Question Unit and an Answer Unit based on the template.

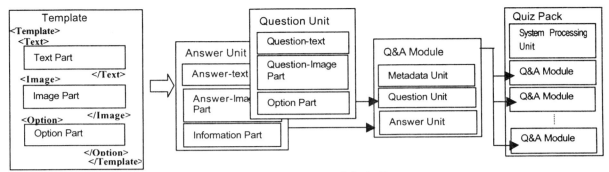

Fig.1 Process of Packaging of Quiz Resources

3) Making a Q&A Module by combining the Question Unit and Answer Unit, and also adding the Metadata Unit, which describes the copyright, the quiz title, and the quiz description based on the Dublin Core [3].

4) Making a Quiz Pack by combining several Q&A Modules based on a certain theme, and also adding the System Processing Unit, which is written as an XML declaration and program code to process the system.

In this way, the Quiz resource is one complete XML file (Fig.1).

To display the quiz resource, four kinds of XSL (Extensible Stylesheet Language) files, one each to view question, answer, review, and hint, were prepared. To choreograph multimedia presentations for synchronizing multiple images, SMIL (Synchronized Multimedia Integration Language) which is written as an XML application, was adopted.

The online quiz system we developed converts XML and XSL into HTML on the Web server by using Cocoon[4], which is a 100% pure Java publishing framework that relies on new W3C technologies such as DOM, XML, and XSL to provide Web content. The system creates four kinds of HTML files (question, answer, review and hint) automatically from one XML file. When a quiz is changed, you have only to move one XML file. Additionally, the system introduced individual authentication, and recording of every user's performance history on the quiz. With the record of the users' history, the feedback from the questions would be available for analysis.

2.2 Result of experiment with the Online quiz

We provided an online quiz, entitled "Challenge! Astronomy Quiz" with the cooperation of the Nagoya City Science Museum Planetarium, under a high speed network experiment which targeted 1,000 households in Nagoya City. In total, 51 gif/jpeg files, 14 Flash files, 6 RealVideo files and 60 RealAudio files were used in these quizzes. A total of 181 people of ages ranging from under 10 years old to over 71 years old, have taken the Astronomy Quiz (Fig.2).

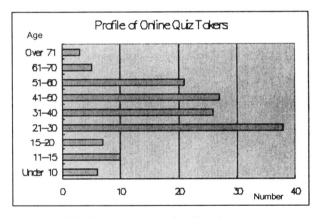

Fig.2 Age group of quiz takers

As for the process of making the quizzes, it was clear that the proposed method described above was effective for corroborating with the curator because it allows each person to take responsibility for only one aspect of the work. For example, the curator thinks of the scenario of the quiz, one of the project members creates an animation, and a designer draws an interface. Also, it was a simple procedure to build multimedia into the quiz appropriate for the question or answer content: We just inserted multimedia materials into the previously determined places. As a matter of fact, the Astronomy quiz has been carried out with six monthly renewals of the quiz based on different themes from November 2000 to May 2001 using this system.

As a result of this experiment, high marks from the users

were given to the following points:
.Providing a friendly resource using multimedia, and
.Providing a comprehensible description by the specialist.
From this viewpoint one may say that this system create it easy to make and provide a "rich" online quiz easily in collaboration with an expert.

3. Future Development

3.1 Overview of development

In the next step of this research we expect to work on the reuse of "rich" resources, especially including multimedia materials. This system was highly evaluated, as mentioned above; however, the following problem and request were stated by participants in the project:
(1) It is hard work to create the multimedia materials.
(2) A comprehensive environment, such as groupware, would be helpful for making quiz on the Web.
  Under the present system, the curator usually sent the quiz scenario and materials that existed in the museum by e-mail, and project members processed the material or made new multimedia. Finally, an organizer composed a Quiz Pack based on the scenario. Therefore, the curator could devote much time to considering the contents or communicating with users, instead of writing HTML or making multimedia materials. Thus, it has been shown that this method is effective and simple for creating resources.
However, the work of making multimedia materials was difficult. It takes much time and money to make multimedia materials, although these are very useful for the users' understanding. As a consequence, we need to consider exchanging parts of the resource with other learning resources or the easy reuse of parts of itself, and effective utilization of a museum or library's multimedia materials.
Considering the feedback from the participants, for creating a comprehensive multimedia online quiz system on the Web, the purposes of this second phase are as follows:
1. Development of an authoring tool that can easily reuse parts of a quiz resource.
2. Development of a collaboration environment, such as groupware, to allow specialists to work together

easily on the Web.

3.2 Developing the comprehensive multimedia online quiz system on the Web

We have already developed a simple authoring tool that helps organizers to compose a quiz without being conscious of XML tags. Now, we are developing a modification function to quiz resources made by this system to easily exchange parts. In the case of making a Quiz Pack, it is not always necessary to make all the questions from the beginning. When making a new Quiz Pack based on the theme of "the Apollo Project," for example, parts of other Quiz Packs of other themes such as the first question of "Moon" and the third question of "Rocket" can be utilized, and so only three new questions need to be created (Fig.3). Thus, with this authoring tool it will be easy to reuse parts of the quiz resource itself, and it is very effective for multimedia learning resources.
Furthermore, we are thinking about how to exchange parts of the resource with other learning resources from other systems and the utilization of resources of a museum or library. It is difficult to make all the resources the target of this exchange; however, there are some specifications for reuse in the world, such as QTI (Question & Text Interoperability Specification) [5].

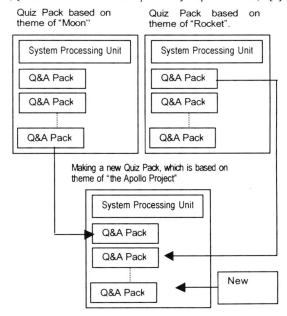

Fig.3 An example of making a new Quiz Pack by combing other Q&A Packs.

These specifications are developing XML structure for designing appropriate learning resources, in order to share, reuse, and interoperate with other systems from the huge amount of learning resources on the Web. We believe that it will be easy to exchange parts of the resource with other learning resources based on QTI specifications. Consequently, we will develop compatibility of our system resources with other standard system resources.

Finally, the point I wish to emphasize is that this system supports the teacher who, instead of doing everything alone, can now work with a team. The teacher thinks of a scenario or lesson to teach, and discusses online with a designer and engineer. Together they pool their expertise to create a work that is better than each one could have created separately.

4. Conclusion

This research aims to create a comprehensive multimedia online quiz system on the Web that makes it easy to create and administer a "rich" online quiz, and to reuse and exchange it efficiency with collaboration from specialists.

At first, we proposed a new method of packaging the multimedia online resource, and developed the Online Quiz System. From the results of the high speed experiment, it was clear that this method was useful for making and providing such a product in collaboration with specialists. As for further steps, we are developing an authoring tool to broaden the availability of online quiz resources. Finally, we are working to create a collaboration online environment where people can make one resource from specialist collaboration.

We intend to use this system at the Nagoya Science Museum and make it available on the Web to improve the system with feedback from users. To collect user opinions, we are planning to provide the online quiz not only on the Web but also at the Nagoya Science Museum. We would like to explore a new way of using the online resource; for example, people using the online quiz for confirming what they have learned at the museum after coming back home. By the end of this research we hope to have created a useful tool that is easy to use, and that can use the wide variety of resources on the Web.

Acknowledgements

This experiment was sponsored by Chubu Electric Company within its FTTH environment. We are indebted to Chubu Electric Company. Also, thanks are due to Katsunori Mouri, curator of Nagoya City Science Museum, for providing us with the content materials. Moreover, we would like to thank Takashi Hara for his cooperation in developing the quiz system, and members of the educational group of our laboratory for their assistance in making the quiz materials. Finally, this research was supported in part by a grant from the Hori Information Science Promotional Foundation.

References

[1] D. Harris, A. DiPaolo, "Advancing Asynchronous Distance Education Using High-Speed Networks," IEEE Transactions on Education, Vol.39, pp.444-450 (1996).

[2] K. Umeda, T. Yasuda, S. Yokoi, "An Online Quiz System Using XML-based Multimedia Resources", Proc. of ICCE/SchoolNet 2001, Vol1. pp481-488

[3] Dublin Core Metadata Initiative: http://www.purl.org/dc/

[4] Apache XML Project,http://xml.apache.org/cocoon/

[5] QTI http://www.imsproject.org/question/index.html

Web-Based Multimedia Teaching Materials for Acoustic Science

Motonobu UCHIMURA*, Hiroshi SUDA**, Yoshiro MIIDA**

Dept. of Computer Science

**Dept. of Information and Network Science*

Chiba Institute of Technology

2-17-1 Tsudanuma, Narashino, Chiba 275-0016, Japan

Tel: +81-47-478-0288 Fax: +81-47-478-0582

E-mail: uchimura@miida.net.it-chiba.ac.jp

Abstract

In the education of acoustic science, it is important how the student imagine the appearances of actual acoustic phenomena. So, for teachers, it is important problems how to model the acoustic phenomena and to provide them to students. It cannot be seen by eyes though sounds are familiar as the phenomena. And that hinders students from studying the acoustic science. Therefore it is worthy for the education of the acoustic science that ties theories to phenomena by simulating acoustic phenomena, and modeling as animations or synthetic sounds on computer. The past multimedia teaching materials, which we made, have been hard to distribute. Then, we are developing web based multimedia teaching materials. They includes presentation slides, simulation programs, movies, and so on... In this paper, we introduce web based multimedia teaching materials, and report the experimental effects of them.

Keywords: WWW-based learning resources/tools, Multimedia, CAI, Simulation, Real time processing

1. Introduction

When students learn acoustic science, they should imagine phenomena by theories, expressions, tables, and figures in textbooks. However figures which have been described to the textbook expresses the moment with phenomena, and it is impossible to express a whole of phenomena. Especially, phenomena caused as sounds need other devices to express them. Therefore, to imagine phenomena, high imagination and wide knowledge are needed for students. On the site of the acoustic education, to improve the student's understanding, it is a problem how teachers model phenomena and present them to students.

Up to now, to improve the understanding of students in the acoustic education, we have modeled by simulating acoustic phenomena with a computer. As results of obtaining by the simulation, the student is made to pseudoexperience the acoustic phenomena by visualizing them as animation or playing them as a synthetic sounds.

These simulation programs, slides which explains each phenomenon, movies which collected actual phenomena and which collected scenes the teacher explains phenomena by using slides, we make them one teaching materials. And we enabled students to inspect, and to use all these teaching materials on Web. We chose existing Web browsers to avoid dependence on a specific OS as the execution environment. And to operate contents on the Web browser, Flash is adopted in slides, and Java is adopted in simulation programs and MPEG-1 is adopted to compress of movies.

2. Example of education which uses multi-media teaching materials

At our university, the lecture which uses explanation-slides, simulation programs, and related movies is executed in the subject of "Acoustic science". Fig1 shows the outline of the composition of education contents, and the educational environment.

The lecture and the exercise of the acoustic science are done to classification by purpose respectively, in the Multi-media room where acoustic education contents are projected to large screen with high brightness projector according to explanation of teacher, or in the multipurpose-room where individual student can access teaching material, and teaching material be operated interactively.

These teaching materials of each theme are composed of the explanation-slides, the simulation programs, the movies which collected actual phenomena and the explanation movies of slides as Fig2 shows.

The number of these slides reaches 100 themes, and the simulation programs, to obtain interactive of changes in the parameter, calculation processing is in real time done.

3. Composition of Multimedia Teaching Materials or Acoustic Science

Our Multi-media Teaching Materials are composed of explanation-slides, simulation programs and movies.

3.1 The Explanation-slide

The explanation-slide is used to explain theories in each theme.

In the explanation-slide, to explain with method, animation has been added. It is possible to explain or study by setting up the theory in the order by gradually displaying each part of the slide. Macromedia

Flash is used for these explanation-slides to enable animation also on the Web browser.

3.2 Simulation Programs

In the simulation program, the computer simulates phenomena whom theory and expression express, and visualizes the result as a graphics or plays as a synthetic sound. In these programs, the calculation of the expression, the display of the graphics, and the play of the sounds, they are in real time all processed. As a result, it has been achieved to present phenomena' changes according to the change in the parameter.

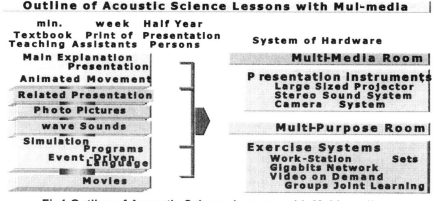

Fig1 Outline of Acoustic Science Lessens with Multi-media

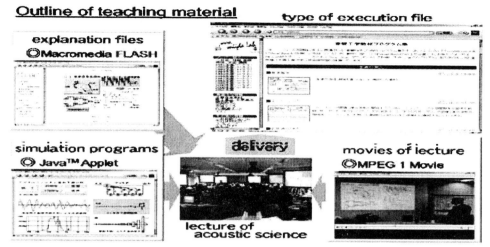

Fig2 Outline of teaching material

Sun Microsystems Java applet is used for the development of the simulation program. By using Java applet, it was able to be achieved to execute the simulation program on Web browser with which Java plug-in is equipped.

Fig3 shows the example of the simulation program made with Java applet.

3.3 Movie

In these teaching materials, movies which collected examples of acoustic phenomena and movies which lecturer is explaining with slide are offered. The former can be related directly to the image of the phenomenon that the student imagines, and can interest students. And by offering the latter, the student can repeatedly audit the explanation outside the lecture until he consents. To make the size of the file smaller in consideration of offering them on Web, these movies are compressed by MPEG-1.

4. Estimation

At our university, the subject of "Acoustic science" is lectured on by using the above-mentioned teaching materials. All explanation-slides are all printed, and being distributed to

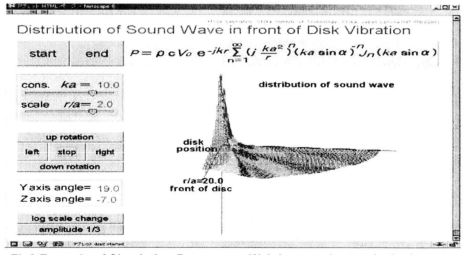

Fig3 Example of Simulation Program on Web browser lecture in the lecture

those who attend a lecture in the lecture.

We investigated the class evaluation by the unsigned class content investigation by those who attended a lecture. The main result by that is shown in Fig4.

The graph of "Satisfaction" of Fig4 shows he evaluation to the class evaluated by five stages; excellent, good, normal, no good, worst. The consciousness value of the degree of the student's understanding is shown in the graph of "Understanding". And it shows that the evaluation goes up compared with the lecture which uses the blackboard.

The graph of "contents necessity" shows the answer to the question which asks the necessity of contents. And, it can be confirmed that the student of 60% or more thinks these teaching materials to be necessary from the graph.

"agreeable movement" shows the operation on personal computers that 15 postgraduates at this university have privately.

"Bad reading" and "Few trouble" show the person who was not able to confirm operation by problems of something. The former is students who were not able to solve the problem by themselves and the latter is students who were able to solve the problem by himself and operate it finally. However, having become a problem in both cases was a difference of the version of

Flash Plug-in or Java Runtime, and it was possible to operate it by updating them.

On the other hand, in the evaluation of the understanding level by examination executed at the end of course, qualitative understanding, that is, the evaluation of the statement type has improved especially. And the remarkable improvement of understanding level was not confirmed in the evaluation by the examination for which calculation by scientific formula is needed.

5. Summary

In this research, we developed the multi-media teaching materials to improve the student's understanding in the acoustic science, and had verified the effectiveness. Consequently, at the understanding level to phenomena, qualitative understanding has improved especially. On the other hand, a remarkable effect was not achieved for mathematical understanding. As a result, how to improve mathematical understanding was clarified as the problem in the future.

However, if we enable the improvement of mathematical understanding, it can be expected that the

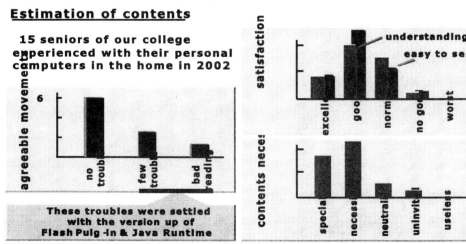

Fig4 Estimation of contents

educative effect is obtained even in other fields which confirmation of phenomena by sight is difficult, and which change in parameter in expression characterizes phenomena.

Reference

[1] Maki SUGIMOTO, Hiroshi SUDA, Masahiro UKIGAI, & Yoshiro MIIDA, "Multimedia-Based Teaching Material For Learning About Voice", ICCE/SchoolNet2001 Enhancement of Quality Learning Through Information & Communication Technology, No.3 pp.1193-1196, (2001)

[2] Tetsuro SHIMAMURA, Hiroshi Suda, Masahiro Ukigai, & Yoshiro Miida, "Multimedia-Based Teaching Material For Learning Digital Signal Processing", ICCE/ICCAI2000 Multimedia and Hypermedia in Education, No.2, pp.984-987 (2000)

[3] Hiroshi Suda, Masahiro Ukigai, & Yoshiro Miida, "Multimedia-Based Acoustical Engineering Education", Journal of the Educational Application of Information Technologies, Vol.2, No.1, pp.13-18, (1999).

[4] Hiroshi Suda, Masahiro Ukigai, & Yoshiro Miida, "Education of Acoustic science with Multimedia-Presentation Style", Proceedings of the International Conference on Computers in Education (ICCE'99), Kisarazu, Japan, November 4-7, pp.2-211-214, (1999).

[5] Harutoyo Ozawa, Hiroshi Suda, & Yoshiro Miida, "The Education System for Acoustic science with Multimedia", Proceedings of the Electoronics, Information and Systems Conference Electoronics, Information and System Society, I.E.E. of Japan, Narashino, Japan, August 30-31, pp.453-456, (1999).

[6] Shuichi Arai & Yoshiro Miida, "Suuchi Keisan Hou", Morikita-Shuppan,(1991).

NORMIT: a Web-Enabled Tutor for Database Normalization

Antonija Mitrovic

Department of Computer Science, University of Canterbury
Private Bag 4800, Christchurch, New Zealand
tanja@cosc.canterbury.ac.nz

Abstract

The paper describes the design and development of NORMIT, an Intelligent Tutoring Systems (ITS) that teaches database normalization to university students. NORMIT is a Web-enabled system, and we discuss its architecture and techniques used to deal with multiple students. We also discuss Constraint-Based Modeling (CBM), the underlying student and domain modelling approach. NORMIT is the first in the series of constraint-based tutors developed at ICTG that teaches a procedural task, and we comment on the suitability of CBM for such tasks. We also discuss the plans for the evaluation of the system and future work.

1. Introduction

Web-enabled educational systems are becoming the dominant type of systems available to students. Web-based systems offer several advantages in comparison to standalone systems. They minimize the problems of distributing software to users and hardware/software compatibility. New releases of systems are immediately available to everyone. More importantly, students are not constrained to use specific machines in their schools, and can access Web-enabled tutors from any location and at any time. The time/location independence is of enormous value for learning environments, as flexibility and accessibility are extremely important for learning.

The Intelligent Computer Tutoring Group (ICTG) has been involved with developing intelligent tutoring systems for a number of years. We have developed two stand-alone systems: KERMIT [12], an ITS that teaches the conceptual database modelinh using the Entity-Relationship data model, and CAPIT [6], a system that teaches English punctuation and capitalization rules. We have also developed two Web-enabled systems: SQLT-Web, an ITS that teaches the SQL database language [8, 9], and LBITS, a tutor that develops the language skills of elementary school children. All these systems use Constraint-Based Modeling [10] to model the domain

knowledge and the knowledge of their students. The instructional domains covered by these systems differ significantly. CAPIT and LBITS cover domains with a small number of rules. SQL is a declarative database language which students find very difficult to master. KERMIT teaches an open-ended design task, and is based on fuzzy knowledge. Therefore, we decided to develop a system that teaches a procedural task, to see how well our existing methodology for building ITSs will support a different kind of tasks. We also decided to develop a Web-enabled system due to reasons discussed earlier.

The paper is organized as follows. In the next section we discuss the process of database normalization and how it is supported in NORMIT. In Section 3, we present the architecture of the system, focusing on the components necessary for dealing with multiple students. The final section presents our plan for the evaluation of the system, and discusses the future work.

2. Learning database normalization in NORMIT

Database normalization is the process of refining a database schema in order to ensure that all tables in a relational database are of high quality [4]. Normalization is usually taught in introductory database courses in a series of lectures that define all the necessary concepts, and later practised on paper by looking at specific databases and applying the definitions. To the best of our knowledge, there are no ITSs that support student learning database normalization, and NORMIT is novel in that respect.

The student needs to log on to NORMIT first, and the first-time user gets a brief description of the system and database normalization in general. NORMIT is a problem-solving environment, and as such provides only limited information about the task itself. We have envisioned the system as a complement to traditional classroom instruction, so the emphasis is on problem solving, not on providing information. However, the system does provide help about the basic domain concepts, when there is evidence that the student does not understand them, or has problem applying knowledge. The system also insists on using the appropriate domain vocabulary; "talking science" has been shown to increase learning and deep understanding of the domain. After logging in, the student needs to select the problem to work on. NORMIT lists all the pre-defined problems, so that the student may select one that looks interesting. In addition, the student may enter his/her own problem to work on.

The database normalization task is a procedural one: the student should go through a number of steps to analyze the quality of the database schema. We require the student to go through the following steps in NORMIT:

1. *Determine candidate keys*: the student needs to analyze the given table and functional dependencies in order to determine all candidate keys. A candidate key is an attribute or a set of attributes that has two properties: uniqueness (its value is unique within the table) and irreducibility (no attribute can be removed from the

key so that each value of the key is still unique. Figure 1 illustrates this task: the student is currently working on a table consisting of 5 attributes, for which five functional dependencies are given. The student enters the candidate keys one at a time, and may ask the system to evaluate the solution at any time.

2. *Determine the closure of a set of attributes*: if the student is unsure whether a set of attributes makes a candidate key, he/she may compute the closure of that set under the given set of functional dependencies.

3. *Determine the prime attributes* (a prime attribute is an attribute that belongs to any candidate key).

4. *Simplify functional dependencies*: if any of the given functional dependencies has more than one attribute on the right-hand side, the student needs to turn it into as many dependencies as there are attributes on its right-hand side (this step is the application of the decomposition rule).

5. *Determine the normal form* the table is in. During this task, when necessary, the student will also be asked to specify functional dependencies that violate one or more normal forms.

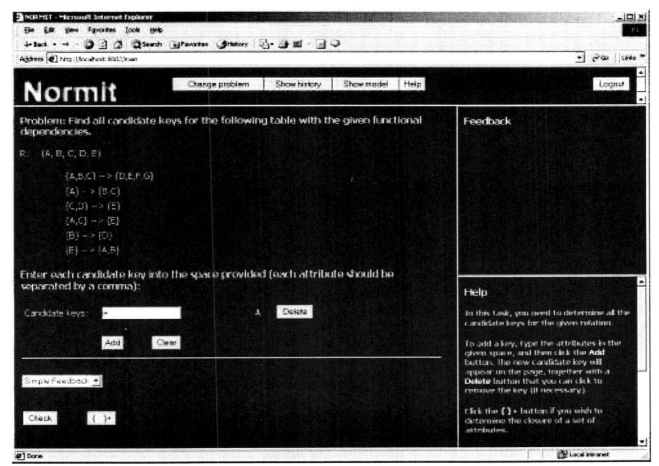

Fig. 1. A screenshot from NORMIT

6. If necessary, *decompose the table* so that all the final tables are in Boyce-Codd normal form.

The sequence of the steps is fixed: the student will only see a Web page corresponding to the current task. However, the student may ask for a new problem at any time during problem solving. In addition to that, he/she may review the history of the current session, or examine a global view of the student model. When the student submits the solution to the current step, the system analyses it and offers feedback. The first submission receives only a general feedback, specifying whether the solution is correct or not. If there are errors in the solution, the incorrect parts of the solution are shown in red. On the second submission, NORMIT provides a general description of the error, specifying what general domain principles have been violated. On the next submission, the system provides a more detailed message, by providing a hint as to how the student should change the solution. The correct solution is only available on student's request.

3. The architecture of NORMIT

Figure 2 illustrates the architecture of NORMIT. As can be seen, NORMIT is based on a centralized architecture, as many other existing Web-enabled ITSs (e.g. ELM-ART [3], AST [11] and SQLT-Web [7]). Centralized tutors perform all tutoring function on the server side, where all student models are also kept. Distributed systems (e.g. ADELE [5], AlgeBrain [2] or Belvedere [13]) also keep the student model on the central server, but some of the tutoring functions are performed on the client.

NORMIT is developed in Allegro Common Lisp (ACL) [1] and uses the AllegroServe Web server, which is an extensible server provided with ACL. At the beginning of interaction, a student is required to enter his/her name, which is necessary in order to establish a session. The session manager requires the student modeller to retrieve the model for the student, if there is one, or to create a new model for a student who interacts

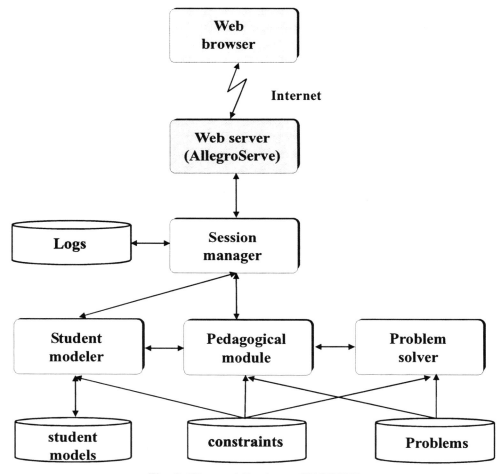

Fig. 2. The architecture of NORMIT

with the system for the first time. A Web-based tutor must be able to associate each request to the appropriate student model. Some Web-enabled systems use cookies or IP numbers to identify the student who made a request. Those two approaches were not suitable in our case. It was not possible to use the IP number, as several students might be using the same machine. We did not want to use cookies for identification purposes because cookies reside on a specific machine and would prevent the student from using the system from different machines. Instead, we identify students by their login name, which is embedded in a hidden tag of HTML forms and sent back to the server. If a student accesses a page by following a link instead of accessing it through a form, then user name is appended to the end of the URL.

It is also necessary to store student-specific data separately from data about other students. All processing is carried out within a single address space, and therefore there must be a uniform mechanism for identifying students and associating requests to corresponding student models. In order to achieve this, we use a hash table that maps the string representing a student name to their student object, which contains all details pertaining to the student.

Each action a student performs in the interface is first sent to the session manager, as it has to link it to the appropriate session and store it in the student's log. Then, the action is sent to the pedagogical module, which decides how to respond to it. If the submitted action is a solution to the current step, the pedagogical module sends it to the student modeller, which diagnoses the solution, updates the student model, and sends the result of the diagnosis back to the pedagogical module. The pedagogical module then generates feedback. If the student has requested a new problem, the pedagogical module consults the student model in order to identify the knowledge elements the student has problems with, and selects one of the predefined problems that feature identified misconceptions.

The domain knowledge is represented as a set of constraints. Constraint-Based Modeling (CBM) is a student modeling approach proposed by Ohlsson [10], as a way of overcoming the intractable nature of student modeling. CBM starts from the observation that all correct solutions to a problem are similar in that they do not violate any of the basic principles of the domain. CBM is not interested in the exact sequence of states in the problem space the student has traversed, but in what state he/she is currently in. As long as the student never reaches a state that is known to be wrong, they are free to perform whatever actions they please. Constraints define equivalence classes of problem states. An equivalence class triggers the same instructional action; hence all states in an equivalence class are pedagogically equivalent. It is therefore possible to attach feedback messages directly to constraints. A violated constraint

signals an error, which translates to incomplete/incorrect knowledge. The domain model is therefore a collection of state descriptions of the form:

"If <relevance condition> is true, then <satisfaction condition> had better also be true, otherwise something has gone wrong."

In other words, if the student solution falls into the state defined by the relevance condition, it must also be in the state defined by the satisfaction condition in order to be correct.

NORMIT currently contains 53 constraints, which are modular and problem-independent; they describe the basic principles of the domain, and do not involve any elements of problems directly. Some constraints check the syntax of the solution, while others check the semantics, by comparing the student's solution to the ideal solution, generated by the problem solver. The semantic constraints check whether the student has specified all the necessary parts of the solution. In order to identify constraints, we studied material in textbooks, such as [4], and also used our own experience in teaching database normalization. Figure 3 shows constraint 5, which specifies one condition the student's solution must satisfy when working on the closure task. The constraints are written in Lisp, and can contain built-in functions as well as specially developed functions. The first two lists of constraint 5 are its relevance and satisfaction condition. The relevance condition is a compound one: it firstly tests whether the current task the student is working is the closure task, and then it checks whether the student has specified the attribute set. Finally, it binds variable *a* to each attribute that appears in this set, thus forming a multiple binding list. The satisfaction part consists of a single test, which is applied to each binding of variable *a* separately. If the attribute appears in the closure, the constraint is satisfied. In the opposite case, the student will be given the appropriate feedback.

There are two feedback messages in the constraint, which are given to the student if his/her solution is incorrect. The first message is shorter, and tells the

```
(5
(and (equalp (current-task sol) 'closure)
     (not (null (attribute-set sol))))
     (bind-all ?a (attribute-set sol) bindings))
(member ?a (closure sol) :test 'equalp)
```
"Each attribute that is an element of the set of attributes we want to compute the closure of must appear in the closure."
"Remember the reflexivity rule? Each attributes determines itself (A -> A).
The general form of the reflexivity rule is:
If X is a superset of Y, or X=Y, then X -> Y"
```
(?a "attribute-set"))
```

Fig. 3. An example constraint

student what needs to be done. If the student still cannot correct the solution after this message, NORMIT will present the second message, which explains the underlying domain principle that has been violated (in this case, it is the reflexivity rule). The final element of the constraint specifies the part of the solution that is incorrect (in this case, that is the attribute to which variable a is bound). This binding is used for highlighting the error.

4.Conclusions and future work

This paper presented the architecture and underlying philosophy of NORMIT, a Web-enabled ITS for teaching database normalization. NORMIT uses Constraint-based modelling to model domain knowledge and the knowledge of its students. However, unlike the previous tutors we developed, NORMIT is the first constraint-based tutor that teaches a procedural task. We have experienced no problems specifying constraints for such a task. The system contains a problem solver, capable of solving normalization problems. The knowledge base contains 53 constraints that check the syntax and semantics of students' solutions, enabling it to analyze all students' submissions. To analyze the semantics of solutions, NORMIT compares the student's solution to the ideal solution produced by the problem solver. The number of constraints is likely to be higher, as we are currently working on the decomposition task.

NORMIT is a Web-enabled system, with a centralized architecture. Student models are kept on the server, and all tutoring functions are also executed on the server. The amount of information that needs to be transferred from the browser to the server is not large, and we believe that such architecture is appropriate. NORMIT is developed in AllegroServe, an extensible Web server that allows the components of the system to be developed in Lisp. A special component of the system called the session manager ensures that a student's actions are associated with her/his student model, thus enabling the system to be used by multiple students simultaneously.

We plan to evaluate NORMIT in a real classroom in September 2002 at the University of Canterbury. The system will be used in an introductory database course, which has more than 170 enrolled students. We plan to compare the students' performance on a pre-test to their performance on a post-test, after using NORMIT. Information about all sessions will be recorded in logs, and we will analyze how students learn constraints, and also evaluate other types of support the system offers, such as the open student model and support for self-explanation.

Acknowledgements

The work presented here was supported by the Computer Science Department, University of Canterbury. We thank Li Chen for developing the interface.

References

1. Allegro Common Lisp, Franz Inc, 1998.
2. S. Alpert, M. Singley, P. Fairweather, Deploying Intelligent Tutors on the Web: an Architecture and an Example. *Int. J. Artificial Intelligence in Education*, 10, 1999, 183-197.
3. P. Brusilovsky, E. Schwarz, G. Weber, ELM-ART: an Intelligent Tutoring System on Wolrd Wide Web. In C. Frasson, G. Gauthier, A. Lesgold (eds), *Proc. 3rd Int. Conf. On Intelligent Tutoring Systems (ITS'96)*, Springer, LCNS 1086, 1996, 261-269.
4. R. Elmasri, S.B. Navathe, *Fundamentals of database systems*. Benjamin/Cummings, Redwood, 1994.
5. W.L. Johnson, E. Shaw, R. Ganeshan, Pedagogical Agents on the Web. Proc. ITS'98 Workshop on Intelligent Educational Systems on the Web, 1998.
6. M. Mayo, A. Mitrovic, Optimising ITS Behaviour with Bayesian Networks and Decision Theory'. *International Journal on Artificial Intelligence in Education*, 12(2), 2001, 124-153.
7. A. Mitrovic, K. Hausler, Porting SQL-Tutor to the Web. Proc. ITS'2000 workshop on *Adaptive and Intelligent Web-based Education Systems*, 2000, 37-44.
8. A. Mitrovic, B. Martin, M. Mayo, Using Evaluation to Shape ITS Design: Results and Experiences with SQL-Tutor. *User Modeling and User-Adapted Interaction*, 12(2-3), 2002, 243-279.
9. A. Mitrovic, S. Ohlsson, Evaluation of a constraint-based tutor for a database language, *Int. J. Artificial Intelligence in Education*, 10(3-4), 1999, 238-256.
10. S. Ohlsson, Constraint-based Student Modeling. In *Student Modeling: the Key to Individualized Knowledge--based Instruction*. Berlin: Springer-Verlag, 1994, 167-189.
11. M. Specht, G. Weber, S. Heitmeyer, V. Schoch, AST: Adaptive WWW-Courseware for Statistics. *Proc. Workshop on Adaptive Systems and User Modeling on the World Wide Web, UM-97*, 1997, 91-96.
12. P. Suraweera, A, Mitrovic, Designing an Intelligent Tutoring System for Database Modelling. In: M.J. Smith, G. Salvendy (eds) *Proc. 9th Int. Conf Human-Computer Interaction International (HCII 2001)*, New Orleans, vol. 2, 2001, 745-749.
13. D. Suthers, D. Jones, An Architecture for Intelligent Collaborative Educational Systems In: B. de Boulay, R. Mizoguchi (eds) *Artificial Intelligence in Education: Knowledge and Media in Learning Systems*. IOS, Amsterdam, 1997, 55-62.

An e-Learning Library on the Web

Shinobu Hasegawa
Center for Information Science, JAIST
1-1, Asahidai, Tatsunokuchi, Ishikawa 923-1292, Japan
hasegawa@jaist.ac.jp

Akihiro Kashihara, Jun'ichi Toyoca
I.S.I.R., Osaka University 8-1,
Mihogaoka, Ibaraki, Osaka, 567-0047, Japan
{kasihara,toyoda}@ai.sanken.osaka-u.ac.jp

Abstract

The main topic addressed in this paper is how to help learners select some instructive hypermedia-based learning resources according to their learning contexts from the Web. Our approach is to provide a digital library for web-based learning called e-Learning Library, which includes learning resource repository, local indexing, and adaptive navigation support. This aims to promote their learning with diverse learning resources involving a certain topic.

1. Introduction

Learning with existing web-based resources has become popular and important. Especially, there are diverse learning resources with the same learning topic, which are designed by different authors [6]. Properly using these web-based resources, learners can learn the topic from diverse points of view. However, most resources do not usually have clear description such as what kind of learners should use, what kind of learning goal can be achieved and so forth. This makes it difficult for learners to select web-based resources suitable for their learning contexts.

Our approach to this issue is to provide a digital library for web-based learning called e-Learning Library in order to promote learning a certain topic from diverse points of view. In the following sections, we propose three key ideas towards realization of the e-Learning Library.

2. e-Learning Library

2.1 Learning with Existing Resources on the Web

In this paper, a learning resource means hyperdocuments, which describe a learning topic within a web site. It provides learners with hyperspace that consists of a number of web pages and their links. Learners can explore the hyperspace to learn domain concepts/knowledge [2]. On the Web, in addition, there are a number of learning resources with the same topic, which could facilitate diverse learning phases such as augmenting or applying domain concepts/knowledge. Properly using these learning resources according to learning contexts, learners can learn the topic from diverse points of view. This paper especially describes a web-based learning that makes use of diverse learning resources embedding a certain topic to promote learning.

Following Bloom's taxonomy, we classify the learning phases into accretion, understanding, and stabilization [1]. We view web-based learning as learning a topic in three phases and as the transition among the phases. The transition among three learning phases is expected to occur according to completion or impasse of learning in a phase. Learners can start learning from any learning phase according to their knowledge states, and are expected to finally stabilize their knowledge.

2.2 Framework

In learning a topic, learners would select a learning resource according to their knowledge states. When learners use search engines or collections of learning resources with a keyword representing the topic, they may get too many resources as search results and such results information do not usually have clear description about which learning phase could be facilitated. Therefore, these make it difficult for learners to select instructive resources according to their learning contexts. One way to resolve these problems is to provide a digital library so that learners can select more proper learning resources.

The digital library is a digitized collection of material that one might find in a traditional library. There currently exist many digital libraries, which collect, store, and organize a large number of multimedia resources on the Web. These libraries are mostly focused on the tools for indexing, retrieval and visualization [3]. In order to construct a digital library for web-based learning discussed in above, especially, indexing and retrieval in the digital library are very important. So, we propose an e-Learning Library, which consists of learning resource repository, local indexing, and adaptive navigation support as shown in Figure 1.

3. Learning Resource Repository

Learning resource repository is a collection and storage module of a great number of web-based learning resources reorganized by indexes called resource indexes representing their characteristics.

3.1 Resource Index

There exist many web sites gathering URLs of web-based learning resources. These sites use resource indexes, which mainly represent learning topics/subjects to classify the learning resources. These indexes allow learners to select learning resources from a "what to learn" point of view. However, such indexes are not enough in selecting learning resources since the learners would

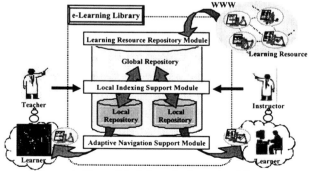

Figure 1. Three Modules of e-Learning Library

usually think of not only "what to learn" but also "how to learn" especially in which learning phase they can learn.

We have consequently provided resource indexes that consist of How To Learn (HTL) indexes in addition to conventional What To Learn (WTL) indexes, and have proposed a way to reorganize learning resources. In helping learners select learning resources proper for the transition between learning phases, learning phases is first most important as HTL indexes. In helping learners continue learning in a phase, second, some HTL indexes are necessary for differentiating some learning resources that could facilitate the phase. Considering web-based learning resources with the same topic, media types (such as text, diagram, chart, illustration, etc.) and communication channels (such as simulation, chat, BBS, etc.) would have an influence on how to learn (See [4] for more detail).

3.2 Global and Local Repositories

An important issue towards the reorganization is how to apply WTL and HTL indexes to web-based learning resources. The resources should be generally indexed with indexes given by the authorities concerned, which indexes public learners can share. However, we have difficulty in following this idea. Although WTL indexes, media type, and communication channel indexes can be shared, it is quite difficult to share learning phase indexes since learning phase specified by a web-based learning resource depends on which knowledge level the learners have.

Following the above discussion, we have proposed a framework for developing the learning resource repository. We have first implemented a global repository whose resources are classified with WTL indexes, media type, and communication channel indexes. The learning resources have been gathered from registrations of learning resource designers and from some resource collection sites on the Web. In our framework, teachers/instructors next take their learners into account to apply learning phase indexes to the global repository, reorganizing a local repository. The way of such indexing is discussed in the next section.

4. Local Indexing

In order to apply learning phase indexes to the local repository, we propose a practical approach that individual teachers/ instructors assess the learning phase indexes from their points of view. We call this approach local indexing. In the local indexing, each teacher/instructor can index learning resources on the assumption that his/her learners use them. Different teachers/instructor may accordingly index a learning resource with different indexes. The local repository built from the global repository with the learning phase indexes helps the learners select more instructive learning resources according to their learning contexts.

In indexing learning resources, teachers/instructors may have difficulty in assessing the learning phase indexes since the indexing often requires careful reading of the contents of learning resources and since there exist a great number of learning resources. This paper accordingly proposes a support module for the local indexing, which allows teachers to assess learning phase indexes in a simple and consistent way.

How to compose learning resources would generally depend on a learning phase assumed by designers of the learning resources. This suggests that the learning phase indexes can be assessed from

the structure/function of learning resources. In order to make this indexing possible, we make clear the correspondence between the structure/function and the learning phase. The items of structure/ function are presented to teachers/instructors in the form of checklist, by which they can assess the learning phase in a simple and consistent way (See [4] for more detail).

5. Adaptive Navigation Support

Although the resource indexes allow learners to search learning resources they want to learn, it is still difficult for them to select a learning resource in accordance with their learning contexts to promote learning from knowledge accretion to knowledge stabilization. We have accordingly proposed a navigation support, which recommends learning resources to be learned next according to learners' knowledge states and needs.

The main aim of this support is to promote learning of a specific topic with diverse learning resources so that learners' knowledge can be stabilized. For this aim, in particular, the support attempts to facilitate the transition among learning phases and to change media types and communication channels for promoting learning in one phase.

In navigation support, we consider two knowledge states: impasses and completion of learning a resource. Learners are asked which knowledge states they reach after learning the resource. If necessary, they can also demand change of media types and communication channels for a learning resource to be learned next as their needs.

The learning resource recommendation uses learners' knowledge states and needs given by them to make a list of learning resources to be learned next. The learning resources are put in the order of priority. The aim of the recommendation is not to give the learners the most instructive resource from the repository. The list provides them with a guide in selecting a learning resource next (See [5] for more detail).

6. Conclusion

In this paper, we have described e-Learning Library with learning resource repository, local indexing, and adaptive navigation support, which makes use of diverse learning resources involving a certain topic to promote web-based learning.

In the future, it is necessary to evaluate the e-Learning Library. We would also like to develop a more practical system and make it public as web-based learning portal site.

References

[1] Bloom, B.S. (1956). Taxonomy of Educational Objectives, David Mckay Company.

[2] Conklin, J. (1988). Hypertext: An Introduction and Survey, Computer 20, 9, 17-41.

[3] Goh, D. & Leggett, J. (2000) Patron-augmented digital libraries, Proc. of the fifth ACM conference on digital libraries 2000, 153-163.

[4] Hasegawa, S., Kashihara, A., & Toyoda, J. (2000). An Adaptive Navigation Support with Reorganized Learning Resources for Web-based Learning, Proc. of ICCE 2000, pp.917-925.

[5] Hasegawa, S., Kashihara, A., & Toyoda, J. (2001). A Local Indexing for Web-based Learning Resources, Proc. of ED-MEDIA2001, pp.687-692.

[6] Kashihara, A., & Toyoda, J. (1998). Report on Experiences of Telelearning in Japan, Informatik Forum, Wien, Vol.12, No.1, 39-44.

Association Rule-Based Immediately Dynamic Demand Matching Search System

Chen-Li Hsu   Yuan-Chen Liu
NATIONAL TAIPEI TEACHERS COLLEGE
Email: liu@tea.ntptc.edu.tw

Abstract

With the explosive growth of the World Wide Web, it is difficult for a user to locate information that is relevant to his need. One of the services on the Internet usually used is search engine. Through search engines, we can get information quickly. Furthermore, search engine is also a learning tool, students use Internet as a primary source to look for more information. In WWW world, too much information is a problem; therefore, searching information on web became a time-consuming task.

1.Introduction

According to Hsiao-tieh Pu (2000), a research in Taiwan about search term logs analysis, some preliminary results including characteristics of on-line users and their searching needs, The findings obviously show that "the search terms used frequently are only few ones". Among 23 ten thousands search terms records, there are only 4.33% search terms which are searched over 20 times, and is equal to the 74.89% of total records. For this reason, we use the association rules in data mining, try to improve the ranking of the search result documents in real time according to the records with the same query goal left by the on-line users.

2. Association rule

An association rule is a rule, which implies certain association relationships among a set of objects in a database. Among a set of transactions, each is a set of items, an association rule express the X-Y related degree. An example of association rule is: 30% of transactions that contain beer also contain diapers; 2% of all transactions contain both of these items. Here 30% is called the confidence level of the rule, and 2% is the support level of the rule. The problem is to find all association rules that satisfy user-demand minimum support level and minimum confidence level.

3. Search system

Step1:

Users put a check into the checkbox in front of each document, and we keep records in our database, as Fig.1.

Fig.1 according to user's demand recommend

Step2:

Analysis what in database:

$$\begin{cases} USER_i : the\ ith\ user, 1 \le i \le u; d_j : the\ jth\ documents \\ d_j \in D = \{d_1, d_2, \ldots\ldots d_k\} \\ c_i : the\ document\ set\ chosed\ by\ the\ ith\ user \\ \therefore c_i = \{d_m, d_n \ldots\}\ , d_m, d_n \in D \end{cases}$$

Step3:

Calculate the support level of each item.

$$Support.d_j = \frac{\sum_{i=1}^{u} d_j^i}{u}; \quad i? \ j \in N;$$

$$d_j^i = \begin{cases} 1; & when \quad d_j \in c_i \\ 0; & otherwise \end{cases}$$

Step4:

Calculate the association confidence level (Conf. d_{mn}) of every two documents, conform to the conditional probability:

$Sup.(d_m \cap d_n)$ express the percentage that someone chose d_m and d_n at the same time.

$$Conf.d_{mn} = P\langle d_n | d_m \rangle$$
$$= \frac{P(d_m \cap d_n)}{P(d_m)} = \frac{Sup.(d_m \cap d_n)}{Sup(d_m)}, m \ne n$$

*This work system supported by National Status Council based on Grant NSC90-2521-S-152-001

we care about that.

What follows is our method:

$$Sup.(d_m \cap d_n) = \frac{\sum_{i=1}^{u}(d_m^i \cap d_n^i)}{u};$$

$$m\,?\,n\,?\,u \in N$$

$$(d_m^i \cap d_n^i) = \begin{cases} 1 \; ; \quad when \quad d_m \in c_i \\ \qquad and \quad d_n \in c_i \\ 0 \; ; \quad otherwise \end{cases}$$

Otherwise, we give three different weights in three different conditions:

Condition1:

If user chose d_m and d_n at the same time, we give the weight a = 1

Condition2:

If user neither chose dm nor d_n, we give the weight ß=o.25

Condition3:

If user chose d_m but exclude d_n, we give the weight ?=-o.5

After reforming, the $Conf.d_{mn}$ we change like this:

$$Conf.d_{mn} = \alpha \times Sup.(d_m \cap d_n) + \beta \times Sup.(d_m' \cap d_n')$$
$$+ \gamma \times Sup.(d_m' \cap d_n) + \gamma \times Sup.(d_m \cap d_n')$$

What follows are our user interface system expressed in Chinese:

Fig.2 When user changes his searching path motives, our recommendation will change.

4.Evaluation

According to our experiments, we invite 51 users to test two terms in our system. At the same time, we evaluation four different methods such as Fig.3 and Fig.4. show.

Finally, we find our system show better than any three ones has a lot of advantages, and two of the most important as what follows:

1. It can help few persons that have special searching motives more quickly and convenient to look for what he want, as Fig.3.

2. And the users that have generality and great majority motives in his searching, he also receive more help via the recommendation of the users on-line, as Fig.4.

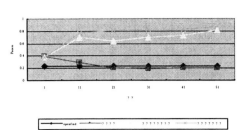

Fig.3. The efficiency evaluation of minority has special searching motives

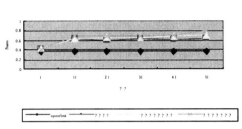

Fig.4. The efficiency evaluation of majority searching

5. Conclusion

In our system, after computing by association rules, when new users with the same goal, we give them searching path recommend, in this way, we can surmount frustrations that students face in searching information, then increase their searching efficiency . On the circle, we improve the documents ranking, it's different from the algorithm only calculating the appropriate of retrieving documents. In the future, we will devote ourselves to automatically detect users' favorite instead of putting a check into the checkbox, so do reduce the quantity of transactions in database.

Reference

[1] Hsiao-tieh Pu(2000), "Exploring Searching Behavior of Network Users in Taiwan", University library, VOL.4,NO.2,23-37, .

[2] Chakrabarti , S. et al.(1999).. "Mining the Web's Link Structure".IEEE Computer.60-67

[3] B.Yuwono & D.Lun Lee(1996). "Wise: A World Wide Web Resource Database System".IEEE Transactions and Data Engineering,VOL. 8,NO. 4, 548-554,

[4] B.Yuwono, S.L.Y.Lam , J.H.Ying &D.L.Lee, "A World Wide Web Resource Discovery System."http://www.w3.org/Conferences/WWW4/Papers/66/.

A Java Based On-line Handwriting Interface
for an Intelligent Algebraic Calculation Tutoring System

Yasuhisa Okazaki*   Xiang Yang Feng*   Masayoshi Okamoto**   Hiroki Kondo*
okaz@ai.is.saga-u.ac.jp   feng@ai.is.saga-u.ac.jp   OKAM038817@dt.sanyo.co.jp   kondo_h@ai.is.saga-u.ac.jp

  *   Saga University   1 Honjo-machi, Saga-shi, 840-8502, Japan
 **   SANYO Electric Co., Ltd.   1-1 Sanyo-cho, Daito City, Osaka 574-8534, Japan

Abstract

This paper describes our on-line handwriting mathematical expression input interface for our Intelligent Algebraic Calculation Tutoring System (ACTS). It consists of a Java-based client, which receives user's handwriting input and displays output, and a C-based server, which recognizes hand-written symbols. Our interface provides simple and easy mathematical expression input environment. Its distinctive features are automatic stroke segmentation based on spatial relationship and time intervals of consecutive strokes, symbol recognition based on DDCPM (Directional and Direction-Change Pattern Matching) method and function buttons that help user's input and correction. Our experiment results show that the recognition rate is 79 % for 91 kinds of symbols and 90 % for 34 kinds of restricted ones for our target domain.

Keywords: Handwriting, On-line, Mathematical Expression, Interface, Intelligent Tutoring System, Java, WWW

1. Introduction

We have been studying a WWW based ITS (Intelligent Tutoring System). We have already developed a system whose input devices are a keyboard and/or a mouse [1]. Although its input is simple and easy, it is difficult for a user (learner) to input his/her own solving process. So we have started to study a handwriting interface with an electronic pen and liquid crystal tablet. Whole architecture of the new system with handwriting input facility is described in [2]. In this paper, we focus on our on-line handwriting mathematical expression input. Our pen-based interface enables a user (leaner) to input mathematical expressions into the tutoring system easily just as he/she writes on papers as he/she does in school.

2. Handwriting interface

Our interface is designed as a notebook for solving

algebraic expression. Figure 1 shows a snap shot of the handwriting interface. The display has following five fields: (1) message field, (2) problem field, (3) answering field, (4) function button field, and (5) candidate list field. Function button field provides 14 kinds of function buttons, such as one character clear, one line clear, all clear, line insert, line delete, etc.

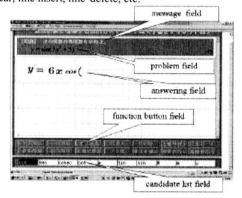

Figure 1: Java based handwriting interface

Candidate list provides 10 recognition candidates as buttons. If the recognition result is wrong, a user (learner) can easily replace the candidate by touching the corresponding button by pen. It enables a user (learner) to write algebraic expressions naturally by using an electronic pen on the WWW client. The Java-based interface runs on WWW client (browser), while C-based symbol recognition module works on the WWW server. A user (learner) can write symbols continuously. The client gets stroke data and segment symbols automatically based on spatial relationships and time interval between two sequential strokes. Grouped strokes are transmitted to the recognition engine in the server. The recognition result is displayed at the same position with a system font.

3. Recognition server

The recognition server consists of recognition engine and

dictionary. Our engine adopts DDCPM (Directional and Direction-Change Pattern Matching) method for hand-written symbols' recognition. This method uses not only directional features of strokes but also directional change features for recognition. The engine calculates resemblance between inputted symbol's feature pattern and standard symbols' feature patterns in the dictionary [3]. The symbol whose resemblance is highest is obtained as the recognition result and top 10 rank candidates are returned to the client.

4. Symbol Recognition Evaluation

Comfortable interface demands high recognition rate and easy error correction. We had evaluated our recognition performance. We have collected 19 sets of on-line handwriting stroke data for 91 kinds of symbols. Eighteen collected data sets were used for dictionaries, and one was used for a recognition test.

Table 1 shows the recognition results. The upper table shows that the recognition rate is 79 % for 91 kinds of symbols and 90 % for 34 kinds of restricted ones for our target domain. The lower table shows the cumulative probability that the correct symbol is included in the candidate list. In almost all (98 %) case, the correct result is included in the top 10 rank candidates for 91 kinds of symbols and it is always included in the top 5 rank candidates for 34 kinds of symbols. The recognition rate of "restricted" was improved significantly, because confusion of resembled symbols decreased. We are going to solve a resembled symbol problem by using contractual information.

5. Conclusion and future works

In this paper, we have presented our on-line handwriting mathematical expression input interface for our WWW based ITS (ACTS). It provides a natural learning environment for solving algebraic expression.

Automatic stroke segmentation of consecutive strokes, efficient handwriting character recognition based on DDCPM method and function buttons that help user's input and correction, contribute to

6th location	95.63 %	100.00 %
7th location	96.03 %	100.00 %
8th location	97.22 %	100.00 %
9th location	98.02 %	100.00 %
10th location	98.02 %	100.00 %

implement a comfortable handwriting interface. We have also evaluated our symbol recognition performance.

The current implementation provides basic functions. We have room to improve symbol recognition in accuracy and speed to complete our interface. After that, we are going to integrate the interface and other systems independently under construction into ACTS.

Acknowledgement

The research reported in this paper was partially supported by the Ministry of Education, Science, Sports and Culture, Grant-in-Aid for Encouragement of Young Scientists, No. 13780123, 2002.

References

[1] Y.Okazaki, K.Watanabe and H.Kondo: "An ITS (Intelligent Tutoring System) on the WWW (World-Wide Web)", Systems and Computers in Japan, Vol.28, No.9, pp.11-16(1997.8).

[2] Y.Okazaki, T.Imafuku and H. Kondo: "Recognition of Handwritten Mathematical Expressions in an ITS for Algebraic Calculations", ADVANCED RESEARCH IN COMPUTERS AND COMMUNICATIONS IN EDUCATION (Proc. of ICCE99), Vol.1, pp.824-827 (1999.11).

[3] M. Okamoto, K. Yamamoto: "On-line Handwriting Character Recognition Method with Directional Features and Direction-Change Features", Proc. of 4th ICDAR, Vol.2, pp.926-930 (1997.8).

Table 1: Recognition results

	All 91 symbols	Restricted 34 symbols
Well recognized	78.57 %	90.00 %
Confused	21.43 %	10.00 %
Rejected	0.00 %	0.00 %

Accumulated recognition rate	All 91 symbols	Restricted 34 symbols
1st location	78.57 %	90.00 %
2nd location	88.10 %	95.55 %
3rd location	92.86 %	97.78 %
4th location	93.65 %	98.89 %
5th location	94.44 %	100.00 %

A Lifelong Learning Support System on Multimedia Networks

Minoru Okada*   Takahiko Mendori**   Akihiro Shimizu***

Kochi University of Technology
Tosayamada-tyou, Miyanoguchi 185, Kochi, 782-8502 Japan
*okada@kcc-kochi.co.jp, **mendori.takahiko@kochi-tech.ac.jp, ***shimizu.akihiro@kochi-tech.ac.jp

1   Introduction

In Japan, there has been a rise in demand for lifelong learning due to an increase in national income, average life expectancy and leisure time. On the Internet, research and development in remote educational systems is prospering which can satisfy the characteristics of the learner's demands.

In the remote educational system, when there are few participants to a certain study, the creation cost of the teaching-material contents becomes high-priced. For this reason, it is difficult to enrich teaching-material contents in all fields of the remote educational system for lifelong learning with a wide range of study fields. On the other hand, the Internet offers many Web pages which can be studied. But the information on the Internet is expanding rapidly, and it is becoming increasingly difficult for us to select required material from this vast information network[1].

We have used the "Kochi-ken multimedia model deployment project" [2] and are building the model which circulates teaching-material contents efficiently. The Kochi-ken multimedia model deployment project has the following four technical elements: (1)A multimedia teaching-materials transmission system [3],[4] (2) An asymmetric communication network system using satellite communication [5] (3) A personalized information navigator[6] (4) An image collaboration system[7]

The multimedia teaching-materials transmission system commissioned the local volunteer creation of the teaching-material contents which used the Web template and realized curtailment of cost. However, the system has few fields of the teaching-material contents which can actually be offered. The number of contents for every field is also restricted. On the other hand, the index is not shown clearly, lifelong learning is difficult for a person with no opportunity to study.

Based on these problems, we created a personalized information navigator using Web teaching materials by way of trial.

2   The new prototype of a personalized information navigator

A personalized information navigator of Kochi Prefecture handles the contents distributed in a satellite. In the new prototype system we created the Web teaching materials on the Internet are used in order to aim at shortage of teaching-material contents and expansion of a field. With the information filtering technology using the contents profile of the Web teaching materials and a learner's individual profile, the Web teaching materials suitable for learners are offered. we propose a three-step filtering system using three filters, in order to offer the Web teaching materials suitable for the individual learner.

This comprises of:(1)a registration filter, (2)an individual filter, and (3)a basic filter in a three-step filtering system. A registration filter is a filter which checks whether the URL is the justification and the detrimental website of the URL, and performs decision of the registration, in case a learner registers the URL of Web teaching materials. An individual filter is a filter which extracts the Web teaching materials suitable for a learner. A basic filter is a filter which extracts the whole student's study tendency. In this study, "the rate of learner action"[9] of data social-life-survey is used as a study tendency of lifelong learning.

This system consists of a Server Client. The function of a prototype system has Registration of the URL, Offering URL, and Feedback processing. Registration of the URL is a function which checks the justification and the detrimental website of the URL by the registration filter. Offering URL is a function which presents learners with the results processed by the three-step filtering system. The number of the URL offered to learners is 10 in consideration of learning time. Feedback processing is a function to improve the precision of the basic filter and the individual filter. Importance is added to a basic filter as conformity evaluation to a learner's URL at a category and URL.

In weighting a category, the user of this system carries out the category chosen when creating an individual profile. For example, when a user in their 20's chooses English, the process adds one to the 20's category of "English", and performs weighting to the 20's category of the higher rank category. In weighting to the URL, to the URL which the student judged to conform, positive weighting is performed, and when incongruent, negative weighting is performed conversely.

Feedback processing leaves the individual filter the history of a conformity judging of the learner to each URL. The history is used in order to extract the feature of the Web teaching materials which are processed by the individual filter and then matched to the learner. The individual filter uses the TF·IDF (Term Frequency·Inverse Document Frequency) method as the extraction technique[8].

3 Evaluation of the prototype system

We experimented in evaluations of the prototype system in order to investigate whether the Web teaching materials based on the study tendency of a certain generation were satisfactory for the other learners of the same generation. For this we used 5 subjects from the 10's category and 27 subjects from the 20's category.

For the evaluation methods, we compared the prototype system with the retrieval by keyword of "Yahoo Japan". The number of the URL of this system and Yahoo to evaluate is 10. If a subject is satisfied for the URL, 1 point is added to the URL. 0.5 points are added if a subject is partly satisfied for the URL. If a subject is not satisfied for the URL, no points are added. The maximum sum total value of the degree of conformity to Web teaching materials is 10 points. Evaluation items consist of two items of [English] and [Foreign language] with the highest study trend being seen in the 20's category. The number of the URL of [Foreign language] detected by Yahoo is 397, the number of [English] is 1283. The number of [Foreign language] registered at this system is 94, the number of [English] is 83.

3.1 The result of evaluation experiments and consideration

(1)Comparison between the prototype system and Yahoo Japan

The evaluation experiment by comparison of this system and Yahoo was conducted on 3 subjects from the 20's category about the degree of conformity of [Foreign language] and [English]. Consequently, the system with the best results can be seen in Table 1.

Table1:Comparison of suitability for conformity(20's:3 subjects)

	Prototype system		Yahoo Japan	
	Foreign language	English	Foreign language	English
User-A	4.5	5.0	0.5	3.5
User-B	6.0	7.5	1.0	4.0
User-C	5.5	4.5	1.0	2.5
Average value	5.3	5.6	0.8	3.3

(2)First Feedback processing to the basic filter

Based on the experiment results of Table 1, Feedback processing performed weighting to the URLs of [English] of which three subjects were judged to be conforming. Then the display order was re-arranged, and this system exposed the same URLs to the same subjects again. Consequently, the average value of [English] was low at 4.7.

(3)Feedback processing to the individual filter

To the URLs of [English] judged to be conforming from the results of (2), the TF·IDF method was used, and the results which performed filtering processing are shown in Table 2.

The URL containing the keywords extracted by the TF·IDF method did not exist in the other URLs. Therefore,

Table2:The feedback processing using the TF·IDF method

	User-A	User-B	User-C
The total number of words	7	5	4
High value	6.7	6.7	6.7
Indexes of the URL	working people, vocabulary	working people	working people
The number of the URLs offered	2	1	1
The suitability URLs	2	1	1

this feedback processing could only offer a few URLs. However, the URLs offered were matched with all subjects.

(4)Second Feedback processing to the basic filter

Based on the experiment results of Table 1, positive weighting was performed on the URLs judged to be conforming, and negative weighting was performed on the URLs judged to be incongruent. They were then subjected to the new participants(20's:24,10's:5). Consequently, the average value of the degree of conformity of [English] from the 20's category showed 5.5. Moreover, in the items of a conformity judging, the incongruent rate of Table 1 is decreasing at the rate of 24% to 31% at this time. On the other hand, the average value of [English] from the 10's category showed 4.5. Thus, we can suggest the validity of this system which presents the Web teaching materials suitable for a certain generation.

4 Conclusion

In this paper, in order to solve the problems of a lifelong learning support system, we collected the URLs of Web teaching materials , and proposed a three-step filtering system and feedback processing system as the technique of extracting URLs suitable for the individual from collected URLs. Furthermore, we developed a prototype system and conducted an evaluation experiment. Consequently, as compared with the prototype system and the similar search engine, suitability for conformity was high, and it was shown that URLs which were further suitable for the individual can be offered by feedback processing. From this, we can conclude that the developed prototype system was able to show that the problems and subjects of a lifelong learning support system were solvable.

References

[1] Masahiro Morita,Haruo Hayami,"Information Filtering System for Information Flood", IPSJ,Vol.37,No.8,pp751-757,1996
[2] Kochi-ken multimedia model deployment project,URL   http://sugar.tao.tosa.net-kochi.gr.jp/
[3] A multimedia teaching material transmission system,URL   http://sugar.tao.tosa.net-kochi.gr.jp/
[4] Hiroo Skai,"The web contents excavation and e-Learning tool from an area",JSEI,Vol.17,pp248-251, 2001.11
[5] Hideo Yamazaki,Hideyuki Shimaoka,Minoru Okada,Akihiro Shimizu, "An evaluation of asymmetric communication network using satellite communication", IPSJ,Vol3,no.2N-6,pp607-608,2001.9
[6] Minoru Okada,Hideo Yamazaki,Hideyuki Shimaoka,Junichiro Tanabe,Akihiro Shimizu,"URL filtering for Personalized information navigation",IPSJ,Vol3,4V-6,pp59-pp60,2001.9
[7] Yoko Uyama,"Group study exchange of joint study using the multi-point simultaneous TV meeting" ,JSEI,Vol.17,pp170-173,2001.11
[8] Minoru Okada, Hideo Yamazaki, Takahiko Mendori, Akihiro Shimizu,"A lifelong learning support system on multimedia networks",TECHNICAL REPORT OF IEICE.ET2001-89,Vol.101,No.609,pp45-52,2002.1
[9] URL:http://WWW.stat.go.jp/index.htm

Evaluation of Japanese-English CALL Tool Supporting Contextual Language Acquisitions

Alexandr Pershin*, Satoru Fujitani**, Kanji Akahori*

*Department of Human System Science, Graduate School of Decision Science and Technology, Tokyo Institute of Technology, 2-12-1, O-okayama, Meguro, Tokyo 152-8552 Japan.
**Mejiro University College, 4-31-1, Naka-ochiai, Shinjuku, Tokyo 161-8539 Japan.
sasha@ak.cradle.titech.ac.jp, fujitani@mejiro.ac.jp, akahori@ak.cradle.titech.ac.jp

Abstract

This paper describes and evaluates the Computer Assisted Language Learning (CALL) Tool, which supports contextual language acquisitions. The CALL Tool searches for and retrieves parallel texts, while aligning unedited Japanese-English parallel texts from the World Wide Web [Pershin, Akahori, 2001]. We compared the proposed tool with an existing system by conducting an experiment that showed our system's effectiveness in phrase acquisition, discourse-structure acquisition and text comprehension. However, this experiment also exposed the drawbacks of the proposed system, such as a poor interface design. We concluded that the proposed system could be used together with existing systems to increase the number of learning strategies available for language learners.

1. Introduction

Everyone of us has acquired language through context, because this way of acquiring language is natural and basic to native language acquisition. We often use the same strategy, also known as Contextual Deduction, in second language acquisition. Researches [1],[5] show that a large percentage of the words acquired by foreign language learners have been incidentally acquired by the Contextual Deduction strategy.

We are proposing here a new tool that automatically aligns and creates first language (L1) hints (glosses) from the dynamically changing Internet content, and that supports contextual acquisition in foreign language (L2) learning.

2. Theory

At present there is no adequate theory clearly explaining contextual language acquisition, but researchers common assert that the learner can apply, among others, the following strategies [9]:

1. Investigate the context and guess at the unknown word or idiomatic expression
2. Refer to a word list or dictionary
3. Skip the unknown word or idiomatic expression

. Laufer and Hill [6] showed that combined L1 and L2 look-up supported Contextual Deduction and improved retention.

Systems that support Contextual Deduction by using dictionary [8] or online dictionaries and human informants [11] have been already applied.

In contrast, we present a system that does not use any dictionary for its L1 glossing. Instead it uses on-line resources to automatically generate authentic L1 paragraph-level hints and expose them to the learner.

However, we are not exactly certain which kind of gloss gives the learner better support for language acquisition. In attempt to answer this question, we decided on an experiment that compares an existing system to our tool, then discussed the results.

3. System

The flow of the Tool is as follows:

Our Tool (hereafter referred as B system) (Fig.1) searches for both a predefined Japanese site (Referred one) and an English site with similar content (Research one), clusters these by date and topic, then translates Japanese articles to English. It then aligns the documents on the paragraph level and stores it to the Translation Memory.

When the learner surfs the web page, where the URL is in the Translation Memory, an agent instantly displays its translation to the learner (Fig 2).
For more detailed information about the system see [7].

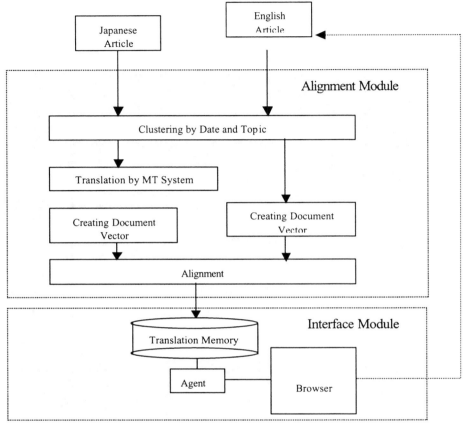

Fig.1.Structure of the system

We summarized the main features of the existing system, Roboword (hereafter referred as R system) and our B system in the following table

special domains

Table 1. Main features of the existing systems and our system

Existing Systems	Our System
Exposure to word translation	Exposure to paragraph level authentic text translation
Can be applied to every site	Application ability is restricted
Has a static vocabulary which can be detrimental in time-sensitive or	Has a dynamic vocabulary

We would also like to emphasize the role of language instructors in selecting the learning content.
They should choose a Referred Site that is:
- Interesting for their learners [2]
- Adjusted to the learner's language levels

4. Experiment

Our hypothesis was that the exposure of the authentic L1 hints will facilitate contextual language acquisition and improve the Contextual Deduction strategy.
We chose the subjects who satisfied the following requirements:
- Possess a large enough vocabulary to effectively use contextual deduction strategy, [4]
- Have high motivation

Our subjects were 10 English-language learners (4 females and 6 males) with intermediate or high English proficiency levels and intermediate Computer skills. Their average age was 29 years.

All subjects had great interest in learning the present content.

The Researched and Referred Sites were the sites of the famous usability guru, Jacob Niels en: www.useit.com and its Japanese translation at www.usability.gr.jp.

The purpose of the experiment was to examine the effectiveness of the proposed hints exposure. Our B(Bear) system (Fig.2) has been compared to another well-known R (Roboword) system (Fig.3).

Fig.2 The screenshot of the Tool

The main difference between these two systems was that R system exposed dictionary-based hints on the word

level, and our B system exposed authentic hints based on the parallel on-line texts

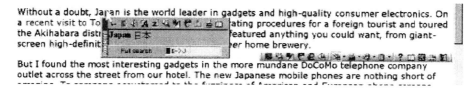

Fig.3 The screenshot of the Roboword system

To avoid subjective judgments, half of the subjects firstly operated R system first, then B system. The other group operated B system first. The flow of the experiment was as following:

1. Filling in the fact sheet.

All subjects were asked to fill in their personal information, English and computer proficiencies etc.

2. Instruction

All subjects had been instructed on how to operate both the B and R systems.

3. Using B and R systems

All subjects were asked to freely operate B and R systems. The order of using B and R systems has been random. The informants were informed about the Questionnaire they would have to fill out after the experiment.

4. Filling in the Questionnaire

The subjects were asked to rate the hints exposure and operation of the systems by 11 criteria on a 5-point scale [Fig. 4]. Subjects were also asked to comment on the systems.

5. Results

The data gained from the questionnaire (Fig.4) was analyzed by a two-tailed t-test. We choose a null hypothesis that these systems did not have any difference

in supporting language acquisition. We found that the proposed B system was better than traditional R for increasing:

- Text comprehension (T(9)= 6.12, p<.01)
- Reading Speed (T(9)=3.24, p<.05)
- New Phrase Acquisition (T(9)=2.84, p<.05)
- Discourse Structure Acquisition (T(9)= 4.24, p<.01)

But the traditional R system was better than proposed B system for new words acquisition (T(9)=5.40,p<0.01), although it seems that this rating of the B system strongly depend on the level of the English proficiency of the subject, i.e. High proficiency subjects tended to evaluate the B system higher than those with intermediate proficiency.

By combining the features of both systems we could get better results and better support learners who use different strategies in their language acquisition.

Questionnaire

Average Rating per Question by System

System:
1.Improves comprehension of the text........................

2.Speeds up reading...

3.Supports new wo rds acquisition......................

4.Supports new phrases, idioms acquisition............

5.Helps understand in what context new word, phrase.............. should be used
6.Glosses are adequate.....................................

7.Glosses is suitable in language acquisition...................

8.Is complete..

9.Is suitable in language acquisition....................

10.Is easy in manipulation..............................

11.Is interesting.......................................

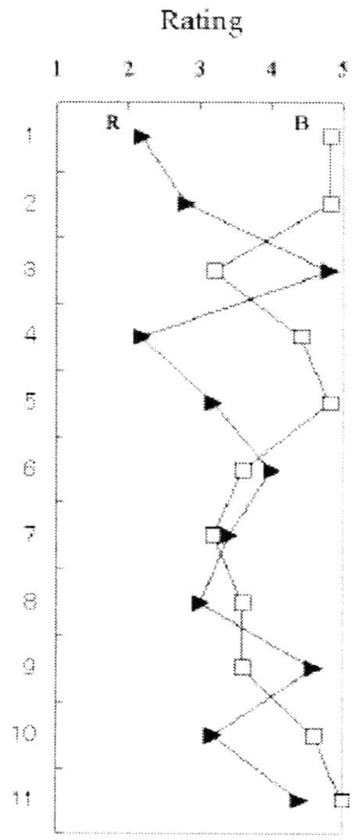

Fig.4 Average Rating per Question by System

6. Discussion

The overall rating of the B system was higher than R system. In text comprehension, reading speed, phrase acquisition, and acquisition of the discourse structure our B system was better than traditional R system.
One of the subjects said:
"Through manipulation of B system the user can grasp a way the natural English is written. I can understand better in what context this word should be appropriately used".
A trend became evident where subjects with high language proficiency tend to rate our system higher than others. But overall rating of the traditional R system was better for word acquisition. Some of the informants also commented about the drawbacks in interface design: some didn't like the bear agent, others were displeased that the hints' pop-up overlapped on the original text. We have to seriously tweak our system to remedy these concerns. Many subjects also mentioned that they wanted to use the two systems simultaneously.

7. Conclusions and Future Work

We compared our proposed system with an existing system by conducting an experiment which compared both systems' effectiveness in phrase acquisition, discourse-structure acquisition and text comprehension. The experiment exposed the drawbacks of our proposed system involved with poor interface design. We conclude that proposed system could be used in tandem with existing systems, enriching the learning strategies available for learners.

In the future, we would like to improve the interface of the system, as well as conduct experiments with combined system, which would allow use of two strategies, Contextual Deduction and Dictionary Look-up, at the same time.

References

[1]Anderson, J. R. (1990). Cognitive psychology and its implications. New York: Freeman.

[2]Frumkina, R.M(2001) Sociolinguistics. Moscow:Academiya Press

[3]Groot.P.J.M(2000)Computer assisted second language vocabulary acquisition.Language Learning&Technology,4,1

[4]Horst, M., Cobb, T., & Meara, P. (1998). Beyond a Clockwork Orange: Acquiring second language vocabulary through reading. Reading in a Foreign Language, 11

[5]Nagy, W.E., & Herman, P.A. (1987). Breadth and depth of vocabulary knowledge: Implications for acquisition and instruction. In M.G. McKeown & M. Curtis (Eds.), The nature of vocabulary acquisition. Hillsdale, NJ: Erlbaum

[6]Laufer,B., Hill. M.(2000) What lexical information do L2 learners select in a CALL dictionary and how it affect word retention? Language Learning&Technology,3,2

[7]Pershin A., Akahori K. (2001), Development and Evaluation of Japanese-English CALL Tool for improving Reading and Listening Skills. *Procedings of ICCE/SchoolNet 2001 International Conference on Computers in Education.*

[8]Roboword (2001) Roboword V5.5 for Window, Technocraft

[9]Schmitt, N. (1997). Vocabulary learning strategies. In Schmitt, N. and McCarthy, M., editors, Vocabulary: Description, Acquisition and Pedagogy. Cambridge University Press.

[10]Schmitt&McCarthy,editors.Vocabulary:Description,Acquisition and Pedagogy.Cambridge University Press,1997

[11]Zernik, Uri, & Dyer, Michael G. (1987), The Self-Extending Phrasal Lexicon, Computational Linguistics 13.

Online Workspaces for Annotation and Discussion of Documents

Toshiyuki Takeda
Center for Information and Media Studies
Kwansei Gakuin University
Uegahara 1-1-155
Nishinomiya, Hyogo, 6628501, JAPAN
takeda@kwansei.ac.jp

Daniel Suthers
Laboratory for Interactive Learning Technologies
Department of Information and Computer Sciences
University of Hawai'i at Manoa
1680 East West Road, POST 309
Honolulu, HI 96822, USA
suthers@hawaii.edu

Abstract

Pink is a system that supports threaded discussions about artifacts (such as source code or security bulletins) by making it easy for users to refer to and annotate parts of the artifacts. Pink supports multiple types of artifacts and annotation patterns while maintaining appropriate separation of content and view through a three-tier architecture. This system is implemented as server-side scripts and operates with any standard WWW browser.

1. Introduction

With the expansion of the Internet, system administrators cannot easily keep up with new viruses and security vulnerability information. As Code Red and the Nimda Worm spread globally in 2001, the understanding of how to prevent such viruses was not sufficiently disseminated from system administrators to users. Although companies like Microsoft and CERT published security information, many users did not take action. Myriad security advisories confused many users because the system environments they covered differed from those of the users. Here, the issue of context sharing comes into play, as many users cannot identify the context of the messages they read, or identify the portions of the messages that are relevant for their own context. Popular tools such as Email, Netnews and the WWW were created to facilitate the sharing of knowledge. However, these tools are sometimes less effective because they do not facilitate context sharing.

1.1. Artifact-Centered Discourse

We call the type of discussion and argumentation that should be supported in the applications just described Ar-

tifact Centered Discourse [9]. Others refer to these applications as Anchored Discourse [4] or Contextualized Discussion [11]. The fundamental requirement in these applications is that the connection between messages and their contexual artifacts be maintained.

We discriminate three types of Artifact Centered Discourse (ACD); Parallel ACD, Embedded ACD and Linked ACD.

In parallel ACD (Figure 1), discussion tools and shared artifacts are displayed on entirely different screens. There is no communication or coordination between the discourse and the artifacts; they are simply displayed in parallel. The advantage of parallel ACD is that a user can change interface as one wants. The disadvantage of it is that a user might lose track of which part of an artifact is being discussed.

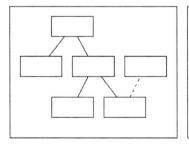

Alice: I couldn't get 1.2.26 from RedHat.
Bob: When is this encoded chunk feature used?
Carol: It's ok. RH releases backward patched 1.2.22.

Figure 1. Parallel Artifact Centered Discourse

An embedded discourse representation embeds comments directly in the artifact under discussion, or achieves a similar effect by inserting comments for display without modifying the original artifact. Because the discourse always takes place in the context of the artifact, embedded ACD (Figure 2) has the advantages that it is easier to refer to parts of the artifact or to recover the portion of the discussion that is concerned with a given part.

The fact that the discourse is distributed across the artifact in embedded ACD leads to one of its disadvantages: it is more difficult to get a sense of the whole discussion or to notice relevant relations between discussions about different parts of the artifact. The artifact may also become cluttered with comments.

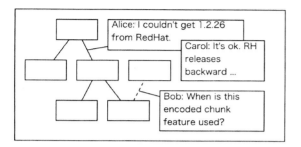

Figure 2. Embedded Artifact Centered Discourse

Linked ACD (Figure 3) can resolve the disadvantages of parallel and embedded ACD. In linked ACD, discourse representations and contextual artifacts are displayed side by side, as in parallel ACD, retaining the reply structure and chronology of the discourse. This approach resolves the tradeoff between the unrelated representations of parallel ACD tools and contextualized yet conversationally fragmented discourse contributions of embedded ACD tools. We believe that linked ACD, properly designed, can improve coherence and convergence of artifact-centered discourse by collecting together topically related contributions. The disadvantage of linked ACD is that it requires a larger screen.

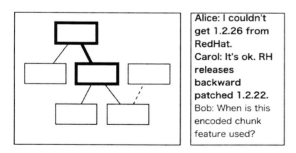

Figure 3. Linked Artifact Centered Discourse

This paper describes the software system Pink, which was created to support Artifact Centered Discourse. Pink supports the understanding and creation of artifacts that reflect intellectual discussions among participants. Since Pink is client server software, it requires only a WWW browser for use.

1.2. Related Work

Previous research has shown that annotating text online enables participators to find relevant information more easily. The Annotation Engine [12], ComMentor [6], CoNote [2], CritLink Mediator [14], and the Journal of Interactive Media in Education [8] are web based online discussion system with similar approaches. Microsoft Share-Point Team Services [7] is one of the out-of-the-box solutions. Kukakuka [10] is under development in the same laboratory as Pink and has many of the same objectives. In Kukakuka, a collection of Java servlets associates web pages with NNTP discussion groups and threads, presenting these together in a web client using frames. Many of the systems described above support only annotations to web pages, whereas Pink supports not only web page annotation but also embedded annotation to documents, such as Wiki-Wiki [5] documents, created within the system.

2. Software Design

Design issues for Pink system are as follows.

1. Artifact Centered Discourse support. The system supports Artifact Centered Discourse, especially linked ACD to discuss the contents of the artifacts. It is important to clarify and share assumptions, background knowledge and limits of applicability, which are not noted in the artifacts. Discussion in a shared context requires support of two functions:

   (a) Artifact to Discussion reference. Enable users who are reading an artifact to access comments on a specific annotated region of an artifact. This allows users to share knowledge with someone who has the same interests.

   (b) Discussion to Artifact reference. Enable users who are reading and responding to a threaded discussion about an artifact to access and refer to the relevant passages of that artifact. Since artifacts such as security advisories are quite large, this function should highlight the portion of the document that is being discussed.

   (c) Building shared knowledge. Summarize and share as a new artifact the created knowledge that becomes clear to participants in a discussion.

2. Extensibility.

   (a) Multiple types of Artifact. Supports artifacts internal to the server (e.g., text documents and WikiWiki [5]), on external servers (e.g., web pages), or offline artifacts (e.g., citations to books or journal articles). The system has meta data with Artifact information.

   (b) Multiple annotation patterns. Proper annotation pattern varies with artifact pattern. For example, software source code should be annotated on line(s) or function(s), and a document should be annotated on sentence(s) or paragraph(s).

   (c) Flexible view. Content and its view should be separated and workspace manager can change to meet their needs.

   (d) Multiple repository platforms. A repository (database) of the system can change to meet their needs, such as performance or other administrative reasons.

3. Multiple client platforms. Enable users of a variety of hardware and software platforms to access the community workspaces (including artifacts and discussions). Objects in the system should be accessible from any standard based WWW browser without client side software, such as Java applet or Active X.

2.1. A Sample User Scenario

The next two sections show how users read and write in the workspace.

2.1.1 Reading and Annotating Artifacts

A user can begin either by reading a document artifact or by reading topic threads of interest. References are displayed as links in both directions. When the user is reading a document and encounters an annotation, the user can click on the annotations reference number in the artifact to read the related discussion. Conversely, a user who is reading a discussion can click on the numbered references to view the referenced artifact. (The referenced artifact may be the document itself, or a link or citation to the artifact in the case of external documents, respectively.)

A user creates a reference to a portion of a plain text or WikiWiki artifact as follows. The user shifts to a page for inserting a special tag when the user clicks a button in the artifact-browsing page. The user then inserts tags to indicate the extent of the reference, and clicks submit. A reference is then created in the repository and threaded discussion menu page.

Once a reference has been created, it shows up as a new thread in the discussion thread view. The user then adds a Note to the Reference by clicking on [Write Comment], which loads a simple form for entering the Note.

2.1.2 Reading and Writing a Comment

The subject of the created Note is displayed in the discussion view and users can reply to the Notes as in a normal threaded discussion.

The Reference is shown as an anchor in the document with the number of the reference. When a user clicks this part, the corresponding part in the threaded discussion is shown and a user can read notes attached to the annotation point. Conversely, if a user clicks the number of a reference on a discussion thread page, the part of the artifact that includes the annotation point is shown.

2.2 Architecture

Pink has a Three-tier architecture (Figure 4) consisting of Presentation, Model and Repository.

Presentation. The Presentation layer generates html using objects in the model layer and parameters from a user. It uses two important objects: WebComponent to wrap model objects and WebTemplate for a template to generate html.

Model. A Model consists of a Workspace, and Artifact, Note and Reference objects derived from the Workspace. There are also objects related to users and access control.

Repository. The Repository is a persistent database in which to store objects. It is designed to use simple interfaces like a space-based repository, TupleSpace [3], so it is easy to implement a Repository in many ways.

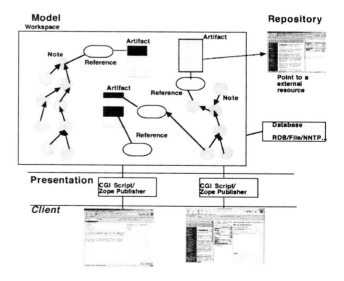

Figure 4. Architecture in Pink System

Workspace. The Workspace is a place to share and exchange knowledge by setting an annotation on an artifact and writing a note to a threaded discussion. A user can add or create an artifact, annotate it, and write a comment about the annotated part of an artifact.

Artifact. The Artifact object is used for representing a text document, web page, a book or journal article, etc. There are two kinds of Artifacts: structured and unstructured. The structured Artifact is composed of parts like W3C DOM [13] and an annotation point can be set on each part of an Artifact. (See Figure 5)

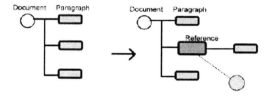

Figure 5. Reference Insertion

Reference. Reference is a pointer object that refers to either a part or whole of an artifact object and is often a root point of a discussion thread. *Note.* A Note object includes a user's writings about something in a workspace and usually has a pointer to either a reference object or another note object.

2.3. Implementation

The current version of Pink is implemented on Zope (web application server and content management system written by Python programming language [15]). All object classes including Artifacts and discussion items and its containers (threads) are defined as Python objects. New Artifact types can be written in Python when needed. Zope supports many database management systems as repository with fine abstract interface so that Pink repository can be changed easily.

Figure 6 shows a sample user interface when a user make an annotation on a structured artifact.

3. Future Work

The current version of Pink allows the user to set an annotation point on an entire external web page. Annotation of parts requires a filtering object that takes in an external page and changes it into a model object. This is a kind of proxy server function, the way CoNote and CritLink Mediator work. Pink already has similar functionality, but there are two reasons not to deploy this function as a service now.

One is the problem of intellectual property rights. Rewriting a certain page and showing this revised page to a user may not be allowed in some cases, even though Pink just appends tags and doesn't change any contents of an artifact. For the Internet community to share knowledge, permissible usage should include at least proper quotation.

Another reason is the problem of version management. The Web page used as a target artifact will be referenced by its structure, which is assumed to be constant. However, Internet documents on active sites do change, especially security advisories. The new version of the artifact may not include all the contents mentioned in the past discussion. When the system detects changes in an external web page or finds that a discussion thread is connected to obsolete content, the simplest approach would be to treat the old annotation and discussion as obsolete, and to only display non-obsolete and new annotations.

However, valuable knowledge may lie in these obsolete discussions. Consider for example a workspace recording design rationale for software revisions, or a learning application in which a student posts a document on a web server, an instructor comments on it, and the student then revises the document accordingly. The discussion for such frequently changed sites needs to include older versions. A better approach is needed. Ideally, the system would enable users to browse the differences between old and new artifacts, and provide access to the old discussion thread generated by the prior versions. On the other hand, there are no problems for the contents created in the Workspace because the system can show the part changed in the artifact easily. Another area for further work is to support structured discussions like IBIS [1]. The IBIS scheme of Issue, Position, and Argument is used to record argumentation while exploring wicked problems. Since our approach focuses on the relationship between artifacts and discourse, further examination is required to introduce discourse-structuring devices.

4. Summary and Conclusions

The Web has fostered explosive growth in a variety of online communities. Many of these communities would benefit from better tools for online discussions that are focused on the interpretation and/or creation of shared documents and other artifacts. Functional requirements of tools for artifact-centered discourse include the ability to move between discourse and artifacts in both directions: retrieving a discussion associated with an artifact or portion thereof; and bringing up an artifact that is referenced by a contribution to the discussion.

This paper described the architecture and interface of Pink, a software system that meets these functional requirements. The system is based on an abstract 3-tier server ar-

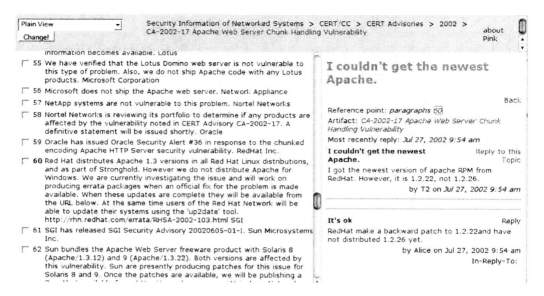

Figure 6. Pink Sample Screen

chitecture that is designed to be extensible and exchangeable. Pink was originally implemented as CGI scripts in the Ruby object oriented language and is currently implemented using the Zope application server. The present implementation is currently under experimental use in our laboratory (including use in preparation of this paper), and has been undergoing testing within an open-source community since March 2002.

The significance of this work and similar work by others goes beyond its potential for improving artifact-centered discourse in online communities. It also represents a better approach to the design of web-based tools for collaboration, in which the design is driven by an understanding of the interactions to be supported.

5. Acknowledgements

The first author was supported by the W. R. Lambuth scholarship of Kwansei Gakuin University. The second author was supported by National Science Foundation grants 9873516 and 0093505. Opinions expressed are those of the authors and do not necessarily reflect policy of the sponsoring organizations.

References

[1] J. Conklin. Hypertext: An introduction and survey. *IEEE Computer*, 20(9), 1987.

[2] J. R. Davis and D. P. Huttenlocher. Shared annotation for cooperative learning. In *Third International World-Wide Web Conference*, 1995.

[3] D. Gelernter. Generative communication in linda. *ACM Transactions on Programming Languages and Systems*, 8(1):80–112, 1985.

[4] M. Guzdial. Information ecology of collaborations in educational settings: Influence of tool. In *In Proceedings of the 2nd International Conference on Computer Supported Collaborative Learning (CSCL 97)*, pages 83–90, 1997.

[5] B. Leuf and WardCunningham. *The Wiki Way*. Addison-Wesley Longman, March 2001.

[6] M. Roscheisen, C. Mogensen, and T. Winograd. Beyond browsing: Shared comments, soaps, trails, and on-line communities. In *Third International World-Wide Web Conference in Darmstadt, Germany*, April 1995.

[7] Sharepoint portal server. http://www.microsoft.com/sharepoint/.

[8] T. Sumner and S. B. Shum. From documents to discourse: Shifting conceptions of scholarly publishing. In *Proc. CHI 98: Human Factors in Computing Systems*, April 1998.

[9] D. Suthers. Collaborative representations: Supporting face-to-face and online knowledge-building discourse. In *Proceedings of the 34th Hawai'i International Conference on the System Sciences (HICSS-34)*, January 2001. http://lilt.ics.hawaii.edu/lilt/papers/2001/Suthers-HICSS-2001.pdf.

[10] D. Suthers and J. Xu. Kukakuka: An online environment for artifact-centered discourse. In *Education Track of the Eleventh World Wide Web Conference (WWW 2002)*, pages 472–480, 2002. http://www.c2.com/cgi/wiki?WikiWikiWeb.

[11] Tecfa newsletter. http://tecfa.unrge.ch/.

[12] The annotation engine. http://cyber.law.harvard.edu/projects/annotate.html.

[13] Document object model (dom) level 1 specification, 1998. The World Wide Web Consortium http://www.w3.org/TR/1998/REC-DOM-Level-1-19981001/.

[14] K.-P. Yee. Critlink: Better hyperlinks for the www. In *Hypertext 98*, 1998. http://www.crit.org/ ping/ht98.html.

[15] Zope (z object publishing environment) community. http://www.zope.org/.

Student use of knowledge building tools in networked communities.

Shaun Nykvist

Abstract

This paper reports on an elective unit of study, offered to undergraduate primary and early childhood education students at the Queensland University of Technology. The course has as its main focus, the notion of online virtual communities, and explores students' current trends and practices with communication tools and networked communities with those currently being offered in a variety of educational contexts. After exploring and using a range of knowledge building tools, students then attempt to develop an online environment that espouses a sense of community amongst its participants. The students participate in the course through the use of various tools including multi user domains and bots, video and audio streaming including live video, chat including comic chat, threaded discussion lists, online gaming environments, email lists and instant messaging.

There is a considerable pressure for teachers to understand the curriculum implications of network communities and to be able to participate in such communities (Williams, 1997). To respond to such imperatives, teachers must have appropriate knowledge, along with the technical and communications skills to participate creatively and critically in such communities. In turn, schools have an expectation that graduating teachers have such skills, and a critical understanding of the educational implications of network communities, so that they are able to take a leadership role in the professional development of peers and in the strategic planning of school resourcing and curriculum activity.

Evidence of the importance of these skills for teachers in Queensland state education schools in Australia can be witnessed from the launch of Education Queensland's Learning Place (http://education.qld.gov.au/learningplace, 2002). The Learning Place was launched at the end of April, 2002 and is intended as a place for staff, students and the community to learn online, participate in online communication and online communities. Some of the tools that Education Queensland has now provided for these members include online chat, comic chat, a MOO (Mud, Object Oriented), and Blackboard

and meeting tools. Hence, the nature of such an online infrastructure reinforces the need for teachers to have a wide range of skills in this field.

This unit of work is called Network Communities and is a work in progress currently being implemented during semester 1, 2002. It aims to provide practical skills and a cultural understanding of the impact of network communities for students in their role as pre-service teachers, professional peers and lifelong learners. In trying to achieve this, the course looks at the notion of community and what it means to be part of a community. Students are introduced to several communities including, Knowledge Forum, the Web-based Inquiry Science Environment (WISE), Tapped In, Oz Teachernet, Learning Circles and Webquests. They are asked to critique a number of the environments according to what they view as an effective learning environment with particular emphasis being placed on the notion of communities of practice. Further the course looks at how students currently use their current Internet connection and how these practices can be likened to that of the various networked communities they explore.

The unit not only presents students with lecture material pertaining to the use of various online virtual community tools, but also immerses the students in the use of these tools as part of the lecture program. This means that students are witness to both face-to-face environments as well as being part of a virtual community. Within this community of practice students also use instant messaging, chat, threaded discussion, MOO's and streaming video and audio to explore and learn about these knowledge building tools. For example students may use a virtual classroom within a MOO to discuss the issues pertaining to hosting an online event or discuss ways in which the use of video or chat is best used in the classroom.

The course is currently being undertaken at the time of writing this paper, however, there are a number of findings and reflections emerging from its implementation. Findings reveal that what students see as a networked community is very much a part of their everyday use of their internet access. Many of the students undertaking the unit are already members of communities such as MSN Communities (http://communities.msn.com, 2002) and Yahoo Groups (http://groups.yahoo.com, 2002). These are communities that an individual can design or join to chat, share files, view pictures and video, use threaded discussion and help each other or even just lurk. Some students are also members of multi-user domains and gaming communities where it is imperative that you are involved in discussions or even various forms of argument. Students within the lecture group are also familiar with tools such as email lists, discussion boards and news groups to solve problems or help each other.

The course is designed so that students complete two pieces of assessment based on the notion of communities of practice in education. The first piece of assessment involves reviewing the literature pertaining to this area of study and evaluating a number of communities of practice and their tools. The second piece of assessment looks at the construction of a community of practice. Students attend lectures or tutorials in environments that are similar to what they are learning about. For example a tutorial or lecture about video conferencing and the tools used in this medium take place using face to face lectures, chat and video conferencing, while a lecture on MOO's will take place using face to face tutorials and using an actual MOO.

While it is still very early to reflect on the overall implementation of the unit it is also interesting to note that the students' familiarity with various knowledge building tools is quite high and their use of tools such as chat is quite mature. Students are currently developing online communities around the Australian theme "Year of the Outback". They have access to a variety of community building tools and have online access to an expert in the field. The expert is the current project officer for the online community Oz TeacherNet (http://rite.ed.qut.edu.au/oz-teachernet, 2002). The students find that this is a beneficial resource to gain access to various tools and to clarify their community ideas.

References

1. Education Queensland, (2002). Learning Place, http://education.qld.gov.au/learningplace, [30/04/02].
2. MSN Communities, (2002). MSN Communities, http://communities.msn.com, [30/04/02].
3. Oz TeacherNet (2002). Oz-TeacherNet, http://rite.ed.qut.edu.au/oz-teachernet, [30/04/02].
4. Williams, M. (1997). Professional associations: Supporting teacher communities. *Computers in New Zealand Schools*, 9(2).
5. Yahoo Groups (2002). Yahoo Groups, http://groups.yahoo.com, [30/04/02].

Digital ShuTong: Reviving the Ancient Form of Learning Support Agents

Isaac Pak-Wah Fung
Institute of Information Sciences & Technology
Massey University
Palmerston North, New Zealand
P.W.Fung@massey.ac.nz

Abstract

Inspired by the practice of studying escort in ancient time, this paper describes an approach to the development of learning support agency. The agency is in fact a team of small agents which embody with clearly defined and domain specific knowledge or skill. The agents are not designed as full blown instructors or tutors but only escorting the students during their study journeys and serve them as their assistants. The students still bear the major responsibility of their own learning but the agency is always at their disposal and can offer help if necessary. Among others, agility is the strongest selling point of this architecture. Whenever a new agent is developed, it simply either joins the team as new member or replaces an old agent that is due to 'retire' without bothering the students and instructors.

Design Philosophy

The idea described in this short paper is inspired by the practice of studying escort, namely ShuTong, in ancient China. Every year hundreds of students from around the country travelled a very long distance to the capital for a public examination run by the emperor's government. Excelling in the examination would bring the top students a promising career and a very prestigious honour to their families or even the entire clan. Throughout their journeys, most students were closely escorted by a male teenage escort – ShuTong who provided all sorts of personal care to their masters. The scope of work covered by the ShuTong was very wide ranging - carrying the luggage, booking motel room, washing the master's clothing, preparing the meals, ensuring the stationery are ready to use and even fighting off road side thieves, to name a few. The students were still responsible for their own study and the ShuTong's work was in no way related to the student's academic pursuit. Nonetheless, the ShuTong's services to the young masters was very instrumental in bringing success to the students. The underlying rationale of this practice was to relieve the master from doing the daily routines and could concentrate on studying. This practice of learning escort was very successful and practiced in ancient China for many centuries.

In today's information era, it seems impractical, if not impossible, to replicate the learning escort system because of the heavy cost involved in hiring a person. In the meantime, most students would not like being closely followed by a person. However, digitalising the practice of learning escort in the form of smart agents is an interesting and promising approach, in the author's view, to the development of learning support tools. As [1] noted, many agent-based learner supporting systems are natural evolution of intelligent tutoring systems, this approach inevitable inherits the legacy of classical tutoring systems architecture which normally includes closely coupled expert model, tutoring model and student model. One major drawback of this approach is the notorious problem of maintaining realistic student models. In the Learning Assistant Agency (or ShuTong) architecture, student modelling was eliminated from the design at the outset. Instead, we concentrate on building smart agents that are small, knowledge-based, domain-specific, learnable and portable. It is our belief that the students have to bear the ultimate responsibility of learning the subject domain. The agents only serve them in the only aspects they were designed such as visualising algorithms or performing complex calculations. As the agents are escorting the students throughout the course, these agents can be called at anywhere and at any time to perform tasks. Ancient escorts reduced the physical loading rested on the students. Digital escorts relieve cognitive loads. One distinguishing feature of the digital escorts is their knowledge-driven task-tackling capability. By watching the escort performing the task, the student could find learning the domain much easier because the escort's action trace would facilitate the assimilation of difficult concepts.

Architectural Consideration

Figure 1 shows the schematic architecture of the Learning Assistant Agency system. As mentioned, we expect the agency and the entire course environment have high agility so that students on different platforms can all access the materials and agents with ease. That should explains why we emphases a loosely coupled small component design.

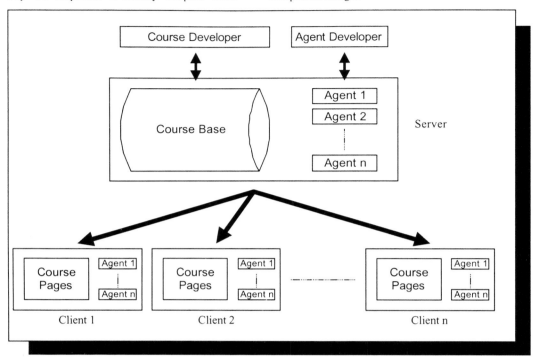

Fig.1: Architectural consideration of the ShuTong system

With this design, different agents can be called upon by the students at any time as long as the student find their skill/knowledge useful in understanding the concepts described in the course pages. When developing the course pages, on the other hand, the developer can choose to tag the pages with appropriate agents. The agency is deployable in a complex multi-user environments which might involves different hardware and software platforms, from handheld devices to workstations, the agent(s) are loaded to the clients on demand. Also worth mentioning is the agent's learnability. By observing the clients logging history, individual agents could learn about the learning style of its master and adapt itself to suit his needs.

[2] O'Riordan C & Griffith J. (1999) *A Multi-agent System for Intelligent Online Education.* Journal of Interactive Learning Research, Vol. 10(3/4), pp. 263-274

References

[1] Aroyo, L & Kommers P (1999) *Intelligent Agents for Educational Computer-aided Systems.* Journal of Interactive Learning Research, Vol. 10(3/4), pp. 235-242.

The Technology Integration Outreach Project: Developing "Best Practices" Curriculum Units

Mary Engstrom, Assistant Professor
LOFTI Coordinator
Division of Technology for Training and Development
School of Education
University of South Dakota
Vermillion, SD USA

Rosanne Yost, Associate Professor
PDC Director
Division of Technology for Training and Development
School of Education
University of South Dakota
Vermillion, SD USA

Ray Thompson, Professor
Division of Technology for Training and Development
School of Education
University of South Dakota
Vermillion, SD USA

Don Versteeg, Instructor
SILDL Coordinator
Division of Technology for Training and Development
School of Education
University of South Dakota
Vermillion, SD USA

Abstract

The Technology Integration Outreach Project (TIOP) is a joint project between the Southeast Interactive Long Distance Learning Consortium (SILDL), and University of South Dakota School of Education's Professional Development Center (PDC) and it's Learning Organizations for Technology Integration Project (LOFTI). Three outcomes guide the projects work: (1) develop partnerships with USD School of Education and K-12 schools; (2) create curriculum models of best practices in technology integration. (3) utilize distance technologies as a communication tool for professional development across the project. Three separate TIOP Projects have taken place. During the Spring Semester of 2001, the fall of 2001 and the spring of 2002 TIOP interdisciplinary teams were assembled and completed the development of best practices curriculum units with technology integration as a key element of the unit.

About four-dozen teachers, faculty and pre-service teachers have participated in completing eight units. Experiences will be shared with text and video.

Introduction

The Technology Integration Outreach Project (TIOP) is a joint project between the Southeast Interactive Long Distance Learning Consortium (SILDL) the University of South Dakota School of Education LOFTI (Learning Organizations for Technology Integration) group and the Professional Development Center (PDC) in the USD School of education. Three outcomes guide the TIOP project: (1) develop partnerships with USD School of Education and K-12 schools; (2) create curriculum models of best practices in technology integration. (3) utilize distance technologies as a communication tool for professional development across the project.

Implementation

Teams of educators have worked together to develop technology enriched curriculum units to be used in their schools. The teams include two or more K-12 teachers from different content areas, one University of South Dakota School of Education faculty member, and two 3rd or 4th year pre-service teachers.

The teams attend five daylong workshop sessions where they work collaboratively to develop their curriculum units. While at the workshops the teams learn about: (1) assessment practices that support student-centered teaching and learning; (2) backwards curriculum design process; and (3) inquiry-based, constructivist theory of teaching and learning. In addition each team is supported with or has available to them: (1) Technology for Training and Development Division (TTD) faculty; (2) content experts from Arts and Science and/or Curriculum and Instruction; and (3) ongoing support to facilitate communication, site visits, and continued learning during the implementation and evaluation phases of the project. A daylong wrap-up session, in which teams share information about the unit implementation and participate in an Action Research process, concludes the project.

The workshops are spread out over a semester long period. Each team uses a video-conferencing system to communicate beyond the on-campus workshop sessions. K-12 teachers are provided with release time to attend the workshop sessions. Funds from a Department of Education TICG grant, the LOFTI project, are used to reimburse the cost of the substitutes. In addition, stipends are provided to all curriculum design team members.

All participant are expected to: (1) demonstrate a willingness to explore, learn and implement new and different teaching and learning strategies; (2) attend all workshops; (3) develop, in collaboration with others, a curriculum unit that incorporates the use of technology to be used in their classroom during the implementation period; (4) participate in project research and assessment activities; and (5) demonstrate a willingness to share their learning with other pre-service and practicing education professionals.

Project Results

Three separate cycles of TIOP projects have been completed over the past three semesters. The resulting "best practices" curriculum units, which incorporate technology integration to support learning for understanding, are implemented in the K-12 classrooms and are used as theory-to-practice examples in teacher education courses at USD. The teams meet on the USD campus and at a distance to collaborate in creating their instructional components. A total of eleven teams were assembled during the three project cycles. Approximately four-dozen teachers, faculty and pre-service teachers have participated in completing the eight instructional units. Most of the units include web sites incorporated into the instruction. A TIOP Project web site is used to disseminate information. The TIOP website also has a discussion board and links to best practices web sites.

As a result of the LOFTI project, the teacher education field experience program at USD is being revised to include more opportunities for pre-service students to work with use technology applications in K-12 classrooms throughout their program. Action Research findings indicated a need to involve school administrators in the TIOP project. By working with the curriculum design teams, administrators to will develop a better understanding of this conceptual framework and be in a better position to support their teachers' efforts. In addition, their involvement affords us an opportunity to strengthen our partnerships and work collaboratively to create structures and practices that will impact student learning via technology integration in K-12 classrooms and in our teacher education program.

Task Design Principles of a Campus-based Communication Skills Course in a Natural-Virtual Learning Community

Carissa Young
The National University of Singapore

Abstract

Many students from non-English speaking backgrounds find it difficult to use English in the virtual learning communities. This paper proposes a task designed for a campus-based English course in a Singapore university and explains the theoretical underpinnings of the design. It is argued that communication skills in both "virtual" and "natural" learning communities need to be learned. As such, communication skills courses should include learning activities that help students polish such skills.

1: Introduction

While English is the most popular medium of communication in the virtual learning communities, many students from non-English speaking countries have found it difficult to express themselves in English. As such, learning tasks should be designed to help students improve their online English communication skills. This paper briefly describes the design of a web-based task proposed for a communication skills course and explains the rationale for the design.

2: The English Course and the Online Task

The communication skills course referred to in this paper is Graduate English Course: a 12-week campus-based program conducted by the National University of Singapore to help graduates improve their written communication skills. While this course has a website in the Integrated Virtual Learning Environment (IVLE, http://ivle.nus.edu.sg), a courseware management system developed by the University, the site only contains a course outline.

The task proposed in this paper is initially a writing activity. The author, who is also the tutor of the course, designed this task to help students polish their report writing skills through a small-scale questionnaire study. The time allocated for the task is 10 hours, with 1 hour spent in the classroom and 9 hours spent in IVLE. Besides, the students are required to work individually to write a report. The IVLE tools used for this task include

Discussion Forum (a CMC tool), Multimedia (an audio/visual resource repository), and Workbin (an assignment repository).

The task begins with a lecture, in which the tutor briefly describes the aims of the task to the class. The lecture focuses on four aspects: (1) how to conduct a small-scale questionnaire study, (2) how to design a questionnaire, (3) how to work collaboratively, and (4) how to communicate effectively in a virtual environment. At the end of the lecture, the students work in small groups to select a survey topic. The recorded lecture, as well as the teaching materials and relevant resources, are uploaded in the IVLE Multimedia and IVLE Workbin respectively.

The students then work collaboratively to draft a 10-itemed questionnaire. They could have discussions in the IVLE Discussion Forum if necessary. To ensure the work is done, each group selects a coordinator, who may set a prearranged time to have the discussion so that the group members could get instant responses from their peers. Each group submits the draft to the tutor and revises it according to his/.her suggestions. The group uploads the questionnaire in the group website to collect data from the respondents. When they have finished analyzing the data, the students work individually to write a report and then upload it to the IVLE course website for peer review purposes. Based on these comments, the students revise their reports and submit the final draft to the tutor. As an optional follow-up activity, each group will give an oral presentation on their project in class.

3: Pedagogical Rationale for the Task Design

The task facilitates English communication in both virtual and natural learning environments. This section explains the rationale for design of the proposed task, focusing on three aspects: course model, students' needs and task aims.

3.1: Course Model

The proposed task uses computer mediated communication (CMC) as a tool to teach communication skills. This design, which involves both readymade print materials and online components, is similar to the "Wrap Around" model [1], "Scenario 1" [2] or "Adjunct mode" [3]. It has been argued that such virtual-natural instruction often fails because the technological infrastructure of an institution cannot support CMC among students. However, problems such as dialup connection charges, backward network system, and inadequate networked computers that might affect the accomplishment of online tasks are not observed in this context. This is because the University has an information technology strategic plan to strengthen her technological infrastructure. Currently, tutors and students can access the campus network through 3,000 networked computers on campus. They also gain free access to the system through 7,000 wired and wireless network access points campus-wide. Since this system is powerful, safe and free-of-charge, it is indeed a good virtual environment for online communication.

In addition, the design of this task conforms to the strategic plan of the University [4]. According to this plan, online instruction should supplement but not replace classroom instruction. For this reason, a course model that allows students to collaborate in the virtual and natural communities appears to be an appropriate and practical model for the course.

3.2: Students' Needs

The online task was designed also because students need to learn how to use English -- the major medium of electronic communication -- to collaborate with others. This is because online discourse, which is neither spoken language nor written language, is itself a new genre [5, 6]. Pincas [6], for example, points out that the spatial and temporal patterns in an online learning environment are different from those in a face-to-face environment. Online "talks", especially when more than two "speakers" are involved, require appropriate turn-taking and referencing skills. Besides, text-based communication in the "virtual world" requires speakers to use text to express their ideas. Whereas paralinguistic cues such as abbreviations or emoticons could also be used, such cues need to be learned before they are used properly. For these reasons, the proposed task allows students to practice online discussion. Besides, tutors can take this opportunity to demonstrate interactions in the natural and virtual communities.

3.3: Task Aims

One of the aims of the proposed task is to allow students to work collaboratively and cooperatively inside and outside of the classroom. In this design, the discussion activity is deliberately put on the Internet and the earlier briefing part conducted in the classroom.

The rationale behind such a design is that at the time of writing, there is still little concrete empirical evidence on the superiority of computer-mediated collaborative work over face-to-face one in the language teaching literature [7-9]. Whereas some claim that computer-mediated collaborative activities help students improve their language learning, others argues that students who have discussions in a classroom setting can focus more on the language task than those who have discussions online.

To avoid the above problem, the present task design is an attempt to make full use of both online and traditional collaborative learning by asking students to have the initial discussion in the classroom and to draft the questionnaire through online discussion. An advantage of this design is that the students could spend more time on thinking about the task and doing library research before drafting the questionnaire items with their classmates.

4: Conclusion

The design principles for an English task have been described. To ensure the success of the course, it is suggested that the task be tested with a few students. Based on their feedback, the task will be revised and more components added to the course. This paper concludes that there is a need for students to do similar tasks in order to improve their English communication skills in virtual and natural learning communities.

References

[1] F. T. Tschang and T. D. Santa, *Access to knowledge: New information technologies and the emergence of the virtual university*, Oxford: Pergamon, 2000.

[2] Centre for Studies in Advanced Learning Technology, *Effective networked learning in higher education: Notes and guidelines*, England: Lancaster University, 2001.

[3] L. Harasim, "A framework for online learning: The virtual-u," *Computer*, vol. 32, pp. 44-49, 1999.

[4] National University of Singapore, *National University of Singapore: Strategic directions for the 21st century*. Singapore: National University of Singapore, 1996.

[5] M. Warschauer, H. Shetzer, and C. Meloni, *Internet for English Teaching*. Alexandria, VA: TESOL, 2000.

[6] A. Pincas, "Features of online discourse for education," unpublished manuscript, London: Institute of Education, 1999.

[7] K. M. Armstrong and C. Yetter-Vassot, "Transforming teaching through technology," *Foreign Language Annals*, vol. 27, pp. 475-486, 1994.

[8] M. Warschauer and R. Kern, *Network-based Language Teaching: Concepts and Practice*. Cambridge: Cambridge University Press, 2000.

[9] N. Dabbagh, "The challenges of interfacing between face-to-face and online instruction," *TechTrends*, vol. 44, pp. 37-42, 2001.

A Knowledge Flow Driven E-Learning Architecture Design: What is its Stratification and How is it Personalized

Qiaozhu Mei   Junrong Shen

Department of Computer Science & Technology, Peking University, 100871, P.R. China

meiqzh@pku.edu.cn   junrongshen@water.pku.edu.cn

Abstract

How to personalize an e-Learning system has become an interesting question. The purpose of this paper is to demonstrate an innovative idea of personalizing an e-Learning system driven by Knowledge Flow and show the stratified architecture and the current progress made in Peking University.[1]

1. Introduction:

E-Learning has become increasingly hot in the past decade but is still on its way to a new acme. However, learning is so highly personalized that a sound e-Learning architecture should guarantee that every participant can get a distinctive guide fitting him best. An e-Learning participant doesn't need to be a skilled computer operator and they aren't expected to be restricted by age or background. These expectations require a computer-based learning system that is easy to handle, clear to be evaluated, free to achieve distinct study goal from distinct start points and learning paths.

We are designing a personalized and internet-based learning system with highly personalized property. We design the architecture with an assumption that an e-Learning system is driven by Knowledge Flow (KF), similar to the Material Flow in e-Business.

2. Knowledge Flow and How it is Involved in an E-Learning System:

2.1 What is Knowledge Flow and Why is it Important:

As an analogy to Material Flow, we can describe an e-Learning model as being driven by Knowledge Flow, which is an abstract of those entities of infor- mation flow between participants, all sorts of knowledge bases, guiders and outside information sources. As an abstract of information transport, it includes information (knowledge content), transport direction, transport methods and density, etc, and functions like information filtration, methods selecting and self–adapting personalization.

2.2 How is Knowledge Flow Involved

We can safely define our Knowledge Flow based

---

[1] This work is supported by a research grant in National Distance Learning Program, Ministry of Education of China.

e-Learning system into a structure of three apparatuses: guiders, learners and Knowledge bases, extended by an apparatus of outside Information source.

This structure is not a static but an interacting system. It contains various entities of Knowledge Flow that connect the four apparatuses. Categorizing these flows by information transport directions, we can safely come to the following structure view:

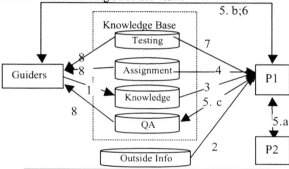

1. Knowledge classification and courseware making
2. Info searching & mining from outside Info base
3. Knowledge learning from knowledge base
4. Applying knowledge to solve problems
5. Learning Interacting
   a. Between participants
   b. Between participant and guider
   c. Between participant and computer
6. Discover new knowledge
7. Evaluating and testing
8. Fetching feedback to guiders
        (P1/P2: short for participant 1/2)

Figure 1: Knowledge Flow Driven Interacting Structure of E-Learning System

3. A Personalized E-Learning Architecture Driven by Knowledge Flow:

3.1 Stratification and System Architecture Design

The goal of our design is to build a highly personalized e-Learning system that fits participants with various backgrounds and study plans. According to the classification of personalized learning by Walberg[1], we design our system based on the "multi-faceted Learning" theory, which means participants can finally reach the same target through personalized paths.

We divide our workflow into four consecutive steps,

---

namely, knowledge classification, personality mining, adapting and learning evaluation /testing.

As the first step, knowledge classification is done by domain experts. Domain knowledge can be classified into hierarchic ranks. Learning objectives of each level depend on the achievements of knowledge and skills of its lower levels. Bloom has divided knowledge into 6 levels from low to high[2], which enables participants to run an object-oriented learning model. All six levels are interwoven which form a network. Participants can choose personalized start points and learning paths, all of which lead to the top target of the network.

The middle two steps of personality mining and personality adapting are simultaneous. On one hand, intelligent agent can discover what a participant prefers and which learning method fits him best based on his background and feedbacks of in-pace tests; on the other hand, it can adapt itself to these personalities. This personalization cannot be made thorough unless the KF are fully concerned. The architecture design of our e-Learning system can be figured as following:

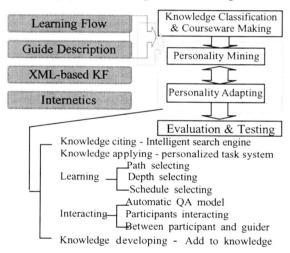

Figure 2: Stratification and Architecture of E-Learning System Driven by Knowledge Flow

The last step in the learning workflow is evaluation and testing, which are vital to define whether a learning method fits a participant. With the feedbacks, computer can find out at which level the participant grasps knowledge, as well as the advantages and disadvantages of his current learning methods. Consequently, system can recommend a learning path or method which seems to fit him better and choose the best way to demonstrate knowledge, or advise him skip a knowledge point. We are designing a reusable Computer Adaptive Testing (CAT) system to run the evaluation and testing step.

3.2 Important Technology Involved and Current Progress

Intelligent Agent, Media Stream, XML and Natural

Language Processing (NLP) are crucial technologies involved. Through training, the agent can attain participants' favorites, filtrate the information and pick out what the user may prefer. Media stream technology enables KF to be transported by means of various combinations of media streams. System can determine which combination is best adapted to each participant and adjust new ways to demonstrate knowledge.

Knowledge Flow also depends on language a lot. We can apply basic NLP principles to the design of a self-adapting QA (question and answer) sect . Computer Science Department of Peking University has done a number of progressive works on Internet based data mining, Intelligent Search Engine, Interactive Courseware Building and has a strong background on Internetics[3], NLP and web service. Now we are making full-scale progress in individual apparatuses discussed in 3.1 and considering an evaluation for personalization.

4. Conclusion:

In summary, we are designing a personalized e-Learning system with a stratified architecture driven by Knowledge Flow. Entities of KF are characterized by standard XML-based messaging. With the support of Internetics and other important computer technologies, this system enables participants to get personalized guiding service and adjust learning methods according to the feedbacks from evaluations and tests.

China has a great potential market of e-Learning projects. Only 10.5%[4] of high school graduated students at the age of 18-21 can go to university. A good e-Learning product will be a storm. Despite a brighter industrial prospect than e-Business, e-Learning has been developed as a subject rather than an industry. Starting with this system, we can find more innovative ideas to promote the industrialization of e-Learning.

5. Acknowledgment:

During the research and designing, Prof. Xiaoming Li gave us a lot of helps and suggestions. Prof. Jinzhong Zhang enlightened our idea of personalization. The authors show special thanks for their help.

6. Reference:

[1] HJ. Walberg, *Improving the Productivity of American School*, in *Education Leadership* (1984, No.8)

[2] Zhiwei Deng, *Personalized Education & Learning*, Shanghai Education Publishing House Press, 2000.6

[3] Bloom Benjamin S. and David R. Krathwohl. *Taxonomy of Educational Objectives: The Classification of Educational Goals, by a committee of college and university examiners.* Handbook I: Cognitive Domain. New York, Green, 1956.

---

[2] Bloom's 6 levels: KNOWLEDGE, COMPREHENSION, APPLICATION, ANALYSIS, SYNTHESIS and EVALUATION

---

[3] Internetics include Internet resultant Infrastructure, service and tools. This concept is first put forward by Prof. Xiaoming Li

[4] Data from Dongping Yang, *2000' Educational Evolution in China* ,http://www.net.edu.cn/20010101/22290.shtml

Development of An Education Tool for Computer System

Yoshiro Imai
Faculty of Engineering, Kagawa University
2217-20 Hayashi-cho Takamatsu, Japan
imai@eng.kagawa-u.ac.jp

Shinji Tomita
Graduate School of Informatics, Kyoto University
Yoshida Hon-machi, Sakyo-ku, Kyoto, Japan
tomita@lab3.kuis.kyoto-u.ac.jp

Haruo Niimi
Kyoto Sangyo University
Kamigamo Honzan, Kita-ku, Kyoto, Japan
niimi@ics.kyoto-su.ac.jp

Hitoshi Inomo, Wataru Shiraki, Hiroshi Ishikawa
Faculty of Engineering, Kagawa University
2217-20 Hayashi-cho Takamatsu, Japan
{inomo, shiraki, ishikawa}@eng.kagawa-u.ac.jp

Abstract

An education tool has been developed to explain internal behavior and structure of computer graphically. It is written in Java Language and designed for students to understand how computer works in the classroom lecture of information science. This paper describes some characteristics of our education tool and improvement of its facilities, especially embedded mail handling module for information exchange between teacher and students.

1. Design Concept for our Education Tool

First of all, we describe design concepts of our visual simulator as education tool and almost these concepts have been realized in the previous version of our simulator as the existing facilities. Our design concepts are summarized as follows:

1) It is used as a practical education tool, which covers from information literacy to computer system. It can illustrate internal structure and behavior of Neumann-style computer together with projector in the classroom lecture[1].

2) It may provide stepwise and continuous execution modes of programs and realize an easily learning environment for assembly programming exercise. It is implemented in a single source code of Java language to support both of stand-alone application and Java applet.

3) It is easily maintained, modified and customized for multiple applications such as demonstration tool, communication one (in other words, collaboration tool) and so on. It is quickly distributed from web server into users who want to utilize through network connectivity.

4) It is equipped with a simple GUI for interactive manipulations which includes initialization, program loading, stepwise execution and continuous (namely automatic) one. It is independent from kinds of operating system and machine specification and available in multiple platform environments. It works on the major web browsers such as Microsoft IE and Netscape Composer/Navigator so that it does not need additional software.

The existing facilities of simulator are illustrated with its characteristics and practical example of use. With our visual simulator, it is demonstrated how computer works: namely, loading program into memory, fetching each instruction of program in the memory, decoding it into several fields such as operation code and address fields, executing accordingly to the result of decoding instructions which includes, for example, data fetching, arithmetic/logical operations, data storing, conditional/unconditional jumping, subroutine call/return and so on. Many of these concepts are not only original ideas for our simulator, because they are efficient ideas for designing education tools and effective methods for utilizing tools in the practical situation. It is our original approach to develop a visual simulator(called "VisuSim") with Java for understanding internal behavior and structure of computer and it is also designed to work as both stand-alone and Java applet in order to use from classroom lecture to after school and/or at home[2].

2. Some Improvements for our Education Tool

From a brief evaluation of VisuSim for a few previous years, it has been decided to improve VisuSim and enhance the following two facilities that can provide help message and its proper communication method through mail sending and receiving. This section explains details of the latest enhanced facilities such as online help/guideline and embedded mail handler. Both of online help message and guideline display are essential to students who manipulate VisuSim after school or at home. The former is helpful to give students some kinds of concrete advices how to describe assembly programs by means of showing instruction set table and some sample program codes, and the later is useful to indicate how to operate VisuSim with mouse-cursor-position sensitive guideline message display. Online help message window can be invoked by pushing "HeLP" bottom, used as an information board and utilized by students who learn from information literacy to assembly programming with VisuSim. By addition of online help and guideline message facilities into VisuSim, its users may obtain more information about operation of VisuSim than the previous version. Its online help mechanism is implemented to make VisuSim read a specific file and display its contents on the newly created window. In the same manner, teacher can rewrite such a specific file, customize the help message of VisuSim for each student, and select suitable files of sample codes according to student's understanding level.

The mail handling facility embedded in VisuSim has been realized with pure Java code and consists of two major parts below: namely, SMTP-based mail sender module and POP3-based mail receiver one.

1) Characteristics of SMTP-based mail sender: This mail sender is different from other general-purpose mailers' sending modules at the following two points. At first, when students who use VisuSim meet some problems and consult such a situation to teacher or friends, they can transfer the current data of all the registers and memory into mail to be sent simply. Data in the content received mail can be analyzed in order to investigate whether student understands or not by teacher who received such a mail. This is a major reason to develop a special-purpose embedded mailer for VisuSim. Secondly, user may specify the e-mail address as not only domain-name oriented notation such as "imai@eng.kagawa-u.ac.jp" but also IP address specific notation such as "imai@#192.168.1.1". Almost temporary (informal) mail server for users of VisuSim should not always be entered on the official DNS and therefore such a mail server must be only specified with IP address.

2) Characteristics of POP3-based mail receiver: As the same functions of SMTP-based mail sender, this mail receiver has the following two characteristics different from others; namely easy restoring data of all the registers/memory in VisuSim from content of the received mail and IP address direct specification of mail server. On the other hand, it has some weaknesses to handle several kinds of mail message. For example, it cannot process mail with attached files. Although it reads out the specified mail from server, it shall not delete that mail from server. So another mailer will be able to process non-deleted mails with attached files. The mail facility of VisuSim may be useful not only for consulting communication between students and teacher but also for online submission of students' reports

to teacher. The mail sender and receiver of VisuSim can handle message in Japanese as well as English.

Figure 1 shows a sample scheme of information exchange between users of VisuSim by means of its mail sending and receiving facility. With such embedded mail handler of VisuSim, students who need some kind of advise can send help mail to others and obtain suitable advises from teacher and/or other students who has understood more than them.

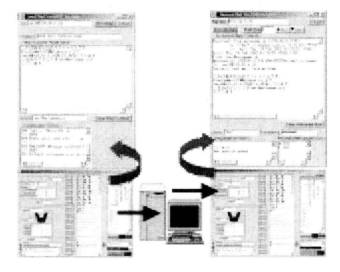

Figure 1. Scheme of Information Exchange through Mail Communication by VisuSim

3. Concluding Remarks

We can conclude our study as follows:
1) With use of our visual simulator, graphical demonstration can be available in classroom lecture on computer system and information literacy, so that it is efficient for even beginners of computer to understand the internal structure and behavior of computer more precisely.
2) Online help and guideline message get useful to users, and embedded mail handling facility can be provided for communication between its users. These facilities will let students manipulate our simulator not only in the classroom lecture but also after school and/or at home.

Acknowledgments
This study is partly supported by grand 12040107 in aid for scientific research from the Ministry of Education, Culture, Sports, Science and Technology.

References
[1] Y.Imai et.al., "A Visual Simulator for Understanding Structure and Behavior of Computer", proc. of ITHET2001
[2] Y.Imai et.al., "Design and Implementation of Web-based Education Tool", proc. of SAINT2002 WebSE02workshop

Past Viewer: Development of Wearable Learning System for History Education

Hiroaki NAKASUGI*1   Yuhei YAMAUCHI*2

Graduate school of Interdisciplinary Information Studies,
The University of Tokyo, Japan*1
Interfaculty Initiative in Information Studies,
The University of Tokyo, Japan*2

keishu@muf.biglobe.ne.jp*1   yamauchi@iii.u-tokyo.ac.jp*2

Abstract

We have developed a system that helps users acquire historical viewpoints using a wearable computer. This is accomplished by overlaying incidents from the past and live scenes from the present on a see-through display. The purpose of this system is to enable history learners to combine past and present information and obtain a significant notion of the continuity of time through viewing part of the series of events which happened in that very place. In evaluating this system, we found out that users could experience and feel history as a reality. We contend that this system is effective in furthering the motivation of history learners, and we have an expectation that it can become a significant new educational media.

Keywords: Wearable Computer, Overlay, History Learning, Motivation, Augmented Reality

1. Introduction
1.1. Research background

A "wearable computer" is a component with a computer attached to a human body and a Head Mounted Display (HMD, Fig1). It had been originally developed for military purposes, such as maintenance of complex equipment. The amount of manuals regarding maintenance of an airplane, for example, was enormous, and it was a herculean task for mechanics to refer to such manuals while working in the bottom of a huge airplane body. By introducing a wearable computer, their work efficiency was drastically improved. Today, with technical innovation, the total weight of a main computer and a display has become less than 1 kg and HMD became almost the same size as a pair of glasses. This made its application to the fields of education, medicine and architecture more practical.

1.2. Prior research

Much research on wearable computers emerged from Augmented Reality (AR). AR is a kind of Mixed Reality that connects extended reality to the real world. A system called KARMA (Feiner 1993) is famous in this field. This is a maintenance support system for laser beam printers. Nakajima (1999) developed a system that enables viewers to see stars on a celestial sphere as a constellation. Past research was emerged from engineering standpoints. Research on educational use of wearable computers has just started.

Ockerman (1997) compared effectiveness between textbooks and wearable computers when non-Japanese learn how to make "Origami", Japanese paper craft art. Bowskill (1999) verified distance communication with ABATA on a wearable display. This study also mentioned that using a wearable display was applicable for scientific experiments and processes of cross-cultural exchange.

2. Development of Past Viewer
2.1 Past Viewer

Past Viewer is designed for history learners to use in front of a historical building. It overlays news films reporting historical events which have occured there on top of the present scene in order to encourage viewers to connect the important events in the past with the present historical monument. With help of a see-though display, they can feel as if they are experiencing a historical incident in front of the historical monument.

Fig.1 Head Mount Display (HMD)

2.2 Historical Objects to be Studied

For this research, Yasuda Auditorium (built in 1925, Fig2) at the University of Tokyo was choosen as a historical object. This place can be traced back to 2000 years ago with archaeological items ,and especially in contemporary history of Japan, it is well known as political battlefield between students and the government in the 1960's. This method of overlaying the past incident and present scenary is applicable, for example, for famous world monuments like the Arch of Triumph in France(Fig3) or the Berlin Wall in Germany.(Fig4)

2.3 Structure of educational scenario with Past Viewer

1. A learner wears a backpack containing a note-type computer, a HMD, a headphone and a mouse. (Fig5)
2. Educational scenario consists of the following three parts:

Part 1   Three minutes of news film clips taken at the place where

learners are standing at present.

Part 2   Six one minute movies of the

Fig.2 Yasuda Auditorium (1969/ 2001)   Fig.3 The Arch of Triumph (1919/2002)   Fig.4 Brandenburg Gate (1989/2001)

University of Tokyo Dispute
in 1969.

Part 3   Ten minutes of movies and photos of scenes between

1927-2001.

In Parts 1 and 2, Users watch the past movies with the navigation shown on HMD. In Part 2, they move to the six different geographical viewpoints with mouse operation In Part 3, still pictures and movies on Yasuda Auditorium from 1927 to 2001 are presented. Users are asked to find out where these pictures were shot. As overlaying pictures, they voluntary perform these tours which deepen their knowledge about history.

3. Implementation

We interviewed ten people aged 10- 40 who used Past Viewer. The purpose of interview is whether they experienced changes about their own historical viewpoints by overlaying past and present information. After using this system, four of ten persons
recognized acquiring new viewpoints which connect the past and present as follows:

A (man in 30's): "I noticed afresh that the place where I stood had been existing for a very long time!"

B (woman in 20's): "It gave me a cue to reflect present situation, I feel as if I entered into history."

C (man in 20's): "I haven't experienced history with feeling. But I can do so now"

D (woman in 20's): "I thought that history was another person's affairs and looked on it from the outside. But (through using Past Viewer), I

could sympathize with people who were here before me

and I was awaked by a new viewpoint."

A, B and C seemed that they already have historical viewpoints from the results of pre-test. These persons are considered to reinforce their own viewpoints in this experiment. On contrary, in the case of D, she could succeed in getting a historical viewpoint because she has never imagined such an interpretation. We consider that

Fig.5 The scenery of practice

she could notice a viewpoint which connects the past and present.

4. Summary and further research

We developed the system using a wearable computer to enhance learners acquiring historic viewpoints with the expectation that this will give stronger motivation to those who study history. Though we admit that the number of subjects is not enough, it is significant that some learners showed their deeper interest on connection between place and its history after they used Past Viewer. We will keep collecting data and analyze patterns of the experience.

5. References

[1]Feiner, S., Macintyre, B., Seligmann, D. (1993)"Knowledge-based augmented reality", Communications of the ACM, vol36 (7), pp52-62

[2] Nakajima, K., Ban, T., Manabe, Y., Sato, K., Chihara, K. (1999) "An Astronomic Observation
Supporting System based on Wearable Augmented Reality", Japan Virtual Reality Society, pp417

[3] Ockerman, J., Najjar, L., Thompson, C. (1997) "Wearable computers and performance support: Initial
feasibility study", ISWC, pp10-17

[4] Bowskill, J., Dyer, N. (1999) "Wearable Learning Tools", Association for Learning Technology Journal, vol 7(3), pp44-51

A Web-based CAL System on
Computer Architecture and Assembly Language Programming

Yip Kit Kuen Raymond, Li Kei Chun Daniel

Department of Information and Applied Technology, Hong Kong Institute of Education

10 Lo Ping Road, Tai Po, New Territories, Hong Kong

hkryyip@ied.edu.hk   danielli@ied.edu.hk

ABSTRACT

This paper introduces a CAL system on Computer Architecture and Assembly Language Programming. The ability of the system is to simulate a computer system that allows the student to understand the whole process from software programming to hardware execution. Multimedia and web-based technologies are applied in the system. The proposed system helps the student to connect theory to practice more easily and can reduce the number of laboratory hours needed.

Keywords: Computer Assisted Learning (CAL), Simulation, Computer Architecture, Assembly Language

1 Introduction

The operating principle of computer system is an important section to all computer, engineering and IT students. It's knowledge usually spread across several modules like Digital Logic Circuit Design, Computer Architecture, Assembly Language Programming and Computer Programming Language. These modules are usually divided into lecture, tutorial and laboratory. Laboratory may be purely hardware implementation (e.g. Digital Logic Circuit Design) or just software implementation (e.g. assembly language programming). Usually, there is no laboratory support for Computer Architecture in small and media size university. This kind of course structure has the following properties

1) The operating principle of computer system is divided into separate pieces (modules). Students are difficult to get an overall picture as there is no laboratory to demonstrates the integration of theories of these modules.

2) The experiments need special hardware (e.g. 68000 microprocessor kit) and software simulator. This leads to difficulties in offering these modules through web-based learning.

3) Student only observes the results rather than the operating process. For example, consider the

following 68000 assembly program

Machine Code			Assembly	
Address	Content		Opcode	Operand
00001000	4240		CLR.W	D0

In traditional experiments, student can only observes the content of register D0 is clear and the Program Counter becomes 00001002 when the machine code 4240 (i.e. CLR.W D0) is executed. However, instead just the software result (assembly language programming), the student needs to know the hardware fetch and execute cycle in Computer and CPU architecture. The fetch and execute process of the above assembly is

1. The address 001000(Hex) is output from the CPU through address buses to the memory (RAM).
2. The content 4240 of memory address 001000 is read from memory (RAM) to the Instruction Register (IR).
3. The content of the Program Counter is increase from 00001000 to 00001002.
4. The content 4240 of the instruction register is decoded by the Control Unit.
5. The Control Unit then activates the Clear signal of the D0 register and the content of D0 becomes zero (clear).

2 The CAL system on Computer Architecture and Assembly Language Programming

In 2002, we began to develop a web-based multimedia CAL system on Computer Architecture and Assembly Language Programming. This system simulates the hardware operating process for different software instructions and program structure. The system aims to demonstrates

1) The relationship between programming language, compiler and machine code
2) The function of ALU, Control Unit, Address Register, Data Register, Address Bus, Data Bus, RAM, etc.

3) The fetch and execute cycle
4) Different addressing mode.
5) Stack pointer, subroutine and branch
6) Input, output and interrupt process

The system is divided into 4 areas,

1) Single Assembly and machine code instruction (include different addressing mode), e.g MOVE, ADD, SUB, NOT, AND, OR, CLR, JMP, BEQ (Branch if equal), BNE (Branch if not equal), BSR (Branch subroutine), RTS (Returns), etc.
2) Simple program structure, e.g. If then else conditions, Loop conditions, Subroutine and Returns (including stack pointer), etc.
3) Simple Input/Output Conditions, e.g. Serial IO, parallel IO, Polling, Interrupt, etc.
4) Some simple assembly programs

User can step-by-step run the instruction or program that select fromeach area and observes both the software and the hardware operating process.

In this project, Flash MX is select as the multimedia-editing tool. This is because it provides a rich supports in graphical, audio, video and script programming. Figure 1 shows the first few steps of a PC boot up of the described system.

3 Conclusion

This paper introduces a web-based CAL system on Computer Architecture and Assembly Language Programming. It simulates both the software and hardware process of a computer system. On further expand, the system will allow

1) The user to input and run their own programs.
2) The user to observe the gate level operating process instead of the block level observation (e.g. ALU).

References

[1] Cheng benmao, Zhao jingcheng, "A Multimedia CAL system on Circuit and Electronic Technology Experiments", ICCE, p215-218, 1999.
[2] Sadaf Alam, Roland N Ibbett, Frederic Mallet, Christos Sotiriou, "Computer Architecture Simulation & Visualisation: HASE & SimJava" Institute for Computing Systems Architecture, *Division of Informatics, University of Edinburgh*. http://www.dcs.ed.ac.uk/home/hase/index.html

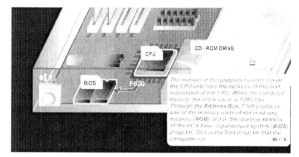

Figure 1a The CPU put the address F000 (Hex) in the address bus that selects one of the memory units of the ROM.

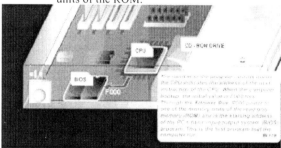

Figure 1b Animation shows the moving direction of F000.

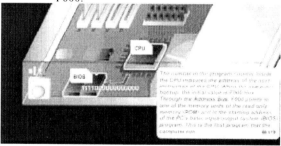

Figure 1c F000 will change to its binary value 1111000000000000 when the mouse is roll over it.

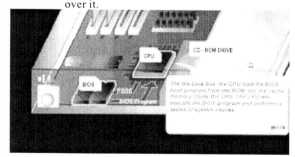

Figure 1d The CPU loads the BIOS program from the ROM.

Utilization of Video Conferencing over the Internet to Facilitate Biological Education and Research at the University of Maine

John Gregory, Executive Director, IT, University of Maine
Andrei Strukov, Instructional Technologies Development, IT, University of Maine

Abstract

The University of Maine has long been involved with the use of instructional television. The recent adoption of video conferencing over the Internet has opened opportunities with other institutions that had not previously used video conferencing. This is possible by leveraging the networking infrastructure in place for data connectivity to the Internet. The University strives to further exploit this technology to extend education and research in the state of Maine.

Problem

Six educational and research institutions in the state of Maine needed to work together and share educational resources in biological studies. The goal of the Maine Biomedical Research Infrastructure Network (BRIN) project was to develop a collaborative partnership and strong network composed of two premiere research institutions - the Mount Desert Island Biological Laboratory and The Jackson Laboratory; two undergraduate and graduate degree granting institutions - The University of Maine and the College of the Atlantic; and two undergraduate degree granting institutions - Bates College, and Colby College.

Overview

This three-year, $5.5 Million project established a Biomedical Research Infrastructure Network (BRIN) among the six Maine institutions. These six institutions formed a network for research training of faculty and students that will be advantageous by virtue of the quality and geographic proximity of the institutions involved.

To facilitate this collaboration a major goal of the project was the development of video conferencing capabilities to enhance training opportunities, research collaborations and administrative function. During the first year of the project, point-to-point (H.323) compressed video conferencing was established. Multipoint video conferencing is planned for the second and third years.

The Bioinformatics Core will direct the development of communication networks for the BRIN institutions. This Core will also be responsible for the development of methods for multi-center research and resource sharing, will provide methods for secure and confidential data sharing, and provide investigators and students with access to technical expertise and assistance in data management and analysis. More about the project may be found on the web at: www.brinme.net

Process

Utilizing the expertise and interests of the Core members has been the primary approach to meeting the Core goals. Dr. John Gregory, The University of Maine's Executive Director of IT and Bioinformatics Core Director, has led the group in surveying existing video conferencing infrastructure across the network and planning ahead for expansion and interoperability with the State of Maine's existing ATM network. Bioinformatics contact people have been identified at each institution. Michael McKernan has led the development of the brinme.net website, and is sharing network administration responsibilities with Glenn Colby, who has dealt with server configuration including file sharing, backups, and security. The Bioinformatics Core is currently hiring a network administrator to supervise the Maine BRIN VLAN and technical aspects of video conferencing.

Results and Findings

Challenges to the project include preparing for multipoint video conferencing over the existing backbone. Not all member institutions have the necessary DS3/ATM circuits. In Maine, circuits take up to 8 months to be installed after the initial order. This may lengthen the time that we

The video conferencing network has proved to be useful to minimize the need for travel from institution to institution. It has also proved useful in allowing larger audiences for educational activities. For example, an electron microscope can be demonstrated at The Jackson Laboratory and faculty and students from all other sites can view the demonstration. What is especially nice about this is that electron microscopes tend to be in small labs that only accommodate five or six people. By using the video conferencing system we are able to demonstrate to a much larger audience.

The conferencing system can also be used for interviews at a distance so that summer interns for the research labs do their interviews from the campuses over the network and avoid the need to travel several hours.

The summer program also includes a number of guest lecturers. These presentations have been available to the resident interns. With video conferencing, we plan to make these lectures available on the campuses to students who may be future summer interns.

An Authoring System for Instructionally Designed Tutoring Processes

Alexander Seitz*, Matthias Dannenberg*, Hubert Liebhart§

*Dept. of Artificial Intelligence, University of Ulm, 89069 Ulm, Germany,
{seitz,dannenberg}@informatik.uni-ulm.de
§Faculty of Medicine, University of Ulm, Albert-Einstein-Allee 7, 89081 Ulm,
hubert.liebhardt@medizin.uni-ulm.de

Abstract

This paper describes the design and implementation of a domain independent authoring tool for tutoring systems. The presented work incorporates standard authoring features, including a hierarchical development of learning material, but also supports users in a didactically suitable design of the tutoring process. Requirements for the realization of Goal Based Scenarios are fulfilled by a number of implemented add-ons.

Introduction

E-Learning plays a significant role in the field of education and training today. In this connection, the success and acceptance of tutoring systems depends on the quality of the mediated knowledge and skills as well as the quality of how these things are mediated. By now, a considerable assortment of authoring systems exists [1], which support authors well in developing high quality tutoring material. Nevertheless authors still ask for special help for a suitable instructional design of their work. This applies particularly in the field of problem-oriented learning. We designed and implemented an authoring tool to fill this important gap.

The theoretical basis of our system is the instructional design theory of Goal Based Scenarios developed by Roger Schank [4]. Referring to this approach, the authoring tool guides case engineers in designing cases to teach procedural knowledge to solve problems on a high level. In a first step the case engineer identifies the target skills and defines concrete learning objectives, which are realized by defining an exact mission and its submissions. The mission is embedded in a realistic, authentic and enriched cover story that supports the learner to associate him with the real case situation. Finally, two main focuses of the cognitive learning process are supported, namely the discovering of information and the explanation of theoretical and procedural knowledge. Concretely, tasks and learning materials are realized by various learning operations. For example, in the medical domain of Docs 'n Drugs [2], those operations include searching information according to diagnostic reasoning, answering questions for relevant examinations and choosing alternatives to find the correct diagnosis.

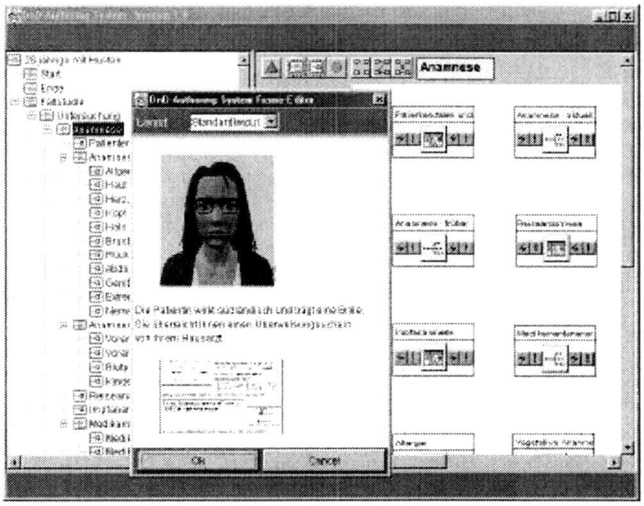

Usually, a tutoring case can be used for different target groups with special learner profiles. Nevertheless, it has to be adapted to the special requirements of each group. Thus we designed our authoring tool to support structuring a tutoring case for allowing the selection of specific case-scenarios and difficulty levels.

Basic authoring features

The basis of a tool for authoring instructionally designed tutoring systems is a set of basic features that allow building appropriate special support modules upon them. We implement a hierarchical system of modules and frames. Frames form the leaves of the hierarchy and contain presentation and interaction elements shown to the learner. See Figure 1 for an example. Contents can be fed into single frame slots on a declarative level, while the author separately specifies the presentation and interaction elements that display these contents. Concrete tutoring system implementations are generated based

Figure 1: The Frame Editor

on these specifications, including web based systems and standalone applications. By this procedure, contents become resistant to individual demands and future technological developments of tutoring systems. The nodes of the hierarchy are modules, consisting of frames or other modules that pertain to each other in content. For each module, common properties of its elements can be defined in attribute editors. In order to specify which other frames or modules are reachable from a given frame or module, the author is able to draw arrows between them. These arrows can be enriched by attribute based conditions, specifying when the associated navigation possibility becomes active. For example, in Docs 'n Drugs the module for a first acquisition of patient data is typically connected to a module where the medical student has to decide which technical examinations have to be done necessarily. The student is not able to reach the second module until he has performed a specified set of anamnesis and body examinations. In a similar manner, an author can create conditional branches within a navigation possibility. For that he draws arrows from a condition node to the possible alternatives for the navigation. A special condition editor feeds the conditions into the system.

Instructional design components

Before an author builds concrete frames of a tutoring case, the learning objectives of that case must be identified. We offer possibilities to formulate learning objectives and assign them to the tutoring case, to modules, or finally to individual frames. Based on the assignments made, the system can build a learning objectives map that helps the author to get an overall view of the didactical structure of his tutoring case.

Learning objectives are realized by a framework of missions and submissions that a learner has to perform. For that, our system allows the definition of instructional design patterns, which form the basis of such frameworks. Instructional design patterns are implemented by configurations of named modules and basic navigation structures, where each module can be supplemented with frames that realize common case aspects. For example, an instructional design pattern that is typical for Docs 'n Drugs includes a module for the standard acquisition of patient data plus frames for a first differential diagnosis, a module for performing specific examinations and making the final diagnosis, and a module for finding the appropriate therapy. Those patterns can be stored, integrated into the user interface of the authoring system, and reused for the design of other tutoring cases.

We support the realization of two important focuses of the cognitive learning process: the discovering of information and the explanation of theoretical and procedural knowledge. For that, frames can be associated with facts like for example patient data. Furthermore, a general rule editor allows relating facts with each other or

with procedural knowledge. Thus, patient data can be related to diagnoses, while diagnoses together with patient circumstances can be related to appropriate therapies. Based on that, tutoring systems can realize facilities to discover and explain the formulated facts and relations. For example, Docs 'n Drugs does this by displaying found relevant patient data in a finding map and asking for the relations in special differential diagnosis and therapy tools.

In order to prepare tutoring cases for the use by different target groups, it has to be kept modular and variable adequately. The use of modules within instructional design patterns and their association with general learning objectives enables a specific selection of those modules by the tutoring system for a given target learner group. Additionally, our system allows formulating different variants of a single frame, frame element, or conditional branch, each of which can be associated with facts like user levels or learning objectives. Those associations together with user preferences or user modeling components allow an individualized configuration of the tutoring case.

Conclusion

The system is implemented in Java and supports jar plugins to extend and adapt its functionality to author needs. An application generator allows different environment realizations like client-server, CD, or web-based products. An XML interface allows the exchange of tutoring data between applications. As far as medical tutoring cases are concerned, we are also involved in standardization efforts [3] for that kind of material.

Ongoing work will focus on the further development of a library of relevant instructional design patterns. This will happen together in corporation with our internal and external application partners.

References

[1] Dean, C. (Ed.): Technology Based Training & Online Learning - An overview of Authoring Systems and Learning Management Systems available in the UK. Sheffield, UK. Department for Education and Skills, Dean Interactive Learning Ltd, Snaithing Grange Annexe, Snaithing Lane, Ranmoor, Sheffield S10 3LF: 2001. URL http://www.deancbt.demon.co.uk/authrep/authrep.pdf. - Updated: June 2001.

[2] Docs 'n Drugs – The Virtual Policlinic. http://www.docs-n-drugs.de.

[3] MedicML. http://www.medicml.de.

[4] Schank, R. (Ed.): Inside Multi-Media Case-Based Reasoning. Mahwah, NJ: Erlbaum Ass, 1998.

Courseware Authoring Tasks Ontology

Lora Aroyo[1] and Darina Dicheva[2]
[1] Technische Universiteit Eindhoven, The Netherlands
l.m.aroyo@tue.nl
[2] Winston-Salem State University, United States of America
dichevad@wssu.edu

Abstract

Authoring of concept-based Web courseware is more complicated than the 'standard' courseware authoring and thus needs more adaptive and intelligent support. In order to provide such support the authoring system itself needs to have understanding about the process of courseware authoring, to be able to decompose it in steps and procedures and reason over it; to provide hints and recommendations to the author, and perform various (semi-) automatic actions. Our goal is to develop a knowledge-based system for concept-based courseware authoring, where the knowledge representation is realized with the help of Courseware Authoring Tasks Ontology (CATO).

1. Introduction

Concept-based courseware employs conceptual domain presentation to link educational materials to a course structure. Therefore concepts are the core building blocks and the main operations in the along going courseware authoring process are grounded around concept manipulation, maintenance and management. The information base of a concept-based course support environment often includes three main components: domain ontology, course structure, and library metadata, which set specific requirements to the supporting authoring tools [3]. Since the authoring of concept-based Web courseware is three-fold [4], including domain-, course-, and library authoring, the process is becoming more complicated and labor intensive than the process of a 'standard' courseware authoring. Apparently this calls for better authoring support for concept-based Web courseware. We envisage such support to include automatic or semi-automatic performance of some authoring activities, intelligent assistance to the authors in the form of hints, recommendations, etc., as well as

supporting the activities of different instructors for collaborative building and/or reuse of domain and course ontologies with templates (eg. based on recognizing different information patterns within domain ontologies or instructional patterns within course structures). A central idea in our approach for providing adequate authoring support for concept-based courseware is to propose a knowledge-based framework for concept-based courseware authoring, where the knowledge representation is realized with the help of Courseware Authoring Tasks Ontology (CATO).

2. Courseware Authoring Tasks Ontology

CATO is functional concept ontology in the sense of [1], where the functional concepts are courseware-authoring tasks. CATO design involves an initial decomposition of the courseware authoring process into a set of basic authoring operations that are used to build an upper-level ontology describing the basic authoring functions and mapping the underlying domain-specific models (such as in AIMS [3] and other instructional systems).

CATO consists of two main layers: *base layer*, which includes hierarchy of atomic authoring tasks, and *meta-layer*, which includes hierarchy of meta-functions. The atomic authoring tasks are primitive functional concepts, which are basic for the concept-based courseware authoring process, for it's understanding and performing. Formal definitions of the atomic tasks are presumed to support their interpretation. This will allow building courseware authoring ontology terminology (vocabulary).

The primitive functions are defined on objects (concepts, documents, course topics and course tasks) within a specific concept-based structure (domain model, course structure, document base). They express a simple functional formalism, where the object changes the structure, or the structure is manipulated. Examples of atomic authoring functions include:

Create (Structure)
Create (Object)
Add (Object, Structure)
Delete (Object, Structure)
Edit (Object, Structure)
Link (Object₁, Object₂, Structure)
Delete (Structure)
Compare (Object₁, Object₂)
Exist (Object, Structure)
List (Objects, Structure)

where *Object* ∈ {{Domain_Concepts} ∪ {Course_Topics} ∪ {Course_Tasks} ∪ {Library_Docs}} and *Structure* ∈ {Domain_Model, Course_Model, Library_Base}. Note that such a definition is independent of the structure - the only prerequisite for it is to be concept-based.

In the meta-layer, we define hierarchy of *meta-functions* to represent conceptual categories of relationship (interdependence) between primitive functions. These present certain aggregation criteria (including causal and other relations among components) that are used for grouping primitive functional concepts into higher-level authoring functions (classes). This way we can construct/identify functional groups of authoring tasks. The meta-functions represent a role of one base-function for another base-function [1]. They are concerned not with the actual change in the objects, but with their actual function in the concept-based courseware authoring process. We define the meta-functions with conditions for their primitive parameters in order to achieve specific authoring goals. This will be based on extracting the functional structure for courseware authoring from existing authoring models (as domain) and their connection to educational information. Examples of meta-functions include:

'is-a-prerequisite-for'
'is-assigned-to'
'is-achieved-by'
'requires'
'follows-from'
'is-followed-by'
'is-preceded-by'
'if-<goal>-then-<action>'

CATO aims at defining formal specifications of conceptualisation to provide a common understanding of the concept-based courseware authoring process (as domain) that can be communicated to support tools for adaptive courseware authoring systems. In order to realise this, we envisage defining of a rule-based model (CATO-

Rules) over the schematic representation of the ontology to

support the understanding of CATO ontological scheme and allow for extracting additional semantics that can be applied in the reasoning strategies of the support tools. CATO-Rules assign interpretations directly to the CATO graph (based on RDF syntax [2]). The vocabulary of the CATO graph is determined by the set of primitive functional concepts (PFC) within the base layer. An interpretation function I is defined over a range (vocabulary V of PFC) and a domain (class of CATO meta-functions).

3. Conclusion

Knowledge representation based on ontologies could be very beneficial in environments, where flexibility is required, thus it can help in meeting the dynamic needs of courseware authoring systems, their maintenance and reuse. We believe that CATO can support common reasoning over the processes accruing in the authoring of the domain model, course structure and information base of concept-based courseware. As additional advantages, CATO can provide for: easy update and altering of knowledge structures; easy change of operation sets without changing the structures; a bird-eye view over the whole authoring process, which can be helpful for process analysis; better understanding of the semantics of the authoring process; good options for visualization, e.g., authoring workflow visualization, visual system feedback, constructing visual authoring wizard, etc.

References

[1] Kitamura, Y., Sano, T. & Mizoguchi, R. (2000). Functional Understanding based on an Ontology of Functional Concepts, Proc. of Sixth Pacific Rim International Conference on AI (PRICAI'00), 723-733.

[2] RDF Model theory. http://www.w3.org/TR/2002/WD-rdf-mt-20020214/.

[3] Aroyo, L., Dicheva, D. & Cristea, A. (2002). Ontological Support for Web Courseware Authoring. *International Conference on Intelligent Tutoring Systems (ITS'02)*, Biarritz, France.

[4] Aroyo, L. (2001). *Task-oriented approach to information handling support within Web-based education*. PhD Thesis, University of Twente, PrintPartners Publishers, Enschede.

Social Integration and Distance Learning Focused on Hospitalized Children with their Habitual Educational Centers and Leisure-Pedagogical Entertainment.

Beatriz Mora Plaza
Diego Pérez Donoso
Alfonso de las Heras de Rivera
Fernando Hervás del Río
Lorena Lebrero Aldegunde

Hospital Universitario de Getafe (University Hospital of Getafe)
Ctra. De Toledo, Km 12,500 CP: 28905 Getafe Madrid (Spain)
info@telesalud.org

Abstract

The continuous progressing of Computing and Communications, along with the increasing number of Internet users, lead us to update the concept of Health Services, being succeeded to offer new and revolutionary functionalities. Derived from this evolution, the supply of Health Attention Services via this media is required from the State Authorities and Administrations.

Internet, as universal net, offers a wide diversity of mechanisms that enable these types of services, from the concept of bibliographic information or as medium, between users of Public heath and Health Staff, or between patient that reside in hospitals and their external family-social environment. In this sense, most demanding areas are the Newborn Children and Paediatrics Services. The position of the children that temporarily reside in hospitals should be emphasized for being somehow excluded from their natural environment, and coexistence with their families and other children. This event can be efficiently surmountable with Technologies that nowadays are used for other purposes. The inclusion of those services using Internet (e-Health) will serve the child during his stay in hospital offering Services of Social Integration with their owns teaching centres keeping contact with their habitual teachers and colleagues; or participating in games, chats, etc defined by experts in children cares.

1. INTRODUCTION

The continuous progressing of Computing and Communications, along with the increasing number of Internet users, lead us to update the concept of Health Services, being succeeded to offer new and revolutionary functionalities. Derived from this evolution, the supply of Health Attention Services via this media is required from the State Authorities and Administrations. The aim of the Project is to develop a Virtual Platform of e-Learning using New Technologies, offering a quality-education and a social inter-relationship with resident children and their educational centers, colleagues, etc.

Children that resides in hospitals have a mayor predisposition towards school failure because, among other reasons, they are somehow excluded from their natural environment and coexistence with their families and other children.

At the same time, Educational centers do not offer at all any kind of help to those children, apart from other problems, because do not have the required technological mechanisms that nowadays are used for other purposes. The inclusion of those services using Internet (e-Health), will serve the child during his/her stage in hospital, offering services of Social Integration with the own teaching center, keeping contact with their habitual teachers and colleagues; or participating in games, chats, etc., defined and supervised by experts in children cares.

2 OBJETIVES:

Continuity in the habitual learning methodology of the children that temporally resides in hospitals and during the recovery period at children's homes.
Increase the participation of Educational Centres in the formation and education of those children.
Ease Social Integration.
Make the best of the already existing Technologies.
Improvement of the teaching quality.
Re-enforcement of the parents confidence about the education of their children and the educational centres.
Improvements of the teaching quality of the stage of the children and an increase of their self-confidence.

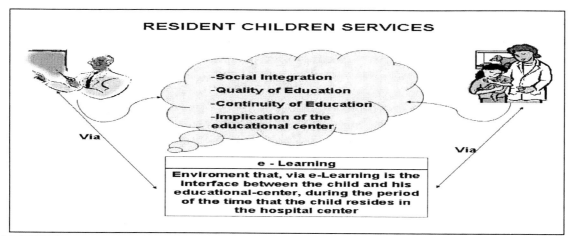

RESIDENT CHILDREN SERVICES

- Social Integration
- Quality of Education
- Continuity of Education
- Implication of the educational center

Via

Via

e - Learning
Enviroment that, via e-Learning is the interface between the child and his educational-center, during the period of the time that the child resides in the hospital center

3 METHODOLOGY:

The Information required for the development of e-Health (Internet for New Health Services), is collected from Health professionals and from direct beneficiaries with this Health interaction with New Technologies. The main data collector element is the University Hospital of Getafe, Nurses, Paediatrics, and collaborators that form the research team. These Health professionals, being a heterogeneous group, have detected the needs and requirements in a wide and exhaustive manner. In the e-Health (Internet for New Health Technologies), a division of the work line has been necessary, because of the detection of different kinds of requirements depending on the population groups. This division, modular structured, represents groups of Services for the groups of necessities detected.

4 RESIDENT CHILDREN SERVICES:

Developed to work for children integration in their familiar-social environments, inter-relationship between children and their educational centers, tutors, colleagues, other children in their same situation via entertainment and educational services (chats, forums, net-games, competitions, etc.).

Children Resident Services pretend to be the intermediates between children and their schools, taking advantages of the e-Learning benefits. This platform would be the mechanism required by educational centers to assure no educational carencies during the period of time that children cannot assist the classes. A more involucration and participation from these centers and parents confidence would be obtained. The children would be supervised by their own teachers and would make practices and laboratories with their classmates; but the most important success is that it would make children feel closer to their family-social environment that is outside the hospitals.

5 GENERAL RESULTS:

Improvement of Health Services via the communication, participation and supervision on-line of patients.
Collaboration among hospitals to reach the objetive of an effective and swift Health Service.
Making resident children getting closer to their habitual environment.
Improvement of the quality of children stage in hospitals.

6 CONCLUSION:

New Technologies at the service of well-defined and well-marked aims, give unique help and benefits.
This type of solutions is well-accepted by resident children, for offering them activities from which they are excluded during the period of time that are in hospital.
The big disadvantage of e-Learning is the loss of humanization because there is no direct human contact. Despite of this, with the participation of the child school centre and the habitual teachers via e-Learning, a reduction of this effect and an enforcement of the child integration is successfully achieved.

7 REFERENCES

1 .- [Butler et al.; 1989] Hernán, San Martín. Manual de salud pública y medicina preventiva. Editorial MASSON, Barcelona (España), 1989.
2 .- Enrique Casado de Frías, Ángel Nogales Espert. Pediatría. Editorial HARCOURT, Madrid (España), 1997.
3 .- [Castillo Luna et al.; 1998] Javier Castillo Luna. Cuidados intensivos en Pediatría. Editorial Colegio Oficial de Diplomados en Enfermería de Madrid, 1998.
4 .- Consuelo Gutiérrez Ortiz. Medicina en Internet. Editorial Anaya Multimedia, Madrid (España), 1997.

Windows Into The Classroom

Anne-Louise Agnew
St Paul's Grammar School
Sydney Australia

Paul's Grammar school in Sydney, Australia, provides a world of exciting and challenging learning experiences for the students. Working from class web pages and with schools from a number of countries around the globe, these students use a wide range of technologies as an integral tool in the classroom.

The students have created discussion boards to assist with assignments, web pages to display their completed work, videos and powerful PowerPoint presentations to broaden their perspective on delivering oral presentations to the class and wider audiences. Each student is also compiling a file of work from different curriculum areas through out the year to create a digital portfolio that will be included with their end of year report.

Technology is enabling these students to develop independence and greater responsibility for their own learning. It has changed the nature of the classroom and has enriched the learning environment exponentially

Since educators first began to use computers in the classroom, researchers have tried to evaluate whether the use of educational technology has a significant and reliable impact on student achievement. It has been acknowledged that technology cannot be treated as a single independent variable, and is most effective when integrated into the curriculum, so that students are encouraged to use higher-order thinking skills, (such as thinking critically, analyzing, making inferences, and solving problems).

The most common - and in fact, nearly universal - teacher-reported effect of using technology in the classroom has been an increase in student motivation. Teachers and students are sometimes surprised at the level of technology-based accomplishment displayed by students who have shown much less initiative or facility with more conventional academic tasks.

Through the use of technology in the classroom, students are developing skills that will help to prepare them for a future world that is ever-changing. Through the use of technology, students are able to handle more complex assignments and do more with higher-order

The address of our class web site is:www.geocities.com/spg7a/7a.html

The idea is to familiarize the students with accessing the web for their class information and to become more independent with regards to their learning. All projects and assignments are published on these class web sites— no hard copies of the tasks are provided. Students are expected to read the information themselves and to access the associated links that have been created to assist with all aspects of the task. In addition to providing the students with this information, it also provides parents with ready-access to what is happening at school and to the assignments that are currently being undertaken by the students – thus preventing loss of important details or misunderstanding of criteria,

requirements etc. Email links have been established so that both students and parents can contact the teachers at any time if they have problems, queries or wish to discuss some aspect of the assignment or associated matter.

Technology is also integrated into the daily routine of the classroom. Students are encouraged to use the computers whenever they feel that this could enhance their work. We have noticed that there has been a greater level of peer tutoring and co-operation within the classroom and students are generally more involved with one another on a practical level. They tend to stimulate one another and encourage others to use more advanced skills as they work through the processes of applying their skills to the tasks.

It is important to realize that technology does not mean using computers alone, but rather that the best uses include a wide range of multi-media technologies, including video, photographs, discussion boards, web development, slide presentations etc. Experiences in developing the kinds of rich, multimedia products that can be produced with technology, particularly when the design is done collaboratively appears to initiate the greatest responses from the students who then experience their peers' reactions to their presentations. Multiple media give students choices about how best to convey a given idea (e.g., through text, video, animation). Greater confidence in preparing presentations is also apparent as students are completing more professional-looking products and the developing skills to use the tools required to manipulate the way information is presented. As a result, students in many technology-using classes are using and developing a wide range of skills previously not experienced in the "regular" classroom, but previously only occurring in specialist classes.

Students are encouraged to develop and work with a rubric that sets out the criteria required for all aspects of every task. In this way, they have ownership over the process of completing the activity and also a greater understanding of accepted responses within the task. This also helps to avoid common pitfalls encountered when using technology ie students sometimes get "carried away" with the creative side of technology and move a way from the content aspect. Because the rubric identifies all the components of the task that will be assessed, students are able to remain focused on the task as a whole. These rubrics are also published on the class web site so that parents have access to the same information – an important issue for those who support their students with their studies. You can view samples of the rubrics if you go to the class web site (spg7a) and visit the assignments links.

Students in the class are also working with schools in a number of countries around the world. They are sharing a range of activities and projects with these students including:

- Travel buddies with a school in Azerbaijan (see 7A web site for details of this project)
- Emails with schools in Austria, Azerbaijan and Finland
- World Project with schools from a number of countries globally – please visit the site for our project: http://www.geocities.com/worldproject2002/home.html
- International School Partnerships through Technology with a school in North Carolina. Please visit the site: http://www.ga.unc.edu/NCCIU/ispt/ to read more information about this project

The work undertaken by the students with other schools around the world not only provides opportunities to develop greater cultural awareness and understanding,but also to provide a springboard for ideas and an audience for completed works.

Throughout the year, all students in year 7 are compiling their own Digital Portfolios. These are a collection of works from all major curriculum areas showing development and accomplishment of a variety of skills and tasks. Each addition includes a reflection written by the student referring to the processes undertaken, approaches to learning and outcomes achieved. Samples of these portfolios can also be viewed on the 7A web site www.geocities.com/spg7a/7a.html

These Portfolios will be used as an adjunct to the written reports given to parents at the end of the school year. Their purpose is to support the report and to provide a more tangible record of the development of skills and the achievement of specified outcomes.

The students at St Paul's Grammar School are using technology as an integrated tool in the classroom. Students and teachers have worked together to create a new learning environment in the classroom that supports flexibility, individual learning needs and styles and a greater level of independence in the learning process.

The results have been quite significant and appear to be having an extremely positive impact on all students – at all learning levels, students have become more interested and more responsible for their own learning; and teachers have taken on new roles as guides, supervisors and tutors rather than holding the central position in the classroom.

The use of technology has assisted the implementation of an inquiry based approach to learning where students are encouraged to become involved in creating, researching, exploring, problem-solving and experiencing the whole process of learning in an exciting and fulfilling manner.

The development and discriminant validity of the computerized dynamic number sense assessment system

Su-wei Lin[1], Pi-hsia Hung[2], Wen-long Cheng[2], Weichung Wang[2]

[1]National Taiwan Normal University, [2]National Tainan Teachers College, Taiwan, R.O.C.

linsuwei@tpts6.seed.net.tw

Abstract

The purpose of this study is to develop a computerized dynamic number sense assessment (CDNSA) system to investigate the issues of elementary students' number sense. Number sense is enriched by meaningful experiences and the performance is situated in specific content or context. Based upon our operational definition, three difficulty levels are developed to assess the students' number sense dynamically. The results show that the three difficulty levels of the CDNSA system could discriminate different ability levels groups successfully. It suggests that there is discriminative power in the CDNSA system for distinguishing different number sense degrees.

1. Introduction

A document from the National Research Council (1989) suggested that major objective of elementary school mathematics is to develop number sense. This strong statement can change the way many teachers' mathematical instructions in today's elementary school. In Taiwan, there is increasing concern about the students' number sense. How to teach? How to learn? How to assist students to develop it? And how to assess? With these important educational issues in mind, the purpose of this study is to develop a computerized dynamic number sense assessment (CDNSA) system to investigate the relevant issues of students' number sense development in the elementary school.

In this study, the operational definition of number sense is following. When an individual faces the life experience-related situations that embedded by numbers and quantities, she/he can access the number knowledge base automatically, be sensitive to it and process it rapidly. Based on this definition, we develop the CDNSA system to investigate the issues of students' number sense development in the elementary school.

2. The design logic of CDNSA

According to the definition of number sense, a series of questions were developed to assess the students' number sense. These questions require students to focus on the relationships among numerical data, complete the numerical data mathematically and contextually. As a capacity to learn, to perceive, and to use, number relationships are implicit in the idea of number-sense. Besides, the assessment drew on Vygotsky's notion of a "zone of proximal development" (ZPD) (Vygotsky, 1978) in order to take learning into account. To assess students' number sense dynamically, the CDNSA system includes a feedback system. After their responses, students have to evaluate the appropriateness of their answers by the feedbacks of the assessment system. If some of the students' answers are wrong, the feedback system will give a hint and ask students to try again. As the number of trials increasing, hints are more concrete and precise toward the solutions. The feedback procedure will not end until answers to the question are all correct. The basic logic of feedback design is as follow:

Hint 1: Providing "right or wrong" feedback.
Hint 2: Reminding students to find the easier blanks.
Hint 3: Reminding students to look for related blanks that have some mathematical relationships.
Hint 4: Presenting related blanks.
Hint 5: Presenting related blanks and relationships.
Hint 6: Presenting partial correct answers.
Hint 7: Presenting all correct answers.

3. The discriminant validity of CDNSA

The CDNSA system required the student to answer each question correct completely. If she/he fails to complete correctly, the system will not proceed to the next question. This study differentiates the students into three ability groups according to their responses on the first question. The ability degrees of Group 1, 2, and 3 were low, middle, and high, respectively. Figure 1 presents the three groups' average pass rates on each question. If we set the correct percentages exceed .70 as the cut point. It then suggests that the first 2 questions, we called Level I, appear to be the easiest for all students. For Group 1, they are able to pass the Level I, but not able to pass the Level II, namely, the question 3. Group 2 could easily pass the Level I and II, but can not overcome the Level III (question 4 and 5.) For Group 3, it should not be too difficult for them to pass all the questions. Having analyzed the number of trials of the three groups, the results also suggest the Gorup1 and 2 had more difficulty than Group3, and all students encountered even more difficulties as the question number increases. To sum up, CDNSA is able to achieve good discriminant effect. Table 1 presents the correlations between the performance on CDNSA and the school grades. The correlation coefficient between correct percentage and math is around .5s, and the coefficient also for language is also .5s. Between the number of trials and school grades, the correlation coefficient is around -.62s for language and -.42s for math. It suggests that the CDNSA has quite reasonable validity.

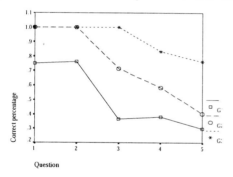

Figure 1. The pass rates of the CDNSA system of three ability groups

Table 1. The correlations between the performance on CDNSA and the school grades

	Language	Math	Correct percentage of CDNSA
Math	.727**		
Correct percentage of CDNSA	.514**	.487**	
Trial Number of CDNSA	-.624**	-.422*	-.726**

**p< 0.01   *p<0.05

4. Conclusion

We offer an innovative approach to assess and promote students' number sense. Although students might experience a lot of realistic number activities, he or she still needs opportunities to challenge their number sense. Simultaneously, an appropriate teacher or instrument support also needed in dealing with challenging tasks that can extend students' mathematical understanding. The CDNSA presented here fulfilled our aims of developing children's number sense to facilitate their understanding of the numerical data material.

This study also points to the affiliated need for testing methodologies and appraisal methods that take students' ability to learn into account, rather than `controlling' for it. The feedback system used in the present study represents one possible step in that direction-one which could also be used to assess students' number activity. This would also render future investigation of whether children's ability to learn in one domain (e.g. number) is or not related to their ability to learn mathematics possible.

References

[1] Brown, A.L. & Ferrara, R.A. (1985) Diagnosing zones of proximal development, in: J.V. Wertsch, (Ed.) *Culture, Communication and Cognition: Vygotskyan perspectives* (pp. 273-305). Cambridge: Cambridge University Press.

[2] Greeno, J.G. (1991) Number sense as situated knowing in a conceptual domain, *Journal for Research in Mathematics Education*, 22, pp. 170-218.

[3] Markovits, Z. & Sowder, J. (1994) Developing number sense: an intervention study in Grade 7, *Journal for Research in Mathematics Education*, 25, pp. 4-29.

[4] National Council of Teachers of Mathematics. (1989). *Curriculum and evaluation standards for school mathematics*. Reston, VA: Author.

[5] National Council of Teachers of Mathematics. (2000). *Principles and Standards for School Mathematics*. Reston, VA: Author.

[6] National Research council. (1989). *Everybody counts*. Washington, D.C. : National Academy Press.

[7] Sowder, J. (1992). Estimation and number sense. In D. A. Grouws (Ed.), *Handbook of research on mathematics teaching and learning* (pp. 371-389). New York: Macmillan.

[8] Vygotsky, L. (1978). *Mind in society: The development of higher psychological processes*. Cambridge, MA: Harvard University Press.

Online Collaborative Learning:
Have We Overcome the Obstacles?

J. M. McInnerney
Bundaberg, Queensland 4670, Australia
cowlrick@bigpond.com
'Phone: +61 7 4155 1649

Tim S Roberts
Central Queensland University
Bundaberg, Queensland 4670, Australia
t.roberts@cqu.edu.au
'Phone: +61 7 4150 7057
fax: +61 7 4150 7090

Abstract

Collaborative learning techniques are still largely disregarded within higher education. This paper investigates the reasons why the practice of collaborative learning within a tertiary environment is still seen as largely problematical.

Introduction

Many educational institutions are currently seeking to re-engineer their degree programs to match the needs of a changing market place. The irony at this time is that as the fierce competitiveness of the market place increases, so too does the collaborative and co-operative nature of work forces in many commercial enterprises. This means that if our educational institutions do not teach their students to work together – collaborate – they may well find their own students marginalized as prospective employees.

Defining the terms

The term "collaborative" means to work in a group of two or more to achieve a common goal while respecting each individuals contribution to the whole: note that one does not have to be on-line to be a part of a collaborative team. Collaborative learning is a learning method that uses social interaction as a means of knowledge building [5].

The term "cooperative" is often used interchangeably with "collaborative", but they have different literal meanings. Cooperative means to work or act together as one to achieve a common goal and tends to de-emphasize the input of particular individuals [3]. The difficult aspect for some, but not necessarily all, students, whether school leavers or mature age, is that collaboration has often been encouraged in their school or workplace, but is not always encouraged at the tertiary level.

On-line Collaborative Learning at the Tertiary Level

As an ever-increasing number of students find that they need to work to pay for their education, universities have had to adapt their courses to enable increased use of the on-line environment to communicate with and educate both their existing and potential student base as well as potential employers.

Populations, whether academic or mainstream, do not grow with any confidence if their members do not embrace and become literate in those technologies that will let them be a part of the growing global village. Educators have to understand that they cannot simply translate current lectures and tutorials to the on-line environment. They have to utilize the latest technologies to the benefit of both the institutions and the students.

In the case of on-line collaborative learning, all the students in a group have to work together to achieve a common goal even though each student is primarily responsible for their own individual effort and assessment [1].

An examination of the existing literature in this area suggests the following basic guidelines for educators seeking to implement collaborative learning techniques:

- Design the on-line flexible course so as to enable collaborative learning,

- Establish rules at the beginning of the course,
- Do not allow individual students to dominate discussion,
- Ask specific questions of the group as a whole and also address questions to specific groups of students,
- Assign the role of gatekeeper to students on a rotational basis so that each student learns to be responsible for the behavior of the group,
- Summarize contributions and ask for comments on the topics being discussed, and
- Conduct a mid-course assessment to ascertain how the course is progressing.

Johnson and Johnson [2] advise of three shortcomings of individual or isolated on-line learning:

- Individual work isolates students,
- Individual instruction limits the resources and the technology available, and
- Individualized instruction greatly increases development and hardware costs.

Panitz [4] lists several reasons why academics may not rush to utilize collaborative learning in their courses, whether on-line or face-to-face, but the top four in our opinion are:

- Possible loss of control in the classroom,
- Possible lack of self confidence,
- Possible fear of the loss of content coverage, and
- Possible damage to the ego.

Student Perspectives

As with most of the research in the area of collaborative learning the vast majority of the written research on student perceptions is from the K-12 perspective. However, much can be extrapolated from this research if it is combined with what little has been written on on-line collaborative learning at the tertiary level. Collaborative learning should teach students to understand the importance of teamwork, and will make it easier for them to be integrated into the workplace. We know that collaborative learning means more preparation for the academic but also that such experiments can be very successful. [2].

One of the more positive effects of on-line collaborative learning is that the student is able to participate in collaboration outside of normal class or work time. This makes it an ideal method for traditional distance students who are unable to attend a campus due to either distance or work. Simply because there is no face-to-face interaction between students it becomes essential that we take the time to teach our students, both distance and on-campus, to communicate in the on-line environment.

Social Relationships

Panitz [4] suggests 59 benefits of collaborative learning. Many of the points apply to the on-line collaborative environment as practices at the tertiary level indicating that the prime objective of collaborative learning is that of enhancing the self-esteem of the students. It also encourages the students to be aware of and interact with each other thereby promoting social and academic relationships.

Should it be the responsibility of tertiary institutions to develop social awareness in their students or is that the prerequisite and mandate of parents? The answer to that question is a resounding yes; it is the responsibility of tertiary institutions to develop social awareness in their students, with the caveat that it is also the parents' responsibility to ensure that their children become socially aware and interact harmoniously with others prior to starting at the tertiary level.

Summary

This paper has described in a relatively informal way a broad outline of on-line collaborative learning at the tertiary level, discussed student perspectives of the process, and the strengths and sometimes the weaknesses of online collaborative learning, and has suggested that much depends upon the student perspectives and social relationships engendered by the structure and content of the courses.

References

[1] Hiltz, R. S. (1998). 'Collaborative Learning in Asynchronous Learning Networks: Building Learning Communities'.
http://eies.njit.edu/~hiltz/collaborative_learning_in_asynch.htm

[2] Johnson, D. W. & Johnson, R. T. (2001). 'Cooperation and the use of Technology'. In The Handbook of Research for Educational Communications and Technology.
http://www.aect.org/Intranet/Publications/edtech/35/index.html

[3] Panitz, T. (1996). 'Collaborative versus cooperative learning- A comparison of the two concepts which will help us understand the underlying nature of interactive learning'.
http://home.capecod.net/~tpanitz/tedsarticles/coopdefinition.htm

[4] Panitz, T. (1997). 'Why more teachers do not use collaborative learning techniques'.
http://home.capecod.net/~tpanitz/tedsarticles/whyfewclusers.htm

[5] Paz Dennen, V. (2000). 'Task structuring for on-line problem based learning: A case study'. In Educational Technology & Society 3[3] 2000.

Assessment Design for Mathematics Web Project-based Learning

Yuen Chen, I-hua Lin, Yann-jiun Tzeng, Pi-hsia Hung, Weichung Wang

National Tainan Teachers College, Taiwan, R.O.C.

eve@m2k.chukps.kh.edu.tw

Abstract

Four mathematics project-based learning activities were carried out on a web environment in this study. Several mindtools such as dynamic geometry scratch pad, concept mapping and powerpoint were also adopted as learning aids. Forty second to fifth grade elementary school students from Tainan and Kaohsiung cities were included. They registered as the collaborative learners for one year. The quality of final reports, collaborating skills and the ability of using mindtools for each group were assessed while they were doing mathematics project learning through internet collaboration. Based upon the process-oriented assessment design, student's learning progresses were discussed in detail. Overall, the inter-rater reliability of the three assignment designs is between .84 and .92. These flexible structured and process oriented assessment designs would be of great potential to monitor the web collaborative learning.

Keywords: Probleming-based learning,
Computer-based learning,
Mathematic learning assessment,
elementary school

1 Introduction

Project-based learning, which focuses on collaboration, multi-subject integration, and technological application, has become a revolutionary trend in recent mathematics education. This learning emphasizes the linkage between authentic experiences as well as the importance of shared goal and mutual support among different learners, hoping to offer a promising alternative for future mathematics educational reform.

Krajcik,Czerniak and Berger(1999)define collaboration as a joint intellectual effort of students, peers, teachers, and community members to investigate a question or a problem. The Internet provides learners with a handy opportunity to cooperate. By lessening each team member's learning load, it also provides better opportunities for learners to develop techniques that everyday life calls for. Collaboration learning on the Internet goes beyond superficial exchanges of information. What's more important, it provides a mutually cooperative and interactive procedure for learners to create and redefine what learning is(Kaye, 1992) . Students can then be cultivated to learn independently and avail themselves of the Internet.(Wu, Hung& Tzou,2000) Project-based learning emphasizes learners' motivation in exploring and follow-up extensive learning that goes beyond their textbooks. It hopes that students' learning can be so full of vitality as to experience the adaptability, challenge and fun of mathematics learning.

2 Research Design

Series of mathematics project-based learning activities were carried out in the " YP Learning Garden." see table2-1, Website: http://yp.ntntc.edu.tw)

Table 2-1: YP Learning Garden and the Assessmnet Enbeded

YP Learning Garden	Public Discussion Chatting Room	
	Digital Portfolio	
	Mind tools Reference	
	Web Post Office	
	Dynamic Assessmnet Center	Web Collaboration (Issue-relation,Self-initiation Collaboration)
		Project Product (Accuracy,Originality, Richness)
		Mind tools (Application,Creativity, Appropriateness)

3 Methods and Procedure of the Experiment

Forty elementary school students from Tainan and Kaohsiung city registered voluntarily for the study. It is agreed consent that participants should abide by the following qualifications. Learning activities in the study proceed from mid December 2000 to the end of December 2001, spanning a one-year period. Students work collaboratively on the Internet. There are three assessment designs in this research. The first one is to assess the product quality of each group. The second one is to evaluate students in the efficiency of web collaboration learning and their progress in project-based learning (PBL). The third one is to evaluate their ability of applying mindtools in PBL.

4. Results and analysis of the experiment

4.1 Project Product

Four series projects were carried out in this study. The final report of each project is rated in regard to originality, accuracy and richness. Table2 presents the results of comparison and correlation of the descriptive statistics of the product ratings. The internal-consistency reliability between scores in originality, accuracy and richness discriminate .76, .80 and .66. Overall, progress in originality, accuracy and richness of PBL at the later stage is better than that at the early stage. Figure 4-1 presents the three-dimensional curves in the products of one single group at both the early and later stages.

Table 4-1: Comparison of the Product Ratings of Different Stages

Report quality	Project 1		Project 2		Inter-rater reliability
	mean	sd	mean	sd	
Originality	7.96	0.72	10.49	0.62	.76
Accuracy	8.06	0.63	11.00	0.63	.80
Richness	7.43	0.71	10.95	0.69	.66

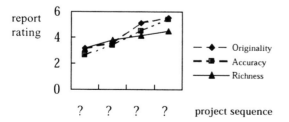

Figure 4-1. The profile of three facets of the series reports of group2

4.2 Web collaboration

This study investigates collaborative project-learning on the Internet. Students' performance in the respect of issue-relation, self-initiation and collaboration are to be studied.or frameworks of the learned courses. Generally speaking, students' discussions appear enthusiastic and active. If conflicts emerge, they will also state their arguments on the Internet so as to maintain collaborative equilibrium.

4.3 Mindtools Application

The research uses the Geometry Scratch Pad (GSP) and PowerPoint as the mindtools in PBL. It also analyzes how creativity, appropriateness and skills are applied in the products.

Table 4-3: Comparisons of Mindtools Application of Different Stages

Report quality	Project ?		Project ?	
	mean	sd	mean	sd
Creativity	4.04	0.43	5.01	0.45
Appropriateness	3.50	0.41	4.76	0.56
Skills	3.00	0.33	5.41	0.66

5. Conclusion

This study looks into mathematics project-related learning activities conducted through the Internet. On the one hand, it keeps track of students' progression on both their project performance and on-line discussion skills. On the other hand, it represents the correlations between participants' assignments and their final achievements. As they grow more experienced in project learning, their work also reflects a better quality of elaborateness and originality, thus proving that project-based learning would be ideal within a long-term time frame. In the aspect of negotiating what learning goals should be and giving feedbacks on what has learned, all the observation records and assessment designs developed in the study also hope to provide some physical help. The collection and design of such framed and systematic data should also greatly benefit the compilation, integration and interpretation of all assessment data in project learning.

References

[1] Balacheff.N,Kaput J.J.(1996).Internation Handbook of Mathematics Education. Kluwer Academic Publishers.

[2] Kaye, A. R.(1992). Collaborative Learning through Computer conferencing. NY:Spronger Verlag.

[3]KrajcikJ.S,CzermiakC.M&Berger,C(1999).Teaching children science:A project-based approach.McGraw-Hill College.

[4] Pi-Hsia Hung,, Yuen Chen(1991).The Assessment and Application of Mathematical PBL Journal.Taiwan Education,604,15-24

[5] Tieh-Hsiung Wu , Pi-Hsia Hung & Hui-Yin Tzou(2000).The Dynamic Assessmnet of Web-based PBL.National Science Council Project research project.

Use of Learner Agents as Student Modeling System and Learning Companion

Teresita Limoanco and Raymund Sison
College of Computer Studies
De La Salle University, Prof. Schools Inc
{tessie, raymund}@ccs.dlsu.edu.ph

ABSTRACT

Instructional systems are computer programs that provide educational support to individual learners. One such system is the intelligent tutoring systems (ITSs). ITSs center on individualized learning and do not consider the situation where learners can learn beyond the teacher-learner relationship. Several learning companion systems (LCS) were implemented to create social learning environments. However these systems are merely extensions of tutor agents and act as "learners". In this paper, we introduce the use of learner agents both as student modeling systems and as peers.

1 Introduction

Intelligent tutoring systems (ITSs) are software systems intended for educational support that have the capability to diagnose problems of individual learners. Aside from individualized instruction, they also cater to peer-supported learning known as learning companions. However, these learning companions are merely variants of tutor models made to "act" as students. They appear to be peers but do not really act as peers for the following reasons: (1) the learning companions' knowledge base is a subset of that of the tutor agent; and (2) the tutor agent controls the learning companions throughout its interaction with the student. This paper, therefore, introduces the use of learner agents as models of human learners and as learning companions. *Learner agents* are software agents whose functions are: (1) to represent and model a human learner; and (2) perform tasks on behalf of human learners. The proposed use of learner agent is intended for intelligent Internet-based learning support [5].

2 Learner Agent Architecture

Figure 1 shows the structure of a learner agent that is based on the INTERRAP agent architecture of Muller [3]. The architecture has three basic components: the *interaction behavior, reasoning behavior* and *knowledge base*. The **interaction behavior** specifies how the agent engages its environment. The **reasoning behavior** is the agent's decision-making process, which is divided into

two subcomponents. The first subcomponent, *local planning and control* allows the learner agent to react accordingly on the environment, and performs tasks that may not require any cooperation with other agents. The *social behavior*, in contrast, handles the cooperative process of the learner agent. The **knowledge base** contains information about the human learner and records all activities conducted (as well as interactions with other agents and entities) by the learner as he navigates and executes applications in the Internet. The World Model, on the other hand, contains knowledge common to all agents or agents belonging to a particular class.

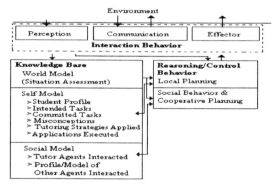

Figure 1: Learner Agent Architecture

3 Learner Agent As Student Modeling System

The traditional ITS structure follows the architecture shown in Figure 2a. It contains 2 major components: the student model and the tutor model. The student model here contains information on how the tutor model sees and represents the learner during learner's interaction with the system. Thus, the ITS is viewed as a tutor agent. The proposed architecture for a learner agent as a student modeling system (Figure 2b) is similar to that of the traditional ITS structure; but it treats the student model component as a separate entity. In this case we call it a *learner agent*. The *social model* (Figure 2b) pertains to information about the tutor agents, other learner agents and entities the learner agent has interacted with.

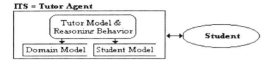

Figure 2a: Intelligent Tutoring System

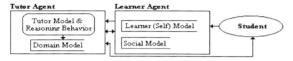

Figure 2b: Learner Agent as Student Modeling & Peer

Treating the learner agent as a student modeling system has several advantages: (a) user modeling is not confined to the tutor agent's perception; and (b) the most current student profile and other related information is considered and carried to the subsequent learning activities with other ITSs. This yields to a more accurate assessment on student's learning. However, several issues need to be considered in this research and some include: (a) a generic framework for the learner agent is need to be defined so that it can work with existing ITSs; (b) the student model component and the adapt strategy component of the tutor agent should follow common formats when it comes to exchanging of information.

4 Learner Agent as a Peer

The learner agent can be in any of the two possible states if the human learner is not interacting with an ITS: (1) perform tasks on behalf of the human learner and (2) provide assistance to other learner agents in the environment. The former involves modeling of human learner while the latter focuses on the cooperative activity involving learner agents.

The concept of a learning companion in this research differs from the learning companion of [1,2,4] in the sense that the latter learning companion is focused on teaching a learner, while the former acts as the learner's peer and may interact with other peers. In [1,2,4] the learning companion is fully controlled by the tutor agent. This means that the tutor agent decides how the companion will interact with the human learner. In contrast, the learning companion proposed in this research (Figure 2b) has the capability to teach or share information of what it knows to other learner agents. In some cases, it is possible that a human learner requires resources on topics of which he is not competent. In this case, the learner agent has the option of seeking assistance from other learner agents in the environment or pursuing the human learner's goal on its own. In addition, while performing search, if a learner agent encounters information that might be useful and helpful to its counterpart human learner, it can take note of the information in its knowledge base (World Model & Self Model, Figure 1).

5 Conclusion

Employing learning companions in ITSs would definitely give assistance in the learning activities of a human learner or better yet increase the learner's competence in topics being learned. But, with the current implementations of learning companions, they suffer from certain common drawbacks (e.g., their knowledge base is rather fixed and predefined; and their behavior is determined by the tutor agent).

In this paper, we introduced the use of learner agents as student modeling systems and as learning companions. It revises what we know as the traditional ITS structure by treating the student model component as a separate entity and allowing it to behave autonomously. However, much work remains to be made towards building learner agents in reality. Particularly, in-depth study of modeling learner agents and implementation of such is needed to see how its interaction with other agents affects its represented beliefs, knowledge and learning behavior of learners. Moreover, careful design of learner agent should be considered when it is used as student model component of ITSs. This is because different ITSs have different implementations and means of modeling learners' profiles.

References

[1] Chan, T. W. & Baskin, A. B. (1990). Learning Companion Systems. In C. Frasson & G. Gauthier (Eds). Intelligent Tutoring Systems: At the Crossroads of Artificial Intelligence and Education, Chapter 1., New Jersey: Ablex Publishing Corporation

[2] Chan, T.W, & Chou, C. (1995). Simulating a Learning Companion in Reciprocal Tutoring Systems. Proceedings of CSCL 1995. The 1st International Conference on Computer Support for Collaborative Learning. October 17-20, 1995. Bloomington, Indiana, Laurence Enbaum Associates, Inc. pp. 49-55.

[3] Muller, J. (1997). A Cooperation Model for Autonomous Agents. In M. Wooldridge and Nicholas Jennings (Eds). Intelligent Agents III: Agent Theories, Architectures and Languages. Springer Verlag 1193. LNCS

[4] Ramirez Uresti, J. (1998). Teaching a Learning Companion. In Halloran, J & Retkowsky, F. (Eds). The 10th White House Papers. Graduate Research in the Cognitive and Computing Sciences at Sussex. CSRP No. 478. School of Cognitive and Computing Sciences, University of Sussex, Brighton, U.K.

[5] Sison, R. (2001). Framework for Intelligent Internet-based Learning Support. In Proceedings of the Ninth International Conference on Computers in Education. Pp. 926-931.

Qualitative Study of Students' Learning Information Technology
via a Cooperative Approach

Shu Ching Yang
shyang@mail.nsysu.edu.tw

Shu Fang Liu
liufang@ms17.hinet.net

Graduate Institute of Education
National Sun Yat-sen University
70 Nein-Hi Rd, Kaohsiung, Taiwan, R.O.C. 80424

1. Introduction

The need for learners to interact cooperatively and work toward group goals undoubtedly increased during the 1990s. Educational researchers and teachers all pressed for a change and accentuated the need for a more student-active, social, as well as cooperative approach to school work. As society changes and information technology becomes more and more important, schools must place an increased emphasis on students' ability to search for information and knowledge, and to study critically. Students must be given opportunities to solve problems, to be creative, and to take initiative on their own. Yet in Taiwan, education traditionally has emphasized individual competition and achievement, an approach that results in winners and losers and sometimes produces outright hostility among learners. Furthermore, research on the instruction of computers in Taiwan reveals that classroom instruction frequently is dominated the use of lectures. A project to design student-centered, and team-based, learning information technology is an important and worthwhile endeavor.

The theoretical advantages of cooperative instruction have long been acknowledged and have been extensively practiced in the classroom. Cooperative learning is a pedagogical technique that has students work together in small, fixed groups on a structured learning task with the aim of maximizing their own and each other's learning (Johnson & Johnson, 1987). Johnson et al. (1991) emphasizes that five basic elements are necessary for effective use of the method: positive group interdependence, individual accountability, face-to-face interaction, social skills training, and group processing.

In the current study, Johnson and Johnson's Learning Together approach is employed for its emphasis on group learning instead of competition. The Learning Together approach involves a more collaborative model in which students are directed to coordinate their efforts toward task completion with less emphasis on competition. The exploratory study investigates the learners' perceptions and attitudes toward the cooperative approach.

2. Methodology

Participants

The participants in the study were thirty-two elementary school students in the third grade. Prior to instruction, a survey was administered to students in order to assess their knowledge of computers and interpersonal relationships. The 17 girls and 15 boys were divided into eight heterogeneous groups of three and four on the basis of their prior knowledge, computer experience, and their interpersonal relationships.

Curriculum Design

There were nine units of programs, including understanding Internet terminology, launching search engines, browsing the Web, downloading, and word processing, as well as a final week of group presentations. The program introduced students to the basic functions of the browser, such as the forward and back buttons, the address bar, and bookmarks. Students learned to scroll through a site and use links to other sites. They learned to use search engines and the rudiments of Boolean logic search tools. They also learned how to find computer files and software, download text and graphic material onto computers to save for future use. Theme activities (Internet Secret Garden) and worksheets were provided.

Data collection and analysis

Data collection consisted of a survey and interview. At the end of the course a survey was given to elicit relevant information on the participants' perception of, and attitudes towards, learning technology via a cooperative approach. The survey included a 5-point Likert-type scale and open-ended questions to encourage student's reflections about the project. It consisted of five dimensions; teaching methods, peer interactions, learning attitudes and motivation, as well as attitudes toward, and perceived learning benefits from, collaborative learning. After the course, interviews with each learner were conducted in order to elicit relevant information on the participants' perception of, and attitudes toward the cooperative approach to information learning.

Results and Discussion

The results obtained from the first part of the survey indicates that, with respect to learning methods, 84 % subjects thought they increased their knowledge and learned more computer skills via group work. 90% subjects preferred learning via group work. With respect to peer interaction, nearly 80% of the subjects were aware that cooperative learning allowed more discussion time with teammates. Nearly 71% reported that classmates were more willing to help; 4 learners disagreed. 87% felt the cooperative approach made them get along much better with others, whereas 3 learners disagreed.

On the learning attitude and interests scale, 87 % reported that they made more effort to practice their skills and report their progress. 77% were more attentive to the lectures and become more interested in learning about computers. 71% of learners tended to express more of their thoughts. On their view of learning IT via cooperative learning, 77% learners hoped that learning via group work would be continued in future information technology courses, with 3 learners disagreeing. Nearly 87% of the students expressed their wish to continue learning via group work in subjects such as math, science, social studies, etc. Finally, 84% of the learners expressed their satisfaction with learning via group work. Two learners, one who did most of work and one who was slow with computers, would rather learn by themselves.

Further examination of learners who preferred working alone revealed that most of them were slower learners who did not contribute to group discussions. One learner had capable computer skills and did more than his fair share of the work. Also, his group often quarrelled and wasted time, which lead to his negativity about peer interaction. With respect to learning gains, more than 90% of learners reported that their computer ability improved significantly along with their motivation to learn technology. Regarding interpersonal communication, cooperative skills, and enhanced classmate relationships, although fairly positive, the learners considered these benefits to be not as high compared to computer skills and interest, with 55% of learners rating them as very beneficial and 45% learners as not very beneficial. This indicates that there is much room for improvement. One explanation for this difference is that this was the first time that the kids where asked to cooperate with others in class, and they need more time to learn how to share and work in a team environment.

The children were interviewed in order to obtain a more comprehensive picture of students' views on cooperative learning. With the open-ended questions regarding their reflections on cooperative learning, it was found that learners saw both benefits and challenges from learning IT collaboratively. Some benefits the students identified clustered around: learning the importance of teamwork; learning more about computer technology and communications; acquiring cooperative techniques; and learning how to undertake a research project.

Most learners enjoyed working with their teammates and felt that although some of the things they learned were not exactly planned, the spontaneity of picking up tips and ideas from others in the group was both helpful and fascinating. In particular, during group presentation of projects to the class, each group conducted a tour of their projects and explained their rationale for the way they constructed them. The learners all engaged in discussion and negotiation of their shared and disparate electronic Web spaces. This highly social, sharing activity was very positive in that it allowed each subject to perceive the multiple perspectives that different learners can bring to the task, and to reflect on these alternative possibilities.

Some shortcomings or challenges found centered more on peer interaction. 25% of learners felt that getting a group to effectively work together on a project was a main problem. They felt angry and helpless about group members who were not good team players, or not willing to contribute their share, or try harder. They felt frustrated, particularly in the earlier stages, when members fooled around, playing computers gaming or chatting without concentrating on the main task. 20% of learners remarked that quarrelling was also a drawback; learners did not appreciate agreeing to differ, easily losing one's temper, egoism or self-centeredness. 10% of learners responded that they were upset when assertive members dominated the interaction, were indifferent to others' thoughts, or occupied the computers most of the time. Furthermore, some children were of the opinion that the division of computer time was unfair since they seldom were given an opportunity to interact directly with the computer.

Summary

Generally speaking, the study showed the positive value of a cooperative approach, when effectively integrated into computer curriculums. Although the positive learning effects on students were quite satisfactory, there are still some issues that need to be further reflected upon. For example, the study showed that not every learner enjoyed teamwork learning, 2-4 learners, it is noted, were not receptive to cooperative learning. Given that students bring different perspectives to the conceptualization of cooperation and have varying personality, those learners with a passive or maladjusted orientation toward cooperative learning need careful guidance. Therefore, providing scaffolding, both in group learning and in orienting the learners to the task, is vital to the successful implementation and integration of cooperative learning into the curriculum.

References Upon Request

AN ANALYSIS OF BRANCHING BEHAVIOR PATTERNS IN AN INTERACTIVE HYPERMEDIA LEARNING

Chiann-Ru Song
The Institute for Secondary School Teachers in Taiwan, Feng-Yuan, Taiwan, R.O.C.
crs0417@isst.edu.tw

Complex learning requires that learners have certain skills to succeed (Recker & Pirolli, 1995; Spiro et. al., 1992; Winne & Perry, 1999). For example they need to be able to reason, solve problems, and synthesize. These skills are not learned by providing information (Jacobson & Spiro, 1994). It requires that procedures be modeled, student efforts be critiqued (coached) (Brown, Collins, & Duguid, 1988), examples (cases) provided (Kolonder, 1993), evaluations made (Butler & Winne, 1995), etc. Thus instruction about complex learning needs to include these kinds of units.

Hypermedia has been used to provide these and other kinds of learning (Lajoie, 1993). Systems that focus on problem solving may consist primarily of a sequence of increasingly complex cases (Burton, Brown, & Fischer, 1984) that model situations, and cases where students solve similar situations and receive feedback on their performance (coaching). The next decision is when to offer these experiences (Kolonder, 1993). Branching, which provides students opportunities to select a variety of instructional units, is one way of structuring learning units. The student judges a unit that seems appropriate to his skills, begins working at this unit, but then, depending on the feedback received, is able to jump to subsequent units that seem best suited for facilitating learning (Butler & Winne, 1995).

User navigation through branching was one type of interaction focused in the study. The use of branch points is one of the innovative characteristics of hypermedia. Branch points are nodes or decision points along the pathway to a particular goal—a set of "buttons" that enable users to be in control of their own learning process (Schank, 1993). Branch points are the place where complex learning skills such as monitoring and decision making are employed to move a learner from branch point to branch point (Bulter & Winne, 1995). When learning complex knowledge, the actions taken at branch points are reflective of the learning process being used by the learner and, hence, provide insights that may allow researchers to form models of branching behaviors.

Students' branching behaviors can be tracked and recorded by the computer as log files for later analysis. By analyzing branching behavior patterns, students' individual learning differences has the potential to be inferred according to a strong learning theory (Song, 2002).

Egan (1988) stated performance measurement has been used popularly to characterize differences between individuals:

Performance differences in human-computer interaction are not random. We can predict and begin to understand what causes performance differences. We can test our understanding and put it to use by designing systems that enable a great variety of people to work productively with computer. (Egan, p. 544)

But, in 1989, Snow concluded that:

We need a theory of the initial properties of the learner which interact with learning - the complex of personal characteristics that accounts for an individual's end state after a particular educational treatment. We do not yet have such a theory. But we are now much closer. (p. 51)

Such an ideal theory should (1) identify individual user differences that are most likely to account for variance of performance in an interactive learning environment and, ultimately, (2) include guidelines for the design of instructional systems that effectively and/or support interact with these differences.

Obviously, if students do not know how to reason through a particular problem individually, how can they be provided with various required supports of modeling, scaffolding, and coaching? In the absence of adequate understanding of hypermedia learning, the challenge of the study is to understand the interaction between branching behavior patterns and learner characteristics in order to identify means for interactive hypermedia learning.

MAPLE (Multimedia Authoring and Production Learning Environment) was used to investigate branching behavior in this study. It is a working experimental hypermedia prototype to learn the complex knowledge, Macromedia Director 6.5 (M.M. Director 6.5, Jason & Roslyn, 1998). MAPLE was created using Macromedia Director 6.5 and designed to direct students to learn how to use the M.M. Director authoring system by producing multimedia / hypermedia. Case level is where the main teaching / learning activities actually happened in MAPLE.

Cases attempt to combine previous learning experiences with specific domain knowledge and general information related to the case. With the completion of each case, students are expected to absorb relevant experiences and obtain an accurate understanding of a complex, new domain. Cases in each unit are arranged in order from simple to complex. Each case consists of five different kinds of learning units. They are Introduction, Challenge, Plan, Experiment, and Reflect. Within a case students can branch to any of these five units or outside the case to the main menu, to Quit, or to Notes. A student can branch to any of these units by clicking on the title at the left of the screen.

Its branching structure was developed according to principles based on studies of cognitive apprenticeships (Brown, Collins, & Duguid, 1988), case-based reasoning (CBR) (Kolonder, 1993), and organizing units as increasingly complex microworlds (ICM) (Burton, Brown, & Fischer, 1984). In this structure a complex knowledge domain was treated as a broad range of cases. Cases are scenarios of problem solving. The expected learning outcomes of these instructional design principles are learning skills.

MAPLE was designed to provide its learners with control of their sequencing of linked available units through branching points (i.e. modest interaction[1]). In its branching structure a particular learning task may be difficult for students with certain aptitudes; thus, a branch point is inserted. The student's response (feedback) to this branch point should be indicative of the student's aptitude and will link the student to a treatment appropriate for his or her aptitude (Corno & Snow, 1986).

In addition, MAPLE itself was designed and used as a research tool for collecting students' data as they work through this hypermedia system. By tracking MAPLE's branching behaviors (navigation activities), variables that accord with select theories of learning that are most likely to account for variance in learning were delineated (Butler & Winne, 1995; Collins, Hawkins, & Frederiksen, 1993; Pirolli & Recker, 1994; Winne, Gupta, & Nesbit, 1994).

In this study, student's branching behaviors were classified; the relationships between their branching behavior patterns and learner variables such as learner's prior knowledge of instructional hypermedia production were explored. In particular the potential influence of learning skills is emphasized (Last, O'Donnell, & Kelly, 1998).

Cluster analysis was used to identify individual

branching behavior and learner characteristics differences (Edelson, 1996; Lawless & Kulikowich, 1996, 1998; Romesburg, 1984). Cluster analysis develops groups whose inter-group behavior significantly differs while intra-group behavior is similar (Lorr, 1983; Martin, 1999), as substantiated by conventional non-parametric analyses. The appropriate statistical analyses were incorporated to further identify the characteristics of each group, such as comparing the differences of variables in means and non-parametric analyses. Data for the two missions were analyzed separately. For investigating these research interests, interview data were used as supplemental material for support quantitative findings (Young, 1993).

Finally, demographic data was used to develop a better understanding of the students' histories of individuals in specific branching behavior patterns and their possible relevancies to learner variable/and performance in a hypermedia environment (Edelson, 1996; Lawless & Kulikowich, 1996, 1998; Recker & Pirolli, 1992).

The results showed that students differ in their branching behaviors and learner characteristics:

In Mission 1, individual differences in branching behavior patterns were related to prior domain knowledge of Director. High prior knowledge students tended to employ the branching behavior pattern, moving linearly; low prior knowledge students tended to employ branching behavior pattern, moving forward and backward; medium prior knowledge students tended to employ branching behavior pattern, skip sub-sections. Other prior knowledge variables (like Software, Programming and Computer system proficiencies), and learner variables (such as: self-regulation, self-explanation, performance and demographic variables) were unrelated to students' branching behavior patterns.

In Mission 2, branching behavior patterns were unrelated to all learning variables.

The result showed that students branching behavior patterns between Mission 1 and Mission 2 are significantly related.

From the interview data, students' differences in goal settings were found:

1)   Student set their learning goals actively with using MAPLE as a reference.

2)   Student set their learning goals actively without using MAPLE as a reference.

3)   Student set their learning goals passively with using MAPLE as a reference.

Moreover, after gaining experience in Mission 1, most students figured out the most effective way to learn with MAPLE was to complete the simple cases then move into the next more complicated cases. Therefore, in Mission 2, the prior knowledge level was insignificant, and almost all students employed the same branching behavior (moving from the simple cases to the next more complicated ones).

---

[1] Payne (1995) defines four levels of hypermedia interaction: "no interaction" refers to a system that provides linear presentation of information, such as slides and videotape; "modest interaction" refers to a system that allows the learner to control sequencing of linked available units through branching points, such as MAPLE (a prototype of the specific hypermedia used in this study); "medium interaction" refers to a system that provides direct, immediate interaction, such as asking the learner to respond to a question, or allowing for the learner to ask a question with the system responding appropriately; "high interaction" refers to a system that provides an intelligent agent to interact with learners on a continuous basis. Highly interactive learning environments are very expensive and difficult to develop, thus, limiting the number of such systems being produced.

Reference:

[1] Brown, J., Collins, A., & Duguid, P. (1988). *Situated cognition and the culture of learning*. IRL Report No. 88-0008, Institute for Research on Learning.

[2] Butler, D., & Winne, P. (1995). Feedback and self-regulated learning: A theoretical synthesis. *Review of Educational Research, 65* (3), 245-281.

[3] Burton, R. R., Brown, J.S., & Fischer, G. (1984). Skiing as a model of instruction. In B. Rogoff and J. Lave (eds). *Everyday cognition: its development in social context.* Cambridge, MA: Harvard Univ. Press.

[4] Collins, A., Hawkins, J., & Frederiksen, J. (1993). Three different views of students: The role of technology in assessing student performance. *The Journal of The Learning Science, 3* (2), 205-217.

[5] Corno, L. & Snow, R.E. (1986). Adapting Teaching to Individual Differences Among Learners. In Merlin C. Wittrock (Editor), Handbook of Research on Teaching. pp. 605-629. New York: Macmillan.

[6] Edelson, D. (1996). Learning from cases and questions: The Socratic case-based teaching architecture. *The Journal of The Learning Science, 5* (4), 357 –410.

[7] Egan, D. (1988). Individual differences in human-computer interaction. In Helander , M. (Ed.), *Handbook of human-computer interaction.* Amsterdam; New York: North-Holland; New York, N. Y., U.S.A.: Sole distributors for the U.S.A. and Canada, Elsevier Science Pub. Co..

[8] Jacobson, M., & Spiro, R. (1994). A framework for the contextual analysis of technology-based learning environments. *Journal of Computing in Higher Education, 5* (2), 3-32.

[9] Jason R., & Roslyn B., (1998). *Director 6 Demystified.* Peachpit Press.

[10] Kolodner, J. (1993). *Case-based reasoning.* San Mateo, CA: Morgan Kaufmann Publishers, Inc.

[11] Lajoie, S. (1993). Computer environments as cognitive tools for enhance learning. In Lajoie, S., & Derry, S. (Eds.), *Computers as cognitive tools* (pp. 201-288). Hillsdale, NJ: Lawrence Erlbaum Associate, Publishers.

[12] Last, D. A., O'Donnell, A. M., & Kelly, A. E. (1998). Using Hypermedia: Effects of Prior Knowledge and Goal Strength. SITE 98: Society for Information Technology & Teacher Education International Conference (9th, Washington, DC, March 10-14, 1998).

[13] Lawless, K., & Kulikowich, J. (1996). Understanding hypertext navigation through cluster analysis. *Journal Educational Computing Research, 14* (4), 385-399.

[14] Lawless, K., & Kulikowich, J. (1998). Domain Knowledge, Interest, and Hypertext Navigation: A Study of Individual Differences. *Journal of Educational Multimedia and Hypermedia,* 7 (1), 51-69.

[15] Lorr, M. (1983). Cluster analysis for social scientists. San Francisco: Jossey-Bass.

[16] Martin, S. (1999). Cluster Analysis for Web Site Organization. ITG Publication. http://www.sandia.gov/itg/newsletter/dec99/cluster_anal ysis.html.

[17] Payne, D. (1995). Unpublished classroom notes in the Cognitive Science II. New York University.

[18] Pirolli, P., & Recker, M. (1994). Learning strategies and transfer in the domain of programming. *Cognition and Instruction, 12* (3), 235-275.

[19] Romesburg, H.C. (1984). Cluster Analysis for Researchers. California:Lifetime Learning Publications.

[20] Recker, M., & Pirolli, P. (1992). *Student strategies for learning programming from a computational environment.* Paper presented at 2nd international conference, ITS'92 (Intelligent tutoring systems), Montreal, Canda.

[21] Recker, M., & Pirolli, P. (1995). Modeling individual differences in students' learning strategies. *The Journal of The Learning Sciences, 4* (1), 1-38.

[22] Schank, R. (1993, May). Learning via multimedia computers. *Communications of the ACM, 36* (5). 54-56.

[23] Snow, R. (1989). Aptitude-treatment interaction as a framework for research on individual differences in learning. In Ackerman, P., Sternbert, R., & Glaser, R. (Eds.), *Learning and individual differences: Advances in theory and research.* New York: W.H. Freeman.

[24] Song, C. R. (2002). The Branching Structure for Individual Learning Skills Differences in Instructional Hypermedia Learning. Online Information Review, 26 (2), 2002

[25] Spiro, R., Feltovich, P., Jacobson, M., & Coulson, R. (1992). Cognitive flexibility, constructivism, and hypertext: Random access instruction for advanced knowledge acquisition in ill-structured domains. In Duffy, T., & Jonassen, D. (Eds.), *Constructivism and the technology of instruction: A conversation* (pp. 57-75). Hillsdale, NJ: Erlbaum.

[26] Winne, P., Gupta, L., & Nesbit, J. (1994). Exploring individual differences in studying strategies using graph theoretic statistics. *The Alberta Journal of Educational Research, XL* (2), 177-193.

[27] Winne, P. & Perry, N. (1999). Measuring Self-Regulated Learning. Unpublished paper. This paper was supported in part by grants from the Social Sciences and Humanities Research Council of Canada.

[28] Young, M., (1993). Instructional Design for Situated Learning, Educational Technology Research and Development, 41, pp.43-58.)

Web Based Peer Assessment Using Knowledge Acquisition Techniques: Tools for Supporting Contexture Awareness

Chen-Chung Liu, Baw-Jhiune Liu, Tzu-An Hui, *Jorng-Tzong Horng
Department of Computer Engineering and Science
Yuan Ze University, Chung-Li, Taiwan
*National Central University, Chung-Li, Taiwan
Email: christia@saturn.yzu.edu.tw

Abstract

Web based peer assessment for portfolios has been used as an innovative assessment methods to reuse students' portfolio for refining learning. However, without sophisticated support to articulate the assessment contexture about portfolios, students can not communicate with explicit learning concepts and think reflectively for refinement of their learning. This study attempts to utilize knowledge acquisition and data mining techniques to solve the problems in support contexture awareness. By way of knowledge acquisition and data mining techniques, web peer assessment systems obtain students' personal theories during assessing portfolios. Thereby, teachers and students can go online to fully exchange personal theories, thus allowing them to think reflectively for refinement of learning.

I. Introduction

Web based peer assessment systems implement a convenient assessment communication channel among teachers and student peers for engaging students in reflection thinking. Schon's conception of *reciprocal reflection - in - action* has emphasized the way to implement the reflective communication channel[2][6]. Through reflectively communicating with peers and teachers, students critically question the result and process with personal experience. However, without the sophisticated support to articulate the assessment contexture about portfolios, students can not communicate with other peers with explicit learning constructs and think reflectively for progressive refinement of their learning through peer assessment.

Peer assessment generally engages students in comparing and classifying portfolios. Such implementation of assessment is accordance to Luhmann's 'autologie' theory of observation. Autologie implies the self-reflection of a student's interpretation framework by which students identify *distinctions* and *indication* to distinguish various portfolios. Lumann's

conception of contexture elucidates the distinctions and how individual students use these distinctions to assess portfolios. However, students would have different assessment contexture since individual students would pose different distinctions and indications to classify portfolios. Many researches [5] has emphasized the use of Web based peer assessment systems for continuously monitoring of review processes. However, the contexture awareness for monitoring students' assessment contexture is not well supported in Web based peer assessment systems. Consequently, students and teachers can not easily articulate and compare students' personal theories [8] of evaluation scheme for enhancing self-reflection during assessment..

Implementing communication with contexture awareness to stimulate reflection entails acquiring evaluators' conceptualization about portfolios. While using web-based peer assessment systems, teachers and students encounter several difficulties in acquiring such conceptualization.

II. Tasks

This study presents a novel methodology to implement the communication channel to support web peer assessment. The methodology utilizes knowledge acquisition [1] [3] [4] [7] and data mining techniques to solve the problems in support contexture awareness. Knowledge acquisition techniques, termed as also knowledge extraction or knowledge elicitation techniques, are used to transfer and transform problem-solving expertise from a knowledge source to expert system program or knowledge base[3]. Deeply affected by personal construct psychology, knowledge acquisition software such as *WebGrid* and *Enquire Within* can facilitate students identify salient concepts by comparing and contrasting portfolios through repertory grid analysis to solve the *concept evoking* problem.

The web peer assessment system is not only designed for assessment purposes but also as a means for to promote students' reflection for refining learning. Engaging students in comparing evaluation concepts between students may help students reflect their approaches from others' perspectives. Although teachers have given student general evaluation dimensions, students poses personal evaluation concepts according to personal experiences to classify portfolios. For instance, a student may identify a vague concept such as *'fast searching'* as evaluation concept of the *searching methodology* dimension while others may identify the concrete concept *'binary searching'* if this student is capable of using *binary searching* methodology. Therefore, teachers and students need supports to eliciting students' evaluation concepts to perceive personal theories and experience.

Students identify evaluation concepts and classify/score others' portfolios by these evaluation concepts. Therefore, a student assesses another's portfolio and represents its feature as a vector. Figure 1 displays the assessment result of a student in an assessment group by a Focus analysis methodology [7]. Each column represents the vector of scores of a student's portfolio in each evaluation concept.

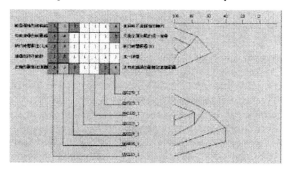

Figure 1 : The concepts and conceptual framework using knowledge acquisition techniques

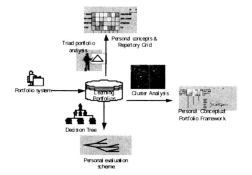

Figure 2. Eliciting assessment contexture with knowledge acquisition techniques

Figure 2 illustrates how knowledge acquisition techniques are used to obtain students' evaluation concepts, conceptual framework, and evaluation scheme. Students initially develop learning portfolios in the web learning system. Meanwhile, the web peer assessment system automatically dispatches students' portfolios to students. The system provides an interactive manner for students to evaluate portfolios. Triadic portfolio analysis is applied herein to elicit students' repertory grids. The repertory grids represent students' personal concepts and evaluation of portfolios. The grids enable the system to automatically probe students' conceptual framework and evaluation scheme. The cluster analysis tools automatically clusters portfolios according to elicited concepts. The cluster analysis displays the relationship among portfolios and concepts with similarity among them. Meanwhile, decision tree software discovers how students reach the decision to mark the final score of portfolios. Therefore, students and teachers can go online to exchanging personal conceptual structure, and hence, enhance self-reflection to refine learning.

References

[1] Ford, K., Bradshaw, J., Adams-Webber, J. & Agnew, N.(1993) Knowledge Acquisition as a constructive modeling activity, International Journal of Intelligent system, Vol. 8, pp.9-32.

[2] S. Hansen, Project assessment as an integrated part of the learning process in the problem-based and project-oriented study at Aalborg university, New Engineering Competencies - Changing the Paradigm, SEFI conference, Copenhagen 12-14 Sep 2001.

[3] Hayes-Roth, F, Waterman, D., Lenat, D.(1983) Building Expert Systems. Reading, MA:Addison-Wesley.

[4] Karen L. M. and Karen H. (1989) Knowledge Acquisition, Principle and Guidelines, Prentice-Hall, Englewood Cliffs, New Jersey.

[5] S. S. J. Lin, E. Z.F. Liu, & S. M. Yuan, Web-based peer assessment: Feadback for students with various thinking styles, *Journal of Computer Assisted Learning (JCAL). 17(2001). 420-432.*

[6] Schon, D.A. (1983) *The Reflective Practitioner.* London: Temple Smith

[7] Shaw M. L. G. and Thomas L. F.(1978) Focus on Education – an interactive computer system for the development and analysis of repertory grid, International Journal of Man-Machine Studies, Vol. 10, pp 138-173.

[8] Tann, S. (1993) Eliciting students' personal theories, in J. Calderhead & P. Gates (Eds)*Conceptualising Reflection in Teacher Development.* London: Falmer Press

Classroom of the Sea: Problem-based learning for the deaf

Scott W. Brown, Ivar Babb, Paula R. Johnson, Peter M. Scheifele,
University of Connecticut

Harry Lang,
Rochester Institute of Technology

Dongping Zheng,
University of Connecticut

Denise Monte, & Mary LaPorta
American School for the Deaf

Abstract

The Classroom of the Sea (COS) Project is an interactive problem-based learning environment embedded in marine science for deaf high school students to assist them in understanding and communicating scientific concepts. COS mixes a real and virtual environment for the students and teachers aboard a research vessel as they gather marine science data to address a problem. The students note the locations of their samples and record them on the ship's LAN. Once the students return to their classrooms, students, faculty and researchers work to place the data they have collected on to web sites enabling students to experiment with real data, generate hypotheses, test these hypotheses and write up their results. Knowledge, attitudes and behaviors (KABs) and self-efficacy measures related to science literacy and procedures of the students are collected to measure changes.

Introduction

For the purposes of this study, constructivism is defined as *meaning making*, rooted in the context of the situation whereby individuals construct their knowledge of, and give meaning to, the external world [1, 2, 3, 4] as a product "shaped by traditions and by a culture's toolkit of ways of thought" [5]. "Consistent with this view of knowledge, learning must be situated in a rich context, reflective of real-world contexts for this constructive process to occur and transfer to environments beyond the school or training classroom." [6].

For learning and transfer to succeed, the educator must design a constructivist learning environment. But, what constitutes a constructivist learning environment, particularly for a project like the Classroom of the Sea simulations? - A learning environment in which students identify and address real problems of acoustics, marine life, changes in the ocean environment and the impact of various parts of the marine environment. An environment was created in which students go to sea on a research vessel several times a year, collect data and present it on the web for others to view (see www.cos.uconn.edu). The others that view and explore this data are predominately hearing students at high schools across the USA as well as other students in schools for the deaf.

A key component in this definition is problem-solving activities. Problem-solving skills are essential for today's workforce. One of the best ways of preparing students for this is through the use of real-world, authentic problem-solving. This method of instruction, commonly called Problem-based Learning (PBL) has been used for decades, starting in medical schools in the 1950s and then adapted for use by business schools, schools of education, architecture, law, engineering, etc.

COS is a model that meets the criteria for PBL in a constructivist environment. It is authentic, complex, substantive, learner empowering, and challenging.

Working through an interdisciplinary team COS combines real and virtual environments by scheduling working class trips for the students and teachers aboard the research vessel *RV Connecticut* for a day. During this period on the ship the students gather marine science data related to addressing a specific component of the problem-based learning environment (PBL).

Once the students return to their classrooms, students, faculty and researchers work together to place the data they have collected on web sites enabling students to experiment with real data and share their data and insights with other students, both hearing and deaf.

Because this is a special population of deaf high school students, there are special challenges of communications among the students, teachers and crew of the ship. A specific challenge of this project is the development of a set of communication signs that represent science concepts for which currently there are not any American Sign Language (ASL) signs/symbols.

Procedures

Each trip out to sea, the students (n=10-12) complete pre- and post- assessment of science knowledge, attitudes and behaviors. Students write about their goals and objectives, as well as their accomplishments.

Knowledge, attitudes and behaviors (KABs) of the students were collected to measure changes related to science literacy, attitudes and things the students can accomplish. The KAB approach is a derivative of Bloom's taxonomy of cognitive, affective and psychomotor skills and has been used effectively in a varied number of research studies [7].

Additionally, self-efficacy measures are collected. Self-efficacy (SE) is a concept developed by Bandura and focuses on a person's belief of self-agency; that a person can attempt and accomplish a specific task successfully. Bandura's work has demonstrated that SE is a good predictor of task commitment and task engagement [8]. In the COS study, the SE is related to science procedures.

Both the KAB and the SE scales used a Likert-type format with two anchors for responses (1=Strongly Agree and 5= Strongly Disagree), where 1 represents the strongest response.

In addition to the scales, students were asked about their reactions to the activities in a written survey. Student interactions were observed during ship as well as classroom activities to examine communication access patterns among these deaf students using scientific concepts.

Results

The pre-test Cronbach reliability for the KA portion of the KAB instrument was .87. The SE scale for scientific procedures was .95.

Mean scores on the KAB indicated that students reported knowing and understanding science concepts, had a positive attitude towards science and believed they could successfully conduct science procures as well as tasks on the ship (Mean's ranged from 1.14 to 1.71, where 1= Strongly Agree and 5 is Strongly Disagree). SE responses were also positive with means ranging from 1.57 to 1.86 regarding students' ability to conduct scientific procedures.

Responses to open-ended questions were also positive, as exemplified by the following two responses: "*I never really liked science before being involved in COS though I've always had good grades*" and "*Science particular made me feel smarter. Though it's not what applies to my future career but it's a great benefit. (sic)* "

Conclusion

The results of the COS project have demonstrated that a PBL environment can be successful in increasing students' KAB and self-efficacy related to science for deaf students. Additional studies are being conducted to examine the long-term impact as well as the effects of transfer of KABs and SE to other academic areas for these students.

References

[1] Brown, J.S., Collins, A., Duguid. (1989). Situated cognition, & the culture of learning, *Educational Researcher* 32-42.

[2] Brown, S. W., & King, F.B., (2000). Constructivist pedagogy and how we learn: Educational psychology meets international studies. *International Studies Perspective 1*, 245-254.

[3] Jonassen, D. , Peck, K.L., & Wilcon, B.G. (1999). *Learning with technology: A constructivist perspective.* Upper Saddle River NJ: Merrill.

[54 Schunk, D.H. (2000). *Learning theories: An educational perspective (3rd edition).* Columbus, OH: Merrill/Prentice-Hall.

[5] Bruner, J.S. (1973) *Beyond the information given: Studies in the psychology of knowing.* NY: Norton.

[6] Bednar, A.K., Cunningham, D., Duffy, T.M, & Perry, J. D. (1992). Theory into practice: How do we link? In T. M. Duffy & D. J. Jonassen (Eds.), *Constructivism and the technology of instruction: A conversation.* Hillsdale, NJ: Lawrence Erlbaum.

[7] Bloom, B.S., Englehart, M.D., Frost, E.J., Hill, W.H., & Krathwohl, D.R. (1956). *Taxonomy of educational objectives, Handbook I: Cognitive domain.* NY: David McKay.

[8] Bandura, A. (1997). *Self-efficacy: The exercise of control.* New York: W.H. Freeman and Company.

A Qualitative study of Mentors' Scaffolding
in a Teacher Professional Development Online Workshop

Shu Ching Yang
shyang@mail.nsysu.edu.tw

Shu Fang Liu
liufang@ms17.hinet.net

Graduate Institute of Education
National Sun Yat-sen University, Taiwan, R.O.C. 80424

1.Introduction

Taiwan's Digital School (DS) was established to suport online K-12 Teacher Professional Development. At the core of the online TPD center is platform-independent, web-based environment designed to meet the needs of a large and diverse community of education professionals. DS provides a powerful set of synchronous and asynchronous communication systems, and support tools. DS offers teaching community a vareity of online TPD activities hosted by universities and educational organizations. Professionals design their own programs, take online courses experiment with new teaching methods, and expand their circle of colleagues by participating in community-wide events.

In this study, we will report findings from the Professional Development Online Workshop for Mathematical Capacity (Mathematical Capacity Workshop, MCW). We analyzed the effects of electronic mentors' scaffolding and the interactive quality of preservice/inservice mathematics teaching at a Web-based professional development workshop. MCW was the first workshop offered by DS to provide teachers online professional development. Three senior elementary mathematics teachers co-mentored the workshop and provided apprenticeship and online mentoring for pre-and in-service mathematics teacher's professional development. The study contributes to an understanding of teaching participants' assessment of the value and efficacy of online workshops as a tool for creating professional learning, and provides a basis for empirical study of the acquisition and maintenance of professional knowledge in Taiwan's web-based professional teaching community. The study identifies several factors essential to delivering effective professional development programs. Insights gained in this pilot study will help teacher-educators continue to refine better intellectual tools to augment professional growth.

2. Methodology

2.1 Professional Development of MCW

The MCW was designed to promote teachers' professional development. A series of 15 weeklong workshops based on a theme of mathematical capacity investigations provided the core activity of this online mathematics workshop. Two weeks comprised face-to-face lectures with the aim of providing students the opportunity to become familiar with each other. The workshops had the explicit aim of enhancing the quality of the teachers' repertoires of substantive knowledge about mathematics capacity and integrative curriculum.

2.2 Instructional Design

Three senior elementary mathematics teachers provided online mentoring for pre-and in-service teachers' mathematics professional development. They were responsible for course design, co-moderating the weekly asynchronous and synchronous discussions, and assessing assignments. There were eleven units in MCW. Learners were required to browse the online-materials and then discuss them on the discussion board.

2.3 Evaluation

The evaluation included individual assignments including at least one weekly entry, one individual final report and 3 group projects including worksheets for parent-child interaction, instructional design, etc. The PD certification diploma was issued based on their involvement in the workshop and calculated hours.

2.4 Data Collection and Analysis

Research methods included content analysis, and brief email interviews. A code for dialogue transcripts was identified for dialogue content, and forms of mentoring from senior teachers. The categorization scheme was adapted from the twelve forms of electronic learning mentoring and assistance (Bonk & Kim, 1988) and Simsek (1992), which included management, questioning, direct instruction, modeling/exampling, feedback/praise, cognitive elaborations/explanations, push to explore, fostering reflection/self-awareness, encouraging articulation/dialogue prompting, and general advice. A brief email interview was given to elicit relevant information on the participants' perception of using online workshop for professional development.

3. Discussion

In order to understand how assistant moderated participants discussion to promote their professional growth, the frequency of assistant scaffolding strategies embedded in electronic discussions was calculated. The results indicate that the assistants mainly employed feedback/praise strategies (n=52, 42.97%), followed by the general advice (n=21, 17.35%), management (n=17, 14.16%), fostering reflection (n=11, 9.09%), encouraging articulation (n=7, 5.78%), with direction, modeling, questioning, cognitive elaborations and effort to explore accounting for less than 10% altogether.

Among the three assistants, M1 post 47 messages, M2 55 messages, and M3 only 18 messages during the conference workshop. Of 11 posts fostering reflection, M2 made 10 posts to foster participants' reflection and self-awareness compared with M1's one post and M3's none. Of 52 feedback/praise posts, M2 offered 32 posts, while M1 11posts, M3 9 posts. Of 17 management posts, M1 offered more organizing and managing conferences, M2 initiated 2 posts, while M3 did not have any. To sum up, M1 relied more on management (32 %), feedback and praise (23 %), direction, dialogue prompting, as well as general advice (each 11 %). M2 resorts more to feedback and praise (58 %), fostering reflection as well as general advice (18 % each). M3 used more feedback and praise as well as general advice.

Paulsen (1995) describes three essential functions of computer conferencing moderators, such as the organisational, social, and intellectual functions. The study showed that while there was much variability in assistants' mentoring styles, the assistants employed most of the social and organizational functions. M1 adopted more organizational functions; and M2 demonstrated more social with some intellectual functions. The assistants created a friendly, social environment, encouraging participation throughout, as well as providing lots of feedback and praise on students' input. They also structured and managed the conferences, including setting the agenda (the objectives of the discussion, the timetable, and procedural rules). As the study showed, the assistants focused more on the social and organisational functions, whereas the intellectual one was less emphasised. Given this, that moderators employed a variety of modes of communication to nurture collegial connections, and reflective conversations, is of major importance.

4. Conclusions

In this project, we offered teachers an online professional development opportunity through the Web. Results indicate that most participants found the online workshop useful. They claimed they benefited emotionally and intellectually by using the telecommunications network for professional development and support. Although the positive learning effects on members were acceptable, there were some issues that needed to be further addressed and reflected upon.

First, while teachers recognized the need for greater professional interaction, they did not bring those concerns to their online colleagues due to the various reasons. The study showed that a number of participants sent bulletin-board-like messages rather than conversational messages, while a small group of teachers became "lurkers", who did not post much messages. Future design might evoke more reflection-stimulating responses by requiring participants' reading and responding to peers and mentors postings, and force them to think and form ideas.

Second, a number of studies emphasize the importance of specific skilled moderators for fostering learning in a CMC environment (Spitzer et al., 1995). In this study, despite participants expressing their gratitude for assistants' socio-emotional support and their efforts in guiding their learning, they expressed the need for more clues to react to messages, as they felt less sure of themselves in their use of sustained online communication skills. With this in mind, future PD workshops should model more reflective practices to provide a clear link between a significant professional development activity and classroom practice.

Third, the study showed that the assistants focused more on the social and the organisational functions, whereas the intellectual function was less emphasised. One explanation for this might be offered. As this study was a first attempt, senior teachers did not receive any formal training with mentoring strategies preceding the workshop. In addition, only 3 senior teachers were responsible for mentoring more than 100 participants, certainly a tremendous task for them. In addition to their daily teaching, they had to provide just-in-time support, initiate chat room discussion, comment on participant's assignments, as well as employ their professional expertise to stimulate reflective dialogues. Our future PD design will recruit more mentors and provide moderators training with manuals to have mentors deliberately employ a variety of modes of communication to nurture collegial connections and reflective conversations.

5. References

Bonk, C. J., & Kim, K. A. (1998). Extending sociocultural theory to adult learning. In M. C. Smith & T. Pourchot (Ed.), *Adult learning and development* (pp. 67-88). Lawrence Erlbaum Associates.

Paulsen, M. F. (1995). An overview of CMC and the online classroom in distance education. In Z. L. Berge & M. P. Collins (Eds.), *Computer-mediated communications and the online classroom* (Vol. III, pp. 31–57). Cresskill, NJ: Hampton Press.

Simsek, A. (1992). The impact of cooperative group composition on student performance and attitudes during interactive videodisc instruction. ERIC Document Reproduction Service No. ED 348-025.

Spitzer, W., & Wedding, K. (1995). LabNet: An international electronic community for professional development. *Computers and Education*, 24(3), 247-255.

Developing Japanese CALL Courseware for Listening Comprehension Practice

Isao MIZUMACHI (Hiroshima University), Shinichiro TAWATA (Hiroshima University)
Emi YAMANAKA (Harvard University)

Abstract

CALL (Computer Assisted Language Learning) courseware was developed for advanced learners of Japanese, entitled "Listening Comprehension: Life in Japan; Dwelling in a Private Apartment." Based on the "Three-step Auditory Comprehension Approach" (Takefuta, 1997), this courseware consists of three STEPs: STEP1 helps learners grasp the outline of the content, STEP2 assists in a more detailed understanding of the conversation, and STEP3 leads learners through comprehensive practice exercises. The CD-ROM in which it is packaged requires QuickTime5 and contains movies with two Japanese students (male and female) talking in informal style to help a non-Japanese student. It offers several types of tasks and provides information about the language, culture and learning strategies. The CD-ROM has four courses on the following topics, each divided into three sublessons: 1) looking for, 2) moving into, 3) living in, and 4) moving out of an apartment. The main directions and explanations are given in Japanese, Chinese, Korean or English. 6 native speakers of Japanese and 6 advanced language learners of Japanese who used part of the CD-ROM as well as 14 Japanese language learners who used all the materials and functions of the CD-ROM in a language course specially designed for the CD-ROM reported a positive attitude toward the courseware and agreed it was effective in helping to learn the language.

1: Introduction[1]

A general survey on Japanese CALL was conducted in 2000 in order to determine what software packages were already available and what kinds still remained to be developed. The results of this survey, links to related web sites, CALL courseware, and research papers on relevant topics can be found at http://home.hiroshima-u.ac.jp/nihongo/kaken/kakenA2/index.html

A follow-up survey was conducted to investigate what needs both Japanese language teachers and learners had

in the area of CALL (Mizumachi, Tawata and Yamanaka 2002[1]).

Analysis of these surveys led to the following three conclusions:
1) Courseware based on a modern language learning theory should be created.
2) Listening comprehension practice for Japanese CALL courseware is needed.
3) "Life in Japan" is an important topic that should be addressed by Japanese CALL courseware for advanced learners of the Japanese language.

2: Purpose of the Study

Based on the findings above, Japanese courseware for listening comprehension skills related to "life in Japan" was created based on a recent language learning theory. The theory used in our courseware is "The Three-step Auditory Comprehension Approach" (TSACA) developed by Takefuta (1997[2]) at Chiba University, Japan. There are very few theories that have been developed for CALL. This particular theory, which concentrates on listening skills, has proven its effectiveness in the acquisition of English as a second language at the college level. Therefore, it was thought worthwhile to investigate if this theory would be effective for Japanese CALL courseware as well. Our purposes were,
1) to apply the theory to our Japanese CALL courseware,
2) to develop Japanese CALL materials targeted specifically for listening comprehension practice, and
3) to find whether or not the Japanese CALL courseware would be effective for learners of Japanese.

3: Courseware

3.1: Focused Skill – Listening Comprehension

As Vandergrift (1999[3]) states, "Listening comprehension is anything but a passive activity. It is a complex, active process in which the listener must discriminate between sounds, understand vocabulary and grammatical structures, interpret stress and intonation, retain what was gathered in all the above, and interpret it

---

[1] The present research is based on the project "Research on Highly Developed CALL Courseware for the Teaching of a Foreign Language" (Group KA, coordinator: Yukio Takefuta (Professor emeritus at Chiba University) Project No.12040205) supported by a Grant-in-Aid for Scientific Research on Priority Areas(A) 2001 of MEXT(Ministry of Education, Culture, Sports, Science and Technology), Japan.

within the immediate as well as the larger sociocultural context of the utterance." Hence, language learners require a variety of tasks in listening comprehension. Brown and Yule (1983[4]) state that listening skills must be targeted in language instruction. They also state that native speakers normally encounter spoken language in the context of situations associated with a set of stereotypical knowledge. Providing context visually and virtually is one of the strengths of CALL. Takefuta (1997[2]) also asserts that, more so than any other language skill, listening skill leads to a positive transfer to other language skills and has developed a theory for CALL listening practice. Therefore, listening skills were chosen as the target for this project.

In the TSACA theory, listening tasks should be divided into three steps. STEP1 focuses on helping the listener grasp an outline of the content. STEP2 concentrates on a more detailed understanding of the meaning of the conversation. Finally, STEP3 leads learners through comprehensive practice. Tasks similar to those in the English version as well as original tasks for the Japanese version are integrated into the present Japanese courseware. These include checking important expressions (STEP1), answering questions for which three HINTs are provided (STEP2), choosing words or phrases to fill in blanks (STEP2), choosing characters (HIRAGANA, KATAKANA, or KANJI) from charts to fill in blanks (STEP3), taking multiple choice quizzes (STEP3), and listening to "telephone conversations" (STEP3) as applied listening practice, along with information about the language, culture and learning strategies. A modified speed (20% slower) version of the movie soundtrack is available for users to confirm the content of the conversation. However, the speed here is no slower than that encountered in natural conversation.

3.2: Topic

"Dwelling in a Private Apartment" was chosen as the topic for this courseware based on the survey stated in the introduction. 72 university students learning the Japanese language in the U.S. and 18 Japanese language teachers in the U.S. and in Japan participated in the survey. The survey responses indicated that it would be highly desirable if CALL could provide information and practice dealing with "Life in Japan." It was also found that the respondents felt it is particularly hard to deal with situations where fluency in all four skills of the language is required, such as dwelling in an apartment in Japan. The courseware has four subtopics: 1) looking for an apartment, 2) moving into the apartment, 3) living in the apartment, and 4) moving out of the apartment. The dialogs are informal conversations between two Japanese students (male and female) who are trying to help an international student. The users of the CD-ROM are able to watch movies of the two students talking.

3.3: System

The CD-ROM for this courseware, requiring QuickTime5, contains movies and several types of controlled tasks that can be answered using a point-and-click interface. The main directions and explanations on the screen are displayed in Japanese, Chinese, Korean or English, which are all stored as graphics. Learners can choose a language by clicking one of the language buttons at any time.

4: Evaluation of the Courseware and Conclusions

In an evaluation we conducted, 6 native speakers of Japanese (NS) and 6 advanced learners of Japanese (AL) used one of the 4 courses in the CD-ROM. The courseware was also integrated in a Japanese language class and 14 Japanese language learners (JL) used all the materials and functions in the CD-ROM. All of them were asked to give their impressions of the courseware by answering 29 question items. Table 1 shows that all three groups indicated positive attitudes toward the courseware and thought it was effective (5 as the highest).

Impressions (question items)	NS	AL	JL
tasks for STEP1 (3)	4.4	4.4	4.3
tasks for STEP2 (6)	4.0	4.1	4.2
tasks for STEP3 (5)	4.4	4.5	4.4
OVERALL (15)	4.1	4.3	4.3

Table 1: Impressions of the users (5 point scale)

The respondents indicated favorable impressions toward the courseware and agreed it was effective in helping to learn the language. However, as Ellis (1997 [5]) states, students' positive ratings in a questionnaire does not necessarily mean that the task works effectively in acquiring the language. Therefore, a response-based evaluation and a learning-based evaluation are needed in future research to closely investigate the effectiveness of this courseware. Learners' responses toward the CD-ROM will be analyzed in future research.

References

[1] Mizumachi I., Tawata S., and Yamanaka E., 2002. 'Discussions for the Development of Japanese CALL Listening Comprehension Materials', in *Bulletin of the Department of Teaching Japanese as a Second Language*, No.12 (Hiroshima University), 17-23.
[2] Takefuta, Y., 1997. *Eigo Kyoiku no Kagaku*, Aruku.
[3] Vandergrift, L., 1999. 'Facilitating Second Language Listening Comprehension: Acquiring Successful Strategies', in *ELT Journal*, Volume 53/3 July, 168-176.
[4] Brown, G. and Yule, G., 1983. *Teaching the Spoken Language*. Cambridge University Press.
[5] Ellis, R., 1997. *SLA Research and Language Teaching*. Oxford University Press.

When the Playing Fields Aren't Even: Personalised Attention in the Multilingual, Varied-Ability Classroom.

Glenda Jacobs, UNITEC Institute of Technology, Auckland New Zealand
Duncan Meyer, Chalksoft Ltd, Auckland New Zealand

Abstract

This paper describes an English-language application developed within an educational system undergoing radical change. Since the mid-1990s, South African education has moved from a dual system favouring one privileged class, to one that embraces integration and equality. This move has been complex and fraught with the difficulties inherent in incorporating disadvantaged pupils from multilingual backgrounds into previously-'advantaged' classrooms with English as principle medium of tuition. In order to cope with widely-varying student needs, an interactive computer-based application has been created to enable students to diagnose their own specific weaknesses and to provide personalised assistance in overcoming them. Results demonstrate that the system is highly effective in improving students' performance, establishing a closer sense of personal attention, and in alleviating the pedagogical stresses experienced by instructors in an extremely demanding educational environment.

Introduction

Since the mid-1990s, South African education has moved from a dual system of education that favoured one privileged class to one that embraces integration and equality. This move has been a complex one, fraught with the difficulties inherent in incorporating disadvantaged pupils from multilingual backgrounds into previously-'advantaged' classrooms in which English is the principle medium of tuition. While educationalists and politicians produced and debated the principles, policies and philosophies underlying the new system, both secondary and tertiary teachers were practically faced with having to teach huge classes and to provide individualised remediation to students of often greatly varied ability.

Although most schools offer special English tuition programmes for these students, these few hours per week have proved inadequate to meet the ongoing linguistic demands of their 'standard' classes; furthermore, most teachers, despite their best intentions, are on the one hand not qualified ESOL practitioners, and on the other, hard pressed to complete already full syllabi. Despite their best efforts, already-disadvantaged students fall further behind, become resentful of a system that seems to place them on the defensive, and the problem is exacerbated.

A further consideration is that, while students need English language skills to participate meaningfully in the learning environment, many fail to understand how niceties such as correct grammar and sentence structure may contribute to their ability to succeed and be competitive in academic or professional arenas. Consequently, little class time is devoted to remediation of these rather politically sensitive communication requirements. At the same time, many instructors feel a responsibility to provide means of achieving some degree of excellence to those students who wanted to strive for it.

English College

English College is a computer-based self-help application designed by secondary and tertiary teaching staff to address the most pressing perceived problems experienced by NESB students with regard to fluent, correct written communication in English.

After consultation with students at the University of Stellenbosch and Simons Town High School (both in South Africa), it was decided to address problems in the following areas:

- Rules of Concord (verb-noun agreement)
- Sentences, Clauses and Phrases
- Sentence types (Simple, Compound and Complex)
- The Apostrophe
- The use of the Comma
- Parts of speech

It is worth noting in passing that struggling students themselves prioritised these areas, particularly in the light of long-standing international trends away from the inclusion of grammar in teaching curricula.

The design brief was to:
1. Identify individual students' problem areas
2. Devise a personalised remediation program
3. Ensure competence in the areas identified
4. Provide students with the means of asking for 'human' intervention where necessary
5. Provide a teacher module, which would facilitate tracking of student progress.

The User Interface:

A further requirement was to create a user interface with which students could identify. Since using the application was voluntary, students needed to 'feel like' doing the test and engaging with the subsequent tutorials.

Over the years a range of strategies has been employed to this end, with the programme requiring constant updating to maintain its contemporary feel. Currently targeted are elements from SMS (phone text messaging) and cartoons (with, for example, speech bubbles instead of the standard 'text book' instruction format).

In addition, students needed to be able to contact their instructor/tutor with specific questions about the programme, or with questions about any of the rules or examples that they might encounter. In order for the instructor to be able to provide appropriate assistance, he/she needed to be able to identify immediately the precise location in the course from which the student sent the question, so that he/she could assess the problem first-hand.

Programme Structure

English College comprises an 'umbrella' diagnostic test which students complete by simply pointing and clicking – no written responses are required – for already-disadvantaged students, it was considered important not to introduce distracters such as typing/spelling errors at this stage. At the end of the diagnostic test, the student is presented with an itemised report, identifying his or her problem areas, and offering the option of either beginning the remedial lessons immediately, or of quitting and returning later. The student's location is recorded, so that (s)he can quit at any time, and return to the same place later.

If a student encounters a problem at any stage while using the application, he/she can click on the question mark icon, and be presented with the following (which can be personalised by the instructor):

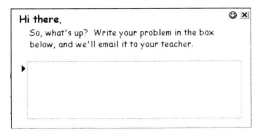

The teacher then receives an email and (optionally) an SMS text message on his/her mobile phone, identifying the student, exactly where in the course (or test) the student is, and giving the text of the SOS message.

The remedial lessons comprise self-contained, dynamic and interactive tutorial modules containing practice exercises on each rule/feature as it is taught. A concluding test is given at the end of the lesson cycle, and if necessary, the remedial content is again modified to accommodate the needs of the student.

When all remedial cycles have been completed, the student is again given a (different) diagnostic test covering all grammar areas, and (if necessary) the process of remediation starts again.

Results:

Results over the past five years have been measured in three ways. Firstly, student progress through the programme has been monitored, with number of attempts and length of time taken on each module recorded. Secondly, a before-and-after sample of students' work has been analysed each year, to identify whether success in the test translates into success in essays and assignments. Thirdly, students have been interviewed and their qualitative feedback noted and acted upon.

Students' progress through the programme varies so widely that meaningful trends are not immediately discernible. A significant improvement in performance has, however, been clear. By definition, when a student completes a module, (s)he will have achieved a 95% competency, so the acid test was seen to be the results of the 'before-and-after' sample. Over 5 years, students' error rate (for those who completed modules) has decreased by 85% on average, with the most impressive results (90% and 95%) being recorded for the concord and apostrophe modules.

A further satisfying outcome has been students' feedback, provided in person, in the end-of-programme survey, or via the Notes function. This feedback reinforces existing studies that advocate the advantage to students of being able to pace themselves and manage their own progress, as well as of being able to repeat errors and learn from them without loss of face. In addition, while benefiting from the electronic patience of the computer, students also praised highly the facility for contacting their instructor... even when they did not make use of this function. On average only 20% of students used the Notes function, but 88% of the feedback received identified it as a positive feature of the programme. It seems that the *notion* of personal attention is in itself considered valuable in the overcrowded classroom contexts in which student frequently find themselves.

Conclusion

While success in a small grammar application may seem like a drop in an ocean when compared with the complex difficulties faced by disadvantaged NESB students within the South African education system, it is felt that providing students with a computer-mediated means of successfully mastering and controlling even one small area of their frequently demoralising educational experience is of value. It is also felt that the principle on which the programme is based could be extended to empower and encourage students in other subject areas where the playing fields (for whatever reason) are overcrowded and less than level.

Old Dogs and New E-Tricks:
Staff Development in a South African Tertiary Institution.

Geoffrey Lautenbach and Duan van der Westhuizen
Department of Curriculum Studies, RAU University, South Africa
gvl@edcur.rau.ac.za and dvdw@edcur.rau.ac.za

Abstract: This paper reports on a study in progress at RAU University (RAU) in Johannesburg, South Africa. Participants in the study are online lecturers at RAU who consider themselves to be experienced face-to-face instructors. Since 1998, progressive updates of WebCT^{TM} have been implemented at RAU to support a growing number of instructors embracing the new multi-modal approach to teaching. In many cases, being able to use the available technologies has become a necessity rather than a matter of choice, but even though technology has found general acceptance at RAU, change has come slowly. This study identifies the central role that staff (faculty) can play in this process of change through a process of action research. This process cannot be seen as a top down process, but rather a complex one in which the online instructor is very active. Initial findings have identified that higher education technology strategies ignore the central role that staff (faculty) can play in the change process.

Introduction and Orientation

Instructors at the Rand Afrikaans University (RAU), Johannesburg, South Africa, are relatively new to web-based education and have used WebCT^{TM} in various ways since its inception in 1998, ranging from *optional online components with a purely administrative function only*, to courses that are presented *exclusively online*. Surrey and Land (2000) point out the potential of technology to change the nature of the teaching and learning process. Bennett, Priest and Macpherson (1999) emphasise that it is not the technology that is important, but rather how it is used by the instructor to create new experiences for the learner. Even though technology has found acceptance at RAU, change has come slowly. One reason for the lack of utilisation of this innovation, as suggested by Surrey and Land (2000), is that most university-level technology strategies ignore the central role that staff (faculty) can play in the change process. Williams and Peters (1997) suggest that faculty members with similar course responsibilities should collaborate and pool their expertise and resources. Unfortunately, as we have found out in this study, many of these faculty members are uncomfortable working with colleagues and are more accustomed to working alone. According to Jennings and Dirksen (1997), the challenge is to assist instructors in making the change. Through a process of action research this study will be used to develop and implement a programme, including a curriculum for web-based teaching with the focus on the creation and use of environments in which learning is facilitated

(Alessi & Trollip, 2001). The curriculum can ultimately be used as a core module in a professional development course within the university, or as a stand-alone course to assist instructors in improving their web-based teaching. This pro-active approach is in line with keeping ahead of, and adapting to, changes in the role of the traditional academic institution as well documented by Porter (1997), Radford (1997), and Palloff and Pratt (1999).

Participants

Two recent studies at RAU have influenced participant selection in this study. Firstly, it was discovered that instructor concerns about the *quality of teaching* and *keeping up with innovative teaching techniques* rated higher than a *general interest in online teaching* (Cronjé & Murdoch, 2000:[Online]). Rogers' theory of innovativeness suggests that innovators and early adopters would adopt a new innovation because they are interested in *any* new innovation, rather than being concerned with its specific use or value (Rogers, 1995:279). A possible explanation for the instructor concern about quality teaching in the above-mentioned study, may be that most of the early adopters of WebCT^{TM} at RAU were from the Faculty of Education and Nursing, where most of the online teaching was implemented, based from the start on what could reasonably be expected to have been informed and professional educational principles (Cronjé & Murdoch, 2000:[Online]). In a more recent study at RAU, novice online instructors with no formal qualifications in any form of educational science, little or no knowledge of pedagogy as a science, and no training in instructional design showed that they too could contribute to design principles for online education (van der Westhuizen & Lautenbach, 2002). This study therefore focuses on a group of early adopters, including novice online instructors.

Methodology

A *qualitative design* was implemented, underpinned by the principles of *action research* as described by Zuber-Skerritt (1996), McNiff, Lomax and Whitehead (1996), and Kuhne and Quigley (1997). Zuber-Skerritt (1992b) sees this as an appropriate approach for evaluating teaching and staff development in higher education (human phenomena in complex relationships), with the aim of effecting change by integrating theory and practice in action research with or by the teachers themselves. Zuber-Skerritt (1992b), points out that there is evidence that curriculum development is an effective way of developing the professional competencies of academic staff in higher education. Action research in this case has proven to be a way to include academics who would not normally discuss and critically reflect upon their courses and programmes with others. Apart from phenomenology, action research has become the most influential and almost certainly the fastest-growing orientation towards educational and staff development at present (compare Webb, 1996). The method of action research as described by Zuber-Skerritt (1992a) can be seen as cyclic moments of *planning*, *acting*, *observing* and *reflecting*. Having completed one such cycle, participants have spiraled into a further series of offshoot cycles (Webb, 1996).

Findings and Conclusions

In the initial cycle of this study, instructors had the opportunity to plan, implement (act) and observe their own web-based teaching. Data was collected in an initial round of *open interviews* with instructors and concurrent analysis, with further rounds of interviews on completion of each new semester to further investigate emerging themes. Initial sampling was purposive to achieve a balance of gender and a variety of subject areas. *Key informant interviews* were held with individuals who we believed possessed special knowledge, status and communicative skills, and who were willing to share their knowledge and skill (LeCompte & Priessle, 1993). Further data was collected using a reflexive journal based on events, comments made by the participants, and our own experiences during the research process. Relevant postings from the discussion forums within the various virtual classrooms were also analysed. This study is a work in progress. The initial data analysis has identified that online instructors at RAU have specific needs in the field of web-based education. It is clear that novice instructors can benefit from the combined knowledge of other online instructors and the exposure to design principles for online learning. The choice of the action research methodology has proven to be a productive and fruitful exercise and has resulted in meaningful contributions from a wide variety of instructors who, in the past, have not been a major source of shared information. Preliminary findings are that the greatest need is for technical assistance and training. There is also an expressed need to discuss online education matters with other instructors and to share ideas. Further cycles of the action research process will be implemented in order to refine the proposed programme for staff development at RAU and it is evident that the instructors themselves have an active role to play in this process.

List of sources

ALESSI, SM & TROLLIP, SR 2001: Multimedia for Learning: Methods and Development. Massachusetts: Allyn & Bacon.

BENNETT, S; PRIEST, A & MACPHERSON, C 1999: Learning About Online Learning: An Approach to Staff Development for University Teachers. Australian Journal of Educational Technology, 15(3), 1999: 207-221. Online. Available: http://cleo.murdoch.edu.au/ajet/ajet15/bennett.html. 12 July 2000.

CRONJÉ, M & MURDOCH, N 2001: Experiences of Lecturers using WebCT, from a Technology Adoption Perspective. (Paper Delivered at the Third Annual Conference on World Wide Web Applications, 5-7 September 2001). Johannesburg: Rand Afrikaans University. Online. Available: http://general.rau.ac.za/infosci/www2001/abstracts/cronje.htm. 3 February 2002.

JENNINGS, MM & DIRKSEN, DJ 1997: Facilitating Change: A Process for Adoption of Web-Based Instruction. (In: KHAN, BH eds. 1997: Web-Based Instruction. New Jersey: Educational Technology Publications. pp. 111 – 116.)

KUHNE, GW & QUIGLEY, A 1997: Creating Practical Knowledge through Action Research: Posing Problems, Solving Problems, and Improving Practice. San Francisco: Jossey-Bass Inc.

LeCOMPTE, MD & PREISSLE, J 1993: Ethnography and Qualitative Design in Education Research. San Diego: Academic Press, Inc.

PALLOFF, RM & PRATT, K 1999: Building Learning Communities in Cyberspace: Effective Strategies for the Online Classroom. San Francisco: Jossey-Bass Publishers.

PORTER, LR 1997: Creating the Virtual Classroom: Distance Learning with the Internet. New York: John Wiley & Sons, Inc.

RADFORD, A: The Future of Multimedia in Education. First Monday, Peer-Reviewed Journal on the Internet. 1997. Online. Available: http://www.firstmonday.dk/issues/issue2_11/radford. 8 July 2000.

ROGERS, EM 1995: Diffusion of Innovations, Fourth Edition. New York: The Free Press.

SURRY, DW & LAND, SM 2000: Strategies for Motivating Higher Education Faculty to Use Technology. Innovations in Education and Training International, 37(2), May 2000. Routledge, London.

VAN DER WESTHUIZEN, D & LAUTENBACH, GV 2002: Novice designers of online learning: A contribution to principles for instructionally effective online learning design. Proceedings of ED-MEDIA 2002, Denver, Co. Norfolk, VA: AACE Publications.

WEBB, G 1996: Becoming Critical of Action Research for Development. (In. ZUBER-SKERRITT, O eds. 1996: New Directions in Action Research. London: The Falmer Press. pp. 137 – 161.)

WILLIAMS, V & PETERS, K 1997: faculty Incentives for the Preparation of Web-Based Instruction. (In: KHAN, BH eds. 1997: Web-Based Instruction. New Jersey: Educational Technology Publications. pp. 107 – 110.)

ZUBER-SKERRITT, 0 1992a: Action Research in Higher Education – Examples and Reflections. London: Kogan Page

ZUBER-SKERRITT, 0 1992b: Professional Development in Higher Education: A Theoretical Framework for Action Research. London: Kogan Page.

ZUBER-SKERRITT, 0 1996: Emancipatory Action Research for Organisational Change and Management Development. (In. ZUBER-SKERRITT, O eds. 1996: New Directions in Action Research. London: Falmer Press. pp. 83 - 105.)

"OKOME" NHK's Full-Digital Material (1): Web Site Design and Log Collection System

Yuuji UJIHASHI*, Takashi MINOWA**, Tadashi INAGAKI***
and Haruo KUROKAMI****

*NHK Educational Cooperation, Japan <y-ujihashi@nhk-edu.co.jp>
**NHK (Japan Broadcasting Cooperation), Japan <minowa@sch.nhk.or.jp>
***Graduate School of Informatics, Kansai University, Japan <slt@mba.sphere.ne.jp>
****Faculty of Informatics, Kansai University, Japan <kurokami@mbc.sphere.ne.jp>

Abstract

"OKOME" or "rice" is the first full-digital course material produced by NHK (Japan Broadcasting Cooperation). Using the familiar subject rice as a teaching resource, this program is designed to provide children with lessons on various integrated issues such as community, the environment, the economy and international understanding, which cannot be simply categorized in the traditional framework of the subjects. "OKOME" full-digital course materials have four main contents: (1) Review the TV Program, (2) Video Clips, (3) Internet, and (4) BBS. All of these four were designed so as to work effectively by relating to each other. To measure the effects of the material, 13 elementary schools were appointed as pilot schools and various researches have been conducted since April 2001. The purpose of this first paper is to introduce the whole picture of the "OKOME" full-digital course material and log collection system supporting its research activities.

1. What is "OKOME"?

"OKOME", which means "rice" in Japanese, is the first full-digital course material for Integrated Study for the fifth to sixth grade children (10 to 12 years old) produced by NHK (Japan Broadcasting Corporation). "OKOME" course material was provided in two ways, through TV broadcasting and through the Internet, which was started in April 2001.

"OKOME" focuses on rice, which is Japanese staple diet and the most important agricultural product. As rice can be discussed in relation to many aspects like science, agriculture, environment, local community, culture, festival, health, cooking and so on, each school or child can choose a specific topic of their interest. The topic "OKOME" was chosen to serve as a common theme for various activities in the "Period for Integrated Study", which was added from April 2002, to Japanese primary and secondary school curricula.

2. The contents of "OKOME"

The overall structure of the "OKOME" full-digital material is shown in Figure 1. There were four main parts in the "OKOME" Web site: (1) Review the TV Program, (2) Video Clips, (3) Internet, and (4) BBS. Each of these parts will be described below:

(1) Review the TV Program: There were 15 minute-long 20 programs throughout the school year. All the "OKOME" TV programs were made available using Real Player on the file server only at the 13 pilot schools during the school year 2001-02. In April 2002, "OKOME" became one of first 5 educational programs that were made available to the general public via NHK's public Web site.

(2) Video clips: Adding to the TV programs provided through the Internet, video database with about 200 video clips on the themes of rice, each about two minutes in length, could be watched on the Web.

(3) Internet: "Try!" provided diverse quizzes and games using many pictures and animation. "Research" had a glossary of about 450 words with photos and links to the other sites. "Click!" contained some questions for children to vote. "Ask questions" allowed children sent their question about rice to get answers from the cooperators or NHK staffs.

(4) BBS "Rice Club": Created to promote large and high quality collaboration between distant classrooms with four types of BBS (Inagaki, et al, 2001).

3. Log Data Collection Mechanism

A log data collection mechanism was built into all the file servers provided for the 13 pilot schools. Each time the Web site was used, all the clicks were recorded so that the names of file (page) and duration of its uses would be kept in record. The purpose of this data collection was to see how much information provided in each file was utilized and in what patterns of combinations. The collected data are being analyzed that will be reported elsewhere (Inagaki, et al, in press).

References

Tadashi INAGAKI, Kenichi KUBOTA, Yuuji UJIHASHI, Haruo KUROKAMI(2001). Designing of a Web Community to Promote Inter-Classrooms Collaborative Learning with a TV Program, ICCE/Schoolnet 2001,pp.217-220

Tadashi INAGAKI, Kenichi KUBOTA, Yuuji UJIHASHI, Haruo KUROKAMI, Kenji KIKUE (in press), Analysis on a Web Community to Promote Inter-Classrooms Collaboration, ED-MEDIA2002

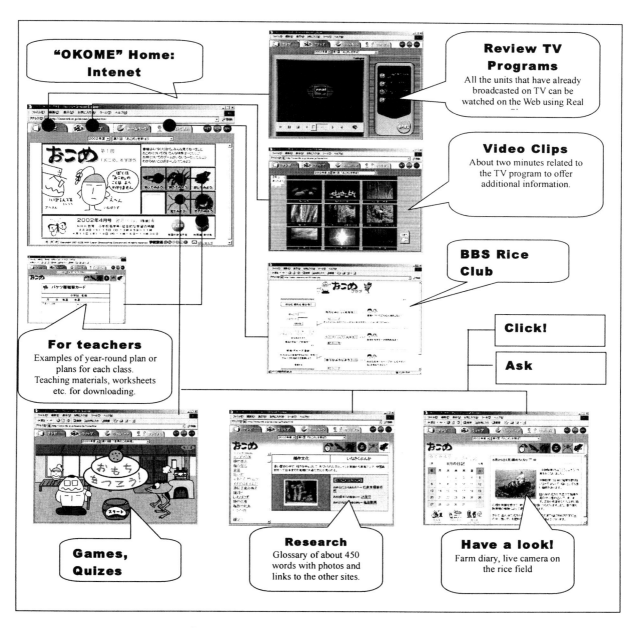

Figure 1 Site map of "OKOME" full-digital material

Developing a Web- Based Heuristic Advisory System
for Instructional Designers

Helmut M. Niegemann
Technische Universitaet Ilmenau
Institute for Media and Communication Studies
98684 Ilmenau (Germany)
helmut.niegemann@tu-ilmenau.de

Abstract

Although there are several dozens of instructional design models and a lot of empirically founded principles of instructional design, there is a lack of integration preventing us from sound recommendations for insructtional designers. The contribution presents a research and development project aiming at the development of a web-based heuristic advisory system for instructional designers. In fact, such an advisory system is a representation of an integrated technological theory. The advisory system contains three modules: an information assessment unit, the knowledge base, and an advisory unit. The most difficult part of the project is the definition of the relations between input information and design options.

1   The Problem

The two most complained problems concerning instructtional design are (a) the very limited practical application and the dissipation of the different ID models, (b) the lack of an integration of theories, models and relevant results of empirical research. Teachers and designers miss hints, which model could be best applicable under given conditions and whether or when it may be more appropriate to blend elements from different ID models.

Necessary prerequisites for any serious recommenddation of this kind are (a) a functional analysis of current instructional design theories, and (b) a technological theory which relates elements or modules from instructtional design models to combinations of instructional objectives and internal and external conditions of learning. Such a theory does not yet exist.

2   ID - Hypertheory

Our work[1] aims to construct such a theory which will be represented by a kind of an expert system (knowledge based advisory system). The idea of representing a technological theory by an expert system is analogous to the representation of a descriptive theory by a simulation system (e.g. J.R. Anderson's ACT-model; [1]). A software system representing a technological theory has to prove it's worth by providing suggestions that are in the average (a) for the short term not worse than decisions made by practicians of ID with less experience and (b) in the long run not worse than recommendations given by ID experts.

Such a theoretical framework – we call it an "ID hypertheory" (Niegemann, 2001) – ideally should contain an integration of empirically founded knowledge relevant for the solution of instructional design problems.

This is clearly a rather ambitious project and there will be continuously new knowledge to be integrated. We don't think we can make it alone after some pioneer work. Thus, the philosophy is to invite researchers to submit their results to be admitted and integrated into the ID hypertheory. Proposals for admittance will be peer-reviewed analogous to the reviewing process for papers to be published in scientific journals. An admittance into this system should be a prove of the practical relevance of a project.

The advantages of building an ID hypertheory are in the beginning more on the side of the theory: Like simulation models representing descriptive theories of memory and thinking, theory makers are forced to formulate unambiguous statements, contradictions between different statements will necessarily be uncovered and lacks of knowledge become evident.

.1 "We" are two cooperating research groups at the Technische Universitaet Ilmenau and the Universitaet Koblenz-Landau at Landau (both Germany) working on this research programm: W. Schnotz, H. M. Niegemann, M. Molz, A. Eckhardt and D. Hochscheid-Mauel

Recommendations produced by the system will not be directive. Rather like an experienced business consultant the system will successively show for every level of design decisions the appropriate design options, connected costs and possible consequences. Similar to expert systems in medicine it should be a decision support system, i.e. the final decision is never made by the software but by the human instructional designer. The architecture of the system contains three modules:

- An information assessment unit
- A knowledge base
- An advisory unit

3   State of the Project

A first phase of the projects has focused on the functional analysis of existing instructional design models [3] to determine (a) main categories of "functional elements" used in ID models and (b) main levels of design decisions.

The second phase has been the provisional definition of the information the system must assess from users: Instructional objectives, including the kind of knowledge or the competencies to be fostered, relevant traits of the target group (knowledge, motivation, composition) and the contextual conditions (time, budget, competencies etc.). The current phase is the core phase and the most difficult one: The definition of relations between instructional objectives and the other input variables on the one hand and the options available on any level of the process of designing multimedia learning environments on the other hand.

References

[1] Anderson, J. R. (1983). The architecture of cognition. Cambridge, MA: Harvard University Press.
[2] Niegemann, H, (2001). ID Hypertheory. Paper presented at the Conference of the European Association for Research on Learning and Instruction 2002, Fribourg (Switzerland).
[3] Reigeluth, C. (Ed.). (1999). Instructional-design theories and models. A new paradigm of instructional theory. Mahwah, NJ: L. Erlbaum Associates, Publishers.

Faculty Reward and Promotion in Distributed Learning Environments - Pedagogy in Implementation

Myrna Sears, Katy Campbell, Cheryl Whitelaw
University of Alberta (Academic Technologies for Learning)

Abstract:

This paper focuses on the scholarship of teaching and the need to implement change in the evaluation practices of post-secondary institutions. The scholarship of teaching is closely linked to the development of instructional technology innovations. The principles underlying teaching excellence are inherent in the effective use of instructional technology innovations.

Increasing the value placed upon teaching and learning is a primary concern of a research project called "Peer Review in Instructional Technology Initiatives" (PRITI). PRITI (2000-2002) is a collaborative initiative to develop a peer review model of evaluation, which will be used to assess instructional technological innovations for faculty reward and promotion. One of the deliverables is a set of evaluative criteria and templates to assist institutional academic program review bodies in the evaluation of existing and proposed offerings in distance & distributed learning environments.

Rationale:

The rapid growth of new information technologies to enhance new and existing post-secondary curriculum through distance and distributed learning models has made it necessary to develop a means to evaluate the effectiveness of learning outcomes from an institutional standpoint. As more and more faculty members place their course materials on the WWW, issues arise concerning academic standards and learning outcomes evaluation. The traditional models for evaluating technology-enhanced curriculum are no longer adequate. Technology-based projects are not included in tenure and promotion policies because of the lack of established criteria necessary to evaluate such projects and the lack of knowledge concerning how to present the projects in a scholarly manner (Seminoff, & Wepner, 1997, [1]).

In this context, instructional technology innovations refer to a wide breadth of educational initiatives that use technology to enhance or deliver learning. Technology-based and enhanced courses, learning objects, and course authoring products are all examples of instructional technology innovations.

Key Issues:

The scholarship of teaching refers to efforts to improve teaching and learning. Therefore it is closely linked to the development of instructional technology innovations. The principles underlying teaching excellence are inherent in the effective use of instructional technologies. These innovations cannot be evaluated outside of the teaching and learning context in which they are used. The scholarly efforts of faculty members who develop and employ the use of instructional technology innovations to improve learning on campuses need to be recognized.

Several facets of teaching with technology create increased demands on instructors. Depending on which instructional technologies are used, the amount of time needed to design and develop a web-enhanced course is often extensively greater than that needed for a traditional face-to-face course. Factors affecting time include the length of the course, the degree to which technology is integrated, and the type of course being offered. There is often an increased need to plan in advance for technology-enhanced courses.

One of the aspects to be considered is a way to value the efforts of instructors who may be contributing significantly higher levels of time and talent to teaching with instructional technology than to teaching traditional face-to-face courses. A universal set of standards used to evaluate the merit of instructional technology innovations does not currently exist.

The delivery of instruction itself has long been regarded as a private activity and therefore difficult to evaluate (Cambridge, 2001, [2]). As a result, little research has been published on what constitutes successful university teaching (Samad et al., 1995, [3]). Similar to the peer-review process of publications, a standard process of evaluation is necessary if instructional technology innovations are to be considered as a form of scholarship within the university reward structure.

Description of the PRITI Project:

PRITI is an acronym for the "Peer Review of Instructional Technology Initiatives". The PRITI research project is a collaborative initiative at the University of Alberta, Canada to develop a peer review model of evaluation, which will be used to assess instructional technological innovations. The PRITI research study arose from the need to provide leadership and advocacy for academic staff members who have developed technology-enhanced instructional resources (e.g. - a WebCT course) and who wish to have this work recognized for tenure and promotion purposes. Currently many Faculty Evaluation Committees do not know how to evaluate instructional technology innovations and are unsure whether they fall under research or teaching, or both.

The PRITI Project attempted to develop a rigorous, evidence-based model for evaluating technology-enhanced curriculum developed by faculty and delivered in flexible, distributed, or alternative learning environments. The PRITI Project is advocating a process of evaluation by peers, self and students. Portfolios, which contain artifacts and relevant information, can be a holistic representation of a faculty member's teaching and research endeavours. Peer and self-evaluations of teaching practices can be artifacts included within the teaching portfolio.

Evaluating the quality of a technology-enhanced course involves not only evaluating how the technology is being used but also determining the technologies' appropriateness to the course objectives. The PRITI Project has created an evaluation template for Faculty Evaluation Committees to pilot in the evaluation of faculty's technology-enhanced curriculum.

Project Deliverables:

The PRITI Project is a first step in the long-term advocacy process to effect change in the university culture. Evaluating technology-enhanced teaching has to be taken to the point of comparing it with traditional classroom instruction for tenure and promotion.

The PRITI Project provides a model and a process for providing peer review of instructional innovations that can be used for the evaluation of faculty and for the evaluation of technology-enhanced curriculum. One of the deliverables is a set of evaluative criteria and

templates to assist institutional academic program review bodies in the evaluation of existing and proposed offerings in distance & distributed learning environments. A folder of resources contributes to the research and implementation.

This poster presentation focuses on the scholarship of teaching and the need to implement change in the evaluation practices of post-secondary institutions. The research used a mixed research design that included a needs assessment at the institutional level and the faculty level, document analysis, interviews, surveys, and personal narratives gathered both before and during the PRITI Project. The PRITI research study is currently in process with a completion date of Fall 2002.

Conclusion

In order for the teaching and learning process to be valued on the same level as research there needs to be a fundamental cultural change within the university (Fairweather, 1996, [4]). Increasing the value placed upon teaching and learning at the University of Alberta campus is a primary concern of PRITI Project collaborators. The current university culture rewards research over teaching. Efforts to promote teaching on campus must be made at the student, faculty and administrative levels and be embraced by the university infrastructure itself. We are, for all intents and purposes, speaking of a University-wide cultural change.

Bibliography:

Fairweather, J. S. (1996). Faculty work and public trust restoring the value of teaching and public service in American academic life. Boston: Allyn and Bacon.

Seminoff, N., & Wepner, S. (1997). What Should We Know about Technology-based Projects for Tenure and Promotion. Journal of Research on Computing in Education, 30 (1), 16p.

Cambridge, B. (2001). Fostering the Scholarship of Teaching and Learning: Communities of Practice. To Improve the Academy, 19, 3-15.

Samad, D., Fraser, I., Fish, T., & Fraser, L. (1995). Teaching Excellence: A Reaction to the Smith Commission Report and its Effect. The Canadian Journal of Higher Education, 25 (1), p. 79-83.

Teaching Methodology for 3D Animation

Muqeem Khan
Assistant Professor of Digital Design
School of Architecture and Design
American University of Sharjah
mukhan@aus.ac.ae
www.muqeemkhan.com

Abstract

The field of 3d animation has addressed design processes and work practices in the design disciplines for in recent years. There are good reasons for considering the development of systematic design processes for the development of 3d animation and it's teaching. Design methodology understood as a general field has developed through cross-disciplinary efforts, primarily involving architecture, engineering design and industrial design. This body of knowledge is not very well known in the development of 3 dimensional animation or computer graphics discipline, but appears to be highly relevant. In this paper, I introduce a number of systematic design methods for teaching and development of 3d animation. I hope that they will prove useful for teachers and professionals in computer graphics. Several methods that I present here are all mainly oriented towards early phases of the design process, where concepts and ideas are the main currencies. The later phases, including implementation and evaluation, are perhaps less problematic. My choice of methods is not meant to be comprehensive, perhaps not even the best possible. Instead I present examples of methods that can be tried out in a very simple ways without putting too much effort into the learning process.

It is every academic's dream that students can hold their place in the job market or in higher education. Furthermore, schools try their best to acquire equipment and human resources to help students excel. But there are many hurdles and constraints that have to be faced in an academic environment as compared to a production house.

The integration of computing, telecommunication, visualization and new interaction techniques will change and expand the paradigm of teacher-student interaction. The role of a teacher in this century will be different and will be based on traditional teaching techniques with technology and its implementation. The use of advanced visualization tools will play a major role in the teaching and learning process in design methodology by providing a new institutional environment. This institutional environment can be characterized as distributed, highly available, portable, dynamic and cooperative.

Muqeem Khan developed digital graphics nearly fifteen years ago by working in BASIC language. This curiosity led first to the National College of Arts, Lahore Pakistan (NCA 1988), and then completion of Bachelor of Science and Masters of Arts in Industrial Design with emphasis on computer graphics from ACCAD Advanced Computing Center for the Arts and Design (1996) at Ohio State University, Columbus Ohio. Muqeem produced the visual effects for movies like Deep Rising, George of the Jungle, Flubber, Armageddon and the newly released Final Fantasy. Currently he is an assistant professor of Digital Design at the American University of Sharjah, UAE, instructing in Computer Graphics.

To see his work visit:
http://www.muqeemkhan.com

Design is a purposeful, systematic, and creative activity, whose aim is produced in limited or mass quantities to satisfy human needs and wants. In that highly active environment, computer visualization will play a very important role and will be an important domain of any teaching aspects of design. Furthermore, a teacher's role and potential in the development of computer visualization will be accelerated in the next century. We observe and see the development of a product in industrial design, in the corporate identity, several phases of spatial decision in the field of interior and architectural design. Similar to these phases, the boundary of design will expand to critically examine the influence of computer and informational visualization. If we are preparing designers for the next century, it would be our responsibility to expand and explore the design thinking and process for a digital visualization.

A carefully examined process or even disclosure of various processes in the field of computer visualization in classroom teaching will be an addition to the embodiment of design knowledge. This activity, or study will help and enhance the elements, academia, and the corporate world.

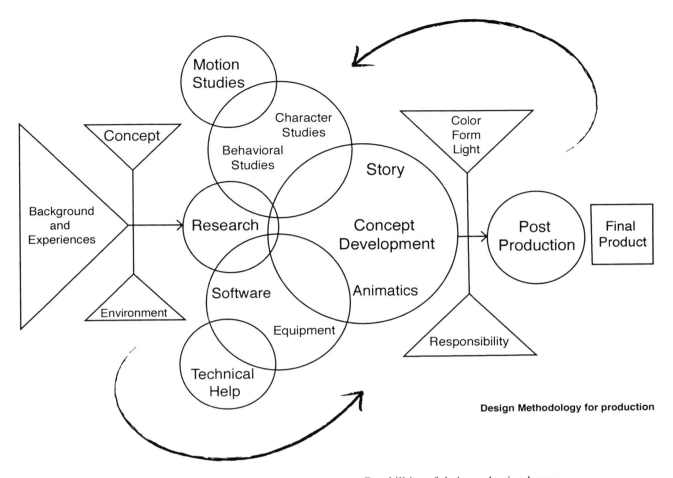

Design Methodology for production

I created exercises based on design methodology that would separate ideation from the implementation process. This is important in any production related pipeline too. Regardless of required software and hardware capabilities, expectations were set in the beginning and were clear to both instructor and students. Consequently, at the end of the term both, educator and learners were satisfied with the result.

Time and money are two important elements in a production house. The important task for higher-level managers in any production house is to deal with the financial matters. Lower level managers mainly deal with project schedules. They are responsible for overseeing the completion of the job with maximum effort in a required time period.

These lower level managers/supervisors can be compared to instructors and educators in any institution responsible for teaching production related material. The following are some of the issues that they are very familiar with:
-Their own strengths and weaknesses.

-Capabilities of their production house.
-Strengths and weaknesses of their staff.
-An overall picture of the project schedule.
-The necessity to meet deadlines

A teacher in a institutional setting may change the above issues in the following manner:

-Instructor's own strengths and weaknesses.
-Capabilities of the institution.
-Strengths and weaknesses of their students.
-An overall picture of the academic term
-The necessity for students to meet required deadlines.

By taking these issues with the production methodology on board, an instructor achieves quality work by the required deadline. This applies to teachers with or without production experiences. An instructor, who either has production experiences or not, can have these states of mind. Therefore, it is important to understand how production houses work with the highest capabilities. Almost every production house, one way or the other, uses very systematic, creative, and purposeful design methodology.

The whole process of bringing design methodology to classroom teaching with the emphasis on systematic design process is to compose cyclical design phases. This process is covered with an ongoing evaluation cycle, as can be seen in the diagram. Furthermore, the origin of this whole process is composed of the following:

a) Definition and analysis of concept statement.
b) Designer's background and experience.
c) Environmental influence.

All of these elements tend to proceed towards a thorough research activity, which then synthesize the major steps and decisions within the process. After such research students can easily understand a number of processes and their expected solutions. Good research leads the designer to a systematic design implementation process where creativity and intuition can be combined with all the other systematic design decisions.

Most of the time students are involved in the use of several computer packages available in a institutional facility. It is also important to minimize the gap between student development and technical production of computer animation. During the project development, I tried to find ways of adjoining student's personal design and technical background in order to simplify a complex process of production from concept development to final presentation of an animation.

1:Concept Design and Procedures

The animation that students completed had several sequential design and technical processes. The whole process of making this computer-generated film is a cyclical, creative, intuitive, and analytic process where inductive and deductive reasoning played an important role. The whole process can be subcategorized into several individual group processes as follows:

1.1:Early Sketches

The first step to start this process was to establish a concept statement for the project. A concept statement sets a goal to direct a student to a particular path. During this process several basic line drawings were created which were not very detailed. These drawings and statements are there to create a personal rapport between the student and his/her own creative thinking. The student's personal experiences and background are important to elaborate and synthesize the creative process. These early sketches will be more purposeful, systematic and creative later in the design process. The main purpose at this stage is just to get a fresh and a meaningful idea for the animation.

Simple shapes within the stories

1.2:Linkage and Development of the Story

In this process of thinking and development, students tried to find a link between the concept statement and story development. As a designer they had to be very sensitive about the importance of a concept and its goal. The ability to think in three dimensions was important in terms of the development of ideas and translating visionary inputs into the design process. In the early stages it is important to consider who would be the audience for this design output.

In the creation of the story, one must clarify the possible hurdles that will be encountered during the implementation process. Most often the challenges were the appearance of objects, texture and lights. There are several issues the student needs to consider before the implementation process:

a) What software is available within the facility?
b) Previous problems related to the software
c) Capabilities of tools
d) Technical Support
e) Previous users
f) Availability of the software in the facility
g) What software libraries are accessible in the facility?
h) Data transfer from other programs and related problems

All of the above issues are relative to each other and dependent on the facility and software available during the design process.

1.3:Story in Segments and time

At this stage, a student should consider the rough duration of time for each of the events within the story. For example, how many seconds a particular scene or movement requires.

It is not very important to estimate a correct time at this stage, however it would be beneficial for future development.

If there is a talking character in the story, a student should estimate the time of its speech. Early detection of these elements will minimize the overall time it will take to complete the story.

1.4: Design Thinking and Evaluation

The Design process in the development of computer animation is also a cyclical process where research, ideation, implementation, and evaluation take place in a parallel fashion. It would be great if the student follows each one after another. In this cyclical process the first step is to complete valuable research related to the story and concept. Several data gathering techniques should be utilized in this process, like literature search, case study, observation, and previous related work. Even during the implementation process, evaluation plays an important role. Important issues related to the primary goal should be considered during the ideation and concept development process.

1.5: Finished Story Board

After completing all of the above stages, a clean and elaborated, but focused storyboard can be generated. Even at this stage, it is not extremely important to consider all the techniques of the development process. A storyboard can show a sequence of events and their linkage to each other. Right numbers of representation of events in the story can be presented in terms of clean and colorful images. A final storyboard can give a feeling of the final product. It can give an idea of space, time, color, camera angle and position. It can also show a rough feeling of camera movement to a particular direction.

The correct number of images should be represented in the storyboard to show an event or events during the particular time duration. The grouping and layout of images can also show a semantic relationship of the storyboard to the final product, the animation.

1.6: Animatics

"Animatics" is a combination of images, from a storyboard, and a time sequence with the possible addition of sound. After having good animatics, timing of major the parts, division within the parts, and transition among the parts can be examined. The minimization of time, sound implementation and synchronization can also be done in the animatics.

Any editing tool can be used in this very important part of the ideation process. Transition from one event to the next can be tested in this stage. Good animatics can also motivate the designer to peruse and implement more ideas in terms of design issues. This stage of ideation is also helpful for the evaluation of the whole process and story. It can raise several questions for the implementation process. Final animatics should result in the following elements:

-Timing of major parts i.e. A, B, C
-Division within A, B, C
-Transition among A, B, C

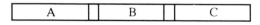

-Minimization of time
-Sound Implementation
-Sound synchronization

1.7: Character Studies

Character studies are the most important element for the development of any character animation. A character in the story is the representation of cultural, social, and psychological realities of living or non-living entities in animation. The very first attempt to tackle this problem is to actually video taped the possible actions and events. In that way the body gesture, the way a character move, and the character interaction within the space can be studied. Different joints and action should be videotaped to categorize and examine the behavior and psychology within the character' personality. Camera angle and framing can be analyzed during this process. After good character movement is recorded on video, important events can be taken out into a file strip using any editing software to find the relationship between time and frames. These frame-captured-images can be utilized as a valuable resource in the production process.

1.8: Frame Studies

Using any editing software, a designer can easily generate action information and see the joints movement and position a certain instance of time. One should not need to see each frame by itself. It should be helpful to see every 15th or 30th frame. Again, all of this information is just for the reference and should help in the implementation process. The method that I thought would work is as follows:

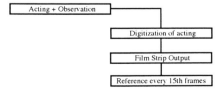

1.9:Pose/Action Sheet

After getting stationary information about the actions, students decided to build their own Pose Sheet, in the cartoon industry known as an Action Sheet. A student can note all the possible sounds, its length and related information in this stage. In the Movement Rate column of the action sheet, the student should depict the rate of the movement. Some students developed their own percentage reading for the related action or movement. For example 95% corresponds to fast movement. All of the columns in the action sheet are controlled by the column "Frame.". One sheet can show all of the above information in addition to the camera movement within fifty frames. The main purpose of making this action sheet was to synthesize the problem to the last stage so the data should be ready for the implementation stage.

2:Implementation of Data

The implementation of data in computer visualization, especially in character animation, is very similar to the traditional design process. Computer visualization is similar to the design stages. For example in design, a designer does the research, gathers all the related information and using creative and intuitive process, passes through the implementation stage. After these stages, the first stage of implementation is to create rough character animation. It is very similar to:

- Form study in Product Design,
or,
- Rough layout in visual Communication Design,
or,
- Spatial relationship within the field of Interior and architecture design.

Like in Product, Visual Communication, Interior Space and architectural design, it is the designer's responsibility to select the right tool for the completion of the project. The completion of computer visualization with the involvement of many software is also very similar to the design implementation process. There were two major factors to complete the process:

a) To reduce the amount of design error, redesign or delay.
b) To make possible a more imaginative and advanced design process.

We can categorize thinking and story development as a creative process and making animation as a systematic design process. Both of these processes are parts of *systematic*, *creative*, and purposeful design activities.

2:Implementation

The method is primarily a means of resolving a conflict that exists between logical analysis and creative thought. The difficulty is that the imagination does not work well unless it is free to alternate between all aspects of the problem, in any order, and at any time, whereas logical analysis breaks down if there is the slightest departure from a systematic step by step sequence. It follows that any design method must posses both kinds of thought to proceed one by one if any progress is to be made.

3:Systematic Design Process

I tried to establish a systematic design process in this particular design problem for students where a student deals with not only a creative thought process, but also handling of a number of advanced visualizations. The selection and research on the tools available in the facility was extremely important to complete the task in the early stages of animation development. For that reason, a systematic design process was essential to adopt. The Systematic Design in the development of computer visualization could be explained as:

1) To leave the student mind free to produce ideas and solutions at any time without confusing the process of analysis.

2) To provide a system of notation which records every item of design information outside the memory, keeping design requirements and solutions completely separate from each other. This means that when students move from problem analysis to solution seeking, they feel the need of the three distinct stages, analysis, synthesis, and evaluation.

The making of Computer Visualization with the elements of design and visual communication should be carefully examined. The identification of the task, elaboration and linkage of visual elements, transition from one visual incident to other, implementation of findings and the overall perceptive and cognitive representation of messages are all important to accomplish the required appropriate goal. A very important role and responsibility of a student is to carefully synthesize the possible problems within all the phases of the development of computer visualization.

Clips of student's animation can be seen at:
http://www.muqeem.com/teaching.html

Web-based Library Instruction for Promoting Information Skills

Lih-Juan ChanLin
Email: lins1005@mails.fju.edu.tw
Fu-Jen Catholic University, Department of Library & Information Science
510 Chung-Chen Road, Hsin-Chuang 24205, Taiwan

Abstract

This article addresses the issues with regards implementing web-based library instruction from cognitive and instructional aspects. With an aim to educate college students to become information literate, a web-based library instruction was developed, implemented and evaluated. Its implications for future implementation were also discussed. From the evaluation results, most students showed a positive attitude towards the WBI and found that it helped them to learn. Students' responses also reflected high value and future expectation on the web-based learning experience. Students' positive attitude toward LibTeach, included the organization of the content and the resources provided in the instruction. Students enjoyed learning with the instructional materials, and would continue learning from it. From the negative aspect of the responses, a need for improvement was revealed. Improvement on issues related to "on-line discussion" and "relating content to other courses".

1. Introduction

As electronic learning has been integrated in various subject areas, the question how to help students to develop the necessary skills, gain experiences and have motivation to learn becomes an important issue. In the advent of World Wide Web (WWW), web-based instruction becomes not only a new way of learning information skills, but also a supplement to traditional mode of face-to-face classroom library instruction. Web-based instruction (WBI) is an appropriate application of the Internet to support the delivery of learning, skills and knowledge in a holistic approach not limited to any particular courses, technologies, or infrastructures [1]. The initiatives of using Internet as a tool for learning have played an increasingly important role in the goals of colleges and universities in recent years, and the trend seems likely to continue [2]. Likewise, information literacy course on the web becomes an emerging trend for providing a different mode in learning information skills. In the advent of World Wide Web (WWW), WBI becomes not only a new way of learning library skills, but also a supplement to traditional mode of face-to-face classroom library instruction.

The Internet has significantly increased the speed of library education activities. It also provides learners more interactive activities and greater exchange of information. Supported by the Internet, WBI allows the instructor or learners to have access at their own convenient times. Therefore, electronically mediated human communication can be achieved easily [3]. Several cases have been reported in employing different forms of web-based library instruction, such as offering fee-based and for-credit web-based courses [4] integrating a web-based library instruction into other courses [5] or using a MOO service for web-based instruction [6].

Web-based library instruction began with simple handouts marked up without any changes from the original text-based materials. It progressed to mini-workbooks and hypertext links to other sources, graphical interfaces including PowerPoint presentations, sound, and video, and finally interactive features [7]. However, to create a learner-centered environment that fosters autonomous learning, scaffold-learning model is widely suggested in integrating many course designs. Scaffold learning is based on a model of conceptual change that involves first expanding the repertoire of ideals held, and then encouraging students to distinguish among these ideas by reflecting and linking ideas into a coherent and cohesive perspective [8].

To transport good library instruction practices into the Web environment, Dewald analyzes several characteristics of good library instruction, including: coursed-related and assignment-related, facilitating active learning, fostering group interaction, offering information in more than one medium, clear instruction objectives, teaching concepts, and including the option of asking the librarian for helps [9]. From these arguments, the elements that constitute good library instruction are not limited to the instruction itself, the strategies to encourage students' involvement, and the opportunities to foster interaction and creative thinking are all essential to success.

Good web-based learning provides opportunity to develop learning-on-demand and learner-centered instruction and training. However, successful implementation of web-based learning requires a systematic understanding of various complex factors. Khan suggested a framework for web-based learning helps to identify and clarify critical issues and complexities of web-based learning. The framework contains several dimensions: pedagogical, technological, interface design, evaluation, management, resources support, ethical, institutional aspects. Each dimension has several sub-dimensions each consisting of items focused on a specific aspect of a web-based learning. Thorough consideration of issues related to learning can help designers create a meaningful and distributed learning environment [10].

2. Development and Evaluation

With an aim to facilitate widespread adoption and foster effective learning of information skills, a web-based library instruction, LibTeach (http://libteach.lins.fju.edu.tw) was designed and implemented in Fu-Jen Catholic University, Taiwan to offer students fundamental information skills. Several attributes essential to learning, including the structure of the instruction, interactivity and feedback, media features, pace of learning, sharing and exchange of information, and flexible course design were considered. From the evaluation results, most students showed a positive attitude towards the WBI and found that it helped them to learn. Students' responses also reflected high value and future expectation on the web-based learning experience. Students' positive attitude toward LibTeach, included the organization of the content and the resources provided in the instruction. Students enjoyed learning with the instructional materials, and would continue learning from it. From the negative aspect of the responses, a need for improvement was revealed. Improvement on issues related to "on-line discussion" and "relating content to other courses".

Students valued the use of Internet in conjunction with the library skills to solve specific academic tasks. However, providing instructional content relevant to students' major courses is needed. To meet students' academic needs, integrating information literacy across-curriculum that incorporates the process of seeking, evaluating, and using information into the curriculum might be a more efficient way of providing students with valuable experience.

In the use of communication tools for obtaining reference help, students expected to get responses from the web as soon as possible. The questions were often posted whenever there was a need from their assignment or project. Since most students prepare their assignment one or two day before the deadline for submission, quick responses to their problems are often required. However, this might be the limitation for the online inquiry. One might never know when his (or her) questions would be answered. And if the inquiry were not clear, or the answers did not satisfy the clients, more time would be spent on clarifying the problems, and identifying solutions.

As it can be observed from the case, even though the on-line reference desk and discussion was used to encourage a person-to-person interaction, students did not use it frequently. Prompt response to students' queries might be needed to ensure that the reference desk is prominently on the web-site. To encourage knowledge sharing and experiencing, allowing students to elect topics or issues and have free discussion opportunities on the web-site is also suggested.

In addition to provide web-based tutorial that covers library instruction, across-curriculum integration of information skills is also important. To promote information literacy and to provide students with valuable learning experience, there is a need to prepare students in locating, managing, critically evaluating and using information, and solving problems. Through the integration of curriculum and information skills, the way of thinking and reasoning regarding varied aspects of subject matter can be facilitated.

3. References

[1] Paul Henry, "E-Learning Technology, Content and Service," Education & Training 43(4/5)(2001): 249-255.

[2] Nancy H. Dewald, Ann Scholz-Crane, Austin Booth, & Cynthia Levine, "Information Literacy at a Distance: Instructional Design Issues" The Journal of Academic Librarianship 26(1) (January 2000): 33-44

[3] Hsiu-mei Huang, "Instructional Technologies Facilitating Online Courses," Educational Technology (July-August 2000): 41-46.

[4] Kimberly B. Kelley, Gloria J. Orr, Janice Houck, & Claudine SchWeber, "Library Instruction for the Next Millennium: Two Web-Based Courses to Teach Distant Students Information Literacy" Journal of Library Administration 32(1/2)(2001): 281-294.

[5] Bruce G. Kocour, "Using Web-Based Tutorials to Enhance Library Instruction," College & Undergraduate Libraries 7(1)(2000): 45-51.

[6] Joanne B. Smyth, "Using a Web-Based MOO for Library Instruction in Distance Education," Journal of Library Administration 32(1/2)(2001): 383-392

[7] Nancy H. Dewald, "Web-Based Library Instruction: What Is Good Pedagogy?" Information Technology and Libraries 18(1) (March 1999): 26-31.

[8] Marcia C. Linn, "Cognition and Distance Learning," Journal of The American Society for Information Science 47(11) (1996): 826.

[9] Nancy H. Dewald, "Transporting Good Library Instruction Practice into the Web Environment: An analysis of Online Tutorials," The Journal of Academic Librarianship 25(1) (Jan. 1999): 26-31.

[10] Badrul H. Khan, " A Framework for Web-based Learning," TechTrends 44(3) (Apr. 2000): 51

Ensuring Academic Integrity in the Age of the Internet: Evaluating a web-based analytic tool

John Gregory, Executive Director, IT, University of Maine
Andrei Strukov, Instructional Technologies Development, IT, University of Maine

Abstract

The following paper details the results of a recent evaluation of TurnItIn.com by The Faculty Development Center at the University of Maine.

Problem

With increasing student reliance upon the Internet for research, educators are aware of the heightened ability to access and extract material from sources unfamiliar to the instructor.

As students download data, ranging from a paragraph to entire papers (including those offered for purchase or in exchange for one of the student's own papers), concern about improper citation or plagiarism grows.

Overview

TurnItIn.com utilizes a proprietary color-coded rating system to assign levels of originality or plagiarized material. Ranging from Blue/Original, through Green, Yellow, Orange, to Red/Matched with other unaccredited sources.

A faculty member at an authorized educational institution uploads papers to the TurnItIn.com site. Documents are analyzed and returned within a specified time period.

Process

Our tests were based on papers ranging in difficulty for detecting plagiarized material. These actual student papers were as follows:

1. 95% of content extracted from three Web sites, one site was password protected
2. Self-written with one appropriate citation
3. 100% self-written, basic literary composition of mediocre quality
4. Entire document was copied from another source and used synonyms and revised sentence order to conceal plagiarism
5. One paragraph copied, without citation, from an on-line PDF file
6. Eight papers in one of the following languages: French, German, Russian, or Spanish
7. Document copied from a low-traffic web site
8. Document copied from a password protected web site

Results

TurnItIn.com had mixed recognition success, using the same document order as above:

1. Orange: Found the two source sites but did not identify the third, password protected site.
2. Green: Found a citation and referred to the Website that contained the cited document.
3. Blue: Despite thousands of similar compositions, the mediocre document was seen as original, which it was.
4. Yellow: TurnItIn found the site from where the paper was copied and modified.
5. Blue. It did not find the borrowed paragraph.
6. Orange. The tool found similar sites in Spanish, other languages are not supported.
7. Blue. The tool did not discover the case of plagiarism.
8. Blue. The tool did not discover the case of plagiarism.

Findings

TurnItIn.com exhibited limitations in its ability to detect and flag plagiarized material from the following source material: password protected sites, PDF files, foreign languages, which the exception of some Spanish.

Faculty using this web-based analytic tool must be aware of its limitations and decide how much weight these limitations must be given.

Most plagiarism is detected and mediocre, but original, students seem not to be penalized for their inadvertent similarity to other papers.

Conclusion

The Faculty Development Center found TurnItIn.com to be a valuable tool that can be trusted. While the service has some flaws, its success rate is significant. Additionally, mediocre matches are not unjustly accused of wrongdoing.

The cost-success ratio is reasonably high to justify the purchase and use of aTurnItIn.com license, particularly if faculty members are made aware of its limitations. Purchasing institutions should market the program to faculty members and provide appropriate training opportunities.

Computer-Assisted Instruction + ? = Earth Science Learning Outcomes: Three Case Studies

Chun-Yen Chang[1] & Chin-Chung Tsai[2]
[1] Department of Earth Sciences, National Taiwan Normal University
[2] Center for Teacher Education, National Chiao Tung University

Abstract

This paper summarizes three companion Computer-Assisted Instruction (CAI) case studies in a series for the last several years. These studies were designed to investigate a various of impacts of an Earth Science Computer-Assisted Tutorial (ESCAT), developed by the research team, on students' Earth science achievement and their attitudes toward Earth science in senior high schools. The pretest-posttest control-group experimental design was adopted by all the three studies. Quantitative data were collected on students' pre- and post-treatment achievement and attitudes toward Earth science measures. The multivariate analysis of covariance (MANCOVA) and analysis of covariance (ANCOVA) revealed that (a) the ESCAT has its promise; (b) the "problem-solving" design of the ESCAT is generally better than the "non-problem-solving" design of the ESCAT; and (c) the "teacher-directed" ESCAT seems producing statistically greater student gains than the "student-controlled" ESCAT. These findings suggested that instruction, such as the ESCAT, should be more broadly developed and widely employed in the secondary earth science classrooms.

1: Introduction

While a number of previous studies and meta analyses have primarily focused on the comparative efficacy of computer-assisted instruction versus traditional instruction (Chang, 2001a, 2001b; Christmann et al., 1997; Fletcherflinn and Gravatt, 1995; Kulik and Kulik 1986, 1991) there are relatively fewer inquiries exploring how various teaching formats or system designs of CAI influence student science learning outcomes in the secondary classroom. Therefore, these studies in a series were designed to investigate a various of impacts of a Earth Science Computer-Assisted Tutorial (ESCAT), developed by the research team, on students' Earth science achievement and their attitudes toward Earth science in senior high schools.

2: Software and instructional methods

Topics covered in the ESCAT included "Typhoon and the Debris-Flow Hazards". At the end of July 1996, Typhoon Herb roared through Taiwan and brought about a huge rainfall over the course of three or four days costing many lives and property damages resulting from flooding, landslides, and a large-scaled debris-flow hazard. The computer program is designed to aid students to become more knowledgeable about the hazards.

The structure of the ESCAT is built upon a virtual, private research office comprising a variety of Learning Sections (LS): tables-and-graphs, news-report, newspaper, bookshelf, computer, virtual-field trip, and Test as the primary interface elements. The LS tables-and-graphs contains mainly graphics and animation including local maps, geological maps, topography maps, animated weather-satellite images, and precipitation data and information for data analysis and interpretation. The LS news-report covers all the relevant TV news reports in the video format on the events of a debris-flow hazard, which occurred in Nan-Tou Province of Taiwan in 1996. The LS newspaper reports the print news in association with the debris-flow hazard. The LS bookshelf consists of science textbooks explaining the occurrences of natural hazards and other matters for further references and readings. The LS computer comprises a series of Video CD presenting the local geological and weather characteristics. The LS virtual-field trip allows students to conduct several geological investigations in order for them to learn facts related to the debris-flow hazard and develop an understanding of the natural events. Finally, the Test Section contains 10 randomly selected test items from a pool of 30 multiple-choice items to examine students' understanding of science concepts.

To summarize, the ESCAT developed and employed in this study emphasized the following characteristics: (1) Large amounts of information and data on the subject of the debris-flow hazards are represented in different formats such as video, graphics, animation, and sound; and (2) The information and data can be accessed through various paths. The detailed design, development, and components of the multimedia CAI can also be found in

Chang (2001b).

3: Instruments

The dependent variables were primarily measured through the use of (1) the *Earth Science Achievement Test* (ESAT) to assess students' Earth science achievement (and (2) the *Attitudes Toward Earth Science Inventory* (ATESI) to measure students' attitudes toward Earth science. The ESAT (Chang 2001a) is a 30-question multiple-choice test designed to measure students' earth science achievement. A panel of specialists, including three university professors and three high school teachers, established the content validity of ESAT. The reliability coefficient of 0.76~0.78 was reported in these studies. The ATESI (Chang and Mao 1999) consists of 30 items intended to investigate students' attitudes toward earth science with three subscales assessing attitudes toward the earth science subject, attitudes toward learning of earth science, and attitudes toward involvement in earth science activities. Internal reliability was shown to be adequate; the Cronbach's alpha was estimated to be around 0.90 in these studies.

4: Research design

A general pretest-posttest comparison-group experimental design (Campbell and Stanley, 1966) was adopted by these studies as shown in the following diagram:
Group 1. R O   X1   O
Group 2. R O   X2   O
R = random assignment
X = experimental treatments
O = pretest or posttest
The first study (n=294) compared "ESCAT versus LIDI (Lecture-Internet-Discussion Instruction)" outcomes; while the second study (n=155) evaluated CAI effectiveness with versus without "problem-solving" design and the third one (n=232) weighed teacher-directed CAI against student-controlled CAI approaches.

5: Data Analysis

A number of variables, such as the involvement of tenth graders and equivalent instructional content and duration, were held constant. The independent variable was the format of instruction or design of CAI and the dependent variables were student achievement and attitudes toward earth science as a subject. A multivariate analysis of covariance (MANCOVA) was performed on the two dependent variables with pre-treatment measures as the covariates to find any significant differences between the experimental and comparison groups. The Wilks's lambda (?) test was employed to test the difference

between these two groups on the set of achievement and attitude adjusted posttest means. The level of confidence was set at a 0.05 level of significance.

6: Results and Discussions

The results indicated that (a) the ESCAT has its promise and is superior to the LIDI method; (b) the "problem-solving" design of CAI is generally better than the "non-problem-solving" design of CAI; and (c) the "teacher-directed" CAI seems producing statistically greater student gains than the "student-controlled" CAI, yet with only practical significance of small to medium effects sizes. As a result, these findings could serve as bases for development of "problem-solving" based computer-assisted instruction. Furthermore, it is also suggested that instruction, such as the ESCAT, should be more broadly developed and widely employed in the secondary earth science classrooms.

7: References

Campbell, D. and Stanley, J. (1966) *Experimental and Quasi-experimental Designs for Research* (Chicago: Rand McNally).
Chang, C. Y. (2001a) Comparing the impacts of a problem-based computer-assisted instruction and the direct-interactive teaching method on student science achievement. *Journal of Science Education and Technology, 10,* 147-153.
Chang, C. Y. (2001b) A problem-solving based computer-assisted tutorial for the earth sciences. *Journal of Computer Assisted Learning, 17,* 263-274.
Christmann, E., Badgett, J. and Lucking, R. (1997) Microcomputer-based computer-assisted instruction within differing subject areas: A statistical deduction. *Journal of Educational Computing Research, 16,* 281-296.
Chang, C. Y. and Mao, S. L. (1999) Comparison of Taiwan science students' outcomes with inquiry-group versus traditional instruction. *The Journal of Educational Research, 92,* 340-346.
Fletcherflinn, C. M. and Gravatt, B. (1995) The efficacy of computer-assisted-instruction (CAI) – A meta analysis. *Journal of Educational Computing Research, 12,* 219-242.
Kulik, C-L. C. and Kulik, J. A. (1986) Effectiveness of computer-based education in colleges. *AEDS Journal, 19,* 81-108.
Kulik, C-L. C. and Kulik, J. A. (1991) Effectiveness of computer-based instruction: An updated analysis. *Computers in Human Behavior, 7,* 75-94.

A Pilot Study of Students' Attitudes Toward and Desired System Requirements of Networked Peer Assessment System

Sunny San-Ju Lin, Eric Zhi-Feng Liu, Shyan-Ming Yuan
National Chiao Tung University
E-Mail: sunnylin@cc.nctu.edu.tw, totem@cis.nctu.edu.tw

Abstract

This study applied NetPeas (networked peer assessment system) in peer assessment activities of graduate level of thesis writing course. Authors wish to discover the students' attitudes toward and desired system requirements of NetPeas in writing course. This study involved 100 electrical engineering graduates from two research-oriented universities at northern Taiwan. Those students were required to attend a weekly thesis writing course and submit eight assignments through four rounds of networked peer assessment, and then authors survey their attitudes and opinions toward NetPeas. In the last, quantitative and qualitative surveys indicated that significantly more students willing to join the networked peer assessment activities via NetPeas in the near future and stand for using NetPeas. Authors also have dug several desirable requirements for NetPeas.

Keywords: NetPeas, networked peer assessment system, peer assessment, thesis writing course

Introduction

Among many alternative assessment methods developed in recent years include extensive use of concept mapping, peer, cooperative and portfolio assessment [1, 2]. This study illustrates the use of networked peer assessment system (NetPeas, referred to 1) in a thesis writing course with same background students. Peer assessment, a natural process used from childhood onwards to evaluate peers, has been extensively studied in higher education in recent decades. Researchers have explored the validity, reliability and practicalities of peer assessment and generally conferred on its acceptability. However, the exploration of students' attitudes and desired system requirements of applying networked peer assessment to thesis writing course has seldom been explored.

If this research would find meaningfully desired system requirements for NetPeas, then the adaptability and receptiveness of NetPeas would be increased in the near future after revising NetPeas according to students' desired system requirements.

Results
Analysis of students' attitudes toward NetPeas

1) *Willingness to join networked peer assessment activities via NetPeas in the near future*: Question 1 showed that 69% (Chi^2 = 14.44***) of the students willing to join networked peer assessment activities via NetPeas in the near future. Feedback from structured interview indicated that majorities of student see networked peer assessment effective and they benefited from using this learning strategy. 2) *Satisfied with NetPeas in sum*: Question 2 showed that 77% (Chi^2 = 29.16***) of the students satisfied with NetPeas in sum. 3) *Ease of use in submitting an assignment via NetPeas*:

Question 3 also showed that 77% ($Chi^2 = 29.16$***) of the students agree with that submitting an assignment via NetPeas is easy. 4) *Satisfied with the presenting interface of assignments*: Question 4 also showed that 91% ($Chi^2 = 67.24$***) of the students satisfied with presenting interface of assignments. 5) *Ease of use in assessing peers' assignment*: Question 5 showed that 69% ($Chi^2 = 14.44$***) of the students agree with that assessing peers' assignment via NetPeas is easy. 6) *Satisfied with the presenting interface of reviewers' evaluation*: Question 6 showed that 81% ($Chi^2 = 38.44$***) of the students satisfied with the presenting interface of reviewers' evaluation.

Analysis of students' desired system requirements of NetPeas

There are 100 qualitative opinions of desired system requirement, but we selected only 34 (34%) meaningful opinions for this study. In these meaningful opinions, there were 15 (44%) opinions about their needs of submitting documents in Microsoft Word other than HTML file format. There were also 14 (41%) opinions about their needs of marking sentences in different colors to distinguish the wrong sentences from those correct ones. This problem could be solved perfectly by allowing students to use the Microsoft Word, because Microsoft Word provided the function of marking the amended sentences. Only 5 (15%) opinions suggested to increasing the number of files in NetPeas's submission form. Under our investigation, results demonstrated that some students need to upload a lot of figures (e.g. bitmap files) in order to illustrate their formula, system architecture and steps of experiment.

Acknowledgments

The authors would like to thank the National Science Council of the Republic of China for financially supporting this research under Contract Nos. NSC 90-2520-S-009-003 and NSC90-2520-S-009-002.

References

1. E. Z. F. Liu, C. H. Chiu, S. S. J. Lin, and S. M. Yuan, "Web-based Peer review: An effective web-learning strategy with the learner as both adapter and reviewer," IEEE Transactions on Education, Vol. 44, 3, 246-251, 2001.

2. E. Z. F. Liu, S. S. J. Lin, and S. M. Yuan, "Design of a networked portfolio system," British Journal of Educational Technology, Vol. 32, 4, 492-494, 2001.

Improving Courseware Evaluation via the Use of a Model

Corina Mulholland & Wing Au
School of Education
University of South Australia

Abstract

To help overcome problems associated with courseware evaluation there are a growing number of support tools being developed, such as models, frameworks, handbooks, and toolkits. This paper presents an overview of a model designed to aid evaluators of courseware. The model evolved from a critical analysis of current and past courseware evaluation methodologies and a detailed examination of factors that may be influential, particularly learning theory and stakeholder interests and biases. The model is structured in three phases – Planning, Conducting *and* Reporting of Results *- each incorporating a number of tools and resources designed to help evaluators consider and address critical issues and make appropriate decisions for their specific circumstances.*

Introduction

With courseware being increasingly utilised in education and training, there is a need to be able to evaluate its quality and suitability. Courseware evaluation, however, is subject to a number of common problems that often limit its usefulness. These shortcomings include methodological problems, inappropriate choices of evaluation questions [1] and methodologies [2], and not accounting for contextual factors [3]. Courseware evaluation can also be adversely affected by the influence of stakeholders [4] and failure to address learning issues [2]. It is becoming increasingly evident that there is a need for courseware evaluators to consider 'the big picture'.

Along with developments in evaluation methodologies [e.g., 5], researchers have recently begun to develop support tools to improve courseware evaluation. These tools include models, frameworks, handbooks, and tool-kits [6], which aim to promote good practice in courseware evaluation by encouraging evaluators to consider a range of issues. They are also designed to allow novices at conducting evaluation to make informed decisions by providing critical information [2].

This paper proposes a model that aims to help courseware evaluators produce useful and accurate evaluations, by minimising the likelihood of encountering the problems listed above. The model consists of a number of components to help evaluators tailor-design evaluations and encourage the examination of important, and often neglected, issues. As such, it is more comprehensive than many of the other support tools available, whilst still aiming to be easy to use for the wide range of people who may wish to conduct courseware evaluation, including teachers and software developers.

Structure and Use of the Model

The model is presented in three phases – *Planning, Conducting* and *Reporting of Results*. The planning phase covers the design of the evaluation from the formation of the initial evaluation questions to the drawing up of the evaluation plan. The conducting phase covers the time of the actual implementation of the evaluation and any ongoing modification during this time, while the reporting phase covers the final analysis, interpretation of data and the dissemination of results. Each phase incorporates a number of components to assist evaluators in clarifying the issues relevant to the specific phase and to help them make appropriate choices, thereby maximising the efficacy of their courseware evaluations.

The model incorporates guidelines, information tables and a set of evaluation categories, all of which aim to clarify issues for evaluators. Critical issues addressed by the model include stakeholder consultation and involvement; selection of appropriate evaluation goals, questions, tools and methodologies; consideration of learning theory and pedagogic design; and identification and reduction of biases.

There are two kinds of components used in the model – *tools* and *resources*. *Resources* offer reference information, such as guidelines or descriptions of important aspects (eg. methodologies, biases), while *tools* are designed to be actively applied by the model user (often in questionnaire or checklist format). Many of the resources support the tools by providing supporting and clarifying information that the model user can refer to when using the tools (eg. descriptions of methodologies, information on incorporating stakeholders, lists of potential biases). By consulting and working through these model components, appropriate and informed decisions can be made in each of the three evaluation phases.

The planning phase of the model is the most complex, as a principal goal of this phase is to aid selection of the most appropriate methodology or methodologies. Owing to the importance of this decision, and the number of potentially influential factors, this phase contains the largest number of components. The components of the conducting phase of the model emphasise reviewing of the data gathering process, ensuring that evaluation goals are being met, and modification of the evaluation if problems are identified. Finally, the reporting phase's components emphasise reduction of bias in the analysis and reporting of the results and propose ways of ensuring appropriate dissemination of results. Table 1 outlines the principal aims of each of the three phases:

Phase:	Aims:
Planning	Provide information on stakeholder involvement in the evaluation design and assist in this decision. Assist in establishing evaluation goals and framing evaluation questions. Assist in the assessment of learning-related issues. Provide information on possible evaluation methodologies and techniques and assist in appropriate choices. Minimise bias in this phase. Assist in the drawing up of the evaluation plan. Provide a checking mechanism to review the evaluation plan.
Conducting	Provide information on stakeholder involvement in the evaluation conduct and assist in this decision. Minimise bias in this phase. Provide a checking mechanism to ensure the evaluation is meeting evaluation needs and advise on how to modify the evaluation if it is not. Encourage suitable documentation of this phase.
Reporting	Provide information on stakeholder involvement in the analysis of the evaluation data and in the reporting of the results and assist in this decision. Minimise bias in the analysis, interpretation, and reporting of the evaluation results. Assist in determining how to best distribute the evaluation results. Provide a checking mechanism to review the evaluation results.

Table 1:   **Principal Aims of the Model Phases**

Aiding the phase-specific components of the model are two general components that have applications for the entire evaluation process. These components are *resources* that can be consulted for information when using other model components. Specifically, the general components offer information on stakeholder involvement and bias identification and reduction. These issues are critical because stakeholders, whether evaluators, participants or consumers, may consciously or

inadvertently affect evaluations [4]. This influence can occur in all three phases of an evaluation as defined in the model. Bias can likewise affect each of the three evaluation phases.

The model will be available as both a hard copy and a hyper-linked HTML version. The HTML version allows users to jump between associated components (eg. resources and tools) and takes users to subsequent components based on their needs (as indicted by certain responses). The HTML version also indicates where users may need to revisit components (e.g., if bias is indicated, earlier decisions may need to be altered).

Conclusion

The model emphasises the presentation of a holistic picture, not only of the courseware and its use, but also of the evaluation itself. The model is also flexible to allow for the wide range of evaluation needs and courseware designs and aims that exist, hence it allows for the use of a range of methodologies and data collection procedures. The actual methodologies used will depend upon the conclusions drawn as a result of applying the model. In addition, the questionnaires, checklists, points for consideration, suggestions and recommendations offered in the model will aid in the addressing of common problems associated with the evaluation of courseware. It should be noted that, although individual phases and components of the model can be consulted to address individual concerns, it is recommended that for optimum outcomes most, if not all, of the phases and components should be utilised.

References

1. Reeves, T. C. (1995). "Questioning the Questions of Instructional Technology Research" in Proceedings of the 1995 Annual National Convention of the Association for Educational Communications and Technology (AECT). (17th, Anaheim, CA, 1995). ERIC Document: ED 383 331.
2. Oliver, M. (1998). "A Framework for Evaluating the Use of Educational Technology". University of North London, England. URL: http://www.unl.ac.uk/latid/elt/report1.htm
3. Atkins, M.J. (1993). "Evaluating interactive technologies for learning" in Journal of Curriculum Studies, Vol. 25, No. 4, pp. 333-342.
4. Mulholland, C. R., Au, W. & White, B. (1998). "Identifying the evaluators of courseware – how agendas, assumptions and ideologies may impact upon evaluation" in Proceedings from Australian Computers in Education Conference ACEC1998 (Adelaide, South Australia, 5-8 July, 1998).
5. Gunn, C. (1997). "CAL evaluation: future directions" in ALT-J, Volume 5, No. 1, pp. 40-47.
6. Conole, G. & Oliver, M. (2001). "Advanced Learning Technology Frameworks and Toolkits"., Madison, USA, 6-8 August, 2001. URL: http://lttf.ieee.org/icalt2001/presentations/workshop_evaluation.doc [Accessed on-line 22/2/2002].

Effects of Negative Information on Acquiring Procedural Knowledge

Masaaki Kurosu[1] and Yousuke Ookawa[2]

[1] National Institute of Multimedia Education, JAPAN

PFD00343@nifty.com

[2] Faculty of Information, Shizuoka University, JAPAN

cs6018@cs.inf.shizuoka.ac.jp

Abstract

Usually, the material for learning is given in a positive form, i.e. xxx is yyy. This type of information will help organize the core of the target knowledge. Instead of this type of information, negative information, i.e. xxx is not zzz, will help sharpen the edge or extent of the target knowledge. Hence, it is expected that the negative information will have an effect of minimizing the chance of making errors and thus making the learning faster.

For the purpose of confirming this hypothesis, we conducted an experiment on the procedural knowledge, i.e. the procedure of application software. We compared the execution time of operation after presenting the positive information (simple explanation) and the negative information (scene of failure and explanation) in terms of the use of software to different subject groups. The result showed that the negative information had a significant effect for a simple operation but had not an effect for a complex operation.

1. Introduction

In a general educational situation, the information is frequently given in a positive form such as "In order to shut down the Windows machine, you will have to push the start button, then select the shut down item from the menu." But sometimes, the negative form of information such as "In order to shut down the Windows machine, do not press the power button of your PC" will help to minimize the risk of making an error.

The purpose of this study was to investigate if such negative information actually has a positive effect for acquiring the specific knowledge.

2. Method

2.1 Material

There are a variety of learning situations that can be used for our study, e.g. learning the foreign language, learning the car driving, learning the programming, etc. We decided to use not the declarative knowledge but the procedural knowledge simply because it was easier for us to provide the negative information material as well as the positive information material for the procedural knowledge. And we used the computer software as the material for our study.

Material used in this experiment was "Home Page Builder (HPB) Ver. 6 (Japanese version)" of IBM.

2.2 Collecting Sample Failures

For the purpose of finding out tasks with moderate difficulty, we conducted the usability testing using this software. Three subjects who were male graduate school students participated in the usability testing.

They had no previous experience of using this software.

They were asked to perform 24 tasks such as to start the software, to name a new page, to set up a background color, to center the logo, etc. From among 24 tasks, 4 difficult tasks were selected based on the number of errors. They were (1) to create the page title, (2) to create the scroll character that moves from left to right, (3) to insert the picture as the background image, and (4) to close the HPB after saving the page data.

2.3 Creating the Instruction Video

Positive information material was created as a video by showing the simple explanation regarding these four tasks. This video showed the screen image while the correct operation is conducted with the narration explaining about the procedure. This was similar to the usual instruction video on the market in terms of the correct use of the software.

Negative information material was created as a video by showing the scene of failure during the usability testing. After the scene of failure, the positive information video described above was concatenated for each of 4 tasks.

2.4 Experiment

Total of ten subjects were used as the subjects who were the graduate students with no previous experience with this software. Five of them were given the positive information video and another 5 subjects were given the negative information video. Then they were asked to accomplish the same task by themselves.

Before and after the experiment, a questionnaire on the subjective evaluation was given to the subjects. Sample items were "This software is easy to use", "It doesn't take much time to learn how to use this software" for the positive information group. The negative information group was given some additional

items such as "By looking at the scene of failure, I would like to know how to use this software correctly".

2.5 Result

The result of the experiment regarding the length of time to achieve the task is shown in Tab. 1.

Task number	Average time in second for positive information group	Average time in second for negative information group	P-value
1	66.0	40.0	*0.027
2	206.8	206.2	0.200
3	182.6	188.6	0.969
4	74.8	90.4	0.387

Tab.1 Result of the experiment (* Significant at 5% level)

As shown in this table, only task #1 showed a significant difference between the positive information group and the negative information group. Because task #1 is an operation with a short sequence compared to other tasks, it was assumed that the negative information had a positive effect on learning the simple procedural knowledge.

Based on the analysis of the additional data by the questionnaire, it was concluded that giving the negative information influenced the subject to think of the task as difficult, but at the same time, influenced them to increase the motivation to overcome the difficulty.

3. Discussion

Although giving the negative information did not increase the level of understanding in all cases, it was effective for the simple task and was useful in increasing the motivation of the learner.

A Conducive Classroom Environment for IT Integration: A Collective Case Study of Primary Schools in Singapore

Cher Ping, Lim; Shanti, Divaharan; Myint Swe, Khine; Ching Sing, Chai; Yiong Hwee, Teo; Philip, Wong, National Institute of Education, Nanyang Technological University (Singapore)

Abstract

This paper discusses the findings of the collective case study of two primary schools in Singapore. It is part of a larger funded research project that examines and analyses where and how IT is integrated in Singapore schools to develop pupils' higher order thinking skills. The focus of this paper is on the IT classroom management issues that create a conducive environment to support the effective integration of IT in the schools. In such an environment, pupils are more likely to be task-oriented and reflective, and hence, more likely to engage in higher order thinking. These issues include the establishment of rules and procedures, availability of IT resources, conduct and management of IT-based activities, and division of labour among participants.

In Singapore, the Master Plan for ICT in Education was launched in April 1997. As part of this plan, all Singapore schools are expected to acquire and integrate ICT in their curriculum so as to develop a culture of thinking, lifelong learning and social responsibility. Based on the implementation progress of the ICT Master Plan, it is an appropriate time to study the integration of ICT in schools as the process of integration has reached a considerable level of maturity and stability for evaluation purposes.

This article reports and discusses the findings of the case study of two primary schools in Singapore. The focus of this article is the discussion of ICT classroom management issues that create a conducive environment that supports the effective integration of ICT in the schools. In such an environment, pupils are more likely to be task-oriented and reflective, and hence, more likely to engage in higher order thinking. These issues include the establishment of rules and procedures, conduct and management of ICT-based activities, and division of labour among participants.

The Case Studies: East Primary School and North Primary School

To provide an in-depth examination of the ICT management issues that support the effective integration of ICT in schools, case study research is the most appropriate tradition of inquiry. The 'cases' for the study in this article were 2 primary schools in Singapore, East Primary and North Primary School. The 2 schools were selected based on their high degree of ICT integration reported in the questionnaire survey distributed to all Singapore schools. To ensure the accuracy of conclusions drawn, the data

from the observations of ICT-based lessons, face-to-face interviews with teachers, head of department (HOD), and principal, focus group discussions with pupils, and pupils' questionnaire were used in the multiple strategies process. Multiple strategies involve gathering accounts of different realities that have been constructed by various groups and individuals in the school; and hence, enhance reliability and validity of the study.

The study in East Primary School, a government-aided school, was carried out between 17 and 27 September 2001. At the time of the study, there were 2118 pupils, consisting of boys and girls with ages ranging from 7 to 12. The school has a teaching staff strength of 80 with 10 support staff, including a computer technician. There were 2 computer rooms where each has been equipped with about 40 computers, data projector, pull-down projector screen and whiteboard. The ICT learning packages used included Midisaurus for Music, I-Micro and RoboLab for Science, and a wide range of CD-ROMs for the other subjects. The school also converted certain areas in the school into free access corners with a total of 12 computers for pupils to engage in independent learning.

The fieldwork in North Primary School, a government-aided school, was carried out from 21 August to 4 October 2001. All 720 pupils were girls between 7 to 12 years old. There were 31 teaching staff and 9 support staff, including with computer technician. There was 1 computer room with about 40 computers, data projector, pull-down projector screen, whiteboard and 2 printers. The ICT learning packages used included Midasaurus for Music, Crayola for Art, and CD-ROMs such as MathBlaster and ZARC for Mathematics.

Establishment of Rules and Procedures

Although the rules and procedures established in a non-ICT based classroom apply in an ICT-based classroom, there are additional rules and procedures to be established in the latter. This is due to the addition of computers, printers, monitors, CD-ROMs and other ICT resources. The rules are generally set up to prevent the abuse of the hardware and software in the computer room. In both schools, the rules of the computer room were clearly displayed on the wall. They included no water bottle or food in the computer room, no unauthorised installation of program, and no unauthorised change to the features of the control panel.

It is also important to establish procedures for pupils to follow, as this will minimise the occurrences of deviant behaviour among pupils and keep the pupils on task.

Some procedures that were observed in both schools included the following:

- Pupils entered and exited the computer room in an orderly fashion according to their class index number. Each of them knew their assigned seats and there was no rushing.
- A procedure of distributing and collecting ICT resources (e.g. CD-ROMs, diskettes) were set up in both schools. Teachers enlisted pupil helpers (they were called group leaders) to carry out this procedure for a conducive learning environment.
- Pupils turned on the computers only when the teacher gave instructions. In North Primary School, some teachers would get the pupils to turn off their monitor when they were explaining a concept or giving instructions at the front of the class. These procedures ensured that the pupils paid attention to the instructions and explanations. When such a procedure was not established, a few pupils in East Primary School were observed to be not paying attention.
- In East Primary School, a red cup was placed beside each computer to allow pupils to signal for help. When pupils encountered a technical or instructional problem, they would place their cups on top of their monitors to request for help. As the use of such cups was absent in North Primary School, the pupils who encountered problems have to raise their hands and that disrupted or delayed the completion of their tasks.

In the pupils' questionnaire, more than 80% of the pupils from both schools strongly agreed or agreed with the rules and procedures established by the teacher in the computer room. Both teachers and pupils in their respective interviews and discussion groups stated that these rules and procedures ensured a more conducive environment for learning.

Conduct and Management of ICT-Based Activities

Pupils cannot be assumed to be 'expert' learners in the ICT-based learning environment. They may lack the technical skills to operate and navigate through the ICT learning package; they may lack the learning skills to learn in such an environment; or/and they may lack the motivation to learn using the ICT learning package. Teachers need to conduct and manage the ICT-based activities such that the assumptions of the 'expert' learners are addressed. Such conduct and management of ICT-based activities were observed in both schools:

- Pre-instructional activities were conducted in both schools. Most of the teachers reviewed previous concepts and made links to the concepts to be covered in the ICT-based lessons. Some teachers highlighted and demonstrated the key features and the navigation buttons of the ICT learning package before allowing pupils to start using the computers.
- Most of the instructions of the ICT-based activities were clear in both schools. When pupils were clear about the tasks that they were to complete, they were more likely to be task-oriented and motivated. When instructions were confusing, as observed in a lesson in North Primary School, pupils were found to display more deviant behaviours.
- Most of the ICT-based lessons observed in both schools were pupil-centred with very little direct teaching. There were only 2 lessons observed in East Primary School where more than two-third of the lesson was spent on direct teaching. In these 2 lessons, many pupils were observed to be distracted and a few were caught fiddling with the keyboards and the mouse.
- Scaffolding activities were present in most lessons observed in both schools. Worksheets and checklists were distributed to the pupils to guide them to complete their tasks. Such scaffolding ensured that pupils were able to successfully engage in the tasks and complete them.

Division of Labour among Participants

The responsibility of ensuring a conducive learning environment should not fall entirely on the teacher. There is a need for the division of labour among the participants in the computer room. The role of the teacher in the 2 schools was to plan for the ICT-based lessons, conduct and manage them, evaluate them and make necessary changes. They moved around the computer room to engage the pupils in dialogues while the pupils were working at the computers. However, it was observed that there were also the crucial roles of the computer technicians and the pupil helpers.

- Role of computer technician: In both schools, the technicians were present in all ICT-based lessons observed. They helped the teachers to address technical problems faced by the pupils. By doing so, the technicians freed the teachers from attending to technical problems and ensured that they focused their attention on the conduct and management of the ICT-based lessons.
- Role of pupil helpers: In both schools, group leaders and assistant group leaders were assigned to collect, distribute and return CD-ROMs, diskettes, worksheets and checklists. Their roles facilitated the smooth running of the lessons that created a conducive learning environment.

Managing ICT-based lessons is not very different from managing non-ICT based ones. The basic classroom management principles apply for both. As the case studies have highlighted, there is a need for the establishment of rules and procedures for the computer room, the proper conduct and good management of ICT-based activities, and the division of labour among teachers, technicians and pupils. It is only then that a conducive learning environment is created to set up the necessary condition for the effective integration of ICT in schools.

To Propose a Reviewer Dispatching Algorithm for Networked Peer Assessment System

Eric Zhi-Feng Liu, Sunny San-Ju Lin, Shyan-Ming Yuan

National Chiao Tung University

E-Mail: totem@cis.nctu.edu.tw

Abstract

Despite their increasing availability on the Internet, networked peer assessment systems lack feasible automatic dispatching algorithm of student's assignments and ultimately inhibit the effectiveness of peer assessment. Therefore, this study presents a reviewer dispatching algorithm capable of supporting networked peer assessment system in order to automatically dispatch student's assignments to their peer reviewers.

Reviewer Dispatching Algorithm

We set four constraints for dispatching reviewers. The first is that author should not review his (or her) own assignment. The second is that how many reviewers per assignment should set up via instructor. The third is that how many reviewers per assignment should equal to how many assignments reviewed by each student. The forth is that the reviewers of first assignment are fixed under k rounds but the reviewers of second or another assignment should be different to maintain the fairness.

Then, we would like to model these constraints via constraint satisfaction problem. In order to illustrate this process in an easy way, we hypothesized that when there are three students. In the first step, we write down a 3x2 matrix (Table 1).

	Col_1	Col_2
$Student_1$	X_1	X_2
$Student_2$	X_3	X_4
$Student_3$	X_5	X_6

Table 1: A 3x2 matrix for modeling the constraints of three students

In the second step, we defined the $X_i = \{1, 2, \text{ or } 3\}$, $\diamond$ should not transitive but symmetric, and the following constraints (C1, C2, and C3):

$$X_1 \diamond 1, \quad X_2 \diamond 1, X_1 \diamond X_2, X_1 \diamond X_3, X_1 \diamond X_5 \ (C1)$$

$$X_3 \diamond 2, \quad X_4 \diamond 2, X_3 \diamond X_4, X_3 \diamond X_5 \ (C2)$$

$$X_5 \diamond 3, X_6 \diamond 3, X_5 \diamond X_6 \ (C3)$$

In third step, we utilized the recursive searching method for constraint satisfaction problem. The answers for this problem could be found in 3^6 (729) steps, also if there are four students then there are twelve variables and the execution steps could equal to 4^{12} (16,777,216). This result would make the dispatching task impossible, so we should seek another ways to solve this problem.

We listed the first possible solution for the constraint graph (left part of Fig. 1), but it is hard to find the regularity. Then, we listed the second possible solution for the constraint graph (right part of Fig. 1), and via observation I concluded a simple formula, $\{X_i=3$ if $((col\# + 1) \bmod 3)=0, X_i=((col\# + 1) \bmod 3)$ if $((col\# + 1) \bmod 3)\diamond 0\}$, for calculating one of the answers of this problem. Surprisingly, dispatching three reviewers using this formula needs only twelve steps and saves 98% execution steps when compared with recursive searching method.

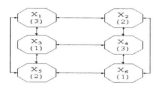 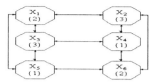

Figure 1: The two possible solution for the constraint graph.

To standardize this algorithm, we have written down a C language like pseudocode (Table 2). The time complexity of this algorithm should be O(n), $T(n) = 1 + 2n \leq c_1 n = O(n)$ for some constant $c_1 > 2$, in the best case, $O(n^2)$, $T(n) = n-1 + 2(n-1)(n) = 2n^2 - n - 1 \leq c_1 n^2 = O(n^2)$ for some constant $c_1 \geq 2$, in the worst case, and $O(n^2)$, , in the average case. The space complexity of this algorithm should be O(1) to O(n), if the program only save some important data (e.g. total number of students and some row numbers), in the best case, $O(n^2)$, $S(n) = k + n(n-1) = n^2 - n + k \leq c_1 n^2 = O(n^2)$ for some constant $c1 \geq 1$, in the worst case, and $O(n^2)$ in the average case. About k what value instructors should set, we suggested set k between three and six, and not set k too large (e.g. > 20) to reduce the resistance from students.

```
/* n is the total number of students*/ /* k is the number of reviewers */
/* p is 1 by k array */ /* s is a n by k array */
Input: n, k, p, s, Result: s

Assessor_Dispatching (n, k,p, s)
1    Choose k different number between 1 to n-1 to p array
2    For i = 1 to k
3    do w = p[i]
4        for j = 1 to n
5        do s[j,w] = (w + 1 mod n), w = w + 1
6    return s
```

Table 2: The pseudocode of dispatching algorithm.

Acknowledgments

The authors would like to thank the National Science Council of the Republic of China under Contract Nos. NSC 90-2520-S-009-003 and NSC90-2520-S-009-002.

References

1. E. Z. F. Liu, C. H. Chiu, S. S. J. Lin, and S. M. Yuan, "Web-based Peer review: An effective web-learning strategy with the learner as both adapter and reviewer," IEEE Transactions on Education, Vol. 44, 3, 246-251, 2001.

2. E. Z. F. Liu, S. S. J. Lin, and S. M. Yuan, "Design of a networked portfolio system," British Journal of Educational Technology, Vol. 32, 4, 492-494, 2001

Computer Game and Educational System

K.Kozuki ,M.Imachi , M.Ueno ,A.Tsubokura and K.Tsushima

(KONAMI Co. , Osaka Electro-Communication Univ.)

The behaviors of players of a computer game called Drum Mania are analyzed from the view point of cognition motion process of human being.

And then we have developed an analyzer called ADMP(Analyzer for Drum Music Player) on the computer to investigate the behavior of our objectives who play various games using dram in which game parameters are easily changed. Andfinally the connection and difference between a trainer used in themusical education and computer game using musical instrument are discussed.

1.Introduction

We have been interested in educational system on the computer for a long time.[1] In old days, the presentation capability of the computer was relatively poor. So,moving pictures and movies could not be used in the educational system on the computer , so it was difficult to stimulate a good environment in which a learner is confined by using realistic images. But ,in the present,we obtain the high computational power, so the educational system responds the learner by presenting realistic response on the multimedia computer. Simulator and trainer become promising educational tool inthe present. But , educational content on the computer does not seem so attractive even in the present. On the other hand, we can see many attractive and exciting contents in computer game. We want to make the educational tools more attractive by referring to the knowledge and skill used in computer game in series of our research.

In many educational systems on the computer a learner can communicate with a system using only mouse and keyboard. We feel there are the lack of communication channels in interaction between educational system and a learner to give attractive educational experience to a learner.

But ,in the present,we obtain the enough computational power, so we can easily detect information concerning human behavior from a learner interacting with educational system. We have introduced Eye Mark Recorder ,datagloves and 3D censors into educational system to obtain human information concerning eye movement , hand , finger motion of a learner and also to give the educational system the capability of multi modal communication. [2,3,4,5,6,7]

But , several computer game systems have used such human information using interface technology already. Several original interfaces such as controller for the computer game are designed and widely used.

Computer games have come into wide use recently. Many creative game contents and ideas about computer games are sent mainly from Japan to the world.

The problem which a educational system on the computer has has been solved partly in computer game already. We analyze the origin of charm of computer game in this paper and we want to build some criterion to produce attrac-

Fig.1 Joint Institute for Advanced Multimedia Study

Fig.2 The Game Laboratory.

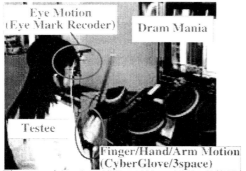
Fig.3 The our objectives put on
Eye Mark Recorder plays Dram Mania

tive educational contents such as trainer system.

We want to design the next generation educational system by introducing moreprecise and multi modal interface than computer game has.

We founded the new research institute between Osaka Electro-Communication University and KONAMI Co. called Joint Institute for Advanced Multimedia Study in our university in 2002 (Fig.1). There is a room called Game Lab. in our new institute. Several computer game machines are introduced in this room. (Fig.2) The cognition action process of the player of the introduced computer game machines are measured and analyzed using several human censors such as Eye Mark Recorder , Data Groves and 3D censors in our Game Lab. (Fig.3)

We measured theplayer of a computer game called Drum

Mania(hereafter DM) , and several results are reported in Chap.2.of this paper(Fig.3) By comparing these results with the results of educational system for musical education about percussion instrument byother authors , we discuss the difference between these results in Chap. 4.

And we developed analyzing and simulation system called ADMP on the computer in which many trainer systems and game systems about percussion instrument are easily generated.

2.Drum Mania and preparatory measurement

There is a computer game machine called Drum Mania (we call it DM hereafter) we can find it in a game center in town.

There are two pads, three drums and one pedal in front of a DM player. There are 6 icons correspond to real pads , drums and pedal on the CRT of DM.(Fig.4)

6 squares are fallen down into these 6 icons in the CRT according to game scenario. The player must beatthe corresponding drums or pads at the moment when each square reaches bottom line synchronized with the movement of the fallen square. After acknowledging the timing of beat by seeing a fallen square and the strength matching with

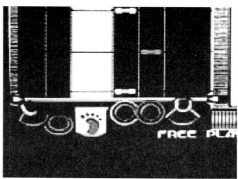

Fig.4 a) Dram Mania Machine   b) Six Icons on the CRT of Dram Mania Machine

tempo of the melody given by DM , a player plays DM. And DM system evaluates the timing and strength of beats of a player and take off points and adds points in his playing.

DM has the fixed evaluation mechanism for a player's performance. Of course, the evaluation mechanism is tuned up carefully to excite aplayer in his playing by a expert engineer of game maker. But, DM is no more than the product delivered to a game center in a town , so its evaluation mechanism is fixed and written on ROM of DM machine , so it is difficult to vary the evaluation mechanism of game.

We measured forty objectives playing DM in our Game Lab. preparatorily. We measured from a novice to an expert of real drum carefully.The behavior of objectives were analyzed by using VTR tape carefully. It was difficult to analyze the behavior of a player shorter than 50 mSec using VTR tape .It is find out from our analysis that an expert of a real drum is not always an expert of DM game. And the reverse is not always true.

3. ADMP----- Analyzer for drum Music Player

The parameters to judge the performance of a player used in DM game are fixed on the ROM in real DM machine , so we cannot change parameters ofDM game. To understand the behavior of a player playing DM in detail from the viewpoint of cognitive science , it is not sufficient to use the measured data from a player playing real DM game only.

So, we have developed an analyzer called ADMP(Analyzer for drum Music Player) on the computer which has the following features .

1) It can simulate completely real DM on the computer.

2) It can simulate modified DM which has different parameters from real DM.

3) ADMP has more I/O data channels than DM , so we can obtain more human behavior data from our objectives playing a game like DM on ADMP.

4)We can design and simulate the different game from DM easily on ADMP.

5)We can analyze our objectives playing a game like DM on ADMP by using time series analysis method embedding in ADMP.

6) ADMP may be used as a good trainer system for percussion instrument.

We can easily make a new game on ADMP in which a player can use key on keyboards instead of drum sticks. Further we can change the number of the used keys from one to six and many games similar to DM can be made on ADMP.

Feedback mechanism to a player is an important factor which influences the processof acquiring the skill of a player. We can easily change feedback condition of the game on ADMP, so we can develop a new computer game which fascinates a player strongly. And we can also design the new trainer system for drum beat musical instruments on ADMP. We discuss the influence of feedback mechanism on our objectives in chap.4 in detail.

The player responds complicatedly on a feedback mechanism given by thegame system , so we want to see the behavior of our objectives playing several games which has different cognitive parameters from DM.

ADMP works on the Macintosh Computer which works on Mac OS X.

This system is written using C language and library SDL(Simple DirectMedia Layer). This system will be developed on the real time OS ART-Linux finally.

We can measure the behavior of our objectives in the accuracy of 10 mSec using the present version of ADMP. If we use the fastest Macintosh computer , we can obtain the accuracyof 2 mSec.

4. Feedback mechanism and the process of acquiring skills

We measured the process of acquiring the skills of pushing a key synchronized with the falling square touching a

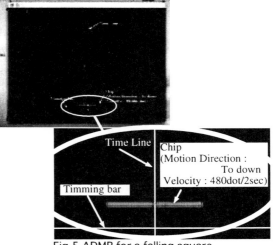

Fig.5 ADMP for a falling square .

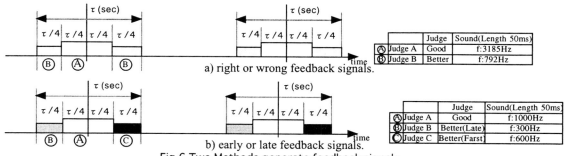

a) right or wrong feedback signals.

		Judge	Sound(Length 50ms)
Ⓐ	Judge A	Good	f:3185Hz
Ⓑ	Judge B	Better	f:792Hz

		Judge	Sound(Length 50ms)
Ⓐ	Judge A	Good	f:1000Hz
Ⓑ	Judge B	Better(Late)	f:300Hz
Ⓒ	Judge C	Better(Farst)	f:600Hz

b) early or late feedback signals.

Fig.6 Two Methods generate feedback signals.

bottom line on the CRT.(Fig.5).We prepared two different feedback mechanisms for our objectives , the one is visual feedback , the other is sound feedback.

If the timing of pushing the key is correct, ADMP system returns blue background color ,otherwise, red background color in visual feedback mechanism.

There are two ways ofgenerating the feedback signals in sound feedback mechanism. As the first way , if the timing of pushing the key iscorrect, ADMP system returns high frequency beep sound ,and if the timing is relatively good, low frequency sound.If the timing of pushing key is completely bad, the signal sound is not generated. (Fig.6a)

As the second way, if the timing of pushing the key is correct , ADMP system returns the highest frequency beep sound and if the timing is early , the lowest frequency beep sound is generated. If the timing is late , then middle frequency beep sound is generated. (Fig. 6b) The every sound beeps for 50 mSec.

É— is the total length of the interval used for judgment of accuracy of timing. We use two length,120 mSec and 80 mSec, for É— in our measurement.The feedback mechanism which use 80 mSec as judgment interval is called "quick feed back environment" , and 120mSec "slow feed back environment". Our objective who is confined in quick feed back environment seems to acquire the skills quickly .And a objective confined in the slow feedback environment acquires the skill moderately. And a objective acquires the skill slowly if there is not feed back

sound(Fig.7).

Real DM uses visual feedback on the CRT.This type of feedback doesn't seem effective for acquiring the skills for our objective , judging from our preliminary analysis reported in this Chapter.

5. Musical Education and computer games

There is a research to evaluate the rhythm aptitude of a learner in musical education by Simuzu et al. [8] in whicha learner beat notes on a push button. They pointout that two measures called "long tempo fluctuation" and"short tempo fluctuation" developed by them are essential to evaluate a learner's rhythm aptitude successfully.These measures can be obtained from a time train of beated note by a learner. They compare these quantities with the evaluation by musical expert ,and conclude that these quantities are useful as a measure.

These evaluation become possible when a learner ends his beats. Instantaneous feed back index for a learner which indicate whether his beat is slow or fast is not given to a learner, so a learner must beat notes by the feel in their measurement.

So, a player is forced to play the drums without real time feedback signal about his performance.The aim of their research seems to be the development of a trainer system or an educational system for musical education. [9]

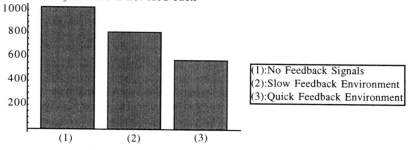

(1):No Feedback Signals
(2):Slow Feedback Environment
(3):Quick Feedback Environment

Fig 7. The Variation of The delay time of objectives

On the other hand , we can generate visual or hearing feed back for our objective in ADMP. We are more interested in computer game rather than in musical educational system , so instantaneousfeed back index for a player are indispensable to maintain a player's interest in the game during his playing.

Point allotted to a player changes in every moment by the results evaluated by

computer game system , and this dynamical interaction between a player and computer gamesystem may excites a player.

A learner who is not an expert of drums is amused not by sound feedback but by visual feedback of his performance.

6.Conclusions

From our preliminary measurement using ADMP , we find that the followingfactors which the computer game has amuse a player.

1⁾ quick response from a game system such as feed back signal for his performance

2⁾ multi modal communication channels

3⁾ apparent high speed skill up

4⁾ feeling to play using a real thing

A learner is forced to obtain the rhythm aptitude in lengthy monotonous musical exercise that uses the real drum in the ordinary school education. It is seems difficult to develop a trainer system on the computer for real drumming which has the above four features. We want to develop the more efficient and exciting training system by investigating computer game systems carefully.We have already developed all-purpose simulator of computer game called ADMP in this research. So several tries and errors for developing more attractive training system on the computer become possible on ADMP following the course proposed in this paper.

references.

1).M.Ueno,H.Imai,N.Nomura and K.Tsushima,"Intelligent Learning Environment using Eye Mark",Proc. of Int.Conf. in MultiMedia in Education ,533,1996.

2).T.Nisiki , A.Tsubokura , M.Ueno and K.Tsushima , "Man-Machine

Communication using Eye Movement",Proc.of ED-MEDIA97, ,1997.

3).T.Nisiki , A.Tsubokura , M.Ueno, K.Higashino,N.Nomura and K.Tsushima,"Human Communication using Eye Movement",Proc.of ED-MEDIA98, ,1998.

4).K.Kohzuki,T.Nisiki,A.Tsubokura,M.Ueno,S.Harima and K.Tsushima, "Man-Machine Interaction Using Eye movement", Proceedings of Human-Computer Interaction International '99 vol1.407,1999.

5).K.Kozuki,N.Ashida,N.Nomura,T.Otsuka,A.Tsubokura and K.Tsushima,"Cognitive Interface for Idea Processor",International Workshop on Advanced Learning Technologies,268,2000.

6).K.Kozuki,N.Ashida,N.Nomura,T.Otsuka,A.Tsubokura and K.Tsushima,"Cognitive Interface for Idea Processor",Proc.of IWALT2000,2000.

7).M.S.Landy,L.T.Maloney and M.Pavel,"Exploratory Vision",Springer,1996.

8)Y.Yoneyama,A.Nishikata,M.Nakayama and Y.Shimizu,"An Evaluation of Basic Rhythm Aptitude Based on Tempo Fluctuation",Japan JournalofEducational Technology,24,3,173-181,2000.

9)Aiello,R.,"Musical Perception",Oxford University Press,1994.

Faculty Support for Online Teaching:
Instructional Design Issues And Beyond

Rowena Santiago, Ed.D.
California State University, San Bernardino, U.S.A.

Abstract

When a faculty member decides to use online technology for teaching, the campus' faculty development center usually becomes one of the sources of support. This presents a great opportunity for the faculty development center to address instructional design issues. However, if faculty members who have done online teaching were the source of support, what issues will they address and what advice would they provide? This presentation summarizes survey responses given by faculty members who used online features for teaching between 1999-2001 at a four-year comprehensive university.

Introduction

When a faculty member decides to use online technology for teaching, support is sought in various ways: self-study/self-help, attending workshops, reading reports and publications, interviewing or listening to an experienced colleague, or going to the faculty development center.

As more and more demand is placed on faculty development centers to provide efficient and effective support for online teaching, finding the right approach and addressing the right issues become very important. Brown [1] reports that using the logical way with educational theories, or providing training on basic technology skills did not work. He reports greater success when support starts with teaching strategies.

While it helps faculty development centers to get reports such as Brown's, or consider guidelines that are reported in the literature, such as Sitze's [6] guidelines for teachers at a distance, there are campus factors and campus culture that need to be taken into consideration. As such, getting input and feedback from one's own faculty may prove to be the more useful source of information for addressing online teaching issues and giving the best possible support to faculty.

Faculty Survey

What issues will experienced online teachers address and what advice would they provide to beginners? To answer this question, 70 online teachers at a four-year comprehensive university (California State University, San Bernardino) were surveyed. Twenty (20) responses were received. Respondents included 5 lecturers, 3 assistant professors, 6 associate professors, and 6 full professors. Age range was from 28-64 years. Ten (10) of the 20 respondents preferred the lecture-discussion-test style of teaching, while 9 taught using lecture plus student activities and tests (1 had no response). In addition to demographic questions, each faculty member was asked what advice they would give to non-technologically oriented individuals who intend to integrate online features in their teaching. They were to give their top three (3) advice on: how to proceed, the best practices to follow, and what should be avoided

Survey Results

The following sections summarize the responses given by faculty.

A. How to Proceed

Faculty respondents were cognizant of the work that needs to take place before actual online course development. Instructional/course design tips that were given for this phase included: finding a course that best fits online teaching, determining the number of class sessions that are needed for that course, locating and selecting material for online posting and that will be read outside of class, having a set policy for grading, and preparing 80% of course materials in advance.

Beyond instructional design, faculty responses advised that beginning online teachers get training before doing course development. In addition to training on specific technology skills (such as HTML, FTP, use of course software, etc), learning about pedagogy was highly recommended. Having students take training on how to use online software was also included among the responses.

Another advice on how to proceed was for the beginning online teacher to get online experience by taking an online class, by team teaching an online class, and/or by talking with an experienced online instructor. The experience of teaching the course face-to-face at least twice prior to teaching it online was considered an important and useful experience. Experience with technology-use included creating one's own webpage and testing/re-testing online equipment.

Embleton's [3] Online Teaching Tips listed Aase's recommendation that faculty need an ongoing relationship with a technical-support person so that students will receive support and the course will be of high quality. Faculty responses to this survey echoed the same advice and the importance of getting to know tech-support persons.

Lastly, beginning online teachers were advised to give themselves a lot of time to prepare. Successful preparation for online teaching requires a lot of time and successful teachers are prepared, organized, well-trained and plan well [4].

During online teaching, beginning teachers are advised to proceed slowly, by trying one or two online features or activities per class. A recommended strategy is to supplement one's face-to-face teaching with online activities before going fully online.

Requesting feedback from students throughout the term was considered useful. Useful feedback include asking how they feel, the course's ease of use, problems encountered, and what changes are needed. Beginning teachers should not hesitate to change midstream if things do not go well. Working closely with tech support was also recommended during online teaching.

B. Best Practices/What To Avoid

Various websites address the do's and don'ts of online teaching (see [5] as example). They list online teaching tips, common mistakes to be avoided, practical lessons, strategies, etc. Faculty who responded to this survey listed some best practices and pitfalls that are similar to what has been reported in these resources. It was noted that these faculty responses focused more on course/instructional design issues than technology issues. This implies that faculty training for online teaching should address instructional design first, before the technology.

The following is a summary of faculty responses on best practices which were related to instructional design. These responses reflect the basic steps given in instructional design models, such as Dick & Carey's [2], which starts with goal/task/content analyses, to formative/summative evaluation.

- Clearly specify what students should do
- Ensure accuracy of materials
- Start small
- Find effective pedagogical approaches for online teaching

- Do not use general teaching techniques you would not use face-to-face
- Provide examples
- Analyze online technology for benefits to class and students
- Include feedback and practice exercises
- Beta test materials with students prior to online use

Best practices related to technology included the effective use of email, being available by phone during the early weeks of the term, and making sure students have access to online course. Doing the work yourself was also recommended.

What to avoid? Experienced faculty advised against doing too much too soon, making too many assumptions on what will make students learn, doing everything the first quarter, and having too many online projects in the beginning. Practical advice included avoiding being too rigid during emergencies, and going solo. Long exams and optional assignments and/or participations were not recommended because students will decide against doing them.

Summary

When it comes to online teaching, faculty development centers could provide more meaningful support to beginners by seeking feedback and input from its own faculty who have taught online. The synergy that results from this could lead to better prepared faculty, better instructional design for online courses, as well as more effective ways of dealing with issues that go beyond instructional design.

References:
[1] Brown, D.G. (2001). Teaching strategies and faculty workshops. *Syllabus: New Dimensions in Education Technology*, Vol. 15 (No. 2), p. 20.
[2] Dick, W. & Carey, L. (1996). *Systematic Design of Instruction*. Addison-Wesley Publishing Company.
[3] Embleton, K. (Dec 1999). *Online Teaching Tips*. http://www.fcs.iastate.edu/computer/tips/onlinetechtips.html
[4] Garrison, S. & Onken, M. H. (Apr 1998). *Practical Lessons on Delivery of Distance Learning: Do's and Don'ts*. Paper presented at the Third Annual TCC Conference, Hawaii. http://leahi.kcc.hawaii.edu/org/tcon98/paper/onken.html
[5] Sample website: http://www.sfu.ca/lidc/instr_development/text/benefits/onlineteachtips.html
[6] Sitze, A. (2000). Teachers at a distance. *Inside Technology Training*. Vol. 4 (no. 4), pp. 40-45.

E-learning and HK School Education

Ka Man PANG

Hong Kong Institute of Education, Hong Kong.

Wing Kee AU

University of South Australia, Australia.

Abstract

E-learning has become increasingly important. The situation in Hong Kong is no exception. Since the implementation of the five-year strategic for information technology in education, there have been substantial changes in the infrastructure in Hong Kong schools in terms of hardware, software and peopleware. These advances are providing a good platform for Hong Kong schools to further develop a better and necessary learning environment for their students. This paper reports some of the recent development of e-learning in Hong Kong and reflects critically of its future.

Introduction

In recent years, educators have witnessed rapid changes in the use of information technology (IT) in education. In incorporating e-learning in the classrooms and other learning scenarios, new possibilities for both learners and educators have emerged. A market survey in USA by i-OP reports that e-learning on current served market for educating technology professionals is estimated to reach 60-65 billion dollars, 96% of the 376 respondents for high-tech engineer community were willing to taking online course [1]. IBM Mindspan Solution also predicts that the e-learning market in business and industry will grow at the compound average growth rate of 83% from 1997 to 2003 [2]. While e-learning may or may not totally replace traditional education and training, it has been widely adapted in the business professional development and training. This paper does not examine e-learning in this area, rather, it focuses on how it relates to current HK primary and secondary education.

There have been substantial changes in HK education after the five-year strategic plan was released in 1998 [3]. This plan contains, among others, a strategy to promote more learner-centred learning through the use of IT in Hong Kong schools. Included in this plan were elements such as massive roll out of IT equipment to the schools, Internet access for all schools, a pilot scheme of 10 primary and 10 secondary schools and preparation for an education-specific intranet. Perhaps most important of all, is the provision of 45000 training places for teachers [4]. The other initiatives by the Hong Kong government included the setting up of the five-billion dollar Quality Education Fund (QEF) which has provided substantial grants for the IT in Education endeavours, development of exemplar software, the IT Education Resource Centre, the development of a portal site "Education City" for all schools, and the formulation of the IT Learning Targets for students [4].

A mid-term review of the five-year strategic plan was conducted in 2001 [see 5]. Some of the findings of this review are significant and will be used in this paper for examining the capacity of Hong Kong schools to adopt Web-based e-learning environment in HK, since these findings form the cornerstone of e-learning. These features are (1) Hardware and network infra- structure, it is significant because e-learning is made possible of exchanged and sharing information, instructions via a computer using standard Internet technology [6]; (2) teacher's ability and the willingness of using computer; and (3) the development of web-based teaching software. The remaining of this paper will concentrate on these aspects and discuss how they can support the implementation of web-based e-learning environment in HK primary and secondary school education.

E-learning in HK education

Hardware and network infrastructure: Student-to-computer-ratio is commonly used for measuring IT provision in schools. There has been a substantial improvement of this ratio from 36:1 to 7.5:1 at secondary level and from 53:1 to 13.4:1 at primary level. The percentage of schools using powerful computers (suitable for multimedia and intensive Internet applications) is above 70%. The improvement of this ratio could also be partly attributed to the additional funding provided by the QEF [4]. It is expected that this ratio will continue to improve although the QEF has now virtually stopped funding the purchase of hardware in schools. In respect to network access, computers in HK primary and secondary schools are networked and serviced by different type of servers (Web server, Ftp server, e-mail server). Moreover, 54% of secondary school and 85% of primary school are using 1 Megabits or over broadband Internet access service while 68% of secondary schools have their own homepages on the WWW. The figure will even be up to 80% if schools using the homepage service set up by HK Government are included.

Teachers' and students' ability and the willingness of using IT: From the mid-term review [4], it was found that senior classes in secondary schools used IT in subject teaching less frequently than the junior classes. It signifies teachers in senior secondary school have less interest in using IT for teaching. It is unlikely that this is related to teachers' IT competence since this scenario is also found in the subject of Computer Studies. Presumably, the limit of teachers' resources and the heavy workload in normal teaching processes may be one of the reasons. Moreover, it could also be surmised that the public examination system in Hong Kong places a lot of pressure on both teachers and students in the senior classes, not to mention a very packed syllabus. However, such scenario becomes better if using website resources reference and supplementary materials. The survey shows that 60% HK teachers' IT competence is sufficient for them to develop simple web-based materials, and over 95% of Hong Kong students have access to the Internet at home. In the teachers' side, 60%~70% in secondary and primary level use website resources for teaching. This phenomenon indicates that teachers are more willing to use website resources rather than in use courseware for teaching. However, the attitude of willingness to use IT including both website resources and IT integrating approach in the teaching is greatly improved. This also can be supported by the figures that 94.5% and 97.1% for HK primary and secondary students have a positive motivation and ability to learn actively and 98.2% and 96.2% are encouraged to be engaged in more collaborative project-based learning.

The development of web-based teaching software: One of the findings of the mid-term review highlights that teachers are more willing to use website resources rather than web-based teaching packages is somewhat related to the difficulty of developing high quality of web-based teaching software and e-learning portals. In fact, there are very few web-based education software and portals that are satisfactorily used [7]. Besides, the improvement of the hardware infrastructure in HK primary and secondary schools is far better than the developing of the teaching software [5]. Besides, it is almost impossible to expect teachers to develop a sophisticated web-based e-learning portal, which meet the satisfaction factors [7], for secondary level on top of their normal teaching loads.

Some problems and issues

While the Hong Kong government has made tremendous efforts to improve its education system since the return of Hong Kong to China in 1997, especially in the use of IT in education, there are a number of problems

and issues faced by the HK schools. A few of these problems are discussed here as examples. First, Hong Kong is facing some serious economic problems and it is unlikely that its economy will improve in the next few years. As a result, Hong Kong schools will face the problem of upgrading its hardware and infrastructure. Second, there have been too many educational reforms in Hong Kong in the last few years. Teachers and school leaders are under immense pressure to cope with the excessive demands. Third, Hong Kong has a relatively small market for the development of traditional Chinese character based web software, which implies that it might not be cost-effective for HK to develop its web-based software.

Conclusion

This paper examines some of the development and capabilities of the web-based environment in HK education midway through the five-year IT strategic plan. It would appear that the fundamental conditions exitst in HK schools, e.g., IT facilities, and teacher and students attitude, to make good use of a web-based e-learning environment for HK school education. However, the support in high quality web-based e-learning software and portals still requires substantial improvement. Moreover, there are quite a few problems and issues that Hong Kong schools have to deal with in order to realise the potential of e-learning.

Reference

1. i-OP (2001). E-learning and professional development in the high tech community. Retrieved April 30, 2002, from the World Wide Web: http://www.cenquest.com/pdf/onlinelearning.pdf
2. IBM Mindspan Solutions. (2001). The future of e-learning: An expanding vision. Retrieved April 30, 2002, from the WWW: http://www-3.ibm.com/software/mindspan/distlrng.nsf/892 97bbbe911d2788525674c00675635/bdeca83a173667d0852 56a0e007771a2/$FILE/LSP-2001-043.pdf
3. Education and Manpower Bureau. (1998). *Information technology for learning in a new era five-year strategy 1998/99 to 2002/03.* Hong Kong: HKSAR.
4. Au, W.K. (2001). The present situation and future prospects of information education on junior high and elementary schools in Hong Kong. *Information and Education, 81, pp. 13-43.*
5. Law, N., Yuen, H.K., Ki, W.W. & Li, S. (2001). Preliminary Study on Reviewing the Progress and Evaluating the Information Technology in Education (ITEd) Project. Hong Kong:. CITE, Hong Kong University: HKSAR
6. Rosenberg, M. (2001) *E-Learning: Strategies for Delivering Knowledge in the Digital Age.* New York: McGraw Hill.
7. Carlson, R.D., & Repman, J. (2002). Activating Web-based E-learning. *Internal Journal on E-Learning, 1(2), 7-10.*

Student Opinions on Web-Enhanced Courses

Poonam Kumar* and Anil Kumar**
*Saginaw Valley State University, United States
**Central Michigan University, United States

Abstract

This study examined student satisfaction with technology enhanced traditional courses. Students were enrolled in two courses where the instructors used Blackboard to supplement the course content. Student responses indicated that students were very satisfied with the technology-enhanced course and liked the availability of lecture notes, links to additional resources and online discussions. Students also provided feedback about face to face and online discussions. Students who preferred online discussions, liked the flexibility and convenience of the medium of communication. Students who preferred face to face discussions felt that online discussions lacked personal touch. Implications of the results for instructors and future research are also discussed.

1: Introduction

In the recent years, the rapid advancements in technology and telecommunications, especially the Internet, have led to an explosive growth of Web-based courses. The World Wide Web (WWW) is emerging as the most popular medium for delivering instruction and an increasing number of instructors are integrating various features of the Web in novel ways to provide exciting learning opportunities for their students. While some instructors use the World Wide Web to offer totally Web-based classes, others use technology to enhance the content of a traditional course. However, there are many challenges associated with incorporating the World Wide Web in instruction. The research examining student feedback about the use of World Wide Web, multimedia and online discussions is varied and mixed [1]. Many students like the convenience and flexibility of Web-based instruction (WBI) as well as the access to large amount of the information in WBI [2]. On the other hand, studies have also reported that students experience feelings of isolation, anxiety and confusion [3]. Students are primary participants in a learning environment, their satisfaction with the learning environment is important for the success of implementing web-based instruction. In addition, student feedback about the use of technology in a course can be valuable for the instructor for designing effective Web-based courses. This study assessed student satisfaction regarding the use of web components in two traditional classes and gathered their feedback to examine the advantages, disadvantages and effectiveness of using the Web course activities to enhance the traditional class content.

2: Procedures

The authors used different features of Blackboard like discussion forums, virtual chatroom, bulletin board, e-mail and group features to enhance the traditional course content of the two courses they were teaching. The learning materials were arranged into small learning units or modules, which included course syllabus, lecture notes, examples, and links to additional reading and resources. The students were required to participate in online discussions in addition to classroom discussions. This allowed the classroom discussion to be ongoing and extended beyond the classroom boundaries. The classroom activities and classroom discussions required that students access the additional readings and resources. Students worked in groups on projects and were encouraged to use group features provided in Blackboard to facilitate group work.

At the end of the semester, students were asked to provide their feedback regarding the use of technology in the courses. The survey was completed by 89 students enrolled in the two classes taught by the authors. Thirty one students were enrolled in a Special Education course and 58 were enrolled in a Management Information Systems course. Out of the 89 students, 17 students were graduate, 72 undergraduate, 61 students were full time and 28 were part-time. Fifty nine students were male and 30 were female. Twenty one students reported that they had taken an online course before they were enrolled in this class. Students reported that they accessed the class web site from home, school or work. All survey questions were on Likert scale, from 1-5, with 1 being strongly disagree and 5 being strongly agree.

3: Results

In general, the students' feedback regarding the use of technology in the class was positive (Table 1). Students liked the fact that the course syllabus was available on the course website for reference. Majority of the students found the lecture notes as being one of the most useful features of using Blackboard. They agreed that having the class presentation available before class on the course website allowed them to focus on the lecture in class rather than taking notes in class.

Items	Mean
Having the course syllabus available on the course website was useful for reference	4.38
Having the class presentation (Lecture Notes) available before class on the website allowed me to focus on the lecture in class rather than taking notes in the class	4.34
Discussion Forums allowed me to participate in discussions at my own pace and gave me time to think and reflect before responding	3.94
I prefer online discussion forum over the traditional in class discussions	2.69
The file exchange in the group account increased the productivity of the group	3.22
The email feature under the group account increased productivity by allowing me to communicate easily with my groups	3.38
The group feature allowed me to collaborate and communicate with other group members using virtual chat rooms available for our groups	2.98
The group feature allowed me to communicate using discussion forums just for my group	3.03
I found the links to resources on the course website useful	4.01
Packages like Blackboard increase overall productivity of students	3.84

Table 1: **Student opinions on web-enhanced courses**

Students also found the links to additional resources useful. A possible reason why students liked this feature is because it was integrated in the lectures, classroom activities and assignments, thus prompting students to explore and access that information. Students also reported satisfaction with using discussion forums in the courses. Students agreed that discussion forums allowed them to participate at their own pace and gave them time to think and reflect upon before responding. It is interesting that although most students believed that online discussions were beneficial, only 40 % of the students preferred online discussions to traditional face to face discussions, 47% preferred face to face and 12% students were neutral about it. Students provided several reasons for their preferences. Students who preferred face to face discussions reported that online discussions were impersonal because they lacked non-verbal cues and body language. For example, one student wrote: "*Online discussions are nice for those individuals who may be reluctant to speak up in class, but you loose some of the*

spontaneity that comes from responding immediately to what others say." Another student commented that "*I think face to face discussion is better in that the person can see and interpret their gestures and reactions to things.*" Similarly another student commented, "*I learn more from listening to people than reading responses online.*" On the other hand, students who preferred online discussions liked it because online discussions allowed enough time to think before responding and were flexible and convenient. For example, a student commented "*I like the online discussions because I had time to thoroughly read and analyze the materials and it gave everyone a chance to participate unlike classroom discussions.*"

Student comments indicate that students had different preferences in terms of how they learn-some learned more through online discussions, others felt they had to listen to people. Students also commented that lack of non-verbal cues in online discussions inhibited communication and therefore they found online discussions impersonal. Research related to the effectiveness of Web-based instruction has focused primarily on the student performance in these environments and has not paid attention to the social processes [3]. This social dimension of the Web-based learning environments needs further investigation. According to Vygostky [4], discussions and social interactions are an important part of the learning process. Therefore effectively facilitating social interactions and communications among students may influence both learning outcomes and student satisfaction. For students who prefer face to face communication, enrolling in an online class could lead to isolation and poor performance.

4: References

[1] Alavi, M. & Leidner, D.E. (2001). Research commentary: Technology-Mediated learning- A call for greater depth and breadth of research. *Information Systems Research, 12*(1),1-10.
[2] Daugherty, M.& Funke, B.L. University faculty and student perceptions of Web-based instruction. *Journal of Distance Education,* 13(1), 21-39.
[3] Hara, N., & Kling, R. (2000). Students' distress with Web-based distance education course: An ethnographic study of participants' experiences. *Information, Communication and Society,* 3(4), 557-579.
[4] Vygotsky, L. (1986). *Thought and Language.* Cambridge: MIT Press.

The JISC SHELL Project: Connecting Learning Environments in Higher and Further Education in the UK.

Jon Yorke

University of Plymouth, United Kingdom
jon.yorke@plymouth.ac.uk

Abstract

This short paper aims to introduce the SHELL project, a UK based JISC-funded project which is part of the JISC "Managed Learning Environments for Lifelong Learning" programme. The project commenced March 2002, and aims to facilitate the smooth transition of lifelong learners as they move between places of study through a student centred record (SCR) database using IMS specifications to transfer data.

1. Introduction

There is a clear need to support learners as they move between institutions in Further (FE) and Higher Education (HE) in a political climate characterised by a sharpening focus on agendas of widening participation and lifelong learning.

The increasing use of managed and virtual learning environments provides a context in which to explore the benefits of interconnected online systems, a context which led the Joint Information Systems Committee (JISC) to call for projects as part of the JISC 1/01 Programme [1].

2. The SHELL Project

The SHELL Project [2] is one of two projects funded by JISC to develop the integration of technologies across a consortium comprising one University and several partner colleges in the UK.

The first phase of this three year project involves the University of Plymouth, Cornwall College, Exeter College, North Devon College and Somerset College of Arts and Technology. In the second phase, involvement will extend to other institutions in Cornwall, Devon, Somerset, Dorset, and Bristol.

The SHELL project aims to develop the integration of online technologies across institutions in support of lifelong learning. IMS standards (such as IMS LIP and Enterprise) will be used to support the automatic transfer of student data between various records systems.

3. Project Aims and Objectives

Currently, students who are enrolled on a HE course in a partner college complete 'dual registration' -registration for both the college and the associated University. The SHELL Project aims to replace this cumbersome process with single registration for all partnership students. This requires a rapid and efficient transfer of student data between consortium members.

This transfer of student data will be achieved through the development of a Student Centred Record Database (see Figure 1). This database will be protected by security measures which will provide authenticated access to the data in the SCR database, shared by partner colleges and students themselves. Transfer mechanisms will be established to ensure that data in the SCR database is not less than 24 hours behind data held in institutions own student record systems.

Working with software suppliers (such as Capita and Campus IT), the project will also work towards the provision of:

- a framework for integration of Managed Learning Environments (MLEs);
- improved efficiency for the administration of partnership students;
- access to partnership Virtual Learning Environments (VLEs) for partnership students;
- a framework for the seamless movement of the learner within FE and between FE and HE;
- a record of lifelong learning within the region for FE and HE students.

A permanent web portal (remaining available even after a student has left the institution) will provide individual students with portal access to online materials from the point of single registration whilst studying.

It will also allow them to have permanent internet based access to their transcripts of formally accredited marks and will facilitate the future storage of other records of achievement, such as personal development records and planning.

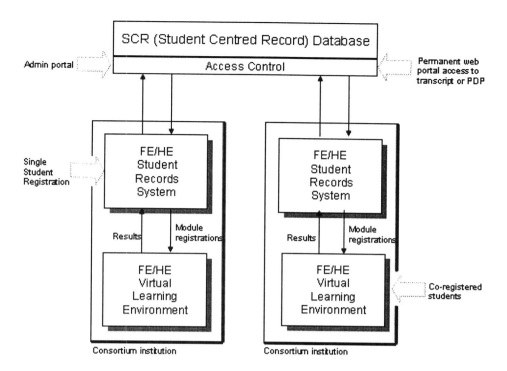

Figure 1: Interconnecting VLE and Student Records Systems

It is recognised that despite automated and/or new business processes, there will be occasional need for administrative staff to correct errors or duplications in the SCR Database. An administration portal (see Figure 1) will provide access to allow this.

4. The SHELL Project Team

The SHELL Project team comprises the Project Director, Manager and four Team Leaders, supported by a range of staff throughout the consortium. For example, the 'Business Analysis and Implementation' team leader focuses on the business processes within the partnership, working closely with the 'Standards' team leader to develop specifications for data transfer.

5. SHELL Project Phases

Phase one covers the period until Summer 2003. In this phase, the focus is on developing the SCR database and its use within the core partners. This will involve the analysis of business processes, and technical specifications for the interfaces and data transfer mechanisms. A multi-institution transcript which sets out what data is recorded will be developed, in addition to the specification of the multi-institution personal development record (PDR).

Phase two starts in July 2003 and runs until February 2005. In this phase the SCR will be available to the wider project partners, and will by that time include the personal development record.

6. Summary

A number of themes of particular interest in this project will be investigated, spanning aspects of technical implementation, IMS standards, issues of organisational change and staff / educational development. The project will explore and disseminate the experiences of implementing large scale change between the partner institutions, with the potential of serving as a model for information exchange at a national level.

At the heart of this investigation lies an interest in the experience of the learner in a changing environment.

7. References

[1] The Joint Information Systems Committee 1/01 Programme (2002) [online] Available from: http://www.jisc.ac.uk/mle/01-01/ [Accessed 08/2002]

[2] The SHELL Project website (2002) [online] Available from: www.shellproject.net [Accessed 08/2002]

Integrating the critical thinking approach with web resources:
An application to history teaching in a junior high school

Shu Ching Yang
shyang@mail.nsysu.edu.tw
Lijung Huang
lijung@ms1.url.com.tw
Graduate Institute of Education
National Sun Yat-sen University, Taiwan, R.O.C. 80424

1. The Research Problem

In line with a shift from transmissional/didactic instructional approaches to constructive/critical activities, the technology mediated history curriculum via critical thinking instruction is constructed to provide students an opportunity to engage in a critical and meaningful investigation of history. Instead of consuming predigested accounts of historical figures, events, and fragmentary information, the project engages students in authentic historical inquiry. Peter Stearns (2000), a leading American historian, wrote about teaching history to young people, saying: "The key to developing historical habits of mind...is having repeated experience in historical inquiry. Such experience should involve a variety of materials and a diversity of analytical problems...What matters is learning how to access different magnitudes of historical change, different examples of conflicting interpretations, and multiple kinds of evidence."

As students often do not see the nature of evidence gathering and interpretation in history and the discursive nature of history texts; thus, they tend to view history texts as "objective truth" that they do not question or otherwise think about critically. The critical thinking modules using major characteristics and theories of Richard Paul's model, Ennis are designed and instruct students how to analyze and interpret primary source documents. The model was integrated into a series of assigned classroom activities, stimulating learners' using sourcing, contextualization, and corroboration as engaged in by historians (Wineburg, 1996). The design of web sources is designed to broaden the students' understanding of events, periods, and themes by offering them the multiple perspectives. In addition, as a knowledge creation tool, the discussion forum is designed to allow students to make visible their constructed representations of what they are learning, giving teachers a means of assessing student understanding as well as giving students a platform for discussion and reflection on their historical thinking. It is hoped that through this history project of integrating the critical thinking approach with web resources, it promotes learners' active learning and development of critical thinking, reasoning, and problem solving.

With this background in mind, the study teaches students to think critically using web resources in history. The study looked at learners' perceptions and learning growth of critical historical thinking as they learn history using advanced technological tools . The project offers students the opportunity to become researchers of history by using technology. It is hoped that the thoughtful and creative use of computer technology in conducting historical inquiries will contribute to learners' historical knowledge, critical thinking skills, and interest in learning history. The insights gained in this study will help teachers' design and implement oral historical projects. Some challenges to the implementation of historical projects will be discussed.

2. Methodology

2.1 Participants

The 33 participants, 9 boys and 24 girls, in this study were students from second grade of Chi-Jin junior high school. They selected the course as an extracurricular activity. They joined the project voluntarily.

2.2 Context of the study

In order to give readers a general sense of the context in which the study took place, this subsection briefly describes the overall course structure. The instructor integrated the Web into the curriculum, and required the students to use it extensively on their projects. The instructor chose the technology and the project assignment and acted as a guide throughout the activities. The instructor aimed to help students develop historical understanding with critical and creative disposition.

Specifically, the instructor's objectives for this endeavor were to: (1) provide students with multiple information about late Chin dynasty, (2) provide students with an information-literate experience in the Web technology; (3) enhance students' discourse synthesis ability, namely, learning how to search, organize, and compose information for a research project, and most importantly, (4) offer critical thinking modules, providing students with a strategy for critical thinking about multiple, conflicting documents, provide them with opportunities to engage in a historian's activities.

2.3 Doing history project

The subjects had to complete several assignments during the semester for the course. The main assignment, Doing history project, was used as the task for the study. Using the resources of Web-Based Historical Curriculum, students can find a range of resources to study the theme of the Opium War and the Sino-Japanese War. Doing history project integrates Hexter's Doing history model and Anderson-Inman & Kessinger Gather Model (2000) to instruct students how to analyze and interpret primary source documents. The students were encouraged to engage their historical inquiry. They are required to compose their we-based projects in a group of 45 by presenting their personal perspectives on a selective topic related to the theme of the Opium War and the Sino-Japanese War. The grades for this project were awarded based on several criteria. The information being communicated, the breadth and diversity of the information, the credentials/ documents used to present the information, as well as the formulation, organization and synthesis of ideas.

2.4 Web-Based Historical Curriculum

The Web-Based Historical Curriculum enhances students learning history through quick and extensive access to primary sources. In this website, we have collected many primary sources not limited to printed documents such as letters, newspapers, diaries, official documents and poems. Artifacts (art, pottery, articles of clothing, tools, documents), places (events, and other buildings and structures), sounds (music, stories, and folklore), and images (paintings, photographs, and videos/movies) can also be considered primary sources. Introducing and using primary sources in the history classroom leads to active learning and to the development of critical thinking and enhancement of the learning process by allowing students to construct their own understandings of people, events, and ideas.

2.5 Critical thinking instructional modules of history

We design critical thinking history modules using major characteristics and theories developed by Richard Paul and colleagues at the Foundation for Critical Thinking, complemented by Ennis's critical thinking model, IMPACT (Improving Minimal Proficiencies by Activating Critical Thinking).

2.6 Questionnaire

After project was done, a questionnaire was given to elicit relevant information on the participants' perception

of, and their attitudes towards Web-Based Curriculum, doing history project. The first part of the survey pertained to background information. The second part consisted of attitude statements about evaluation of Historical Website, such as leaning content, screen design, interface design, system usage as well as learning effect. The third part specifically focused on the learners' self-evaluation of their Historical learning Website. The fourth part included 5 opening questions depicting their reflections about the project.

3. Discussion and Summary

The goal of our research and development is to offer students the opportunity to become researchers of history by using technology. The project is to enrich students' historical understanding by providing multiple perspectives and contextualized environment. The study found that our Web-Based Historical Curriculum Critical thinking instructional modules of history and doing history project have the potential to scaffold construction of an integrated understanding of historical content and context. The study demonstrated that students' perception of the subject of history is changed – they no longer see history as a static-descriptive subject. With the learning modules designed to nurture students' capability of critical thinking in learning history, students do not only know what happened in the past, but also realize how to make inquiries and search for answers.

Moreover, the implementation of critical thinking instruction modules of history shows that students' capability of thinking of history in a critical way is enhanced to different degrees– some realize better techniques while the other less so. As a result, it is important to design a long-term project with aims to developing such techniques for long-lasting effect.

4. References

Anderson-Inman, L., & Kessinger, P. (2000). Promoting historical inquiry: GATHER model.

Ennis, R. H. (1985). A logical basis for measuring critical thinking skills. *Educational Leadership, 43*(2), 45-48.

Paul, R. W. (1984). Critical thinking: Fundamental to education for a free society. *Educational Leadership, 42*(1), 4-14.

Paul, R., & Elder, L. (2001). *Critical thinking: Tools for taking of your learning and your life*. NJ : Upper Saddle River.

Stearns, P. N. (January 2000). Why study history? American Historical Association. Available online at http://www.theaha.org/pubs/stearns.htm

Wineburg S. S. (1991) *Historical problem solving: A study of the cognitive processes used in the evaluation of documentary and pictorial evidence. Journal of Educational Psychology 83*(1), 73-87.

Constructing Internet Futures Exchange for Teaching Derivatives Trading in Financial Markets

An Sing Chen
finasc@ccunix.ccu.edu.tw
Department of Finance

Jyun-Cheng Wang
jcwang@mis.ccu.edu.tw
Department of Mangement
Information Systems

Shu Ching Yang*
shyang@mail.nsysu.edu.tw
Graduate Institute of Education

National Chung-Cheng University, National Sun Yat-sen University*, Taiwan, R.O.C.

1. Introduction

Simulations and games are widely accepted as a powerful mode of teaching and learning. This is especially so in the field of finance in teaching students the intricacies of stock market trading. Stock market simulations complement more traditional methods of teaching finance by encouraging learning by doing, by generating motivation and enjoyment, and by engaging the business student in a simulated experience resembling the "real world." Although there exist numerous stock market simulation games on the Web, they are all "secondary simulations" in that the players cannot affect the prices of the traded securities but must take the security prices "as given" and base the trading simulation on these given prices. Such secondary simulations, however, lose an important dimension of market realism in that in the real stock market, players, especially "big" players such as major banks and large institutional investors, can influence the price of the traded securities. Secondly, being secondary simulations, existing internet stock market simulation games focus almost exclusively on stock trading and cannot realistically simulate the trading of derivatives. Compared to stock trading the trading of derivatives is a lot more complex both conceptually and from a teaching point of view. In this study, we leverage the power of internet technology and design a fully functional internet futures exchange. In our internet futures exchange, the prices of the futures contracts being traded is directly determined by the market participants (players). Additionally, our designed website tackles the difficult task of teaching derivative (futures) trading via learning by doing in a realistic trading environment with realtime feedback where traders can influence the price. Conceptually, this is superior to the use of secondary simulators (existing web market simulation games) where players must take the security prices as given and cannot influence its value through strategic behaviors. This is especially of importance for the teaching of derivative trading in as much as in the real world, powerhouses (large institutional traders) often exert significant influence on the observed derivative prices.

With respect to academic research, we provide an example of the use of our internet futures exchange as a research platform to address the issue of market transparency and front runners. This, in itself is an important research question since market transparency level lies at the heart of controversial debates. Empirical data gathered from a controlled laboratory setting may help resolve the controversy. Previous laboratory studies addressing this issue use simplified representations of financial exchanges based on simulated securities whose values are chosen randomly form some predetermined distribution. For our study, we construct a fully functional futures exchange based on real underlying securities on the internet and conduct our experiments on this exchange. Our obtained results should be more robust than those obtained from simplified financial exchanges used in previous studies. We also analyze the relation between market transparency and front runners. No previous research has been done analyzing this issue in detail. In our study, we make use of our constructed fully functional internet futures exchange and gather empirical data under alternative exchange designs and varying levels of transparency and front-runner participation. The effect of varying levels of front runner participation on the bid-ask spread and on trading gains and losses can be tested for. Additionally, the effect of varying levels of front runner order quantity (order size) can be tested for.

2. Front-runners and Market Transparency

Front runners can be defined as traders who infer security values from the displayed order (quantity). An example of a front runner (in a market where all price quantity pairs of the entire supply and demand schedule is observable to all market participants) is a trader who would enter a buy (sell) order at a price that is 1 cent above (below) the currently displayed buy (sell) price if an order quantity of greater than a certain set threshold is observed. The existence and effect of front runners on the market is intricately related to the issue of market transparency. However, currently, no research has been done analyzing this issue in detail.

Market transparency level lies at the heart of controversial debates. In theory, a totally transparent regime leads to greater popularization of information and consequently to a reduction of adverse selection. Therefore, increasing market transparency will enhance market liquidity and improve price efficiency. Several studies, however, show that a lack of transparency can sometimes provide lower spreads (e.g. Bloomfield and O'Hara (1999), Porter and Weaver (2000)). Empirical data gathered from a controlled laboratory setting may help resolve controversy. In this study, we construct a fully functional futures exchange and gather empirical data under alternative exchange designs and varying levels of transparency and front-runner participation. Given the rapid advances in internet technology and the growing numbers of newly emerging economies starting to develop advanced financial markets, detailed analysis and research concerning the issue of market transparency under controlled laboratory conditions is timely and important.

Liquidity and transparency are two essential qualities for any financial market. Liquidity essentially reflects trading conditions and is often interpreted in the market microstructure literature as the ability for a trader to buy or sell any amount of the tradable asset immediately and at a price very near the current market price. Market transparency is the ability of market participants to observe information about the trading process (Madhavan (1996) and O'Hara (1995)). In this context, information can refer to knowledge about prices, quotes, the sources of order flow and the identities of market participants.

Transparency, furthermore, has many dimensions. Two important dimensions are the pre- and post trade dimensions (Madhavan (2000)). Pre-trade (Quote) transparency refers to the dissemination of limit order book content such as current bid and ask quotations, depths and possibly also information about limit orders away from the best prices. Post-trade (Trade) transparency refers to the public transmission of information on past trades such as execution time, volume, price and possibly information about buyer and seller identifications.

In the real world, no market is actually fully transparent and existing markets usually attempt to maintain a degree of opacity. The most often implemented means of creating opacity (or decreasing transparency) are the delayed dissemination of information (trades delayed reporting) and the use of hidden orders.

3. Experimental Market

In our research, we manipulate transparency by altering the amount of information traders can observe about other trader's activity, and examine how this manipulation affects the efficiency of the prices. In the fully transparent setting, the entire supply and demand schedule of the futures contracts are observable by all the traders. That is, all traders see the bid price, ask price, the quantity (number of contracts) corresponding to each price order. In the semiopaque setting, a certain percentage of traders are given the option to make use of hidden orders, thereby hiding the quantity portion of their order submission from other traders. In the fully opaque setting, all traders see

only the price but not the associated quantity.

4. Interface Design

By leveraging the power of internet technology, this project will construct and design a fully functional internet futures exchange, creating a real-time, authentic and supportive environment for students engaging in stock inquiry. A* Trade Online website is built with M$ SQL Server2000. The Web server uses the MS Internet Information Server (IIS) 4.0, and the database uses the MS Access 2000. DreamWeaver4.0 and Photoshop6.0 are used to create basic page layout and hyperlink architecture for web pages and Flash 5.0 is used as an additional tool for system function development. ASP (Active Server Page) programming is employed in web-front end complemented by JavaScript. The monthly and daily schedules are based on VB, agents developed by Java.

5. Effect of front runners

The entire experiment is repeated with varying levels of automated 'front runners' introduced into the market. Front runners are defined in this case as traders who infer security values from the displayed order (quantity). An example of an automatic front runner is to automatically enter a buy (sell) at a price that is 1 cent above (below) the displayed buy (sell) price if an order quantity of greater than a certain set threshold is observed. In detail, suppose we can currently observe the entire demand schedule and suppose the auto front runner threshold quantity is 100 shares. In this case, suppose a trader issues a limit order to buy 120 shares of say CISCO at 100 dollars, the auto front runner would kick in and issue an order to buy say F shares of CISCO at 100.01 dollars, thereby front-running the trader who originally issued the buy order at 100 dollars. The effect of varying levels of front runners on the bid-ask spread and on trading gains and losses will be tested for statistical significance. Additionally, the effect of varying levels of the threshold F will be tested for statistical significance.

Our the internet futures exchange is ideal for research in several diverse fields: 1) research in behavioral finance 2) research in high frequency economics 3) questions about cognitive behavior 4) inquiry into learning agents and evolutionary environment they inhabit 5) research in human and computer interface design

Our obtained results should be more robust than those obtained from simplified financial exchanges used in previous studies. We make use of our constructed fully functional internet futures exchange and gather empirical data under alternative exchange designs and varying levels of transparency and front-runner participation. The effect of varying levels of front runner participation on the bi-ask spread and on trading gains and losses can be tested for. Additionally, the effect of varying levels of front runner order quantity (order size) can be tested for.

Gender Education through Creating Internet Theatre in Education

Shu Ching Yang
shyang@mail.nsysu.edu.tw

Chia-Chieh Huang
hjjjay101@yahoo.com.tw

Graduate Institute of Education
National Sun Yat-sen University, Taiwan, R.O.C. 80424

1. Introduction

In Taiwan, gender equity and gender issues in education recently beginning to open up and become a hot topic in education. Curriculum materials are now being developed, professional publications are beginning to cover gender equity issues, a serious of professional workshops are devoting time to it, and individual teacher educators are starting to become concerned about it.

In response to the educational policy of our country, the Internet theater gender program is designed to achieve gender equity for K 5-6 primary school students. The Internet theatre project takes advantage of computer support learning community and theater education. The introduction of Internet theatre into the gender education presents both an opportunity to expand the power of teaching and learning gender issues through electronic facilitation of the Internet technology to exploit the enhanced features of interactive hypermedia and the educational, entertaining value of theatre education. It intends to give learners a safe, entertaining, intellectual and supervised opportunity to examine their own attitudes, behaviors and living experience regarding gender issues through interactive drama and discussion.

2. Rationale for Internet Theater Gender Program

The design rationales of the project are based upon a set of theory-based design principles, such as theater in education, cognitive flexibility theory (Spiro et al., 1992), situated learning (Brown, Collins, & Duguid, 1989), and cooperative learning, anchored instruction with features of video-based format, narrative with realistic problems, generative format (CTGV, 1992).

It is well-documented that the educational effectiveness of drama or theater in education, such as enhancing motivation and interest, developing children's literacy, supporting cognitive and constructive learning, enriching affective learning concerning subject matter, promoting collaborative learning through teamwork as well as exploiting Gardner's multiple intelligences (Christie, 1980; Lillard, 1993; O'Neill, 1989; Vedeler, 1997; Winston, 1998; Wolf, 1994, 1995). The participatory nature of drama, coupled with its ability to encourage students to explore their beliefs and attitudes toward the characters and plot, evidently provides a wealth of pedagogical possibilities for developing students' awareness of gender inequity and how to cope with them.

For the purpose of gender education, whether improvised in the classroom or scripted for the stage, the performance enactments, scenarios, or cases are well-crafted and designed to represent some situations occurring gender inequity and have learners act out a situation through role play, which further serve as the anchor for open-ended discussion for further inquiry about gender issues. The dramatic dialogue does more than simulate talk or argument between two or more children, it set the stage for learners' immersion and interactivity in the authentic situation, and further, think about how the characters see themselves and others, their situation and crucially their future actions.

As having appropriate understanding about and attitudes toward gender-equity issues for young learners is a challenging task, learning about gender-equity issues by simply reading or hearing about them in single, simple, or abstract presentations offers little assurance that students will achieve a deep level of conceptual understanding. Spiro and his colleagues argue that multiplicity provides learners with multiple "traversal routes" or perspectives with which to "criss-cross" the topic, and enables them to highlight the complexities of certain issues and skillfully negotiate these landscapes, therefore, learners can come to understand the ill-structured concepts and flexibly apply them by experiencing them in different cases or contexts (Jacobson & Spiro, 1995).

As the gender-equity issues are often subtle, ill structured, value-laden and complex, it requires situated learning that is case-based and experienced learning in authentic contexts, rather than the simple presentation of abstract descriptions of the issues, involved (Bransford, Sherwood, Haselbring, Kinzer, & Williams, 1990). Furthermore, the instructional activities require to bridge the gap from hypothetical or theoretical to real understanding if learning is to occur and any changes in behaviors are to be made, or appropriate (attitude, behavior problem-solving) action to be taken or dealt with regarding gender equity in classrooms or social context.

3. Design Framework

The program presents various interactive scenarios or drama enactments that illustrates inequities in classroom or social interaction patterns, language, gender expectations, and curriculum etc., which have learners use the knowledge learned to think about the inequities presented in various interactive scenarios and invite students to compose, act out, reflect on and provide an online discussion-lead for further exploration. The focus of this project is to create a computer-support collaborative learning environment through theater education capable of hosting instructional activities related to gender issues.

The interface design includes stage area, role-playing platform as well as discussion form. In the stage area, the drama enactments include "situation play" and "problem-solving play", which can be created in IT (Internet Theater) by children working individually or collectively based on the scrip written by teachers or students themselves. After completion, the plays can be transmitted through the Internet which allows access by learners. An unfinished play or case can be transmitted through the Internet to be updated or extended by other students, establishing a process of collaborative creation through the Internet. In the role-play platform, the user can inhabit the IT interface world in different ways (or roles): as an author, a director, an actor or a spectator of plays. Inhabiting IT as an author, the learners can write the scripts about any themes for gender issues, post their line/script for each role, or give suggestion for particular role.

As the stage program, it provides a variety of video-based, script-format or animation, picture, multimedia presentation "anchors", accompanied by the learning materials, for learners' discussion. A follow-up different theme of discussion is designed and structured to have learners reflecting and commenting on the episodes or scenarios with the best solution for the situation or puzzled questions inviting further discussion. Spectators can provide their opinions aimed at director's scripts, come up with their best solution for the situational play or reply to other learners' opinion toward the gender issues.

4. Future Directions

The goal of this project is to offer students the gender education by using computer-mediated drama activity. The project intends to enrich students' understanding of gender issues by providing multiple perspectives and contextualized environment through action-oriented, dramatic approaches on the web. In this project, Internet Theater Gender Program is conceived as situated, dialectical, and cultural tools which are intended to diminish gender stereotyping and build self-esteem,

raise gender-consciousness, inspiring learners toward reflective and constructive understanding of the gender issues, and further used the knowledge learned resolve inequities in their living world. It is noted that IT Gender teaching is not a pre-package instructional tool rather than more properly a set of informational resources, which designs for teachers to plan, enact, tailor and adapt for their course, and allow teachers to ink multiple sections of the same course or similar courses in different schools or areas for interesting cross-cultural discussions and collaborations. The Internet Gender Teaching Theater has been developed through a number of design cycles, creating a version, evaluating it with the help of colleagues/students, revising it and will be expanding the content and refining the interface design in the near future.

5. References

Brown, J., Collins, A., & Duguid, P. (1989). Situated cognition and the culture of learning. *Educational Researcher, 18*(1), 32-42.

Christie, J. F. (1980). Play for cognitive growth. *The Elementary School Journal, 81*(2), 115-118.

Cognition and Technology Group At Vanderbilt (1992). The Jasper Series as an example of anchored instruction: Theory, program description, and assessment data. *Educational Psychologist, 27*(3), 291-315.

Gardner, H. (1983) *Frames of mind: The theory of multiple intelligences*. New York, Basic Books.

Jacobson, M. J., & Spiro, R. J. (1995). Hypertext learning environments, cognitive flexibility, and the transfer of complex knowledge: An empirical investigation. *Journal of Educational Computing Research, 12*(4), 301-333.

Lillard, A. S. (1993). Pretend play skills and the child's theory of mind. *Child Development, 64*(2), 348-371.

O'Neill, C. (1989). Dialogue and drama: The transformation of events, ideas, and teachers. *Language Arts, 66*(5), 528-540.

Vedeler, L. (1997). Dramatic play: A format for "literate" language? *British Journal of Education Psychology, 67*,153-167.

Winston, J. (1998). *Drama, narrative and moral education*. London, Falmer.

Wolf, S. A. (1994). Learning to act/acting to learn: Children as actors, critics, and characters in classroom theatre. *Research in the Teaching of English, 28*(1), 7-44.

Wolf, S. A. (1995). Language in and around the dramatic curriculum. *Journal of Curriculum Studies, 27*(2), 117-137.

Helping Teachers implement Experience Based Learning

Jayashree Roy, Debbie Richards, Yusuf Pisan

Department of Computing
Division of Information and Communication Sciences
Macquarie University
Sydney, Australia
Email: richards@ics.mq.edu.au

Abstract

Experience Based Learning (EBL) is a process in which real world problems are used to help and motivate students to identify, apply, collaborate and communicate their knowledge effectively. However, implementation of EBL requires substantial effort on the part of teacher involving new teaching strategies and significant course restructuring. Also, coming up with suitable problems and solutions in sufficient detail that still allow for creativity and individuality is time consuming and difficult. This project focuses on facilitating the development of a problem-based repository of teaching resources. We are developing a web-based system to capture valuable teaching resources that may otherwise be lost and provide a searchable repository of problems and solutions that can be reused in a number of different units, possibly being expanded on each reuse, to implement EBL.

Keywords

Experience Based Learning, Problem Based Learning, Intra-net use in conventional universities

1. Introduction to Experience Based Learning

Experience Based Learning (EBL), also known as problem-based learning (PBL), is a process in which real world problems are used to help and motivate students to identify, apply, collaborate and communicate their knowledge effectively [2]. This strategy helps promote life-long habits of learning. The modern history of problem-based learning began in the early 1970s at the medical school at McMaster University in Canada. Though its intellectual history can be traced earlier than this. Thomas Corts, president of Samford University, sees PBL as "a newly recovered style of learning" [1]. In his view, it embraces the question-and-answer dialectical approach associated with Socrates as well as the Hegelian thesis-antithesis-synthesis dialectic. As John Cavanaugh puts it: "It's like discovery-based learning in the 1960s. We knew about it; we didn't do it. Dewey talked about it when he talked about 'engagement.' Dewey had it right on the abstract level. We do the details better now, that's all, and that's because of advances in cognitive science and in technology." [1] EBL has found 80% acceptance in medical schools where it is used to teach students about clinical cases, either real or hypothetical [5]. However successes are reported in the in other fields such as the Humanities and Physics. Universities like University of Delaware [3] and Samford University in Alabama [4] have received grants for restructuring their teaching methods.

The interest in PBL is growing because research shows a higher quality of learning and it also feels right intuitively. PBL appears to reflect the way the mind actually works, not a set of procedures for manipulating students into learning. Hence in a problem-based approach to teaching and learning, both teachers and student interact where the intellectual commonalities between research and teaching can be noted. Apart from equipping students with a more lateral approach to problem solving so that they are able to handle the unstructured and unexpected problems of normal life, PBL fosters group work, social skills, independent investigation, high level of comprehension and mobilises prior knowledge more readily.

2. Issues in Implementing Experience Based Learning

The implementation of EBL requires substantial effort on the part of teacher. Coming up with suitable problems and solutions that allow for creativity and individuality is time consuming and difficult. EBL typically involves groupwork which requires managing the teams and training the tutors. Just providing a problem and a solution does not encourage the tutor or the student to engage with the problem and to guide without seeming to be hiding the answer. It also a difficult task to pose authentic problems with certain open-endedness about them. This approach helps to keep a constant interaction between teacher and student. [1]. When it comes to creating problems, John Cavanaugh says: "One place to start is to take your exams and work backwards. Take those word problems and essay questions and make cases out of them." [1] Loreta Ulmer, who teaches psychology at Delaware Technical and Community College, says it's hard work revamping a course into problems, "but after you've done it, the whole course becomes so exciting, you'd never go back." [3]

3. Facilitating the Development of Problem Based Resources

This project does not solve all of the problems identified above. This project is a first step to assist and encourage teachers in managing and accessing various teaching resources within the Computing Department that can be used in problem based teaching. The project will develop a web-based system to archive and retrieve teaching resources. As part of the project we have interviewed each teacher to discover what teaching resources they have and to raise awareness of the benefits of EBL. The goals of the project are:

1. Capture valuable teaching resources that may otherwise be lost.
2. Facilitate cohesion within a unit from one semester to the next.
3. Provide a searchable repository of problems and solutions that can be reused in a number of different units, possibly being expanded on each reuse.
4. Encourage a forum for discussion between teachers to implement EBL across a number of units.

The third and fourth goals are focused on providing a complete and integrated program of study for students that encourages them to develop complete and workable to real problems as opposed to toy or oversimplified problems often used in lectures. For example, a problem could be introduced in an Introductory Programming unit and code developed to solve part of it. In a Database unit a database can be built to support and improve the original solution. In another unit more efficient data structures and alternative algorithms could be explored. In a Communications unit students could look at network issues for this problem. A Web Design unit could build a web-based solution. A Human Computer Interaction unit could develop an interface to be used by the other units. Currently this scenario is not possible because these problems and solutions are not known or available across units in the department. We do not want students to rote learn solutions but to learn concepts. Expanding on and exploring alternatives to problems/solutions already seen should complement the concept building process. As each resource is archived it will be indexed according to the type of resource and keywords entered by the depositor. Problem statements, assignments, teacher worked solutions, selected assignment submissions, implemented systems, executables, case studies, reports, analysis and design models, lecture notes, code, databases, etc are all candidates for the repository.

For the project to achieve its goals teachers will need to occasionally add to the repository and be encouraged to use the resources. Currently we have a Master's student building the system. Further development will require a programmer, allocation of equipment, disk space, technical support and possibly purchase of software. Maintenance and appropriate procedures to handle access, version control, etc will need to be put in place. This involves an ongoing commitment at the department level as any major shift in teaching practice requires. These are the costs.

In summary we believe the benefits will outweigh the costs. These benefits are difficult to measure but can be broken into three main categories.

1. The benefit to lecturers are:
   a. A systematic way of storing a resource that a lecturer would like to keep track of and maybe make available to others.
   b. Problems can be explored in greater depth and more interesting issues considered since students are familiar with aspects of the problem already.
   c. A potential source of ideas, code, etc that can be used in implementing EBL.
2. The benefit to students are:
   a. They will be encouraged to solve problems for themselves.
   b. Selective material from prerequisite units can be made available to students who have transferred from other institutions or who have done the units many years prior.
   c. They gain a more comprehensive and deeper understanding of real problems and their solutions.
3. The benefits to the department:
   a. Resources may be reused requiring less duplication of effort.
   b. Greater cohesion of a program of study
   c. Greater consistency in unit content across semesters.

REFERENCES

[1] Rhem, J. (1998) Problem based learning : An Introduction *The National Teaching & learning forum* December 1998 Vol. 8 No.1 (www.ntfl.com)

[2] Savery, J. (1994, May). *What is problem-based learning?* Paper presented at the meeting of the Professors of Instructional Design and Technology, Indiana State University, Bloomington, IN.

[3] University of Delaware: Problem Based Learning Site http://www.udel.edu/pbl/

[4] University of Alabama http://www.ua.edu

[5] Vernon, D. T., & Blake, R. L. (1993). *Does problem-based learning work? A meta-analysis of evaluative research.* Academic Medicine, *68*(7) 550-563.

Knowledge Management and Reusability in Internet Based Learning

Bhavani Sridharan & Kinshuk
Department of Information Systems
Massey University, Palmerston North
New Zealand

ABSTRACT

The unparalleled advancement in information and communication technology has led to extensive use of Internet in learning environment. Creation and distribution of knowledge on such a phenomenal basis has in fact has trapped the learner's ability to digest and filter the superabundance of knowledge. In this background, this paper looks at the applicability of knowledge management in learning environment to enhance the learning systems and efficient use and reuse of available information.

1. Introduction

Use of the Internet in learning has increased many-folds in recent years, not only in distance education settings, but also in more traditional learning venues. This phenomenon can be attributed to the vast information available on the Internet all over the world, and its quick and easy availability with few mouse clicks. This ocean of information has created several concerns about the quality of the learning process.

In the following section we give brief account of the key concepts and components related to knowledge management. The second section examines the technology's role in knowledge management and Internet based knowledge management. The third section of this paper concentrates on the methodology and the architecture of knowledge management system in Internet based learning. Implementation aspects are discussed in the fourth section. The fifth section looks at the benefit of the proposed system and follows with the conclusion.

2. Key Concepts and Components in Knowledge Management

2.1 Knowledge Management in Business Process And Learning Process

There is no single unanimously accepted definition of knowledge management prevalent in the literature. To quote some representative sample, "Knowledge management is the explicit and systematic management of vital knowledge and its associated processes of creating, gathering, organizing, diffusion, use and exploitation. It requires turning personal knowledge into corporate knowledge that can be widely shared throughout an organization and appropriately applied" [1].

2.2 Components of Knowledge Management

The important components of knowledge management are people, content, culture, process, and technology [2]. People are the ones to produce, use and share knowledge. Content include knowledge, information and data about the subject to be shared and managed. Culture of sharing is crucial to the success of knowledge management and Internet based learning. Process and technology are integral part of knowledge management.

2.3 Link between Knowledge Management and Information Technology

Knowledge management is a synergy between data and information processing capacity [3] of information technology and the creative and innovative capacity of human being. No doubt, that the success of Internet based knowledge management depends on the Internet, intranets, relational databases, data warehouses, groupware and other high value technologies. Hybrid knowledge management [3] is expected to bring the best results. Technologies like communication technology, collaborative technology, artificial intelligence and business intelligence [4] could augment chances of success of knowledge management.

2.4 Internet Based Knowledge Management in Learning

The phenomenon of overloading of information to learners results in the learners inability to cope with the processing of increased amount of information availability. This is especially true during the training of application of complex concepts with steep learning curve, where initial mistakes by students are not corrected immediately hence leading to wrong neural connections and eventual failure. The problems are aggravated at high magnitude when learning takes place in a distant environment. Internet based knowledge management systems can prove to be efficient solution to manage these problems.

3. Methodology

3.1 Internet Based Knowledge Management Learning System's Architecture

The architecture for the knowledge management system is as follows: First step is to identify what exactly is the user looking for in terms of area of discipline, context of the query, type of resources, preferred format etc. The second step is to create a learner's profile with parameters like key interests, level of expertise in the subject, level of expectations, preferred method of learning and other relevant parameters will help to identify the critical factors for success. The third phase is to synthesis user query and user profile and its intended context. The fourth step is to get the results from the local knowledge base. If the search is not able to come up with appropriate results, the global web is searched for the appropriate links and resources. After the relevant materials are found from the global search, it's accuracy and authenticity needs to be established in the fifth step. The next phase, namely the sixth phase, is to organize newly found knowledge in such a way it can be accessed very fast before it can be appended to the local knowledge base. The last but the most important part is to presentation of knowledge with user adaptability.

4. Prototype/Implementation

Based on the architecture, a prototype system developed which will aim to guide the learners a guided discovery learning process. The guidance will be individualized, based on the behavioral attributes of the learner. The components of the prototype would be domain knowledge base, user knowledge base, knowledge engine, inference engine and Internet based interface. Domain knowledge base would contain local information, reference to Internet based remote information, and cache of frequently accessed information. Knowledge engine would help to

manipulate the acquired information and effective indexing and storage. Inference engine would enable retrieval of knowledge as per individual learner. Internet-based interface will provide adaptive representation of the knowledge to the learner. The discipline selected to test the prototype system was database concepts and tools. The choice of this domain stems from the fact that application of requires familiarization with numerous procedures.

5. Benefits of knowledge Management for Internet Based Learning

Knowledge management system in internet based learning would not only augment the teaching abilities of the provider and foster the learning abilities of students but also open new ways of integrating knowledge management concepts in the learning systems development process. This would definitely result in efficient use of time and other resources facilitating better reusability, sharing, pooling and collaboration in the learning process.

6. Conclusion

Synergy between knowledge management system and Internet based learning will bring forth a lot of untapped benefits in academic institutions, as there has not been much research in this area. Also, with the increasing popularity of on line learning, the use of knowledge management system in Internet based learning will have multiplier effect on reusability with large size classes.

References
[1] Skyrme, D. (1997). Knowledge management: Making sense of an Oxymoron. *Management Insight*, 2nd series, No.2, URL: http://www.skyrme.com/insights/22km.htm.
[2] Phillips, J. T. (2000). Will KM alter information managers' roles? *Information Management Journal*, 34 (3), 58.
[3] Malhotra, Y. (1998). Knowledge Management, Knowledge Organizations & Knowledge Workers: A view from the Front Lines. *Mail Business Newspaper*, February19, URL: http://www.brint.com/interview/maeil.htm.
[4] Knowledge Management through I-Nets. (1999). URL: http://www.indiainfoline.com/bisc/sskm.html.

Development of a Visualization System of Relationships among Papers

Youzou MIYADERA[1,] Sho TANABE[1], Kayoko OYOBE[1], Norifumi SUNAOKA[1], Setsuo YOKOYAMA[1] and Nobuyoshi YONEZAWA[2]

1) Tokyo Gakugei University, 4-1-1 Nukuikita, Koganei, Tokyo 184-8501, Japan
miyadera@u-gakugei.ac.jp
2) Kogakuin University, 2265-1 Nakano, Hachiouji, Tokyo 192-8822, Japan

Abstract

This study has developed a support system that can retrieve papers by using the paper-relationship diagrams (PRDs) that express the relationships among papers. The system has the following functions: (1) users can see various relationships among papers by visualizing of PRDs and (2) the visualization patterns can be changed dynamically by users' point of view.

1 Introduction

There are many ways of searching for scientific papers, for example, by checking published sources (including journals, conference proceedings, etc.), reviewing lists of references in the target paper, or by using various search engines including those available on the Web. However, all these methods have a number of problems. First, all are time-consuming. Second, the relationship between the paper you are looking for and other papers is not always clear. Third, it is impossible to find papers that do not include any keywords the user has specified.

To solve these problems, we developed a visualization system of the relationships among papers. The system provides to users various visualization patterns that are requested by their own point of view.

2 Development of the visualization system

Our system was developed by using Java/Swing for visualization and by using Perl and MySQL for database construction. The user can use our visualization system by using a web browser connected to a network. The system consists of two subsystems, a visualization database construction subsystem and a paper retrieval/paper-relationship visualization subsystem, as shown in Figure 1

Figure 2 shows the user interface. The interface is divided into the drawing part and the operating part. The operating part consists of a keyword input part, a text window for displaying information, a drawing constraints selection part, and a scaling slider.

By inputting words in the word input part, the user can retrieve papers that have the input word. In the drawing constraints selection part, the user can choose those by using buttons. The slider enables expansion and contraction of diagram coordinates making it easy for the user to understand the relationship between papers. Text panel displays detailed information about the paper. By clicking on the drawn node, the user can obtain the title of the paper, the year of its publication, the authors, its keywords and index words that are common between papers. By placing the cursor on the paper node, the user can obtain five index words that characterize the target paper. After the user's adjusting of the slider, the drawing conditions, and the others in the operation part, the relationship among papers can be visualized under the changed conditions by pushing the re-draw button. The target paper can be changed by double-clicking on the other nodes.

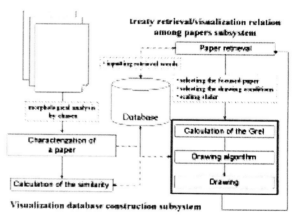

Figure 1. System Structure

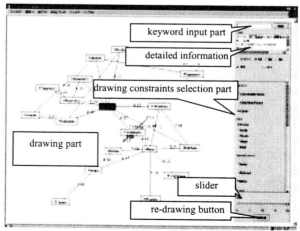

Figure 2. Interface

3 Search activities by using the system

Figure 3 is a pattern with the target paper in the center and reference papers arranged in the shape of a concentric circle around the target paper in the order of strength of the relationship. In the pattern, the user can find reference papers that the target paper was affected by, and determine the strength of the relationship between the target paper and the other papers.

Figure 4 express the refer/referred relationship between papers hierarchically with the target paper in the center. In Figure 4, the papers are arranged according to the year of publication, and the user can find the year when most of the papers were written.

Figure 5 shows the target paper and referenced papers arranged hierarchically, which enables the user to understand in what way the target paper contributes to the other papers. By following the reference chain, the user can see what field the target paper comes from.

Thus, the relationship between various papers can be visualized by using a combination of drawing constraints. By using the visualization system, users can see various relationships among papers by changing their own point of view, and can be supported their efficient search activities. Currently, there is no system for supporting research activities like our developed system. Our system can be therefore expected to widely use in the research field.

4 Conclusions

To implement the visualization of the relationship among papers, we formalized user requirements for visualization as a set of conditions on the graph drawing problem, and developed a system that visualizes the relationship among papers by combining various formalized constraints

In the future, we will improve the user interface and add a function to automatically convert user requirements for visualization into a combination of constraints.

References

[1] Miyadera, Y., Taji, A. and Yaku, T., Methods of Visualizing Paper-Relation Diagrams Based on the Viewpoints of Users, *Proc. Int. Conf. Human-Computer Interaction (HCI2001)*, pp.775-779, 2001.

[2] Anne Bruggemann-Klein, Rolf Klein: BibRelEx: Exploring Bibliographic Database by Visualization of Annotated Content-Based Relations, *Proc. IEEE Int. Conf. IV2000*, pp.19-24, 2000.

[3] Tanabe, S., Oyobe, K., Sunaoka, N., Yokoyama, S. and Miyadera, Y., A Visualization System of Relationships among Papers Based on the Graph Drawing Problem, *Proc. IEEE Int. Conf. IV2002*, 2002.

[4] http://www.cs.orst.edu/~burnett/vpl.html

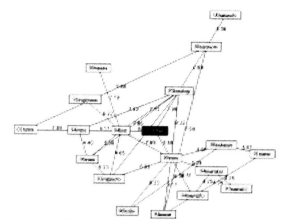

Figure 3. Drawing pattern 1

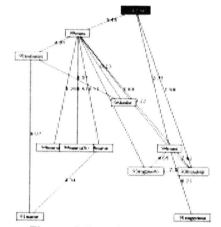

Figure 4. Drawing pattern 2

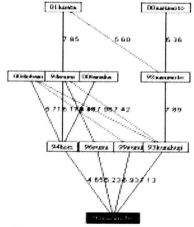

Figure 5. Drawing pattern 3

Proposal of an Adaptive Chinese Keyboard Typing Learning Environment

Peng-Wen Chen

Department of Computer Science and Information Engineering
Tamkang University, Taipei, Taiwan, R.O.C.
csviolet@tpts5.seed.net.tw

Abstract

Chinese keyboard typing is fundamental training at school in Taiwan. For the sake of sharp learning curve, many CAI systems have been used to help teaching and learning. However, these CAI systems highly focus on learning results (say speed, accurate rate, etc) rather than learning process. In this paper, we use adaptive learning strategy and agent-based technology to propose an adaptive Chinese-typing learning system and its relative course organization. We hope to help typing skill refinement according to one's personal learning condition.

Keywords: Adaptive Learning System, Keyboard Typing, Teaching Agent

1. Introduction

In the digital era, keyboard typing is fundamental training, which can help people do information processing. However, mapping 40 keys (except control and number keys) to more than 10,000 Chinese characters becomes an obstacle for Chinese to go into the computer world. For this reason, Chinese Keyboard Typing (CKT) is a basic course in almost every university in Taiwan. From our teaching experience of CKT in Tamkang University, Taiwan, we can find:

- The general CAI systems used today only can measure learning achievement (such as speed, accurate rate). They can not provide too much feedback according to each learner's learning condition.
- A teacher is hard to superintend so many students (60 on average) at the same time.
- Some students may lose learning motivation and interest when falling behind learning schedule.
- According to the questionnaire at keyboard typing class, more than 50% students feel that CKT is difficult. Even hard-working students make low progress if they make efforts in mechanical practice rather than refine skill according to their "stuck" points.

From our researches, Chinese keyboard typing is highly depended on mapping rules cognition, personalized practice and skill refinement. When someone tries to input a Chinese character, he or she does not only hit the right keys but also think about how to decompose this word. In such skill training, people fetch information, think, repeat, store, and interact with learning material and environment. These series of events reflected on each learner are the processes of mental transformation and behavior modification [1]. Therefore, the effects of CKT are influenced by personal learning process. From the pedagogy viewpoint, adaptive learning strategy is sufficient to support this personalized learning requirement [2]. However, we can find it is hard to achieve adaptive CKT in traditional teaching environment (with only one teachers and 60 students on average).

Hence, we propose and design an Adaptive Typing Learning and Assessment System (ATLAS) according to the highly "tracking and interaction" properties of computer systems.

2. Methodology

2.1. Analysis

We need some tracking items which can be used as decision rules in "adaptation process". After analyzing the actual learning activities, we can get several evaluation factors of CKT which include: confusing root (root is the smallest unit being used to compose a Chinese character), error key's position, decomposition order (getting code failed), miss-match key stroke, miss-applied decomposition rules, skipped words, etc.

2.2. Adaptive Course Organization

We use tree structure as fundamental skeleton to organize all learning information. In this learning tree, tree nodes represent the topics in the course material. Each leaf node is the smallest learning unit. Tree traversal will build a learning path that reflect each learner's learning state and sequence.

Besides content, we also include extra learning information in each node as we call it "learning requirement". Learning requirement is used to describe learning condition such as starting behavior, learning target, and mastery degree, etc. Figure1 is an example of a tree node in our course. In figure1, we can find practice will be bound within particular learning time, range of content, sequence and mastery level. System will give different practice content at the same level till one passes through the "threshold". We use XML mechanism to describe the whole course information. Using XML description will facilitate integrating into automatic system.

Figure 1. Example of course node

Course Level: fundamental
Request Time: 20 min
Range and Ratio:
      code1: ASDF=40%
      code2: JKL;=40%
      code3: GH=20%
Pre-Request: Node0015~Node0022
Post-Request: Node0024+
Behavior Target: (Typing Rate = 40+, Accurate Rate = 96%+)
Mastering Target: (Speed, Accuracy Rate, Action)
      Low=(30%,70%,Supplement)
      Mid=(65%,85%,Grade)
      Threshold=(80%,75%,Next)

2.3. ATLAS system

Several researches have pointed out agent-based technology can be used to construct personal learning environment [3,4]. Therefore, we design a teaching agent in the Adaptive Typing Learning and Assessment System (ATLAS). The functionalities of teaching agent are guided by:

- Teaching agent must keep track of personal learning records such as online persistent time, valid learning time, idle time, topic repetition times, interaction records, online assessment results and times, key strokes records, mastery degree, etc.
- Learners can fetch his or her personal course material and learning state at any time and any place. In other words, it can achieve "learning on demand".
- It can control each topic's mastery degree along the pre-define learning path.
- It can dynamically provide adaptive examination. The content of tests will follow instructor's teaching target and each learner's learning condition.
- It can do analysis of learning behavior and process. System will adjust teaching material and modify learning path to fit personal one's need according to these analyzed data. Online learning does not just reading electronic books page by page. The most important is finding stuck points and do modification.

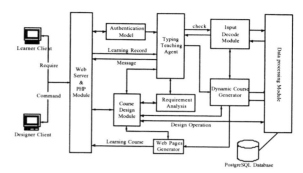

Figure 2. Software Architecture of ATLAS

ATLAS is an online learning and assessment platform based on client/server architecture. We use FreeBSD as course material server and use HTTP protocol to communicate between client and server. It means that client site can cross platform if there is a browser in it. In ATLAS, we use PHP scripts language with Apache web server and PostgreSQL database to design teaching agent. Each HTTP request will be kept by teaching agent for further analysis. System architecture is illustrated in figure 2. In addition, ATLAS server also provides functionalities for management purpose. Instructors can manage course material and learners' records online

3. Conclusion

In this paper, we explore the current difficulties of Chinese keyboard typing. We also provide an adaptive learning environment and its course organization. The assessment and management part of ATLAS has completed and used in class since summer, 2001. We still continuously work on the Typing Teaching Agent module in figure 2. The learning activities of keyboard typing are simpler than other curricula. Does the adaptive course organization and agent architecture provided in this paper suit for other curricula needs further research.

4. Reference

[1] Robert E. Slavin, "Educational Psychology", 4ed, Allyn and Bacon, 1994.
[2] Keller, "Personalized System of Instruction", 1968.
[3] Serengul Guven, "ML Tutor: A Web-based educational adaptive hypertext system", IEEE, 1999.
[4] Koyama, Barolli, etc. "An Agent-based Personalized Distance Learning System", IEEE, 2001.

Manga University:
Web-based Correction System for Artistic Design Education

Takeshi Sugiyama, Tsuneko Kura, Naoyuki Kakehi, Tokiichiro Takahashi
NTT Cyber Solutions Laboratories
3-9-11, Midori-cho, Musashino-shi, Tokyo, Japan, 180-8585
{sugiyama.takeshi, kura.tsuneko, kakehi.naoyuki, toki.takahashi }@lab.ntt.co.jp

Abstract

In Artistic design education, the teacher instructs each student individually face to face. As a result, it is difficult to share coaching with a third party or to teach distantly. To solve these problems, we have developed Manga University, which is a web-based application to aid artistic design education. It enables distant teaching or shared teaching and provides learning portfolio for collaboration. It is applicable several other types of artistic design education, such as fashion design or GUI design for software or the web.

1. Introduction

We have developed Manga University, which is a web-based correction system for artistic design education. It enables students to easily submit their contents and enables teacher to directly coach by drawing something on the web. It also enables teachers and other students to look back at students' histories and lets other students share the correction. These days, there are many web-based education systems. However, there are few systems for artistic design education. It is difficult to aid it by information technology because it has some unique features, such as face-to-face coaching. We made a prototype and used it to aid lessons on how to creating Manga, which is Japanese cartoons or comics, by forty students and four teachers at Kyoto Seika University (KSU) from May to September 2001. The results of that experiment show that our prototype was effective for artistic design education [1]. But, it did not have enough functions, such as to handle multiple contents. We consider the features of artistic design education and picked up its problems. Manga University solves these problems. This paper explains the problems of artistic design education and describes how Manga University solves them.

2. Problem

Artistic design education has three main features.

- **Individual face to face coaching**
  The teacher instructs each student individually face to face because the instruction points depend on the student's level or personality. It enables adaptive coaching. However, it is impossible for other persons to see other coaching. As a result, it is difficult to share coaching with a third party, such as other teachers or other students.

- **Teachers usually create objects**
  Some teachers are professional artists. However, they do not have much time available for teaching and must travel from their studios to the student's school. So, it sometimes is difficult to coach face to face.

- **Direct Coaching through the creations**
  Usually the teacher directly corrects the student through his creations. It directly lets the student understand important points or how he should re-create. However, it needs face to face coaching.

3. Solution

To satisfy these requirements, we propose a web-based application to aid artistic design education. It uses the Internet, a database and an electronic drawing board. Using the Internet, it is possible for the teacher to coach the students remotely anytime, anywhere, at his convenience. The database allows everyone to easily share the coaching. This has a multiplying effect for students because they can be exposed to viewpoints

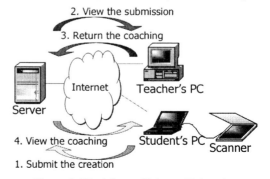

Figure 1: Workflow of Manga University

other than their own. Moreover, the database enables them look back over the past and refer their history as a personal portfolio. It supports the management of individual histories and shared coaching. Finally, to solve the problem caused from direct coaching through creations, we propose using drawing tools running on a web browser. This lets the teacher directly coach the students through their creations via the web. We developed a web-based correction system for artistic design education, which is called "Manga University". Figure 1 shows its workflow. The student submits his scanned creations to a server via the Internet. The teacher looks at them and coaches directly using a drawing board in a browser. After coaching, the teacher uploads the corrections to the server.

4. System Configuration

We employed the following approach to develop Manga University to satisfy the above requirements.

- **Web-based archiving system**

As a web-based archiving system, we employed CyberPedia, which is a multimedia archiving system [2]. We modified CyberPedia by adding some features, such as history management, to handle multiple contents and bulletin boards for each submission. It lets students archive and manage their submissions and acts as a personal portfolio and supports collaborative creation with peers. It overcomes temporal/spatial restriction, shares the teacher's coaching and stores the coaching history. Figure 2 shows a sample of a submission in teacher site. You can see plural thumbnails of contents.

Figure 2: Details of Submission

- **Available Drawing Tool on the Web**

As an available drawing tool, we employed CollaBoard, which is an ActiveX component for drawing images on the web [3]. It lets teachers correct through the contents on the web using Scalable Vector Graphics (SVG) [4]. It enables objects to be drawn directly. It also enables several teachers to correct individually because CollaBoard provides multi-layer control. Figure 3 shows an example of correction using CollaBoard.

We paid considerable attention to design of the

graphical user interface because it should be easy for anyone to use. For example, to enable easy browsing of the contents, we developed WebComic, which is a book-like browser.

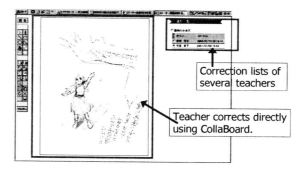

Correction lists of several teachers

Teacher corrects directly using CollaBoard.

Figure 3: Correction using CollaBoard

4. Experiment and Discussion

We ran an experimental Manga University in KSU from October to December 2001. We found that Manga University improved the efficiency of instruction, allowed coaching anytime and anywhere, made creative activity compatible with instruction, reflected teaching or learning history, and allowed peers to share the coaching. Additionally, it raised students' motivations to create, such as submitting many extra creations besides homework assignments.

5. Conclusion

Manga University can assist artistic design education effectively. It not only improves the efficiency of instruction but also improves students' motivations to create. It also enables shared teaching and provides learning portfolio for collaboration. It is applicable not only to Manga but also several other types of artistic design education, such as fashion design or GUI design for software or the web. It can also assist coaching about creating animation or movie, submitting storyboard and video contents. Moreover, it can be used for collaborative design work by distant creators.

6. References

[1] T. Kura et al., "Development of Web-based Correction System for Design", proceedings of IEICE, 2002 (Japanese)
[2] T. Kura et al., "CyberPedia", Proceedings of WebNet2001, pp. 730-731, 2001.
[3] T. Sugiyama and T. Takahashi, "CollaBoard", Proceedings of WebNet2001, pp. 1190-1191, 2001.
[4] W3C Scalable Vector Graphics (SVG)[ON-LINE] "http://www.w3.org/Graphics/SVG/ "

How Electronic Portfolios Add Coherence to Educational Programs

David Georgi and Penny Swenson
dgeorgi@csub.edu, pswenson@csub.edu
California State University, Bakersfield
9001 Stockdale Highway
Bakersfield, California 93311

Abstract

CSU Bakersfield has been implementing electronic portfolios into several of its programs. This poster will showcase applications in online Educational Technology Master's program and in a technology proficiency certification program for K-12 and university instructors. Master's program was begun in fall, 2001 and is being developed in partnership with Connected University. Selected classes include a digital exhibit that addresses the a program theme. A capstone class assists students in assembling the exhibits and creating a portfolio demonstrating program objectives, which is given a public presentation much like a doctoral defense. The certification program has been in place for three years using hard copy portfolios, resulting in dramatic changes in the teaching learning process in local schools. At this time more than 3000 educators have been certified. An electronic version was developed recently and will be demonstrated. Copies of the instruments used are available online

Introduction

CSU Bakersfield has found electronic portfolios (e portfolios) have enhanced its educational programs by adding coherence and addressing some issues unique to the institution. CSUB is the only comprehensive regional university in a service area that is larger than several New England states. The population is largely rural and in poverty. Electronic portfolios address such needs as:

- Serving the needs of working students who often have to take time off for financial and personal reasons
- Adding perceived coherence to programs by having a single system encompass all courses, serve as connection threads throughout the programs, and allow the program objectives to be seen as unified by the completion of all required exhibits
- Emphasizing the application of knowledge and skills on real-world problems
- Using an assessment system in which rubrics clearly demonstrate the skill levels attained
- Providing access to wide-ranging students

E Portfolios in Graduate Programs

CSUB had a Curriculum and Instruction Masters Program in Education that was a traditional face to face model. The size of the service area created a hardship for many students in rural locations. CSUB partnered with Connected University in fall, 2001 to begin an online MA program with a technology emphasis. CSUB was able to apply some of CUs class modules and instructors to its program, adding richness and versatility that was lacking because of the few CSUB instructors available. CU also makes the program available to its world-wide audience, ensuring full sections of classes. By being accessible anytime/anywhere, students in distant locations or with frenetic work schedules can be served.

CSUB had a Curriculum and Instruction Masters Program in Education that was a traditional face to face model. The size of the service area created a hardship for many students in rural locations. CSUB partnered with Connected University (CU) in fall, 2001 to begin an online MA program with a technology emphasis. CSUB was able to apply some of CUs class modules and instructors to its program, adding richness and versatility that was lacking because of the few CSUB instructors available. CU also makes the program available to its world-wide audience, ensuring full sections of classes. By being accessible anytime/anywhere, students in distant locations or with frenetic work schedules can be served.

CSUB has developed a plan to use electronic portfolios to provide students with a sense of coherence as they move through it. Four classes will include assignments to create an electronic exhibit reflecting the objectives of the class. A capstone class will help students assemble their exhibits and add a final exhibit that synthesizes the program objectives. The portfolios will be publicly presented in this class, with students having the option of coming to a central location or participating in a video conference. The interaction among the students is expected to provide a depth of reflection that would not be attainable by traditional means.

CSUB is currently piloting the use of TaskStream < www.taskstream.com >, an online application provider, to house e portfolios that demonstrate the standards that must be met in teacher credential programs.

E Portfolios for Technology Proficiency Certification

In 1997, California adopted a new technology standard for teachers. CSUB collaborated with California Technology Assistance Project Region 8 (CTAP8), a state agency that provides technology resources for teachers. The collaboration resulted in a system of technology proficiency certification based on the state standard, but going beyond it. The state listed two sets of skills, one for students entering a credential program (Level I) and one for teachers earning their credential (Level II). CTAP8 developed a rubric for each of these two levels and went on to develop skill sets for Level III, which could be earned in two areas: Mentoring and Leadership.

The system was adopted by all school districts in the county and by CSUB's School of Education. All instructors are expected to earn Levels I and II. Coherence was added to professional development activities because training sessions could target skills at either level. In addition, skills were seen as part of a holistic continuum of skills by the portfolio assessment process. Teachers completing a portfolio had proof that they had mastered a range of skills. As the process became widely used in schools, a change in culture could be detected. Once a significant minority of teachers attained Level II, the majority were motivated to catch up. Schools offered incentives of stipends and frequent trainings to assemble the portfolios. Two federal grants (StarTEC <www.startecproject.org/>and Project TNT <www.projecttnt.com>) provided trainings, equipment and stipends for attaining proficiencies. There are currently over 3000 certified educators in the service region and CTAP8 has plans on getting a majority of local educators to Level II within three years.

The existence of Level III provided acknowledgement of those teachers who had advanced technology skills. Other teachers could go to them for support, addressing the need for widespread and quick assistance. Level III teachers are empowered to certify those at Level I and II, thus providing the staffing capacity to make the system efficient. Further, Level III teachers could be paid to conduct workshops, write technology grants and provide other technological services.

The hardcopy portfolio system has been very successful in raising the level of technology proficiency among local educators. The development of an electronic model is bringing the system to the next level. Placing portfolios on a web site or CD makes them easily accessible from any location in the county. The contents can be easily adapted to other uses, such as demonstration of skills in job interviews or having a rich vita with many electronic examples.

A model portfolio including the html file structure is available at <http://www.csub.edu/~dgeorgi/pres_refs/ctap8georgiIIIportfolio/index.htm>. Examples of the CTAP8 system, including online examples of exhibits at each proficiency level, can be seen at <http://www.ctap.org/ctc/>

CSUB is in the process of integrating e portfolios in the programs described in this paper, which can be accessed at<http://www.csub.edu/~dgeorgi/pres_refs/366geo.doc> with active links.

A Strategic Analysis of the Online Learning Community for Continuing Professional Development of University Faculty in Taiwan: A SWOT Analysis

Tzy-Ling Chen, Assistant Professor
Agricultural Extension Education
National Chung-Hsing University
250 Kao-Kung Rd., Taichung, Taiwan
Email: tlchen@nchu.edu.tw

Tzu-Jung Chen, Graduate Student
Department of Human Resource Education
University of Illinois-Urbana-Champaign
United States of America
Email: txchen@uiuc.edu

Abstract

This paper delineates an instrumental multi-case study conducted in Taiwan with university faculty. The study explores higher education teachers' standpoints concerning adoption of online learning community (OLC) as a strategy for continuing professional development (CPD) taking advantage of the technique frequently applied to program planning or decision making analyses on internal effects of Strength and Weakness as well as external possibilities of Opportunity and Threat (SWOT). In the end, discussions of use of OLC for CPD of university faculty in Taiwan are elaborated.

CPD of University Faculty as a Shared Concern

By definition, CPD is stated as the systematic maintenance, improvement and broadening of knowledge and the process of developing personal qualities necessary for professional services and technical duties throughout practitioners' working lives through continuing education[1]. In the context of education, today's constantly evolving educational environment has resulted in great demands on teachers of all levels and in all areas to engage themselves in CPD. Besides imperatives of survival, maintenance, and mobility, it is also pivotal to comprehend the concept of "worthwhileness" interpreted by Jarvis (1983) as the underlying motivation for CPD [2]. For example, to improve competences and promote the feeling of self-worth within the current role, to become qualified for career progression as well as learn how to learn effectively and engage in learning its intrinsic worth and so on.

In Taiwan, there emerges a boost in number of practicing teachers of all levels engaging themselves in CPD for the purpose of professional growth, and meanwhile, meeting the requirements of institutional performance evaluations. However, of all efforts made to explore teachers' CPD, seldom there exist less than few inquiries to probe and discuss issues emphasizing on CPD of university faculty as a target group. Basically, almost all universities in Taiwan have a ternary mission, involving teaching, research, and extension services. As for university faculty members, not only they need to carry on interdisciplinary research in relate to their expertise and/or of their interests, but also it is required of them to engage in the effective transfer of innovative knowledge and technology to meet public needs by integrating research findings and collaborating with experts from different field as well as peer colleagues from different programs, departments, and colleges within or outside universities they serve. In consequence, university teachers commonly work with other practitioners of various kinds, which may raise their awareness of alternative ways of working and additional areas of knowledge and be classified as informal, project-based, or self-directed learning of CPD. The value of shared understanding between professionals from different fields and disciplines may further serve as the infrastructure upon which learning communities are established. It is also true that meanings pertaining to such interactions and dialogues have been long recognized as important in meeting the needs of college students and adult learners with a wide range of personal experiences and backgrounds. But, due to a lack of efforts to transform and include them as a set of criteria in the performance evaluation system for faculty's tenure as well as promotion review, CPD practice of university faculty in Taiwan seems restricted and limited in terms of variance in activities and methods, and effectiveness.

Strategic analysis of OLC for CPD of University Faculty

With the advent of Internet technologies, the process of conveying information and knowledge has become overtly different comparing to what used to be decades ago. In addition, not only synchronous online learning events possible have been made possible, but also they encourage the development of learning communities where individual learners can create their own lifelong learning plans by taking advantage of the strengths of all forms of learning opportunities. It has been also evidenced that interactive online learning contributes to unique benefits those traditional formal, face-to-face-based CPD methods can impossibly achieve (Miller & Smith, 1998[3]; Oelrich, 2001[4]). As confirmed, much of the success of OLC comes from productive, online threaded discussions through which learners involved are able to construct their own understanding[5]. In this sense, OLC is assumed in this paper that it can provide university faculty with an alternative to initiate and pursue CPD for successfully meeting the concomitant needs for individuals to update themselves, to remain competent and continue to contribute themselves to universities as valued and productive members, and to enhance their mobility in the labor market. As a four-part approach of SWOT analysis aims to explore strengths, weaknesses, opportunities, and threats of a strategy or plan for action, overall it is viewed as a very effective tool designed to be employed in the preliminary stages of decision-making and as a precursor to strategic planning in various kinds of applications (Dugger, 1995[6]; Collett, 1999[7]). It is, thus, utilized as a decision-making aid for analysis when OLC is suggested as a strategy for use to engage university faculty in CPD in this study.

Qualitative Case Study Methodology

Built upon the framework of SWOT analysis, an acronym in which four letters of strength, weakness, opportunity, and threat stand for, this study utilized an instrumental, multiple-case method as the primary research design. For a fundamental characteristic of the instrumental case study is attributed to its focus on an issue with the case used instrumentally to illustrate the issue (Creswell, 1998[8]), it was adopted to help better capture research participants' perceptions in regard to the OLC used as a current strategy for CPD. The major objectives of this research are twofold. First, the research aimed to identify strengths and weaknesses of the application of OLC as the CPD strategy among university faculty. The second objective then involved an examination of where these participants can and should go from there. The data collection of a case study research design is extensive, drawing on multiple sources of information, including observation, interview, questionnaire survey, documentation, archival record, and physical artifact, etc. The data collection strategy employed in this research is semi-structured interview. In accordance with qualitative methodology, three participants were selected based on criterion-oriented purposeful sampling. Not only the richness of information an individual case can provide was taken into account, but to be included in the study, the participants have to meet the following requirements: from the four-year universities in Taiwan with a ternary mission, involving teaching, research, and extension services, from any OLC, such as listserv or Web-based discussion group, etc., and consented to be interviewed. Participants all represented the field of agriculture. A more detailed description of three selected participants is illustrated in Table 1, below.

Table 1 Profiles of Three Taiwanese University Faculty

Code	Job Title	Age	Teaching	OLC Joined
Mr. A	Associate Pro.	42	9yrs	4
Mr. B	Pro.	47	12yrs	1
Miss C	Assistant Pro.	30	3yrs	3

Participant codes were assigned to each interviewee to protect anonymity during analysis. An open-ended interview guide was used for each audio taped face-to-face interview. The interview guide consisted of questions that explore participants' perceptions regarding application of OLC for their CPD. Interview questions included:

1. What is "golden" about the OLC in terms of CPD?
2. What kind of learning experiences do you have in participating in OLC?
3. What looks a bit rusty about OLC in terms of CPD?
4. What do you think OLC can be improved for helping attain better learning experiences?
5. What new needs of learners can OLC meet?
6. What are the emerging trends that benefit the development of OLC?
7. What are the negative trends?
8. Where is OLC vulnerable?

All interviews were subsequently transcribed and analyzed for key ideas, key participant comments, discrepancies in responses, and reactions to questions covered in the interview guide. Miles and Huberman (1994) illuminate that an audit trail as a method of logging and describing our procedures and data clearly enough so that others can understand, reconstruct, and scrutinize them[9]. The truthworthiness is contingent upon the audit trail being complete, comprehensible, and systematically related to methodological approaches[10].

Conclusion

Overall, the participants viewed OLC predominantly as a beneficial and useful strategy for CPD for its convenience, easy-to-use, interactive, and resource richness if resources and contents provided can ensure faculty to return and use them regularly. Findings further revealed that participation of OLC is highly related to faculty involvement in CPD. In other words, when faculty members have voluntarily dedicated themselves more to the pursuit of learning for updating their competencies and for professional growth, more likely they may become an active member of a professional OLC, which can be recognized as "integral or adept participants." A lot of these integral participants are also highly literate in terms of skills of using online technologies. If the case is that they engage in CPD as only by required to maintain certain level of knowledge and skills to become equipped for the job, it is suitable to classify them as "involved participants" of OLC. Other than these two types of participants, the rest of faculty is considered as "potential participants" for OLC is, in fact, perceived as a valuable strategy for faculty to participate in CPD. Many potential participants may eventually become so-called "lurkers" in OLC because some of them are satisfied with getting involved in this way. In this sense, the development of OLC will be faced and challenged with the needs of a variety of participants' types and learning styles as well. Constraints in use of OLC for engaging faculty in CPD as evidenced according to the analysis include a lack of reward and support systems for facilitating faculty participation, computer illiterate and phobic as well as distrust and uncertainty of network relations.

Reference

[1] Guest, G. (1999). Towards lifelong professional learning, Adult Learning, 11(4): 23-25.
[2] Jarvis, P. (1983). Professional education. Beckenham: Croom Helm.
[3] Miller, C., & Smith, C. (1998). Professional development by distance education: Does distance lend enhancement? Cambridge Journal of Education, 28(2): 221-230.
[4] Oelrich, K. (2001). Virtual schools: A 21st century strategy for teacher professional development, Journal of Technological Horizons in Education, 28(11): 48-50.
[5] Johnson, D. W., & Johnson, R. (1999). Learning together and alone: Cooperative, competitive, and individualistic learning. Needham, MA: Allyn and Bacon.

Rest of Reference is Available from Authors Upon Request

Minimum computer literacy at tertiary institutions – who's responsibility is it?

Matthew C. F. Lau, Rebecca B. N. Tan
Gippsland School of Information Technology, Monash University, Victoria 3842, Australia
Email: Matthew.Lau@infotech.monash.edu.au, Rebecca.Tan@infotech.monash.edu.au

Abstract

The widespread use of information and communication technology in education and in the community has led to a higher expectation of prospective students' level and type of computer competency. Currently, most higher education institutions in Australia do not require a minimum entry requirement in computer skills. This applies even to computing degrees. For most undergraduate degrees, entry depends on students' meeting the minimum TER (Tertiary Entry Requirements) score of the respective degree including passes in English and Mathematics. Lecturers, especially those lecturing in first level programming subjects, cannot assume any prior computer knowledge for either on-campus (full-time) or distance education (DE) (part time) students although many of the latter courses are frequently highly dependent on computers. This paper focuses on the difficulties facing teachers in the higher education sector, most notably due to the variable computer abilities of students coming in to tertiary institutions, the issue of equity and resources, and special issues related to mature age students.

INTRODUCTION

The use of information and communication technology (ICT) is becoming more widespread in education and in the wider Australian workforce and community (Australian Education Council 1990, Australian Government Publishing Service, 1997). There is an assumption that school leavers are a generation of computer literate individuals but the level of skill is not uniformly high (Meredyth et al, 1999, Lim and Lee, 2000)

This paper focuses on the difficulties facing lecturers in the higher education sector, most notably the variable computer abilities of students and their differing access to computer facilities. Four main questions were analysed:

1. Should there be a minimum tertiary entrance computer ability requirement?
2. Should higher education or secondary education be responsible for a minimum standard of computer skills?

3. What are the implications of this in terms of equity and resourcing?
4. How would this effect mature age students?

1. Should there be a minimum tertiary entrance computer ability requirement?

A decade ago the introduction of minimum compulsory formal school based computer courses was not considered urgent. However, in this Internet age, there seems to be clear and widespread agreement among the public and educators that computer usage for a range of learning tasks is now as much a part of a student's basic learning toolkit, as taking notes or reading texts though computer competency requirements may vary from discipline to discipline. A proposed computer competency course could include topics like basic computer concepts, use of basic application packages and tools, and basic knowledge of the Web or the Internet. This is in line with the syllabus used in the International Computer Driving License Scheme (ICDL) introduced to Australia in 2000 by the Australian Computer Society (ACS).

Whatever the reasons, schools and universities have to deal with the current reality and must work towards removing it as an issue. Therefore, the answer to the above question is – Yes, there should be a minimum tertiary entrance computer requirement although obtaining a consensus among the universities would almost be impossible to achieve.

2. Is it the responsibility of higher education or secondary education to equip students with a minimum standard of computer skills?

Where does the responsibility lie? This is contentious issue. It is too late for students and irresponsible of secondary schools to shift the responsibility to higher education institutions. It is the responsibility of secondary education to equip students with a minimum standard of computer skills, with optional of a higher-level courses for students keen on pursuing a computer-related tertiary programs. The government must ensure that there is a consistent long-term policy on objectives of information technology in secondary schools. Tertiary institutions, generally better equipped in terms of physical, financial and academic resources, should be responsible for identifying the need for generic computer literacy training for all commencing students.

University lecturers must not assume any prior computer knowledge among students involved in first year programming subjects. However, lecturers could quickly bring up to speed the computer background knowledge required within the first two-three weeks, thereby satisfying the needs of the majority of the students.

3. What are the implications of this in terms of equity and resourcing?

It might not be possible for every secondary school to have adequate resources to provide students with the minimum standard of computer literacy skills. The government must ensure that there is a consistent funding policy for IT in secondary schools. Again the minimum standard is often not static. IT changes rather quickly. The goal posts keep shifting. Topics like multimedia and Internet were not even thought of until a few years ago. Few schools would have teachers proficient in the newer applications of computer technology. Hopefully, tertiary institutions can do the rest.

4. How would this effect mature age students?

Mature age students cannot be assumed to have prior knowledge or exposure to computers at either primary or secondary schools although a significant number of the working adults could be highly computer literate. Those who have no prior computer knowledge and who would have not undertaken any computer literacy classes could experience anxiety (Glass & Knight, 1988). A separate program for these mature age students would provide the lecturer with more opportunity to cater for individual needs, although this would only be appropriate for on-campus students. Alternatively, incoming students could be provided with a WebCT CD-ROM and/or on-line computer literacy program. Many universities have adopted this approach.

CONCLUSION

The questions posed do not seem to have a simple answer for secondary and tertiary students as far as computer training is concerned, although there is agreement that tertiary students require a basic level of computer competency. How this competency is achieved is still open to debate. In an ideal world, students would all enter tertiary institutions with well-developed skills in reading, writing, critical analysis, basic mathematics and computer applications. However, the reality is that with a very broad spectrum of secondary schools, some schools

prepare students very well whilst others do less well. There are a few affluent, well-resourced private schools where IT is well integrated into the curriculum and skills are well developed. This contrasts with some less affluent, government schools that struggle for resources. Given that not all secondary schools are likely to receive a massive boost in funding in the near foreseeable future, it would be hard to mandate yet another tertiary entrance requirement that could further marginalise less fortunate secondary school students.

One solution is for tertiary institutions to become more sensitive, sympathetic, and aware of the varying degree of ability of prospective students and provide a range of specifically tailored bridging courses, on-campus or on-line, for the various student cohorts including mature age students. Indeed, this appears to be a common approach taken by most universities. Perhaps our questions cannot really be answered. If it is accepted that it is the responsibility of the tertiary sector to provide computer education to new students, this could potentially be interpreted as relieving the secondary school sector of its duties in this area. Perhaps it should be seen as a shared responsibility.

REFERENCES :

Australian Computer Society Inc: http://www.acs.org.au/icdl/index1.htm

Australian Education Council (1990) *A National Statement on Mathematics for Australian Schools* Carlton (Vic): Curriculum Corporation (Australia)

Australian Government Publishing Service (1997) *Business Use of Information Technology* Canberra: Australian Government Publishing Service

Glass, C. R., Knight, L. A., (1988) *Cognitive Factors in Computer Anxiety,* Cognitive Therapy and Research, 12(4), 351-366.

Lim, K.F. and Lee, J. (2000). *IT skills of university undergraduate students enrolled in a first year unit.* Australian Journal of Educational Technology, 16(3), 215-238

Meredyth, D., Russell, N., Blackwood, L., Thomas, J., and Wise, P. (1999). *Real Time: Computers, Change and Schooling.* Canberra: Department of Education, Training and Youth Affairs

Cultural Change for the E-World.

Professor Dawn Forman,
University of Derby, UK

In the transition to e-learning, many institutions provide some face to face delivery alongside their e-learning delivery. The spectrum ranges from the traditional face to face delivery, with lecturing through to full e-learning, and it is anticipated for the next 5 years, at least, that the majority of delivery will be in the middle of the spectrum and provide a mixed mode of delivery. Nevertheless, there will be some programmes, which can be delivered purely in e-learning mode, and some e-learners who want to study purely by this method. It is this end of the spectrum with which the design factors of e-learning need to be considered.

In order to think through all the elements of e-learning delivery, one has to consider what McKey (2000) describes as the "total student experience". McKey lists 4 key factor for consideration. The first factor to ensuring the e-learners experience is a positive one, is ensuring the **administration** is geared to support the e-learners through all aspects of their on-line experience. Administration, in this context, takes on board the traditional roles of enrolment and monitoring an e-learner performance, plus the link with the tutor but in the e-learning context administrators also have a key role in communicating with: quality assurance departments; the marketing department; the learning resource centre; the technology provider. Last but certainly not least, administrators need to ensure there is a good communication link to the e-learners themselves who will expect, an almost immediate feedback on the queries or concerns they may have.

The second factor of McKey's model is that of the **education provision.** The provision of e-learning programmes to e-learners can be thought of in 2 stages:

1. Designing the materials

In looking at the design of the materials, it is clear that the e-learners will study, in different ways to that of a traditionally taught student. To appropriately design materials, which will stimulate and encourage the e-learners to study, the designer must park most of their traditional ways of portraying information and reconsider what e-learners expectations and ways of studying will be.

2. Support from the academic

In order to achieve what Pollard and Hillage (2001) described as cost effective advantage of e-learning delivery, the support from the academic or e-

moderator must be both effective and appropriate, but limited. In order to ensure that this is the case, administrative and technical support is provided for the majority of e-learner enquiries. Nevertheless, the e-moderators involvement in supporting the e-learner is vital but again different to that involved in the traditional delivery.

Salmons Five Step Model

Salmon (2000) has described the support from the academic, as a model for e-moderators involving with five steps. Ironically, the first steps start even prior to the e-learners enrolling and are a clear example of why the Marketing and Finance Departments need to be fully aware of the impact of the e-learning within the institutions.

The first step of Salmon's model is **access and motivation.** This stage has been found to be crucial, in order to allay the e-learners fears of the e-learning experience, therefore what is needed at this stage is a high level of rapid, timely and empathetic support which facilitates engagement and access to the new learning environment. Evidence shows from Salmon's work, that if this first stage is achieved, the retention of e-learners through out the programme is much higher than if this stage is ignored.

The second step is **on-line socialisation.** E-learning does not have verbal and visual clues, which is the norm in traditional delivery. It is always been the norm that in traditional delivery, the e-learner will learn as much from fellow e-learners and independent study as they do from the tutor. Without the on-line socialisation taking place this learning cannot be achieved in an e-learning environment.

The next step Salmon's model is **information exchange**. At this step, the e-learners are encouraged to look at a variety of resources where information can be provided, and are reminded not to rely purely on the information, which is provided in the programme. The moderators role at this stage is therefore to ensure that the e-learners concentration is on discovering and exploring issues.

The fourth step is **knowledge construction**. The e-learner should now have acquired the norms of interaction and be coming independent of the e-moderator. Dialogue will occur with other e-learners with whom they have found empathy and mutual understanding. The e-moderators role therefore is to ensure that the e-learners are grasping the concepts and theory.But overall the locus of power is moving to the e-learner and it is necessary to explain that this will be the case to them.

By step 5, **the development stage,** the participants are responsible for their own learning. This stage is for further exploration, synthesis and conceptualisation purposes. Learning at this stage will take place not only with regard to the topic, but also about the fellow e-learners' experiences. At this stage little or no additional support is required. If we now reconsider the McKey model and the third factor which is **functionality**, we see that this relates very much to the quality assurance and methods that are necessary to ensure that the materials and the methods of delivery are consistent and of a high standard.

The final factor of McKey's model is that of **presentation**. This not only relates to the professional presentation, nor merely to the support given from various departments interacting with the e-learner. The presentation internationally of the institutions provision must be appropriate, and this is where the Marketing Department's analysis of what e-learners are requiring and promote e-learning at the Institution, is paramount.

Conclusion

The cultural change, which is necessary within our higher education institutions in order to support the new E-World, is apparent throughout this paper. Such is a pace of change that no one higher education

institution can hope to achieve the benefits of this move in isolation. We need to learn from each other in partnership relationships, not only between the higher education institutions but also partnership with industry, commerce, public sectors and local communities. The provision of what was once described by Davies et al (1998), of a virtual University cannot be achieved in isolation.

Forman, D., (2001) The University of Derby E-Learning Manual. University of Derby.

Huws, U., Jaggar, N. Bates, P., Where the Butterfly Alights: the Global Location of E Work. IES Report 378, ISBN 1-85184-307-8

McKey, P. (2000) The Total Student Experience. White Paper, NextEd.

Pollard, E., Hillage, J., (2000) Exploring e- learning. IES Report 376, IBSN 1-85184-305-1

Salmon, G. (2001) E-Moderating - The Key to Teaching and Learning On Line, Kogan Page, London.

Teare, R., Davies, D., Sandelands, E., (1998) The Virtual University: An Action Paradigm and Process for Workplace Learning. Cassell. London.

**Diagram 1.
Modes of E learning**

**Diagram 2.
McKey Total Student
Experience Model**

**Diagram 3.
Salmons Five Step Model**

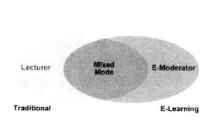

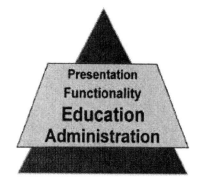

Learner Experiences in Online Courses

Angela D. Benson
University of Illinois at Urbana-Champaign

Abstract

This qualitative case study explored learner experiences in online courses. The study identified three categories of challenges that online learners face: learning perspective, technology, and course design; four coping strategies that learners used to address the challenges: Transform, Resist, Revise and Apply; and three categories of learning outcomes: skill acquisition, transformed learning perspectives, and revised learning perspectives.

Introduction

Online learning advocates position online education as superior to and distinctly different from traditional face-to-face education and distance education. These advocates also suggest that learners and instructors moving from either face-to-face education or distance education must undergo a transformation in their epistemic meaning perspectives (how they learn, what they think about the learning process) in order to experience the full benefits of online education [3][4].

Harasim [3], Eastmond [2] and Harasim, Hiltz, Teles,and Turoff [4] all agree that the traditional frameworks, or perspectives, that learners hold about learning may be inadequate for the online learning environment. Their discussion of changing frameworks and perspectives is similar to the concepts and terminology Mezirow [6] uses in his theory of perspective transformation. Mezirow [6] contends that learners can have distorted or undeveloped meaning perspectives which lead them "to view reality in a way that arbitrarily limits what is included, impedes differentiation, lacks permeability or openness to other ways of seeing, [and] does not facilitate an integration of experience" (p. 188). Mezirow's remedy for the distorted or undeveloped meaning perspective is the eleven-phase process of perspective transformation.

Purpose

The purpose of this qualitative study was: 1) to describe the learning experiences of students enrolled in an online graduate-level library media course, and 2) to identify their individual learning outcomes. Three

questions guided this study:
1. What challenges do learners face in online courses?
2. What coping strategies do learners adopt in online courses?
3. What are the learning outcomes for the students in online courses?

Background

The Instructional Technology Department at a southeastern Research I institution went online in 1999-2000 for four pre-service graduate-level school library media courses. This study includes the first two of these courses: Reference Materials (offered Fall 1999), and Administration (offered Winter 2000). The Reference Materials course was conducted fully online using the TopClass courseware system. The Administration course met face-to-face each week and was supplemented by a TopClass bulletin board discussion list.

Methodology

A collective qualitative case study design was used [7]. The unit of analysis was the individual participant who had completed both the Reference Materials and Administration courses [5].

Four participants (Barbara, Diane, April and Carolyn) were chosen using criterion-based sampling [5]. The selection criteria were: 1) the Reference Materials course was their first online course; 2) they completed both the Reference and the Administration courses; and 3) they had less than two years' Internet experience prior to enrollment in the Reference course. Carolyn had one and one-half years of Internet experience, Barbara and Diane had less than one year, and April had none. Each participant was enrolled in a master's program in Instructional Technology with the goal of beginning or continuing careers as school library media specialists.

A variety of data collection methods were used to enhance the comprehensiveness of the students [1]. On the first night of the Reference course, the students submitted written statements of their course expectations. Focus group interviews were conducted at the end of the each course. After both courses were completed, semi-structured one-on-one interviews were conducted with the four participants. In addition, a document analysis was conducted of the archived bulletin board messages from both courses and the archived e-mail messages between the instructor and the students in the Reference course.

The data analysis proceeded in two phases. Phase 1 was a within-case analysis of data from each participant. The data were open-coded, grouped into natural groupings, and categorized. Phase 2 was a cross-case analysis of the data from all four participants. During this phase, the categories were aggregated and their inter-relationships identified. During both phases, the emerging findings were reviewed with the course instructor, a senior researcher and two research peers.

Findings

What challenges do learners face in online courses?

This study identified three categories of challenges that online learners face: learning perspective challenges, technology challenges, and course design challenges. Each participant's personal history and pre-course learning perspectives were major factors in determining which challenges she faced.

What coping strategies do learners adopt in online courses?

This study identified four coping strategies that learners used to address the challenges they face in the online course: Transform, Resist, Revise and Apply. Each participant applied each of the strategies at some point during the course. The Transform strategy was used least often, while the Revise strategy was used most often.

In addition, each participant's course experience can be characterized by a single strategy. Barbara's predominate strategy was Transform as she was able to identify an instance in which her pre-course learning perspectives were transformed. Diane's predominate coping strategy was Resist as exemplified by her decision to cease participating in the discussion list. April's predominate coping strategy was Revise as indicated by her ability to revise (but not transform) her learning perspectives as she encountered and solved problems in the online course. Carolyn's predominate coping strategy was Apply as her pre-course learning perspectives were most compatible with the online learning environment.

What are the learning outcomes for the students in online courses?

This study identified three categories of learning outcomes for online learners: skill acquisition, transformed learning perspectives, and revised learning perspectives. Each of the participants experienced skill

acquisition, one experienced transformed learning perspectives, and two experienced revised learning perspectives. The Transform strategy resulted in transformed learning perspectives, while the Resist, Revise and Apply strategies led to skill acquisition or revised learning perspectives.

At the end of the course, all four participants had mastered the course content requirements as demonstrated by their all receiving a grade of "A." Diane, Barbara and April--the three participants with the least amount of Internet experience--gained competence and confidence in their use of Internet technologies. Diane and April demonstrated their competence by assisting others with lesser skills. In addition to gaining technical competence, Barbara also experienced a transformation of her learning perspectives and learned independence. Her application of this independence in interactions with her fellow teachers and with her students is evidence of the transformation. While Carolyn, the participant with the most Internet experience, gained content knowledge, she did not express any gain in technical competence or any transformation in learning perspectives.

Implications

This research suggests that online educators can use learners' pre-course learning perspectives to design online learning experiences which support transformative learning, and thus improve the student experience in the online course. Future research should seek to verify the challenges, coping strategies, and learning outcomes categories identified in this study.

References

1. Bogdan, R. C., & Bilken, S. K. (1982). Qualitative research for education: An introduction to theory and methods. (1st ed.). Boston: Allyn and Bacon.
2. Eastmond, D. V. (1995). Alone but together: Adult distance study through computer conferencing Cresskill, New Jersey: Hampton Press, Inc.
3. Harasim, L. (1989). On-line education: A new domain. In R. Mason & A. Kaye (Eds.), Mindweave: Communication, computers and distance education (pp. 50-62). Oxford: Pergamon Press.
4. Harasim, L., Hiltz, S. R., Teles, L., & Turoff, M. (1995). Learning networks: A field guide to teaching and learning online. Cambridge, MA: The MIT Press.
5. Merriam, S. B. (1998). Qualitative research and case study applications in education. (Second ed.). San Francisco, CA: Jossey-Bass Inc.
6. Mezirow, J. (1991a). Transformation theory and cultural-context - a reply to Clark and Wilson. Adult Education Quarterly, 41(3), 188-192.
7. Stake, R. E. (1995). The art of case study research. Thousand Oaks, CA: Sage Publications.

A Model for Shaping the Learning Environment for Effective Web Based Courses: Pepperdine's Online Master's in Educational Technology Program

Mercedes M. Fisher; Pepperdine University
Bonita Coleman; Bellflower Christian Schools

Abstract

Investigating the pedagogical strategies of a program that promotes dialogue and collective intellect in a community model could benefit course designers and contribute to significant development of online course delivery. This paper summarizes the study of a program that has a proven track record in offering learners powerful and substantial change in their practice. The community model is utilized with students in the Online Master of Arts Educational Technology program at Pepperdine University. In this summary we conducted a detailed case study using a mixture of quantitative and qualitative methods - including observation, focus groups, transcripts from synchronous and asynchronous discussions, questionnaires, and interviews, as well as statistical data from enrollment records - to identify perceptions of effective online collaboration and performance, and also to show the overall program success rate. Community formation, support, and sustainability were also explored.

Corporate and educational institutions have rushed to provide online courses; however, too often they have discovered the difficulty in transferring effective teaching strategies from the classroom to an online environment. According to a report prepared by International Data Corporation, there were approximately 700,000 students enrolled in distance learning classes in the United States in 1997-1998. By the end of 2002, that number could reach 2.23 million. In a knowledge-driven society, high-quality online instruction relies heavily on effective collaboration to create meaningful learning environments that contribute positively to learning outcomes. Making changes to how we interact with students or business colleagues and developing a more collaborative, 'community of learner' approach will have a major impact in what we do with or without technology.

In well-structured learning environments delivered via the web, learners actively participate in projects, planned research, synchronized active discussions, and even "live editing" of documents and projects with shared viewing made possible using the web. Course design demands attention toward such successful transfer of knowledge, with the Internet as a delivery option. Learning in a constructivist context is "action technology" in a computationally rich environment. Students create their own content based on individual need. Students document what they are doing and their understanding, allowing greater capacity for reflection and self-correction. They apply what they learn to their workplace in a practice related circumstance.

Based on the collected research, in the past four years over 200 students or 92% of students (Table 1), who take their coursework online in a community model, valued their education through the online program and graduate. Cohort members have come together online to explore and examine course content, share their viewpoints of the material, develop ideas and create solutions all with the single purpose of learning from each other. When compared to traditional face-to-face classroom instruction students have found web-based learning an authentic learning experience that fosters productive interaction between students. Pepperdine makes its program dynamic by using an action research project with real world application of coursework, which is an apprenticeship in making change - a year-long effort that is the backbone of the entire program

A most recent focus group of 85 students and 15 alumni explored and examined program development recommendations, trends, and global implications (see Table 2). In analysis of these data sources from the past four years across the online Master's in Ed Tech program, we were able to widen the research sample and increase the confidence level of results in identifying and describing several key elements and patterns of learning and growth that are important to student performance achievement and what students attribute to part of their growth during the program.

To set up an effective online environment we found the following elements must be considered:

Learning model needs to be collaborative and approached as a team effort
Professors act as guides, mentors and even co-learners
Student opinion and experience is valued by professors and peers
Students are challenged to apply new knowledge and share what happened as a result. This challenge piece changes knowledge into something owned not memorized.
Select tools for both synchronous and asynchronous communication
Include learning technologies: Chat rooms, threaded discussions, video streaming, audio streaming, simulations and laboratories
Decide on activities/projects (a.k.a., What to do where?)
Make projects and assignments open-ended. Interactive set-up includes distributed collaborators, web-based inquiry, case

application, rich media and public demonstration of learning

- Determine how work will be evaluated (i.e., peer review, % on collaboration) and communicate it to students
- Determine how you will provide feedback (i.e., emails, privacy, frequency)
- Set schedule for synchronous meetings. Consider student input
- Set expectations for asynchronous discussion every day, several times per week
- Limit Group size (i.e., 20 – 25 for newsgroups 3 – 5 for group projects)
- Provide orientation if required (i.e., Tech Camp, tech remediation, community help)

Unlike a traditional classroom that moves in lockstep to a well-defined syllabus (that is measured by minutes and hours) learning is sometimes difficult to observe—even by those involved in the collaborative effort. The advantage to a collaborative community is the direct involvement that is required for the acquisition of knowledge. One student observed, "Ideas are out there for all to see and comment on, which lends itself to our examining of what we are doing and learning…we get to see the big picture." There was a shift from an emphasis on the individual learner to one of a shared community. Rather than being subjected to being told what to do they are being guided in how to accomplish something that they have decided upon. Giving students choices in layers of communication for synchronous communication (i.e., chat, videoconferencing, instant messaging and telephone conversations), allows students a greater amount of ownership and confidence when working in collaboration with other students. Their vested interest in the outcome is an important factor when it comes to motivation because the learning is no longer an external manifestation that is held inside a textbook, rather the learning is internal and depends on their decisions of what to include or exclude. As one student reflected, "How rewarding it is to read an article, feel a strong reaction, type this into NG (newsgroup), and read someone else's reaction in a few hours! In a traditional setup, I'd have to wait until next week's class."

It is difficult to be a non-participant without falling back into the traditional mode of learning-by-rote and explicit isolation of sharing knowledge. "The assignments utilizing technology are not just busy-work, but are thought provoking and challenging – much more so than any undergraduate or graduate classes that I've ever had. Always before the learning has been self-contained…[now] we rely on cadre members for help, support, information and feedback. That makes a world of difference. The technology involved makes that possible."

Both instructors and students prosper when instructors initiate and facilitate their learning environment with dynamic communication methods to foster and support student-to-student communication and collaboration. Specifically, 1) It aids college faculty in designing courses; 2) Guides teacher education students in integrating educational technology in K-16 courses; and 3) Helps instructional trainers in developing web-based training materials. Our goal is that educators will benefit by developing an awareness and knowledge of the potential in online teaching.

An essential piece in planning for online courses is in thinking about WHEN is technology the best tool to accomplish the work involved. The fact is, tools may change over time. Things that continually have presence in learning are the learning process, dialogue, idea of apprenticing, culture, shared knowledge or co-creation of knowledge, and an authentic context. The connecting factor of a learning community, we found, is a common goal (i.e. project within the learning group), which is essential for complete success.

Enrollment Yr.	Education	Business	Total Yr.	Drop	Graduated	Percentages
1998	14	10	24	1	20	83.33%
1999	37	25	62	1	58	93.55%
2000	48	26	74	2	67	90.54%
2001	35	28	63	1	61	96.83%
2002	42	31	73		TBD	
Totals to date	223				206	92.37%
5 Yr. Total	296					Grad. rate

(Table 1) **Compiled Enrollment Data**

Benefits & Sustained Results (in order of popular idea & preference as stated from participants)	1) Networking & relationships 2) Mentoring & leadership 3) Communication 4) Knowledge sharing & management 5) Ethics 6) Diversity education (connecting across barriers)
Global Thinking and World Trends	1) Project based learning; hands on approach 2) Community action; seeing results 3) Transcends barriers & expands walls 4) Education worldwide
Implications	Collaboration; establishes partnerships
Suggestions	Expand existing courses to include international collaboration

(Table 2) **Program Participant Feedback**

The Authors
Mercedes Fisher is an Associate Professor and Co-Director of the Master of Arts Program in Educational Technology Pepperdine University, CA USA mmfisher@pepperdine.edu 310.568.5671 PH 310.568.5755 FAX http://gsep.pepperdine.edu/~mmfisher/main/home.html
Bonita Coleman is Director of Technology Integration & Teacher Training at Bellflower Christian Schools Cerritos, CA USA bcoleman@bcschools.org or bgcolema@pepperdine.edu 562.865.6519 PH http://www.bcschools.org/

The Practical Use of Email Lists as Class Discussion Forums in an Advanced Course

Michael L. Turnbull
Faculty of Informatics and Communications,
School of Computing and Information Systems,
Central Queensland University

Abstract

In 1999 Central Queensland University's School of Computing and Information Systems offered a computer programming course in a totally online delivery mode. Academic support from the lecturer was provided, in total, by means of email lists to which all class members were expected to subscribe. It was found that a single class email list was insufficient to cater for the needs of advanced students. This two-year study of the course email list usage demonstrates the benefit of providing advanced online students with an advanced topic discussion forum so that the general class email forum can be freed up for core business. It also demonstrates that totally on line students tend to use the class email list as a primary workroom for assignment preparation.

INTRODUCTION

This paper examines the usage of class email lists over a two-year period, in a class of 200 students. It demonstrates that overuse of a general class email list by enthusiastic advanced students can be avoided by providing an alternative email list for them, on which to discuss advanced topics. It also demonstrates that class email lists can provide students with an effective *workroom* during major assignment preparation periods.

YEAR 1999 CLASS EMAIL LIST USAGE

At the beginning of the term a general email list was made available for the students and the course coordinator to use. The objective of the list subscription policy was to encourage class members to openly discuss any aspects of the course topics with one another, and to encourage peer help within the class. Students could actively participate in the discussion or passively *listen* to the traffic.

Figure 1 displays the usage of the class list as a **5-day running average** of the number of messages posted to the list per day.

The following features can be seen in Figure 1:

A. The beginning of term where the activity on the list commences at a low level.
B. A rapid rise in activity over the first 4 weeks of the term. **This rapid increase was caused by advanced students taking control of the email list.**
C. The introduction of a second email list to cater for students wishing to discuss advanced concepts of the course topic.
D. Reduction in the traffic subsequent to the introduction of the advanced list, during a period when two minor assignments were due.
E. The end of the period when minor assignments were due.
F. A period that typified *background* activity. During this period no assignment submissions were imminent and the mid-term vacation was ahead.
G. Start of the mid-term vacation period.
H. The mid-term vacation period. During this period no messages were posted to the class list!
I. The end of the mid-term vacation period.
J. Traffic associated with preparation of the first major assignment. There is a rapid increase in traffic, followed by a rapid decline.
K. Due date for the first major assignment.
L. Background traffic between the two major assignments.
M. Traffic associated with preparation of the second major assignment. As with the first major assignment there is a rapid increase in traffic, followed by a rapid decline.
N. The due date for the second major assignment; and also the end of term.

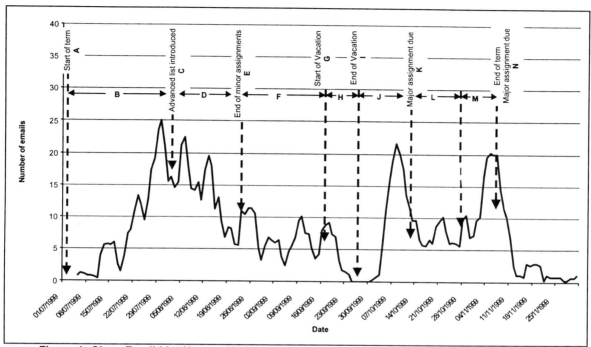

Figure 1: Class Email List Usage, 1999

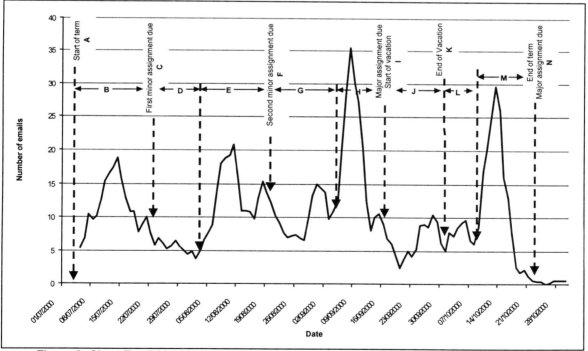

Figure 2: Class Email List Usage, 2000

YEAR 2000 CLASS EMAIL LIST USAGE

At the beginning of the term both general and advanced discussion email lists were provided. Figure 2 displays the usage of the class list as a **5-day running average** of the number of messages posted to the list per day

The following features can be seen in Figure 2:

A. The beginning of term where the activity on the list commences at a low level.
B. Traffic associated with preparation of the first minor assignment. There is a moderate increase in traffic, followed by a decline down to background level.
C. The end of the period when the first minor assignment was due.
D. A period of background discussion activity.
E. Traffic associated with preparation of the second minor assignment. There is a moderate increase in traffic, followed by a decline down to background level.
F. The end of the period when the second minor assignment was due.
G. A period of elevated discussion activity.
H. Traffic associated with preparation of the first major assignment. There is a dramatic increase in traffic, followed by an equally rapid decline.
I. Due date for the first major assignment, and start of a 2 week vacation period.
J. The mid-term vacation period.
K. End of mid-term vacation period.
L. Background discussion activity.
M. Traffic associated with preparation of the second major assignment. There is a dramatic increase in traffic, followed by an equally rapid decline.
N. Due date for the second major assignment, and end of term.

It is noted that during the term the general class email list did not get out of control as it did during the previous year. The use of the general email list as a workroom for preparation of the four assignments is clearly in evidence.

SUMMARY AND CONCLUSIONS

In 1999, based on previous experience, only one general discussion email list was provided. It was expected that one list would cater for all students' needs. Unexpectedly a few students, discussing topics far too advanced for the course content, intimidated most other students and effectively displaced them from the class discussion process. This result indicates that, for advanced courses, a single class discussion email list cannot be assumed to cater for all students' needs.

To rectify the problem a second email list was made available especially for discussion of advanced topics. This allowed the traffic on the main class list to revert to core topics, and the less advanced students returned to active class discussion. This confirmed that, in order to nurture the needs of advanced students and at the same time ensure that general class activity continues, an alternative forum for discussion of advanced topics is required.

In 2000 both email lists were made available to the class from the start of term. This resulted in the activity on the main list being much more orderly for the whole term.

Increasing Student Technology Skills through a Technology-Intensive Syllabus

Diane Heller Klein, Ph.D.   Indiana University of Pennsylvania, USA

Abstract

It is critical for all students to become skilled users of a variety of software and hardware applications. It is particularly important for students training to become educators because their employers will expect them to be more knowledgeable and comfortable with instructional technologies than the students they teach.

To facilitate skill development, a syllabus was designed to incorporate all of the software applications used in the MS OfficeSuite package. This software was selected because it is used by the majority of students on their personal computers as well as in all of the university computer labs.

Students were expected to use each of the Office Suite components to fulfill their assignment requirements. In addition, students also developed skill in the use of SmartBoard, projection systems, and the manipulation and use of digital sound and picture files.

After completing this course, students met all of the ISTE [1] standards for technology competency.

Introduction

The Education of Persons with Hearing Loss Program at Indiana University of Pennsylvania (IUP) is one of only 68 programs in Deaf Education in the United States. It is critically important that students who graduate from this program are well-schooled in the specific knowledge base and pedagogical skills required for successfully teaching deaf and hard of hearing children, and are more than minimally accomplished in the used of basic educationally related hardware and software applications.

To facilitate the development of these skills, a technology-intensive syllabus was constructed for one course that is taken by all students in the deaf education major during their final semester prior to student teaching. The course is not only technology-intensive, but also designated a 'Writing Intensive" course by the university. This means that the vast majority of work done in the class and the subsequent grade is based primarily on written products rather than examinations.

The Course

The course selected for this activity was the three-credit EDHL 351 –Teaching Reading to Persons with Hearing Loss. The course is 14 weeks in length and typically meets twice per week for ninety-minute class sessions. The class is held in a 'technology' classroom that contains a SmartBoard and a complete projection system connected to a computer that is online and fully networked with the various university systems. Since flexibility is a hallmark trait of a good teacher, the classroom also includes the old standby standard low-technology equipment often utilized by teachers in public school settings (VCR and monitor, overhead projector and screen).

Communicating with the Class

Communication in the class was maintained in a variety of ways. Several of the required writing tasks involved what became the most popular method of communicating in class, a WebCT instructional site. WebCT is an online course tool package utilized at IUP. Students are enrolled in the course by the instructor and then have full capabilities to converse either synchronously or asynchronously with the instructor or other students enrolled in the class.

The students participated in biweekly dialogue journals with the instructor and discussed a variety of 'hot' topics with each other through a threaded discussion on the bulletin board. Any questions related to the technology assignments were answered on the bulletin board, through email, or through a specified chatroom. The instructor even maintained regular office hours while out of town by using the chatroom feature of the WebCT site. The 20 students in the class 'hit' the WebCT site over 800 times in one semester alone. Since online communication was one of the course objectives, clearly, the use of the WebCT site enabled all of the students in the class to meet these objectives.

Technology-Based Assignments

The assignments were evenly spread over the entire course to allow for instructional/tutorial time. Students who were not already familiar with some of the components of MS OfficeSuite (Word, Access, Excel, PowerPoint) were provided with tutorials in the Course Content section of the WebCT module to assist them in self-directed learning tasks. In addition, peer tutors volunteered to help those unfamiliar with the software.

MS Word

Students had two major papers and an authentic piece of childrens' literature to write using Word software. The students worked in randomly selected editorial dyads. The formal use of a 'process writing' strategy was expected and the dyads edited each other's work electronically using the Word editing features. Students learned to track text and insert comments. They also utilized the various tools available in this software. Students were required to edit each other's work at least twice. The work was all shared electronically, as attachments, through the email feature of the WebCT site.

In addition to word processing, students learned how to take and manipulate a variety of digital images. These were used as a part of the childrens' literature assignment. Each story was a minimum of 1,000 words and produced entirely with desktop publishing strategies. Each student produced a hardcopy of his/her book and created an archive copy by burning the electronic file onto a CD-R disk.

MS Access

In order to write their stories, students were required to locate and read a variety of childrens' literature. Each student selected a grade level, researched books written at the identified level, then created a database using MS Access. The database was used in a variety of ways. Its primary purpose was to provide a form of bibliographic evidence supporting the research completed for the book. The database was also used to teach students how to use queries to sort information.

MS Excel

In addition to flexibility, organization is a trait that is critical for a teacher to experience success in the classroom. Spreadsheet applications allow a teacher to manage their everyday academic and administrative tasks in a relatively quick and efficient manner.

Students were required to use MS Excel to create any form of spreadsheet with classroom applications. Some students chose to create a grade book page while others created data charts that were also converted to graphs. Some students used Excel to create databases. The most rewarding part of the activity occurred when each student presented his/her spreadsheet. Students

were amazed at the various applications of the software and the creativity with which the spreadsheets were designed.

MS PowerPoint and SmartBoard

All of the students are well acquainted with creating presentations using PowerPoint software by the time they take the EDHL 351 course. In this course, however, the students are expected to teach an entire segment of the textbook using a PowerPoint presentation that is projected onto a SmartBoard. The SmartBoard is a touch sensitive electronic whiteboard that links to a computer. The board is calibrated when turned on to respond to the slightest touch on its surface. The student can present an entire PowerPoint presentation simply by touching different parts of the SmartBoard.

Like the Excel presentations, the PowerPoint presentations were often enlightening for all students. Many students had very sophisticated production abilities that resulted in nearly professional presentations. Their peers did not hesitate to ask, "How did you DO THAT?" Invariably, much was taught and learned by all in the class regarding both the subject content and the use of PowerPoint as a presentation tool.

Project Evaluation

All of the projects were evaluated using rubrics. Each project had its own rubric with the task parameters clearly provided. Students received points within three possible categories of performance; exceptional achievement, adequate achievement, needs improvement. The criterion for each level of performance for each task was defined. Students received a copy of the rubric along with the assignment.

Outcomes

The students who complete this course are expected to be fluid in their use of basic instructional technologies. Without exception, every student demonstrated the appropriate level of ability in the use of MS OfficeSuite software applications and in their use of digital cameras, the SmartBoard, and other pieces of instructional hardware. The teacher education accrediting organizations require that students meet ISTE standards. Students who completed this course met and surpassed all standards.

[1] International Society for Technology in Education. (n.d.). Retrieved July 31, 2002, from http://www.iste.org/standards/index.html

Using Technology to Improve the Quality of Classroom Instruction

David Ripley, University of Canterbury

This short paper is a case study describing the introduction of a computer-mediated dialogue process in support of classroom instruction in two graduate courses in the Management Department at the University of Canterbury. The R9 dialogue process was introduced using the WebCT platform. Course quality, both as perceived by the instructor and as indicated by student course and teaching evaluations, increased in both courses. Results are discussed and changes based on this experience are noted.

1. Introduction

In 2001, the R9 process [1] using WebCT was introduced in two face-to-face (FTF) graduate courses in the management department at the University of Canterbury. The objective was to improve quality by increasing the extent of critical thinking and reflection by students in these classes, and to enhance the perceived quality of the classes, as measured by student evaluations. The evaluations for both classes showed significant improvement over previous years.

2. The Courses

Both FTF courses were human resource management (HRM) courses. One was an MBA HRM course and the other was a BCom (honours) Strategic HRM course. In previous years, both courses were taught using a combination of lecture and discussion. The composition of each class varied, both in number and in experience. The MBA class was the largest (over 30 students), and the students generally had between 5 and 10 years of managerial experience. The honours class was smaller, with 16 students. This group had all completed undergraduate work in various disciplines, but as a group generally had little or no significant work experience.

Given the different levels of the students in the two courses, and the different purpose of the courses, course content was focused at different levels. For example, the MBA class was very application-focused, while the strategic HRM honours course was theory-based to a much greater degree. In both courses, previous evaluations had been adequate but not at the level desired.

3. Critical Thinking and Reflection

The R9 process was first developed in response to concerns that first arose during my experience teaching on-line in an asynchronous format. My primary concern was that students' participatory responses tended to be quite superficial, indicating a lack of critical thinking and reflection. I experienced the same concerns with my graduate FTF classes at Canterbury.

In looking at perspectives on critical thinking one can start with the limited perspective of a highly focused problem-solving approach (i.e. a quality program manual). Beyond that would lie the broader – but still skill-based – approach that is more about the "how and what" of critical thinking. This is more in keeping with the informal logic movement (ILM) [2,3]. One can then broaden the objectives of critical thinking with a more "socially conscious" perspective. To use Alvesson's and Willmott's [4] term, a "softer" approach (p. 432) that shows some concern for higher-order human needs. Finally, we have those perspectives that suggest the goal of critical thinking should be social emancipation. This latter position is more in keeping with the ideas of critical pedagogy and critical practice [5], and moves toward critical theory [6] and critical social science [7].

R9 is positioned somewhat in the middle of these perspectives -- going beyond the ILM by stressing critical thinking in the context of domain-based learning (in this case HRM), but not attempting to move to the socially conscious perspective or the critical theory and social science areas.

At the same time, we want to emphasise reflection and see students progressing toward becoming the reflective practitioners envisioned by Schon [8], who think and rethink some of their positions and assumptions, and practice "reflection-in-action" (p. 50).

4. The R9 Process Used On-Line

R9 as originally developed for on-line work basically involves an iterative process of reading, reflecting, and responding to material related to the learning objectives three separate times during a learning module. The first iteration requires small groups of students (normally not more than 4 or 5) to respond individually to one of the module's questions. It is critical that these questions require thought, not just repetition of assigned material. The second iteration requires students to review and critique individual responses of other students (who were assigned other questions). The final iteration requires the

0-7695-1509-6/02 $17.00 © 2002 IEEE

small groups who had each question to reflect upon their initial responses and the critiques they received from others, and as a group, developing a "definitive response" (DR). In on-line classes, all this work is done on the platform being used to support the class, with the DR being the last posting for the learning module. The process activities are shown below.

Step	Description
R1	Read the assignment for basic understanding
R2	Reflect on the contents
R3	Respond to the question (post)
R4	Read the responses of others as assigned
R5	Reflect on those responses
R6	Respond with critiques that will expand others' thinking on their questions (post)
R7	Receive the critiques of others relating to one's own initial response
R8	Reflect on the responses of others who had the same question and on the critiques that were received by all who had that question
R9	Respond by posting the DR to the question, developed in conjunction with others who had the question.

Table 1. The Basic R9 Process Activities

5. WebCT and R9 in Classroom Instruction

WebCT is the platform adopted by the University of Canterbury for computer support of classroom instruction. It has the primary component needed for using the R9 process, which is a threaded bulletin board-type posting feature. It also has many other features, such as e-mail, chat rooms, and provision for other course resources.

In the two classes mentioned, initial questions were posted on WebCT immediately following each class. Each was assigned to a specific group of students. During the week between class meetings, the students posted individual responses to the questions they were assigned, and other students posted critiques of the responses of those students. Each group of students assigned a particular question then presented their DR in class (rather than posting), where it served as a basis for discussion. The instructor at this time ensured that all desired learning points had been covered. Using this process significantly increased class involvement, since each week, all students had to be involved in the process. As one MBA student put it, "There's no place to hide".

6. Results

Using the R9 process ensured broad participation and the quality of the dialogue in terms of critical thinking

and reflection by students was significantly greater than in previous classes. In addition, student evaluations of the two courses improved significantly over the previous year – in the honours class, on the order of 20%. Since there were no control groups, we cannot say with certainty that all the improvement in student evaluations was due to the addition of the computer-mediated R9 process. However, from our experience with these two (and subsequent) courses, we feel there is good reason to believe this approach can enhance the quality of classroom instruction. Other management instructors at Canterbury have adopted R9 and are enthusiastic about their results.

The method seemed to be more effective with the honours class of 16 students than with the much larger MBA class so, as one would expect, class size may be an effectiveness factor. In response to a statement related to the effectiveness of the method in helping them learn, the honours students indicated a degree of agreement of 4.6 out of 5.0. In contrast, there were a number of comments from MBA students to the effect that they liked the methodology but would like to have heard more from the instructor. In response to this concern, the MBA format was modified so that only half the groups presented in class each week in 2002, which allowed more time for both discussion and instructor comments.

References

1. Ripley, D. E (2000). Using technology to foster critical thinking and reflection: The R9 process. *The International Journal of Vocational Education and Training* 9 (2): 17-32.
2. Ennis, R. (1987). A taxonomy of critical thinking dispositions and abilities. In J. Baron & R. Sternberg (Eds.), *Teaching Thinking Skills: Theory and Practice*. New York: W. H. Freeman and Company.
3. McPeck, J. (1990) (Ed.). *Teaching critical thinking*. New York: Routledge.
4. Alvesson, M. & Willmott, H. (1992). On the idea of emancipation in management and organisation studies. *Academy of Management Review 17* (3): 432-464.
5. Mezirow, J. (1990). *Fostering critical reflection in adulthood: a guide to transformative and empancipatory learning*. San Francisco: Jossey-Bass.
6. Foucault, M. (1994). *Power*. New York: The New Press.
7. Fay, B. (1987). *Critical social science*. Cambridge: Polity Press.
8. Schon, D. (1983). *The reflective practitioner: how professionals think in action*. New York: Basic Books, Inc.

A Workshop Teaching Tool For Rapid Mobile Information Service

T.T. Goh, B Troughton
Victoria University of Wellington, New Zealand
tiong.goh@vuw.ac.nz

Abstract

This paper intends to help users understand the design methodology of a workshop tool used for a rapid mobile information service development. This tool is aimed at students with limited programming skill. The objective is to guide the students experience the end product and in the process develop others mobile information service applications rapidly.

Introduction

One of the ways to teach students with limited knowledge of programming skill to design a mobile information service application is to do it by example [1] [2]. This teaching tool aims to serve that purpose. The programme is written using four ASP (Active Server Page) pages [3] and a corresponding database table for that page. The four ASP pages are new.asp, test.asp, course.asp and name.asp. The database were developed using Access 2000 and is named Test.mdb. There are four headings with a database table that relates to that heading. The general design methodology for the rapid mobile information service uses a modular approach as shown in figure 1.

Architectural Design

WML[4][5] does note use pages instead its applications comprise of one or more decks that contain a collection of cards. The cards contain the content that is displayed to the user via a micro browser on their WAP enabled device. The other content on the card controls the way the user moves from one card to the next. The use of decks and cards overcomes the problems of bandwidth, limited battery power, and limited processing power that WAP devices such as cell phones have. The cards can be bundled together and sent several at a time to the micro browser so that it does not have to ask for new cards from the server every time the user tries to move from one to another.

Page Number One: NEW.ASP

Due to space constraint of the paper, only page one which carries the code of NEW.ASP is presented in full details. Other codes can be obtained from the authors. Figure 2 shows the output of the mobile timetable service.

Guide 1.1: This block states that WML is based on XML version 1.0 and gives the location of the document type definition against which this document will be validated. The document type declaration identifies the DTD (document type definition) for version 1.1 of the WML specification.

The DTD can be found at www.wapforum.org/DTD/wml_1.1.xml. The ASP code "text/vnd.wap.wml" text tells the server what MIME type it should send to the browser, which is the type we associated with the .wml extension.

```
<% Response.ContentType =
"text/vnd.wap.wml" %><?xml
version="1.0" encoding="iso-8859-1"?>
<!DOCTYPE wml PUBLIC "-
//WAPFORUM//DTD WML 1.1//EN"
"http://www.wapforum.org/DTD/wml_1.1.
xml" >
```

Guide 1.2: There is one deck in this programme used to select the degree of choice (enclosed by <wml> </wml>).

```
<wml>
```

Guide 1.3: This is the Splash card of the deck (enclosed by <card> </card>).

The micro browser pulls up the logo and text to be displayed on the splash page. There is a timed navigation of 50 micro seconds before the micro browser displays the heading text and the records extracted from the database table.

```
<card                    id="card_logo"
ontimer="#MainCard" >
           <timer value="50" />
<p              align="center"><img
src="vuw_logo.wbmp"
alt="vuwlogo"/></p>
<p          align="center"><b>VICTORIA
UNIVERSITY</b></p>
<p          align="center"><b>TIMETABLE
</b></p>
</card>
```

Guide 1.4: This is the "MainCard" of the deck (enclosed by <card> </card>)
The micro browser displays the choice of degrees the user can select.

```
<card id="MainCard">
<p align="left"><b>DEGREE</b></p>
```

Guide 1.5: The <% %> syntax delimits the enclosed code to return WML text in the micro browser window.

```
<%
```

Guide 1.6: This block of code provides the path of the file to locate the Access Database called "test". It sets the connection type (ADO ActiveX Data Object) and generates a record set that will be queried in the next block.

```
strconn = "DRIVER=Microsoft Access
Driver (*.mdb);DBQ=" &
Server.MapPath("test.mdb") & ";"
set conn =
server.createobject("adodb.connection
")
conn.open strconn
set rs =
server.createobject("adodb.recordset"
)
```

Guide 1.7: This block is where the query is performed. The query retrieves all records and passes them to the Recordset object (DEGREE_ID). This enables the user to access all the data in the table labelled "Degree". The data is displayed in the micro browser ordered by the "Degree_ID" number. The recordset object then allows the user to step through each of the records until the EOF (end of file) market is reached. The values of DEGREE_NAME column are written out for each record.

```
Query = "Select * from DEGREE ORDER
BY DEGREE_ID"
rs.open Query, conn
if not rs.eof Then
rs.movefirst
Do While NOt rs.EOF
DEGREE_ID = rs("DEGREE_ID")
%>
```

Guide 1.8: This is the anchor navigation block. This WAP programme uses anchors that have hyperlink references to navigate from one ASP page to the next. Once the user selects the record source "DEGREE_NAME" the test.ASP page is opened on the micro browser and the deck on that page is displayed.

```
<p
align="left"><anchor><%=rs("DEGREE_NA
ME")%><go
href="test.asp?DEGREE_ID=<%=DEGREE_ID
%>"/></anchor></p>
```

Guide 1.9: The record source movenext command ends the query loop. If this command is not in the coding the ASP process will continue to loop for 900 seconds (by default) before it closes. This will cause the programme to slow to a crawl.

```
<%
rs.movenext
```

```
Loop
End if
%>
```

Guide 1.10: The card and the deck are closed.

```
</card>
</wml>
```

Summary

This workshop tool details the design methodology of a rapid mobile information service. It serves as a workshop tool in WAP development for students with limited programming skill typically in an internet database course. The teaching tools enhance their understanding and motivate them to develop similar application such as a mobile parking fine database search service, a mobile restaurant menu service, a mobile truck stop service and a mobile netball schedule service.

Acknowledgement

The authors wish to thank Sunjay, Dianne, and Jan for their contributions in the project.

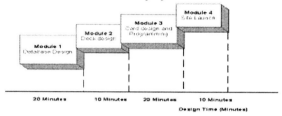

Figure 1 Modular approach in rapid mobile information service development

Figure 2 Output after selecting course

References

1. Graham Gibbs, "Learning by doing: A guide to teaching and learning methods", www.glos.ac.uk/el/philg/gdn/gibbs/index.htm
2. Dan Carnevale, "Scholar Says Learning by doing is the key to quality instruction", The Chronicle of higher education, May 30, 2000.
3. A tutorial on learning WAP www.ASPfree.com
4. Ericsson developer package www.Ericsson.com
5. Wei Meng Lee et al; " WAP, WML, and WML Script ", Wrox Press Ltd, 2000.

Promoting Reflective Thinking in Teacher Candidates : Are Digital Video/Multimedia Portfolios a Useful Tool?

Sheila Spurgeon, Ph.D., Northwestern Oklahoma State University

James L. Bowen, Ed.D. Northwestern Oklahoma State University

Abstract

This research examined the effects of a process of digital video editing used to create multimedia portfolio has on the quality of teacher candidates' critical reflections. Subjects were randomly assigned to one of three groups: control, experimental – reflection, and experimental – reflection with multimedia production. The difference between the control group and the experimental groups indicate that digital video editing does have an impact on teacher candidate's ability to reflect.

Teacher preparation programs throughout the United States are requiring teacher candidates to reflect critically on his/her actions. As Dewey observed, reflective thinking involves a state of doubt, hesitation, perplexity, mental difficulty, however this discomfort leads to reflection which is the act of searching, hunting, and inquiring to find material that will resolve the doubt and settle and dispose of the perplexity (Dewey, 1933, p 12).Although the usefulness of reflection in teacher education appears to be established, teacher educators may want to consider the fairness and appropriateness of its use before the conclude its validity and advocate mandating this requirement. Requiring teacher candidates to reflect on their activities may not be "developmentally appropriate".

If reflection entails a high level of adult cognitive development, as Kitchener (1983) and has argued, then what teacher educators are assessing in candidates portfolios is their level of cognitive development and not necessarily their mastery of the program competencies. Critical thinking skills may be necessary for the development of higher-level thinking but are not in themselves sufficient to guarantee that development. On the other hand, if reflection is viewed as a form of critical inquiry, then what is asked of teacher candidates may be conceptualized as a metacognitive approach to problem solving. This metacognitive approach to problem solving entails a systematic strategy that can and probably should be taught to teacher candidates.

Subjects were randomly assigned to one of three groups: control, experimental – reflection, and experimental – reflection with multimedia production. During the student teaching seminar course, the two experimental groups met for explicit instruction in reflection. Subjects in the reflection and multimedia production group received field-based (on site) one-on-one instruction in video editing. Inquiry oriented instruction focused on the process of understanding and improving one's teaching by using video as a tool to facilitate critiquing performance.

The instrument used to measure the dependent variable, teacher candidate's critical reflections, was based on a 7-part framework developed by Sparks-Langer, Simmons, Pasch, Colton, & Starko (1991). The data were analyzed using 3 separate t-tests for independent samples. The data were analyzed using 3 separate t-tests for independent samples. The first test assessed the difference between the average rater score for Group 1 (control) and Group 2 (reflection). The mean of 63.19 for Group 2 was not significantly larger ($p = .718$) than the mean of Group 1 ($m = 59.22$). The second test looked for a difference between Group 1 and Group 3 (reflection/video ed). The largest difference was between these 2 groups (Group 1 $m = 59.22$; Group 3 $m = 70.96$) which is what we anticipated. However,

the difference was not significant ($p = .17$). The third test assessing the difference between Group 2 ($m = 63.19$) and Group 3 ($m = 70.96$) also found no significant difference ($p = .53$).

Although the difference between groups was not significant, the large difference between the control group and the experimental group (reflection/video ed) is encouraging. Our hypothesis was that multimedia portfolio development increase the teacher candidate's critical reflections.

References

Dewey, J.(1933). *How we think*. Boston: D.C. Heath.

Kitchener, K. (1983). Cognition, metacognition, and epistemic cognition. *Educational Forum, 13*, 75 – 95.

Sparks-Langer, G. M., Simmons, J. M., Pasch, M., Colton, A., & Starko, A. (1991). Reflective pedagogical thinking: How can we promote it and measure it? *Journal of Teacher Education, 45,* 310 – 318.

A Measure of Dissimilarity between the Structure of Instructional Material and the Structure of the Learner's Understanding

Nobuyoshi YONEZAWA [1], Kazuhito HIRAI [1], Shizuaki TAKAHASHI [1],
Youzou MIYADERA [2] and Keizo NAGAOKA [3]

1)Department of Computer Science and Communication Engineering, Kogakuin University,
2665-1 Nakano-machi, Hachioji-shi, Tokyo 192-0015, Japan. E-mail: ct72058@ns.kogakuin.ac.jp
2)Department of Mathematics and Information Science, Tokyo Gakugei University
3)National Institute of Multimedia Education, Ministry of Education and Science

Abstract

The present paper investigates the construction of a navigation system that assists the learner in linking learning tasks so that the structure of the learner's understanding will conform to the structure of instructional material. As an initial step, a measure of the dissimilarity between two digraphs expressing the structure of instructional material and the structure of learner's understanding, respectively, is defined. Details concerning the navigation will be reported at a later date.

1. Introduction

The structure of instructional material is expressed via a digraph having no directed cycles conceptually. The vertex v_i and the directed edge (v_i, v_j) of the digraph correspond to the learning task and the order relation of the learning task, respectively. A topological order for the structure of instructional material is a sequential listing of learning tasks.

The system doesn't show the structure of instructional material to the learner and presents only the learning tasks in order of the sequential listing. The learner then solves the tasks in the order in which they were presented. After learning, the learner constructs a digraph, referred to as the structure of the learner's understanding, by linking the learning tasks.

The learner's degree of understanding is measured based on the difference between the structure of the learner's understanding and the structure of the instructional material.

2. Digraph

Let G_T be the structure of the instructional material designed by a teacher. Figure 1 shows an example of G_T. The vertex without the output edge is called a root, whereas the vertex without the input edge is called a leaf. The root is a learning target, whereas the leaf is the most basic learning task. The structure of the learner's understanding as constructed by the learner after learning is designated as G_S. Figure 2 shows an example of G_S. The two digraphs G_T and G_S have the same vertices, and are respectively given as

$$G_T = [V(G_T), E(G_T)], \quad G_S = [V(G_S), E(G_S)]$$
$$V(G_T) = V(G_S), \quad V(G_T) = \{v_1, v_2, \ldots, v_n\}$$

Members of a set $E(G_T)$ are the edges of G_T. If $E(G_T) = E(G_S)$, then G_T is equal to G_S. If the number of members in a set, A, is expressed as $N(A)$, then $N(V(G_T)) = n$.

The dissimilarity between G_T and G_S is defined in Section 3. As the dissimilarity is made smaller, the similarity between G_T and G_S increases. If the dissimilarity is 0, then $E(G_T)$ is equal to $E(G_S)$, that is, $G_T = G_S$.

3. Dissimilarity between two digraphs

A sequence of directed edges

$$(v_{j_{c-1}}, v_{j_c}) \quad c = 1, 2, 3, \ldots, x$$

from v_{j_0} to v_{j_x} in G_T is called a path. Let P< - v_j - >^{T} be the set of all paths from a number of leaves to a root, which passes through a vertex v_j. P< - v_j - >^{T} is divided into two sets P< - v_j>^{T} and P< v_j - >^{T}, where P< - v_j >^{T} and P< v_j - >^{T} are the set of all paths from a number of leaves to v_j and the set of all paths from v_j to a root, respectively. Let E< - v_j >^{T} be a set in which the members are the edges that form P< - v_j >^{T}, and let $E< v_j ->^T$ be a set in which the members are the edges that form $P< v_j ->^T$.

In the same way, $P< -v_j ->^S$, $P< v_j >^S$, $P< v_j ->^S$, $E< -v_j >^S$ and $E< v_j ->^S$ for G_S is defined.

We define the distance between $v_i \in V(G_T)$ and $v_j \in V(G_T)$ as follows:

$$d_{ij}^{TT} = N(E< -v_i >^T \nabla E< -v_j >^T) + N(E< v_i ->^T \nabla E< v_j ->^T)$$

where ∇ is the symmetric difference $(A \cup B) - (A \cap B)$.

In the same way, the distance between $v_i \in (G_T)$ and $v_j \in V(G_S)$ is given by

$$d_{ij}^{TS} = N(E< -v_i >^T \nabla E< -v_j >^S) + N(E< v_i ->^T \nabla E< v_j ->^S)$$

For example,

$E< -v_2 >^T = \phi$, $E< v_2 ->^T = \{(v_2,v_3), (v_3,v_5)\}$

$E< -v_3 >^T = \{(v_1,v_3), (v_2,v_3)\}$, $E< v_3 ->^T = \{(v_3,v_5)\}$

$E< -v_2 >^S = \phi$, $E< v_2 ->^S = \{(v_2,v_3), (v_3,v_5),(v_2,v_4),(v_4,v_5)\}$

$E< -v_3 >^S = \{(v_1,v_3), (v_2,v_3)\}$, $E< v_3 ->^S = \{(v_3,v_5)\}$

$d_{22}^{TT} = 0$, $d_{22}^{TS} = N(\{(v_2,v_4), (v_4,v_5)\}) = 2$

$d_{23}^{TS} = N(\{(v_1,v_3), (v_2,v_3)\}) + N(\{(v_2,v_3)\}) = 3$

$d_{32}^{TS} = N(\{(v_1,v_3), (v_2,v_3)\}) + N(\{(v_2,v_3),(v_2,v_4),(v_4,v_5)\}) = 5$

As the difference between G_T and GS increases, the value of d_{ij}^{TS} increases.

All d_{ij}^{TT} of G_T are expressed in a $n \times n$ square matrix d^{TT} having the components d_{ij}^{TT}. d^{TT} is a symmetric matrix having diagonal components equal to 0. All d_{ij}^{TS} between G_T and G_S are expressed in a $n \times n$ square matrix d^{TS} having the components d_{ij}^{TS}. d^{TS} is an asymmetric matrix, and the diagonal components are not necessarily 0.

We define the dissimilarity between G_T and G_S as follows:

$$D^{TS} = \frac{1}{n^2} \sum_{i=1}^{n} \sum_{j=1}^{n} \left| d_{ij}^{TS} - d_{ij}^{TT} \right|$$

where $n = N(V(G))$.

4. Conclusions

d^{TT} and d^{TS} are shown in Tables 1 and 2. The dissimilarity D^{TS} between G_T and G_S is 0.8. The shape of the digraph and the dissimilarity visually coincide approximately. The navigation system, which assists the learner in linking learning tasks based on the dissimilarity, will be reported in a future study.

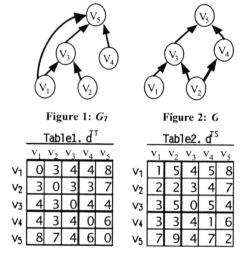

Figure 1: G_T Figure 2: G

Table1. d^T

	v_1	v_2	v_3	v_4	v_5
v_1	0	3	4	4	8
v_2	3	0	3	3	7
v_3	4	3	0	4	4
v_4	4	3	4	0	6
v_5	8	7	4	6	0

Table2. d^S

	v_1	v_2	v_3	v_4	v_5
v_1	1	5	4	5	8
v_2	2	2	3	4	7
v_3	3	5	0	5	4
v_4	3	3	4	1	6
v_5	7	9	4	7	2

Reference

[1] R.J. Shavelson, "Some aspects of the correspondence between content structure and cognitive structure in physics instruction", Journal of Educational Psychology, vol.63, no.3, 225-234,1972.
[2] M. Takeya and H. Sasaki, "An Evaluation Method for Students' Understanding Using Their Cognitive Map", IEICE, vol.J80-D-2, No.1, pp.336-347, 1997.

Ten Years of Junior Professors

Matthew M. Maurer, Associate Professor, Butler University
Laura Baker, Teacher, Indianapolis Public Schools
Jacqueline Noel, Teacher, Indianapolis Public Schools

Abstract

The Junior Professor project has been in operation for ten years. It is a project in which elementary school children teach lessons in a college level class on computers in education. The project requires little in the way of funding, and only reasonable arrangements and effort to organize. The elementary school students have benefited substantially as have the college students and the university program.

History

The project was initiated after it was noticed that a number of college students would complete the introductory class, and make comments like, "this is hard for me, so it must be even harder for little kids." A powerful experience was needed that would make the point that many aspects of using computers is actually easier for children than it is for adults. Over the ten years of the project, that objective has been met consistently. In the process, other benefits have been derived, for the college students, for the elementary students and for the teacher preparation program.

The project has consistently worked with children from the inner city. Many of them have little knowledge of colleges and what attending college entails. The children selected were from a school with which the professor has a strong relationship. Over the years of the project, the professor, has developed a strong relationship with the classroom teachers.

The content the elementary school students taught was selected on the basis of what they knew best. In the earlier years of the project, younger students (first through third graders) taught a simple graphic program (Kid Pix) and the older students (fourth and fifth graders) taught a hypermedia program (Hyperstudio). Later in the evolution of the project, we switched the graphics work to younger students (kindergarteners and first graders) and we switched the older children to teaching web page design. The primary reason these topics were taught was because it provided a reasonable teaching opportunity for the children to teach the young adults. The children intimately knew the software and processes they were teaching and the college students did not.

Flow of Instruction

Prior to the children coming to campus to teach, the professor would meet with them to outline the task and to discuss some specific issues related to teaching college students. The children would be instructed to allow the college students to do their own work, and that the children must always "help with their mouths, not with their hands." This was a point that had to be enforced actively during the instruction time. We sometimes had to enlist "sit on your hands" activities, or "hands in pockets" activities.

Depending on the way classes were scheduled, the day flowed somewhat differently. The class is scheduled either just before lunch, just after, or both. Regardless, the students would eat lunch on campus. Lunch on campus was considered their primary "payment," and was always well received. After lunch, the students are taken on a short tour of the campus.

During instruction, the task was introduced briefly by the professor and the children showed examples of their finished work. Then the children began tutoring the college students through the required task. As the children needed help, their teacher and the professor stepped in to fulfill that need. During the tutoring session, there was ample opportunity for the children and the college students to interact informally.

Upon completion of the task, the college students and the children had an opportunity for further sharing. The children were asked to give the future teachers advice on teaching and the college students were asked to tell the children one thing they enjoyed about college.

Outcomes

Beyond the primary outcome of demonstrating the abilities of young children, several other benefits were derived. Possibly the most important outcome it provided was the opportunity for the children to demonstrate their technical skills and develop teaching skills. In the ten years, the ability of each group of children has varied, but never has a group failed to be able to accomplish the task. The impact of that accomplishment has been powerful over the years. It has noticeably raised the attitudes of the children, giving them a concrete source of pride.

The visit to campus, the campus tour, the informal and formal discourse with the college students all contributed to a new awareness of the possibility of college for the children. Many of the children had little or no experience with college life. They frequently asked questions about what life in a dorm or a sorority house was like (e.g., "Do they have TV?"). They were curious about schedules and rules (e.g., "You can really sleep until noon some days?"). During the visit, many children said things like, "I am going to go to college here." This was clearly a new thought for many of them.

The tutorial session provided the professor with an early observation of the college students' interactions with children. This was a useful way to begin to see the future teachers' dispositions toward children. More than once, experiences like a small child climbing into a college student's lap prompted them to rethink their decision about teaching or the grade level they were considering. The few college students who simply could not appropriately interact with the children were identified and counseled.

Over the ten years of this project, the results have vastly outweighed the time, money, and effort needed to accomplish it. The relationships that have formed have been invaluable for all involved, professor, teachers, college students, and children.

Multimedia Mathematics Tutor : Matching Instruction to Student's Learning Styles

Nor Azan Mat Zin, Halimah Badioze Zaman and Shahrul Azman Mohd. Noah
Department of Information Science
Faculty of Technology and Information Science
National University of Malaysia. 43600 UKM BANGI
azan@sun1.ftsm.ukm.my

Abstract

Mathematics is an important subject for science and technological careers but many children still have difficulties and failures in mathematics learning. Therefore, educational design for effective learning and teaching environment is important in the prevention and remediation of mathematical learning difficulties. Since individuals differ in cognitive ability (intelligence), prior knowledge and the way they perceive and process information or learning styles, adapting instruction to these differences will facilitate learning and thus help increase learning gains especially for low and moderate achieving students. Information Technology, in the form of courseware can be used effectively to individualize instruction. We are developing a learning style inventory to identify student's learning styles and propose a multimedia tutor that can adapt instruction to learner's styles and ability level for secondary school mathematics.

1: Introduction

Mathematics is an important subject for science and technological careers but many children still have difficulties and failures in mathematics learning. School children who fail to master basic arithmetic and algebra continue to have problems later on in related college subjects that require the use of these basic literacy in their problem-solving activities. Most observed failures and substandard performance in mathematics are due to insufficient teaching-learning environment. Learning difficulties due to deficiency or developmental delay of cognitive components are also reinforced and shaped by environmental influences, for example, insufficient measures taken by the instructional and educational support system [1]. Therefore, educational design of effective learning and teaching environment should be considered a key factor both in the prevention and remediation of a wide class of mathematical learning difficulties. Adapting instruction to individual learner's differences such as learning styles (LS), and prior knowledge will help maximise learning gains especially for low and moderate achieving students.

Computer-aided instructional (CAI) software which has been around for some times and proven effective can be used for students who fail to learn through normal classroom instruction and need individualized tutoring. Under the Malaysian smart school project, CAI software are being developed and used in participating schools. However, these traditional CAI software which are costly to produce have limitations, they cannot be tailored for individual learning since they are not able adapt to student's different traits such as learning styles which affect learning outcomes. Students are not given any informative feedback or remedial tutoring if he makes mistakes such that wrong knowledge is inadvertently reinforced. Thus a model for an intelligent CAI that can adapts instruction to student's ability and learning styles is proposed to help overcome limitations of the current mathematics software. In this paper, we discuss the first part of our research, the development of LS conceptual framework and instrument to diagnose student's LS.

2: Learning Style

Individuals vary in their aptitudes for learning, their willingness to learn and the styles and preferences for learning. Traits that affect learning outcomes include intelligence, cognitive controls and cognitive styles, learning styles, personality and prior knowledge. Intelligence is the aggregate of mental abilities that individual possesses and can use in interacting with instruction and accomplishing learning outcomes [2]. Intelligence form a foundation for cognitive control and cognitive styles which in turn determine learning styles. Cognitive styles reflect an individual's perceptual habit and approach to organizing and representing information. Learning style is a consistent way an individual acquires, retains, and retrieves information in a learning environment, based on his cognitive styles.

Learning performance is affected by an interaction between cognitive style and the structure of instructional material, its mode of presentation and type of content [3], therefore different structural design of instructional material will facilitates different styles of learning and thus influences learning achievement. Matching instruction to learner's learning preferences will facilitates acquisition and processing of information. If information is in the preferred mode then processing load is less. For some learners additional processing load result in a longer time being required to learn the information or at worst the load may exceed capacity and the information will not be learned at all. Matching instructional styles to LS can significantly enhance academic achievement, student attitudes, and student behaviour. Previous researches on LS showed numerous varied models with their own measuring tools, used in different situations such as for training or teaching and different target population such as school children or adults. We propose a perceptual modality and cognitive LS model shown in figure 1.

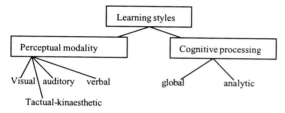

Figure 1. Conceptual model of Learning Style

Based on this model, we have designed an inventory to identify learner's most preferred modality and cognitive processing. This will be used with the courseware, an intelligent CAI for the domain of percentage in mathematics for secondary school students.

3: Intelligent CAI

Intelligent CAI or Intelligent Tutoring Systems (ITSs) are computer-based instructional systems with common elements of 1)tutoring strategy (pedagogical module), 2) learner model 3) knowledge base (domain knowledge), and 4) learner interface or communication module [4]. Multimedia elements which are useful to facilitate different LS modality will be incorporated to provide a context for learning during problem-solving, concept presentation [5] or to provide attractive learning environment such as presenting hints to guide student's problem solving [6]. The functional diagram of the proposed tutor is shown in figure 2.

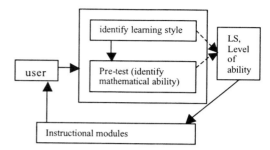

Fig. 2 Functional diagram of the proposed tutor

Conclusion

Individual traits such as ability and LS can affect learning outcomes. Different LS includes perceptual modality of visual, auditory, verbal and tactile-kinaesthetic while styles of cognitive processing are analytic, global or in between. An intelligent CAI which can adapt instruction to these different styles provide an individualised instruction that can help low and moderate achieving students understand difficult mathematical concepts better. Matching instructions to learner's style will facilitate acquisition and processing of information to be learned. The proposed tutoring system will help teachers in giving remediation to weak and average students.

References

[1] Reusser, K. (2000). "Success and Failure in School mathematics: Effects of Instruction and School Environment." European Child & Adolescent Psychiatry 9(Suppl.2): 11/17-11/26.
[2] Jonassen, D. &Grabowski, B. 1993. Handbook of Individual Differences: Learning & Instruction. Hillsdale, New Jersey: Lawrence Erlbaum Associates.
[3] Riding, R. dan Rayner, S. 1998. Cognitive Style and Strategies. London: David Fulton Publishers Ltd.
[4] Y.D.Yoo. PITS: An Intelligent Tutoring System Loosely Coupled to External DataBase Systems in *Intelligent Systems*, E.A.YfantisT(ed.):79-728.
[5] Ilart, et al. (1999). WhaleWatch: An Intelligent Multimedia Math Tutor.
[6] Beal, et al. (2000). Gaining Confidence in Mathematics: instructional technology for Girls. 2000. (at ftp:// queequeg.cs.umass.edu/public/papers/mset2000.ps)

Teachers' Professional Development in Vocational Education with Technology Integration

Chien-Chih (James) Lee, Assistant Professor/ Director of Instructional Media Center
Wenzao College of Languages, Kaohsiung, Taiwan, R.O.C

Abstract

Vocational teachers today face the challenge of utilizing and integrating computers and related technologies into their instruction in a manner that enhances student learning and achievement. Based on International Society for Technology in Education (2000) standards, teachers should demonstrate understanding of technology operation and concepts, implement curriculum plans to maximize student learning, and use technology to enhance productivity and professional practices. This teaching unit is designed for teachers' and school personnel' professional development in vocational education system. The unit is designed to meet all six facets of understanding including explanation, interpretation, application, perspective empathy, and self-knowledge. In the paper, several issues also will be considered to incorporate a technology component into the activity when design this teaching unit.

I. Introduction

Vocational teachers today face the challenge of utilizing and integrating computers and related technologies into their instruction in a manner that enhances student learning and achievement. Modeling appropriate uses of these resources by teachers in the classroom can help teachers with the necessary knowledge and skills to use these tools effectively in their classrooms. Dyrli and Kinnaman (1994) stated, "Technology has transformed every segment of American society--except education . . . schooling today remains much the same as it was before the advent of the personal computer" (p. 92). Barriers to using technology in education include lack of teacher time, limited access and high costs, lack or vision or rationale for technology use, lack of training and support, and current assessment practices that may not reflect what has been learned with technology (OTA, 1995). Competencies focus on the ability of vocational teacher to utilize and integrate a wide variety of educational computing and technology applications to enhance student learning and to increase teacher productivity. Saye (1998) stated that four general factors must be considered before teachers will accept and use technology: time, preparation for future, knowledge, and availability. This course is designed as a professional development course for use with classroom teachers and school personnel in vocational education system. Upon completion of the course, the participants will be able to integrate technology into classroom instruction and feel prepared to use technology for instructional and personal use.

II. Get ready to integrate technology

U.S. Secretary of Education Richard W. Riley released the nation's first educational technology plan in 1996. In 2000, he announced a new plan showing "where progress has been made, where new opportunities exist, and where challenges remain" and included news of five new national goals and a link to the plan. Integrating technology can seem like a formidable task to the vocational teacher. But what if there was a way to bring computers into the curriculum while saving time and engaging the learner? Technology can enhance learning---and calls on teachers to take a leadership role in determining the ways in which technology is used to support educational goals. Based on International Society for Technology in Education (2000) standards, teachers should demonstrate understanding of technology operation and concepts, implement curriculum plans to maximize student learning, and use technology to enhance productivity and professional practices. Technology benefits teachers by not only providing information, but the real advantage is that these tools can save time and energy in order to offer guidance for research and communication. Teachers need to be able to use technology in the classroom in order to prepare students for the 21st century.

III. Design principles of understanding

The unit is designed to meet all six facets of understanding according to principals of understanding by design (Grant Wiggins & Jay McTighe, 1998). The first facet is explanation. Participants will relate current research to classmates. The second is interpretation. Upon learning about the Internet, participants will interpret the information to brainstorm ways to integrate the Internet into the classroom on an understanding level. Participants will interpret current research to synthesize it for classmates. The third is application. Participants will search the Internet, utilize e-mail, create a web page, compose a biography paper (Word), compose a biography presentation (PowerPoint), compare student performance (Excel), and conduct and synthesize research. The next is perspective. The teachers must evaluate the sites for use by other teachers. They must take into consideration the needs of others. Participants will determine if research information. The fifth facet is empathy. Participants will discuss perceptions of technology (fears, failures, successes. Participants will discuss amounts of technology available in their own school districts. The last is self-knowledge. The teachers must evaluate the sites for use in their own classrooms and instruction. They must consider what they will and will not use and why.

When design this teaching unit, the following issues need to be considered. The first issue is to consider what enduring understandings are required. Teachers will understand that technology can improve both teaching and learning. In addition, teachers will understand the importance of technology integration in the classroom. The second issue is to review what the overarching "essential" questions are such as what do you know about the importance of technology in the 21st century and "how can technology affect the efficiency of school personnel". The next issue is to look at what teachers understand as a result of this unit will. The purposes are that teachers will understand how to use the Internet to search, to use e-mail, to use Instant Messenger and to design a class and/or personal web page. Teachers will understand how to use Microsoft Office applications (Word, PowerPoint, and Excel) to increase efficiency of classroom organizational tasks. Teachers will understand the importance of technology integration in the classroom to improve teaching and learning. The fourth issue is to consider what "essential" and "unique" questions will focus this unit. Some samples are (1) What is the Internet? (2) How can the Internet be a useful classroom tool? (3) How can Microsoft Office applications be useful to teachers? and (4) What does current educational research say about the integration of technology in the classroom? The last issue is, "What evidence will show that students understand technology integration?"

IV. Incorporate a technology component into the activity

This activity will allow teachers to start thinking about technology integration. Though they may be aware of technology, some teachers are not aware of the benefits of technology integration. Teachers will read the article and discuss it in small groups. The article will be used to facilitate a large group discussion of technology integration. Teachers would love to incorporate a technology component into the activity. The fist procedure is to distribute copies of the article "Computers, Creativity, and the Curriculum: The Challenge for Schools, Literacy, and Learning" (Sefton-Green, 2001). Then the participants will read the article. While reading the article, the teachers will note uses for technology in the classroom as well as barriers of technology use in the classroom. In groups of 3 to 5, the teacher will discuss their thoughts. Each group will share their thinking in a brief oral presentation. Based on the comments of the groups, a large group discussion will be facilitated. The following topics for discussion are: (1)Why do you think technology

can be scary? (2) Why do teachers integrate technology?" (3) Why do teachers not integrate technology? (4) What could be done to make teachers more likely to integrate technology? (5) What differences do you see in the amounts of technology present in various school districts? and (6) How and why do I integrate technology in the classroom? Finally, the teachers will write reflectively according to the following prompt. The teachers will understand the goal of the workshop through reading and discussion and begin to think about the role of technology in the classroom. The materials will be copies of the article, writing prompt. The instructor will read the reflection of each teacher and will be looking for positive and negative aspects of current technology integration, or lack thereof. In addition, follow-up will occur on an individual and large group basis. The follow-up will depend on changes in thinking from the first day writing prompt to the mid-unit writing prompt.

V. Conclusion

It was created to prepare teachers to use technology in the classroom for vocational education. In order for this unit to be successful, each participant will need access to a computer, the Internet, Netscape, Microsoft Office, and a printer. The goal of the unit is to give teachers an understanding of technology uses and applications that will benefit instruction and organization in the classroom. Also, teachers will understand the importance of technology integration. Any instructor using this unit must be highly skilled in technology use. The developers recommend that a district Technology Coordinator be the instructor for this unit. Additionally, the instructor should show knowledge of current educational research concerning technology integration.

References

Dyrli, O. E., & Kinnaman, D. E. (1994). Preparing for the integration of emerging technologies. Technology & Learning, 14(9), 92-100.

Grant Wiggins and Jay McTighe , 1998. Understanding by design. Association for Supervision and Curriculum Development http://www.ascd.org/readingroom/books/wiggins98book.html

International Society for Technology in Education. (2000). ISTE national technology standards (NETS) and performance indicators. Retrieved July 17, 2001, from the World Wide Web: http://cnets.iste.org/teachstand.html.

Saye,J. W. (1998). Technology in the classroom: The role of disposition in teacher gatekeeping. Journal of Curriculum and Supervision, 13 (3), 210-234.

Sefton-Green, J. (2001). Computers, creativity, and the curriculum: The challenge for schools, literacy, and learning. Journal of Adolescent & Adult Literacy, 44 (8), 726-728.

Office of Technology Assessment. (1995). Teachers and technology: Making the connection, Washington D.C.: U.S. Government Printing Office.

Computers in Teaching-Learning of Physics Discipline: Investigating Different Methodologies

Eliane Regina de Almeida Valiati
evaliati@inf.ufrgs.br
Renato Heineck
reheck@uol.com.br
Universidade de Passo Fundo
Instituto de Ciências Exatas e Geociências
Passo Fundo - RS, Brasil Caixa Postal: 611
CEP 99001-970 Telefone: 054-316-8351

Abstract

Nowadays, the use of the computer science is an unquestionable fact in all sections of our society. In the last years, in Brazil, some public and private incentives have been permitting to take for some teaching institutions a little of this reality. Therefore what we can question today is not if the computer has out not to enter schools, since this is unavoidable but how technology has to be incorporated to the school context in order to provide the learning process and universalization of knowledge. In this sense, a great deal still needs to be developed and investigated in way to guarantee that the new technologies do not just arrive at schools, but that they are appropriately used in classroom. This article shows the results obtained in a research work that had for objective to evaluate the use of different methodologies and resources in teaching learning in physics discipline.

Keywords: learning process, educational softwares, Physics.

1. INTRODUCTION

Today, technology invades great space of our quotidian. Different from this reality it is in most of Brazilian schools, which should offer to students the use of computers as one more didactic-pedagogic resource, exploring its advantages in order to enrich the educational process.

There are incentives but for that it happens, there is much to be done for new technologies be appropriately developed and used in classroom. So, this article presents a research work, that has as main objective develop an educational software for teaching-learning contents of Physics and to evaluate its use in classroom, looking for question the different methodologies used in Physics teaching, its pedagogical inferences, its didactic resources, as well as, its implications in its use, as on students' part as on teacher's part.

In section 2 we discuss the teaching-learning process of Physics and the experimental method; in section 3 we present the proposed software; in section 4 it is described the methodology used for the software evaluation in classroom and, finally, in section 5 we report some results and conclusions.

2. TEACHING-LEARNING OF PHYSICS DISCIPLINE

On research results, published by Yager [4], it is verified by didactic investigation that certain number of students disinterest themselves for Physics discipline (and other sciences) during the schooling period.

This perhaps happens because of the teaching manner presented for them, where many times the concepts worked are far away from the practice. They present a little or no one relation to the facts of the quotidian. They don't use appropriate didactic resources that motivate and help the learning process.

According to Heineck [2], Physics classes with support of experimental, organized and adapted methods, provide the incentive, favor the learning, increase expectations that students develop during investigation techniques, stood out by Vygotsky as the zone of proximal development [3].

Even so, unhappily, most of schools do not have or can't acquire materials for Physics laboratories, because of their very high costs, or they do not offer physical space for their assembly and use.

Due to such difficulties, many teachers adopt traditional methodologies of simple repassing contents (with the use of resources as blackboard, chalk and didactic books) couldn't make it possible to use methodologies in which students can practice the knowledge they've got from theoretical contents.

3. EDUCATIONAL SOFTWARE WITH CONTENTS OF PHYSICS

The Passo Fundo University Department of Physics, during more than 20 years, elaborates tests and adapts equipment for laboratories of Physics from instructional materials. Those, for its time, have also been tested, appraised and approved by teachers from regional schools, in systematic meetings promoted by Physics area.

The software that was developed, in partnership between Physics and Computer science areas, is an educational multimedia software composed of Physics contents (based on the equipment and experiments produced in laboratory), organized in different modules. Each module has: specific conceptual explanations about the studied content, additional information related to the content, a video with explanations that reproduce the equipment and experiment done in laboratory, an interactive experiment based on the experimentation accomplished on the video and interpretation exercises and comprehension of the content.

This way, we searched through this educational software to supply schools with a didactic resource for their teaching learning of Physics contents with experimental methods.

4. METHODOLOGY OF THE RESEARCH

The concern of this research was not just in obtaining quantitative data, which become insufficient to achieve the essential, but as the teachers see their formation and how it interferes in their pedagogic practice. Therefore, the accomplishment of a study centered in the educational practice of a qualitative approach was proposed and that in agreement with Bardin "falls back upon indicators not frequencies susceptible of allowing inferences" [1].

Thus, the research activities accomplished at the target-school happened in the following way and under these conditions:

a) the research had as objective two groups from high school from the same grades and from the same teaching institution;

b) in group A, the teacher of Physics discipline worked the content on Newton's Laws just using the traditional methodology (Blackboard, chalk, bookish and theorization);

c) at the same period of time, the teacher of Physics discipline taught the same content using the educational software with his students from group B;

d) after the two groups have worked the same content with the same teacher, even so using different methodologies and didactic resources, we collected the data with the Physics teacher and students from both groups;

The instruments used to collect data were characterized

for containing 10 driven questions, that they looked for to collect information on the use of the didactic resources adopted in classroom, the understanding of the worked content, the influence of the different methodologies adopted about the same theme for the same teacher and the relationships of Physics content with daily routines.

After finishing the collect of the data with the educator and students from the two groups of the school-target, the analysis of content of that information was accomplished.

5. SOME RESULTS AND CONCLUSIONS

Thus, among the main results and conclusions obtained with this research, we can mention:

1) students great majority, of both investigated groups, were unmotivated in concerning physics discipline, regarding the methodology and resources used in classroom;

2) the teacher drove the classes, in general, with many theorical explanations and formulas, little practice and use of experiments, demonstrating a very strong dependence of an only didactic book;

3) even so, analyzing specifically group B, in which the students used the software for their teaching-learning of Newton's Laws content, we could notice that:

- there were more motivation and interest for all the students in learning this content;

- some students could to understand the content well and others presented learning difficulties, using the educational software as only resource in classroom;

- a considerable number of students pointed to the use of a hybrid approach (of methodologies and resources), springing here up indicatives for new subjects to be investigated;

Therefore, we can notice through these results and conclusions that many of our objectives were reached, as well as, spring up strong indicatives that new researches need to be accomplished as continuation of this work.

On the other hand, we hope that the software here proposed as well as the results to be obtained with this research can help in the reflection of the use of the new technologies at schools and to contribute, positively, to the teaching of Physics contents becomes more joyful and stimulant for the students.

6. REFERENCES

[1] BARDIN, L. **Análise de conteúdo**. Lisboa: Edições 70, 1988.
[2] HEINECK, R. **Relações entre as disciplinas de Física e de Didática de Ciências no curso de magistério-ensino médio**. Dissertação de Mestrado. Universidade de Passo Fundo, 1999.
[3] VYGOTSKY, L. S. **A formação social da mente**. 6. ed. São Paulo: Martins Fontes, 1984.
[4] YAGER, R. E. Perceptions of four age groups toward science classes: Teachers and the value of science. In: **Actividades Exploratórias-Experimentales en la Educacion Cientifica em Edad Infantil y Primaria**. Universutat de Valencia, 1991.

New Business Model for Universities – Impact of Metacapitalism

Pedro Paraíso
pparaiso@crb.ucp.pt
International Institute for Applied Informatics and Flexible Learning
Viseu - Portugal

Abstract

In the old economy educational organizations and their executives played the role of gatekeepers. In the 21st century the tables have turned. ICT produced a Metamarket focus from customer-centric to customer-driven. The new model must design new strategies to "compete aggressively".

Introduction

In the old economy, if something was scarce it was valuable. Educational organizations and their executives played the role of gatekeepers, shoring up the boundaries of the institution both internally, by creating hierarchies, and externally, by remaining largely unconnected with the outside world. The institution was free to function at the center of its universe.

In the 21st century the tables have turned. It is openness and availability that drive value. The more people who have access to a product or an idea, the better. Success is achieved through alliances with partners, direct contact with all types of "customers" and collaboration with competitors.

There is a new importance around connections between different institutions and customers target, the right orientation can mean the difference between success and failure.

The leaderships of such institutions are daily forced to face the following question: "Is our organizational structure ready to interact with such kind of information, made possible by the Internet era?"

The focus consists to know more, to learn faster at finally and operate at lower costs.

The " new learning products" will be centered on the "client" side and, in this sense, present the following features: - it should provide the information wanted, in order to obtain the previously defined aims; - it should include features of permanent actualization and adaptation to the profile of the user; - it should have a modular structure; - the accessibility should constitute one of the mains concerns at the creation base; - the evaluation should be previously defined, foreseeing the possibility of interaction with experts on the subject at stake.

A New Management Model for Universities

With this integration process, people in general and organizations in particular seek to fond connection ways, in order to materialize new contact points, characterized in their essential by the multi-directionality of a network independently they establish one synchronous or asynchronous connection. In this context new fluxes are identified and their essential constitution involves people, objects and information. [1]

A new temporal measure represents essentially abstraction and the complete separation between human experience and the rhythms of nature. Information became instantly or simultaneously available at any location. In this context, knowledge implies an increasing process of "de-territorialization", generically changing into bits of information. [2]

The functional methodology of the university institutions will necessarily move from the well-known teaching/learning periods, semesters, credit units and academic years, to new organization strategies, which take into consideration the dimension of global time. [3]

The university institutions are relatively weak in establishing and sustaining cooperation networks, which allow the same "pedagogical product" to be introduced in the same way, reflecting the same standard. "Is the teaching staff ready to interact with a new academic environment?" "Has the possibility of being replaced by someone with a better and more competitive socio-professional frame ever been considered at any point in the career of this teaching staff?" Questions like these lead us to question the new mission of "university" institutions with frames included in an increasingly global world and with an institutional competition more and more differentiated.

Strategic Position in a new Economy – the Innovation

The opportunities within the education market today are quite distinct of those of a few years ago, essentially in what concerns the inversion that occurred in the positioning of the pre-graduate studies relatively to the post-graduate studies, and more recently concerning life long learning.

The essential market condition has changed each year for the most part of the university institutions, particularly concerning the following aspects: the number of candidates, the typology and expectations of the candidates towards the offer. With the globalization process previously mentioned, some concerns arose related with the efficiency and synchronization of the new distribution channels, the planning of organization resources corresponding to an adaptation of the ERP, the increased use of technology for the process of decision-making and Internet, as a means of integration of both academy dimensions.

The same changes, however, also produce new opportunities for more attentive and better-equipped organizations.

This organizations should therefore provide a fast response to the impact of these changes, in order to maximize the creation of value and a corresponding more attractive offer.

The traditional departments of university institutions will have to assume a new position of greater creativity and innovation, in order to provide a response to the new market demands. They can do so by identifying new academic programs, pedagogical methodologies or by using new pedagogical equipment based on ICT. This will lead them to materialize differentiation factors, which generate a positive attractively in all organization dimensions. [4]

The activity oriented for the consumer, or for the market in a general way, has forced to create new management models, where the new methods for raising value are quite distinct from the ones identified before.

The competitive advantage of the new university organizations derives from the use of new strategies and processes, which allow the organization to act in face of change in the framing market, and to do so in a fast and flexible way.

Universities should even be prepared to restructure their own organization, and thus be ready to create or extinct pedagogic-scientific units.

Simultaneously, university organizations need more than ever to adopt company management models, in order to better identify and apply the best options, which continuously emerge for the organization, and thus to apply them in such a way that allows them to generate the necessary value.

The majority of students, now regarded as clients, prefer to choose degrees with great professional visibility, and which are socially relevant and productive.

In the present context the academic products to be offered to an increasingly demanding market, should explicitly be related to a specific domain, reflecting a holistic vision of this selected domain.

In this frame, four essential factors are identified in order to enable the model to operate:

1)   The clear change into organizations based on Internet;

2)   Focus on the "client";

3)   The adoption of flattened structures as a privileged way of company organization;

4)   Establishing of a clear separation between educational organizations and research organizations.

These four great factors imply the revision of the future universities as strategic business units in the education market, characterized by only two levels of decision and where from the first step the organizational mission and vision are identified and included in a well-defined business plan. In this sense, the creation and development of innovative ideas require strong discipline and the excellency of processes, which originate multiple conditions, such as: understanding business as such, understanding products and identifying the life cycle associated to them.

Conclusion

The discontent of most university students, the permanent pressure of the new ICT tools draws the university each time closer to the meta-capitalist model.

This proximity hypothetically designs the solution for the greatest problem the sector faces as the moment – the decrease in demand as the result of transformations occurring in the physiological balance. With the specific orientation of this orientation, the demand will exponentially increase with the opening of new academic institutions and products, related to the global market in the present operational conditions.

The recognition of university education as meta-market will develop a new role for the university, where net-based audiences will be larger than those, which typify the sector nowadays. This meta-market will be characterized by a great consolidation among different institutions it includes. It will also demand the slow decapitalization of university structures, where the need for a set of great physical infrastructures will progressively decrease. The organization and management of this meta-market will be the task of some universities, which sooner and best realize need for change.

Main References

[1] Albrow, .M., "*The Global Age.*", Cambridge: Polity, 1996.
[2] Delanty, .G., "*The idea of the university in the global era: from knowledge as an end to an end of knowledge*", Social Epistemology, 12: 3-25, 1998.
[3] Cooper, .W. E., "*Restructuring the university.*", Science **282**, 1047, 1998.
[4] Gazzaniga, .M. S., "*How to change the university.*", Science **282**, 237,1998.

Connecting Context and Creating Relevant Pedagogy: Deep Viewing of an Online Learning Community

Cynthia C. Choi, Ph.D.
Department of Education
Le Moyne College
Syracuse, NY
choicc@lemoyne.edu

Abstract

With a massive connectivity movement occurring throughout American schools, these learning networks present suitable environment for peer learning activities. While the prevalence of these networked communication tools tend to encourage formation of online learning communities, effective assessment strategies of such

Keywords: Peer Learning; Assessment; Online Learning Communities

INTRODUCTION

During the past several decades, analytical techniques to analyze the cognitive processes that are generated by the students' interaction have deepened our understanding of peers discourse and its impact on student learning. While researchers have learned much about the ways in which interactions among students in groups promote learning (Chinn, O'Donnell, & Jinks, 2000), discussion on effective assessment strategies for learning outcomes and learning processes of online small group discussion have been limited. As these networked communication tools tend to encourage formation of online learning communities, peer learning activities are more widespread among various learning settings, in particular, online learning environments. Although much of the investigation on peer-learning relationships is directed toward face-to-face interactions, with the increasingly prevalent application of technology in various learning environments, more attention is necessary to examine this strategy in online context.

In this investigation, "Virtual Classroom," an online activity developed for preservice and inservice teachers enrolled in an educational technology course of a teacher preparation program was examined. The learning objective of this activity is two fold: content knowledge and creation of a strong collaborative learning environment. Using the deep viewing methodology

learning remain to be addressed. In this investigation, Deep Viewing methodology (Watts Pailliotet, 1998) was applied to assess learning outcomes and learning processes of online small group discussion among preservice and inservice teachers. As a result of this critical viewing, the need for connecting context and creating relevant pedagogy is shared.

(Watts Pailliotet, 1998), applied in the field of media literacy, learning outcomes and learning processes of three content driven online small group discussions were examined. Data source for this investigation includes online exchanges generated by nine small groups of 5 to 7 students, as well as written documentation of each group's process.

FRAMEWORK and METHODOLOGICAL APPROACH

Deep viewing's theoretical basis is from the premises shared among literacy researchers, media analysts, and critical theorists, embodying many intermedial principles and processes. Combined with a heuristic framework (Lusted, 1991), understanding print and visual information is guided by semiotic codes (Barthes, 1974; Saint-Martin, 1990), and three leveled comprehension models (Herber & Herber, 1993; Himley, 1991). Extended from Himley's (1991) notions of "Deep Talk" to visual text, this method have been used to analyze electronic media, print media, as well as for observation and of instruction and social interactions in classrooms and schools. This three-leveled deep viewing process, *Literal, Interpretation, and Synthesis*, offered as a systematic process guided critical analysis of archived online dialogue generated by preservice and inservice teachers in its natural setting.

Extending the following deep viewing categories outlined by Watts Palliotet (1998), series of guiding questions were developed to analyze the data and to collect evidence of learning outcomes and processes:

Deep Viewing Categories*	Guiding Questions for Assessment of Online Discourse
Action/Sequence ...to look at what occurs, when, and for how long	**Description of Events** ▪ When during the allowed time period did discussion occur? ▪ Did every member participate? ▪ How was turn taking structured? ▪ How long were the discussions?
Semes/Forms ...to record visual forms then examines their characteristics	**Examination of Instructional Environment** ▪ Who/what is pictured? ▪ Characteristics of folders, icons, graphics, and other visuals?
Actors/Discourse ...to examine what texts say	**Content Analysis** ▪ Who talks to whom? ▪ How main ideas or themes articulated and conveyed? ▪ How is it communicated? ▪ How is it heard or understood?
Proximity/Movement ...to record what sorts of movements occur	**Flow of Interaction** ▪ How is the learning space used? ▪ What types of communication (asynchronous/synchronous) is used?
Culture/Context ...to note symbolic and discourse references to cultural knowledge	**Critical Analysis** ▪ Any references to cultural knowledge? ▪ Any assumptions related to understanding based on "common" knowledge ▪ How stereotypes, issues of control, and equity represented?
Effects/Processes ...to examine how production elements and quality affect meaning	**Effectiveness of the Process** ▪ How production What is seen? ▪ What is missing? ▪ What is the quality?

* Watts Palliotet, 1998

DISCUSSION and CONCLUSION

To facilitate the process, "Blackboard 5," the institutionally adapted platform with comprehensive and flexible course management tools was employed as the interaction medium to foster online learning communities. This software allowed students to navigate to different areas, such as announcements, course information, assignments, communication, discussion board, groups, and tools.

For each "virtual class", in-class planning time is provided and suggested process guidelines are offered as follows:

Phase 0   Strategizing a plan – organize
          All members share in developing an action plan.
Phase 1   Sharpening the focus – summarize/synthesize
          1-2 members provide an overview of the article.
Phase 2   Deepening the dialogue – moderate

          1-3 members develop and pose discussion questions.
Phase 3   Documenting the process – record
          1-2 members document group process – timeline, effectiveness, challenges, frustrations, aha moments.

Each group had the option to interact both asynchronously by using the "Discussion Board" feature and synchronously through live chat titled "Group Virtual Classroom". For those group selecting the Discussion Board, they are directed into a webpage where discussion forums are posted. The following excerpts model content discussion related to personal experiences and applications of the assigned reading among three students.

Student 1   [The Author] says children under the age of 7 don't need to use computers. Do you agree? Thoughts?

Student 2   I do agree with her for the most part. . . .While I agree that some of the games are good at building eye/hand coordination, I think there are many other activities that would achieve the same end result that do not involve sitting in front of a computer terminal. I think that children, under the age of 7 especially, have a great opportunity to use their imaginations. Therefore, using computer games as a form of entertainment at that age is unnecessary. If computer programs can be used effectively to teach spelling, reading, or math, then I would encourage its usage, but in a limited dose.

Student 3 . . . From my own personal experience I have found that many software programs that are beneficial for kids at a 7th grade level are fairly complicated. A number of the activities that I have done have involved the teacher guiding the students through most of the activity on the computer or require a tutorial for them to look at when they got stuck. ... I don't know how user-friendly programs are for younger kids but I would imagine this would cause a problem with younger kids. Are any of the group members elementary teachers that have a little more information on this?

Overall, student feedback and archived interactions show that small communities of learners were indeed established. Students referred to each other by name and appeared to feel comfortable enough to openly share personal comments and perspectives. Archived interactions demonstrate a high level of critical inquiry of content through constructive challenges of one's responses. In addition, the general tone of discussion is with respect and encouragement. These peer learning groups shared responsibility of achieving mutual goals to successfully complete each virtual discussion.

In facilitating the development of collaborative learning relationships, collaborative effort among the learners help them achieve a deeper level of knowledge generation while moving from independence to interdependence. The development of collaborative skills requires a means of study and an environment for study that (a) lets a group of students formulate a shared goal for their learning process; (b) allows the students to use personal motivating problems, interests, and experiences as springboards; and (c) takes dialogue as the fundamental way of inquiry (Collison, Elbaum, Haavind, & Tinker, 2000). While

online peer learning effectively support content learning, it was also extended to facilitate discussions of real-life concerns and applications.

REFERENCES

Berge, Z. & Collins, M. (1995). Computer-mediated communication and the online classroom. Cresskill, NJ: Hampton Press.

Chinn, C. A., O'Donnell, A. M., & Jinks, T. S. (2000). The structure of discourse in collaborative learning. The Journal of Experimental Education, 69(1), 77-97.

Collison, G., Elbaum, B., Haavind, S., & Tinker, R. (2000). Facilitating online learning: Effective strategies for moderators. Madison, WI: Atwood.

Herber H. L., & Herber, J. N. (1993). Teaching in content areas with reading, writing, and reasoning. Boston: Allyn and Bacon.

Himley, M. (1991). Shared territory: Understanding children's writing as works. New York: Oxford University Press.

Jonassen, D., Davidson, M., Collins, M., Campbell, J., & Bannan-Haag, B. (1995). Constructivism and computer-mediated communication in distance education. American Journal of Distance Education, 9(2), 7-26.

Watts Pailliotet, A. (1998). Deep viewing: A critical look at texts. In S. Steinberg & J. Kincheloe (Eds.), Unauthroized methods: Strategies for critical teaching (pp. 123-136). New York: Routledge.

Mentoring in Online Learning Communities

Lynnette R. Porter
Humanities and Social Sciences Department
Embry-Riddle Aeronautical University
Daytona Beach, Florida, USA

Abstract

Learners in university-level communication or technical communication web-enhanced classes should benefit from an online mentoring program. Mentors from several disciplines, geographic locations, and companies should be selected. An online mentoring program should provide learners with practical experience in communicating online with professionals, as well as provide learners with new perspectives and accurate information. Learners, mentors, and teachers should benefit from the program.

Because Internet resources are often general, and anyone can put anything on the web without peer review or content editing, information gathered by online learners may be false, misleading, outdated, incomplete *or* insightful, current, and effectively researched. However, learners, on their own, may not be able to tell the difference between a legitimate argument or high-quality research and biased or inaccurate data that support their or their peers' preconceptions about a subject.

Problems in evaluating Internet resources and expanding learners' views beyond their preconceptions may be exacerbated when learners take online or web-enhanced courses. Adult learners tend to be highly focused on career preparation and have little time to examine alternative perspectives about each topic that they encounter in a class. In-class or online discussions may be limited; if the discussion isn't required, many adults won't take time just to chat with others or debate topics of mutual interest, especially online.

How, then, can online learning communities foster true education and expose learners to a wider range of resources and ideas that are more likely to represent current theory and practice? How can learners be lured into more active participation in learning communities?

One way that university-level learners may gain more correct information, as well as access to a wider range of resources and perspectives, is through mentors who are subject matter experts. Online mentors who share professional insights, examples, and project critiques help learners better understand the complexity of a subject. These mentors can guide discussions, provide "outside" opinions, and introduce learners and teachers to Internet resources that they may not have previously discovered. When several subject experts are actively involved in the course, learners are exposed to perspectives that most likely are different from their peers' in the classroom.

Career-oriented learners more often value learning communities when the members include not only their peers or teacher, but also professionals who can provide insights into what learners need to know and must be able to do in order to be successful. Learners can expand their network of contacts, and mentors often are willing to help learners outside of the established parameters of the class.

Online communities allow teachers to involve mentors outside regular business hours and from a variety of locations. Online mentoring is an ideal way for teachers to bring more mentors from different technical/scientific specializations into learning communities and give learners practical experience in writing communication that will be evaluated by professionals, a requirement for learners planning to enter communication professions.

Online mentoring is not a new process, but it hasn't been widely used throughout technical or general communication classrooms. The benefits described in previous studies of high school and university students [1, 2] also should be found when mentoring is introduced in web-enhanced classes. Online learning communities can help nurture learners and build their self-esteem through online learning communities [3]. Learners may ask more questions of mentors, who don't give them a grade and can't see them through print e-mail. Visual anonymity and synchronous communication that can be edited before it is sent can encourage learners to work more often and more closely with mentors. Formal online mentoring has seldom been used to create a "real world" atmosphere, although teachers agree that simulating the workplace is important [4, 5, 6]. My plan for fall 2002 classes includes the following steps: 1. Establish a group of online mentors, representing different subject areas, job titles, and companies, who have agreed to respond to learners' e-mail messages throughout the course; 2. Set up rules and expectations for myself (the teacher), mentors, and learners; 3. Facilitate online messaging and assignments; 4. Monitor the mentoring process; 5. Solicit feedback from learners and mentors.

Some steps were completed several months before the classes' scheduled starting date. For example, early on I requested help from possible mentors at conferences and professional associations' meetings, as well as from advisory board members and colleagues. I hope to establish a group of potential mentors, from which I may request assistance for different classes throughout the year. The guidelines and expectations for mentors were agreed upon before learners were introduced to the mentoring plan. Mentoring activities were incorporated into required web-based assignments. Because computer requirements currently need to be low tech, e-mail and posted website information initially have been established as the methods of communication. Netiquette, mentoring procedures, and e-resources for technical communicators [7] should be covered within the first two weeks of class. Mentoring and learning-community activities should take place during 12 of the 15 weeks of the course, with the last week of class given to feedback.

In the past year, I've linked some learners with mentors for professional advice about careers and specific writing projects. Mentors and learners exchanged e-mail, and both groups benefited from the association. For my web-enhanced classes during fall 2002, I set up a program to expand and formalize mentoring with whole classes of communication and technical writing students. Mentors and small groups of learners should create online learning communities for the duration of the course.

Learners should benefit by exposure to ideas directly from the workplace and professionals' comments, resources, and advice. They gain practical communication experience in working with mentors from different companies and cultures, as well as receive feedback about their course projects.

Mentors gain information from learners who plan to enter their profession and are studying the latest theories and practices. Learners' questions, expectations, and biases can provide new insights to mentors who are familiar with their areas of expertise, but may also need a fresh perspective about the subject area and its perceived relevance to learners. Mentors support teachers and serve as colleagues; teachers and mentors should learn from each other.

Mentoring helps teachers update materials and supplement course links and textbooks. It helps teachers offer learners a wider range of relevant ideas and practices. It also allows teachers to keep up with changing technology and information available throughout business and industry but perhaps not as readily in academia. The benefits to the web-enhanced classes should increase as the use of online mentors is expanded, both technically and in the number of mentors, in future semesters.

As the mentoring program is expanded and additional technology used in web-enhanced classes, chat sessions, mailing lists, bulletin board posts, whiteboard examples, and videoconferencing should be incorporated, along with e-mail and website information. Ideally, both synchronous and asynchronous mentoring activities should be used by online learning communities. Asynchronous activities help connect learners and mentors who have busy schedules or work from widely separated locations, and synchronous communication provides the immediacy of a "real" classroom or workplace experience. Learning communities can then be created by a series of exchanges, asynchronous or synchronous, throughout the course. The learning becomes more personal, as mentors take the time to correct misinformation, share additional links or resources to supplement course materials, and provide feedback about learners' ideas and class projects.

The benefits of using mentors with individual learners for brief periods of time have encouraged me to set up the framework for an expanded mentoring program in communication classes. As I learn from setting up a low-tech mentoring system, I hope to expand the program to involve more learners and mentors and more synchronous forms of communication.

References

1. Bennett, D., Kallen, T., Hupert, N., Meade, T., & Honey, M. (September 1998). *The benefits of online mentoring for high school girls: Telementoring young women in science, engineering, and computing project, year 3 evaluation.* Report for the Center for Children and Technology, funded by the National Science Foundation. [Online web site.] Available http://www.edc.org/CCT/telementoring

2. Shimazu, H., Shibata, A., & Nihei, K. (2001). Expert Guide: A conversational case-based reasoning tool for developing mentors in knowledge spaces. *Applied Intelligence, 14,* 33-48.

3. Jonassen, D. H., Peck, K. C., & Wilson, B. G. (1998). *Creating technology-supported learning communities.* [Online web site.] Formerly available at http://www.cudenver.edu/~bwilson/learn comm.html. Currently not available.

4. Eiler, M. A., Feinberg, S., & Murphy, M. (2001). Curriculum re-design for web-based and distance learning: The "search" for online models. 14-18. *Proceedings of the Society for Technical Communication's 48th Annual Conference.* Arlington, VA: Society for Technical Communication.

5. Kryder, L. G. (2001). Crossing the chasm: The quest to bring the best of academia and industry to the technical communication profession. 9-13. *Proceedings of the Society for Technical Communication's 48th Annual Conference.* Arlington, VA: Society for Technical Communication.

6. Lau, L. (2000). *Distance learning technologies: Issues, trends and opportunities.* Hershey, PA: Idea Group Publishing.

7. Smith, E. O. (2002). E-resources for technical communicators. *Proceedings of the Society for Technical Communication's 49th Annual Conference.* 111-113. Arlington, VA: Society for Technical Communication.

Technology & Education

Dale L. Cook, Ed.D. - Kent State University

An interactive CD-ROM

Produced by the Research Center for Educational Technology at Kent State University, the CD-ROM, TECHNOLOGY & EDUCATION: THE RESEARCH ON WHERE WE HAVE BEEN • A VISION OF WHERE WE ARE GOING, is designed for staff developers in a K-12 environment, university faculty working with preservice educators, and practicing teachers. The purpose of this session is to demonstrate the use of an interactive CD-ROM that was developed to actively engage teachers in reflective dialogue regarding best practice research, their teaching philosophies, and instructional practices.

The Research on Where We Have Been

If we want teachers to create exciting and engaging learning contexts which respects all students' right to learn, the best way to do this might just be to create exciting and engaging learning contexts for teachers that respects their ability to shape education.
(Riel, 2001, [1])

One major finding of the 1998 *Teaching, Learning, and Computing* Study (Becker & Riel, 2000, [2]) was that the role of the student as a learner in the classroom mirrored the role of the teacher in the larger educational community. Students in classes taught by teachers who were engaged in a range of professional development endeavors were asked to think deeply about issues, generate heir own ideas, work collaboratively on projects, share and evaluate their own work in a public forum, and use technology to support these types of activities. This finding points to the need to create learning experiences for educators that reflect the learning environment we want for our children

The CD takes an in-depth look at current research findings on the impact of technology on teaching and learning. Dr. Henry J. Becker & Dr. Margaret Riel (University of California at Irvine), who conducted the research on the *Teaching, Learning, and Computing* study, talk about the significant findings of this work. Dr. Rob Tierney (University of British Columbia), one of the researchers in the *Apple Classroom of Tomorrow* (ACOT) project, shares results from his ACOT research. Dr. Nancy Padak (Kent State University) describes her research in the SBC Ameritech Classroom and cites major studies that recognize the increase in motivation by

students who are immersed in a technology-rich learning environment.

Vignettes of real teachers, students, and classrooms that exemplify what the research describes follow each research retrospective. The CD-ROM offers suggestions for professional development activities based on the information presented. The *Teaching, Learning, and Computing* study overview leads into an I-Search activity. The ACOT piece offers a dynamic simulation activity. The motivation studies lead into discussion opportunities about instructional frameworks. Content of the CD crosses all disciplines.

A Vision of Where We Are Going

The CD-ROM also illustrates how technology is changing our lives and our schools. A video message by Dr. Thomas Carroll, former director of the *Preparing Tomorrow's Teachers for Technology* program, addresses the issue of teachers and their changing role in the classroom. Dr. Linda Roberts, former Director of the Office of Educational Technology for the United States Department of Education, speaks to the importance of research in educational technology.

The CD-ROM takes the viewer inside the SBC Ameritech Classroom on the campus of Kent State University. Teachers and their students come to the classroom for a half-day every day for six weeks while researchers use the attached observation room to conduct studies in the technology rich environment.

The Research Center for Educational Technology (RCET), housed at Kent State University in Kent, Ohio, was founded in 1999 to provide a collegial network for university researchers and preK-16 educators committed to studying the impact of technology on teaching and learning.

1. Riel, M. (2001). Research, stories, and ideas: Section 1(a) - Teaching, learning, and computing study. Technology and education: The research on where we have been - A vision of where we are going [CD-ROM]. Research Center for Educational Technology, Kent State University, Kent, OH.

2. Becker, H.J., Riel, M. (2000). The beliefs, practices, and computer use of teacher leaders. (Teaching, Learning, and Computing-1998 National Survey, Special Report). Center for Research on Information Technology and Organizations, University of California, Irvine.

Virtual Laboratory Course in Chemical Engineering and Unit Operations (VIPRATECH)
Tutorials, Simulations and Remote Process Control

R. Moros, F. Luft, H. Papp, Institut of Chemical Technology, University Leipzig
Institut für Technische Chemie, Universität Leipzig, 04103 Leipzig, Germany

Abstract

Being part of the major project "Vernetztes Studium Chemie" VIPRATECH aims at developing Internet based teaching aids to provide the means for a virtual laboratory course in chemical engineering and unit operations.

With VIPRATECH students and other people have the possibility to inform themselves about the theoretical background and the experimental setup before going ahead with the experiment. Additional, VIPRATECH helps to visualize fundamental processes as well as to clarify theoretical concepts needed for the evaluation of the received experimental data. One major advantage is the possibility to deepen one's understanding of the underlying concepts while surfing the net.

VIPRATECH consists of three parts: multimedia text books, interactive simulations and interfaces for observing/controlling real laboratory experiments via the Internet by using a standard web-browser.

The poster discusses the structure and the advantages of VIPRATECH.

Introduction

Being part of the major project "Vernetztes Studium Chemie" VIPRATECH aims at developing Internet based teaching aids to provide the means for a virtual laboratory course in chemical engineering and unit operations.

While VIPRATECH is meant primarily for students taking chemistry, contents are also available for people interested in furthering their chemical knowledge. With VIPRATECH students have the possibility to inform themselves about the theoretical background and the experimental setup before going ahead with the experiment.

Secondly, VIPRATECH helps to visualize fundamental processes as well as to clarify theoretical concepts needed for the evaluation of the received experimental data. One major advantage is the possibility to deepen one's understanding of the underlying concepts while surfing the net.

VIPRATECH consists of three parts: multimedia text books, interactive simulations and interfaces for observing/controlling experiments via the Internet for each element of the laboratory course (heat transfer, adsorption and others).

Multimedia Text Books

Multimedia text books present the underlying theoretical concepts, explain the experimental setup and give detailed instructions on how to use the equipment.

Multimedia elements such as videos, animated films and interactive graphics support the accompanying text.

Interactive Simulations

Interactive simulations for each real experiment has been developed. These simulations can be executed – independent of the location – in shorter time as the real experiment, at any moment during the day.

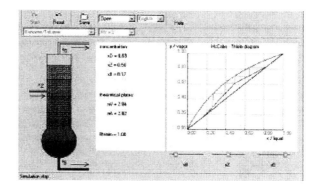

simulation for the rektification experiment

Another advantage is the possibility to simulate processes which otherwise could not be realized – due to financial reasons or because of the risks involved.

Remote Process Control Interface

For the third part of VIPRATECH, a remote access to selected real experiments of our laboratory course via the Internet has been realized including the possibility of remote controlled execution of these experiments.

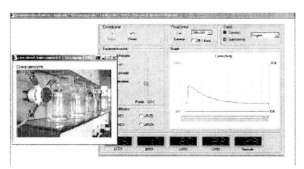

remote control for the resident time experiment

The student controls the experiment using only a standard web browser. Critical data will be collected and evaluated online. It is also possible to observe the experiment live using real-time video.

Based on these innovative methods it should be possible to create a network of remotely controlled experiments.

VIPRATECH:
> http://leipzig.vernetztes-studium.de/

Vernetztes Studium Chemie:
> http://www.vernetztes-studium.de/

Institut of Chemical Technology Leipzig:
> http://techni.chemie.uni-leipzig.de/

> moros@chemie.uni-leipzig.de

an Agent-based Model of Virtual Experiment

Ruimin Shen, Liping Shen, Dazheng Wang
Department of Computer Science ,Shanghai Jiaotong Univ.
{rmshen,lpshen}@mail.sjtu.edu.cn, dzwang@dlc.sjtu.edu.cn

Abstract

This paper analyzes the architecture of virtual experiment and discusses the possibility of building a standard interface for it.We also introduces an agent-based VE system ,which can integrates easily apparatus developed independently and using which a teacher can just focus on his own field even without any programming technique.This model may greatly eliminate many problems involved in software engineer and make distributed experiment possible.

Key words-- Virtual Experiment,COM ,Agent

I. INTRODUCTION

Virtual Experiment(VE) is kind of efficient means of e-learning, it can save money due to expensive apparatus , ensure safety because of dangerous chemical powders and so on. However,nowadays many VEs are developed in different entities though their functions are same.

The components of VE,virtual apparatus,are difficult to reuse.On the other hand,the border between teacher and developer is not clear and it is usually not possible for a teacher to design an experiment with his own knowledge.So it is an urgent requirement for us to devise a standard interface of virtual apparatus and an intelligent mechanism for teacher to design a VE without much unnecessary effort.

II. ARCHITECTURE OF VIRTUAL EXPERIMENT

There is no doubt that VE is a complex system,so different people may have different perspectives on it.These people relevant to VE can be roughly divided into three groups:teachers ,programmers and students. On the basis of top-down analysis,VE consists of three parts:programming by programmers,designing by teachers and experimenting by students (see Figure1).We should keep in mind the fact that not all of the teachers are programmers at the same time,which implies that different people with different background shoud have different responsibilities.A successful VE system must ensure

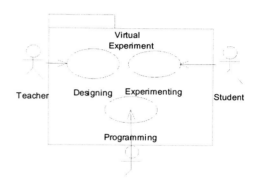

Figure 1 – Different Perspectives

that designing an experiment would be as simple as to such an extent that the teacher can design VE using no other expertise but his own instructional field .

III. VIRTUAL APPARATUS

VE is made up of many virtual apparatus.To make them reusable and easy to integrate,the best technology to adopt might be Component Object Model. Though COM has many merits of independece,scripting skill is still needed to glue these virtual apparatus together.The aim of our VE framework is to gain the advantage of two features:

1.   A standard programming interface
2.   Minimum interference into the inner structure of each virtual apparatus

If we achieve this goal,we will never be trapped into the embarrassment of software engineer.The basic appearance of each virtual apparatus is shown in figure 2[1].

Figure 2 – Virtual Apparatus

Each virtual apparatus is implemented as a COM object with some interfaces exposed to the ouside and a self-described XML file for registration.One of the interfaces ,called IDropSource,must be inherited to enable the teacher to interact with the apparatus.The IAgent interface will be discussed shortly. The special XML file is in fact a media for the virtual apparatus and VE to interact and has two sections:one is a readable section for VE to obtain the information of the COM object including its dynamic library file name,CLSID and IID,etc;the other is a writable section filled by VE ,where the object can get the necessary run-time information such as its agent identity number , server name and port number.

IV. AGENT STRUCTURE

Since only minimum interference is done to each apparatus,it must do lots of work its own ,such as changing its behavior according to the environment condition.This character makes an apparatus look like an agent,so every one should implement the IAgent interface.Though several characteristics of agents have been discussed in the literature, we assume that agents exhibit the following three important properties in our modeling approach[2][3].

1. Autonomy - an agent can make decisions about what to do based on its own state, without the direct intervention of other entities.
2. Adaptation - an agent can perceive its environment,and respond to the changes in the environment in a timely fashion.
3. Cooperation - an agent can interact with other agents through a particular agent-communication language,and typically has the ability to engage in collaborative activities to achieve its goal.

Once activated by the environment,the agent goes into the adaptation state.Then it receives messages from other agents,judges the condition variables and sees if they are relevant.After the sense phase,it can produces some plan by arranging a series of actions,which may result the changed appearance or its inner states.The agent can also give feedback to the environment by changing the experiment parameters.The agent comes to the end of its life cycle if deactivated by the outside.

V. COMMUNICATION

Only a minimum number of functions in an agent are exposed to the environment,such as Activate and Deactivate,but they cannot be accessed by other agents.The messages between agents are passive ,i.e.,they do not contain methods because agents never know each other's structure.Once activated ,an agent just sends out massages containing measurement parameters according to its own state transitions,which are sent to another agent connected to it or to the environment.The parameters might be temperature,pressure and so on.Because the message is

different from traditional method invocations,we name it as passive message or PMessage. The communication mechanism is implemented on the basis of socket technique. At the beginning of its life cycle ,every agent must create a listening socket with the server address and port number assigned by the environment on registration. Those who want to communicate with it must bind to that address and port number.Such a email-like communication mechanism can make distributed experiment possible. If agents want to have a conversation ,they must send their identity numbers to each other via run-time environment.Figure 3 [4]shows such scenario.

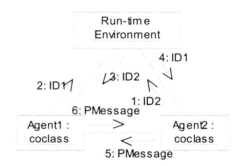

Figure 3 – Conversation scenario

VI. CONCLUSION AND FUTRUE WORK

Since our virtual apparatus component is highly autonomous and possesses a clean programming interface,potential trouble for integrating them into a virtual experiment system is avoided.At the same time,we have achieved the feature for teacher to design an experiment with little effort.Futrue work will focus on the concurrency and responsiveness of our agent model.We will also pay much attention to the analysis of heterogeneous experiment platforms and realize the distributed virtual experiment system.

VII. REFERENCES

1. COM Specification http://www.microsoft.com
2. F. J. Garijo, M. Boman. *Multi-Agent System Engineering.* Proceedings of MAAMAW'99.Springer, ed., 1999.
3. C. M. Jonker, J. Treur. *Compositional Verification of Multi-Agent Systems: a Formal Analysis of Pro-activeness and Reactiveness.* Proceedings of International Workshop on Compositionality (COMPOS'97), Springer, 1997.
4. B. Bauer. *Extending UML for the Specification of Interaction Protocols.* submission for the 6th Call for Proposal of FIPA 99, 1999.

Mechatronic Experiment via the Internet

K.K. Tan, K.N. Wang
Department of Electrical and Computer Engineering
National University of Singapore
4 Engineering Drive 3
Singapore 117576

Abstract

This poster paper reports on a specific experiment in the mechatronic program which is set up to provide hands-on experience in the use of the Internet to implement remote monitoring and fault diagnosis for machines from a long distance, using only low cost and easily available components. Both hardware and software configuration will be highlighted.

1. Introduction

The term *"Mechatronics"* was first introduced and registered in 1969 by an engineer called Tesuro Mori of Yaskawa Electric [1] to provide a semantic reference to the phenomenon of increasing interaction between the mechanical and electronics engineering disciplines. *Mechatronics* was mainly coined to refer to simplified mechanisms with sophisticated functions in electronics. The importance of a mechatronic approach in the design of new products and processes, through a seamless synergy of associated technological disciplines, is becoming increasingly recognized worldwide as a mean towards effective manufacturing to maximize economic gains [2]-[5]. As the benefits associated with applications of mechatronics become more evident, the education systems in many countries also evolve to reflect the need for a cross-disciplinary curriculum. At the National University of Singapore, a new program leading to the award of a Master of Science in Mechatronics was recently introduced. A specific focus of the mechatronic program is on real hands-on laboratory practice. Experiments of specially designed themes are to be systematically carried out by the students enrolled in the program as a core part of the program.

This paper will report on a specific experiment in the mechatronic program which is set up to provide hands-on experience in the application of an mechatronic device (accelerometer) and digital signal processing techniques to vibration monitoring and fault diagnosis of machines [6]. The accelerometer will provide directly vibration measurements, and an intelligent algorithm (to be programmed by the students) will carry out the fault inferencing procedures. The approach adopted in the experiment is based on capturing machine-specific vibration signatures and comparing these signatures to real-time vibration patterns to determine if possible faults have occurred. In addition, students are introduced to how the Internet may further shape the operations of mechatronic systems. Via remote laboratory access approaches, the students will implement remote monitoring and diagnosis of a single axis shaker to which they have earlier instrumented with the accelerometer. Thus, from a remote site, using only a regular web browser, they will be able to characterize the vibration signatures of machine, monitor their health, tune their thresholds and initiate alerts when abnormal conditions are encountered. This will be achieved using only existing extensible TCP/IP infrastructure.

2. Main Principles

The main idea behind the approach is to construct a vibration signature based on pattern recognition of "acceptable" or "healthy" vibration patterns, against which the actual vibration pattern is compared. Figure 1 highlights the key steps involved. The key components necessary are shown in Figure 2. An accelerometer, mounted on the machine being monitored, is used to provide measurements of the vibration signals in an electrical form. These signals can subsequently be digitized and acquired into a micro-processor based system in which resides the intelligent vibration analysis program. The vibration analysis program can work in two modes: the learning and monitoring mode. The learning mode is to be initiated to identify the normal vibration characteristics of the machine, i.e., the vibration signature. The mode can be re-initiated at any time when the operator feels a re-learning/re-training is necessary (for example, after the machine has undergone modifications/retrofitting). Thus, normal vibration signatures can be extracted in this way automatically through only a pushbutton on the software interface. Thereafter, the monitoring system can enter a continuous monitoring mode. In the monitoring mode, the vibration signals are continuously acquired and compared to the pre-acquired "normal" signatures. If the deviation from the signature exceeds a certain specified threshold, an alarm can be raised to alert the operator of possible machine malfunction.

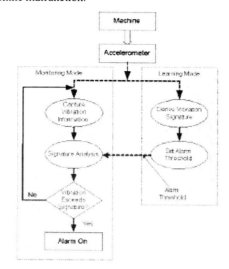

Figure 1: Key operational steps of the intelligent vibration monitoring system

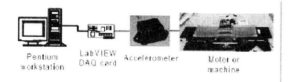

Figure 2: Vibration signal acquisition system

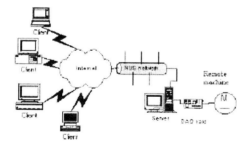

Figure 3: Hardware connections of the remote monitoring system

3. Hardware and Software Configuration

The hardware that is necessary and used in the development of the remote monitoring at the server's end, is the server itself, consisting of a data acquisition (DAQ) card installed in a PC. The PC which is linked to the Internet, is used primarily for data acquisition and control of the remote machine. The accelerometer acts as an interface between the motor (or machine) and the data acquisition card. It converts mechanical acceleration into electrical signals. The analog

electrical signals from the accelerometer are then acquired by the DAQ card as raw data and stored in the PC for further conditioning and analysis. The hardware connection is depicted in Figure 3. The software configuration for the remote monitoring system is shown in Figure 4. The user interface is shown in Figure 5.

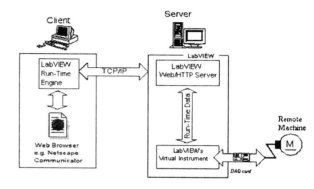

Figure 4: Software requirements and interactions

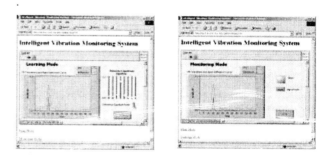

Figure 5: Snapshot of the interface

References

[1] N. Kyura and H.Oho, Mechatronics - an industrial perspective. *IEEE/ASME Transactions on Mechatronics* **1**(1), 10-15 (1996).

[2] R.W. Daniel, and J.R. Hewit, Editorial, *Mechatronics*, **1**(1), i-ii (1991).

[3] V. A. Job and J. Wim, Mechatronics in the Netherlands. *IEEE/ASME Transactions on Mechatronics* **1**(2), 106-110 (1996).

[4] S.Vesa, Ten years of mechatronic research and industrial applications in Finland. *IEEE/ASME Transactions on Mechatronics* **1**(2), 103-105 (1996).

[5] K.K. Tan, T.H. Lee, H.F. Dou and S.Y. Lim, Various developments in mechatronics in Asia, Mechatronics, **8**, 777-791, (1998).

[6] Clarence W. de Silva, Vibration, Fundamentals and Practice, CRC Press LLC: Washington DC, (1999).

Interactive Animation of Chemical Reactions Based on Quantum Chemical Calculations -Computer Microscope 2002-

IKUO Akira*, TAMURA Shyunsuke*, KOJIMA Yousuke*, BUQUERON S. Samson**,
Rahmat Setiadi***, and TERATANI Shousuke*

*Department of Chemistry, Tokyo Gakugei University,
4-1-1 Nukuikita-machi, Koganei-shi, Tokyo 184-8501, Japan.
Phone/FAX: +81-42-329-7510, E-mail: ikuo@u-gakugei.ac.jp
** Regional Science High School, SMBA, Olongapo City, Region III, Philippines.
*** Chemistry Department, Faculty of Science and Math, Indonesia University of Education,
Jl. Setiabudi 229, Bandung 40154 Indonesia.

Abstract

CG animations of chemical reactions based on quantum chemical calculations were produced. The reactions include hydration of CO_2, SO_3, N_2O_4, and phthalic anhydride. User-interface of the animation was studied.

1. Introduction

We have produced CG animations of chemical reactions based on quantum chemical calculations. We call these animations the "Computer Microscope"[1]. The Computer Microscope is an effective tool for better understanding how and why chemical reactions occur. As a useful teaching material, however, the Computer Microscope needs to be more user-friendly and appealing. We have revised the original animations to interactive animations of chemical reactions, the "Computer Microscope 2002", that gives students the chance and means of molecular manipulation.

2. Method

In this work, the *ab initio* calculation software, Gaussian 98W (Gaussian, Inc.), was used to find the transition states and the reaction path of chemical reactions according to the intrinsic reaction coordinate (IRC) theory[2]. The calculations were then used for such reactions as hydration of CO_2, SO_3, N_2O_4, phthalic anhydride and others. The Quick Time (Apple Computer, Inc.) movie was produced by DIRECTOR 8.5J (Macromedia, Inc.) following the display of bond order or molecular orbital of the structure in the each reaction stage which was drawn by CAChe MOPAC (Fujitsu, Inc.). Quick Time VR Authoring Studio (Apple Computer, Inc.) was used for the production of the three-dimensional (3D) rotation.

3. Features of the Computer Microscope 2002

The introduction section of the Computer Microscope has been revised to explain the basics of reaction path

studies. The goal of the revision is to help students understand the reaction profile. To explain the reaction profile, the reaction path of a simple reaction such as chlorine molecule attacked by a hydrogen atom is shown on a 3D potential energy surface. The most probable pathway is demonstrated by the movement of a ball along the steepest fall line from a transition state on the potential surface. Theoretically, the reaction profile shown by the most probable pathway representing the relation between potential energy and IRC is obtained and used for various complex reactions.

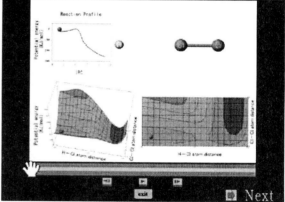

Figure 1 The reaction profile of the reaction of hydrogen atom and chlorine molecule

The CG animation is synchronized with the movement of the ball so that the degree of reaction progress and structural alignment of the molecules of all stages are shown at the same time. A Quick Time (QT) control bar

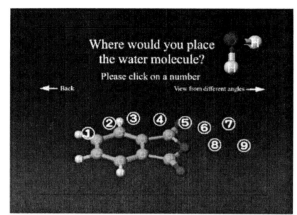

Figure 2 The transition state search simulator

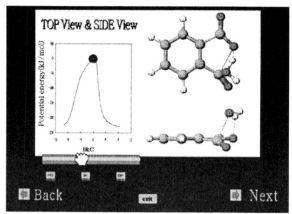

Figure 3 The reaction profile of hydrolysis of phthalic anhydride

for the movie is placed just under the reaction profile to allow the student to move the reaction back and forth along the IRC with a computer mouse. This type of "virtual hands-on" experience helps students look into the process of chemical reactions.

The updated version includes a transition state search simulator. This is a trial-and-error simulator in which students select initial configurations and orientations of the reactants for given molecules. Correct choices lead to the next step, while incorrect choices bring the students back to the beginning. Finding the true transition state and reaction path give students basic information about reaction path studies based on quantum chemical calculation.

The 3D display of the chemical change is shown by two viewpoints; Top view and Side view of the CG animation of the reaction process. Thus it is easy to see that a reactant approaches a substrate from a certain direction and with a specific orientation to produce a product(s). The approaching route and molecular orientation should help the student understand the chemical change on the basis of atomic orbital. The QT-VR allows the student to rotate the molecules of the reactant, transition state, and product. The rotating HOMO and LUMO combinations also help the student

understand which atomic orbital plays an important role in bond formation and scission.

4. Conclusion

The CG animations of chemical reactions based on quantum chemical calculations were produced which gives students the chance and means of molecular manipulation.

An English version of *"Computer Microscope 2002"* is available on CD-ROM. For enquiries, please contact Akira Ikuo at: ikuo@u-gakugei.ac.jp

Acknowledgement
This work was partly supported by a Grant-in-Aid for Scientific Research (C)(No. 12680173) from the Japan Society for the Promotion of Science (JSPS). The Ministry of Education, Culture, Sports, Science and Technology of Japan provided the scholarship for Mr. BUQUERON as a Teacher Training Student. JICA provided funding for Mr. Rahmat Setiadi as an IMSTEP Trainee.

References
[1] a) A.Ikuo, T.Ichikawa, A.Yoshimura, and S.Teratani,"Computer Microscope-Dynamics of Chemical Reactions" Proceedings of ICCE 99, 7th International Conference on Computers in Education, Chiba, Japan, **2**, 916-917, IOS Press,1999; b) Ikuo, A., Ichikawa, T., Teratani, S., "Chemical Reaction Observed with Computer Microscope", *J. Chem. Software*, **6**, 45-54(2000); c) S.Teratani,"COMPUTER MICROSCOPE - CG ANIMATED CHEMICAL REACTIONS", 16th International Conference on Chemical Education, Budapest, Hungary, August 5-10 (2000), Book of Abstracts, 313; d) A. Ikuo, A.Yoshimura, S.Tamura, S.Teratani"WHAT DO YOU FIND WITH THE COMPUTER MICROSCOPE DISPLAYING CG ANIMATED CHEMICAL REACTIONS?", 2000 International Chemical Congress of Pacific Basin Societies, Honolulu, USA, December 14-19 (2000), Book of Abstracts, 1, COMM4-129; e) S.Teratani, S.Tamura, A.Yoshimura, A.Ikuo,"COMPUTER MICROSCOPE – CG ANIMATION FOR BETTER UNDERSTANDING OF CHEMICAL REACTIONS-" World Chemistry Congress Journal, IUPAC 38th Congress, Brisbane, Australia, 1-6 July 2001, 351;
[2] Fukui, K., "A Formulation of the Reaction Coordinate", *J. Phys. Chem.*, 74, pp. 4161-4163(1970).

A Method to Support Learning on Structures of Chemical Substances for Intelligent Educational System of High School Chemistry

Satoshi Yukimoto, Kiyoshi Yoshikawa, Isamu Takahashi, Tatsuhiro Konishi, Yukihiro Itoh
Faculty of Information, Shizuoka University
E-mail: cs8093@cs.inf.shizuoka.ac.jp

Abstract

In this paper, we discuss an intelligent educational system for high-school chemistry that helps learners who do not understand structures of chemical substances. In order to help such learners, it is not enough to merely display the relevant structures. We propose a method taking advantage of virtual phenomena representing how the substances are composed. In order to deal with virtual phenomena, we improve our prototype system by extending the chemical reaction simulator and the problem solver for exercises. We also illustrate implementation of our extended system and the experimental evaluation of it.

1. Introduction

In this research, we have extended our prototype system for high-school chemistry to be practical for actual scenes of education. More concretely, we are trying to make our system handle every topic written in a practical textbook of high-school chemistry.

Generally, main topics of high-school chemistry can be classified into two types: One is structures of the chemical substances such as atom or molecular. The other is the causation of chemical reaction such as acid and base. In precedence research[1][2][3], our system deals with causation in acid and base. Therefore, in this research, we propose a method to support learning on structures of chemical substances in order to make our system be able to cover the whole of high school chemistry. We also illustrate implementation of our extended system and the experimental evaluation of it.

2. Our basic method to support learning on structures of chemical substances

In the learning of a structure of a substance, it is important to let learners imagine the structure. But it is almost impossible to observe structures of atom or molecular in real laboratories in usual high-schools. Therefore a virtual laboratory in a computer is one of the effective tools for learning structures of chemical substances. However, we think simple visualization of the structures is insufficient, because it is more essential for the learner to understand the rules for determining the structures of atoms, than to memorize the structures of substances.

We propose a method supporting learners in understanding such rules. Firstly, the system shows a learner components of a substance. Then the learner tries to construct the substance by combining the components

each other. In the constructing process, the system explains the reason why some combinations are possible and others are impossible on the basis of the rules on the structure of the substance. Note that such a constructing process would not occur in the real world. Nevertheless, such a virtual process will be effective to help the learner understand why the target substance has such a structure, because the learner can start learning from relatively small structures, then proceed to global structures step by step. We call the phenomena that don't occur in the real world "*virtual phenomena*". Our system provides the following learning environments in which the virtual phenomena are dealt with.

(1) The virtual laboratory

In the environment, learners can construct a substance by themselves in order to understand rules for determining the structure of the substance.

(2) The tutor for exercises on structures of substances

In the environment, the system provides exercises on structures of substances, and supports the learner to understand essentially the rules and other types of knowledge necessary to solve the exercise (such as causal relation, numerical relation, etc).

3. Extension of our system

3.1 Extension of the simulator in order to deal with virtual phenomena

In the virtual laboratory, our system lets learners construct substances by using a graphical interface, so that the learners learn the rules for determining structures of the substances by themselves. In order to realize such a discovery learning, our system has the following three levels of teaching strategies for the virtual laboratory.

Level 1: The learner operates freely.

Level 2: The system displays feedback messages in response to learner's operation.

Level 3: The system shows the ideal process to achieve the goal.

In order to realize such supports, the system has to simulate a constructing process of a substance in a virtual phenomenon.

The existing simulator of our system uses forward reasoning based on knowledge of causal relations. In our existing knowledge representation of causal relations, chemical concepts have been represented by using classes of substances (ex. "acid", "base"). It is because usual chemical reaction can almost be determined by only the combinations among classes of chemical substances. However, in order to represent virtual phenomena, representation of substances has to specify constraints on structures of chemical concepts, such as "electrons on the most outside shell".

In order to apply such knowledge, the simulator has to identify a chemical concept in the knowledge. For this, it has to interpret the constraints and to determine the corresponding substance in virtual laboratory. Therefore we extend our knowledge representation: a procedure identifying the chemical concept can be attached to knowledge representation of causal relation. We call such procedures *"procedures identifying chemical concepts"*.

3.2 Extension of process of solving exercise

It is insufficient for a learner who cannot solve an exercise to show merely a solving process. It is desirable that the system can solve the exercise by itself, construct problem solving process model in order to diagnose the learner's problem solving process by comparing with it.

In our precedence research [3], our system can solve exercises which ask an attribute value of a chemical concept in a chemical reaction. It uses knowledge of numerical relations among attributes of chemical concepts in a chemical reaction. However, it does not support how to calculate attribute values of chemical concepts in virtual phenomena (ex. Number of the electron of Na ion is calculated by observing a virtual phenomenon that the Na ion is generated by removing electron(s) from a Na atom). Such a calculation process is important for learning of structures of chemical substances.

So we extend the problem-solving unit in order to deal with virtual phenomenon. We prepare knowledge of numerical relations among attributes of chemical concepts in a virtual phenomenon. As mentioned above, some attached procedures are necessary for identifying concepts in knowledge representation on virtual phenomena. So we introduce procedures which identify chemical concepts in the knowledge representation and calculate an attribute value from the virtual phenomenon. We call such procedures *"procedures calculating attributes"*. By verbalizing the procedures, the system can explain how an attribute value of a chemical substance is determined by its structure.

4. Implementation

By using the above mentioned methods, we implement an extended system which can support learning of structures of chemical substances. The system is implemented by using Tcl/Tk and LISP(GNU Common Lisp).

When the system sets the exercise "Make the electron configuration of Na atom in the virtual laboratory" but a learner cannot operate it correctly, the system sets its pedagogical strategies to level 2. Fig 1 shows a snapshot of the environment provided by the system with the level 2 strategy. In the environment, if the learner puts an electron on an invalid area, the system shakes the electron to let the learner notice that the electron's position is invalid. The learner is allowed to move the shaken electron to another place. If the learner asks the system for more help, the system changes its strategy

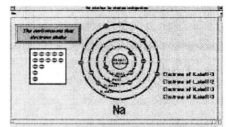

Fig. 1: Level 2 environment

into level 3 and prepares a new environment. In the new environment, the system operates electrons and achieves the goal by itself.

5. Experimental Evaluation

To evaluate an efficacy of our system, we have examined our system experimentally. Generally, evaluation by learners is the better way, but we adopt such a way that we explain our system to actual teachers and interview them. Firstly, we explained the outline of our system. Then we showed them five exercises and let the teachers operate our system to solve them. Finally, we let the teachers evaluate our system by seven grades (good:7 – bad:1) from some viewpoints and describe the reasons. Table 1 shows the result of the evaluation.

The average scores of every term are over 5.0. Totally, we think that they have good impression on our system. However, some of them suggested that the user interface of our system is not easy to manipulate. So, in the near future, we are going to improve the usability of our system from the viewpoint of easiness of operations, response time, clarity of visual design and so on.

Table1:Evaluation contents & Average score

No	Evaluation contents	Average
A	Educational efficacy of our designing policy	6.0
B	How well our system reflects the designing policy	5.5
C	Educational efficacy of the virtual phenomenon	5.3
D	Educational efficacy of the supports by our system	5.0

6. Conclusion

In this research, we implemented an educational system that covers the field of "structures of chemical substances" and evaluate it experimentally. The framework proposed in this paper covers almost all of the topics of high-school chemistry. Therefore, we will implement more knowledge and educational contents in order to make our system to be practical.

Reference
[1] Takahashi,I., Konishi,T., Itoh,Y., "On a Framework of an Educational System which Acts both images and texts for Micro World", Proc. of ICCE'99, Vol.1, pp954-957(1999)
[2] Yoshikawa,K., Takahashi,I., Konishi,T., Itoh,Y., "Generating interactive explanations by using both images and texts for Micro World", Proc. of ICCE2000, Vol.1, pp.643-650(2000)
[3] Yoshikawa,K., Inoue,U., Takahashi,I., Konishi,T., Itoh,Y., "An Intelligent Learning Environment for calculation of exercise high-school chemistry", Proc. of ICCE2001, Vol.3, pp.1739-1740(2001)

The Effects of Synchronized Presentation Model:
New Type of Web Based Learning System

Hiroyuki AKAMA , Tomotaka OSUMI, Nobuyasu MAKOSHI (Tokyo Institute of Technology)
Toshihiko ODA (Toyota Digital Cruise, Inc.)

Abstract

This paper presents for a web-based learning system two models we have named the patterned frame model (PFM), and the synchronized presentation model (SPM).

1 : Introduction

Our vision is to create and evaluate several types of remote education in a live setting comparable to that of traditional classroom teaching. In this study we try to present two types of Web content model, each with a frame interface, the patterned frame model (PFM) and the synchronized presentation model (SPM).

2 : Two Models

PFM is a rapidly developing model that can be operated with a Web browser. With well-known authoring tools such as "Click2learn" and "Microsoft Producer," we have been able to create a template for the composition of windows by situating at least two frames. Figure 1a illustrates one such model with the teacher's live performance movie frame on the left side and his PowerPoint documents on the right side.

In general, this type of web presentation sometimes lacks for a dynamic sensation of unity because the synchronization of each side is limited by the events generated in the ppt (PowerPoint) files.

This is the case even if we replace the background using Chroma Key (a blue screen behind the teacher), with virtual and neat images representing an artificial classroom and its unified components (e.g., the teacher's body, a textual space, or other ornamental elements).

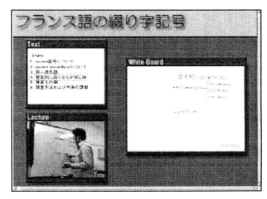

Figure I-b: the synchronized presentation model (SPM)

In order to overcome some of the weak points of the PFM, namely a lack of liveliness (presence) and high costs, our team devised a synchronized presentation model (SPM). Our innovation consists of a compound and dynamic presentation of the lesson scene. Instead of well-made but static presentation materials prepared in advance, we include a special window next to the lesson movie window to represent anything the teacher might wish to write. The script inside that window comes from a whiteboard (on the right side) and is perfectly synchronized with his voice and writing motions (on the lower left in Figure I-b).

We accomplish this using an authoring time-line tool to manually interlock the moving images representing the teacher in the classroom directly with the emerging document interpreted by a whiteboard capture device (such as eBeam, Mimio, etc). The result is that our synchronized presentation model (SPM) is better capable of transmitting the live atmosphere of the classroom to distance education participants.

3 : Evaluation and Comparison

In order to test the above hypothesis, we carried out an experiment to compare the two types of Web Based Learning (WBL) systems. A short lecture about the usage of French spelling letter marks was adapted for multimedia contents transmission to evaluate both PFM and SPM.

We demonstrated the two models to 51 graduate and undergraduate students who were then asked to mark assessment sheets on a scale of one to five to rate each of some factors we selected to evaluate the models. The data was examined by means of a Student's t-test to compare the mean of evaluation rates. This investigation revealed that on the whole PFM was a little more highly evaluated than SPM, perhaps because of the usage of Chroma Key which improved the quality of our PFM sample.

However, when one considers the basal conditions necessary to the online live classroom, it seems undeniable that SPM reproduces them more effectively than PFM as a browsing environment for the Web. As is shown in Figure II where we isolate assessment categories that clearly contrast the two models, SPM was favorably evaluated for "Presence," "Hand-made Feeling," and "Liveliness" with each registering a highly significant difference, ($p<0.01$).

On the contrary, PFM was judged to be a "Good-looking," "Useful to preparation," but "Formal" and "Artificial."

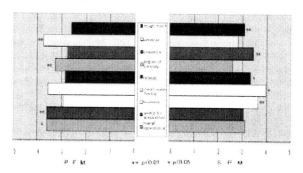

Figure II :Evaluation of the two models

3 : Conclusion

By analyzing these results, we conclude that the SPM is characterized by its capacity to simulate real classroom education by digitalizing the blackboard, an element of classroom experience that has been familiar from as far back as elementary school education.

But in reality, most Web contents used for distance learning fit the PFM. It cannot be denied that, in the final analysis there remains an educational trade-off between the advantages of PFM and those of SPM.

Further investigations will aim at measuring the effects of SPM by considering physiological indicators (such as using eye cameras or brain wave monitors). But on the other hand, using text-mining tools to analyze the free speech of SPM users might be also fruitful.

References

Kimihiro SHIRATO, Hitoshi SASAKI and Makoto TAKEYA(1999), *Development of a virtual school with Internet*, Proceedings of THE 1999 CONFERENCE of JET, 665-666

Liu Wei (1998), *Distance Learning*, Proceedings of The International Conference on Distance Education, Distance Learning and 21st Century Education Development, 340-347

A Research on the Types of the Web Based Corrective Feedback

JangHyeon Baek*, Sehee Jang *, and Yungsik Kim *
* Dept. of Computer Education, Korea National University of Education
Email: lousuk@chollian.net, shjang@blue.knue.ac.kr, kimys@mail.knue.ac.kr

Abstract

We have designed and realized a formation evaluation system which provide two types of corrective feedback to understand the difference in the study achievement degree and to find the best appropriate method in accordance with the types of the web-based corrective feedback at this point of time when the importance of feedback is being clearly brought out, as well as the formation evaluation, in the teaching-learning process. In this research work, we have designed and realized a corrective feedback which suggest similar questions repetitively' and a 'corrective feedback which suggest the results', leading to apply the two types to real lectures to verify the effects. It is expected that the two types can be used effectively in correcting students' errors and providing them with correct information in the web-based formation evaluation process.

1. Introduction

After the evaluation is accomplished, appropriate feedbacks should be made for the performance. Appropriate feedbacks are different in accordance with the evaluation areas. In the case of knowledge, only the suggestion of right-wrong answers can be a sufficient feedback. In the case of intellectual function, however, the suggestion of right-wrong answers is not sufficient, and the information to correct the error should be provided.

to find the right answer repeatedly. Since the excessive requirement for the right answer for a learner can make him experience frustration. We need to let the learner to study through repeated practice for the part of which the learner i77s supposed to experience problems in understanding or fail to learn.

2. Designing of the Web Based Corrective Feedback

2.1 The Corrective Feedback, Suggesting Similar Questions Repeatedly

The repeated type corrective feedback in the formation evaluation process is a feedback that has similar concept with the wrong answered question and provide the same level of questions repeatedly until a right answer is made. This corrective feedback is a process of problem solving through repeatedly studying of similar level concept, rather than providing information pertaining to the correct answer, to solve the suggested question. [Diagram 1] is showing a feedback design providing similar questions repeatedly in the event a wrong answer has been made for the suggested question.

2.2 Result Suggesting Corrective Feedback

This method is not providing a feedback immediately or the question after solving it. It's a method of providing

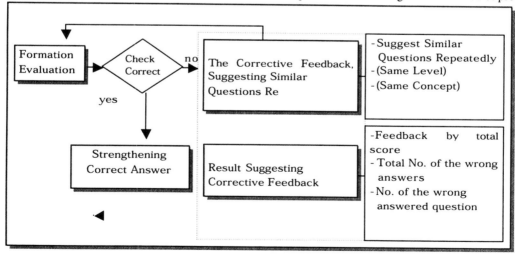

[Figure 1] Type of Corrective feedback

Also, the timing for the feedback should be appropriate. It is important to decide when the correct answer should be provided, after allowing a learner to try

a feedback for a learner to study by himself for the wrong answered question by visiting the related unit through suggesting the total numbers and the specific number of questions for the wrong answered questions after solving specific numbers of questions. [Diagram1] is showing a feedback design to suggest the evaluation result to learners.

3. Effect Analysis for the Types of the Web Based Corrective Feedback

3.1 Study Object

We selected two classes of the first grade of N High School in Ulsan. First, we selected the two same quality groups by analyzing the records of the interim test for Information Industry subject in the previous semester for all 10 classes of the first grade statistically. The two groups can be said as a same quality group since there is no significant difference between G1, G2 before treatment in accordance with<Table1>. (p>0.05)

Group	N	M	SD	t	p
G1	39	61.15	16.18	-1.439	0.154
G2	39	56.15	13.88		

<Table 1> Feedback Application Object by Type

3.2 Experiment Design

To verify the effect of the feedback, <Table 2> was designed.

G1	O1	X1	O2
G2	O3	X2	O4

<Table 2> Experiment Design Model

O1, O3 : preliminary inspection
O2, O4 : ex post facto inspection,
G1, G2 : experiment group
X1 : corrective feedback, suggesting similar questions repeatedly
X2 : result suggesting corrective feedback

4. Result of the Research and its Interpretation

We have implemented the T-inspection to check the influence of the types of feedback on the study performance by the following three methods. The result of analysis is as shown on <Table 3>

Inspection time	Group	N	M	SD	t	p
Before	G1	39	61.15	16.68	-1.439	0.154
	G2	39	56.15	13.88		
After	G1	39	71.41	15.47	-3.075	0.003
	G2	39	60.26	16.54		

<Table 3> The result of analysis

The average performance of before-after in G1 increased

by 10.26 and that of G2？ increased by 4.11. As a result of applying the corrective feedback, suggesting similar questions repeatedly and the result suggesting corrective feedback on the experiment group 1(G1) and the experiment group 2(G2) respectively, the average difference of the two groups showed 11.15. After we implemented the T-inspection to check if the difference in score has the meaningful value, it turned out that it was meaningful. (p<0.05)

According to the result of this research, the corrective feedback, suggesting similar questions repeatedly was more effective than the result suggesting corrective feedback in enhancing the students' study performance.

5. Conclusion and Suggestion

Based on the result of this research work, it turned out that the corrective feedback, suggesting similar questions repeatedly in the web based formation evaluation is pretty effective in enhancing the study performance of students. The result suggesting corrective feedback, on the other hand, has no significant effect.

Accordingly, the corrective feedback, suggesting similar questions repeatedly, is more superior in enhancing the study performance of students than the result suggesting corrective feedback type.

This study is expected to be of much help to design and develop the corrective feedback system to provide opportunity to correct study method, study direction and study error in the web based teaching-learning process.

However, we need to compare and analyze the system based on various variate, as well as researching and developing various types of corrective feedback to meet the individual study level and the characteristics of learners. Besides, we are required to control the variate affecting the study performance of students more strictly and to verify the mechanism more precisely.

6. Reference

[1] Kim Ok Hwan, etc. (1996). Education Evaluation. Seoul : Education Publishing
[2] Park Sung Ik (1995). The Principle and Application of the Instructional Design. Seoul : Educational Science.
[3] Lee Byung Seok (1999). Principle and Practice of Teaching. Seoul : Wonmi Publishing.
[4] Won Jong Mun (1993). The Effect of Feedback Types to he Scholarly Achievement, according to the Study Style of students. A Master's Degree Thesis, KNUE.
[5] Sun Jong Man (1996). The Effect of the Types of the correction Feedback to the Scholarly Achievement of Students with Different Recognition Styles. A Master's Degree Thesis KNUE.
[6] Lee Young Mi (1986). The Effect of Feedback in the Course of Teaching-Learning to the Scholarly Achievement. A Master's Degree Thesis, Ewha Women's University.

WebCord - A Visualizing Tool for Enhancing Web-Based Learning

Kei-Chun Li   Wai-Ming Yip   Kit-Kuen Yip
Department of Information and Applied Technology
Hong Kong Institute of Education,
10 Lo Ping Road, Tai Po, New Territories, Hong Kong
danielli@ied.edu.hk   wmyip@ied.edu.hk   hkryyip@ied.edu.hk

Abstract

Web browser bookmarks (also known as "favorites") predominate as the current approach to managing URLs. Yet these bookmarking schemes exhibit deficiencies that hinder effective organization and access to URLs. This paper describes WebCord, a visualizing tool for enhancing Web-based learning that allows the user to organizing and managing their URLs of interest by creating categories.

1. Introduction

More and more students and lecturers are then turning to the Internet when teaching and learning. However, the availability of such great quantities of information has left some users bewildered and overwhelmed. Finding appropriate information on the Web is a significant problem in itself, but once the information is found, a secondary problem surfaces. The uniform resource locators (URLs) associated with the found information must be organized and stored in a manner that enables rapid and effective access for individuals. Web browser bookmarks (also known as "favorites") predominate as the current approach to managing URLs. Yet these bookmarking schemes exhibit deficiencies [2] that hinder effective organization and access to URLs.

Several systems have been developed to manage useful URLs. WebMap [1] shows a 2D graphical relationship between visited Web pages. PadPrints [3] takes screen grabs of visited pages and organizes them as nodes in a single tree for visualization. Domain Tree Browser (DTB) [4] is a visualization tool that keeps track of all visited Web pages within a domain in the form of a tree hierarchy.

In this paper, we propose a personal Web history visualization tool, known as WebCord, to organizing and managing URLs. This tool differs from the ones described above in several important ways. First, we are not just keeping track of all visited Web pages within domains like DTB [4] but also organizing all the links into categories based on the user's criteria. Second, we do not attempt to construct a map of the Website. We construct a tree of the actual pages visited in a domain. Third, unlike WebMap [1] and PadPrints [3], we do not have a single tree modeling the entire history. Instead, we organize the visited pages into different domains and categorize them into different topics.

2. Visualization of navigation

WebCord is a Web navigation visualization tool that is used as a browser companion. It receives events from the browser whenever hyperlinks on a Web page are clicked and uses those events to create and maintain Web histories. It automatically keeps track of all visited URLs within a domain in the form of a tree hierarchy and creates categories under which to group URLs. Figure 1 shows a screenshot of a sample example from WebCord.

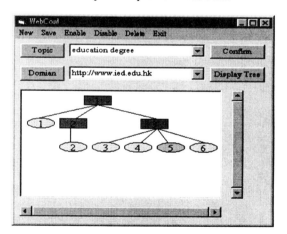

Figure 1: Sample session with WebCord.

When you click the down arrow of the combo box of the *Topic* field, a pull down menu appears where the created topics will be display in alphabetic order for you to select. After click the confirm button, the combo box of the *Domain* field will then display the visited domain names list under the selected topic. You can then select one of the domains and a corresponding URL tree is displayed on the lower tree panel.

The URL tree hierarchy is displayed in a top-down manner. The rectangle node in the tree corresponds to a sub-directory of the domain and the oval node corresponds to a visited URL. Whenever the mouse is moved over a node, a label pops up at the cursor, displaying the sub-directory or URL that the node represents. When clicking an oval node, the corresponding page is displayed in the browser window and that node is marked as the current node of the tree with orange color.

For ease of description, let the tree displayed in the tree panel be called *current tree*, the domain corresponding to the tree as *current domain* and the last visited node as *current node* in that domain. When a Web page is navigated in the browser, there are two cases. In the first case, under that category, the page has been already visited. If the corresponding tree is the current tree, the node is made the current node and is colored orange, otherwise the corresponding tree is made current and is displayed on the tree panel and the corresponding domain becomes the current domain. In the second case, under that category, the page has not been visited before. In this case, a new node is created according to the path of the URL. If the user has already visited the domain, this new node is added in that domain. If not, a new tree corresponding to the domain is created, and the new node is added as the only visited child of this tree.

To prune a tree, the user may select (click on the node) any node (rectangle or oval) and then select the Delete button on the top. For a rectangle node, the sub-tree rooted at the node will be deleted. For an oval node, only the node will be deleted. WebCord also provides the ability to enable or disable the option of saving history. This may be useful in cases where the user temporarily does not want the histories to be recorded.

3. Layout strategies

WebCord uses a tree layout algorithm similar to that in WebMap [1] to draw the URL tree for visualization. The characters of the URL tree have been defined as: the horizontal distance between two neighboring leaves is H; the vertical distance between two layers (parent and child nodes) is V; the parent node locates one level above its children and in the middle between its leftmost and rightmost descendant.

When a new node x_b is to be inserted into an URL tree, the following algorithm is used to calculate x_b's coordinates and also recalculate the coordinates of the affected nodes (above and to the right of x_b). $X(x_b)$ and $Y(x_b)$ represents x_b's x-coordinate and y-coordinate respectively.

Step 1: If x_b is inserted as a root node, then $X(x_b) = 0$, $Y(x_b) = 0$. Exit, else Next step.

Step 2: If x_b is to be inserted as child node of node x_a, $Y(x_b) = Y(x_a) + V$. Next step.

Step 3: If x_b is the only child of x_a, then $X(x_b) = X(x_a)$, else $X(x_b) = X(x_r) + H$ where x_r is the rightmost descendant of x_a. Next step.

Step 4: If $R(x_b)$ is the set of right sidling nodes of x_b (parent node is not x_a) and is not empty set, $X(x_i) = X(x_i) + H$ where $x_i \in R(x_b)$. Next step.

Step 5: $X(x_a) = X(x_a) + \dfrac{H}{2}$ Next step.

Step 6: If x_a is not the root node, set x_b as x_a and x_a as its parent node and go to Step 4, else Exit.

4. Conclusion

We have proposed a visualization tool, known as WebCord, to organizing and managing their URLs of interest by creating categories. Rather than display the entire history in a single tree, it automatically constructs and visualize a tree of the actual pages visited in a domain. Our future work will include providing services that allows users to share their URLs within groups and provides dynamically updated ranking of resources based on incremental user feedback.

References

[1] P. Doemel, WebMap – A Graphical Hypertext Navigation Tool, *Proc. 2nd Int'l Conf. on the World Wide Web Conference*, USA, 1994, p785-789.

[2] R.M. Keller et al., A Bookmarking Service for Organizing and Sharing URLs, *Proceedings of Sixth International World Wide Web Conference*, Santa Clara, CA, 1997.

[3] R. Hightower et al., Graphical Multiscale Web Histories: A Study of PadPrints, *ACM Conference on Hypertext*, 1998.

[4] R. Gandhi, G. Kumar, B. Bederson, and B. Shneiderman, Domain Name Based Visualization of Web Histories in a Zoomable User Interface, *Proc. 2nd Int'l Workshop on Web-Based Information Visualization*, UK, 2000.

Examining Self-efficacy and Self-Regulation Levels Across Gender in Business Distance Education Courses

Lori B. Holcomb, Scott W. Brown, University of Connecticut
& Fredrick B. King, University of Hartford

Abstract

The purpose of this study was to examine the roles self-efficacy, specifically technology self-efficacy and distance education self-efficacy, and self-regulation play in students' learning via distance education. Participants were undergraduate and graduated students enrolled in business distance education courses at a university in northeastern USA. Prior to the completion of the semester, students were asked to complete an on-line survey that was designed to measure technology self-efficacy, distance education self-efficacy, and self-regulation. In addition, students responded to three short answer prompts concerning the benefits and drawbacks of distance education. Their self-efficacy and self-regulation levels were compared across gender to see if there were in fact gender gaps in technology, distance education, and self-regulation.

Introduction

The rationale for this study was to examine the roles self-efficacy, specifically technology self-efficacy and distance education self-efficacy, and self-regulation play in students' learning via distance education. Both undergraduate and graduated students enrolled in business distance education courses at the University of Connecticut participated in this study. Prior to the completion of the semester, students were asked to complete an on-line survey that was designed to measure technology self-efficacy, distance education self-efficacy, and self-regulation. In addition, students responded to three short answer prompts concerning the benefits and drawbacks of distance education. Previous research has demonstrated that self-efficacy and self-regulation are two constructs that have a significant effect on achievement in education [1,3]

The post Distance Education Survey (DES) was developed and administered to students enrolled in a distance education course. All participants involved in this study were enrolled in the School of Business at the University of Connecticut. The same set of surveys (Appendices A, B, and C) were completed by the one group of participants during the eleven day time period. The dependent variable for this study was gender, with technology self-efficacy, distance education self-efficacy, and self-regulation as the independent variables.

Comprised of 53 questions, all based on a five point Likert-type scale, the DES asked participants to rate the degree to which they agreed or disagreed with the given statements. Questions 1-30 focused specifically on technology self-efficacy, while questions 31-44 focused specially on distance education self-efficacy. The remaining nine questions, 45-53, addressed self-regulatory skills. Participants were not required to respond to any of statements (questions one through fifty-three) and therefore were allowed to skip responses, leaving them blank. In addition to the 53 questions, participants were asked to respond and comment to a set of three questions directed towards the benefits and drawbacks of distance education. Like the prior section of the survey, responses were strictly voluntary and were not required. The only required responses on the survey pertained to demographic information.

Analysis

A Principle Components Analysis (PCA), with Varimax Rotation, was conducted on the 53 statements in the DES. Due to the design of the instrument, the pilot study findings [11,12] and the theoretical foundations of the study, three factors were forced in this PCA. The three factors accounted for 71.35% of the total variance. The three factors were labeled: Technological Self-Efficacy; Distance Education Self-Efficacy; and Self-Regulation.

Factor loading patterns were carefully examined for each of the three factors. Items with a factor loading of less than .3 were removed from the factor. In turn, factor 1 was reduced from 30 items to 19 items resulting in an alpha reliability of $\alpha = .89$. The 12 items comprising Factor 2, reduced from the original 14, had an alpha reliability of $\alpha = .91$. The third factor produced an alpha reliability of $\alpha = .82$ after being reduced from 9 items to 6 items. Each of the factors proved to have good reliability for attitudinal measures as defined by Gable and Wolf [4], ranging from .82 to .91. Individual factors scores were then computed for each participant using the arithmetic average of the individual items in that factor. A one-way ANOVA was run with the dependent variable being technology self-efficacy, distance education self-efficacy, and self-regulatory skills respectively. The results indicated no statistically significant gender differences (p>.05) on any of the three factors: technology self-efficacy, distance education self-efficacy, or self-regulatory skills. Therefore, there does not appear to be an effect of gender on the manner in which students responded to the factors related to technology self-efficacy, distance education self-efficacy, and/or self-regulation.

Additional three one way ANOVAs revealed that previous experience with distance education did have a significant impact on both distance education self-efficacy and self-regulation skills ($p < .05$), but no significant impact on technology self efficacy ($p > .05$). A series of three one-way ANOVAs with the independent variable previous distance education experience and the dependent variables as technology self-efficacy, distance education self-efficacy, and self-regulatory skills demonstrated that prior distance education impacted distance education self-efficacy and self-regulation.

Conclusions

Based on previous research [5,6] it was expected that there would be gender differences with respect to technology self-efficacy. Prior studies have demonstrated that males, as a whole, have higher technology self-efficacy levels than females [8]. In addition, previous findings have shown that the gap between male and female achievement and attitudes toward computers was small in the early grades, but males were at significantly higher achievement levels by high school [9]. The present research, conversely, found no statistically significant differences between the genders, counter to the previous research. However, this finding is of value. The perception of technology self-efficacy among these students may be due, in part, to the type of students that took these courses. Students who participated in the study were either graduate or upper classmen undergraduate students. In addition, all of the students were enrolled in a business program. Majority of business students are apt to be more experienced with computer technology than the average student. However, there was no significant difference between genders on technology self-efficacy measures for this study. It was not surprising that there were significant findings regarding the effect prior distance education experience had on distance education self-efficacy and self-regulation. This concurs with previous studies and literature written on distance education and self-efficacy. Previous success with distance education provides students with a positive experience, which according to Bandura [2], allows for self-efficacy to increase in addition to increasing the willingness to repeat the experience of taking future courses at a distance. Likewise, self-regulation is a

critical component of distance education success [10]. Having successfully completed a distance education course would reinforce and enhance the individual's self-efficacy for self-regulation [3].

Students enrolled in the distance education courses identified both the benefits and drawbacks of taking a course via distance education, as well as provided recommendations and necessary changes. Females, as a whole, identified more of the benefits of distance education than their male counter parts. Flexibility and convenience were among the benefits mentioned by both genders. These two benefits are reflective of the large learning population that is emerging from the workforce [13]. Distance education allows for students to maintain full time jobs while enrolling in courses. Students are no committed to learning in a specific location at a specific time [7]. In addition, distance education also allows for students with unique needs, be it location or personal needs, to learn at a distance.

The overall findings of this study could have significant implications in the field of distance education. Studies such as this one provide more insight into the characteristics of learners enrolled in distance education courses. As more is learned about learner characteristics and the effects they have on successful distance education learner, the manner in which distance education courses are constructed and the pedagogy used in their delivery may change. Further research is needed in the area of what makes learners successful in distance education. This research might result in the development of an instrument that could reasonably predict a student's success in a distance education course prior to their enrollment. Moreover, this research could also result in the development of interventions that would aid students, and contribute to their success, in taking courses at a distance.

Findings from this study can only be generalized to those with similar traits as participants in the study: undergraduate or graduate students enrolled in business distance education courses. Although no significant differences were found between genders on technology self-efficacy, distance education self-efficacy, and self-regulation measures and conflicted with prior research, the findings are still of value. One reason for the different results may have been the sample characteristics, business students. Participants in this study identified convenience and flexibility as two of the benefits of distance education courses. Drawbacks of distance education were identified as lack of human interaction, deadlines, and clarification issues. When asked to provide recommendations for future distance education courses, participants expressed the need for more human interaction and greater professor accessibility. Further research in the area of distance education is still necessary.

The Studies to Develop Integrated Database for Supportinginter-school Activities

Mr. Hitoshi NAKAGAWA

Center for Educational Research and Training Faculty of Education, Kanazawa University, Japan

Abstract

We developed "Integrated database for supporting inter-school activities" which content is to support for cooperative & collaborative learning; the database functions not only as a "registration" and "search" tool for schools looking for a eager partner to work together in a collaborate learning program, but also is designed to assist schools in "finding a subject of study" or "case example," to help their earlier stage indeterminating a program to start for.

In our study to develop this database system, we tried to integrate the following features;

1) to find a partner school for interactive study, based on learning subjects and themes.

2) to encourage interactive study.

3) to cultivate a relationship between partner schools, through sessions of the studying objective.

And we also had teachers actually use the database to improve the usability of it.

Presentation of the studies to develop "Integrated database for supporting inter-school activities" that assists to find a collaborate learning partner among schools, which aims to work together on certain programs and subjects.

1. The basic concept and objective in developing the program

Today, there are plenty of websites that support children in studying activities. However, there are very few sites that assist interaction of students, working on the same field but from different regions, as they collect information they want. And, even though some exist, they often restrict the scope of the project, or restrict free entry into the community.

Our study ultimately tries to acheive, a system that provides the opportunity for each and every school in Japan to participate and colaborate. This project like ours, which provides a device to find a collaborative partner wide-spread, may help give us the chance to reconstruct the schools aproach or curriculum of classrooms in studying. Teachers in schools that are used to utilizing the network environment, have a clear image of the curriculum and collaborate studying program using the net, but many teachers with less experience, is better off to cultivate these images through dialogs with their counterparty in this collaborative studying process. In these cases, it is often hard to start a program with a given studying theme to start with.

In our study, we tried to set up a sytem in which,

a collaborative program can start off without a clear theme, but instead with a vague activity plan, by accessing this site and through dialogues with teachers in charged of the prospective school partners. In addition, to free the teachers and schools from the daily maintenance duties of the servers and sysytems, we will concentrate the server to one location, so the operation staff can take care of the system. Thus, the teachers can concentrate their efforts in the studying activity using the internet.

２．Target of users, grades, and schools.

1) Activities between Elementary and Junior high schools, without distinctions between grades and school types.

2) For teachers setting up studying plans and curriculums. For students utilization of research for their study.

３．Targeting area of education

The target covers each school subject, integrated study, and et alia (morality, extracurricular activity, school activities at large.) Each elementary and junior high school curriculum subject, unit and area is categorized into themes and linked to webpages with related studying objectives.

In regards of integrated study, here again, we try to categorize them in themes and studying methods and link them to websites providing information with related studying objectives.

４．The structure and envisioned utilization of the interaction supporting database system.

We designed the interface, so that each

function can be used organically and consistently, considering the use in the following stages, in the planning of interactive learning classes.

1) In the stage of determinating the subject. [Database of integrated study examples, and database of studying program examples, based on carriculum subject units]

fig.1

· Click the navigation button, "Search for studying program examples," and the top page for Studying program examples apear.

· To change elementary and junior high school programs, just click the top page tab.

· In terms of integrated study, subjects are arranged into 19 categories, such as "hometown" and "expression and production." You can search for your objective page, through narrowing down the list through "Category, Sub-category, and Region."

·

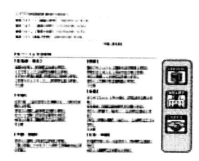
fig.2

2) The stage of finding useful information for the learning subject.

[Webpage database useful for investigative study]

- Our website provides categorized linkage, based on learning subjects, to sites that provide useful support for investigative studying.
- "Carriculum unit examples" directory provides "integrated study" in 19 categorys and 9 other sub-directorys for each other curriculum subjects.
- On the bottom of the "carriculum unit examples" directory page, there is a category and sub-category directory guiding tool.

3) The stage of expressing interest in interactive studying.

[Bullletin board for searching for an interactive studying partner]

- The user registration page blocks registration by an outside party by an ID and password authentication.
- ID's and passwords are delivered to schools by e-mails (aprrox. 3200 schools).
- We accept application, by a given format, on the schools official homepage and

learning examples page.

- The management office confirms the content of the applied websites, and adds it to the database, if it has no conceivable problem.
  - The format also provides for space for modification on registered website contents.

4) To investigate about your partner school, before or after your interchange with the school.

[Database on general information of the schools]

- Click "search for schools" on the navigation button, and you will be on the top page of general information of schools.
- Select the prefecture of the school on the map navigation.

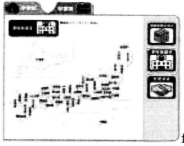
fig.3

5) The stage when teachers correspond to discuss their interactive studying plan.

[Bullletin board for searching for an interactive studying partner]

- There are bulletin boards for each interactive study subjects. (classified into19 categories)

fig.5

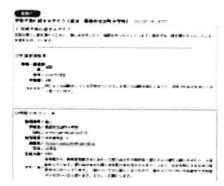

fig.6

6) The stage of reporting the results of the interactive program.

[Questionares (includes application for registration of studying program examples.)]

Click either "Studying program examples," "school search," and "referencial homepage search," which is another way of searching for information. We provide for students use, as well, after a inter-school and inter-class collaboration program is in tact.

We also provide for individual investigative study in using our database. In addtion, we are ready for students voluntarily corresponding with the students of their interactive partner, in their usual course of there curriculum and extracurricular activity.

5. The significance of using the interaction database

1) The solution of finding a partner

The most difficult part of interactive study, is that it is hard to find a partner. If you are not a teacher that participates in many national workshop programs, you almost have no idea how tosearch for a partner in inter-scholl activities. Regional school boards sometime provide for assistance, but many boards themselves are in a trial and error stage. As a matter of fact, there will be more opportunity for interchange between schools, with this kind of community on the web. This is a breakthrough event.

2) The solution of determinating whether the school could be a constructive partner, even with the same studying subject. Even if the two schools share the same subject of study, it is a different story whether they can develop a fruitful interactive studying program. This is because there are differences in the intents of the teachers and which part of the studying programs are to be planned for interactivity. And if your school partner is selected through the introdution of the school board or through your partner's school homepages, it is hard to decline the relationship, and you must work on with an awkward situation in the studying program. But with the interactive database, you have a picture of the content of the activity, and after correspondence with your counterpart teacher, you can enter into a

collaborative program.

3) Support for derterminating the content of the studying program.

In interactive studies, most of the time, the content of the studying activities are not that clear to begin with. With the interactive database, you can well-define your objectives in the curriculum through dialogues with fellow teachers.

4) To provide a platform for schools throughout the nation, that can be freely accessed and free to participate.

As we assure a platform for schools to participate and interchange, we can expect for better information literacy and manners to live in a informational society, through discipline of communication with other school students. In addition, the scope of education can be broadened, from the conventional library study and class discussion, to using the open internet database.

6. Future issues to address

We need to continuely address the following issues of this database system.

1) To check whether the interactive subjects match the schools educational needs.

2) To examine how we can keep up with the expectedly growing numbers of school homepages, how to register the pages, check the link and maintain the overall operation of the network.

3) To maintain the operation for proper ID issuance.

4) To work to improve the system to link this bulletin board system with regional community bulletin boards, and maintain the ID and password system.

5) To examine PR and announcement measures to enhance usage of this database content.

6) To improve the interface to be more friendly for pupils to use.

7) To align with various educational contents that exist in many ways.

An Analysis of Image Retrieval Behavior for Metadata Type Image Database

Toru FUKUMOTO and Kanji AKAHORI

Department of Human System Science, Graduate School of Decision Science and Technology

Tokyo Institute of Technology, 2-12-1 Ookayama, Meguro-ku, Tokyo, JAPAN

+81-3-5734-3233

fukumoto@ak.cradle.titech.ac.jp

Abstract

A large number of digital images are stored on the Internet. From an educational perspective the fact that a vast number of images on a number of topics are readily available and are in some cases free is a very helpful thing. With the rapidly expanding nature of the net however, it is becoming increasingly difficult to search out and retrieve relevant images. The aim of this study was to analyze users' behavior during image retrieval exercises. Results revealed that users tend to follow a set search strategy: firstly they input one or two keyword search terms one after another and view the images generated by their initial search and after they navigate their way around the web by using the 'back to home' or 'previous page' buttons. These results are consistent with existing Web research. Many of the actions recorded revealed that subjects' behavior differed depending on if the task set was presented as a closed or open task. In contrast no differences were found for the time subjects took to perform a single action or their use of the AND operator.

Keywords Image Retrieval, Metadata, Keyword, Searching Behavior

1: Introduction

The number of images being stored in the Internet is increasing due to an increase in affordable digital recording devices, such as digital cameras and scanners. In order to effectively manage these digital images, an image album or an image filing system has become the subject of study. As the Internet grows so the task of image retrieval becomes more complicated. From an educational perspective the role of images as important educational aids is unquestionable. Images not only serve to support curriculum and extra curricular subjects but can, if used properly, enhance students understanding of concepts and issues and in some cases provide the teacher with an alternative and inexpensive source of study materials.

There are now accepted ISO (International Standards Organization) regulations governing the structure contents description of metadata for multimedia known as MPEG-7

2: The Purpose of our Research

Over the past years a considerable number of studies have been conducted on information retrieval studies for information over the Internet. More recently there has been a new method proposed for assessing information searching behavior on WWW however this only deals with text information not image based information. The Internet is rapidly expanding and the number of stored images on sites has increased therefore we argue that effective retrieval methods aimed at retrieving stored images from a database have become significantly more important. However there have not been many studies that have attempted to assess user's behavior on image information retrieval tasks. The aim of this study was to analyze user's behavior on image retrieval tasks.

3: Method

20 undergraduate students participated in this study. All were accustomed to using search engines on the Internet such as Google and Yahoo! We developed the image database based on previous research]. The number of images in this database was 1700 with the contents being varied. Subjects were shown an image and asked to retrieve it so that they could become accustomed to the system. We repeated this procedure twice with a different image on each trial. These initial tasks were labeled Task 1-1 and Task 1-2, respectively. We then issued instructions to the subjects asking them to search for images that would be suitable for a "Summer Greetings Card"and to retrieve an image/s from the database. We did not impose a time limit on this exercise nor did we restrict the number of images that subjects could retrieve, this task was labeled Task 2. During both tasks subject's behavior was recorded on video.

Results

Categorization of Actions: Table 1 shows the ratio of subjects' actions.

Table 1:Categorization of Subject's Actions

		Task1-1	Task1-2	Task2
Keyword	Input	50.48%	55.03%	40.29%
Operation	Add	1.67%	3.13%	1.49%
	Delete	7.60%	2.50%	1.11%
	Replace	1.00%	0.71%	0%
Web page Operation	Magnify	7.75%	10.28%	8.78%
	Select Link	0%	0.56%	0.29%
	Select Pull-down	0%	0.42%	0.19%
Browser Operation	Forward	0%	12.56%	10.66%
	Back	25.65%	9.56%	30.01%
	Home	0%	0.79%	4.88%
	Jump	0%	0%	0%
	Subtotal	96.14%	98.66%	97.71%
Other	Other	3.86%	0.71%	2.29%

Process of Search: Table 2 shows the ratio of subjects' search processes. For set actions such as inputting a keyword or going back to a previous page no significant time differences in the execution of these tasks was found. We believe that this characteristic is not dependent on the task but is instead a personal characteristic.

Table 2: Ratio of Search Processes

	Task1-1	Tast1-2	Task2	Signify
Pages	1.00	2.80	5.55	t=3.27**
Actions	4.70	4.95	22.40	t=4.83**
Time (MM:SS)	01:20	01:30	06:30	t=4.90**
Time/Action	00:21	00:19	00:18	t=0.98

Keywords of Search: Table 3 shows the ratio of subjects' keyword operations

Table 3: Ratio of Keyword Operation

	Task1-1	Task1-2	Task2	Signify
Inputting	2.60	1.85	9.30	t=4.35**
Unique	2.50	1.80	7.65	t=4.06**
Depth of AND	1.45	1.25	1.25	t=1.25

Expansion of the i-mode Drill "The World of Kanji" with Review Functions for m-learning

Aya Ichinohe, Katsuaki Suzuki
Faculty of Software and Information Science,
Iwate Prefectural University, 020-0193, Japan
E-mail: ksuzuki@soft.iwate-pu.ac.jp

Abstract

This study suggested some ways to improve "The world of Kanji," a Web site for mobile phone users, which provides many features to support users to learn Kanji (One of three ways of Japanese writing which originated in Chinese). To strengthen review functions of the present version, the expanded version of "The world of Kanji" was designed and developed by adding/changing the following functions: (1) mail delivery of the drill, (2) correctness of response in feedback, (3) more user control over areas and number of items for reviewing. User reactions in formative evaluation studies were favorable of the expanded version.

Keywords: Mobile phone, Web-based learning environment, Drill delivery, Kanji proficiency test, m-learning

1. Introduction

There are many Web sites in Japan for i-mode[1] users that offer learning materials. Web site "The world of Kanji" that helps users to prepare for the Kanji proficiency test[2] is an good example of such an advanced learning environment by using E-mails and Web browsing for mobile learning. Although the screen is not suitable for displaying large contents, mobile phones will make learning-on-demand possible whenever the users want regardless of the user's location.

Learning Kanji, one of three ways of Japanese writing which originated in Chinese, is classified in the domain of verbal information. Suzuki (1989) pointed out that it is effective for learning verbal information to eliminate the items that has mastered, so that the learner can concentrate the items that have not yet mastered. In this study, the expanded version of "The world of Kanji" was designed and developed in order to suggest more effective learning environment on the mobile terminal.

2. Design and Development

A registered user of "The world of Kanji" can choose a level and take an exam. After finishing the exam consisting of fifty questions from five sections, the result (pass/ fail) will be sent by an E-mail. On the Web, such pages as "See your rank", "See the answers", "Your points", "Your studying history" and "Advises" will be made available. After taking the exam, "the personalized drill" will become available, which consists of thirty questions. It contains more questions from the area that the user missed more in the exam.

Although "The world of Kanji" has many features to support learning, it has some limitations. E mails were used only to receive the result of the exam, which could be done by using the next screen of the Web. There was no information of the correctness of user's responses for each item of the exam, although the correct answers are given. There are no functions to concentrate on the missed items, even in the personalized drill, nor to change the order of the items for reviewing.

The present version of "The world of Kanji" was first recreated using Perl and HTML, and it was placed on the Web server with restricted access. The movement was checked by an i-mode mobile phone while developing. After having developed the present version, the expanded version was developed by adding or changing functions as follows:

1) Mail delivery of the drill: URLs for the drills of

---

[1] Internet connecting service for mobile phones by NTT Docomo. The number of the user is about 30 million as of December 2001.
[2] A test aimed at Japanese to certify the level of Kanji (one of three types of Japanese letters which has its origin in Chinese). Knowledge of 6,000 Kanji characters is required to pass Level 1, the highest level.

each area depending on the days of the week are sent by e-mails, starting on the day after taking an exam. The drills of the weak areas are delivered again in the same week. More frequent learning is to be signaled by not only waiting the access from the user, but by pushing from the learning site.

2) Correctness of responses on the explanation page (Figure 1): The user can select to see "Only wrong items", "First wrong items and next correct items" or "In the order of the exam" when checking his/her answers.

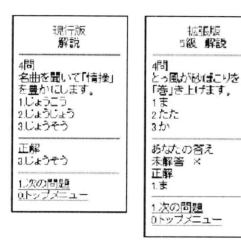

Figure 1. Comparison of the "Explanation" pages in the present version and the expanded version

3) Announcement of the test result on Web: No e-mail is used to announce the test result to make the user free from changing from Web to email screen only to know the result.

4) Personalization of the personalized drill: the style of the personalized drill was changed so that the user can choose only the areas with difficulties. Also, the number of the question is not limited so that the user can practice as much as wanted. The questions in the drill are at first presented in the same order as in the exam when reviewing. The question that is answered correctly twice will be eliminated from the review drill. When all the questions in the exam are finished, new questions will be given from the item pool.

3.   Formative Evaluation and Conclusion

To compare reactions for the original and the expanded version, one college student was asked to use the expanded version for fifteen minutes after studying with the original version for forty minutes. Favorable reactions were given for the functions of the expanded version, and some advises for further improvement were also obtained. After some improvement were made, two more college students were asked to try the improved expanded version for one week. The original version was shown on the last day and their opinions after comparison were collected. Favorable views were given about the function of the expanded version.

In this research, the expanded version of "The world of Kanji" was developed so as to make m-learning by i-mode mobile phone system as effective as possible. Data from formative evaluation studies supported that the expansion. Our future tasks are to conduct further evaluation studies to compare the original version and the expanded version for supporting learning in longer terms.

References

1)   ZAPPALLAS, INS, Association for Kanji proficiency test. URL=http://kanjikentei.com/

2)   Suzuki, K. (1989). A study of CAI drill design to complement learning foreign language through TV program, *Japanese Journal of Radio and Television Education Research*, No.17 pp.21-37

Development of the WBL System to Complement Lectures for Teacher Professional Development

Yusuke Morita
Nagasaki University
Faculty of Education
1-14 Bunkyo, Nagasaki 852-8521, Japan
ymorita@i.edu.nagasaki-u.ac.jp

Norifumi Mashiko
Naruto University of Education
Faculty of School Education
748 Takashima, Naruto 772-8502, Japan
mashiko@naruto-u.ac.jp

Naoto Sone
Naruto University of Education
Information Processing Center
naosone@naruto-u.ac.jp

Ayako Kawakami
Naruto University of Education
Faculty of School Education
kawakami@naruto-u.ac.jp

Abstract

In this study, a Web Based-Learning system to complement lectures for teacher professional development was developed and evaluated by five points of view. The WBL courses using prior inference task were developed by Mashiko (2001) to exploit the lectures. The system including the courses had three function modes, (1) administrator mode, (2) learners mode and (3) instructor mode, are integrated using RDBMS. The learners estimated usefulness and practicability of the system for professional development of teachers especially the interaction in the online asynchronous forum with the face pictures of learners was valued.

1. Introduction

It is important to develop quality courses for professional development of teachers as in-service training in distance education. Mashiko *et al.* [2] developed Web-Based Learning courses using "prior inference task" to retrain teachers in the Graduate School of Education at Naruto University of Education(NUE), one of the public institutions providing retraining programs for teachers in Japan. This WBL system was also developed to complement lectures.

Levin *et al.* [1] identified five dimensions that contributed to effective online learning for teachers' professional development as follows: (a) relevant and challenging assignments, (b) coordinated learning environments, (c) adequate and timely feedback from instructors, (d) rich environments for student-to-student interaction, and (e) flexi-

bility in teaching and learning. The purpose of this research was to develop WBL system where teachers can discuss online their practical experience and knowledge about computers and other subject areas. They can access information and make inquires to develop the best practice.

2. Development

The WBL system was constructed from free software (OS: Debian GNU/Linux kernel 2.4.14, HTTP Server: Apache 1.3.17, Streaming Server: RealServer 8, RDBMS: PostgreSQL7.0.2, Script Language: PHP4.0 and Perl5) for "(e) flexibility in teaching and learning." In the system, three function modes, (1) administrator mode, (2) learners mode and (3) instructor mode, are integrated using RDBMS.

(1) **Administrator mode**: In the administrator mode, a WBL system administrator can register personal information about learners and instructors, and can also open or close the courses when learners access or leave the system through the Internet/Intranet.

(2) **Learner mode**: In the learner mode, a learner can access some course materials, see profiles of other learners who attend the same course, discuss assignments using online asynchronous forum, and transmit reports to instructors. Special features are following. The system automatically identifies successful transmission when the learner submits a report to an instructor using the system. And a still digital picture of each learner is displayed on the forum pages to give the discussions a more personal feeling. Therefore, the forum provides

"(d) rich environments for student-to-student interaction."

(3)**Instructor mode**: In the instructor mode, an instructor can survey data records of each learner in the courses covered by the instructor on this system. Instructors can also evaluate learners' reports, and the instructor can input comments which appear in each learner's private feedback box.

The instructor needs the instructor mode to "(b) coordinate learning environment" and to provide "(e) flexibility in teaching and learning." The WebCT, the most famous WBL system, has a designer mode which assists instructors in constructing online courses, however, instead of our system replaces the designer mode.

3. Evaluation

3.1 Method

Subjects: 11 subjects (8 teachers and 3 graduate students) participated in this test.

Lectures: From October to November 2001, the system using prior inference tasks for "(a) relevant and challenging assignments" complemented the lecture, 'Practical contents development.' One of the in-service teachers at Nagasaki University took the lecture through the Internet using live streaming video and NetMeeting for interactive communication with other learners on another campus. The instructor led them to accomplish tasks using text, pictures, and/or multimedia contents by SMIL (*Synchronized Multimedia Integration Language*). All of the learners connected to the system through the Internet/intranet after the lecture, in order to browse complementary instruction and discuss asynchronously with other learners in the forum. The instructor provided "(c) adequate, timely and meaningful feedback" and also promoted learners' discussion about the assignments.

Data: A questionnaire was used and data of learning records were analyzed to evaluate the system. The mean scores were calculated on the total number of 11 responses on a scale of 1-4, with 1 representing "strongly disagree" and 4 indicating "strongly agree."

3.2. Results

Figure1 shows the items of the questionnaire and the mean scores. All scores were higher than 2.5 (mid value on a scale of 1-4). "Intelligibility of the instructor's explanations" scored 3.41. Furthermore, learners evaluated instruction in the forum, usefulness of showing face pictures, and effectiveness of displaying the information of leaning records.

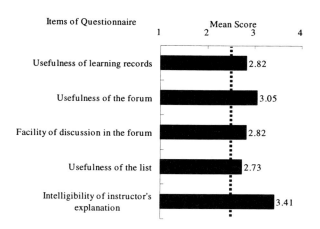

Figure 1. Evaluation of WBL System

On the other hand, Pearson's correlation coefficients between the number of ideas input by each learner, teaching careers, and access time from login to logout were calculated to analyze learners' behavior in the forum. The number of ideas on the forum correlated significantly with the careers in teaching ($r=0.44$), and also correlated with the access time ($r=0.86$). The instructor suggested many ideas and guided the discussion more than learners did in the forum.

4. Conclusion

In this study, we developed a WBL system for professional development of teachers. The system was evaluated from five points of view, which were as follows: (a) relevant and challenging assignments, (b) coordinated learning environment, (c) adequate and timely feedback from instructors, (d) rich environments for student-to-student interaction, and (e) flexibility in teaching and learning by Levin *et al* [1]. The learners estimated usefulness and practicability of the system for teacher professional development.

References

[1] S. R. Levin, G. L. Waddoups, J. Levin, and J. Buell. Highly interactive and effective online learning environment for teacher professional development. *International Journal of Educational Technology*, 2(2):http://www.outreach.uiuc.edu/ijet/v2n2/slevin/index.html, 2001.

[2] N. Mashiko, H. Sako, M. Umezawa, K. Nishioka, Y. Morita, and H. Kuzukami. Linking educational practice research and university lecture improvement under promoting it education in public schools. *Research Bulletin of Educational Sciences in Naruto University of Education*, 17:57–64, 2002.

Development and Evaluation of Distance Learning Courses for Professional Development of Teachers: Effects of Web-Based Learning Using Prior Inference Tasks

Norifumi Mashiko
Naruto University of Education
Faculty of School Education
748 Takashima, Naruto 772-8502, Japan
mashiko@naruto-u.ac.jp

Yusuke Morita
Nagasaki University
Faculty of Education
1-14 Bunkyo, Nagasaki 852-8521, Japan
ymorita@i.edu.nagasaki-u.ac.jp

Naoto Sone
Naruto University of Education
Information Processing Center
naosone@naruto-u.ac.jp

Ayako Kawakami
Naruto University of Education
Faculty of School Education
kawakami@naruto-u.ac.jp

Abstract

In this study, a new type of Web-Based Learning (WBL) courses for professional development of teachers was developed. We set up "inference tasks" as the core of our WBL courses. These tasks were expected to be effective in reflecting learners' various experience on learning process and in keeping learners' highly-motivated learning. The developed test courses were generally evaluated as useful by subjects. However, it was also suggested that inference activity was more effective in the case of presenting simple information than that of complicated one.

1. Introduction

Distance learning programs on the WWW are very useful for professional development of teachers as off-campus training systems. However, it is pointed that the quality of learning contents and courses highly matters for effective learning in such programs. In this paper, we report a new type of distance learning courses that we developed for professional development of teachers.

2. Development

In distance learning environments, the positive participation in learning courses of learners is indispensable to effective learning. Therefore, it is important to facilitate the interaction between learners and the instructor or among learners in learning process. In order to encourage such interaction and maintain strong motivation of learners, we included the following points as necessary conditions in designing the courses of WBL.

1) As learning contents material, concrete practical cases collected in several schools as a result of our field study (e.g., Mashiko & Kagawa, 1999 [1]; Mashiko et al.,

2001 [2]) are used.

2) The learning courses show definite practical skills that teachers can apply at their school.

3) The learning courses show theoretical and universal knowledge linking with practical skills.

4) Instructors are well acquainted with those contents.

Further, we set up "inference tasks" in process of WBL. In this task, learners are presented a practical case that is the solution of a problem in a certain school (e.g., a photo of learning material developed by one teacher with some intentions), and are requested to reason about the meaning or effect of the case and to present a short report about it. Those inference tasks were expected to be effective in reflecting learners' various experience on learning process and in keeping learners' highly-motivated learning. Each of learners' reports is evaluated by the instructor and the result of evaluation is informed to each learner. After the evaluation and feedback of reports, the instructor explains the practical meaning and theoretical knowledge linking with that case. Finally, learners verify the acquired knowledge by applying it to their class in school.

In learning process, learners can interact each other and with the instructor on the occasion of reading other learner's report, asking the instructor about his/her explanation and discussing about the new knowledge and the application of it on on-line forum. Figure 1 shows the process of WBL courses that we developed.

3. Evaluation

3.1 Method

Test courses: We designed three types of courses (A, B, and C) according to three different cases collected in our field study. Each theme of course A, B, and C is "the developing process of learning materials", "the designing

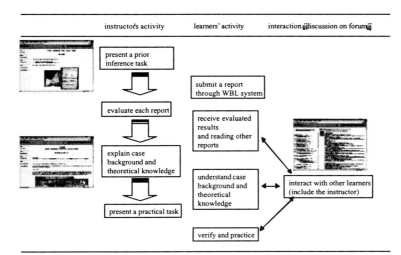

| | instructor's activity | learners' activity | interaction ｉｊｄiscussion on forumｊｊ |

Figure 1. Learning process including a prior inference task.

of learning environment", and "the promoting of active learning", respectively.

Subjects: 11 subjects (8 teachers and 3 graduate students) were participated in this test.

Procedure: The test was conducted as a part of on-campus lecture. On each test course, subjects were presented the inference task one week in advance of the

	Course A	Course B	Course C
motivation	3.50 (.50)	3.64 (.45)	3.41 (.38)
comprehension	3.36 (.55)	3.55 (.52)	3.41 (.38)
a sense of participation	3.59 (.49)	3.64 (.50)	3.45 (.42)

Table 1. Evaluation of prior-inference acvitity.

on-campus lecture and provided the feedback of

	Course A	Course B	Course C
motivation	3.23 (.61)	3.45 (.52)	2.82 (.46)
comprehension	3.32 (.64)	3.41 (.49)	3.05 (.47)
effectiveness for improvement	3.23 (.61)	3.09 (.94)	2.86 (.55)
verifiable	3.14 (.32)	3.09 (.54)	3.00 (.49)

Table 2. Evaluation of the effectiveness as the off-campus training course.

evaluation of his/her report before the lecture. The instructor gave his lecture with pictures in the WBL course. After that, subjects and the instructor had a discussion about the case and theoretical knowledge and the new inference task in the next course was presented. When all courses finished, subjects were asked to fill out a questionnaire for each test course. The questionnaire was consisted seven items: 3 items about the effectiveness of prior inference activity and other 4 items about the effectiveness of those courses as the off-campus training course. All items had a 4 point scale with 1 representing strongly disagree to 4 indicating strongly agree.

3.2 Results

Table 1 shows mean scores of the items about the effectiveness of prior inference activity. All scores were higher than 2.5 (mid value on a scale of 1-4). The result of an ANOVA demonstrated no significant effect between courses on any item. Table 2 indicates mean scores of the items about the effectiveness of those courses as the off-campus training course. All scores were higher than 2.5. As the result of an ANOVA, there was a significant effect on only "motivation" item $F(2,30)=4.02$, $p<.05$). This effect was due to the difference between course B and C. In course C, the streaming video was presented at the inference task while in other two courses one picture was used. It would seem that too much information from the video decrease learner's motivation.

4. Conclusion

In this study, we developed a new type of WBL courses with prior inference task for professional development of teachers. Though the courses were generally evaluated as useful by subjects, it was also suggested that inference activity was more effective in the case of presenting simple information than that of complicated one.

References

[1] N. Mashiko and T. Kagawa. Analysis and conceptualization of teaching strategies for computer operation skills: Teaching strategies of computer operation for primary school children (A case analysis). *Research Bulletin of Educational Sciences in Naruto University of Education,* 14:71-80, 1999.

[2] N. Mashiko et al. Tryout of constructing school-university partnerships through information education at local area: Virtual professional development schools at Naruto-city. *Research Bulletin of Educational Sciences in Naruto University of Education,* 16:55-63, 2001.

Constructing Web-based Japanese Text Reading Support System and Its Evaluation

MOCHIZUKI Hajime
Faculty of Foreign Studies
Tokyo University of Foreign Studies
3-11-1 Fuchu Tokyo 183-8534 Japan
motizuki@tufs.ac.jp

TERA Akemi
Japanese Course
Hokuriku University
1-1 Taiyogaoka Ishikawa 920-1180 Japan
tera@jaist.ac.jp

Abstract

In this paper, we describe a design for our system and report the current status of the system. We also present the result of preliminary examination to evaluate an interface of the system.

1 Introduction

A variety of methods and systems to support for Japanese text reading have already been proposed[2, 4]. In our project, we design a web-based system which can be able to show various supporting information for any texts flexibly to a learner. In this paper, we explain our system and have an experimentation for comparing two different interfaces to show the information. From result of the examination, we evaluate our current system and discuss good or bad points about the interface.

2 System Overview

Fig.1 gives an overview of our system, DL-MT.

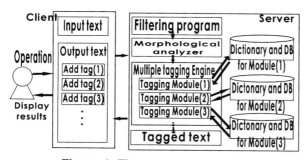

Figure 1. The systerm overview

First, a learner inputs or pastes a text that he or she wants to read and understand. Next, the text is sent to the main program on a WWW server via CGI. Then the main program filters the input text and decomposes it into morphemes by Japanese morphological analyzer ChaSen[1]. The system analyzes the text and adds some advice functions for the learner to the text as tags. Finally, a learner can read the text with some advice for understanding it. In our system architecture, all advice functions are implemented as modules. Therefore we can add new functions to our system easily.

Fig.2 shows a snapshot of the current system. In the current version, if a learner puts a mouse cursor on a word in a text, a small window called a pop-up window, **PU-W** will come up around the word and some advice are shown into the window. A learner can also see the same information in a right side frame on a main window by clicking that word.

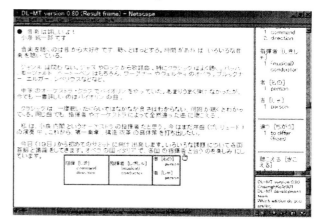

Figure 2. A snapshot of the DL-MT

The following information can be shown by our current prototype system.
- EDICT[3] dictionary information about simple words and complex words in a text.
- Information and pronunciation of proper nouns.
- Information to understand Japanese syntax.

Our system also can change all Kanji in a text to Hiragana or Katakana.

3 Experiment

To evaluate an interface of our system mainly, we use human subjects and make an evaluation examination. We use 2 systems, 8 texts and 18 subjects. One of the systems is **DL-MT** with **PU-W** and other one is **DL'** without **PU-W**. Eight texts are selected from a Japanese examination book and Japanese newspapers each 4 texts. We attached two types of exam questions to all texts.[1] 18 subjects consists of three regions by

---

[1]The type one question is a relevance judgment question. 5 exam questions which are written about the text are shown to a

Table 1. The results of the examination

DLMT	K1L1	K1L2	K1L3	ave	K2L1	K2L2	K2L3	ave	K3L1	K3L2	K3L2	ave
act	3.38	1.38	3.75	2.83	46.38	11.12	8.75	22.08	61.62	42.12	51.38	51.71
time(sec.)	263	281	328	291	375	398	289	354	632	511	646	596
cor	0.911	0.840	0.822	0,857	0.750	0.875	0.911	0.845	0.660	0.714	0.911	0.762
DL'	K1L1	K1L2	K1L3	ave	K2L1	K2L2	K2L3	ave	K3L1	K3L2	K3L2	ave
act	0.88	0.00	2.38	1.08	5.38	6.88	1.50	4.58	47.62	18.62	14.75	27.00
time(sec.)	260	296	334	297	431	392	301	375	640	436	672	583
cor	0.750	0.785	0.857	0.797	0.875	0.804	0.911	0.863	0.678	0.660	0.892	0.744

Table 2. The results of the question

	K1L1	K1L2	K1L3	sum	K2L1	K2L2	K2L3	sum	K3L1	K3L2	K3L2	sum
good	0	0	1	1	1	1	0	2	2	2	2	6
so so	1	1	0	2	0	0	1	1	0	0	0	0
no good	1	1	1	3	1	1	1	3	0	0	0	0

the difference of the similarity with Japanese and each subject's native language; **K1** is a Chinese native class, **K2** is a Korean native class and **K3** is a class of other languages.[2] They are also divided into three stages, L1, L2 and L3 according to their Japanese skill degrees. The subjects are required to read texts and to answer exam questions. We also record time for finishing the task, logs for using **PU-W** by each subject and logs for clicking words by each subject. All subjects are also required to answer questions about the system. The results are shown as table 1 and table 2.

In table1, 'cor' and 'time' indicate the average score of the subjects and the time required for the task respectively. 'act' means the average number of the information reference actions by clicking words or using PU-W. About time, there is no significant difference between DL' and DL-MT. About scr, DL-MT are higher than DL' in K1 and K3 group but in K2 group, the result is upset. However the differences of the results are not enough to be significant. About act, in all three groups DL-MT has higher numbers than DL' has.

From these results, it is difficult to say that the difference of interfaces between DL-MT and DL' will affect the subjects to read texts. However it can be considered that the interface of DL-MT can stimulate the subjects to refer a lot of information about the texts. We expect the reason why PU-W interface in DL-MT is easier than click to refer information.

Table2 shows the results of the question about PU-W. All of the subjects in K3 group answered 'good.' In the contrary, each three subjects answered 'no good' in K1 and K2 group. The main reasons of 'no good' as follows; 'It feels obstructive because PU-W appears soon when the mouse cursor is put on a word,' 'It feels unconvenient because PU-W disappears before the content is read when the mouse cursor is moved out from a word,' 'It feels that eyes are tired.' The main reasons

---

subject and the subject is required to judge if each description is correct or incorrect to a content of the text. The type two question is a selecting answer question. 2 exam questions which have 4 selections each are shown to a subject and the subject is required to choose correct one.

[2]In this examination, subjects in this class are from Poland, Germany, Russia, and India.

to say good as follows; 'It is possible to be able to read no separation of eyes from the text,' 'It is easy to use just put on the mouse cursor on a word.' From the results, it seems that the value of PU-W depends on the user. Especially in our current implementation, reading support information is shown in English in PU-W. Therefore, the user who is familiar with English tends to feel good for PU-W.

4 Conclusion

In this paper, we described a design for our system for Japanese reading support. We also presented the result of preliminary examination to evaluate an interface of the system. From the results, it can be said that our current system helps the learner because the many subjects reference much information provided by our system. We also compared PU-W and non PU-W. There is no significant difference between two interfaces at times and scores. However many subjects who use PU-W referenced information frequently. Therefore, PU-W will be more helpful than the non PU-W.

As a future work, we should extend the system which can be able to show much information with a good interface for each learner flexibly.

Acknowledgment

A part of this research has been subsidized by the Telecommunications Advancement Foundation.

References

[1] Matsumoto Y. et al. *Morphological Analysis System ChaSen version version 2.2.9 Manual*, 2002.

[2] Totsugi N. et al. A Study on the Display of the Results of a Parser and Particle Equivalents, and the Use of the History Data (in Japanese). *Journal of Technical Japanese Education*, 2(2):22–29, 2000.

[3] The Electronic Dictionary Research and Development Group. *EDICT -JAPANESE/ENGLISH DICTIONARY FILE.* ftp://ftp.cc.monash.edu.au/pub/ nihongo/ edict_doc.html, 2000.

[4] Kitamura T. and Komori S. A Reading Support System using Multimedia Data . In *CASTEL/J '99*, pages 173–184, 1999.

Mathematic Guide-Learning System to the Misconception of Elementary Students

Yuan-Chen Liu, Hong-Yan Lee, and Wei-Kai Wang
Graduate School of Mathematics and Science Education,
National Taipei Teachers College

ABSTRACT

In the process of mathematics learning, most elementary students never think but receive all the methods their teachers have taught. In other word, they don't catch the basic concept in every unit. Based on the Petri-Net theory, this paper designs a guided learning system to correct the misconception of elementary students. We expect to achieve the best effect of computer-assisted instruction through the internet.

Key words: Petri-Net , misconception

1. Background

In recent years, the application of the CAI plays an important role to guide students' study and resolve traditional problems of teaching [1],[2]. However, students might produce many misconceptions, which would lead them to neglect present hints that need to be used when they solve problems . They might lose interests and confidence for mathematics. How to develop the CAI tool and help students to study become the most important research lesson of CAI. Accordingly, to understand students' misconceptions and to draft out the project of the solutions are the main keys that mathematics CAI can smoothly accomplish [3]-[6]

2. Purposes of the paper

• We Apply Petri- Net theories to record the learners' solution process and analyze learners' mistake types [7], [8], [9]. By making use of instant sketch, we promote the student's study results since the application produce a solving system of mathematics that is adapted to the individual difference.

3. System application

We can analyze the mistake and misconception of the student.

Figure 1 is an example: "How big do you think is the area of the triangle in?" The correct answer is " 6 $\times 5 \div 2 = 15$

The calculation process can be inputted by students and analyzes its mistake type through this system, then give appropriate guidance and feedback further. However Petri-Net recorded the solution process and guidance of the students .It will make the study process of the students much more clear. When student input computation, the system not only analyze their study condition, but also provide the instant diagram. That make the student can control their solving condition and sense of vision to study results. And give them appropriate help and feedback at appropriate time will make the student acquire the study result that is like the classroom teaching. Figure 2 shows for its instant graphic assisted tools.

If students input the false calculating type, system will immediately generate graph that students input equations by the graphic assisted tools. Students then could understand their misconceptions of the equations they input: triangle area miscalculated rectangular area, and then they will further understand the basic concept and know how to revise the mistake type. More co-operate with the appropriate teaching hint inside system, student acquire the correct and basic concept from mistake type.

4. Conculsion

The main purpose of this paper is based on Petri-Net theories to record the solving process and to analyze the mistake types of students. It designs an fitting pupil mathematic system that have guide functions to correct the wrong thinking and misconception of pupils . It will make them understand mathematic idea and study targets. Through the convenient network environment, we can attain the best result of CAI. By applying Petri-Net theory, the system provides guiding and solving functions. It uses the instant graphic assisted tools to promote the student's learning.

References

[1] Rong Gui H.&yan ping Z.(1995),The CAI software establishment technique references,Taipei: Ministry of Education computer center.
[2] Rong Zhao H.&Ming Zhou L.(1992),The design principle and application of the CAI,book of National Taiwan Teacher University.
[3] Shi Yi C.(1997), the learning and teaching research of Taiwan elementary school, Taichung teacher's college thesis.
[4] Yu SuY. translate(Polya,G.)(1991).How to solve problems,Jiu Zhang press
[5] Ning Jun T.(1995), the area concept study, the nation educate, volume 35 ,7,8 period, P.14~19?

[6]   Ning Jun T (1998),The analyzing research of misconceptions of area pupils,The journal of National Taipei teacher college 11 periods,573-602?

[7]   Christopher M.Hoadley (2000). Teaching science through online, peer discussions: SpeakEasy in the Knowledge Integration Environment. International Journal of Science Education,vol.22, No.8, 839-857.

[8]   Peterson, J. L.,(1981).Petri net theory and the modeling of systems. Prentice-Hall,Englewood Cliffs, N. J

[9]   Berend P.Stellingwerf & Ernest C.D.M.Van Lieshout.(1999). Manipulatives and number sentences in computer aided arithmetic word problem solving. Instructional Science 27: 459-476.

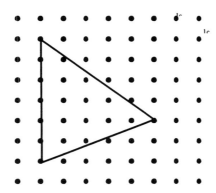

Figure 1: the example of the area of the sideway triangle

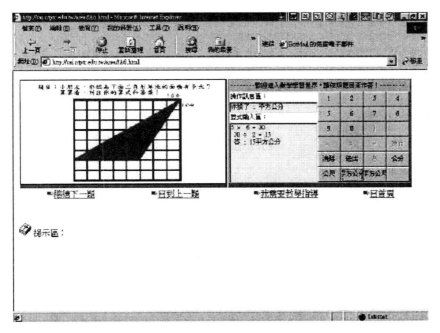

Figure 2: Instant graphic assisted tools.

Digital Repatriation: Virtual Museum Partnerships with Indigenous Peoples

Paul Resta, The University of Texas at Austin
Loriene Roy, The University of Texas at Austin
Marty Kreipe de Montaño, Smithsonian National Museum of the American Indian
Mark Christal, The University of Texas at Austin

The University of Texas and the Smithsonian National Museum of the American Indian have had experience working together on virtual museum projects that bring indigenous people to the museum for the purpose of "digitally repatriating" important cultural items. The initial virtual museum project provided a strategy for cultural responsive teaching in American Indian schools. They also provided a forum for cultural revitalization and cultural collaboration. The university and the museum are currently developing proposals to further develop the digital repatriation concept to include more tribal community participation international indigenous participation.

The richness of indigenous cultures is widely recognized and of great interest to Native and non-Native people alike. Many cultural and historical artifacts of indigenous life are spread across the collections of museums and private holdings. Such holdings may be viewed on site or, increasing, electronically through virtual museums. Still, many indigenous people have limited access to their own cultural heritage and may be excluded also from interpreting these objects even when publicly displayed.

Around the world indigenous people have been struggling to reclaim their cultural rights and maintain their languages. In the United States, one legal tool, the Native American Graves Protection and Repatriation Act of 1990 (NAGPRA), has been used by American Indian tribes to reclaim important cultural artifacts from museums. The law provides for the return of human remains, funerary objects, sacred items, and "objects of cultural patrimony" to the tribes of their origin. Initially, the law alarmed many museum professionals who were afraid their Native American collections would be gutted, but this has not occurred. Since NAGRA became law, outside of a few controversial instances, museums have become very cooperative with Native communities in the repatriation process. In many cases, items that fall under this law have not been repatriated because the tribes do not have facilities to care for them. Most American Indian museum items do not fall under this law, and remain inaccessible to Native Americans who live far from the museums that own them.

In 2000, two partners in the Four Directions project, the Smithsonian National Museum of the American Indian and the University of Texas at Austin, began a unique collaboration that created partnerships with the museum and American Indian schools for the purpose of creating virtual museums of American Indian cultures. The experience has led us to explore a middle ground of cultural reclamation for indigenous peoples that we call "digital repatriation."

The Four Directions project was a major education initiative funded by a U.S. Department of Education Challenge Grant (see http://www.4directions.org) . The partners in the project, which included four universities and two museums with important American Indian collections, worked with nineteen American Indian K-12 schools to develop technology-supported approaches to culturally responsive teaching. The initial virtual museum project brought teams of students, teachers, and tribal community members from three Four Directions schools to New York City to create a Virtual Tour of the National Museum of the American Indian. The result of this effort is the virtual tour at http://www.conexus.si.edu/VRTour/.

Since that initial effort the Four Directions participants at the University of Texas and the Smithsonian Museum of the American Indian have worked on nine other virtual museum projects that included ten American Indian schools, six regional museums, two tribal museums, a university anthropology department, and a Canadian provincial archeological service. These experiences are providing an evolving concept for museum-school-community collaboration that serves the missions and needs of all participants—what we are calling the Four Directions model for virtual museum collaborations. Three aspects of our experiences with virtual museum projects guide the Four Directions model:

- *Cultural Responsive Teaching* – Virtual museum projects are culturally responsive, because they teach to and through the culture of the child and bring community concerns and values to the center of the teaching-learning process. Students are motivated to excel because they are doing important, authentic work to recover and preserve their heritage. They gain from the knowledge of museum professionals and the wisdom of community elders. They develop skills in research, writing, social studies, science, mathematics, information literacy, and twenty-first century information technology.

- *Cultural Revitalization* – A common concern among Native American peoples is the recovery and preservation of cultures and languages. Much of what remains of traditional material cultures resides in museum collections far from Native American communities. Virtual museum projects provide a way for communities to digitally repatriate precious items of cultural heritage. In the Four Directions Model,

virtual museum activities also take place in the Native American communities, where students research and record local materials that supplement the museum's resources for the virtual museum. Local resources such as oral histories, cherished heirlooms, traditional stories, dances, and songs, native language and contemporary arts get combined with museum materials to present the vision of a vital, living culture.

- *Cultural Collaboration* – Museums exist to preserve heritage and educate the public, but Native Americans sometimes object to the way museum exhibitions appropriate cultural property. Native Americans want the public to have access to authentic knowledge of their histories and cultures, but they believe that some aspects of their cultures should not be shared with outsiders. Virtual museum collaborations provide a venue where thorny issues of cultural property rights may be addressed and protocols for cultural collaboration may be designed and levels of accessibility decided.

Since our Four Directions experiences, the University of Texas and the National Museum of the American Indian have been seeking ways to expand this model of digital repatriation so that it will apply to more tribal institutions, such as tribal colleges, tribal museums, and tribal culture centers. We have submitted grant proposals to the Institute of Museums and Library Services and the National Science Foundation that expand on our initial experiences with the Four Directions model and seek international partnerships.

The purpose of our poster session is to demonstrate some of the virtual museum projects we have developed, share our progress in creating new virtual museum partnerships with indigenous peoples, and make contact with conference-goers who are interested in similar collaborations.

Knowledge Capture at Source. Developing collaborative shared resources

Michael Verhaart
Eastern Institute of Technology, Hawkes Bay
New Zealand
mverhaart@eit.ac.nz

Abstract

Today's organisations have well developed systems for capturing financial data and producing reliable and accurate information. An area that is often overlooked is the importance of knowledge held by individuals associated with the organisation. This is also true in an educational setting, where learners can often contribute real-world and personal experiences.

The difficulty of capturing this knowledge provides many challenges, in both business and educational settings. In order to be of any use, this knowledge has to be captured at its source and easily disseminated among those who will be interested or affected by this knowledge. The World Wide Web may be a potential technology platform.

The research in progress looks at whether this data/information can be effectively and efficiently captured, managed and retrieved, in an educational context. It will further look at whether generalisations can be made across different domains, including Business and Government.

1. Introduction

As an educator in a Tertiary Institution for many years the author has been involved in building a substantial knowledge base built around the subjects being delivered. Currently the static web based system has about 4,000 individual web pages, and the maintenance and updating of the material has become practically impossible. Further, the students involved often have knowledge either through their own research or from life experiences that would make a significant contribution to the quality of the resources being studied.

The shortfalls of the current system and its unwieldy nature required a different approach.

So research into alternative methods was undertaken. A simple database prototype that would replace the static pages was developed. This was completed and the prototype was able to deliver the resources in both printed and overhead form.

The requirement to deliver on a web platform was investigated. So at this point the author undertook a *knowledge interrupt*, and developed skills in developing database systems on the Internet.

The next requirement was to enable capturing of the student knowledge. Adding the ability to annotate and to open up the database for the addition of new material by the student was next developed. So, source data capture became possible.

Many new issues now surfaced. Pedagogical considerations became important, and the ability to provide scaffolding and Exploration Space Controls became necessary.

In developing the system it became apparent that the technologies being investigated could be generalised into commercial applications. It is anticipated that the research will develop into this area.

2. Knowledge capture at source

In the book Knowledge Management [1] it is stated that "the way these [modern successful] companies create wealth has precious little to do with the physical assets they own and almost everything to do with the people who work for them and the systems they have in place to enable these people to be creative and innovative".

From the author's observation in an educational setting, students can provide valuable resources in one of two ways. Firstly, from their own "real-world" experiences. For example, while teaching coding systems a student who was also a bank employee discussed how account numbers were codified. Secondly, students are often researching the topic whether in a learner directed mode or discovery learning mode. This contribution to the topic knowledge base is often held by the individual and most often lost to their peers.

A second and equally important part of that the students can play is that of moderation of resources. In one instance recently, a resource indicated that a "modern computer that would support multimedia was a 486 with a large 20MB Hard Drive!". Clearly, the ability to indicate that this information is in dire need of updating becomes important to maintain the credibility of the whole resource. Hence the ability to add "annotations" directly to the offending resource is desirable.

3. A database solution

Davidson, C. & Voss, P[1] further discuss that the "obvious ways that information technologies can support knowledge management is through the creation of a database to store explicit knowledge." and goes further and indicates that "done well, such databases can pay big returns".

As indicated in the introduction, with a static web site of in excess of 4,000 pages, a database approach was considered, and a prototype developed. In the first instance the ability to replace the static pages was required. The concept of a small logical piece of knowledge evolved. In some systems (for example, Hyperskript) this is known as a fragment but to enable a progressive definition, the term **sniplet** has been coined. The second phase of the prototype was to add the ability to add new sniplets and add annotations to the sniplets.

Once information became available in the prototype database, retrieval becomes an issue. In an education setting, the way data is displayed and retrieved is an issue. The ability to incorporate pedagogical concepts such as, scaffolding and Environmental Space Control [2], and others is being explored. Design issues such as cognitive loading will need to be explored, and the possibility of providing an adaptive interface. This needs to be generalised to other settings to determine if the same systems can be adapted to a different environment.

4. Web based collaboration of Knowledge capture

Once the knowledge was stored and organised in a database, the issue of multiple users needs to be explored. The initial prototype was developed in MS-Access so web development was undertaken using Microsoft's Active Server Pages.

5. Education applications

To test the workability of the database solution, a literature review database is currently one of the trials in progress. Issues that this has highlighted are those of knowledge source recognition and copyright. This is both from the creator of the knowledge (using a Dublin Core term rather than author), and any reference that may have been used (such as a journal article). While not attempting to reach the sophistication in applications, such as *end-notes* it has been shown that an efficient collaborative system is possible.

A second trial involves the theory component of an Internet theory and design course.

At this stage the ability for the prototype to perform the same functions as the original static pages has been successfully trialled, and the collaborative features of users adding additional material and annotating current material is being investigated.

5.3 Transferability to a non-education setting

As indicated earlier, databases that can capture institutional knowledge (explicit, tacit and the knowledge held by specific individuals but required in their absence , termed missing knowledge) well can pay big returns. Can the meta-data schema developed for the sniplet database be generalised into a non-educational setting. To answer this question two areas need to be researched. The first is the current state of knowledge capture in organisations. In order to keep the scope of this research manageable and relevant, it is proposed that focus will be on New Zealand based companies and government. The second is to apply the model developed to a non-educational setting.

6. Conclusion

The focus of the proposed research is in knowledge capture at its source. The initial development is set in an educational context and early research indicates that this is both achievable and workable. As knowledge and knowledge capture is important to organisations, the ability to transfer this research to a commercial setting needs to be carried out.

Preliminary feedback of the concept has been positive, with many additional features and considerations such as alternative user interfaces surfacing. The research is still in its formative stages and needs to be clarified further to avoid the scope expanding too far.

References
[1] Davidson, C. & Voss, P. (2002) Knowledge Management. An introduction to creating competitive advantage from intellectual capital, Tandem Press. http://www.tandempress.co.nz. ISBN 1-877178-94-2
[2] Akiihiro Kashihara, Kinshuk, Reinhard Oppermann, Rossen Rashev and Helmut Simm (2000) A Cognitive Load Reduction Approach to Exploratory Learning and Its Application to an Interactive Simulation-based Learning System. Journal of Educational Multimedia and Hypermedia , 9(3), 253-276, (ISSN 1055-8896)

An Agent-based Approach to Support Formative Assessment

Joice Lee Otsuka, Heloísa Vieira da Rocha (advisor)
Institute of Computing – University of Campinas (Unicamp)
Caixa Postal 6176   CEP: 13083-970 - Campinas, SP – Brazil
{joice, heloisa}@ic.unicamp.br

Abstract

The formative assessment process and the difficulties found in online assessment overloads the educators activities. The doctoral research presented in this paper aims to reduce this overload through a formative assessment support based on interface agents.

1   Research Goals

The goal of the doctoral research presented in this paper is to propose a formative assessment support to TelEduc[1], a web based distance education environment. The TelEduc Project has been developed since 1997 by the Nucleus of Informatics Applied to Education and the Institute of Computing, both from University of Campinas [1].

The formative assessment has been used as an alternative to the traditional assessment based on exams, and allows the continuous monitoring and orientation of the learning process [2]. In distance education, the formative assessment is even more important since the online assessment has some intrinsic difficulties, such as the absence of the face-to-face interactions feedback, the lack of instructor control over the assessment and the authentication problem (who is performing the assessment?).

In this context, the instructors need to take extra steps to monitor learners' performance and comprehension, and the formative assessment helps instructors to ensure that the learners are on the right track and to detect learning problems [3]. An advantage

---

[1] Teleduc is an open source software, with free distribution at http://www.nied.unicamp.br

to be explored in online formative assessment is the possibility of saving all interactions for later analysis. Formative assessment also offers some control over the authentication problem, since the instructor becomes familiar with the writing styles and the abilities of individual students, so that changes on writing styles would be an alert. So the interest on formative assessment supports research.

Nevertheless, the formative assessment has high costs, making necessary to explore the development of intelligent and automatic mechanisms to help collecting and analysing assessment relevant data and making decisions based on these data, aiming to reduce the instruct overload and consequently, the formative assessment costs.

It is not possible to predict an ideal set of assessment methods and criteria on formative assessment that supplies the pedagogical goals of any teacher in any course because they change according to the context. Thus the formative assessment demands a flexible support, that is, it should be adaptable to different contexts. This is the present doctoral research's specific goal.

2   Partial Results

Actually the formative assessment on TelEduc is supported through the monitoring of its communication tools logs (**Discussion Forums, Chat, Portfolio, Mail, Bulletin Board**) and the analysis of the data generated by the **Accesses** and **InterMap** tools. The **Accesses** tool allows the generation of reports on student access (to the course or tools), and the **InterMap** tool uses visualisation techniques to map the interactions, making easier to visualise the students' participation [4].

A recent participation on a teachers' distance preparation course based on formative assessment, using the TelEduc support, allowed us to evidence the instructor overload using this assessment approach [5].

The teacher's main roles on this process are explained briefly: (1) **Tasks elaboration:** to define the learning goals and to elaborate appropriate assessment tasks that orientate learners to achieve those goals; (2) **Monitoring:** to monitor and analyse the learner behaviour, to detect problems and to generate reports based on this monitoring; (3) **Orientation:** to motivate the active participation and to incentive the collaboration through the continuous and constructive interventions on learning process; (4) **Learning quality analysis:** to collect and to analyse useful information in order to verify the learning quality during the requested tasks development.

The assessment support model that has been developed in this research aims to reduce the instructor overload. The initial proposed model explores the software agents technology, specifically, interface agents based on machine learning techniques [6], that observes and learns with the instructor, trying to provide a flexible and customised assistance to the teacher's particular necessities. The interface agents are going to explore the distance courses' interaction records and filter, search and analyse important information, according to the teacher's pedagogical goals.

Initially the model has three modules, whose functionalities are presented briefly here:

- **Monitoring Module:** (1) to monitor the learners interaction and the ongoing tasks; (2) to select and present the relevant monitoring information (based on instructor's interests); (3) to detect the possible problems on learning process (access and interaction absence, late tasks) and make decisions (for example send messages to learners, alert the instructor); (4) to generate learner monitoring reports, according to the instructor's interests;

- **Learning Quality Analysis Module:** (1) to select and present the relevant information (based on instructor's interests) in order to help the learning quality analysis, developed during the learner's task performance; (2) to assist grading, through the instructor's criteria observation;

- **Validation Module:** (1) to construct dynamic learners profiles, reflecting the actual knowledge on topics and subtopics of the course; (2) to validate the previous grades by promoting learners collaboration (for example, asking them to respond doubts posted on **Discussion Forum** tool, according to their profiles).

3 Concluding Remarks

Recently TelEduc Project's researchers have obtained promising results with the interface agent technology on chat's log adaptive filtering [7]. These results seem to indicate that this technology is appropriate to provide an effective and flexible formative assessment support.

The research presented in this paper is at initial stage and actually we are involved in the modules specification and in the viability analysis of integrating them to the TelEduc Project.

4 Acknowledgements

We would like to thank the Institute of Computing (IC - Unicamp), the Nucleus of Informatics Applied to Education (NIED - Unicamp) and the "*Coordenação de Aperfeiçoamento de Pessoal de Nível Superior*" (CAPES) that have been making this research possible.

5 References

[1] Rocha, H. (2002) O ambiente TelEduc para Educação à Distância baseada na Web: Princípios, Funcionalidades e Perspectivas de desenvolvimento. In: Moraes, M.C. (Org). Educação à Distância: Fundamentos e Práticas. Campinas, SP:Unicamp/Nied, 2002, 197-212.

[2] Perrenoud, P. (1999) Avaliação: da excelência à regulação das aprendizagens entre duas lógicas. Porto Alegre: Artes Médicas, 1999.

[3] Thorpe, M. (1998) Assessment and 'Third Generation' Distance Education. Distance Education 19, no. 2, pp. 265-286, 1998.

[4] Romani, L. (2000) InterMap: Ferramenta para Visualização da Interação em Ambientes de Educação a Distância na Web. Master Thesis, Institute of Computing/Unicamp, December, 2000.

[5] Otsuka, J. L. (2002). Análise do processo de avaliação contínua em um curso totalmente à distância. In: Virtual Educa Conference, Valencia, Spain, 2002.

[6] Maes, P. (1994) Agents that Reduce Work and Information Overload. *Communications of the ACM*. 37 (7), 1994.

[7] Otsuka, J. L.; Lachi, R. ; Ferreira, T.; Rocha, H. V. (2002) Suporte à Avaliação Formativa no Ambiente de Educação à Distância TelEduc. In: VI Congresso Iberoamericano de Informática Educativa, Vigo, Spain, 2002.

Towards a Distance Education Model in Maldives

Ali Fawaz Shareef and Kinshuk
Information Systems Department, Massey University
Palmerston North, New Zealand

Abstract

This research looks into developing a distance education model for Maldives. This paper gives an overview of the literature that leads to the model and a brief discussion on the design of the model at its current phase.

Since the introduction of distance education in 19th century, several research work have been undertaken to outline the different perspectives of distance education. Several considerations have to be made in order to provide an efficient and effective distance-learning package. Some of the main aspects to focus are the media choice, needs of the market, characteristics of the consumers, size and technology, and the institutional framework. This research will aim at finding a viable way to provide distance education in Maldives. The research will look into the possibilities of using distance education in Maldives to move towards the goal of "Education for ALL".

An overview of literature is carried to understand the research problem. A background into Maldives is done in order to rationalise the research as well as find out how and where distance education can be used. The background information included the demography of Maldives, current physical infrastructure and planned developments, and some aspects of social infrastructure. The small population sizes of the islands inhibit infrastructure developments as this cause diseconomy of scale and transport limitations between islands makes it impossible to capitalise on the use of regional centres. Hence the research cannot be based on assumptions of infrastructure developments but rather should exploit the current infrastructure. An overview of current infrastructure is included to realise the options with planned developments that can be used. The current infrastructure analysis with planned developments helped in identifying the media choices for the proposed model. One aspect of social infrastructure is also considered in this research, which is education. Since the research is about distance education in Maldives it is essential to identify the issues like access to education, enrolment and drop out rates by level as well as regions to rationalise the use of a distance education model in the country.

Further literature research is done to understand what media is used in distance education and how they are used in different parts of the world. Media discussion covers all the media used in distance education outlining their strengths and weaknesses. Furthermore investigations into specific distance learning institutions are carried out to understand what features are suitable for which situations. This investigation is focussed into delivery systems, media use, support systems, and target population. The countries from which these institutions are selected have similar economic, social and cultural conditions as Maldives.

The literature overview provided insights into deciding on the attributes of the model as well as the media choice. The current distance education programmes also provided an understanding of what media has been used in the islands of Maldives. These include print, radio, audiocassettes, face-to-face tutorials, and teleconferencing. In addition to focussing on the strengths and weaknesses of different media, Maldives has to capitalise on the available media at different levels. For example computer-based instruction with Internet could be used in parts where possible, while computer based instruction using computer networks at schools and other planned kiosks could compensate in other areas. Consequently Maldives should look into developing a system where media is selected according to availability and which allows easy transfer from one medium to another if and when more advanced telecommunications capability is introduced. The use of teleconferencing in previous distance education programmes and the increasing number of computers in schools and other government owned kiosks leads to a combination of these media a good choice. Teleconferencing cannot be used, as it needs human resources at the regional level. The model looks at ways of minimising human resources however it is unreasonable to totally eliminate it. Hence computer networks, Internet wherever possible, and CD ROMs will be used as media choices.

The model will be developed as three different modules. These include the student module, the regional module, and the headquarters module. The student module will be sent to each student, the regional module will be set up in each of the regional centres, and the headquarters module resides at the central location.

The student module will be burnt into CD ROMs and sent to students. The students can either install the software into their own computer or use computers at the regional centres. Once the software is installed a profile for the student will be created. This will be stored in the hard disk or the regional computer network depending on where the student installed it. The profile will be used to record the student's progress and give feedback. Other components of the module include the subject matter, database, and engine. The subject matter resides on the CD ROMs or on the network. The database which resides in students' computer or network will have many functions including recording student behaviour, providing navigation suggestions, recording problems, solutions. All these components will be integrated through the engine that will also provide the interface for the student. The student will have the flexibility of recording their profile on to a floppy disk. They could then take the floppy disk to the regional centre and upload the data. Any feedback could then be downloaded from the regional centre's network to the floppy and back to student's computer. If the students are using the regional centres computers then they will logon to the network and their profile will be automatically updated as they progress.

The regional module will be the intermediary between the student module and the headquarters module. All the updates from the headquarters module will be uploaded into the regional module, which will then be transferred into the student module and vice versa. The specific components of this module have yet to be formulated that will focus into how communication will be done between these three module and what components used.

The headquarters module controls the whole system and provides feedback and solutions, which are not built-in to the other two modules. The headquarters module will have human intervention to assess the students' progress and provide feedback, which are not built into the system. The headquarters module will have an authoring tool that will enable the subject matter experts or tutors build the intelligent tutoring system for the student module. As the study progresses more specific components of this module will be formulated. The intelligent tutoring system will include answers to standard questions, identifying student's weaknesses using built-in assessment, etc. An authoring tool is developed for the subject matter experts. The authoring tool will have the flexibility of allowing the subject matter expert to design their subject in different formats. It will allow the use of different media with limitations based on the capability of regional networks.

Once the model is developed it will be tested in Maldives. Since computer networks and Internet already exist in Maldives the system can be tested at different parts of the country. The headquarters module will be installed in the capital at the Centre for Open Learning in Maldives College of Higher Education. Regional modules will be installed in the two ends of the country. One in the regional centres of the Centre for Open Learning in the southern most atoll and the one in the Northern Secondary School. Since there are no regional centres in the northern most atoll Northern Secondary School will be used as a test centre.

Bibliography

1. ADB, *Report and Recommendation of the President to the Board of Directors on a Proposed Loan to the Maldives for the Information Technology Development Project*, November 2001.
2. Eastmond, D. 2000 "Realizing the Promise of Distance Education in Low Technology Countries", Educational Technology, Research and Development, 48(2), pp 100++
3. Mason, R, 1998, Using Communications Media in Open and Flexible Learning, London: Kogan Page.
4. Mason, R. 1999, "The Impact of Telecommunications" in K. Harry (eds) Higher Education through Open and Distance Learning, New York: Routledge.
5. Ministry of Communications, Science and Technology (MCST), *Ministry of Communications, Science and Technology Website*, [Online], Available: http://www.mcst.gov.mv/ [20th August 2001]
6. Ministry of Education, 2001, *Providing for Basic Computer Literacy Project Papers*
7. Ministry of Education, Maldives, *Ministry of Education Website*, [Online], Available: http://www.thauleem.net/ [20th August 2001]
8. Perraton, H. 2000, Open and Distance Learning in the Developing World, London: Routledge.
9. UNDP, *Maldives Poverty and Vulnerability Assessment 1998*.

Enhancing Critical Thinking in Language Learning through Computer-Mediated Collaborative Learning: A Preliminary Investigation

Janpha Thadphoothon
School of Languages and International Education
University of Canberra, Australia

ABSTRACT

This paper investigates a framework for computer-mediated collaborative learning and critical thinking in language learning. It is based mainly on the notions of awareness, autonomy, and achievement posited by Lian (1993). Central to its argument are two assertions. Firstly, computer-mediated collaborative learning requires a high level of autonomy in learners. Secondly, thinking critically in language learning can only occur in learners after they have become aware of the critical elements or " things that matter" in language learning. Hence, the more they are aware of such elements, the more they think critically in language learning. This framework argues against the idea of grouping learners so as to make them work together using a common means toward a common goal. This alternative model of computer-mediated collaborative learning is one in which learners have more control over their own learning. Their needs will arise when they engage in reality. In addition, the paper suggests positive roles that teachers should play in this context. An initial investigation of this framework will be presented.

1: Background

Language teachers in general are concerned with the use of the Internet to enhance language learning. Many of its features have been utilized to foster collaborative learning (Warschauer, 1997). Many studies have reported such learning to be desirable. In the ELT context, the Internet provides ample opportunities for learners to engage in reality by using English as a global language with people from other countries around the world. More importantly, several contemporary concepts such as Vygotsky's Zone of Proximal Development, Krashen's input hypothesis, Bandura's social learning theory support the notion of collaborative learning in many respects (Vygotsky, 1935; Krahen, 1982; Bandura, 1977). Computer-mediated collaborative learning has been found to have positive effects on learners by empowering them

to explore and experience new possibilities. Though there is some evidence supporting that collaborative learning enhances critical thinking and problem-solving, little research in ELT has been carried out to find the relationships between computer-mediated collaborative learning and critical thinking in language learning.

2: Framework

In a broader sense, thinking is all about being aware of something. Thinking critically in language learning and being aware of the " things that matter" in using the language are highly correlated. The paper hypothesizes that the more learners become aware of the critical element, the more they think critically. Traditionally, such things that matter often include grammar, vocabulary, and pronunciation. Little attention has been paid to context and circumstances in which the language is used. However, in complex real-life situations, learners, to function properly, need more than just grammatical rules and memorized words or sentences. If learners have to communicate face-to-face, when spontaneity is a crucial matter, they often run into the problem of having insufficient time to refer to such rules (Lian, 1993). What learners should be able to do, rather than simply learning grammatical rules and memorizing words, is to engage reality. In reality, a broad range of phenomena and circumstances provides learners with massive opportunities to confront, contrast, and contest their existing perceptions with that of the real world (Lian, 2000).

The Internet is the 'global market' where people do things, for example, buying, bargaining, negotiating, and talking to each other. It is the place of work and play. Contexts can be created so as to enable learners to do things together for mutual benefit. On the Internet, learners can learn anytime and anywhere. They can also 'talk to people' when they 'do things at the market.' By talking to people, this paper means something as simple as greeting, thanking, apologizing, etc as seen from email exchanges or chat-rooms, for instance. Also, it refers to situations when learners, upon carrying out their duties, are regulated by their own desires and the demands of the task to talk to one another. This situation can be seen in the real world. In the past, because of the limitations, most learners lacked the opportunities to be immersed in the target language communities, which is one of the best ways to become proficient in such a language. Nowadays, however, virtual worlds have been created, and it has empowered learners. Experience has taught us that we can learn from indirect experience as well (e.g. through reading or listening). Thus language learning can be viewed as a by-product of our awareness.

Upon doing things at the 'market' together, as learners 'walk and talk' with friends and acquaintances, they also talk to strangers and those with whom they have to do business. Little by little, they develop the 'feeling for the market.' Gradually, they have become familiar with the market. One can think of one's favourite shopping mall in which one knows the whereabouts of things and people, of whom to ask for information, or of the quality of the products. Upon carrying out their enterprise, learners become aware of the things at that market, including the people of the market, and the language they use, and their social norms ---- of what does matter and what doesn't. Bourdieu (1991), in the context of cultural practices, calls this awareness the "feel for the game (*sens du jeu*) --- a sense of what is appropriate and what is not" (p.13). Unless having severe perception problems, as learners do things together online, they sensitize themselves/are sensitized to the real world, including the language and its environment. They gradually develop their feel of the language: its context and circumstances. Our feelings of language exist. Krashen (1981), in proposing his Monitor model, has pointed out that: " Adults often demonstrate a 'feel' for grammaticality for some aspects of grammar in a second language, in some cases without ever having known a conscious rule" (p. 156).

3: Preliminary Investigation

At present, a website, www.geocities.com/janphauc, is being developed. Under part 3 of the site, Bamboo Enterprise has been created as a center where everybody involved, including learners, teachers, and helpers, can discuss and create a number of joint projects. The collaboration is of two levels: the teacher and the students. The projects are also open to the public.

In addition, the Microsoft online community Bamboo Forum, http://groups.msn.com/BambooForum, has been built as a meeting place for all members to discuss and to decide upon new projects. So far (as of July 30th, 2002), 11 volunteers have joined. The support system comprises of humans (teachers, peers, and other helpers), other resources available online, and resources produces by the researcher. In addition to several intermediate stages, the finished product will also be included in the overall study.

At this conference, I would like to discussed the following questions:

- Under certain conditions whereby learners jointly work on a real life project e.g. creating a radio program or publishing a magazine etc, when does " critical thinking in language learning" occur in learner?
- During the intervention, what data should be considered as relevant, and how should the information be interpreted?

References

Bandura, A. (1977). *Social Learning Theory*. New Jersey: Prentice-Hall.

Bourdieu, Pierre (1991). *Language and symbolic power*. Cornwall: Polity Press.

Krashen, S. (1982) *Principles and Practice in Second Language Acquisitio* . Oxford: Pergamon Press.
Lian, A.-P. (1993). " Awareness, Autonomy and Achievement in Audio-Video Computer Enhanced Language Learning and the Development of Listening Comprehension Skills, " (ed. Lian, A-P. Hoven, D. L. and to an Intellectual Framework for Language-Learning" *On-Call*: May 1997 pp. 2-19.

Lian, A-P (2000) " From First Principles: Constructing Language-Learning and Teaching Environment." In *Selected Papers from the Ninth International Symposium on English Teaching*, Crane Publishing Co., Ltd., November 2000, pp. 49-62.

Thadphoothon, J. (2002). 'Enhancing Critical Thinking in Language Learning through Computer-Mediated Collaborative Learning: A Proposed Intellectual Framework'. In press, *Asia CALL 2002 Conference Proceedings*.

Vygotsky, L. (1935). *Mind in Society*. Massachusetts: Harvard University press.

Warschauer, M. (1997)." Computer-mediated collaborative learning: Theory and practice." in *Modern Language Journal*. 81(3), p. 470-481.

LEARNING IN ASYNCHRONOUS ENVIRONMENTS FOR ON CAMPUS STUDENTS

Philippa Gerbic
Faculty of Business
Auckland University of Technology
NEW ZEALAND

Abstract

Computed mediated conferencing (CMC) into asynchronous form, offers potential benefits for learning through its text based nature and space and time to reflect. The project investigates student approaches to learning (deep surface) and learning strategies, in this environment. The research is sited in a degree course where flexible learning models are available for n campus students. The relationship between CMC and face-to-face activity in terms of student learning will be a part of the research. The project takes a student perspective, which is explored through a case study design.

Context for the Research

The central role of the internet in the world, especially its communication capability, raises major issues for universities. How should graduates be prepared for this networked world? How can universities use the communication capability to improve the quality of learning outcomes? Computer mediated conferencing (CMC) (Salmon, 2000) in its asynchronous form has two particular features which are beneficial to learning. These are the text based nature of the communication and space and time to think. Together these features have the potential to produce better and more careful development of ideas and deeper understanding (Hammond, 1998; Harasim, 1989; Garrison and Anderson, 2000). Neither of these features occur naturally in a face-to-face environment and for this reason CMC is potentially a good compliment for on campus learning.

Once the province of distance education, CMC is now being mainstreamed as universities blend face-to-face and on line learning activities (mixed mode or flexible learning). (Taylor, Lopez and Quadrelli , 1996). A key issue is how students learn in this new environment. How does learning happen in an asynchronous environment and how is this learning affected by regular face-to-face contact with their peers and teachers?

Objectives of the Research

The purpose of the research is to investigate approaches to learning and learning strategies that undergraduate students in business use when they are working in an asynchronous environment in a course that uses a mixture of asynchronous and face-to-face activities. In particular, it focuses on the ways in which students interact with and use the identified features of CMC to develop their understanding and capabilities in their subject area. It examines this in the context of one kind of flexible learning environment ie on campus students learning through face-to-face and asynchronous activity.

Research questions are grouped in three areas and relate to

- Student approaches to learning in an asynchronous environment (eg how, student ideas about learning, deep and surface approaches)
- Student learning strategies in an asynchronous environment (eg what strategies, where do they come from, adaption and change in new environments
- Relationships between asynchronous and face-to-face activity (eg impact of face-to-face contact, motivation, student value perspectives)

Methodology

Because the aim of the research is descriptive and explanatory, a qualitative approach will be taken. A case study design, (Bassey, 1999) will focus on undergraduate students enrolled in three selected modules using a blended approach of face-to-face and on line learning. This design has been chosen because it supports investigation which is sited in the real world, and can address "complexity and embeddedness" and "discrepancy and conflict", illustrate (Adelman, Kemmis, & Jenkins, 1976) on page 151 as well as multiple viewpoints and interdependencies and patterns. (Sturman, 1994, in Bassey, 1999)). Data for the case study will comprise

CMC discussions, student interviews, systems data and secondary information eg module evaluations. Currently, I am obtaining Ethics Committee approvals, designing a content analysis framework and an interview structure. I intend to begin gathering data from the first module in the second part of this year.

Significance of the Research

The literature to date eg Eastmond, 1994; Berge, 1994) indicates that much of the substantive research in the CMC field has focused on distance learning. However, more recently, accounts of the use of CMC for on campus students have started to appear, eg Rimmershaw (1999). My reading of the literature to date indicates that there is a paucity of in depth research on student approaches to learning and learning strategies, particularly in a mixed mode environment. There is a need for further research on student perspectives (Laurillard, 1993) and for qualitative research in this area (Windschitl, 1998). There is a need to examine student learning from an ecological perspective (Entwistle, 1997) ie students interacting with the wider environment and vice versa.

This research will:
- add to the current body of research in the field of
  - asynchronous learning
  - approaches to learning and learning strategies
  - flexible or mixed mode learning
- provide new insights for teachers and those responsible for curriculum and programme development
- inform my own practice and potentially, practice within my workplace.

References

1. Adelman, C., Kemmis, S., & Jenkins, D. (1976), 'Rethinking Case Study : Notes from the Second Cambridge Conference 'Cambridge Journal of Education, 6(3), 139-150.
2. Bassey, M. (1999), Case Study Research in Educational Settings. Open University Press Buckingham.
3. Berge, E. (1994), 'Learning in Computer Conferenced Contexts : The Learners Perspective' Journal of Distance Education, 4(1), 19-43.
4. Eastmond, D. (1994), 'Adult Distance Study through Computer Conferencing ' Distance Education, 15(1), 128-152.
5. Entwistle, N. (1997), 'Contrasting Perspectives on Learning'. In F. Marton & D. Hounsell & N. Entwistle (Eds.), The Experience of Learning. Scottish Academic Press: Edinburgh.
6. Garrison, R., & Anderson, T. (2000), 'Transforming and Enhancing University Teaching : Stronger and Weaker Influences'. In T. Evans &
D. Nation (Eds.), Changing University Teaching : Reflections on Creating Educational Technologies (pp. 24-33). Kogan Page: London.
7. Hammond, M. (1998), 'Learning Through On-Line Discussion : what are the opportunities for professional development and what are the characteristics of on-line writing' Journal of Information Technology for Teacher Education, 7(3), 331 - 346.
8. Harasim, L. (1989), 'On-Line Education : A New Domain'. In R. Mason & A. Kaye (Eds.), Mindweave. Pergamon Press: Oxford, England.
9. Laurillard, D. (1993), Rethinking University Teaching. Routledge London and New York.
10. Rimmershaw, R. (1999), 'Using Conferencing to Support a Culture of Collaborative Study' Journal of Computer Assisted Learning, 15(3), 189 - 200.
11. Salmon, G. (2000), E-Moderating : The Key to Teaching and Learning Online. Kogan Page London.
12. Taylor, P., L, L., & C, Q. (1996). Flexibility, Technology and Academics' Practices : Tantalising Tales and Muddy Maps (96/11). Canberra: Department of Employment, Education and Training and Youth Affairs, Evaluations and Investigations Programme, Higher Education Division,.
13. Windschitl, M. (1998), 'The WWW and Classroom Research : What Path Should WeTake? 'Educational Researcher, 27(1), 28-33.

Using Virtual Learning Environments: Lecturers' Conceptions of Teaching and the Move to Student-Centred Learning.

Sue Morón-García, Institute of Educational Technology, The UK Open University, Walton Hall, Milton Keynes, MK7 6AA s.d.moron-garcia@open.ac.uk

Abstract

This paper reports on doctoral research investigating whether Virtual Learning Environments (VLEs) are being used to facilitate student-centred learning in UK Higher Education (HE). The focus is on lecturers (HE teachers) teaching in a face-to-face context. It is claimed that the use of Web or Internet-based technology can facilitate the creation of a student-centred learning environment [1] and the adoption of a student-centred method of teaching [2]. It is argued that student-centred learning and learning environments designed with reference to constructivist theories of learning will produce in students the critical and cognitive skills that Higher Education aims to develop [3], [4], [5]. However, there are barriers that prevent the integration of technology into teaching [6] and elements in the teaching environment [7] that affect whether a student-centred approach to teaching is adopted. The conception of teaching held by the lecturer [8] is one such element.

1: Introduction

The aim of this research is to examine whether lecturers are using Virtual Learning Environments (VLEs) to support student-centred methods. VLE is the term used to describe the package of integrated software (content management and presentation, synchronous and asynchronous communication tools) that make use of Web or Internet-based technologies and are used to put courses online [9]. Examples are commercial packages such as WebCT, Blackboard, Learning Space and Learnwise. Some VLEs are based on specific pedagogic models, for example COSE [10], which emphasise the importance of communication and collaboration tools and encourage a move away from the uploading of large amounts of content and electronic page turning which is not considered the best use of VLEs. The research questions are:

- Can VLEs support student-centred learning and how does the functionality of the system affect lecturers?
- What are the motivating factors for lecturer use of VLEs and what prevents them being used?
- How are lecturers using VLEs, what methods are they using, and how does this fit into their overall pedagogy?

2: Approaches to teaching and technology use

It is widely argued that student-centred teaching approaches encourage students to adopt higher quality approaches to learning – what Biggs and Moore [11] among others call a deep approach to learning - and aid the development of critical abilities. It is argued that student-centred learning and learning environments designed with reference to constructivist theories of learning will produce in students the critical and cognitive skills that Higher Education aims to develop [3], [4], [5]. However, there may be pressures on lecturers to use particular approaches in their teaching. Trigwell and Prosser [7] found that lecturers who felt that they had more control over their teaching (what is taught and how) were more likely to adopt student-focused approaches. These approaches were affected detrimentally if the class size was thought to be too large, student diversity too great and workload too heavy.

Lecturers' beliefs about teaching and learning and how to create the most effective learning environments are fundamental to improving student learning. Research has shown that lecturers' conceptions of teaching correlate with teaching approaches that in turn correlate with student learning approaches and learning outcomes (see [8] for an overview and [12]). Murray and MacDonald [13] argue that there is a disjunction between lecturers' conceptions of teaching and their claimed educational practice; Prosser and Trigwell [14] developed the Approaches to Teaching Inventory (ATI) as a way of overcoming this.

Elements in the institutional environment, such as access to equipment, training and support, may also affect lecturer usage of the Web and Internet-based technology. Barnard writes about an obstacle course of barriers that have to be overcome if teachers are to move "from being non-users of technology to being fluent users who could integrate technology into their teaching" [6], pg. 352). These include anxiety, unfamiliarity with the technology, resourcing, perceived usefulness, personal philosophy, the influence of colleagues and classroom dynamics [6].

3: The pilot study

A semi-structured interview was used to collect data from twelve lecturers at four different UK universities.

The aim was to find out what was actually happening in Higher Education (as distinct from what the literature indicates may be happening): Were lecturers using Web and Internet-based technology? What sort of technology and how? Was pedagogy influencing the use of the technology? Were lecturers aware of their pedagogy? Consideration was given to the possibility that some lecturers may be more comfortable with the use of Web and Internet-based technology and that some lecturers may be more able to explain and justify their pedagogy. For this reason education lecturers and those teaching computer science were interviewed. The third category of lecturer interviewed was those in social science or humanities, because they had no obvious reason to feel comfortable with the technology or a reason to be familiar with pedagogic terms. The findings indicated that:

- The use of VLEs is not widespread, even within those universities that support use. The post-1992 universities are more likely to have an institutionally supported VLE and have a strategy that encourages use.
- Use was restricted by access issues, student and lecturer IT literacy, student expectations and colleague use, time available to create resources and to become familiar with technology.
- The 'electronic filing cabinet' was thought to be valuable, it was a time saver for lecturers and convenient for students.
- Use of e-mail was widespread, discussion lists were used in some cases, but there was some resistance from students and lecturers were unsure; 'chat' was only used by one lecturer
- The technology was used to support group work, reflection, contact with the lecturer, sharing of work and engagement with materials and content outside class time.
- Teaching methods adopted by lecturers were dependent on class size and influenced by the way they had been taught, observing others and any training they had received.

4: Designing the main study

The pilot study indicated that the following issues should be borne in mind when designing the main study:
- Asking about teaching methods did not help identify a lecturer's teaching model, the same method can mean different things to different people: use of the ATI [14] may give a better indication of their intentions and strategies.
- Talk about technology use was often confused with talk about general teaching: asking a lecturer to focus on specific examples and the reason for technology use may clarify this.

- Trying to compare use across discipline areas is difficult; there are differences that impact on technology use and teaching method used. Choosing a particular discipline area may help in this case.

The interview schedule was revised in the light of these issues and individual interviews were conducted with thirty-two lecturers across ten universities. All lecturers were also asked to complete the ATI. The data collected is being analysed at the time of writing.

References
[1] B. Collis, *Tele-learning in a Digital World*. London: Thomson Computer Press, 1996.
[2] W. Westera, "Paradoxes in Open, Networked Learning Environments: Toward a Paradigm Shift," *Educational Technology*, vol. 39, pp. 17-23, 1999.
[3] CNAA, "Case studies in student-centred learning," The Council for National Academic Awards, London 36, 1992.
[4] D. Jonassen, T. Mates, and R. McAleese, "A Manifesto for a Constructivist Approach to Uses of Technology in Higher Education," in *Designing Environments for Constructivist Learning*, T. M. Duffy, J. Lowyck, and D. H. Jonassen, Eds. Berlin: Springer-Verlag, 1993, pp. 231-247.
[5] M. Thorpe, "Pedagogical implications of flexible learning," in *Flexible Learning, Human Resource and Organisational Development: Putting theory to work*, V. Jakupec and J. Garrick, Eds. London: Routledge, 2000, pp. 175-192.
[6] J. Barnard, "Factors Affecting the Use of Computer Assisted Learning by Further Education Biology Teachers," in *The Institute of Educational Technology*. Milton Keynes, UK: Open University, 1999.
[7] K. Trigwell and M. Prosser, "Towards an understanding of individual acts of teaching and learning," *Higher Education Research and Development*, vol. 16, pp. 241-252., 1997.
[8] D. Kember, "A Reconceptualisation of the Research into University Academics' Conceptions of Teaching," *Learning and Instruction*, vol. 7, pp. 255-275, 1997.
[9] S. Moron-Garcia, "Are Virtual Learning Environments being used to facilitate and support student-centred learning in Higher Education?," in Proc. 5th Human Centred Technology Postgraduate Workshop - Information Technologies and Knowledge Construction: bringing together the best of two worlds, 2001, pp. 9-11.
[10] M. J. Stiles, "Effective Learning and the Virtual Learning Environment," in Proc. EUNIS 2000: Towards Virtual Universities: INFOSYSTEM 2000, pp.171-180.
[11] J. B. Biggs and P. J. Moore, *The Process of Learning*, 3rd ed. Sydney, Australia: Prentice Hall, 1993.
[12] K. Trigwell, M. Prosser, and F. Waterhouse, "Relations between teachers' approaches to teaching and students' approaches to learning," *Higher Education*, vol. 37, pp. 57-70, 1999.
[13] K. Murray and R. MacDonald, "The disjunction between lecturers' conceptions of teaching and their claimed educational practice," *Higher Education*, vol. 33, pp. 331-349, 1997.
[14] M. Prosser and K. Trigwell, *Understanding Learning and Teaching: The Experience in Higher Education*. Buckingham: SRHE and Open University Press, 1999.

Application of Knowledge Management in Reusable Web-based Learning Systems

Bhavani Sridharan & Kinshuk
Department of Information Systems
Massey University, Palmerston North
New Zealand

Abstract

This research is focused on the use of knowledge management techniques to develop reusable web-based intellectual assets to leverage the learning process for individual learners. The literature review reveals that corporate solutions of knowledge management are not directly applicable due to the lack of adaptivity needed to provide individualized feedback to the learner, and their localized nature that does not directly deal with authentication and verification of distributed information. Architecture has therefore been formulated for the knowledge management system that specifically supports web-based learning.

1. Introduction

Current educational process indicates that learners are mostly overloaded with information but, at the same time, they are not able to grasp the fundamental concepts behind the theory. This generally results in learning-by-rote. This phenomenon is especially true during the training of application of complex concepts with steep learning curve, where initial mistakes by students are not corrected immediately hence leading to wrong neural connections and eventual failure. This erroneous learning process is repeated year after year by different student groups and the entire process recurs resulting in frustration and inefficiency. The problems are aggravated at high magnitude when learning takes place in a distant environment.

Internet based knowledge management systems can prove to be efficient solution to manage these problems. It seems, therefore, important in this competitive environment to make the best use of the technological explosion and improve the productivity through achieving reusability and enhancing educational services to the learners. In this context, this research is concerned with the alternative ways of knowledge acquisition, integration, management, retrieval and dissemination of intellectual assets among wide variety of audience to leverage their learning.

2. Work in Progress

As part of the PhD research, a comprehensive literature review has been conducted in the area of knowledge management, with particular focus on its applicability in academia. The report looks at the concepts related to knowledge management namely acquisition, elicitation, representation and retrieval of knowledge. Also, comparison is made between knowledge management and other related areas like information management, document management, artificial Intelligence, etc. This gives an idea of how this field is different from other related fields. The report examines the difference between data, information and knowledge. Success of knowledge management and its links with Information technology is also investigated in the report. Distinguishing tacit knowledge and explicit knowledge helps in identifying the special role of transforming these in knowledge management system. Important issues related to knowledge management like cultural, structural and process issues are discussed in this part of the report. Finally this report looks at the challenges to its success.

Available knowledge management systems and knowledge management tools in academic environment has been evaluated and a preliminary report has been written. Various knowledge management systems and tools like Wincite 5.0, FuzzyClips, Grapewine, and KnbowledgeX etc. are investigated in the report. Further examination needs to be made to see the availability and use of commercial knowledge management system in the market.

The applicability of knowledge base structure and Internet based learning has also been examined. This part of the report investigates the types of knowledge base structure used in Internet based learning scenarios and looks at the adaptability of these structures in knowledge management in learning environment. Considering the information and knowledge available in the Internet is in heterogeneous format, the report looks at what kind of knowledge base structure is appropriate for the knowledge management in learning situation.

Work is also progressing on an ABRF project which looks at one of the aspects of knowledge management in learning environment namely query aspect of knowledge management. The aim is to develop a knowledge management system for Internet based intellectual assets to leverage the learning process for individual learners. Since the literature review reveals that corporate solutions of knowledge management are not directly applicable due to the lack of adaptability needed to provide individualized feedback to the learner, and their localized nature that does not directly deal with authentication and verification of distributed information. This project aims to integrate the users profile and users to query to search for the required result. One of the special features of the system is to authenticate the reliability of the information. The discipline selected to test the prototype system was database concepts and tools. The choice of this domain stems from the fact that application of requires familiarization with numerous procedures. Most Internet based sources provide very generalized instruction of these procedures without effectively relating them to the individual learner's attributes, hence resulting in learning-by-rote due to no reflection possibilities on the part of the learner. This makes this domain one of the best candidates to test the effectiveness and efficacy of the prototype, which is meant to provide individualized instruction.

3. Methodology

A conceptual framework will then be formulated to understand the processes involved in creating and development of knowledge management systems in distant academic environment. Based on this theoretical research work, a prototype system will be developed which will aim to guide the learners either in a guided discovery learning process or in an exploratory learning process, based on the behavioral attributes of the learner. Needs of the learners will be surveyed and categorized into various levels. Knowledge base will then be developed to test the system, the result will be interpreted, and a generalized recommendation set will be developed. We plan to use the discipline of "database tools and associated concepts" for our prototype.

4. Benefits and Conclusion

The results of this research should not only augment the teaching abilities of the provider and foster the learning abilities of students but also open new ways of integrating knowledge management concepts in the learning systems development process. Outcomes of this research are expected to result in better reusability, sharing, pooling and collaboration in the learning process. Quality of knowledge transformation should also be enhanced, giving a strategic and competitive edge to the academic institutions involved in distant learning, and eventually reengineering the academic atmosphere to enhance quality and productivity with the application of

technology. There is a lot of scope for developing knowledge management for learning environment, in particular web based learning, as there has not been much research in this area of knowledge management.

Selected References

1. Angus, J., Patel, J., and Harty, J. (1998), Knowledge Management: Great Concept...But What is it? InformationWeek, March 16, 1998, Issue: 673, Section information Week Labs, URL: http://www.techweb.com/.
2. Barclay, O. R., Murray, C. P, What is Knowledge Management? Knowledge Praxis, URL: www.media-access.com/what is.html
3. Corrall, S., (1999), Knowledge Management: Are we in the Knowledge Management Business? URL: http://www.ariadne.ac.uk/issue18/knowledge-mgt/
4. Couldwell, Clive (1999), A Little Knowledge is a Dangerous Thing, Document World, Boulder, Nov/Dec, Volume 4, Issue 6, Page 24-27.
5. Davenport, T.H., Prusak, L., Working Knowledge: How Organisations Manage What they Know, Ma: Harvard Business School Press, Boston, 1998, Page 5.
6. Duffy, Jan (2000), Knowledge Exchange at Glaxo Wellcome, Information Management Journal, Prairie Village, Jul 2000, Volume 34, Issue 3, Page 64.
7. Gothca --Guide to KM, (1999) The Knowledge Management Resource Centre, URL: http://www.kmresource.com/exp university.htm/
8. Schwartz, David G., Divitini, Monica, Brasethvik, Terje (2000), Internet-Based Organizational Memory and Knowledge Management, Hershey: USA, Idea Group Publishing.
9. Sveiby, E. Karl (2000), What is knowledge Management, URL: http://www.sveiby.com.au/KnowledgeManagement.html

Computer Assisted Learning Applications for Teaching Language Technology
– A view on the pedagogical aspect

Tina Nielsen, Ph.D. student, tina@cbs.dk
Department of Computational Linguistics, CBS, Denmark

Abstract

This paper consists of a discussion about the pedagogical aspect of developing a Computer Assisted Learning application for the discipline Language Technology. It discusses the influence of cognitive and behavioral learning theories on the development.

The Pedagogical Aspect

According to the results of research in the effectiveness of CAL compared to traditionally taught classes, it is difficult to prove which is more or less effective. Some empirical studies show that CAL is as effective as traditional education, but especially many earlier studies claim that CAL is not nearly as effective. One reason for this can be the fact mentioned by Brahler and Johnson [1], who state that many computer assisted instructional materials are developed by technical professionals who have the technical skills necessary for successful implementation but lack knowledge of educational principles. I would like to add that it is also very likely that the technical professionals lack thorough knowledge of the discipline that the CAL application covers.

The Discipline "Language Technology"

Language Technology (LT) is a subject that consists of both technological and linguistic aspects. During a course in language technology, the students learn how to work with language for special purposes (LSP) for improved understanding and translation. They learn to create concept diagrams and ontologies for difficult areas in professional communication and how to search for information when definitions and translations for concepts cannot be found in dictionaries. In order to save the results of their work, they learn to use and develop terminology databases such as MultiTerm 95+ from Trados and DANTERM^{CBS}, an Access database application developed at the Copenhagen Business School.

The Pedagogical Aspect of CAL for LT

It is important to clarify the educational goals of the computer assisted learning program, and then use the learning theories to reach these goals through the development of the program. Choosing between the learning theories during the development does not have to be a matter of total commitment to one learning theory or the other. When developing a computer assisted learning program the developing team can choose between implementing the use of the different learning theories for the different partial educational goals of the program. When it comes to the computer's role in CAL there exists a basic difference between cognitive and behavioral learning. In behavioral learning the computer is seen as an instrument for instructing the students, whereas in cognitive learning the computer is seen as a tool that the students can actively use for retrieving and building knowledge. Introductions to the two educational theories are available in several textbooks e.g. those mentioned in the references.

Use of Cognitive Learning

The main purpose of cognitive learning is to make the student reflect on the subject of the CAL application. One way to obtain this is to reduce the role of the instruction as much as possible in the learning situation. This forces the student to think for him-/herself. In cognitive learning the student is supposed to be an active participant in his/her own learning. This can be done by providing a learning situation where the student learns by means of unrestricted exploration of the instructional material in the CAL application. The CAL application should also include questions that lead to cognitive conflicts for the student so the student realizes that a disequilibrium exists (something he/she did not understand or misunderstood). This way, the student accommodates the relevant cognitive schemes into the existing cognitive schemes that contain the knowledge that he/she already has. When posing a question, it is also important not to give the student the right answer up front, this will encourage the students to think actively [2]. Cognitive learning is suitable for learning topics that the students later have to reflect on in order to use the learned language technology theory on their own.

Use of Behavioral Learning

Behaviorism is often associated with trial and error exercises. The classical example of an operant behavioral learning application is the self-instructing and self-rewarding learning programs where the student is learning a subject through varying exposures to learning material and controlling questions. Typically the application is divided into sections. Each section represents a level of learning and the levels increase from one level to the next. The function of the controlling questions is to determine whether the student is ready for the next level or not.

In CAL, the main purpose of behavioral learning is to equip the student with rote competencies within a subject. According to Hermansen [3], the most suitable topics for behavioral learning are technical, conceptual and definitory topics. Language Technology includes all three topics and they should become rote competencies for the student. Therefore, there is also justification to include behavioral learning in the CAL application for the discipline.

Content of the CAL application

At this early stage, I intend to implement an application that combines the two basic educational theories mentioned above. The educational goals of the application are to give the students rote competencies and teach them to work with the language technology tools and to give them the capability to work with the theory of language technology in an independent and creative manner. The content of the application is going be:

- Introduction
- Theory sections
- Examples
- Exercises
- Self-tests
- Help

The application is not going to demand that the students follow a specific path through the material. This means that the student can explore the instructional material unrestrictedly. In this way each student controls the progression of the learning situation at any given point in the application. This is a cognitive aspect and it is chosen because the student then has to consider and be aware of what he/she needs to learn. Because there is no given path through the material, the design has to be very comprehensible in order for the students to grasp the perspective of the application

The exercises will also be developed with consideration to cognitive learning. The exercises are meant for triggering accommodation of the assimilated knowledge accumulated when going through the theory sections. An exercise could for example be to construct a simple concept system with ten concepts related to the concept "bicycle". To use the theory on a well-known object will presumably create a realization of how to actually implement the theory.

The self-tests will be developed according to the behavioral educational theory. The self-tests will be a set of multiple choice questions for each section of the theory. When the student has answered the questions connected to one section, he/she will receive a reply from the application that indicates which answers are correct and which are wrong together with the right answers for the section. Furthermore, the student will receive positive reinforcement for the correct answers and be encouraged to continue with a section of the theory that reflects the

level of correctly answered questions. It is however, very important to consider the reinforcement carefully. The Danish mentality does not take kindly to praise, unless it is of very moderated character. Therefore, too much reinforcement will have the exact opposite effect on a Danish student than anticipated by the behavioral educational theory. It is also important to consider what will function as reinforcement for the target group. As the target group for this application is students at university level, it must be assumed that the students, as a minimum, have an interest in learning the skills required by the study board in order to pass an exam. Therefore, this will be used as reinforcement in the CAL application.

The introduction contains a motivational aspect. This is intended to motivate the students to become interested in learning the theory of language technology. The motivational aspect can for example be video clips of experts telling how they use language technology.

To help the students cope with both academic and technological problems, a number of opportunities will be available. In the program there will be a Help function to help the students overcome minor technical problems that might occur. For major technical problems, the students can contact the local IT Support. For academic problems, the students can ask each other for help or contact the teacher in charge of the course e.g. by email.

Concluding Remarks

In this paper I have pointed out that many of the problems that seem to be connected with CAL are a consequence of the lack of a pedagogical foundation. However, until the CAL application for language technology has been developed and empirical studies have been conducted on a group of students, it is not possible to evaluate the actual effect of involving the pedagogical aspect into a CAL application.

I have justified the use of both the cognitive learning theory and the behavioral learning theory in the development of a CAL application and furthermore, that they can be used for specific partial educational goals in the development. Cognitive learning can be used for knowledge that the student is required to reflect on, while behavioral learning can be used for obtaining rote competencies within the subject.

References

[1] (Brahler 2000): C. Jayne Brahler and Emily C. Johnson: Pedagogy: A Primer on Education Theory for Technical Professionals, Washington State University, Pullman, Washington, USA

[2] (McCormick 1997): Christine B. McCormick, Michael Pressley: Educational Psychology, Learning, Instruction, Assessment. Longman 1997

[3] (Hermansen 1996): Mads Hermansen: Læringens univers. Forlaget Klim, 1996

Task-based learning for pronunciation

Kyehyoung Lee
School of Languages and International Education
University of Canberra, Australia

Abstract

The aim of this paper is to create a task-based model for L2 learners to reach native-like pronunciation using technology. The model is based on three major principles. Firstly, language-learning system is that it need to give learners an opportunity to make sense for themselves. Secondly, Build up the modified 3Ms (Meaning Making Mechanisms), (Lian, A.P. 2000) which is operating in the heads of each and every human being as they go about their daily lives. Thirdly, learners must engage reality as it presents itself to them in the course of this engagement and through the means that are available learners interrogate reality in order to achieve the goal they want to achieve. Against the background of these statements, this paper seeks to establish a task-based model that would assist in teaching pronunciation and explore the ways in which technology could be used in providing practical solutions implied by these principles. A technological program, which is a part of the model, will be presented in the end.

Principles

1. Language-learning system

A fundamental principle for constructing a language-learning system is that it needs to give learners an opportunity to make sense for themselves, in the context of their internal logical and representational systems, of the new communicative world with which they are trying to engage. (Lian, 2000)

2. The 3Ms (Meaning-Making Mechanisms) & B.I.M (Bumping, Interacting, Moderating)

If learners were put in a new environment, they would start to *Bump* with the new world with which learners are not familiar or even do not know at all. Here, learners would experience some problems. To solve these problems learners must *Interact* and *Moderate* while they try to put their former knowledge (or history) into a new situation and compare and contrast all their information, which is relevant.

As Lian, (1996) has said this process will not necessarily enable the learner to perform the whole interaction, rather, it would provide a small but significant platform of stability on which to build new understandings i.e. new relationships. Through this process, learners will develop their 'Meaning-Making Mechanisms' (Lian, 2000).

3. Authentic task - Radio Program

The reason why a radio program has been chosen is to teach second language to learners using an authentic method not contrived for the purpose of teaching. Lian.A.B (2001, in the class) defined the criteria of authentic task that you engage reality as it presents itself to you in the course of this engagement and through the means that are available you interrogate reality in order to achieve the goal that you want to achieve.

On these views, using a radio program as a task-based methodology is an authentic methodology.

Strategies for radio program

1. "One-stop learning"

Once learners come into this learning place, they should not need to move to other places to solve problems they may encounter there. This place can be named "one-stop learning". In other words, almost all necessities are provided, which saves time and prevents learners from losing interests. Hence, the program seeks to provide all facilities such as watching videos, listening, speaking while recording learners' voice, and dictionary etc.

2. Learner-centred approach

The major point of a learner-centred approach is that the understanding of the learner and the learning needs which are necessitated by the differences between learners. "One learns by engaging the world."

The principle is as follows. Nobody knows anything; therefore all knowledge is social i.e. constructed against the principle that historically, and not logically, makes sense.

So, learners do task which is anything that arises in response to reality and in order to affect reality (Lian A.B., 2001) and learner himself or herself engage in reality not teacher engage in it.

3. Self-directed learning

One of the premises of this model is pursuing the self-directed learning. Self-directed learning has been described as "a process in which individuals take the initiative, with or without the help of others," to diagnose their learning needs, formulate learning goals, identify resources for learning, select and implement learning strategies, and evaluate learning outcomes (Knowles 1975).

4. Providing diversity to learners

The major reason that the language is not simple but complicated is because a complicated world makes language. The second major reason is different language groups, which belong to a large society is different at least slightly. Moreover, language has different shapes according to different type of groups-their division criteria might be generation, social level and gender etc even in one language using country. Hence the database is required to be diverse.

Model of task-based Program

It requires four periods of five weeks.
First week, students select a topic (mean) through negotiation between learners and their feeling of reality, and form a group according to their task e.g. parody, interview and news.
Second week, students make a script while accessing the various relevant authentic resources which teacher provided or from the outside world and collect data.
Third week, the teacher needs to teach pronunciation in various ways with technological support.
Fourth week, the class needs final pronunciation correction before broadcasting their program.
Fifth week, students evaluate the program with feedback from various sources such as peers, teacher, audience etc. After one term is finished, the process is repeated with different topics and rotated the roles among learners

One of the technological program

1. To make the model seems like real world it was devised for learners to be able to hear the sound faster or slower.

2. Rather than clear recording, some noise is included a background for making the environment more like the real world. Listening to perfect, clear sounds without noise is impossible in real world.
3. Providing scripts synchronised with the screen and sound helps learners to catch up the speed, emotional situation and body movement of authentic text.
4. Teaching intonation and rhythm as well as sounds at the same time and with meaningful sentences.
5. Providing a database, which is able to make learners access as many various resources as they need.

Conclusion

The current paper has established a pronunciation-teaching model using an authentic task, a radio program, suggesting technology program for its implementation. Achieving native speaker pronunciation must be a goal of all second language learners. Also, it is perhaps the most difficult goal. Although it is not easy for a single model to cover the theories, learners need to have a model in learning L2 area. Hopefully, the suggested model and program will make a small contribution to help learners achieve native-like pronunciation.

References

1. Bourdieu, P., 1995, *The logic of practice.* (Translated by R. Nice), Stanford University Press, Stanford, CA
2. Lian, A-P. 1980 - 1998, *Intonation Patterns of French.* Teacher's Book. River Seine Publications, Melbourne, Digitised version begun in 1998
3. Lian, A. B. and Lian A-P., 1997 "The Secret of the Shao-Lin Monk: Contribution to an intellectual framework for language-learning", <http://www.ace.jcu.edu.au/llc/mod-lang/dmlstaff/mlapl/shaolin/Psupre2.htm>
4. Lian, A. P., 2000, "From First Principles: Constructing Language-Learning and Teaching Environments", University of Canberra http://comedu.canberra.edu.au/~andrewl/mlapl/first_principles/
5. Runyon K 1977 *Consumer Behavior and the Practice of Marketing*, Charles Merrill Publishing Company, Chapter 13.
6. Knowles, M. 1975 Self-Directed Learning: A guide for Learners and Teachers. New York: Association Press

Explanations for the Differential Use of ICT in the New Zealand Secondary School Classroom

Lorrae Ward; Centre for Child and Family Policy Research;
School of Education; The University of Auckland

Abstract

This paper is based on a research project currently being undertaken. The aim of the project is to find, and validate, possible explanations for the differential level, manner and patterns of use of ICT (Information and Communication Technologies) as learning tools in the New Zealand Secondary School classroom both within and between schools. Currently the government, and our schools, are spending large amounts of money on both ICT infrastructure and staff professional development. Yet, despite the high level of implementation that has resulted the level of integration into the classrooms and the use of ICT as a learning tool is still disappointing at best.

Introduction

This study focuses on the impact of teacher philosophies, values and practices on their use of ICT and what Cuban (2001) calls the "contextually constrained choices" they make. Even though there is some validity in the slow revolution theory, in that ICT usage is increasing, questions need to be asked as to whether the level of change and the quality of use justifies the expenditure by the government, schools, and in some instances private corporations. Similarly there is no denying there are issues with the structure and traditions of our secondary school system such as the division into subjects and the rigid timetable. However, neither of these arguments explain why, or how, some teachers have managed to overcome any obstacles and are using technology in exciting and innovative ways while others are using it for administration only.

The rationale for the study therefore lies in the need to understand why teachers have made the decisions they have regarding the use of ICT in their classroom as a learning tool in order to explain the differential use apparent in other studies undertaken. It cannot be refuted that many secondary schools have made enormous strides in terms of the implementation of ICT. ERO reports show that both the ratio of computers to students and the level of connectivity in our schools have improved considerably; they also show that Boards of Trustees see ICT as their highest priority in terms of in-service training. Their 2000 ICT report stated that 76% of all schools had committed financial resources to ICT training. Given this level of commitment, the question then needs to be asked why there has not been a greater level of integration of ICT into the curriculum in Secondary Schools and why current patterns of use still suggest that the dominant use of computers is in teaching computer skills rather than enhancing the learning in curriculum areas. [4]

Both Becker and Cuban, in very different studies in the United States, raise the issue of type and quality of use rather than quantity of use. It is Cuban's contention that:

> "When it comes to higher teacher and student productivity and a transformation of teaching and learning, [however] there is little ambiguity. Both must be tagged as failures. Computers have been oversold and underused". [3]

While a proponent of the slow revolution theory, which claims that over time, and with improvements in hardware and software, the integration of ICT will increase, Becker also expresses some concerns over the current use of computers. In 1999 he surveyed more than 4100 teachers in over 1100 schools in the United States. A substantial body of his survey data supported Cuban's claims that there has been, in reality, limited impact in the classroom from computers in education. [1] A study by the National Center for Education Statistics showed similar results with 78% of teachers using computers to create instructional material and only 36% using them to present to the class using multi-media. [5] From his study of schools in the Silicon Valley, where infrastructure was not a major issue Cuban found that only 2 out of 10 secondary school teachers were what he described as "serious users" of ICT, with 4 out of 10 using computers once a month and the rest never using them. [3]

Clark in a review of early work on teachers' thoughts and beliefs and their impact on their actions claims that

> "a complete understanding of the process of teaching is not possible without an understanding of the constraints and opportunities that impinge upon the teaching process". [2]

This emphasis is echoed by Becker who states that:

> "the final and critical piece may yet turn out to be teachers' philosophies of learning and teaching and whether they can be brought around to be supportive of constructivist applications of computer technology". [1]

The Study

The project takes a case study approach and is in two phases using multiple data collection methodologies such as questionnaires, interviews, observation and document analysis. Data collected during the first phase will be used to purposefully select participants and areas of focus for Phase Two as well as the development of data collection tools. During Phase One a questionnaire will be used to study the following areas:

- The level of infrastructure in the school
- ICT use by teachers
- School contextual factors
- Teacher values and beliefs

The findings from this questionnaire provide the foundation for Phase 2 during which the constraints and opportunities that exist for teachers to use ICT will be probed more deeply using a problem based methodology approach. That is it will attempt to determine the reasoning behind what Cuban (2001) calls the "constrained choices" teachers make as to how and why they use ICT with their students. Dialogue with the teachers selected will be the primary source of data collection for this phase.

The results of phase 1 will be written up as case studies of the use of ICT in schools and will add to the current literature, which describes this and considers the barriers to further use.

It is intended that phase 2 will provide a more in-depth understanding of the factors that impact on why teachers use ICT as they do and will ultimately be discussed in terms of the variables that account for the different patterns of usage within a school as well as those implicated in the different patterns across schools.

References

1. Becker, H. J. and J. L. Ravitz (2001). Computer Use by Teachers: Are Cuban's Predictions Correct? Annual Meeting of the American Educational Research Association, Seattle.
2. Clark, C. M. and P. L. Peterson (1986). Teachers' Thought Processes. Research in Teaching and Learning. A. E. R. Association. New York, Macmillam Publishing Company.
3. Cuban, L. (2001). Oversold and Underused Computers in the Classroom. London, Havard University Press.
4. Lai, K.-W., K. Pratt, et al. (2001). Learning with technology: Evaluation of the Otago Secondary Schools Technology Project. Dunedin, The Community Trust of Otago.
5. Smerdon, B., S. Cronen, et al. (2000). Teachers' Tools for the 21st Century., The National Center for Education Statistics.

Models for the Development of Learning Contexts: Managing Learning and Knowledge in Virtual Environments through Learning Communities

Ana Paula Afonso*

Institute of Cognitive Psychology, Faculty of Psychology and Education Sciences, University of Coimbra; Apartado 6153; 3000 Coimbra – Portugal / Phone&Fax: +351239851467 / e-mail: apa@ci.uc.pt

This work has been partly supported by the Portuguese Foundation for Science and Technology (FCT) under grant SFRH/BD/3289/2000.

Abstract

This project addresses the design of a framework for the development of learning contexts through virtual learning communities, based on the development of learning activities.

It endeavours to establish a framework to rethink the management of learning and knowledge as processes of social participation within virtual contexts of collective learning. It builds on the conviction of the importance of creating a model that may represent a guideline for the design of systems for the management of knowledge and learning in educational sites and, ultimately, for building learning contexts for virtual environments.

Introduction

We are now evolving towards a different level of consciousness and understanding of human development, human motivation and human learning, brought up, in part, by the development and dissemination of new information and communication technologies, mainly driven by the internet in all its forms. Our main interest, within the scope of this project, is the web and its potential as a medium for the promotion and development of a new educational paradigm, assuming that the development of web-based educational servers represents one of the most significant contributions of information technologies to the transformation of the processes of knowledge representation and of learning itself [1].

How can the web be more than just another way of delivering content to students? How can mankind profit from existing millions of bytes of information? How can we give a human touch to the technological world? Probably the answer is not easy to find, but it may lay somewhere in the articulation of pedagogic, psychological and sociologic theories, along with the contribution of organisational practice and theory.

In an attempt to find an answer to these and other questions, this project addresses a framework for the development of virtual learning communities, based on the development of learning activities. It endeavours to establish a framework to rethink the management of learning and knowledge as processes of social participation within virtual contexts of collective

learning, that is, to build a model that may represent a guideline for the management learning in educational sites and to build learning contexts for virtual environments.

With these background ideas, we will be able to: state strategies required for the construction and management of virtual learning communities; clearly identify the roles and responsibilities of the members; identify and promote the structures involved in the construction of collective knowledge; develop the activities necessary for the management of knowledge/learning and for the construction of learning contexts.

Discussion of issues

Recent practice in organisations is showing that learning communities are privileged contexts for the acquisition and creation of knowledge, and the development of decentralised information resources encouraged by information and communication technologies are bringing a new light on this issue.

This reflection supports the view that individuals learn when engaged in communities in which knowledge is built through interaction (within collaborative activities, either social exchange activities or self-discovery activities), discourse and consensus. Thus, learning communities constitute an important alternative to traditional learning and organisational contexts, supported by new information and communication technologies, and are becoming more tangible today than a decade ago. In this way, the concept of learning communities emerges as an alternative to traditional teaching/learning models, under the shape of decentralized groups of people that self-organize as functional and stable communities with the aim of scaffolding each other in the development of constructive learning activities [2].

It might be said that the greatest advantage and the biggest challenge of web-based learning is that of building context rich virtual communities that foster individual and collective learning, where learners are responsible for the collaborative construction of a culture where collective knowledge develops. If we accept that web environments are new tools for the creation of this kind of communities, and that psychological tools deeply influence the sense we make of the world, it's crucial to recognize the need for a new perspective on the creation of learning contexts [3]. In fact, researchers rarely pay attention to the framework of the learning contexts and activities, or to the social interactions they promote. This may be because defining context is neither easy nor consensual. Thus, the need of developing research on this domain is getting clearer every day.

The development of virtual learning environments through sophisticated technologies supporting learning seems to be increasingly gaining shape. However, solutions that have been deployed until now carry a perspective of learning and education that emphasizes content neglecting, almost completely, context. These solutions lack the capacity to set free from learning paradigms inherited from the mechanistic tradition of Industrial Society that still rule over the majority of the initiatives taking place to improve learning and education. We consider that part of the solutions for open learning will concern the development of learning activities – that is, of contexts – that provide sense and structure to content.

Methodological issues

Influenced by these ideas, one can no longer neglect the role of context in any attempt at building web-based learning environments for e-learning. There lays the importance and urgency in discussing the concept of and construction of learning contexts, in what may be a contribution to understanding the influence of contextual issues in learning. Our interest lies in the interactions among members, and between them and the context itself: how do they relate and develop, how to they influence learning, how can we foster their creation?

There are several strategies for the study of contexts. The one we intend to use consists on creating systematised contexts and acting within them, in this way important elements might be provided by context itself, through the interactions between members and between these and the system. To this end, learning communities are, in themselves, the object and the process of research.

This research will contemplate theorization about learning contexts and learning communities, the identification of roles and responsibilities, the classification of learning contexts according to different variables, and the design of learning activities for the construction of learning contexts.

The first goal is the creation of a framework for the development of virtual learning communities. In this area, alongside work previously completed, there is plenty of literature available from consolidated domains such as Organisational Learning, Knowledge Management, Flexible Cognition, Situated Learning, Communities of Practice, and so on. This literature will be reviewed and analysed, in order to consolidate the theoretical reflection on learning communities and learning contexts.

Following the principles of distributed constructionism and the socio-constructivist models for instructional design, as well as other psycho-pedagogic learning theories, we have proposed earlier [4] some models for the management of learning in virtual environments, based on three kinds of strategies: interaction, action and presentation. The use of these strategies is illustrated through a variety of concrete learning activities that might promote the construction of contexts for collective learning.

The project will resource to diverse methodologies, considered suitable for its different features: a)action-research in all phases to ensure a reflexive evolution; b)case studies for those phases focusing on existing communities; c)action-research on the community to be developed.

Concluding remarks

This reflection suggests that individuals learn when engaged in communities in which knowledge is built through interaction, discourse and consensus. They constitute an important alternative to traditional learning and organisational contexts, and are more tangible today than a decade ago.

The challenge underlying the project of building learning contexts is that of achieving a balanced combination of all the dimensions and components of the learning architecture, where the need for one dimension cannot be fulfilled at the expense of the others. A framework for the design of learning contexts is needed to provide a deeper understanding of how a specific design serves the different requirements of the learning architecture of a learning community.

Having in mind situated learning, where learning is viewed as a social process and conceived as a situated activity, the main characteristic of the framework is the underlying conviction that individuals engage in learning communities, looking for participation in their social practices. It focuses on the crucial relationships between incoming members and existing members, as well as on the existing interactions between activities, artefacts, knowledge and practice.

This project is still at an early stage, namely the analysis of cases and the conceptual construction of the framework; by the time this conference takes place we believe there will be some results and improvements to share with the audience.

References

[1] A. Afonso & A. Figueiredo. Web-Based Learning and the Role of Context. In Kinshuk et al. (Eds.). *Proceedings International Workshop on Advanced Learning Technologies 2000*. Los Alamitos, CA: IEEE, 2000, pp. 270-271.
[2] E. Wenger. *Communities of practice – Learning, meaning, and identity*. Cambridge: Cambridge University Press, 1999.
[3] A. Figueiredo. Web-Based Learning – Largely Beyond Context. In F. Restivo & L. Ribeiro (Eds.). *Proceedings European Conference Web-Based Learning Environments 2000*. Porto: FEUP Edições, 2000, pp. 85-88.
[4] A. Afonso. *Models for the management of learning in virtual environments*. M.Sc. Thesis. Coimbra: University of Coimbra, 2000.

For further references, feel free to contact the author.

Voice Recognition Software as a Compensatory Strategy for Postsecondary Students with Learning Disabilities

Kelly D. Roberts
University of Hawai`i Center on Disability Studies

Abstract

Research indicates that persons with disabilities who obtain some level of postsecondary education are more likely to be employed compared to those who have no postsecondary education experience. The problem is that often people with disabilities are not able to overcome the barriers that exist in obtaining postsecondary education. When they do enroll in postsecondary education they often experience difficulty staying in, and completing their programs.

The purpose of this research was to determine if assistive technology, in the form of voice recognition software, could assist in overcoming some of the barriers that exist for people with learning disabilities. The study sought to determine if voice recognition software was an effective compensatory strategy for students with learning disabilities in postsecondary education and the experiences of these students in relationship to their use of the software. Follow-up data will be collected to determine if the software is an effective compensatory strategy for the participants in their future employment.

Introduction

Over the past twenty years changes in the nation's labor market have increased the importance of having a postsecondary education to be able to compete in the job market. Whether it is college; adult and continuing education; or technical preparation; postsecondary education plays a major role in preparing persons for employment and career opportunities (HEATH-VR, 1996). Students who continue their education after high school maximize their preparedness for careers in today's changing economy as they learn the higher order thinking and technical skills necessary to take advantage of current and future job market trends.

Employment rates for persons with disabilities demonstrate a stronger positive correlation between level of education and rate of employment than we see in statistical trends for the general population (Stoddard, 1998). In 1996, the U.S. Bureau of Census statistics indicated labor force participation rates at 75.4% for persons with less than a high school diploma, 84.6% for those with a diploma, 87.8% for persons with some

postsecondary education, and 89.7% among persons with at least four years of college. Proportionately, these labor force participation rates increase even more sharply when compared to increasing levels of education and persons with disabilities. Deplorably, only 15.6% of persons with disabilities with less than a high school diploma currently participate in today's labor force. However, this participation doubles to 30.2% for those who have completed high school, triples to 45.1% for those with some postsecondary education, and climbs to 50.3% for disabled people with at least four years of college (Reskin & Roos, 1990; Yelin & Katz, 1994). As Gajar (1998) cautions, "[f]or individuals with disabilities, a university education is highly correlated with vocational options and financial success. Therefore, the cost of failure, both to these individuals as well as to society is a pressing concern" (p.384-85).

Research indicates that the academic difficulties experienced by students with learning disabilities in elementary and secondary settings persist into adulthood (e.g. Gerber, Ginsberg, and Reiff 1992) yet an increasing number of secondary students are choosing to continue their education (Higgins and Zvi, 1995). In 1991, 8.8% of full-time college freshmen reported having some form of disability, compared with 2.6% in 1978. Of the types of disabilities reported, learning disabilities were the fastest growing group, increasing from 15% to 25% of all students with disabilities over the 13-year period (Blackorby, & Wagner, 1996). While these findings indicate an increase in the number of people with learning disabilities attending college they do not indicate the number of students graduating or the length of time it takes for them to graduate as Vogel and Adelman, (1992) indicate, people with learning disabilities tend to take longer to complete their program of study compared to their peers without disabilities.

Even though people with learning disabilities often form their own compensatory strategies through "trial and error" or via "training" which then help them to compensate for their learning disabilities (Schumaker, Deshler, & Ellis, 1986) there are still persistent areas of difficulty. Estimates of the number of adults with learning disabilities who exhibit written language disorders range from 80% to 90 % (Blalock, 1981). For these individuals assistive technology in the form of voice recognition may offer a new strategy to be utilized in the writing process while increasing access and success in postsecondary and subsequent employment settings.

Raskind (1993) indicates that although both remedial and compensatory strategies are beneficial for adults with learning disabilities, the compensatory approach "may offer the most expeditious means of addressing specific difficulties within particular contexts" (p 159). Raskind (1993) also points to the frustration and burnout adults with learning disabilities experience as a result of years of remedial instruction that yielded little benefit, and the appeal of immediate solutions to particular problems as reasons to support the use of assistive technology by adults. Under these circumstances the current study sought the answer the following research questions:

1. Is assistive technology, in the form of voice recognition software, a statistically significant compensatory strategy for person with learning disabilities in postsecondary settings?

2. What are the experiences of persons with learning disabilities who use voice recognition software?

Methods

Participants were recruited from three postsecondary institutions over a period of two semesters. Criteria for participation included postsecondary students who were eligible for services, at the institution in which they were enrolled, under the category of learning disabled. Participants were trained on the use of VRS and were requested to use the software as appropriate, provide three writing samples, keep track of the number of hours they used the software, and complete pre and post surveys. Participants were instructed to call this researcher if additional instruction or assistance was needed. The VRS was available on each campus and Learnout and Hauspie, the makers of Dragon Naturally Speaking (the VRS used), provided 5 complete programs for participants to install on their personal computers.

Writing samples were graded using Fry's Readability Graph. Post semester focus groups were held to obtain qualitative data.

Results

VRS is not a statistically significant compensatory strategy for postsecondary education students with learning disabilities. But, out of the fifteen participants who were trained on the use of the software two are using it on a regular basis and one is using it intermittently. One participant loves the VRS "it cut my work load in half". Three others dropped out and five participants found learning a new software program too time consuming while meeting their academic demands. Four persons who were trained on the software did not respond to numerous inquires from this researcher.

Discussion

After training the VRS it does not recognize the persons voice accurately and quickly enough to be helpful to all persons. One person with the most severe dysgraphia is using the software consistently and finds it very useful. One assumption that can be drawn from this is that the more severe the person's dysgraphia and the fewer or less advanced their other compensatory strategies the more likely the person is to use the software. Based on feedback from the participants this researcher anticipates that several of them will use the software at a later date. One person who did not use the software during the semester in which they were trained telephoned and asked for additional support.

References

1. Blackorby, J., & Wagner, M. (1996). Longitudinal postschool outcomes of youth with disabilities: Findings from the National Longitudinal Transition Study. Exceptional Children, 62, 399-413.
2. Blalock, J. (1981). Persistent problems and concerns of young adults with learning disabilities. In W. Cruickshank & A. Silvers (Eds.), Bridges to tomorrow: The best of ACLD, 11, 31-45.
3. Gajar, A. (1998). Postsecondary education. In F. Rusch, & J. Chadsey (Eds.). Beyond high school: Transition form school to work. Belmont, CA: Wadsworth.
4. Gerber, P. J., Ginsberg, R., & Reiff, H. B. (1992). Identifying alterable patterns in employment success for highly successful adults with learning disabilities. Journal of Learning Disabilities, 25, 475-487.
5. Higgins, E., & Zvi, J. (1995). Assistive technology for postsecondary students with learning disabilities form research to practice. Annals of Dyslexia, 45, 123-142.
6. Raskind, M. (1993). Assistive technology and adults with learning disabilities. Learning Disabilities Quarterly, 16, 185-196.
7. Reskin, B., & Roos, P. (1990). Job queues, gender queues. Philadelphia: Temple University Press.
8. Schumaker, J., Deshler, D. & Ellis, E. (1986). Intervention issues related to the education of LD adolescents. In J. Torgesen & B. Wong (Ed.), Psychological and educational perspectives on learning disabilities (pp. 329-360). Orlando, Florida: Academic Press.
9. Stoddard, S. (1998). Chartbook on work and disability in the United States: An InfoUse report. Washington DC: National Institute on Disability and Rehabilitation Research.
10. Vogel, S., & Adelman, P. (1992). The success of college students with learning disabilities: Factors related to educational attainment. Journal of Learning disabilities, 25, 430-441.
11. Yelin, E., & Katz, P. (1994). Labor force trends of persons with and without disabilities. Monthly Labor Review, 117, 36-42.

Mathematics Tutor: Matching Instruction to Student's Learning Styles

Nor Azan Mat Zin
Department of Information Science
Faculty of Technology and Information Science
National University of Malaysia. 43600 UKM BANGI
azan@sun1.ftsm.ukm.my

1: Introduction

Computer-aided instruction (CAI) has been around for sometimes and has been proven effective for learning as was reported in various research findings [1, 2]. However, these traditional CAI and multimedia software which are costly to produce have limitations, they cannot be tailored for individual learning since they lacked the ability to adapt to the student's different learning styles or different academic ability such as relating his incorrect answers to the correct ones. Furthermore, the practice or problems presented in CAI were usually limited to simple drill-and-practice questions after which the student is then given the next module depending on his score in the evaluation of the module. Therefore there is a need for 'intelligence' in these systems so that inferences about student's mastery of topics or tasks and traits such as learning styles can be made in order to dynamically adapt the content or style of instruction. Adaptation of instructional materials to students ability and learning style should facilitate learning.

2: Research objective

The main objective of this research is to design a model of an intelligent multimedia mathematics tutoring system that can automatically adapt instruction to student's learning style and ability, for use in Malaysian secondary school. Other related objectives are to develop a learning style diagnostic tool, to develop a pre-test questions to assess students prior knowledge related to the chosen topic and to develop a prototype of the system in order to evaluate the design of the proposed instructional model.

3: Research Questions and Methodology

Following the research objectives mentioned above, the main research question is:

Does matching instruction to student's learning styles increase his/her performance in the tutored topic?

Related question is, what are the different learning styles of learners in learning mathematical concepts and solving problems?

The research methodology follows the design of instructional courseware as discussed in [3, 4]. User or learner analysis has been completed. Domain percentage of secondary school mathematics syllabus is found to be the most difficult topic for first year students, so this topic is chosen for the content of the courseware.

4: Findings

Currently I'm working on learning styles diagnostic tool for mathematics learning. The tool consists of three parts to assess perceptual and cognitive learning styles and the style of mathematics problem solving. At the same time I'm working on the design of instructional modules based on learning styles characteristics.
Framework for the proposed tutoring system is shown in figure 1.

References

[1] Rosser, J. 1996. CD-ROM Multimedia- The Step before Virtual Reality. Surgical Endoscopy (1996) 10: 1033-1035

[2] Scholten, I. And Russel, A. 2000. Learning about the Dynamic Swallowing.ProcessUsing an Interactive Multimedia Program. Dysphagia. 15: 10-16

[3] Jonassen, D. 1988. *Instructional Design for Micro-computer Courseware*. New Jersey: Lawrence Erlbaum Associates Publishers

[4] Robyler, M. 1988. Fundamental Problems and Principles of Designing Effective Courseware Dlm. Jonassen, D.(ed.) *Instructional Design for Micro-computer*

Courseware, pp.7-33. New Jersey: Lawrence Erlbaum Associates Publishers.

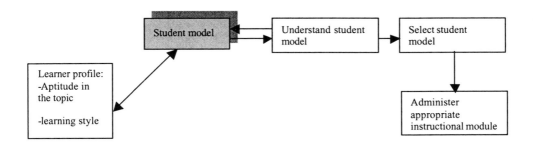

Fig.1. Framework for the instructional system

The Internet Communication Environment (ICE) - Virtual University as Virtual Community

Birgit Feldmann
University of Hagen
58084 Hagen, Germany
birgit.feldmann@fernuni-hagen.de

Abstract: Our Experiences and research in the field [1,2,3,4,5,6,7,8,9] have shown, that students working collaboratively are more successful than students working alone. Therefore, it should be a logical consequence to install collaboration as key factor in distance study environment. That is not as easy as spoken, because the classical distance study institutions struggle with a bundle of different problems. E. g. in Germany no study fees are allowed. How to finance highly interactive, small classes? Another problem are the professional restrictions of distance students, their time budget is limited. The consequence is, that normally students have nearly no contact to their peers and their tutors until the final examinations. The drop-out rates are extremely high (more than 90%) and a lot of students study more than six years to reach a degree. The deployment of virtual teaching improved the situation substantially, but not enough.
The following paper tries to show a solution for the mentioned problems.

Introduction:

The above mentioned problems are typical, not only for the University of Hagen, which is specialized in distance teaching, but for all similar institutions. To improve the situation Hagen developed in 1996 a Virtual University (VU). Part One shortly describes this University. Part two develops a vision of an improved VU – the virtual university as virtual community. To build up this community meaningful communication tools like the described Internet Communication Environment (ICE) are necessary. The paper concludes with prospect to future needs.

Part One: The Virtual University Project

The University of Hagen has an experience and a tradition of distance education since more than 20 years. Therefore, it was a logical consequence to use the Internet for learning and teaching purposes. The benefits of distance education, time- and location independence and the advantages of the Internet (fast information, easy communication and co-operation possibilities) were combined in the project Virtual University, Germany's first university to offer all its services in the Internet.
The project is experimenting with and evaluating different forms of teaching and learning in the Internet. When the project started a suitable software platform was not available for our purposes, so a platform was built based on Internet technologies and

a commercial database system. It is a virtual university system that integrates all functions of a university into a complete, homogeneous, extensible system with an easy to use and intuitive student-centered user-interface. The VU started with only a few courses of electrical engineering and computer science, however, courses and events from all departments were moved to the system over time. For instance, after the first year more than half of the courses came from humanities. This clearly contradicts the original assumption that web-based learning would be accepted easily by the technical departments and their students, but would be accepted very slowly in non-technical departments. Currently, more than 20.000 students are using the Virtual University of Hagen. Since the beginning of the Virtual University more than 1000 virtual learning events took place. The home page of the Virtual University offers the following functions:
education - for participation in courses, seminars, practical training and exercises; *news* - a campus wide blackboard containing all sorts of up-to-date information relevant to the users of the Virtual University; *office* - the component including administrative functions; *research* - offers access to all research-related activities in the university; *cafeteria* - a forum for social contacts between students; *library* - offers access to both traditional and digital libraries , *information* - provides general information about the university; *shop* - offers all material that can be purchased from the university.
The experiences are positive throughout.
It turned out, that the most efficient teaching events were highly interactive events like virtual seminars, practical training and online exercises [1,2].

The new virtual university – virtual university as virtual community

As the most popular teaching events are the ones with a high grade of interactivity and collaboration we thought about improving the running VU. The main aspect is to improve the contact possibilities for the students to build a students community.
One step on the way to a learning community is the Internet Communication Environment (ICE), an instant messaging service for students developed by our department of computer science.
The ICE is a complex client-server system to manage users, communication profiles and communication technologies. The primary objective of ICE is to support the peer-to-peer communication process: The

student is able to look online for matching communication partners, contact them easily and reach them with the correct communication tool as soon as possible, especially with synchronous means like chat, audio- and videoconferencing. However, our users have less technical and organizational problems in using internet communication technologies to enhance their learning success. Problems can be solved in direct dialogues with tutors or other students of the course. Organizational questions can be asked on a broad basis to be answered equally fast as directly.

Another important impact is that the building of communities (e.g. beginners, special interest, etc.) will be improved highly.

The secondary objective is the collection of data to analyze the communication processes between users. This information is essential to develop the system with regard to users needs and to moderate efficiently the community building process.

Technically, we are able to add new technologies into the ICE repository and monitor how much these technologies are used by the users. This will allow us to adapt communication tools to users needs. Furthermore, we are able to create new communication possibilities with progressing technologies like new mobile communication technologies. Our expectation is that students built up communities more efficient than before and because of that they will be able to solve their problems faster and easier. We hope that students are more motivated and work more effective than before.

Prospect

The last five years have shown that the traditional distance teaching will more and more succeed by modern e-learning environments. The new electronic communication possibilities have the quality to break down the students' isolation, to enable long-lasting learning communities [3, 4, 6] with completely new communication qualities that are fundamentally different from traditional ways of teaching and learning. Students using electronic communication within the virtual university are much more motivated than before; the dropout rate is decreasing and the feedback is entirely positive [5].

The Internet Communication Environment is an instrument to improve students situation to create a
[9]
[10]   The Virtual University of Hagen: http://vu.fernuni-hagen.de
Basic Support for Cooperative Work (BSCW): http://bscw.gmd.de

virtual university's community.

It's hard to imagine our everyday life without electronic communication. Email, news, mobile phone, mobile data-exchange will become more and more integrated. Mobile Internet is not just a catchword for some future thing to happen. The ICE is ready for these new facilities.

These developments will have a major impact on e-learning. Depending on the situation a message will be received as email, SMS, instant message, or contribution in a newsgroup. Learning communities will exchange data in a mobile way, and workspaces will not require stationary PCs.

Be it mobile phone, PC, laptop, or PDA, mobile learning will be part of life-long learning. The virtual university as a virtual community is one step on the way to future e-learning environments.

Acknowledgements

[1]   Feldmann-Pempe, B., Schlageter, G. (1999) *Internet-based Seminars at the Virtual University: A Breakthrough in Open and Distance Education.* Proceedings of the ED-Media 99, Seattle, AACE.

[2]   Feldmann, B. Schlageter, G. (2001). *Five Years Virtual University – Review and Preview.* Proceedings of the WebNet01, Orlanda: AACE.

[3]   Leh, Amy S. C. (2001*). Computer-Mediated Communication and Social Presence in a Distance Learning Environment.* International Journal of Educational Telecommunication 7 (2). 109-128.

[4]   Mason, R. *Using Communications Media in Open and Flexible Learning.* Kogan Page.

[5]   Ogata, H., Yano, Y. (1998): *Supporting awareness for augmenting participation in collaborative learning.* Proceedings of the WebNet98, Charlottesville: AACE.

[6]   Palloff, Rena M.; Pratt K. (1999) *Building Learning Communities in Cyberspace. Effective Strategies for the Online Classroom.* Jossey-Brass, San Francisco.

[7]   Preece, J. Online Communities. Designing Usability, Supporting Sociability.

[8]   December, J. (1996) *Units of Analysis for Internet Communication.* Journal of Communication 46 (1) Winter. 0021-9916.

A CAL Wizard

Wasana Ngaogate
Under supervisor - Dr. Steve Matthews
Department of Computer Science,
The University of Warwick, Coventry, CV4 7AL, UK
wngaogate@dcs.warwick.ac.uk

Abstract

The project is to design and implement a 'wizard' with the following functionality to support a traditional CAL learning environment. To continually monitor and collect data on individual and group student performance, to perform statistical analysis, to provide feedback for teachers, to enable students to contribute to the wizard's experience, and to provide advice to the individual student.

Motivation

Based on my experience, I believe in student imagination. If I give them a clear and simple example program, most students have fun with adding more functions into my original. Their programs considerably enhance my own.

This is my inspiration of wanting an easier CAL tool for teachers to build on-line lessons. Allowing students to get basic knowledge on their own would let more able students to get more advance knowledge as soon as they can. Moreover, average students can repeat a lesson as many times as they want. What students need is a highly flexible, customisable, supportive CAL tool.

The Learning Process

Separating one lesson into several topics is a typical method of teaching. Students can focus on each topic that has predefined objectives and take some exercises at the end of topic. Topics should have some relative points to connect them. It might be 'the next step of doing something', 'another part of something', 'why this step is like this', etc. A person walking along a path needs to know where he or she is going and his current progress.

During this process, teachers cannot predefine everything students should know. My idea is that teachers can learn from students' obstacles as we all learn from our mistakes. It would be wonderful if this process could be automatic improved using its own experience. This means arrangement of students, teacher, topics and history of user interaction. The teacher predefines an initial learning track, and then students follow or repeat the track. Topics in the track could be moved, added, deleted or changed in content. This may be done either by the teacher, or by a wizard learning from students experience of the track.

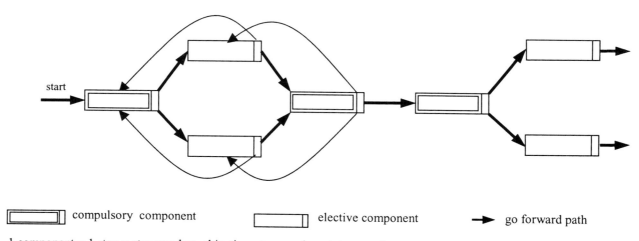

compulsory component   elective component   → go forward path

1 component = 1 step = step number, objective, story, and next step number

Students start at the entry component and study until the end of each subsequent component that might have a small formative assessment exercise, and then allows students to make a decision to move on or to guide them to the next topic if they prefer otherwise. Moreover,

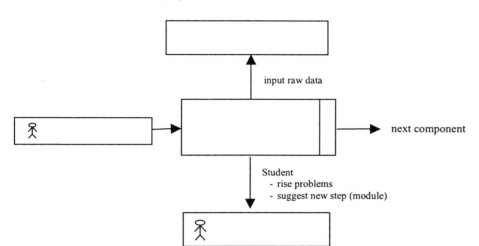

students can go back to repeat the same component as often as they wish.

All information since students have logged in the system would be recorded – where and when they log in, which topic they choose to start learning and which topic they continue, which topic they repeat and how many times repeated. Until the end of learning, students can suspend a lesson and continue a later date.

Moreover, students can raise their problems or suggest new steps to be added into the system. During the learning process, gaming-like themes would apply to each lesson – fighting with devils, collecting golden medals – these themes would be automatically created by the system.

The Learning Hierarchy

As students execute each learning module (driven by JSP and MySQL) observation and analysis module would produce and leave information in the right place. This hierarchy shows working relevance between humans and machine. The more repetition in a module, the more attention the teacher should pay.

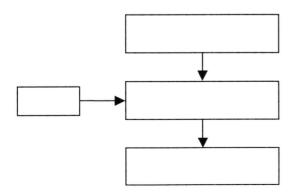

My Questions

My objective is to build a web-based tool including all functions for teachers and students to get involved with basic knowledge, in particular as many subjects as they want. This action leaves a lot of useful raw data. Inside the learning hierarchy, neat analysis methods would be used to interpret students' behaviour and represent their behaviour in an understandable way. Hopefully, a learning pattern could be generated. Analysis of student progress is a major challenge.

Possibilities

The mechanics of this model could be supported by current web technologies, for instance, getting IP addresses that automatically sent to the server allowing the system to know where the student is and to verify the same student who is learning at that time. Obviously, JSP (Java Server Page) is the most convenience language for web-based application. Moreover, MySQL is a well-known database engine and it is free. Any operating systems are available to be server or client. Nice and easy is the main feature of all applications.

Guiding the system for users both student and teacher would be built-in – how to create lessons and examinations for the teacher, how to follow lessons for students. Generally, students can learn from anywhere-anytime-on any system.

Bibliography

1. Evando de Barros Costa, Angelo Perkusich: Modeling the Cooperative Interactions in a Teaching/Learning Situation, *ITS 3rd International Conference* (1996) 168-176
2. Martina Angela Sasse, Christopher Harris, et Al.: Support for Authoring and Managing Web-based Coursework: The TACO Project, *The Digital University: Reinventing the Academy*, Springer-Verlag
3. Ramzan Khuwaja, Vimla Patel: A Model of Tutoring: Based on thte Behavior of Effective Human Tutors, *ITS 3rd International Conference* (1996) 130-138
4. Stephen Farrel, Paul P. Maglio, et Al., *How to teach a fish to swim*. <http://www.buzwords.com/~ccampbel/pbe-fish.pdf> Accessed 17 May 2002
5. Tom Murray: Authoring Intelligent Tutoring Systems: An Analysis of the state of the art, *International Journal of Artifitial Intelligence in Education* (1999), Vol. 10, pp.98-129

A discussion on mobile agent based mobile web-based ITS

T.T. Goh, Kinshuk
Victoria University Wellington
Massey University
Tiong.goh@vuw.ac.nz   kinshuk@massey.ac.nz

Abstract

Currently there is no ITS application tailored to the need of mobile users. This paper provides a pioneering work in mobile ITS which intents to address the competency framework of a mobile ITS. The competency framework includes the mobile device identification, users device preference adaptation, content adaptation, and user model adaptation.

Introduction

Currently there is no ITS system or web based learning environment that is capable of adapting to mobile device user agents such as mobile phone, PDA, CE, or automobile Internet devices. Most of the ITS systems are targeted and optimised towards PC users [1]. With the increasing popularity of mobile devices and the availability of high bandwidth infrastructure such as GPRS, 3G and UMTS networks, there is a need to look into the requirements for mobile access into ITS system or web based learning environment. The purpose of the research is to investigate and to construct a competency framework and implementation of a mobile agent based mobile intelligent tutoring system. While there are mobile agent based ITS system currently available, none truly support mobile devices. A mobile agent based mobile ITS is one that is capable of code migration from host to host and requires an agent platform.

Framework

The keys trust in the research is not to re-invent an ITS system or web based learning environment, but to develop a framework for such system to fit into the framework of mobile access with maximum efficiency and minimum effort.

Though a mobile agent based mobile ITS might look rather similar to traditional ITS, it is far more complex. We identify a mobile agent based mobile ITS should have the following four core competencies.

1. Mobile Device identification
2. Users Device preference adaptation
3. Content adaptation
4. User model adaptation

Other components such as knowledge modules, data mining modules, teacher modules and assessment which are part of a traditional ITS can be used in conjunction with item 3 and 4 above and will not be discussed.

Mobile Device Identification

While traditional ITS or web based system assume access is from PC, it is more complicated for mobile access. The question here is how a web server know a mobile device such as a mobile phone has made a request instead of a PDA. Another question is that a user might send an agent to pre-fetch module using one device type and receive using another device type because environment has changed. How can the service be rendered? Mobile agent can fit into these using interface agent that communicates with web services by either directly communicate with a server agent or a repository agent that contain device ID database. While a repository system allows user to frequently switch to other mobile devices without necessary updating the device itself, it increases the number of communication between agents. There is a need to further investigate the effectiveness of each technique.

Users Device preference adaptation

Once the device has been identified, the system must be able to adapt to user preferences any time. For example a user might like to turn off sound while half way through working on a module. Again agent technology can be used and track users device preference to be adapted anytime without sending content that is consuming bandwidth and is not required. Traditional ITS or web based learning environment might not have such a requirement.

Content adaptation

Content adaptation is unique in mobile intelligent tutoring system or web-base learning environment. Two fundamentals questions arise in content adaptation. First, the content must be translated to the correct mark-up such as wml, xhtml or chtml and divide into correct size that the mobile device is capable of render. Agent based XML/XSLT architectures [2] would likely to achieve such adaptation effectively for a heterogeneous network that constitutes both fixed and mobile devices. Second, not every part of the ITS will be useful to mobile devices. For example a mobile phone user access might be useful to view bullet type revision and take multiple-choice quizzes and a PDA user access might be meaningful to take a short answer quiz and a guided tutorial. Again content adaptation is more tricky in mobile access as compared to traditional ITS or web based learning. The correct content adaptation will be one of the critical success and motivation factors for the adoption of mobile web based learning environment.

User model adaptation

The purpose of user model adaptation is to match user with appropriate challenge and enhance motivation for using the system. The ultimate aim is to achieve best user satisfaction and performance in understanding of the subject domain. While there exist several matching model such as individual model, group model or expert model, the pre-assumption in traditional ITS or web based learning environment that these models being derived might be different from mobile access ITS. For example, if full multimedia content is delivered to achieve an individual or group model, a partial content delivery through mobile device might not result in the same model. Do we then get a sub-optimal model? How do we adapt user model with both sub and optimal model when the access can be both fixed PC and mobile access? On the other hand, a full multimedia delivery might contain redundant information [3] that does not improve learning. On a contrary, a "monomedia" delivery through mobile device might end up being more precise and focus and help people learn.

Current Mobile Agent Technology

While there are many mobile agent platforms such as Telescript, AgenTCL, Aglet [4] and Bee-gent [5] available in the past, none of them is capable of running on mobile devices such as PDA or mobile phone. However current technology such as LEAP [6], a lightweight and extensible agent platform, makes possible for agent to run seamlessly on both fixed PC and wireless mobile devices. LEAP is also an open source software and FIPA compliance. Other commercial mobile agent software such ADK and Enago Mobile which will be releasing mobile devices capability edition this year are also capable of developing a mobile agent based mobile web based learning environment.

Their capabilities and usability will need to be evaluated.

Summary

We present a competency framework for implementing a mobile agent based mobile web-based ITS that can be accessed from either fixed or mobile devices. We also highlighted areas of possibilities for implementations and identify questions need to be answered. Our next step is to work on implementing the above four competencies on available web-based ITS.

References

1. Kinshuk, A Patel, D Russell,"Hyper-ITS: A Web-Based Architecture for evolving and configurable learning environment", staff and educational Development international Journal, 3(3), 265-280.

2. Mark H.Butler, " Current Technologies for Device Independence", Publishing Systems and Solutions Laboratory, HP Laboratories Bristol, HPL-2001-83, April 4th, 2001.

3. Lawrence J.Najjar," Multimedia Information and Learning". http://mime1.marc.gatech.edu/MiME/papers/multimedia_and_learning.html

4. http://www.agentlink.org/resources/agent-software.html

5. Bee-gent, http://www.toshiba.co.jp/beegent/whatsbge.htm

6. Federico Bergenti, Agostino Poggi " LEAP: A FIPA Platform for handheld and mobile devices". Dipartimento di Ingegneria dell'Ingformazione, Universita degli Studi di Parma, Parcro Area delle Scienze 181A, 43100 Parma, Italy

A Story about Learning

Alfred Bork
Information and Computer Science
University of California
Irvine, Ca 92697-3425
bork@uci.edu
www.ics.uci.edu/~bork

Let me tell you a story. It has three parts.

1989 (this really happened)

Mary, twelve, went into a public library in Irvine, California, in the United States. She was looking for books to read. She noticed a device that looked like a television set with a typewriter keyboard. She sat on a chair in front of the screen. There are some pictures on the screen and text. It said, press any key to begin. Just as she did that, John, 11, started watching.

A question appeared on the screen about thermometers. John became interested and sat down. Mary typed an answer, and more questions followed: 'How long do you leave it in your mouth for accurate temperature reading.' Mary and John discussed this, and then Mary typed 'I would leave it in for several minutes'. The message on the screen agreed with her, and another question was presented. The questions were frequent, every few seconds.

This process continued for some time, with questions followed by typed responses, both in ordinary English. They were absorbed with the process, and often talked about what to respond to a question. Sometimes John did the typing. It was like having a conversation with a knowledgeable friend.

Mary and John could have left at any time they were not interested. No exam was going to follow, as their teachers did not even know they were using this material. But they stayed for a long time, until Mary had to go home for supper. When they did leave, they agreed to continue where they left off, so they arranged to meet again the next day. They were playing a constantly active role in creating their own knowledge.

A few days later they used other learning programs. One helped them discover the laws of genetics, one the laws of simple electric circuits.

2003

Laboratory xyz announced that it is conducting a global experiment in highly interactive tutorial learning, through the use of the computer, to determine if this method should be widely employed. Several cultures and languages will be involved. The experiment will include very poor students. Both distance learning and classrooms will be tried. Thousands of students will participate.

The primary mode of interaction will be through questions from the computer, and free-form answers from the student, all in the students' native languages. Both voice and typewriter input will be used, so that they can be empirically compared. Student responses to these questions will be in intervals of less than twenty seconds.

Almost all students will be successful learners. The results of the experiment will guide future development and delivery of material in many other areas of learning.

2020

We are in the center of a town in India with about 100,000 people, in a room that contains many screens that again look like television sets. But unlike the library in Irvine, there are no keyboards. Many people all ages are in the room intently interacting with the material on the screen. The interaction is entirely by voice in the native language of the students, except when they are learning another language.

Again as in Irvine students are free to say anything they wish, and they do.

Their slightly older brothers and sisters bring Maya, Asha, and Gopal, each four, to the center. This is their first visit.

They sit down at one of the screens, and begin a voice-based conversation: The learning device talks to the students, mostly asking questions, and the students talk to the learning device, answering the questions. Our three young heroes sit down, and often discuss what they will say.

The learning aid asks the children what their names are. Then it suggests that Maya tell a story. Children love to tell stories. As the child tells a story print appears on the screen in the child's native language. These young children may not know how to read. Pictures illustrate the story. The learning device adds periods where appropriate. We are beginning even in this early stage both to get children to write, and to understand the connection between speech and the funny symbols that appear on the screen.

The learning device asks the student to read back the story, determining just what they can read. The learning aid reads back the story slowly, using the voice of the student, and other voices, emphasizing each word on the screen as it is read. The story will be presented again to the student.

Our students come back often, eventually learning to read and to compose stories and other documents. Student information is saved frequently, and used in the dialog. Occasionally the learning device suggests that they work with other students, so they become familiar will many children.

There are many groups in the room, working on many things. Some learn about nonviolent ways to resolve disputes. A group of 10-year-olds is learning to differentiate a function. An older group of children is working on quantum electrodynamics. Some are learning how to build and operate a small factory. Several 80 year olds are striving to understand Beethoven's ninth Symphony.

No one is in charge, The room belongs to the learners. Learners work on a topic until they succeed in learning, as determined by the learning device. Since all succeed, no tests and grades are given. Any subject is possible at any time and at whatever pace the students want or need. The learning device assists with choosing new subjects based on what is known about the student. If more learning devices are needed, because of heavy use, they are shipped automatically.

The learners mostly work in groups of about three or four. They come and leave when they want to; they are free learners, working because they are in a highly interactive motivating environment, and because they have always enjoyed learning. Many of the children spend much of the day in the center. They may also work on projects outside the Center. If special help is needed, the learning aid suggests several people to assist, and asks those people if they are willing, when they are in the Center.

The learners in this village understand that learning is a lifelong process. They love to learn. Even at a young age they understand the power of learning, and this encourages lifelong learning.

Their own village has changed greatly since the learning aids were available. Everyone has a comfortable place to live, enough food, and enough water. People enjoy life.

They know too that billions of people on earth are engaged in similar activities, and they understand this helps them avoid violence, and to help solve the major problems of the world, such as too many people, poverty, and limited food and water.

This story was dictated with Dragon NaturallySpeaking Version 5. Thanks to Stephen Denning, George Leonard, and Arthur Clarke.

For details see Tutorial Distance Learning -- Rebuilding our educational system, by Alfred Bork and Sigrun Gunnarsdottir, Kluwer, 2001.

Anywhere, Any Time, Any Kind
Towards a Sustainable Learning System

Hock-Beng Cheah
School of Economics and Management, University College
The University of New South Wales, Australia
h.cheah@adfa.edu.au

Forms of learning: from apprenticeship to sustainable learning

Womack, et al., (1990) identified an evolutionary process from the craft production system to the mass production system to a lean production system. It is argued here that the next stage in this evolutionary process will lead to a sustainable production system. Furthermore, we may identify corresponding learning systems associated with the different production systems.

Individual apprenticeship in a craft learning system may be described as a form of learning in which knowledge and understanding are acquired principally through individual 'learning by following'. There is significant scope for individual attention and guidance, but the learning is constrained by the specificity of the location, limited resources, and the limited numbers of learners that can be accommodated.

Mass schooling in a mass learning system disseminates knowledge and understanding through 'learning by instruction' in relatively large groups. It is location bound and constrained by narrow limits on learning methods and resources, and severe limits on individual attention and guidance.

Mass customised learning in a lean learning system promotes knowledge and understanding through 'learning by tailored instruction' on an individual or group basis. There are greater possibilities for individual attention and guidance, and a wider range of opportunities, methods, settings and resources available to individuals or groups, that are less constrained by location.

Sustainable learning in a sustainable learning system is a form of learning in which knowledge and understanding are acquired principally through 'learning by choice', based on a wide range of sustainable opportunities, methods, settings and resources available to every individual or group, unconstrained by location. Most significantly, it will be based on a learning system that also seeks to be cost effective, environmentally friendly, ethically responsible and focused on enhancing societal well-being (see Cheah, 2002).

Towards a Sustainable Learning System

Learning systems have evolved from the craft learning system (CLS) dominant in pre-industrial economies, to the mass learning system (MLS) that has dominated the industrial economies. In the 21st century, the imperatives of sustainability will contribute to further changes that will evolve eventually into what may be termed as a sustainable learning system (SLS).

The SLS will benefit from the use of the new information and communication technology. This will change the dynamics of the learning and communication process radically. It will provide the capacity for decentralised learning, de-scaling, better use of local resources and skills, reduced environmental harm, improved energy efficiencies, and lower capital/labour ratios. In combination these benefits will be revolutionary. The outcomes for product or service delivery in this shift from MLS to SLS will be manifested in at least eight distinct dimensions: (a) location (b) time, (c) variety, (d) material, (e) price, (f) provider, (g) scale, and (h) focus. Specifically:

Location: In the 21st century, the possibility for large and relatively rapid capital, technology and other resource flows to various locations in the world mean that learning opportunities and activities can be more widely diffused. One important consequence will be the progressive shift from isolated or stand-alone systems to inter-connected systems. This leads to the emergence of distributed networks, which are both fully functional as well as connected. The emergence and diffusion of distributed learning networks is leading to a tendency where flexible learning systems can potentially be set up anywhere and reach everywhere.

Time: In the SLS the desired learning opportunity, resource or service will be available at any time. To facilitate this possibility, the learning system will need to create "real-time structures; structures that change continually in tiny increments, not in large static quantum jumps. Each change is so minute that the overall effect is one of a structure in constant, seamless motion" (Davis, 1987, p.41). In this situation, flexible learning services and opportunities would become available anytime and all the time.

Variety: The SLS will also feature an increasing range and diversity of learning options, resources and services that evolve into mass customised learning. In the ultimate, learners will be able to access any kind of learning opportunity, resource or service tailored to their specific desires or specifications. This will be associated with the ability of diversified learning providers to offer a large range of niche learning services and opportunities.

Material: The SLS will also be associated with the development of learning options, resources and activities that use less or no physical material. This may be illustrated by the encapsulation of the 32-volume contents of Encyclopaedia Britannica (plus dictionary and world atlas) within one DVD-ROM. This spatial contraction has generally been accompanied by increased product capability, functionality, sophistication and, consequently, value. Miniaturisation, increased portability and online delivery mean that transportation constraints are reduced tremendously, such that learning products and services can be delivered more flexibly.

Price: The SLS will benefit from a deflationary tendency, and from a growing number of products and services becoming available at no charge. This will have major significance for widening access to learning opportunities, because cost barriers can be lowered significantly and, in a growing number of cases, eliminated completely. In this context, learning will become an 'public good'.

Provider: In the SLS, an increasing range of learning materials and options will be self-made or self-serviced; that is, there will be a growing capacity to shift from 'do (make) it for me' to 'do (make) it yourself', when information, knowledge and production and learning capabilities become more widely diffused. This tendency would also lower significantly the minimum scale for learning activities, increase flexibility and responsiveness, increase competition and innovation. enhance the capabilities of small learning providers, and strengthen their ability to organise learning 'anywhere', 'anytime', of 'any kind'.

Scale: The SLS will be significantly more scalable, both upwards and downwards. The former will enhance the ability to cater better to large numbers of learners, where this is necessary. The latter will help to increase tremendously the number of learning providers. Furthermore, decreasing economies of scale, increasing economies of scope and other processes, described above, will contribute to the lowering of barriers to entry for small learning providers. This will also lead away from dominance by large mega-institutions, and towards a tendency for learning to be organised and managed by smaller diversified learning providers.

Focus: In the SLS, the economic imperative will be complemented by the ecological imperative, the social imperative and the ethical imperative. These will constitute the quadruple bottomline that will set new benchmarks for behaviour, performance and expectations in the learning process. The consequence will be a more balanced approach to learning, to include a focus on more environmentally friendly, more socially conscious and more humane learning objectives. Learning to improve economic prospects will be balanced by learning to promote a capacity for 'sustainable abundance' (see Cheah and Cheah, 2002).

Conclusion

The principal outcomes of the new learning system will lead to learning opportunities that are potentially available 'anywhere', at 'anytime', of 'any kind', with 'no matter', at 'no charge', and you can 'do-it-yourself'. These systems will be highly scalable and sustainable. They will have the potential to resolve many of the difficulties that, until now, have impeded learning for a large proportion of the world's population.

To effect this evolution from mass schooling to sustainable learning, the first major challenge is to be able to visualise these possibilities ex ante, when they are still at an early or embryonic stage. The next major challenge is to work for the metamorphosis that will transform the possibility for widely accessible, flexible, affordable, effective and sustainable learning opportunities into reality.

References

Cheah, H. B. (2002), "Small is beautiful in a sustainable production system," in C. Harvie and B-C. Lee eds., Sustaining SME Innovation, Competitiveness and Development in the Global Economy: Conference Proceedings, Wollongong: Centre for SME Research and Development.

Cheah, H. B. and M. Cheah (2002), "Sustainable development and sustainable management: Promoting economic, ecological and social sustainability in post-crisis Asia," in U. Haley and F-J. Richter eds., Asian Post Crisis Management: Corporate and Governmental Strategies for Sustainable Competitive Advantage, New York: Palgrave.

Davis, S. (1987), Future Perfect, Reading, MA: Addison-Wesley.

Womack, J., D. Jones and D. Roos (1990), The Machine that Changed the World, New York: Harper.

The future for learning

Sigrun Gunnarsdottir
Iceland Telecom - Research and Development
Armuli 25, 150 Reykjavik, ICELAND
sigrung@simi.is

Introduction

My grade school was an experimental school and was one of a kind in Iceland where I was born and raised. What this school had to offer was a new and experimental approach to teaching - personalization it was called. The school celebrated its 30th anniversary this year. Through the years the school has been forced to move towards more traditional forms of teaching although there are still remnants of the "old" way of teaching within the school.

Today, the term personalization is gaining more and more attention. Research efforts during the past several years have yielded various tools to enable learners to participate in more personalized learning environments – however, further research and development is still needed. Although we have come closer to our ultimate goal, we still have some barriers to cross in order to provide our learners with acceptable personalized learning environments. The most compelling barrier is that we need to build more highly interactive learning models. This position paper discusses the importance of creating an environment for the mass, where creation and sharing of highly interactive learning modules is made easy and where each learning module provides mastery for certain objectives, whether they be one or many.

Individualization and Interaction

In my opinion, individualization or personalization is a fundamental factor in making learning more effective and efficient. Everyone needs to set their personal goals and actively work towards those goals by conquering some objectives. These objectives need to be measurable. Having worked as a teacher and having been a student for a number of years, I know that most teachers are basically practicing this today. The problem is that the learning goals are created for a classroom full of students and not on an individualized basis. This situation needs to be altered. We are all both similar and different in our unique way and there is no guarantee that learning material that works well for one learner will work equally well for the other. Hence there is a compelling need to create an abundance of learning models to cope with the personal differences of our learners.

Interaction is another basic factor that will play an important role in the personalized learning environments of the future. There are many forms of interaction and we can divide them into two categories:

- interaction with other human beings
- computer assisted tutoring

Both of these categories are important when discussing learning. Terry Mayse [3] has constructed a framework for learning technology, which he divides into three stages, conceptualization, construction and dialogue. For dialogue he states:

> "In education, the goal is testing of understanding, often of abstract concepts. This stage is best characterised in education as *dialogue* . The conceptualisations are tested and further developed during conversation with both tutors and fellow learners, and in the reflection on these" [3]

Grades or Mastery

The modern school system is driven by grades, and a common assumption is that the grades are normally distributed. This is a very narrow approach and the question is why the practice of assigning grades has been so widely used.

According to Benjamin Bloom and others [2], almost all students are able to learn through a tutorial approach, with human tutors. This method is called *Mastery learning*. The major difference between grades and mastery is the roles of the examinations or the students assessment. In mastery courses, evaluation determines which learning material is presented to the student in the next phase. This approach is very important when assessing learners towards certain objectives and in our book [1], Alfred Bork and I explain how this approach could be easlily included in tutorial learning.

How do we get there?
Today most educational ministries and/or educational institutes have created a list of objectives where they follow the basic principle that "One size fits all". In fact they should be considered lucky if these objectives fit anyone at all. These objectives are in most cases based on the age of the learners rather than their level of knowledge and skills. The creation of these objectives is not the criticism and is in fact a necessary source for our future learning enviroments, but it is the means of how they are used in the school today that can be criticised.

My vision is that each learner will have a personalized learning profile, which includes the already mastered learning objectives, the goals for future objectives and how to achieve those goals. Through our learning profiles we will talk to a networks of systems, through standardisation, which keeps information, actual learning moduls and objectives databases, learning styles etc.

Conclusion
The future for learning will involve personalized learning environments with access to highly interactive learning modules as well as advanced communication environments.
To make this dream a reality, we need to create an abundance of learning resources, which have to be shared and be accessible to those who need to use them. The resources need to be created according to standards that can track which objectives they relate to and what to do when the learners have fulfilled their objectives.

References
[1] Bork, A. & Gunnarsdottir, S. (2001) *Tutorial distance learning: Rebuilding our education system*, Kluwer Academic/ Plenum publishers.
[2] Bloom, B. (1984) The 2 sigma problem: The search for Methods for group instruction as effective as one-to-one tutoring. Educational Researcher, 13(6), 4-16.
[3] Mayse, T. (2000) Pedagogy, Lifelong Learning and ICT, A Discussion Paper for the Scottish Forum on Lifelong Learning, 28 Feb. 2000.

The Linguistic Divide, Autolinguals, and the Notion of Education-For-All

Fusa Katada
School of Science and Engineering
Waseda University, Japan
katada@mn.waseda.ac.jp

Abstract

Education-For-All (EFA), understood as an 'equal education opportunity for every single person on the globe', is a challenge of this century that cannot be met without advanced information technologies and instructional computing. One question we must address is whether EFA is a force that will advance social welfare and equality on a global scale or institutionalize differences in social class outlook. EFA comes to achieve its principled reality only when the former is the case. This paper clarifies that a possible factor that may affect EFA negatively will be found in linguistic disparity, whose effect is characterized here as the 'linguistic divide'.

The paper nonetheless reports that the emergence of automatic portable multilingual mediators (translators and interpreters), which I wish to call 'autolinguals', is forthcoming at an affordable cost in the very near future, and that logically this should overcome the linguistic divide.

Given that EFA is a technical reality, the paper then directs its discussion to implications for the future of schooling.

1. Technical powers

The advancement of instructional computing has made tutorial learning a reality. Two projects in which I participated in the very early stage (1980's) of the field for language instruction (i.e. the Project Upgrade under the US Federal Funding developed at the Calif. State Univ., Long Beach with the Compton Unified School District [4], and Understanding Spoken Japanese developed at the Educational Technology Center, the Univ. of Calif., Irvine [1]) already realized four basic and vital functions for tutorial learning: (1) bidirectional, as opposed to unidirectional, capacities, (2) individualized, as opposed to group-oriented, teaching, (3) immediate remedial, as opposed to non-immediate or never remedial, capacities, and (4) variable rate, as opposed to constant rate, of instruction.

On the other hand, the advancement of worldwide communication systems in more recent years has made the world knowledge and information accessible by anyone, at anytime, and from anywhere. This advanced technology added the dimension of 'long distance' to 'tutorial learning', which together made the idea of 'global scale tutorial learning' a technical reality. Education is then freed from time and space restrictions, leading to the notion of EFA.

2. Eminence of English as a global lingua franca

In reality, however, education with structured information and knowledge as its base is not possible without a unified form of language. For geographical-historical and socio-cultural reasons, English has achieved its pre-eminent status as a global language in nearly all areas of human social activities [3], including international politics, economic activities, academic conferences and data bases, and the media. Under the given 'linguistic diversity', that is, among more than 6,000 languages of the world [2], English has also been functioning as a lingua franca paramount [6]. English, in other words, is a global lingua franca for education transmitted via a worldwide information network. The more the eminent status of English advances, the more is spent for mastering English. This is what is happening in the nonnative-English world.

3. Three Ds of linguistics

Countries in the nonnative-English world are investing tremendous amount of social cost, time and money for English. Take Japan as an example. English is virtually a mandatory subject of higher education required not only for proper curricula but also for various levels of entrance examinations; consequently, it is also a main subject taught in cram-schools throughout the country. English is now seriously considered as a subject of elementary education. Even out of school, English is a big subject; to be promoted business men are often required to achieve scores of at least 80% on the TOEIC (Test of English for International Communication); it is the current fashion to teach English to preschool children. The issue of

English becoming Japan's second official language, though controversial, keeps coming up among opinion leaders. Various education materials for English occupy good parts of the book stores. One estimate reports that the annual social cost spent on English is never under 30 billion dollars in Japan alone. Such a situation is more or less true in many other nonnative-English countries.

Despite such zeal and efforts for mastering English, it is unrealistic to expect that the nonnative-English world achieves a level of competence similar to that of the native-English world; hence the 'linguistic disparity'. If English is taught early enough, powerful bilingualism may be achieved, and we may expect it to be a possible solution. However, this expectation may even be questionable as we see in California Spanish-English bilingual education which, everyone seems to agree, did not work very well (ABC World News Tonight 6/1/98), even in the English speaking world.

Here, linguistic disparity seems unavoidable, and education delivered in the form of English via a worldwide network will institutionalize differences in social class outlook between those who have good access to English and those who have not, if no solution comes forth; hence the 'linguistic divide', akin to the notion of 'digital divide' (e.g. [5]).

It is worth noting that half of the world population will be competent in English by the year of 2050, by one estimate. Ironically, however, because of its overwhelming success, English will be diversified into many dialects that are mutually unintelligible. I suspect that this direction is evidenced by such examples as Singlish spoken in Singapore, Ebonics spoken in African-American communities, and Spanglish spoken in Hispanic communities.

Three Ds of linguistics—i.e. linguistic diversity, linguistic disparity, and linguistic divide—seem to remain recurring problems to any issue of globalization.

4. Emergence of autolinguals

Under the emergence of other advanced information technologies, the linguistic divide as a possible barrier to EFA may largely disappear. Among such notable technologies advancing day by day, I report the two which came to my immediate attention. For one, the Universal Networking Language developed by the UNL project at the United Nations University in Tokyo is a possible global lingua franca of computers which mediates between any language pairs. It was announced in 1997 by The Nikkei (Japan Economy) Newspaper that by 2006, UNL would be able to handle any language of about 180 countries and areas of the world. It would no longer be a dream that papers written in French are directly read in Swahili on the Internet.

For another, portable multilingual automatic interpreters with listening competency will be a genuine breakthrough for real time language processing. Such a technology looks forthcoming, at the Advanced Telecommunications Research Institute (ATR) in Kyoto, for example, reminding us of the now widespread cellular phones.

It is likely that the emergence of affordable, portable machine interpreters and translators, characterized here as 'autolinguals' of this century, is just a matter of time, perhaps 5 to 10 years in the future. Linguistic disparity against the nonnative-English world will then disappear, and the idea of EFA becomes a practical reality.

5. Implications for the future of schooling

Application of EFA to the future of learning leads us to ask about the effect on the notion of school in the traditional sense: If ideal tutoring with free access to information and knowledge is available to everybody, can schools be unnecessary and hence eliminated, at least in principle? This is a question which involves philosophical value judgments for education.

The answer may not be all positive if we remember some neglected goals of education: to nurture creativity, to understand how worlds and humanities are connected, to develop emotions. Often, if not always, these aspects of education cannot be met without human contact. We may even articulate that human contact itself is the goal of education. It seems, then, that the advanced educational technologies used for EFA and local schools where teachers and students meet face to face will play complementarily shared roles of education in the future.

References

[1] Bork, A., and S. Gunnarsdottir, *Tutorial Distance Learning: Rebuilding Our Education System*, Kluwer Academic, New York, 2001.

[2] Comrie, B., S. Matthews, and M. Polinsky, *The Atlas of Languages*, Facts On File, New York, 1996.

[3] Crystal, D., *English as a Global Language*, Cambridge University Press, Cambridge, 1997.

[4] Hertz, R., *Computers in the Language Classroom*, Addison-Wesley, Menlo Park, 1987.

[5] Kimura, T., *What Is Digital Divide? Toward Consensus Community* (in Japanese), Iwanami, Tokyo, 2001.

[6] McArthur, T., *The Oxford Guide to World Englishes*, Oxford University Press, Oxford, 2002 (to appear).

Does intelligent tutoring have future!

Kinshuk
Massey University, New Zealand

Abstract

Decades of intelligent tutoring systems research has only produced hopes and potential prototypes; in reality, such systems have failed to prove their usefulness in wider academic environment. There seems to be a gap between the delivered research output and the needs of actual educational process. This discussion recommends that a paradigm shift is required in the research and design process of intelligent tutoring systems to involve implementing teachers, and to design these systems as tools for teachers rather than as replacements.

The research on intelligent tutoring systems now spans over three decades, with millions of dollars put in, mostly in America and Europe, with hope that computer systems would be able to teach the students without any further intervention from human teachers. It is somewhat surprising that this research area could attract so much sponsorship from government funding organisations in different countries even when very few industries were interested in putting any money on it.

As on today, the result of this abundant funding and research is that many potential intelligent tutoring system prototypes are out there. Various evaluation studies also seem to confirm that individual students can benefit in their learning process using these systems.

But we do not find any such systems in the actual learning environment. There does not seem to be any enthusiasm on the part of educators, outside computing related disciplines, to adopt these systems in their curriculum. There is also no evidence that commercial organisations are eager to take this research and turn into profitable products. On a closer look, one can find that most evaluation studies were actually done either by the developers of the systems, or by those who evaluated the systems for the developers.

It only seems reasonable to stop for a moment and think, why so much funding and decades of research has resulted in something that has not been used in actual environment for which it was intended? And more so, why such a research could still get funding from here and there (mostly from non-profit avenues such as government agencies) and continues to do so? Is it that people still see this area of research very important for future and therefore non-profit agencies still provide support, but

profit-driven organisations hesitate to put money in it because they do not find the current way of research in this area convincing for getting results that could be used in real environment!

One could argue many reasons for the failure of the adoption of intelligent tutoring systems research. On the outset of it, one thing is very evident: the intelligent tutoring systems research has been driven mostly by the computer scientists. There has been very little or no input in the process from academics of other disciplines. One can readily verify this fact by looking into the author list of the journals and conferences in this area. The academics from other disciplines have been brought from time-to-time in the process of developing these systems, but mostly to elicit their knowledge so that the system could replace them!

Once a system is developed, it becomes like a black box to any outsider (including the academics of the disciplines for whom that particular system is developed). There is very little possibility of customisation in the system on the part of the implementing teacher (the one who is expected to use it in his/her curriculum) except perhaps few pedagogical rules and the chunks of knowledge (learning objects). System designers (primarily computer science academics) somehow perceive that because they teach their students, they know how to teach, and therefore the systems developed by them would and should be acceptable by any other teacher, regardless of the discipline.

The reality is that there have been no major efforts to reverse the cycle and start from looking into the needs of the teaching and learning process of various disciplines. The academics of other disciplines are subjected to "take or leave" situation with no feeling of ownership of the process. The 'Not Developed Here' syndrome prevails, especially when the underlying philosophy of the intelligent tutoring system follows the preferred teaching style of the developer teacher and may not match with that of implementing teacher.

Many people argue that intelligent tutoring systems are expected to be used in self-learning, and therefore should not require any intervention from a teacher. In other words, there should not be any implementing teacher; the systems should be delivered directly from designer teacher to the students. In practice, this is rarely the case, because of both organisational and pedagogical reasons.

Even in highly constructivist environments, the teacher plays various roles including those of providing context, selecting and scheduling other educational technologies, managing the curriculum, and overseeing the learning progression. It is unlikely that a student will use an educational system that is not recommended by the teacher, more so if the teacher actually has negative views about such a system. There are also some issues regarding student's cognitive abilities. The mix of rapidly changing technology and increasing amount of available information, especially the richness of the contextual information, can overload the novice students. It is the implementing teacher who ensures that the learning process is constrained to suit the level at which a particular discipline is learnt. Different teachers would prefer to constrain the learning process in different ways, including defining an appropriate grain size of learning, learning in a situational context or abstract learning that is applied to problems of varied context.

The ongoing debates suggest that the success of intelligent tutoring systems depends to a great extent on how they become powerful tools in the hands of the teachers, and not in the fact that how they could replace the teachers and take over the learning process. Unless intelligent tutoring systems have some mechanism to distinguish between the teaching styles of designing teacher and implementing teacher and facilities to configure the content to suit the implementing teacher's style, they will not find easy acceptance. We suggest that a *human teacher model* should formally be incorporated in the design of an ITS and indeed in any educational system: to recognise the different teaching styles, record the teaching style/s adopted in the design and preferably enable adaptation to suit the implementing teacher. An explicit explanation of the teaching style adopted in the design will not only enable an implementing teacher to understand the designer's rationale but will also help in dealing with the cognitive dissonance arising from any differences in the teaching styles. Similar to student model research, human teacher model will enable the intelligent tutoring systems to adapt themselves to implementer teacher's style, leading to better possibilities of adoption in real academic environments.

Bibliography

1. Kinshuk, Patel, A., Oppermann, R., & Russell, D. (2001). Role of Human Teacher in Web-based Intelligent Tutoring Systems. *Journal of Distance Learning*, 6 (1), 26-35.
2. Patel, A. Kinshuk & Russell, D. (2000). Intelligent Tutoring Tools for Cognitive Skill Acquisition in Life Long Learning. *Educational Technology & Society*, 3 (1), 32-40.
3. Patel, A., Russell, D., Kinshuk, Oppermann, R. & Rashev, R. (1998). An initial framework of contexts for designing usable intelligent tutoring system. *Information Services and Use*, 18 (1-2), 65-76.
4. International Forum of Educational Technology & Society, http://ifets.ieee.org/

Technology Enabled Life Integrated Learning Environments (TELILE)

M.O. Thirunarayanan
Florida International University
Miami, Florida, USA

Abstract

The author dreams of a future, one in which learning is integrated with a people's lives. Technology of the future in the form of a "Technology Enabled Life Integrated Learning Environments" (TELILE) makes such integration possible. The TELILE is itself is a sub-system of the "Worldwide Information, Transactions, and Communications System" (WITCS). In the paper the author provides some examples of how the TELILE tailors education and learning to fit the lives of people.

The WITCS

I had a dream.

In my dream, I was living the good life in the future, one in which practically every device invented by human beings was connected to the "Worldwide Information, Transactions, and Communications System" (WITCS, pronounced the "wits").

The world of the future was divided into two groups, one that had access to the WITCS (the "wits") and the other without (the "witless") such access. I was fortunate to be among the group that had access to the WITCS.

I had just finished my high school requirements and was enrolled as an undergraduate student in a college in a university without any walls. Access to the WITCS made it possible for me to pursue higher education without having to disrupt the routines of my daily life. I did use the WITCS during my elementary, middle, and high school years as well, and my earlier experiences with WITCS will be discussed in another paper.

The WITCS made it possible for me to learn any time of the day or night, and from any place that I happened to be. It was possible for me to learn whenever and I felt the need to learn. It did not matter where I was at that point in time when the urge to learn manifested itself. I did not have to go to college. I did not have to spend many hours every week safely driving to college and spend many more anxious moments trying to find a parking space. There are still buildings that house schools, but students can earn their degrees without ever having to set foot into one. Only those without access to the WITCS go to schools that are geographically confined to one or more buildings.

The college came to me, and it followed me everywhere that I went. All I had to do was enroll in college and continue on with my everyday life. Since my car was WITCS enabled, during the drive to and from the beach, or wherever else I chose to go to telecommute to work, I could be immersed in learning experiences that my professors had prepared just for me. My whole degree program was specifically tailored to meet my needs, and I could complete the requirements for my degree at my own pace. Every other aspect of the world, such as economics, politics, religion, commerce, and leisure, were personalized to meet my needs and suit my interests. How can education be any different?

The TELILE

A sub-system of the WITCS was known as the "Technology Enabled Life Integrated Learning Environments" or TELILE. It was the TELILE that made my education a dream come true. While it was WITCS that made it possible for me to learn anytime from anywhere, and made it possible for school to come to me, instead of me having to go to school, it was TELILE that made it possible for education and learning to be tailored to fit my life.

Since I was fortunate enough to have access to the WITCS, I could use the capabilities of TELILE to learn and educate myself as I lived my everyday life. Unlike my ancestors, I did not have to make a big sacrifice and devote a few years of the prime of my life to higher education. Higher education was integrated into my daily life.

The other day I decided to go skiing. Since my helmet and ski poles were WITCS and TELILE enabled, I could learn a lot of things as I skied down the slopes at 80 miles an hour. By the time I reached the bottom of the mountain, I was able to learn about gravity, friction, motion, force, and air pressure, to name a few topics. During the numerous times that I skied down the slope and the times when I went up the ski lift, I was also able to immerse myself in several virtual, but very realistic learning experiences. These learning experiences were tied to the leisure activity that I had chosen to undertake this particular weekend, namely skiing. My life experiences provided me with the context for the content that I was learning.

The following weekend I learned a lot about geology. I learned to identify different kinds of rocks, conducted incredibly realistic virtual experiments, and was involved in other powerful learning experiences. Guess where I spent that weekend? I was hiking and camping in the mountains. My hiking boots and my backpack were WITCS enabled, thus making it possible for me to access the TELILE.

On another occasion as I was getting a much deserved massage to relieve my stress and soothe my tired muscles, I was able to learn about the human body, and the various systems that comprise the human body. My anatomy and physiology lessons continued during my visits to the dentist, barber, masseuse, and while playing tennis, basketball, or whatever other sport that interested me on any given day and time.

The flexible nature of TELILE made it possible for me to start and stop my learning experiences at will. If necessary, I could also repeat my learning experiences any number of times until I was confident that I could demonstrate my learning on assessment tasks in order to earn and accumulate credit towards my degree requirements.

Human instructors or technological surrogates thereof, were also available 24/7/365 in case I had some questions or felt the need to interact with an instructor-figure. Since the degree program was geared towards my life, and since I was learning at my own pace, I really did not have many classmates. However, it was always possible for me to communicate with other students, who were also completing similar courses around the same time that I was also completing those courses. These classmates were spread all over the world and spoke different languages, but the translation capabilities of TELIE made it possible for classmates to see and speak to each other in their own native tongues. I spoke in my native tongue and TELILE translated my words into as many languages as necessary to make sure that people who were communicating with me understood what I was saying.

TELILE also made it possible for me to search for any information that I needed, just by moving my lips, eyelashes, or other parts of the body depending on the type of WITCS enabled device that I was using at any given point in time. Using speech, body movement or even just thought waves, I could also view, print, and save the information for future use.

Conclusion

As my interests and choice of daily activities changed, TELILE would recognize such changes and start gearing my learning experiences based on my newly developed tastes. TELILE evolved and grew with me, while giving me the opportunity to integrate my living and learning. I did not have to give up one for the sake of the other.

That, in short, was my dream. Or was that a nightmare?

Worldwide Literacy

Frank B. Withrow, Ph.D.
President
A Better Learning Experiences Company
Washington, DC.

The foundation of learning is the development of literacy skills. The National Reading Panel in the United States in reviewed the research on developing reading skills and has provided a list of essential elements in teaching people to read. This list includes phonemic awareness, phonics, fluency, and comprehension. The RAND Reading Study Group developed a program for research and development program in reading comprehension.

One of the key questions is how can computers enhance the teaching of reading? The computer has the flexibility of being able to mix sounds, images and text under the users demand. It is this ability to provide an association of visual and auditory stimuli that makes the computer a potentially effective tool for teaching reading.

Voice activation provides a great leap forward in the ability to associate speech with words. If a young child can speak and the computer transfers that speech to printed words then the child can associate his known vocabulary with the printed word.

If the young child has a computer reading tutor the range of interactions could be limitless. When the child tells the computer a story and it transposes the speech into print the child has a library of his own works,

However, the computer has the potential for even more exciting speech to print interactions. If the computer has on its screen the sentence THE BUTTERFLY FLEW AROUND THE FLOWER the computer can morph the words into images as the child reads aloud the sentence. If the child can not read it they can ask the computer to read it. As the words are said they morph into the images they represent.

Within the computer's dictionary words can appear on the screen. If the word "football" appears the child can ask the computer to "Say it." "Sound it." "Spell it" or Show me." When asked to "Sound it." The computer will give the phonic elements and the appropriate letters will flash. Likewise when the learner asks the computer to "Spell it" the letters will flash as they are named. The "Show me" request results in the word being said and morphing into an image of the word.

I have experimentally developed in the past a series of games that the child can play using these techniques. Within the computer I have created a world of animals and things that the learner can ask to do things. The animated world adheres to scientifically correct aspects of the real world. For example, if the learner asks the frog to swim across a frozen lake the frog will refuse to do so.

The learner has a set number of animals that she can play with and a there are a set of environments that can be used to build stories and animated programs. In my original experiment entry by the learner was through the keyboard. Today with voice activated systems the entry will be by voice. The design of the program is such that we have a limited computer generated environment within the program. The program introduces the animated animals and environments. The learner can call for frogs; elephants and giraffes to interact with the things and objects in the computer stored environments. A learner could ask the elephant to go into the backyard and jump over the trashcan. As the learner requests the character to do something words pop on the screen as they are said. The elephant would refuse to do this and will argue with the learner. Elephants are simply too heavy to jump. Between the learner and the computer there is a voice dialog that takes place with respect to each action. When the desired action is negotiated the computer will summarize with a printed version of what the learner requested. In addition, there will be an animated sequence of the actions requested.

The program is designed to be highly tutorial and interactive with young children using their natural speech patterns as the computer interface.

The design of the program takes advantaged of the young child's natural speech patterns. The four-year-old child has a spoken vocabulary of 2,500 words. This is a doable size for the creation of this program. The program will have a noun dictionary of 300 words that can morph into images, be sounded out phonetically, and spelled. There will be fifty interactive stories that can be activated by voice in the program. Voice, image or text can be used to enter each section of the program. General voice commands will include "Show Me.," Spell it," "Sound it," "Say it" and "Read it to me." The program also includes games and puzzles that are voice activated.

Once the program is developed and tested in English we are working with a group of linguist in Mexico City to transfer this concept to Spanish. Transfers to other languages and cultures will require modification of the artwork and input from linguists sophisticated in the new language. However, we believe that once the program is developed we will have a template that allows us to transfer it to other languages.

The original work will be done with desktop computers, but once we have demonstrated its effectiveness we think it can be transferred to a "GameBoy" handheld device.

Interactions in Computer Aided Instruction Systems to Meet The Changing Goals of Higher Education

Rika Yoshii
Computer Science Department
California State University, San Marcos
(ryoshii@csusm.edu)

Abstract

Goals and challenges in higher education have been changing in recent years. There are more interests in employment-oriented majors such as computer science and bio-technology. More employers want their employees to go back to school to refresh their knowledge in fast changing fields. With these changes, our students are becoming more aware of the importance of developing specific skills and knowledge that employers require. I expect these changes to continue well into the future. This position paper discusses how Computer Aided Instruction (CAI) systems with "high-quality" interactions centered around a reasoning tool will help us meet the changing goals of higher education.[1]

1: CAI: high-quality interactions = learning outcomes + assessment

Several years ago, the California State University system developed ten principles which were designed to form the basis of strategic planning for the University [1]. Teaching in an employment-oriented field in which students seek to advance their skills and knowledge, I was particularly struck with the first of the ten principles - "award the baccalaureate on the basis of demonstrated learning as determined by our faculty." This involves defining the learning objectives for students and evaluating or assessing student learning. Although many feel that this principle should already be part of any education system, it is surprisingly difficult to enforce clear learning objectives as instructors change. University catalogues usually list a number of topics instead of learning outcomes. Assessment of student learning is also a difficult issue. I argue that we should be using assessment tools for two reasons: 1) to understand where the student is having problems so that we can remedy the situation, and 2) to determine whether he/she has mastered the material. Assignments and exams are

---

[1] The author acknowledges that her views expressed in this paper do not necessarily represent those of the California State University.

designed mostly for the second goal. When there are more than ten students in a classroom, it is difficult to use exam results to help each student. Also, in order to cover the required topics within a term, instructors cannot slow down for a small group of students. Moreover, even when the instructor knows that a student has not mastered the material, the student passes the course with incomplete knowledge. The next course will try to build on top of this incomplete foundation.

What changes are required for us to focus on assessment of student learning for the right reasons? Are these changes feasible? I propose a certain kind of Computer Aided Instruction (CAI) as a possible solution. Not all CAI systems can address this problem. However, with CAI, we can embed the learning objectives into the material itself by constantly assessing the student's skills and/or knowledge. Sequences of exercises can be tailored for each student based on the assessment results. No student will move onto the next material until the system is satisfied with her performance. Interactions that obtain enough information about the student to make such assessments are "high-quality" interactions.

2: Development, changing roles, changing reward systems

Is it feasible to create a "high-quality" CAI system for every course? Will it be possible to update it frequently? If we can develop an "authoring tool" that ensures high-quality interactions and little programmer involvement, the answer is "yes." In fact, the Script Editor and Script Interpreter in the Irvine-Geneva strategy [2][3] were designed with this goal. However, more research is needed to allow a variety of pedagogical features.

How will the instructors' roles change? Instead of preparing written documents for their courses, they will prepare pedagogical designs for their CAI systems. Instead of lecturing, they will be supplementing their systems through additional human-to-human interactions with the students. They will share their experiences and views which are not part of specific learning objectives.

They will also advise students based on the system's evaluation of the students. Students will see their instructors more as mentors and advisors than as just a knowledge source.

Will reward systems need to change? Yes, although this is difficult, the administrators will have to develop criteria and tools to evaluate and reward the instructors not only for the hours they spend in their classrooms but for the quality of the systems they have designed and for their effectiveness as mentors and advisors.

3: Importance of reasoning tools

There is one essential ingredient that controls the success of these systems: the teachers who design the materials. The teachers themselves must have clear learning objectives, must be able to create interactive conversational exercises, must believe in assessing the students to help the students, and must know how to assess student learning.

In our experience in designing CAI systems with good teachers, we often hear anecdotes about some teachers not being able to explain to their students why something works the way it does. In many cases, they themselves learned the material through drill and practice without understanding the fundamental concepts. They can pass on the steps to their students but cannot explain why these steps work. This problem manifests itself in introductory Computer Science classrooms. The students know how to solve algebra problems as presented in math textbooks but do not know how to use the knowledge to analyze computer algorithms. When the students understand only the steps but not the underlying concepts, they cannot apply the knowledge to new situations. With fast changing fields, it is more important than ever for our students to be able to apply knowledge to new situations.

I propose that we always give our students "reasoning models", tools with which they can understand how something works the way it does. I have incorporated the use of reasoning tools in all of the recent systems I have developed. In DaRT (Diagrammatic Reasoning Tool for learning English articles), situational diagrams are used as reasoning tools to explain when to use definite versus indefinite articles [4]. In the ELM Preparation System, diagrams depicting situations as described in word problems are used as reasoning tools to explain how to solve distance-rate-time problems. In the C++ Tracer System, the memory content changes visibly

as each line of a C++ program is executed [5], training the student to view a program as an executor of instructions. We are currently developing a reasoning tool to help ESL students learn countability of nouns: when an ESL student encounters a brand new word, how will she be able to tell whether it is countable or non-countable?

The reasoning tools were designed with the following goals: 1) We want the students to develop reasoning skills so that they can apply the skills in brand new situations they had not encountered before. 2) The reasoning tools can be used as common communication tools for students and teachers (or CAI systems) to discuss and explore their understanding of the material. 3) The CAI systems can assess not just the surface-level performance but the in-depth understanding of the material. 4) The students will be able to explain their understanding, or reasoning, to the next generation of students.

4: Conclusion

To focus on student learning outcomes for fast changing fields, future CAI systems for higher education must have the following ingredients 1) interactions to allow individualization, 2) assessment of mastery, and 3) interactions centering around reasoning tools. With reasoning tools, we can foster the next generation of teachers who will help us develop CAI systems with high-quality interactions.

5: References

[1] California State University, "Cornerstones Report", http://www.calstate.edu/Cornerstones, 1998.

[2] A. Bork, et al., "The Irvine-Geneva Course Development System", *Proceedings of IFIP*, Madrid, Spain, September, 1992, pp. 253-261.

[3] R. Yoshii, X.Wu, and Y.Miao, *Tools in Java for Conversational Tutoring : Script Editor and Script Interpreter*, California State University, San Marcos, 2001.

[4] R. Yoshii, "DaRT: A CALL System to Help Students Practice and Develop Reasoning in Choosing English Articles", *CALICO Journal*, Fall 1998, vol. 16, no. 2, pp. 121-155.

[5] R. Yoshii, and A. Milne, "C++ Tracer for CS111", http://courses.csusm.edu/cs111am/ Tracer/CppTraceProMain.html, 2002.

Critical Elements of Successful Faculty Development
In Information and Communication Technology

Mario A. Kelly
Hunter College of the City University of New York

The almost infinite potential educational uses of information and communication technology (ICT) will only be realized when most teachers have sufficient knowledge and skills to truly integrate ICT into their curricula, utilizing it to make teaching and learning more effective and efficient. For this to be accomplished teachers must experience the integration of ICT into their own pre-service learning as well as into the pedagogical skills they are taught. Teacher education faculty responsible for the pre-service experience of teachers must themselves develop high levels of knowledge, integrative skills, and comfort with ICT. It is the professional development of teacher education faculty that is the focus of this paper. The critical elements of successful faculty development in ICT presented here are drawn from the experiences and evaluation of roughly a year and a half of providing development activities for the faculty of a large, public, urban school of education in the Eastern United States.

At the start of the project the most common uses of technology reported by faculty were word processing and accessing e-mail. Due to lack of knowledge most required assistance to complete a modified version of the School Hardware Technology Survey [1] describing the basic features of their office computer hardware and software.

The principal immediate goal of the project was for the faculty to acquire specific basic knowledge and skills regarding computer hardware and software. The principal medium-range goal was that faculty would develop technology related products or projects that would result in more effective and/or efficient teaching and learning of a unit of a teacher education course. A long range-goal was the modification of the teacher education curriculum to reflect greater integration of technology and to meet technology standards of various professional organizations and government agencies.

The main focus of the intervention was the provision of staff development activities to increase the faculty's level of ICT proficiency and enable faculty to integrate technology into coursework. Development activities followed a constructivist model that included the following elements: hands-on workshops, project-based learning, and learning teams of mutually supportive

members. Central to the model was the requirement that each faculty member develop a technology product to improve the effectiveness and efficiency of teaching and learning one unit of a course they were currently teaching. On the basis of a range of data—survey questionnaires, focus group discussions, individual interviews—the following have been identified as critical elements to successful faculty development in ICT.

1. Clear, Specific, ICT Standards-Based Objectives

Development activities work best when they are tied to meeting ICT state, national and/or professional organization standards and these are articulated in terms of performance outcomes. In the case of our project we focused on the standards of the International Society for Technology in Education (ISTE), and required that faculty develop technology projects to assist faculty and pre-service teachers to meet ISTE standards for teachers and help K-12 students meet their respective standards.

2. Basic Knowledge about Hardware and Software

For faculty with very limited knowledge about ICT the fear of damaging equipment can be high. The result can be great hesitance to engage in trial and error experimentation which is one of the best ways to learn. It is therefore important that development activities start by providing basic knowledge and skills about the hardware and software to minimize the fear of experimentation. In our project, following numerous requests for individual assistance by faculty who lacked the most basic knowledge about hardware and software we developed several tutorials.

3. Project/Problem Based Learning

Faculty are most likely to acquire ICT knowledge and skills when it is tied to their content areas of teaching and research, when they identify specific ways in which ICT can be used to improve teaching and learning in their own content area, and when they are assisted to identify, modify or create specific products that are tailored to their unique needs. In our project faculty were provided with a set of guidelines to facilitate this process. Perhaps the most important of these was that they identify a specific course and component of the course, the teaching and learning of which would be made more effective and/or more efficient by the incorporation of ICT.

4. Hands-On Workshops and Ongoing Technical Support

Hands-on workshops that engaged the faculty at the start of their development activities were very important. Even more important however, was ongoing technical support as they engaged in identifying their ICT needs and creating their projects. Of particular importance in our project was having an ICT specialist who was not only very knowledgeable about technology, but was an effective and patient teacher who made faculty feel comfortable from the standpoint of their limited technology knowledge as he helped them acquire new skills.

5. Effective Incentives

In many respects the "rewards" provided to faculty for developing ICT knowledge and skills may be the most critical element. Of the range of possible rewards the most effective may be psychological and social ones (e.g. meeting state, national and professional organization standards, or keeping up with colleagues who are using technology), rather than the economic ones (e.g. being released from teaching a course during or following the acquisition of ICT skills). In our project the first of two groups of faculty who signed up for ICT development activities did so largely out of interest in keeping abreast of changes in the field of education and the desire to improve their teaching and professional knowledge. The fact that we offered the incentive of a course release at the end of the process did not seem to be their primary motivation, since many were not even aware of the incentive when they first agreed to participate. The salience of the psychological and social incentives was even greater for the second group of faculty. Having directly and indirectly heard about the experiences of the first group for an entire semester, the 2nd group was so eager to participate that many engaged in precursor activities such as taking workshops on their own so that they would be better prepared when the development activities started.

References

The project described here was funded by a grant from the U.S. Department of Education.

1. U.S. Department of Education (1998). An educator's guide to evaluating the use of technology in schools and classrooms. Washington, DC: Office of Educational Research and Improvement.

Designing Enhanced Learning Environments on the Web – the challenge

Kar Tin Lee
Hong Kong Institute of Education
Email: ktlee@ied.edu.hk

Abstract

Creating enhanced learning environments based on the opportunities offered by the Internet has become a hotly debated topic among educators. It is certainly true that many educational research and ICT projects have reported a variety of outcomes and lessons learned with regard to these powerful new media and how teachers can effectively integrate technology into learning and teaching, but there has been little public debate about the nature of these opportunities or how they might most effectively be introduced.

1. Introduction

This contribution offers some early experience from a project conducted in Hong Kong schools and is designed to stimulate such a debate.

Initial experiences of the project demonstrates that ICT can be used to enhance students' learning experiences. However, it confirms that many questions have to be answered first before we could even contemplate the use of ICT in all its' forms to encourage teachers, students and parents to tap into the potential for learning.

The Challenge

In this paper three key questions are posed for discussion.

- *Creative Teachers* - How can teachers become creative instructional designers when teaching on the web?
- *Change* – Are teachers willing to change their current traditional practice to incorporate collaborative learning strategies and online communities into their web-based learning environment?
- *Control* - How will teachers "let-go" and encourage their students to be more self-directed and highly motivated learners?

Creative Design of Online Learning Environments

In the past few years many schools in Hong Kong have gained greater access to ICT due to government support, but, in essence they have changed little as yet, in their basic approach to teaching and learning. Students rarely use computers either for content-area learning tasks in general or for a large portion of the time spent on any single learning task. When used in any subject area for instance Chinese, English, mathematics or general studies, ICT is likely to be focused on the acquisition of factual information rather than higher-order thinking and problem-solving. To a great extent teachers are still using the ICT tool as the equivalent of a glorified blackboard or as a replacement for paper-based charts and materials.

When probed about how teachers used ICT with their students, they were more likely to describe the use of software applications as enrichment or remediation rather than regular instruction. For students, skills in using IT are developed in Computer Literacy classes (skills like keyboarding, Chinese character input, basic computer operations, using email, searching the WWW, using the intranet), but students spend little time applying these skills in meaningful projects or cross-curricular activities.

With the commencement of the project teachers were consistently steered away from the one-size-fits-all approach and all activities were focused specifically on catering for individual students. It adopted the framework that ICT has the potential to cater for differing learning styles and individual learners' experiences and could in time enhance the learning opportunities of all students. It is a model in which learning is enabled by the most appropriate means and modes, whether it is face–to–face in a traditional classroom with one computer, in a computer laboratory or learning online from home. This model makes accessing learning easier, providing a range of content materials and learning activities at any time and accessible from any place.

Therefore in order to facilitate true integration of ICT across the curriculum it was vital that teachers had to, firstly, appreciate that integration has rich potential for enabling more effective learning where the technology is subordinated to the learning goals of the school. Secondly, teachers had to reach this level of understanding before they would critically and creatively select the appropriate digital content based on the needs and learning styles of their students and infuse it into the curriculum. If and when this paradigm occurred, teachers would then be more sensitive to the kinds of learning that students engage in and can critically examine the implications for the management of learning and the effects on students' attitudes and perceptions of the task in hand.

The project has persistently tried very hard to make teachers think about classrooms without walls so that they are ready to realize the potential of the online learning environment. However, at the present time, despite the technology changes teachers in schools are still to a great extent using the same approach and acting as the information giver. Breaking away from traditional approaches to instruction means taking risks and it has indeed taken a long time for teachers to recognize the value of using ICT and to become fully committed to the view that information is available from sources that go well beyond textbooks and themselves. As change agents teachers must proactively help students understand and make use of the many ways in which they can gain access to information and how to make use of this information in a meaningful way. At the very least teachers increasingly need to employ a wide range of technological tools and software as part of their own instructional repertoire. Teachers need to "think outside of the box".

The following were found to be particularly important. When introducing the online environment in schools, all teachers needed to:

- emphasize content and pedagogy not the level of sophistication with hardware and technical skills;
- engage students in meaningful and relevant learning;
- allow students to construct knowledge;
- devise alternative ways of assessing student work; and
- cater for individual learning differences.

Teachers had to realize that use of this environment must go hand in hand with the integrative approach and must be accompanied by the teacher's keen interest in expanded paradigms as they relate to the roles of teachers and students. Learners must be encouraged to construct, evaluate, manipulate, and present their ideas while demonstrating understanding of curriculum concepts and innovate constructs.

Clearly all educators are convinced that teachers need to inculcate the willingness to learn, to rethink and re-structure teaching and learning. But are teachers ready to be creative, be prepared to change and most importantly, to give up control? They must first learn enough about the relevant technologies to apply them in their professional live, and to translate them to their students as part of the integrated learning of the subject matter. In

this knowledge-base age teachers and students need to learn how to learn in an ICT rich environment.

In discussions with teachers another focal point was the methods used to assess learning in and out of class. When using the online environment teachers could assess learning as it is occurring, rather than separating assessment from learning. It was important for teachers to reconceptualize their ways of assessing, in order to focus not only on what students have learned (their knowledge), but also on the ways that students learn. Assessing the strategies and tactics that students use to learn will assist teachers to predict how well they will be able to learn and solve problems in new situations. This aspect was not easy to do.

Since the announcement of the Five-Year Information Technology Strategy [1], there is no doubt, that this, coupled with the recent education reform agenda calls for fundamental changes in teaching practices on the part of all teachers. However, at present the constraints of the classroom and the curriculum are still very evident, and the demands made on teachers extremely high. Many issues are being dealt with at present but many conflicts between the old and the new are only starting to surface and may not be resolved so quickly. Teachers may have to rationalize the content of their syllabus and may have to admit that some of the old content will just have to go.

A final word

The online integrated learning environment created in these Hong Kong primary schools has so far provided teachers with an option that will allow them to shift from a culture of textbook based teaching and learning to an online environment where students are motivated and want to learn. It is a model that we hope students will use and see it as second nature. It is about opening up options for parents, teachers and students to see the potential and the impact of new technologies. As Dale Spender suggested 'new technologies provide the learner (or customer) with an extraordinary range of choices that they can 'do things with' rather than simply memorise or learn" [2].

References

[1] Education Manpower Bureau (1998), Information Technology for Learning in a New Era - Five-Year Strategy 1998/99 to 2002/03, Education Department Hong Kong.

[2] Spender, D. at the Global Summit, Adelaide, 4th March, 2002.

New Ways of Learning Mathematics: Are we Ready for it?

Rod Nason
Queensland University of Technology
Australia

Earl Woodruff
OISE-University of Toronto
Canada

Abstract

In this paper, we report on a research project in progress in which we are attempting to establish and maintain an ICT-mediated math knowledge-building community. The paper first identifies why math knowledge-building communities are very difficult to establish and maintain and then provides evidence to support that these difficulties can be overcome by the inclusion of model-eliciting problems and new iconic math representation tools into the CSCL environment.

One of the most promising new ways of learning that has been ushered in by Information and Communication Technology (ICT) has been the Bereiter and Scardamalia's [1] notion of schools as knowledge-building communities where students are engaged in producing conceptual artefacts (e.g., ideas, models, principles, relationships, theories, interpretations etc.) that can be discussed, tested, compared, hypothetically modified and so forth and the students see their main job as producing and improving such objects, not simply the completion of school tasks.

Anecdotal evidence from teachers and from formal evaluation studies indicates that the notion of schools as knowledge-building communities has been successfully applied in many subject areas such as social studies, art, history, geography, language arts and science [1]. However, during the course of our seven-year research program in which we have been investigating ICT-mediated mathematics knowledge-building communities [2], we have identified two major reasons to explain why the establishment and maintenance of knowledge-building communities has not been successful in the area of mathematics.

First, there is the inability of most "school" math problems to elicit ongoing discourse and other knowledge-building activity either <u>during</u> or <u>after</u> the process of solving the problem. Most "school" math problems require the students to produce "an answer" and not a complex conceptual artefact such as that generally required by most authentic math problems found in the world outside of school. Most school math problems thus do not require multiple cycles of designing, testing and refining that occurs during the production of complex conceptual artefacts. School math problems therefore do not elicit the collaboration between people each with special abilities that most authentic math problems outside of the school elicit. Another factor that limits the potential of school math problems for eliciting ongoing discourse and other knowledge-building activities is the nature of the answer produced by these types of problems. Unlike complex conceptual artefacts that provide students with much stimuli 6r ongoing discourse and other knowledge-building activity, the answers generated from school math problems do not provide students with much worth discussing. Once they have produced the answer, they feel it is time to move onto the next problem.

Second, there are the limitations of ICT-based mathematical representation tools. Unlike almost every other discipline, mathematics relies on a variety of interacting systems (e.g., concrete models, pictorial models, natural language and mathematical symbols) to represent its corpus of knowledge. Therefore, in order to be able to solve mathematical problems and then be able to adequately communicate their reasoning processes and justification of solutions to others in an ICT-based math learning community, students need to have recourse to tools that enable them to:

1. Dynamically represent a problem in concrete, pictorial, natural language and math symbolic forms; Transparently and dynamically translate within and between representation modes during problem solving; and

2. Utilise multiple forms of representation when engaging in ICT-mediated discourse with other students and their teachers. Unfortunately, most current ICT-based mathematical representation tools do not meet these three criteria.

Therefore, if mathematics educators are to be ready to exploit the potentially powerful new ways of learning mathematics being provided by ICT-mediated knowledge-building communities, we would argue that the following artefacts need to be designed and integrated into Computer-Supported Collaborative Learning (CSCL) Environments such as *Knowledge Forum*®:

1. Model-eliciting problems that involve students in the production of models or other conceptual tools for constructing, describing, explaining, manipulating, predicting and controlling complex systems. And

2. Iconic mathematical representation tools that: (a) enable students to adequately represent mathematical problems and to translate within and across representation modes during problem-solving, and (b) facilitate student-student, and teacher-student hypermedia-mediated discourse.

In the Hypatia research project [3], we are designing and evaluating such artefacts and integrating them into the *Knowledge Forum®* CSCL environment. In this project, students in an Australian and a Canadian school are being posed similar model-eliciting problems. Then via the means of *Knowledge Forum®*, the Canadian and Australian students are presenting their models, commenting on one another's models, and iteratively revising their models based on these comments. This is providing us with opportunities to evaluate and modify our math problems and iconic tools and also to engage in the analysis of inter-group data--with a condition that looks at cross-country/cultural configurations as a means of assisting us in refining our pedagogical approach.

References

[1] Scardamalia, M. & Bereiter, C. (1996). Adaption and understanding: A case for new cultures of schooling. In S. Vosniadou, E. De Corte, R. Glaser, & H. Mandel (Eds.), *International perspectives on the psychological foundations of technology-based learning environments* (pp. 149-165). Mahwah, NJ : Lawrence Erlbaum.
[2] Nason, R.A., Brett, C., Woodruff, E. (1996). Creating and maintaining knowledge-building communities of practice during mathematical investigations. In P. Clarkson (Ed.) *Technology in mathematics education* (pp. 20-29). Melbourne: Mathematics Education Research Group of Australasia.
[3] Nason, R, Woodruff, E, & Lesh, R. (2001-03). *Overcoming the impasse: Creating computer-supported collaborative-learning (CSCL) environments that actually facilitate sustained discourse and knowledge-building in the domain of mathematics.* Research Project funded by the Australian Research Council Large Grants Scheme.

Comprehensive Learning Interactive and Group Activities as New Ways of Learning

Toshio Okamoto

The Graduate School of Information Systems, University of Electronics and Communications
okamoto@ai.is.uec.ac.jp

1. Responsible Assignment study as group project for Learning

At first, it is basic to memorize/understand technical knowledge/concept related to Information Technology and acquire fundamental skills of IT, but still more basic and important objective is to foster children's/students' active study attitude with which they cope with assignment study with interest and curiosity to solve as group project.

The main purpose of "**Assignment study**" is to make students think actively the given assignment-appropriate assignment related to subjects crossing various fields and daily events-through long period. They set, seek and solve a problem, which draws their curiosity and interest, with information techniques so that they naturally increase their problem solving ability and creativity, and eventually master the thinking of information science and problem solving methods. As this responsible assignment study aims at the students active thinking, it is desirable to go through the following steps.

(1) Finding and setting a problem.
(2) Giving the problem a good thinking(awareness/ consciousness).
(3) Drawing a strategy/ tactic to solve the problem.
(4) Formalization (modeling).
(5) Corresponding the problem with an actual event.
(6) Processing and handling.
(7) Analysis, testing and verification.
(8) Judgement
(9) Summarizing and report/ presentation.

Going through each step actively, students are expected to increase their study activity in which they cope with a problem and do a final report with their own responsibility. Also, it is expected that through these activities they put on the information science viewpoint, thinking, research ability and skills based on information science.

Presentation is no less important as it shows the level of skill with which students summarize what they have been doing with their assignment study. Presentation can be graded by the contents, manner/form, attitudes of the presentation, etc.

In this assignment study, it is required to increase such skills and attitudes of students as follows. The presentation which shows the result of the assignment study appropriately is included naturally.

a. the skill to analyze the problem and to build a system to achieve the goal.
b. the skill to build/implement a system appropriate to a given specification.
c. the skill and attitude to evaluate one's own system or others' objectively.
d. the skill to describe what should be reported with correctness.
e. the attitude to probe the problem and to manage to solve it.

It is highly required to build such information science research skills based upon the above points of view. As stated above, there are various opinions from various standpoints about how IT-education should be and what should be basic views. However, we live in a society where we have more chance than ever in our history to face varieties of technology due to the information technology growing so much in our everyday life. Also, the advancement of IT-education is a worldwide trend so much that we should acknowledge the utmost importance of this trend to give the future generation the power to survive in this information society internationally. And to do our best to make it is an important stepping stone.

2. Comprehensive Study

Varieties of knowledge will be taking a form of multimedia in a highly technological, network society. And this knowledge can be obtained through so-called VOD(Video On Demand). Moreover, wide varieties of educational applications and teaching systems will be provided. The problem, however, is that we need ability to grasp the essence of that knowledge. Also this knowledge should not be enclosed just in a human understanding of the existent world. An ability to create a new knowledge out of that understanding is sought now. The knowledge in a closed text book will be transferred to this real world. It is important to form a live knowledge. To make science and technology attractive to the youth needs a synthesizing pipe, that is, a systematic resource to totally canalize scientific minded to that new knowledge.

This view is reflected in the revolution of educational curriculum in countries like Britain, the United States, Canada, Australia, New Zealand, etc. In this Post-Modern age, our new learning viewpoint is as follows.

(1) Group modeling and collaboration for social activities.
(2) Exploration-minded experimental learning.
(3) Learning (urged) by asking, explaining and teaching to make a new insight.
(4) Interactive diagnosis and open learning model.

These points had better be integrated in IT-education. Also, it is assumed that there are well-structured world (the world inside a text book) and ill-structured world (the world outside a text book). The important thing here is learning outside a text book, that is learning without any assumption, and learning (modal logic of thinking) with no guarantee of linearity (ever changing with time and environmental element) in a self-fixed assumption. A curriculum which synthesizes knowledge to do scientific cogitation and knowledge to explore the unknown is needed. The place and resource to grow and teach this kind of knowledge is a crucial point for us. "How", "Why", and "What", the soliloquy, the self pursuing, and the self explaining learning give an opportunity to present scientific cogitation. It is significant to create such a new, comprehensive and information science subject on the threshold of the twenty

first century.

To summarize the thinking view for the comprehensive subject;

(1) topic oriented structure : contents are synthesized according to topics. Many topics are organized systematically, and make comprehensive contents as new learning ways.
(2) scenario oriented structure: making scenario-like contents, and offering well balanced unit subjects.
(3) minimum essentials: extracting minimum, essential unit subjects as "informatics for all" and making comprehensive subject together with other common subjects.
(4) comprehensive subject based on existential subjects: integrated subject, making comprehensive section taking units as thought necessary from other subjects such as math, science and so on.

These are views to make comprehensive subject. Therefore, it is hard to say what is best. Information technology, however, is a familiar matter so that it should be something attractive to children/ students' mind. It should not be something which sounds fictitious.

Fig.1 shows the Knowledge Mining oriented Learning Model as New Ways of Learning.

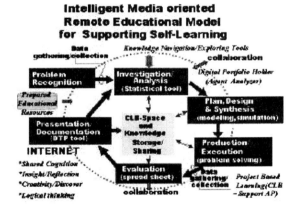

Fig.1 Learning Model

Organisational Critical Success Factors for Managing eLearning Implementation

Maggie McPherson
Department of Information Studies, University of Sheffield

Abstract

Since all formal eLearning programmes exist within an organisational context, such as universities, corporations or virtual learning institutes, it is clear that the organisation has the power to facilitate or to control development of eLearning courses. By imposing corporate views on course philosophies, learning models and strategies, it can restrict feasible pedagogical models. Through management of the educational setting, and decisions regarding the availability of resources, the organisational context also influences the design of courses and may restrict possible modes of evaluation. Therefore, the organisational context is critical to the success of the eLearning setting in which tutors, learners, courses and ICT are integrated.

Introduction and Background

The purpose of this paper is to discuss issues relating to the management of online distance education programmes. The term 'distance education' is normally associated with courses that are not wholly delivered using traditional face-to-face, on-campus lectures within HE (Higher Education). Nowadays, the use of new Information and Communication Technologies (ICT) as a delivery vehicle has led to the term being interchangeably used with terms such as: *Open Learning, Networked Learning, Virtual Learning* and the very recent *eLearning*.

The Use of ICT to Support Learning

Numerous authors [1, 2, 3] have discussed the benefits of ICT course delivery for learners, tutors and institutions. Technology has been used as a means of electronically distributing course material; allowing flexibility for students' favoured learning styles, pace, etc. and giving greater access to information; as well as enabling remote communication between students and tutors, and between student peer groups. On the course management side, it can allow greater communication with the course team and provides flexibility to maintain and up-date course material and documentation.

Research Approaches to Facilitate Educational Management

Action research is thought to be an appropriate approach for investing issues relating to the management of distance learning. In order to accommodate the new challenges posed by eLearning, McPherson and Nunes [4] reflected on work by authors such as Coghlan and Brannick [5], who suggest action research results from spiral research cycles, starting with a process of identifying a problem area – a *pre-step* often based on the previous experience in the field of the researcher. The actual cycle comprises *Diagnosis* (data gathering, analysis and representation), *Action Planning, Action Taking*, and *Action Evaluation* as shown in Fig. 1.

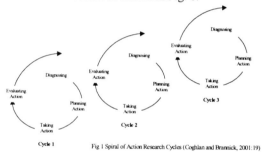

Fig 1 Spiral of Action Research Cycles (Coghlan and Brannick, 2001:19)

An important step in the creation of a specific model for educational management was that of an initial framework proposed and discussed by Goodyear [6] and Khakhar [6]. However, as Goodyear acknowledged, this was merely a preliminary model for discussion that did not address some of the numerous complex relationships and processes involved since it did not accommodate evaluation and persistent improvement vital to successful eLearning programmes. An important point to note is that assessment, although generally an integral part of any programme, it is only part of evaluation and should not be considered as evaluation *per sé* [7].

Accordingly, building on work by Goodyear and Khakhar, and based on seven years of action research at the University of Sheffield, McPherson and Nunes developed a new model to incorporate the essential element of evaluation (Fig.2 overleaf). The Educational Management Action Research (EMAR) model is based upon ongoing evaluation of the MA in

Information Technology Management programme offered by the Department of Information Studies.

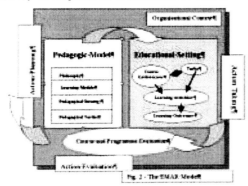

Fig. 2 - The SMAI Model

Organisational Context

Research into online and distance education indicates that the use of ICT learning approaches has generated a number of new issues relating to course delivery, and more importantly, to programme management. However, since most academics involved in setting up distance education programmes have tended to concentrate on teaching and learning issues, rather than on management issues, as yet there is very little research incorporating this important facet of eLearning implementation.

For example, through the means of decisions made at an executive level, organisations have the power to facilitate or to control development of eLearning courses by imposing administrative or financial procedures. Corporate views on course philosophies, learning models and strategies can also either enable or constrain the development of feasible pedagogical models.

At a departmental level, the organisational context also influences the design of courses. For example, through decisions regarding the availability of resources, management of the educational setting can be affected and may restrict possible modes of delivery or evaluation.

Conclusions

To conclude, experiences of managing the MA in IT Management show that the organisational context is critical to the success of the eLearning setting in which tutors, learners, courses and ICT are integrated..

Nevertheless, it is important to reflect whether the lessons learned from this particular programme can be relevant to other distance learning courses, as a generalisation from one single case study.

Theory is usually based on a multiple set of experiments, which have replicated the same phenomenon under different conditions. It is now necessary to conduct further research on other comparable courses in order to verify these initial findings, since scientific facts are rarely based on single experiments Yin [9].

Bibliography

[1] Stamatis, D.; Kefalas, P. & Kargidis, T. (1999) "A Multi-Agent Framework to Assist Networked Learning", *Journal of Computer Assisted Learning*, 15(3), 201-210.

[2] Nunes, J. M. and Fowell, S. P. (1996) "Hypermedia as an experimental learning tool: a theoretical model", *Information Research New,* 6(4), 1996, 15-27.

[3] Eisenstadt, M. and Vincent, T (Eds) (1998) *The knowledge web: Learning and collaborating on the Net.* London: Kogan Page

[4] McPherson, M., and Baptista Nunes, J.M.; "An Action Research Model for Persistent Improvement of Continuing Professional Distance Education (CPDE) Programmes" (2002) In *Proceedings of the Second Research Workshop of the European Distance Education Network (EDEN) on Research and Policy in Open and Distance Learning*, University of Hildescheim, Hildescheim, Germany, 21-23 March 2002, 7-11.

[5] Coghlan, D. & Brannick, T. (2001) *Doing Action Research in Your Own Organisation.* London: Sage Publications, Ltd.

[6] Goodyear, P. (1999) *Pedagogical Frameworks and Action Research in Open and Distance Learning*, Lancaster Univ.: CSALT, Working Paper 99-4-1, http://domino.lancs.ac.uk/edres/csaltdocs.nsf

[7] Khakar, D. (2000) *Guidelines for Evaluation of the Framework.* In Wills, C.; Quirchmayr, G.; Pernul, G. & Khakhar, D. (eds.) *Evaluation of Frameworks for Open and Distance Learning*, Socrates Project Report 3, 56605-CP-1-99-SE-ODL-ODL.

[8] McPherson, M. and Baptista Nunes, J.M. (2001) "The role of evaluation processes in professional continuing education programmes: a case study" In *Proceedings of the University of the 21st Century: an International Conference* sponsored by UNESCO, Muscat, Sultanate of Oman, 17-19 March 2001.

[9]Yin, R. 1989, *Case Study Research: Design and* Methods, Revised Edition, London, Sage Publications

Learning Technologies Critical Success Factors for eLearning Implementation: Educational Technology Interoperability Standards

Sarah Currier & Lorna M. Campbell
University of Strathclyde

Abstract

As communications and information technology becomes ubiquitous in the delivery and management of education, the need for interoperability standards has become a high priority. Standards facilitate the description, packaging, sequencing and delivery of educational content, learning activities and learner information, to enable their sharing and reuse, and their compatibility with future technologies As such, standards are arguably the key critical success factor for enabling technologies in elearning. Development of these standards is an iterative process, requiring testing and feedback from implementers and end users. The UK's CETIS offers a model for educational community engagement with the emerging standards.

1: Introduction

The evolution of learning technologies has gone through many phases in recent decades, from early mainframe based systems, through CD-ROM based resources, to the current Internet explosion, which has brought web-based systems and virtual learning environments. For much of this time, little thought was given to enabling learning resources to survive the continual, rapid changes in technology. For example, many excellent learning materials are locked into CD-ROM based delivery. Additionally, sharing and repurposing of elearning resources has not been much considered, until recently. These factors have meant that much valuable content is underused. Those offering technology-supported learning sometimes waste precious time and money reinventing the digital wheel.

Other educational applications of technology suffer similarly. For instance, student records are often stored in proprietary formats, making it difficult or impossible to transfer them between different suppliers' systems.

Ultimately, teachers want to find content easily wherever it might be, and incorporate it into their courses according to their own pedagogical approach. They also wish to deliver elearning with good information support from administrative systems. Learners want to move between institutions taking their learning records with them. Under increasing pressure, they need efficient access to all the resources they require for their learning. And educational administrators wish to join the global education marketplace, and reach a widening audience of diverse learners, in the most economical ways possible. The development of international standards, which enable these requirements to be met is, arguably, the key critical success factor for enabling technologies.

2: Interoperability standards

IEEE defines interoperability as: "The ability of two or more systems or components to exchange information and to use the information that has been exchanged" [1].

Standards are often confused with specifications. A standard is a recognized technology, format or method that has been ratified by a recognised standards body, e.g. international bodies ISO (International Standards Organisation), CEN (Comité Européen de Normalisation) or IEEE, or national bodies such as BSI (British Standards Institute).

Specifications have not been ratified by these official bodies, but can be useful in achieving de facto standardisation in the interim between identifying a need, and the relevant standard being ratified. IMS is a key developer of interoperability specifications. For instance, they developed the IMS Learning Resource Meta-data specification, which contributed to the IEEE Learning Object Metadata, which has recently become a standard.

3: Challenges

There are challenges involved in encouraging uptake of these standards and specifications, particularly in these early days of their development.

One is that implementation represents a cost for suppliers of learning technologies and resources. Enabling reuse or sharing of materials is a commercial issue for them. A user may, for instance, wish to buy a content management system. If the system is standards compliant, the user's content will not be locked into it, and they will be free to choose a different standards compliant system in the future.

The second challenge arises from the concerns of teachers regarding control over the pedagogical delivery of learning materials. The priorities that different specifications and standards make can represent a bias towards one educational approach. Moreover, the evolving learning object economy implied by the use of standards [2], where learning resources are disaggregated and shared, equivalent to the industrial age, which made inexpensive goods available to many, raises similar concerns, particularly in higher education.

Thirdly, there are challenges at the level of developing an elearning resource. At a time when budgets are tight, some may see using standards as an altruistic act, which they don't have time or money for. Others may feel that the use of specifications which are under development is unnecessarily difficult while problems are still being ironed out. Until critical mass is reached in the use of standards and specifications, and until users of standards can clearly see that they are enabling seamless sharing and reuse, encouraging their uptake is a challenge.

4: Meeting the challenges

In each of the above three areas of difficulty, potential solutions may be found in the engagement of, and cooperation within, educational communities in the development of standards.

In the case of supplier compliance, pressure applied to businesses by a significant number of customers is an effective way of ensuring that user needs are prioritised. If those customers are confused about what they need, or fail to ensure that a similar message is relayed across the board, suppliers will be understandably unable to make valid commercial decisions.

Secondly, where the concerns of teachers are an issue, it should be emphasised that the design of learning technology specifications and standards is an iterative process. Developing standards must be tested in the real world of elearning, and the experiences and needs of implementers and end users must be fed back into the development process. Ultimately, standards should make teachers' jobs easier, not take control of their teaching away from them.

Finally, implementing standards requires planning, time, and an understanding of what is required and why. Quick, reliable access to information about the appropriate standards and their implementation, including access to expert advice and exemplars of good practice, is vital.

5: Engaging user communities: CETIS

CETIS (Centre for Educational Technology Interoperability Standards) was set up by government funding body JISC to support and advise UK higher and further education, and to represent these communities on learning technology standards and specifications bodies.

CETIS has a small central organisation, with six special interest groups (SIGs): Accessibility; Assessment; Educational Content; Metadata; Learner Information & Enterprise; and Further Education. The SIGs are coordinated by individuals based throughout the UK, but their real value lies in the wide networks of interested parties that make up their membership,

which includes learning technologists, teachers, librarians, computer programmers, etc. The SIGs run discussion forums where questions can be put to the most appropriate expert; they hold regular events, with practical demo's of implementations, discussion of issues, and reports from standards bodies; and they fund small scale tasks. The CETIS website, which received a glowing review in Technology Source, covers international news, provides definitions of terminology and acronyms, and gives open access to the results of CETIS funded work.

CETIS as a model is dependent to some extent on the structure of education in the UK. However, it has successfully used the SIG structure to build and support communities of practice, providing a basis for meeting the challenges outlined above.

6: Conclusion: Critical Success Factors

Many factors contribute to successful delivery of elearning. However, in thinking about what is critical to successful use of enabling technologies, think first about buying a new toaster, and taking for granted that when it is plugged in, it will receive the right kind and amount of electricity- a situation brought about by standards. Now imagine taking a CD-ROM based tutorial from last year, and putting its assessment section into a newly purchased learning environment, linking it to student records and new content. This is the world that interoperability standards are taking us towards. The engagement of those involved in elearning, at whatever level is appropriate for their work, is vital to speed the day.

References

[1] IEEE 90: Institute of Electrical and Electronics Engineers. IEEE Standard Computer Dictionary: A Compilation of IEEE Standard Computer Glossaries. New York, NY: 1990

[2] Downes, S. Learning Objects. Unpublished essay. 23 May 2000. URL: http://www.atl.ualberta.ca/downes/naweb/Learning_Objects.doc

Curriculum Development Critical Success Factors for eLearning Implementation

Timothy Brook Hall
Ulim-EMRC, University of Limerick, Ireland

Abstract

Curriculum development for classroom learning is often heavily dependant upon the experience of the teacher and is iterated over a number of delivery cycles to an optimum solution. The higher resource commitment required by eLearning demands an in depth curriculum development phase and a team effort, taking into account the needs of a more diverse learner group. The curriculum must be in sufficient detail for the content to be developed out of sequence and by different specialist members of the team. The project management task becomes more critical and complex and the host organization must be supportive.

CSFs eLearning Curriculum Development

Curriculum development for classroom based learning primarily involves the subject matter expert/teacher in tasks that require them to act variously as instructor, author, project manager, designer, desktop publisher, editor and instructional designer. The process is often heavily dependant upon the past experience of the participants and is iterated over a number of delivery cycles to an optimum solution.

The considerably higher resource commitment required by eLearning demands an expanded and in depth curriculum development phase, which is much more a team effort. Needs analysis must take into account the requirements and aspirations of a more diverse learner group and their employers/parents. The curriculum must be planned and documented in sufficient detail for the content to be developed out of sequence and by different members of the team applying their own specialist skills. The project management task becomes more critical and complex.

A typical team will consist of a project manager, the curriculum expert who preferably should have IT skills, web designer with complementary educational skills, IT services representative, administrative support and access to an outside reviewer. An iterative process of design, develop, review, revise should be followed, with as much emphasis as possible on the initial design phase (the natural tendency is to rush onto the development phase). The key elements to keep in mind are:

1. The student and behind them parents, employers or government agency.
2. The curriculum framework and how it fits to institutional objectives, standards and aspirations.
3. The teacher, tutor, mentor or facilitator who will work with the students during delivery their skills and training. 4. The enabling technology and how it can be exploited to meet the needs of the curriculum without demanding unavailable skills and resources.

The proposed curriculum outline must meet certain criteria to be suitable for on-line delivery, it must be based on knowledge transfer and the development of cognitive skills (on-line learning is less adaptable to the development of interpersonal and altitudinal skills). Content can be complex and require time to assimilate and rely heavily on project work to engage and interact with the learner. On-line learning is less suited to skills practice except in the special case where intelligence in the software can be exploited such as basic language learning or keyboard skills, where group work is necessary specialist resources in the Learning Management System, LMS, are required. Similarly special features are needed for learner testing and assessment, and if progress tracking is important again an LMS must be used.

The students themselves must have access to the technology and be skilled in its use (for learning) they need high motivation if they are to be lone learners, and must have sufficient time to follow the course. The decoupling of time and place between teacher and learner must be exploitable with multiple delivery, multiple locations or large numbers of students.

The organization in which the on-line course is to be developed must be supportive, there must be a distance learning strategy, skilled support personnel, recognition of a realistic time frame, realistic expectations, managerial support.

The curriculum must be designed to match the available technology at both the development and delivery stage and any special demands must be identified early and properly resourced. The connection and bandwidth available to the learners will influence the choice of media and tools and there are small differences between the capability and behaviour of browsers that must be taken account of. Is there a need for on-line formal assessment, the security demands are formidable. What authoring tools will be used, which image, sound, video editing software is available and are there skilled practitioners? Are the designers and subject matter experts knowledgeable about the concepts of page design, layout, navigation, and the acceptable levels of complexity to match the available technology? Will there be technical support for delivery? Technical issues should not interfere with the learning process.

In many cases, an on-line learning variant of an existing conventional face-to-face curriculum is being considered this is a good opportunity to review the teaching and learning methodology – lecture, discussion, self-directed learning, self-organized learning, small group work, projects, and case studies all have their place in the on-line world and are subtly different than their face-to-face counterparts.

A framework for the course material development must be established based on good design principles: good structure and navigation: clear objectives: small units of learning: planned learner interactions: repetitions or summaries: synthesis to tie ideas together: learner stimulation and engagement through interesting format, engaging content, non-passive navigation, self test quizzes, assignments and problems which are open-ended so learners can adapt the material to their own circumstances: regular feedback. This framework can then be fleshed out at the course development phase.

This wealth of front-end activity needs to be planned and managed using good project management practices so that it doesn't usurp the detailed activity required later in the project either in content development or technical support.

Bibliography:

[1] Aussserhofer, A. Ael-Smooth Integration of eLearning onto Traditional Teaching Concepts. Kplus 2001 Available online at: http://www.kplus.at

[2] Price, D & von Schlag, P. Bringing Classroom Curriculum up to Speed. ASTD 2000. Available online at: www.learningcircuits.org/2001/sep2001/price.html

[3] Oliver, C.M. Curriculum Design for eLearning. TechLearn April 2002. Available online at: www.techlearn.ac.uk/NewDocs/LTSN_workshop_Oliver.doc

[4] Hayes Jacobs, H. (ed) Interdisciplinary Curriculum Available online at: www.ascd.org/readingroom/books/jacobs89book.html

[5] www.learnweb.harvard.edu/alps/bigideas/q4.cfm

Instructional versus Educational Systems Design (ESD): Is there a difference?

J. M. Baptista Nunes
Department of Information Studies, University of Sheffield

Sue Morón-García
Institute of Educational Technology, The Open University

Abstract

Systems and environments to support eLearning require detailed specification of learning needs, materials, activities and delivery methods and needs. The complexities of integration of the different ICT components according to these learning needs and sound pedagogical approaches, demand frameworks not too dissimilar to information systems design and development methodologies. These have been traditionally denominated Instructional Design (ID) methodologies. However, the term "Instructional" has strong connotations with the behaviourist school of thought and could indicate a focus on teaching centred approach rather then a less objectivist learner-centred view of education. This paper will explore Educational Systems Design (ESD) as a thorough method of design of educational applications or environments and proposes and discusses the CSFs associated with such an approach.

Introduction

The World Wide Web (WWW or just the web) is a particular powerful form of hypermedia and is slowly becoming one of the most popular of educational technologies (EdT). Nevertheless, and in order to be effective, web applications, be it Virtual Learning Environment (VLE) enabled or simple HTML sites, need to be tailored to suit the particular learner needs, curriculum designs and planned learning activities. In order to do this, the learning process itself must first be analysed and understood. Learning is a complex process involving a large range of activities, some active, some passive, some creative, some reactive, some directed, some exploratory [1]. Furthermore, as proposed by Nunes and Fowell [2], academic learning should be seen as the process of construction of knowledge and the development of reflexive awareness, where the individual is an active processor of information. This type of learning occurs through interaction with rich learning environments, and results from engaging in authentic activities, and by social interaction and negotiation.

This complexity of the learning process suggests the need for situated learning, social negotiation and multiple perspectives on the different aspects of the subject matter, the implication being that a number of different learning strategies must be adopted to assist the learner in the construction of knowledge. The adoption of these different strategies creates learning environments that Grabinger and Dunlap [3] term *Rich Environments for Active Learning* (or *REALs*). REALs promote learning within authentic contexts, and encourage the growth of learner responsibility, initiative, decision-making, intentional learning and ownership over the acquired knowledge. Additionally, REALs should provide an atmosphere, which encourages the formation of knowledge building learning communities that assist collaborative social negotiation of meanings and understandings among the members of the community (peers, tutors, and subject matter experts). Current web based applications, namely those implemented using web based management systems should therefore be conceived as instances of REALs.

These applications must essentially support interactions between the tutor, the learner and her/his peers, subject matter specialists and the learning materials. All these interactions may, or may not, be computer mediated. Furthermore, and as defined by Nunes and Fowell [2], an educational hypermedia application is a software application specifically produced for a particular educational use, built using the hypermedia philosophy. They are developed in order to resolve a particular educational purpose or learning need, and are thus limited to the solution of the problems arising from that need. This means that although they might be linked with other hypermedia applications, other software applications, databases or even computer mediated communications facilities, they have clearly established boundaries.

An educational web application can therefore be seen as an instructional system, in the sense put forward by Nervig [4]: as sets of interacting, interrelated, structured experiences that are designed to achieve specific educational objectives, but organised into a unified dynamic whole. Hence, the design of such an hypermedia application should result from the design specifications emerging from the process of analysing curricular problems. To design and implement these web based REALs, instructional systems design (ISD) should be used. The importance of this overall ISD rests in assuring that the whole REAL is implemented using the same learning theory. In fact, if not carefully planned, the REAL could result in a mix of eventually conflicting techniques from different theoretical perspectives. Accordingly, Bednar *et al.* [5] defend the notion that effective instructional design and development is only possible if it emerges from deliberate application of a particular theory of learning. Furthermore, the developers must have acquired reflexive awareness of the theoretical basis underlying the design. This will ensure that instruction design, hypermedia design and development, and the hypermedia conceptual models selected are compatible and all use the same learning philosophy.

Constructivist Instructional Design

Traditionally, ISD is seen as a process approached from a systems strategy, based on the purpose of the system, using a systematic, objective based process for analysing curricular and instructional problems in order to develop tested, feasible solutions [4]. Conversely, constructivist Educational Systems Design (ESD) focuses on the learner and on the learning process rather than solely on the subject matter. Note, that the term *Instructional* is deliberately not being used, as it has strong connotations with the behaviourist school of thought. In fact, since knowledge is constructed, the learning of a concept must be embedded in the use of the concept and not in the transmission of knowledge through instruction. The educator provides the curriculum design including the course syllabus, content and educational setting, but not instruction. Constructivist ESD requires the separation of method and content, educational systems designers develop learning environments rather than packaged instruction [6].

In the design and development of our web based application the ESD model shown in Fig. 1 was used. Since according to the constructivist philosophy, knowledge domains are not readily separated in the world, information from many sources bears on the analysis of any particular subject matter and it is not possible to isolate units of information. A *central core body of information* must thus be defined in the *curriculum design*, but boundaries of what may be relevant should not be strongly imposed. Instead of dividing the subject matter into logical analysis of dependencies, the constructivist approach turns toward a consideration of what users of that knowledge domain do in real life contexts. The ultimate goal of this approach is to move the learner into thinking in the knowledge domain as if he/she were an expert user of that domain [5]. Curriculum designers should therefore identify the variety of experts on the subject matter and the activities they do. The designer should

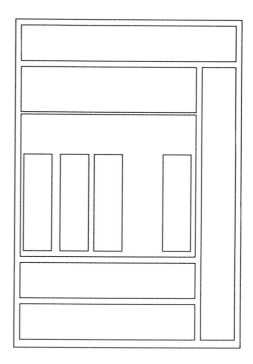

then define simplified but still authentic tasks to be experienced by the learner. The goal is to portray authentic learning activities, not to define the structure of learning to achieve the tasks, since it is the process of constructing a perspective or understanding that is important and no meaningful construction is possible if all relevant information is pre-specified [5].

Additionally, curriculum design must ensure that activities are situated in real world contexts, are authentic, and provide multiple perspectives on the subject matter. Some degree of *coaching* or guidance must be provided, by including meaningful examples and the different perspectives of experts and peers. A central strategy for achieving this consists in providing collaborative learning environments where computer mediated communication (CMC) facilities is available. CMC allows both peer-to-peer and peer-to-tutor communication. Access to extra information sources must also be provided to allow different learner's needs to be satisfied whenever needed.

It is in the *design phase* that all the components of the learning environment required by the curriculum design are defined and specified. During the *development phase* the learning environment is implemented according to the specifications coming from the design phase. Since different types of educational technologies may be needed, to implement all the planned activities, examples and communication channels, different development methodologies may then be applied. Finally the hypermedia application must be system tested and field tested as an embedded component in the overall learning environment.

In summary, in a constructivist approach, the curriculum design of the ESD establishes a core body of information crucial for the subject matter, identifies the type of experts that use it and the authentic learning activities required. The design phase specifies a comprehensive set of educational technology tools required to support the learning process and the function of each one of these tools. During the development phase, the different educational applications and tools are developed in parallel and then system tested and field tested together.

Conclusions

The production of educational hypermedia involves collaboration between subject matter and education experts involved in the ESD, and technical development experts involved in the application implementation. Hence, the communication between these agents becomes paramount. These groups usually speak different "languages" and do not readily understand the problems of the other [8]. An efficient design must thus integrate and support the dialogue between these different groups. However, the gap between expert/professional and non-expert/non-professional developers is narrowing, due to the increasingly more comprehensive and easy-to-use authoring facilities, such as VLEs and *drag&drop* authoring tools. Current authoring tools aim to support both professional quality and do-it-yourself endeavours, so that the developer of an educational application is now often the educator her/himself. Nevertheless, the need for an adequate conceptual view of the process of design and development should always be present.

Bibliographic References

[1] Hammond, N. (1992) Tailoring hypertext for the learner. In: Kommers, P.; Jonassen, D. & Mayes, J. (Eds.) *Cognitive Tools for Learning*. Berlin: Springer Verlag, 149-160.

[2] Nunes, J. M. and Fowell, S. P. (1996) Hypermedia as an experimental learning tool: a theoretical model. *Information Research New*, 6(4), 1996, 15-27.

[3] Grabinger, R. & Dunlap, C. (1995) Rich environments for active learning. *Association for Learning Technology Journal*, 3(2), 5-34.

[4] Nervig, N. (1990) Instructional systems development: a reconstructed ISD model. *Educational Technology*, November, 40-46.

[5] Bednar A., Cunningham, D., Duffy, T. & Perry, J. (1992) Theory into practice: how do we link? In Duffy, T. & Jonassen, D. (Eds.) *Constructivism and the Technology of Instruction: A Conversation*. New Jersey, USA: Lawrence Erlbaum Associates, Inc, 17-34.

[6] Kember, D. (1991) Instructional design for meaningful learning. *Instructional Science*, **20**, 289-310.

[7] Nunes, J. M. (1999) The experiential Dual Layer Model (EDLM): A conceptual model integrating a constructivist theoretical approach to academic learning with the process of hypermedia design, PhD Thesis. Sheffield; University of Sheffield

[8] Moonen, J. (1986) Toward an industrial approach to educational software development. In: Bork, A. and Weinstock, H. (Eds.) *Designing Computer-Based Materials*. Berlin: Springer Verlag, 119-151.

Critical Success Factors for eLearning Delivery

Patrick G. Coman
Department of Electronic Engineering
Institute of Technology Tallaght, Dublin 24, Ireland
Tel: 353-1-4042502
Email: pat.coman@it-tallaght.ie

Abstract

This paper will focus on issues relating to the delivery of elearning, using the delivery of a technology based college course to students in the workplace. The issues addressed include on-line learner skills and support, the effective and appropriate use of multimedia, the use of simulation, ICT requirements and tutor skills and training. On-line learning's opportunities for more personalised learning using simple testing and feedback tools and student use of sophisticated specialist software will be explored along with more mundane factors such as scheduling, student tracking and assessment.

1. Introduction

The determination of Critical Success Factors for eLearning Delivery is influenced by a number of distinct dimensions. The design of any delivery environment must be pedagogically rooted, reflecting the transposition of an abstract pedagogic model to a tangible system design. The learning dynamics of the subject domain provide the data points needed to define the specifics of system design and implementation. The final dimension that must be considered relates to the learning environment and its associated interactions.

This paper addresses each in turn in the context of the e-delivery of a third year telecommunications module to part-time, industry based students completing a National Diploma in Electronic Engineering. Critical Success Factors are identified for each dimension. The treatment is presented independent of any specific learning management system and does not address Critical Success Factors in that regard.

2. Pedagogy of System Design

The pedagogic model adopted for system design is derived from Cognitive Flexibility theory. Cognitive Flexibility theory is a conceptual model for designing learning environments that is based upon cognitive learning theory. Its intention is to facilitate the advanced acquisition of knowledge to serve as the basis for expertise in complex and ill-structured knowledge domains [1]. Cognitive flexibility represents an evolution of classical constructivism. Very closely allied to the model of constructivism is the notion of cognitive

apprenticeship [2]. The apprentice-master model of traditional crafts inspires the model but it is adapted to "cognitive" or intellectual domains.

2.1 Design Realisation and CSF derivation.

The fusion of these concepts enables the definition of the following Critical Success Factors:
1. The design should enable deep learning - all aspects of content should closely interrelate as a whole. Module content is implemented as a hierarchy of units, lessons, and topics.
2. The learning process should be student cantered - the implementation is open and allows the student total flexibility as to how they access or sequence any of the courseware materials or utilities.
3. The learning process should be student directed. A learning plan is provided to allow the student map out their schedule of activities. Data from module delivery suggests that while students may want to be able to asynchronously access module units, synchronisation is preferred within units, each unit typically requiring eight to ten hours of effort.

3. The Subject Domain

The subject domain in this context presents the particular dynamic that many of the concepts require practical demonstration in order to be fully understood by the students. The student is expected to develop certain practical capabilities, with circuits and also with instrumentation. The student is also expected to develop analytical and problem solving capabilities. Influenced by cognitive apprenticeship these cannot be fully developed by simply accessing courseware and tutorials, without actual interaction with circuits and systems. The deterministic behaviour of such associated circuits can be presented with simulation tools, in this case Orcad PSpice, using Citrix [3] as a bandwidth effective on-line access tool. Analytical capability can be developed by providing simulations that present unexpected outcomes, such as circuit behaviour as a result of using modified device timing models.

Real laboratory behaviour and instrumentation form such an integral part of mastering the subject domain that eLearning provision without them is incomplete. A hybrid can be created using tools such as LabView [4] to build virtual instruments, and present those instruments with simulation output data cases, presenting the opportunity for significant asynchronous student access to such cases. Additionally LabView can be used to provide complete remote IP based access to and control of both instruments and hardware, enabling the remote student the full spectrum of activity and experience that a "hands-on" regular student would have.

Extrapolating concepts presented in previous research [5] regarding student-active science education is useful in identifying a set of critical success factors here:

1. Laboratories should be fundamentally investigative, encouraging active learning by actually doing it.
2. Formats used should include active collaboration among students, and between students and lecturers.
3. Laboratories and problem assignments should be based on complex, real-world problems.
4. Exercises and laboratories should inculcate higher order thinking skills, and intellectual maturity.

4. The Learning Environment

The learning environment in this case refers to the interactive dynamics that exist, and how they are enabled in this learning context. One of the most critical factors is the sense of disconnection and isolation that net users may experience. The development of a "knowledge family" is an important element in addressing this. Asynchronous communications are supported using a Spinnaker based bulletin board and MSN Messenger messaging. Synchronous communications such as tutorial sessions are supported with Messenger and MS NetMeeting. The "knowledge family" must be actively promoted and stimulated by tutors and lecturers, through bulletin boards and discussion groups.

MSN Messenger is Microsoft's answer to ICQ for instant messaging. Once Messenger is open on a desktop it will let the user know what members of their contact list are on-line, and which ones are not. Using Messenger alone, a far more community based communications environment can be created for distant learners, addressing some of the concerns regarding sense of place, and isolation in distance learning. Using MS NetMeeting any desktop application can be opened and shared between selected members of the MSN Messenger contact list. This makes it an ideal platform for providing support to students, addressing issues that arise with interactive course elements such as laboratory exercises. It also provides the capability to remotely deliver tutorial sessions, to individuals or groups, with the voice conferencing capability enhancing the communications process.

Streaming media, in this case Real, can be used to provide bandwidth efficient tutorial support that can be accessed in a completely asynchronous manner by students. Video is not required, with a combination of Real Audio and image animation using tools such as Real Pix or Flash providing a more effective support environment.

The student must also be able to benchmark their own progress and level of understanding as they progress through the course. The test strategy is to provide individual formative tests for each lesson, and a single summative test for each unit. Formative assessment is used primarily to help the student and the tutor to monitor progress in the development of skills and understanding in each lesson. The student can take a lesson test at any time, and may retake that test as many times as they wish. Each lesson test will comprise of, typically, ten to twelve questions, selected at random from a question bank. The Unit Test is used both in a formative, but primarily summative manner. The performance from the Unit test can be used as part of the formal assessment process for the student. The Unit test is randomly generated from the same question bank, but can be taken only once, however feedback and support can be provided if specific weaknesses are identified.

5. Conclusions

It is seen that the subject domain heavily influences the determination of Critical Success Factors in eLearning. However the desired pedagogy, and learning environment define the dimensions, and success factors, of the general infrastructure that must be created to support the domain specific presentation. Further work is required to develop and model these processes so that they are better defined, and can become more repeatable, and transportable from application to application cases.

References

[1] Spiro, R.J, Feltovich, P.J, Jacobson, M.J, Coulson, R.L (1992) Cognitive Flexibility, Constructivism, and Hypertext: Random Access Instruction for Advanced Knowledge Acquisition in Ill-Structured Domains.

[2] Berryman, S. E. (1991) Designing effective learning environments: Cognitive apprenticeship models. http://www.ilt.columbia.edu/ilt/papers/berry1.html

[3] CITRIX, Application Serving White Paper, http://www.citrix.com.

[4] National Instruments, Distance Learning http://www.ni.com/academic/distance_learning.htm

[5] McNeal, A. & D'Avanzo, C. (1997). Student-active science: Models of innovation in college science teaching. Fort Worth: Saunders College Publishing.

Concepts and Ontologies in Web-based Educational Systems

Lora Aroyo[1] and Darina Dicheva[2]
[1]Technische Universiteit Eindhoven, The Netherlands
l.m.aroyo@tue.nl
[2]Winston-Salem State University, United States of America
dichevad@wssu.edu

1. Introduction

Web-based Educational Systems (WBES) is one of the fastest growing and challenging areas in educational technology research. To meet the high expectations and requirements of educational community, a present challenging goal is the development of advanced intelligent WBES that adapt their behavior to the learner's state of understanding. Concept-oriented (ontology-based) architectures come as a promising solution in the development of such systems. Conceptual (ontological) structures, such as concept maps, topic maps, and conceptual graphs have a great deal of potential for organizing, processing, and visualizing subject domain knowledge and for building learner models in WBES. Concept-based courseware employs conceptual domain presentation to link educational materials to a course structure. This allows for concept-based course sequencing that supports adaptive courseware generation [1,2], concept-based information retrieval, visualization, and navigation that help students to get oriented within a subject domain and build up their own understanding and conceptual association [3,4], etc.

The information base of a concept-based course support environment aimed at assisting students in retrieving, evaluating, and comprehending information when performing open-ended learning tasks, often includes three main components: domain ontology, course model, and library metadata, which set specific requirements to the supporting authoring tools [5,6]. As a result, authoring of concept-based Web courseware is more complicated than the 'standard' courseware authoring and needs more adaptive and intelligent support.

Consequently, an even more challenging goal for WBES designers is the development of advanced WBES that offer adaptivity and intelligent support not only to learners but also to courseware authors and developers. This goal implies reusing and sharing both courseware functional components and content/knowledge. A well-founded and agreed system of concepts –ontology– would significantly advance interoperability, knowledge sharing and applicability in various areas. Ontology research as part of the Semantic Web initiative is expected to provide the enabling technology for reusable, sharable and exchangeable components, knowledge, content, and design principles. This way the educational information will be given a 'well-defined meaning' [7] as an explicit representation of data semantics.

The goal of ontological engineering is effective support of ontology development and use throughout its life cycle. For the purposes of ontology usage in Web-based educational systems the following phases of the ontology engineering process are considered as most relevant: design, maintenance, integration, sharing, re-using, and evaluation [8]. Ontological engineering of instructional design is believed to significantly contribute to overcoming some common drawbacks of intelligent instructional systems [9]. It will provide the basis for interoperability support to authors and system developers with respect to cost-effective extending and upgrading of WBES, especially in complex domains.

In order to provide intelligent and adaptive support a WBES authoring system needs to have *understanding* of the process of courseware authoring, to be able to decompose it in steps and procedures and reason over it; to provide hints and recommendations to the author and perform various (semi-) automatic actions. A key step in this direction is the proposal in [10] for defining domain ontology and task ontology as a necessary part of ITSs. An application of this idea, aimed at providing common understanding of the concept-based courseware authoring process that can be communicated to support tools for adaptive courseware authoring systems, is found in [11], which proposes specification of a set of generic atomic authoring tasks for the main modules of the concept-based courseware architectures. It is believed that an authoring task ontology can support efficiently common reasoning over the processes accruing in concept-based courseware authoring, which can be applied in the reasoning strategies of the authoring support tools.

The goal of this workshop is to explore issues concerned with the design of concept/ontology-based WBES and to outline the state-of-the-art in the development of ontology-aware systems that facilitate the reuse, sharing, and exchange of knowledge and components with respect to both their creating and authoring. We hope that it will contribute to defining the path towards a new generation authoring strategies, which will meet the complex requirements of concept-based WBES authoring.

2. Current Trends in Ontology-based WBES

The benefits and implications of using ontologies in educational systems could be viewed from various angles. By providing common vocabulary for domain knowledge representation they can support interoperability of learning material, abstract representation of learners and user/group interactions, etc. Moreover, numerous general and specialized task and topic ontologies are already available and need to be shared, reused, and easily maintained [9,12]. Finally, ontologies are expected to facilitate the process of WBES authoring. All these require development of new methods for knowledge organization and processing including combining, merging, reusing, and sharing of knowledge structures. The latter is closely linked to metadata (XML) and reusable components.

The papers accepted for presentation in this workshop are diverse and address many of the above mentioned issues thus giving a good view of what are the current tendencies in concept/ontology-aware WBES research.

An important research direction is related to the ease of construction and use of ontologies in WBES. The paper by Kay & Holden discusses an automatic extraction of ontological structures from teaching document metadata. It proposes a minimalist approach to metadata requiring the author to specify only the concepts, which each document teaches, requires, and uses. Apted & Kay describe a system, which automatically constructs an extensive ontology of Computer Science based on existing reliable resources. The system includes tools for querying the ontology (single- and multiple-concept queries and merging ontological structures) and visualizing the results.

Ontological knowledge representation facilitates building scrutable learner models. Abraham & Yacef's XML Tutor uses XML as an ontological structure to represent an overlay student model, open for inspection by the student. This simple structure allows creating stereotypical models, which from one side are more representative as initial student models, and from another, can be inspected by the students for comparison with their own models. However, a critical problem in using concept maps for student modeling is related to verifying the maps before using them for reasoning about student knowledge. The paper by Cimolino & Kay proposes an approach to verifying concept maps for eliciting learner's understanding of a domain. They have developed a tool that allows a student to construct a concept map, which is then checked against the teacher's map and the student is prompted to reflect on and confirm or revise elements of his/her map.

With respect to the design and implementation aspects of WBES there is quite an extensive effort toward facilitating the reuse and sharing of educational components, knowledge and conceptual structures. Mitrovic & Devedzic present a model for building multitutor ontology-based environments in which Web-based intelligent tutors share ontologies, i.e. meta-knowledge, as opposed to sharing knowledge. Their goal is to create a unifying framework for enabling interpretability of multiple ITSs on the Web. In the same direction, Seta & Umano propose an ontology-based framework for planning of problem solving workflow in learning processes, where the domain independent problem solving tasks are modeled separately from the domain-dependent components (knowledge and resources) thus allowing their sharing and reuse for various domains. Sicilia et al.'s work focuses on the reusability of learning resources. They propose the concept of 'learning link' as an independent and reusable resource that can be annotated with terms defined in link ontology.

As a key direction to a new generation authoring strategy comes the ontology engineering approach for construction of theory-aware authoring environments proposed by Mizoguchi & Bourdeau. This is an effort towards building good learning support systems, well justified by basic instructional theories. In order to support system designers with theory-based help the authors have the ambitious plan to systemize learning / instructional / instructional design science knowledge from engineering point of views through ontological engineering.

References

[1] Brusilovsky, P. & Vassileva J. (2002). Course Sequencing Techniques for Large-Scale Web-Based Education, Int. J. Cont. Eng. Education and Lifelong Learning, 13 (in press).

[2] De Bra, P., Brusilovsky, P., Murray, T. & Specht, M., (2001). Adaptive Web-based Textbooks. (Panel introduction) Proc. of the WebNet Conference, pp. 269-271.

[3] Aroyo L. & Dicheva D. (2001). AIMS: Learning and Teaching Support for WWW-based Education. Int. J. Cont. Eng. Education and Lifelong Learning, 11 (1/2), 152-164.

[4] Hübscher, R. & Puntambekar, S. (2002). Adaptive Navigation for Learners in Hypermedia Is Scaffolded Navigation, In Proc. of AH'2002 Conference, 184-192.

[5] Masthoff, J. (2002). Towards an Authoring Coach for Adaptive Web-Based Instruction, Proc. AH'2002, 415-418.

[6] Aroyo, L, Dicheva, D. & Cristea, A. (2002). Ontological Support for Web Courseware Authoring, Int. Conf. on Intelligent Tutoring Systems (ITS'02), France, 270-280.

[7] Berners-Lee, T. Hendler, J. & Lassila, O. (2001). The Semantic Web. In Scientific American, 17 May 2001.

[8] Dicheva, D. & Aroyo, L. (2002). Concept-based Courseware Authoring: An Engineering Perspective, ICALT'2002.

[9] Mizoguchi, R. & Bourdeau, J. (2000). Using Ontological Engineering to Overcome Common AI-ED Problems, Int. J. AI in Education, v.11, 1-12.

[10] Kitamura, Y., Sano, T. & Mizoguchi, R. (2000). Functional Understanding based on an Ontology of Functional Concepts, Proc. of PRICAI'00, 723-733.

[11] Aroyo, L. & Dicheva, D. (2002). Courseware Tasks Ontology for Adaptive Authoring, Proc. ICCE 2002 (to appear).

[12] T. Murray, Authoring Knowledge-Based Tutors: Tools for Content, Instructional Strategy, Student Model, and Interface Design, J. Learning Sciences, 7(1), 1998, 5-64.

Theory-aware Authoring Environment
-- Ontological Engineering Approach --

Riichiro Mizoguchi[1] and Jacqueline Bourdeau[2]
[1] ISIR, Osaka University, 8-1 Mihogaoka, Ibaraki, Osaka, 567-0047 Japan
miz@ei.sanken.osaka-u.ac.jp
[2] Tele-universite,4750 Henri-Julien, Montreal (Quebec), H2T 3E4 Canada
bourdeau@teluq.uquebec.ca

1. Introduction

In AI in education research community and related academic communities such as learning science (LS), instructional science (IS) and instructional design science (ID), a lot of research results have already accumulated and many sophisticated learning support systems have been built to date. The problem, however, is that it is not easy to build a good learning support system well-justified by such basic theories because they are not easily accessible for system designers/developers nor ready for engineering use. Imagine a theory-aware authoring environment, which can help designers/developers find, understand and utilize necessary LS/IS/ID theories to build a theory-justified learning support system. It must give a great impact on our community.

The next problem is how to realize it. On one hand, we need to articulate and organize the knowledge hidden in LS/IS/ID theories and to implement it in a computer for engineering use. On the other hand, knowledge of the architecture and building process of various types of learning support systems also must be declaratively modeled and implemented. And then, the correspondence and relationship between both of the knowledge is explicitly represented declaratively. This is what such a theory-aware authoring environment has to have. In AI research, ontological engineering, which tells us how to extracts and organize concepts in a target world declaratively in a computer-understandable form is becoming available. This is why ontological engineering approach could play an important role in our research.

2. Proposed Approach

The authors have some experience in building ontologies for learning support systems and LS/IS/ID knowledge as well as a road map towards a theory-aware authoring system. On the basis of development of a general framework of an ITS, we first designed a comprehensive ontology [1] for ITS whose top-level categories are (1) Goals of education, (2) Learner's state, (3) System's functionality, (4) Learner-system interaction, (5) Teaching material knowledge [1]. The ontology has developed into the following SmartTrainer task ontology [2] shown in Fig. 1, which contributed to realization of an ontology-aware authoring tool for a training system.

The next ontology we built is one for Opportunistic Group Formation (OGF), which dynamically form a group for collaborative learning based on learning theories. The OGF ontology [3] shown in Fig. 2 succeeded in making some Learning theories available to engineers.

```
- Generic structure of material
    - Traning scenario
    - Backbone stream
    - Rib stream
    - Instruction
- Learning contents
    - Teaching contents
        o  Problem
        o  Solution item
        o  Explanation contents
        o  Simulation contents
    - Concrete material
        o  Card
        o  Dialog
    - Learning item network
        p/o@n "nodes": Learning item
        p/o@n "links": Learning item link
    - Learning item
    - Learning item link

- Process related concept
    - Interactive process related concept
        o  Goal
        o  Teaching activity
        o  System action
    - Internal process related concept
        o  Update learner model
        o  Diagnose learner's answer
        o  Control

- Teaching strategy
        p/o "Goal": Goal
        s/o "Subgoals": Goal  Teaching
        action

- Learner modelling concept
    - Modelling
    - Knowledge
```

Figure 1. Some upper-level categories of a training task ontology

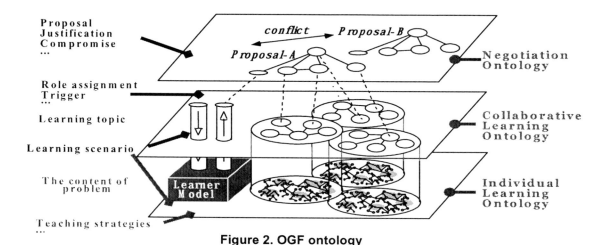

Figure 2. OGF ontology

The one the authors currently design is a bit more ambitious and comprehensive in that the ontologies will cover learning, instruction and instructional design theories [4]. These ontologies are being designed based on the nesting structure of the three theories, which gives effective guidelines (Fig. 3).

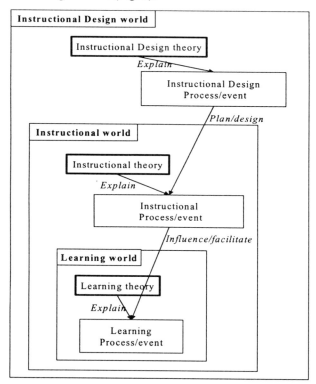

Figure 3. Nested structure of the three

The authors are going to build ontologies not for theorists but for engineers who need effective help based on the theories when they build a learning support system. This requires the ontologies be operational to organize these theories *from engineering point of views*. This is the

key point of the success of the enterprise, which is otherwise almost impossible to achieve, since each theorist has his/her own specific views and terminologies incompatible to others.

The engineering point of view enables us to employ what engineers have about learning and training, which is used for specifying their needs for it and contributes to establishing the common conceptual background on which the ontologies can be designed. Another merit of the viewpoint is that it allows us to approximate each theory to put it into the engineering system framework. This is also one of the success factors of the enterprise, since too fine-grain theories are not necessary in engineering settings and they are sometimes the causes of the argumentations among theorists.

3. Conclusions

In the position paper, we first summarize our approach and then review what we have done thus far followed by the future plan which might suggest that our enterprise could be said "LS/IS/ID knowledge systematization from engineering point of views through ontological engineering" as well as intermediate results.

References

[1] Mizoguchi, R. et al. (1996). Task Ontology Design for Intelligent Educational/Training Systems, *Workshop proc. on 'Architectures and Methods for Designing Cost-Effective and Reusable ITS'*, *ITS'96*, Montreal, Canada, 1-21.

[2] Jin, L., et al. (1999). An Ontology-Aware Authoring Tool: Functional structure and guidance generation, *AIED'99 Proc.*, 85-92.

[3] Supnithi, T., et al. (1999). Learning Goal Ontology Supported by Learning Theories for Opportunistic Group Formation, *AIED'99 Proc.*, 67-74.

[4] Bourdeau, J. & Mizoguchi, R. (2002). Collaborative ontological engineering of instructional design knowledge for an ITS authoring environment, *Proc. of ITS2002*, 399-409.

Automatic Extraction of Ontologies from Teaching Document Metadata

Judy Kay and Sam Holden
School of Information Technologies
University of Sydney, Australia

Abstract

SITS (Scrutable Intelligent Teaching System) is designed to make use of existing learning items in flexible and effective learning interactions. The reuse of pre-existing resources is important since creating new learning resources is a time consuming task which requires a skilled author. The Internet also provides a large number of resources for reuse. A major hurdle for reuse is metadata, especially epistemological metadata since different teachers or courses may have different ontologies for a given domain. SITS takes a minimalist approach to metadata. It requires only that the author of a teaching environment should define document metadata specifying the concepts which each document teaches, requires, and uses.

1. Introduction

Reusing available teaching resources is valuable as the resources are non-trivial and time consuming to create. The World Wide Web is potentially a source for a large number of teaching resources for a diverse range of topics. Reuse of those resources should allow for faster creation of a course and a richer coverage of areas of the course.

For example, when creating a course to teach the C++ Standard Template Library, there are many high-quality and varied teaching resources which can be reused. These range from the "Standard Template Library Programmer's Guide"[1], to introductory tutorials such as "An introduction of STL for beginners"[2], and entire books such as "Thinking In C++"[3].

The potential value of these pre-existing resources is increased if the teaching system has some form of ontology for the domain and the resources have suitable markup in terms of that ontology. This can then be exploited by a teaching system which has a model of the student's knowledge and their learning goals within this ontology.

For example, in the C++ Standard Template Library domain a student may wish to learn about the concepts 'unique' algorithm. If the teaching system has an ontology that indicates that the concepts 'iterator' and 'remove' are

prerequisite knowledge for the concept 'unique' and the system believes the student understands the concept 'iterator' but not the concept 'remove', then it can create a teaching plan starting with the concept 'remove' and then moving to 'unique'.

The creation of such an ontology is non-trivial as it involves enumerating the concepts and relationships between the concepts being taught. Many methodologies have been used for representing such domain knowledge, ranging from rule based expert systems to genetic graphs. In general, a domain expert must create the ontology in terms of the representation approach.

2. SITS Approach to Creating Ontologies

In SITS, the ontology is constructed from the document metadata. A course in SITS requires the definition of the vocabulary of concepts; each document in SITS has metadata specifying the concepts that the learner needs to know if they are to understand the document (prerequisites), the concepts the document teaches (learning outcomes), and the concepts it uses (where the use of these concepts does not require the learner understands them, as is the case for prerequisites). We refer to these three types as *prerequisites*, *shows*, and *uses*.

SITS uses this metadata to construct the inherent ontology for the course composed of the collection of documents put together by the creator of the learning environment. This ontology is dependent on the teaching strategy. For example, one teaching strategy might treat uses-metadata in the same way as prerequisite-metadata. This would result in a different ontology from that generated using a teaching strategy which did not treat uses-metadata in such a restrictive way. Teaching Strategies in SITS are separate modules and their implementation is not restricted, students select the teaching strategy they wish to use, and can change their selection at any time.

For a student wishing to learn about the concept 'unique' algorithm, SITS examines the metadata of the documents which show 'unique'. Suppose we have the following pair of documents that teach the same concept:

---

[1] http://www.sgi.com/tech/stl
[2] http://www.mindcracker.com/mindcracker/c_cafe/stl/stlt1.asp
[3] http://www.mindview.net/Books/TICPP/ThinkingInCPP2e.html

Document1:
> *prereqs*: iterator, remove, binarypredicate;
> *shows*: unique;
> *uses*: vector, copy, sort

Document2:
> *prereqs*: iterator, binarypredicate;
> *shows*: remove, remove_if, remove_copy,
> remove_copy_if, unique, unique_copy;
> *uses*: container, sort, vector, generate, set

Suppose SITS believes the student understands the following concepts: 'iterator', 'binarypredicate', 'vector', 'remove', and 'copy'. A teaching strategy, which treated *uses* concepts as non-essential could select either document to use to teach the 'unique' concept. The decision would be dependant on other factors (such as the extra concepts in *shows* for the second document, and the other metadata such as author and style). A teaching strategy which treated the concepts in *uses* as if they were prerequisites would have to first teach the student those concepts and in effect would be choosing between two ontologies:

> *(iterator, remove, binarypredicate, vector, copy, sort)*
> *-> unique*
> *(iterator, binarypredicate, container, sort, vector,*
> *generate, set)   -> unique*

SITS represents student knowledge using an evidence based student model in which the concepts used in the document metadata are the items for which evidence of knowledge is collected.

3. SITS Evaluation

The main testing domain for SITS is the C++ Standard Template Library (STL). The course has approximately 200 concepts and 600 documents. We have created metadata for documents from four independent sources: an introductory, tutorial-style on-line textbook; parts of a higher level textbook; the standard C++ reference materials; and a collection of small, focussed examples which was developed for testing for STL implementations.

We have begun artificial experiments, with a range of different teaching strategies and we are experimenting in combining these with various student models. We compare the outcome of this SITS minimalist approach against expert definitions of good selections of teaching documents. We are also assessing the quality of the ontologies that are inferred from the metadata.

The ontologies are to be assessed by comparing the order of concept introduction they result in with the order used by a number of textbooks in the area, as well as comparing the ontologies directly with hand crafted ontologies of the area, and by having an expert in the area examine the generated ontology itself.

4. Conclusions

It is important to note that SITS' metadata is the representative of the document in the system. In combination with the teaching strategy, it is used to infer the ontology for the domain.

In addition, SITS makes use of other metadata, such as the author of a resource and the style of the resource (eg. tutorial, reference, exercise, etc). This is imported from metadata sources, which are independent of SITS and are external to it. This forms an independent ontology of learning object type.

By contrast, the metadata, which relates the resource to the concepts being taught is part of SITS and its creation is the essential task for adding a new resource to a SITS teaching environment. It provides this mechanism that relates resources to concepts. In general, a SITS learning environment is created by defining the set of concepts before any documents are added to the environment. A major attraction of this approach is that the addition of the hundredth or thousandth resource is as easy as adding the first.

The one change that one expects over time is that teachers will become aware of the need for additional concepts after they have marked up some of the documents. SITS allows the creation of new concepts at any stage. This poses problems since such concepts could not be part of the metadata of documents already in the learning environment. Ideally, the teacher would revisit the coding of all existing documents to ensure that new concepts have been added to their metadata where this is relevant. However, at worst, the new concepts can simply be used for future document's metadata.

SITS is being tested with the quite substantial STL domain. It remains to perform experiments to evaluate the quality and effectiveness of the ontologies generated by SITS. The SITS approach seems promising for the automatic and pragmatic construction of ontologies from modest collections of metadata that a teacher creates for each of the documents that are to be used or reused for a rich teaching environment.

A Model of Multitutor Ontology-Based Learning Environments

Antonija Mitrovic[1] and Vladan Devedzic[2]
[1]Department of Computer Science, University of Canterbury
Private Bag 4800, Christchurch, New Zealand
tanja@cosc.canterbury.ac.nz
[2]Department of Information Systems, FON - School of Business Administration
University of Belgrade, POB 52, Jove Ilica 154, Belgrade, Yugoslavia
devedzic@galeb.etf.bg.ac.yu

Abstract

The paper proposes the M-OBLIGE model for building multitutor ontology-based learning environments. We show how the model can be applied to tutors in the database domain. The proposed model can be used as a framework for integrating multiple tutors on the Web.

1. Introduction

Once a team of ITS developers builds a successful ITS that helps students learn a part of some knowledge domain efficiently, chances are that they may want to extend and upgrade the system later on. If the domain is complex enough, chances are also that the developers may want to build other tutors to cover other parts of that domain. In such cases, developers will want to reuse parts of knowledge built into existing tutors. Moreover, two different teams may develop two different tutors that partially overlap in expertise. Therefore, the need for automatic knowledge sharing, reuse, and exchange among several tutors in the same complex domain is highly likely to arise. This is especially the case in Web-based education, where different tutors may be distributed across a number of sites.

This paper analyzes the role and cost-effectiveness of using ontologies in such settings. We first look at some relevant ontology-related work in the domain of ITS in Section 2. We present the model of a Multitutor *Ontology-Based LearnInG Environment* (M-OBLIGE) in Section 3. In Section 4 we discuss how that model would be applied in the context of database tutors [3]. Finally, we present conclusions in Section 5.

2. ITS and Ontology-related Work

The way we consider ontologies in our work is best described by Swartout and Tate's definition: ontologies provide the necessary armature around which knowledge bases should be built [6]. In other words, ontology contains reference knowledge for making two or more related intelligent systems *knowledge-consistent*. Our emphasis is on the role of ontologies in knowledge sharing among related Web-based educational systems. We put our research in the context of the emerging *Semantic Web*, a huge network of machine-understandable and machine-readable human knowledge, not just ordinary information [2]. The Semantic Web is expected to provide explicit representation of the semantics of data in the form of various domain theories stored on many Web-servers as a myriad of shareable ontologies, as well as advanced, automated, ontology-supported, and agent-ready reasoning services.

Mizoguchi et al. [4] point out that *ITS ontology* consists of a *domain ontology*, which characterizes the domain knowledge, and a *task ontology*, which characterizes the computational architecture of knowledge-based systems. They also make an important contribution to the hierarchy of ontologies in the domain of education, and study how ontologies can contribute to ITSs and authoring tools. They identify limitations of current authoring tools, all of which pertain to tools for building Web-based educational systems as well. Murray [5] defines the important *topic ontology*, based on topic types (e.g., concept, fact, principle etc), link types (e.g., is-a, part-of, prerequisite, context-for), and topic properties (e.g., importance, difficulty). More recently, Devedzic discusses educational services and servers in the context of ontologies on the Semantic Web [1].

3. The OBLIGE Model

Two or more Web-based ITSs can refer to a common, shared part of their knowledge as in Figure 1. Note that both tutors (App1 and App2) have their own private knowledge and reasoning mechanisms. The Web pages corresponding to any single tutor in this scenario must contain pointers to ontologies the tutor uses as its meta-knowledge. Such *semantic markup* of the tutor's Web pages enables an external agent or application to recognize the "armature" part of the tutor's knowledge. The ontologies themselves are stored in a machine-readable form at possibly different locations on the Web. They can point to each other as well, since the knowledge from one ontology can refer to the knowledge in another ontology. For example, the ontology of, say, *fraction*, can refer to the ontology of *number*, which in turn may be stored at another location on the Web.

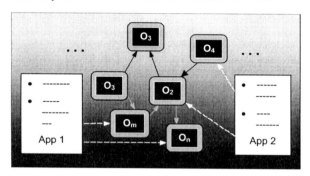

Figure 1. Two Web-based ITS applications sharing ontologies (O_i - ontologies)

We also want to stress that this model of knowledge sharing significantly differs from Web-based collaborative learning environments, shared knowledge bases, and shared student models. What is shared here is meta-knowledge, i.e. the static part of the tutors' knowledge that only makes each tutor aware of the knowledge models used by the other tutors.

4. Ontology-based Database Tutors

We now illustrate how M-OBLIGE would be applied to a suite of database tutors. At the moment, three of these tutors are operational: KERMIT is a database design tutor, based on the ER model, SQL-Tutor teaches SQL, and NORMIT is a database normalization tutor [3]. Other planned tutors include a tutor for converting ER schemas to relational ones, and tutors for other query languages. The existing systems are not ontology-based.

Each of these tutors will have its own local ontology, supporting the tasks being taught. Although the domains are not identical, there is overlap between them: there may be several fairly general DB ontologies as a basis for knowledge reuse in all tutors. For example, a DB design that comes out of KERMIT is expressed as an ER schema, which may be converted into the corresponding relational schema. SQL-Tutor (and other query language tutors) may refer to this relational schema when the

student builds queries. Local ontologies are specific to each tutor, as each tutor focuses on particular domain aspects. On the other hand, the external ontologies are general, describing the whole domain, and may be used by external tutors and other applications. For example, the architecture of KERMIT will be extended as in Figure 2. Its local ontology refers to the idiosyncrasies of the implemented ER model. On the other hand, the ontologies of the ER model, data models, and databases are general enough to be used by other DB tutors and other intelligent DB applications alike. Ontology processor will help the pedagogical module to make instructional decisions and enable external agents find out about KERMIT's instructional focus.

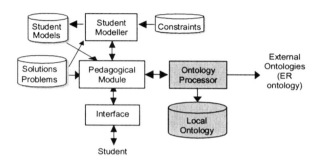

Figure 2. Ontology extension for KERMIT

5. Conclusions

There is a growing need for applying ontologies in the field of ITS. Artificial tutors often need to exchange and reuse their knowledge, and ontologies provide infrastructure for that. The M-OBLIGE model proposed in this paper is our first step towards a unifying framework for enabling interoperability of multiple tutors on the Web.

References

[1] V. Devedzic, "Next-Generation Web-Based Education", *Int. J. EE&LLL*, 2003 (to appear).

[2] J. Hendler, Agents and the Semantic Web, *IEEE Intelligent Systems*, 16(2), 2001, 30-37.

[3] A. Mitrovic et al. Constraint-based tutors: a success story. *Proc. IEA/AIE-2001*, 2001, 931-940.

[4] R. Mizoguchi, J. Bourdeau, Using Ontological Engineering to Overcome Common AI-ED Problems, *Int. J. AI in Education*, 11, 2000, pp. 1-12.

[5] T. Murray, Authoring Knowledge-Based Tutors: Tools for Content, Instructional Strategy, Student Model, and Interface Design, *J. Learning Sciences*, 7(1), 1998, 5-64.

[6] W. Swartout, A. Tate, "Ontologies," Guest Editors' Introduction, *IEEE Intelligent Systems*, 14(1), 1999, 18-19.

XMLTutor – an Authoring Tool for Factual Domains

David Abraham and Kalina Yacef
School of Information Technologies
University of Sydney
kalina@it.usyd.edu.au

Abstract

The XMLTutor is an Authoring Tool that generically delivers personalised teaching on an arbitrary domain, which must be specified in Extensible Markup Language (XML). The tool was built to explore the consequences of using XML as the main ontological structure in an Intelligent Tutoring System (ITS).

1. Domain Knowledge Module

Constructing domain knowledge can be a time intensive task [4]. Often it is difficult for a domain expert to translate their knowledge and thinking into a foreign format. A promising solution to this difficulty is the XML format. XML has a natural hierarchical structure similar to the contents section of a book. This allows XML to store both structural and semantic information about the domain. Mizoguhi [3] describes a set of XML tags more formally as a kind of *level 1* ontology.

XML is used extensively outside the Intelligent Tutoring field as a data markup language and so many people would already be familiar with it. Furthermore, the language is very simple, making it an ideal format for non-computer experts to encode their factual knowledge[1] in.

The XMLTutor can read in an arbitrary XML file and deliver a personalised tutorial on the material inside it. There are already XML descriptions of almost everything from Geography to Stock Prices. With little or no work, a tutorial can be constructed on any of these areas.

The XMLTutor can do this because the knowledge is expressed in a common format. There is nothing immediately special about XML - if this knowledge were encoded in a semantic network then the equivalent *Semantic Network Tutor* would be able to automatically generate tutorials as well. Having said that, there are real advantages to using XML for knowledge reuse over other possible formats. This paper will attempt to highlight some of these advantages.

2. Student Model

For each student, the XMLTutor maintains a separate instance of the domain knowledge, overlayed with some additional personalised information (see Fig. 1). This information is stored in attributes of the XML nodes and includes the student's number of correct and incorrect answers, as well as their confidence in their last answer.

```
<country UK correct="3" incorrect="2" confidence="60">
  <capital correct="4" incorrect="1" confidence="90">London</capital>
</country>
```

Figure 1. Example Student Model

Although the Student Model used by the XMLTutor is simplistic, it contains the essential information needed by the Pedagogical Module to intelligently personalise teaching for each student. The model can easily be extended to include more information.

The XMLTutor allows the student to visualise and edit all aspects of their student model. This has two main advantages. Firstly, visualising the Student Model encourages students to reflect on their learning and identify any areas of weakness. Secondly, the student may also correct any inaccurate information in the Student Model (see Section 3.3 for an example). This can help the Pedagogical Module deliver higher quality teaching.

The XMLTutor contains an XML viewer similar to the one built into the Internet Explorer browser. This viewer allows the student to explore different aspects of their model by expanding and collapsing whole trees of nodes. Alternative XML viewers, some of which are quite powerful, are already available in the Database community [1]. These viewers, like many other XML tools, can often be plugged into an ITS. This is one of the main benefits of using XML.

The XMLTutor allows the ITS designer to create stereotypical student models [5, 2]. The ITS designer can then supply a set of questions and answers that helps to classify a new student in terms of the stereotypes. Therefore, when a new student uses the XMLTutor, their Student Model can be set to some combination of the existing stereotypes. This model should be more representative of the student than the alternative - a blank Student Model.

Students can inspect these stereotypes and compare them with their own model (for instance, how their knowledge of British Geography compares with a stereotypical European). These comparisons involve performing a sequence of basic Student Model operations. For instance, the difference between two Student Models

---

[1] Procedural knowledge is better represented by a more powerful format, such as an expert system or programming language.

is calculated by taking the difference between attributes (e.g. confidence) in each node common to both models.

Because the stereotypes and student models are XML documents, these operations essentially involve a single traversal of the tree structure. This functionality is packaged as a small intuitive language inside the XMLTutor allowing the student to make arbitrarily complex comparisons with ease.

3. Pedagogical Module

The Pedagogical Module in the XMLTutor uses information in the Student Model, along with the domain knowledge, to deliver personalised instruction to a student. All sequencing of the instruction (topic selection) is done automatically using the structure of the underlaying XML. The module also generates natural language materials to present to the student.

Each XML node in the student model is placed in a priority queue. The Pedagogical Module repeatedly removes the node with the highest priority, delivers a question on it, and places the node back on the priority queue with an altered priority (based on the correctness and confidence of the student's answer). Because nodes with higher priorities are more likely to be presented to the student, the problem of topic selection reduces to controlling the priorities of each node.

The basic parameters for computing the priority of a node are its *correct, incorrect, confidence* and *relevance* attribute values. By using these values, the Pedagogical Module is able to implement the four following topic selection principles.

Knowledge Relevance. Domain experts can associate a *relevance* value with each node in the initial domain knowledge. This value specifies the importance of the knowledge contained inside the node. The Pedagogical Module assigns a higher priority to nodes with a higher relevance value, meaning that important knowledge is more likely to be taught to the student.

Students can change the relevance value of any nodes in their Student Model. Therefore, after determining which parts of the domain are important for them, the students can influence the delivery of questions from the Pedagogical Module.

Exploration. After focusing on the important areas, the student needs to explore other parts of the domain. To this end, the priority of a node is partially based on the total number of questions the student has answered for the node (correctly or otherwise). When the total is small (i.e. the student has seen few questions on the node) the priority is assigned a relatively higher value, making it more likely the node will be selected as the next node to present to the student.

Reinforcement and Revision. The Pedagogical Module balances the exploration of new material with the reinforcement of material previously covered. With a complete student model, it is usually very easy to decide which pieces of knowledge need reinforcement and how urgently it is required. Nodes with higher *incorrect* values identify knowledge that the student has consistently failed to master. Nodes with lower *confidence* values highlight areas that the students know themselves to need revision in. Both of these attributes contribute to higher priority values.

Coherence and Learning by Association. As much as possible, the domain should be presented to the student in a series of coherent subtopics. This enables the student to learn not only individual concepts in the domain knowledge, but also associations between these concepts. The Pedagogical Module determines these subtopics through the structure of the XML encoded domain knowledge. The selection of a node from the priority queue increases the priority of all the nodes in its *neighbourhood*. A neighbouring node (one with some connection to the previous node) is then more likely to be selected next.

Natural Language Questions. Once a node is selected, the Pedagogical Module needs to present it to the student. This is done by automatically generating a question for the student to answer. The hierarchical and descriptive structure of XML makes it a straightforward task to describe a node in natural language.

The Pedagogical Module has a number of template natural language questions. These templates are instantiated by substituting actual tag names and data values from the XML structure. This template design is extendable, allowing the designer to easily add new question constructions.

4. Conclusion

The XMLTutor demonstrates the power of using XML to encode domain ontological knowledge. By defining a standard representation format, the program is able to deliver personalised instruction in any domain. Non-computing experts should find it much easier to translate their knowledge into the simple XML format. Once this ontology is built, the XMLTutor is able to automatically generate student models and instruct students in a way that maximises their personal learning.

References

[1] Desclefs, B. & Soto, M. XML and Information Visualization. http://citeseer.nj.nec.com/328420.html

[2] Kay, J. (1998). Stereotypes, Student Models and Scrutability. In *J. of Intelligent Tutoring Systems*, 19-30.

[3] Mizoguchi, R. & Bourdeau, J. (2000). Using Ontological Engineering to Overcome Common AI-ED Problems. In *Int.J. of Artificial Intelligence in Education*, Vol 11.

[4] Murray, T. & Woolf, B. (1992). Results of Encoding Knowledge with Tutor Construction Tools. In *Proceedings of the Tenth National Conference on Artificial Intelligence*, 17-23.

[5] Rich, E. (1989). Stereotypes and User Modelling. In *User Models in Dialog Systems*, 1989, 35-51.

Verified Concept Mapping for Eliciting Conceptual Understanding

Laurent Cimolino, Judy Kay
School of Information Technologies
University of Sydney, Australia, 2006.
{laurent,judy}@it.usyd.edu.au

Abstract

Concept mapping is a valuable technique for education evaluation. This paper describes a system which supports teachers in creating concept mapping tasks which are intended to capture the student's understanding of the ontology of a small domain. A novel feature of our work is that the system verifies that the student intended the map elements that will be used to infer student understanding and misconceptions.

1. Introduction

Concepts maps [2,5] have become a common tool for externalising learner conceptions of a domain. There are many available tools for learners to draw concept maps, such as those summarised at [4,6]. Concept mapping has strong foundations in theories of learning and in empirical studies of brain activity [6]. The approach has many potential roles in education.

We are concerned with the use of concept maps as a mechanism for determining the way that a learner conceptualises a domain. From this, we aim to build accurate and detailed learner models of the learner's conceptual knowledge of a domain. Since our research focuses on scrutable learner modelling and strong learner control, the concept map is a natural tool for eliciting learner models.

In line with our philosophy of learner control, our current work explores approaches to building *verified* concept maps for the purpose of modelling the student's knowledge. We consider it critical to verify concept maps before using them as a basis for reasoning about the student's knowledge. This is because it is very easy for a student to accidentally link the wrong concept or omit a concept or a link from their concept map. Moreover, Novak emphasises that revision of concept maps is a normal and important part of the concept mapping process: he comments 'it is always necessary to revise [the original map] ... Good maps usually undergo three to many revisions.' [6]

2. Overview of System Use

Our system allows the student to construct a map and then, once they decide that it is complete, they indicate this at the interface. The system then checks the map and prompts the user to check elements of it to see if they are correct. In particular, it can prompt the user to check if certain concepts should be added to the map. It also can ask the user to check if a particular concept should have any other links. Similarly, it can ask the user to check if they actually intended certain propositions in the map (as indicated by the two concepts and their link). This phase of the mapping activity can help the learner check that they have not made careless mistakes. It also helps them think about additional links and conceptual relationships that they actually do know about but may have failed to include in the initial map. Since concept mapping is such a cognitively demanding activity, it is highly likely that the learner will forget some of the map elements that they might have included. This prompting phase helps them to return to the task and focus on elements they have forgotten.

Another important part of our prompting process is that the system can help the learner examine parts of the map that suggest misconceptions. Where the map has been accidentally created to suggest a misconception, the prompting phase can help the learner correct that. Equally, if the learner really does hold the misconception, the prompting phase ensures that the final map has captured this misconception. This is somewhat similar to the approach of comparing student and expert maps as in [1] although we do not wish to use it as summative assessment of the student but rather to capture the conceptual understanding of the student where each element of this is then captured in a student model.

Essential to the operation of this concept mapping tool is the teacher interface. It is here that the system captures the essential knowledge needed for the prompting phase. The teacher first constructs a map. Then they interact with the interface to define the associated actions to occur at the prompting phase of the student map building. We might consider the student's completed concept map as a form of student model. However, we prefer to use it as one source of information about the student's conceptual knowledge and this can be kept in our generic user model framework [3]. This can then be combined with various other sources of information about the learner, such as their performance on various other learning activities.

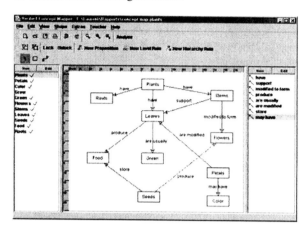

Figure 1. Example of a concept mapping task

Figure 1 shows an example of the concept mapping interface as it would be seen by the teacher creating a task. This map is adapted from those in [5]. At the left is the list of concepts that will be available to the student. The student will also be able to create their own concepts. The interface allows but does not encourage this since the teacher will have built an ontology for the task and this will only use the concepts that the teacher has defined. Similarly, the right hand window of Figure 1 provides the list of links which are the relationships that can relate concepts. The teacher uses these concepts and links to create a map like that shown in the main window. This interface is similar to that the student will see. Indeed, the teacher can mark parts of the map to be provided for the student as they start the mapping task. This much of the interface provides similar functionality to that of many other concept mapping interfaces.

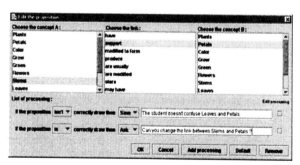

Figure 2. Teacher's rule creation interface

The checking of student maps is performed by a set of rules created by the teacher. The interface for creating one such rule appears in Figure 2. This allows the teacher to define a proposition that will be matched by the rule: in this case, the proposition is `Stems support petals`. The teacher then can construct actions to be applied when the student's map has this proposition. One type of action is the inference about the student's knowledge. This will be saved at the completion of the mapping task. Another type of action, also shown in the window, will prompt the student to reflect on aspects of their map. In cases where the student has accidentally created an unintended proposition, this improves the chances that he student will realise this and correct the map. If the student actually did intend the proposition, the system will conclude that the student has a misunderstanding. In either case, the inferences based on the student's final map are more likely to be valid than in an unverified mapping task. At the same time, careful construction of the rules can provide students with assistance in reflecting about their conceptualisation of a domain.

3. Conclusions

We have constructed a system for eliciting student understanding of a domain. We believe that our approach has considerable promise for modelling student's personal ontologies. User trials will be needed to assess the effectiveness of the interface and the approach.

References

[1] Fife, B. (1996), Computer Assisted Concept Mapping, http://www-personal.umich.edu/~cberger/compmapanalysis.htm (visited 2002).

[2] Kay, J. (1991), An explicit approach to acquiring models of student knowledge, in Lewis, R and S Otsuki (Eds) *Advanced Research on Computers and Education*, Elsevier, North Holland, 263-268.

[3] Kay, J. (1995), The um toolkit for cooperative user modelling, *User Modeling and User-Adapted Interaction*, Kluwer 4(3), 149-196.

[4] Lanzing, J. (1997), The Concept Mapping Homepage, http://users.edte.utwente.nl/lanzing/cm_home.htm (visited 2002).

[5] Novak, J. & Gowin, D. (1984), *Learning how to learn*, Cambridge University Press.

[6] Novak, J. (2002), The Theory Underlying Concept Maps and How To Construct Them, http://cmap.coginst.uwf.edu/info/ (visited 2002).

Automatic Construction of Learning Ontologies

Trent Apted and Judy Kay
School of Information Technologies,
University of Sydney, Australia, 2006

Abstract

This paper describes a system which automatically constructs an extensive ontology of computer science. This can serve as a basis for making inferences about student models and other reasoning within a teaching system. The system enables a user to select a focus concept and then see the most closely related concepts.

1. Introduction

A software representation of an extensive computer science ontology may be used in a variety of roles in a teaching system. It enables a system to infer from a minimal knowledge base about a student to a quite extensive model of what their knowledge. Teaching goals can then be inferred by studying this model and expanding concepts the student is modelled as knowing – working with those that are closely related. It is also possible for a learning goal to be established, with the ontology identifying aspects that need to be taught as a foundation for this goal (eg if they are prerequisites).

Rather than creating the ontology by hand, we have built a tool for automatically constructing the ontology. It uses an existing, reliable resource to ensure appropriate coverage of computer science terms. This saves a considerable amount of effort and helps minimise errors while maximising breadth of coverage. The generated ontology may also serve as a basis for refinement by hand. For example, it is often easier to categorise an 'unknown' relationship (that is, a relationship known to exist for which there is not enough information to categorise it) by examining the automatic construction than it is to identify a relationship independently. Our approach to the ontology construction overcomes some of the limitations of existing ontology tools and representation formats such as OilEd [1] and DAML [2]. To accomplish this, the resource chosen was the Free On-Line Dictionary Of Computing (FOLDOC) [3]. This is a free web resource that currently contains definitions for 13,590 computer science terms in over 4.8 megabytes of text; it is quite extensive. The off-line version encloses significant words (eg words defined elsewhere) in braces and uses standard conventions in the layout and grammar of each definition; this makes it feasible to perform automatic analysis of the definitions.

2. Ontology Construction

Currently, the ontology is generated by processing an off-line image of the FOLDOC computer science dictionary. Individual definitions are parsed, looking for a categorisation for that word and to identify words that are related to it. Grammatical conventions in the dictionary are also used to provide additional information to the relationships wherever possible. For example, 'synonym', 'antonym', 'child' and 'parent' relationships can be extracted if certain keywords are present, otherwise an 'unknown' relationship is created.

The keyword-relationship mapping itself is read from a text (configuration) file, so it is easily customisable. This also makes it possible to process a similarly formatted dictionary in a different, or more specific domain (eg a description of courses and subjects offered at a university). This may then be used to perform similar queries, or to merge (see Sec. 3.3) the generated ontology with another domain for amalgamation or comparison.

The output of the parsing process is a weighted digraph. Heuristics based on the type of relationship (and the position within the definition that the relationship was identified) are used to assign a weight to each edge. The nodes are the words defined in the dictionary, as well as words used in definitions that are not defined themselves but are identified to be significant. Categories found also become nodes to facilitate querying.

3. Ontology Queries

The ontology generated is very large – in excess of 20,000 nodes. Tools have been written to query the ontology from a specific concept, or a set of concepts (for example in a user model). This results in a subgraph of the original ontology graph being generated. As a useful side-effect, nodes (as well as edges) are assigned a weight that reflects how closely each node matches the original query.

3.1. Point Queries

A query can be executed from a single node in the original graph, or in any graph generated as the result of a previous query. This results in a concept map of all things related to the query node (a word or category) within a certain 'distance'. The distance is specified in the query and its reach is determined by the edge weights corresponding to the relationships between nodes. This is useful for browsing the ontology and for general information retrieval.

3.2. Multipoint Queries

A set of nodes can similarly be specified. This results in a model being generated, represented by an underlying graph. Any computer science entity can be modelled in this way, provided it can be translated into a set of key concepts. The ontology determines the relationships between those concepts and allows the model to be extended to include related concepts.

In the future the generation of a graph this way will be more automated. Any arbitrary textual input could be processed to generate a model. For example an email, personal web page or call for papers could be processed in order to create a model of that entity.

3.3. Merge Queries

Any two graphs (models) can be merged, resulting in a new graph. This type of query can be used either to combine the information they represent or to compare and contrast two models. The merge operation records the source of each node in the new graph and can use this information to provide clustering and formatting specifications as input to the visualisations, along with relationships within and between the clusters.

4. Results and Discussion

Using an image of the dictionary obtained on 2002-03-12, the following statistics were obtained:

```
Definitions = 13536
Category links = 8998
Plus other links = 54830
Keywords processed = 33297
Preparse: 13536 defs for 153 categories
Graph Size: 23095, Density: 61926
```

The reason for the graph size being greater than the number of definitions is due to links being identified for words not actually defined, as well as for 'category' nodes. A tiny snapshot of the ontology is shown in Fig. 1 as a graph. This shows a point query with a distance of 1.5 from the 'declarative language' node and with a minimum of ten peers[1]. Bolder edges indicate a stronger relationship between nodes, and nodes are positioned vertically to indicate their closeness to 'declarative language'. For example, should a relationship be classified as a 'synonym' or with a keyword indicated as being 'very strong', it is given a bold edge in the graph. The other line styles (normal, dashed, dotted) indicate progressively weaker relationships as indicated by the edge weight (see Sec. 3).

Formal evaluation of the effectiveness is currently being conducted. Todate, informal evaluation has indicated

that the ontology construction has been effective and accurate.

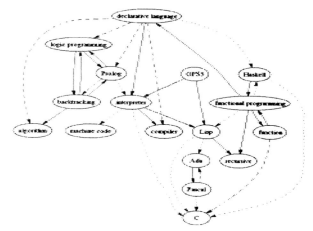

Figure 1. Concepts near 'declarative language' with a minimum of 10 peers

This was conducted by examining output similar to Figure 1, but with greater scope and detail, and from a number of different focal points.

5. Supplementary Visualisation

For small models (less than one hundred concepts) a traditional graph output is able to provide useful information to the user. To facilitate this, automatic output to the dot language [4] is provided. This output is useful for simulating concept maps generated from models or individual concepts. It also includes information regarding the relationship strengths (edge line style), and positions nodes vertically, according to how closely they match the query used to generate the initial graph.

6. Conclusion

The generation of an intuitively accurate and complete ontology has been successfully accomplished. However, the it remains to perform more systematic and thorough evaluation. The querying tools provide an effective way to focus on individual concepts or a collection of concepts representing a model, or models (for comparison).

References

[1] OilEd – Ontology Interface Layer Editor, at http://oiled.man.ac.uk/ (*visited 2002-03-12*)
[2] DAML – DARPA [Defense Advanced Research Projects Agency] Agent Markup Language, at http://www.daml.org (*visited 2002-03-12*)
[3] FOLDOC – the Free On-Line Dictionary Of Computing, at http://www.foldoc.org/ (*visited 2002-03-12*)
[4] The DOT Language, by AT&T Labs; (*visited 2002-04-18*) at http://www.research.att.com/~erg/graphviz/info/lang.html

---

[1] The peers themselves are not shown unless they also have a minimum of ten peers.

A Support System for Modeling Problem Solving Workflow

Kazuhisa Seta and Motohide Umano
Department of Mathematics and Information Sciences, Osaka Prefecture University,
1-1, Gakuen-cho, Sakai, Osaka, 599-8531 Japan

1. Introduction

Novice learners in a problem solving domain build up their own understanding of its target area and make plans to solve a problem based on their understanding. Our goal is to develop a system for supporting those processes and the reuse, sharing and inheritance of expertise acquired by suffering troubles.

Ontology is a key technique to achieve this goal [1]. In this paper, we mainly focus on supporting learners' planning processes and describe our modeling framework for effective and efficient planning of problem solving workflow that includes learning processes.

2. Learners' Work and Task Structures

Consider an example of a learner who is not very familiar with Java and XML programming and tries to develop an XML based document retrieval system. He/she explores web space, gathers useful information and plans learning and problem solving processes. In our scenario, novice learners in a problem solving domain try to gather information from web sources, build up their own understanding of the target area and make plans to solve the problem in hand. Needless to say, complete plans cannot be made at once but gradually detailed by iterating spirally those processes with trial and error.

Problem solving knowledge, in general, can be decomposed into a task-dependent but domain-independent portion and a task-independent but domain-dependent portion. The former is called task knowledge, e.g. diagnosis, planning, learning and so on, and the latter domain knowledge, e.g. device models, mathematics and so on [2]. This idea is known as "knowledge decomposition."

By analyzing learners' work using this idea, we can understand that their work is very complicated task, that is, a problem solving task in planning is decomposed into a type of a planning task and subject domain. Subject domain, in our case, consists of learning and problem solving activities. Furthermore, learning and target problem solving activities are decomposed into a type of learning and target problem solving and their target domain. Since this nested structure of learners' tasks puts

heavy loads on the learners, they tend to fall into utter confusion and lose their way. Based on the above task analysis, we propose a framework where learners can make effective and efficient plans with explicit awareness of the structures of their work and distinction among their activities

3. Structure of the Model

By problem solving workflow we mean all the required knowledge for problem solving and its flow, i.e., meaning and roles of target concepts, learning activities, problem solving procedures and so on.

Figure 1 shows our proposed framework for representing problem solving workflow. The framework is composed of a knowledge map and a task flow model. Furthermore, the knowledge map is divided into a knowledge resource and domain map.

- *Knowledge Resource (KR)* is a collection of knowledge sources such as web pages, electronic texts and human resources.
- *Domain Map (D-Map)* is a collection of the target domain concepts and relationships among them using basic semantic links such as "is-a" and "part-of" and plays a role of annotation of KR. D-Map expresses the meaning, roles and manners of the problem solving processes, for example, "JBuilder *is-a* integrated development environment which *includes* a debugger, XML-parser and Tomcat," "DOM and SAX *is-a* XML processing system," "the XML-parser *supports* both DOM and SAX system," "Tomcat *provides* an environment for running servlet program" and so on. D-Map represents the state of learner's understanding of each concept, e.g. what is DOM is 'known'. Thus, D-Map is considered to be a user model of the target domain.

The task flow is a model of a series of learner's activities along time axis (each activity is represented by a combination of verb and noun in natural language). The task flow model is divided into a problem solving process model and a learning process model.

- *Problem Solving Process Model (PSPM)* is a model of problem solving processes needed to solve the target problem, for example, "install JBuilder," "choose DOM

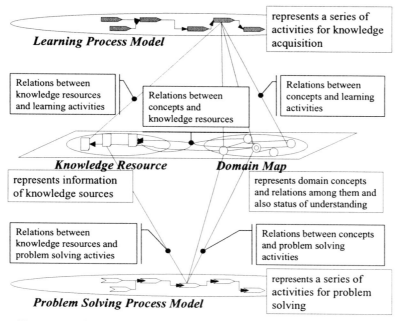

Figure. 1. A framework for representing problem solving workflow

Learning Process Model

represents a series of activities for knowledge acquisition

Relations between knowledge resources and learning activities

Relations between concepts and knowledge resources

Relations between concepts and learning activities

Knowledge Resource

Domain Map

represents information of knowledge sources

represents domain concepts and relations among them and also status of understanding

Relations between knowledge resources and problem solving activies

Relations between concepts and problem solving activities

Problem Solving Process Model

represents a series of activities for problem solving

or SAX system," and so on.

- *Learning Process Model (LPM)* is a model of a series of learning activities that is recognized as a problem solving in acquiring the knowledge needed for performing the target task,. for example, "gather information on DOM and SAX system," "understand the characteristics of DOM and SAX," and so on.

The difference between PSPM and LPM is in the type of their effects. Activities in LPM affect learners' states of understanding while those in PSPM affect the real world and contribute directly to solving the problem.

We have three reasons to define LPM and PSPM separately. The first is that the preparation of the models gives learners' explicit awareness of their task structures. It prevents learners from losing their way and helps them to have awareness of the purpose of what they do and what they should do next. The second is shareability and reusability of models. PSPM can be widely shared and reused in performing similar tasks. LPM, however, may not be reused or shared even in performing similar tasks, since their activities depend on the learners' expertise and states of understanding of the target domain concepts. Of course, learners whose states of understanding are similar to this of the creator of the model can share and reuse the LPM. The third is that not only problem solving processes but also design rationales behind them might be shared effectively by successive learning activities.

4. Kassist: A System for Supporting Problem Solving Workflow

It is quite time consuming work for learners to make effective and efficient plans of problem solving processes.

To help the learners', we are developing Kassist, which is a *modeling –methodology-aware tool*. The tool can provide useful information for learners' work. Kassist is an environment for planning, sharing and evolving problem solving workflows. Because of the space limitation, we will concentrate on its functional advantages.

Support for planning:
- If a learner has not acquired knowledge needed for problem solving, the system suggests performing learning activities for acquiring that knowledge prior to the problem solving activities requiring it.

Support for sharing and inheritance of problem solving workflow:
- The system suggests learning processes for understanding the design rationales of the problem solving workflow.

Support for evolving problem solving workflow:
- If the problem-solving context changes, we need to adapt the model. Since problem-solving workflow represents the problem-solving context, the system can provide the scope needed reviewing by tracing the links. As a simple example, when a learner doesn't use JBuilder, he doesn't need learning activities related to it, e.g. how to install it, how to use the debugger, etc. Instead, they need to learn how to install XML-parser and Tomcat in JBuilder.
- We can view D-Map as valid domain ontology [3] sufficient for performing the problem solving processes. Thus users and the system can collaboratively retrieve useful information from the WWW using the semantic information.

5. Concluding Remarks

We outlined the framework for representing problem solving workflow. We are currently implementing Kassit based on the design principle in this paper.

References

[1] Mizoguchi, R. & Bourdeau, J. (2000). Using Ontological Engineering to Overcome AI-ED Problems, *Int.J. of Artificial Intelligence in Education*, Vol.11, (2), 107-121.

[2] Mizoguchi, R., Tijerino, Y. & Ikeda, M. (1995). Task Analysis Interview Based on Task Ontology, *Expert Systems with Applications*, Vol. 9, (1), 15-25.

[3] Fensel, D. (2001). *Ontologies: A Silver Bullet for knowledge Management and Electronic Commerce*, Springer.

LEARNING LINKS: Reusable Assets with Support for Vagueness and Ontology-based Typing

Miguel A. Sicilia[1], Elena García[2], Paloma Díaz[1] and Ignacio Aedo[1]

[1]DEI Laboratory, Carlos III University. Avd. Universidad, 30, 28911 Madrid, Spain
[2]Computer Science Dept., Alcalá University. Cta. Barcelona km. 33.6, 28871 Madrid, Spain
{msicilia@inf, pdp@inf, aedo@ia}.uc3m.es; elena.garciab@uah.es

Abstract

Existing approaches to ontological support in courseware are focused on the annotation of hypermedia nodes or contents, while links are described only by classifying them into a set of predefined types. In this work, we describe the concept of Learning-Link as an independent and reusable learning resource that can be annotated with terms defined in a link ontology. The computational semantics of that ontology, combined with fuzziness to specify graded relations, enables the implementation of extended adaptive behaviors that entail inferences and approximate reasoning.

1. Introduction

Existing approaches to using ontologies (or similar knowledge representation formalisms) in learning resources are focused in mapping concepts to hypermedia nodes or contents, while links are constrained to a number of predefined interpretations, which are in some cases derived from the meta-structure of nodes. For example, in [1] the system derives connections of two types (*priority* and *relatedness*) from terms that are used to annotate contents, and in [2], concepts in a network are related to nodes. But *link ontologies* can be used to annotate the links themselves, so that richer and unified models of linking can be exploited to design adaptive behaviors, as sketched in [3]. Furthermore, current proposed standards for the interoperability and reusability of learning resources (and specially, the SCORM model [4], that aims at being a unified reference model) are organized around the concept of *learning object* (*Sharable Content Object*, SCO, in SCORM), defined as structured, context-independent aggregations of Web assets, which are also oriented towards metadata annotation of contents. In fact, in SCORM, links are derived from *content structures,* and they are limited to internal sequencing inside learning objects [1]. In this work, we describe the novel concept of *learning link* as a first-class citizen in educational technology reference models, and how XLINK[1] and straightforward

extensions to the SCORM model can be used to describe learning links. These links can be reused independently of the contents they associate, and ontologies can be used to provide them with semantically rich *types*. In addition, imprecision in the implicit assertions contained in links is considered a key characteristic that may enhance the implementation of adaptive behaviors that are supported by learning links.

2. A *Learning Link* Model Supporting Types and Fuzziness

The annotation of links with ontology terms is a generalization of the concept of link type [5] that has been used in hypermedia models [6] for diverse purposes. Web-enabled ontology definition languages [7] enhance simple link types with arbitrary relationship definitions between types and with full expressive power for the definition of axioms that can be used for subsequent reasoning processes. In consequence, applications that rely on link typing [8] may take advantage of these extensions. In addition, *vagueness* is an inherent property of many link types, since they convey semantic structures that are essentially vague. For example, weights in [1] are an implicit form of quantifying grades in relatedness connections. The concept of *fuzzy link* [9] can be used to model that vagueness depending on the learner and the semantics of the link type. As a result, a link can be defined in an abstract manner as a triple $L=(S, T, \Lambda)$, where S and T are the sets of sources and targets, respectively, and Λ is a set of membership functions in the form:

$$\mu_{(L,p)}:(S, T, U) \rightarrow [0..1]$$

where p denotes the *type* or purpose of the link, and U is the set of users of the system. An arc that belongs to the link L in the form $(a, b) \in S \times T$ with a specific type is thus described by the corresponding membership function, which allows the definition of partial matching with specific users (this is essentially a generalization of the abstract link model of XLINK). For example, the relative density level of a set of nodes D that give details about a node k in S along with the mastery level of the user (in the corresponding concept) can be used to derive a membership grade in a link so that:

$$\mu_{(L,\ detail)}(k,\ d,\ u) = f(density(d), mastery_k(u)),\ d \in D$$
where f is a function that should be empirically adjusted.

If we use a term in a link ontology as a link type designator, we can take advantage of ontology-defined predicates. For example, we know that an *analogy* link is a kind of *argument* link, which is related to a *work-part* according to [10]. Designer-defined links can be defined on existing ontologies, for example, the *"where in the world?"* link cited in [8] could be considered a subtype of *apply* link in [10].

3. Extending SCORM for Learning Links

A fourth type of SCORM learning resource (current ones are assets, SCOs and content aggregations) can be defined to introduce learning links as sharable elements. Independent links or link-bases expressed in XLINK format can be described with the same metadata items used for the other kinds of resources, thus not breaking the current restriction which requires that "learning resource sequencing is defined in the content structure and is external to the learning resource"[4]. The annotation of the links should be defined on metadata items rather than in the link itself, to be Learning Management System (LMS)-visible. Basically, the *meta-metadata* section should include references to the ontology, and the *classification* section can be used to annotate the link (or set of links) with specific classes. As a proof of concept, we have developed a link ontology derived from Trigg's taxonomy of scientific writing [10], and a preliminary prototype based on the "SCORM sample run-time environment 1.2"[2], which uses the DAML+OIL RDFS-based markup generated by OILEd[3]. A link in a SCORM manifest describes a set of arcs (sources and targets) between assets or SCOs. Membership grades can be specified in the meta-data, as hard-coded values or functions or they can be internal to the LMS. The class *LMSManifestHandler* was extended to read the extended manifest syntax, and storing learning links in the relational database. After that, the JSP script file *sequencingEngine* was modified to add LMS-controlled links on the fly, depending on the current knowledge status of the learner, described by the SCORM data model. For example, *detail* links (and links of any of its subclasses) may only be showed by default if `cmi.core.lesson_status` is 'passed', and the inverse may occur with *summarization* links. Extensions to the `cmi.student_preference` data item can be used also for adaptation (for example, to hide or show *formalize* links depending on the student's mathematical background). In addition, membership values can be used also as sorting or highlighting criteria in adaptive link sorting or annotation.

4. Conclusions

A model of learning links as reusable learning resources has been described, with support for vagueness and semantic typing. Our current approach can be situated at *level-2* according with the computational semantics described in [11] and complements existing approaches that use ontologies or concept maps to provide semantic interpretation to hypermedia nodes or contents. The link model can be mapped to XLINK structures and integrated in existing learning technology standards.

References
[1] Cristea, A. and Okamoto, T. (2001). Object-oriented Collaborative Course Authoring Environment supported by Concept Mapping in MyEnglishTeacher. *Educational Technology and Society*, **4**(2).

[2] Weber, G. and Brusilovsky, P. (2001). Elm-Art: An adaptive versatile system for Web-based instruction. *Intl. Journal of Artificial Intelligence in Education* **12**(4).

[3] Sicilia, M.A. and García, E. (2002). Link Types as Enablers of Semantic Navigation in Standard-Based Web Learning Systems. *IEEE Learning Technology Newsletter* **4**(3).

[4] Advanced Distributed Learning (ADL), Sharable Courseware Object Reference Model (SCORM) Ver. 1.2. Oct. 1, 2001. http://www.adlnet.org/ [Viewed 6 June, 2002].

[5] Kopak, R.W. (1999). A proposal for a taxonomy of functional link types. *ACM Computing Surveys*, **31**(4).

[6] Díaz, P., Aedo, I. and Panetsos, F. (1997). Labyrinth, an abstract model for hypermedia applications. Description of its static components. *Information Systems*, **22**(8), 447–464.

[7] Fensel, D. (2002). Language standardization for the Semantic Web: The long way from OIL to OWL. *Proc. of the 4th Int. Conf. on Distributed Communities on the Web*.

[8] Murray, T. (2002). MetaLinks: Authoring and Affordances for Conceptual and Narrative Flow in Adaptive Hyperbooks *Intl. Journal of Artificial Intelligence in Education*, **13**.

[9] Sicilia, M.A., Díaz, P., Aedo, I. and García, E. (2002). Fuzziness in Adaptive Hypermedia Models. *Proc. of North American Fuzzy Information Processing Society*, 268-273.

[10] Trigg, R. H. and Weiser, M. (1986). TEXTNET: A Network-Based Approach to Text Handling. *ACM Transactions on Office Information Systems*, **4**(1), 1-23.

[11] R. Mizoguchi, and J. Bourdeau (2000). Using Ontological Engineering to Overcome Common AI-ED Problems. *Intl. Journ. Artificial Intelligence in Education*, **11**, 107-121.

---

[2] Available at http://www.adlnet.org/
[3] Available at http://oiled.man.ac.uk/

Author Index

International Conference on Computers in Education — ICCE 2002